# Rick

# ITALY

## 2020

# CONTENTS

# Welcome to Rick Steves' Europe

Travel is intensified living—maximum thrills per minute and one of the last great sources of legal adventure. Travel is freedom. It's recess, and we need it.

I discovered a passion for European travel as a teen and have been sharing it ever since—through my tours, public television and radio shows, and travel guidebooks. Over the years I've taught thousands of travelers how to best enjoy Europe's blockbuster sights—and experience "Back Door" discoveries that most tourists miss.

This book offers you a balanced mix of Italy's lively cities and cozy towns, from brutal but *bella* Rome to *tranquillo,* traffic-free Riviera villages. And it's selective—rather than listing dozens of hill towns, I recommend only the best ones. My self-guided museum tours and city walks give insight into the country's vibrant history and today's living, breathing culture.

I advocate traveling simply and smartly. Take advantage of my money- and time-saving tips on sightseeing, transportation, and more. Try local, characteristic alternatives to expensive hotels and restaurants. In many ways, spending more money only builds a thicker wall between you and what you traveled so far to see.

We visit Italy to experience it—to become temporary locals. Thoughtful travel engages us with the world, as we learn to appreciate other cultures and new ways to measure quality of life.

Judging from the positive feedback I receive from readers, this book will help you enjoy a fun, affordable, and rewarding vacation—whether it's your first trip or your tenth.

*Buon viaggio!* Happy travels!

Rick Steves

# ITALY

*Bell'Italia!* Italy has Europe's richest, craziest culture—bubbling with emotion, traffic jams, strikes, rallies, religious holidays, crowds, and irate ranters shaking their fists at each other one minute and walking arm-in-arm the next. Promise yourself to relax and accept it all as a package deal—the exquisite and the exasperating. If you take Italy on its own terms, you'll experience a cultural keelhauling that actually feels good.

After all, Italy is the cradle of European civilization—established by the Roman Empire and carried on by the Roman Catholic Church. As you explore Italy, you'll stand face-to-face with some of the world's most iconic images from this 2,000-year history: Rome's ancient Colosseum and playful Trevi Fountain, Pisa's Leaning Tower, Florence's Renaissance masterpieces (Michelangelo's *David* and Botticelli's *Venus*), and the island city of elegant decay—Venice.

Beyond these famous cities, there's even more: German-flavored Alps, timeless hill towns, peaceful lakes lined with 19th-century villas, the business center of Milan, and Mediterranean beaches. Italy is reasonably small and laced with train lines and freeways, so you're never more than a half-day's journey from any of these places.

Wherever you go, Italy's top sights are its people. They're outgoing and social. They have an endearing habit of speaking Italian to foreigners, even if they know you don't speak their language—and it somehow works. If a local starts chat-

*Interact with the people you meet—in the streets and in the shops.*

tering at you in Italian, don't resist. Go with it. You might understand more than you'd expect.

Italian food is a cut above. If America's specialty is fast food, Italy's is slow food—bought daily, prepared with love, and enjoyed convivially. Three-hour restaurant meals are common; dinner is the evening's entertainment. To "eat and run" is seen as a lost opportunity. Wine complements the meal; Italy is the world's number-one wine producer (just ahead of France). For just a quick sandwich or a coffee, Italians stop by a bar. The bars aren't taverns, but cafés…good for a light meal anytime, with all ages welcome.

Early evening is the time for the ritual promenade—called the *passeggiata*—up and down main street. Shoppers, people watchers, families, and young flirts on the prowl stroll and spread their wings like peacocks. You might hear sweet whispers of *"bella"* (pretty) and *"bello"* (handsome). You can be a spectator, sipping a drink at a sidewalk table, or better yet, join the promenade, with a gelato in hand.

As you stroll, it's fun to window-shop. While no longer a cheap country, Italy remains a hit with shoppers for glassware and Carnevale masks in Venice; gold, silver, leather, and prints in Florence; and high fashion in Rome and Milan.

## Buon Appetito!

Italian cuisine is sightseeing for your palate. The recipe: Start with fresh ingredients and talented cooks, mix in the owner's personality, and add a happy restaurant crowd. Eating in Italy is a joy you can't get anywhere else. Be adventurous, and try the regional specialties and culinary customs. You can eat well, even on a budget.

In Florence and the hill towns of Tuscany, enjoy hearty farmer's food: grilled meats, beans, fresh herbs, and high-quality seasonal vegetables. Popular dishes are *ribollita,* a savory bean-and-bread soup, and *bistecca alla fiorentina,* a grilled T-bone steak. Forage through Florence's gourmet food hall. For light fare, try an *enoteca* (wine bar), where appetizers and salads are paired with fine wine. For dessert, decide for yourself if Florence really does have Italy's most flavorful gelato.

Venetian cuisine features catch-of-the-day fish and shellfish, risotto, polenta, and some exotic choices. *Nero di seppia* is squid in its own black ink, served over pasta. Tourists are drawn to the pricey, romantic, canalside eateries (Hint: Pizza is the least expensive item on the menu). But I prefer to dine on the cheap, dropping into atmospheric *cicchetti* bars to munch bite-size appetizers that add up to a fun, tasty meal. Try both!

*Take your taste buds for a spin, from Florence's* bistecca alla fiorentina *(grilled steak) and Venice's* nero di seppia *(inky squid over pasta) to this popular pairing in Milan:* risotto alla milanese *and* ossobuco *(saffron risotto with veal).*

Trendsetting Milan claims to have created the *aperitivo* happy hour—a drink with free appetizers—that's catching on elsewhere in Italy. In stylish Milan, even the deli food is photogenic. The most famous dish is *risotto alla milanese* paired with *ossobuco* (saffron risotto with veal shank). The Lake District features ▶▶▶

▶▶▶ whitefish on the menu with sublime views included in the cost. In the mountainous Dolomites, the hearty cuisine is Germanic, with pork, game, potatoes, dumplings, and strudel. Passersby will wish you a *"Guten Appetit!"*

In coastal regions such as the Cinque Terre, Riviera, and Amalfi Coast, seafood is the specialty (add pesto and focaccia for the Cinque Terre). For that quintessential beach experience, settle in at a waterfront café on a sunny day. Sample *antipasti frutti di mare*—a plate of mixed "fruits of the sea"—with a glass of wine as the Mediterranean shimmers before you.

Roman cuisine, strongly flavored and unpretentious, features meats, fish, some fried foods, and fresh vegetables. Numerous food-and-wine tasting tours, offering an insider's look, can fill you in and fill you up. Roman specialties are *spaghetti alla carbonara* (with an egg-and-bacon sauce created here) and *saltimbocca alla romana* (literally "jump in the mouth" veal). Dine at a sidewalk café with the rust-colored facades of Rome as your backdrop.

Italians say the best pizza is in Naples, its birthplace. The soft, chewy crust is topped with mozzarella and tomato sauce, and baked in a wood-burning oven. At a Neapolitan pizzeria, pizza is often the only thing on the menu. Go for it!

For an affordable splurge anywhere in Italy, have a glass of wine or cup of coffee in an elegant café or on a classic square. If you sip your pricey drink slowly in a prime people-watching zone, it's an excellent value. Raise a toast: *La vita è bella!* Life is good. ▨

*In coastal towns, seafood is always on the menu. When in Rome, eat what the Romans eat:* saltimbocca alla romana *(veal with prosciutto). Pizza is best in its hometown, Naples.*

Italy's biggest business is tourism—the country is considered the world's fifth-most-visited tourist destination.

Culturally, there are two Italys: The North tends to be industrial, aggressive, and "time is money" in its outlook (though Venice is a world apart). The South is hotter and more crowded, poor, relaxed, farm-oriented, and traditional; families usually live in the same house for many generations. Loyalties are to family, city, region, soccer team, and country—in that order.

Italians are obsessed with soccer (called *il calcio*). Star players are treated like movie stars, and fans are passionate. On big game nights, bars are packed with fans watching TV screens. After a loss, they drown their sorrows. After a victory, fans celebrate by driving through the streets honking horns and waving team flags.

Home of the Vatican, Italy is still mostly Catholic. Although Italians will crowd into St. Peter's Square with rock-concert energy to catch a glimpse of *"il Papa,"* they're not particularly devout. They baptize their kids at the local church (there's one every few blocks), but generally don't attend church regularly and hold modern opinions on social issues, often in conflict with strict Catholic dogma. Italy is now the land of legalized abortion, a low birth rate, nudity on TV, socialist politics, and a society whose common language is decidedly secular. The true dominant religion is life: motor scooters, fashion, girl-watching, boy-watching, good

**Left:** *Swiss Guards have protected the Vatican since the 1500s.*
**Right:** *Soccer games draw devout crowds.*

**Left:** *Venice's Carnevale is celebrated with masks, costumes, and revelry.*
**Right:** *Imagine Roman life 2,000 years ago.*

coffee, good wine, and *il dolce far niente* (the sweetness of doing nothing).

Italians are stylish. They strive to project a positive image in manner and dress—a concept they call *la bella figura*. They'd rather miss their bus than get sweaty and mussed-up rushing to catch it. And no matter how hot it gets, Italian men wear long pants—not shorts (except at the beach).

Traditions remain important. On festival days, locals still dress up in medieval or fanciful garb to celebrate Carnevale (Venice), play soccer (Florence), or race horses (Siena). Traditional ways are carried on by choice. Italians are wary of the dangers of a fast-paced global lifestyle. Their history is long, and they're secure in their place in the world.

Zero in on Italy's fine points and don't dwell on the problems (just call them "cultural experiences"). Savor your cappuccino, dangle your feet over a canal (if it smells, breathe through your mouth), and imagine what it was like centuries ago. Ramble through the rabble and rubble of Rome and mentally resurrect those ancient stones. Sit silently on a hill-town belvedere and get chummy with the winds of the past. Write a poem over a glass of local wine in a sun-splashed, wave-dashed Riviera village. Italy is for romantics.

# Italy's Top Destinations

*Mamma mia!* There's so much to see in Italy and so little time. This overview breaks the country's top destinations into must-see sights (to help first-time travelers plan their trip) and worth-it sights (for those with extra time or special interests). I've also suggested a minimum number of days to allow per destination.

# MUST-SEE DESTINATIONS

Italy's major cities are Rome, Florence, and Venice. Each has a distinctly different flavor, from ancient Roman to Renaissance art to a romantic island. If you have just two weeks for your first Italian trip, include these cities, add the coastal Cinque Terre and the town of Siena, and you'll get an unforgettable introduction to the best (if most touristy stops) that Italy has to offer. Here they are, listed north to south, as they appear in this book:

### ▲▲▲Venice (allow 1-2 days)
Venice is Italy's dreamy island city, powerful in medieval times, and famous today for St. Mark's Basilica, the Grand Canal, and singing gondoliers. Idling on St. Mark's Square—best at night while the orchestras play—is one of Italy's grand experiences.

### ▲▲▲Cinque Terre (2-3 days)
The lovely Cinque Terre is a string of five idyllic Riviera hamlets tucked along a rugged coastline, connected by scenic hiking trails and boats, and dotted with beaches. The region is revered by hardy hikers, sun-worshippers, and photographers.

### ▲▲▲Florence (1-2 days)
If you love art, you'll enjoy Florence. This surprisingly compact city, which Michelangelo called home, was the cradle of the Renaissance. You'll marvel at the Uffizi Gallery's priceless paintings (starring Botticelli's ethereal *Birth of Venus,* shown above), Brunelleschi's dome-topped cathedral, and Michelangelo's *David.* And anyone can appreciate Italy's best gelato.

*Gliding through Venice, a parade in Siena, Florence's shop-lined Ponte Vecchio, hiking in the Cinque Terre*

### ▲▲▲Siena (1 day)

Nearby Siena is Florence's smaller and (some say) more appealing Tuscan rival, with its magnificent Il Campo square, striking striped cathedral, and medieval pageantry, spurred by its Palio horse race. On any night, if you hear the low throb of drumming signaling a parade in a proud neighborhood—seek it out!

### ▲▲▲Rome (2-3 days)

Rome is Italy's capital, the sprawling Eternal City, studded with impressive Roman ruins: the Forum, Colosseum, and Pantheon. It's home to Vatican City and the astonishing Sistine Chapel. Wandering through Rome's floodlit-fountain squares at night, happening upon the Trevi Fountain... you won't be the only romantic tossing in a coin with a wish to return.

*Rome's Trevi Fountain, Padua's Scrovegni Chapel, Rome's Colosseum at night*

## WORTH-IT DESTINATIONS

You can weave any of these destinations—rated ▲ or ▲▲—
into your itinerary. It's easy to add some destinations based
on proximity (if you're going to Florence, Pisa is next door),
but other out-of-the-way places can merit the journey, depending on your time and interests.

### ▲▲Milan (1 day)

Many travelers arrive in Milan in northern Italy. With three
airports, it's a major transit hub. This powerhouse city of
commerce and fashion boasts the prestigious La Scala opera
house, pink-marble Duomo, and Leonardo's *Last Supper*.

### ▲The Lakes (1 day)

For a lakeside stop just an hour from Milan (as a day trip or
overnight), consider the Lakes—ideally the quaint village
of Varenna on Lake Como, where you can cruise the lake,
wander, sunbathe, and dine al fresco. If relaxation is on your
agenda, so is Lake Como. Another popular stop is Lake
Maggiore and the town of Stresa, where tourists come to see
manicured islands and elegant villas.

### ▲Near Venice (1 day)

Near Venice are several intriguing towns: Padua, known for
Giotto's gloriously frescoed Scrovegni Chapel; little Vicenza
for its Palladian architecture; and Verona for its ancient
Roman amphitheater and Romeo and Juliet sights. Each
town is an easy, quick stop on the main train line between
Venice and Milan.

### ▲The Dolomites (1-2 days)

The Dolomites are Italy's mighty Alps, featuring Bolzano,
home of Ötzi the Iceman; the charming village of Castel-

*Dolomites, lovely Lake Como, fashionable Milan, view of Lucca*

rotto; and Alpe di Siusi, a vast alpine meadow laced with lifts and hiking trails. Near Austria, the region is sausage-and-sauerkraut Germanic and can be time-consuming to reach, but if the weather's good, hikers will be in paradise.

### ▲Riviera Towns (1 day)
You're near Riviera Towns when you're in the Cinque Terre. The coastal towns are little Levanto, double-beached Sestri Levante, the larger Santa Margherita Ligure, gem-like Portofino, and resorty Porto Venere. Choose one—or more!

### ▲Pisa and Lucca (1.5 days)
These towns make two good stops or day trips from Florence. Pisa has the iconic Leaning Tower, set in the stunning Field of Miracles. The pleasant town of Lucca, a delight for window-shoppers, has an inviting old center, encircled by a wide medieval wall you can stroll or bike.

### ▲Volterra and San Gimignano (1.5 days)
In Tuscany, these villages are tempting: Volterra is vibrant and rustically real, while multitowered San Gimignano is more photogenic and touristy.

### ▲▲Heart of Tuscany (1-3 days)
Italy's many hill towns, as sleepy as if they've been caught napping, are popular for good reason. From Florence or Siena, several hill towns are within striking range by public transportation. Those with a car can discover far more. Wine lovers savor a cluster of picturesque, wine-soaked villages amid rolling hills in the Heart of Tuscany: mellow Montepulciano, Renaissance Pienza, and Brunello-fueled Montalcino.

### ▲▲Assisi (1 day)
Perched on a hilltop, Assisi is the hometown of St. Francis, with a divinely Giotto-decorated basilica dedicated to the humble saint who extolled the virtues of love and simplicity. Assisi is located between Florence and Rome, but will always feel off the beaten track.

### ▲▲Orvieto and Civita (1 day)
Near Rome, Orvieto offers more hill-town adventures, featuring classic views, Classico wine, and an ornate cathedral, plus nearby Civita di Bagnoregio, a pint-sized hill town reachable only by a narrow, steep bridge.

### ▲▲Naples (half-day)

A swing south from Rome, from Naples to Paestum, gives you the best of southern Italy. Naples, a good stop en route to the genteel home base of Sorrento, is a gritty port city with nonstop street life and a top archaeological museum starring the treasures from ancient Pompeii.

### ▲▲Pompeii and Nearby (half-day)

South of Naples are the ruins of famous Pompeii (worth ▲▲▲) and smaller Herculaneum, with their nemesis, Mount Vesuvius, looming on the horizon. The ancient sites are an easy stop between Naples and Sorrento; of the two, Pompeii is better.

### ▲Sorrento and Capri (1.5 days)

Sorrento is a seaside resort port—a well-located home base for the many sights in the region, including the jet-set island getaway of Capri (worth ▲▲) with its eerie Blue Grotto, just a short cruise away. Also nearby is the...

### ▲▲Amalfi Coast and Paestum (1-2 days)

From Sorrento, you can travel the cliff-hanging road along the Amalfi Coast, overlooking the sparkling Mediterranean, to visit villages spilling down to beaches.

South of the Amalfi Coast is a site so ancient it predates most Roman sites—Paestum, crowned with well-preserved Greek temples from a time this storied land was Magna Graecia, or Great Greece.

*Naples' vibrant street life and the hilltop perch of Civita di Bagnoregio*

# Planning Your Trip

To plan your trip, you'll need to design your itinerary—choosing where and when to go, how you'll travel, and how many days to spend at each destination. For my best advice on sightseeing, accommodations, restaurants, and using transportation, see the Practicalities chapter.

## DESIGNING AN ITINERARY

As you read this book and learn about your options...

### Choose your top destinations.

My recommended itinerary (on the next page) gives you an idea of how much you can reasonably see in 21 days, but you can adapt it to fit your own interests and timeframe. If you like Renaissance art, linger longer in Florence. Exploring Italy's hill towns could soak up a week. For mountains, make tracks to the Dolomites. And if you've always wanted to ascend Pisa's Leaning Tower, now's the time for the climb.

### Decide when to go.

Italy's best travel months are May, June, September, and October. They're also the busiest and most expensive time to visit (with the north remaining busy straight through the summer). Crowds aside, these months combine the convenience of peak season with pleasant weather.

The heat in July and August can be grueling, particularly in the south, where temperatures hit the 90s. Fortunately

## Italy's Best Three-Week Trip by Public Transportation

| Day | Plan | Sleep in |
|-----|------|----------|
| 1 | Arrive in Milan | Milan |
| 2 | Milan to Lake Como | Varenna |
| 3 | Lake Como | Varenna |
| 4 | To Dolomites via Verona | Bolzano/Castelrotto |
| 5 | Dolomites | Bolzano/Castelrotto |
| 6 | To Venice | Venice |
| 7 | Venice | Venice |
| 8 | To the Cinque Terre | Vernazza |
| 9 | Cinque Terre | Vernazza |
| 10 | To Florence via Pisa | Florence |
| 11 | Florence | Florence |
| 12 | Florence, late to Siena | Siena |
| 13 | Siena | Siena |
| 14 | To Assisi | Assisi |
| 15 | To Orvieto and Civita | Orvieto |
| 16 | To Sorrento via Naples | Sorrento |
| 17 | Capri | Sorrento |
| 18 | Amalfi Coast | Sorrento |
| 19 | Morning to Rome via Pompeii | Rome |
| 20 | Rome | Rome |
| 21 | Rome | Rome |
| 22 | Fly home | |

**Notes:** If you have less time, drop the out-of-the-way Dolomites or save the Amalfi Coast for another trip. With extra time, add a day to sight-filled Florence or Rome, or slow down in the countryside with more hill towns (check public transportation options first—not all towns are well-served).

most midrange hotels come with air-conditioning. August is also when many Italians take their summer vacations; big cities tend to be quiet (with discounted hotel prices), but beach and mountain resorts are jammed (with higher hotel prices).

Winter offers cooler temperatures and fewer tourists, except on major holidays. Expect shorter hours for sights and fewer activities. Beach towns are nearly shut down and battered by waves; skip the Cinque Terre and Amalfi Coast.

For weather specifics, see the climate chart in the appendix.

**To modify for drivers:** Tour most of Italy by train, then use a car to explore a region or two (even if it means backtracking a few hours by train or car). These stops are easier by train than by car: Venice, the Cinque Terre, Florence, Rome, and the cluster south of Rome (Naples, Pompeii, Sorrento, Capri, and the Amalfi Coast). Drivers will find a car most helpful for exploring the hill-town region. Major car-rental agencies have offices in many towns.

## Connect the dots.

Link your destinations into a logical route. Determine which cities you'll fly into and out of. Begin your search for transatlantic flights at Kayak.com.

Decide if you'll travel by car, public transportation, or a combination. A car is particularly helpful for exploring the hill-town region (where public transportation can be sparse), but is useless in big cities (park it). Trains are faster and more expensive than buses (which don't run as often on Sundays).

To determine approximate transportation times between your destinations, study the driving chart in the Practicalities chapter or consult train schedules (www.trenitalia.it). Com-

*Savor Italy's astonishing cathedrals and the joys of sharing your journey with friends. Happy travels!*

pare the cost of any long train ride in Europe with a budget flight; check Skyscanner.com for intra-European flights.

## Write out a day-by-day itinerary.

Figure out how many destinations you can comfortably fit in your timeframe. Don't overdo it—few travelers wish they'd hurried more. Allow enough days per stop (see estimates in "Italy's Top Destinations," earlier). Minimize one-night stands, especially consecutive ones. It can be worth taking a late-afternoon train ride or drive to get settled into a town for two nights. Include sufficient time for transportation; whether you travel by train or car, it'll take you a half-day to get between most destinations.

Staying in a home base (like Florence or Sorrento) and making day trips can be more time-efficient than changing locations and hotels.

Take sight closures into account. Avoid visiting a town on the one day a week its must-see sights are closed. Check if any holidays or festivals fall during your trip—these attract crowds and can close sights (for the latest, visit Italy's tourist website, www.italia.it).

Give yourself some slack. Every trip, and every traveler, needs downtime for doing laundry, picnic shopping, people-watching, and so on. Pace yourself. Assume you will return.

# Trip Costs Per Person

Run a reality check on your dream trip. You'll have major transportation costs in addition to daily expenses.

**Flight:** A round-trip flight from the US to Milan or Rome costs about $1,000-2,000, depending on where you fly from and when.

**Public Transportation:** For a three-week trip, allow $550 for buses and second-class trains ($750 for first class). You'll usually save money buying train tickets in Italy, rather than buying a rail pass before you leave home. In some cases, a short flight can be cheaper than taking the train.

**Car Rental:** Allow roughly $250 per week, not including tolls, gas, parking, and insurance (theft insurance is mandatory in Italy).

AVERAGE DAILY EXPENSES PER PERSON

**$175**
Applies to cities, figure on less for towns

**Lodging**
Based on two people splitting the cost of a $160 double room with breakfast.
★★★★
$80

**Meals**
$15 for lunch, $30 for dinner, and $5 for gelato
$50

**City Transit**
Buses, Metro, or *vaporetti* (in Venice)
$10

**Sights and Entertainment**
This daily average works for most people.
$35

# Budget Tips

You can cut my suggested daily expenses by taking advantage of the deals you'll find throughout Italy and mentioned in this book.

City transit passes (for multiple rides or all-day usage) decrease your cost per ride.

Avid sightseers buy combo-tickets or passes that cover multiple museums. If a town doesn't offer deals, visit only the sights you most want to see, and seek out free sights and experiences (people-watching counts).

Some businesses—especially hotels and walking-tour companies—offer discounts to my readers (look for the RS% ▶▶▶

▶▶▶ symbol in the hotel listings in this book).

Book your rooms directly with the hotel. Some hotels offer discounts if you pay in cash and/or stay three or more nights (it pays to check online or ask).

Rooms cost less outside of peak season (roughly November through March). And even seniors can stay in hostels (some have double rooms) for about $30 per person. Or check Airbnb-type sites for deals.

It's no hardship to eat cheap in Italy. You can get tasty, inexpensive meals at delis, bars, takeout pizza shops, ethnic eateries, and Italian restaurants, too. Cultivate the art of picnicking in atmospheric settings.

When you splurge, choose an experience you'll always remember, such as a food-tasting tour or a gondola ride. Minimize souvenir shopping—how will you get it all home? Focus instead on collecting wonderful memories. ▢

*Getting tourist information, stairs at Vatican Museums, the joy of advance tickets*

## BEFORE YOU GO

You'll have a smoother trip if you tackle a few things ahead of time. For more info on these topics, see the Practicalities chapter (and www.ricksteves.com, which has helpful travel tips and talks).

**Make sure your travel documents are valid.** If your passport is due to expire within six months of your ticketed date of return, you need to renew it. Allow up to six weeks to renew or get a passport (www.travel.state.gov). Beginning in 2021, you may also need to register with the European Travel Information and Authorization System (ETIAS).

**Arrange your transportation.** Book your international flights. It's worth thinking about buying essential train tickets online in advance, getting a rail pass, renting a car, or booking cheap European flights. (You can wing it once you're there, but it may cost more.) Drivers: Consider bringing an International Driving Permit (sold at AAA offices in the US, www.aaa.com) along with your license.

**Book rooms well in advance,** especially if your trip falls during peak season or any major holidays or festivals.

**Reserve or buy tickets in advance for major sights.** In Florence, reserve ahead for the Uffizi Gallery (Renaissance paintings), Accademia (Michelangelo's *David*), and to climb the cathedral dome (mandatory). For Pisa, you can book a time to climb the Leaning Tower. For Milan, reserve three months ahead for Leonardo's *Last Supper.* For Padua, book at least two days in advance for Giotto's Scrovegni Chapel. In Rome, book several days ahead for the Borghese Gallery (Bernini sculptures). Reservations are essential for the Vatican Museums (Sistine Chapel) and for quick entry into the Colosseum and Forum.

**Consider travel insurance.** Compare the cost of the insurance to the cost of your potential loss. Check whether your existing insurance (health, homeowners, or renters) covers you and your possessions overseas.

**Call your bank.** Alert your bank that you'll be using your debit and credit cards in Europe. Ask about transaction fees, and get the PIN number for your credit card. You don't need to bring euros for your trip; you can withdraw euros from cash machines in Europe.

**Use your smartphone smartly.** Sign up for an international service plan to reduce your costs, or rely on Wi-Fi in Europe instead. Download any useful apps you'll want on the road, such as maps, translators, transit schedules, and Rick Steves Audio Europe (see sidebar).

**Rip up this book!** Turn chapters into mini guidebooks: Break the book's spine and use a utility knife to slice apart chapters, keeping gummy edges intact. Reinforce the chapter spines with clear wide tape or use a heavy-duty stapler.

**Pack light.** You'll walk with your luggage more than you think. I travel for weeks with a single carry-on bag and a daypack. Use the packing checklist in the appendix as a guide.

## Rick's Free Video Clips and Audio Tours

Travel smarter with these free, fun resources:

**Rick Steves Classroom Europe,** a powerful tool for teachers, is also useful for travelers. This video library contains over 400 short clips excerpted from my public television series. Enjoy these videos as you sort through options for your trip and to better understand what  you'll see in Europe. Check it out at Classroom.RickSteves.com (just enter a topic in the search bar to find everything I've filmed on a subject).

The **Rick Steves Audio Europe** app makes it easy to download my audio tours and listen to them offline as you travel. For this book (look for the 🎧), these audio tours cover sights  and neighborhoods in Venice, Milan, Florence, Siena, Assisi, Rome, Naples, and Pompeii. The app also offers interviews from my public radio show with experts from Europe and around the globe. Find it in your app store or at RickSteves.com/AudioEurope.

# Travel Smart

Many people think Italy is a chaotic mess and any attempt at efficient travel is futile. This is dead wrong—and costly, in terms of time and money. Italy, which seems as orderly as spilled spaghetti, actually functions quite well. If you have a positive attitude, equip yourself with good information (this book), and expect to travel smart, you will.

**Read—and reread—this book.** To have an "A" trip, be an "A" student. As you study up on sights, note opening hours, closed days, crowd-beating tips, and whether reservations are required or advisable. Check the latest at RickSteves.com/update.

**Be your own tour guide.** As you travel, get up-to-date info on sights, reserve tickets and tours, reconfirm hotels and travel arrangements, and check transit connections. Visit local tourist information offices. Upon arrival in a new town, lay the groundwork for a smooth departure; confirm the train, bus, or road you'll take when you leave.

**Outsmart thieves.** Pickpockets abound in crowded places where tourists congregate. Treat commotions as smokescreens for theft. Keep your cash, credit cards, and passport secure in a money belt tucked under your clothes; carry only a day's spending money in your front pocket. Don't set valuable items down on counters or café tabletops, where they can be quickly stolen or easily forgotten.

**Minimize potential loss.** Keep expensive gear to a minimum. Bring photocopies or take photos of important documents (passport and cards) to aid in replacement if they're lost or stolen. Back up photos and files frequently.

**Beat the summer heat.** If you wilt easily, choose a hotel with air-conditioning, start your day early, take a mid-day siesta at your hotel, and resume your sightseeing later. Churches offer a cool haven (though dress modestly—no bare shoulders or shorts). Take frequent gelato breaks. Join the *passeggiata,* when locals stroll in the cool of the evening.

**Guard your time and energy.** Taking a taxi can be a good value if it saves you a long wait for a cheap bus or an exhausting walk across town. To avoid long lines, follow my crowd-beating tips, such as making advance reservations, or sightseeing early or late. Buy combo-tickets at less-visited sights to get quickly into popular sights.

**Be flexible.** Even if you have a well-planned itinerary, expect changes, strikes, closures, sore feet, bad weather, and so on. Your Plan B could turn out to be even better.

**Attempt the language.** Many Italians—especially in the tourist trade and in cities—speak English, but if you learn some Italian, even just a few phrases, you'll get more smiles and make more friends. Practice the survival phrases near the end of this book, and even better, bring a phrase book.

**Connect with the culture.** Interacting with locals carbonates your experience. Enjoy the friendliness of the Italian people. Ask questions; most locals are happy to point you in their idea of the right direction. Set up your own quest for the best piazza, bell tower, or gelato. When an opportunity pops up, make it a habit to say "yes."

Italy...here you come!

# VENICE

*Venezia*

Soak all day in this puddle of elegant decay. Venice is Europe's best-preserved big city. This car-free urban wonderland of a hundred islands—laced together by 400 bridges and 2,000 alleys—survives on the artificial respirator of tourism.

Born in a lagoon 1,500 years ago as a refuge from barbarians, Venice is overloaded with tourists and is slowly sinking (not because of the tourists). In the Middle Ages, the Venetians became Europe's clever middlemen for East-West trade and created a great trading empire. By smuggling in the bones of St. Mark (San Marco) in AD 828, Venice gained religious importance as well. With the discovery of America and new trading routes to the Orient, Venetian power ebbed. But as Venice fell, her appetite for decadence grew. Through the 17th and 18th centuries, Venice partied on the wealth accumulated through earlier centuries as a trading power.

Today, Venice is home to fewer than 55,000 people in its old city, down from about twice that number just three decades ago. While there are about 270,000 people in greater Venice (counting the mainland, not counting tourists), the old town has a small-town feel, and locals seem to know everyone.

Venice is expensive for residents as well as tourists because everything must be shipped in and hand-trucked to its final destination. I find that the best way to enjoy Venice is to succumb to its charms, accept that prices are higher than on the mainland, and blow through a little money. It's a unique place that's worth paying a premium to fully experience.

Escape the Rialto-San Marco tourist zone and savor the town early and late, without the hordes of vacationers day-tripping in

VENICE

**Venice Overview**

To Mestre & Mainland: Treviso Airport, Padua, Vicenza & Verona

JEWISH MUSEUM ■

GHETTO

CANNAREGIO

PARKING GARAGE

TRAIN STN. & ℹ

GUGLIE BRIDGE

Grand

TRONCHETTO

CA' PESARO ■

Term. #103

BUS STN.

SANTA CROCE

SAN POLO

Term. #117

STAZIONE MARITTIMA

CALATRAVA BRIDGE

FRARI

Term. #107

Piazzale Roma

SCUOLA SAN ROCCO

Canal

500 Yards

500 Meters

Term. #106

Term. #123

CA' REZZONICO

SAN MARCO

MAIN CRUISE PORT

SAN SEBASTIANO

Santa Marta Dock

San Basilio Dock

ACCADEMIA

DORSODURO

ZATTERE

Express Boat (To San Marco)

PEGGY GUGGENHEIM COLLECTION

MOLINO STUCKY (HILTON)

Lagoon

REDENTORE

LA

from cruise ships and nearby beach resorts. A 10-minute walk from the madness puts you in an idyllic Venice that few tourists see.

## PLANNING YOUR TIME

Venice is worth at least a day on even the speediest tour. Sleep in the old center to experience Venice at its best: early and late. For a one-day visit, cruise the Grand Canal, do the major sights on St. Mark's Square (the square itself, Doge's Palace, and St. Mark's Basilica), enjoy the action at the Rialto Bridge and Rialto Market, see the Frari Church for art, and wander the back streets of the Dorsoduro district to the Accademia Bridge and back to St. Mark's Square. Enjoy an evening gondola ride and then a drink with the orchestras on St. Mark's Square. Venice's greatest sight is the city itself. While doable in a day, Venice is worth two. It's a medieval cookie jar, and nobody's looking. Make time to simply wander.

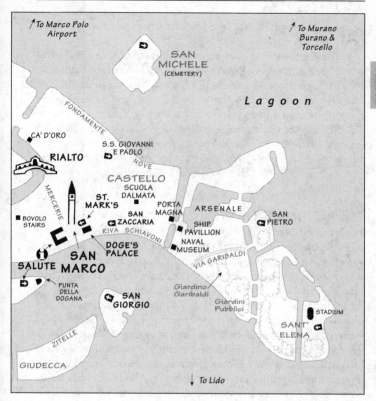

# Orientation to Venice

The island city of Venice is shaped like a fish. Its major thorough-fares are canals. The Grand Canal winds through the middle of the fish, starting at the mouth where all the people and food enter, passing under the Rialto Bridge, and ending at St. Mark's Square (Piazza San Marco). Park your 21st-century perspective at the mouth and let Venice swallow you whole.

## VENICE: A VERBAL MAP

Venice is a carless kaleidoscope of people, bridges, and odorless canals. It's made up of more than a hundred small islands—but for simplicity, I refer to the whole shebang as "the island."

Venice has six districts known as *sestieri:* San Marco (from St. Mark's Square to the Accademia Bridge), Castello (the area east of St. Mark's Square—the "tail" of the fish), Dorsoduro (the "belly," on the far side the Accademia Bridge), Cannaregio (between the train station and the Rialto Bridge), San Polo (west of the Rialto

VENICE

Bridge), and Santa Croce (the "eye" of the fish, across the canal from the train station).

The easiest way to navigate is by landmarks. Many street corners have a sign pointing you to *(per)* the nearest major landmark, such as San Marco, Accademia, Rialto, and Ferrovia (train station). Obedient visitors stick to the main thoroughfares as directed by these signs...and miss the charm of back-street Venice.

Beyond the city's core lie several other islands, including San Giorgio (with great views of Venice), Giudecca (more views), San Michele (old cemetery), Murano (famous for glass), Burano (lace-making), Torcello (old church), and the skinny Lido (with Venice's beach).

## TOURIST INFORMATION

With this chapter, a free city map from your hotel, and the events schedule on the TI's website, there's little need to make an in-person visit to a Venice TI. That's fortunate, because though the city's TIs try to help, they're understaffed and have few free printed materials to hand out. To check or confirm something, try phoning the TI information line at 041-2424 or visit www.veneziaunica.it; this website can be more helpful than the actual TI office. Other useful websites are www.visitmuve.it (city-run museums in Venice), www. unospitedivenezia.it/en (sights and events), www.veniceexplorer.net (detailed maps), www.veniceforvisitors.com (general travel advice), www.venicelink.com (travel agent selling public and private transportation tickets), and www.theveniceinsider.com (transportation tips and current events).

If you must visit a TI, you'll find four convenient branches (all are open daily): St. Mark's Square (in the far-left corner with your back to the basilica), airport, bus station (inside the huge white Autorimessa Comunale parking garage), and train station (across from track 2).

Be wary of the travel agencies or special information services that masquerade as TIs but serve fancy hotels and tour companies. They're in the business of selling things you don't need.

**Maps:** Of all places, Venice demands a good map. Hotels give away freebies (similar in quality to the small color one at the front of this book). TIs and vaporetto ticket booths sell decent €3 maps—but you can find a wider range at bookshops, newsstands, and postcard stands. The cheap maps are pretty bad, but if you spend €5, you'll get a map that shows all the tiny alleys. It may be the best money you spend in Venice. But know you'll still spend some time "exploring" (read: lost). Also consider a mapping app for your mobile phone. (City Maps 2Go and Google Maps cover Venice well.)

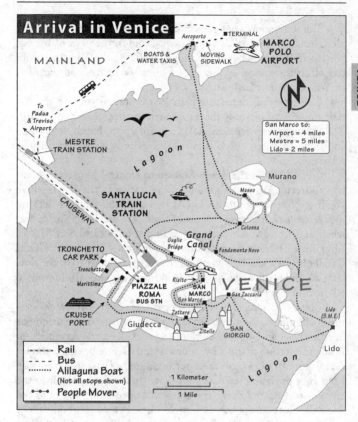

# Arrival in Venice

MAINLAND

*Aeroporto*  ■ TERMINAL

BOATS & WATER TAXIS

MOVING SIDEWALK

**MARCO POLO AIRPORT**

To Padua & Treviso Airport

MESTRE TRAIN STATION

*Lagoon*

San Marco to:
Airport = 4 miles
Mestre = 5 miles
Lido = 2 miles

Murano

*Museo*

CAUSEWAY

SANTA LUCIA TRAIN STATION

*Colonna*

*Fondamente Nove*

TRONCHETTO CAR PARK

*Guglie Bridge*

*Grand Canal*

*Tronchetto*

*Marittima*

PIAZZALE ROMA BUS STN

*Rialto*

**SAN MARCO**

*San Marco*

V E N I C E

*San Zaccaria*

CRUISE PORT

*Zattere*

Giudecca

*Zitelle*

**SAN GIORGIO**

*Lido (S.M.E.)*

Lido

*Lagoon*

Rail
--- Bus
······ Alilaguna Boat (Not all stops shown)
•─• People Mover

1 Kilometer

1 Mile

## ARRIVAL IN VENICE

A two-mile-long causeway (with highway and train lines) connects Venice to the mainland. Mestre, the sprawling mainland section of Venice, has fewer crowds, cheaper hotels, and plenty of inexpensive parking lots, but zero charm. Don't stop in Mestre unless you're changing trains, parking your car, or sleeping there.

### By Train

All trains to "Venice" stop at Venezia Mestre (on the mainland). Most continue on to **Santa Lucia Station** (a.k.a. Venezia S.L.) on the island of Venice itself. If your train happens to terminate at Mestre, you'll need to buy a €1.25 Mestre-Santa Lucia ticket and validate it before hopping any nonexpress, regional train (with an R or RV prefix) for the ride across the causeway to Venice (6/hour, 10 minutes).

Santa Lucia train station plops you right into the old town on the Grand Canal, an easy vaporetto ride or fascinating 45-minute walk (with a number of bridges and steps) to St. Mark's Square.

The station has a **baggage check** (daily 6:00-23:00, no lockers; along track 1). Pay **WCs** are at track 1 and in the back of the big bar/cafeteria area inside the station. You'll find the **TI** across from track 2. If the station TI is crowded when you arrive, visit the TI at St. Mark's Square instead.

Confirm your departure plan (at the station you can use the ticket machines or study the *partenze*/departures posters on walls). The banks of user-friendly ticket machines are handy (but cover Italian destinations only). They take euros and credit cards, display schedules, and issue tickets.

**Getting from the Train Station to Central Venice:** It's best by **vaporetto.** Walk straight out of the station to the canal, where you'll see five vaporetto docks (A, B, C, D, and E), each serving different boats. Electronic signboards show which boats are leaving when and from which dock (for example, boat #2 to San Marco, from dock B). Most tourists want the fast boat #2 down the Grand Canal to Rialto and San Marco (generally from dock B) or the slow boat #1 down the Grand Canal, making every stop all the way to Rialto and San Marco.

Buy a €7.50 ticket before you board. If ticket-window lines by the docks are too long, you can also buy from self-service machines nearby (English-language option, major credit cards accepted), or inside the station at the TI or a newsstand. Before buying a single-ride vaporetto ticket, consider getting a transit pass (see page 42). Find your dock and validate your ticket/pass by touching it to the circular pad on the dock; the gates will open to let you onto the dock. Because docks serve multiple lines, before you hop on the vaporetto, confirm with the conductor that this particular boat is going to your stop ("Rialto?").

A **water taxi** from the train station to central Venice costs about €60-80 (the taxi dock is straight ahead).

## By Bus

Venice's "bus station" is an open-air parking lot called Piazzale Roma. The square itself is a jumble of different operators, platforms, and crosswalks over busy lanes of traffic. But bus stops are well-signed. The ticket windows for ACTV (including #5 to Marco Polo Airport) are in a building between the bridge and vaporetto stop. The ATVO ticket office (express buses to Marco Polo and Treviso airports and to Padua) is at #497g in the big, white building, on the right side of the square as you face away from the canal (office open daily 6:45-19:30).

Piazzale Roma also has two big parking garages and the People Mover monorail (€1.50, links to the cruise port and then the parking-lot island of Tronchetto). A baggage-storage office is next to the monorail at #497m (€7/24 hours, daily 6:00-21:00).

If you arrive here, find the vaporetto docks (just left of the modern bridge) and take #1 or the faster #2 down the Grand Canal to reach the Rialto, Accademia, or San Marco (St. Mark's Square) stops. Electronic boards direct you to the dock you want. Before buying a single-ride vaporetto ticket, consider getting a transit pass (see page 42). If your hotel is near here or near the train station, you can get there on foot.

(see page 42).

## By Car

The freeway (monitored by speed cameras) dead-ends after crossing the causeway to Venice. At the end of the road you have two parking-garage choices: Tronchetto or Piazzale Roma. As you drive into the city, signboards with green and red lights indicate which lots are full.

**Parking at Tronchetto:** This big garage is a bit farther out, but it's a little cheaper and well-connected by vaporetto (€3-5/hour, €21/24 hours, tel. 041-520-7555, www.veniceparking.it).

From the garage, cross the street to the brick building and go right to the vaporetto dock (not well-signed, look for *ACTV*). At the dock, catch vaporetto #2 in one of two directions: via the Grand Canal (more scenic, stops at Rialto, 40 minutes to San Marco), or via Giudecca (around the city, faster, no Rialto stop, 30 minutes to San Marco).

Don't be waylaid by aggressive water-taxi boatmen. They charge €100 to take you where the vaporetto will for far less. Also avoid the travel agencies masquerading as TIs; deal only with the ticket booth at the vaporetto dock or the VèneziaUnica public transport office. If you're going to buy a local transit pass, do it now.

If you're staying near the bus or train station, you can take the €1.50 **People Mover** monorail, which brings you from Tronchetto to the bus station at Piazzale Roma. From there, it's a five-minute walk across the modern Calatrava Bridge to the train station (buy tickets with cash or credit card from machine, 3-minute trip).

**Parking at Piazzale Roma:** The two garages here are more convenient but a bit more expensive and likelier to be full. Both face the busy Piazzale Roma, where the road ends. The big white building on your right is the Autorimessa Comunale city garage (€26/24 hours, TI office in payment lobby open daily 7:30-19:30, tel. 041-272-7211, www.avmspa.it). In a back corner of the square is the private Garage San Marco (€32/24 hours, tel. 041-523-2213, www.garagesanmarco.it). At either, you'll have to give up your keys. Near the Garage San Marco, avoid the Parcheggio Sant'Andrea, which charges higher rates.

## By Plane or Cruise Ship

For information on Venice's airport and cruise ship terminal, see the end of this chapter.

## HELPFUL HINTS

**Sightseeing Tips:** Venice offers plenty of sightseeing passes, but only a few—like the Doge's Palace and Correr Museum combo-ticket—are worth the money. For more on passes and other sightseeing advice, see page 62.

**Theft Alert:** The dark, late-night streets of Venice are generally safe. Even so, pickpockets (often elegantly dressed) work the crowded main streets, docks, and vaporetti. Your biggest risk of pickpockets is inside St. Mark's Basilica, near the Accademia or Rialto bridges (especially if you're preoccupied with snapping photos), or on a tightly packed vaporetto.

A handy *polizia* station is on the right side of St. Mark's Square as you face the basilica (at #63, near Caffè Florian). To call the police, dial 113. The Venice TI handles complaints—which must be submitted in writing—about local crooks, including gondoliers, restaurants, and hotel rip-offs (complaint.apt@turismovenezia.it).

It's illegal for street vendors to sell knockoff handbags, and it's illegal for you to buy them; both you and the vendor can get big fines.

**Medical Help:** Venice's Santi Giovanni e Paolo hospital (tel. 118) is a 10-minute walk from both the Rialto and San Marco neighborhoods, located behind the big church of the same name on Fondamenta dei Mendicanti (toward Fondamente Nove). You can take vaporetto #4.1 from San Zaccaria, or #5.2 from the train station or Piazzale Roma, to the Ospedale stop. Also, a first-aid station staffed by English-speaking doctors is on St. Mark's Square, on the right-hand side as you face the basilica (at #63 next to Caffè Florian—same address as *polizia* station, daily 8:00-20:00, tel. 041-2960-784).

**Behave in Venice:** Remember that Venice is a community of about 50,000 people who welcome visitors but feel violated when tourists don't respect the city they love. The vast majority of visitors are day-trippers stampeding in, seeing the famous stuff, and stampeding out. Venetians ask a few simple rules are followed: Dress decently, don't swim in the canals, don't litter, stay on the right as you walk, and treat things as if they are both historic and fragile...because they are.

**Dress Modestly:** When visiting St. Mark's Basilica or other major churches, men, women, and even children must cover their shoulders and knees. Remove hats when entering a church.

**Picnics:** Picnicking is illegal anywhere on St. Mark's Square, and offenders can be fined. The only place nearby for a legal picnic is in Giardinetti Reali, the small bench-filled park along the waterfront west of the Piazzetta near St. Mark's Square. Elsewhere in Venice, picnicking is no problem.

**Bookstores:** In keeping with its literary heritage, Venice has classy and inviting bookstores. The small **Libreria Studium,** a block behind St. Mark's Basilica, has a carefully chosen selection of new English books, including my guidebooks (Mon-Sat 9:00-19:30, shorter hours Sun, on Calle de la Canonica at #337, tel. 041-522-2382).

Used-bookstore lovers will appreciate the funky **Acqua Alta** ("high water") bookstore, whose quirky owner Luigi has prepared for the next flood by displaying his wares in a selection of vessels, including bathtubs and a gondola. Look for the "book stairs" in his back garden (daily 9:00-20:00, large and classically disorganized selection includes prints of Venice, just beyond Campo Santa Maria Formosa on Lunga Santa Maria Formosa, Castello 5176, tel. 041-296-0841). For a solid selection of used books in English, visit **Marco Polo,** on Calle del Teatro o de l'Opera, close to the St. Mark's side of the Rialto Bridge, behind the church (daily 9:30-19:30, Cannaregio 5886a, tel. 041-522-6343).

**Public Toilets:** Handy pay WCs are near major landmarks, including St. Mark's Square (behind the Correr Museum and at the waterfront park, Giardinetti Reali), Rialto, and the Accademia Bridge. Or use free toilets at any museum you're visiting, or any café you're eating in.

**Laundry:** Across the Grand Canal from the train station is the coin-operated **Orange Self-Service Lavanderia** (daily 7:30-22:30, on Ramo de le Chioverete, Santa Croce 665b—see map on page 90, mobile 346-972-5446).

see map on page 90

VENICE

VENICE

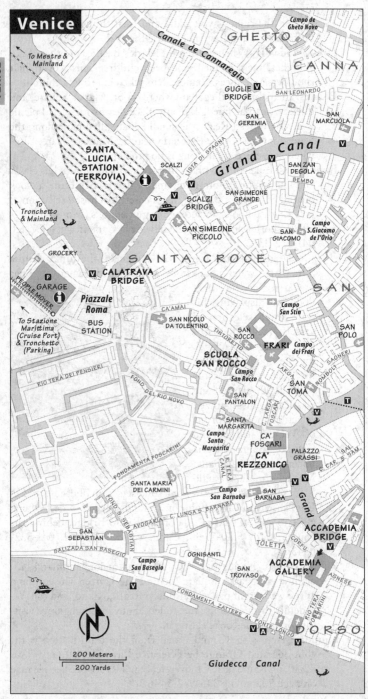

# Venice

GHETTO

Campo de
Gheto Novo

Canale de Cannaregio

CANNA

To Mestre &
Mainland

GUGLIE
BRIDGE

SAN LEONARDO

SAN
MARCUOLA

SAN
GEREMIA

Grand Canal

SANTA
LUCIA
STATION
(FERROVIA)

SCALZI

LISTA DI SPAGNA

SCALZI
BRIDGE

SAN ZAN
DEGOLA

BEMBO

To
Tronchetto
& Mainland

SAN SIMEONE
GRANDE

SAN SIMEONE
PICCOLO

SAN
GIACOMO

Campo
S.Giacomo
de l'Orio

GROCERY

SANTA CROCE

SAN

GARAGE

PEOPLE MOVER

Piazzale
Roma

CALATRAVA
BRIDGE

CA'AMAI

Campo
San Stin

To Stazione
Marittima
(Cruise Port)
& Tronchetto
(Parking)

BUS
STATION

SAN NICOLO
DA TOLENTINO

TINTORETTO

SAN
ROCCO

FRARI

Campo
dei Frari

SAN
POLO

RIO TERA DEI FENSIERI

FOND. DEL RIO NOVO

SCUOLA
SAN ROCCO

Campo
San Rocco

LARGA

ROMBOLI

SAGNERI

SAN
TOMA

SAN
PANTALON

C. LARGA
FOSCARI

T

FONDAMENTA FOSCARINI

SANTA
MARGARITA

Campo
Santa
Margarita

CA'
FOSCARI

CA'
REZZONICO

PALAZZO
GRASSI

C. CAR. B. SAM.

SANTA MARIA
DEI CARMINI

R. TERA
CANAL

Campo
San Barnaba

SAN
BARNABA

Grand

FOND. S. SEBASTIAN

AVOGARIA

C. LUNGA S. BARNABA

ACCADEMIA
BRIDGE

SAN
SEBASTIAN

OGNISANTI

TOLETTA

CORFU

ACCADEMIA
GALLERY

SALIZADA SAN BASEGIO

Campo
San Basegio

SAN
TROVASO

AGNESE

FONDAMENTA ZATTERE AL PONTE LONGO

RIO TERA
FOSCARINI

N

DORSO

A

200 Meters

200 Yards

Giudecca Canal

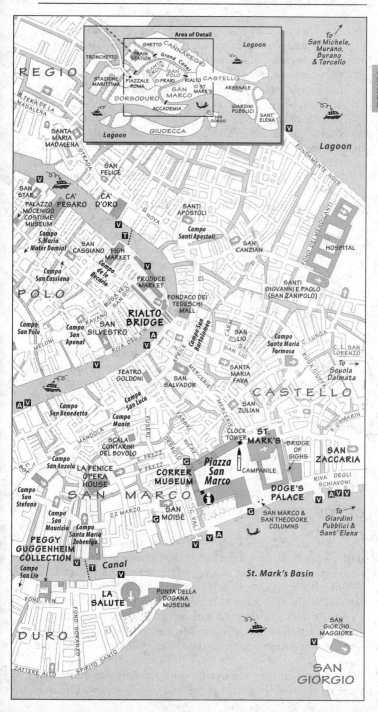

VENICE

These laundry places are near St. Mark's Square (see page 90 for locations): Self-service **Effe Erre** is off Campo Santa Maria Formosa (daily 6:30-23:30, on Ruga Giuffa, Castello 4826, mobile 349-058-3881). **Lavanderia Gabriella** offers full-service laundry, a few streets north of St. Mark's Square (drop off Mon-Fri 8:00-12:30, closed Sat-Sun; pick up 2 hours later or next working day, on Rio Terà de le Colonne, San Marco 985, tel. 041-522-1758, friendly Elisabetta).

**Best Views:** A slow vaporetto ride down the **Grand Canal**—ideally very early or just before sunset—is a shutterbug's delight. On St. Mark's Square, enjoy views from the soaring **Campanile** or the **balcony of St. Mark's Basilica** (both require admission). The **Rialto and Accademia bridges** provide expansive views of the Grand Canal, along with a cooling breeze. The luxury mall **Fondaco dei Tedeschi,** just north of the Rialto Bridge, has even better views, especially around sunset (free but book a reservation; see details on page 79). Or get off the main island for a view of the Venetian skyline: Ascend **San Giorgio Maggiore's bell tower** (admission fee), or venture to Giudecca Island to visit the swanky bar of the **Molino Stucky Hilton Hotel** (the free-to-"customers" shuttle boat leaves from near the San Zaccaria-B vaporetto dock).

**Water:** I carry a water bottle to refill at public fountains. Venetians pride themselves on having pure, safe, and tasty tap water piped in from the foothills of the Alps. You can actually see the mountains from Venice's bell towers on crisp, clear winter days.

**Pigeon Poop:** If your head is bombed by a pigeon, resist the initial response to wipe it off immediately—it'll just smear into your hair. Wait until it dries, and it should flake off cleanly. But if the poop splatters on your clothes, wipe it off immediately to avoid a stain.

## GETTING AROUND VENICE
### On Foot

The city's "streets" are narrow pedestrian walkways connecting its docks, squares, bridges, and courtyards. To navigate, look for signs on street corners pointing you to *(per)* the nearest major landmark. The first landmarks you'll get to know are San Marco (St. Mark's Square), Rialto (the bridge), Accademia (another bridge), Ferrovia ("railroad," meaning the train station), and Piazzale Roma (the bus station). Determine whether your destination is in the direction of a major, signposted landmark, then follow the signs through the maze.

As you get more comfortable with the city, dare to disobey these signs, avoid the posted routes, and make your own discoveries. While 80 percent of Venice is, in fact, not touristy, 80 percent of the tourists never notice. Escape the crowds and explore on foot. Walk and walk to the far reaches of the town.

Don't worry about getting lost—in fact, get as lost as possible. When it comes time to find your way, just follow the arrows on building corners or simply ask a local, *"Dov'è San Marco?"* ("Where is St. Mark's?") Most Venetians speak some English. If you're lost, refer to a map, or pop into a hotel and ask for their business card—it probably comes with a map and a prominent "You are here."

Every building in Venice has a house number. The numbers relate to the district (each with about 6,000 address numbers), not the street. Therefore, if you need to find a specific address, it helps to know its district, street, house number, and nearby landmarks.

Some helpful street terminology: *Campo* means square, a *campiello* is a small square, *calle* (pronounced "KAH-lay" with an "L" sound) means "street," and a *ponte* is a bridge. A *fondamenta* is the embankment along a canal or the lagoon. A *rio terà* is a street that was once a canal and has been filled in. A *sotoportego* is a covered passageway. *Salizzada* literally means a paved area (usually a wide street). The abbreviations S. and SS. mean "saint" and "saints" respectively. Don't get hung up on the exact spelling of street and square names, which may sometimes appear in Venetian dialect (which uses *de la, novo,* and *vechio*) and other times in standard Italian (which uses *della, nuovo,* and *vecchio*).

## By Vaporetto

Venice's public transit system, run by a company called ACTV, is a fleet of motorized bus-boats called vaporetti. They work like city buses except that they never get a flat, the stops are docks, and if you jump off between stops, you might drown. For the same prices, you can purchase tickets and passes at docks and from ACTV affiliate VèneziaUnica (ACTV—tel. 041-2424, www. actv.it; VèneziaUnica—www. veneziaunica.it).

### Tickets and Passes

**Individual Vaporetto Tickets:** A single ticket costs €7.50 (kids under 6 travel free). Tickets are good for 75 minutes; you can hop on and off at stops and change boats during that time. Your ticket (a paper ticket embedded with a chip) is refillable—don't toss it

# Handy Vaporetti from San Zaccaria, near St. Mark's Square

Several vaporetti leave from the San Zaccaria docks, located 150 yards east of St. Mark's Square. The four docks are spaced about 70 yards apart, with six different berths, lettered A to F. Check the big electronic board (next to the C/D dock), which indicates the departure time, line number, destination, and berth letter of upcoming vaporetti. Once you've figured out which boat you want, go to that letter berth and hop on.

**Line #1:** This vaporetto goes up the Grand Canal, making all the stops, including San Marco, Rialto, Ferrovia (train station), and Piazzale Roma (but it does not go as far as Tronchetto). In the other direction, it goes from San Zaccaria to Arsenale and Giardini before ending on the Lido (dock E).

**Line #2:** This vaporetto zips over to San Giorgio Maggiore, the island church across from St. Mark's Square (5 minutes, €5 ride). From there, it continues on to stops on the island of Giudecca, the parking lot at Tronchetto, and then down the Grand Canal (dock B). Note: You cannot ride the #2 up the Grand Canal (for example, to Rialto or the train station) directly from this stop—you'll need to walk five minutes along the waterfront, past St. Mark's Square, to the San Marco-Giardinetti dock and hop the #2 from there.

**Line #4.1:** This boat goes to San Michele and Murano (45 minutes, dock D).

**Line #7:** This is the summertime express boat to Murano (25 minutes, dock D).

**Molino Stucky Shuttle Boat:** This takes even non-guests to the Hilton Hotel, with its popular view bar (20-minute ride, 3/hour, from its own dock near the San Zaccaria-B dock).

**Lines #5.1** and **#5.2:** These are the *circulare* (cheer-koo-LAH-ray) lines, making a loop around the perimeter of the island, with a stop at the Lido—perfect if you just like riding boats. Line #5.1

after the first use. You can put more money on it at the kiosks and avoid waiting in line at the ticket window. It's also smart to keep your receipt (in case you're checked and your ticket is faulty).

**Vaporetto Passes:** You can buy a pass for unlimited use of vaporetti: €20/24 hours, €30/48 hours, €40/72 hours, €60/7-day pass (the clock starts ticking the first time you use it). Because single tickets are pricey, these passes pay for themselves in a hurry. Think through your Venice itinerary before you step up to the ticket booth to pay for your first vaporetto trip. The 48-hour pass pays for itself with five rides (for example: to your hotel on your arrival, on a Grand Canal joyride, into the lagoon and back, to the train station...and that spur-of-the-moment moonlight cruise). It's fun to be able to hop on and off spontaneously, and avoid long ticket lines.

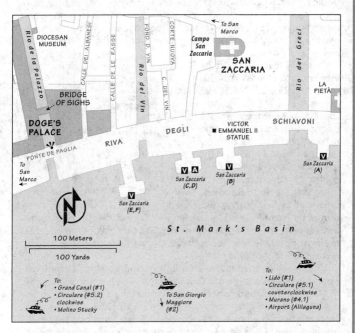

goes counterclockwise, and #5.2 goes clockwise. Both run less frequently in the evenings (#5.1 leaves from dock D, #5.2 from dock C).

**Alilaguna Shuttle Boat:** This runs to and from the airport (dock D).

Because some smaller and outlying stops are unstaffed, that's another reason to buy a pass.

Travelers between ages 14-29 can get a 72-hour pass for €22 if they also buy a **Rolling Venice** discount card for €6 (see page 63).

Passes are also valid on some of ACTV's mainland buses, including bus #2 to Mestre (but not the #5 to the airport nor the airport buses run by ATVO, a separate company). Pass holders get a discounted fare for all ACTV buses that originate or terminate at Marco Polo Airport (see page 120).

**Buying and Validating Tickets and Passes:** Purchase tickets and passes from the machines at most stops (English-language option, major credit cards accepted), from ticket windows (at larger

# Is Venice Sinking?

Venice has battled rising water levels since the fifth century. But today, the water seems to be winning. Several factors, both natural and man-made, cause Venice to flood dozens of times a year—usually from October until late winter—a phenomenon called the *acqua alta.*

On my last trip I asked a Venetian how much the city is sinking. He said, "Less than the sea is rising." Venice sits atop sediments deposited at the ancient mouth of the Po River, which are still compacting and settling. Early industrial projects, such as offshore piers and the railroad bridge to the mainland, affected the sea floor and tidal cycles in ways that made the city more vulnerable to flooding. Twentieth-century industry worsened things by pumping massive amounts of groundwater out of the aquifer beneath the lagoon for nearly 50 years before the government stopped the practice in the 1970s. In the last century, Venice has sunk by about nine inches.

Meanwhile, the waters around Venice are rising, a phenomenon that's especially apparent in winter. The highest so far was in November of 1966, when a huge storm (the same one that famously flooded Florence) raised Venice's water level to more than six feet above the norm. The notorious *acqua alta* happens when an unusually high tide combines with strong sirocco winds and a storm. Although tides are minuscule in the Mediterranean, the narrow, shallow Adriatic Sea has about a three-foot tidal range. When a storm—an area of low pressure—travels over a body of water, it pulls the surface of the water up into a dome. As strong sirocco winds from Africa blow storms north up the Adriatic, they push this high water ahead of the front, causing a surging storm tide. Add to that the worldwide sea-level rise that's resulted from recent climate change (melting ice caps, thermal expansion of the water, more frequent and more powerful storms) and it makes a high sea that much higher.

If the *acqua alta* appears during your visit, you'll see the first puddles in the center of paved squares, pooling around the lime-

stops), or from the VèneziaUnica offices at the train station, bus station, and Tronchetto parking lot.

Before you board, validate your ticket or pass by touching it to the small white pad on the dock until you hear a pinging sound. With passes, you need to touch the pass each time you board a boat. The machine readout shows how long your ticket is valid—and inspectors do come by now and then to check tickets. If you're

stone grates at the square's lowest point. These grates cover cisterns that long held Venice's only source of drinking water. That's right: Surrounded by the lagoon and beset by constant flooding, this city had no natural source of fresh water. For centuries, residents carried water from the mainland with much effort and risk. In the ninth century, they devised a way to collect rainwater by using paved, cleverly sloped squares as catchment systems, with limestone filters covering underground clay tubs. Venice's population grew markedly once citizens were able to access fresh water by simply dropping buckets down into these "wells." Hundreds of cisterns provided the city with drinking water up until 1884, when an aqueduct was built (paralleling the railroad bridge) to bring in water from nearby mountains. Now the wells are capped, the clay tubs are rotted out, and rain drains from squares into the lagoon—or up from it, as the case may be.

So, what is Venice doing about the flooding? After the 1966 flood, officials knew something had to be done, but it took about four decades to come up with a solution. In 2003, a consortium of engineering firms began construction on the MOSE Project. Named for the acronym of its Italian name, Modulo Sperimentale Elettromeccanico, it's also a nod to Moses and his (albeit temporary) mastery over the sea.

Underwater "mobile" gates are being installed on the floor of the sea at the three inlets where the open sea enters Venice's lagoon. When the seawater rises above a certain level, air will be pumped into the gates, causing them to rise and shut out the Adriatic. The first gates are already installed and on the verge of becoming operational. But, in good Italian fashion, greedy government officials were unable to resist the opportunity for personal enrichment and a corruption scandal has stranded the entire project for the foreseeable future.

unable to purchase a ticket before boarding, seek out the conductor immediately to buy a single ticket (or risk a €60 fine).

### Important Vaporetto Lines

For most travelers, only two vaporetto lines matter: **line #1** and **line #2.** These lines leave every 10 minutes or so and go up and down the Grand Canal, between the "mouth" of the fish at one end and St. Mark's Square at the other. Line #1 is the slow boat, taking

45 minutes and making every stop along the way. Line #2 is the fast boat that zips down the Grand Canal in 25 minutes, stopping only at Tronchetto (parking lot), Piazzale Roma (bus station), Ferrovia (train station), Rialto Bridge, San Tomà (Frari Church), San Samuele (opposite Ca' Rezzonico), Accademia Bridge, and San Marco (west end of St. Mark's Square, end of the line).

Take time to study the maps at docks before you board. Some boats run on circular routes, in one direction only (for example, lines #5.1 and #5.2, plus the non-Murano sections of lines #4.1 and #4.2). Line #2 runs in both directions and is almost, but not quite, a full loop. The #2 boat leaving from the San Marco stop goes in one direction (up the Grand Canal), while from the San Zaccaria stop—just a five-minute walk away—it goes in the opposite direction (around the tail of the "fish"). Make sure you use the correct stop to avoid taking the long way around to your destination.

To clear up any confusion, ask a ticket-seller or conductor for help (sometimes they're stationed on the dock to help confused tourists). Get a copy of the most current ACTV map and timetable (in English and Italian, download from www.actv.it, theoretically free at ticket booths but often unavailable). System maps are posted at stops, but it's smart to print out your own copy of the map from the ACTV website before your trip.

## Boarding and Riding

Once you know which line you want, you need to find the right departure platform (many stops have more than one). At these larger stops, check the electronic departure board to see which boats are coming next, when, where they're going, and from which platform they leave (for example, "Line 2 to San Marco, from platform B"). At smaller

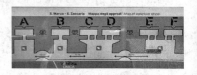

stops without electronic displays, signs on each platform show the vaporetto lines that stop there and the direction they are headed. Once you find your platform, be aware that other boats may also be leaving from the same platform. When the boat arrives, confirm the direction posted on the bow ("Line 2, San Marco"). To double-check, ask the conductor when you board ("San Marco?").

## Crowd-Beating Tips

For fun, take my self-guided Grand Canal Cruise. But be warned: Grand Canal vaporetti can be absolutely jam-packed, especially during the tourist rush hour (during mornings heading in from Piazzale Roma, and in evenings heading out to Piazzale Roma). Riding at night, with nearly empty boats and chandelier-lit palace interiors viewable from the Grand Canal, can be a highlight of your Venetian experience.

## By *Traghetto*

Only four bridges cross the Grand Canal, but *traghetti* (shuttle gondolas) ferry locals and in-the-know tourists across the Grand Canal at three additional locations (see the map on page 38). Just step in, hand the gondolier €2, and enjoy the ride—standing or sitting. Some *traghetti* are seasonal, some stop running as early as 12:30, and all stop by 18:00. *Traghetti* are not covered by any transit pass.

## By Water Taxi

Venetian taxis, like speedboat limos, hang out at busy points along the Grand Canal. Prices are regulated: €15 for pickup, then €2 per minute; €5 per person for more than four passengers (boats can carry around 10 people); and €10 between 22:00 and 6:00. If you have more bags than passengers, the extra ones cost €5 apiece. (For information on taking the water taxi to/from the airport, see page 119.) Despite regulation, prices can be soft; negotiate and settle on the price or rate before stepping in. For travelers with lots of luggage or small groups who can split the cost, taxi boat rides can be a worthwhile and time-saving convenience—and skipping across the lagoon in a classic wooden motorboat is a cool indulgence. For about €120 an hour, you can have a private, unguided taxi-boat tour. You may find more competitive rates if you prebook through the Consorzio Motoscafi water taxi association (tel. 041-522-2303, www.motoscafivenezia.it).

## By Gondola

If you're interested in hiring a gondolier for your own private cruise, see page 84.

# Tours in Venice

Local guides and tour companies offer plenty of walking tours that cater to a variety of interests.

🎧 To sightsee on your own, download my series of free audio tours that illuminate some of Venice's top sights and neighborhoods (see the sidebar on page 26 for details).

VENICE

**VENICE**

# Venice at a Glance

▲▲▲**St. Mark's Square** Venice's grand main square. See page 63.

▲▲▲**St. Mark's Basilica** Cathedral with mosaics, saint's bones, treasury, museum, and viewpoint of square. **Hours:** Mon-Sat 9:30-17:00, Sun 14:00-17:00 (Sun until 16:30 Nov-Easter). See page 66.

▲▲▲**Doge's Palace** Art-splashed palace of former rulers, with prison accessible through Bridge of Sighs. **Hours:** Sun-Thu 8:30-21:00, Fri-Sat until 23:00, Nov-March daily until 19:00. See page 70.

▲▲▲**Rialto Bridge** Distinctive bridge spanning the Grand Canal, with a market nearby. **Hours:** Market—souvenir stalls open daily, produce market closed Sun, fish market closed Sun-Mon. See page 79.

▲▲**Correr Museum** Venetian history and art. **Hours:** Daily 10:00-19:00, Nov-March 10:30-17:00. See page 73.

▲▲**Accademia** Venice's top art museum. **Hours:** Tue-Sun 8:15-19:15, Mon until 14:00. See page 76.

▲▲**Peggy Guggenheim Collection** Popular display of 20th-century art. **Hours:** Wed-Mon 10:00-18:00, closed Tue. See page 77.

▲▲**Frari Church** Franciscan church featuring Renaissance masters. **Hours:** Mon-Sat 9:00-18:00, Sun from 13:00. See page 79.

▲▲**Scuola San Rocco** "Tintoretto's Sistine Chapel." **Hours:** Daily 9:30-17:30. See page 81.

▲▲**Ca' Rezzonico** Posh Grand Canal palazzo with 18th-century Venetian art. **Hours:** Wed-Mon 10:00-18:00, Nov-March until 17:00, closed Tue year-round. See page 78.

## Avventure Bellissime Venice Tours

This company offers several small-group, English-only tours, including a basic two-hour St. Mark's Square introduction called the "Original Venice Walking Tour" (€25, includes church entry, most days at 11:00, Sun at 14:00), a 65-minute boat tour of the Grand Canal (€48, daily at 16:00, 10 people maximum), a Rialto Market-area food-and-wine tour (€69, in summer 3/week at 11:15), and mainland excursions (RS%—10 percent discount, contact them

**VENICE**

▲**Campanile** Dramatic bell tower on St. Mark's Square with elevator to the top. **Hours:** Daily 8:30-21:00, Sept-mid-Oct until sunset, mid-Oct-April 9:30-17:30. See page 73.

▲**Bridge of Sighs** Famous enclosed bridge, part of Doge's Palace, near St. Mark's Square. **Hours:** Always viewable. See page 73.

▲**La Salute Church** Striking church dedicated to the Virgin Mary. **Hours:** Daily 9:30-12:00 & 15:00-17:30. See page 78.

▲**Punta della Dogana** Museum of contemporary art. **Hours:** Wed-Mon 10:00-19:00, closed Tue. See page 78.

▲**Fondaco dei Tedeschi View Terrace** Rooftop terrace atop luxury mall, with views over the Grand Canal. **Hours:** Daily 10:15-19:30, June-Aug until 20:15, Nov-March until 19:15. See page 79.

## Nearby Islands

▲▲**Burano** Sleepy island known for lacemaking and lace museum. **Hours:** Museum open Tue-Sun 10:30-17:00, Nov-March until 16:30, closed Mon year-round. See page 84.

▲**San Giorgio Maggiore** Island facing St. Mark's Square, featuring dreamy church and fine views back on Venice. **Hours:** Daily 9:00-19:00, Nov-March 8:30-18:00. See page 76.

▲**Murano** Island famous for glass factories and glassmaking museum. **Hours:** Glass Museum open daily 10:30-18:30, Nov-March until 16:30. See page 83.

▲**Torcello** Near-deserted island with old church, bell tower, and museum. **Hours:** Church open daily 10:30-18:00, Nov-Feb 10:00-17:00, museum closed Mon. See page 84.

before booking for a promo code; details at www.tours-italy.com, tel. 041-970-499, info@tours-italy.com).

## Alessandro's Classic Venice Bars Backstreets Tours

Alessandro Schezzini is a connoisseur of Venetian *bacari*—classic old bars serving wine and traditional *cicchetti* snacks. He organizes two-hour Venetian bar tours (€35/person, most nights at 18:00) that include sampling *cicchetti* with wines at three *bacari*. (If you think of this tour as a light dinner with a local friend, it's a particularly good value.)

Alessandro is not a licensed guide, so he can't take you into sights. But his 1.5-hour Backstreets Tour gets you into offbeat Venice (€20/person, most nights at 16:30).

Both tours depart almost daily in season when six or more sign up. They meet 50 yards north of the Rialto Bridge under the big clock on Campo San Giacomo. (Book via email, alessandro@schezzini.it, or by phone at 335-530-9024; www.schezzini.it.)

### Venice Bites Food Tours

Adam and Maya Stonecastle are expats from Los Angeles who enjoy sharing their adopted community and their love for *cicchetti* culture with travelers. Their two 3.5-hour food tours—usually led by both Adam and Maya—include lots of walking and fun insights. On their lunch tour, you'll munch and drink at 7 spots from the Accademia to the Rialto Bridge (€105/person, most days at 11:00, 10 people maximum). The dinner walk loops out and back from the Rialto Bridge, stopping at 5 or 6 places (€112/person, RS%—€15 off if you book online with discount code "RICKSTEVES"; tours run most nights at 18:00, 8 people maximum, tel. 800-656-0713, www.venicebitesfoodtours.com).

### Venicescapes

Michael Broderick's private, themed tours of Venice are intellectually demanding and engrossing for history buffs. Michael, a passionate teacher, has spent nearly 30 years living and studying in Venice. He's an instinctive "dot connector," so his tours intertwine history, art, politics, economics, culture, and religion (various 4- to 6-hour itineraries, 2 people—$280-320 or the euro equivalent, $60/person after that, admissions and transport extra, tel. 041-850-5742, mobile 349-479-7406, www.venicescapes.org, info@venicescapes.org).

### Local Guides

Plenty of licensed, trained guides are available (figure on €75/hour with a 2-hour minimum). I've enjoyed working with the following guides and groups:

**Walks Inside Venice** is enthusiastic about teaching (€280/3 hours per group of up to 6, RS%; Roberta: mobile 347-253-0560; Sara: mobile 335-522-9714; www.walksinsidevenice.com, info@walksinsidevenice.com).

**Elisabetta Morelli** and **Corine Govi,** who run **2Guides4Venice,** are informative and reliable (Elisabetta: mobile 328-753-5220, bettamorelli@inwind.it; Corine: mobile 347-966-8346, corine_g@libero.it; www.2guides4venice.com).

**Venice with a Guide,** a co-op of eight good Venetian guides, offers a range of tours (€75/hour, www.venicewithaguide.com).

**BestVeniceGuides.it** offers a smartly organized online catalog of about 100 local guides, with information to help you pick the right guide for you. Note that Italy allows all licensed guides to lead tours anywhere in the country, so it behooves the thoughtful traveler to book a Venetian guide for the best Venetian experience (family-friendly guides, shared group tours available, most guides about €75/hour, www.bestveniceguides.it).

# Grand Canal Cruise

Take a joyride and introduce yourself to Venice by boat, an experience worth ▲▲▲. Cruise the Canal Grande all the way to St. Mark's Square, starting at the train station (Ferrovia) or the bus station (Piazzale Roma, where you're more likely to find an empty seat). Consider topping it off with my self-guided tour of St. Mark's Basilica (later, under "Sights in Venice").

If it's your first trip down the Grand Canal, you might want to stow this book and just take it all in—Venice is a barrage on the senses that hardly needs narration. On the other hand, these notes give the cruise meaning and help orient you to this great city.

This tour is designed to be done on the slow boat #1. The express boat #2 travels the same route, but it skips many stops, making this tour hard to follow and hop-on/hop-off sightseeing impossible.

To help you enjoy the visual parade of canal wonders, the tour is organized by boat stop. I'll point out both what you can see from the current stop, and what to look forward to as you cruise to the next stop. Because it's hard to see everything in one go, you may want to do this tour twice (perhaps once in either direction).

You can break up the tour by hopping on and off at various sights—but remember, a single-fare vaporetto ticket is good for just 75 minutes (passes let you hop on and off all day).

**Length of This Tour:** Allow 45 minutes.

**Tours:** ∩ Download my free Grand Canal Cruise audio tour.

**Seating Strategies:** As the vaporetti can be jammed, strategize about where to sit—then, when the boat pulls up, make a beeline for your preference. You're more likely to find an empty seat if you catch the vaporetto at Piazzale Roma—the stop *before* Ferrovia.

A few remaining older vaporetti have seats in the bow (in front of the captain's bridge), the perfect vantage point for spotting sights left, right, and forward. With a standard boat and normal crowds, I'd head for the open-air section in the stern and grab the middle

VENICE

# Grand Canal

**Vaporetto Stops**
1. Ferrovia
2. Riva de Biasio
3. San Marcuola
4. San Stae
5. Ca' d'Oro
6. Rialto Mercato
7. Rialto
8. San Silvestro
9. Sant'Angelo
10. San Tomà
11. Ca' Rezzonico
12. Accademia
13. Santa Maria del Giglio
14. Salute
15. San Marco
16. San Zaccaria

**Traghetto Stops**
A. Traghetto Santa Sofia
B. Traghetto San Tomà
C. Traghetto Santa Maria del Giglio

Lagoon

FONDAMENTE NOVE

NOVA

200 Meters

200 Yards

N

PALAZZO MARCELLO

PALAZZO MOLIN

PALAZZO ZULLAN

**4**

CANNAREGIO

PALAZZO GIUSTI

PALAZZO SAGREDO

PALAZZO MICHIEL COLONNE

**SAN STAE**

PALAZZO BARBARIGO

PALAZZO FONTANA

PALAZZO DONÀ

CA' PESARO

PALAZZO FAVRETTO

CA' D'ORO

STRADA NOVA

**5**

**A**

T

PALAZZO VALMARANA

PALAZZO CA' DA MOSTO

PALAZZO CORNER DELLA REGINA

PALAZZO BRANDOLIN

**FISH MARKET**

**6**

PALAZZO CIVRAN

**PRODUCE MARKET**

POLO

FONDACO DEI TEDESCHI MALL

**RIALTO BRIDGE**

**A**

SAL. S. LIO

S. MARIA FORMOSA

**7**

PALAZZO PAPADOPOLI

PALAZZO BARZIZZA

PALAZZO DOLFIN-MANIN

PALAZZO BEMBO

MERCERIE

**8**

PALAZZO DONÀ

PALAZZO CORNER-CONTARINI

PALAZZO FARSETTI-DANDOLO

CASTELLO

PALAZZO BERNARDO

PALAZZO BENZON

PALAZZO MARTINENGO

PALAZZO GRIMANI

PALAZZO CORNER-SPINELLI

FABBRI

MERCERIE

**CAMPANILE**

**ST. MARK'S BASILICA**

BRIDGE OF SIGHS

**SAN MARCO**

**DOGE'S PALACE**

**16**

SAN MARCO

CALLE LARGA XXII MARZO

SAN MARCO & SAN TEODORO COLUMNS

HARRY'S AMERICAN BAR

**15**

**A**

To Lido

CA' GRANDE

**GRITTI PALACE HOTEL**

PALAZZO FLANGINI

**13**

**C**

Grand

T

Canal

St. Mark's Basin

PALAZZO DARIO

PALAZZO GENOVESE

**14**

LA SALUTE CHURCH

**PEGGY GUGGENHEIM COLLECTION**

PUNTA DELLA DOGANA MUSEUM

To San Giorgio Maggiore & Giudecca

seat. While views directly ahead are obliterated by the boat's cabin, you'll have a good view of my described sights on both sides of the boat. If it's not crowded, you can hang out in the middle (loading zone) and bop from side to side (especially easy after dark). Your worst option is sitting inside and trying to look out the window.

## OVERVIEW

The Grand Canal is Venice's "Main Street." At more than two miles long, nearly 150 feet wide, and nearly 15 feet deep, it's the city's largest canal, lined with its most impressive palaces. It's the remnant of a river that once spilled from the mainland into the Adriatic. The sediment it carried formed barrier islands that cut Venice off from the sea, forming a lagoon.

Venice was built on the marshy islands of the former delta, sitting on wood pilings driven nearly 15 feet into the clay (alder was the preferred wood). About
25 miles of canals drain the city, dumping like streams into the Grand Canal. Technically, Venice has only three canals: Grand, Giudecca, and Can- naregio. The 45 small waterways that dump into the Grand Canal are referred to as rivers (e.g., Rio Novo).

Venice is a city of palaces, dating from the days when the city was the world's richest. The most lavish palaces formed a grand architectural cancan along the Grand Canal. Once frescoed in reds and blues, with black-and-white borders and gold-leaf trim, they made Venice a city of dazzling color. This cruise is the only way to truly appreciate the palaces, approaching them at water level, where their main entrances were located. Today, strict laws prohibit any changes in these buildings, so while landowners gnash their teeth, we can enjoy Europe's best-preserved medieval/Renaissance city—slowly rotting. Many of the grand buildings are now vacant. Others harbor chandeliered elegance above mossy, empty (often flooded) ground floors.

## ❷ SELF-GUIDED CRUISE

This tour starts at the Ferrovia vaporetto stop (at Santa Lucia train station). The #1 boat to San Marco generally leaves from dock E (far to the right).

**❶ Ferrovia:** This site has been the gateway into Venice since 1860, when the first train station was built. The Santa Lucia sta- tion, one of the few modern buildings in town, was built in 1954. The "F.S." logo above the entry stands for "Ferrovie dello Stato,"

the Italian state railway system. Consider that before the causeway was built in the mid-1800s, Venice was an island with no road or train access and no water system. With the causeway the city got a train line, an aqueduct, and a highway.

VENICE

More than 20,000 people a day commute in from the mainland, making this the busiest part of Venice during rush hour. The nearby Calatrava Bridge, spanning the Grand Canal between the train station and Piazzale Roma upstream, was built in 2008 to alleviate some of the congestion.

❷ **Riva de Biasio:** Venice's main thoroughfare is busy with all kinds of boats: taxis, police boats, garbage boats, ambulances, construction cranes, and even brown-and-white UPS boats. Somehow they all manage to share the canal in relative peace.

About 25 yards past the Riva de Biasio stop, look left down the broad Cannaregio Canal to see what was the Jewish Ghetto. The twin, pale-pink, six-story "skyscrapers"—the tallest buildings you'll see at this end of the canal—are reminders of how densely populated the world's original ghetto was. Set aside as the local Jewish quarter in 1516, this area became extremely crowded. This urban island developed into one of the most closely knit business and cultural quarters of all the Jewish communities in Italy, and gave us our word "ghetto" (from *geto,* the copper foundry located here).

❸ **San Marcuola:** At this stop, facing a tiny square just ahead, stands the unfinished Church of San Marcuola, one of only five churches fronting the Grand Canal. Centuries ago, this canal was a commercial drag of expensive real estate in high demand by wealthy merchants. About 20 yards ahead on the right (across the Grand Canal) stands the stately gray Turkish Exchange (Fondaco dei Turchi), one

of the oldest houses in Venice. Its horseshoe arches and roofline of triangles and dingle balls are reminders of its Byzantine heritage. Turkish traders in turbans docked here, unloaded their goods into the warehouse on the bottom story, then went upstairs for a home-style meal and a place to sleep. Venice in the 1500s was very cosmopolitan, welcoming every religion and ethnicity, so long as they carried cash. (Today the building contains the city's Museum of Natural History—and Venice's only dinosaur skeleton.)

Just 100 yards ahead on the left (the tallest building with the red canopy), Venice's Casinò is housed in the palace where German composer Richard *(The Ring)* Wagner died in 1883. See his distinct, strong-jawed profile in the white plaque on the brick wall. In the 1700s, Venice was Europe's Vegas, with casinos and prostitutes everywhere. *Casinòs* ("little houses" in Venetian dialect) have long provided Italians with a handy escape from daily life. Today they're run by the state to keep Mafia influence at bay. Notice the fancy front porch, rolling out the red carpet for high rollers arriving by taxi or hotel boat. Across the canal, the plain brick 15th-century building was a granary. Now it's a grade school.

**❹ San Stae:** The San Stae Church sports a delightful Baroque facade. Opposite the San Stae stop is a little canal opening—on the second building to the right of that opening, look for the peeling plaster that once made up frescoes (you can barely distinguish the scant remains of little angels on the lower floors). Imagine the facades of the Grand Canal at their finest. Most of them would have been covered in frescoes by the best artists of the day. As colorful as the city is today, it's still only a faded, sepia-toned remnant of a long-gone era, a time of lavishly decorated, brilliantly colored palaces.

Just ahead (on the right, with blue posts) is the ornate white facade of Ca' Pesaro (which houses the International Gallery of Modern Art). *"Ca'"* is short for *casa* (house).

In this city of masks, notice how the rich marble facades along the Grand Canal mask what are generally just simple, no-nonsense brick buildings. Most merchants enjoyed showing off. However, being smart businessmen, they only decorated the sides of the buildings that would be seen and appreciated. But look back as you pass Ca' Pesaro. It's the only building you'll see with a fine side facade. Ahead (about 100 yards on the left) is Ca' d'Oro, with its glorious triple-decker medieval arcade (just before the next stop).

**❺ Ca' d'Oro:** The lacy Ca' d'Oro (House of Gold) is the best example of Venetian Gothic architecture on the canal. Although a simple brick construction, its facade is one of the city's finest. Its three stories offer different variations on balcony design, topped with a spiny white roofline. Venetian Gothic mixes traditional

VENICE

Gothic (pointed arches and round medallions stamped with a four-leaf clover) with Byzantine styles (tall, narrow arches atop thin columns), filled in with Islamic frills. Like all the palaces, this was originally painted and gilded to make it even more glorious than it is now. Today the Ca' d'Oro is an art gallery.

Look at the Venetian chorus line of palaces in front of the boat. On the right is the arcade of the covered fish market, with the open-air produce market just beyond. It bustles in the morning but is quiet the rest of the day. This is a great scene to wander through—even though European Union hygiene standards have made it cleaner and less colorful than it once was.

Find the *traghetto* gondola ferrying shoppers—standing like Washington crossing the Delaware—back and forth. While once

much more numerable, today only three *traghetto* crossings survive along the Grand Canal, each one marked by a classy low-key green-and-black sign. Piloting a *traghetto* isn't the normal day job of these gondoliers. As a public service, all gondoliers are obliged to row a *traghetto* a few days a month. Make a point to use them. At €2 a ride, *traghetti* offer the cheapest gondola ride in Venice (but at this price, don't expect them to sing to you).

❻ **Rialto Mercato:** This stop serves the busy market. The long, official-looking building at the stop is the Venice courthouse. Directly ahead (on the left), is the Fondaco dei Tedeschi—the former German Exchange (a trading center for German merchants in the 16th century). Later the central post office, it's now a luxury shopping mall with great rooftop views. Rising above it is the tip of the Campanile (bell tower), crowned by its golden-angel weathervane at St. Mark's Square, where this tour will end.

You'll cruise by some trendy and beautifully situated wine bars on the right, but look ahead as you round the corner and see the impressive Rialto Bridge come into view.

A major landmark, the Rialto Bridge is lined with shops and

tourists. Constructed in 1588, it's the third bridge built on this spot. Until the 1850s, this was the only bridge crossing the Grand Canal. With a span of 160 feet and foundations stretching 650 feet on either side, the Rialto was an impressive engineering feat in its day. Earlier bridges here could open

to let big ships in, but not this one. By the time it was completed in the 16th century, Venetian trading power was ebbing. After that, much of the Grand Canal was closed to shipping and became a canal of palaces.

When gondoliers pass under the fat arch of the Rialto Bridge, they take full advantage of its acoustics: *"Volare, oh, oh..."*

**❼ Rialto:** A separate town in the early days of Venice, Rialto has always been the commercial district, while San Marco was the religious and governmental center. Today, a winding street called the Mercerie connects the two, providing travelers with human traffic jams and a mesmerizing gauntlet of shopping temptations. This is one of the only stretches of the historic Grand Canal with landings upon which you can walk. Boats unloaded the city's basic necessities here: oil, wine, charcoal, iron. Today, the quay is lined with tourist-trap restaurants.

Venice's sleek, black, graceful gondolas are a symbol of the city. With about 500 gondoliers joyriding amid the churning vaporetti, there's a lot of congestion on the Grand Canal. Pay attention—this is where most of the gondola and vaporetto accidents take place. While the Rialto is the highlight of many gondola rides, gondoliers understandably prefer the quieter small canals. Watch your vaporetto driver curse the better-paid gondoliers.

Ahead 100 yards on the left, two gray-colored palaces stand side by side (City Hall and the mayor's office). Their horseshoe-shaped, arched windows are similar and their stories are the same height, lining up to create the effect of one long balcony.

**❽ San Silvestro:** We now enter a long stretch of important merchants' palaces, each with proud and different facades. Because ships couldn't navigate beyond the Rialto Bridge, the biggest palaces—with the major shipping needs—line this last stretch of the navigable Grand Canal.

Palaces like these were multifunctional: ground floor for the warehouse, offices and showrooms upstairs, and living quarters above, on the "noble floors" (with big windows to allow in maximum light). Servants lived and worked on the very top floors (with the smallest windows). For fire-safety reasons, kitchens were also located on the top floors. Peek into the noble floors to catch a glimpse of their still-glorious chandeliers of Murano glass.

The Palazzo Grimani (across from the San Silvestro dock) sports a heavy white Roman-style facade—a reminder that the Grimani family included a cardinal and had strong Roman connections.

The Palazzo Papadopoli, with the two obelisks on its roof (50 yards beyond the San Silvestro stop on the right, with the blue posts), is the very fancy Aman Hotel where George and Amal Clooney were married in 2014.

❾ **Sant'Angelo:** Notice how many buildings have a foundation of waterproof white stone *(pietra d'Istria)* upon which the bricks sit high and dry. Many canal-level floors are abandoned as the rising water level takes its toll.

The posts—historically painted gaily with the equivalent of family coats of arms—don't rot underwater. But the wood at the waterline, where it's exposed to oxygen, does. On the smallest canals, little "no motorboats" signs indicate that these canals are for gondolas only (no motorized craft, 5 kph speed limit, no wake).

❿ **San Tomà:** Fifty yards ahead, on the right side (with twin obelisks on the rooftop) stands Palazzo Balbi, the palace of an early-17th-century captain general of the sea. This palace, like so many in the city, flies three flags: Italy (green-white-red), the European Union (blue with ring of stars), and Venice (a lion on a field of red and gold). Today it houses the administrative headquarters of the regional government.

Just past the admiral's palace, look immediately to the right, down a side canal. On the right side of that canal, before the bridge, see the traffic light and the fire station (the 1930s Mussolini-era building with four arches hiding fireboats parked and ready to go).

The impressive Ca' Foscari, with a classic Venetian facade (on the corner, across from the fire station), dominates the bend in the canal. This is the main building of the University of Venice, which has about 25,000 students. Notice the el-

egant lamp on the corner—needed in the old days to light this intersection.

The grand, heavy, white Ca' Rezzonico, just before the stop of the same name, houses the Museum of 18th-Century Venice. Across the canal is the cleaner and leaner Palazzo Grassi, the last major palace built on the canal, erected in the late 1700s. It was purchased by a French tycoon and now displays part of Punta della Dogana's contemporary art collection.

**⓫ Ca' Rezzonico:** Up ahead, the Accademia Bridge leads over the Grand Canal to the Accademia Gallery (right side), filled with the best Venetian paintings. There was no bridge here until 1854, when a cast-iron one was built. It was replaced with this wooden bridge in 1933. While meant to be temporary, it still stands today, nearly a century later.

**⓬ Accademia:** From here, look through the graceful bridge and way ahead to enjoy a classic view of La Salute Church, topped

by a crown-shaped dome supported by scrolls. This Church of St. Mary of Good Health was built to ask God to deliver Venetians from the devastating plague of 1630 (which had killed about a third of the city's population).

The low, white building among greenery (100 yards ahead, on the right, between the Accademia Bridge and the church) is the Peggy Guggenheim Collection. The American heiress "retired" here, sprucing up a palace that had been abandoned in mid-construction. Peggy willed the city her fine collection of modern art.

Two doors past the Guggenheim, Palazzo Dario has a great set of characteristic funnel-shaped chimneys. These forced embers through a loop-the-loop channel until they were dead—required in the days when stone palaces were surrounded by humble wooden buildings, and a live spark could make a merchant's workforce homeless. Three doors later is the Salviati building, which once served as a glassworks. Its fine Art Nouveau

mosaic, done in the early 20th century, features Venice as a queen being appreciated by the big shots of society.

**⓭ Santa Maria del Giglio:** Back on the left stands the fancy

Gritti Palace hotel. Hemingway and Woody Allen both stayed here.

Take a deep whiff of Venice. What's all this nonsense about stinky canals? All I smell is my shirt. By the way, how's your captain? Smooth dockings?

**⑭ Salute:** The huge La Salute Church towers overhead as if squirted from a can of Catholic Reddi-wip.

As the Grand Canal opens up into the lagoon, the last building on the right with the golden ball is the 17th-century Customs House, which now houses the Punta della Dogana contemporary art museum. Its two bronze Atlases hold a statue of Fortune riding the ball. Arriving ships stopped here to pay their tolls.

**⑮ San Marco:** Up ahead on the left, the green pointed tip of the Campanile marks St. Mark's Square, the political and reli-

gious center of Venice...and the final destination of this tour. You could get off at the San Marco stop and go straight to St. Mark's Square. But I'm staying on the boat for one more stop, just past St. Mark's Square (it's a quick walk back).

Survey the lagoon. Opposite St. Mark's Square, across the water, the ghostly white church with the pointy bell tower is San Giorgio Maggiore, with great views of Venice. Next to it is the residential island Giudecca, stretching from close to San Giorgio Maggiore past the Venice youth hostel (with a nice view, directly across) to the Hilton Hotel (good nighttime view, far right end of island).

Still on board? If you are, as we leave the San Marco stop look left and prepare for a drive-by view of St. Mark's Square. First comes the bold white facade of the old mint (in front of the bell tower) marked by a tiny cupola yet as sturdy as Fort Knox, where Venice's golden ducat, the "dollar" of the Venetian Republic, was made. Next door is the library, its facade just three windows wide. Then comes the city's ceremonial front door: twin columns topped by St. Theodore standing on a crocodile and the winged lion of St. Mark, who've welcomed visitors since the 15th century. Between the columns, catch a glimpse of two giant figures atop the Clock Tower—they've been whacking their clappers every hour since 1499. The domes of St. Mark's Basilica are soon eclipsed by the lacy facade of the Doge's Palace. Next you'll see many gondolas with their green breakwater buoys, the Bridge of Sighs (leading from the palace to the prison—check out the maximum-security bars), and finally the grand harborside promenade—the Riva.

Follow the Riva with your eye, past elegant hotels to the green area in the distance. This is the largest of Venice's few parks, which hosts the annual Biennale festival. Much farther in the distance is the Lido, the island with Venice's beach. Its sand and casinos are tempting, though given its car traffic, it lacks the medieval charm of Venice.

**⑯ San Zaccaria:** OK, you're at your last stop. Quick—muscle your way off this boat! (If you don't, you'll eventually end up at the Lido.)

At San Zaccaria, you're right in the thick of the action. A number of other vaporetti depart from here (see page 42). Otherwise, it's a short walk back along the Riva to St. Mark's Square. Ahoy!

# Sights in Venice

Venice's greatest sight is the city itself. As well as seeing world-class museums and buildings, make time to wander narrow lanes, linger over a meal, or enjoy evening magic on St. Mark's Square. One of Venice's most delightful experiences—a gondola ride, worth ▲▲▲—is covered later, under "Experiences in Venice."

When you see a 🎧 in a listing, it means the sight is covered in a free audio tour (via my Rick Steves Audio Europe app—see page 26).

## SIGHTSEEING STRATEGIES
### Avoiding Lines and Crowds

The city is inundated with cruise-ship passengers and tours from mainland hotels daily from 10:00 to about 16:00. Major sights are busiest in the late morning, making this a smart time to explore the back lanes. Sights that have crowd problems get even more packed when it rains.

To avoid the worst of the crowds at St. Mark's Basilica, go early or late. To bypass the ticket line, reserve a time online— or if you have a large day bag, you can usually avoid the line by checking it (see the St. Mark's Basilica listing for details). For the Doge's Palace, purchase your ticket at the Correr Museum across St. Mark's Square (see next page). You can also visit later in the day, when crowds thin out. For the Campanile, ascend first thing in the morning or go late, or skip it entirely if you're going to the similar San Giorgio Maggiore bell tower.

## Sightseeing Passes

Venice offers a dizzying array of combo-tickets and sightseeing passes. For most people, the two best options are the combo-ticket for the Doge's Palace and Correr Museum or the Museum Pass (which covers those two plus more). Note that many of the most visit-worthy sights in town (the Accademia, Peggy Guggenheim Collection, Scuola San Rocco, Campanile, and the three sights within St. Mark's Basilica that charge admission) are not covered by any pass.

All the passes described here are sold at the TI (except for the combo-ticket). Most are also available at participating sights.

**Doge's Palace/Correr Museum Combo-Ticket:** A €25 combo-ticket covers both of these sights. To bypass the long line at the Doge's Palace, buy your combo-ticket at the never-crowded Correr Museum (or online—€1 surcharge). The two sights are also covered by the Museum Pass.

**Museum Pass:** Busy sightseers may prefer this more expensive pass, which covers these city-run museums: the Doge's Palace; Correr Museum; Ca' Rezzonico (Museum of 18th-Century Venice); Palazzo Mocenigo Costume Museum; Casa Goldoni (home of the Italian playwright); Ca' Pesaro (modern art); Museum of Natural History in the Santa Croce district; the Glass Museum on the island of Murano; and the Lace Museum on the island of Burano. At €35, this pass is the best value if you plan to see the Doge's Palace, Correr Museum, and one or two of the other covered museums. You can buy it at any participating museum or via their websites (€1 surcharge).

**Rolling Venice:** If you're under 30, this youth pass offers discounts at dozens of sights and shops, but its best deal is for transit. It lets you buy a 72-hour transit pass for just €22—about half price (€6 pass for ages 14-29; sold at TIs, vaporetto ticket offices, and VèneziaUnica shops).

## SAN MARCO DISTRICT
## ▲▲▲St. Mark's Square (Piazza San Marco)

This grand square is surrounded by splashy, historic buildings and sights: St. Mark's Basilica, the Doge's Palace, the Campanile bell tower, the Clock Tower, and the Correr Museum. The square is filled with music, lovers, pigeons, and tourists by day, and is your private rendezvous with the Venetian past late at night, when Europe's most magnificent dance floor is *the* romantic place to be.

For a slow and pricey evening thrill, invest €15 or so (including service and cover charge for the music) for a drink at one of the

VENICE

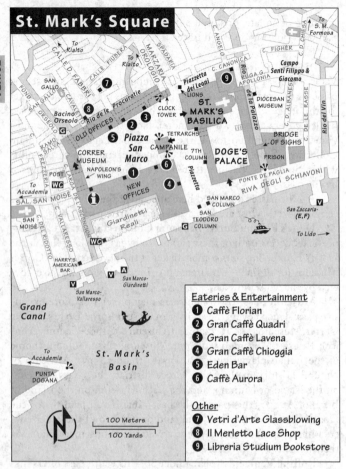

## St. Mark's Square

To Rialto
To Rialto
To S. M. Formosa

CALLE D'FABBRI
CALLE FIUBERA
SPADARIA
MARZARIA OROLOGIO
C. ANGELO
C. FIGHER
C. D. CHIESA

SAN GALLO
FOND. ORSEOLO
RAMO SALVA
FREZZERIA
C. CAVALETTO
Bacino Orseolo
Rio de le Procuratie
OLD OFFICES
Piazzetta dei Leoni
LIONS
CLOCK TOWER
C. CANONICA
Ruga G. APOLLONIA
Rio de la Palazzo
Campo Santi Filippo & Giacomo
DIOCESAN MUSEUM
C. D. ALBANESI
C. DE LE RASSE
Rio del Vin

ST. MARK'S BASILICA

CORRER MUSEUM
NAPOLEON'S WING
Piazza San Marco
TETRARCHS
CAMPANILE
7TH COLUMN
DOGE'S PALACE
BRIDGE OF SIGHS
PRISON
PONTE DE PAGLIA
RIVA DEGLI SCHIAVONI

To Accademia
POST
WC
SAL. SAN MOISE
C. DEL RIDOTTO
C. VALLARESSO
SAN MOISE
NEW OFFICES
Piazzetta
SAN MARCO COLUMN
SAN TEODORO COLUMN

San Zaccaria (E,F)
To Lido →

Giardinetti Reali
WC

HARRY'S AMERICAN BAR
San Marco-Giardinetti
San Marco-Vallaresso

Grand Canal

To Accademia
PUNTA DOGANA

St. Mark's Basin

100 Meters
100 Yards

### Eateries & Entertainment
1 Caffè Florian
2 Gran Caffè Quadri
3 Gran Caffè Lavena
4 Gran Caffè Chioggia
5 Eden Bar
6 Caffè Aurora

### Other
7 Vetri d'Arte Glassblowing
8 Il Merletto Lace Shop
9 Libreria Studium Bookstore

elegant cafés with the dueling orchestras (see "Cafés on St. Mark's Square" sidebar, later). For an unmatched experience that offers the best people-watching, it's worth the splurge.

For more on the square, the Clock Tower, the Campanile, and other sights on the square, download my free 🎧 audio tour.

**Visiting the Square:** St. Mark's Basilica dominates the square with its Eastern-style onion domes and glowing mosaics. Mark Twain said it looked like "a vast warty bug taking a meditative walk." (I say it looks like tiara-wearing ladybugs copulating.) To the right of the basilica is its 325-foot-tall Campanile. Behind the Campanile, you can catch a glimpse of the pale pink Doge's Palace. Lining the square are the former government offices *(procuratie)* that administered the Venetian empire's vast network of trading outposts, which stretched all the way to Turkey.

With your back to the church, survey one of Europe's great urban spaces, and the only square in Venice to merit the title "Piazza." Nearly two football fields long, it's surrounded by the offices of the republic. On the right are the "old offices" (16th-century Renaissance). At left are the "new offices" (17th-century High Renaissance). Napoleon called the piazza "the most beautiful drawing room in Europe," and added to the intimacy by building the final wing, opposite the basilica, that encloses the square.

The arcade ringing the square provides an elegant promenade—complete with drapes to provide relief from the sun.

Imagine this square full of water. That happens every so often at very high tides *(acqua alta)*, a reminder that Venice and the sea are intertwined. (Now, as one sinks and the other rises, they are more intertwined than ever.)

Watch out for pigeon speckle. Venetians don't like pigeons, but they do like seagulls—because they eat pigeons. In 2008, Venice outlawed the feeding of pigeons. But tourists—eager for a pigeon-clad photo op—haven't gotten that message.

**Campanile:** The original Campanile (bell tower) was an observation tower and a marvel of medieval and Renaissance architecture until 1902, when it toppled into the center of the piazza. It had groaned ominously the night before, sending people scurrying from the cafés. The next morning...*crash!* The golden angel on top landed right at the basilica's front door, standing up.

The Campanile was rebuilt 10 years later complete with its golden archangel Gabriel, who always faces the breeze. You can ride an elevator to the top for the best view of Venice. It's crowded at peak times, but well worth it.

**Clock Tower:** Built during the Renaissance in 1496, the Clock Tower (Torre dell'Orologio) marks the entry to the main shopping drag, called the Mercerie (or "Marzarie," in Venetian dialect), which connects St. Mark's Square with the Rialto Bridge. From the piazza, you can see the bronze men (Moors) swing their huge clappers at the top of each hour. In the 17th century, one of them knocked an unsuspecting worker off the top and to his death—probably the first ever killing by a robot. Notice one of the world's first "digital" clocks on the tower facing the square (with dramatic flips every five minutes).

You can go inside the Clock Tower with a pre-booked guided tour that takes you close to the clock's innards and out to a terrace with good views over the square and city rooftops (€12 combo-ticket includes Correr Museum—where the 45-minute tour starts—but not Doge's Palace; reservations required; tours in English Mon-Wed at 11:00 and 12:00, Thu-Sun at 14:00 and 15:00; no kids under age 6; tel. 848-082-000, http://torreorologio.visitmuve.it).

**Piazzetta and Doge's Palace:** *The small square between the basilica and the water is the* Piazzetta. This "Little Square" is framed by the Doge's Palace on the left, the library on the right, and the waterfront of the lagoon. In former days, the Piazzetta was closed to the public for a few hours a day so that government officials and bigwigs could gather in the sun to strike shady deals.

The pale pink Doge's Palace is the epitome of the style known as Venetian Gothic. Columns support traditional, pointed Gothic arches, but with a Venetian flair—they're curved to a point, ornamented with a trefoil (three-leaf clover), and topped with a round medallion of a quatrefoil (four-leaf clover). The pattern is found on buildings all over Venice and on the formerly Venetian-controlled Croatian coast, but nowhere else in the world (except Las Vegas).

The two large 12th-century columns near the water were (like so much else) looted from Constantinople. Mark's winged lion sits on top of one. The lion's body (nearly 15 feet long) predates the wings and is more than 2,000 years old. The other column holds St. Theodore (battling a crocodile), the former patron saint who was replaced by Mark. I guess stabbing crocs in the back isn't classy enough for an upwardly mobile world power. After public ridicule, criminals were executed by being hung from these columns in the hope that the public could learn its lessons vicariously.

## ▲▲▲St. Mark's Basilica (Basilica di San Marco)

Built in the 11th century to replace an earlier church, this basilica's distinctly Eastern-style architecture underlines Venice's connection with Byzantium (which protected it from the ambition of Charlemagne and his Holy Roman Empire). It's decorated with booty from returning sea captains—a kind of architectural Venetian trophy chest. The interior glows mysteriously with gold mosaics and colored marble. Since about AD 830, the saint's bones have been housed  on this site. The San Marco Museum within holds the original bronze horses (copies of these overlook the square), and a balcony offering a remarkable view over St. Mark's Square.

**Cost and Hours:** Basilica entry is free, though you can pay €3 for an online reservation that lets you skip the line (see next). Three separate exhibits within the church charge admission: Treasury-€3, Golden Altarpiece-€2, and San Marco Museum-€5. Church and all exhibits open Mon-Sat 9:30-17:00, Sun 14:00-17:00 (Sun until 16:30 Nov-Easter), interior brilliantly lit Mon-Sat 11:30-12:45. Tel. 041-270-8311, www.basilicasanmarco.it.

**Avoiding Lines:** There's almost always a long line to get into St. Mark's, but you can avoid it. The easiest way is to reserve an entry time online, even for the same day (€3, April-Oct only, book at www.venetoinside.com).

Or, if you have a large day bag (bigger than a purse), you can check it and skip the line (larger bags and backpacks are not allowed inside the church). Check above-limit bags for free for up to one hour at the nearby church called Ateneo San Basso, 30 yards to the left of the basilica, down narrow Calle San Basso (see the map; daily 9:30-17:00). Once you've checked your bag, take your claim tag to the basilica's tourist entrance. Keep to the left of the railing where the line forms and show your tag to the gatekeeper.

For shorter lines and fewer crowds in general, visit early or late.

**Tours:** Free, hour-long English tours (heavy on the mosaics' religious symbolism) are offered many days at 11:30 (meet in atrium, schedule varies, see schedule board just inside entrance). Audioguides are on sale as you enter.

∩ Download my free St. Mark's Basilica audio tour.

### ⊙ Self-Guided Tour

Start outside in the square, far enough back to take in the whole facade. It's a riot of domes, columns, and statues, completely unlike the towering Gothic churches of northern Europe or the heavy Baroque of much of the rest of Italy. Inside is a decor of mosaics, colored marbles, and oriental treasures that's rarely seen elsewhere. The Christian symbolism is unfamiliar to Western eyes, done in the style of Byzantine icons and even Islamic designs. Older than most of Europe's churches, St. Mark's feels like a remnant of a lost world.

The church is encrusted with materials looted from buildings throughout the Venetian empire. Their prize booty was the four bronze horses that adorn the balcony, stolen from Constantinople during the Fourth Crusade (these are copies); the atrium you're about to enter was added on to the church as their pedestal. Later, it was decorated with a mishmash of plundered columns. The architectural style of St. Mark's has been called "Early Ransack."

Now zero in on the details.

**❶ Exterior—Mosaic of Mark's Relics:** The mosaic over the far left door shows two men (in the center, with crooked staffs) entering the church bearing a coffin with the body of St. Mark.

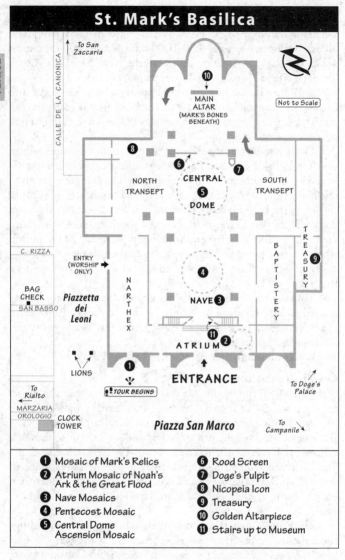

# St. Mark's Basilica

To San Zaccaria

CALLE DE LA CANONICA

Not to Scale

⑩ MAIN ALTAR (MARK'S BONES BENEATH)

⑧

⑥ CENTRAL ⑤ DOME ⑦

NORTH TRANSEPT

SOUTH TRANSEPT

C. RIZZA

ENTRY (WORSHIP ONLY) ➤

BAG CHECK
SAN BASSO

Piazzetta dei Leoni

NARTHEX

④

NAVE ③

BAPTISTERY

TREASURY ⑨

⑪ ②

ATRIUM

① LIONS

ENTRANCE

To Doge's Palace

To Rialto

MARZARIA OROLOGIO

CLOCK TOWER

TOUR BEGINS

Piazza San Marco

To Campanile

| | |
|---|---|
| ① Mosaic of Mark's Relics | ⑥ Rood Screen |
| ② Atrium Mosaic of Noah's Ark & the Great Flood | ⑦ Doge's Pulpit |
| ③ Nave Mosaics | ⑧ Nicopeia Icon |
| ④ Pentecost Mosaic | ⑨ Treasury |
| ⑤ Central Dome Ascension Mosaic | ⑩ Golden Altarpiece |
| | ⑪ Stairs up to Museum |

Eight centuries after Mark's death, his holy body was in Muslim-occupied Alexandria, Egypt. In AD 829, two visiting Venetian merchants "rescued" the body from the "infidels" and spirited it away to Venice.

• *Enter the atrium of the basilica and find a place to view its ceiling mosaics. Start by finding a golden arch overhead with scenes of Noah's Ark.*

❷ **Atrium Mosaic of Noah's Ark and the Great Flood:** Of all the famous mosaics of St. Mark's, this Flood scene is one of the oldest (13th century) and finest. The scenes show Noah and his sons sawing logs to build the Ark. Below that are scenes of Noah putting all species of animals into the Ark, two by two. Then the Flood hits in full force, drowning the wicked. Noah sends out a dove twice to see whether there's any dry land where he can dock. He finds it, leaves the Ark with a gorgeous rainbow overhead, and offers a sacrifice of thanks to God.

• *Climb a few steps, and into church. Just inside the door, step out of the flow and survey the church.*

❸ **The Nave—Mosaics Above and Below:** These golden mosaics are in the Byzantine style, though many were designed

by artists from the Italian Renaissance and later. The often-overlooked lower walls are covered with green-, yellow-, purple-, and rose-colored marble slabs, cut to expose the grain, and laid out in geometric patterns. Even the floor is mosaic, with mostly geometrical designs. It rolls like the sea. Venice is sinking and shifting, creating these cresting waves of stone.

• *Find the chandelier in the nave (in the shape of a cathedral space station), and run your eyes up the support chain to the dome above. This has one of the church's greatest mosaics.*

❹ **Pentecost Mosaic:** In a golden heaven, the dove of the Holy Spirit shoots out a pinwheel of spiritual lasers, igniting tongues of fire on the heads of the 12 apostles below, giving them the ability to speak other languages without a Rick Steves phrase book. You'd think they'd be amazed, but their expressions are as solemn as...icons. One of the oldest mosaics in the church (c. 1125), it has distinct "Byzantine" features: a gold background and apostles with halos, solemn faces, almond eyes, delicate blessing hands, and rumpled robes, all facing forward.

• *Shuffle along with the crowds up to the center of the church.*

❺ **Central Dome Ascension Mosaic:** Here at the center of the church, notice the layout: the church has four equal arms, each topped with a dome, radiating out to form a Greek cross (+). The symmetrical floor plan symbolizes perfection, rather than the more common Latin cross of the Crucifixion (emphasizing man's sinfulness).

Now gape upward into the central dome, the very heart of the church. Christ—having lived his miraculous life and having been crucified for man's sins—ascends into the starry sky on a rainbow. In Byzantine churches, the window-lit dome represented heaven, while the dark church below represented earth—a microcosm of the hierarchical universe.

**Under the Ascension Dome:** Look around at the church's furnishings and imagine a service here. The ❻ **rood screen** (like the iconostasis in a Greek church), topped with 14 saints, separates the congregation from the high altar, heightening the "mystery" of the Mass. The ❼ **pulpit** (the purple one on the right) was reserved for the doge, who led prayers and made important announcements.

• *In the north transept (left of the altar), is an area usually reserved for prayer. The worshippers are facing a big stone canopy, which houses a small painting of the Virgin Mary.*

❽ **Nicopeia** (North Transept): Venetians then and now pray to a painted wooden icon of Mary and Baby Jesus known as Nicopeia, or Our Lady of Victory. For centuries, Nicopeia was venerated by the Byzantines, who asked Mary to protect them in battle. When Venetian Crusaders captured it, the icon came to protect Venice.

**Additional Sights:** The ❾ **Treasury** (Tesoro) and ❿ **Golden Altarpiece** (Pala d'Oro) are the easiest ways to see the glories of the Byzantine Empire outside of Istanbul or Ravenna. The treasury is a beautiful collection of chalices, reliquaries, and jewels, most of them stolen from Constantinople. As you view these treasures, remember that some are nearly 2,000 years old. Beneath the high altar lies the body of St. Mark ("Marce") and the Golden Altarpiece, made of 250 blue-backed enamels with religious scenes, all set in a gold frame and studded with 15 hefty rubies, 300 emeralds, 1,500 pearls, and assorted sapphires, amethysts, and topaz.

Upstairs, in the ⓫ **San Marco Museum** (Museo di San Marco) you can see an up-close mosaic exhibition, more religious objects that once adorned the church, a fine view of the church interior, a view of the square from the balcony with bronze horses, and (inside, in their own room) the original horses. The staircase up to the museum is in the atrium, near the basilica's main entrance.

## ▲▲▲Doge's Palace (Palazzo Ducale)

The seat of the Venetian government and home of its ruling duke, or doge, this was the most powerful half-acre in Europe for 400 years. The Doge's Palace was built to show off the power and wealth of the Republic. The doge lived with his family on the first floor up, near the halls of power. From his once-lavish (now sparse) quarters, you'll follow the one-way tour through the public rooms of the top floor, finishing with the Bridge of

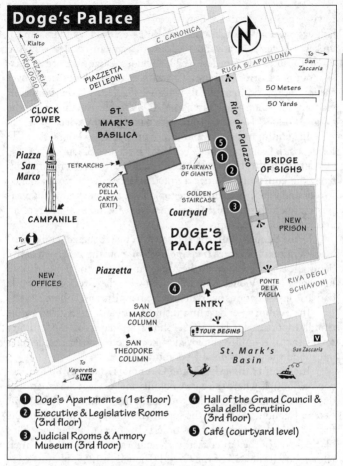

Doge's Palace

- ❶ Doge's Apartments (1st floor)
- ❷ Executive & Legislative Rooms (3rd floor)
- ❸ Judicial Rooms & Armory Museum (3rd floor)
- ❹ Hall of the Grand Council & Sala dello Scrutinio (3rd floor)
- ❺ Café (courtyard level)

Sighs and the prison. The place is wallpapered with masterpieces by Veronese and Tintoretto.

**Cost and Hours:** €25 combo-ticket includes Correr Museum, also covered by Museum Pass; Sun-Thu 8:30-21:00, Fri-Sat until 23:00, Nov-March daily until 19:00; café, next to St. Mark's Basilica, just off St. Mark's Square, vaporetto stops: San Marco or San Zaccaria, tel. 041-271-5911, http://palazzoducale.visitmuve.it.

**Avoiding Lines:** If the line is long at the Doge's Palace, buy your combo-ticket at the Correr Museum across the square; then you can go directly through the Doge's turnstile without waiting in line. Or, you can buy your ticket online. Crowds tend to diminish after 16:00.

**Tours:** The fine **Secret Itineraries Tour** follows the doge's footsteps through rooms not included in the general admission ticket. Though the tour skips the palace's main hall, you're welcome to visit the hall afterward on your own. Three 75-minute English-language tours run each morning. Reserve ahead, as tours can fill up several weeks in advance—although you can try just showing up at the information desk (€28, includes Doge's Palace admission but not Correr Museum, €15 with combo-ticket; reserve over the phone or online: tel. 041-4273-0892, http://palazzoducale. visitmuve.it, €1 online surcharge). Don't confuse this with the Doge's Hidden Treasures Tour, which isn't worth its fee.

The **audioguide** is dry but informative (€5, 1.5 hours, need ID for deposit). Guidebooks are available in the bookshop.

**Visiting the Doge's Palace:** You'll see the restored facades from the **courtyard.** Notice a grand staircase (with nearly naked Moses and Paul Newman at the top). Even the most powerful visitors climbed this to meet the doge. This was the beginning of an architectural power trip.

In the **Senate Hall,** the 120 senators met, debated, and passed laws. Tintoretto's large *Triumph of Venice* on the ceiling (central painting, best viewed from the top) is an allegory of the city in all her glory. Lady Venice is up in heaven with the Greek gods, while barbaric lesser nations swirl up to give her gifts and tribute.

The **Armory**—a dazzling display originally assembled to intimidate potential adversaries—shows remnants of the military might that the empire employed to keep the East-West trade lines open (and the local economy booming).

The giant **Hall of the Grand Council** (175 feet by 80 feet, capacity 2,600) is where the entire nobility met to elect the senate and doge. It took a room this size to contain the grandeur of the Most Serene Republic. Ringing the top of the room are portraits of the first 76 doges (in chronological order). The one at the far end that's blacked out (in the left corner) is the notorious Doge Marin Falier, who opposed the will of the Grand Council in 1355. He was tried for treason, beheaded, and airbrushed from history.

On the wall over the doge's throne is Tintoretto's monsterpiece, *Paradise,* the largest oil painting in the world. Christ and Mary are surrounded by a heavenly host of 500 saints. The painting leaves you feeling that you get to heaven not by being a good Christian, but by being a good Venetian.

Cross the covered **Bridge of Sighs** over the canal to the **prisons.** Circle the cells. Notice the carvings made by prisoners—from olden days up until 1930—on some of the stone windowsills of the cells, especially in the far corner of the building.

Cross back over the Bridge of Sighs, pausing to look through the marble-trellised windows at all of the tourists.

VENICE

## More Sights on the Square
### ▲▲Correr Museum (Museo Correr)

This uncrowded museum gives you a good overview of Venetian history and art. The doge memorabilia, armor, banners, statues (by Canova), and paintings (by the Bellini family and others) re-create the festive days of the Venetian Republic. And it's all accompanied—throughout the museum—by English descriptions and views of St. Mark's Square. But the Correr Museum has one more thing to offer, and that's a quiet refuge—an elegant Neoclassical space—in which to rise above St. Mark's Square when the piazza is too hot, too rainy, or too overrun with tourists.

**Cost and Hours:** €25 combo-ticket includes Doge's Palace, also covered by Museum Pass; daily 10:00-19:00, Nov-March 10:30-17:00; bag check free and mandatory for bags bigger than a large purse, elegant café, enter at far end of square directly opposite basilica, tel. 041-240-5211, http://correr.visitmuve.it.

### ▲Campanile (Campanile di San Marco)

This dramatic bell tower replaced a shorter tower, part of the original fortress that guarded the entry of the Grand Canal. That tower crumbled into a pile of bricks in 1902, a thousand years after it was built. Ride the elevator 325 feet to the top of the bell tower for the best view in Venice (especially at sunset). For an ear-shattering experience, be on top when the bells ring. The golden archangel Gabriel at the top always faces into the wind. Beat the crowds and enjoy the crisp morning air at 9:00 or the cool evening breeze at 18:00. Go inside to buy tickets; the kiosk in front only rents audio guides and is operated by a private company.

**Cost and Hours:** €8; daily 8:30-21:00, Sept-mid-Oct until sunset, mid-Oct-April 9:30-17:30, last entry 45 minutes before closing; may close during thunderstorms, audio-guide—€3, tel. 041-522-4064, www.basilicasanmarco.it.

## Behind St. Mark's Basilica
### ▲Bridge of Sighs

This much-photographed bridge connects the Doge's Palace with the prison. Travelers popularized this bridge in the Romantic 19th century. Supposedly, a condemned man would be led over this bridge on his

## Cafés on St. Mark's Square

In Venice's heyday, it was said that the freedoms a gentleman could experience here went far beyond what any true gentleman would actually care to indulge in. But one extravagance all could enjoy was the ritual of publicly consuming coffee: showing off with an affordable luxury, doing something trendy, while sharing the ideas of the Enlightenment.

Exotic coffee was made to order for the fancy café scene. Traders introduced coffee, called the "wine of Islam," from the Middle East (the plant is native to Ethiopia). The first coffeehouses opened in the 17th century, and by 1750 there were dozens of cafés lining Piazza San Marco and 200 operating in Venice.

Today, several fine old cafés survive and still line the square. Those with live music feature similar food, prices, and a three- to five-piece combo playing a selection of classical and pop hits, from Brahms to "Bésame Mucho."

You can wander around the square listening to the different orchestras, or take a seat at a café. At any place with live music, it's perfectly acceptable to nurse a cappuccino for an hour—you're paying for the music with the cover charge. Or you can sip your coffee at the bar at a nearly normal price. The prices are clearly posted. If you sit outside and get just an espresso (your cheapest option), expect to pay €12.50—€6.50 for the coffee and a €6 cover charge when the orchestra is playing (which is most of the day). Service is included (no need to tip).

---

way to the prison, take one last look at the glory of Venice, and sigh. Though overhyped, the Bridge of Sighs is undeniably tingle-worthy—especially after dark, when the crowds have dispersed and it's just you and floodlit Venice. In the middle of the day, however, being immersed in the pandemonium of global tourism (and selfie sticks) can be a fascinating experience in itself.

**Getting There:** The Bridge of Sighs is around the corner from the Doge's Palace. Walk toward the waterfront, turn left along the water, and look up the first canal on your left. You can walk across the bridge (from the inside) by visiting the Doge's Palace.

For locations of the following cafés, see the "St. Mark's Square" map, earlier.

**Caffè Florian** (on the right as you face the church) is the most famous Venetian café and was one of the first places in Europe to serve coffee (daily 9:00-24:00, shorter hours in winter, www.caffeflorian.com). It was originally named "Triumphant Venice" (Venezia Triomfante). But under French occupation, in the early 19th century, that politically incorrect name was changed.

The Florian has been a popular spot for a discreet rendezvous in Venice since 1720. Each room has a historic or artistic theme. For example the "Room of the Illustrious Men" features portraits of great Venetians from Marco Polo to Titian. The outside tables are the main action, but do walk inside through the richly decorated old-time rooms where Casanova, Lord Byron, Charles Dickens, and Woody Allen have all paid too much for a drink. The café's orchestra—the most serious on the square—plays daily from 10:00 to 24:00. Each hour comes with a musical theme (operetta, Latin, Romantic, jazz, Venetian, and so on—you can ask for the program).

**Gran Caffè Quadri,** opposite the Florian and established in 1780, has another illustrious roster of famous clientele.

**Gran Caffè Lavena,** near the Clock Tower, is less storied—although it dates from 1750 and counts composer Richard Wagner as a former regular—so it's less intimidating than the more formal cafés here. It was the hangout of gondoliers and lantern bearers for local bigwigs. Drop in to check out its dazzling but politically incorrect chandelier.

**Gran Caffè Chioggia,** on the Piazzetta facing the Doge's Palace, has no cover and one or two musicians playing—usually a pianist (€7 cocktails, music from 10:30 to 23:00—jazz after 21:00).

**Eden Bar** and **Caffè Aurora** are less expensive and don't have live music.

## Church of San Zaccaria

This historic church is home to a sometimes-waterlogged crypt, a Bellini altarpiece, a Tintoretto painting, and the final resting place of St. Zechariah, the father of John the Baptist.

**Cost and Hours:** Free, €1.50 to enter crypt, €0.50 coin to light up Bellini's altarpiece; Mon-Sat 10:00-12:00 & 16:00-18:00, Sun 16:00-18:00 only; two canals behind St. Mark's Basilica.

## ACROSS THE LAGOON FROM ST. MARK'S SQUARE

### ▲San Giorgio Maggiore

This is the dreamy church-topped island you can see from the waterfront by St. Mark's Square. The striking church, designed by Palladio, features art by Tintoretto, a bell tower, and good views of Venice.

**Cost and Hours:** Church—free, open daily 9:00-19:00, Nov-March 8:30-18:00; bell tower elevator—€6, runs until 20 minutes before the church closes, does not run during Sun services; tel. 041-522-7827.

**Getting There:** To reach the island from St. Mark's Square, take the one-stop, five-minute ride on vaporetto #2 from San Zaccaria (€5 special vaporetto ticket, runs every 12 minutes from dock B, direction: Piazza Roma).

## DORSODURO DISTRICT

### ▲▲Accademia (Galleria dell'Accademia)

Venice's top art museum, packed with highlights of the Venetian Renaissance, features paintings by the Bellini family, Titian, Tintoretto, Veronese, Tiepolo, Giorgione, Canaletto, and Testosterone. It's just over the wooden Accademia Bridge from the San Marco action.

**Cost and Hours:** €15; Tue-Sun 8:15-19:15, Mon until 14:00, last entry one hour before closing; dull audioguide-€6, vaporetto: Accademia, tel. 041-522-2247, www.gallerieaccademia.it.

**Avoiding Lines:** Just 400 people are allowed into the gallery at one time, so you may have to wait. It's most crowded on Tue mornings and whenever it rains; it's least crowded Wed, Thu, and Sun mornings (before 10:00) and late afternoons (after 17:00). While it's possible to book tickets in advance (€2/ticket surcharge; either book online or call 041-520-0345), it's generally not necessary if you avoid the busiest times.

**Renovation:** The museum is nearing the end of a major multi-year expansion and renovation. As a result, rooms close, paintings come and go, and the actual locations of the pieces are hard to pin down. If you can't find paintings in the rooms listed below, ask a museum guard to point you in the right direction.

**Visiting the Accademia:** The Accademia offers a good overview of painters whose works you'll see all over town. Venetian art is underrated and, I think, misunderstood. It's nowhere near as famous today as the work of the florescent Florentines, but—with historical slices of Venice, ravishing nudes, and very human Madonnas—it's livelier, more colorful, and simply more fun. The Venetian love of luxury shines through in this collection, which starts in the Middle Ages and runs to the 1700s. Look for grand canvases of colorful, spacious settings, peopled with happy locals in extravagant clothes having a great time.

Medieval highlights include elaborate altarpieces and golden-haloed Madonnas, all painted at a time when realism, depth of field, and emotion were considered beside the point. Medieval Venetians, with their close ties to the East, borrowed techniques such as gold-leafing, frontal poses, and "iconic" faces from the religious icons of Byzantium (modern-day Istanbul).

Among early masterpieces of the Renaissance is Mantegna's studly *St. George* (Room 4). As the Renaissance reaches its heights, so do the paintings, such as Titian's magnificent *Presentation of the Virgin* (Room 24). It's a religious scene, yes, but it's really just an excuse to display secular splendor (Titian was the most famous painter of his day—perhaps even more famous than Michelangelo). Veronese's sumptuous *Feast in the House of Levi* (Room 10), pictured below, also has an ostensibly religious theme (in the middle, find Jesus eating his final meal)—but it's outdone by the luxury and

optimism of Renaissance Venice. Life was a good thing and beauty was to be enjoyed. (Veronese was hauled before the Inquisition for painting such a bawdy Last Supper...so he fine-tuned the title.)

End your tour in the largest room in the museum, Room 23. This giant hall is the upper half of an old Gothic church. The nave was divided under Napoleon's rule, and this became the fine arts academy—the Accademia. It's now home to fine temporary exhibitions, and where art displaced by the gallery's ongoing renovation often ends up.

## ▲▲Peggy Guggenheim Collection

The popular museum of far-out art, housed in the American heiress' former retirement palazzo, offers one of Europe's best reviews

**VENICE**

of the art of the first half of the 20th century. Stroll through styles represented by artists whom Peggy knew personally—Cubism (Picasso, Braque), Surrealism (Dalí, Ernst), Futurism (Boccioni), American Abstract Expressionism (Pollock), and a sprinkling of Klee, Calder, and Chagall.

**Cost and Hours:** €15; Wed-Mon 10:00-18:00, closed Tue; audioguide-€7, pricey café, 5-minute walk from the Accademia Bridge, vaporetto: Accademia or Salute, tel. 041-240-5411, www.guggenheim-venice.it.

### ▲La Salute Church (Santa Maria della Salute)

This impressive church with a crown-shaped dome was built and dedicated to the Virgin Mary by grateful survivors of the 1630 plague.

**Cost and Hours:** Church-free; Sacristy-€4; both open daily 9:30-12:00 & 15:00-17:30; 10-minute walk from the Accademia Bridge, at vaporetto: Salute, tel. 041-274-3928, www.seminariovenezia.it.

### ▲Punta della Dogana

Housed in the former Customs House at the end of the Grand Canal, this museum features cutting-edge 21st-century art in spacious rooms. This isn't Picasso and Matisse, or even Pollock and Warhol—those guys are ancient history. But if you're into the likes of Jeff Koons, Cy Twombly, Rachel Whiteread, and a host of newer artists, the museum is world class. The displays change completely about every year, drawn from the museum's large collection—so large it also fills Palazzo Grassi, farther up the Grand Canal.

**Cost and Hours:** €20 (varies depending on exhibit); Wed-Mon 10:00-19:00, closed Tue, last entry one hour before closing; small café, tel. 199-112-112 within Italy, 041-200-1057 from abroad, www.palazzograssi.it.

**Getting There:** Punta della Dogana is near La Salute Church (vaporetto: Salute). Palazzo Grassi is a bit upstream, on the east side of the Grand Canal (vaporetto #2: San Samuele).

### ▲▲Ca' Rezzonico (Museum of 18th-Century Venice)

This Grand Canal palazzo offers the most insightful look at the life of Venice's rich and famous in the 1700s. Wander under ceilings by Tiepolo, among furnishings from that most decadent century, enjoying views of the canal and paintings by Guardi, Canaletto, and Longhi.

**Cost and Hours:** €10; Wed-Mon 10:00-18:00, Nov-March until 17:00, closed Tue year-round; ticket office closes one hour before museum, audioguide—€5 or €6/2 people, café, at vaporetto: Ca' Rezzonico, tel. 041-241-0100, http://carezzonico.visitmuve.it.

## SAN POLO DISTRICT
### ▲▲▲Rialto Bridge

One of the world's most famous bridges, this distinctive and dramatic stone structure crosses the Grand Canal with a single confident span. The arcades along the top of the bridge help reinforce the structure...and offer some enjoyable shopping diversions, as does the market surrounding the bridge (produce market closed Sun, fish market closed Sun-Mon).

### ▲Fondaco dei Tedeschi (German Exchange) View Terrace

In the Middle Ages, Venice was the world's trading center, hosting scores of nationalities, each with its own caravanserai-like center. The most famous is the home of the Tedeschi (German) traders, just off the Rialto Bridge. It was recently purchased by the Benetton family and turned into a luxury mall. The ground floor features gourmet food shops and ritzy cafés.

The mall's top floor terrace offers a unique perspective over the roofs of Venice and an unforgettable view of the big bend in the Grand Canal. Four times an hour, 80 people are allowed onto the roof for 15 minutes. As you ride the red-carpet elevator to the top floor, notice how the old architectural bones of the structure survive.

**Cost and Hours:** The terrace is free but access requires a reservation (15-minute timeslots, book online at www.dfs.com/en/info/t-fondaco-rooftop-terrace; you can attempt to show up and reserve, but no guarantees). Terrace open daily 10:15-19:30, June-Aug until 20:15; east side of Rialto Bridge, tel. 041-314-2000.

### ▲▲Frari Church
### (Basilica di Santa Maria Gloriosa dei Frari)

My favorite art experience in Venice is seeing art in the setting for which it was designed—as it is at the Frari Church. The Franciscan "Church of the Brothers" and the art that decorates it are warmed by the spirit of St. Francis. It features the work of three great Re-

## A Dying City?

Venice's population (fewer than 55,000 in the historic city) is half what it was just 30 years ago, and people are leaving at a rate of a thousand a year. Of those who stay, 25 percent are 65 or older.

Sad, yes, but imagine raising a family here: Apartments are small, high up, and expensive. Humidity and occasional flooding make basic maintenance a pain. Home-improvement projects require navigating miles of red tape, and you must follow regulations intended to preserve the historical ambience. Everything is expensive because it has to be shipped in from the mainland. You can easily get glass and tourist trinkets, but it's hard to find groceries or get your shoes fixed. Running basic errands involves lots of walking and stairs—imagine crossing over arched bridges while pushing a child in a stroller and carrying a day's worth of groceries.

With millions of visitors a year (150,000 a day at peak times), on any given day Venetians are likely outnumbered by tourists. Despite government efforts to subsidize rents and build cheap housing, the city is losing its residents. The economy itself is thriving, thanks to tourist dollars and rich foreigners buying second homes. But the culture is dying.

Greedy residents could sink Venice long before the sea swallows it up. Locals happily rent apartments to tourists a few times a month rather than affordably to local families, and shopkeepers sell trinkets to tourists before pots and pans to the local population. Even the most hopeful city planners worry that in a few decades Venice will not be a city at all, but a museum, a cultural theme park, a decaying Disneyland for adults.

naissance masters: Donatello, Giovanni Bellini, and Titian—each showing worshippers the glory of God in human terms.

**Cost and Hours:** €3; Mon-Sat 9:00-18:00, Sun from 13:00; audioguide-€2, modest dress recommended, on Campo dei Frari, near San Tomà vaporetto and *traghetto* stops, tel. 041-272-8611, www.basilicadeifrari.it.

**Tours:** You can rent an **audioguide** for €2, or download my free ∩ Frari Church **audio tour.**

**Visiting the Church:** In **Donatello's wood statue of St. John the Baptist** (in the first chapel to the right of the high altar), the prophet of the desert—emaciated from his breakfast of bugs 'n' honey and dressed in animal skins—announces the coming of the Messiah. Donatello was a Florentine working at the dawn of the Renaissance.

**Bellini's** *Madonna and Child with Saints and Angels* painting (in the sacristy farther to the right) came later, done by a Venetian in a more Venetian style—soft focus without Donatello's harsh realism. While Renaissance humanism demanded Madonnas and saints that were accessible and human, Bellini places them in a physical setting so beautiful that it creates its own mood of serene holiness. The genius of Bellini, perhaps the greatest Venetian painter, is obvious in the pristine clarity, rich colors (notice Mary's clothing), believable depth, and reassuring calm of this three-paneled altarpiece.

Finally, glowing red and gold like a stained-glass window over the high altar, **Titian's** *Assumption of the Virgin* sets the tone of exuberant beauty found in the otherwise sparse church. Titian the Venetian—a student of Bellini—painted steadily for 60 years... you'll see a lot of his art. As stunned apostles look up past the swirl of arms and legs, the complex composition of this painting draws you right to the radiant face of the once-dying, now-triumphant Mary as she joins God in heaven.

Feel comfortable to discreetly freeload off passing tours. For many, these three pieces of art make a visit to the Accademia Gallery unnecessary (or they may whet your appetite for more). Before leaving, check out the Neoclassical pyramid-shaped Canova monument flanking the nave just inside the main entrance and (opposite that) the grandiose tomb of Titian. Compare the carved marble *Assumption* behind Titian's tombstone portrait with the painted original above the high altar.

## ▲▲Scuola San Rocco

Sometimes called "Tintoretto's Sistine Chapel," this lavish meeting hall (next to the Frari Church) has some 50 large, colorful Tintoretto paintings plastered to the walls and ceilings. The best paintings are upstairs, especially the *Crucifixion* in the smaller room. View the neck-breaking splendor with the mirrors available in the Grand Hall.

**Cost and Hours:** €10, daily 9:30-17:30, tel. 041-523-4864, www.scuolagrandesanrocco.org.

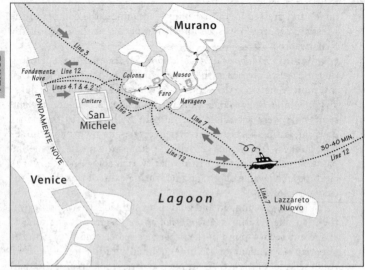

## VENICE'S LAGOON

With more time, venture to some nearby islands in Venice's lagoon. While still touristy, they offer an escape from the crowds, a chance to get out on a boat, and some enjoyable diversions for fans of glass-making, lace, and sunbathing.

### Lagoon Tour

The islands of San Michele (cemetery), Murano (glass), Burano (lace), and Torcello (oldest church in Venice) make a good, varied, and long day trip that you can do on your own.

**The Plan:** You can travel to any of the four islands by vaporetto. Since single vaporetto tickets (€7.50) are only valid for 75 minutes, getting a vaporetto pass for a lagoon excursion makes more sense (for details on tickets and passes, see page 42). Confirm vaporetto times by downloading the latest schedule from www.actv.it.

Start your journey at the **Fondamente Nove** vaporetto stop, on Venice's north shore (the "back" of the fish). Fondamente Nove is a pleasant 15-minute walk from Rialto or St. Mark's. Alternatively, you could reach Fondamente Nove by vaporetto: From San Zaccaria (near St. Mark's), take the #4.1 (35 minutes). From the train or bus station, take #4.2 (30 minutes).

From Fondamente Nove, take the #4.1 or #4.2 vaporetto for Murano (about every 10 minutes). On the way, get off at the Cimitero stop on the island of San Michele to see the cemetery (6-minute ride). Continue on to Murano, arriving at the Murano-Colonna stop (3-minute ride). Sightsee Murano as you make your way to the Murano-Faro stop, where you board vaporetto #12 for the trip to Burano (30-40 minutes). From Burano, you can side-trip to Tor-

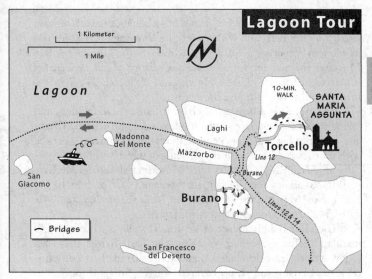

cello (on the #12, 5-minute trip each way). To return to Venice from Burano, take vaporetto #12 all the way back to Fondamente Nove (45 minutes). For a longer, more scenic return past even more lagoon islands, take the #14 from Burano to the San Zaccaria dock near St. Mark's Square (70 minutes).

Note that during summer, there are (slightly faster) express vaporetti that go directly to Murano-Colonna (if you're OK with skipping the cemetery on San Michele): From San Zaccaria, catch the #7, or from the train/bus stations catch the #3.

**San Michele** (a.k.a. Cimitero): This island is the final resting place of Venetians and a few foreign VIPs, from poet Ezra Pound to composer Igor Stravinsky. It's also full of flowers, trees, scurrying lizards, and birdsong, and has an intriguing chapel (cemetery open daily 7:30-18:00, Oct-March until 16:30).

**Murano:** Famous for its glassmaking, this ▲ island is home to several glass factories and the Glass Museum. From the Col-

onna vaporetto stop, skip the glass shops in front of you, walk to the right, and wander up the street along the canal, **Fondamenta dei Vetrai** (Glassmakers' Embankment). The Faro district of Murano, on the other side of the canal, is packed with factories *(fab-riche)* and their furnaces *(fornaci)*. You'll pass dozens more **glass shops** along the canal. Early along this promenade, at #47, is the high-class **Venini** shop, with glass that's a cut above much of what else is on offer here, and with an interior showing off the ultimate in modern Venetian glass design (closed Sun). Murano's **Glass Museum** (Museo del Vetro) traces the history of this delicate art (€14, daily 10:30-18:30, Nov-March until 16:30, tel. 041-739-586, http://museovetro.visitmuve.it).

**Burano:** This ▲▲ island's claim to fame is lacemaking, and (along with countless lace shops) it offers a delightful pastel village alternative to big, bustling Venice. The tight **main drag** is packed with tourists and lined with shops, some of which sell Burano's locally produced white wine. Its **Lace Museum** (Museo del Merletto di Burano) shows the island's lace heritage (€5, Tue-Sun 10:30-17:00, Nov-March until 16:30, closed Mon year-round, tel. 041-730-034, http://museomerletto.visitmuve.it).

**Torcello:** The birthplace of Venice, Torcello is where the first mainland refugees settled, escaping the barbarian hordes. Yet today, it's the least-developed island (pop. 20) in the most natural state, marshy and shrub-covered. There's little for tourists to see except the **Santa Maria Assunta Church,** the oldest in Venice, which still sports some impressive mosaics, a climbable **bell tower,** and a modest **museum** of Roman sculpture and medieval sculpture and manuscripts (10-minute walk from the dock, €12 combo-ticket covers museum, church, and bell tower; museum only-€3; church and bell tower-€5 each; church open daily 10:30-18:00, Nov-Feb 10:00-17:00, museum and bell tower close 30 minutes earlier, museum closed Mon year-round; museum tel. 041-730-761).

### Lido Beach

Venice's nearest beach is the Lido, across the lagoon on an island connected to the mainland (which means car traffic). The sandy beach is pleasant, family-friendly, and good for swimming. You can rent an umbrella, buy beach gear at the shop, get food at the self-service café, or have a drink at the bar. Everything is affordable and in the same building (vaporetto: Lido S.M.E., walk 10 minutes on Gran Viale S. Maria Elisabetta to beach entry).

# Experiences in Venice

### Gondola Rides

Riding a gondola is simple, expensive, and one of the great experiences in Europe. Gondoliers hanging out all over town are eager to have you hop in for a ride. While this is a rip-off for some, it's a traditional must for romantics.

The price for a gondola starts at €80 for a 35-minute ride during the day. You can divide the cost—and the romance—among up to six people per boat, but only two get the love seat. Prices jump to €100 after 19:00—when it's most romantic and relaxing. Adding a singer and an accordionist will cost an additional €120. If you value budget over romance, you can save money by recruiting fellow travelers to split a gondola. Prices are standard and listed on the gondoliers' association website (go to www.gondolavenezia.it, click on "Using the Gondola," and look under "charterage").

Dozens of gondola stations *(servizio gondole)* are set up along canals all over town. Because your gondolier might offer narration

or conversation during your ride, talk with several and choose one you like. You're welcome to review the map and discuss the route. Doing so is also a good way to see if you enjoy the gondolier's personality and language skills. Establish the price, route, and duration of the trip before boarding, enjoy your ride, and pay only when you're finished. While prices are pretty firm, you might find them softer during the day. Most gondoliers honor the official prices, but a few might try to scam you out of some extra euros, particularly by insisting on a tip. (While not required or even expected, if your gondolier does the full 35 minutes and entertains you en route, a 5-10 percent tip is appreciated; if he's surly or rushes through the trip, skip it.)

If you've hired musicians and want to hear a Venetian song *(un canto Veneziano),* try requesting "Venezia La Luna e Tu." Asking to hear "O Sole Mio" (which comes from Naples) is like asking a Chicago lounge singer to sing "Swanee River."

Glide through nighttime Venice with your head on someone's shoulder. Follow the moon as it sails past otherwise unseen buildings. Silhouettes gaze down from bridges while window glitter spills onto the black water. You're anonymous in the city of masks, as the rhythmic thrust of your striped-shirted gondolier turns old crows into songbirds. This is extremely relaxing (and, I think, worth the extra cost to experience at night). Suggestion: Put the camera down and make it a point for you and your partner to enjoy a threesome with Venice. Women, beware...while gondoliers can be extremely charming, locals say that anyone who falls for one of these Venetian Romeos "has slices of ham over her eyes."

For cheap gondola thrills during the day, stick to the one-minute ferry ride on a Grand Canal *traghetto.* At night, vaporetti are nearly empty, and it's a great time to cruise the Grand Canal on the slow boat #1. Or hang out on a bridge along the gondola route and wave at romantics.

## Festivals

Venice's most famous festival is **Carnevale,** the celebration Americans call Mardi Gras (February; www.carnevale.venezia.it). In Carnevale's heyday—the 1600s and 1700s—you could do pretty much anything with anybody from any social class if you were wearing a mask. These days, tourists and Venetians—from kids to businessmen—gather for parades, parties, and masquerade balls. In drawing such big crowds, Carnevale has nearly been a victim of its own success, driving away many Venetians (who skip out on the craziness to go skiing in the Dolomites). Unless you're interested in joining the fun, any other day this time of year will be much less chaotic, and less expensive.

Every year, the city hosts the Venice **Biennale International Art Exhibition,** a world-class contemporary fair alternating between art in odd years (the main event) and architecture in even years (much smaller). The exhibition spreads over the Arsenale and Giardini park. When the Biennale focuses on visual art, representatives from 80-plus nations offer the latest in contemporary art forms: video, digital art, performance art, and photography, along with painting and sculpture (take vaporetto #1 or #2 to Giardini-Biennale; for details and an events calendar, see www.labiennale.org). The actual exhibition usually runs from June through November, but other events loosely connected with the Biennale—film, dance, theater—are held throughout the year (starting as early as February) in various venues on the island.

# Shopping in Venice

Popular souvenirs and gifts include Murano glass, Burano lace, Carnevale masks, prints of Venetian scenes, traditional stationery (pens and marbled paper products of all kinds), calendars with Venetian scenes (and sexy gondoliers), and plenty of goofy knickknacks (Titian mouse pads, gondolier T-shirts, and little plastic gondola condom holders).

In touristy areas, shops are typically open from 9:00 to 19:30 (sometimes with a break at midday), and some stores are open on Sunday. If you're buying at a market, bargain—it's accepted and almost expected. In shops, you may save by offering to pay cash.

Popular Venetian glass is available in many forms: vases, tea sets, decanters, glasses, jewelry, lamps, mod sculptures, and on and on. Shops will ship it home for you, but you're likely to pay as much or more for the shipping as you are for the item(s), and you may have to pay duty on larger purchases. Make sure the shop insures their merchandise *(assicurazione),* or you're out of luck if it breaks.

Some visitors feel that because they're in Venice, they ought to grab the opportunity to buy glass. Remember that you can buy fine glass back home, too (Venice stopped forbidding its glassblowers from leaving the republic a few centuries ago)—and under less time pressure.

You'll want to avoid the cheap glass you'll see—most of it is imported from China or Mexico. Genuine, high-end Venetian glass comes with the signature of the artist etched directly into the glass, along with a number if it's a limited edition piece (for example, 14/30—number 14 of a total of 30 pieces made).

If you're serious about glass, visit the island of Murano, its glass museum, and its many shops—you'll find greater variety on the island.

To learn more about glass art, consider a free glassblowing demo at the **Vetri d'Arte** showroom in Palazzo Rota. Tour groups come and go all day long for the entertaining little demonstration followed by a sales pitch, but individuals are welcome to sit in on the show. From Gran Caffè Quadri on St. Mark's Square, Sottoportico dei Dai leads over a bridge and, 30 yards later, directly into a lobby (it's unsigned, look for the ATM) where stairs lead up to the showroom (RS%–20 percent discount on glass with this book, daily 8:30-17:00, San Marco 834—see the map on page 64 for location, tel. 041-241-2664).

# Nightlife in Venice

You must experience Venice after dark. The city is quiet at night, as many tour groups (not mine) stay in the cheaper hotels of Mestre on the mainland, and the masses of day-trippers return to their beach resorts and cruise ships.

Venice has a busy schedule of events, church concerts, festivals, and entertainment. Check at the TI or the TI's website (www.veneziaunica.it) for listings. The free monthly *Un Ospite di Venezia* lists all the latest happenings in English (free at fancy hotels, or check www.unospitedivenezia.it).

### Baroque Concerts

Venice is a city of the powdered-wig Baroque era. For about €25, you can take your pick of traditional Vivaldi concerts in churches throughout town. Homegrown Vivaldi is as ubiquitous here as Strauss is in Vienna and Mozart is in Salzburg. In fact, you'll find frilly young Vivaldis hawking concert tickets on many corners.

Most shows start at 20:30 and generally last 1.5 hours. You'll see posters in hotels all over town (hotels sell tickets at face value).

Tickets for Baroque concerts in Venice can usually be bought the same day as the concert, so don't bother with websites that sell tickets with a surcharge. The general rule of thumb: Musicians in wigs and tights offer better spectacle; musicians in black-and-white suits are better performers.

The **Interpreti Veneziani orchestra,** considered the best group in town, generally performs 1.5-hour concerts nightly at 21:00 inside the sumptuous San Vidal Church (€28, church ticket booth open daily 9:30-21:00, north end of Accademia Bridge, tel. 041-277-0561, www.interpretiveneziani.com).

### Other Performances

Venice's most famous theaters are **La Fenice** (grand old opera house, box office tel. 041-2424), **Teatro Goldoni** (mostly Italian live theater), and **Teatro Fondamenta Nuove** (theater, music, and dance).

*Musica a Palazzo* is a unique evening of opera at a Venetian palace on the Grand Canal. You'll spend about 45 delightful minutes in each of three sumptuous rooms (about 2.25 hours total) as seven musicians (generally three instruments and four singers) perform. With these kinds of surroundings, and under Tiepolo frescoes, you'll be glad you dressed up. As there are only 70 seats, you must book by phone or online in advance (€85, nightly at 20:30, Palazzo Barbarigo Minotto, Fondamenta Duodo o Barbarigo, vaporetto: Santa Maria del Giglio, San Marco 2504, mobile 340-971-7272, www.musicapalazzo.com).

### St. Mark's Square

For tourists, St. Mark's Square is the highlight, with lantern light and live music echoing from the cafés. Just being here after dark is a thrill, as **dueling café orchestras** entertain. The ultimate Venetian music scene is at the venerable Caffè Florian. But Gran Caffè Chioggia (facing the Doge's Palace) doesn't charge extra for music and has good jazz nightly (see the sidebar on page 74). Every night, enthusiastic musicians play the same songs, creating the same irresistible magic. Hang out for free behind the tables (allowing you to move easily on to the next orchestra when the musicians take a break), or spring for a seat and enjoy a fun and gorgeously set concert. If you sit a while, expect to pay €15 and up (for a drink and the cover charge for music)—money well spent. Dancing on the square is free—and encouraged.

Several venerable cafés and bars on the square serve expensive drinks outside but cheap drinks inside at the bar. The scene in a bar like **Gran Caffè Lavena** (despite its questionable chandelier) can be great. You'll hear people talking about the famous **Harry's**

**American Bar,** which sells overpriced food and American cocktails to dressy tourists near the San Marco-Vallaresso vaporetto stop. But it's a rip-off...and the last place Hemingway would drink today. It's far cheaper to get a drink at any of the hole-in-the-wall bars just off St. Mark's Square; you can get a bottle of beer or even prosecco-to-go in a plastic cup.

Wherever you end up, streetlamp halos, live music, floodlit history, and a ceiling of stars make St. Mark's magic at midnight.

# Sleeping in Venice

I've listed rooms in these areas: St. Mark's bustle, the Rialto action, the quiet Dorsoduro area behind the Accademia art museum, and near the train station.

Hotels in Venice can be tricky to locate. The website Venicexplorer.net allows you to search using a hotel's address number and district, which I've included in my listings (click "Venice Civic Number" on the website to open the search window); it's better than Google Maps, which can choke on Venetian addresses. Remember that Venice has six districts: San Marco, Castello, Cannaregio, San Polo, Santa Croce, and Dorsoduro.

**Hotel Tips:** I rank accommodations from $ budget to $$$$ splurge. For the best deal, contact my family-run accommodations directly by phone or email. When you book direct, the owner avoids a commission and may be able to offer a discount. Book well in advance for peak season or if your trip coincides with a major holiday or festival (see the appendix).

As many hotels in central Venice are in historic buildings, rooms tend to be small and stairs are often plentiful. Unless noted, these listings do not have an elevator. For some travelers, short-term, Airbnb-type rentals can be a good alternative; search for places in my recommended hotel neighborhoods.

For more details on reservations, short-term rentals, and more, see the "Sleeping" section in the Practicalities chapter.

## NEAR ST. MARK'S SQUARE

To get here from the train station or Piazzale Roma bus station, ride the slow vaporetto #1 to San Zaccaria or the fast #2 (which also leaves from Tronchetto parking lot) to San Marco. Consider using your ride to follow my tour of the Grand Canal (earlier in this chapter); to make sure you arrive via the Grand Canal, confirm that your boat goes *"via Rialto."*

### East of St. Mark's Square

Located near the Bridge of Sighs, just off the Riva degli Schiavoni

VENICE

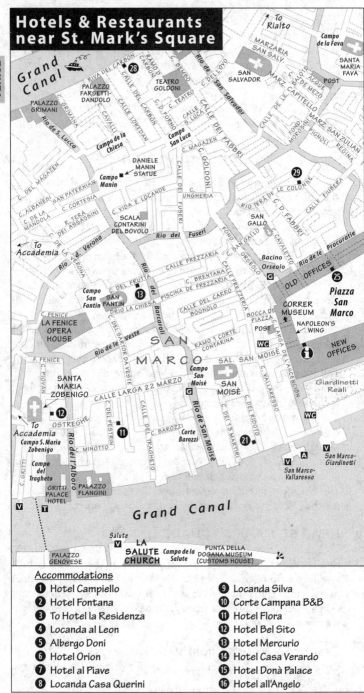

# Hotels & Restaurants near St. Mark's Square

## Accommodations

1. Hotel Campiello
2. Hotel Fontana
3. To Hotel la Residenza
4. Locanda al Leon
5. Albergo Doni
6. Hotel Orion
7. Hotel al Piave
8. Locanda Casa Querini
9. Locanda Silva
10. Corte Campana B&B
11. Hotel Flora
12. Hotel Bel Sito
13. Hotel Mercurio
14. Hotel Casa Verardo
15. Hotel Donà Palace
16. Hotel all'Angelo

VENICE

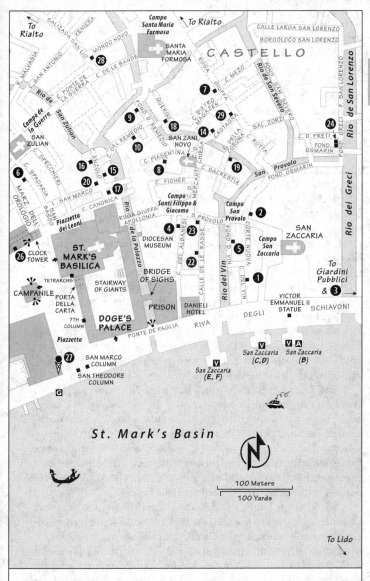

waterfront promenade, these places rub drainpipes with Venice's most palatial five-star hotels.

**$$$$ Hotel Campiello,** lacy and bright, was once part of a 19th-century convent. Ideally located 50 yards off the waterfront on a tiny square, its 16 rooms offer a tranquil, friendly refuge for travelers who appreciate comfort and professional service (RS%, air-con, elevator, just steps from the San Zaccaria vaporetto stop, Castello 4647; tel. 041-520-5764, www.hcampiello.it, campiello@hcampiello.it; family-run for four generations, currently by Thomas, Nicoletta, and Monica). They also rent three modern, upscale, and quiet family apartments for up to six people, under rustic timbers just steps away from the hotel.

**$$$$ Hotel Fontana,** two bridges behind St. Mark's Square, is a pleasant family-run place with 15 sparse but classic-feeling rooms overlooking a lively square (RS%, several rooms with terraces, family rooms, air-con, elevator, closed Jan, on Campo San Provolo at Castello 4701, tel. 041-522-0533, www.hotelfontana.it, info@hotelfontana.it, cousins Diego and Gabriele).

**$$$$ Hotel la Residenza** is a grand old palace facing a peaceful square. It has 16 rooms on three levels (with no elevator) and a huge, luxurious lounge. This is a good value for romantics—you'll feel like you're in the Doge's Palace after hours (air-con; from the Riva, go down Calle del Dose to Campo Bandiera e Moro at Castello 3608, tel. 041-528-5315, www.venicelaresidenza.com, info@venicelaresidenza.com, Giovanni).

**$$$ Locanda al Leon,** which feels a little like a medieval tower house, is conscientiously run and rents 12 rooms just off Campo Santi Filippo e Giacomo (RS%, some view rooms, family rooms, air-con, one- and two-bedroom apartments, Campo Santi Filippo e Giacomo, Castello 4270, tel. 041-277-0393, www.hotelalleon.com, leon@hotelalleon.com, Giuliano and Marcella). Their annex down the street, **B&B Ca' Marcella,** has three newer, classy, and spacious rooms for the same rates (check in at main hotel).

**$$ Albergo Doni,** situated along a quiet canal, is dark and quiet. This time-warp—with creaky floors and 13 well-worn, once-classy rooms—is run by friendly Tessa and her two brothers, Barnaba and (now "retired") Italian stallion Nikos (RS%, cheaper rooms with shared bath, family rooms, ceiling fans, a few rooms have air-con, Wi-Fi in common areas, on Fondamenta del Vin at Castello 4656, tel. 041-522-4267, www.albergodoni.it, albergodoni@hotmail.it). The hotel also has three nice overflow apartments at the same prices (but without breakfast).

## North of St. Mark's Square

**$$$$ Hotel Orion** rents 21 simple, welcoming, pricey rooms in the center of the action (you're paying a premium for the location).

Steep stairs (there's no elevator) take you from the touristy street into a peaceful world high above (RS%—use code RSTEVES, air-con, 2 minutes inland from St. Mark's Square, 10 steps toward St. Mark's from San Zulian Church at Calle Spadaria 700a, tel. 041-522-3053, www.hotelorion.it, info@hotelorion.it).

$$$ **Hotel al Piave,** with 25 rooms above a bright, tight lobby and breakfast room, is comfortable and cheery, and you'll enjoy the neighborhood (RS%, family rooms, lots of narrow stairs, air-con, on Ruga Giuffa at Castello 4838, tel. 041-528-5174, www.hotelalpiave. com, info@hotelalpiave.com; Mirella, Paolo, Ilaria, and Federico).

$$$ **Locanda Casa Querini** rents six bright, high-ceilinged rooms on a quiet square tucked away behind St. Mark's. You can enjoy your breakfast or a sunny happy-hour picnic sitting at their tables right on the sleepy little square (RS%, family rooms, in-room fridges, air-con, halfway between San Zaccaria vaporetto stop and Campo Santa Maria Formosa at Castello 4388 on Campo San Za-ninovo/Giovanni Novo, tel. 041-241-1294, www.locandaquerini. com, info@locandaquerini.com; Patrizia and Caterina).

$$$ **Locanda Silva** is a well-located hotel with a functional 1960s feel and a small terrace. It rents 23 simple rooms with small bathrooms (RS%, a few cheaper rooms with shared bathrooms, closed Dec-Jan, family rooms, air-con, lots of stairs, on Fonda-menta del Remedio at Castello 4423, tel. 041-522-7643, www. locandasilva.it, info@locandasilva.it; Sandra and Katia).

$$ **Corte Campana B&B,** run by enthusiastic and helpful Riccardo and his Californian wife Grace, rents three quiet, spa-cious, characteristic rooms in a homey flat just behind St. Mark's Square. For one room, the private bath is down the hall (cash only, 2-night minimum, family rooms, air-con, elevator, on Calle del Remedio at Castello 4410, tel. 041-523-3603, mobile 389-272-6500, www.cortecampana.com, info@cortecampana.com).

## Near Campo Santa Maria Formosa

A bit farther north of the options listed above, these are in the quiet, somewhat less touristy Castello area, beyond the inviting Campo Santa Maria Formosa (for locations, see the map on page 103).

$$$ **Locanda la Corte** is perfumed with elegance with-out being snooty. Its 14 attractive, high-ceilinged, wood-beamed rooms—Venetian-style, done in earthy pastels—circle a small, sun-drenched courtyard and a ground-level restaurant (RS%, fam-ily rooms, air-con, on Calle Bressana at Castello 6317, tel. 041-241-1300, www.locandalacorte.it, info@locandalacorte.it).

$$ **Alloggi Barbaria,** a good budget choice, rents eight sim-ple, characterless rooms on one floor around a bright but institu-tional-feeling common area. Beyond Campo San Zanipolo/Santi Giovanni e Paolo, it's a fair walk from the action, but in a pleas-

ant residential neighborhood. The Ospedale vaporetto stop is two minutes away on foot, with no steps (RS%, family rooms, limited continental breakfast, air-con in summer, Wi-Fi in common areas, on Calle de le Capucine at Castello 6573, tel. 041-522-2750, www.alloggibarbaria.it, info@alloggibarbaria.it, friendly Fausto). You can reach the Ospedale stop on vaporetto #5.2 from the train or bus stations, or via the Alilaguna blue line from the airport.

## West of St. Mark's Square

These more expensive hotels are solid choices in a more elegant neighborhood.

$$$$ **Hotel Flora** sits buried in a sea of fancy designer boutiques and elegant hotels almost on the Grand Canal. It's formal, with uniformed staff and grand public spaces, yet the 40 rooms have a homey warmth and the garden oasis is a sanctuary for well-heeled, foot-weary guests (RS%, air-con, elevator, great family-size apartment, on Calle Bergamaschi at San Marco 2283a, tel. 041-520-5844, www.hotelflora.it, info@hotelflora.it).

$$$$ **Hotel Bel Sito** offers pleasing Old World character, 34 smallish rooms, generous public spaces, a peaceful courtyard, and a picturesque location—facing a church on a small square between St. Mark's Square and the Accademia (RS%, some view rooms, air-con, elevator; near Santa Maria del Giglio vaporetto stop—line #1, on Campo Santa Maria Zobenigo/del Giglio at San Marco 2517, tel. 041-522-3365, www.hotelbelsitovenezia.it, info@hotelbelsitovenezia.it, graceful Rossella).

$$$$ **Hotel Mercurio,** a lesser value a block in front of La Fenice Opera House, offers 29 peaceful, comfortable rooms (some view rooms, family rooms, air-con, lots of stairs, on Calle del Fruttariol at San Marco 1848, tel. 041-522-0947, www.hotelmercurio.com, info@hotelmercurio.com).

## NEAR THE RIALTO BRIDGE

These places are on opposite sides of the Grand Canal, within a short walk of the Rialto Bridge. Express vaporetto #2 brings you to the Rialto quickly from the train station, the Piazzale Roma bus station, and the parking-lot island of Tronchetto, but you'll need to take the "local" vaporetto #1 to reach the minor stops closer to the last two listings. To locate the following hotels, see the map on page 103.

$$$$ **Hotel al Ponte Antico** is exquisite, professional, and small. With nine plush rooms, a velvety royal living/breakfast room, and its own dock for water taxi arrivals, it's perfect for a romantic anniversary. Because its wonderful terrace overlooks the Grand Canal, Rialto Bridge, and market action, its rooms without a canal view may be a better value (air-con, 100 yards from Rialto Bridge at Cannaregio 5768, use Rialto vaporetto stop, tel. 041-241-

1944, www.alponteantico.com, info@alponteantico.com, Matteo makes you feel like royalty).

**$$$ Pensione Guerrato,** right above the colorful Rialto produce market and just two minutes from the Rialto Bridge, is run by friendly, creative, and hardworking Roberto, Piero, Monica, and Matilde. Their 800-year-old building—with 22 spacious, charming rooms—is simple, airy, and wonderfully characteristic. It's a great value considering the location and charm (RS%, cheaper rooms with shared bath, family rooms, air-con, on Calle drio la Scimia at San Polo 240a, take vaporetto #1 to Rialto Mercato stop to save walk over bridge, tel. 041-528-5927, www.hotelguerrato. com, info@hotelguerrato.com). My tour groups book this place for 60 nights each year. Sorry. The Guerrato also rents family apartments in the old center (great for groups of 4-8).

**$$$ Hotel al Ponte Mocenigo** is off the beaten path—a 10-minute walk northwest of the Rialto Bridge—but it's a great value. This 16th-century Venetian palazzo has a garden terrace and 15 comfy, beautifully appointed, and tranquil rooms (RS%, air-con, take vaporetto #1 to San Stae stop, head inland along right side of church and find Santa Croce 1985, tel. 041-524-4797, www.alpontemocenigo. com, info@alpontemocenigo.com, Sandro and Valter).

## NEAR THE ACCADEMIA BRIDGE

As you step over the Accademia Bridge, the commotion of touristy Venice is replaced by a sleepy village laced with canals. This quiet area, next to the best painting gallery in town, is a 15-minute walk from the Rialto or St. Mark's Square. The fast vaporetto #2 to the Accademia stop is the typical way to get here from the train station, Piazzale Roma bus station, Tronchetto parking lot, or St. Mark's Square (early and late, #2 terminates at the Rialto stop, where you change to #1). For hotels near the Zattere stop, vaporetto #5.1 or the Alilaguna speedboat from the airport are good options.

## South of the Accademia Bridge, in Dorsoduro

**$$$$ Pensione Accademia** fills the 17th-century Villa Maravege like a Bellini painting. Its 27 comfortable, elegant rooms gild the lily. You'll feel aristocratic gliding through its grand public spaces and lounging in its wistful, breezy gardens (family rooms, air-con, no elevator but most rooms on ground floor or one floor up, on Fondamenta Bollani at Dorsoduro 1058, tel. 041-521-0188, www. pensioneaccademia.it, info@pensioneaccademia.it).

**$$$$ Hotel la Calcina,** the home of English writer John Ruskin in 1876, maintains a 19th-century formality. It comes with three-star comforts in a professional yet intimate package. Its 25 nautical-feeling rooms are squeaky clean, with nice wood furniture, hardwood floors, and a peaceful waterside setting facing

VENICE

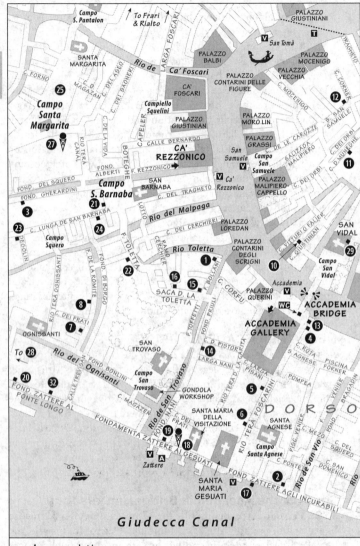

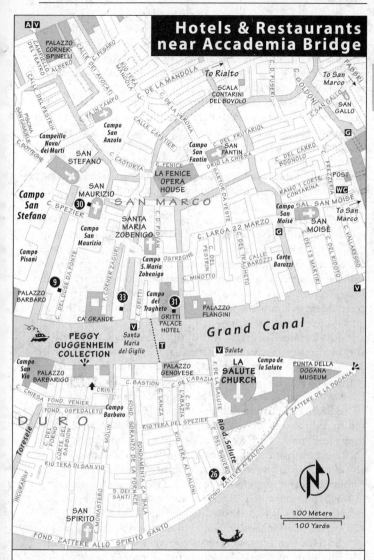

17 Pizzeria Zattere
18 Nico Gelataria
19 Terrazza dei Nobili
20 Pizzeria Oke
21 Ristoteca Oniga
22 Osteria Enoteca Ai Artisti
23 Pizzeria al Profeta
24 Enoteca e Trattoria la Bitta
25 Campo Santa Margarita
   Eateries & Nightlife

26 Ristorante Lineadombra
27 Gelateria Il Doge
28 To Supermarket

Nightlife
29 Interpreti Veneziani Concerts
30 Music Museum
31 Musica a Palazzo
30 El Chioschetto alle Zattere
33 Venice Jazz Club

Giudecca Island (some view rooms, air-con, no elevator and lots of stairs, rooftop terrace, buffet breakfast outdoors in good weather on platform over lagoon, near Zattere vaporetto stop at south end of Rio de San Vio at Dorsoduro 780, tel. 041-520-6466, www. lacalcina.com, info@lacalcina.com).

**$$$$ Casa Rezzonico,** a tranquil getaway far from the crowds, rents seven inviting, nicely appointed rooms with a grassy private garden terrace. All the rooms overlook either the canal or the garden (RS%, family rooms, air-con, near Ca' Rezzonico vaporetto stop—line #1, a few blocks past Campo San Barnaba on Fondamenta Gherardini at Dorsoduro 2813, tel. 041-277-0653, www.casarezzonico.it, info@casarezzonico.it, brothers Matteo and Mattia).

**$$$$ Hotel Galleria** has nine old-fashioned and velvety rooms, half with views of the Grand Canal. Some rooms are quite narrow, but you can open your window to watch boats pass by at any time. It's run with a family feel by Luciano (one cheaper room with detached private bath, breakfast in room, ceiling fans, 30 yards from Accademia art museum, next to recommended Foscarini pizzeria at Dorsoduro 878a, tel. 041-523-2489, www.hotelgalleria.it, info@hotelgalleria.it).

**$$$$ Hotel Belle Arti,** with a stiff, serious staff, lacks personality but has a grand entry, an inviting garden terrace, and 67 heavily decorated rooms (air-con, elevator, 100 yards behind Accademia art museum on Rio Terà A. Foscarini at Dorsoduro 912a, tel. 041-522-6230, www.hotelbellearti.com, info@hotelbellearti.com).

**$$$$ Don Orione Religious Guest House** is a big cultural center dedicated to the work of a local man who became a saint in modern times. With 80 rooms filling an old monastery, it feels cookie-cutter-institutional (like a modern retreat center), but is also classy, clean, peaceful, and strictly run. It's beautifully located, comfortable, and supports a fine cause: Profits go to mission work in the developing world (family rooms, groups welcome, air-con, elevator, on Rio Terà A. Foscarini, Dorsoduro 909a, tel. 041-522-4077, www.donorione-venezia.it, info@donorione-venezia.it).

**$$$ Ca' San Trovaso** rents six pleasant rooms in a little three-floor, formerly residential building. The location is peaceful, on a small, out-of-the-way canal (RS%, some view rooms, breakfast in your room, tiny roof terrace, apartments available with 3-night minimum, near Zattere vaporetto stop, off Fondamenta de le Romite at Dorsoduro 1350, tel. 041-241-2215, mobile 349-125-3890, www.casantrovaso.com, info@casantrovaso.com, Anna and Alessandra).

**$$$ Casa di Sara,** a colorfully decorated B&B, is hidden in a leafy courtyard in a humble back-street area overlooking a canal. Their four quiet rooms and tiny roof terrace offer the maximum

in privacy (air-con, along Fondamenta de le Romite at Dorsoduro 1330, mobile 342-596-3563, www.casadisara.com, info@
casadisara.com, Emanuele).

### North of the Accademia Bridge

These places are between the Accademia Bridge and St. Mark's
Square.

**$$$$ Novecento Hotel** rents nine plush rooms on three
floors, complemented by a big, welcoming lounge, an elegant living
room, and a small breakfast garden. This boutique hotel is nicely
located and has a tasteful sense of style, mingling Art Deco with
North African and Turkish decor (air-con, lots of stairs, on Calle
del Dose, off Campo San Maurizio at San Marco 2684, tel. 041-
241-3765, www.novecento.biz, info@novecento.biz).

**$$$$ Foresteria Levi,** run by a foundation that promotes research on Venetian music, offers 32 quiet, institutional yet comfortable and spacious rooms—some are loft quads, a good deal for
families (RS%, air-con, elevator, on Calle Giustinian at San Marco
2893, tel. 041-277-0542, www.foresterialevi.it, info@foresterialevi.
it). From the base of the Accademia Bridge, it's just over the tiny
Ponte Giustinian.

**$$$ Domus Ciliota** is a big, efficient, and sparkling-clean
place—well-run, well-located, church-owned, and plainly fur-
nished—with 30 dorm-like rooms and a peaceful courtyard. If you
want industrial-strength comfort with no stress and little charac-
ter, this is a fine value. During the school year, half the rooms are
used by students (air-con, elevator; just off Campo San Stefano at
San Marco 2976; tel. 041-520-4888, www.ciliota.it, info@ciliota.
it).

**$$$ Hotel San Samuele** rents 10 tidy rooms in an old *palazzo*
near Campo San Stefano. Antique furniture and restored original
floors give this place a homey feel. It's in a great locale, and the
rooms with shared bath can be a good deal (RS%, no breakfast,
fans, some stairs, on Salizada San Samuele at San Marco 3358, tel.
041-520-5165, www.hotelsansamuele.com, info@hotelsansamuele.
com, Judith).

# Eating in Venice

While touristy restaurants are the norm in Venice, you can still
make the most of your meal by dining at one of my recommended
listings and following these tips. First trick: Walk away from tri-
ple-language menus or laminated pictures of food. Second trick:
For freshness, eat fish. (But remember that seafood can be sold by
weight—per 100 grams or *etto*—rather than a set price.) Many seafood dishes are the catch-of-the-day. Third trick: Eat later. A place

may feel touristy at 19:00, but if you come back at 21:00, it can be filled with locals...or, at least, Italian visitors.

## EATING TIPS

Venetians often eat a snack—*cicchetti* or *panini*—while standing at a bar. (You'll usually pay more if you sit.)

Unique to Venice, *cicchetti* bars specialize in finger foods and appetizers that combine to make a speedy and tasty meal. *Cicchetti* (the Venetian version of tapas) was designed as a quick meal for working people. The selection and ambience are best on workdays—Monday through Saturday for lunch or early dinner (see "The Stand-Up Progressive Venetian Pub-Crawl Dinner" sidebar, later).

Sandwiches are sold fast and cheaply at bars everywhere (order a *panini, piadini,* or *tramezzini*). A great "sandwich row" of cheap cafés is near St. Mark's Square. You can eat your sandwich at the bar or take it with you.

A favorite Italian tradition is the *aperitivo* (predinner drink). The dominant *aperitivo* among Venetians is the *spritz* (white wine, soda, and ice with a liquor of your choice). When you order, you'll be asked if you'd like your *spritz con Campari* (bitter) or *con Aperol* (sweeter).

## NEAR THE RIALTO BRIDGE
### North of the Bridge

These restaurants and wine bars are located near or beyond Campo Santi Apostoli, on or near the Strada Nova, the main drag going from Rialto toward the train station.

**$$$ Trattoria da Bepi,** bright and alpine-paneled, feels like a classic, where Loris carries on his mother's passion for good, traditional Venetian cuisine. Ask for the seasonal specialties: The seafood appetizer plate and crab dishes are excellent. There's good seating inside and out. If you trust Loris, you'll walk away with a wonderful dining memory (Fri-Wed 12:00-14:30 & 19:00-22:00, closed Thu, reservations recommended, half a block off Campo Santi Apostoli on Salizada Pistor, Cannaregio 4550, tel. 041-528-5031, www.dabepi.it).

**$$$ La Cantina** is a rustic yet sophisticated *enoteca*—you won't find a menu here. Rather than cook (there's no kitchen), they serve *cicchetti* and gourmet cold plates of meat, cheese, and fish. Though short on smiles and expensive (meat-and-cheese plates—€18/person, seafood plates—€35/person), you'll enjoy good ingredients paired with fine wines. You can sit inside and watch the preparation scene or enjoy the parade of passersby from great seats right on the Strada Nova (Mon-Sat 11:00-22:00, closed Sun, facing Campo

San Felice on Strada Nova near Ca' d'Oro, Cannaregio 3689, tel. 041-522-8258).

**$$$$ Vini da Gigio,** a more expensive option, has a traditional Venetian menu and a classy but unsnooty setting that's a pleasant mix of traditional and contemporary (Wed-Sun 12:00-14:30 & 19:00-22:30, closed Mon-Tue, 4 blocks from Ca' d'Oro vaporetto stop on Fondamenta San Felice, behind the church on Campo San Felice, Cannaregio 3628a, tel. 041-528-5140, www. vinidagigio.com).

## East of the Rialto Bridge

The next few places hide away in the twisty lanes between the Rialto Bridge and Campo Santa Maria Formosa. Osteria da Alberto is a tad farther north of the others.

**$ Bacarando Bar** has a youthful feel, with clearly marked and priced little dishes at the counter and table seating (daily 11:00-24:00, tel. 342-800-3823). It's behind Campo San Bartolomeo (if the statue turned around, walked to the far right-hand corner, and explored the back lanes there, he'd find Bacarando in Corte dell'Orso).

**$$ Osteria al Portego** is a small and popular neighborhood eatery near Campo San Lio. Carlo serves good meals, bargain-priced house wine, and excellent €1-3 *cicchetti*—best enjoyed around 18:00 (picked over by 21:00). The *cicchetti* here can make a great meal, but consider sitting down for a dinner from their menu. From 12:00-14:30 & 17:30-21:30, their six tables are reserved for those ordering from the menu; reserve ahead if you want a table (daily 11:30-15:00 & 17:30-22:00, on Calle de la Malvasia, Castello 6015, tel. 041-522-9038, Federica). From Campo San Bartolomeo, continue over a bridge to Campo San Lio, turn left, and follow Calle Carminati straight 50 yards over another bridge.

**$$ Osteria da Alberto,** up near Campo Santa Maria Novo, is one of my standbys, with locals at lunch and tourists at dinner. They offer up excellent daily specials: seafood dishes, pastas, and a good house wine in a woody and characteristic interior. It's smart to reserve at night—I'd request a table in front (daily 12:00-15:00 & 18:30-22:00; on Calle Larga Giacinto Gallina, midway between Campo Santi Apostoli and Campo San Zanipolo/Santi Giovanni e Paolo, and next to Ponte de la Panada bridge, Cannaregio 5401; tel. 041-523-8153, www.osteriadaalberto.it, run by Graziano and Giovanni).

## Rialto Market Area

The north end of the Rialto Bridge is a great area for menu browsing, bar-hopping, drinks, and snacks; it also has fine sit-down restaurants. As with market neighborhoods anywhere, you'll find lots

VENICE

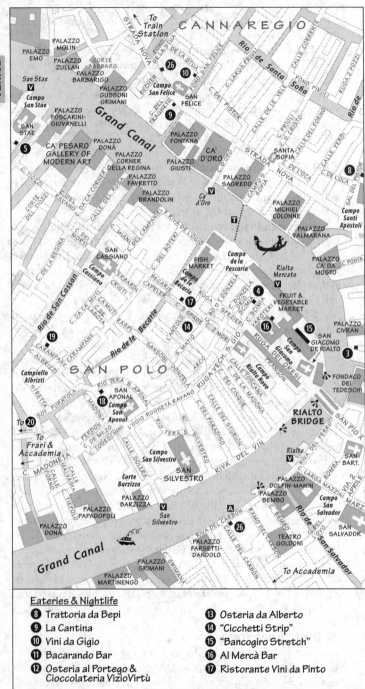

## Eateries & Nightlife

- 8 Trattoria da Bepi
- 9 La Cantina
- 10 Vini da Gigio
- 11 Bacarando Bar
- 12 Osteria al Portego & Cioccolateria VizioVirtù
- 13 Osteria da Alberto
- 14 "Cicchetti Strip"
- 15 "Bancogiro Stretch"
- 16 Al Mercà Bar
- 17 Ristorante Vini da Pinto

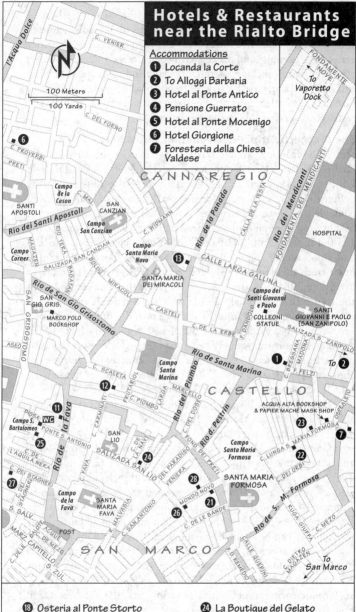

## Hotels & Restaurants near the Rialto Bridge

**Accommodations**

1. Locanda la Corte
2. To Alloggi Barbaria
3. Hotel al Ponte Antico
4. Pensione Guerrato
5. Hotel al Ponte Mocenigo
6. Hotel Giorgione
7. Foresteria della Chiesa Valdese

18. Osteria al Ponte Storto
19. Trattoria Antiche Carampane
20. To Antica Birraria la Corte
21. Osteria alle Testiere
22. Osteria al Mascaron
23. Peter Pan Kebabs & Pizza
24. La Boutique del Gelato
25. Gelatoteca Suso
26. Supermarket (3)
27. Devil's Forest Pub
28. Inishark Pub

of hard-working holes-in-the-wall with a line on the freshest of ingredients and catering to local shoppers needing a quick, affordable, and tasty bite. This area is very crowded by day, nearly empty early in the evening, and packed with young, trendy Venetians later.

My listings include a stretch of dark and rustic pubs serving *cicchetti* (Venetian tapas), a strip of trendy places fronting the Grand Canal, a few little places on the market, and a couple of "normal" restaurants serving solid pasta, pizza, and *secondi*.

### The *Cicchetti* Strip: Four Venetian Tapas Bars

The 100-yard-long stretch starting two blocks inland from the Rialto Market (along Sotoportego dei Do Mori and Calle de le Do Spade) is beloved among Venetian *cicchetti* enthusiasts for its delightful bar munchies, good wine by the glass, and fun stand-up conviviality. These **$** places serve food all day, but the spread is best at around noon (unless otherwise noted, generally open daily 12:00-15:00 & 18:00-20:00 or 21:00). Each place offers a fine bar-and-stools scene, and a couple can be treated like a restaurant— order from their rustic menu and grab a table. Scout these places in advance (listed in the order you'll reach them, if coming from the Rialto Bridge) to help decide which ambience is right for the experience you have in mind. Then pick one, dig in, and drink up.

At each place, look for the list of snacks and wine by the glass at the bar or on the wall. When you're ready for dessert, try dipping a Burano biscuit in a glass of strawberry-flavored *fragolino* or another sweet dessert wine. Most bars offer glasses of house wine for €1, better wine for around €3, and *cicchetti* for €1.50-2.

**Bar all'Arco,** a bustling one-room joint, is particularly enjoyable for its *cicchetti* (Mon-Sat 10:00-17:00, closed Sun, San Polo 436; Francesco, Anna, Matteo).

**Cantina Do Mori** has been famous with locals (since 1462) and savvy travelers (since 1982) as a convivial place for wine. They serve a forest of little edibles on toothpicks and *francobolli* (a spicy selection of 20 tiny, mayo-soaked sandwiches nicknamed "stamps"). Go here to be abused in a fine atmosphere—the frowns are part of the shtick—and be aware that prices can add up quickly (closed Sun, can be shoulder-to-shoulder, San Polo 430).

**Osteria ai Storti,** with a cool photo of the market in 1909, is more of a sit-down place (tables inside and on street). It's run by Alessandro, who speaks English and enjoys helping educate travelers (around corner from Cantina Do Mori on Calle San Matio, San Polo 819).

**Cantina Do Spade** is run by Francesco, who clearly lists the *cicchetti* (mostly deep fried) and wines of the day. It's also good for sit-down restaurant-style meals (30 yards down Calle de le Do Spade from Osteria ai Storti at San Polo 860, tel. 041-521-0583).

## The Bancogiro Stretch: Five Places Overlooking the Grand Canal

Just past the Rialto Bridge, between Campo San Giacomo and the Grand Canal, this strip of popular places in a recently renovated old building has some of the best canalside seating in Venice. I call this the "Bancogiro Stretch" (the restaurants front a former banking building called Bancogiro).

Each place has a unique character and formula. Unless otherwise noted, all are open daily and serve drinks, *cicchetti,* and somewhat pricey sit-down meals. While you can get a drink anytime, dinner is typically served only after 19:00 or 19:30. During meals, they charge more and limit table seating to those ordering full lunches or dinners; but between mealtimes you can enjoy a drink or a snack at fine prices. After dinner hours, the Bancogiro Stretch— especially in the surrounding alleys that house low-rent bars—becomes a youthful and trendy nightspot. Before or after dinner, this strip is one of the best places in town for a *spritz.*

Here's the rundown (in the order you'll reach them from the Rialto Bridge): **$$$ Bar Naranzaria** serves Italian dishes with a few Japanese options. **$$ Caffè Vergnano** is your cheapest option—especially during mealtimes (vegetarian dishes and a busy microwave oven). **$$$ Osteria al Pesador** has a friendly staff and serves local specialties. **$$$ Osteria Bancogiro** has the best reputation for dinner, a passion for the best cheese, and good *cicchetti* options at the bar (nice cheese plate, closed Mon, tel. 041-523-2061, www.osteriabancogiro.it). The more modern **$$ Bar Ancòra** seems to be most popular with the local bar crowd, with a live piano player crooning lounge music during busy times (*cicchetti* at the bar).

## Other Good Eateries near the Rialto Market

**$ Al Mercà Bar** ("At the Market"), a few steps away and off the canal, is a lively little nook with a happy crowd, where law-office workers have lunch and young locals gather in the evening for drinks (quality wine by the glass) and little snacks (€2 mini-sandwiches). The price list is clear, and the youthful crowd seems to enjoy connecting with curious tourists (stand at bar or in square— there are no tables and no interior, Mon-Sat 10:00-14:30 & 18:00-21:00, closed Sun, on Campo Cesare Battisti, San Polo 213).

**$$ Ristorante Vini da Pinto** is a tourist-friendly eatery facing the fish market, with a large menu and relaxing outdoor seating (and easily confused with the restaurant next door to it). Owner Giorgio visits the market each morning to select the day's best catch. Enjoy the lunch-only, fixed-price, three-course seafood meal for €18, including a pasta, seafood sampler plate, veggies, and dessert. Grander versions cost €20-25. Rick Steves readers receive

# The Stand-Up Progressive Venetian Pub-Crawl Dinner

My favorite Venetian dinner is a pub crawl (*giro d'ombra*)— a tradition unique to Venice, where no cars means easy crawling. (*Giro* means stroll, and *ombra*— slang for a glass of wine—means shade, from the old days when a portable wine bar scooted with the shadow of the Campanile bell tower across St. Mark's Square.)

Venice's residential back streets hide plenty of characteristic bars (*bacari*), with countless trays of interesting toothpick munchies (*cicchetti*) and blackboards listing the wines that are uncorked and served by the glass. This is a great way to mingle and have fun with the Venetians. Bars don't stay open very late, and the *cicchetti* selection is best early, so start your evening by 18:00. Many bars are closed on Sunday. For a stress-free pub crawl, consider taking a tour with the charming Alessandro Schezzini (see page 49).

## The *Cicchetti* Experience

*Cicchetti* bars have a social stand-up zone and a cozy gaggle of tables where you can generally sit down with your *cicchetti* or order from a simple menu. In some of the more popular places, the crowds happily spill out into the street. Food generally costs the same price whether you stand or sit. I've listed plenty of pubs in walking order for a quick or extended crawl.

Look for a place that's more "bar" than "restaurant." Make sure they have *cicchetti* on display. Bar-hopping Venetians enjoy an *aperitivo*, a before-dinner drink. You may have to pay for it up front (but probably not—it varies). Then chill. Sip your drink and

a welcoming prosecco and a farewell *limoncello* and homemade cookie (daily 11:00-23:00, Campo de le Becarie, San Polo 367a, tel. 041-522-4599).

**$$ Osteria al Ponte Storto,** a little family-run place on a quiet canalside corner a block off the main drag, is worth seeking out for its good-value main dishes, daily specials, and peaceful location. Rather than a romantic place, it feels like the corner favorite of the neighborhood (Tue-Sun 12:00-15:00 & 18:00-21:45, closed Mon, down Calle Bianca from San Aponal church, San Polo 1278, tel. 041-528-2144, Nicola is the chef/owner).

make the scene while standing at the bar. Next, order a *cicchetti* or two by pointing. Chill some more, while munching and sipping. Then order another one or two. Find a stool or table nearby where you can sit (but don't sit at tables with tablecloths—those are for diners). Pay when you're ready to leave. If you've crawled enough, most of my recommended bars make a fine one-stop, sit-down dinner.

### What to Eat (and Drink)

While you can order a plate, Venetians prefer going one-by-one... sipping their wine and trying this...then give me one of those... and so on. Try deep-fried mozzarella cheese, gorgonzola, calamari, artichoke hearts, and anything ugly on a toothpick. Crostini (small toasted bread with a topping) are popular, as are marinated seafood, olives, and prosciutto with melon. Meat and fish (*pesce;* PESH-ay) munchies can be expensive; veggies (*verdure*) are cheap, at about €3 for a meal-sized plate. In many places, there's a set price per food item (for example, €1.50). To get a plate of assorted appetizers for €8 (or more, depending on how hungry you are), ask for *"Un piatto classico di cicchetti misti da €8"* (oon pee-AH-toh KLAH-see-koh dee chee-KET-tee MEE-stee dah OH-toh eh-OO-roh). Bread sticks (*grissini*) are free for the asking.

For drinks, start with an *aperitivo:* Order a Bellini, a *spritz con Aperol,* or a prosecco, and draw approving looks from the natives. Enjoy the house wines with the food. An *ombra* ("shadow") is a small glass of wine often offered with *cicchetti.* An *ombra rosso* (red) or *ombra bianco* (white), or a small beer (*birrino*) costs about €1. The house keg wine is cheap—€1 per glass, about €4 per liter. *Vin bon,* Venetian for fine wine, may run you from €2 to €6 per little glass. There are usually several fine wines uncorked and available by the glass. A good last drink is *fragolino,* the local sweet wine—*bianco* or *rosso.* It often comes with a little cookie (*biscotto*) for dipping.

## Between the Rialto Bridge and Frari Church

**$$$$ Trattoria Antiche Carampane** is a dressy, family-run place with an open kitchen and a local following. They have a passion for fish (and make a point: no pizza) and serve traditional Venetian dishes with a fresh twist that change with the season. It's small—there are just 30 seats with six tables on the street (Tue-Sat 12:45-14:30 & 19:30-22:30, closed Sun-Mon, reservations necessary, Rio Tera delle Carampane, San Polo 1911, tel. 041-524-0165, www.antichecarampane.com, Francesco).

**$$ Antica Birraria la Corte** is an everyday eatery on the de-

VENICE

lightful Campo San Polo. Popular for its huge array of pizza—and smaller selection of hearty salads, pasta, and *secondi*—it fills the far side of this cozy, family-filled square. Although the interior is sprawling and modern, it's a joy to eat on the square, where metal tables teeter on the cobbles, the wind plays with the paper mats, and children run free (daily 12:00-15:00 & 18:00-22:30, on Campo San Polo at #2168, tel. 041-275-0570).

## NEAR ST. MARK'S SQUARE

Other than the first place, a more serious restaurant, the other eateries listed here are cheap-and-cheery options convenient to your sightseeing. For locations, see the map on page 90.

**$$$$ Ristorante Antica Sacrestia** is a classic restaurant where the owner, Pino, takes a hands-on approach to greeting guests. His staff serves creative fixed-price meals (€35, €55, or €80), a humdrum *menù del giorno*, and wonderful pizzas. You can also order à la carte; their antipasto spread looks like a lagoon aquarium spread out on a plate. My readers are welcome to a free *sgroppino* (lemon vodka after-dinner drink) upon request (Tue-Sun 11:30-15:00 & 18:00-23:00, closed Mon, behind San Zaninovo/Giovanni Novo Church on Calle Corona, Castello 4463, tel. 041-523-0749, www. anticasacrestia.it). There's no wine by the glass. Order carefully. Pizza is your only budget escape.

**$$ Rossopomodoro Pizzeria** is a big, fun, and practical pizzeria offering top quality, good prices, and a very handy location. They cook Naples-style pizzas in their wood oven and also offer a selection of hearty salads and pastas (long hours daily, Calle Larga San Marco 404, tel. 041-243-8949).

**$$$ L'Ombra del Leone** is a big, modern, and classy bar (with attached restaurant) featuring an outdoor terrace right on the Grand Canal. It's in the Biennale offices and is popular with gondoliers. Its bar menu of salads and sandwiches has reasonable prices for the elegance and location (long hours daily, in Ca' Giustinian, behind San Moisè Church at the end of Calle Ridotto, tel. 041-241-3519).

**Sandwich Row:** On Calle de le Rasse, just steps away from the tourist intensity at St. Mark's Square, is a handy strip I call "Sandwich Row." Lined with several **$ sandwich bars,** it's the closest place to St. Mark's to get a decent sandwich at an affordable price with a place to sit down (most places open long hours daily, about €1 extra per item to sit; from the Bridge of Sighs, head down the Riva and take the second lane on the left). They all sell the *tramezzino* local-style sandwiches. **Birreria Forst** serves busy local workers a selection of meaty sandwiches with tasty sauce on wheat bread, or made-to-order sandwiches (daily 9:30-23:00, air-con, rustic wood tables, Castello 4540, tel. 041-523-0557). **Bar Verde**

is a more modern sandwich bar with fun people-watching views from its tables outside on the corner (also splittable salads, fresh pastries, at the end of Calle de le Rasse facing Campo Santi Filippo e Giacomo, Castello 4526).

**Picnicking:** Though you can't picnic on St. Mark's Square, you can legally take your snacks to the nearby Giardinetti Reali, the small park along the waterfront west of the Piazzetta.

## North of St. Mark's Square, near Campo Santa Maria Formosa

For a (marginally) less touristy scene, walk a few blocks north to the inviting Campo Santa Maria Formosa.

**$$$$ Osteria alle Testiere** is my top dining splurge in Venice. Hugely respected, Luca and his staff are dedicated to quality, serving up creative, artfully presented market-fresh seafood (there's no meat on the menu), homemade pastas, and fine wine in what the chef calls a "Venetian Nouvelle" style. With only 22 seats, it's tight and homey, with the focus on food and service. They have daily specials, 10 wines by the glass, and one agenda: a great dining experience. This is a good spot to let loose and trust your host. They're open for lunch (12:00-15:00), and reservations made via email only are a must for their two dinner seatings: 19:00 and 21:30 (plan on spending €60 for dinner, closed Sun-Mon, on Calle del Mondo Novo, just off Campo Santa Maria Formosa, Castello 5801, tel. 041-522-7220, www.osterialletestiere.it, info@osterialletestiere.it).

**$$$ Osteria al Mascaron** is a rustic little bar-turned-restaurant where I've gone for years to watch Gigi, Momi, and their food-loving band of ruffians dish up rustic-yet-sumptuous pastas with steamy seafood to salivating foodies. The *antipasto misto* fish-and-vegetable plate—have fun pointing—and two glasses of wine make a terrific light meal (Mon-Sat 12:00-15:00 & 18:00-23:00, closed Sun, reservations smart Fri-Sat; on Calle Lunga Santa Maria Formosa, a block past Campo Santa Maria Formosa, Castello 5225; tel. 041-522-5995, www.osteriamascaron.it).

**Fast and Cheap Eats:** The veggie stand on Campo Santa Maria Formosa is a fixture. For *döner kebabs* and pizza to go, head down Calle Lunga Santa Maria Formosa to **$ Peter Pan** at #6249 (daily 11:30-23:00, Castello).

## DORSODURO

All of these recommendations are within a 10-minute walk of the Accademia Bridge (for locations, see the map on page 97). This area, called Dorsoduro, is great for restaurants and well worth the walk from the more touristy Rialto and San Marco areas. The first listings, near the Accademia, are best for lunch. The places in Zattere overlook the Giudecca Canal. Best for dinner are the restau-

# Venetian Cuisine

Even more so than the rest of Italy, Venetian cuisine relies heavily on fish, shellfish, risotto, and polenta. Along with pizza and pasta, here are some typical foods you'll encounter. For more on Italian food, see the "Eating" section of the Practicalities chapter.

## Sandwiches

*Panini:* Sandwiches made with rustic bread, filled with meat, vegetables, and cheese, served cold or toasted *(riscaldato)*.

*Piadini:* Flatbread or wrap-like sandwiches.

*Tramezzini:* Crustless white sandwiches, served cold (various fillings, such as egg, tuna, or shrimp mixed with mayonnaise).

## Antipasti (Appetizers)

Venetians start a meal with a light *antipasti* or some *cicchetti*—finger-food appetizers sold in many bars.

*Antipasto di mare:* Marinated mix of chilled fish and shellfish.

*Asiago cheese:* A regional specialty, this cow's-milk cheese is either *mezzano* (young, creamy) or *stravecchio* (aged, pungent).

*Sarde in saor:* Sardines marinated with onions.

## Risi (Rice), Pasta, and Polenta

*Bigoli in salsa:* Long, fat, whole-wheat noodle in anchovy sauce.

*Pasta alla buzzara:* Pasta in a rich seafood-tomato sauce, generally with shrimp.

*Pasta al pomodoro:* Pasta in a simple tomato sauce.

*Pasta al vongole:* Pasta with clams.

*Pasta e fagioli:* Bean-and-pasta soup.

*Polenta:* Thick cornmeal porridge served soft or cut into firm slabs and grilled.

*Risi e bisi:* Rice and peas.

*Risotto:* Short-grain rice simmered in broth and flavored with seafood, meat, or veggies. *Risotto nero* is made with squid and its ink.

## Frutti di Mare (Seafood)

Venetian fish are generally smaller than American salmon and trout (think sardines and anchovies). The weirder the seafood (eel, octopus, frogfish), the more local it is.

*Baccalà:* Atlantic salt cod that's rehydrated and served with polenta; or chopped up and mixed with mayonnaise as a topping for *cicchetti* (appetizers), called *baccalà mantecato*.

*Branzino:* Sea bass, grilled and served whole.

*Calamari:* Squid, often cut into rings and deep-fried or marinated.

*Cozze:* Mussels, often steamed in an herb broth with tomato.

*Gamberi:* Shrimp—*gamberetti* are small, and *gamberoni* are large.

*Moleche col pien:* Fried soft-shell crabs.

*Orata:* Sea bream (usually farmed).

*Pesce fritto misto:* Deep-fried seafood (often calamari and prawns).

**Pesce spada:** Swordfish.

**Rombo:** Turbot, a flatfish similar to flounder.

**Rospo:** Frogfish, a small marine fish.

**Salmone:** Salmon (typically farm-raised).

**Seppia:** Cuttlefish, a squid-like creature. *Nero di seppia* is the squid served in its own ink, often over spaghetti.

**Sogliola:** Sole, served poached or oven-roasted.

**Vitello di mare:** "Sea veal," like swordfish—firm, mild, and grilled.

**Vongole:** Clams, often steamed with fresh herbs and wine, or served as *spaghetti alle vongole.*

**Zuppa di pesce:** Seafood stew.

## Dolci (Desserts)

Rather than order dessert in a restaurant, I like to stroll with a cup or cone of gelato from one of Venice's popular *gelaterie.* Cookies are also popular. The numerous varieties are due perhaps to Venice's position in trade (spices) and love of celebrations.

**Bisse:** Seahorse-shaped cookies.

**Bussola:** Ring-shaped cookies made for Easter.

**Croccante:** Toasted almond confection, similar to peanut brittle.

**Fritole:** Tiny doughnuts associated with Carnevale (Mardi Gras).

**Pinza:** Rustic cornmeal and wheat-flour cake filled with dried fruit; made for Epiphany, January 6.

**Tiramisù:** Spongy ladyfingers soaked in coffee and Marsala, layered with mascarpone cheese and bitter chocolate.

## Cocktails and Local Wines

**Amarone:** Rich and intense red, made from dried Valpolicella grapes that yield a wine high in alcohol—often around 15 percent.

**Bardolino:** Beaujolais-like wine made from Valpolicella grapes.

**Bellini:** Cocktail of prosecco and white-peach puree (invented at the pricey Harry's American Bar near St. Mark's Square).

**Fragolino:** A sweet, slightly fizzy dessert wine made from a strawberry-flavored grape.

**Prosecco:** Sparkling white wine. Connoisseurs say the best hails from Valdobbiadene.

**Recioto:** Dessert wine made with dried, aged Valpolicella grapes.

**Sgroppino:** Traditional after-dinner drink of squeezed lemon juice, lemon gelato, and vodka.

**Soave:** Crisp, dry white wine, great with seafood.

**Spritz:** White wine and soda or prosecco mixed with Campari (bitter) or Aperol (sweeter), over ice.

**Tiziano:** Grape juice and prosecco.

**Valpolicella:** Light, dry, fruity red wine, often served as the *vino della casa* (house wine).

rants near Campo San Barnaba. Last are a handful of pizzerias and *cicchetti* bars on Campo Santa Margarita. My top Dorsoduro listing, **Ristorante Lineadombra,** is described later in "Splurging on a Water (or Otherwise Great) View."

## Near the Accademia Bridge

**$$ Bar Foscarini,** next to the Accademia Bridge and Galleria, offers decent pizzas and *panini* in a memorable Grand Canal-view setting. The food is forgettable and drinks are pricey. But you're paying a premium for this premium location. On each visit to Venice, I grab a pizza lunch here while I ponder the Grand Canal bustle. They also serve breakfast (daily 8:00-23:00, Nov-April until 20:30, on Rio Terà A. Foscarini, Dorsoduro 878c, tel. 041-522-7281, Paolo and Simone).

**$ Enoteca Cantine del Vino Già Schiavi,** with a wonderfully characteristic *cicchetti*-bar ambience, is much loved for its inexpensive *cicchetti,* sandwiches (order from list on board), and wine. You're welcome to enjoy your wine and finger food at the bar, in the back room surrounded by wine bottles, or out on the sidewalk (specify "*fuori*" to sit outside and they'll provide plastic cups; please don't sit on the bridge). This is primarily a wine shop with great prices for bottles to go (Mon-Sat 8:30-20:30, closed Sun, 100 yards from Accademia art museum on San Trovaso canal; facing the Accademia, take a right and then a forced left at the canal to the second bridge—it's at Dorsoduro 992, tel. 041-523-0034; they have no WC).

**$ Bar al Maraveje** is handy for a sandwich, with quiet, comfy tables just minutes from the Accademia. They serve a range of fresh sandwiches, from less expensive *topolini* (four-bite sandwiches) and *tramezzini* to heartier ciabatta sandwiches (daily, 100 yards west of the Accademia, just over a bridge on Calle de la Toletta, Dorsoduro 1185, tel. 041-523-5768). **$ Bar Toletta,** a few doors down (#1191), has similar offerings and better *tramezzini*. Like other bars around

town, avoid their frozen, microwaved pasta, as evidenced by the laminated pictures out front.

**$$$ Al Vecio Marangon Ristorante** glows like a dream come true on its corner tucked away from the frenzy of Venice, about 100 yards west of the Accademia. This stylishly rustic restaurant serves *cicchetti*-style dishes and pastas within its tight and picturesque interior or at a line of outdoor tables. It's super romantic. Consider their splittable *piatto di cicchetti misti,* a sampler of sardines, octopus, codfish, and seafood salad. As they take no reservations, arrive early or be prepared to wait (daily 12:00-22:00, on Calle de la Toletta, Dorsoduro 1210, tel. 041-277-8554).

## Zattere

The far south side of Dorsoduro has a wide promenade along the canal that, on warm summer evenings, has a special charm. Next to the Zattere vaporetto stop is **Pizzeria Zattere,** where you can enjoy your pizza on a floating dining barge. Nearby is the popular **Nico Gelateria** (also with floating seating on the canal). These two places are also worth consideration:

$$$ **Terrazza dei Nobili** takes full advantage of the warm, romantic evening sun. They serve regional specialties and pizza at tolerable prices. The breezy and beautiful seaside seating comes with formal service and the rumble of vaporetti from the nearby stop. The interior is bright and hip (daily 12:00-24:00; at the Zattere vaporetto stop, turn left to Dorsoduro 924; tel. 041-520-6895).

$$ **Pizzeria Oke** is playful, with casual tables on the embankment and a sprawling pizza-parlor interior. It's a hit with young Venetians for its fun atmosphere. While the energy and food are great, be careful to understand the bill—and be warned that  dishes presented as free may end up on your check (daily 11:30-23:00, a couple hundred yards from the Zattere vaporetto stop, Dorsoduro 1414, tel. 041-520-6601).

## On or near Campo San Barnaba

This small square is a delight—especially in the evening. As these places are within a few steps of each other—and the energy and atmosphere can vary—I like to survey the options before choosing (although reservations may be necessary to dine later in the evening).

$$$ **Ristoteca Oniga** has an eclectic yet cozy interior, great tables on the square, and is run by the enthusiastic Raffaele. The menu has a few vegetarian and meat dishes but focuses on fresh fish and other sea creatures, highlighted by their specialty, *bucintoro*—a pan full of mussels, clams, prawns, calamari, and spaghetti (daily 12:00-14:30 & 19:00-22:30, reservations smart, Campo San Barnaba, Dorsoduro 2852, tel. 041-522-4410, www.oniga.it).

$$$ **Osteria Enoteca Ai Artisti** serves well-presented quality dishes, with seating within its tight little wine-snob interior or at a

few petite, romantic canalside tables. They serve good wines by the glass. When reserving, make sure they know your preference—a table on the canal or inside (Mon-Sat 12:45-14:30 & 19:00-22:00, closed Sun, Fondamenta de la Toletta, Dorsoduro 1169a, tel. 041-523-8944, www.enotecaartisti.com, Vicenzo and chef Francesca).

**$$ Pizzeria al Profeta** is a casual place popular with tourists for great pizza. Its sprawling interior seems to stoke conviviality, as does its leafy garden out back (daily 12:00-14:30 & 19:00-23:30; from Campo San Barnaba, a long walk down Calle Lunga San Barnaba to #2671; tel. 041-523-7466).

**$$$ Enoteca e Trattoria la Bitta** is dark and woody, with a soft-jazz bistro feel, tight seating, and a small back patio. They serve beautifully presented, traditional Venetian food with—proudly—no fish. Their helpful wait staff and small, handwritten daily menu are focused on local ingredients (including rabbit) and a "slow food" ethic. As it has an avid following, they do two dinner seatings (19:00 and 21:00) and require reservations (dinner only, closed Sun, cash only, just off Campo San Barnaba on Calle Lunga San Barnaba, Dorsoduro 2753a, tel. 041-523-0531, Debora and Marcellino).

## On Campo Santa Margarita

For a fresh, youthful neighborhood vibe away from the tourist crowds and cutesy Venice, hike out to Campo Santa Margarita, where you'll find a multigenerational slice-of-life scene by day and a trendy college-bar scene after dark. The square is ringed by bakeries, pubs, pizzerias, and fruit stands offering options for everything from picnics to finer dining. If slumming, a picnic or takeout pizza on this square (with fine benches and trees) is great. The area gets a little sketchy late at night.

**$$ Osteria alla Bifora** is a former butcher shop, serving creative plates of mixed cold cuts in their candlelit woody interior and at tables on the square. For rustic *cicchetti* plates ranging from sardines, anchovies, and cod to platters of fine salamis and cheeses, this is a good choice (daily, #2930, tel. 041-523-6119, Franco and Mirella).

**$$$ Osteria Do Torri** is a family affair delightfully situated with tables overlooking the square. Loretta and Paolo offer classic Venetian dishes (daily, #3408, tel. 041-522-0686).

**$$ Pier Dickens Ristorante-Pizzeria,** next door, also has good tables on the square and serves a selection of pizzas as well as three-course fixed-price meals (daily, #3410, tel. 041-241-1979).

Various **hole-in-the-wall** *cicchetti* **bars** (on the square and just off it) serve drinks and *cicchetti* plates to local eaters with a contagious love of life. For the best gelato on the square, find Gelateria Il Doge.

## SPLURGING ON A WATER (OR OTHERWISE GREAT) VIEW

**Overlooking the Giudecca Canal:** Peacefully situated on the Giudecca Canal, **$$$$ Ristorante Lineadombra,** immediately behind La Salute Church, has commanding lagoon views from their big floating terrace and a spacious, modern, and dressy interior. This is a gourmet treat, with gorgeously presented dishes that are local and modern at the same time. Each dish is a memory, and even though plates are pricey, you are welcome to share. The appetizers especially are big and are happily served on two smaller plates. Reserve ahead and choose seating inside or on their terrace. Service is friendly yet professional (daily 12:00-15:00 & 19:00-22:00, closed Tue off-season, a short walk behind La Salute Church, directly across the island from the Salute vaporetto stop, Dorsoduro 19, tel. 041-241-1881, www.ristorantelineadombra.com).

**On Fondamente Nove, with a Lagoon View:** Handy to the islands of Murano and Burano, **$$$$ Ristorante Algiubagiò** is a good place to eat as you look over the northern lagoon. The name joins the names of the four owners—Alberto, Giulio, Barbara, and Giovanna—who strive to impress visitors with quality, creative Venetian cuisine made with the best ingredients. Reserve a waterside table or sit in their classy cantina dining room (daily 12:00-15:00 & 19:00-22:30, between the two sets of vaporetto docks on Fondamente Nove, Cannaregio 5039—see map on page 97, tel. 041-523-6084, www.algiubagio.net).

**On Giudecca Island:** Sit canalside with a view of St. Mark's Square at **$$$ I Figli delle Stelle Ristorante,** which offers a delightful dining experience and an excuse to ride the boat from St. Mark's Square to the island of Giudecca. While they have inside seating, the reason to venture here is to enjoy fine views of Venice across the broad Giudecca Canal and all the water traffic. Reserve ahead to specify "first line" seating along the water, "second line" seating a few steps away, or a table inside (daily 12:30-14:30 & 19:00-23:00, 50 yards from Zitelle vaporetto dock—from San Marco, ride line #4.2, #4.1, or #2, Giudecca 70/71, tel. 041-523-0004).

A bit farther west on Giudecca Island (around the Palanca vaporetto dock), several **$$$** eateries offer similar canal views, even if St. Mark's Square isn't in the panorama. These are often less touristy (take vaporetto line #2 from Zattere to Palanca). Listen to the hum of the boats with a glass of wine.

**On St. Mark's Square:** For fancy dining on Venice's famous square, **$$$$ Gran Caffè Quadri** (a.k.a. Bistro ABC Quadri) is the place to go. Upstairs is their Michelin-star restaurant, but this bistro, also dressy and a bit pretentious, shares the same kitchen, with a more traditional and accessible menu, and prices that won't ruin your appetite. While its 15 tables are all inside, the orchestra is just out the window (daily 12:00-15:00 & 19:00-22:30, reservations smart, San Marco 121, tel. 041-522-2105, www.alajmo.it/grancaffe-quadri).

## PICNICS AND SWEETS
### Picnicking

You're legally forbidden from picnicking anywhere on or near St. Mark's Square except for Giardinetti Reali, the waterfront park near the San Marco vaporetto docks. Though it's legal to eat outdoors elsewhere around town, you may be besieged by pigeons who are, in turn, besieged by aggressive seagulls.

Venice has one main produce market and several convenient supermarkets:

**Outdoor Market near the Rialto Bridge:** Assemble a fun picnic at the **fruit and vegetable market** that sprawls for a few blocks to the north of the Rialto Bridge (best Mon-Sat 8:00-13:00, liveliest in the morning, closed Sun). The adjacent **fish market** is wonderfully slimy (closed Sun-Mon). Side lanes in this area are speckled with fine hole-in-the-wall munchie bars, bakeries, and cheese shops. The Rialto Mercato vaporetto stop is convenient to both.

**Produce Stands:** Many larger squares have a produce stand. To find the one nearest St. Mark's Square, face St. Mark's Basilica, then walk along its left side, heading east down Calle de la Canonica. Cross the bridge and turn left at Campo Santi Filippo e Giacomo. There are also stands on Campo Santa Maria Formosa and Campo Santa Margarita.

**Supermarket near St. Mark's Square:** A handy **Co-op** supermarket is between St. Mark's and Campo Santa Maria Formosa, on the corner of Salizada San Lio and Calle del Mondo Novo at Castello 5817. It has a deli counter and a great selection of picnic supplies, including packaged salads and fresh sandwiches (daily 8:30-22:00).

**Other Supermarkets:** The largest supermarket in town is the **Co-op** at Piazzale Roma, next to the vaporetto stop at Santa Croce 504. It's an easy walk from the train station, as is a smaller **Co-op** on Campo San Felice (along the Strada Nova between the train station and Rialto area, Cannaregio 3660). A **Conad** supermarket is convenient for those staying in Dorsoduro: It's at #1492, as far west as possible on the Zattere embankment, by the San Basilio vaporetto stop and the cruise-ship docks. And just beyond the Rialto vaporetto stop is another handy **Co-op** (facing the Grand Canal on Riva del Carbon). All are open long hours daily. They cater to huge Airbnb demand with ready-to-eat packaged meals.

## Good Gelato and Chocolate Spots

Venice isn't known for its quality gelato but you'll still find good *gelaterie* in every neighborhood, typically offering one-scoop cones for about €2 (€1 per extra scoop). The words *artigianale* or *produzione propria* indicate that a shop makes its own gelato, although sometimes from powder or paste bases (avoid brightly colored gelato or places that have overflowing tubs). The following places are all open long hours daily.

**St. Mark's Side of the Rialto Bridge:** A gourmet gelato shop, **Gelatoteca Suso,** serves delectable flavors in bowls you can eat (next to Campo San Bartolomeo on Calle de la Bissa, San Marco 5453a).

**St. Mark's Square:** Both **Gran Caffè Lavena** at #134 and **Todaro** (on the corner of the Piazzetta at #5, near the water just under the crocodile-topped column) are cafés that have gelato counters in summer. They won't win any awards, but they are convenient if you want something to lick while enjoying the San Marco orchestras.

**On Campo Santa Margarita and Campiello San Tomà:** Along with all the regular flavors, **Gelateria Il Doge,** with two locations, has Sicilian-style *granita*—slushy ice flavored with fresh fruit.

**Near Campo Santa Maria Formosa:** On Salizada San Lio is the popular **La Boutique del Gelato** (next to Hotel Bruno, run for many years by Alessandra). And nearby is a hit with chocolate lovers: **Cioccolateria VizioVirtù** (Vice and Virtue). Across from the recommended Osteria al Portego, it's a modern lab of deliciousness with fine gelato as a bonus (closed Mon, Castello 5988).

# Venice Connections

## BY TRAIN

**From Venice by Train to: Padua** (30 minutes, Trenitalia: 2/hour, Italo: hourly), **Vicenza** (45 minutes, Trenitalia: 2/hour, Italo: 7/day), **Verona** (1.5 hours, Trenitalia: 2/hour, Italo: 7/day), **Ravenna** (roughly hourly, 3 hours, transfer in Ferrara or Bologna), **Florence** (Trenitalia: hourly, 2-3 hours, may transfer in Bologna, often crowded—reserve ahead; Italo: 4/day, 2 hours, reservations required), **Bolzano/Dolomites** (to Bolzano about hourly, 3 hours, transfer in Verona; catch bus from Bolzano into mountains), **Milan** (Trenitalia: 2/hour, most direct on high-speed ES trains, 2.5 hours; Italo: 7/day, 2.5 hours), **Cinque Terre/Monterosso** (5/day, 6 hours, change in Milan), **Rome** (Trenitalia: hourly, 4 hours; direct night train, 7 hours, reserve ahead; Italo: 4/day, 3.5 hours, reservations required), **Naples** (Trenitalia: almost hourly, 5.5 hours, some change in Bologna or Rome, reserve ahead; Italo: 3/day, 5.5 hours, reservations required), **Brindisi** (5/day, 9 hours, change in Rome or Bologna).

**International Destinations: Interlaken** (4/day, 6 hours with 2 changes), **Munich** (1/day direct, 6.5 hours, more with change in Verona; reservable only at ticket windows or via www.bahn.com), **Innsbruck** (1/day direct, 5 hours, more with change in Verona; reservable only at ticket windows or via www.bahn.com), **Salzburg** (4/day, 6.5 hours with change in Villach), **Paris** (2/day, 11 hours, change in Turin; 1 direct night train, 14.5 hours, reserve up to 4 months in advance, no rail passes accepted, www.thello.com), **Geneva** (1/day direct, 2/day with change in Milan, 7-8 hours), **Vienna** (2/day direct, 8 hours; direct night train, 11 hours), **Ljubljana** (4/day, 5 hours, train to Trieste, then bus or train to Ljubljana). To Ljubljana, there's also a direct DRD bus from Mestre (1/day, 3 hours, www.drd.si) and a private shuttle service (www.goopti.com).

## BY PLANE
## Marco Polo Airport
Venice's surprisingly large, modern airport is on the mainland shore of the lagoon, six miles north of the city (code: VCE, tel. 041-260-9260, www.veniceairport.it). There's one sleek terminal, with a TI (daily 9:00-20:00), car-rental agencies, ATMs, a bank, and plenty of shops and eateries.

### Getting Between the Airport and Venice
You can get between the airport and central Venice in any of four ways: by Alilaguna boat, water taxi, airport bus, or land taxi.

| Type | Speed | Cost | Notes |
| --- | --- | --- | --- |
| Alilaguna boat | Slow | Moderate | No transfer |
| Water taxi | Fast | Expensive | No transfer |
| Airport bus to Piazzale Roma | Medium | Cheap | Transfer to vaporetto |
| Land taxi to Piazzale Roma | Medium | Moderate | Transfer to vaporetto |

Alilaguna boats reach most of this chapter's recommended hotels very simply, with no changes. Hotels near the train station, however, are better served by the bus to Piazzale Roma.

Both Alilaguna boats and water taxis leave from the airport's boat dock, an eight-minute walk from the terminal, following signs along a sleek series of (indoor) moving sidewalks. Ticket offices are at the docks.

When flying out of Venice, allow plenty of time to get to the airport. From your hotel to the airport can take two hours. Alilaguna boats are small and can fill up. In an emergency, you can always hop in a water taxi and get to the airport in 30 minutes.

## Alilaguna Airport Boats

These boats make the scenic journey across the lagoon, shuttling passengers between the airport and the island of Venice (€15, €27 round-trip, €1 surcharge if bought on boat, includes 1 suitcase and 1 piece of hand luggage, additional bags—€3 each, roughly 2/hour, 1-1.5-hour trip depending on destination). Alilaguna boats are not covered by city transit passes, but they do use the same docks and ticket windows as the regular vaporetti. You can buy Alilaguna tickets online for a slight discount, but it does not ensure a reservation as you must still exchange the voucher for a ticket (www. alilaguna.it or www.venicelink.com).

There are three key Alilaguna lines for reaching St. Mark's Square. From the airport, the **orange line** *(linea arancio)* runs down the Grand Canal, reaching Guglie (handy for Cannaregio hotels, 45 minutes), Rialto (1 hour), and San Marco (1.25 hours). The **blue line** *(linea blu)* heads first to Fondamente Nove (40 minutes), then loops around to San Zaccaria and San Marco (about 1.5 hours) before continuing to Zattere and the cruise terminal (almost 2 hours). In high season, the **red line** *(linea rossa)* runs to St. Mark's in just over an hour. It circumnavigates Murano and then runs parallel to the blue line, ending at Giudecca Zitelle.

For a full schedule, see www.alilaguna.it, visit the TI, call 041-240-1701, ask your hotelier, or scan the schedules posted at the docks.

**From the Airport to Venice:** Buy Alilaguna tickets at the ticket windows at the docks. Any ticket seller can tell you which line to catch to get to your destination. Blue- and orange-line boats from the airport run roughly twice an hour and go all day (until about midnight); red goes once an hour (runs 9:40-18:40). Ask your hotelier (when you reserve your room) which stop in Venice is best.

**From Venice to the Airport:** Ask your hotelier which dock and which line is best. Blue-line boats start leaving Venice as early as 3:50 in the morning. Scope out the dock and buy your ticket in advance to avoid last-minute stress. Get there 10 minutes early to assure yourself a seat.

## Water Taxis

Luxury taxi speedboats zip directly between the airport and the closest dock to your hotel, getting you within steps of your destination in about 30 minutes. The official price is €110 for up to four people; add €10 for every extra person (10-passenger limit). You may get a higher quote—politely talk it down. A taxi can be a smart investment for small groups and those with an early departure.

From the airport, arrange your ride at the water-taxi desk or with the boat captains at the dock. From Venice, book your taxi trip the day before your departure, either through your hotel or

VENICE

directly with the Consorzio Motoscafi water taxi association (tel. 041-522-2303, www.motoscafivenezia.it).

## Airport Shuttle Buses

Buses between the airport and Venice are fast, frequent, and cheap. They drop you at Venice's bus station, at the square called Piazzale Roma. From there, you can catch a vaporetto down the Grand Canal—convenient for hotels near the Rialto Bridge and St. Mark's Square. If you're staying near the train station, you can walk from Piazzale Roma to your hotel.

Two bus companies serve this route: ACTV and ATVO. ATVO buses take 20 minutes and go nonstop. ACTV buses make a few stops en route and take slightly longer (30 minutes), but you get a discount if you buy a Venice vaporetto pass at the same time (see page 42). The service is equally good (either bus: €8 one-way, €15 round-trip; ACTV bus with transit-pass discount: €6 one-way, €12 round-trip; runs about 5:00-24:00, 2/hour, drops to 1/hour early and late, check schedules at www.atvo.it or www.actv.it).

**From the Airport to Venice:** Buses leave from just outside the arrivals terminal. Buy tickets from the TI, the ticket desk in the terminal, the kiosk near baggage claim, or ticket machines. ATVO tickets are not valid on ACTV buses and vice versa. Double-check the destination; you want Piazzale Roma. If taking ACTV, you want bus #5.

**From Venice to the Airport:** At Piazzale Roma, buy your ticket from the ACTV windows (in the building by the bridge) or the ATVO office (at #497g) before heading out to the platforms (although sometimes an attendant sells tickets near the buses). The newsstand in the center of the lot also sells tickets.

## Land Taxi or Private Minivan

It takes about 20 minutes to drive from the airport to Piazzale Roma or the cruise port. A **land taxi** can do the trip for about €50. To reserve a private minivan, contact **Treviso Car Service** (minivan—€55, seats up to 8; car—€50, seats up to 3; mobile 338-204-4390 or 333-411-2840, www.trevisocarservice.com).

## Treviso Airport

Several budget airlines use Treviso Airport, 12 miles northwest of Venice (code: TSF, tel. 042-231-5111, www.trevisoairport.it). The fastest option into Venice (Tronchetto parking lot; convenient if taking vaporetto line #2) is on the **Barzi express bus,** which does the trip in just 40 minutes (€12, buy tickets on board, every 1-2 hours, www.barziservice.com). From Tronchetto, hop on a vaporetto, or take the People Mover monorail to Piazzale Roma for €1.50. **ATVO buses** are a bit more frequent and drop you right at Piazzale Roma (saving you the People Mover ride), but take nearly twice as long (€12 one-way, €22 round-trip, about 2/hour, 70 minutes, www.atvo.it; buy tickets at the ATVO desk in the airport and stamp them on the bus). **Treviso Car Service** offers minivan service to Piazzale Roma (minivan—€75, seats up to 8; car—€65, seats up to 3; for contact info, see listing earlier).

## BY CRUISE SHIP

Most cruise ships dock at Venice's Stazione Marittima, at the west end of town. From the cruise port, the most direct way to reach St. Mark's Square is to take the Alilaguna **express boat** (2/hour in each direction, 30 minutes, www.alilaguna.it). Another option is to take the **People Mover** monorail from the port to Piazzale Roma, then hop on a **vaporetto.** It's about a five-minute walk to the People Mover, then a three-minute ride to Piazzale Roma, where you'll find a stop for vaporetti to Rialto, Accademia, or San Marco (boat #1 or the faster boat #2). Or, take an expensive **water taxi** ride (at least €70-80).

For more details, see my *Rick Steves Mediterranean Cruise Ports* guidebook.

# NEAR VENICE

*Padua • Vicenza • Verona*

Venice is just one of many towns in the Italian region of Veneto (VEHN-eh-toh), but few visitors venture off the lagoon. That's a shame, as there's much to see within a very short hop of Venice. The trip from Venice westward to Milan is a route strewn with temptations: the Dolomites peaks, Italy's famous lakes, and—closer to Venice—the important and worthwhile towns of Padua, Vicenza, and Verona.

If you can't make it to all three, pick the one that interests you most. Art lovers will want to head to **Padua** to see Giotto's celebrated Scrovegni Chapel. History buffs should see **Verona**'s impressive Roman ruins. Verona is also the pick for star-crossed lovers retracing Romeo and Juliet's steps. Architecture fans could consider a quick stop in Palladio-designed **Vicenza,** located about halfway between Padua and Verona.

If you're Padua-bound, remember that you need to reserve ahead to see the Scrovegni Chapel. Don't bother visiting Vicenza on a Monday, when many of the top sights are closed; in Verona, several sights are only open in the afternoon on Mondays.

Spending a day at one of these towns as a side trip from Venice or town-hopping between Venice and Milan is exciting and efficient. Padua, Verona, and Vicenza are on the same train line. Connected by at least two trains per hour, they're easy to visit.

Trenitalia operates Regional (R), "Fast Regional" (RV) and Frecce (Express) trains. Italo runs their own trains equivalent to the Frecce, but these don't work with Eurail passes. Train travelers find that the "fast regional" trains (marked with an RV prefix on schedules and ticket machines) offer the best mixture of speed, convenience, and savings. Frecce and Italo trains cost quite a bit

**Towns near Venice**

more—and though rail-pass holders don't have to pay the fare, they do have to commit to a time and pay to reserve a seat. Regional trains don't require (or even accept) seat reservations. The regular regional trains (R prefix) offer the same savings as the RV ones but are much slower.

# Padua

This inexpensive, easily appreciated city is a fine destination on its own and a convenient base for day trips all around the region. Nicknamed "the brain of Veneto," Padua (*Padova* in Italian) is home to the prestigious university (founded in 1222) that hosted Galileo, Copernicus, Dante, and Petrarch. Pilgrims know Padua as the home of the Basilica of St. Anthony, where the reverent assemble to touch his tomb and ogle his remarkably intact lower jaw and tongue. And lovers of early Renaissance art come here to make a pilgrimage of their own: to gaze at the remarkable frescoes by Giotto in the Scrovegni Chapel. But despite the fact that Padua's museums and churches hold their own in Italy's artistic big league, its hotels are reasonably priced, and the city doesn't feel touristy. Padua's old town center is elegantly arcaded, filled with students, and sprinkled with surprises, including some of Italy's most inviting squares for lingering over an *aperitivo* as the sun slowly dips low in the sky.

NEAR VENICE

From Padua, architecture fans can ride by train (15-25 minutes) to Vicenza and its celebrated Palladian buildings. And Venice is just a half-hour away in the other direction.

## PLANNING YOUR TIME: PADUA IN A DAY

Day-trippers can do a quick but enjoyable blitz of Padua—including a visit to the Scrovegni Chapel—in as little as six hours. Trains from Venice are cheap, take 30 minutes, and run frequently. Once in Padua, everything is a 10-minute walk or a quick tram ride apart.

To see Giotto's Scrovegni Chapel, you need to make a reservation; your entry time will dictate the order of your sightseeing (see "Reservations" on page 137). When planning your day, also consider these factors: The station has a reliable baggage-check desk; the open-air markets are vibrant in the morning; student life is best at the university late in the day; and the Basilica of St. Anthony is open all day, but the reliquary chapel closes midday, from 12:45 to 14:30.

Ideally, I'd do it this way: 9:00—market action and sightseeing in town center, 11:00—Basilica of St. Anthony, 13:00—lunch, 15:00—Scrovegni Chapel tour. Then, cap off your day with a *spritz* on the main square.

# Orientation to Padua

Padua's main tourist sights lie on a north-south axis through the heart of the city, from the train station to Scrovegni Chapel to the market squares (the center of town) to the Basilica of St. Anthony. It's roughly a 10-minute walk between each of these sights, or about 30 minutes from end to end. Padua's wonderful single tram line makes lacing things together quick and easy (see "Getting Around Padua," later).

## TOURIST INFORMATION

Padua has two TIs: in the **center** (in the alley behind Caffè Pedrocchi at Vicolo Cappellatto Pedrocchi 9, Mon-Sat 9:00-19:00, Sun 10:00-16:00) and at the **train station** (same hours, tel. 049-520-7415, www.turismopadova.it).

The **Padova Card** includes entry to all my recommended sights—except the university's Anatomy Theater and the Oratory of St. George—plus unlimited tram rides (€16/48 hours, €21/72 hours, buy at either TI, the Scrovegni Chapel, or online at www.padovacard.it). If you go through the chapel website (www.cappelladegliscrovegni.it), you can buy the card and make a chapel reservation at the same time. Show your receipt to collect your pre-purchased card at either TI or at the chapel. Also, there's a chance

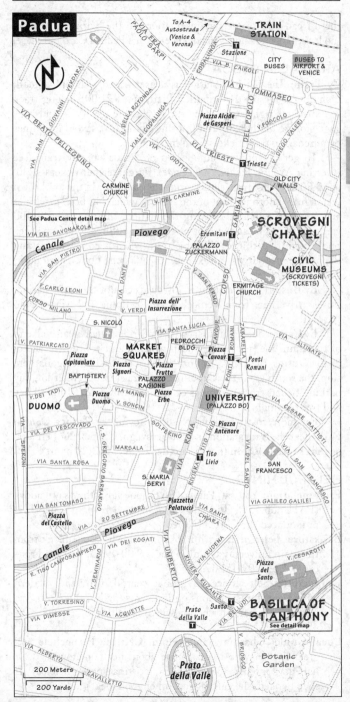

**NEAR VENICE**

the TI can book same-day reservations to the Scrovegni Chapel (no less than three hours in advance) with a Padova Card purchase.

## ARRIVAL IN PADUA

**By Train:** The efficient station is a user-friendly shopping mall, including a Despar supermarket (daily until 21:00). Along track 1, on the far right as you face the tracks, are pay WCs and baggage storage (daily 6:30-20:00, bring photo ID). Avoid long lines by purchasing train tickets from machines.

To get downtown, simply hop on Padua's handy **tram** (see "Getting Around Padua," next page). Purchase your ticket (€1.30, or €3.80 day pass) from shops inside the station or in the low brown rectangular booth in front of the station, which has both machines and a staffed window. Leaving the station, the tram stop is 100 yards to the right at the foot of the bridge (direction: Capolinea Sud). Note that thieves like this tram when it comes to picking the pockets of tourists. A **taxi** into town (a good option after dark) costs about €8-10.

**By Bus:** The bus station is 100 yards east of the train station. Buses arrive here from Venice's Piazzale Roma and Marco Polo Airport.

**By Car:** Padua has a smart park-and-ride system near each end of the tram line, providing cheap parking and convenient access to town using the tram. The north lot is at the Pontevigodarzere stop, the south lot at the Capolinea Guizza stop. At either lot, buy parking tickets from machines or at the nearby café (€1 for all day and free overnight).

For more costly parking closer to town, try **Padova Centro Park** (near the train station and the Scrovegni Chapel, €6/24 hours) or **Piazza Isaac Rabin** (near Prato della Valle, €12/24 hours).

## HELPFUL HINTS

**Pronunciation:** You say Padua (PAD-joo-wah), they say Padova (PAH-doh-vah). The city's top sight, Scrovegni Chapel, is pronounced skroh-VEHN-yee.

**Bookstore: Feltrinelli,** with books in English, is one block from the main university building (daily 9:00-19:45, Via San Francesco 7, tel. 199-151-173).

**Launderette:** Self-service **Lavami** is central, tiny, and modern with English instructions on flip cards (daily 7:00-21:30, Via Marsala 22 near intersection with Via dell'Arco, tel. 049-876-4532).

**Local Guide:** Charming and helpful **Cristina Pernechele** is a great teacher who is passionate about her hometown (€120/half-day, mobile 338-495-5453, cristina@pernechele.eu). If she's booked, she can suggest other good local guides.

## GETTING AROUND PADUA

Ignore the city buses; pretend there is only the **tram** and rely on it. There's just one line, which efficiently and without stress connects everything you care about. With a Padova Card you get unlimited tram use; just show the card to security upon request. Or, buy tickets from tobacco shops, newsstands, or the booth on the square in front of the train station and validate them on board; there are also ticket machines at some stops, but they sell only single tickets and don't give change (€1.30 single ticket good for 75 minutes, €3.80 *biglietto giornaliero* good for one calendar day; departs every 8 minutes during the day Mon-Sat, every 20 minutes evenings and Sun). The rubber-wheeled trams run on a single rail.

Before boarding, note the tram direction on posted schedules and above the front window (Pontevigodarzere is northbound, Capolinea Sud is southbound). Stops that matter to tourists include Stazione FS (train and bus stations), Eremitani (Scrovegni Chapel), Ponti Romani (old town center, market squares, university), Tito Livio (ghetto, old town center, Hotel Majestic Toscanelli), and Santo (both for Basilica of St. Anthony and neighborhood hotels).

Padua's **hop-on, hop-off tour buses** are not worth the time or money.

# Sights in Padua

## IN THE CENTER

Padua's two main sights (Basilica of St. Anthony and Scrovegni Chapel) are, respectively, at the southern and northern reaches of downtown. But its atmospheric, cobbled core—with bustling markets, vibrant student life, and inviting sun-and-café-speckled piazzas—is its own ▲▲▲ attraction. You could simply stroll the area aimlessly or seek out some of the following spots.

### ▲▲Market Squares

The stately Palazzo della Ragione (described later) provides a dramatic backdrop for Padua's almost exotic-feeling produce market,

which fills the surrounding squares—**Piazza delle Erbe** and **Piazza della Frutta**—each morning and all day Saturday (Mon-Fri roughly 8:00-13:00, Sat 8:00-19:00 but a bit quieter in the afternoon, closed Sun). Second only to the produce market in Italy's gastronomic capital of Bologna, this market has been renowned for centuries as having the freshest and greatest selec-

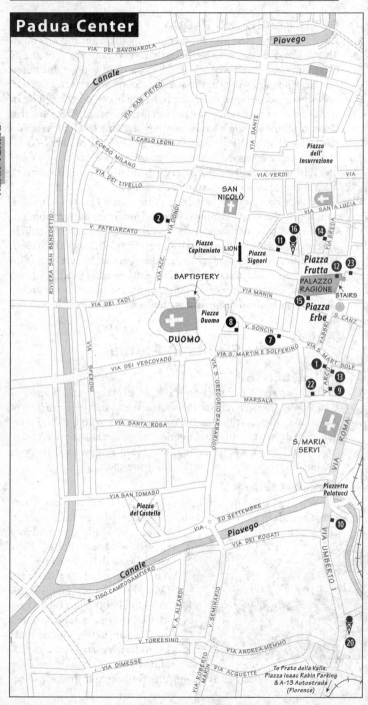

**Padua Center**

NEAR VENICE

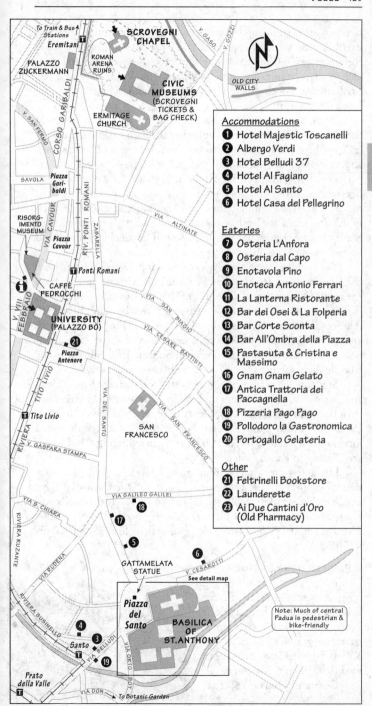

**NEAR VENICE**

To Train & Bus Stations
Eremitani

**SCROVEGNI CHAPEL**

V. GASO
V. GOZZI

PALAZZO ZUCKERMANN

ROMAN ARENA RUINS

OLD CITY WALLS

CORSO GARIBALDI

V. SAN FERMO

**CIVIC MUSEUMS**
(SCROVEGNI TICKETS & BAG CHECK)

ERMITAGE CHURCH

SAVOLA

Piazza Garibaldi

RIV. PONTI ROMANI — ZABARELLA

VIA CAVOUR

VIA ALTINATE

RISORGIMENTO MUSEUM

Piazza Cavour

Ponti Romani

CAFFÈ PEDROCCHI

VIA SAN BIAGIO

V. VIII FEBBRAIO

**UNIVERSITY**
(PALAZZO BÒ)

Piazza Antenore

VIA CESARE BATTISTI

TITO LIVIO

Tito Livio

RIVIERA V. GASPARA STAMPA

VIA DEL SANTO

SAN FRANCESCO

VIA SAN FRANCESCO

RIVIERA S. CHIARA

VIA GALILEO GALILEI

RIVIERA RUZZANTE

VIA EUDENA

VIA S. CHIARA

GATTAMELATA STATUE

See detail map

RIVIERA BUSINELLO

Santo

BELLUDI

Prato della Valle

VIA DON

To Botanic Garden

**Piazza del Santo**

**BASILICA OF ST. ANTHONY**

VIA ORTO BOT.

Note: Much of central Padua is pedestrian & bike-friendly

### Accommodations
1. Hotel Majestic Toscanelli
2. Albergo Verdi
3. Hotel Belludi 37
4. Hotel Al Fagiano
5. Hotel Al Santo
6. Hotel Casa del Pellegrino

### Eateries
7. Osteria L'Anfora
8. Osteria dal Capo
9. Enotavola Pino
10. Enoteca Antonio Ferrari
11. La Lanterna Ristorante
12. Bar dei Osei & La Folperia
13. Bar Corte Sconta
14. Bar All'Ombra della Piazza
15. Pastasuta & Cristina e Massimo
16. Gnam Gnam Gelato
17. Antica Trattoria dei Paccagnella
18. Pizzeria Pago Pago
19. Pollodoro la Gastronomica
20. Portogallo Gelateria

### Other
21. Feltrinelli Bookstore
22. Launderette
23. Ai Due Cantini d'Oro (Old Pharmacy)

tion of herbs, fruits, and vegetables. The presentation is an art in itself. As you wander, appreciate the local passion for good food: Residents can tell the month by the seasonal selections, and merchants share recipe tips with shoppers. You'll notice quite a few Sri Lankans working here (Italy took in many refugees from Sri Lanka's civil war).

Don't miss the **indoor market** zone on the ground floor of the Palazzo della Ragione. Wandering through this H-shaped arcade—where you'll find various butchers, *salumerie* (delicatessens), cheese shops, bakeries, and fishmongers at work—is a sensuous experience. For centuries, this was a market for luxury items (furs, fine fabrics, silver, and gold—notice the imposing iron gates used to lock it up each evening). Then, the devastating loss to the French in 1797 marked the end of good times, and with no market for luxury items, the arcade was used to sell perishables—meat and cheese—out of the sun.

The building with the flags overlooking Piazza delle Erbe is the Renaissance City Hall with a Rationalist (fascist-era) wing on the right. (Notice the relief from the 1930s celebrating Mussolini's pathetic little empire—Libya, Albania, Somalia, and Ethiopia.) And opposite the big Palazzo della Ragione is the Jewish quarter and a charming zone of arcaded lanes (some of about 15 miles of lanes in the city that provided protection from sun and rain in the Middle Ages, giving the city an extra boost of elegance).

Students gather in the squares after the markets have closed, spilling out of colorful bars and cafés, drinks in hand (see sidebar). Bars and food stalls offer plenty of refreshments and fun food. Pizza by the slice is dirt-cheap. For pointers on a recommended local sandwich stand, **Bar dei Osei,** and a neighboring squid stand, see "Eating in Padua," later.

Just a few steps away from these is a classic old pharmacy that dates to 1841: The licorice-perfumed **Ai Due Cantini d'Oro,** which stocks retail items like it did before World War II, sells odd foods and specialty items for every dietary need (Tue-Sun 9:00-13:00 & 16:00-19:30, closed Mon, Piazza della Frutta 46, tel. 049-875-0623).

## ▲Palazzo della Ragione

Looming over Padua's two big central market squares (Piazza delle Erbe and Piazza della Frutta), this grand 13th-century palazzo—commonly called *il Salone* (the great hall)—once held the medieval law courts.

**Cost and Hours:** €6; Tue-

## Drinking a *Spritz* with the Student Crowd

Each early evening, before dinner, students enliven Padua by enjoying a convivial drink in their favorite places. Piazza dei Signori is trendier, with people of all ages, while the scene on Piazza delle Erbe is more bohemian and alternative. Or you could sit in front of the university, nurse your drink, and watch the graduates get roasted with their crazy gangs of friends.

The drink of choice is a *spritz,* an aperitif generally made with Campari (a red liqueur infused with bitter herbs), white wine or prosecco, and sparkling water, and garnished with a blood-orange wedge. Another version is a sweeter and lighter *spritz* made with Aperol (an orange-flavored liqueur), which has a lower alcohol content and is not as bitter as the heavier Campari *spritz.* Padovans brag that Aperol was created here in 1919.

Grab a table and be part of the scene. This is a classic opportunity to enjoy a real discussion with smart, English-speaking students who see tourists not as pests, but as interesting people from far away. For an instant conversation starter, ask about the current political situation in Italy, the right-wing party's policy on immigrants, or the cultural differences between Italy's North and South. A question they might ask you: "What the hell is the electoral college?"

Sun 9:00-19:00, Nov-Jan until 18:00, closed Mon year-round; Ponti Romani tram stop, tel. 049-820-5006.

**Visiting the Palazzo:** Facing the palazzo from Piazza delle Erbe, climb the grand staircase on the palazzo's far right side, buy your ticket (and pick up the English info flier), and go to the loggia overlooking Piazza delle Erbe. Enjoy the view and the fine vaulting that was painted in the 1300s to celebrate the city's wealth when Padua was an independent city-state (one of many little states in "the land of a thousand bell towers" that ultimately formed Italy).

Step into the great hall and head right, to the back of the room opposite the giant horse to take it all in. This huge hall—265 feet by 90 feet—was at one time adorned with frescoes by Giotto. A fire in 1420 destroyed those paintings, and the palazzo was redecorated with the 15th-century art you see today: a series of 333 frescoes depicting the signs of the zodiac, labors of the month, symbols representing characteristics of people born under each sign, and, finally, figures of the 12 apostles and favorite saints to legitimize the power of the courts in the eyes of the Church.

The hall is topped with a hull-shaped roof, which helps to support the structure without the use of columns—quite an architectural feat when built in 1306, considering the building's dimensions.

The biggest thing in the hall is the giant, very anatomically correct horse. Its prominent placement represents the pride locals feel for the Veneto's own highly respected breed of horse. (After the bronze ones in St. Mark's Basilica in Venice, these are the favorite horses in the region.)

The curious black stone in the corner (behind you on the right) is the "Stone of Shame," which was the seat of debtors being punished during the Middle Ages. It was introduced as a compassionate alternative to prison by St. Anthony in 1230. Instead of being executed or doing prison time, debtors sat upon this stone, surrendered their possessions, and denounced themselves publicly before being exiled from the city.

Behind it on the left is a Foucault pendulum that demonstrates the rotation of the earth (well-described in English). Computers display information that helps give meaning to the building. After enjoying the paintings and getting a closer look at the horse, leave through the door you entered.

## Piazza dei Signori

Just a block away from Palazzo della Ragione, this square is a busy clothing market in the morning and the most popular gathering place in the evening for students out for a drink. The circa-1400 clock decorates the former palace of the ruling family. The aggressive lion with unfurled wings on the column was a reminder of the Venetian determination to assert its control. Today that lion can be seen as representing the Veneto region's

independence from Rome: Italy's North (Veneto and Lombardy) is tired of subsidizing the South. Grumbling about this issue continues to stir talk of splitting the country.

## ▲Caffè Pedrocchi

The white-columned, Neoclassical Pedrocchi building is much more than just a café on the ground floor. A complex of meeting rooms and entertainment venues, it stirs the Italian soul (or the patriotic Italian soul, at least). Built in 1831 during the period of Austrian rule, Caffè Pedrocchi was inaugurated for the fourth Italian Congress of Scientists, which convened during the mid-19th century to stir up nationalistic fervor as Italy struggled to unite as a single country. In 1848, this symbol of patriotic hope was the target (no surprise) of those repressing a student uprising that was being plotted here. (For more on the story of Italy's unification, visit the upstairs Museum of the Risorgimento; see the next listing.)

**Cost and Hours:** Café interior free, daily 8:00-23:00, across from Via VIII Febbraio near Ponti Romani tram stop, tel. 049-878-1231, www.caffepedrocchi.it.

**Visiting the Café:** Each of the café's three dining rooms is decorated and furnished in a different color (denoted by the hue of velvet on the chairs): red, white, or green—representing the colors of the Italian flag. In the outer, un-heated **Sala Verde** (Green Room), people are welcome to sit and relax without ordering anything or having to pay. This is where Italian gentlemen read their newspapers and gather with friends to chat about the old days. In the **Sala Rossa** (Red Room), the clock over the bar is flanked by marble reliefs of morning and night, a reminder that, back in the 19th century, the room was open 24 hours a day. In the rooms on either side, the maps of the hemispheres with south up top reflect the anti-conventional spirit of the place. In the **Sala Bianca** (White Room), where one of the revolutionaries in that ill-fated 1848 uprising was killed, you can see a bullet hole in the wall (framed in tarnished silver).

The menu offers teahouse fare, including sandwiches and ice-cream sundaes, a variety of breakfast combos, and the writer Stendhal's beloved *zabaglione*, a creamy custard made with Marsala wine. A shiny new bar in the center of the building has a pastry counter and serves sandwiches at outdoor tables. Remember that in Italy, you can order a basic coffee standing up at the bar of any place, no matter how fancy, and pay the same low, government-regulated price.

## ▲Museum of the Risorgimento

Upstairs in Caffè Pedrocchi, this small museum tells the stirring story of Italy's unification in a series of fine 19th-century rooms. With good English descriptions, the museum traces Padua's role in Italian history, from the downfall of the Venetian Republic (1797) to the founding of the Republic of Italy (1946).

**Cost and Hours:** €4; Tue-Sun 9:30-12:30 & 15:30-18:00,

closed Mon; entrance up staircase on Piazza Cavour side of café; tel. 049-878-1231.

**Visiting the Museum:** You'll pass through a series of rooms—all in different styles, such as Greek, Etruscan, or Egyptian—that were intended to evoke memories of the glory of past epochs, which a united Italy had hopes of reliving. Exhibits include uniforms, medals, weaponry, old artillery, fascist propaganda posters, and a 30-minute propagandistic video in Italian that also contains a lot of fascinating footage with no narration (runs on a loop in a small theater). The video is a "Luce" production (meaning a Mussolini production) and features great scenes of the town in the 1930s, including clips of Il Duce's visit and later WWII bombardments.

The war and propaganda posters in the last room are haunting. An old woman (what we would call a "gold star" mother) wears the medal of a son lost in battle and pleads to those who question the fascist-driven war effort: "Don't betray my son." Another (with a Nazi soldier offering a handshake) declares, "The Germans are truly our friends." And yet another asks, "And you...what are *you* doing?"

### ▲University of Padua

The main building of this prestigious university, known as Palazzo Bò, is adjacent to Caffè Pedrocchi. Founded in 1222, it's one of the first, greatest, and most progressive universities in Europe. Back when the Church controlled university curricula, a group of professors and students broke free from the University of Bologna to create this liberal school, which would be independent of Catholic constraints and accessible to people of other faiths.

A haven for free thought, the university attracted intellectuals from all over Europe, including the great astronomer Copernicus, who realized here that the universe didn't revolve around him. And Galileo—notorious for disagreeing with the Church's views on science—called his 18 years on the faculty here the best of his life.

Anyone can stroll through its two courtyards for free. And tours are given in English several times a day for a deeper look that includes the famed Anatomy Theater.

**Cost and Hours:** Grounds—free, closed Sun; University and Anatomy Theater tour—€5 (English tours Mon-Sat generally at 10:30, 12:30, 14:30, and 16:30, fewer tours in winter, no tours on Sun, maximum 40 people per tour); Via VIII Febbraio 7 (Ponti Romani tram stop), tel. 049-827-3939, www.unipd.it/en/guidedtours. Confirm tour times and availability on website or by phone, or stop by the ticket desk (in passage between two courtyards).

**Visiting the Courtyards on Your Own:** You can poke into two of the university's courtyards (or peer through the gate on Sunday when it's closed). Find the entrance on Via VIII Febbraio under the "Gymnasium" inscription (30 yards from Caffè Pedrocchi, facing City Hall). You'll pop into a 16th-century courtyard, the school's historic core. It's littered with the coats of arms of important faculty and leaders of the university over the ages. Classrooms, which open onto the square, are still used. Today, students gather here, surrounded by memories of illustrious alumni, including the first woman in the world to receive a university degree (in 1678).

A passageway leads from here to an adjacent second courtyard, dating from the fascist era (c. 1938). The relief celebrates heroic students in World War I. Off this courtyard, notice the richly decorated stairway, frescoed fascist-style in the 1930s with themes celebrating art, science, and the pursuit of knowledge.

The tiny Da Mario Bar, just under the WWI mural in the second courtyard, is fun for its photos of the crazy rituals of university life (run by 80-year-old Mario, famed for his strong *spritzes,* open Mon-Fri only).

**University and Anatomy Theater Tour:** Students give 45-minute tours of the university that include a look at Europe's first great Anatomy Theater (from 1595). Despite the Church's strict ban on autopsies, more than 300 students would pack this theater to watch professors dissect human cadavers (the bodies of criminals  from another town). This had to be done in a "don't ask, don't tell" kind of way, because the Roman Catholic Church only started allowing the teaching of anatomy through dissection in the late 1800s.

## ▲Baptistery

Located next to Padua's skippable Duomo, this richly frescoed little building was once the private chapel of Padua's ruling family, the Carraresi. In the 1370s, they hired Florentine artist Giusto de' Menabuoi to do a little interior redecoration. Later, in 1405, Venice conquered Padua and deposed the Carraresi; the building was turned into a baptistery, but the decorations survived.

## Graduation Antics in Padua

With 60,000 students, Padua's university always seems to be hosting graduation ceremonies. There's a constant trickle of happy grads and their friends and families celebrating the big event.

During the school year, every 20 minutes or so, a student steps into a formal room (upstairs, above the university courtyard) to officially meet with the leading professors of his or her faculty. When they're finished, the students are given a green laurel wreath. They pose for ceremonial group photos and family snapshots. It's a sweet scene. Then, craziness takes over.

The new graduates replace their somber clothing with raunchy outfits, as gangs of friends gather around them on Via VIII Febbraio, the street in front of the university. The roast begins. The gang rolls out a giant butcher-paper poster with a generally obscene caricature of the student and a litany of *This Is Your Life* photos and stories. The new grad, subject to various embarrassing pranks, reads the funny statements out loud. The poster is then taped to the university wall for all to see. (Find the plastic panels to the right of the main entry, facing Via VIII Febbraio. Graduation posters are allowed to stay there for 24 hours. The panels are emptied each morning, but by nighttime a new set of posters is affixed to the plastic shields.)

During the roast, the friends sing the catchy but obscene local university anthem, reminding their newly esteemed friend not to get too huffy: *Dottore, dottore, dottore del buso del cul. Vaffancul, vaffancul* (loosely translated: "Doctor, doctor. You're just a doctor of the a-hole...go f-off, go f-off"). After you've heard this song (with its fanfare and oom-pah-pah catchiness) and have seen all the good-natured fun, you can't stop singing it.

The crazy show is usually staged late in the afternoon. Outdoor café tables afford great seats to enjoy the spectacle.

**Cost and Hours:** €3, daily 10:00-18:00, on Piazza Duomo.

**Visiting the Baptistery:** The Baptistery's frescoes, like those in St. Mark's Basilica in Venice, show Byzantine influence. Almighty Christ, the Pantocrator, is in majesty on top, while approachable Mary and the multitude of saints provide the devout with access to God. Find the world as it was known in the 14th century (the disk below Mary's feet). It kicks off a cycle of scenes illustrating Creation (clockwise from the creation of Adam). The four evangelists (Matthew, Mark, Luke, and John) with their books and symbols fill the corners. A vivid Crucifixion scene faces a gorgeous Annunciation. And the altar niche features a dim, blue-toned, literal Apocalypse from the book of Revelation.

While the Baptistery was created 70 years after Giotto, it feels older. Because de' Menabuoi was working for a private family, he needed to be politically correct and not threaten or offend the family's allies—especially the Church. While still mind-blowing, the Baptistery's art seems relatively conservative compared to Giotto's Scrovegni Chapel. Giotto, supported by the powerful Scrovegni family and the Franciscans, could get away with being more progressive and bold.

## ▲▲▲SCROVEGNI CHAPEL AND CIVIC MUSEUMS

Wallpapered with Giotto's beautifully preserved cycle of nearly 40 frescoes, the glorious Scrovegni Chapel holds scenes depicting the lives of Jesus and Mary. You must make reservations in advance to see the chapel. To protect the paintings from excess humidity, only 25 people are allowed in the chapel at a time. Every 20 minutes, a new group is admitted for a 15-minute video presentation in an anteroom, followed by 20 minutes in the chapel.

With a Scrovegni Chapel ticket you can also visit the adjacent Civic Museums (archaeology and paintings).

**Cost and Hours:** €13, covers the Scrovegni Chapel and Civic Museums. Reserve a timed-entry slot when you buy your ticket—see "Reservations," below. The **chapel** is open daily 9:00-19:00; the **museums** are open Tue-Sun 9:00-19:00, closed Mon. Special evening visits to the chapel are available in peak season (see below).

**Information:** Tel. 049-201-0020, www.cappelladegliscrovegni.it.

**Reservations:** Prepaid reservations are required, and your smartest move is to reserve your ticket well in advance online (or by phone). Select the day you want to visit, then the time. Remember that for just a bit more, you can get the Padova Card that includes the Scrovegni plus other Padua sights and the tram—just make your chapel reservation when you buy the card online.

Unfortunate souls arriving in Padua without a Scrovegni reservation can sometimes buy a same-day ticket, but don't count on it. You could drop by the ticket office to see if anything is available. Or, check at the TI; with a Padova Card purchase they may be able to make same-day reservations no less than three hours (and up to

# Giotto di Bondone (c. 1267-1337)

Although details of his life are extremely sketchy, we know that the 12-year-old shepherd Giotto was discovered painting pictures of his father's sheep on rock slabs. He grew to become the wealthiest and most famous painter of his day. His achievement is especially remarkable because painters at that time weren't considered anything more than craftsmen—and weren't expected to be innovators.

After making a name for himself by painting frescoes of the life of St. Francis in Assisi, the Florentine tackled the Scrovegni Chapel (c. 1303-1305). At age 35, he was at the height of his powers. His scenes were more realistic and human than anything that had been done for a thousand years. Giotto didn't learn technique by dissecting corpses or studying the mathematics of 3-D perspective; he had innate talent. And his personality shines through in the humanity of his art.

The Scrovegni frescoes break ground by introducing nature—rocks, trees, animals—as a backdrop for religious scenes. Giotto's people, with their voluminous, deeply creased robes, are as sturdy and massive as Greek statues, throwbacks to the Byzantine icon art of the Middle Ages. But these figures exude stage presence. Their gestures are simple but expressive: A head tilted down says dejection, an arm flung out indicates grief, clasped hands indicate hope. Giotto created his figures not just by drawing outlines and filling them in with single colors; he filled the outlines in with subtle patchworks of lighter and darker shades, and in doing so pioneered modern modeling techniques. Giotto's storytelling style is straightforward, and anyone with knowledge of the episodes of Jesus' life can read the chapel like a comic book.

The Scrovegni represents a turning point in European art and culture—away from scenes of heaven and toward a more down-to-earth, human-centered view.

48 hours) in advance. You might also see local tour guides, who have to book blocks of tickets, trying to unload unneeded tickets. But why waste time hunting around for tickets when you can reserve in advance?

**Evening Visit:** Special 20-minute evening visits to the chapel only (not the Civic Museums) are available for €8 (April-Oct daily 19:00-22:00). To book this, go to the Scrovegni website and choose "Giotto Under the Stars."

**Helpful Hint:** If you packed binoculars, bring them along for a better—and more comfortable—view of the uppermost frescoes.

**Getting There:** From either the town center or the train station, it's a 10-minute walk, or a quick tram ride to the Eremitani stop.

**Getting In:** To reach the chapel, enter through the Eremitani building, where you'll find the Civic Museums, ticket office, and the free and mandatory bag check. Though you're instructed to pick up your tickets at the ticket office one hour before your visit, in practice, 30 minutes is enough to weather any commotion at the desk. Present your confirmation number at the ticket desk, verify your time, pick up your ticket, and check any bags or purses.

While waiting for your reserved time, blitz the Pinacoteca and Multimedia Room (described later). Read the chapel description below before you enter, since you'll only have a short time in the chapel itself.

From the ticket office, follow the signs, go outside, and walk 100 yards down the path, passing some ruins of Roman Padua. Be at the chapel doors at least five minutes before your scheduled visit. The doors are automatic, and if you're even a minute late, you'll forfeit your visit with no recourse.

At your appointed time, you first enter an anteroom to watch an instructive 15-minute video (with English subtitles) and to establish humidity levels before continuing into the chapel. Although you have only a short visit inside the chapel, it is divine. You're inside a Giotto time capsule, looking back at an artist ahead of his time.

**NEAR VENICE**

## Scrovegni Chapel (Cappella degli Scrovegni)

Painted by Giotto and his assistants from 1303 to 1305 and considered by many to be the first piece of modern art, this work makes it clear: Europe was breaking out of the Middle Ages. A sign of the Renaissance to come, Giotto placed real people in real scenes, expressing real human emotions. These frescoes were radical for their 3-D nature, lively colors, light sources, emotion, and humanism.

The chapel was built out of guilt for white-collar crimes. Reginaldo degli Scrovegni charged sky-high interest rates at a time when the Church forbade the practice. He even caught the attention of Dante, who placed him in one of the levels of hell in his *Inferno*. When Reginaldo died, the Church denied him a Christian burial. His son Enrico tried to buy forgiveness for his father's sins by building this superb chapel. After seeing Giotto's frescoes for the Franciscan monks of St. Anthony, Enrico knew he'd found the right artist to decorate the interior (and, he hoped, to save his father's soul). The Scrovegni residence once stood next to the chapel, but it was torn down in 1824.

NEAR VENICE

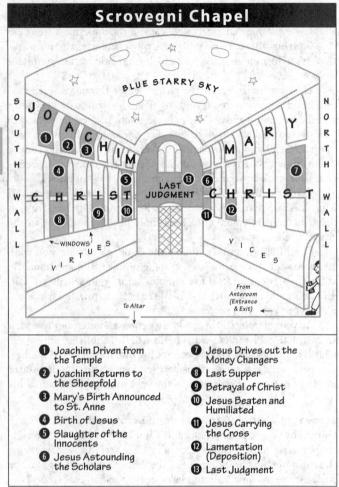

# Scrovegni Chapel

1. Joachim Driven from the Temple
2. Joachim Returns to the Sheepfold
3. Mary's Birth Announced to St. Anne
4. Birth of Jesus
5. Slaughter of the Innocents
6. Jesus Astounding the Scholars
7. Jesus Drives out the Money Changers
8. Last Supper
9. Betrayal of Christ
10. Jesus Beaten and Humiliated
11. Jesus Carrying the Cross
12. Lamentation (Deposition)
13. Last Judgment

**Giotto's Frescoes:** Giotto painted the entire chapel in 200 working days over two years, but you'll get only 15 minutes to see it.

As you enter the long, narrow chapel, look straight to the far end—the rear wall is covered with Giotto's big *Last Judgment*. Christ in a bubble is flanked by crowds of saints and by scenes of heaven and hell. This is the final, climactic scene of the story told in the chapel's 38 panels—the three-generation history of Jesus, his mother Mary, and Mary's parents.

The story begins with Jesus' grandparents, on the long south wall (with the windows) in the upper-left corner. ❶ In the first frame, a priest scolds the man who will be Mary's father (Joachim, with the halo) and kicks him out of the temple for the sin of being childless. ❷ In the next panel to the right, Joachim returns dejectedly to his sheep farm. ❸ Meanwhile (next panel), his wife is in the bedroom, hearing the miraculous news that their prayers have been answered—she'll give birth to Mary, the mother of Jesus.

From this humble start, the story of Mary and Jesus spirals clockwise around the chapel, from top to bottom. The top row (both south and north walls) covers Mary's birth and life.

Jesus enters the picture in the middle row of the south (windowed) wall. ❹ The first frame shows his birth in a shedlike manger. In the next frame, the Magi arrive and kneel to kiss his little toes. Then the child is presented in the tiny temple. Fearing danger, the family gets on a horse and flees to Egypt. ❺ Meanwhile, back home, all the baby boys are slaughtered in an attempt to prevent the coming of the Messiah *(Slaughter of the Innocents)*.

Spinning clockwise to the opposite (north) wall, you see (in a badly damaged fresco) ❻ the child Jesus astounding scholars with his wisdom. Next, Jesus is baptized by John the Baptist. His first miracle, at a wedding, is turning jars of water into wine. Next, he raises a mummy-like Lazarus from the dead. Riding a donkey, he enters Jerusalem triumphantly. ❼ In the temple, he drives out the wicked money changers.

Turning again to the south wall (bottom row), we see scenes from Jesus' final days. ❽ In the first frame, he and his followers

gather at a table for a Last Supper. Next, Jesus kneels humbly to wash their feet. ❾ He is betrayed with a kiss and arrested. Jesus is tried. ❿ Then he is beaten and humiliated.

⓫ Finally (north wall, bottom row), he is forced to carry his own cross, crucified, and prepared for burial, while his followers mourn (⓬ *Lamentation*). Then he is resurrected and ascends to heaven, leaving his disciples to carry on.

⓭ The whole story concludes on the rear wall, where Jesus reigns at the Last Judgment. The long south wall (ground level) features the Virtues that lead to heaven, while the north wall has the (always more interesting) Vices. And all this unfolds beneath the blue, starry sky overhead on the ceiling.

Some panels deserve a closer look:

*Joachim Returns to the Sheepfold* (south wall, upper left, second panel): Though difficult to appreciate from ground level, this oft-reproduced scene is groundbreaking. Giotto—a former shepherd himself—uses nature as a stage, setting the scene in front of a backdrop of real-life mountains and adding down-home details like Joachim's jumping dog, frozen in midair.

*Betrayal of Christ*, a.k.a. *Il Bacio*, "The Kiss" (south wall, bottom row, center panel): Amid the crowded chaos of Jesus' arrest, Giotto skillfully creates a focus upon the central action, where Judas ensnares Jesus in his yellow robe (the color symbolizing envy), establishes meaningful eye contact, and kisses him.

*Lamentation*, a.k.a. *Deposition* (north wall, bottom row, middle): Jesus has been crucified, and his followers weep and wail over the lifeless body. John the Evangelist spreads his arms wide and shrieks, his cries echoed by anguished angels above. Each face is a study in grief. Giotto emphasizes these saints' human vulnerability.

*Last Judgment* (big west wall): Christ in the center is a glorious vision, but the real action is in hell (lower right). Satan is a Minotaur-headed ogre munching on sinners. Around him, demons give sinners their just desserts in a scene right out of Dante...who was Giotto's friend and fellow Florentine. Front and center is Enrico Scrovegni, in a violet robe (the color symbolizing penitence), donating the chapel to the Church in exchange for forgiveness of his father's sins.

Before the guard scoots you out, take a look at the actual altar. Though Enrico's father's tomb is lost, Enrico Scrovegni himself is in the tomb at the altar. The three statues are by Giovanni Pisano—Mary (in the center) supports Baby Jesus on her hip with a perfectly natural, maternal S-shape. She's flanked by anonymous deacons.

**Nearby:** Between the museum and the chapel are the scant remains of **Roman Padua.** The remnants are from the wall of an arena (with a reconstructed grand entry gate) and include nicely fitting pipes that once channeled water so that the arena could be flooded for special spectacles.

## Civic Museums (Musei Civici agli Eremitani)

The Eremitani, the building that functions as the entry for the adjacent Scrovegni Chapel, was once an Augustinian hermit's monastery and now houses the Civic Museums: archaeology on the ground floor and paintings upstairs in the Pinacoteca (all included with your Scrovegni Chapel ticket).

**Archaeology Museum:** Filling the ground floor around the monastery's cloister courtyard is an impressive collection of ancient statues and artifacts—Egyptian, Venetian, and Roman. Sadly, there are no English descriptions.

**Pinacoteca:** The entire upper floor of the monastery, also facing the cloister, is the Pinacoteca (picture gallery). The collection has 13th- to 18th-century paintings by Titian, Tintoretto, Giorgione, Tiepolo, Veronese, Bellini, Canova, and other Veneto artists.

Start your visit by going directly to its highlight: the **Giotto crucifix.** Climb to the top of the stairs, take a few steps to the right through the cloister's gallery, and into a room featuring a precious crucifix. Ask for *"La Croce di Giotto?"* (lah KROH-cheh dee JOH-toh?)

The remarkable crucifix, painted by Giotto on wood, originally hung in the Scrovegni Chapel between the Scrovegni family's private zone and the public's worshipping zone. If you kneel on the floor and look up, the body really pops. The adjacent "God as Jesus" *(L'Eterno)* was the only painting in the otherwise frescoed chapel. (The original hangs here for conservation purposes; its copy is the only nonoriginal art in the chapel.) Studying these two masterpieces affirms Giotto's greatness.

Behind the crucifix room is a collection of 14th- and 15th-century art. While the works here are exquisite—and came well after Giotto—they're clearly done by artists without the genius of Giotto.

**Rest of the Civic Museums:** The **Multimedia Room** in the basement (take stairs down from the cloister) is a children's exhibit giving more meaning to the Scrovegni Chapel frescoes with a 15-minute video in a small theater (pick up headphones for English), and fun computer teaching programs. Across the busy street is the **Palazzo Zuckermann,** with a commotion of applied and decorative arts (clothing, furniture, and ceramics) from the Venetian Republic (1600s and 1700s) and a collection of 19th-century coins and local Impressionist paintings.

## ▲▲▲BASILICA OF ST. ANTHONY

Friar Anthony of Padua, "Christ's perfect follower and a tireless preacher of the Gospel," is buried here. Construction of this impressive Romanesque/ Gothic church (with its Byzantine-style domes) started immediately after St. Anthony's death in 1231. As a mark of his universal appeal and importance in the medieval Church, he was sainted within a year of his death. Speedy. And for nearly

NEAR VENICE

# St. Anthony of Padua (1195-1231)

One of Christendom's most popular saints, Anthony is known as a powerful speaker, a miracle worker, and the finder of lost articles.

Born in Lisbon to a rich, well-educated family, his life changed at 25, when he saw the mutilated bodies of some Franciscan martyrs. Their sacrifice inspired him to join the poor Franciscans and dedicate his life to Christ. He moved to Italy and lived in a cave, studying, meditating, and barely speaking to anyone.

One day, he joined his fellow monks for a service. The appointed speaker failed to show up, so Anthony was asked to say a few off-the-cuff words to the crowd. He started slowly, but, filled with the Spirit, he became more confident and amazed the audience with his eloquence. Up in Assisi, St. Francis heard about Anthony and sent him on a whirlwind speaking tour.

Anthony had a strong voice, knew several languages, had an encyclopedic knowledge of theology, and could speak spontaneously as the Spirit moved him. It's said that he even stood on the shores of the Adriatic Sea in Rimini and enticed a school of fish to listen. Anthony also was known as a prolific miracle worker.

In 1230, Anthony retired to Padua, where he founded a monastery and initiated reforms for the poor. An illness cut his life short at 36. Anthony said, "Happy is the man whose words issue from the Spirit and not from himself!"

800 years, his remains and this glorious church have attracted pilgrims to Padua.

**Cost and Hours:** The **basilica** is free and open daily 6:20-19:45 (Nov-March Mon-Fri closes at 18:45). The **Chapel of the Reliquaries** is also free and keeps the basilica's hours but closes for lunch (12:45-14:30). The nearest tram stop is Santo.

**Information:** Tel. 049-822-5652, www.santantonio.org.

**Other Basilica Sights:** A €7 combo-ticket gets you into the basilica's museum, Oratory of St. George, and Scuola del Santo. These sights are generally open daily 9:00-13:00 & 14:00-18:00. Tickets are sold at the info desk at the cloisters (just to the right of the church entry) and include an excellent audioguide that covers the basilica and all related sights (you must provide your own earbuds).

**Dress Code:** A modest dress code is enforced.

**Church Services:** The church hosts six separate Masses each morning (the last at 11:00), as well as at 17:00 and 18:00 in summer and on Sunday year-round, plus additional Sunday services at 12:15, 16:00, and 19:00.

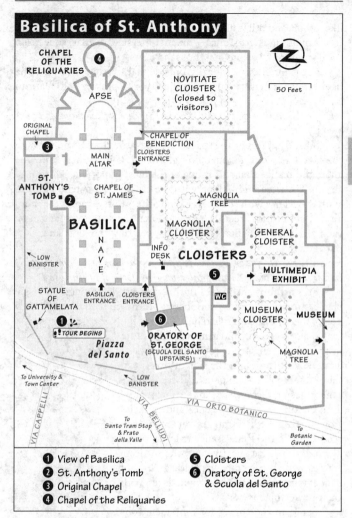

# Basilica of St. Anthony

CHAPEL OF THE RELIQUARIES
4
APSE
NOVITIATE CLOISTER (closed to visitors)
50 Feet
ORIGINAL CHAPEL
3
CHAPEL OF BENEDICTION
CLOISTERS ENTRANCE
MAIN ALTAR
ST. ANTHONY'S TOMB
2
CHAPEL OF ST. JAMES
MAGNOLIA TREE
MAGNOLIA CLOISTER
GENERAL CLOISTER
BASILICA
N A V E
INFO DESK
CLOISTERS
LOW BANISTER
5
MULTIMEDIA EXHIBIT
WC
STATUE OF GATTAMELATA
BASILICA ENTRANCE
CLOISTERS ENTRANCE
6
MUSEUM CLOISTER
MUSEUM
1
TOUR BEGINS
ORATORY OF ST. GEORGE (SCUOLA DEL SANTO UPSTAIRS)
MAGNOLIA TREE
Piazza del Santo
To University & Town Center
LOW BANISTER
VIA CAPPELLI
VIA BELLUDI
VIA ORTO BOTANICO
To Santo Tram Stop & Prato della Valle
To Botanic Garden

NEAR VENICE

1 View of Basilica
2 St. Anthony's Tomb
3 Original Chapel
4 Chapel of the Reliquaries
5 Cloisters
6 Oratory of St. George & Scuola del Santo

## ⊙ Self-Guided Tour

Stand outside to view the basilica's red-brick facade. St. Anthony looks down and blesses all. He holds a book, a symbol of all the knowledge he had accumulated as a quiet monk before starting his preaching career.

A golden angel—the weathervane atop the spire—points her trumpet into the wind. (While you can never really be sure with angels, locals say they know it's a woman because she always tells the truth.)

Guarding the church is Donatello's life-size equestrian statue of the Venetian mercenary general, Gattamelata. Though it looks like a thousand other man-on-a-horse statues, it was a landmark in Italy's budding Renaissance—the first life-size, secular, equestrian statue cast from bronze in a thousand years.

The church is technically outside Italy. When you pass the banisters that mark its property line, you're passing into Vatican territory.

• *Enter the basilica and grab a pew in the center of the nave. Let your eyes adjust.*

Sit and appreciate the space. Gaze past the crowds and through the incense haze to Donatello's glorious crucifix rising from the altar, and realize that this is one of the most important pilgrimage sites in Christendom. Along with the crucifix, Donatello's bronze statues—Mary with Padua's six favorite saints—grace the high altar. Late in his career, the great Florentine sculptor spent more than a decade in Padua (1444-1455), creating the altar and Gattamelata.

• *Head to the left side of the nave to find the gleaming marble masterpiece that is the focus of the visiting pilgrims—the tomb of St. Anthony.*

**St. Anthony's Tomb:** Pilgrims file slowly through this side chapel around the tomb, so focused on the saint that they hardly notice the nine fine marble reliefs. (While the  long queue looks intimidating, these folks are just waiting their turn to touch the tomb; you can easily skirt around the side of this group for a closer look at each panel.) These Renaissance masterpieces were carved during the 16th century and show scenes and miracles from the life of the saint. As you enjoy each scene, notice the Renaissance mastery of realism and 3-D perspective and the intricate frames, which celebrate life with a burst of exuberance. Note also the vivid faces with their powerful emotions.

Stand in the corner for a moment, observing the passionate devotion that pilgrims and Paduans alike have for Anthony. Touching his tomb or kneeling in prayer, the faithful believe Anthony is their protector—a confidant and intercessor for the poor. And they believe he works miracles. Believers leave offerings, votives, and written prayers to ask for help or to give thanks for miracles they believe Anthony has performed. By putting their hands on his tomb while saying silent prayers, pilgrims show devotion to Anthony and feel the saint's presence.

Popular Anthony is the patron saint of dozens of things: travelers, amputees, donkeys, pregnant women, infertile women, and flight attendants. Most pilgrims ask for his help in his role as the "finder of things"—from lost car keys to a life companion. You'll see dozens of photos posted on his tomb in prayer or as thanks, including many of fervently wished-for newborns.

Before leaving, pause to appreciate how the entire chapel is an integrated artistic wonder.

• *Leave the chapel and step into the oldest part of the church. This is the...*

**Original Chapel:** This is where Anthony was first buried in 1231. To the left of the altar, note the fine (and impressively realistic for the 1380s) view of medieval Padua, with this church outside the wall (finished by 1300 and looking like it does today). Below the cityscape, in a circa-1380 fresco, Anthony on his cloud promises he'll watch over Padua.

As you exit this chapel, you'll notice many tombs nearby. People wanted to be buried near a saint. If you could afford it, this was about the best piece of real estate a dead person could have. (The practice was ended with Napoleonic reforms in 1806.)

• *Continue your circuit of the church by going behind the altar into the apse, to the Chapel of the Reliquaries. Just before that is the Polish chapel with its ornate bronze gate and a painting of St. John Paul II (canonized in 2014). At busy times, you may have to line up and trudge slowly up the stairs past the reliquaries.*

**Chapel of the Reliquaries:** The most prized relic is in the glass case at center stage—Anthony's tongue. When Anthony's remains were exhumed 32 years after his death (in 1263), his body had decayed to dust, but his tongue was found miraculously unspoiled and red in color. How appropriate for the great preacher who, full of the Spirit, couldn't stop talking about God.

Entering the chapel, join the parade of pilgrims working their way clockwise around the chapel and up the stairs. First, on the left, look for the red, triangular vestment in which Anthony's body was wrapped. Next is his rough-hewn wood coffin. Then, up the stairs, is his pillow—a comfy rock (chest level in first glass case). The center display case contains (top to bottom) the saint's lower jaw with all his teeth impressively intact (*il mento*, located about 8 feet high), his uncorrupted tongue (*lingua*, at about eye level), and, finally, his vocal chords (*apparato vocale*, at about waist level) discovered intact when his remains were examined in 1981. In the last display case, a fragment of the True Cross *(la croce)* is held in a precious cross-shaped reliquary. Finally, descend the stairs and pass St. Anthony's holy, and holey, tunic *(tonaca)* in the center of the room. Pilgrims stop at a desk to pick up a small card with a tiny piece of blessed cloth that touched Anthony's tongue.

Above the relics, decorating the cornice, is the *Glorification of St. Anthony*. In this Baroque fantasy—made in 1691 of carved marble and stucco—a cloud of angels and giddy *putti* tumble to the left and right in jubilation as they play their Baroque-era musical instruments to celebrate Anthony's arrival in heaven.

• *Leaving this relic chapel, continue circling the apse. You'll come to the* **Chapel of Benediction.** *Here, under a powerful modern fresco of the Crucifixion (by Pietro Annigoni, painted in 1982), a priest is waiting to bless anyone who wishes to be blessed.*

*Next, past the sacristy (where you can peek in at priests preparing for Mass), is a door leading to the cloisters. But before heading out, walk just beyond this passage to the...*

**Chapel of St. James:** Exactly opposite the tomb of St. Anthony, this chapel features an exquisite 14th-century fresco by Altichiero da Zevio. Study the vivid commotion around the Crucifixion, clearly inspired by Giotto (this was created 70 years after the Scrovegni Chapel). The faces are real—right off the streets of 14th-century Padua. From this chapel, look across the nave and appreciate how Anthony's massive tomb is so beautifully integrated into the church architecturally.

• *Next, exit out into the cloisters. From the right side of the nave as you face the altar, follow signs to* chiostro.

**Cloisters:** Of the four cloisters at the basilica, you can wander in three. The main cloister is dominated by an exceptionally bushy **magnolia tree,** planted in 1810 (the magnolia was exotic for Europe when it was imported from America in 1760). Also in the cloister are the graves of the most illustrious Paduans, such as Gabriel Fallopius, the scientist who gave his name to his discovery, the Fallopian tube. When Napoleon decreed that graves should be moved out

of cities, this once grave-covered courtyard was cleared of tombstones. But the bodies were left in the ground, perhaps contributing to the magnolia tree's fecundity. Today the tree remains an explosion of life.

In another cloister, the **multimedia exhibit** tells about the life of St. Anthony and the Franciscan mission in a slow, thoughtful, and evangelical way (free, 20 minutes, entry every 10 minutes). You move two times as you use headphones to listen to the story of each tableau.

At the far end of the cloister, a small **museum** (shares combo-ticket with the oratory and scuola) is filled with votives and folk art recounting miracles attributed to Anthony. The abbreviation *PGR* that you'll see on many votives stands for *per grazia ricevuta*—for answered prayers.

**Other Basilica Sights:** There are two other sights, covered by the same combo-ticket as the museum. The small but sumptuous

**Oratory of St. George** faces the little square in front of the basilica. The oratory ("ora" means prayer) is not actually a church, though it's certainly a fine place to pray—it's filled with vivid, circa-1370 frescoes showing scenes not of Anthony but from the life of St. George, St. Lucia, and St. Catherine. Because many lovers credit St. Anthony with finding them their partners—and this is the closest place to St. Anthony where you can be married—it's popular for weddings.

Next door and upstairs is the skippable **Scuola del Santo** (a.k.a. La Scoletta), the former meeting hall of the Confraternity of Anthony. It has frescoes and paintings by various artists—including some by Titian.

## NEAR THE BASILICA
### Prato della Valle

The square is 150 yards southwest of the basilica (down Via Beato Luca Belludi). Once a Roman theater and later Anthony's preaching grounds, this square claims to be the largest in Italy. It's a pleasant, 400-yard-long, oval-shaped piazza with fountains, walkways, dozens of statues of Padua's eminent citizens, and grass. It's also a lively **market** scene (though smaller than those previously listed): fruit and

vegetables (Mon-Fri 8:00-13:00), clothing, shoes, and household goods (Sat 8:00-19:00), and antiques (third Sun 8:00-19:00). This place is often busy with special events and festivals. Ask at the TI or your hotel if anything's going on at Prato della Valle.

### ▲Botanic Garden (Orto Botanico)

Green thumbs, science fans, and anyone who wants a break from art or religious sights can appreciate this historic botanical garden, which contains the university's vast collection of rare plants. Founded in 1545 for the cultivation and study of medicinal plants, it's the world's oldest existing academic botanical garden. Because of the Venetian Republic's vast reach through trade and commerce, and the university's renown, exotic plants from all over the world made their way to Padua. It's believed that the first potato, sesame, lilac, and sunflower in Europe were planted in this city.

**Cost and Hours:** €10; daily 9:00-19:00, closes earlier off-season, last entry one hour before closing; the garden's free app is best suited to plant and science buffs; entrance 150 yards south of

Basilica of St. Anthony—with your back to the facade, take a hard left; Santo tram stop, tel. 049-201-0222, www.ortobotanicopd.it.

**Visiting the Garden:** The botanical garden's original 16th-century square-within-a-circle configuration remains intact. Inside its circular wall, the garden is filled with elegant, geometrical plant beds. Wandering the paths, visitors can also admire a 340-year-old Oriental plane tree, a Southern magnolia that's only 10 years younger than the United States, and the garden's oldest specimen—a St. Peter's dwarf palm that was planted in 1585, and inspired Goethe to write his essay on the "Metamorphosis of Plants."

From the south end of the enclosed garden, find the path over a footbridge that leads to the striking and enormous **Biodiversity Garden.** The five greenhouse biomes take you on a journey through the world's major climate zones. Panels provide superb English descriptions of the environments and offer insight into how plant life has influenced the development of humankind—and vice versa.

## Sleeping in Padua

Rooms in Padua's hotels are more spacious and a better value than those in Venice. I've listed a couple of hotels in the center and a group of accommodations near the basilica. All are reachable from the station by tram; only Albergo Verdi is more than a five-minute walk from the nearest tram stop.

### IN THE CENTER

**$$$ Hotel Majestic Toscanelli,** an old-fashioned, ornate, family-run hotel with 34 rooms, owns a perfectly convenient location right in the town center—buried in the characteristic ghetto with wonderful cobbled ambience. At night, this area is popular with noisy students; request a quiet room on the back side (RS%, spacious attic "loft" rooms with kitchenettes and low beams, air-con, elevator, pay parking, Via dell'Arco 2, Tito Livio tram stop, tel. 049-663-244, www.toscanelli.com, majestic@toscanelli.com, Mario Morosi and family). From the tram stop, follow the passageway next to #26, then jog left down Via Marsala and turn right on Via dell'Arco.

**$$ Albergo Verdi,** an outdated Ikea-esque little place, is crammed into an old building on a small back street beyond Piazza dei Signori. While public spaces are tight, the 14 rooms are sufficient (air-con, tiny elevator, Via Dondi dall'Orologio 7, Ponti Romani tram stop, tel. 049-836-4163, www.albergoverdipadova.it, info@albergoverdipadova.it). From Piazza dei Signori, walk through the arch under the clock tower and go to the far end of Piazza del Capitaniato; the hotel is on the side street to your right.

## NEAR THE BASILICA OF ST. ANTHONY

Santo is the nearest tram stop for the following hotels.

**$$$ Hotel Belludi 37** is a slick, stylish place renting 16 chic rooms in an old building. The decor is dark, woody, and crisp. Owners Andrea and Mauro are friendly and attentive, as is their staff (RS%, some rooms with basilica view, air-con, lots of stairs with no elevator, apartments available nearby, a block from the Santo tram stop at Via Beato Luca Belludi 37, tel. 049-665-633, www.collezionebelludi.it, info@belludi37.it).

**$$ Hotel Al Fagiano** feels like an art gallery with crazy, sexy, modern art everywhere. The hotel is all about the union of a man and a woman (quite romantic). They rent 37 bright and cheery rooms, each uniquely decorated with Rossella Fagiano's creations (RS%, air-con, elevator, pay parking, 50 yards from the Santo tram stop at Via Antonio Locatelli 45, tel. 049-875-0073, www. alfagiano.com, info@alfagiano.com; Anita, Rossella, and Amato).

**$ Hotel Al Santo,** run with charm by Valentina and Antonio, offers 15 spacious rooms with essential comforts on two floors above their restaurant, a few steps from the basilica. Given the warm welcome and pleasant location, it's a fine value (family rooms, double-paned windows, quieter rooms off street, some rooms with basilica views, air-con, elevator, pay parking, Via del Santo 147, tel. 049-875-2131, www.alsanto.it, alsanto@alsanto.it).

**$ Hotel Casa del Pellegrino,** with 148 spotless, cheap, bare rooms and straight pricing, is owned by the friars of St. Anthony. It's home to the pilgrims who come to pay homage to the saint in the basilica next door. Any visitor to Padua is welcome, making it popular with professors and students. Some rooms with basilica views also come with more noise—both from the street and, starting at 6:00 in the morning, the church bells—while others are in *dipendenza,* the hotel's modern wing (cheaper rooms with shared bath, family rooms, ask for a room off the street, breakfast extra, air-con, elevator, pay parking, Via Melchiorre Cesarotti 21, tel. 049-823-9711, www.casadelpellegrino.com, info@casadelpellegrino.com).

# Eating in Padua

The university population means cheap, good food abounds. My recommended restaurants are all centrally located in the historic core. You'd think there would be fine dining on the charming market squares, but on the piazzas it's a takeout-pizza and casual-bar scene (dominated by students after dark). La Lanterna, at the neighboring Piazza dei Signori, is the best on-square option—but they only offer functional Italian classics. The dreamily atmospheric ghetto neighborhood (just two blocks off the market squares) thrives after dark with trendy bars and a lively student *spritz* scene.

I've listed several serious restaurants (each with a distinct personality), plus a good pizzeria and a good gelateria at each end of town. And, if you want a fun and mobile multi-stop meal of bar food capped with some fine gelato, string together my recommendations under "Cheap Eats and Bars with Tapas in the Center."

## DINING NEAR THE CENTER

**$$ Osteria L'Anfora** is a colorful if chaotic place serving classic dishes in an informal, fun-loving space. Don't be put off by the woody, ruffian decor, the squat toilet, and the fact that it's a popular hangout for a premeal drink. They take food seriously and serve it at good prices, and the fun energy and commotion add to the dining experience (meals served Mon-Sat 12:30-15:00 & 19:30-22:30, bar open 9:00-24:00, closed Sun, reservations smart for dinner, Via dei Soncin 13, tel. 049-656-629).

**$$ Osteria dal Capo** is a tight and jumbled little bistro with chandeliers and white tablecloths serving classic Veneto meat and fish dishes, home-cooking style (closed Sun-Mon, inside only, reserve for dinner, Via degli Obizzi 2, tel. 049-663-105, www.osteriadalcapo.it).

**$$$ Enotavola Pino** (*enotavola* means "wine table") is, in the front, a dressy, hip wine bar where owner/chef Pino offers scores of wines by the glass—each with a little plate of mortadella. The back is a sleek and youthful fish-only restaurant with a busy, open kitchen and bright, spacious seating. If you like the energy in the wine bar, you can order from the menu there, too (closed Mon like any serious fish restaurant, Via dell'Arco 37, tel. 049-876-2385).

**$$$ Enoteca Antonio Ferrari** is a top-end wine bar serving near-gourmet-level meat and cheese boards to a smart, young, and local foodie crowd. It's pricey but a good value and feels bright and youthful (daily, Via Umberto 1, tel. 049-666-375).

## CHEAP EATS AND BARS WITH TAPAS IN THE CENTER

**$$ Pizza on Piazza dei Signori:** Though **La Lanterna** has a forgettable interior and a predictable menu of pizzas, pastas, and *secondi*, its prime location provides a rare-in-Padua chance to sit in a grand square under the stars, surrounded by great architecture. Locals know it as the first pizzeria in town (Fri-Wed 12:00-15:00 & 18:00-24:00, closed Thu, Piazza dei Signori 39, tel. 049-660-770, www.lalanternapadova.it).

**$ Squid, *Porchetta*, and *Spritz* on Piazza della Frutta:** Just a simple sandwich place, **Bar dei Osei** has some of the best outdoor seats in town. While Paduans love their delicate *tramezzini*—white-bread sandwiches with crusts cut off, I'd choose their *porchetta*—savory roasted pork sandwiches. You'll find a two-foot-long mother lode waiting on the counter for you; tell friendly Betty how big a slice you'd like. Wines are listed on the board (Mon-Sat 7:00-21:00, closed Sun, Piazza della Frutta 1, tel. 049-875-9606). In the evenings, just a few feet away, **La Folperia squid stand** sells mostly boiled and spiced plates of squid by the weight—indicate small (€6) or big (€12) and request bread. Crowd your way up to the bar, and Massimiliano and Barbara will take care of you (Mon-Sat 17:00-20:30, closed Sun). Even with a plate of La Folperia seafood, you're welcome to grab a Bar dei Osei table and order a drink from the roaming server.

**$ *Cicchetti* Bars Popular with Students:** Surrounding Palazzo della Ragione you'll find lots of atmospheric bars jammed with students marked by the glowing orange glasses of *spritz*. These bars also serve little €1 and €2 bites (mostly fried gut bombs and enticing open-face sandwiches). While the tapas aren't advertised, the walls are scribbled with the various wines, vermouths, and cocktails for sale. Two classy holes-in-the-wall are particularly atmospheric (each about a block off the market squares): **Bar Corte Sconta** (across the street from the recommended Hotel Majestic Toscanelli, at Via dell'Arco 9) and **Bar All'Ombra della Piazza** (100 yards off Piazza della Frutta, down the tiny Via Pietro D'Abano at #16).

**$ Pasta and Vegetarian on Piazza della Erbe: Pastasuta** is a minimalist little pasta joint tucked away in the Palazzo della Ragione arcade (Piazza delle Erbe side). Choose your pasta and sauce combo or enjoy prepared options from their little *tavola fredda*. Seating is limited, but all of their dishes can be packed to go. Just say, *"Per portare via, per favore"* (Mon-Sat 8:00-21:00, closed Sun). **Cristina e Massimo,** just a few doors down from Pastasuta, serves seasonal and creative vegetarian dishes, from fancy salads to muffins to tarts (Mon-Sat 7:00-20:00, closed Sun).

**Gelato:** For your best dessert in the market square area, enjoy a high-end gelato at **Gnam Gnam** (that means "yum yum") on Piazza dei Signori (Via San Clemente 18).

## NEAR THE BASILICA OF ST. ANTHONY

**$$ Antica Trattoria dei Paccagnella,** the most serious restaurant near the basilica, serves nicely presented, seasonal local dishes with modern flair and an impressive attention to ingredients. The place has friendly service, modern art on the walls, and no pretense. It's thoughtfully run by two brothers, Raffaele and Cesare (daily 12:00-14:00 & 19:00-22:00 except dinner-only on Sun-Mon, Via del Santo 113, tel. 049-875-0549).

**$ Pizzeria Pago Pago** dishes up wood-fired Neapolitan pizzas (a local favorite) and daily specials depending on what's in season. They also have good salads, non-pizza dishes, and beer on tap in a bright and high-energy dining area (Wed-Mon 12:00-14:00 &

19:00-24:00, closed Tue; 2 blocks from basilica, up Via del Santo and right onto Via Galileo Galilei to #59; tel. 049-665-558, Gaetano and Modesto).

**$ Pollodoro la Gastronomica,** my pick of the takeout delis near the basilica, sells roast chicken, pastas, pizza, and veggies. They'll also make sandwiches (Wed-Mon 9:00-14:00 & 17:00-20:00, closed Tue, 100 yards from basilica at Via Belludi 34, tel. 049-663-718).

**Gelato: Portogallo Gelateria** is considered the best gelateria in town, with amazing and creative flavors (Via Umberto 1, Alberto).

## Padua Connections

Unless otherwise specified, the following connections are for Trenitalia.

**From Padua by Train to: Venice** (2/hour, 30 minutes; Italo: hourly, 30 minutes), **Vicenza** (at least 2/hour, fewer on weekends, 15-25 minutes), **Milan** (1-2/hour, 2-3 hours; Italo 7/day, 2 hours), **Verona** (2/hour, 40-80 minutes), **Florence** (4/day direct, 2 hours, require reservations; otherwise 3 hours with connections). When taking the train to Venice, Vicenza, or Verona, buy a ticket on a regional train (R or RV). The Trenitalia Frecce or Italo express trains cost more and get you there only marginally faster (especially when compared to an RV train).

**By Bus to: Venice's Marco Polo Airport** (65 minutes, €8.50 from ticket windows, €10 on board, hourly at :25 past the hour from 6:25 to 21:25, leaves from platform 11 at Padua's bus station, next to the train station; recheck times at www.fsbusitaliaveneto. it). If flying into the airport, take this bus to get directly to Padua (buy tickets at windows in arrivals hall or at airport TI).

**By Minibus to Airports:** An Air Service minibus runs from Padua to **Marco Polo Airport** (€35/person) or **Treviso Airport** (€42/person, reservations required, tel. 049-870-4425, www. airserviceshuttle.it).

# Vicenza

To many architects, Vicenza (vee-CHEHN-zah) is a pilgrimage site. Entire streets look like the back of a nickel. This is the city of Andrea Palladio (1508-1580), the 16th-century Renaissance architect who defined the Palladian style that is now so influential in countless British country homes. But as grandiose as Vicenza's Palladian facades may feel, there is little marble here because the

city lacked the wealth to build with much more than painted wood and plaster.

If you're an architecture buff, Vicenza merits a quick day trip on any day but Monday, when major sights are closed. If you're packing light, it's an easy stop, located on the same train line as Padua, Verona, and Venice. However, because you can't store bags at the train station, it's not worth stopping here if you have lots of luggage (though in a pinch, the TI may be willing to store bags for you while you walk around town).

**Tourist Information:** The TI is next to the Olympic Theater at Piazza Matteotti 12 (daily 9:00-13:30 & 14:00-17:30, tel. 0444-320-854, www.visitvicenza.org). Ask for the free brochure on Palladio's buildings. Architecture fans appreciate the booklet titled *Vicenza and the Villas of Andrea Palladio.*

**Arrival in Vicenza:** From the **train station,** I'd head straight for the most distant sight, the Olympic Theater (with a TI next door) and then see other sights on the way back. Go straight out the train station's front door, and use the crosswalk on the right side of the roundabout. From here, it's a five-minute walk straight ahead up wide Viale Roma to the PAM supermarket at the bottom of Corso Palladio; turn right through the gate, and then it's a good 10 minutes more down the Corso to the Olympic Theater (a taxi costs €8). **Drivers** can park in one of the cheap parking lots (Parcheggio Bassano and Parcheggio Cricoli) and catch a free shuttle bus to the center.

# Sights in Vicenza

Helpful bilingual signs in front of Palladio's buildings explain their history. Arrows around town point you to his major works.

All the sights mentioned (except the villas outside town) are covered by the **Museum Card** combo-ticket (€15, €18 family pass, good for 3 days, sold at Olympic Theater and Palazzo Leoni Montanari Galleries).

### ▲▲Olympic Theater (Teatro Olimpico)

Palladio's last work, one of his greatest, shouldn't be missed. This indoor theater is a wood-and-stucco festival of classical columns, statues, and an oh-wow stage bursting with perspective tricks. When you step back outside, take another look at the town's main drag—named after Palladio. It's the same main street you saw on the stage of his theater.

**Cost and Hours:** €12.50; Tue-Sun 9:00-17:00, closed Mon, very occasionally closed when theater is in use; audioguide available, entrance to left of TI at Piazza Matteotti 11, info tel. 0444-222-800, tickets tel. 044-496-4380, www. teatrolimpicovicenza.it.

### ▲Church of Santa Corona (Chiesa di Santa Corona)

A block away from the Olympic Theater, this "Church of the Holy Crown" was built in the 13th century to house a thorn from the Crown of Thorns, given to the Bishop of Vicenza by the French King Louis IX. The church has two artistic highlights: Paolo Veronese's *Adoration of the Magi* (1573) and Giovanni Bellini's fine *Baptism of Christ* (c. 1502).

**Cost and Hours:** Free, Tue-Sun 9:00-12:00 & 15:00-18:00, closed Mon, Contrà Santa Corona 2, tel. 0444-323-644.

### Archaeological and Natural History Museum (Museo Naturalistico Archeologico)

Located next door to the Church of Santa Corona, this museum's ground floor features Roman antiquities (mosaics, statues, and artifacts excavated from Rome's Baths of Caracalla, plus swords) and a barbarian warrior skeleton complete with sword and helmet.

Prehistoric scraps are upstairs. Look for English description sheets near exhibit entryways throughout.

**Cost and Hours:** €3.50, Tue-Sun 9:00-17:00, closed Mon, Contrà Santa Corona 4, tel. 0444-222-815, www.museicivicivicenza.it.

### Palazzo Leoni Montanari Galleries
### (Gallerie di Palazzo Leoni Montanari)

Across the street from the Church of Santa Corona, this small museum is a palatial riot of Baroque, with cherub-cluttered ceilings jumbled like a preschool in heaven. A quick stroll shows off Venetian paintings and a floor of Russian icons.

**Cost and Hours:** €8.50, Tue-Sun 10:00-18:00, closed Mon, Contrà Santa Corona 25, tel. 800-578-875, www.palazzomontanari.com.

### Piazza dei Signori

Vicenza's main square has been the center of town ever since it was the site of the ancient Roman forum. The commanding **Basilica Palladiana,** with its 270-foot-tall, 13th-century tower, dominates the square. This was once the meet-

ing place for local big shots. It was young Palladio's proposal—to redo Vicenza's dilapidated Gothic palace of justice in the Neo-Greek style—that established him as the city's favorite architect. The rest of Palladio's career was a one-man construction boom. The basilica hosts special exhibitions that sometimes involve a fee, but you can often pop in for a free look.

### Villas on the Outskirts of Vicenza

Vicenza is surrounded by dreamy Venetian villas. Venice's commercial empire receded in the 1500s when trade began to pick up along the Atlantic seaboard and dwindle in the Mediterranean. Venice redirected its economic agenda to agribusiness, which led to the construction of lavish country villas, such as **Villa la Rotonda,** the inspiration for Thomas Jefferson's Monticello (www.villalarotonda.it), and **Villa Valmarana ai Nani** (www.villavalmarana.com). Located southeast of the town center, both houses are furnished with period pieces (closed Mon). Pick up the free brochure on Palladio's villas from the TI if you plan to visit.

## Vicenza Connections

**From Vicenza by Train to: Venice** (Trenitalia: 2/hour, 45 minutes; Italo: 7/day, 45 minutes), **Padua** (at least 2/hour, fewer on weekends, 15-25 minutes), **Verona** (2/hour, 30 minutes), **Milan** (1-2/hour, 2 hours). You'll save money by taking the slow R or the faster RV trains to Vicenza instead of the speedy Freccia or ES trains.

# Verona

Romeo and Juliet made Verona a household word. Alas, a visit here has nothing to do with those two star-crossed lovers. You can pay to visit the house that falsely claims to be Juliet's (with an almost believable balcony and a courtyard swarming with tour groups), join in the tradition of rubbing the breast of Juliet's statue to help find a lover (or to pick up the sweat of someone who can't), and even make a pilgrimage to what isn't "La Tomba di Giulietta."

Fiction aside, Verona has been an important crossroads for 2,000 years and is, therefore, packed with genuine history. R&J fans will take some solace in the fact that two real feuding families, the Montecchi and the Cappellos, were the models for Shakespeare's Montagues and Capulets. And, if R&J had existed and were alive today, they would still recognize much of their "hometown."

Verona's main attractions are its wealth of Roman ruins; the remnants of its 13th- and 14th-century political and cultural boom brought about by its leading family, the Scaligeri; its 21st-century, pedestrian-only ambience; and its world-class opera festival, held each summer. After Venice's festival of tourism, the Veneto region's second city is a cool and welcome sip of pure Italy, where dumpsters are painted by schoolchildren as class projects and public spaces are primarily the domain of locals, not tourists. If you like Italy but don't need blockbuster sights, this town is a joy.

## Orientation to Verona

Verona's old town fills an easy-to-defend bend in the River Adige. The vibrant and enjoyable core of Verona lies along Via Mazzini between Piazza Brà (pronounced "bra") and Piazza Erbe, Verona's market square since Roman times. Each evening the two main streets from Piazza Brà to Piazza Erbe, Via Mazzini and Corso Porta Borsari, are enlivened by a wonderful *passeggiata*...bustling with a slow and elegant parade of strollers. For a good day trip to Verona, take my self-guided walk, beginning with a visit to the Roman Arena.

## TOURIST INFORMATION

Verona's helpful TI is just off **Piazza Brà**—from the square, head to the big yellow building with columns and cross the street to Via degli Alpini 9 (Mon-Sat 9:00-19:00, Sun 10:00-18:00, shorter hours off-season, tel. 045-806-8680, www.turismoverona.eu). If you're staying the night, ask the TI about concerts.

**Sightseeing Passes:** The **Verona Card** covers city transportation and entry to all recommended Verona sights. The card can save day-trippers quite a bit if you're intent on blitzing the city's sights (€20/24 hours, €25/48 hours, sold at TI and at participating sights, www.turismoverona.eu).

The €6 **Church Card,** sold at four churches that require admission (San Zeno, Duomo, Sant'Anastasia, and San Fermo, normally €3 each), pays for itself if you visit two (www.chieseverona.it).

**Walking Tours:** The TI organizes 90-minute tours in English (€12/person, Sat-Sun at 11:00, none in winter). Tours meet inside the Piazza Brà TI and stroll all the way through the old town (confirm schedule, no reservation necessary).

## ARRIVAL IN VERONA

**By Train:** Verona's main train station is called Verona Porta Nuova. In the main hall, you'll find pay WCs and a baggage-check office (daily 8:00-20:00). Buses and taxis are immediately outside.

Avoid the boring 15-minute walk from the station to the center. Buses are cheap, easy, and leave every few minutes (although taxis are smart after sundown). Buy a ticket from the tobacco shop inside the station (€1.30/90 minutes, €4 day pass valid until midnight), or buy one on board using coin-op machines for €0.70 more. Leaving the station, angle right across the street to the bus stalls: For **Piazza Brà** (near the Roman Arena) and **San Fermo** (near the Ponte Navi bridge), find platform B1 and hop on a bus (#11, #12, #13, #51, and #52 run Mon-Sat until 20:00; #90, #92, and #98 run after 20:00 and all day Sun). For **Porta Borsari** (ancient city main gate), find platform D2 (buses #21, #22, #23, #24, #41, and #61 run Mon-Sat; #93, #94, and #95 run evenings and Sundays). If in doubt, confirm that your bus is headed to the city center by asking, *"Per il centro?"* (pehr eel CHEN-troh). Validate your ticket by stamping it in the machine on the bus.

If getting off at Piazza Brà, you'll see the can't-miss-it Roman

**NEAR VENICE**

# Verona

## Accommodations

1. Hotel Antica Porta Leona
2. Hotel Aurora
3. Casa Coloniale
4. To L'Ospite Apartments
5. Protezione della Giovane
6. Hotel Giulietta e Romeo & Hotel Milano
7. Hotel Colomba d'Oro
8. Aparthotel Verona House
9. To Pepita Lodge
10. Albergo Arena

## Eateries & Other

11. Cangrande Ristorante & Enoteca
12. Darì Ristorante & Enoteca
13. Trattoria al Pompiere
14. Antico Caffè Dante
15. Bottega del Vino
16. Ristorante Torcolo
17. Osteria Caffè Monte Baldo
18. La Piazzetta
19. Osteria Sottoriva
20. Osteria del Bugiardo
21. Osteria Vini Zampieri
22. Pizzeria da Salvatore
23. Pizzeria Du de Cope
24. Döner Kebab Shop
25. Supermarket (2)
26. Salumeria Caliari & Salumeria Albertini
27. Gelateria Savoia
28. L'Arte del Gelato
29. Launderette

Piazza Vittorio Veneto

VIA ROVERETO
VIALE NINO BIXIO
VIA DEI MILLE
V. CARLO EDERLE
VIA MARIO TODESCHINI
VIA MARIO DEL RISORGIMENTO
VIA IV NOVEMBRE
VIA G. ABBA
VIA PRATO SANTO
V. MONTE PASUBIO
VIA TONALE
VIALE DELLA REPUBBLICA
VIA ISONZO
LUNG

River

ARSENALE

PONTE VITTORIO

Piazza Arsenale

LUNG. CAMPAGNOLA

Adige

SAN LORENZO

PONTE SCALIGERO

ARCO DI GAVI
CORSO CAVOUR
SANTI APOSTOLI

VIC. DISC.

CASTELVECCHIO MUSEUM

VIA ROMA
VIA CATTANEO
VIC. DIETRO LISTON
LISTON

STR. PROVOLO
VIA BOSCO

To San Zeno

STR. PORTA PALIO
VIC. SAN SILVESTRO
VIA MANIN

WC

PORTONE DEL BRÀ

V. MUTILATI

B

To Porta Palio & Train Station

VIA MARCONI

200 Meters
200 Yards

To Train Station

Piazza Pradaval

CORSO PORTA NUOVA

To Porta Nuova, Train Station & Parking

P

**NEAR VENICE**

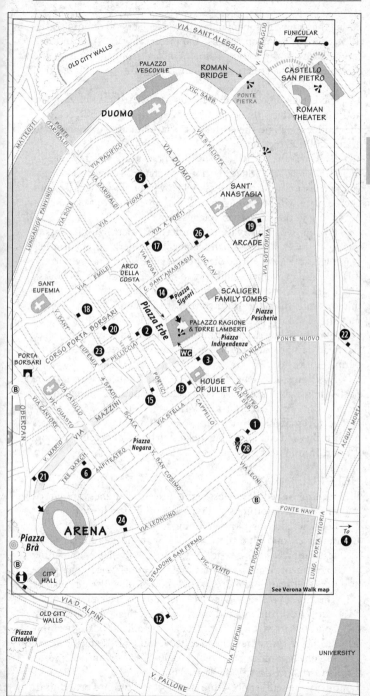

Arena (bus stops in front of big, yellow, Neoclassical building). The TI is near the bus stop, against the medieval wall. You can catch return buses to the station (same numbers) from the stop on the piazza side of the street, or from another bus stop on Piazza Brà, near the WCs.

**Taxis** pick up only at taxi stands (at Piazza Brà, Piazza Erbe, and the train station) and cost €10-12 for the quick ride between the train station and the center of town (€2 more on Sundays and after 22:00, €1/big bag).

**By Car:** The old town center (where nearly all my recommended hotels are located) is closed to traffic. Your hotel can get you permission to drive in—ask when you book. Otherwise your license plate will be photographed, and an expensive ticket might be waiting in the mail when you get home.

Drivers will find reasonably priced parking in well-marked lots and garages just outside the center. The underground **Cittadella garage,** at Piazza Cittadella (a block off Piazza Brà, behind the TI), is huge, convenient, and easy to find (€2/hour, €16/24 hours). The **Città di Nimes/Parking Stazione** lot is near the wall, a five-minute walk from the train station (€1.50/hour, €7/day). **Street parking** is limited to two hours and costs €1/hour (spaces marked with blue lines, buy ticket at a tobacco shop or ticket machine, place ticket on dashboard; some hotels can give you a free street-parking permit—ask).

**By Plane:** Efficient AeroBus shuttles connect Verona's airport (known as Catullo or Verona-Villafranca, 12 miles southwest of the city, airport code: VRN, tel. 045-809-5666, www.aeroportoverona.it) with its train station (€6, valid for 75 minutes on AeroBus and city buses, buy tickets on board or at tobacco shop, 3/hour, 15 minutes).

## HELPFUL HINTS

**Sightseeing Schedules:** Most sights (except churches) are closed on Monday mornings and typically open after lunchtime. The churches are closed Sun morning to sightseers.

**Opera:** From mid-June through early September, Verona's opera festival brings the city to life, with 15,000 music fans filling the Roman Arena for almost nightly performances (cheap upper-level seats—€25-30, day-of-show tickets often available). The city is packed and festive—restaurants have prescheduled seatings for dinner, and hotels jack up their prices. You can book tickets at the TI or through the official box office (buy online at www.arena.it or call 045-800-5151; during opera season, box office open daily 10:00-17:45, or until 20:30 on performance days; Via Dietro Anfiteatro 6B).

**Laundry:** The self-service **Oblò** is a short walk from Porta Borsari in a tranquil neighborhood (daily 8:00-22:30, Via Mario Todeschini 18).

**Private Guides:** Three enthusiastic Verona guides give private tours of the town and region tailored to specific interests—villas, wine tasting, and so on (€125/2 hours, €265/5 hours). They are **Marina Menegoi** (mobile 328-958-1108, www.marinamenegoi.com, mmenegoi@gmail.com), **Valeria Biasi** (mobile 348-903-4238, www.aguideinverona.com or www.veronatours.com, valeria@aguideinverona.com), and **Franklin Baumgarten** (mobile 347-566-6765, franklin_baumgarten@web.de).

# Verona Walk

This walk covers the essential sights in the town core, starting at Piazza Brà and ending at the cathedral. Allow two hours (including the tower climb and some dawdling).

## ❶ Piazza Brà

If you're wondering about the name, it comes from the local dialect and means "big open space." A generation ago this piazza was noisy with cars. Now it's open and people friendly—it's become the community family room and natural festival grounds.

Grab a bench near the central **fountain** called "The Alps." This was a gift from Verona's sister city Munich, which is just over

the mountains to the north. You'll see in the middle of the fountain the symbols of the two cities separated by the Alps, carved out of pink marble from this region. In general, Verona has a bit of an alpine feel; historically it was the place where people rested and prepared before crossing the mountains, and to this day it's the place where the main west-east, Milan-Venice train line meets the north-south line up to Bolzano, the Dolomites, and Austria.

The ancient **arena** looming over the piazza is a reminder that the city's history goes back to Roman times. On this walk, we'll meander across what was the ancient city, from the arena on this side to the theater across the river.

With the fall of Rome in the fifth century, Verona became a favored capital of barbarian kings. In the Middle Ages, noble families had to choose sides in the civil struggles between emperors (Ghibellines) and popes (Guelphs). During this time (1200s),

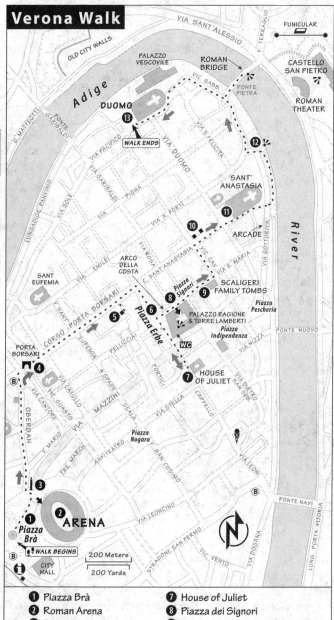

# Verona Walk

1. Piazza Brà
2. Roman Arena
3. Devotional Column
4. Porta Borsari & Corso Porta Borsari
5. Enoteca Oreste
6. Piazza Erbe
7. House of Juliet
8. Piazza dei Signori
9. Tombs of the Scaligeri Family
10. Groceries (2)
11. Church of Sant'Anastasia
12. Ponte Pietra & River View
13. Duomo

the town bristled with several hundred San Gimignano-type towers, built by different families to symbolize their power. When the Scaligeri family rose to power here in the 14th century, they established stability on their terms and made the other noble families lop off their proud towers—only the Scaligeri were allowed to keep theirs. To add insult to injury, the Scaligeri paved the city's roads with bricks from the other families' toppled towers. But interfamily feuds made it impossible for the Scaligeri to maintain a stable government, and in 1405 the town essentially gave itself to Venice, which ruled Verona until Napoleon stopped by in 1796. During the 19th century, a tug-of-war between France and Austria actually divided the city for a time, with the river marking the border of each country's domain. Eventually Verona, like Venice, fell into Austrian hands.

Reminders of Austrian rule remain: The huge, yellow, Neoclassical **City Hall** facing Piazza Brà (look for the flags) was built by the Austrians to serve as their 19th-century military headquarters. Their former arsenal stands just across the river, and an Austrian fortress caps the hill looking over the city. But the big **equestrian statue** is of Italy's first king, Victor Emmanuel II, celebrating Italian independence and unity, which was won in the 1860s. The **statue of a modern soldier** striking a *David* pose, with a machine gun instead of a sling over his shoulder, honors Verona's war dead.

Apart from all its history, Piazza Brà is about strolling—the evening *passeggiata* is a kind of national sport in Italy. The broad, shiny sidewalk (named "Liston" after a Venetian promenade; note the fine, Venetian-style marble pavement slabs) was built by 17th-century Venetians, who made it big and wide so that promenading socialites could see and be seen in all their finery.

## ❷ Roman Arena

The Romans built this stadium outside their town walls, just as modern stadiums are usually located outside downtown districts. With 72 aisles, this elliptical, 466-by-400-foot amphitheater is the third largest in Italy (and it was originally 50 percent taller). Most of the stone you see is original. Dating from the first century AD, it looks great in its pink marble. Over the centuries, crowds of up to 25,000 spectators have cheered Roman gladiator battles, medieval executions, rock concerts, and modern plays, all taking advantage of the arena's famous acoustics. This is also

where the popular opera festival is held every summer. Started in 1913, the festival has run continuously ever since, except for brief breaks during both World Wars, when the arena was used as a bomb shelter. While there's little to see inside except the impressive stonework, it's memorable to visit a Roman arena that is still a thriving concert venue. If you climb to the top, you'll enjoy great city views.

The gladiators posing with tourists out front are mostly from Albania and part of a local gang; they're notorious for overcharging for photos. While they're a nuisance, the police say it's better that they're scamming a living here than finding even more disreputable ways to get by.

**Cost and Hours:** €10, don't bother with the combo-ticket that includes the unimpressive Maffei Museum; Tue-Sun 8:30-19:30, Mon from 13:30, closes earlier—likely around 16:00—during summer opera season, last entry one hour before closing; WC near entry, tel. 045-800-3204.

• *As you exit the arena, look to your right. Where the street splits you'll see the...*

### ❸ Devotional Column

In the Middle Ages, this column blessed a marketplace held here. Ten yards in front of it, a bronze plaque in the sidewalk shows the Roman city plan—a town of 20,000 placed strategically in the bend of the river, which provided protection on three sides. A wall enclosed the peninsula. The center of the grid was the forum, today's Piazza Erbe. (Look down Via Mazzini, the busy main pedestrian drag—the bell tower in the distance marks Piazza Erbe.)

• *After viewing the bronze plaque, turn with your back to the arena and head down Via Oberdan (bearing left at the fork). Continue a couple of blocks (passing a derelict fascist-era theater, the Astra, set back from the street on the left, at #13) until you see an ancient gate to your right.*

### ❹ Porta Borsari and Corso Porta Borsari

You're standing before the main entrance to Roman Verona; back then, this gate functioned as a tollbooth (*borsari* means purse, referring to the collection of tolls that once took place here). Carved into the rock below the spiral, fluted columns (which parents nickname "*tortiglioni*"—a pasta kids can relate to), is a tribute to the emperor who restored this gate. Outside the adjacent Caffè Rialto, the stone on the curb is from a tomb: In Roman times,

the roads outside the walls were lined with tombstones, because burials were not allowed within the town itself. Turn around, look down Corso Cavour, and imagine it in Roman times, leading away from the city gate and lined with tombs. Step into the café. A glass panel in the floor shows the original Roman foundations and pavement stones.

Back outside, cross under the Roman gate and head into the ancient city. Walk down Corso Porta Borsari, the Roman main drag, toward what was the forum. Make it a scavenger hunt. As you walk, discover bits of the town's illustrious past—chips of Roman columns, medieval reliefs, fine old facades, fossils in marble—as well as its elegant present of fancy shops, in a setting that prioritizes pedestrians over cars. On the right, you'll pass the recommended Osteria del Bugiardo, a popular wine bar and a good place to take a break and hang out with Verona's young and trendy.

• *Between Corso Porta Borsari 13 and 15, detour right down Vicolo San Marco in Foro, following the Pozzo dell'Amore sign. Twenty yards ahead on your right, you'll find...*

### ❺ Enoteca Oreste

This funky wine-and-grappa bar is still run by Oreste (with his Chicagoan wife, Beverly) like a 1970s, old-style *enoteca*. Browse and sample and clown around with Oreste. This historic *enoteca* was once the private chapel of the archbishop of Verona. Traces of the past hide between the bottles—ask Beverly to tell you the story (light food, Vicolo San Marco in Foro 7, tel. 045-803-4369).

• *Return to Corso Porta Borsari and continue one block until you hit a big square.*

### ❻ Piazza Erbe

This bustling market square is a photographer's delight. Its pastel buildings corral the fountains, pigeons, and people who have congregated here since Roman times, when this was a forum. Notice the Venetian lion hovering above the square atop a column, reminding locals of the conquest of 1405. Wander into the market, to the fountain in the middle. A fountain has bubbled here for 2,000 years.

The original Roman statue lost its head and arms. After a sculptor added a new head and arms, the statue became Verona's Madonna. She holds a small banner that reads, roughly, *"The city of Verona de-*

*serves respect and justice."* During medieval times, the stone canopy in the center of the square (past the fountain) held the scales where merchants measured the weight of goods they bought and sold, such as silk and wool.

If you were standing here in the Middle Ages, you would have been surrounded by proud noble-family towers. Medieval nobles showed off with towers. Renaissance nobles showed off with finely painted facades on their palaces. Find remnants of the 16th-century days when Verona was nicknamed "the painted city."

Locals like to start their evening with an *aperitivo* here. Each bar caters to a different market segment. Survey the scene and, if or when the time is right, choose the terrace that suits you and join in the ritual. It's simple: Grab a spot, adjust your seat for the best view, and order a *spritz* to drink (€4 with a plate of olives and chips).

• *At the far end of Piazza Erbe is a market column featuring St. Zeno, the patron of Verona, who looks at the crazy crowds flushing into the city's silly claim to touristic fame: the House of Juliet (100 yards down Via Cappello to #23, on the left—just follow the crowds). Side-trip there now (but watch your wallet—it's a pickpocket's haven).*

## ❼ House of Juliet

The tiny, admittedly romantic courtyard is a spectacle: Tourists from all over the world pose on the balcony, while those hoping for love wait their turn to polish Juliet's

bronze breast. Residents marvel that each year, about 1,600 Japanese tour groups break their Venice-Milan ride for an hour-long stop in Verona just to see this courtyard (free, gates open roughly 8:30-19:30 or longer). It's fun to stand in the corner and observe the scene, knowing that all this commotion was started by a clever tour guide in the early 1970s as a way to attract visitors to Verona.

The courtyard walls have long been filled with amorous graffiti. The latest trend is to affix a paper note to the gates or walls with chewing gum. The wall of padlocks is another gimmick, enabling lovers to blow money in an attempt to prove that their hearts are thoroughly locked up. (The shop that sells the locks also sells pens to write on them.) The red mailbox is for love letters to Juliet. There's actually a Juliet Club that reviews these—and all the letters mailed from around the world to "Juliet, Verona, Italy." Each year, the club awards the author of the sweetest letter a free vacation to Verona.

Even those who milk their living out of this sight freely admit,

"While no documentation has been discovered to prove the truth of the legend, no documentation has disproved it either." The "museum," which displays art inspired by the love story, plus costumes and the bed from Franco Zeffirelli's film *Romeo and Juliet,* is certainly not worth the entry fee.

Was there ever a real Juliet Capulet? You just walked down Via Cappello, the street of the cap makers. Above the courtyard entry (looking out) is a coat of arms featuring a hat—representing a family that made hats and which would be named, logically, Capulet.

The public's interest in a fictional Romeo and Juliet—or at least Juliet—is a sign that there's a hunger for a Juliet in our world. Observing the mobs clamoring to polish her breast or blow kisses from her bogus balcony, I try to appreciate what she means to people, and to psychoanalyze what she provides to those who come to Verona specifically for this: the message that love will prevail. In love, you can lose, and still be a winner. Juliet is brave, tragic, honest, outspoken, timeless, and passionate. She's a mover and a shaker, a dreamer and a fighter. In a way, this is a pagan temple where the spirit of Juliet gives people something to believe in...or maybe it's just a bunch of baloney appreciated by a simple-minded crowd.

• *Return to Piazza Erbe. From the middle of the piazza, head right on Via della Costa and into the big square.*

## ❽ Piazza dei Signori

Literally the "Lords' Square," this is Verona's sitting room, quieter and more harmonious than Piazza Erbe. The buildings—which span five centuries—define the square and are all linked by arches. From one arch dangles a whale's rib. It was likely a souvenir brought home by a traveling merchant from a trip to the Orient, reminding the townspeople that there was a big world out there. The long portico on the left is inspired by a building in Florence: Brunelleschi's Hospital of the Innocents, considered the first Renaissance building.

Locals call the square Piazza Dante for the statue of the Italian poet **Dante Alighieri** that dominates it. Dante—always pensive, never smiling—seems to wonder why the tourists choose Juliet over him. Dante was expelled from Florence when that city sided with the pope (who didn't appreciate Dante's writing) and banished its greatest poet. Verona and its ruling Scaligeri family, however, were at odds

with the pope (siding instead with the Holy Roman Emperor), and granted Dante asylum.

With the whale's rib behind you, you're facing the brick, crenellated, 14th-century Scaligeri residence. Behind Dante is the yellowish, 15th-century Venetian Renaissance-style Portico of the Counsel. At Dante's two o'clock is the 12th-century Romanesque Palazzo della Ragione.

Looking back the way you came, follow the white *toilette* signs into the courtyard of the **Palazzo della Ragione.** The impressive stairway is the only surviving Renaissance staircase in Verona. Within the palazzo you can visit the Gallery of Modern Art (skippable) and climb the 13th-century **Torre dei Lamberti** for a grand city view. The elevator saves you 243 steps—but you'll still need to walk up 46 more to get to the tower's first viewing platform (€8 ticket covers tower and Gallery of Modern Art, €4 for just the gallery, no individual tower tickets sold; Mon-Fri 10:00-18:00, Sat-Sun 11:00-19:00; ticket office next to staircase, tel. 045-800-1903, www.palazzodellaragioneverona.it).

• *Exit the courtyard the way you entered and turn right, continuing downhill. Within a block, you'll find the...*

## ❾ Tombs of the Scaligeri Family

These exotic and veritable 14th-century Gothic tombs, with their fine, original, wrought-iron protective cages, evoke the age when one family ruled Verona. The Scaligeri were to Verona what the Medici family was to Florence. These were powerful people. They changed the law so that they could be buried within the town. They forbade the building of any noble family's new towers but their own. And, by building tombs atop pillars, they arranged to be looked up to, even in death.

• *Continue 15 yards to the next corner and take the first left on Vicolo Cavalletto. At the first corner, turn right along Corso Sant'Anastasia toward the big, unfinished brick facade of Verona's largest church. For a fragrant and potentially tasty diversion, pop into* ❿ *two classic grocery stores: Salumeria Caliari (at #33, closed Sun afternoon) and Salumeria Albertini (#41).*

## ⓫ Church of Sant'Anastasia

This church was built from the late 13th century through the 15th century. Although the facade was never finished (the builders ran out of steam), the interior was—and still is—brilliant. Step inside to see the delightful way this region's medieval churches were

painted. Note the grimacing hunchbacks holding basins of holy water on their backs (near main entrance at base of columns). And don't miss Pisanello's fresco of *St. George and the Princess of Trebizond* (1438; at the tip of the arch, high above chapel to right of altar). Once colorful, it has oxidized over time to its current monochrome state. For a closer look at its wonderful detail, check out the images on the computer terminal below the fresco. Ask for the English brochure, which describes the story of the church.

**Cost and Hours:** €3; Mon-Sat 9:00-18:00, Sun from 13:00, shorter hours in winter; www.chieseverona.it.

• *Leaving the church, make two lefts, and walk along the right side of the church to Via Sottoriva. To the right, the Sottoriva arcade was once busy with colorful wine bars and osterie, some of which still exist (see "Eating in Verona," later). But for now, head to the left on Via Sottoriva. In a block, you'll reach a small riverfront area with stone benches that usually have a few modern-day Romeos and Juliets gazing at each other rather than at the view. Belly up to the river view.*

## ⑫ Ponte Pietra and River View

The white stones of the Ponte Pietra footbridge are from the original Roman bridge that stood here. After the bridge was bombed

in World War II, the Veronese fished the marble chunks out of the river to rebuild it. From here, you can see across the river to the Roman Theater, built into the hillside behind the green hedge (see "Sights in Verona," later). Way above the theater (behind the cypress trees) is the fortress, Castello San Pietro. The nearby funicular can take you there.

The wide spot in the river here was called the "Millers' Widening," where boats stopped and unloaded grain to be milled. Water wheels once lined the river and powered medieval Verona, employing technology imported from the Holy Land by 10th-century Crusaders.

Continue up the river toward the bridge. Walk to its high point and enjoy the view.

• *From the bridge, look back 200 yards at the tall white spire...that's where you're heading. Walk back off the bridge, then turn right, keeping an eye on the left for the steeple of the...*

## ⑱ Duomo

Started in the 12th century, this church was built over a period of several hundred years. Before entering, note the fine Romanesque carvings on its facade.

**Cost and Hours:** €3, Mon-Sat 10:00-17:00, Sun from 13:30, shorter hours off-season.

**Visiting the Church:** Step inside, pick up the leaflet that explains the church's highlights, and head to the back-left corner of the church. In the last chapel on the left is Titian's 16th-century *Assumption of the Virgin*. Mary calmly rides a cloud—direction up—to the shock and bewilderment of the crowd below. Notice a handful of tombs embedded in the walls about 15 feet above floor level—an unusual feature. (Generally, tombs are found in the floor of the church or in crypts below.)

Now head up the aisle to the last door on the left (left of high altar), where you'll find the **ruins** of an older church. These are the 10th-century foundations of the Church of St. Elena, turned intriguingly into a modern-day chapel featuring exposed fourth-century mosaic floors from the Roman church that originally stood here.

From there, pass through the little open-air courtyard into the adjacent **baptistery,** with its clean Romanesque lines, hanging 14th-century crucifix, and fine marble font. Try to identify the eight biblical scenes carved on its panels before referring to my answers. (Answers, starting with the panel just to the right of center and working counterclockwise: Annunciation; first Christmas, with animals licking Baby Jesus and giving him a barnyard welcome; announcement to shepherds of Jesus' birth, with their flock stacked on one side; Epiphany, with the Three Kings giving their gifts to Baby Jesus; Herod commanding that all male infants be killed; Slaughter of the Innocents; flight to Egypt; and finally, facing the entry door, John the Baptist baptizing Christ.)

Finally, after leaving the church, circle around its left side (as you face the main facade) to find the peaceful Romanesque **cloister** *(chiostro),* with mosaics from a fifth-century Christian church exposed below the walk.

# Sights in Verona

Several of Verona's main sights, including the Roman Arena, Church of Sant'Anastasia, and Duomo, are covered in my Verona Walk.

### ▲▲Evening *Passeggiata*

For me, the highlight of Verona is the *passeggiata* (stroll)—especially in the evening. Make a big circle from Piazza Brà through the old town on Via Mazzini (one of Europe's many "first" pedestrian-only streets) to the colorful Piazza Erbe, and then back down Corso Porta Borsari to Piazza Brà. This is a small town, where people know each other, and they're all out on parade. Like peacocks, the young and nubile spread their wings. The classy shop windows are integral to the *passeggiata* as, for many of the ladies, shopping is a sport. Their never-finished wardrobes are considered a work in progress, and this is when they gather ideas. If you're going to complement your stroll with a stop in a café or bar, the best plan is to enjoy a *spritz* drink—not on Piazza Brà, but on Piazza Erbe (the oldest and most elegant bars are on the end farthest from Juliet's balcony).

### ▲Castelvecchio

Verona's powerful Scaligeri family built this castle (1343-1356) as both a residence and a fortress. The castle, located west of Piazza Brà and the Roman Arena, has two parts: the family palace and the quarters for their private army (separated, for the nervous family's security, by a fortified wall and an internal moat). Today, it houses the city's art gallery, with an extensive, enjoyable collection of sculpture and paintings.

**Cost and Hours:** €6, Tue-Sun 8:30-19:30, Mon from 13:30, last entry 45 minutes before closing, Corso Castelvecchio 2, tel. 045-806-2611. Info sheets are available throughout, but the €4 audioguide (€6/2 people) is still worthwhile.

**Visiting the Castle:** Religious statues were Verona's medieval forte, while paintings were the city's Renaissance forte. From the entrance, you'll head right toward the **statues,** once brightly painted. Cross to the next wing and head upstairs to walk through two floors that trace the evolution of **painting** from the 13th through the 17th century, including minor works by many major masters (such as Bellini, Mantegna, and Veronese). You'll also pass by a small armory collection.

En route, watch for the chance to roam the **ramparts** with fine views of the city, river, and Ponte Scaligero. Kids (and kids at heart) enjoy scrambling across the delightfully crenellated parapets. Verona was an independent city-state from 1176 to 1387. Then came a long period of subjugation under other powers which, in more modern times, included the Austrians. From the ramparts you can see remnants of Austrian rule: the arsenal across the river and the castle atop the distant hill.

**Nearby:** Next to Castelvecchio, the picturesque red-brick bridge called **Ponte Scaligero**—fortified and crenellated, as if a continuation of the castle—is free, open to the public, and fun to stroll across. Destroyed by the Germans in World War II, it was rebuilt in the 1950s using many of its original bricks, which were dredged out of the river. Today it's understandably a favorite for wedding-day photos.

## OUTSIDE THE CITY CENTER
### ▲Basilica of San Zeno Maggiore

This church, a 15-minute walk upriver beyond Castelvecchio, is dedicated to the patron saint of Verona, whose remains are buried in the crypt under the main altar. In addition to being a fine example of Italian Romanesque, the basilica features Mantegna's *San Zeno Triptych* (1456-1459) with its marvelous perspective, peaceful double-columned cloisters, and a set of 48 paneled 11th-century bronze doors nicknamed "the poor man's Bible." Pretend you're an illiterate medieval peasant and do some reading. Facing the altar, on the walls of the right-side aisle, you can see frescoes painted on top of other frescoes and graffiti dating from the 1300s. These were done by people who fled into the church in times of war or flooding and scratched prayers into the walls. Druidic-looking runes are actually decorated letters typical of the Gothic period, like those in illuminated manuscripts.

**Cost and Hours:** €3; Mon-Sat 8:30-18:00, Sun from 12:30, shorter hours off-season; on Piazza San Zeno, www.chieseverona. it.

### Roman Theater
### (Teatro Romano)

Dating from about the time of Christ, this ancient theater—located across the Roman Bridge, north of the city center—was discovered in the 19th century and restored. Admission includes

the Roman Museum, located high in the building above the theater (reach it via elevator—start at the stage and walk up the middle set of stairs, then continue straight on the path through the bushes).

The museum displays a model of the theater, a small chapel, and Roman artifacts, including mosaic floors, busts and other statuary, clay and bronze votive figures, and architectural fragments. There's not much to see. Unless you've never seen a Roman ruin, I'd skip it.

**Cost and Hours:** €4.50, Tue-Sun 8:30-19:30, Mon from 13:30, last entry one hour before closing, theater located across the river near Ponte Pietra footbridge, tel. 045-800-0360. From mid-June through August, the theater stages Shakespeare plays—only a little more difficult to understand in Italian than in Elizabethan English.

### Giusti Garden (Giardino Giusti)

You'll see this picturesque Renaissance garden capping the steep hilltop just across the Roman Bridge at the northern edge of the city. It's a little oasis with manicured box hedges, towering cypress trees, and a city view from the top of its hill. For most people, however, it's not worth the hike, time, or money.

**Cost and Hours:** €8.50, daily 9:00-19:00, across the river, beyond Ponte Nuovo.

# Sleeping in Verona

Hotel prices soar from mid-June through early September (opera season), in early April (during the Vinitaly wine festival—see "The Wines of Verona" sidebar, later), and during big trade fairs or major holidays. Unless your goal is opera, consider coming outside the summer months. For hotel locations, see the Verona map, earlier.

## NEAR PIAZZA ERBE

**$$$$ Hotel Antica Porta Leona** exudes refined elegance and is worth the splurge. Each of its 23 rooms is uniquely decorated, with some named for famous operas. Use of pool, gym, and spa facilities are included (air-con, elevator, some rooms in nearby annex, valet garage parking, Corticella Leoni 3, tel. 045-595-499, www.anticaportaleona.it, info@anticaportaleona.it).

**$$ Hotel Aurora,** at the corner of Piazza Erbe and Via Pelli-

**NEAR VENICE**

ciai, has friendly family management, attention to detail, a welcoming terrace with wonderful piazza views, and 18 straightforward rooms (family rooms, air-con, elevator, Piazzetta XIV Novembre 2, tel. 045-594-717, www.hotelaurora.biz, info@hotelaurora.biz, Rita).

**$$ Casa Coloniale** is just a stone's throw from Piazza Erbe. The four rooms all have balcony views and are furnished with a simple yet bright and stylish flair. Energetic owner Lucca runs the nearby Caffè Coloniale (Piazza Viviani Francesco 12), where breakfast is provided, along with B&B check-in after 15:00 (air-con, no elevator, Via Cairoli 6, tel. 393-940-8687, mobile 337-472-737, www.casa-coloniale.com, info@casa-coloniale.com).

**$$ L'Ospite,** a 10-minute walk across the river from Piazza Erbe, has six cozy, immaculate, fully equipped apartments and lots of stairs. The rooms, warmly managed by English-speaking Federica De Rossi, sleep two to four (family rooms, no reception or daily cleaning, air-con, Via XX Settembre 3, tel. 045-803-6994, mobile 329-426-2524, www.lospite.com, info@lospite.com). Coming from the station by bus (ride same buses as those headed downtown; see "Arrival in Verona," earlier), get off three stops past Piazza Brà, just after crossing the bridge, at the XX Settembre stop (across the street from the apartments).

**¢ Protezione della Giovane,** run by an association that houses poor women, also rents rooms and dorm beds to female tourists (and their children, up to age 12 for boys). Buried deep in the old town and up several flights of stairs, this place offers 10 cheap beds in a clean, institutional, and peaceful setting (women only, no breakfast, 23:00 curfew, reception open 9:00-20:00, Wi-Fi in common areas, Via Pigna 7, tel. 045-596-880, www.protezionedellagiovane.it, info@protezionedellagiovane.it).

## NEAR PIAZZA BRÀ

You'll find several options in the quiet streets just off Piazza Brà. From the square, white or yellow signs point you to the hotels. Most of these are big, fairly impersonal business-class places. Albergo Arena and Pepita Lodge are a little farther out, but still within a short walk to Piazza Brà.

**$$$ Hotel Giulietta e Romeo** is on a quiet side street 100 yards behind the Roman Arena. It's stylish and well-managed; 10 of its 37 sexy, ultra-modern rooms have balconies (air-con, elevator, free loaner bikes, fitness room, pay parking in garage or ask for free street-parking permit, Vicolo Tre Marchetti 3, tel. 045-800-3554, www.hotelgr.it, info@hotelgr.it).

**$$$ Hotel Colomba d'Oro** is a sprawling place with old-school elegance, renting 50 spacious rooms with Baroque flourishes. It has generous public spaces, including a courtyard, and overlooks a quiet and central street (air-con, elevator to every other floor, stairs between the rest, Via C. Cattaneo 10, tel. 045-595-300, www.colombahotel.com, info@colombahotel.com).

**$$$ Hotel Milano** is an arty hotel with 56 rooms. The lobby and fancier rooms are tricked out in black and chrome. It has a wonderful terrace and hot tub overlooking the Roman Arena (air-con, elevator, pay parking in garage, Vicolo Tre Marchetti 11, tel. 045-596-011, www.hotelmilano-vr.it, info@hotelmilano-vr.it).

**$$ Aparthotel Verona House** is a good option if you want hotel amenities and residential comfort. The 23 apartments are swanky and stylish (some can fit up to eight people). The bright, spacious breakfast room has great views onto Castelvecchio and doubles as an honor bar in the afternoon and evening (air-con, elevator, pay parking, loaner bikes, Stradone Provolo 3, tel. 045-205-0366, www.veronahouse.com, info@hotels2go.it).

**$$ Pepita Lodge** is convenient for train travelers and a 10-minute walk from Piazza Brà. The artful and spacious rooms have a calm, contemporary, clean-lines vibe. Breakfast is provided across the street at a *pasticceria* (family rooms, air-con, elevator, pay parking, Corso Porta Nuova 103, reception at #99B, tel. 045-800-1393, www.pepitalodge.it, info@pepitalodge.it).

**$$ Albergo Arena,** with a contemporary feel and few frills, is just this side of dreary but a good value for those on a budget. Located in a peaceful courtyard off a busy street a few blocks from Piazza Brà, it offers 16 basic, quiet rooms (air-con, elevator, just west of Castelvecchio at Stradone Porta Palio 2, tel. 045-803-2440, www.albergoarena.it, info@albergoarena.it, Francesco and Elena).

# Eating in Verona

Every restaurant listed here is within a 10-minute walk of the others. They're mostly small and intimate and found along side streets. It's tempting to grab a table next to the *passeggiata* action along Piazza Brà, but you'll be sacrificing service, value, and quality for your view of the floodlit Roman Arena and Verona on parade (perhaps a fair trade-off). Restaurants on the piazza tend to charge a cover and service fee, making even pizza a pricey choice. For restaurant locations, see the Verona map, earlier.

## FINE DINING

**$$$$ Cangrande Ristorante & Enoteca** offers seating in an outdoor garden or in a plush little dining area inside. The star offering is a €49.50 set menu including *antipasti*, pasta, a meat or fish course, and dessert. They also offer a light à la carte menu at lunch (Wed-Mon 12:30-14:30 & 18:30-22:00, closed Tue, also closed Mon during opera season; a block off Piazza Brà at Via Dietro Liston 19D—if the equestrian statue jogged slightly right, he'd head straight here; tel. 045-595-022, www.cangranderistorante.it).

**$$$$ Darì Ristorante & Enoteca,** run by longtime Verona restaurateurs Corinna and Giuliano, has a lovely setting inside and out and beautifully presented food (Wed-Mon 12:00-15:00 & 18:30-22:30, closed Tue, Vicolo Cieco San Pietro Incarnario 5, tel. 045-595-022, www.ristorantedari.com).

**$$$ Trattoria al Pompiere,** which has a commitment to regional traditions, has formal waiters weaving among its tight tables and walls plastered with photos of big shots from the area. This bustling place is a favorite of local foodies. Marco and his gang serve gourmet meats and cheeses as *antipasti* from their larger-than-life back counter, ideal for a mixed plate to complement the huge selection of fine wines. Reservations are wise (Mon-Sat 12:40-14:00 & 19:40-22:30, closed Sun, chivalry lives—ladies' menus come without prices; halfway between Piazza Erbe and Juliet's courtyard—head down narrow side street next to Via Cappello 8 to Vicolo Regina d'Ungheria 5; tel. 045-803-0537, www.alpompiere.com).

**$$$ Antico Caffè Dante** is a high-end place with a 19th-century pedigree and elegant service on the coziest and classiest square in town. You can enjoy a memorable meal of classic Veneto cuisine either at romantic tables on the square or inside. While it's not cheap, if you want to dress up and enjoy a slow, romantic, memorable meal, this can be a good value. The kitchen has limited hours, but the café is open throughout the day (daily 12:00-15:00 & 18:00-23:00, closed Sun afternoon off-season; Piazza dei Signori 2, tel. 045-800-0083, www.caffedante.it).

**$$$ Bottega del Vino** is pricey, venerable, and a bit pretentious. Under a high ceiling and walls of wine bottles, brisk, black-vested waiters match traditional dishes (polenta, duck, game) with glasses of fine wine. Choose from 50 open bottles. The waitstaff, ambience, and food have deep roots in local culture. I like their front room best. Reservations are smart for dinner (good daily specials, daily 11:00-23:00—kitchen closed 14:30-19:00, bar open later, off Via Mazzini at Via Scudo di Francia 3, tel. 045-800-4535, www.bottegavini.it).

## MODERATE RESTAURANTS

**$$ Ristorante Torcolo** is a family restaurant, with mom (Paola) running the kitchen, and father and son (Roberto and Luca) serving the meals. While it feels a bit dressy, it lacks pretense. They serve all the classics but with modern twists, and have an accessible menu and extensive wine list. Eat in their dining hall or on the tiny courtyard outside (daily 12:30-14:30 & 19:00-22:30, dinner from 17:00 in opera season, just behind the Piazza Brà scene on a quiet street, Via Carlo Cattaneo 11, tel. 045-803-3730).

# The Wines of Verona

Wine connoisseurs love the high-quality wines of the Verona area. The hills to the east are covered with grapes to make Soave; to the north is Valpolicella country; and Bardolino comes from vineyards to the west.

Valpolicella grapes, which are used to make the fruity, red Valpolicella table wine (found everywhere), are also the basis for full-bodied red Amarone and the sweet dessert wine Recioto. To produce Amarone, grapes are partially dried *(passito)* before fermentation, then aged for a minimum of four years in oak casks, resulting in a rich, velvety, full-bodied red. Recioto, which in local dialect means "ears," uses only the grapes from the top of the cluster (so they sort of look like the "ears" of the cluster's "head"). Because these grapes get the most sun, they mature the fastest and have the highest concentration of sugar. Before pressing, the grapes are dried for months until all moisture has gone out; the wine is then aged for one to three years.

Bardolino, from the vineyards near Lake Garda, is a light, fruity wine, like a French Beaujolais. It's a perfect picnic wine.

Soave, which might be Italy's best-known white wine, goes well with seafood and risotto dishes. While Soave can vary widely in quality, the best are called "Soave Classico" and come from the heart of the region, near the Soave Castle. Soave is sometimes aged in oak casks, giving it a mellow, rounded flavor.

Sample these and many others at the numerous *enoteche* (wine-tasting bars) or at any restaurant around town. In early April, Verona hosts Vinitaly, the most important international convention of domestic and international wines. Vintners vie for prestigious awards for the past year's vintage. Tourists are welcome to attend at the end of the week and are shuttled to the convention hall from Piazza Brà. Hotels book up months in advance. Check with the TI and Vinitaly.com for details.

If you're visiting the area in the fall, consider a day trip to nearby Monteforte d'Alpone, east of Verona. The town hosts a fun, raucous wine festival in September—ask at the TI for more information on this and other regional wine festivals.

**$$ Osteria Caffè Monte Baldo** has cafè-style bites plus a full menu with dishes typical of Verona like *risotto all'Amarone* for two or potato-less *gnocchi di malga*. If you want to share, go with the cold cuts and cheese boards. Or just pop into this cozy, rustic spot for a drink and snack on some *tartine* (small open-faced sandwiches; open daily 12:00-23:00, Via Rosa 12, tel. 045-803-0579). Their sister eatery, **La Piazzetta,** offers the exact same menu but in a more relaxed, boho-chic environment with terrace seating (daily

12:00-15:00 & 19:00-22:30, Corte San Giovanni in Foro 4/A, tel. 045-591-099).

## EATING IN OSTERIE (OLD BARS)

Wandering around the old town, you'll see plenty of Verona's thriving little watering holes. While these traditional old bars focus more on wine than on food, most serve memorable, characteristic, and affordable plates. Menus are simple and rustic—sometimes just bar munchies and the daily pasta. Service is relaxed and the clientele is young and local. For drinks it's mostly wine or water—fine wines are served by the glass, with bottles open and prices listed on blackboards. (I saw one sign suggesting that patrons "don't drive too much to drink.")

I've listed three places below: a classic antique osteria with more of a menu; a trendy, more modern place in the old center; and a small one-man show just off Piazza Brà, where you're most likely to make a new friend.

**$$ Osteria Sottoriva** (not to be confused with nearby Ostregheteria Sottorviva 23) survives from an era when Verona's river served as the town thoroughfare, and business deals could be made over a glass of wine at rustic riverside eateries. Located in a fine old covered arcade (the portico of Via Sottoriva), with both cozy indoor and outdoor seating, Sottoriva serves simple Veneto fare that changes seasonally and with the owner's whim (daily 11:00-15:00 & 18:00-22:30—but open all day long in summer, closed Wed in winter, behind the Church of Sant'Anastasia at Via Sottoriva 9, tel. 045-801-4323).

**$$ Osteria del Bugiardo** is jammed with a hip young crowd that spills out into the pedestrian-filled Corso Porta Borsari. They have a buffet of little sandwiches, can whip up a plate of top-quality cheeses, and serve a good pasta-of-the-day. They showcase their own Buglioni wines and are proud to tell you more about them (daily 11:00-24:00, Corso Porta Borsari 17a, tel. 045-591-869).

**$$ Osteria Vini Zampieri,** with a tiny bar and a few tables, keeps a tradition of stoking conviviality with good wine since 1937. Its young and energetic manager, Leo, is passionate about organic wines, slow food, and his own home-brewed beer. As the drinks are their priority, they don't serve much food—just some bar munchies and a nice *antipasti* plate. Locals go for horse's balls *(polpettine di cavallo)*, which are procured from the butcher down the street (daily 11:00-14:00 & 17:00-late except closed Mon for lunch, a few steps off Piazza Brà and next to Via Mazzini at Via Alberto Mario 23, tel. 045-597-053). You're welcome to play foosball downstairs on what Italians call the *calcio balilla* ("the little boy soldiers of Mussolini").

## A Mobile Feast Through Verona

Verona is a great town to sample the *aperitivo* ritual. All over town, locals enjoy a refreshing *spritz*, ideally on Piazza Erbe between 18:00 and 20:00. Choose a nice perch, and then, for about €4, you'll get the drink of your choice and a few nibbles (olives and/or potato chips) and a chance to feel very local as you enjoy the *passeggiata* scene.

Consider this for a fun sampling of many dimensions of the Verona eating and socializing scene: Start with an *aperitivo* on **Piazza Erbe,** then walk across Ponte Nuovo to **Pizzeria da Salvatore** and enjoy the town's best pizza. If you have to wait for a table, have another *spritz* at the neighboring bar. Then stroll along the river to **Osteria Sottoriva,** and enjoy a little sampling of bar food with a glass of Amarone (wine to meditate with) under the old arcade. Finish by meandering through the old center back to Piazza Brà for a gelato at **Gelateria Savoia.** *Buon appetito!*

## PIZZA, CHEAP EATS, AND SWEETS

**$ Pizzeria da Salvatore,** Verona's first pizzeria, opened in 1963, when pizza was considered a foreign food...from Naples. They serve the best pizza in town, and a visit here offers a nice excuse to stroll across the river into a part of town with no tourists. It's family-friendly, not fancy or romantic, and you'll squeeze into a tight row of tiny tables, rubbing elbows with your neighbors. While it's not quite Naples, it's justifiably popular—come early, or plan to leave your name on the list and wait awhile (Tue-Sat 12:30-14:30 & 19:00-23:00, Sun 19:00-23:00 only, closed Mon, no reservations, across Ponte Nuovo to Piazza San Tomaso 6, tel. 045-803-0366).

**$$ Pizzeria Du de Cope** is a colorful, high-energy, informal place (with paper placemats) that buzzes with smartly attired young waiters and locals who keep coming back for the pizza (daily 12:00-14:30 & 19:00-23:00, flamboyant desserts, families welcome, no reservations, at Galleria Pelliciai 10, tel. 045-595-562).

**$ *Döner kebab*** shops all over town serve hearty, cheap kebabs to munch on from a stool or to take out (most open daily roughly noon-midnight). *Piadine* (pita-bread) kebabs are worth the €4, and the super-sized kebabs can fill a couple on a very tight budget for a total of €7. The best kebabs, according to local assessments, are behind the Roman Arena at Via Leoncino 44. There's another good place on the other side of Piazza Brà at Via Teatro Filarmonico 6b. The benches in the center of Piazza Brà are handy for a scenic place to munch your cheap meal.

**Groceries:** The large **PAM supermarket chain** has two helpful locations (both generally open 8:00-21:00 with shorter hours on

Sun). One is just outside the historic gate on Piazza Brà (exit Piazza Brà through the gate and take the first right to Via dei Mutilati 3). The other one is across the Adige River, beyond Ponte Vittoria (Via IV Novembre 6A). Near the Church of Sant'Anastasia are two classic grocery stores, **Salumeria Caliari** and **Salumeria Albertini** (as mentioned in the town walk, earlier).

**Gelato:** The venerable **Gelateria Savoia** has been in business since 1939. It's in an arcade just off Piazza Brà, marked by a crowd licking their distinctive *semi-freddo*—a specialty of bitter-almond amaretto, cream, and cookie (just off Piazza Brà at Via Roma 1b). Just next to the Porta Leoni Roman gate (and in front of an excavation of the foundations of the gate) is **l'Arte del Gelato.** The gelateria prides itself on using organic ingredients. Their Sicilian *granite* and their *semi-freddo* are nearly as popular as their gelato (Via Leoni 3).

# Verona Connections

You have several options for getting train tickets in Verona: the standard station ticket office (with slow-moving lines, daily 6:00-21:00), a bank of modern machines (good English descriptions, cash and credit cards accepted), or the Deutsche Bahn ticket office (20 yards from baggage check office in the tunnel, offering tickets at the same cost as the station office but with German efficiency and no lines, Mon-Sat 8:00-18:00, closed Sun). Or you can buy tickets online with the train companies—Trenitalia or Italo (either via their websites or apps).

Every hour, at least two trains connect Verona with Venice, Padua, and Vicenza. Choose one of the cheaper regional trains (R or RV) instead of the faster Italo or Frecce express trains, which get you there slightly sooner but cost much more. Unless otherwise specified, the following connections are for Trenitalia.

**From Verona by Train to: Venice** (2/hour, 70 minutes-2 hours), **Padua** (2/hour, 40-80 minutes), **Vicenza** (2/hour, 30-60 minutes), **Florence** (*Firenze*, about hourly, 1.5 hours direct or 2.5 hours with transfer in Bologna; Italo: 4/day, 1.5 hours), **Bologna** (hourly, 1.5 hours), **Milan** (2/hour, 1.5-2 hours; Italo: 7/day, 1.5 hours), **Rome** (at least hourly, 4-5 hours, often with transfer in Bologna, also 1 direct night train, 6.5 hours; Italo: 4/day, 3.5 hours), and **Bolzano** (about hourly, 2.5 hours).

# THE DOLOMITES

*Bolzano • Castelrotto • Alpe di Siusi*

Italy's dramatic rocky rooftop, the Dolomites, offers some of the best mountain thrills in Europe. The city of Bolzano—blending Austrian tidiness with an Italian love for life—is the gateway to the Dolomites. And the village of Castelrotto is a good home base for your exploration of Alpe di Siusi (Seiser Alm), Europe's largest alpine meadow. Dolomite, a sedimentary rock similar to limestone, gives these mountains their distinctive shape and color. The bold, light-gray cliffs and spires flecked with snow, above green, flower-speckled meadows and beneath a blue sky, offer a powerful and memorable mountain experience.

A hard-fought history has left the region bicultural, with an emphasis on the German. In the mountains and closer to the border, most locals speak German first, and some wish they were still part of Austria. In the Middle Ages, as part of the Holy Roman Empire, the region faced north. Later, it was firmly in the Austrian Habsburg realm. By losing World War I, Austria's South Tirol became Italy's Alto Adige. Mussolini did what he could to Italianize the region, including giving each town an Italian name and building a severely fascist-style new town in Bolzano. But even as recently as the 1990s, secessionist groups agitated violently for more autonomy—with some success.

The government has wooed locals with economic breaks, which have made this one of Italy's richest areas (as local prices attest), and today all signs and literature in the province of Alto Adige/Südtirol are in both languages. Some include a third language, Ladin—an ancient Romance language still spoken in a few traditional areas. (I have listed both the Italian and German, so the

confusion caused by this guidebook will match that experienced in your travels.)

The Dolomites are well-developed, and the region's most famous destinations suffer from après-ski fever. But in spite of all the glamorous resorts and busy construction cranes, the regional color survives in a warm, blue-aproned, ruddy-faced, felt-hat-with-feathers way. There's yogurt and yodeling for breakfast. Culturally, as much as geographically, the area is reminiscent of Austria. In fact, the Austrian region of Tirol is named for a village that is now part of Italy.

## PLANNING YOUR TIME

One night in the Dolomites will give you a feel for the South Tirol's alpine culture. But it's best to stay at least two nights so you have at least one full day to hike. Pretty Castelrotto is the best base for hiking in the spectacular Alpe di Siusi alpine meadow, but ___ flavored Bolzano, down in the valley, is also in easy reach of ___-mountain lifts.

___ m either town, plan an early start up to Compatsch, the

gateway to the high Alpe di Siusi meadow. Tenderfeet stroll and ride the lifts from there. For serious mountain thrills, do an all-day hike. And for an unforgettable memory, spend a night in a mountain hut. With a second day, do more hiking or spend time in Bolzano, where you can stroll the old town and visit Ötzi the Iceman at the excellent archaeology museum (best to get tickets a few days in advance, especially if you expect to visit on a rainy day). Always check local transportation timetables before you set out.

Hiking season is mid-June through mid-October. The region is particularly crowded, booming, and blooming from mid-July through mid-September (but once you're out on the trails, you'll leave the crowds behind). It's packed with Italian vacationers in August. Spring is usually dead, with lifts shut down, huts closed, and the most exciting trails still under snow. Many hotels and restaurants close in April and November. By mid-May, most businesses reopen, some lifts start running (check dates at www.seiseralm.it), and—if you luck into good weather—a few rewarding hikes are already possible. Ski season (Dec-Easter) is busiest—and most expensive—of all.

**DOLOMITES**

# Bolzano

*Willkommen* to the Italian Tirol! If Bolzano ("Bozen" in German) weren't so sunny, you could be in Innsbruck. This enjoyable old city is the most convenient gateway to the Dolomites, especially if you're relying on public transportation. It's just the place to take a Tirolean stroll.

Bolzano feels like a happy castaway between the Germanic and Italian worlds. The people are warm and friendly, but organized. One person greets you in Italian, the next in German. But everyone can agree the city has a special verve, with lively shopping arcades, a food-and-flower market more bustling than anything you'll find north of the border in Austria, and a tidy main square with a backdrop of colorful churches and wooded foothills.

The town has only one museum worth entering, but it's world class, offering the chance to see Ötzi the Iceman—a 5,300-year-old Tirolean found frozen on a mountaintop—in the (shriveled, leathery) flesh. Beyond that, Bolzano is made for strolling, relaxing, and hiking in the nearby hills—and works well as a home base for venturing deeper into the mountains (though Castelrotto is prettier and closer to the high-mountain lifts).

# Orientation to Bolzano

Virtually everything I mention in Bolzano (pop. 107,000) is in the compact and strollable old town, which radiates out from the main square, Piazza Walther/Waltherplatz. Those curious about fascist architecture can head 10 minutes west of the center to see Mussolini's "New Bolzano" development.

## TOURIST INFORMATION

Bolzano's TI, just down the street from the train station, is helpful (Mon-Fri 9:00-19:00, Sat 9:30-18:00, Sun 10:00-15:00 except Nov-April closed Sun, Via Alto Adige/Südtiroler Strasse 60, tel. 0471-307-000, www.bolzano-bozen.it).

**Discount Card:** The **Museummobil Card** covers most museums in the South Tirol (including the archaeology museum, with its famous Iceman), plus local trains, buses, the Funivia del Renon/Rittner cable car *(Seilbahn)* to Oberbozen, and more (€30/3 days, doesn't cover the gondola or chairlifts in Alpe di Siusi, available at local TIs and the train station baggage storage office, www.mobilcard.info). It pays for itself only if you're very busy (for example, if you visit the Iceman, ride the Renon cable car, and take the bus round-trip from Bolzano to Castelrotto). A transit-only version, the **Mobilcard,** covers the same trains, buses, and lifts (€15/1 day, €23/3 days, sold at TIs and transit offices).

**Walking Tours:** The TI offers a guided town walking tour in English on Tuesdays in season (€6, April-Oct at 10:30, departs from TI).

## ARRIVAL IN BOLZANO

**By Train:** Bolzano has two train stations—you want *Bolzano,* not *Bolzano Süd.* WCs are in the underground passage by track 1, and luggage storage is just upstairs (see "Helpful Hints," next). To reach the **TI,** exit the station, turn left, and walk two long blocks. To get **downtown,** jog left through the park and go two blocks up the tree-lined Viale della Stazione/Bahnhofsallee to Piazza Walther/Waltherplatz and the start of my self-guided walk.

**By Car:** Some areas of Bolzano are ZTL zones (marked with a red circle), where you'll be automatically ticketed. The most convenient parking lot for a short visit is the P3 garage, right under the main square (€2.70/hour, cheaper overnight; to find it, make your way to the train station, then drive up Viale della Stazione/Bahnhofsallee, watching for the *P3/Piazza Walther* entrance on your right). For longer stays or to save a few euros, try P8 (Parking Centro/Mitte), just south of the ring road and west of the train sta-

## *Ich bin ein Italiener*

With the exception of Bolzano, where Italian has become the primary language, you'll hear mostly German in Dolomite villages. Overall, seven in ten Italians living in the South Tirol speak German as their mother tongue. Many are fair-skinned and blue-eyed and prefer dumplings and strudel to pasta and gelato. Most have a working knowledge of Italian, but they watch

German-language TV, read newspapers *auf Deutsch,* listen to jaunty oompah music, and live in Tirolean-looking villages.

At the end of World War I, the region was ceded by Austria (loser) to Italy (winner). Mussolini suppressed the Germanic cultural elements as part of his propaganda campaign to praise all things Italian. Many German speakers hoped that Hitler would "liberate" them from Italy, but Hitler's close alliance with Mussolini prevented that from happening. Instead, in June of 1939, residents were given six months to make a hard choice: Move north to the Fatherland and become German citizens, or stay in their homeland *(Heimat)* under Italian rule. The vast majority (212,000, or 85 percent) decided to leave, but with the outbreak of World War II, only 75,000 actually moved.

After the war, German speakers were again disappointed when the Allies refused to grant them autonomy or the chance to become Austrian citizens. Instead, the victors decided to stick with the prewar arrangement. The region rebuilt and the two linguistic groups patched things up, but for the remainder of the 20th century, German speakers were continually outvoted by the Italian-speaking majority in the regional government (comprising two provinces, Italian-speaking Trentino and German-speaking Alto Adige/Südtirol).

German speakers lobbied the national government for more control on the provincial (not regional) level, even turning to demonstrations and violence. Over the years, Rome has slowly and grudgingly granted increased local control. The country's 2001 constitution gave Alto Adige/Südtirol a large measure of autonomy—similar to Sicily and Sardinia—though it's still officially tied to Trentino. Roads, water, electricity, communications, and schools are all under local control, including the Free University of Bozen-Bolzano, founded in 1998.

A good way to sum it all up: In many ways, the people of the Dolomites feel a closer bond with their Austrian ancestors than with their countrymen to the south. But when Italy plays Austria in a big soccer match, who do locals root for? Italy.

tion—about a 10-minute walk from the main square (€1.50/hour, cheaper overnight, enter from Via Josef Mayr Nusser).

## HELPFUL HINTS

**Sleepy Sundays:** This small, culturally conservative city is dead on Sunday (young locals add, "and during the rest of the week, too").

**Markets:** Piazza delle Erbe/Obstplatz hosts an ancient and still-thriving open-air produce market (Mon-Sat all day, generally closed Sun). Wash your produce in the handy drinking fountain in the middle of the market. Another market (offering more variety, not just food) runs Saturday mornings on Piazza della Vittoria.

**Baggage Storage:** You can store bags at **Base Camp Dolomites,** at the train station by track 1 (daily 8:30-18:30, they also rent bikes, tel. 0471-971-733, Lukas).

**Laundry: Ecomatic** is at Via Rosmini/Rosministrasse 39, southwest of the South Tirol Museum of Archaeology (daily 7:00-22:30, doors lock automatically at closing time, tel. 0474-832-204).

**Bike Rental:** The city has a well-developed bike-trail system and cheap, city-subsidized rental bikes (€2/6 hours, €5/6-24 hours, €10 refundable deposit, ID required, Mon-Sat 7:30-19:50, closed Sun and Nov-March, just off Piazza Walther/Waltherplatz on the road to the station). For a higher-quality mountain bike or electric bike, try Base Camp Dolomites at the station (see "Baggage Storage," above).

# Bolzano Walk

This brief self-guided walk will help you get your bearings in central Bolzano.

• *Start the walk in...*

**Piazza Walther/Waltherplatz:** The statue in the center honors the square's namesake, Walther von der Vogelweide, a 12th-century politically incorrect German poet who courageously stood up to the pope in favor of the Holy Roman (German) Emperor. Walther's spunk against a far bigger power represents the Germanic pride of this region. The statue is made of marble quarried in the village of Laas, north of Bolzano. (The US chose this same marble for the 86,000  crosses and Stars of David needed to mark the WWII dead buried at Normandy and other battlefields across Europe).

When not hosting Bolzano's Christmas market, flower market (May Day), or Speck Fest (a spring ham festival), Piazza Walther/Waltherplatz is simply the town's living room. And locals care about it. It was the site of Italy's first McDonald's, which, in the early 1990s, became the first McDonald's to be shut down by locals protesting American fast food. Today the square is home to trendy cafés such as Café Walther, where (outside of meal times) you're welcome to nurse a local "Hugo" aperitif (see sidebar on page 199), "Venetian" *spritz,* or a pricier cocktail as long as you like.

• *Cross the street to the big church.*

**The Cathedral:** The cathedral's glazed-tile roof is typical of the Germanic world—a reminder that from the sixth century until 1919, when Italy said *benvenuti* to the Südtirol, German was the region's official language. The church was flattened in World War II (a common consequence of being located near a train station in 20th-century Europe).

Walk around to the right, to the Romanesque Lion's Gate entrance (at the far end), and step inside. The place feels Teutonic, rather than Italian, with a mostly Gothic interior that's broken at the front by an impressive Baroque tabernacle. Partway down the nave, the sandstone pulpit (c. 1500)—with its reliefs of the four Church fathers whose presence gave credibility to sermons preached here—is reminiscent of Vienna's St. Stephen's Cathedral. Most of the art is by Bavarian artists.

• *Leaving the church, return to Piazza Walther/Waltherplatz and cross it diagonally, heading up the street to the right of the big Sparkasse bank building. Follow this for one block, to...*

**Piazza del Grano/Kornplatz:** Nine hundred years ago, this was Bolzano's main square. The building to your right was the bishop's castle. The traditional food stand selling *Vollkornbrot* (dense, whole-grain bread) and pretzels is another reminder of German heritage. At the top of the square, look for the flower bed with a big, chunky rock. A bronze relief embedded in the rock shows Bolzano's street plan in the 12th century: a one-street arcaded town huddled within a fortified wall.

• *Jog right and continue straight ahead into the original medieval town, passing a* Wurstel *(frankfurter) stand on your left. You'll pop out in the middle of...*

**Via dei Portici/Laubengasse:** This was the only street in 12th-century Bolzano. Step into the center (dodging bikes). Looking east and west, you see the width of the original town.

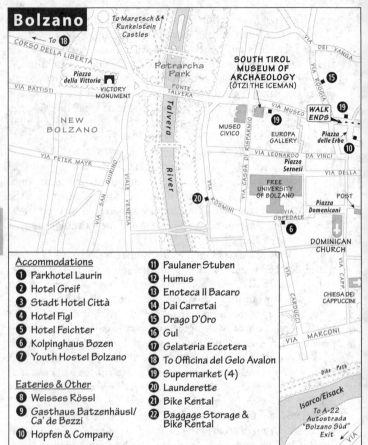

**Bolzano**

To Maretsch &
Runkelstein
Castles

To 18

CORSO DELLA LIBERTA

VIA DEI YANGA

Piazza
della Vittoria

VIA BATTISTI

VICTORY
MONUMENT

Petrarcha
Park

SOUTH TIROL
MUSEUM OF
ARCHAEOLOGY
(ÖTZI THE ICEMAN)

VIA RUGGA

15

NEW
BOLZANO

VIA PETER MAYR

VIALE VENEZIA

VIA SAN QUIRINO

Talvera
River

PONTE
TALVERA

MUSEO
CIVICO

VIA MUSEO

19

EUROPA
GALLERY

VIA CASSA DI RISPARMIO

VIA LEONARDO DA VINCI

Piazza
Sernesi

FREE
UNIVERSITY
OF BOLZANO

VIA ROSMINI

20

VIA OSPEDALE

6

WALK
ENDS

19

Piazza
delle Erbe

10

VIA DELLA

Piazza
Domenicani

POST

DOMINICAN
CHURCH

VIA CAPP

CHIESA DEI
CAPPUCCINI

VIA CARDUCCI

VIA MARCONI

Bike Path

Isarco/Eisack

To A-22
Autostrada
"Bolzano Süd"
Exit

VIA

**Accommodations**
1 Parkhotel Laurin
2 Hotel Greif
3 Stadt Hotel Città
4 Hotel Figl
5 Hotel Feichter
6 Kolpinghaus Bozen
7 Youth Hostel Bolzano

**Eateries & Other**
8 Weisses Rössl
9 Gasthaus Batzenhäusl/
   Ca' de Bezzi
10 Hopfen & Company

11 Paulaner Stuben
12 Humus
13 Enoteca Il Bacaro
14 Dai Carretai
15 Drago D'Oro
16 Gul
17 Gelateria Eccetera
18 To Officina del Gelo Avalon
19 Supermarket (4)
20 Launderette
21 Bike Rental
22 Baggage Storage &
   Bike Rental

Turn left and stroll a bit, watching on the right for the frescoed, pointed arches of the old City Hall—the street's only Gothic building (at #30). Notice that the other buildings, with uniform round arches, are all basically the same: Each had a storm cellar, cows out back, a ground-level shop, and living quarters upstairs. Bay windows were designed for maximum light—just right for clerks keeping track of accounts and for women doing their weaving. The arcades (*Lauben*, pictured on previous page), typical of Tirol, sheltered merchants and their goods from both snow and sun. Narrow passages between shops lead to neighboring streets.

A bit farther along on the left, the only balcony marks the street's lone Baroque building—once the mercantile center (with a fine worth-a-look courtyard), now a skippable museum.

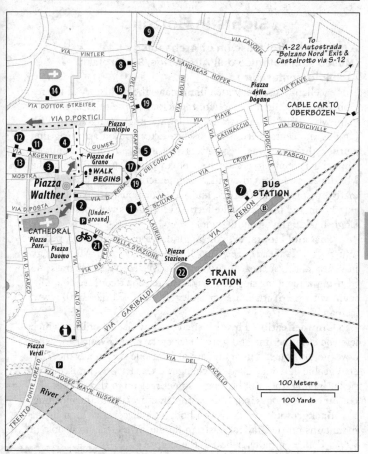

• *Continue to the end of the street, where you'll find a bustling market generally every day but Sunday.*

**Piazza delle Erbe/Obstplatz:** This square hosts an open-air produce market, liveliest in the morning. The historic market fountain gives Bolzano its only hint of the sea—a 17th-century statue of Neptune. Stroll around and see what's in season. All the breads, strudel, and hams *schmecken sehr gut.*

• *From the market, Via Museo/Museumstrasse (called "Butcher Street" until the 19th century, when a museum opened) leads straight ahead to Frozen Fritz.*

DOLOMITES

# Sights in Bolzano

### ▲▲▲South Tirol Museum of Archaeology (Museo Archeologico dell'Alto Adige/Südtiroler Archäologiemuseum)

This excellent museum, which illuminates the prehistory of the region, boasts a unique attraction: the actual corpse of Ötzi the Iceman, who spent more than five millennia stuck in a glacier. With Ötzi as the centerpiece, the museum takes you on an intriguing journey through time, recounting the evolution of humanity—from the Paleolithic era to the Roman period and finally to the Middle Ages—in vivid detail. The interactive exhibit offers informative displays and models, and video demonstrations of Ötzi's extraction and his personal effects. Everything's well-described in English (skip the €4 audioguide).

**Cost and Hours:** €9, €37.50 guided tour for up to 15 people (must reserve ahead), Tue-Sun 10:00-18:00, closed Mon except July-Aug and Dec, near the river at Via Museo/Museumstrasse 43 (if using a mapping app to navigate here, don't confuse this museum with the Naturmuseum Südtirol), tel. 0471-320-100, www.iceman.it.

**Crowd-Beating Tips:** It's smart to buy tickets online, which lets you skip the line and guarantees entry during your time window (no extra fee, must purchase at least one day in advance, exchangeable if your schedule changes). Capacity is limited, and ticket-buying lines can be long—sometimes up to three hours. It's busiest on rainy days in July and August, especially in the morning.

**Background:** Ötzi's frozen body was discovered high in the mountains on the Italian/Austrian border by a German couple in 1991. Police initially believed the corpse was a lost hiker, and Ötzi was chopped roughly out of the glacier, damaging his left side. But upon discovering his pre-Bronze Age hatchet, officials realized what they had found: a 5,300-year-old, nearly perfectly preserved man with clothing and gear in excellent condition for his age. Austria and Italy squabbled briefly over who would get him, but surveys showed that he was located 100 yards inside Italian territory. Tooth enamel studies have now shown that he did grow up on the Italian side. An Austrian journalist dubbed him Ötzi, after the Ötztal valley, where he was discovered.

**Visiting the Museum:** The permanent exhibit is smartly displayed on three floors (plus temporary exhibits on the top floor).

First you'll learn about Ötzi's discovery, excavation, and preservation. Upstairs, you'll walk through displays of his incredibly well-preserved and fascinating clothing and gear, including a finely stitched two-color coat, his goat-hide loincloth, a fancy hat, shoes, a well-crafted hatchet, 14 arrows, a longbow, a dagger, and shreds of his rucksack (which held fire-making gadgets and a tree fungus used as a primitive antibiotic). And finally, you'll peek into a heavily fortified room to see Ötzi himself—still kept carefully frozen.

One floor up, exhibits focus on the Copper Age. The discovery of Ötzi helped researchers realize that the use of copper occurred in this region more than a millennium earlier than previously thought. There's also a complete medical workup of Ötzi, including an interactive flatscreen where you can zoom in on different parts of his body to see the layers of skin, muscle, and bone. And you'll learn how researchers have used modern forensic science techniques to better understand who Ötzi was and how he died. (Think of it as a very, very, very cold case.)

From all of this, scientists have formed a complete picture of the Iceman: In his mid-40s at the time of his death, Ötzi was 5 feet, 3 inches tall, with brown hair and brown eyes. He weighed about 110 pounds, was lactose-intolerant, ate too much animal fat, and likely had trouble with his knees. And they've even determined the cause of death: an arrowhead buried in Ötzi's left shoulder. (Discoveries still make the news every few years—in 2018, for example, scientists were able to deduce what he'd eaten for his last meal.) At the end of the exhibit, you'll see an eerily lifelike reconstruction of how Ötzi may have looked when he was alive. If you're interested in learning more about Ötzi, *National Geographic* and the public-television program *Nova* have covered the evolving story.

### Dominican Church
### (Chiesa dei Domenicani/Dominikanerkirche)

Art lovers can drop by this mostly stark and sterile 13th-century church to see its Chapel of St. John (San Giovanni/St. Johannes; chapel is through the archway and on the right), frescoed in the 14th century by the Giotto School. While you're here, take a moment to also enjoy the Baroque ceiling of the "deep chancel" that connects the front of the church with the Chapel of St. John.

**Cost and Hours:** Free, €0.50 coin lights dim interior, Mon-

DOLOMITES

**DOLOMITES**

Sat 10:00-17:00 (often until 18:00), Sun 12:00-18:00, on Piazza Domenicani, two blocks west of Piazza Walther/Waltherplatz.

## Lift to Oberbozen and Renon/Ritten

The **Funivia del Renon/Rittner cable car** *(Seilbahn)* whisks you over the hills from Bolzano to the touristy resort village of Oberbozen on the high plateau of Renon/Ritten. The reasonably priced, 12-minute cable-car ride itself is the main attraction, offering views of the town, surrounding mountains, made-for-yodeling farmsteads, and 18-wheelers downshifting along the expressway from Austria. While the cable car is fun, it's no replacement for a trip to Castelrotto and Alpe di Siusi. But if you're here off-season and unable to go any higher, or staying in Bolzano in summer and up for an evening excursion, this lift gives you a taste of the Alpine wonderland that lies above the valley floor. From Oberbozen you can ride a narrow-gauge train to the village of Klobenstein and back (if you do, allow about 2 hours for the whole outing).

**Cost and Hours:** €10 round-trip, cash only; ticket machine on ground floor to the right of the stairs, validate tickets in blue box upstairs just before the gates; departures every 4 minutes year-round Mon-Sat 6:30-22:45, Sun 7:10-22:45; every 12 minutes after 21:00 in low season; for info call regional transport toll tel. 840-000-471 or visit www.sii.bz.it.

**Getting There:** The cable car's valley station is a five-block walk east from the Bolzano train station along Via Renon/Rittner Strasse or from Piazza Municipio/Rathausplatz in the old center.

**At the Top: Oberbozen** (elevation 4,000 feet) is mostly a collection of resort hotels, most famous as the place where Sigmund Freud and his wife once celebrated their wedding anniversary. From Oberbozen, a narrow-gauge train makes the 16-minute trip to **Klobenstein,** a larger and slightly less touristy village at 3,800 feet (€3.50 one-way, €6 round-trip, €15 round-trip for both Oberbozen cable car and train, daily departures every 30 minutes—reduced to hourly early and after 19:00). The local TI has branches in both villages (www.ritten.com).

The lift station has brochures suggesting short walks. More interesting than Oberbozen itself (though not a must-see) are the nearby **"earth pyramids"**—Bryce Canyon-like pinnacles that rise out of the ridge, created by eroding glacial debris dumped at the end of the last ice age. Some of these are visible from the Oberbozen cable car (on the right as you're riding up), but are challenging to hike to; an easier-to-reach area is a 15-minute walk from Klobenstein. Another walk is the **Freudpromenade,** a fairly level, 1.5-hour stroll between Oberbozen and Klobenstein (you can take the train back).

### New Bolzano (Nuova Bolzano)

Just across the river from the Museum of Archaeology, the fascist-style **Victory Monument** (Monumento alla Vittoria) glistens in white Zandobbio marble. It marks the beginning of the "new" city built by the fascist government in the 1920s to Italianize the otherwise Germanic-looking city. Indeed, you won't hear much German spoken in the shops and bars along the colonnaded Corso della Libertà—it feels a world away from the old town. A visit to New Bolzano comes with a delightful stroll over the river and the inviting, parklike Talvera promenade (described later).

In the basement of the arch-like structure, you'll find a small but well-done **exhibit** about the history of the monument itself, the Italianization of the South Tirol, and the efforts of local people to keep their language, culture, and traditions alive (monument always viewable, exhibit free and open April-Sept Tue-Sun 11:00-13:00 & 14:00-17:00, Thu 15:00-21:00, shorter hours off-season, closed Mon year-round, good information in English, www.monumenttovictory.com).

The grand plans for this part of the city were never fully realized. But several blocks of buildings were constructed in a repetitive Modernist design, following the idea of imperial monumentalism trumpeting the dawn of a new era in Italy. Most of the structures were intended to house state institutions and highly desirable apartments for state employees. (A few blocks south on Piazza Tribunale, you can still find the somewhat faded image of Mussolini waving from one of the buildings.)

While in the neighborhood, consider a stop at **Officina del Gelo Avalon,** a gourmet, organic gelato shop tucked under the arches of Corso della Libertà. Try the pistachio or one of the half-dozen flavors of chocolate (daily 13:00-21:30, shorter hours off-season, closed Tue in Jan, Corso della Libertà 44).

### Bolzano Walks

Pick up the good map at the TI for scenic, accessible strolls that provide a different perspective on the region.

One popular option is the easy, shaded **Talvera promenade** just west of the Museum of Archaeology, following the river embankment north. This route has great people-watching in the summer, with views of vineyards and Maretsch Castle (Castello Mareccio/Burg Maretsch) to the right. In about 25 minutes, you'll reach the Bridge of St. Antonio, where you can cross (look for *Runkelstein*

**DOLOMITES**

signs), loop under onto the pedestrian path, and follow the river for another 15 minutes to the impressive **Runkelstein Castle** (Castel Roncolo/Schloss Runkelstein; be aware that the last 10 minutes are up a steep, unevenly cobbled path). Inside this 13th-century "illus-trated manor" is an impressively large collection of secular medieval frescoes, with scenes from the everyday lives of knights and ladies (€8, Tue-Sun 10:00-18:00, until 17:00 off-season, closed Mon, perched above the river north of town on Kaiser-Franz-Josef Weg, tel. 0471-329-808, www.runkelstein.info).

To extend your hike, go back to the Bridge of St. Antonio and head up the hill about 45 minutes for the **St. Oswald** walk. This route takes you to the church of Santa Magdalena (with its 14th-century frescoes), offering great views back to the city.

## Sleeping in Bolzano

All the places listed here are in the city center, within walking dis-tance of the train and bus stations. Bolzano has no real high or low season. Most hotels have the same rates all year, but they're most likely to make deals in March and November.

**$$$$ Parkhotel Laurin** is a fancy Old World hotel near the train station, with 100 tastefully decorated rooms, marble bath-rooms, a chic dining room and terrace, a swimming pool (summer only), an extensive and luxurious garden, and attentive staff. Fres-coes throughout the grand lobby and atmospheric bar depict the legend of King Laurin (air-con, elevator, pay parking, Via Laurin/Laurinstrasse 4, tel. 0471-311-000, www.laurin.it, info@laurin.it).

**$$$$ Hotel Greif,** a luxury boutique hotel, is right on Piazza Walther/Waltherplatz. Each of the 33 individually designed rooms makes you feel like you're in an avant-garde art installation (its website gives a room-by-room tour). It's not exactly "cozy," but it is striking, and a stay here comes with one of my favorite breakfasts in Italy (family rooms, air-con, elevator, pay parking at P3/Parking Walther under main square—enter hotel directly from level 1 of the garage, Via della Rena/Raingasse 28, tel. 0471-318-000, www.greif.it, info@greif.it).

**$$$ Stadt Hotel Città,** a venerable old hotel with 99 mod-ern, straightforward rooms and serving an uncommonly good breakfast, is ideally situated on Piazza Walther/Waltherplatz. The hotel's café spills out onto the piazza, offering a prime spot for people-watching (family rooms, air-con, elevator, pay parking at P3/Parking Walther under main square—enter hotel directly from level 1 of the garage, Piazza Walther/Waltherplatz 21, tel. 0471-975-221, www.hotelcitta.info, info@hotelcitta.info, Francesco and Hannelore, plus son Fabio and daughter Sandra). This place is an especially good value if you spend an afternoon in their free-for-guests Wellness Center (generally open mid-Sept-June Mon-Sat 16:00-21:30, closed Sun and in summer; Turkish bath, whirlpool, Finnish sauna, biosauna, massage by appointment)—a fine way to unwind.

**$$$ Hotel Figl,** warmly run by Anton and Helga Mayr, has 23 comfy, bright, good-value rooms. It's situated over a popular-with-locals café on a pedestrian square located a block from Piazza Walther/Waltherplatz (breakfast extra, air-con, elevator, pay parking at P3/Parking Walther under main square—take the escalator to the square and walk a couple of minutes, Piazza del Grano/Kornplatz 9, tel. 0471-978-412, www.figl.net, info@figl.net, include a phone number if you email).

**$$ Hotel Feichter** is a solid value: an inexpensive, well-kept, family-run place with simple but sufficient amenities in a great location. Most of the 34 rooms are a little tight, but pleasantly renovated, and some share a communal terrace overlooking the rooftops of Bolzano. Papà Walter, Mamma Hedwig, Hannes, Irene, and Wolfi Feichter have run this homey hotel since 1969, and are a good source of local advice (family rooms, air-con, pay parking, 18 steps up to reception and elevator from entrance, ground-floor café serves lunch Mon-Fri 11:30-14:00; from station, walk up Via Laurin/Laurinstrasse, which becomes Via Grappoli/Weintraubengasse—hotel is on the right at #15; tel. 0471-978-768, www.hotelfeichter.it, info@hotelfeichter.it).

**$$ Kolpinghaus Bozen,** modern, clean, and church-run, has 50 rooms that feel like a renovated college dorm (doubles have two twin beds placed head to toe). Though institutional, it makes me feel thankful for no-nonsense budget rooms (weak air-con, elevator, pay laundry, pay parking, 4 blocks from Piazza Walther/Waltherplatz near Piazza Domenicani at Largo A. Kolping/Adolph-Kolping-Strasse 3, tel. 0471-308-400, www.kolpingbozen.it, info@kolpingbozen.it). The line of people out front at lunchtime consists mainly of office workers waiting for the cafeteria to open (generally Mon-Fri 11:45-14:00, Sat 12:00-13:30, closed Sun).

**¢ Youth Hostel Bolzano Youth Hostel Bolzano** is the most comfortable and inviting hostel that I've seen in Italy. It has 17 four-bed rooms (each with two bunk beds and a full bathroom; fifth bed possible) and 10 delightful singles with bath. The bright, clean, modern rooms make it feel like a dorm in a fancy university (family discounts, no age limit, elevator, pay laundry, 9:00 checkout, 100 yards to the right as you leave the train station at Via Renon/Rittner Strasse 23; tel. 0471-300-865, easy online reservations at www.ostello.bz, bolzano@ostello.bz).

# Eating in Bolzano

All my recommendations are in the center of the old town. Prices are consistent (you can generally get a good plate of meat and veggies for €10). While nearly every local-style place serves a mix of German/Tirolean and Italian fare, I favor eating Tirolean here in Bozen. Many restaurants have no cover charge but put a basket of bread on the table; as in Austria, if you eat the bread, you'll be charged a small amount. Bolzano's restaurants tend to stay open all day, but at a few places the kitchen closes in the afternoon with only snacks available.

**$$ Weisses Rössl** ("White Pony") offers an affordable mix of pasta and Tirolean food with meat, fish, and fine vegetarian options. Located in a traditional woody setting, it's good for dining indoors among savvy locals (Mon-Fri 11:00-24:00, Sat 10:00-15:00, closed Sun, 2 blocks north of Piazza Municipio at Via Bottai/Bindergasse 6, tel. 0471-973-267).

**$$ Gasthaus Batzenhäusl/Ca' de Bezzi** is Bolzano's oldest inn, with two Teutonic-feeling upper floors; by contrast, the patio and back room are refreshingly modern and untouristy. They make their own breads, pastas, and beer, and serve traditional Tirolean fare—stick-to-your-ribs grub (daily 9:00-late, one of the rare places open on Sun, Via Andreas Hofer/Andreas-Hofer-Strasse 30, tel. 0471-050-950).

**$$ Hopfen and Company** fills an 800-year-old house with happy eaters, drinkers, and the beer lover's favorite aroma: hops *(Hopfen)*. A tavern since the 1600s, it's a stylish, fresh microbrewery today. This high-energy, boisterous place is packed with locals who come for its homemade beer, delicious Tirolean food, and reasonable prices (great salads, limited menu outside of mealtimes, daily 9:30-24:00, Piazza delle Erbe/Obstplatz 17, tel. 0471-300-788).

**$$ Paulaner Stuben** is a restaurant-pizzeria-*Bierstube* serving good food (more Italian than German) and a favorite Bavarian beer. It has good outside seating and a take-me-to-Munich interior (Mon-Sat 11:00-24:00, closed Sun, Via Argentieri/Silbergasse 16—or use back entrance at Via dei Portici/Laubengasse 51, tel. 0471-980-407).

**$$ Humus** is a trendy eatery packed with locals enjoying a hearty mix of Italian and Middle Eastern dishes. With an emphasis on organic food, this place feels fresh, lively, and inviting (Mon-Sat 8:00-20:00, closed Sun, Silbergasse/Via Argentieri 16D, tel. 0471-971-961).

**Drinks and Light Food: $ Enoteca Il Bacaro,** a hole-in-the-wall wine bar, is an intriguing spot for a glass of wine and bar snacks amid locals. Wines available by the glass are listed on the blackboard (Mon-Fri 8:00-14:00 & 17:00-21:00, Sat 8:00-14:00,

# Tirolean Cuisine

During your visit to the Dolomites, take a break from Italian-style pizzas and pastas to sample some of the region's tradi-

tional cuisine...with a distinctly Austrian flavor. For simplicity, I've generally listed Italian names here, though local menus are in both Italian and German (and usually also English).

Wurst and sauerkraut are the Tirolean clichés. More adventurous eaters seek out *speck,* a raw (prosciutto-style) ham smoked for five months then thinly sliced and served as an antipasto or in sandwiches. *Canederli*—large dumplings with bits of *speck,* liver, spinach, beets, or cheese—are often served in broth, or with butter and cheese. (Never cut a dumpling with a knife—it'll destroy the chef.) *Merenda* is a platter of cured meats and hard cheeses. Pastas aren't an integral part of the local cuisine, but you will see *mezzelune*—half-moon-shaped ravioli.

The stars of Tirolean cuisine are the hearty meat dishes—which, unlike traditional Italian main courses, are nearly always served with side dishes of doughy dumplings or vegetables and potatoes. Try *stinco di maiale* (roasted pork shank, usually garnished with potatoes) and *crauti rossi* (a sweetish sauerkraut made from red cabbage). *Carrè affumicato* is pork shank that is first smoked, then boiled. *Selvaggina,* or wild game, comes in the form of *capriolo* (fawn), *cervo* (venison), or *camoscio* (chamois/antelope). Game is eaten smoked and thinly sliced in antipasti; in meat sauce (*ragù*) with fresh pasta or as ravioli stuffing; or in entrées, as tender chunks grilled or roasted in a rich sauce (*spezzatino).*

For dessert, strudel is everywhere, filled with the harvest from this region's renowned apple orchards. Cakes and pies are loaded with other locally grown fruits, raisins, and nuts. *Kaiserschmarrn* is an interesting alternative: a thick, fluffy, caramelized crêpe that's pulled apart into pieces; usually prepared with raisins and topped with powdered sugar and red currant jam.

*Bier (birra)* is king in the Alto Adige (the best-known brand, Forst, is brewed in nearby Merano), but the wines of the area are well-matched to the local fare. *Magdalener* is a light, dry red made from Schiava grapes. *Lagrein scuro* is a full-bodied red, dry and fruity, similar to a cabernet sauvignon or merlot. *Gewürztraminer* is a dry white wine with a spicy fruit flavor. For a local aperitif, try the popular and refreshing Hugo, made with sparkling wine, elderflower syrup (stir your drink), sparkling water, and a sprig of mint. For something stronger, try grappa made from Williams pears (and served with a wedge of fresh pear), or *grappa nocino*—a darker, sweeter brew similar to Jägermeister. *Guten Appetit und Prost!*

**DOLOMITES**

closed Sun, located a half-block east of Hopfen and Company on a hidden alley off Via Argentieri/Silbergasse 17, look for *vino/Wein* sign next to fountain on south side of street and enter courtyard, tel. 0471-971-421). **$ Dai Carretai** is a popular *cicchetti* bar where locals meet after work over a glass of wine—the crowd spills out onto the street. Browse the array of toothpick snacks at the counter, or order a bruschetta from the menu (also serves hot lunches, Mon-Fri 7:00-14:00 & 16:30-21:00, Sat 7:00-14:00, closed Sun, Via Dr. Streiter/Dr.-Streiter-Gasse 20b, tel. 0471-970-558).

**International Food: $ Drago D'Oro** is a good and afford-able Chinese restaurant on a pleasant old-town lane, with plenty of shaded seating out back (Mon 11:30-15:00, Tue-Sun 11:30-15:00 & 18:00-23:00, Via Roggia/Rauschertorgasse 7a, tel. 0471-977-621). **$$ Gul** has Indian-Pakistani standards (Mon-Sat 12:00-14:30 & 18:00-23:00, closed Sun, at Via Dr. Streiter/Dr.-Streiter-Gasse 2, tel. 0471-970-518). Both are takeout-friendly, as are several small pizzerias in the same area.

**Gelato:** At the tip of a city block less than five minutes from Piazza Walther/Walther Platz is **Eccetera...,** a tiny gelato coun-ter with no seating, just excellent (and excellently priced) gelato. They often have more flavors available than what's right under your nose—check the sign overhead for today's selection (daily 11:00-23:00, Via Grappoli/Weintraubengasse 23).

**Picnics:** Assemble the ingredients at the **Piazza delle Erbe/Obstplatz** market and dine in the park along the Talvera River (the green area with benches past the museum). Or visit one of the four **Despar supermarkets:** The largest is just before the museum at Via Museo/Museumstrasse 39 (daily 9:00-19:00). Another is a little more centrally located at the end of the Galleria Greif arcade (enter arcade from Piazza Walther/Waltherplatz by Hotel Greif and walk to far end—the supermarket is downstairs; same hours as the big store but closes Sun at 13:00). Smaller branches are on Pi-azza delle Erbe/Obstplatz and at Via Bottai/Bindergasse 29 (both open Mon-Sat 8:30-19:30, closed Sun).

# Bolzano Connections

Most trains from Bolzano are operated by Trenitalia (departures marked *R* or *RV* on schedules; ticket windows open daily 6:30-20:30, www.trenitalia.com). But some long-distance trains on the Innsbruck-Bolzano-Verona line are run by the German (or Austri-an) railways—DB/ÖBB for short (trains marked *Eurocity, EC,* or *Trenord*). With your back to the Trenitalia ticket counter, the DB *Reisebüro* ticket office is located near the left exit (open Mon-Fri 10:00-17:00, closed Sat-Sun; www.oebb.at). Because the German and Italian systems don't cooperate very well, it's best to book tickets through the company that's running your specific departure.

**From Bolzano by Train to: Milan** (about hourly, 4 hours, change in Verona), **Verona** (about hourly, 2.5 hours, take the regional/"R" trains—avoid fast trains that take same time for double the cost), **Venice** (about hourly, 3.5 hours, change in Verona), **Florence** (every 1-2 hours, 5 hours, change in Verona and/or Bologna), **Innsbruck** (1/hour, 2.5 hours, some regional connections change in Brennero), **Vienna** (4/day, 7 hours, change in Innsbruck), **Salzburg** (at least hourly, 4 hours, change in Brennero/Brenner, Innsbruck, and/or Rosenheim), **Munich** (called "Monaco" in Italy, 5/day direct, 4 hours).

**By Bus:** Bus #170 connects Bolzano with the gondola to **Compatsch** (putting you at the gateway to all the Alpe di Siusi hikes in about an hour) and the town of **Castelrotto** (direction: Kastelruth/Castelrotto, 2/hour Mon-Sat, hourly on Sun, last departure at 20:12—may run until later in summer, free schedule at bus station, €4 each way, buy tickets from driver, toll tel. 840-000-471, www.sii.bz.it).

The bus leaves from Bolzano's bus station (just north of the train station) and then winds high into the mountains. For the Alpe di Siusi, ask the driver to let you off at the "Bergbahn" station (Seiser Alm Bahn gondola, 40 minutes from Bolzano), then ascend to Compatsch. Otherwise, stay on the bus another 10 minutes to reach the center of Castelrotto.

# Castelrotto

Castelrotto (altitude: 3,475 feet) is the ideal home base for a day of hiking at Alpe di Siusi/Seiser Alm. Relax on the traffic-free main square, surrounded by a mountain backdrop and a thousand years of history, with an oversized (and hyperactive) bell tower above you. You'll feel almost lost in another world. (Stay at least two nights.) Easy bus and cable-car connections bring you up to the trails at Alpe di Siusi and down to Bolzano.

With a population of around 2,300, Castelrotto is a combination of real town, ski resort, and administrative center for surrounding villages. Tourism has become increasingly important here; while farming occupied most of the population in the 1960s, it's a small part of the economy nowadays. Castelrotto's good lodging and services help make your stay trouble-free. Though I've used the town's Italian name, life here goes on almost entirely in German, and locals call their town Kastelruth. (Fewer than 5 percent of Castelrotto's residents are native Italian speakers.)

# Orientation to Castelrotto

## TOURIST INFORMATION

The helpful TI is on the main square, facing the church (Mon-Sat 8:30-12:30 & 14:00-18:30, closed afternoons in Nov and sometimes April, closed Sun except July-Aug 9:00-12:00, tel. 0471-706-333, www.seiseralm.it). If you plan to hike, pick up the TI's free *Living the Dolomites* pictorial hiking map, which includes estimated walking times and trail numbers. For longer hikes, 1:25,000 maps are worthwhile (about €5).

If visiting the TI, pop upstairs for a minute to see the free **Trachten Museum,** where traditional costumes are displayed beside paintings and photos of the same styles worn by locals in centuries past (no English descriptions, hours similar but shorter than the TI).

**Transit Deals:** If you're sleeping anywhere in the Castelrotto/Alpe di Siusi area (but not in Bolzano), ask your hotel for a free **Südtirol Guest Pass** (a.k.a. the **Seiser Alm Live Card**). It covers local buses between Castelrotto and places like Bolzano and the base of the Seiser Alm Bahn gondola. It doesn't cover anything above the gondola base (at Seis/Siusi). You'll only get the card if you ask...so ask.

The TI also sells the pricey **Combi Card** transit pass, which only makes sense if you're here several days and/or take at least three round-trip rides on the Seiser Alm Bahn gondola.

## HELPFUL HINTS

**Annual Events:** The Oswald-von-Wolkenstein Riding Tournament, held on a spring weekend (between mid-May and mid-June), features medieval-style equestrian tournament games, followed by a feast. The town also holds religious processions with locals dressed in traditional costumes, usually on the Sunday after Corpus Christi (June 14 in 2020); on the feast day of the village protectors, Sts. Peter and Paul (nearest Sunday to June 29); and on the local Thanksgiving (first Sun in Oct). In mid-October, the town is packed for the Kastelruther Spatzenfest, a concert weekend for the local musical heartthrobs, the Kastelruther Spatzen.

## Castelrotto

CALVARY HILL STROLL

100 Meters
100 Yards

KOFELGASSE

BÜHLWEG

CHURCH

(Underground)

PLATTENSTR.

Main Square

BELL TOWER

WC

B

BUS STN.

P

BANDSTAND

DOLOMITEN-

MENDEL HAUS

VON WOLKEN

PANIDERSTR.

(MAIN ROAD)

PANIDERSTRASSE

TIOSLERWEG

KASTELRUTHER SPATZEN-LADEN

STR.

WEGSCHEID

VOGELWEIDERGASSE

P

OSWALD VON WOLKENSTEIN STR. (MAIN ROAD)

MARINZENWEG

PUFL

PANIDERWEG

MARINZEN CHAIR LIFT

To Pool, Alpe di Siusi, Siusi Village (Cable Car to Alpe di Siusi) & Bolzano via S-12

SP-64

KLEINMICHLWEG

POST

To ⑩ & St. Valentin Church

To San Michele, Val Gardena & Sella Pass →

GRÖDNI BODEN

SP-64

FORTLWEG

**DOLOMITES**

### Accommodations
1. Hotel Cavallino d'Oro (Goldenes Rössl)
2. Hotel/Rest. zum Turm (alla Torre)
3. Hotel zum Wolf (Hotel al Lupo)
4. Residence Trocker
5. Pension Lantschner

### Eateries & Other
6. Saalstuben Restaurant
7. Café Restaurant Bachler
8. Gasthof Toni
9. Zur Alten Schmiede Pizzeria
10. To Ristorante Liftstüberl
11. Hotel Schgaguler Bar
12. Supermarket (2)
13. Alpin Sport

**Spring and Fall Closures:** The periods between ski season and hiking season (April–mid-May and Nov) are quiet, with lifts closed for maintenance and most hotels and restaurants shuttered (this is when locals take their own vacations).

**Business Hours:** Shops in Castelrotto close between 12:30 and 15:30—a good time for a long lunch, a hike in the hills...or a siesta.

**Launderette:** There's none in the area.

**Recreation:** A heated outdoor **swimming pool** with alpine views and nearby tennis courts is in the hamlet of Telfen, between

Castelrotto and Seis/Siusi (mid-May-mid-Sept 9:00-21:00, tel. 0471-705-090). You can **rent a horse** at Unter-Lanzinerhof in Telfen (mobile 339-868-6868, www.reiterhof-oberlanzin. com, Karin speaks some English). For more excitement, tandem **paragliding** flights—you and the pilot—depart from Alpe di Siusi and land either there or in Castelrotto (mobile 335-603-6400, www.tandem-paragliding.com, Ruben). You can rent **skis and snowboards** at both the bottom and top stations of the Alpe di Siusi lift, or at Alpin Sport in Castelrotto (also has hiking gear in summer, near the Marinzen lift at Paniderstrasse 10, tel. 0471-711-079, Robert—mobile 339-293-9725).

## ARRIVAL IN CASTELROTTO

The **bus station** *(Busbahnhof)* is 100 yards below the town's main square. It's unstaffed, but there's a shelter with timetables and a ticket machine (cash only). Free WCs are in a building at the tip of the bus loop. Take the stairs (by the tiny elevator) to get to the main square and TI.

**Drivers** can park in one of the two underground parking lots: One is near the bus station, and the other is on Wolkensteinstrasse, next to the recommended Saalstuben Restaurant (€1.80/hour, €20/day, cash only). Each of the recommended hotels also has free parking (ask for details when you book).

Coming from the south, drivers exit the expressway at *Bolzano Nord*. Coming from Innsbruck and points north, exit (earlier than you would expect) at *Chiusa/Klausen* and continue five miles toward Bolzano along the secondary road (SS-12) before crossing the river (signed *Waidbruck/Ponte Gardena*) and following signs for *Kastelruth/Castelrotto*.

# Castelrotto Walk

Castelrotto is a great place to sleep but has only a little sightseeing of its own—the surrounding mountains and hikes are the attractions here. This quick self-guided walk will get you oriented and trace the town's history.

• *Start in the...*

**Main Square** (Piazza Kraus): This square is named for the noble family who ruled the town from 1550 to 1800. Their palace, now the City Hall, overlooks the square and sports the Kraus family coat of arms.

Castelrotto puts its square to use. A farmers market takes place here on Friday mornings in the summer, and a clothing/craft market fills the square most Thursday mornings. Before and after Sunday Mass, the square is crowded with villagers and farmers (who fill the church) dressed in traditional clothing. The main Mass (Sat at 20:00 and Sun at 10:00) is in German. In July and August, when Italian tourists visit, another Mass takes place in Italian (at 11:30).

• *A landmark in the square is the...*

**Bell Tower:** At 250 feet, the freestanding bell tower dominates the town. It was once attached to a church, which burned down in 1753. While the bell tower was quickly rebuilt, the gutted church was torn down, and the church you see today was constructed farther back, enlarging the square.

When you feel the pride that the locals have in their tower—which symbolizes their town—you'll better understand why Italy has been called "the land of a thousand bell towers." The bells of Castelrotto, which are a big part of the town experience, ring on the hour from 6:00 until 22:00. While sleepy tourists may wonder why the bells clang so very early in the morning, locals who grew up with the chimes find them comforting. The beloved bells mark the hours, summon people to work and to Mass, announce festivals, and warn when storms threaten. In the days when people used to believe that thunder was the devil approaching, the bells called everyone to pray. (Townspeople thought the bells' sound cleared the clouds.) Bells ring big at 7:00, noon, and 19:00. The biggest of the eight bells (7,500 pounds) peals only on special days. When the bells ring at 15:00 on Friday, it commemorates Christ's sacrifice at the supposed hour of his death—a little bit of Good Friday every Friday. The colorful poles in front of the church (yellow-and-white for the Vatican, red-and-white for Tirol) fly flags on festival days. The towering May Pole, a Bavarian tradition, was a gift from Castelrotto's sister city in Bavaria.

• *Also on the square is the...*

**Church:** Before entering, notice the plaque on the exterior. This commemorative inscription honors the tiny community's WWI dead—*Fraktion Dorf* means from the village itself, and the other sections list soldiers from the surrounding hamlets. Stepping into the church, you're surrounded by harmonious art from about 1850. The church is dedicated to Sts. Peter and Paul, and the paintings that flank the high altar show how each was martyred (crucifixion and beheading). The pews (and smart matching confessionals) are carved of walnut wood.

• *Back outside, belly up to the...*

**Fountain:** Opposite the church, Castelrotto's fountain dates from 1884. St. Florian, the protector against fires, keeps an eye on it today as he did when villagers (and their horses) first came here for a drink of water.

• *With your back to the church and the fountain on your left, walk a half-block down the lane to see the finely frescoed...*

**Mendel Haus:** This house, with its traditional facade, contains a woodcarving shop. Its frescoes (from 1886) include many symbolic figures, as well as an emblem of a carpenter above the door—a relic from the days when images, rather than address numbers, identified the house. Notice St. Florian again; this time, he's pouring water on a small painting of this very house engulfed in flames. Inside Mendel Haus

are fine carvings, a reminder that this region—especially nearby Val Gardena—is famous for its woodwork. You'll also see many witches, folk figures that date back to when this area was the Salem of this corner of Europe. Women who didn't fit society's mold—including midwives, healers, and redheads—were sometimes burned as witches.

• *Continue downhill to the left of Mendel Haus, then before the underpass, climb the stairs on your right. At the top of the stairs, turn left on Dolomitenstrasse. In 50 yards, on the left at #21, is a shop dedicated to Castelrotto's big hometown heroes.*

**Kastelruther Spatzen-Laden:** The ABBA of the Alps, the folk-singing group Kastelruther Spatzen (literally "sparrows") is a gang of local boys who put Castelrotto on the map in the 1980s. They have a huge following here and throughout the German-speaking world. Though he's now in his late 50s, the lead singer, Norbert Rier, remains a Germanic heartthrob. You'll see his face on ads all over town—in the recommended Saalstuben Restaurant, suggesting what to order for dessert, or in the Co-op supermarket, reminding you to drink lots of Tirolean milk. The group's feel-good folk-pop style—an alpine version of German *Schlager* music—is popular with the kind of conservative, working-class Germans who like to vacation in the South Tirol. (Younger, more progressive Germans cringe at this stuff, with its nationalistic overtones.) At a big festival in Castelrotto on the second weekend in October, the band puts on a hometown concert, filling this place with fans from as far away as the Alsace, Switzerland, and the Netherlands. They also hold an open-air concert here in June and a Christmas concert.

Browse the store, which is part souvenir shop and part insignia and apparel outlet. Downstairs is a sprawling, folksy museum slathered with gifts, awards, and gold records. The group

# The Dramatic Dolomites

The Dolomites have been called the most beautiful mountains on earth, and certainly they are among the most dramatic.

They differ from the rest of the Alps because of their dominant rock type, dolomite, which forms sheer vertical walls of white, gray, and pink that rise abruptly from green valleys and meadows. Many parts of the mountains (including the Alpe di Siusi/Seiser Alm) are protected as regional or national parks, where development is restricted. Still, rail lines, roads, good bus routes, and innumerable lifts make this group of mountains very accessible.

Once dubbed the "Pale Mountains" or the "Venetian Alps," this mountain range was named after French mineralogist Dolomieu, who in the late 1700s first described the rock type responsible for the region's light-colored bluffs and peaks.

These sedimentary rocks (similar to limestone) were formed in warm tropical seas during the Triassic Period (about 250 million years ago). The marine sediments, along with the fossilized remains of coral reefs and other animals, were buried, hardened, and later scooped upward along with the rest of the Alps by the tectonic-plate action of Africa slowly smashing into Europe. Today, marine fossils are found atop the region's highest peaks, including the skyscraping, nearly 11,000-foot-high Marmolada.

During World War I, the front line between the Italian and Austro-Hungarian forces ran through these mountains, and many paths were cut into the range for military use. Today mountaineers can still follow these networks of metal rungs, cables, and ladders (called *via ferrata*). One famous wartime trail is the "Strada delle Gallerie," near Rovereto, which passes through 52 tunnels *(gallerie)*.

A paradise for hikers, cyclists, and climbers in summer, the Dolomites are even better known as a top skiing destination. A popular winter activity for intrepid skiers is the "Sella Ronda"—circling the Sella massif using a system of lifts and 28 miles of ski runs. The 1956 Winter Olympics in Cortina d'Ampezzo brought the Dolomites to the world's attention, and the 2026 Winter Olympics (shared between Cortina and Milan) are set to do it all over again.

Whether you experience the Dolomites with your hand on a walking stick, a ski pole, or an *aperitivo* while mountain-gazing from a café, it's easy to enjoy this spectacular region.

**DOLOMITES**

has won 13 Echo Awards..."more than Robbie Williams." Watch the continuously playing video (€2 museum entry, refunded with €5 purchase in the shop, Mon-Fri 9:00-12:00 & 14:00-18:00, Sat 9:00-12:00, closed Sun).

• *Leaving the shop, cross the street for a...*

**Fine Mountain View of the Schlern:** This bold limestone outcropping—so typical of the Dolomites—is a symbol of the Südtirol. Witches are said to live there, and many locals climb it yearly (it's actually an easy—if long—walk up the back side).

Look left—the street points to a ridge in the distance. That's Puflatsch (a high meadow with a popular trail called the "Trail of the Witches"—see "Activities in the Alpe di Siusi," later).

• *Continue up the hill 50 yards, cross left at the crosswalk, pass the little parking lot square, and find two stones marking the top of a cobbled pedestrian lane that leads downhill back into town. Look up at the top of the bell tower. Ahead stands the elegant...*

**Hotel zum Wolf Facade:** This was painted by the same artist who did the Mendel Haus. St. Florian is still pouring water on burning houses and locals are busy enjoying the local wine.

As you head left, uphill back to the town square, enjoy windows filled with traditional Südtirol formal wear—delightful dirndls. You'll pass an old hotel, which, by the looks of its street sign, must be called The Golden Pony (*Cavallino d'Oro* or *Goldenes Rössl*). Ahead of you is the inviting sound of a refreshing drink from the town fountain.

• *Our walk is over. Ahead (through a white arch just to the right of the TI) are two big pictorial maps showing the region in summer and in ski season, as well as a modern café with ice cream and a nice terrace. The arch that's closer to the church leads up to Calvary Hill for a fine little loop walk, described next.*

## Activities in Castelrotto

### Calvary Hill (Kalvarienberg) Stroll

For an easy stroll to Castelrotto's finest postcard views—the giant bell tower with a dramatic alpine backdrop—take a 15-minute mini hike around the town's hill, Kalvarienberg/Calvario (Calvary). Originally, this was the site of the ancient Roman fortress, and later the fortified home of the medieval lord. One lane circles the hill while another spirals to the top past seven little chapels, each depicting a scene from Christ's Passion and culminat-

ing in the Crucifixion. Facing the church, take the road under the arch to the left, and then follow signs to *Kofelrunde* (to go around the hill) or *Kofelkapelle* (to get directly to the top). The light is best late in the day, and the stroll is also great after dark—romantically lit and under the stars. (The lead singer of the Kastelruther Spatzen enjoyed his first kiss right here.) For a longer walk back into town, take the Friedensweg (Peace Trail) from the top of the hill. This 30-minute forest walk is decorated with peace-themed artwork by local elementary students.

### Marinzen Lift

The little Marinzen chairlift trundles you up above town in two-person seats to the Marinzenhütte café (at 4,875 feet), which has a playground and animal park for kids (open when the lift runs). The views from the top are nothing special, but several hikes leave from here—and as you ride back down, you'll enjoy pleasant panoramas over Castelrotto. Or skip the return ride—it's a sce-

nic one-hour hike back down; to extend the walk, detour to St. Valentin church, described next. While the chairlift doesn't com-pare with going up to the Alpe di Siusi, it's still a nice activity. Catch it right in town, up the lane behind the Co-op/Konsum-Markt supermarket.

**Cost and Hours:** €8 one-way up, €7 one-way down, €11.50 round-trip, daily mid-May-mid-Oct 9:00-17:00, until 18:30 July-Aug, slow and scenic 22 minutes each way, closed off-season and rainy mornings, tel. 0471-707-160, www.marinzen.com.

### Hillside Walk to St. Valentin Church

On a clear summer evening, my favorite post-dinner activity is the gentle 40-minute walk above town to the picture-perfect St. Valen-tin Church, perched on a hillside high above Seis/Siusi. Although the church is rarely open, on the way there you'll enjoy uninter-rupted views of the stern Schlern, the smell of hay (and cows), and the distinct clang of Castelrotto's church bell.

From Castelrotto's town center, walk uphill along Marinzen-weg, passing the driveway to Ristorante Liftstüberl. Stay on the road until you reach a signpost for *St. Valentin* and *Seis*. Follow the path (and signs to *Seis*) past a few farmhouses to a well-kept shrine to the Virgin Mary. Just after the shrine, take the path to the right and into the grass (on the #7 trail). Crossing a road, you'll head down a paved driveway and take the far-left fork between a barn and a white building (marked *za Oberzonn*) to find the church standing proudly under the mighty Schlern.

From the church you can either retrace your steps back to Castelrotto (my preference), walk another 15 minutes steeply downhill to Seis/Suisi and catch a bus back to Castelrotto (#3, #4, or #170; last departure around 20:45), or split the difference and head more gently downhill to the main road to catch the bus back.

This walk can be combined with a walk down from the top of the Marinzen chairlift, but it's a steep descent to the church. Instead I'd walk down toward Castelrotto until the path leaves the forested hillside, then head left to follow the gentle, mostly level walk toward the church.

## NEAR CASTELROTTO
### Pflegerhof Herb Farm

On a narrow country road a little outside the nearby town of Seis/Siusi, you'll find an organic farm that grows dozens of varieties of herbs. Walk among the scent-filled, fully labeled beds and browse the wide variety of herbal products in the shop. To reach the farm from Castelrotto, drive through Seis/Siusi, pass the turnoff for the cable car on your left, and after about a half-mile, turn right following *St. Oswald* and *Pflegerhof* signs.

**Cost and Hours:** Free, Mon-Sat 10:00-18:00, Sept-March until 17:00, closed Sun year-round, St. Oswald 24, tel. 0471-706-771, www.pflegerhof.com.

# Nightlife in and near Castelrotto

In summer, traditionally costumed groups offer free band concerts on Thursday evenings at the bandstand near the bus station (usually at 21:00 and kicked off with a procession from the main square).

For a more contemporary scene, the recommended **Zur Alten Schmiede Pizzeria** in Castelrotto is a fun spot that's open late. **Hotel Schgaguler** in Castelrotto has a fancy bar, and **Sasso's,** on Schlernstrasse in the nearby town of Seis/Siusi, is a trendy wine bar. A popular hangout for the younger crowd in Seis/Siusi is **Santners** (the only dance club in the area), at the Seiser Alm Bahn station. If you're here on the weekend, the "Nightliner" shuttle bus can bring you home in the wee hours (Fri-Sat roughly hourly 20:40-2:40, schedules at www.silbernagl.it).

# Sleeping in and near Castelrotto

Castelrotto has the largest selection of accommodations and is the only truly convenient option for those traveling in this region by public transport. If you've come to hike on the Alpe di Siusi, you could also stay in one of the hotels there (in or around Compatsch)—I've listed two less expensive options—or even in a mountain hut.

Dozens of farmhouses in the area also offer accommodations, usually practical only if you have a car. (There's a full list on the TI website.) Some are working farms; others have been converted to tourist accommodations. I've listed a few that are willing to accept guests for two or three nights (the typical American stay here). German and Italian tourists—who make up the bulk of the area's business—are more likely to stay for a week and to rent apartments with a kitchen but with no breakfast or daily cleaning service—which can save a great deal of money, especially for families.

Rates skyrocket in July, August, and around Christmas. Accommodations often close in November and from April to mid-May. I've assigned categories based on the price of a double room in June or September.

If sleeping in this area, you're entitled to the **Südtirol Guest Pass**—a free pass for many local buses (described earlier, under "Tourist Information"). Be sure to ask your hotelier for one.

## IN CASTELROTTO VILLAGE

These listings are within 300 yards of the bus station. The first three are in the traffic-free area of the old town; hotel guests are allowed to drive in to park. All have free parking.

**$$$ Hotel Cavallino d'Oro** (in German, **Goldenes Rössl**), right on the main square, is plush and welcoming, with the best Tirolean character in town. Run by helpful Stefan, Susanne, and Sophia, the entire place is dappled with artistic, woodsy touches—painted doors, carved wood, and canopy beds in many rooms—and historical photos. If you love antiques by candlelight, this nearly 700-year-old hotel is the place for you (elevator, free self-service laundry, open all year, Piazza Kraus 1, tel. 0471-706-337, www. cavallino.it, info@cavallino.it). Stefan converted his wine cellar into a Roman steam bath and Finnish sauna (free for guests, great after a hike, can book an hour for exclusive use)—complete with heated tile seats, massage rooms, a solarium for tanning, and tropical plants.

**$$ Hotel zum Turm** (in Italian, **Albergo alla Torre**) is comfortable, cozy, and warmly run by Gabi and Günther. The 15 rooms are woody and modern. If you're staying at least three nights, the €12/person half-board option is a great value (family rooms, el-

**DOLOMITES**

evator, free passes for Marinzen chairlift, closed April-mid-May and late Oct-Nov, Kofelgasse 8, tel. 0471-706-349, www.zumturm. com, info@zumturm.com). From Castelrotto's main square, walk (or drive) through the upper of the two archways. If coming on a Wednesday, let them know your arrival time in advance.

**$$ Hotel zum Wolf** (in Italian, **al Lupo**) is pure Tirolean, with all the comforts in 23 neat-as-a-pin rooms, most with balconies (elevator, coin-op laundry, closed April-late May and Nov-mid-Dec, a block below main square at Wolkensteinstrasse 5, tel. 0471-706-332, www.hotelwolf.it, info@hotelwolf.it, Malknecht family).

**$$ Residence Trocker** is run by the Moser family, who rent 11 great rooms in a place that's bomb-shelter solid yet warm-wood cozy. While the family is shy and less welcoming than others listed here, their compound is beautifully laid out—with a café-bar (a popular, often-smoky local hangout), garden, sauna, steam bath, roof deck with Jacuzzi, and coin-op laundry (family rooms, apartments available, elevator, closed Nov, Föstlweg 3, tel. 0471-705-200, www.residencetrocker.com, garni@residencetrocker.com, Stefan). If arriving on Sunday (the family's day off), be sure to let them know in advance what time you'll arrive.

**$ Pension Lantschner** is family-run and a good budget value. Its 10 rooms—on the two upper floors of a large traditional house—are a little smaller, simpler, and older than at my other listings, but all are comfortable and have balconies with views (Kleinmichlweg 8, tel. 0471-706-025, www.garni-lantschner.com, info@garni-lantschner.com).

## FARM STAYS NEAR CASTELROTTO

Dozens of working farms around Castelrotto take in visitors, mostly in apartments with a kitchen and a minimum stay of five to seven nights (the TI has a complete list). A few farms also accept guests for short stays—even one night—and serve breakfast. Expect rustic doubles with bath for about €70. Staying in these places is practical only if you have a car. Consider the following (all **$**): **Goldrainerhof** (a 10-minute uphill trudge from Castelrotto, Tioslerweg 10, tel. 0471-706-100, www.goldrainerhof. com); **Tonderhof** (a fruit farm in a dramatic hillside setting along the road down to Waidbruck/Ponte Gardena, Tisens 25, tel. 0741-706-733, www.tonderhof.com) and their neighbor, **Schiedhof** (Tisens 23, mobile 345-583-7278, www.schiedhof. it); and **Formsunhof** (along the road up to Alpe di Siusi, before the checkpoint, 4-night minimum stay, St. Valentin 12, tel. 0471-706-015, www.formsunhof.com).

## IN ALPE DI SIUSI/SEISER ALM, NEAR THE HIKING TRAILS

There are more than two dozen hotels up on the Alpe di Siusi, most in Compatsch (where the gondola from Seis/Siusi arrives) but some farther into the park. Most are quite expensive, four- and five-star affairs, with doubles from €200 and up in July and August. The two hotels listed here cost less—because Compatsch and the park entrance are a 10-minute uphill walk away. These are most practical for drivers (though they can reached by the Seiser Alm Bahn gondola and bus #10). Half-board is wise here, as there's nowhere else to eat dinner (except other hotels). The main advantage: Staying here, you can hike all day without concern for catching the last gondola down. Serious hikers should consider staying at the park's high-altitude mountain huts (mentioned under "Activities in Alpe di Siusi," later).

**$$$ Hotel Schmung** is along the road and has fine, recently renovated rooms (most with balconies). During the day, the Seiser Alm Bahn gondolas float through the air just outside the front balconies (dinner available, free sauna, closed mid-April-May and Nov-mid-Dec, Compatsch 12, tel. 0471-727-943, www.schmung.com, info@schmung.com).

**$$ Hotel Seelaus** is a friendly, mellow, family-run, creekside place a little off the road to Compatsch. About 20 of its 30 rooms have been smartly renovated with a modern look, but the hotel still has an Austrian feel (family rooms, hearty €25 dinners, free wellness area with sauna, hydro-massage, and minipool; closed mid-April-mid-May and mid-Oct-early Dec, Compatschweg 8, tel. 0471-727-954, www.hotelseelaus.it, info@hotelseelaus.it, Roberto). Roberto offers free rides from the bus or cable-car station, and affordable transfers to/from Bolzano—arrange in advance.

## Eating in Castelrotto

**$$$$ Hotel zum Turm** tries hard to up the culinary bar in town, focusing on locally sourced ingredients and serving good, meaty fare—including venison—and inventive vegetarian options. You can sit in the humdrum breakfast room, the cozy and very traditional *Stube*, or out on the oasis of a back terrace (salad bar, Thu-Tue 12:00-13:45 & 18:00-20:45, closed Wed, closed April-mid-May and late Oct-Nov, tel. 0471-706-349, www.zumturm.com).

**$$$ Saalstuben Restaurant** serves a selection of hearty and tasty Tirolean classics, including lots of grilled meats, indoors or on their terrace (Fri-Wed 11:30-14:00 & 18:00-21:00, may also open Thu in July-Aug, Wolkensteinstrasse 12, tel. 0471-707-394, www.saalstuben.com).

**$$ Café Restaurant Bachler**'s selling point is its stunning view—easily the best in town—of the Schlern from its outdoor seating. The focus is pizza, but they also serve local standards like schnitzel, and offer a decent salad bar. For casual dining, this is the place to be on a sunny evening (Wed-Mon 11:00-14:00 & 17:00-21:00, closed Tue, Dolomitenstrasse 4, tel. 0471-705-161). From the main square, pass the Mendel Haus, cross the upper street, enter the doorway labeled *Panorama-Terrasse,* then head downstairs.

**$$ Gasthof Toni,** along the main road at the town's main intersection, pleases hungry locals with huge €17 two-course meals served at both lunch and dinner (pick one pasta and one meat course, includes side salad). It's cozy inside but the outdoor tables are just off a noisy street. They also have good pizza (Mon-Sat 12:00-14:00 & 17:00-21:00, pizza until 23:00, closed Sun, Wolkensteinstrasse 15, tel. 0471-706-306).

**$$ Zur Alten Schmiede Pizzeria** is a great place to enjoy an evening drinking Forst, the local beer, and playing darts. They offer a wide range of nothing-fancy grub—pizzas, pastas, meaty dishes, and *wurst* meals (Tue-Sun 12:00-14:00 & 17:30-21:00, pizza until 23:00, closed Mon, outdoor seating, near bus station entrance at Paniderstrasse 7, tel. 0471-707-390).

**$$ Ristorante Liftstüberl** is a good bet on a nice day if you'd like to eat in nature rather than in town. It's a charming local favorite offering good traditional dishes and three-course dinners for less than €20. The classic woody interior is nothing special, but the picnic benches come with sweeping views, and there's a mini playground for the kids. Find it in a meadow about a half-mile hike south of town (Mon-Sat 11:30-14:00 & 17:30-20:30, closed Sun, Marinzenweg 35, tel. 0471-706-804).

**Picnics:** Castelrotto has two supermarkets in the center, both with a decent selection of useful items beyond groceries. **Eurospar** is the handiest, at the town's main intersection, and has the longest hours (Mon-Sat 8:00-19:30, closed Sun, on Wolkensteinstrasse). The **Co-op/Konsum-Market** has the best selection of locally produced food, and a hardware section where you can pick up a bell for your cow—no joke (Mon-Sat 7:30-12:30 & 15:00-19:00, closed Sun, Paniderstrasse 24).

## Castelrotto Connections

**From Castelrotto by Bus to: Seiser Alm Bahn gondola station** (#3 and #4, frequent departures—see "Getting There," later), **Bolzano** (#170, 2/hour Mon-Sat, hourly Sun, 50 minutes, last departure around 19:00—may run until later in summer, covered by Südtirol Guest Pass; if you're connecting to a train in Bolzano, give yourself about 10 minutes to get to your platform at the train station). From Bolzano, you can easily connect to **Verona, Venice, Innsbruck, Munich,** and beyond. Get bus schedules at the TI, toll tel. 840-000-471, or check www.sii.bz.it or www.silbernagl.it.

# Alpe di Siusi

This grassy mountain plateau above the village of Seis/Siusi (the next over from Castelrotto) is the largest high meadow—and summer pastureland—in the Alps. It's a premier hiking and skiing area,

and also home to hundreds of cows every summer. Undulating rather than flat, broken by rushing streams, and dappled with shapely evergreens, what makes the Alpe di Siusi (Seiser Alm in German) really spectacular are the views of the surrounding Dolomite peaks. Well-kept huts, trails, and lifts make hiking here a joy. It's family-friendly, with lots of playgrounds. Being here on a sunny summer day comes with the ambience of a day at the beach.

The cows munching away in this vast pasture all summer after a winter huddled in Castelrotto produce two million gallons of milk annually, much of which is sent to Bolzano to make cheese. After tourism, dairy is the leading industry here.

To enjoy the Alpe di Siusi, you'll need a full day and decent weather. Arrive in Compatsch (the main entry point) as early as you can, then hike (or bike) as much as you please. Bring a picnic (or buy lunch at a high mountain hut), and aim to wrap up the day in midafternoon—many upper lifts close at 17:00, and thunderclouds tend to gather even on days that start out sunny.

The hiking season runs roughly from mid-June through mid-October (though if the weather's good, you can hit some of the trails as early as mid-May). The trails are pretty dead in April, early May, and November. For a fragrant festival of wildflowers suited to growing at 6,000 feet, come in June.

With additional time, you can explore more of the park or overnight in one of the mountain huts as a base for more remote and challenging hikes. You're more than a mile high here, so take it easy and give yourself frequent breaks to catch your breath.

Get to know the park's mountains by sight. The jagged peaks called **Langkofel** (Sasso Lungo, "Long Stone") and **Plattkofel** (Sasso Piatto, "Flat Stone") together form an "M" at the far end of Alpe di Siusi—providing a storybook Dolomite backdrop. The

DOLOMITES

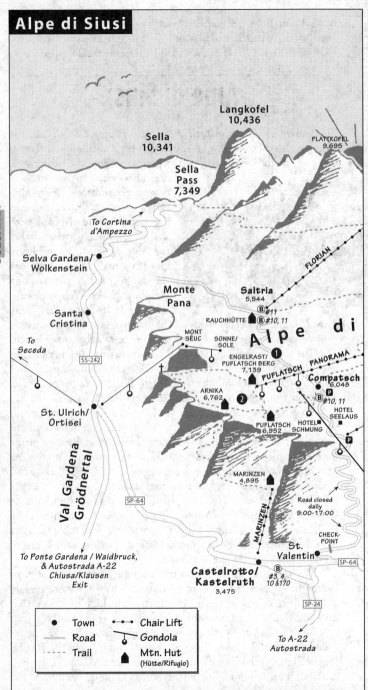

Alpe di Siusi

Langkofel 10,436

Sella 10,341

PLATTKOFEL 9,695

Sella Pass 7,349

To Cortina d'Ampezzo

Selva Gardena/ Wolkenstein

Santa Cristina

FLORIAN

Monte Pana

Saltria 5,544

RAUCHHÜTTE  (B) #11
(B) #10, 11

MONT SËUC

SONNE/ SOLE

To Seceda

SS-242

Alpe   di

PANORAMA

ENGELRAST/ PUFLATSCH BERG 7,139

(1)

PUFLATSCH

Compatsch 6,048

(B) #10, 11

†

ARNIKA 6,762

(2)

HOTEL SEELAUS

St. Ulrich/ Ortisei

PUFLATSCH 6,952

HOTEL SCHMUNG

P

MARINZEN 4,895

Val Gardena Grödnertal

SP-64

MARINZEN

Road closed daily 9:00-17:00

CHECK-POINT

To Ponte Gardena / Waidbruck, & Autostrada A-22 Chiusa/Klausen Exit

St. Valentin

Castelrotto/ Kastelruth 3,475

(B) #3, 4, 10 &170

SP-64

SP-24

To A-22 Autostrada

| | | | |
|---|---|---|---|
| ● | Town | •••• | Chair Lift |
| ﹏﹏ | Road | ⚬—⚬ | Gondola |
| ---- | Trail | ▲ | Mtn. Hut (Hütte/Rifugio) |

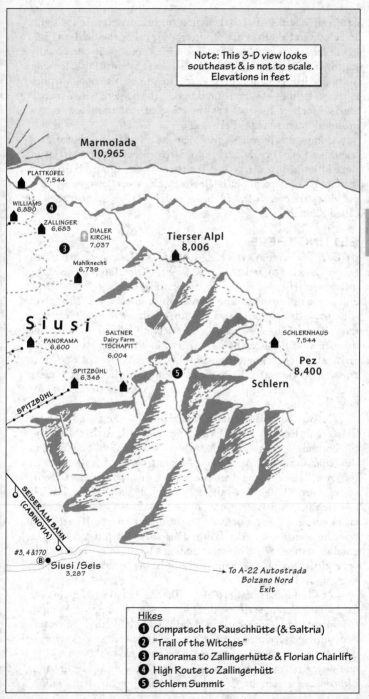

Note: This 3-D view looks southeast & is not to scale. Elevations in feet

Marmolada
10,965

PLATTKOFEL
7,544

WILLIAMS
6,890 ④

ZALLINGER
6,683

DIALER
KIRCHL
7,037

③

Mahlknecht
6,739

Tierser Alpl
8,006

Siusi

PANORAMA
6,600

SALTNER
Dairy Farm
"TSCHAPIT"
6,004

SCHLERNHAUS
7,544

Pez
8,400

SPITZBÜHL
6,348

⑤

Schlern

SPITZBÜHL

SEISER ALM BAHN
(CABINOVIA)

#3, 4 &170

Ⓑ Siusi /Seis
3,287

→ To A-22 Autostrada
Bolzano Nord
Exit

DOLOMITES

Hikes
❶ Compatsch to Rauschhütte (& Saltria)
❷ "Trail of the Witches"
❸ Panorama to Zallingerhütte & Florian Chairlift
❹ High Route to Zallingerhütt
❺ Schlern Summit

dark, eerie saddle between them fires the imagination. To the right, and closer to Compatsch, the outcropping called the **Schlern** (Sciliar in Italian) is a long, flat ridge that ends in spooky crags boldly staring into the summer haze. The Schlern's Santner Peak, looking like a devilish *Winged Victory,* gave ancient peoples enough willies to spawn legends of supernatural forces. The Schlern witch, today's tourist-brochure mascot, was the cause of many a broom-riding medieval townswoman's fiery death.

Compatsch provides great views of the Schlern, but only a truncated look at Langkofel and Plattkofel. For better views, gain some altitude on a lift, or hop the bus (or hike) toward **Saltria,** at the far end of Alpe di Siusi. (Because Saltria sits down in a valley, the views are even better from the road just above it, near the hut called Rauchhütte.)

## GETTING THERE

**By Car:** The winding, six-mile road up to Compatsch starts between Castelrotto and Seis/Siusi (at San Valentino). To keep the meadow serene, it's closed to cars during the day (9:00-17:00), unless you're staying in one of the hotels in the park. (The road is unblocked, but you'll likely be stopped by roving traffic monitors—be ready to show your hotel reservation confirmation.) But if you're an early riser, there's no reason not to drive up if you can arrive at the checkpoint before 9:00. (You can drive back down at any time.) Compatsch has a huge parking lot (€18/day—the same price as one round-trip cable-car ticket, so groups of at least two save by driving).

**By Bus from Bolzano or Castelrotto to the Gondola near Seis/Siusi:** Regular buses from Bolzano and Castelrotto link to the bottom of the gondola that whisks visitors from Seis/Siusi to the Alpe di Siusi. Buses #3 and #4 run from Castelrotto (4/hour July-Aug in morning and afternoon peak times, otherwise 2/hour; 10 minutes, €1.50 ticket valid for the whole day, use machine, if no machine pay driver, covered by Südtirol Guest Pass). Be sure to check your bus's direction before boarding (or ask the driver)—you want buses to Seiser Alm Bahn. These buses stop directly at the gondola station. Some buses, including #170 to/from Bolzano (see page 201), stop on the main road just below the station—a steep five-minute hike up.

**By Gondola from Seis/Siusi:** The Seiser Alm Bahn gondola (in Italian, Cabinovia Alpe di Siusi) runs hikers and skiers up to Compatsch (mid-May-early Nov daily 8:00-18:00, mid-June-mid-Sept until 19:00, closed most of Nov and mid-April-mid-May, runs continuously during open hours, 15-minute ride to the top, €11.50 one-way, €18 round-trip, tel. 0471-704-270, www.seiseralmbahn. it). You can reach the valley station either by car (free outdoor parking; garage parking—€3/day) or by bus (see earlier). The lower cable-car station is a slick mini shopping mall, with lots of outdoor outfitters and a tempting local-products store.

**By Bus from Castelrotto:** "Express" bus #10 runs from Castelrotto all the way to Compatsch. It costs the same as the more memorable—and environmentally friendly—gondola, takes the same amount of time, and runs less frequently. The only advantage to the bus: It runs in some shoulder season periods when the gondola doesn't, and in high season leaves Compatsch 10 minutes after the gondola stops running—useful if you're a little late getting back to Compatsch (9 buses/day mid-June-mid-Oct, 20 minutes, fewer mid-May-mid-June and late Oct, www.silbernagl.it). Round-trip gondola tickets aren't good on the bus (or vice versa). Note that the Südtirol Guest Pass does not cover this bus (or other buses that run above Seis/Siusi).

**Transit Passes:** For short-time visitors, most passes don't make sense. If you're here for three or more days, the Combi Card pass covering the Seiser Alm Bahn gondola and area buses can be worthwhile. Consider the Seiser Alm Card Gold pass only if you're staying for a week. Ask at a TI or your hotel for details.

**Missed the Last Gondola Down?** If you don't make the last gondola off the meadow, you can walk about 2.5 hours to Castelrotto (via St. Valentin) or about 2 hours to Seis for buses to Bolzano—or call a taxi (about €35 to Castelrotto; the *Living the Dolomites* booklet has mobile numbers for taxi services—call one of those listed for the Seiser Alm).

## GETTING AROUND THE ALPE DI SIUSI

**Shuttle Buses:** The plateau is essentially car-free, except for guests staying at a few hotels inside the park. The #11 shuttle bus takes visitors to and from key points along the tiny road between Compatsch—the gateway to the Alpe di Siusi—and Saltria, at the foot of the postcard-dramatic Kofel/Sasso peaks and the base of the Florian lift (2-3/hour mid-June-mid-Oct, fewer mid-May-mid-June and in late Oct, runs about 8:40-18:40—but double-check before heading out, 15 minutes from Compatsch to Saltria, €2, not covered by Südtirol Guest Pass, buy ticket at vending machines at the station or pay driver, www.silbernagl.it). At the end of the day, buses back from Saltria can be jam-packed, and may be too full to pick up passengers between Saltria and Compatsch. Bus #14 serves some hotels on the meadow but isn't helpful for points in this chapter.

**Gondolas and Chairlifts:** Five upper lifts (marked on maps) are worth the €7-12 per ride to get you into the higher and more scenic hiking areas expeditiously (or back to the shuttle buses quickly). The Puflatsch lift takes credit cards, but as of my last visit, the others are cash only. Keep in mind that the upper lifts stop running fairly early (typically at about 17:00; the Seiser Alm Bahn gondola from Compatsch down into the valley runs until 18:00 most of the year—and until 19:00 in high season). Check schedules locally and plan your day accordingly.

# Orientation to Compatsch Village

Compatsch (about 6,000 feet), at the entrance to Alpe di Siusi, isn't quite a "village," but rather a collection of hotels and visitor services. The upper station of the Seiser Alm Bahn gondola has WCs and a few shops and eateries, but most services cluster around a parking lot about five minutes away (including the TI, ATMs, restaurants, bike rental, small grocery store, and shops; from the top of the gondola, it's to the right).

Make a point to stop by the **TI,** which sells maps and has the latest on snow conditions and trail openings. If considering a demanding hike, review your plan here (Mon-Fri 8:15-12:30, Sat until 12:00, closed Sun, tel. 0471-727-904, www.seiseralm.it).

## HELPFUL HINTS

**Trekking-Pole Rental:** Most of the hikes here have at least some bits with uneven or gravely footing—poles can be nice to have along (rentals—€4-5/day, used poles available to buy for about €10, at nearly every sport shop on either end of the Seiser Alm Bahn gondola).

**Bike Rental:** Two shops offer standard, performance, and electric bikes, along with helmets, maps, and trail advice, and have roughly similar prices (standard bike—€14/1 hour, €28-30/day; performance or electric bike—€43-49/day). **Sporthaus Fill** is by the cable-car station (tel. 0471-729-063, www.sporthausfill.com) and **Sport Hans** is across from the parking lot, and is slightly pricier (tel. 0471-727-824, www.sporthans.com, Hans and son Samuel). There's a world of tiny paved and gravel lanes to pedal. Pick up their suggested routes and consider the ones I describe later. Rentable baby buggies are popular for those hiking with toddlers.

**Groceries:** **Onkel Eugen's,** a tiny store across from the parking lot, has necessities (open early June-mid-Oct and Dec-Easter 9:00-17:30).

**Horse-Drawn Carriage Rides:** These are available next to the TI (May-Oct 9:00-16:00, from €55/hour, from €80 to Saltria, price depends on size of carriage).

# Activities in the Alpe di Siusi

## HIKING

Easy meadow walks abound on the Alpe di Siusi, giving novice hikers classic Dolomite views from manicured trails. Experienced hikers should consider the tougher, more exciting treks. Before attempting a hike, call or stop by the TI to confirm lift schedules and check your under-standing of the time and skills required. As always, when hiking in the mountains, assume weather can change quickly, and pack accordingly (wear good shoes and carry water and an extra layer). Meadow walks, for flower lovers and strollers, are pretty—

but for advanced hikers, they can be boring. Chairlifts are spring-boards for more dramatic and demanding hikes. Upper lifts generally close at 17:00.

Trails are very well-marked with wooden signposts pointing to mountain huts (*Hütte* in German, *rifugi* in Italian), which offer food and, often, beds. The number on the arrow is the number of the trail; the number near the destination name is the approximate time in minutes. In theory, the trail numbers are keyed into local maps. In practice, trail numbers on signs don't always match the numbers shown on maps. Instead, navigate by knowing your huts, which are clearly labeled on all signage and maps. (When asked for directions, most locals will know the trail by the huts it connects rather than its number.) For simple hikes, you can basically string together three or four names off the free pictorial map in the *Living the Dolomites* brochure. For anything more serious, invest in a good 1:25,000 map from the TI (about €5). The Alpe di Siusi website (www.seiseralm.it) has more information (click on "Summer," then "Hiking").

**Low-Exertion Excursions:** Besides hiking, there are fun ways to bask in the high-alpine beauty with minimum huffing and puffing. From the two lift stations near Compatsch you could ride the Puflatsch and/or Panorama lifts up on a round-trip ticket, look at the views, enjoy a restaurant meal or picnic at the top, and simply ride back down. You could also ride the #11 shuttle bus from Compatsch to Saltria (or walk there, described later) and take a round-trip ride on the Florian chairlift before riding back to Compatsch.

**Shoulder-Season Strategies:** The Seiser Alm Bahn gondola up to Compatsch starts running in mid-May, but upper lifts begin operating a few weeks later; there's a similar gap at the end of the season (mid-Oct–early Nov). But even during these shoulder seasons, the Alpe di Siusi can still be worth visiting (and busy with hikers) in good weather. Many of the hikes listed here are doable without a lift—but only if you're willing to hike to the trailhead (most realistic for the "Trail of the Witches" and the Panorama-to-Zallingerhütte route). Get local advice about snow levels and which hikes are possible. The simplest option is to hike trail #30 or ride bus #11 along the valley floor between Compatsch and Saltria, enjoying the views along the way.

**Hiking Club:** If you're headed up into the mountains, the Alpenverein Südtirol, a local hiking club, provides good, free trail maps for the whole region on its website (www.trekking.suedtirol.info).

## Easy Hikes

### ▲Compatsch to Rauschhütte (and Saltria)

Bus #11 connects Compatsch to Saltria (at the far end of Alpe di Siusi, tucked under Langkofel and Plattkofel) in about 15 minutes—zipping past some impressive scenery en route. For a very easy, mostly level walk, follow this same route by foot, in about one hour one-way (returning on the bus) or 1.5 hours round-trip (using trail #30, which parallels the route). To begin, leave the top gondola station via the stairs to the road that leads under the view terrace to the TI. From the TI, follow the road for a few minutes (with the gondola station behind and to your right) to the modern wood chapel, then follow signs pointing off the road to the #30 trail.

The last stretch—into Saltria—is steeply downhill and has less impressive views; consider going only as far as **Rauchhütte** (a charming old hut serving good food, spectacular views, closed Wed), located where the road starts to switchback down. Bus #11 stops at various points along this route (including Rauchhütte and Ritschhütte)—making it easy to do as much or as little of this by foot as you like. (Saltria is not a good destination on its own: It's a steep walk below Rauchhütte and has hotels, trailheads, and a bus stop, but no shops.)

### ▲▲▲The "Trail of the Witches"

This three-hour loop trail—past the legendary stone "witches' benches" *(Hexenbänke)*—is popular with first-time visitors and can be crowded in peak season. You'll enjoy ever-changing views as you get a handy 360-degree panorama of the peaks and valleys that ring the Alpe di Siusi. It's mostly downhill, with a few brief uphill stretches.

From the top of the Seiser Alm Bahn gondola, ride the €6.50 Puflatsch gondola (or chairlift, depending on weather) up to Puflatsch Berg (6,952 feet). A two-minute walk above the lift, an engraved map at the Engelrast ("Angel's Rest") observation point identifies the surrounding mountains. The counterclockwise hike follows *PU/Puflatsch* signs around the rim of the Puflatsch plateau. First you'll have Langkofel and Plattkofel on your right as you hike gently but steadily uphill. Eventually you'll hit a little cross overlooking the valley village of St. Ulrich/Ortisei (far below in Val Gardena), then hook left and trace the dramatic rim of the plateau. Soon tiny Castelrotto pops into view, then you'll pass Arnikahütte (with a café), and finally you'll head back toward the Schlern. Near the end of the loop, you can either hike steeply back up to the Engelrast/Puflatsch Berg lift, or—better and easier— keep going downhill all the way into Compatsch, with fine valley views the entire time.

**Note:** If you're here when the upper lifts aren't running (or even in the early evening, assuming you're staying in Compatsch or have a car for returning to the valley after the main lift stops running), this is your most realistic and rewarding option. But be ready for a very steep 30-minute uphill hike to the top of the Puflatsch lift to begin the hike.

## Moderate Hikes
### ▲▲▲Panorama to Zallingerhütte and Florian Chairlift

This walk on well-marked trails is a great introduction to the Alpe di Siusi. While it starts and ends at about the same altitude, it includes plenty of ups and downs. It comes with fine vistas, changes of scenery (meadows, woods, and high valleys), fun stops along the way, and lifts up and down on each end. Though signs rate it at three hours without stops, allow five or six hours (including the lift from Compatsch, lift down to Saltria, and bus back to Compatsch) so you'll have time to dawdle, yodel, and eat.

Start by riding the Panorama chairlift (€6.50) from its base near Compatsch (the Panorama lift is on your right as you walk down the gravel path from the Seiser Alm Bahn's terrace). From the Panorama hut (6,600 feet), find the signpost pointing toward trail #2, and follow it across the meadow to the paved road, and then join trail #7. You'll pass the rustic Edelweisshütte (snacks only), and the Almrosenhütte (hot food); after about 1.5 hours total you'll reach the Mahlknechthütte (6,739 feet, hot food and plenty of outside seating).

From the Mahlknechthütte, you'll cross two streams (one on stepping stones, another by bridge). Shortly after the bridge, you hit the highest point of the walk, just below a small wooden church (Dialer Kirchl, 7,037 feet) that makes a good picnic spot. Continuing on trail #7 from just below the church, you'll go gently through woods, mostly downhill, for another hour and a quarter to Zallingerhütte (6,683 feet). From here it's a serious 10-minute climb to Williamshütte (6,890 feet, full restaurant), where you catch the Florian chairlift (€11.50 one-way) to Saltria and the shuttle-bus stop (return to Compatsch on bus #11).

**High Route to Zallingerhütte:** For a more thrilling, demanding version of the previous hike—longer by two hours—branch off at the wooden church (Dialer Kirchl) following trail #4B and then the high #4 ridge trail, with commanding views both left and right, to the Plattkofelhütte/Rifugio Sasso Piatto hut (7,544 feet, excellent lunches, tel. 0462-601-721). Then descend steeply to Zallingerhütte and Williamshütte (6,890 feet). No special experience or gear is needed for this trail, and it richly rewards those who take it.

Serious hikers can hike a steep and satisfying hour from the Plattkofelhütte to the peak of Plattkofel/Sasso Piatto.

## Challenging Hikes
### ▲▲▲Schlern Summit
For a serious 12-mile hike—with a possible overnight in a traditional mountain refuge (generally open mid-June-Sept)—consider hiking to the summit of Schlern (Sciliar). This route, which takes about eight hours round-trip (including lunch) from Compatsch, is popular with hardy hikers; some call it the best hike in the region.

Start at the €6.50 Spitzbühl chairlift, a 20-minute walk below Compatsch (5,659 feet, free parking, Castelrotto-Compatsch bus stops here), which brings you up to 6,348 feet. Trail #5 takes you through a high meadow, down to the Saltner dairy farm (6,004 feet—you want the Saltner dairy farm at Tschapit, not the one near Zallingerhütte), across a stream, and steeply up the Schlern mountain. About three hours into your hike, you'll meet trail #1 and walk across the

rocky tabletop plateau of Schlern to the **Schlernhaus** mountain "hut," really a simple restaurant and 120-bed hostel (7,544 feet, called "Rifugio Bolzano" in Italian). From this dramatic setting, you can enjoy a meal and get a great view of the Rosengarten range. Hike 20 more minutes up the nearby peak (Monte Pez, 8,400 feet), where you'll find a lofty meadow, cows in the summer, and the region's ultimate 360-degree alpine panorama. Unless you're staying overnight, hike back the way you came.

**Overnight Option:** To do the Schlern summit hike as an overnight, either sleep at the ¢ **Schlernhaus** (bunks and private rooms, open early June-mid-Oct, coin-op shower, summer-only tel. 0471-612-024, off-season tel. 0471-724-094, can reserve by email before

DOLOMITES

hut opens in June, www.schlernhaus.it, info@schlernhaus.it) or walk two hours farther along the Schlern to the hut at ¢ **Tierser Alpl,** at 8,006 feet (bunks and private rooms, open June-late Oct, tel. 0471-727-958, mobile 333-654-6865, www.tierseralpl.com, info@tierseralpl.com). From Tierser Alpl, you can descend to Saltria or Compatsch by any of several different scenic routes.

## TRAIL RUNNING

The Running Park Seiser Alm includes 46 miles of signed running trails in the meadow. The clean air and high mountain altitude attract many international runners/masochists. During a one-day, scenic half-marathon on the first Sunday of July, they invite the public to run with them...or at least try. Contact the Compatsch TI for trail info and maps, or go to www.seiseralm.it and click on "Summer," then "Running."

## BIKING

Bikes are easy to rent (including electric ones—see "Helpful Hints," earlier), welcome on many lifts for free or a small fee, and permitted on many of the trails and lanes in Alpe di Siusi. The Compatsch TI has a good information flier that lists the best routes. You can also go to www.seiseralm.it and click on "Summer," then "Bike," then "MTB Trails." Get local advice to confirm difficulty levels and your plan before starting any ride; the TI hands out helpful bike-route cards. Those with a bike don't need to worry as much about lifts shutting down early.

For a fairly easy, 2.5-hour ride that gives you the same scenic thrills as the "Panorama to Zallingerhütte and Florian Lift" hike recommended earlier, try this: Start from Compatsch (6,048 feet), bike or ride the lift to Panorama (6,600 feet), and take road #7, which runs generally uphill to Goldknopf and then follows a series of hills and dips to Mahlknechthütte (6,739 feet). Then take road #8 downhill to Saltria (5,544 feet) and back to Compatsch (6,048 feet). About 60 percent is paved and 40 percent is gravel lanes.

# More Sights in the Dolomites

### ▲▲Mountain Drive from Venice to Bolzano

Between Venice and Bolzano, most drivers just take the expressway through Verona. But going across the mountains gives you the definitive Dolomite experience. You'll take the Venice-Belluno autostrada, then this route: Belluno-Cortina-Pordoi Pass-Val di Fassa-Bolzano (about 125 miles). If you aren't traveling in summer, check road conditions before you depart (call 0471-200-198, in Italian or German only).

## ▲▲Short Dolomite Loop Drive

You could spend a day from Bolzano or Castelrotto driving a loop over the scenic Sella Pass (Sellajoch, Passo di Sella)—it's about 70

miles on windy roads, so allow four hours. Note that on certain summer days, traffic on the pass may be limited to buses and bikes. Confirm the route is open to drivers by talking to a local TI or your hotelier before heading out.

Going clockwise, you drive first through a long valley, the Grödner Tal/Val Gardena, which is famous for its skiing and hiking resorts, traditional Ladin culture (notice the trilingual road signs), and woodcarvers (the woodcarving company ANRI is from the town of St. Cristina). You'll first reach the large town of St. Ulrich/Ortisei, with base stations for two different cable cars. One heads up to the Alpe di Siusi; the other—among the most dramatic experiences in the Dolomites—rides up to Seceda, where you're dropped at the edge of a thrilling cliff with unforgettable ridge walks and jaw-dropping views. A ski area in winter, Seceda is a meadow in summer, with lots of enticing trails (www.seceda.it).

An hour beyond St. Ulrich/Ortisei, you'll reach Sella Pass (7,349 feet). After a series of tight hairpin turns a half-mile or so over the pass, you'll see some benches and cars. Pull over and watch the rock climbers. Over the pass is the town of Canazei, with nice ambience and altitude (4,642 feet).

If you'd like to take a ridge hike, a gondola runs from Canazei to a hillside shelf called "Pecol"; from there a cable car runs up to Col dei Rossi Belvedere. From the top cable-car station you can hike the Viel del Pan trail past Rifugio Belvedere and Rifugio Fredarola along an easy-but-breathtaking ridge to Rifugio Viel del Pan. This three-hour round-trip hike has views of the highest mountain in the Dolomites—the Marmolada—and the Dolomighty Sella range.

From Canazei, you can either follow very twisty roads (via St. Zyprian and Tiers) back to Castelrotto, or take the easier and slightly faster route via Welschnofen and Birchabruck back to Bolzano and the main valley highway.

**Bus Option:** It's possible to experience the Sella Pass without a car by riding a bus from Castelrotto via St. Ulrich/Ortisei and

Plan to the base of the Col dei Rossi cable car (about 2 hours one-way). Get details at the TI.

### Brixen (Bressanone)

This charming small city (pop. 20,000), on the highway between Bolzano and Innsbruck, is a worthwhile pit stop (park at garage P2 and take the pedestrian underpass into the old town; the main square is a 5-minute stroll away). With an illustrious history of powerful bishops—and a sleepy present—Brixen feels like a charming, mini Bolzano with a bit more Germanic character. It has a sprawling, traffic-free old town; a big main square with two stately churches (connected by a fine cloister); arcaded shopping streets; and plenty of al fresco cafés and restaurants. Explore the lanes beyond the main square to find a beautiful waterside walking and biking path.

**Near Brixen:** More impressive than any sight in Brixen itself, the **Kloster Neustift** (Abbazia di Novacella)—just two miles north—is an Augustinian monastery complex that's open to the public. The centerpiece is a basilica with the region's most glorious Bavarian-style Baroque interior—slathered with decadent white and pink stucco, frilly curlicues, twisty columns, and pudgy winged babies everywhere. While a quick stroll through the grounds and a look at the church interior is plenty satisfying, you can also take a guided tour or try the monk-made wines in the *enoteca* (tel. 0472-836-189, www.kloster-neustift.it).

### ▲Reifenstein Castle (Castel Tasso)

Reifenstein Castle, with one of my favorite castle interiors in Europe, is just off the highway at the town of Sterzing/Vipiteno. While easy for drivers, it's not worth the trouble for those without wheels—it's unique and interesting but only open for a few tours a day. The castle is privately owned and has not been developed for tourism (no gift shop, no café—and no photos). Its layout and decor have changed little since the 15th century, when it passed into the hands of the Teutonic Knights. Since 1813, a branch of the noble Thurn and Taxis family has owned the castle. The current heads of the family (an elderly brother and sister) live in Innsbruck, and have chosen to keep the castle just as it was when they spent summer vacations here in the 1940s as children. On your tour, you'll see most of the building, including bedrooms with original wall paneling and decorations, a real dungeon, wooden boxes knights slept in, and a medieval kitchen with a roof that is black with centuries of soot.

**Cost and Hours:** €8 for required guided tour, German/Italian tours run April-Oct Sun-Fri usually at 10:30, 14:00, and 15:00, with 16:00 tour added mid-July-Aug; no tours on Sat (call ahead to confirm tour times; 4-person minimum or you can pay the extra admission prices). English speakers can join any tour (using promised audioguide—confirm availability) or book an English tour in advance (offered Sun and Wed at 15:00, call number below to reserve). Show up punctually at drawbridge at your tour time (mobile 339-264-3752—call between 8:00-10:30, 11:30-14:00, or 17:00-20:00; www.sterzing-ratschings.com, choose "Activities," then "Sightseeing"). The castle caretaker-guides (Herr Splendori and Frau Steiner) also offer one-hour private tours in English by appointment for a reasonable price.

**Getting There:** By car, the castle is about 45 minutes from Bolzano, Castelrotto, and Innsbruck. Exit the Innsbruck-Bolzano expressway at Sterzing/Vipiteno (just on the Italian side of the Brenner Pass and Austrian/Italian border), and carefully follow brown *Reifenstein* signs. Park at the base of the castle's rock (in the spot right off the road from the bridge) and hike up the castle drive (10 minutes). Of the two castles here, Reifenstein is the one to the west of the expressway.

### ▲High-Alpine Route Between Como and the Dolomites

Between the Dolomites and Lake Como, the scenic high road (SS-38, via Meran and Bormio) is about 1.5 hours slower than the expressway through Verona. The high point is the incredible 9,045-foot Stelvio Pass (Passo dello Stelvio; Stilfser Joch in German), which makes the extra time worthwhile, at least for thrill-seeking drivers (the 48 hairpin curves on the Lake Como side are not for the faint of heart). The pass is generally open June-October, but can close in bad weather (check road conditions at www.bormio.eu). The pass also closes to vehicles except bikes one Saturday in August or September. On the way, you can stop for a meal in the cute, untouristed little town of Glurns (Glorenza in Italian, 45 minutes west of touristy Meran, www.glurns.eu). Glurns still lives within its square wall on the Adige River, with a church bell tower that has a thing about ringing, typical Tirolean arcaded streets, and real farms rather than tourist boutiques.

# THE LAKES

*Lake Como • Varenna • Bellagio • Lake Maggiore*

Commune with nature where Italy is joined to the Alps, in the lovely Italian lakes district. In this land of lakes, the million-euro question is: Which one? For the best mix of accessibility, scenery, and offbeatness, Lake Como is my choice—and I stay in the village of Varenna. The town of Bellagio on the same lake is a good second choice. And Lake Maggiore is a suitable backup. Enjoying either place, you'll get a complete dose of Italian-lakes wonder and aristocratic-old-days romance.

You could spend a busy day side-tripping from Milan (about one hour away by train) to either lake, do some island- and villa-hopping, and be home in time for dinner. But the lakes are an ideal place to slow down and take a break from your busy vacation. Settle in here, and bustling Milan doesn't even exist. Now it's your turn to be *chiuso per restauro* (closed for restoration). If relaxation's not on your agenda, the lakes shouldn't be either.

## Lake Como

Lake Como (Lago di Como)—lined with elegant 19th-century villas, crowned by snowcapped mountains, and busy with ferries, hydrofoils, and slow, passenger-only boats—is a good place to take a break from the intensity and turnstile culture of central Italy. It seems like half the travelers you'll meet have tossed their itineraries into the lake and are actually relaxing.

Lake Como is Milan's quick getaway, and the sleepy mid-lake village of Varenna is the handiest base of operations. With good

connections to other mid-lake towns (and Milan), Varenna is my favorite home base for exploring the lake. While Varenna has a village vibe, beautiful Bellagio has earned its ritzy allure and feels a bit more like a resort.

The hazy, lazy lake's only serious industry is tourism. In fact, every day lots of lakeside residents commute to work in Lugano, just across the border in Switzerland, for a good paycheck. The lake's isolation and flat economy have left it pretty much the way the 19th-century Romantic poets described it: heaven on earth.

## PLANNING YOUR TIME

Even though there are no essential activities, plan for at least two nights so you'll have an uninterrupted day to see how slow you can get your pulse. Spend some time exploring your home base town, take my self-guided ferry tour to view the scenery (with visits to the lake's two main villas), and hop off the boat to poke around the town you're not staying in. With additional time, visit more lakeside villas or go for a hike.

Lake Como is also workable as a day trip from Milan. Take a

morning train to Varenna, ride the boat to Lenno (and tour Villa Balbianello), then take a boat to Villa Carlotta to tour the gardens. From there, head either to Bellagio or back to Varenna to linger and explore (or, with more time and energy, see a little of both) before taking the train back to Milan from Varenna. Start early to pack everything in; otherwise, you'll have to be more selective (with time to see just one of the villas).

## GETTING TO LAKE COMO

**By Train via Varenna:** From any destination covered in this book, you'll reach Lake Como via Milan. The quickest, easiest, and cheapest way to get from Milan to any mid-lake town is to take the train to Varenna. From Varenna you can hop on a boat to Bellagio.

At Milano Centrale train station, catch a train heading for Sondrio or Tirano—sometimes the departure board also says "Lecco/Tirano." (Tirano is often confused with Torino...wrong city.) All Sondrio-bound trains stop in Varenna, as noted in the fine print on the *partenze* (departures) schedule posted at Milan's train station. Trains leave Milan nearly hourly at :20 past most hours (confirm times at station or at www.trenitalia.com). Get a second-class ticket, since most of these trains don't have first-class cars. If you plan to head back to Milan on the train, also buy a return ticket. Stamp your ticket or risk a fine.

Leaving Milan, sit on the left for maximum lake-view beauty. Get off at Varenna-Esino-Perledo. (Train schedules list just Varenna or Varenna-Esino, but *Varenna-Esino-Perledo* is what you'll see at the platform.) The long trains that serve Varenna's tiny station stop only briefly—be ready to hop out. The platform is very short, and your car may actually stop before or after the platform. Look out the window. If even part of the train is at the station, you'll need to get out and walk. Tips: Board midtrain to land next to a platform. Leave from the door through which you entered, since you know it's working. If necessary, pull hard on the red handle (or push the button) to open the door.

**By Train and Boat via Como:** For a less convenient, slower, but more scenic trip, you can get to Varenna or Bellagio from Milan via the town of Como. Trains take you from Milan to Como (2/hour, 45 minutes). From the station in Como, it's a 10-minute walk to the dock, where you catch either the speedy hydrofoil or the leisurely *battello* (slow boat—great for enjoying the scenery) for the ride up the lake to Bellagio or Varenna. Boats leave Como about every 2 hours (*battello:* €11.60, 2.5 hours, last departure about 15:20; hydrofoil: €16.20, 1 hour, last departure about 19:00, fewer on Sun, www.navigazionelaghi.it).

**By Plane via Milan's Airports:** To reach Milan's Centrale train station, take the Malpensa Express train from Malpensa

LAKES

---

## Boat Schedule Literacy

**Boats**
*Traghetto* or *autotraghetto:* Car and passenger ferry
*Aliscafo* or *servizio rapido:* Hydrofoil (pricier, faster, enclosed, and less scenic)
*Battello ship:* Slow passenger-only boat going all the way to Como
*Battello navetta:* Shuttle serving mid-lake only

**Schedules**
*Feriali:* Monday-Saturday
*Festivi:* Sundays and holidays
*Partenze da:* Departing from

---

Airport, an airport express bus from Linate Airport, or any of the buses from Bergamo's Orio al Serio Airport (see "Milan Connections" at the end of the next chapter), and then transfer to a Varenna-bound train (see earlier).

**By Taxi:** Taxis between Varenna and Milan or its airports won't save money over the train, even for groups, but can be worth it for the convenience. **Marco Barili** (and his wife Nelly) don't charge extra for baggage or early/late departures (€170 to central Milan for up to 4 people, €220 for 5-8 people in a minivan, €160/€210 to Linate Airport, €170/€220 to Malpensa Airport, tel. 0341-815-061, mobile 348-550-0787, taxi.varenna@tiscali.it).

## GETTING AROUND LAKE COMO

**By Boat:** Boats go about every 30-45 minutes between Varenna and Bellagio (€4.60/hop, cash only, 15-minute ride, daily approximately 7:00-22:30). If you're staying in one of these towns, you'll probably limit your cruising to this scenic mid-lake area. Express boats cost a little more and save only a couple of minutes per leg. Because boats are frequent and the schedule is hard to read, I just show up, buy a ticket for the next boat, and  wait. Always ask which slip *(pontile)* your boat will leave from—it's not posted, and Bellagio has several docks (boat info: tel. 031-579-211, www.navigazionelaghi.it). On sunny days, long lines can form at ticket booths; don't dillydally, and consider buying your tickets in advance at a quieter time. The one-day €15 mid-lake pass makes

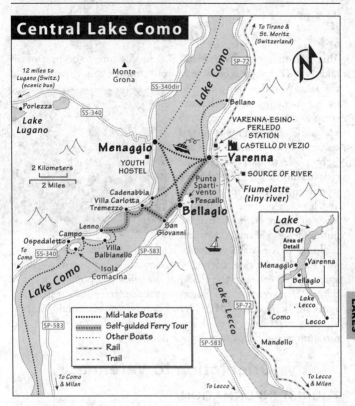

sense if you take four or more rides—unlikely (pass does not cover fast hydrofoils).

If you're making more complex plans, pick up a free **boat schedule** and ask for help to decipher it. It's a good idea to ask your hotelier to review your possible connections before you set out so you can pace your day smartly. You'll find the schedule at hotels and boat docks. Confusingly, the schedule requires you to scan four different timetables to know all the departures; for key terms, see the sidebar.

**By Car:** With scarce parking, traffic jams, and expensive car ferries, Lake Como is no place to drive. While it's possible to drive around the lake, it's not a scenic loop: The road is narrow, congested, and lined with privacy-seeking walls, hedges, and tall fences. If you do have a car, park it in Varenna's big underground garage, and use the boat to get around. Parking in Bellagio is more difficult than in Varenna.

While you can rent cars in Bellagio, for most travelers, it's best to take the train to Milan and pick up a car there, either at the central train station or at one of Milan's three airports.

# Varenna

This well-manicured village of 800 people offers the best of all lake worlds. Easily accessible by train, on the less-driven side of the lake, Varenna has a roman-  tic promenade, a tiny harbor, steep and narrow stepped lanes, and some scenic sights (a ruined castle and two villas). It's just the right place to savor a lakeside cappuccino or *aperitivo*. There's wonderfully little to do here, and it's very quiet at night...unless you're here during one of the hundred-or-so annual American wedding parties. The *passerella* (lakeside promenade, well-lit and inviting after dark) is adorned with caryatid lovers pressing silently against each other in the shadows. Varenna is a popular destination with my readers and European vacationers—book well in advance for high season (May-Oct). From November to mid-March, Varenna practically shuts down: Hotels close for the winter, and restaurants and shops reduce their hours.

## Orientation to Varenna

### TOURIST INFORMATION

The TI is near the **main square** (Tue-Sun 10:00-13:00 & 14:00-18:00, closed Mon, shorter hours off-season, just past the bank at Via IV Novembre 7, tel. 0341-830-367, www.varennaturismo. com). The Tivano travel agency, located in the **train station,** also operates as a TI (see "Helpful Hints"). At either TI (or your hotel), pick up a town map and lake info.

### ARRIVAL IN VARENNA

Varenna is small, and pretty much everything is within a 15-minute walk.

**By Train:** From Varenna's train station, follow the blue-painted pedestrian lane down to the main road. If you're heading for the ferry to Bellagio, go straight to the water and turn left; otherwise, turn left along the main road, Via Corrado Venini, and keep rolling uphill into town (a 15-minute walk from the station). If you have a bag with wheels, use the high road rather than the lakeside promenade, which ends in stairs and cobbles.

A **taxi** from the station costs about €10. Reliable Marco Barili (or his wife Nelly) can meet you at the train station if you know your exact arrival time. Look for a flashing sign with your name (tel. 0341-815-061, mobile 348-550-0787, taxi.varenna@tiscali.it).

**By Boat:** The boat dock is close to the train station and a 10-minute stroll north of Varenna's main square and old town.

**By Car:** Don't even try to park on the streets of Varenna; the few spots are mostly reserved for residents. The easiest parking option is the multilevel lot at the south end of town, across from the entrance to Villa Monastero (€2/hour 6:00-22:00, otherwise €1/hour, €20/24 hours).

Parking at Varenna's train station is free overnight, but you'll pay from 8:00 to 20:00 most of the year (€1.50/hour, €13/day, feed coins into meter in center of lot and put ticket on dashboard).

## HELPFUL HINTS

**Travel Agency:** Varenna's travel agency, **I Viaggi del Tivano,** is conveniently located in the train station. In addition to acting as a TI, they sell train tickets and book planes and automobiles (daily 9:00-13:00 & 14:30-18:30; good place to pick up boat schedules, tel. 0341-814-009, www.tivanotours.com, helpful Gaia, Martina, Cristina, and Eleonora). They also offer baggage storage (€5/day), rent e-bikes (€15/2 hours, €30/day), and sell half-day and daylong sightseeing bus and boat tours (including day trips looping through Switzerland).

**Train Tickets:** The train station doesn't have ticket windows. Buy tickets at the **I Viaggi del Tivano** travel agency there (see above). Don't cut it too close, in case there's a line. You can also buy tickets on the town square at the **Barilott** bar/tobacco shop, which is also a lively place to buy a *panino* and/or a glass of wine (daily 7:00-20:00, closed Sun Oct-April, next to Hotel Royal Victoria at Via IV Novembre 6, tel. 0341-815-045, Claudia and Fabrizio).

**Laundry: Lavanderia Pensa Barbara** can wash and dry your laundry in 24 hours with morning drop-off (priced by weight, no self-service, Mon-Fri 9:00-12:00 & 15:00-19:00, Sat 9:00-12:00, closed Sun, Via Venini 31, tel. 340-466-2977). A self-service machine is tucked in the back of the little **"Il Bottaio"** shopping gallery facing the harbor (you'll pay for laundry plus a €1 entry voucher every time you go in/out, voucher covers WC or can be used toward food or drinks at nearby Bar il Molo, daily 8:00-24:00). Another self-service option is just off the **main square,** between the recommended Albergo del Sole and the post office ("change" machine dispenses only tokens, Bar Il Molo can break bills for you, daily 24 hours, Contrada del Prato 10).

**Nightlife?** None. Here your time is better spent taking a lakeside stroll and watching the moonlight dance on the water.

**LAKES**

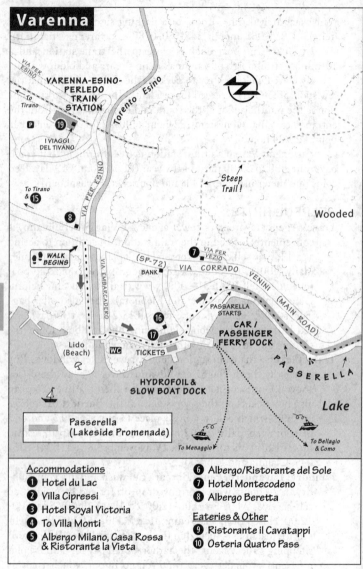

## Varenna

**VARENNA-ESINO-PERLEDO TRAIN STATION**

VIA PER ESINO

To Tirano

P

**19**

I VIAGGI DEL TIVANO

Torento Esino

Steep Trail!

Wooded

To Tirano & **15**

**8**

VIA PER ESINO

👣 **WALK BEGINS**

VIA EMBARCADERO

(SP-72)

BANK

**7** VIA PER VEZIO

VIA CORRADO VENINI (MAIN ROAD)

**16**

**17**

PASSARELLA STARTS

CAR / PASSENGER FERRY DOCK

PASSERELLA

Lido (Beach)

WC

TICKETS

**HYDROFOIL & SLOW BOAT DOCK**

Lake

To Menaggio

To Bellagio & Como

Passerella (Lakeside Promenade)

**Accommodations**
- **1** Hotel du Lac
- **2** Villa Cipressi
- **3** Hotel Royal Victoria
- **4** To Villa Monti
- **5** Albergo Milano, Casa Rossa & Ristorante la Vista
- **6** Albergo/Ristorante del Sole
- **7** Hotel Montecodeno
- **8** Albergo Beretta

**Eateries & Other**
- **9** Ristorante il Cavatappi
- **10** Osteria Quatro Pass

LAKES

## Varenna Walk

Since you came here to relax, this short self-guided walk gives you just the town basics.

• *Begin by standing in the little piazza next to the...*

**Bridge Just Below Train Station:** This main bridge spans the tiny Esino River, which divides two communities: Perledo (which

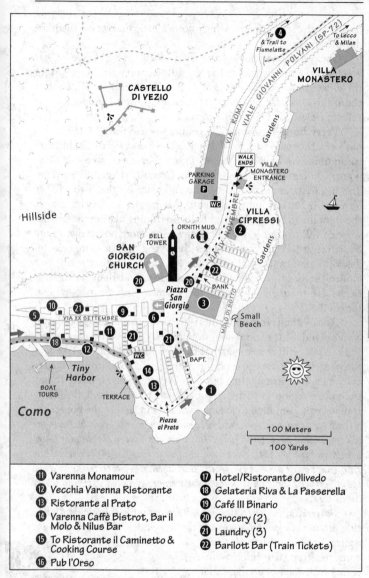

| | | | |
|---|---|---|---|
| ⑪ | Varenna Monamour | ⑰ | Hotel/Ristorante Olivedo |
| ⑫ | Vecchia Varenna Ristorante | ⑱ | Gelateria Riva & La Passerella |
| ⑬ | Ristorante al Prato | ⑲ | Café III Binario |
| ⑭ | Varenna Caffè Bistrot, Bar il Molo & Nilus Bar | ⑳ | Grocery (2) |
| ⑮ | To Ristorante il Caminetto & Cooking Course | ㉑ | Laundry (3) |
| ⑯ | Pub l'Orso | ㉒ | Barilott Bar (Train Tickets) |

sprawls up the hill—notice the church spire high above) and the old fishing town of Varenna (huddled around its harbor). The train station, called Varenna-Esino-Perledo, gives due respect to both, as well as to the village of Esino, eight miles higher in the hills.

Go down the tree-lined promenade on the right (north) side of the river. You'll run into the entrance to the town's public beach—the lido (small fee to enter)—and then cross the cute pedestrian bridge to the small square, which hosts a little market on Wednesday mornings.

The yellow inn facing the ferry dock, Hotel Olivedo, has greeted ferry travelers since the late 19th century and is named for the olive groves you can see growing halfway up the hill. Natives claim this is the farthest north that olives grow in Europe.

• *Across from Hotel Olivedo is Varenna's...*

**Ferry Landing:** Since the coming of the train in 1892, this has been the main link to Milan and the world for the "mid-lake" communities of Bellagio, Menaggio, and Varenna. From this viewpoint, you can almost see how Lake Como is shaped like a man. The head is the north end (to the right, up by the Swiss Alps). Varenna is the left hip (to the east). Menaggio, across the lake, is the right hip (to the west). And Bellagio (hiding behind the smaller wooded hill to your left) is the crotch—or, more poetically, Punta Spartivento ("Point That Divides the Wind"). In a more colorful description, a traditional poem says, "Lake Como is a man, with Colico the head, Lecco and Como the feet, and Bellagio the testicles." (In the regional dialect, this rhymes—ask a native to say it for you.)

Across the lake, the farthest high ridges mark the border of Switzerland. This region's longtime poverty shaped the local character. Many still remember that the Varenna side of the lake was the poorest, because those on the Menaggio side controlled the lucrative cigarette-smuggling business over the Swiss border. Today, the entire region is thriving—thanks to tourism (and the many Italians who commute to jobs in Switzerland, across the border).

• *Walk past the ferry dock, past the small playground, and check out the old traditional boat (on the left). This is an example of the standard lake utility and fishing boat. Men would stand to row (see the oarlocks). The frame supported a canopy—giving some shelter to fishermen who spent the night net fishing. Just beyond is Varenna's elevated shoreline walk, called the...*

**Passerella:** A generation ago, Varenna built this elegant lakeside promenade, which connects the ferry dock with the old town center. Strolling this lane, you'll come to a tiny, two-dinghy, concrete breakwater of a villa. Lake Como is lined with swanky 19th-century villas; their front doors face the lake to welcome visitors arriving by boat. At this point, the modern *passerella* cuts between this villa's water gate and its private harbor. Just  around the bend, enjoy a good Varenna town view. These buildings are stringently protected by preservation laws; you can't even change the color of your villa's paint.

Just over the hump (which allows boats into a covered moorage), look back and up at another typical old villa—with a private *passerella*, a lovely veil of wisteria, and a prime lake-view terrace. Many of these villas are owned by the region's "impoverished nobility." Bred and raised not to work, eventually they were unable to pay for the upkeep of their sprawling houses. Some of these villas have now been bought by the region's nouveau riche.

• *At the community harbor, walk to the end of the pier for a town overview, then continue under the old-time arcades—with chestnut beams and a fishing heritage going back to the 1600s—toward the multihued homes facing the harbor.*

**Varenna Harborfront:** There are no streets in the old town— just the characteristic stepped lanes called *contrade*. Varenna was

originally a fishing community. Even today, old-timers enjoy Lake Como's counterpart to Norwegian lutefisk: *missoltino*, air-dried and salted lake "sardines."

LAKES

Imagine this harbor 200 years ago: The "Il Bottaio" gallery is named for the cooperage—once active with coopers fitting chestnut and oak staves into barrels. Stoneworkers were busy carving the black marble that was quarried just above town. Fishermen dragged boats onto the sloping beach and unloaded their goods onto carts for horses to carry up Contrada dei Cavalli (named for those horses, with gentler, more horse-friendly steps than other lanes) to the market square above. The little stone harbor dates from about 1600. Today, the fishing boats are just for recreation.

At the south end of the harbor, belly up to the banister of Bar il Molo's upper terrace for a colorful town view. Another traditional ditty goes, "If you love Lake Como, you know Bellagio is the pearl...but Varenna is the diamond."

• *Continue straight, leaving the harbor. A lane curves around Hotel du Lac, where you can check out its fine lakeside terrace (it welcomes even nonguests for drinks—try the afternoon happy hour—and has an amazing view). Then climb the stairs (opposite the hotel) on a lane called Contrada Oscura to...*

**Piazza San Giorgio:** Varenna's town square, historically the market square, faces what for centuries has been the lakeside highway. In earlier eras it was busy with traders and pilgrims.

The sycamore, or plane, trees, groomed to provide shade, are planted to make a V for Varenna. The street plan survives from Roman times, when gutters flowed down to the lake. The little church on the lake side of the square is the baptistery. Dating from the ninth century, it's one of the oldest churches on the lake (but rarely open).

The Hotel Royal Victoria, also on the main square, recalls the 1839 visit of Queen Victoria, who registered herself as the Countess of Clare in an attempt to remain anonymous.

**Church of San Giorgio** (Chiesa di San Giorgio): Varenna is an understandably popular spot for weddings—rice often litters the church's front pavement. The main church was built in the 1200s. Imagine being a 13th-century wayfarer and coming upon the fresco of St. Christopher, patron saint of travelers, on the church's facade. With a backpacker—just like you—at his feet, he welcomes you to step inside.

You'll find a Romanesque interior with a few humble, centuries-old bits of carving and frescoes. The black floor and chapels are made from local marble. On the right, a beautifully carved walnut confessional is ornamented with symbols reminding worshippers that in death, all are equal. And the fresco on the back wall, dating from the same century as Dante's *Inferno* (the 14th), makes the horrors of hell all too clear.

• *Leaving the church, turn left to find the TI and the Ornithology and Natural Science Museum, with a small collection of stuffed birds and other wildlife (small fee).*

**Lake and Garden View from Villa Monastero:** Finish your walk a hundred yards farther down the street (past the Villa Cipressi). Across from the big parking garage, step through the door of the Villa Monastero (on the right) and up to the balcony overlooking the garden and the lake: Here you can savor an ultimate Lake Como view.

Lake Como is lined with aristocratic 19th-century villas. In the Romantic Age, a villa came with a charming lakeside kiosk and an extravagant garden. People loved exotic trees, and here—at the latitude of Boston—they could grow palms and oranges. A promenade through this mix of gardens and architecture was enjoyed as an art form.

Your tour is over, and now you have options. You can pay to explore the Villa Monastero gardens (described next page). You can catch the steep trail nearby up to the castle (also described next). Or you can return to the square and head downhill to enjoy the Varenna waterfront. Either of the lanes flanking the Hotel Royal Victoria go down to the humble beach, and farther along, lanes go to the café-lined harborfront.

LAKES

# Sights and Activities in Varenna

### ▲Hike to Vezio Castle (Castello di Vezio)

A steep and stony trail leads to Varenna's ruined hilltop castle, located in the peaceful, traffic-free, one-chapel hamlet of Vezio. It was built on the remains of an ancient Roman fort that was part of a defense system spanning the entire lake. In the sixth century, after the fall of Rome, the barbarian Longobards settled here and needed a fortress on this strategic spot. Today, the castle itself is barren—a courtyard protecting an empty tower, where you can cross a drawbridge and climb 60 steps to earn 360 degrees of Lake Como panoramas.

**Cost and Hours:** €4, Mon-Fri 10:00-18:00, Sat-Sun until 19:00, June-Aug stays open one hour later, March and Oct closes one hour earlier, closed Nov-Feb and in bad weather, mobile 333-448-5975, www.castellodivezio.it, Nicola.

**Visiting the Castle:** To get to the castle, hike up Via per Vezio, the small road near Hotel Montecodeno (figure on a 20-minute steep climb one-way). Arriving in Vezio, follow *castello* signs. You'll reach a bar (with drinks, light food, and WCs) that serves as the castle's ticket desk.

Once inside the grounds, the views are the main attraction: Follow the little loop trail on the lake side of the castle for vistas down on Varenna's rooftops and the adjacent lakefront community of Pino.

The parklike terrace has birds of prey chained to little stakes (an owl, a buzzard, a hawk, and a falcon), each with a medieval name.

**Falconry Shows:** The castle hosts low-key falconry shows (by Nicola, free, for about an hour), usually around 15:00—but check the website or call in the morning for times.

**Hiking Back Down:** Leaving the castle grounds you'll see a sign indicating two ways back to Varenna. You can hike back the way you came or make a loop by continuing down to the east end of Varenna, on a steeper, narrower, less-manicured trail. To do that, from the castle gate turn right and follow signs for *Varenna Scabium* and *Sentiero del Viandante*. You'll wander past some backyards and some scenic tennis courts, then gradually descend, popping out at the parking garage for the Hotel Eremo Gaudio. From here, head down to the right to walk back into Varenna, passing the entrances for both Villa Cipressi and Villa Monastero (described next) on your way to the main square.

### Gardens

Two separate manicured lakeside gardens sit next door to each other just a short distance from Varenna's main square. While the villas and gardens elsewhere on the lake are more magnificent (see

LAKES

"More Sights on Lake Como," later), these are a good option if you're staying around Varenna. An €11 combo-ticket covers the gardens at both villas but not the museum at Villa Monastero.

**Villa Cipressi:** First are the small but lush terraces of Villa Cipressi, which stretch to the nearby Hotel Royal Victoria. The gardens were principally built between 1400 and 1800, and have been carefully restored and embellished. The lakeside climate is amenable to species not otherwise common in northern Italy. Look for agaves, myrtles, and a rare California cypress (€6, €11 combo-ticket includes Villa Monastero gardens but not museum, garden brochure dryly details 56 different trees and shrubs, daily 8:00-sunset, closed Dec-April, www.hotelvillacipressi.it).

**Villa Monastero:** Just beyond are the more interesting grounds of Villa Monastero, which also admits visitors into the former residence of the De Marchi family, now a museum filled with overly ornate furnishings from the late 1800s. It offers the handiest look inside one of the old villas that line the lakeshore, but the lack of information makes the place feel sterile. The gardens feature cypress trees, several varieties of palms, a citrus garden, and a wisteria garden that is delightful when in bloom (gardens-€6, gardens and museum-€9; €11 combo-ticket covers gardens here and at Villa Cipressi but not museum; gardens open daily 9:30-19:00, closed Nov-Feb; museum open Fri-Sun 9:30-19:00, closed Mon-Thu except open daily in Aug; garden bar serves snacks, tel. 0341-295-450, www.villamonastero.eu).

### Swimming

There are three spots to swim in Varenna: the free little beach behind the Hotel Royal Victoria off Piazza San Giorgio, the central lakefront area by Nilus Bar, and the lido (best-equipped for swimmers). Just north of the ferry dock, it's a wide concrete slab with sand and a swimming area off an old boat ramp. It has showers, bathrooms, a restaurant, a bar, and lounge chairs and umbrellas for rent (€3 entry, tel. 0341-815-3700). Swimming by the ferry dock is strictly forbidden for safety reasons.

### Boat Tours (or Rent Your Own)

You can explore the lake either by taking a boat tour with a captain who narrates the views as you skirt elegant villas and the homes of famous neighbors (1-3 hours, 6-10 people on a fast boat) or by renting your own boat (with a 40-hp engine). Renting a boat requires no license. It's not realistic to stop anywhere, so you'll just putter around the mid-lake region trying to stay out of the ferry's path.

**Taxi Boat Varenna** organizes hour-long central-lake tours (€30/person), plus a 2.5-hour version that adds a stop at Villa Balbianello (€60/person, price includes villa entry and one-hour tour). They also offer hour-long romantic private tours (€180 for up to 6 people) and a three-hour tour. Book directly on the website (mid-March–mid-Nov only, mobile 389-949-9104, www.taxiboatvarenna.com). A similar company works out of Bellagio.

**Nautica Varenna,** for those who want to be their own skipper, rents motorboats (from €70/hour, up to 6 people) and zero-horsepower kayaks (€10/hour). You'll find them at the harbor in front of the Nilus Bar (mobile 392-417-0347, www.varennaboatrental.com).

**Varenna Rent a Boat** is a more serious boat-rental shop with a fleet just beyond the ferry dock. Roberto's a mechanic, so you know things are in good shape, and his boats come with GPS systems, so he always knows where you are (from €80/hour, mobile 338-140-7424, www.varennarentaboat.com).

### Hiking

**Wayfarers' Path:** The best three-hour hike from Varenna is along the Wayfarers' Path from Bellano to Varenna. Take the train (or boat) to Bellano and hike steeply up and then along the hill and back into Varenna on the well-marked trail. (Get details from your hotel or the TI.)

**Fiumelatte:** The town of Fiumelatte, about a half-mile south of Varenna, was named for its "milky river." Promoted as the shortest river in Italy (at 800 feet), it runs—like the area's tourist industry—only from April through September (though even then it may be dry, depending on the weather). The *La Sorgente del Fiumelatte* brochure, available at Varenna's TI, lays out a walk from Varenna to the Fiumelatte, then to a castle, and back. It's a 30-minute hike to the source *(sorgente)* of the river (at Varenna's monastery—take the high road, drop into the tranquil and evocative cemetery, and climb steps to the wooded trail leading to the peaceful and refreshing cave from which the river spouts).

**Central Lake Boat, Food, and Villas Tour:** Lake Como Food Tours, run by creative team Laura and Elena, has a selection of guided activities. For a well-organized and very experiential day, consider their "Central Lake Boat, Food, and Villas Tour" (runs most mornings at 10:30 from Varenna). You'll load into a van to visit an old mill for an olive oil tasting, take a guided walk through Varenna with an included lunch, hop in a boat for an hour-long tour of the lake, see Villa Balbianello with a local guide, and finish in Bellagio with a walk through the botanical gardens at Villa Melzi.

**LAKES**

This leaves you in Bellagio at about 17:00 free for the evening and a convenient ferry ride away from your Varenna starting point (€255, RS%—use code "ricksteves" for 15 percent discount on anything they offer, mobile 349-560-0603, www.lakecomofoodtours.com).

### Cooking Course

Charming chef Moreno of the recommended Ristorante il Caminetto picks you up in Varenna, zips you 10 minutes up the mountain to his restaurant, and then teaches you some basics of Italian cooking. Gathered around a big table with a dozen or so other English-speaking travelers, you'll learn how to make fresh pasta and prep regional specialties. Classes cover three recipes and last about three hours, plus time to *mangiare* (€67 includes transfers from and back to Varenna, lesson, recipes, and lunch complete with wine, cookies, and coffee; Mon, Tue, Thu, and Fri; 10:00 pickup from Varenna ferry landing or parking garage, return by 16:00; reservations required, tel. 0341-815-127, www.ilcaminettoonline.com, info@ilcaminettoonline.com).

## Sleeping in Varenna

Reservations are tight in August, snug May through October, and wide open most of the rest of the year. Many places close in winter. High-season prices are listed here; prices get soft off-season.

**$$$$ Hotel du Lac,** filling a refined and modernized 19th-century villa, is classy and dignified. From its exclusive private perch on the point, it offers a quiet lakefront breakfast terrace; genteel public spaces; a friendly, professional staff; and 16 delightful rooms—all but three with lake views (air-con, some rooms with elevator access, pay parking, Via del Prestino 11, tel. 0341-830-238, www.albergodulac.com, info@albergodulac.com, Valleria).

**$$$$ Villa Cipressi** is a sprawling, centuries-old lakeside mansion with 31 rooms (some in a courtyard annex) that have a sophisticated simplicity. The villa sits in a huge, quiet, terraced garden that nonguests pay to see. Its elegant but understated public spaces are often busy with wedding parties. Guests can use their free shuttle service to and from the train station or ferry dock between 9:00 and 16:00 (RS%, some view rooms, family rooms, streetside rooms can be noisy, air-con, elevator in main building, pay parking, Via IV Novembre 22, tel. 0341-830-113, www.hotelvillacipressi.it, info@hotelvillacipressi.it).

**$$$$ Hotel Royal Victoria,** a central splurge facing the main square, has a classic, grand-hotel lobby, an inviting terrace with a swimming pool just above the lake, and 43 richly furnished rooms with modern amenities (RS%, some view rooms, air-con, elevator, pay parking, Piazza San Giorgio 2, tel. 0341-815-111, www. royalvictoria.com, info@royalvictoria.com).

**$$$$ Villa Monti** has six apartments (most with lake views, two with balconies) perched along Via Roma. Each is styled with a modern coziness, sleek kitchenette, and beautiful artwork. The pool is petite but has impeccable views and lots of deck chairs along a terraced garden (family rooms, air-con, no breakfast, check-in 14:00-18:00 or by appointment, Via Roma 11, tel. 0341-168-0161, www.visitvarenna.com, villamonti@vistivarenna.com).

**$$$ Albergo Milano,** right in the old town, is graciously run by Egidio and his Swiss wife, Bettina. Fusing the best of Italy with the best of Switzerland, this well-run, romantic hotel has eight comfortable rooms with extravagant views, balconies, and big terraces (ceiling fans, no elevator; from the station, take main road to town and turn right at steep alley where sidewalk and guardrail break; Via XX Settembre 35, tel. 0341-830-298, www.varenna.net, reservations@varenna.net). This place whispers *luna di miele*—honeymoon (see website for honeymoon deal). Nearby is **$$$ Casa Rossa,** an annex with five comfortable rooms and an apartment that works well for families (breakfast served at main hotel, non-view rooms are more budget-friendly). Their recommended Ristorante la Vista is worth considering for dinner.

**$$$ Albergo del Sole** rents eight simple, comfortable rooms (with partial-lake or piazza views) above a restaurant right on the town square, which can be lively at night. It's run by fun-loving Enzo and Francesco (family rooms, air-con, hardwood floors, shiny bathrooms, elevator, open all year, Piazza San Giorgio 17, tel. 0341-815-218, www.solevarenna.altervista.org, albergo.sole@ virgilio.it).

**$$ Hotel Montecodeno,** with 11 decent rooms and no views, is a functional concrete box along the main road, next to the northern trailhead to Vezio Castle. It's a five-minute walk from the train station and ferries (RS%, air-con, no elevator, attached restaurant, Via Venini 146, tel. 0341-830-123, mobile 340-356-7688, www. hotelmontecodeno.com, info@hotelmontecodeno.com, Marco).

**$ Albergo Beretta,** on the main road a block below the station, has 10 small, basic rooms, several with balconies (and street noise). Second-floor rooms are quietest. Above a coffee shop that doubles as the reception, it feels dated and lacks lakeside glamour but is a decent budget option (elevator, pay parking nearby, Via per Esino 1, tel. 0341-830-132, hotelberetta@iol.it, Barbara).

**LAKES**

# Eating in Varenna

*Lavarello,* a lake whitefish, is popular on menus. For something more adventurous, consider *missoltino,* which are salted little fish often served with pasta or local-style polenta (buckwheat is mixed in with the corn). *Pizzocchere* is a regional pasta dish made with buckwheat noodles, boiled potatoes, greens, and lots of melty cheese—a carb lover's dream. As with Varenna's hotels, many of these restaurants close off-season (generally November through February or March).

## FINEST DINING

**$$$$ Ristorante la Vista,** at Albergo Milano, feels like a private hotel restaurant but also welcomes nonguests. On a balmy evening, its terrace overlooking the town and the lake is hard to beat. Egidio (or Egi—pronounced "edgy") and his staff give traditional cuisine a creative twist, and his selection is great for foodies with discerning tastes. While you can order à la carte, I'd go with his €40 three-course fixed-price dinner (Mon and Wed-Sun 19:00-22:00, closed Tue; reservations required, Via XX Settembre 35, tel. 0341-830-298, www.varenna.net).

**$$$ Ristorante il Cavatappi** serves honest, unpretentious yet beautifully presented dishes grounded in classic Italian cuisine. It's a classy little place on a quiet lane, with only seven tables, so the cook-and-waiter team can connect personally with diners. It's both elegant and intimate with tight and convivial seating under a single vault and three tables outside on the stony lane. The chef is vegetarian, so there's always a good veggie course (Thu-Tue 12:00-14:00 & 18:30-21:00, closed Wed, closed Oct-March, reserve for dinner, Via XX Settembre 10, tel. 0341-815-349, www.cavatappivarenna.it).

## MORE DINING OPTIONS

**$$$ Osteria Quatro Pass** is a welcoming bistro known for its homemade pasta, lake fish, and meat. It offers 18 candlelit tables under picturesque vaults, plus sidewalk seating. Its fun energy lets you know that it's a popular spot (daily 12:00-14:00 & 18:30-22:00, closed Mon-Wed in winter, Via XX Settembre 20, tel. 0341-815-091, Chiara serves while her husband Giuseppe cooks).

**$$$ Varenna Monamour**'s split-level interior, done up with stone and beams, feels sleek but casual. Its menu has a nouvelle-cuisine flair, and the restaurant prides itself on specializing not in lake fish but in seafood (late May-Sept daily 12:00-15:00 & 18:00-23:30, shorter hours off-season, closed mid-Nov-Feb, Contrada Scoscesa 7, tel. 0341-814-016, www.varennamonamour.it).

**$$$ Vecchia Varenna Ristorante,** the only classy restaurant right on the water, is under the old stone arcade in the center of town. Its menu is creative, offers a fine value, and seems to taste even better if you sit on the terrace. Chef Luca takes no reservations (Tue-Sun 12:30-14:00 & 19:30-21:30, closed Mon, Contrada Scoscesa 14, tel. 0341-830-793).

**$$$ Ristorante al Prato,** tucked onto a quiet square a block off the harbor, does regional specialties and international dishes with local ingredients and influences. Chef Giulio's joy of cooking shows through in the meals, and good-natured owner Giovanni enjoys interacting with the guests (daily 12:00-14:00 & 19:00-21:00, Piazza del Prato 6, mobile 348-712-4389).

## FAST FOOD WITH A LAKE VIEW
Beautifully situated along the waterfront in Varenna's old section are three simple eateries: **Varenna Caffè Bistrot, Bar il Molo,** and **Nilus Bar.** All are crowd-pleasers for their great lakefront seating and ideal for lingering over affordable food in a stunning setting. Each serves salads, sandwiches, pizzas, and pastas for around €10 and cocktails between meals. All are open daily; Il Molo and Varenna Caffè Bistrot are also open at 9:00 for breakfast. While Il Molo and Nilus have nicer terraces, the food at Varenna Caffè Bistrot is a bit more serious.

## EATING SIMPLY WITHOUT A LAKE VIEW
**$$ Ristorante del Sole** is an old-school place facing the town square that feels like it was here before tourism. It serves respectable, well-priced meals and Neapolitan-style pizzas. This family-friendly restaurant provides a fun atmosphere, a cozy, walled-in garden in back, and tables on the square. Try their hearty *pizzoc-chere,* a handmade buckwheat pasta with melted cheese, potatoes, and greens (daily 11:00-16:00 & 18:30-late, Piazza San Giorgio 17, tel. 0341-815-218, www.solevarenna.altervista.org; Francesco and Enzo).

**High Above Town: $$$ Ristorante il Caminetto** is a homey, backwoods mountain trattoria in Gittana, a tiny town in the hills above Varenna. Getting there entails a curvy 10-minute drive (they'll pick you up for free at 19:00 or 19:30 at the ferry dock or the parking garage and bring you home after dinner). Moreno and Rossella take pride in their specialties, including grilled meats and risotto with porcini mushrooms and berries. They serve 22 diners a night and that's it. Plan on the €32 three-course fixed-price meal and spending the evening—you won't regret it (open Thu-Tue 19:30-21:30, Sat-Sun also 12:30-14:30, closed Wed, reservations mandatory to confirm pickup from Varenna, Viale Progresso 4, tel. 0341-815-127, mobile 347-331-2238, www.ilcaminettoonline.com).

LAKES

## OTHER EATERIES

**By the Ferry Dock: $$ Pub l'Orso,** filling a renovated former joiner's workshop, is a fun bar that serves cheap salads and sandwiches (at the ferry dock, behind Hotel Olivedo). **$$$ Hotel Olivedo,** a fine old hotel facing the ferry dock, serves diners in a classic Grand Tour hall.

**Gelato:** Side-by-side places on the harborfront compete with good gelato and pillows on the adjacent stone steps. At **Gelateria Riva,** Duilio prepares his gelato fresh every day (ask the day before if you want to watch it being made). Try his *nocciola* (hazelnut) before making your choice (daily 11:00-19:00, later in summer). A few doors down, Giulia at **La Passerella** makes tasty gelato, as well as refreshing fruit sorbets. Also on the menu is an enticing array of pastries and sweets (daily 10:00-20:00, later in summer).

**Scenic *Aperitivo:*** The Hotel du Lac has the most beautiful lakeside setting in town. Anyone is welcome to enjoy its garden or terrace, which literally hangs over the lake, for a happy hour *aperitivo* (daily 15:00-20:00). An €8 *spritz* or glass of wine comes with a plate of meat and cheese. They also have wine tasting on the menu.

**Picnics:** Varenna's two little grocery stores have all you need for a tasty balcony or breakwater picnic. The *salumeria* on the main square is best for meats, cheese, and bread; try their homemade salami (Tue-Sat 8:30-12:30 & 16:00-19:30, Sun-Mon 8:30-12:30 only, Via IV Novembre 2). The **grocery store** just north of the main square by the pharmacy stocks fresh fruits, veggies, and a few essentials (Tue-Sat 8:30-19:00, Sun-Mon until 12:30, shorter hours off-season, Via Venini 6).

**At the Train Station: $ Café III Binario** is both charming and classy, offering fresh salads, homemade pizza, sandwiches, pasta, pastries, and even breakfast. Enjoy your food on their terrace or take it to go (daily 6:00-21:00, closes earlier off-season).

**Breakfast in Varenna:** For a leisurly start to your day on the lakefront, Varenna Caffè Bistrot and Bar il Molo each have a breakfast menu. (They get up and running at about 9:00.) Hotel Royal Victoria and Hotel du Lac offer buffet breakfasts with eye-popping views to nonguests for about €20 (check with reception that morning for availability). If you're catching an early train, Café III Binario offers a good breakfast right at the station. To feel as though you're staying in a boutique guesthouse (with an amazing view terrace overlooking the lake), break your fast at Albergo Milano, which offers visitors the same fine breakfast it serves its guests for €15 (reserve the night before).

# Varenna Connections

## BY TRAIN

Before leaving Varenna, buy your tickets from the I Viaggi del Tivano travel agency in the station. (Or, to avoid lines and stress at the station, buy tickets in advance in the town center at the Barilott bar/tobacco shop just off the main square.) Stamp your ticket in the yellow machine at the station before boarding. If the office is closed and you can't buy tickets, win the sympathy of the conductor and buy your ticket as soon as you get on board for a small additional fee. (Find him before he finds you—or you'll face a €50 fine.)

**Varenna to Milan:** Trains from Varenna to Milano Centrale take about an hour and leave at :37 past most hours (confirm schedule at the station or online at www.trenitalia.com). Additional connections require a change in Lecco and an extra 30 minutes.

**Varenna to Stresa** (on Lake Maggiore): You'll have to take the train back to Milano Centrale, then connect from there to Stresa (3-4 hours).

**Varenna to Lugano** (Switzerland): Catch the ferry to Menaggio and then the bus (about hourly, 1 hour, €6). It's a 10-minute walk into town from the ferry dock and then a bit confusing (buy bus tickets in front of the main church at the La Provincia bar; the bus stop is 100 yards uphill from there).

**Varenna to St. Moritz** (Switzerland): Take the train from Varenna to Tirano (1.5 hours), where you'll have a layover before boarding the scenic Bernina Express train to St. Moritz (another 2.5 hours, 3 connections/day in summer, 1/day late Oct-early May, www.rhb.ch). A quicker, more frequent, but less scenic route is to take the train to Chiavenna (changing in Colico), then transfer to the bus, which takes you over the Maloja Pass to St. Moritz (5-6/day, 3.5 hours total). For times and tickets, stop by the I Viaggi del Tivano travel agency (see "Helpful Hints," earlier). Don't forget your passport for trips into Switzerland. For more about St. Moritz and scenic trains, consider my guidebook *Rick Steves Switzerland*.

LAKES

# Bellagio

The self-proclaimed "Pearl of the Lake" is a classy combination of tidiness and Old World elegance. If you don't mind that "tramp in a palace" feeling, it's a fine place to shop for ties and umbrellas while surrounding yourself with the more adventurous posh travelers. Heavy curtains between the harborfront arcades create welcome shade and keep visitors and their poodles from sweating. Thriving yet still cute, Bellagio is a much more substantial town than Varenna.

## Orientation to Bellagio

### TOURIST INFORMATION

The TI is at the slow boat/hydrofoil dock (daily 9:30-17:30, shorter hours Nov-March, tel. 031-950-204, www.bellagiolakecomo.com). The TI has free brochures for several walking tours, varying from one to three hours. They also sell a hiking map that shows hikes with a range of difficulty and duration.

### ARRIVAL IN BELLAGIO

Bellagio is best reached by boat from Varenna or Como.

**By Boat:** Bellagio has two docks a couple hundred yards apart. One serves slow boats and hydrofoils; the other is for faster car ferries. When you depart, be sure you're at the right dock—ask when you buy your ticket. For details on boat schedules, see "Getting Around Lake Como" near the beginning of this chapter.

**By Car:** Having a car in Bellagio makes little sense. Parking is difficult and the center of town is a no-traffic "ZTL" zone 10:00-18:30—pay attention to signed restrictions. Spaces marked with white lines are always free, yellow lines are for residents only, and blue lines are pay-to-park (use pay-and-display machines—€1.50/hour 8:00-23:00, free overnight). Looking for a free spot is likely a waste of time and energy. Plan on just paying and displaying.

### HELPFUL HINTS

**Laundry: Lavanderia Vecchia** is handy. Don't be discouraged if it looks closed; the lights come on automatically when you enter (daily 8:00-23:00, Salita Carlo Grandi 21, mobile 333-659-9074). You can pass the time at the fun Angelo DiVino wine bar across the way.

**Bellagio to Como by Bus:** An hourly bus runs from the Como

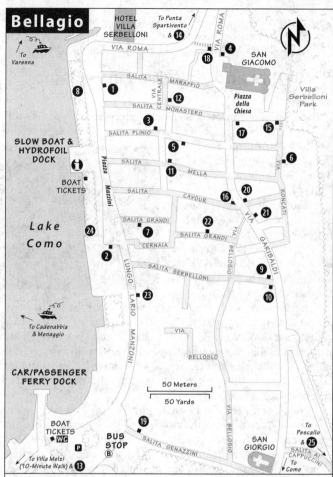

## Accommodations

1. Hotel Florence
2. Hotel/Rist./Snack Bar Metropole
3. Hotel Centrale
4. Albergo Europa
5. Il Borgo Apartments
6. Albergo Giardinetto
7. Hotel Bellagio

## Eateries & Other

8. The Florence Ristorante
9. Trattoria San Giacomo
10. Bilacus Ristorante & Aperitivo Et Al
11. Rist. Terrazza Barchetta
12. La Fontana Ristorante Pizzeria & Antichi Sapori
13. To Alle Darsene di Loppia
14. To La Punta Ristorante
15. Torre del Borgo & Villa Serbelloni Park Tickets
16. Vecchio Borgo
17. Daisy's Bar
18. Albergo Europa Restaurant
19. Enoteca Cava Turacciolo
20. Gelateria del Borgo
21. Grocery
22. Launderette
23. Bar Sanremo (Bus Tickets)
24. Bellagio Water Limousines
25. To Bellagio Water Sports

train station to Bellagio. In Bellagio, buy tickets at Bar San-remo (midway between the two docks, facing the water at Via Lungo Lario Manzoni 40) or pay more from the driver.

# Sights and Activities in Bellagio

### Strolling

Bellagio was built below a medieval fortress that capped its hill (today's Villa Serbelloni Park). The town's chic image was stoked by the Rockefellers (who purchased Villa Serbelloni in 1927) and by John F. Kennedy (who visited in 1961).

The harborfront is mostly fancy shops and cafés designed for visitors. Café Rossi, with a 1905 interior, faces the ferry dock. While Johnnie Walker and jewelry sell best at lake level, the natives shop up the hill.

Explore the steep-stepped lanes rising from the harborfront. Piazza della Chiesa, near the top of town, has an 11th-century church that's worth a look. It's dedicated to Saint James and has a dark, typically Romanesque interior with small windows, a marble pulpit carved with symbols of the four evangelists, and a golden altarpiece under glittering mosaics (pick up the English handout that describes its art).

**North of Town:** The de facto capital of the mid-lake region, Bellagio is located where the two legs of the lake split off to the south. For an easy break in a park with a great view, wander right on out to the crotch. Meander behind the rich-and-famous Hotel Villa Serbelloni, and walk 10 minutes up a concrete alley to **Punta Spartivento** ("Point That Divides the Wind"). You'll pop out to find a Renoir atmosphere complete with an inviting bar-restaurant (see "Eating in Bellagio," later), a tiny harbor, and a chance to sit on a park bench and gaze north past Menaggio, Varenna, and the end of the lake to the Swiss Alps.

**South of Town:** For another stroll, head south from the car-ferry dock down the tree-shaded promenade. Ten minutes later, you'll pass the town's "beach." The Lido di Bellagio is actually a terrace with sand and rentable lounge chairs, a youthful cocktail bar, a concrete pool, and a swimming platform in the lake. Just beyond the lido is **Villa Melzi Gardens** (€6.50, daily 9:30-18:30). While the actual villa is not open to the public, the gardens are, and visitors enjoy a long and lovely lakeside promenade with exotic plants, flowers, and trees (all labeled—pick up the botanical guide at the entry) and Neoclassical sculpture that was assembled by the vice president of Napoleon's Italian Republic in the early 19th century. Although not as elaborate as some of the lake's finer gardens, it offers a pleasant, tree-shaded lakefront stroll. Gaze across the lake at the Villa Carlotta (straight over, surrounded by greenery—described later, under "More Sights on Lake Como") and imagine the time when aristocrats tried to outdo each other (and showcase their wealth) by creating unique and immense horticulture collections.

At the far end of the garden you can exit at the tiny harbor of Loppia, where you'll be tempted by the recommended Alle Darsene di Loppia restaurant. About 15 minutes farther south, you'll reach San Giovanni, with a pebbly public beach (no showers).

### Villa Serbelloni Park

If you need a destination, you can visit this park (accessible only with guided tour), which overlooks the town. The villa itself, owned by the Rockefeller Foundation, is not open to the public.

**Cost and Hours:** €9, required tour Tue-Sun at 11:00 and 15:30; no tours Mon, Nov-mid-March, or when rainy; 1.5 hours, first two-thirds of walk is uphill, show up at the little tour office in the medieval tower on Piazza della Chiesa 15 minutes before tour time to buy tickets, confirm time at office, tel. 031-951-555.

### Boating and Water Sports

**Bellagio Water Limousines,** with a small stand adjacent to the slow boat/hydrofoil dock, is run by Australian Jennine and Italian Luca, who offer tours and private service in their shiny mahogany Venetian water taxi. Consider their one-hour mid-lake tour (€40, most days) or their 2.5-hour mid-lake tour with a stop at Villa del Balbianello (€60, RS%, check blackboard for day's offerings or call mobile 338-524-4914, www.bellagiowaterlimousines.com, bellagiowaterlimousines@gmail.com).

**Bellagio Water Sports** is where Michele offers two-hour kayaking tours (€40, most days at 10:00, weather dependent). He's a 15-minute hike over a hill and down on Pescallo Bay near Hotel la Pergola at Via Sfondrati 1, mobile 340-394-9375, www.bellagiowatersports.com, info@bellagiowatersports.com).

## Sleeping in Bellagio

This is a "boom or bust" lake resort, with high-season prices straight through from May to September, plus a brief shoulder season (with discounted prices) in April and from October to November. Bellagio closes down almost completely from December to February and is only half-open in March.

**$$$$ Hotel Florence** has a prime lakefront setting in the center of town. The 160-year-old place, run by the German Ketzlar family, features 30 rooms, hardwood floors, bold earth tones with splashes of bright colors, and a rich touch of Old World elegance (RS%, some rooms with view and balcony, air-con, elevator, Piazza Mazzini 46, tel. 031-950-342, www.hotelflorencebellagio.it, info@hotelflorencebellagio.it).

**$$$ Hotel Metropole,** dominating Bellagio's waterfront between the ferry docks, is a grand old place with plush public spaces. Its tranquil rooms have classic flair and all the comforts. All 42 rooms have lake views, either side or full (family rooms, air-con, elevator, enormous roof terrace, Piazza Mazzini 1, tel. 031-950-409, www.albergometropole.it, info@albergometropole.it).

**$$ Hotel Centrale,** managed with pride and care by Giacomo Borelli, warmly welcomes its guests into a true-blue family operation: Signore Borelli's two sons help out, his mama painted the art, and grandpa crafted much of the Art Deco-era furniture. Look for old family photos near the stairwell. The 17 bright, comfortable rooms lack views, but the public spaces are generous, including the balcony terrace (air-con, elevator, Salita Plinio 7, tel. 031-951-940, www.hc-bellagio.com, info@hc-bellagio.com).

**$$ Albergo Europa,** run with low energy by a kindly family, is in a concrete annex behind a restaurant, away from the waterfront. Its nine basic rooms (most with balcony) are harmlessly behind the times but get the job done (no elevator, free reserved parking, Via Roma 21, tel. 031-950-471, info@hoteleuropabellagio.it, Marchesi family).

**$$ Il Borgo Apartments** offers seven efficient, spacious units in the old center. Equipped with kitchenettes, these are a great deal for families or small groups. Easygoing Flavio and Silvia are available for check-in daily 11:00-14:00 or by appointment (RS%, cash preferred, no breakfast, air-con, elevator, Salita Plinio 4, tel. 031-952-497, mobile 338-193-5559, www.borgoresidence.it, info@borgoresidence.it).

**$$ Albergo Giardinetto** has 10 simply furnished rooms, barren hallways, and no breakfast, but guests may picnic in the large garden. Most rooms have lake and mountain views. Mother Laura and daughter Chiara (who speaks beautiful English) run the place with gentleness and gratefully welcome guests (air-con, no elevator, closed Oct-April, Via Roncati 12, tel. 031-950-168, www.albergogiardinetto.com, giardinetto@aol.it).

**$$ Hotel Bellagio** is stylish but unpretentious, with 28 airy rooms and parquet floors (some with balconies, most with views). The rooftop deck has sun chairs, and the basement gym is small but mighty (air-con, elevator, pay parking, Salita Grandi 6, tel. 031-952-202, www.hotelbellagio.it, info@hotelbellagio.it).

# Eating in Bellagio

As with Bellagio's hotels, many of these restaurants close off-season (generally December through February or March). Two places associated with hotels serve food on the lakefront in the town center (the Florence and Hotel Metropole's Terrazzo Ristorante). The service won't make you smile, and the price will dent your wallet. But the setting will be unforgettable. Rather than eat on the lakefront, I'd hang out there with a drink and find a better-value restaurant at a higher altitude.

## IN THE OLD TOWN, WITHOUT LAKE VIEWS

**$$ Trattoria San Giacomo** is a high-energy place with traditional North Italian cuisine, such as *riso e filetto di pesce* (rice and perch fillet in butter and sage). It has seasonal specials and inviting €28 fixed-price meals (meat or fish) based on regional specialties. It offers fun seating on a steep, cobbled lane or tight seating inside (Wed-Mon 12:00-14:30 & 19:00-21:30, closed Tue, Salita Serbelloni 45, tel. 031-950-329, www.trattoriabellagio.it).

**$$ Bilacus Ristorante,** across the street, has a brighter, more open dining room, a fine garden terrace, an emphasis on wine (including some top-quality vintages by the glass), and a menu of traditional Italian dishes (Tue-Sun 11:30-15:00 & 18:30-22:00, closed Mon, Salita Serbelloni 32, tel. 031-950-480, www.bilacusbellagio. it). Aurelio is happy to give those with this book a complimentary vin santo and biscotti for dessert.

**$$$ Ristorante Terrazza Barchetta,** set on a terrace with no lake view and bedecked with summery colors, puts a creative twist on regional favorites such as lake fish, but is a little pricey (Wed-Sun 12:00-14:30 & 19:00-22:15, closed Tue, Salita Mella 13, tel. 031-951-389, www.ristorantebarchetta.com). Its simpler and less expensive sister, Terrazza Barchetta, is downstairs (described below).

## GOOD VALUES IN THE OLD TOWN

You'll find these places a short climb above the harbor.

**$$ Ristorante Terrazza Barchetta** is popular for its fun and accessible menu of quality, fairly priced pizza and pasta, and simple indoor and outdoor seating (daily 12:00-22:00, Salita Mella 13, tel. 031-951-389).

**$$ La Fontana Ristorante Pizzeria,** near the top of the old center, serves classic Italian dishes at a great price. It has a tight interior with the ambience of a cafeteria, and a nice terrace (go up Salita Monastero to Via Centrale 7, 031-950-283).

**$$ Antichi Sapori,** next door, is another good budget alternative—a favorite for salads, pizza, and pasta with a warm and cozy

**LAKES**

interior and a fine terrace (daily 11:30-22:00, Via Centrale 5, tel. 031-950-431, Julia and Nico).

## GOURMET SPLURGE SOUTH OF TOWN

**$$$$ Alle Darsene di Loppia,** the kind of place you'd expect jet-setters to dress up for, is a romantic gourmet restaurant serving Mediterranean cuisine with a Michelin rating. Consider their seared scallops and their tasting menu. It's a 15-minute walk south of town (through the exquisite Villa Melzi Gardens—worth paying for if dining here to avoid the walk along the street). While seating indoors is OK, dining out on a historic little harbor under their *pergolato* is more memorable (Tue-Sun 12:00-14:30 & 19:00-21:30, closed Mon, on the far side of the Villa Melzi Gardens at Via Melzi D'Eril in Loppia, tel. 031-952-069, www. ristorantedarsenediloppia.com).

## OTHER OPTIONS

**Dining North of Town: $$$ La Punta Ristorante** is a good bet for a lakeside meal a 10-minute walk north at the dramatic Punta Spartivento. Set in a peaceful park, this family-run, white-tablecloth place has reasonable prices and very fresh fish (daily 12:00-22:00, tel. 031-951-888, www.ristorantelapunta.it).

**Breakfast:** If your hotel or B&B doesn't provide breakfast, consider these options. Clustered near Piazza della Chiesa are several cafés that offer either full breakfast menus or à la carte options at tourist pricing: Pick from **Torre del Borgo, Vecchio Borgo,** and **Daisy's Bar.** Down the street at **Albergo Europa**'s restaurant, you'll find a good-value breakfast for €8.50. **Hotel Metropole** serves a €15 buffet breakfast and waterfront views to nonguests (reserve the night before). For a more reasonably priced buffet breakfast with a view (€8), walk-ins are welcome at **Hotel Bellagio.**

**Wine Tasting: $$ Enoteca Cava Turacciolo** is a classy-for-a-troll vaulted stone cellar wine bar. This fun-loving place run by Norberto and Rosy is great for a last drink before catching your ferry, or a simple meat-cheese-wine meal. They offer my readers a €19 taste of three regional wines with a sampling of cheeses, meats, and breads (Thu-Tue 11:00-24:00, closed Wed, Salita Genazzini 3, tel. 031-950-975, www.cavaturacciolo.it).

**$$ Aperitivo Et Al,** slick and jazzy, is a trendier wine bar; it also offers mixed *salumi* and *formaggi* plates and light lunches paired with the right wine. Andrea serves a great selection of wines by the glass (daily 11:30-24:00, Salita Serbelloni 34, tel. 031-951-523).

**Gelato:** Residents agree that you won't find the best *gelateria* in town among the sundaes served on the waterfront. Instead, climb to the top of town to **Gelateria del Borgo** (daily 10:00-20:00, longer hours July-Aug, Via Garibaldi 46, tel. 031-950-755, Stefania and Gianfranco).

**Picnics:** You'll find benches at the park, along the waterfront in town, lining the promenade south of town, and a 10-minute walk north in the lovely park at the tip of the peninsula (Punta Spartivento). **Butti Macelleria e Salumeria,** on the upper street near the *gelateria*, makes sandwiches and sells a few prepared foods (Tue-Sun 8:00-13:00 & 16:00-19:00, closed Mon, Via Garibaldi 42, tel. 031-950-333).

# More Sights on Lake Como

For the best one-day look at Lake Como, take my self-guided ferry tour to get your bearings, and hop off at the towns and villas of your choice. The two main villas worth considering (described after the tour) are Villa Carlotta—with a sterile, museum-like interior and gorgeous, sprawling gardens—and Villa del Balbianello, a bit harder to reach but with a more striking setting, gardens that are more architectural than botanical, and a fascinating tour of the lived-in interior. If you have time, visit both—they're complementary. In this section, I also describe two other lake towns—Menaggio and Como—plus how to side-trip to Lugano in Switzerland.

### ▲▲Self-Guided Ferry Tour

The best simple day out is to take the *battello navetta* (mid-lake ferry) on its entire 50-minute Varenna-Bellagio-Villa Carlotta-Tremezzo-Lenno route (€9.20 without stops, or buy the €15 one-day pass and make it hop-on, hop-off; generally departs Varenna at 9:23, 10:23, 11:32, 12:13, 15:23, 16:25, and 17:33, confirm times locally; for more informa-tion, see page 232). On the  return trip, hop off at any sights that interest you: Lenno (to see Villa del Balbianello), Villa Carlotta, and/or Bellagio. This com-mentary describes what you'll see along the way, leaving from Va-renna, though it's doable from Bellagio too.

**Leaving Varenna:** Looking back at Varenna from the lake, you'll see Vezio Castle rising above the town, with new Varenna on the left (bigger buildings and modern ferry dock) and old Varenna on the right (tighter, more colorful buildings). The big develop-ment high on the hillside is an ugly example of cronyism (without the mayor involved, this would never have happened). Under the castle is a grove of olives—reputedly the northernmost ones grown in Italy. Because the lake is protected from the north wind, exotic flowers grow well in the lake's many fine gardens. To the right of Varenna's castle are the town cemetery, a lift up to Hotel Eremo Gaudio (a former hermitage), and a spurt of water

gushing out of the mountain just above lake level. This is the tiny Fiumelatte, Italy's shortest river.

• *On your way across to Bellagio, take a look around.*

**Mid-Lake:** The Swiss Alps rise to the north. Directly across the lake from Varenna is Menaggio, and just over the ridge from there are Lugano and the "Swiss Riviera." The winds alternate between north and south. In preindustrial times, traders harnessed the wind to sail up and down the lake. Notice the V-shaped, fjord-like terrain. Lake Como is glacier-cut. And, at more than 1,200 feet deep, it's Europe's deepest lake. You'll cruise past the Punta Spartivento, the bulbous point that literally "splits the wind" and where the two "legs" of the lake join (Lake Lecco is on the left/east, and Lake Como on the right).

• *Before long, you'll be...*

**Approaching Bellagio:** Survey the park at Punta Spartivento—it's a pleasant walk from town. Bellagio has three times the number of hotel rooms as Varenna, as you can see upon approach. The town, with its strip of swanky hotels, is bookended by Grand Hotel Villa Serbelloni (five stars) on the left, dominating the lakefront, and the sprawling Grand Hotel Bretagne (four stars) on the right. In the 19th century, aristocratic Rus-

sians hung out in the Serbelloni, and well-heeled English chose the Bretagne. These days, the Serbelloni is the second-most luxurious hotel on the lake after Villa d'Este, while Bretagne is mired in a long renovation project.

• *Leaving Bellagio, you'll pass Villa Melzi and its gardens, then the tiny harbor at Loppia. About half the boats make a stop at **San Giovanni**, a small, nondescript lakefront community just down the shore from Bellagio. Whether your boat stops here or not, soon you'll head across the lake for a stop at...*

**Villa Carlotta:** Because of lake taxes and high maintenance costs, owners of once-elite villas have been forced to turn them into hotels or to open their doors to the paying public. Since 1927, this has been an example of the latter. One of the finest properties on the lake, Villa Carlotta has some good Neoclassical sculpture (including works by Canova) and one of the lake's lushest gardens (see listing below).

• *The shortest hop on this route (you could walk it in less than 10 minutes) takes you along to the town of...*

**Tremezzo:** As you leave the dock at Villa Carlotta, notice the Grand Hotel Tremezzo, with its striking Liberty Style (Art Nouveau) facade and swimming pool floating on the lake. Above the town is a villa built in the 19th-century Romantic Age to resemble a medieval castle (next to the stub of a real one).

After the Tremezzo stop—and just before the Tremezzo church—you'll see a public park with a fountain and balustrade. When the road separated this land from its villa, its owners gave it to the community. Here the lake is dotted by a string of old villas with elegant landings and gated boathouses. Built in the days before motors, they are now too small for most modern lake boats.

**Lenno:** This pleasant resort town—with a long, arcing bay sheltering lots of little docks, and a generously shaded promenade—is the boat's last stop.

It's decision time: To see the recommended Villa del Balbianello, hop off here and turn to the next page. Return boats depart hourly; check the schedule before you set off. If you'd prefer to sail back to Villa Carlotta, Bellagio, or Varenna, you can probably stay put—this is the end of the line, so the boat's going to turn around and head back that way (but for some departures, you may be evicted and need to wait for the next boat).

### ▲Villa Carlotta

For gardens and flowers (its forte), this is the best of Lake Como's famed villas—especially in spring, when the many flowers are in bloom. For gardeners, it's worth ▲▲▲. I see the lakes as a break from Italy's art, but if you need a culture fix, Villa Carlotta also offers an elegant Neoclassical interior with a sculpture gallery, including works by Antonio Canova.

**Cost and Hours:** €10 includes villa/museum and gardens, daily 9:00-19:30, last ticket sold at 18:30, museum closes at 19:00, shorter hours last 2 weeks of March and Oct, closed Nov-mid-March, tel. 034-440-405, www.villacarlotta.it.

**Getting There:** Villa Carlotta, at the southern end of the town of Tremezzo, has its own ferry dock (served by the *battello* passenger ferries). It's also less than a 10-minute walk from the Tremezzo and Cadenabbia docks (each served by a variety of boats). In a pinch, you can also use bus #C10 to zip along the lakefront to Lenno, near Villa del Balbianello (1-2/hour, pay driver, bus stop to the right as you exit Villa Carlotta).

**Visiting the Villa:** When buying your ticket, pick up the map that identifies the rooms in the house and the major plant groups in the gardens.

From the entrance, hike up the grand staircase and enter the **villa** itself. The main floor is filled with Neoclassical sculpture, including Antonio Canova's *Maddalena Penitente* and *Palamede* and works by his students (look for the impressive replica of Canova's famous *Love and Psyche Reclining*). There are also pieces by the great Danish sculptor Bertel Thorvaldsen. On the next floor up are generally well-presented special exhibits, and on the top floor are painstakingly appointed period rooms with elegant Empire Style (early-19th-century French) furniture.

Then explore the main attraction, the **gardens,** which sprawl in both directions from the villa. To the south (toward Tremezzo) is the classical Old Garden. To the north, things get more interesting: pretty camellias, luscious azaleas, a maze of rhododendrons, a bamboo garden, and the gasp-worthy Valley of the Ferns—a lush jungle gorge with a river coursing through it.

### ▲▲Villa del Balbianello

The dreamiest villa on the lake perches on a romantic promontory near Lenno, overlooking Lake Como and facing Bellagio. Built at the end of the 18th century on the remains of an old Franciscan church, today the villa reflects the exotic vision of its last owner, explorer and mountaineer Guido Monzino, who died in 1988— leaving his villa and everything in it to the state. It's well worth paying extra to tour the interior to get to know Monzino, who  led the first Italian expedition to climb Mount Everest in 1973. But the real masterpiece here is the terraced garden and elegant loggia, where the land fits the architecture and landscaping in a lovely way. This is a favorite choice for movie directors when they need a far-out villa to feature; this is where James Bond recovered from a particularly bruising experience in *Casino Royale,* and where Anakin first kissed Padmé (and later married her) in *Star Wars: Episode II—Attack of the Clones.*

**Cost and Hours:** Garden only—€10, garden with villa tour—€20, Thu-Sun and Tue 10:00-18:00, closed Mon and Wed and mid-Nov-mid-March, last entry to garden 45 minutes before closing, tel. 034-456-110, www.visitfai.it/villadelbalbianello.

**Tours:** The only way inside the villa is with an English tour. Limited to 15 people per tour, these depart at least hourly (more frequently with demand); the first tour is usually at 11:00 and the last at 16:30.

**Getting There:** It's at the end of a hilly point next to the town of Lenno. From the Lenno ferry dock, turn left and stroll around to the far end of the harbor (about 10 minutes). Here, you can either pay for a **speedboat shuttle** (€5 one-way, €7 round-trip, 2/hour, mobile 333-410-3854, www.taxiboat.net) or carry on by foot. If you choose to **walk,** continue past the boat dock and through the gate marked *Villa Balbianello,* where two options are clearly sign-posted in kilometers: a 20-minute, 1-kilometer (half-mile) hike (including some up and down), or a more challenging 45-minute, 2.5-kilometer (about 1 mile) huff over the top.

**Visiting the Villa:** Your visit includes two parts: the villa and the gardens. If walking from the boat and back (taking the shorter 20-minute path), allow a leisurely three hours total for the walk and garden/villa visit.

Poke around the **gardens** while waiting for your villa tour to begin. On the Bellagio-facing side, you'll find a tranquil terrace with sweeping lake views. Along the path, notice the circular stone shed. Originally used for refrigeration (they used ice from the mountains to keep things cool), today this shed houses the tomb of Guido Monzino. On the opposite side of the point, you'll  find a terrace in front of the original Franciscan church (now a gift shop selling overpriced drinks). A WC is nearby, and just down the steps is the dock for the speedboat return to Lenno.

The 50-minute tour of the **villa** is as fascinating as its larger-than-life former owner. You'll tour the loggia (with a library and a study), then spend the rest of the time seeing 18 of the main building's 25 rooms. While finely decorated, these feel cozy, lived-in, and not too extravagant. Each one gives you a bit more insight into Monzino—from his personal living quarters, to his extensive collection of prehistoric artifacts from around the world, to the top-floor museum of his expeditions, with memorabilia from his North Pole and Mount Everest adventures. You'll see secret passages, learn why his furniture came with handles, and find out what's hiding behind the faux bookcase.

## Menaggio

Menaggio—the third of the "big three" mid-lake towns (along with Varenna and Bellagio)—has more urban bulk than its neighbors, but visitors are charmed by its lovely lakefront park. Since many find Lake Como too dirty for swimming, consider spending time in Menaggio's fine public pool (look for the *lido*). This is the starting point for a few hikes. (Just a few decades ago, cigarette smugglers used these trails at night to sneak back into

Italy from Switzerland with their tax-free booty.) The TI has information about mountain biking and catching the bus to trailheads on nearby Mount Grona. Ask for the free *Walking in the Province of Como* booklet, with information on 18 different walks detailing historical, artistic, and natural features (**TI** on Piazza Garibaldi, tel. 034-432-924, www.menaggio.com, infomenaggio@tiscali.it).

**Sleeping in Menaggio: ¢ La Primula Youth Hostel** is a classic, old-school hostel, offering sailing lessons, Italian-language courses, cooking classes, kayak and bike rentals, and a great location on the lake, a two-minute walk from the ferry dock (Via IV Novembre 106, tel. 0344-32356, www.lakecomohostel.com, info@lakecomohostel.com).

**Menaggio Connections:** In addition to being connected to Varenna and Bellagio by all the regular boats, bus #C10 connects Menaggio to **Como town** in about an hour (1-2/hour). Menaggio is also a springboard for visiting Switzerland. In summer, the yellow Palm Express bus runs once daily to **St. Moritz** (3.5 hours; off-season runs only weekends; reservations are required, www. postauto.ch or PostBus app)—remember to bring your passport. A bus (#C12) goes to **Lugano** (nearly hourly, 1 hour, €7). It's a 10-minute or so walk into town from the ferry dock and then a bit confusing (buy bus tickets in front of the main church at La Provincia bar; the bus stop is 100 yards uphill from there).

## Como Town

On the southwest tip of the lake, Como has a good, traffic-free old town, an interesting Gothic/Renaissance cathedral, a cable car up to a mountaintop viewpoint, and a pleasant lakefront with a promenade (**TI** at Piazza Cavour 17, tel. 031-269-712, www.lakecomo.it). It's an easy 10-minute walk from the boat dock to the train station (trains to Milan depart about twice per hour, 45 minutes). For details on boats connecting Como to Bellagio and Varenna, see page 232.

### All-Day Lugano Side Trip

From Varenna or Bellagio, you can make a loop that lets you nip into Switzerland to see the elegant lake resort of Lugano, pass through the town of Como, and cruise a good part of Lake Como. Here's a good day plan (times are approximate—confirm schedules locally): about 9:30—ferry to Menaggio (15 minutes from Varenna); 10:30—bus to Lugano (1 hour, bring your passport); 11:30—explore Lugano; 16:00—train to Como (45 minutes); 17:00/18:00/19:00—fast hydrofoil from Como to Varenna (1 hour). For more information on Lugano, see www.ricksteves.com/lugano.

# Lake Maggiore

Lake Maggiore is ringed by mountains, snowcapped in spring and fall, and lined with resort towns such as Stresa. Although Lake Maggiore lacks the cozy charm of Lake Como, a visit here may be worth the trouble for two islands, both with exotic gardens and lovely villas built by the Borromeo family.

The Borromeos—through many generations since 1630—lovingly turned their islands into magical retreats, with elaborate villas and fragrant gardens. Isola Bella has a palace and terraced garden; Isola Madre has a villa and sprawling English-style (more casual) garden. A third island, Isola Superiore (a.k.a. Isola Pescatori), is simply small, serene, and

residential. The Borromeos, who made their money from trade and banking, enjoyed the arts—from paintings (hung in lavish abundance throughout the palace and villa) to plays (performed in an open-air theater on Isola Bella) and marionette shows (you'll see the puppets that once performed here). Although it's a characterless resort, the town of Stresa is a handy departure point for exploring Lake Maggiore's exotic garden islands.

Tourists flock here in May and June, when flowers are in bloom, and in September. Concerts held in scenic settings draw music lovers, particularly during the summer Stresa Festival (get details from Stresa TI). For fewer crowds, visit in April, July, August (when Italians prefer the Mediterranean beaches), or October. In winter, the snow-covered mountains (with resorts a 1.5-hour drive away) attract skiers.

## PLANNING YOUR TIME

This region is best visited on a sunny day, when the mountains are clear, the lake is calm, and the heat of the sun brings out the scent of the blossoms. The two top islands for sightseeing are Isola Bella and Isola Madre (if tight on time, focus on Isola Bella). Isola Superiore has no sights but is a peaceful place for lunch. You can stay the night in Stresa, but a day trip is sufficient for most.

**Day Trip from Milan:** Catch the one-hour, early train from Milan to the town of Stresa (usually at 8:25, which may require reservations, and likely also at 9:29—but check times carefully, as there's often a midmorning gap until 11:25). Upon arrival in Stresa, walk 10 minutes downhill to the boat dock, and catch a boat to Isola Madre. Work your way back to Isola Superiore for a lazy lunch, and then go on to Isola Bella for the afternoon, before returning to Stresa and back to Milan (trains leave about hourly—jot down your departure options upon arrival in Stresa).

## GETTING AROUND LAKE MAGGIORE

Boats link the islands and Stresa, running about twice hourly. Allow roughly 10 minutes between stops. Buy a **free circulation ticket,** which allows you to get off and on at intermediate stops between your departure and arrival ports (€13.80 includes Bella and Superiore, €16.90 covers all the islands, and €20.70 includes the islands and Villa Taranto).

Boats run daily April through September. The map on page 266 shows most of the route: Stresa, Carciano/Lido (at the base of the cable car—but most boats skip this stop), Isola Bella, Isola Superiore, Baveno (lakeside town), Isola Madre, Pallanza, and Villa Taranto. This route is part of a longer one. To follow the boat schedule (free, available at boat docks and the TI), look at the Arona-Locarno timetable for trips from Stresa to the islands, and the Locarno-Arona timetable for the return trip to Stresa. Off-season, the boats cover a shorter route (public boat info: tel. 0322-233-200, www.navigazionelaghi.it).

Buy boat tickets directly from the dock ticket booth under the gallery to the left of the TI. On the promenade to the boat dock, don't be fooled by the private taxi-boat drivers, most dressed in sailor outfits—they'll try to talk you into paying way too much for private tours on their smaller boats.

# Sights on Lake Maggiore

Don't linger in Stresa—it's just a functional springboard. The main attractions are the islands and gardens.

## STRESA

The town of Stresa—which means "thin stretch"—was named for the original strip of fishermen's huts that lined the shore. Today, grand old hotels run along that same shore.

**Arrival in Stresa:** At the train station, ask for a free city map at the newsstand (to the far right of the tracks as you exit the train). To get downtown, exit right from the station and take your first left (on Viale Duchessa di Genova). This takes you straight down to the lake (once you're there, the boat dock is about four blocks to your right; ask for boat schedule at ticket window). The helpful **TI** is located to the right of the ticket window at the boat dock (daily 10:00-12:30 & 15:00-18:30, off-season closed Sat afternoon and all day Sun, Piazza Marconi 16, tel. 0323-31308, www.stresaturismo. it). Taxis charge a fixed rate of €11 for even the shortest ride.

**Visiting Stresa:** The **old town**—basically a traffic-free touristy shopping mall—is just a few blocks deep, stretching inland from the main boat dock. Stresa's stately 19th-century lakeside hotels date back to the days when this town was on the Grand Tour circuit.

In any Romantic Age resort like Stresa, hotels had names designed to appeal to Victorian aristocrats...like Regina Palace (rather than Palazzo), Astoria, Bristol, and Victoria.

The **Grand Hotel des Iles Borromees** was the first (built in 1862). In 1918, 19-year-old Ernest Hemingway—wounded in Slovenia as an ambulance driver for the Italian Red Cross—was taken to Stresa's Grand Hotel des Iles Borromees, which served, like its regal neighbors, as an infirmary during World War I. Hemingway returned to the same hotel in 1948, stayed in the same room (#205, now called the "Hemingway suite"—you can stay there for a couple thousand dollars a night), and signed the guest book as "an old client." Another "old client" was Winston Churchill, who honeymooned here.

A fine waterfront promenade leads past the venerable old hotels to the Lido, with the Carciano boat dock and the **Stresa-Alpino-Mottarone cable car.** This cable car takes you up—in two stages and a 20-minute ride—to the top of Mount Mottarone (€11.50 one-way, €20 round-trip, daily 9:30-17:30 in summer, shorter winter hours, 2-3/hour, bar midway up, tel. 0323-30295, www.stresa-mottarone.it). From the top (about 5,000 feet), you get great panoramic views of neighboring peaks and, by taking a short

LAKES

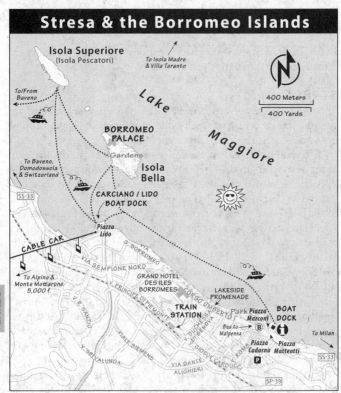

# Stresa & the Borromeo Islands

**Isola Superiore**
(Isola Pescatori)

To Isola Madre
& Villa Taranto

To/From
Baveno

Lake

Maggiore

400 Meters

400 Yards

**BORROMEO PALACE**

Gardene

To Baveno,
Domodossola
& Switzerland

**Isola Bella**

SS-33

**CARCIANO / LIDO BOAT DOCK**

Piazza Lido

CABLE CAR

VIA G. BORROMEO

VIA SEMPIONE NORD

To Alpino &
Monte Mottarone
5,000 f.

V. PRINCIPE DI PIEMONTE

V. R. SANZIO

**GRAND HOTEL DES ILES BORROMEES**

CORSO UMBERTO I

VIALE SIEMENS

**TRAIN STATION**

V. DUCHESSA DI GENOVA

LAKESIDE PROMENADE

Park Piazza
Marconi

Bus to
Malpensa

B

**BOAT DOCK**

Piazza
Cadorna

Piazza
Matteotti

To Milan

SS-33

VIA DANTE
ALIGHIERI

VIA GIOSUE CARDUCCI

V. SEGLIALUNGA

P

SP-39

hike, a bird's-eye view of the small, neighboring Lake Orta (de-scribed later).

Halfway up the cable car line are the **Alpine Gardens,** which come with fine lake views and picnic spots, but can't compare with what you'll see on the islands. To visit the gardens, get off at the midway Alpino stop and walk 10 minutes (turn left as you leave; €4, daily 9:30-18:00, closed Nov-March). If you plan to hike down, pick up the *Trekking* map from the TI and allow four hours from the top of Mount Mottarone, or two hours from the Alpine Gar-dens (mountain biking also possible—ask at TI).

**Sleeping in Stresa:** Because Stresa's town generally lacks ap-peal, I'd day-trip from Milan. But if you'd like to stay, here are some options: **$$$ Hotel Milan Speranza au Lac** is a big, group-oriented hotel facing the boat dock (www.milansperanza.it); **$$ Hotel Saini Meublè** is a small, homey, affordable choice in the old town center (www.hotelsaini.it); and **$$ Hotel Moderno** is a midsize, midrange option in the old town (www.hms.it).

**Eating in Stresa:** The main square, **Piazza Cadorna,** is one big tourist trap, yet it does have a certain charm. (At night, it seems anyone who claims to be a musician can get a gig singing for diners.) For a (slightly) less touristy alternative, seek out one of these options: **$$ Osteria degli Amici,** tucked away under a vine trellis on a forgotten square a couple of blocks beyond Piazza Cadorna (Via Bolongaro 33); **$$ La Botte,** with an old-school diner vibe on the main street between the port and the square (Via Mazzini 6); or **$$$$ Il Clandestino,** a fancier, romantic, modern splurge specializing in fish (Via Rosmini 5).

## ISLANDS AND GARDENS
### ▲▲Isola Bella

This island, nearest Stresa, has a formal garden and a fancy Baroque palace. Looking like a stepped pyramid from the water,

the island was named by Charles Borromeo (sponsor of Milan's Duomo) for his wife, Isabella. The island itself is touristy, with a gauntlet of souvenir stands and a corral of restaurants. A few back streets provide evidence that people actually live here. While the Borromeo family now lives in Milan, they spend a few weeks on Isola Bella each summer (when their blue-and-red family flag flies from the top of the garden).

**Cost and Hours:** Palace and garden—€17, €24.00 combo-ticket includes villa at Isola Madre, daily 9:00-18:00, shorter hours for palace's picture gallery, closed late Oct-late March, tel. 0323-30556, www.isoleborromee.it.

**Tours:** A fine €4 audioguide describes the palace, which also has posted English descriptions. A €1.50 booklet explains the gardens.

**Eating:** Several restaurants cluster between the boat docks and the villa. Picnicking is not allowed in the garden, but you can picnic in the pebbly park at the point of the island, beyond the villa (free and open to the public).

**Visiting the Island:** There are two docks on this island, one for each direction. It's a short walk from the boat to the hulking villa (turn left from the dock; on the way, you'll pass a public WC). Once inside, your visit is a one-way tour, starting with the palace and finishing with the garden. (There's no way to see the garden without the palace.)

In the lavishly decorated Baroque **palace,** stairs lead up under stucco crests of Italy's top families (balls signify the Medici, bees mean the Barberini, and a unicorn symbolizes the Borromeos' motto: Humility). You'll loop through the picture gallery, contain-

**LAKES**

ing 130 beautifully restored 16th-century paintings from the Borromeo family's private collection, hung wall-to-ceiling in several cramped rooms. Then you'll get a peek at the canopied bedchambers and ogle the ornate throne room. Continue through the dining room, with a portrait of the first Borromeo, and into a richly stuccoed grand hall, with an 80-foot-high dome and featuring an 18th-century model of the villa, including a grand water entry that never materialized.

Next comes the music room, the site of the 1935 Stresa Conference, in which Mussolini met with British and French diplomats in a united attempt to scare Germany out of starting World War II. Look for a copy of the treaty with Mussolini's signature on the wall next to the exit. Unfortunately, the "Stresa Front" soon fizzled, when Mussolini attacked Ethiopia and joined forces with Hitler.

Napoleon's bedroom comes with an engraving that depicts his 1797 visit (Napoleon is on a bench with his wife and sister enjoying festivities in his honor). Continue through several more opulent halls, many of which display souvenirs and gifts that the Borromeo family picked up over the generations.

Downstairs, many of the famous Borromeo marionettes are on display. (A larger collection is on Isola Madre.) The 18th-century, multiroom grotto, decorated from ceiling to floor with shell motifs and black-and-white stones, still serves its original function of providing a cool refuge from Italy's heat. The dreamy marble statues are by Gaetano Monti, a student of Antonio Canova. Climbing out of the basement, look up at the unique, cantilevered, spiral stairs; they're from a 16th-century fortress that predates this building.

Pass through the mirrored corridor and follow the route through more rooms until you come to the ornate hall of 16th-century Flemish tapestries. This leads to the finale of this island visit: the beautiful **garden,** complete with Chinese white peacocks, which give it an exotic splash. (Before continuing to the garden, consider heading up the stairs near the WC to stroll through Elisa's Greenhouse, named for Napoleon's sister and home to tropical plants.)

From the palace, head straight up the stairs into the main part of the garden. Baroque—which is exactly what you see here—is all about controlling nature. The centerpiece is a pyramid-shaped outdoor grotto, crowned by the Borromeo family unicorn. Up the stairs and behind this fanciful structure is a vast terrace with views over the lower gardens and Stresa. Back downstairs, follow the signs (hidden in the bushes) to the café and bookshop, which anchor the far points of the island, to see the terraces behind the "pyramid." Finally, follow *exit* signs to pop out a side gate at the top of a twisty, stepped lane back through town to the boat docks.

### ▲Isola Superiore (Pescatori)

This sleepy island—home to 35 families—is the smallest and most residential of the three. It has a few good fish restaurants,

ample pizza-by-the-slice take-out joints, picnic benches, views, and, blissfully, nothing much to do—all under arbors of wisteria. Simply stroll the narrow, cobbled lanes, or relax at the long, skinny, pebbly park/beach at the tip of the island. A delight for photographers and painters, the island is never really crowded, except at lunchtime.

### ▲Isola Madre

Don't come to this island unless you intend to tour the sight, because that's all there is: an interesting furnished villa (with a few sparse English descriptions) and a lovely garden filled with exotic birds and plants. Garden lovers can invest a few euros in a booklet about the plantings.

**Cost and Hours:** Villa and garden—€13.50, €24.00 combo-ticket includes Isola Bella, daily 9:00-18:00, closed late Oct-late March, tel. 0323-31261, www.isoleborromee.it.

**Visitor Services:** A WC is next to the chapel. You'll also find a café/bookshop (selling basic sandwiches) just outside the villa. While eating is best on Isola Superiore, Isola Madre has one real restaurant, **La Piratera Ristorante Bar,** which owns a big, beautiful terrace over the lake. You'll run into this immediately after leaving the villa/garden complex (good-value fixed-price tourist meal, daily 8:00-18:00, sit-down meals 12:00-15:30, simple sandwiches and slices of pizza-to-go anytime, picnic at the rocky beach a minute's walk from the restaurant, just to your right as you exit the gardens, tel. 0323-31171).

**Visiting the Island:** Visiting is a one-way affair. From the boat dock, walk up the stairs to the ticket desk for the villa. Then, once through the gate, take the level path to the right to loop around the gardens and end at the villa (*ingresso al giardino* signs). Or, if you're in a rush, take the stairs to the left instead to go straight to the villa.

First you'll circle all the way around the **gardens.** Eight gardeners (with the help of water continually pumped from the lake) keep this English-style garden paradise lush. It's a joy, even for those bored by flowers and foliage. You'll see trees from around the world, and an exotic bird menagerie with golden and silver pheasants and Chinese peacocks. (You'll see and hear them roaming wild; also look for the bird cages partway up the main staircase to the villa, on the left.)

In front of the villa, a once-magnificent **Himalayan cypress tree** paints your world a streaky green. The 150-year-old tree, knocked down by a tornado in 2006 but successfully saved, is an attraction in its own right, with steel guy-wires now anchoring it firmly in place.

The 16th-century **villa** is the first of the Borromeo palaces, dating from the Renaissance. A century older than the Isola Bella villa, it's dark and somber. The clever angled hinges keep the doors from flapping in the lake breeze. The family's huge collection of dolls, marionettes, and exquisite 17th-century marionette theater sets—painted by a La Scala opera set designer—fills several rooms. A corner room is painted to take you into an 18th-century Venetian Rococo sitting room under a floral greenhouse.

Some of the garden's best flowers are in view immediately after leaving the villa. Walk down the stairs to the terrace in front of the chapel, with WCs tucked around the left side. Stairs lead directly down to the boat dock from here. Or you can loop past the villa to exit at the far end, just above La Piratera restaurant. From there, you can walk through the shop to reach a terrace path that leads you back to the boat dock.

### Villa Taranto Botanical Gardens

Garden lovers will enjoy this large landscaped park, located on the mainland across the lake from Stresa. Although it's the most sprawling garden in the area, and enjoyable for a stroll in a park, it's a bit underwhelming. The gardens are a Scotsman's labor of love. Starting in the 1930s, Neil McEacharn created this garden of delights—bringing in thousands of plants from all over the world—and here he stays, in the small mausoleum. The park's highlight is a terraced garden with a series of cascading pools. Villa Taranto is directly across the street from the boat dock.

**Cost and Hours:** €11, daily 8:30-18:30, Oct 9:00-16:00, closed Nov-mid-March, tel. 0323-404-555, www.villataranto.it.

**Getting There:** It's two stops (about 15 minutes) past Isola Madre. On the way, you'll pass a scenic promontory speckled with villas. Note that only about half of the lake boats stop here, which means an hour between return departures—check schedules carefully.

## DAY TRIP FROM STRESA
### ▲Lake Orta

Just on the other side of Mount Mottarone is the small Lake Orta. The lake's main town, Orta San Giulio, has a beautiful lakeside piazza ringed by picturesque buildings. The piazza faces the lake with a view of Isola San Giulio. Taxi boats (€4 round-trip) make the five-minute trip throughout the day. The island is worth a look for the Church of San Giulio and the circular "path of silence," which takes about 10 minutes. In peak season, Orta is anything but silent, but off-season or early or late in the day, this place is full of peace and magic (TI on Via Panoramica next to the parking lot downhill from the train station, www.orta.net, tel. 0322-905-163; there's another near the town center at Via Bossi 11, tel. 0322-90155).

**Getting There:** The train ride from Stresa to Orta-Miasino (a short walk from the lakeside piazza) takes 1.5-2 hours and requires a change or two (5/day). Public buses from Stresa's Piazza Marconi to Orta depart from near the TI (around €10 round-trip, about 1 hour, 2-3/day mid-June-mid-Sept, confirm schedule at TI or at www.safduemila.com).

LAKES

# MILAN

*Milano*

For every church in Rome, there's a bank in Milan. Italy's second city and the capital of the Lombardy region, Milan is a hardworking, style-conscious, time-is-money city of 1.3 million. A melting pot of people and history, Milan's industriousness may come from the Teutonic blood of its original inhabitants, the Lombards, or from its years under Austrian rule. Either way, Milan is modern Italy's center of fashion, industry, banking, TV, publishing, and conventions. It's also a major university town, a train hub, and host to two football (soccer) teams and the nearby Monza Formula One racetrack. And as home to a prestigious opera house, Milan is one of the touchstones of the world of opera.

Artistically, Milan can't compare with Rome and Florence, but the city does have several unique and noteworthy sights: the Duomo and the Galleria Vittorio Emanuele II arcade, La Scala Opera House, Michelangelo's last pietà sculpture (in Sforza Castle), and Leonardo da Vinci's *The Last Supper*.

Founded by the Romans as Mediolanum ("the place in the middle"), by the fourth century AD it was the capital of the western half of the Roman Empire, the namesake of Constantine's "Edict of Milan" legalizing Christianity, and home of the powerful early Christian bishop, St. Ambrose.

After some barbarian darkness, medieval Milan became a successful mercantile city, eventually rising to regional prominence under the Visconti and Sforza families. The mammoth cathedral, or Duomo, is a testament to the city's wealth and ambition. By the time of the Renaissance, Milan was nicknamed "the New Athens," and was enough of a cultural center for Leonardo da Vinci to call it home. Then came 400 years of foreign domination

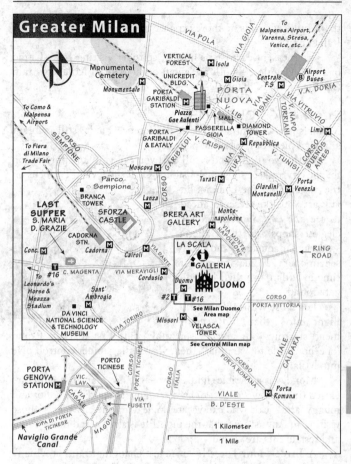

Greater Milan

(under Spain, Austria, France, more Austria). Milan was a focal point of the 1848 revolution against Austria and helped lead Italy to unification in 1870. The impressive Galleria Vittorio Emanuele II and La Scala Opera House reflect the sophistication of turn-of-the-20th-century Milan as one of Europe's cultural powerhouses.

Mussolini left a heavy fascist touch on the architecture here (such as the central train station). His excesses also led to the WWII bombing of Milan. But the city rose again. The 1959 Pirelli Tower (the skinny skyscraper in front of the station), while a trendsetter in its day, now seems quaint considering Milan's glassy new high-rise developments. Today, Milan is people-friendly, with a great transit system and inviting pedestrian zones.

Many tourists come to Italy for the past. But Milan is today's Italy. In this city of refined tastes, window displays are gorgeous, cigarettes are chic, and even the cheese comes gift-wrapped. Yet, thankfully, Milan is no more expensive for tourists than any other Italian city.

For pleasant excursions nearby, consider visiting Lake Como or Lake Maggiore—both are about an hour from Milan by train (see the previous chapter).

## PLANNING YOUR TIME

Milan isn't as charming as Venice or Florence, but it's still a vibrant and vital piece of the Italian puzzle.

With two nights and a full day, you can gain an appreciation for the city and see most major sights. On a short visit, I'd focus on the center. Tour the Duomo, hit any art you like (reserve ahead to see *The Last Supper*), browse elegant shops and the Galleria Vittorio Emanuele II, and try to see an opera. To maximize your time in Milan, use the Metro to get around.

For those with a round-trip flight into Milan: I'd recommend starting your journey softly by going first to Lake Como (one-hour ride to Varenna). Then, with jet lag under control, dive into Milan.

Monday is a terrible sightseeing day, since many museums are closed (including *The Last Supper*). August is oppressively hot and muggy, and locals who can vacate do, leaving the city quiet. Those visiting in August find that the nightlife is sleepy, and many shops and restaurants are closed.

**A Three-Hour Tour:** If you're just changing trains at Milan's Centrale station (as, sooner or later, you probably will), consider catching a later train and taking this blitz tour: Check your bag at the station, ride the subway to the Duomo, peruse the square, explore the cathedral's rooftop terraces and interior, drop into the Duomo Museum, have a scenic coffee in the Galleria Vittorio Emanuele II, spin on the floor mosaic of the bull for good luck, maybe see a museum (most are within a 10-minute walk of the main square), and return by subway to the station. A practical way to make the most of this quick visit is to use my free ∩ Duomo neighborhood audio tour—see page 26.

# Orientation to Milan

My coverage focuses on the old center. Most sights and hotels listed are within a 15-minute walk of the cathedral (Duomo), which is a straight eight-minute Metro ride from the Centrale train station.

## TOURIST INFORMATION

Milan's TI, at the La Scala end of the Galleria Vittorio Emanuele II, isn't worth a special trip (Mon-Fri 9:00-19:00, Sat-Sun until 18:00, Metro: Duomo, tel. 02-884-55555, www.turismo.milano. it).

## ARRIVAL IN MILAN

For arrival by plane, see "Milan Connections" at the end of this chapter.

### By Train

Visitors disembark at one of three major train stations: Milano Centrale, Porta Garibaldi, or Cadorna. Centrale handles most Trenitalia and Italo trains as well as airport buses. Porta Garibaldi receives trains from France and some Trenitalia trains from elsewhere in Italy. Both Centrale and Cadorna are terminals for trains from Malpensa Airport.

#### Milano Centrale

This huge, sternly decorated, fascist-built (in 1931) train station is a sight in itself. Notice how the monumental halls and art make you feel small—emphasizing that a powerful state is a good thing. In the front lobby, heroic people celebrate "modern" transportation (circa-1930 ships, trains, and cars) opposite reliefs depicting old-fashioned sailboats and horse carts.

Moving walkways link the station's three main levels: platforms and eateries on top, shops and more food on a small mezzanine, and most services at ground level (including pay WCs and ATMs). For baggage check *(deposito bagagli)*, taxis, or buses to Linate Airport, head toward the ground-level exit marked *Piazza Luigi di Savoia*. For buses to Malpensa Airport, head to the exit marked *Piazza IV Novembre*. Outside the station's front entrance, under the atrium, are car-rental offices for Avis, Budget, and Maggiore, and a post office-run ATM. You'll also find escalators down to the Metro and a fourth basement level with a few shops, including a Sapori & Dintorni supermarket.

To **buy train tickets,** follow blue signs to *Biglietti* and use the Trenitalia or Italo machines for most domestic trips. For international tickets or complicated questions, join the line at the Trenitalia ticket office on the ground floor. There's also an Italo office on the ground floor.

**Getting to the Center:** "Centrale" is a misnomer—the Duomo is a 35-minute walk away. But it's a straight shot on the **Metro** (8 minutes). Buy a ticket at a kiosk or from the machines, follow signs for yellow line 3 (direction: San Donato), and go four stops to the Duomo stop. You'll surface facing the cathedral.

## Rome vs. Milan: A Classic Squabble

In Italy, the North and South bicker about each other, hurling barbs, quips, and generalizations. All the classic North/South traits can be applied to Milan (the business capital) and Rome (the government and religious capital). Italians like to say that people come to Milan to sin, and they go to Rome to ask for forgiveness.

The Milanesi say the Romans are lazy. Government jobs in Rome come with short hours—made even shorter by multiple coffee breaks, three-hour lunches, chats with colleagues, and phone calls to friends and relatives. Milanesi contend that "Roma *ladrona*" (Rome, the big thief) is a parasite that lives off the taxes of people up North. There's still a strong Milan-based movement promoting secession from the South.

Romans, meanwhile, dismiss the Milanesi as uptight workaholics with nothing else to live for—gray like their foggy city. But Romans do admit that in Milan, job opportunities are better and based on merit. And the Milanesi grudgingly concede the Romans have a gift for enjoying life.

**MILAN**

**Taxis** to the center are a good value for two or more people or if you don't want to lug bags on the Metro (€12-15, departing taxis are to the left of the train station).

### Milano Cadorna
You're most likely to use this commuter station if you take the Malpensa Express airport train, which uses track 1. The Cadorna Metro station—with a direct connection to the Duomo on Metro red line 1—is directly out front.

### Milano Porta Garibaldi
Some Trenitalia trains and the high-speed TGV from Paris use Porta Garibaldi station, north of the city center. Porta Garibaldi is on Metro green line 2, two stops from Milano Centrale, and purple line 5.

## By Car
Leonardo never drove in Milan. Smart guy. Driving here is bad enough to make the €30/day fee for a downtown garage a blessing. And there's a €5 congestion fee if you drive in the city center

While Rome is more of a family city, Milan is the place for high-powered singles on the career fast track. Milanese yuppies mix with each other...not the city's longtime residents. Milan is seen as wary of foreigners and inward-looking, and Rome as fun-loving, tolerant, and friendly. In Milan, bureaucracy (such as social services) works logically and efficiently, while in Rome, accomplishing even small chores can be exasperating. Everything in Rome—from finding a babysitter to buying a car—is done through friends.

Milanesi find Romans vulgar. The Roman dialect is considered one of the coarsest in the country. Much as they try, Milanesi just can't say "Damn your dead relatives" quite as effectively as the Romans. Still, Milanesi enjoy Roman comedians and love to imitate the accent.

The Milanesi feel that Rome is dirty and Roman traffic nerve-wracking. But despite the craziness, Rome maintains a genuine village feel. People share family news with their neighborhood grocer. Milan lacks people-friendly piazzas, and entertainment comes at a high price. But in Rome, *la dolce vita* is as close as the nearest square, and a full moon is enjoyed by all.

on weekdays. Do Milan (and Lake Como) before or after you rent your car, not while you've got it, and use the park-and-ride lots at suburban Metro stations such as Cascina Gobba. These are shown on the official Metro map, and full details are at www.atm.it (select English, then "Car Parks," then "Parking Lots").

## HELPFUL HINTS

**Theft Alert:** Be on guard. Milan's thieves target tourists, especially at the Centrale train station, getting in and out of the subway, and around the Duomo. They can be dressed as tourists, businessmen, or beggars, or they can be gangs of too-young-to-arrest children. Watch out for ragged people carrying newspapers and cardboard—they'll thrust these at you as a distraction while they pick your pocket. If you're ripped off and plan to file an insurance claim, fill out a report with the police (main police station, "Questura," Via Fatebenefratelli 11, Metro: Turati, open daily 24 hours, tel. 02-62261).

**Medical Help:** Here are two medical clinics with emergency care facilities (both closed Sat-Sun): the **International Health**

**Center** in Galleria Strasburgo (also does dentistry, between Via Durini and Corso Europa, at #3, third floor, Metro: San Babila, tel. 02-7634-0720, www.ihc.it), and the **American International Medical Center** at Via Mercalli 11 (Metro: Missori or Crocetta, call for appointment, tel. 02-5831-9808, www.aimclinic.it).

**Bookstores:** The handiest major bookstore is **La Feltrinelli,** under the Galleria Vittorio Emanuele II (daily, tel. 02-8699-6903). The **American Bookstore** is at Via Manfredo Camperio 16, near Sforza Castle (closed Sun, Metro: Cairoli, tel. 02-878-920).

**Events and Entertainment:** HelloMilano.it, WantedinMilan.com, and Turismo.milano.it are decent websites for info on what's happening in the city.

**Soccer:** For a dose of Europe's soccer mania (which many believe provides a necessary testosterone vent to keep Europe out of a third big war), catch a match while you're here. A.C. Milan and Inter Milan are the ferociously competitive home teams. Both teams play in the 85,000-seat **Meazza Stadium** (a.k.a. San Siro) most Sunday afternoons from September to June (ride Metro purple line 5 to San Siro Stadio, bring passport for security checks, www.acmilan.com or www.inter.it).

## GETTING AROUND MILAN

**By Public Transit:** It's a pleasure to use Milan's great public transit system, called ATM ("ATM Point" info desk in Duomo Metro station, www.atm.it). The clean, spacious, fast, and easy **Metro** zips you nearly anywhere you may want to go, and trams and city buses fill in the gaps. The handiest Metro line for a quick visit is the yellow line 3, which connects Centrale station to the Duomo. The other lines are red (1), green (2), and purple (5). The Metro shuts down at about midnight, but many trams continue until 1:00 or 2:00. With 100 miles of track, Milan's classic, century-old yellow **trams** are both efficient and atmospheric.

A **single ticket,** valid for 90 minutes, can be used for one ride, including transfers, on Metro, bus, or tram (€1.50; sold at newsstands, tobacco shops, shops with *ATM* sticker in window, at machines in subway stations, and at many hotel reception desks). Other ticket options include a **24-hour pass** (€4.50) and a **48-hour pass** (€8.25). Tickets must be run through the machines at Metro turnstiles when you enter and again when you leave the station. On buses and trams, the machines are at the front and rear and you need only validate upon entry. You also need to validate if transferring.

**By Taxi:** Small groups go cheap and fast by taxi (drop charge—€3.30, €1.10/kilometer; €5.40 drop charge on Sun and

MILAN

Milan Metro

LINE 5 PURPLE — Bignami

LINE 1 RED — Sesto FS

LINE 3 YELLOW — Comasina

Zara

Not to scale & not all lines or stations shown

Isola

Sondrio

Buses and trains to Malpensa airport; bus to Linate & Bergamo airports
**CENTRAL TRAIN STATION**
*Centrale F.S.*

Lambrate FS

Monumentale

**PORTA GARIBALDI TRAIN STN.**

Gioia

PORTA NUOVA

Loreto

To Cologno Nord & Gessate

Cenisio

Garibaldi FS

Moscova

Repubblica

Lima

To San Siro

Gerusalemme

**BRERA GALLERY**

Turati

Porta Venezia

To RHO, QT8, Lotto, Molino Dorino & Bisceglie

**SFORZA CASTLE**

Lanza

Montenapoleone

Cadorna

**GALLERIA**

**DUOMO**

Palestro

Conciliazione

Cairoli

Cordusio

Duomo

San Babila

**LAST SUPPER**

Sant' Ambrogio

**SANT' AMBROGIO**

**CENTRAL MILAN**

Missori

Sant' Agostino

Crocetta

Porta Genova FS

**NAVIGLIO GRANDE**

METRO LINES
LINE 1 (RED)
LINE 2 (GREEN)
LINE 3 (YELLOW)
LINE 5 (PURPLE)

Assago & Abbiategrasso
LINE 2 GREEN

S. Donato
LINE 3 YELLOW

MILAN

holidays, €6.50 from 21:00 to 6:00 in the morning). It can be easier to walk to a taxi stand than to flag down a cab. Handy stands are at Piazza del Duomo and in front of Sforza Castle. Hotels and restaurants are also happy to call one for you (tel. 02-8585 or 02-6969). The **MyTaxi** app (www.mytaxi.com) lets you summon and pay for a taxi. **Uber** Black and UberLux also operate in Milan.

By Bike: Public BikeMi stations are generally near Metro stations. Download the BikeMi app to see available bikes and parking spots (subscription is €4.50/day, €9/week; first 30 minutes free, then €0.50/30 minutes up to 2 hours, after that €2/hour, www.bikemi.com).

# Milan at a Glance

▲▲▲**Duomo** Milan's showpiece cathedral, with an amazing ▲▲ roof you can walk on. **Hours:** Church—daily 8:00-19:00; archaeological area and rooftop terraces—daily from 9:00. See page 285.

▲▲**Duomo Museum** Church art and original sculptures from Milan's cathedral. **Hours:** Thu-Tue 10:00-18:00, closed Wed. See page 292.

▲▲**Galleria Vittorio Emanuele II** Glass-domed arcade on the main square, perfect for window shopping and people-watching anytime. See page 296.

▲▲**Pinacoteca Ambrosiana** Oldest museum in Milan, with works by Raphael, Leonardo (including some of his sketches and notes in the Biblioteca), Botticelli, Titian, and Caravaggio. **Hours:** Pinacoteca—Tue-Sun 10:00-18:00, closed Mon; Biblioteca—Mon-Fri 9:00-17:00, closed Sat-Sun. See page 302.

▲▲**Basilica di Sant'Ambrogio** Historic, art-packed church dating to early Roman times. **Hours:** Mon-Sat 10:00-12:30 & 14:30-18:00, Sun 15:00-17:00. See page 305.

▲▲*The Last Supper* Leonardo da Vinci's masterpiece, displayed in the Church of Santa Maria delle Grazie (viewable only with a reservation). **Hours:** Tue-Sun 8:00-18:45 (last entry), closed Mon. See page 307.

▲▲**Brera Art Gallery** World-class collection of Italian paintings (13th-20th century), including Raphael, Caravaggio, Gentile da Fabriano, Piero della Francesca, Mantegna, and the Bellini brothers. **Hours:** Tue-Sun 8:30-19:15, closed Mon. See page 310.

▲▲**Sforza Castle** Milan's castle, highlighted by an unfinished Michelangelo pietà. **Hours:** Museum—Tue-Sun 9:00-17:30, closed Mon; grounds—daily 7:00-19:30. See page 312.

▲▲**Porta Nuova** Sleek, futuristic neighborhood of condo towers and shopping mall boulevards. See page 315.

▲**La Scala Opera House and Museum** The world's most prestigious opera house. **Hours:** Museum daily 9:00-17:30. See page 299.

MILAN

▲**Piazza del Duomo** Milan's main square, full of energy, history, and pickpockets. See page 295.

▲**Museo del Novecento** Milan's 20th-century art collection, housed in the fascist-era City Hall. **Hours:** Tue-Sun 9:30-19:30 (Thu and Sat until 22:30), Mon from 14:30. See page 297.

▲**Piazza dei Mercanti** The evocative medieval heart of the city. See page 298.

▲**Gallerie d'Italia** Three adjacent palaces filled with 19th- and 20th-century Italian art. **Hours:** Tue-Sun 9:30-19:30, Thu until 22:30, closed Mon. See page 301.

▲**Church of San Maurizio** The "Sistine Chapel of Lombardy," gorgeously frescoed by Bernardino Luini, a follower of Leonardo. **Hours:** Tue-Sun 9:30-19:30, closed Mon. See page 304.

▲**Leonardo da Vinci National Science and Technology Museum** Leonardo's designs illustrated in wooden models, plus a vast collection of historical and technological bric-a-brac and machines. **Hours:** Tue-Fri 10:00-18:00, Sat-Sun until 19:00, shorter hours off-season, closed Mon. See page 306.

▲**Via Dante** Human traffic frolics to lilting accordions on one of Europe's longest pedestrian-only boulevards. See page 315.

▲**Risorgimento Museum** Italy's rocky road to unification on one floor. **Hours:** Tue-Sun 9:00-13:00 & 14:00-17:30, closed Mon. See page 311.

▲**Naviglio Grande** Milan's old canal port—once a working-class zone, now an atmospheric nightspot for dinner or drinks. See page 317.

▲**Monumental Cemetery** Final resting spot with tombs showcasing expressive art styles from 1870 to 1930. **Hours:** Tue-Sun 8:00-18:00, closed Mon. See page 318.

MILAN

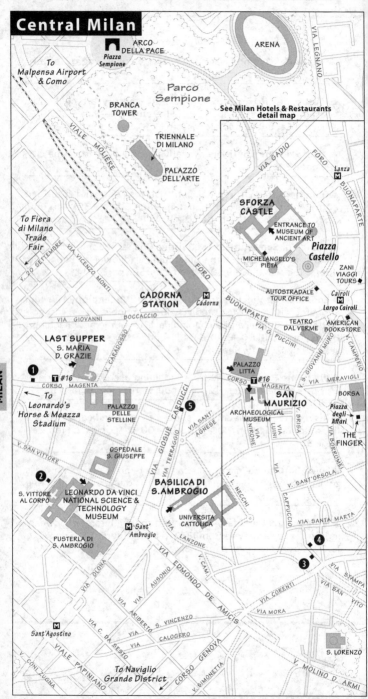

**Central Milan**

MILAN

ARCO DELLA PACE
Piazza Sempione
ARENA

To Malpensa Airport & Como

Parco Sempione

BRANCA TOWER

VIALE MOLIERE

TRIENNALE DI MILANO

PALAZZO DELL'ARTE

See Milan Hotels & Restaurants detail map

VIA GADIO
FORO
Lanza M
VIA BUONAPARTE

SFORZA CASTLE

ENTRANCE TO MUSEUM OF ANCIENT ART

Piazza Castello

MICHELANGELO'S PIETA

ZANI VIAGGI TOURS

To Fiera di Milano Trade Fair

V. 30 SETTEMBRE
VIA VICENZO MONTI

FORO BUONAPARTE

AUTOSTRADALE TOUR OFFICE

Cairoli M

Largo Cairoli

CADORNA STATION
M Cadorna

VIA GIOVANNI BOCCACCIO

TEATRO DAL VERME

VIA G. PUCCINI

AMERICAN BOOKSTORE

VIA CAMPERIO

LAST SUPPER
S. MARIA D. GRAZIE

V. CARADOSSO

PALAZZO LITTA

CORSO MAGENTA

T #16

VIA MERAVIGLI

❶

T #16

CORSO MAGENTA

SAN MAURIZIO

BORSA

To Leonardo's Horse & Meazza Stadium

PALAZZO DELLE STELLINE

VIA GIOSUE CARDUCCI

VIA SANT' AGNESE

ARCHAEOLOGICAL MUSEUM

VIA NIRONE

VIA LUINI

BRISA

Piazza degli Affari

VIA BOERCHIO

VIA BORROMEI

THE FINGER

❺

V. SAN VITTORE

OSPEDALE S. GIUSEPPE

VIA TERRAGGIO

V. SANT'ORSOLA

❷

S. VITTORE AL CORPO

LEONARDO DA VINCI NATIONAL SCIENCE & TECHNOLOGY MUSEUM

BASILICA DI S.AMBROGIO

UNIVERSITA CATTOLICA

V. L. NECCHI

VIA CAPPUCCIO

VIA SANTA MARTA

M Sant' Ambrogio

PUSTERLA DI S. AMBROGIO

VIA LANZONE

❹

❸

VIA STAMPA

VIA OLONA

VIA EDMONDO DE AMICIS

V. CAMI

VIA SAN VITO

M Sant'Agostino

VIA ARIBERTO

VIA C. DA SESTO

S. VINCENZO

VIA CALOGERO

VIA COFENTI

VIA MORA

S. LORENZO

V. CONI ZUGNA

VIALE PAPINIANO

CORSO GENOVA

VIA SIMONETTA

V. MOLINO D. ARMI

To Naviglio Grande District

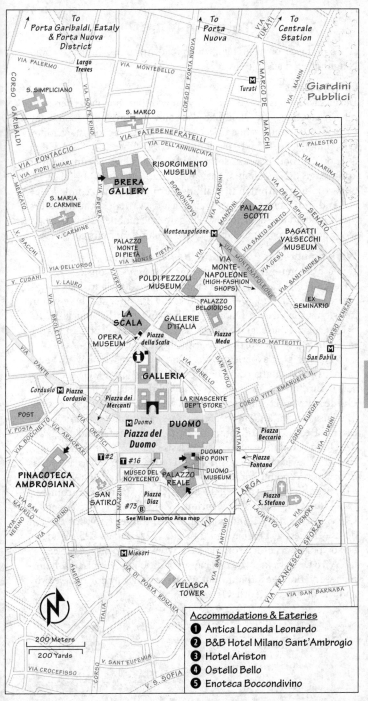

MILAN

To Porta Garibaldi, Eataly & Porta Nuova District

To Porta Nuova

To Centrale Station

VIA PALERMO

Largo Treves

VIA MONTEBELLO

VIA TURATI

V. MARCO DE

V. MANIN

CORSO GARIBALDI

S. SIMPLICIANO

VIA SOLFERINO

S. MARCO

Turati

Giardini Pubblici

CORSO DI PORTA NUOVA

VIA MARCO DE MARCHI

VIA FATEBENEFRATELLI

V. PALESTRO

VIA PONTACCIO

VIA DELL'ANNUNCIATA

VIA MARINA

VIA FIORI CHIARI

RISORGIMENTO MUSEUM

VIA DELLA SPIGA

VIA SENATO

V. MERCATO

BRERA GALLERY

VIA BORGONUOVO

VIA GIARDINI

PALAZZO SCOTTI

S. MARIA D. CARMINE

VIA BRERA

VIA MANZONI

VIA SANTO SPIRITO

BAGATTI VALSECCHI MUSEUM

V. SACCHI

V. CARMINE

Montenapoleone

VIA GESÙ

PALAZZO MONTE DI PIETA

VIA MONTE PIETA

VIA MONTENAPOLEONE

VIA SANT'ANDREA

V. CUSANI

VYVERDI

POLDI PEZZOLI MUSEUM

VIA MONTE-NAPOLEONE (HIGH-FASHION SHOPS)

EX SEMINARIO

V. LAURO

VIA DELL'ORSO

CORSO VENEZIA

PALAZZO BELGIOIOSO

V. BROLETTO

LA SCALA

GALLERIE D'ITALIA

OPERA MUSEUM

Piazza della Scala

Piazza Meda

CORSO MATTEOTTI

San Babila

VIA DANTE

GALLERIA

VIA AGNELLO

VIA SAN PAOLO

VIA SAN PAOLO

Cordusio

Piazza Cordusio

Piazza dei Mercanti

LA RINASCENTE DEP'T STORE

CORSO VITT. EMANUELE II.

CORSO EUROPA

POST

V. FOSTA

VIA BOCCHETTO

VIA ARMORARI

VIA OREFICI

Duomo

Piazza del Duomo

DUOMO

Piazza Beccaria

CORSO DI PORTA

PINACOTECA AMBROSIANA

V. MAURILIO

VIA NERINO

SAN SATIRO

T #2

T #16

MUSEO DEL NOVECENTO

#73 B

PALAZZO REALE

DUOMO INFO POINT

DUOMO MUSEUM

Piazza Fontana

LARGA

Piazza S. Stefano

VIA SIGNORA

VIA TORINO

VIA MAZZINI

Piazza Diaz

See Milan Duomo Area map

VIA LAGHETTO

Missori

VIA SANT'ANTONIO

VIA DI PORTA ROMANA

VELASCA TOWER

VIA FRANCESCO SFORZA

VIA SAN BARNABA

N

200 Meters

200 Yards

VIA CROCEFISSO

V. AMEDEI

VIA ITALIA

V. S. EUFEMIA

V. S. SOFIA

# Tours in Milan

🎧 To sightsee on your own, download my free Milan's Duomo Neighborhood audio tour.

### Local Guides

**Lorenza Scorti** is a hardworking young guide who knows her city's history and how to teach it. She also enjoys leading Lake Como day trips (€160/3 hours, same price for individuals or groups, evenings OK, mobile 347-735-1346, lorenza.scorti@libero.it). **Sara Cerri** is another good licensed local guide who enjoys passing on her knowledge (€195/3 hours, then €50/hour, mobile 380-433-3019, www.walkingtourmilan.it, walkingtourmilan@gmail.com). **Valeria Andreoli,** smart and fun-loving, leads a variety of themed tours (highlights tour—€60/hour, €180/half-day, mobile 338-301-2220, www.bellamilanotours.com, valeria@bellamilanotours.com).

### Walking and Bus Tours with *The Last Supper*

If you can't get a reservation for *The Last Supper,* consider joining a walking or bus tour that includes a guided visit to Leonardo's masterpiece. These €60-75 tours (usually 3 hours) also take you to top sights such as the Duomo, Galleria Vittorio Emanuele II, La Scala Opera House, and Sforza Castle. Ideally book at least a week in advance, but it's worth a try at the last minute, too.

For the best experience, I'd book a walking tour with **Veditalia** (www.veditalia.com) or **City Wonders** (www.citywonders. com). Both have good guides and solid reputations. **Get Your Guide** (www.getyourguide.com) is another worthwhile option. The bus-and-walking tours are less satisfying, but you can try **Autostradale** ("Look Mi" tour, offices in passage at far end of Piazza del Duomo and in front of Sforza Castle, tel. 02-8058-1354, www. autostradaleviaggi.it) or **Zani Viaggi** (office disguised as a "tourist information" point, corner of Foro Buonaparte and Via Cusani at #18, near Sforza Castle, tel. 02-867-131, www.zaniviaggi.com).

**Hop-On, Hop-Off Option:** Zani Viaggi also operates **CitySightseeing Milano** hop-on, hop-off buses (look for the red buses—easiest at Duomo and La Scala, €22/all day, €25/48 hours, buy on board, recorded commentary, www.milano.city-sightseeing. it). With a bus ticket, you can pay an additional €44 for a *Last Supper* reservation—exorbitant but worth considering for the wealthy and the desperate (April-Oct only).

# Sights in Milan

Milan's core sights—the Duomo, Duomo Museum, and Galleria Vittorio Emanuele II—cluster within easy walking distance. Also in the Duomo area are the Piazza della Scala and La Scala Opera House.

The city's other main sights—*The Last Supper*, Basilica di Sant'Ambrogio, Sforza Castle, and Brera Art Gallery—are scattered farther afield. It's easiest to reach them by public transportation.

### ▲▲▲DUOMO (CATHEDRAL)

The city's centerpiece is the third-largest church in Europe (after St. Peter's Basilica in Rome and Sevilla's cathedral). At 525 by 300

feet, the place is immense, with more than 2,000 statues inside (and another thousand outside) and 52 100-foot-tall, sequoia-size pillars representing the weeks of the year and the liturgical calendar. If you do two laps, you've done your daily walk. The church was built to hold 40,000 worshippers—the entire population of Milan when construction began.

A visit here has several elements. First, take in the overwhelming exterior from various angles, admiring its remarkable bulk and many spires and statues. Then go inside to see the church's vast nave, stained glass, historic tombs, basement archaeological area, and a quirky, one-of-a-kind statue of a flayed man. A visit to the adjacent Duomo Museum lets you see the church's statues and details up close. Finally, take an elevator ride (or long stair climb) up to the Duomo rooftop for city views and a stroll through a forest of jagged church spires.

**Cost:** Cathedral-€3, museum-€3, rooftops by elevator-€14. The archaeological area is free with any ticket. Of the various combo-tickets, the best is the €17 Duomo Pass, which includes the cathedral, rooftop terraces by elevator, archaeological area, and Duomo Museum.

**Hours:** Cathedral open daily 8:00-19:00, archaeological area and rooftop from 9:00; Duomo Museum Thu-Tue 10:00-18:00, closed Wed; last entry one hour before closing.

**Information:** Church tel. 02-7202-2656, museum tel. 02-860-358, www.duomomilano.it.

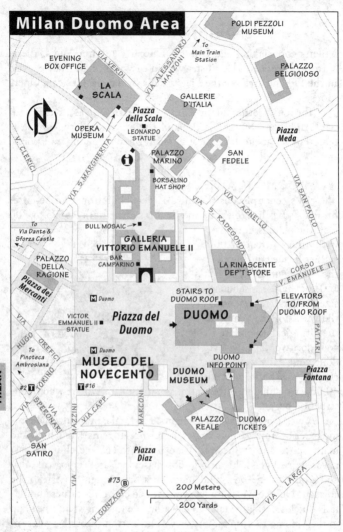

## Milan Duomo Area

POLDI PEZZOLI
MUSEUM

EVENING
BOX OFFICE

VIA VERDI

VIA ALESSANDRO MANZONI

To
Main Train
Station

PALAZZO
BELGIOIOSO

LA
SCALA

GALLERIE
D'ITALIA

Piazza
della Scala

LEONARDO
STATUE

Piazza
Meda

OPERA
MUSEUM

V. CLERICI

VIA S. MARGHERITA

PALAZZO
MARINO

SAN
FEDELE

BORSALINO
HAT SHOP

VIA S. RADEGONDA

VIA S. AGNELLO

VIA SAN PAOLO

To
Via Dante &
Sforza Castle

BULL MOSAIC

GALLERIA
VITTORIO EMANUELE II

PALAZZO
DELLA
RAGIONE

BAR
CAMPARINO

LA RINASCENTE
DEP'T STORE

CORSO
V. EMANUELE II

Piazza dei
Mercanti

Ⓜ Duomo

STAIRS TO
DUOMO ROOF

ELEVATORS
TO/FROM
DUOMO ROOF

VICTOR
EMMANUEL II
STATUE

Piazza del
Duomo

DUOMO

PATTARI

VIA HUGO

V. OREFICI

Ⓜ Duomo

To
Pinoteca
Ambrosiana

MUSEO DEL
NOVECENTO

DUOMO
INFO POINT

Piazza
Fontana

#2 Ⓣ

Ⓣ #16

DUOMO
MUSEUM

V. TORINO

VIA SPERONARI

VIA MAZZINI

VIA CAPP.

V. MARCONI

PALAZZO
REALE

DUOMO
TICKETS

SAN
SATIRO

Piazza
Diaz

VIA LARGA

#73 Ⓑ

200 Meters

200 Yards

V. GONZAGA

**Buying Tickets and Avoiding Lines:** There are two ticket booths (each with ticket machines): the big ticket center with info office (on the south side of the cathedral across from the Duomo's right transept at #14a) and at the Duomo Museum.

You can avoid the occasionally very long ticket lines by simply buying your tickets online; if buying on-site, the museum often has shorter lines. Security lines can also be long. You can avoid the church security line by doing the rooftop first and descending from there directly into the church. Or visit late in the day, when there are generally fewer people.

**Dress Code:** Modest dress is required to visit the church. Keep shoulders and knees covered, and don't wear sports T-shirts or shorts.

**Tours:** A €6 audioguide for the church is available at a kiosk inside its main door (no rentals Sun).

## ◐ Self-Guided Tour

### Exterior

Stand facing the main facade. The Duomo is huge and angular, with prickly spires topped with statues. The style, Flamboyant Gothic, means "flame-like," and the church seems to flicker toward heaven with flames of stone. The facade is a pentagon, divided by six vertical buttresses, all done in pink-white marble. The dozens of statues, pinnacles, and pointed-arch windows on the facade are just a fraction of the many adornments on this architecturally rich structure.

For more than 2,000 years, this spot has been the spiritual heart of Milan: In 2014, archaeologists probing for ancient Roman ruins beneath the Duomo discovered the remains of what might be a temple to the goddess Minerva. A church has stood on this site since the days of the ancient Romans and St. Ambrose (4th century), but construction of the building we see today began in 1386. Back then, the dukes of Milan wanted to impress their counterparts in Germany, France, and the Vatican with this massive cathedral. They chose the trendy Gothic style coming out of France, and stuck with it even after Renaissance-style domes came into vogue elsewhere in Italy. The cathedral was built not from ordinary stone, but from expensive marble, top to bottom. Pink Candoglia marble was rafted in from a quarry about 60 miles away, across Lake Maggiore and down a canal to a port at the cathedral—a journey that took about a week. Construction continued from 1386 to 1810, with final touches added as late as 1965.

The statues on the lower level of the facade—full of energy and movement—are early Baroque, from about 1600. Of the five bronze doors, the center one is biggest. Made in 1907 in the Liberty Style (Italian Art Nouveau), it features the Joy and Sorrow of the Virgin Mary. Sad scenes are on the left, joyful ones on the right, and on top is the coronation of Mary in heaven by Jesus, with all the saints and angels looking on. (High above that is what looks like the Statue of Liberty, dating from the 1820s—decades before Frédéric-Auguste Bartholdi designed the one Americans know and love. Hmmm.)

Topping the church (you may have to back up to see it) is its tallest spire. It rises up from the center of the Duomo to display a large golden statue of the Madonna of the Nativity, to whom the church is dedicated.

**MILAN**

**A Closer Look:** Along the right side of the church are interesting views from every angle: the horizontal line of the long building, the verticals of the spires, and the diagonals of the flying buttresses supporting the roof. Get close to the facade's right corner to appreciate the many intricate details: a nude Atlas holding up the corner buttress, robed saints, relief panels of Bible scenes, and tiny faces—angry, smiling, happy, sad.

Stroll a little farther down the right to see the range of statues, from placid saints to thrashing nudes. These statues were made between the 14th and 20th centuries by sculptors from all over Europe. There are hundreds of them—each different. Midway up are the fanciful gargoyles (96 in total) that functioned as drain spouts. Look way up to see the statues on the tips of the spires...they seem so relaxed, like they're just hanging out, waiting for their big day.

The back end of the church (if you make it that far) is the oldest part, with the earliest stones, laid in the late 1300s. The sun-in-rose window was the proud symbol of the city's leading Visconti family. It's flanked by the angel telling Mary she's going to bear the Messiah. Nearby, find the shrine to the leading religion of the 21st century: soccer. The Football Team store is filled with colorful vestments and relics of local soccer saints.

### Inside the Church

**Nave:** It's the fourth-longest nave in Christendom, stretching more than 500 feet from the entrance to the stained-glass rose window at the far end. The apse at the far end was started in 1385. The wall behind you wasn't finished until 1520. The style is Gothic, a rarity in Italy. Fifty-two tree-sized **pillars** rise to support a ribbed, pointed-arch ceiling, and the church is lit by glorious stained glass. At the far end, marking the altar, is a small tab-

ernacle of a dome atop columns—a bit of an anomaly in a Gothic church (more on that later). Notice the little red light on the cross high above the altar. This marks where a nail from the cross of Jesus is kept. This relic was brought to Milan by St. Helen (Emperor Constantine's mother) in the fourth century, when Milan was the capital of the western Roman Empire. It's on display for three days a year (in mid-Sept).

Notice the two single-stone pillars flanking the main door—each is made from a single stone. Now, facing the altar, look high to the right, in the rear corner of the church, and find a tiny pinhole of white light. This is designed to shine a 10-inch sunbeam at noon

# Milan Duomo

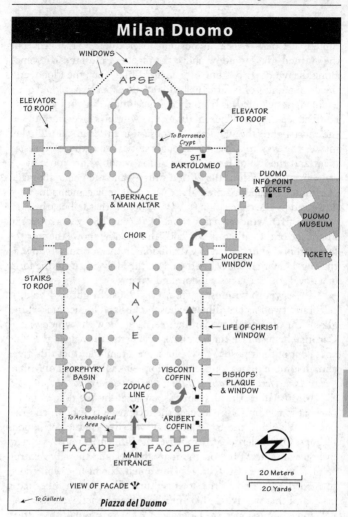

WINDOWS

APSE

ELEVATOR
TO ROOF

ELEVATOR
TO ROOF

To Borromeo
Crypt

ST.
BARTOLOMEO

DUOMO
INFO POINT
& TICKETS

TABERNACLE
& MAIN ALTAR

DUOMO
MUSEUM

TICKETS

CHOIR

MODERN
WINDOW

STAIRS
TO ROOF

N
A
V
E

LIFE OF CHRIST
WINDOW

PORPHYRY
BASIN

VISCONTI
COFFIN

BISHOPS'
PLAQUE
& WINDOW

ZODIAC
LINE

To Archaeological
Area

ARIBERT
COFFIN

FACADE         FACADE

MAIN
ENTRANCE

VIEW OF FACADE

20 Meters

20 Yards

To Galleria

*Piazza del Duomo*

MILAN

onto the **bronze line** that runs across the floor, indicating where we are on the zodiac calendar.

This 600-year-old church is filled with history. It represents the continuous line of bishops who have presided over Milan, stretching back to the days of St. Ambrose (c. 340-397). Let's see some of the earliest artifacts.

• *Before wandering deeper into the church, head to the end of the...*

**Right Aisle:** The first recess along the right wall has the 1,000-year-old gray-stone coffin of **Archbishop Aribert,** a formidable figure in 11th-century Milan. A couple of steps farther along, you'll see a red coffin atop columns belonging to the noble **Visconti** family who commissioned this church.

The third bay has a plaque where you can trace the uninterrupted rule of 144 local archbishops back to AD 51. Check out the **stained-glass window** above the plaque. Find familiar scenes along the window's bottom level: Cain killing Abel, the Flood, and the drunkenness of Noah. The brilliant and expensive colored glass (stained, not painted) is from the 15th century. Bought by wealthy families seeking the Church's favor, the windows face south to get the most light. The windows' purpose was to teach the illiterate masses the way to salvation through stories from the Old Testament and the life of Jesus. Many of the windows are more modern—from the 16th to the 20th century—and are generally made of dimmer, cheaper painted glass. Many are replacements for ones destroyed by the concussion of WWII bombs that fell nearby.

The **fifth window** dates from 1470, "just" 85 years after the first stone of the cathedral was laid. The window shows the story of Jesus, from Annunciation to Crucifixion. In the bottom window, as the angel Gabriel tells Mary the news, the Holy Spirit (in the form of a dove) enters Mary's window and world.

The **seventh window** is from the 1980s. Bright and bold, it celebrates two local cardinals (whose tombs and bodies are behind glass). The memorials to Cardinal Ferrari (below the window) and Cardinal Schuster (in the next bay), who heroically helped the Milanese out of their post-WWII blues, are a reminder that this great church is more than a tourist attraction—it's a living part of Milan.

• *Now take a few steps back into the nave for a view of the...*

**Main Altar:** The altar area is anchored by the domed tabernacle atop columns. This houses the receptacle that holds the Eucharist. Flanking the tabernacle are two silver statues of famous bishops. On the left is **St. Ambrose,** the influential fourth-century bishop who put Milan on the map and became the city's patron saint. The other is **St. Charles Borromeo,** the bishop who transformed the Duomo in the 16th century. Charles had inherited a cathedral that was barely half-finished. He re-energized the project, and commissioned the tabernacle. Above are four 16th-century pipe organs.

While the rest of the church is Gothic, the altar is Baroque—a dramatic stage-like setting in the style of the Vatican in the 1570s. Borromeo was a great champion of the Catholic church, and this powerful style was a statement to counter the Protestant Reformation that was threatening the Roman Catholic Church. Look up into the dome above the altar—a round dome on an octangular base, rising 215 feet. **Napoleon** crowned himself king of Italy under this dome in 1805. It was Napoleon who sped up construction, so that in 1810—finally—the church was essentially completed.

• *Before moving on, look to the rear, up at the ceiling, and see the fancy "carved" tracery on the ceiling's ribs. Nope, that's painted. It looks ex-*

MILAN

*pensive, but paint is more affordable than carved stone. Now continue up the right aisle and into the south (right) transept. Find the bald statue.*

**St. Bartolomeo Statue:** This is a grotesque 16th-century statue of St. Bartolomeo, an apostle and first-century martyr skinned alive by the Romans. Examine the details (face, hands, feet) of the poor guy. He piously holds a Bible in one hand and wears his own skin like a robe. Carved by a student of Leonardo da Vinci, this is a study in human anatomy learned by dissection, forbidden by the Church at the time. Read the sculptor's proud Latin inscription on the base: "I was not made by Praxiteles"—the classical master of beautiful nudes—"but by Marco d'Agrate."

• *Walk toward the altar, checking out the fine 16th-century inlaid-marble floor. The black marble (quarried from Lake Como) is harder and more durable, while the lighter colors (white from Lake Maggiore, pink from Verona) look and feel more worn. At the altar, bear right around the corner 15 steps. You'll see a door marked Scurolo di S. Carlo. This leads down to the...*

**Crypt of St. Charles Borromeo:** Steps lead under the altar to the tomb of St. Charles Borromeo (1538-1584), the economic power behind the church. You can still see Charles' withered body inside the rock-crystal coffin. Charles was bishop of Milan, and the second most important hometown saint after St. Ambrose. Tarnished silver reliefs around the ceiling show scenes from Charles' life.

• *Now resurface and continue around the apse, looking up at the...*

**MILAN**

**Windows:** The apse is lit by three huge windows, all 19th-century painted copies. The originals, destroyed in Napoleonic times, were made of precious stained glass. Each window has 12 panels and 12 rows, creating 144 separate scenes.

• *From the apse, head back through the church toward the main entrance. Near the entrance stands a large basin of expensive purple porphyry. Made by Borromeo's favorite architect, Pellegrini, it was used to baptize infants. Now find the entrance and stairs that lead down to the...*

**Archaeological Area:** The church's "basement" is a maze of ruined brick foundations of earlier churches that stood here long before the present one. Milan has been an important center of Christianity since its beginning. In Roman times, Mediolanum's streets were 10 feet below today's level. The stones and mosaics you see, the pavement you walk on, and the artifacts in the glass case date from the time of the Edict of Milan (AD 313) when Emperor Constantine, ruling from this city, made Christianity legal in the Roman Empire.

The highlight here is the scant remains of the eight-sided **Paleo-Christian Baptistery of San Giovanni.** It stands alongside the remains of a little church. Back then, since you couldn't enter the church until you were baptized (which didn't happen until age 18), churches had a little baptistery just outside for the unbaptized.

This humble baptistery was where St. Ambrose was baptized. Ambrose went on to become bishop here, and to mentor a randy and rebellious Roman named Augustine. On this spot in AD 387, Ambrose baptized the 31-year-old **Augustine of Hippo,** who later became one of Christianity's (and the world's) most influential thinkers, philosophers, and writers. And the rest—like this tour— is history.

## More Duomo Sights

For information on tickets and opening times for these sights, see the cost and hours for the Duomo, earlier.

### ▲▲Duomo Museum (Museo del Duomo)

This museum, to the right of the Duomo in the Palazzo Reale, helps fill in the rest of the story of Milan's cathedral, and lets you see its original art and treasures up close. The collection is much more meaningful with the audioguide (€6, with standard earbud jack).

**Visiting the Museum:** Just after the ticket taker, notice (on the wall to your right) the original **inlaid-marble floor** of the Duomo. The black (from Lake Como) marble is harder. Go ahead, wear down the white a little more.

Now follow the roughly chronological one-way route. Among the early treasures of the cathedral is a 900-year-old, Byzantine-style **crucifix.** Made of copper gilded with real gold and nailed onto wood, it was part of the tomb of the archbishop of Milan. A copy is in today's cathedral.

You'll pass a big, wooden model of the church (we'll get a better look at this later, on the way out). Then you'll step through a long room with paintings, chalices, glass monstrances, and lifelike reliquary busts of Sts. Charles, Sebastian, and Thecla.

Look for the big, 600-year-old statue of **St. George.** Among the cathedral's oldest statues, it once stood on the front (and first constructed) spire of the Duomo. Some think this is the face of Duke Visconti—the man who started the cathedral. The museum is filled with statues and spires like this, carved of *marmo di Candoglia*—marble from Candoglia. The duke's family gave the entire Candoglia quarry (near Stresa) to the church for all the marble it would ever need.

You'll pop into a long room filled with more statues. On your left, gaze into the eyes of the big gilded bust of **God the Father.** Made of wood, wrapped in copper, and gilded, this giant head covered the keystone connecting the tallest arches directly above the high altar of the Duomo.

Continue into a narrow room lined with grotesque **gargoyles.** When attached to the cathedral, they served two purposes: to scare away evil spirits and to spew rainwater away from the building.

Twist through several more rooms of 14th- and 15th-century statues big and small that embellished the church's many spires. In one long, brick-walled hall, watch on the left for **St. Paul the Hermit,** who got close to God by living in the desert. While wearing only a simple robe, he's filled with inner richness. The intent is for pilgrims to commune with him and feel at peace (but I couldn't stop thinking of the Cowardly Lion—"Put 'em up! Put 'em up!").

A few steps beyond Paul, look for the 15th-century dandy with the rolled-up contract in his hand. That's Visconti's descendant, Galeazzo Sforza, and if it weren't for him, the church facade might still be brick as bare as the walls of this room. The contract he holds makes it official—the church now owns the marble quarry (and it makes money on it to this day).

In the next room, study the brilliantly gilded and dynamic statue *God the Father* (1554). Five steps farther is a sumptuous Flanders-style **tapestry,** woven of silk, silver, and gold in 1468. Half a millennium ago, this hung from the high altar. In true Flemish style, it weaves vivid details of everyday life into the theology. It tells the story of the Crucifixion by showing three scenes at once. Note the exquisite detail, down to the tears on Mary's cheeks.

Next you'll step through a stunning room with 360 degrees of gorgeous **stained glass** from the 12th to 15th century, telling the easily recognizable stories of the Creation, the Tower of Babel, and David and Goliath. Take a close look at details that used to be too far above the cathedral floor to be seen clearly—again, designed for God's eyes only.

Farther on, you'll reach a display of **terra-cotta panels** juxtaposed with large **monochrome paintings** (1628) by Giovanni Battista Crespi. After Crespi finished the paintings, they were translated into terra-cotta, and finally sculpted in marble to decorate the doorways of the cathedral. Study Crespi's *Creation of Eve (Creazione di Eva)* and its terra-cotta twin. This served as the model for the marble statue that still stands above the center door on the church's west portal (1643). You'll pass a few more of these scenes, then hook into a room with the original, stone-carved, swirling *Dancing Angels,* which decorated the ceiling over the door.

• *When you reach the doors leading into the museum shop, make a U-turn to see the final exhibits.*

After passing several big tapestries, and a huge warehouse where statues are stacked on shelves stretching up to the ceiling, you'll reach the *Frame of the Madonnina* (1773). Standing like a Picasso is the original iron frame for the statue of the Virgin Mary that still crowns the cathedral's tallest spire. In 1967, a steel re-

**MILAN**

placement was made for the 33 pieces of gilded copper bolted to the frame. The carved-wood face of Mary (in the corner) is the original mold for Mary's cathedral-crowning copper face.

Soon you'll get a better look at that **wooden model** of the Duomo. This is the actual model used in the 16th century by the architects and engineers to build the church. This version of the facade wasn't built, and other rejected facades line the walls.

On your way out, you'll pass models for the Duomo's doors. And stepping outside, as your eyes adjust to the sunlight, you'll see the grand church itself—looking so glorious thanks to the many centuries of hard work you've just learned about.

### ▲▲Duomo Rooftop

Strolling between the frilly spires of the cathedral rooftop terraces is the most memorable part of a Duomo visit. You can climb the stairs or take the elevators. On the left side, the stairs are in front of the transept, and the elevator is behind it. (Even those taking the elevator will have to climb a lot of stairs.) On the right side, look for the "fast-track" elevator behind the transept.

Once up there, you'll loop around the rooftop, wandering through a fancy forest of spires with great views of the city, the square, and—on clear days—the crisp and jagged Alps to the north. And, 330 feet above everything, La Madonnina overlooks it all. This 15-foot-tall gilded Virgin Mary is a symbol of the city.

**Visiting the Rooftop:** As you emerge from the stairs or lift, you first walk along the **lower side-terrace.** You'll enjoy close-ups of fanciful gargoyles, statue-topped spires, and ever-changing views of the rows of flying buttresses (which, on this lavishly ornamented Gothic church, are both decorative and functional).

Take a moment to appreciate the detail. Keep in mind that the stairs you climbed were designed not for the public but for workers. The exquisite figures carved in stone around you—every face and every glower all different—were unseen by the public for over 400 years. They were all carved as a gift to God.

Next you climb a richly carved staircase to the sloping **roof-top**—directly above the nave. As you wander among the spires, pick any one and appreciate its details. At the **spires'** base is the marble "fence" that surrounds the entire rooftop, with its pointed arches topped with pinnacles, which themselves are mostly crowned with crosses. Each spire is supported by blocks of Candoglia marble, with its pink-white-green-blue hues (which blend into gray).

On the next level up, the spires have vertical ribs and saints in cages. Continuing up, they get more ornate, with flamboyant flames that flicker upward toward still more saints posing beneath church-like awnings. Finally, the spire tapers into a slender point, topped with a lifelike **saint** who gazes out over the city. The church has 135 spires—all similar, yet each different. No wonder it took 600 years to carve it all.

At the **counter-facade** (the back side of the church's false-front facade), find a few 20th-century details that are among the last things done. To the left (as you face toward the Piazza del Duomo), find carved reliefs with boxing scenes. Just above and to the right of the boxing scenes is a relief of carved foliage. The proud-looking face peering out from the leaves is none other than the WWII dictator Benito Mussolini.

Before leaving, check out the great **views** of the city. To the east, you can peer down into the Piazza del Duomo, 20 stories below.

To the south of the Duomo is the red-brick, octagonal, statue-topped bell tower of San Gottardo Church, built in the 1300s by the same Visconti family that began the Duomo. The hard-to-miss Velasca Tower (Torre Velasca) is a top-heavy skyscraper from the 1950s (modeled on medieval watchtowers such as those at the Sforza Castle), which became a symbol of Milan's rise from the ashes of World War II.

Looking north, there's a skyline of a dozen-plus skyscrapers. At the far right of the group is the 32-story Pirelli Tower, a slender rectangle with tapering sides, which proclaimed Italy's postwar "economic miracle." The UniCredit Tower (from 2011), with its 750-foot-high rocket-like spire, is Italy's tallest building, and represents Milan's future. (This marks the Porta Nuova neighborhood, described later and worth a visit.)

Remember, as you leave you'll find two descending staircases giving you two options: directly back to the street or into the church.

## AROUND THE DUOMO
### ▲Piazza del Duomo
Stand in the center of Milan's main square and take in the scene. Before you rises the massive, prickly facade of Milan's cathedral, the Duomo. The huge equestrian **statue** in the center of the piazza is Victor Emmanuel II, the first king of Italy. He's looking at the grand **Galleria** named for him. The words above

the triumphal arch entrance read: "To Victor Emmanuel II, from the people of Milan." This grand square is ground zero for public events, marches, and spectacles in Milan.

To the right of the Duomo are the twin fascist buildings of the Arengario Palace. Mussolini made grandiose speeches from the balcony on the left. Study the buildings' relief panels, which tell—with fascist melodrama—the history of Milan. Today the palace houses the **Museo del Novecento** (described later).

Directly to the right of the Duomo is the historic ducal palace, the Palazzo Reale, which now houses the **Duomo Museum** (described earlier). The palace was redone in the Neoclassical style by Empress Maria Theresa in the late 1700s, when Milan was ruled by the Austrian Habsburgs.

Behind the Victor Emmanuel II statue (opposite the cathedral, about a block beyond the square), hiding in a small courtyard, is **Piazza dei Mercanti,** the center of medieval Milan (described later).

And all around you in Piazza del Duomo is a classic European scene and a local gathering point. Professionals scurry, fashion-forward kids loiter, and young thieves peruse.

### ▲▲Galleria Vittorio Emanuele II

This breathtaking four-story glass-domed arcade, next to Piazza del Duomo, is a symbol of Milan. The iron-and-glass shopping mall (built during the age of Eiffel and the heady days of Italian unification) showcased a new, modern era. It was the first building in town to have electric lighting, and since its inception it's been an elegant and popular meeting place. (Sadly, its designer, Giuseppe Mengoni, died the day before the gallery opened.) Here, in this covered piazza, you can turn an expensive cup of coffee into a good value by enjoying some of Europe's best people-watching.

The venerable **Bar Camparino** (at the Galleria's Piazza del Duomo entry), with a friendly staff and a period interior surviving from the 1870s, is the former haunt of famous opera composer Giuseppe Verdi and conductor Arturo Toscanini, who used to stop by after their performances at La Scala. It's a fine place to enjoy a drink and people-watch (€4 for an espresso is a great deal to take a seat, relax and enjoy the view, or pay €1.50 at the bar just to experience the scene). The café is named after the Campari family (its first owners), originators of the famous red

Campari bitter. You can enjoy a Campari or a Campari *spritz* at this unforgettable perch for €13 (Tue-Sun 7:30-20:00, closed Mon and Aug, tel. 02-8646-4435).

Wander around the Galleria. Its art celebrates the establishment of Italy as an independent country. Around the central dome, patriotic mosaics symbolize the four major continents (sorry, Australia). The mosaic floor is also patriotic. The white cross in the center is part of the king's coat of arms. The she-wolf with Romulus and Remus (on the south side—facing Rome) honors the city that, since 1870, has been the national capital. On the west side (facing Torino, the provisional capital of Italy from 1861 to 1865), you'll find that city's symbol: a *torino* (little bull). For good luck, locals step on his irresistible little testicles. Two local girls explained to me that it

works better if you spin—two times, and it must be clockwise. Find the poor little bull and observe for a few minutes...it's a cute scene. With so much spinning, the mosaic is replaced every few years.

Luxury shops have had outlets here from the beginning. Along with Gucci, Louis Vuitton, and Prada, you'll find Borsalino (at the end near Piazza della Scala), which has been selling hats here since the gallery opened in 1877.

If you cut through the Galleria to the other side, you'll pop out at Piazza della Scala, with its famous opera house and the Gallerie d'Italia—all described later. (While you may be tempted to walk the Highline Galleria, which hangs among the Galleria Vittorio Emanuele II rooftops, it's not worth the time or money.)

### ▲Museo del Novecento

Milan's art of the 1900s *(Novecento)* fills the two buildings of the Arengario Palace, Mussolini's fascist-era City Hall. In the beautifully laid-out museum, you'll work your way up the escalators and through the last century, one decade at a time. Each section is well-described, and the capper is a fine panoramic view over Piazza del Duomo through grand fascist-era arches. The museum makes it clear that Milan—a trendy city today—has been setting design trends since the start of the Novecento.

**Cost and Hours:** €10; Tue-Sun 9:30-19:30 (Thu and Sat until 22:30), Mon from 14:30; last entry one hour before closing, audioguide—€5, facing Piazza del Duomo at Via Marconi 1, tel. 02-8844-4072, www.museodelnovecento.org.

**Visiting the Museum:** As you spiral up the ramp, pause at the large painting, *The Fourth Estate,* to gaze into the eyes of proud workers getting off their shift. Painted in 1901, the work was a bold manifesto of a new era, and is a good introduction to the revolutionary spirit of the museum.

On the **second floor,** minor works by Picasso, Matisse, Mondrian and others are a snapshot of "Modern Art" trends around Europe as the 1900s began. Next you see how they inspired Italy's artists. Boccioni followed northern Europe's lead, evolving from a placid painter of realistic portraits to a bold sculptor of swirling forms. He captured a world in high-tech motion—i.e., "Futurism."

Escalate up to the **third floor** to see Giorgio de Chirico's brooding canvases of long shadows and empty architecture—Italy's great contribution to the movement called Surrealism.

The **fourth floor** focuses on the actual Novecento Italiano movement of the 1920s, which was based in Milan. These artists tried to merge Italy's classic roots (of monumental ancient Roman art and geometrically solid Renaissance art) with abstract styles and the revivalist spirit of the Mussolini years.

Continuing up to the **fifth floor,** you emerge into a glass-walled space (often hosting temporary installations) with great views over Piazza del Duomo. Find the stairs up to the top room, with canvases by Lucio Fontana. In the 1950s and '60s, Fontana made his mark by slicing and puncturing canvases to transform a two-dimensional "painting" into a three-dimensional "sculpture." Fontana also did the room's textured ceiling and a large neon sculpture elsewhere on floor 5.

### ▲Piazza dei Mercanti

This small square, the center of political power in 13th-century Milan, hides one block off Piazza del Duomo (directly opposite the cathedral). A strangely peaceful place today, it offers a fine smattering of historic architecture that escaped the bombs of World War II.

The arcaded, red-brick building that dominates the center of the square was the City Hall (Palazzo della Ragione); its arcades once housed the market hall. Overlooking the wellhead in the middle of the square is a balcony with coats of arms—this is where new laws were announced. Eventually two big families—Visconti and Sforza—took power, Medici-style, in Milan; the snake is their symbol. Running the show in Renaissance times, these dynasties shaped much of the city we see today, including the Duomo and the fortress. In 1454, the Sforza family made peace with Venice while enjoying a friendship with the Medici in Florence (who taught them how to become successful bankers). This ushered in a time of stability and peace, when the region's major city-states were run by banking families, and money was freed up for the Renaissance generation to make art, not war.

This square also held the Palace of Justice (the 16th-century courthouse with the clock tower), the market (not food, but crafts: leather, gold, and iron goods), the bank, the city's first university, and its prison. All the elements of a great city were right here on the "Square of the Merchants."

## ON PIAZZA DELLA SCALA

To reach these sights, cut through the Galleria Vittorio Emanuele II from Piazza del Duomo.

### Piazza della Scala

This smart little traffic-free square, between the Galleria and the opera house, is dominated by a statue of Leonardo da Vinci. The statue (from 1870) is a reminder that Leonardo spent his best 20 years in Milan, where he found well-paid, steady work. He was the brainy darling of the Sforza family (who dominated Milan as the Medici family dominated Florence). Under the great Renaissance genius stand four of his greatest "Leonardeschi." (He apprenticed a sizable group of followers.) The reliefs show his various contributions as a painter, architect, and engineer. Leonardo, wearing his hydro-engineer hat, reengineered Milan's canal system, complete with locks. (Until the 1920s, Milan was one of Italy's major ports, with canals connecting the city to the Po River and Lake Maggiore. For more on this footnote of Milan's history, read about the Naviglio Grande on page 317.)

The statue of Leonardo is looking at a plain but famous Neoclassical building, arguably the world's most prestigious opera house (described next).

### ▲La Scala Opera House and Museum

Milan's famous Teatro alla Scala opened in 1778 with an opera by Antonio Salieri (Mozart's wannabe rival). Today, opera buffs can get a glimpse of the theater and tour the adjacent museum's extensive collection, featuring Verdi's top hat, Rossini's eyeglasses, Toscanini's baton, Fettuccini's pesto, original scores, diorama stage sets, busts, portraits, and death

masks of great composers and musicians. For true devotees, La Scala is the Mecca of the religion of opera.

**Cost and Hours:** €9, daily 9:00-17:30, Piazza della Scala, tel. 02-8879-7473, www.teatroallascala.org.

**Visiting the Museum:** The main reason to visit the museum is the opportunity to peek into the theater (on many mornings you'll see the orchestra practicing). The stage is as big as the seating area on the ground floor. (You can see the towering stage box from Piazza della Scala across the street.) A renovation corrected acoustical problems caused by WWII bombing and subsequent reconstruction. The royal box is just below your vantage point, in the center rear. Take in the ornate red-velvet seats, white-and-gold trim, the huge stage and orchestra pit, and the massive chandelier made of Bohemian crystal.

The museum itself is a handful of small rooms with low-tech displays. Room 1 has antique musical instruments—some are familiar-looking keyboards and guitars, some are strange and weirdly shaped. Room 2 takes you to the roots of opera in *commedia dell'arte*—those humorous plays of outsized characters and elaborate costumes, like clever harlequins and buffoonish doctors in masks. Room 3 features Liszt's grand piano, still in playing condition.

Room 4's paintings lead you through opera's heyday in Milan. There's a street scene of La Scala in 1852, with fancy carriages and well-dressed ladies and gents. Find portraits of great opera composers like portly Rossini, sideburned Donizetti, and thick-bearded Verdi (flanked by his three loves: two wives and a piano). In the glass case are miniature portraits of famous opera composers and singers, as well as Napoleon's sword. Pass through Room 5 and into Room 6, with a glass case holding a snip of Mozart's hair and a cast of Chopin's slender hand. (The stairs lead up to temporary exhibits.)

Room 7 features many of opera's all-stars. In the glass case is a snip of Verdi's hair, scores by Verdi and Puccini, and batons of the great conductor (and music director of La Scala) Toscanini, who's practically a saint in this town. The room's portraits bring opera into the modern age. There's the great composer Puccini whose accessible operas seem to unfold like realistic plays that just happen to be sung. The great early-20th-century tenor Enrico Caruso brought sophisticated Italian opera to barbaric lands like America. There are portraits of renowned sopranos (and world-class divas) Maria Callas and Renata Tebaldi.

## Performances in the Opera House

The show goes on at the world-famous La Scala Opera House, which also hosts ballet and classical concerts. There are performances every month except August, and showtime is usually at 20:00 (for information, check online or call Scala Infotel Service, daily 9:00-18:00, tel. 02-7200-3744). On the opening night of an opera, a dress code is enforced for men (suit and tie).

**Advance Booking:** Seats sell out quickly. Online tickets go on sale two months before performances (www.teatroallascala.org).

**Same-Day Tickets:** On performance days, 140 sky-high, restricted-view, peanut-gallery tickets are offered at a low price (generally €15) at the box office (located down the left side of the theater toward the back on Via Filodrammatici, and marked with *Biglietteria Serale* sign). It's a bit complicated: Show up at 13:00 with an official ID (driver's license or passport) to put your name on a list (one ticket per person; for popular shows people start lining up long before, weekends tend to be busiest), then return at 17:30 for the roll call. You must be present when your name is called to receive a voucher, which you'll then show at the window to purchase your ticket before the performance. Also, one hour before showtime, the box office sells any remaining tickets at a 25 percent discount.

## ▲Gallerie d'Italia

This museum fills three adjacent buildings on Piazza della Scala with the amazing art collections of a bank that once occupied part

of this space. The bank building's architecture is early-20th-century Tiffany-like Historicism, with a hint of Art Nouveau; it's connected to two impressive palazzos that boast the nicest Neoclassical interiors I've seen in Milan. They are filled with exquisite work by 19th- and 20th-century Italian painters.

**Cost and Hours:** €5, more during special exhibits, includes audioguide, free first Sun of the month; open Tue-Sun 9:30-19:30, Thu until 22:30, closed Mon, last entry one hour before closing; across from La Scala Opera House at Piazza della Scala 6, toll-free tel. 800-167-619, www.gallerieditalia.com.

**Visiting the Museum:** Enter through the bank building facing Piazza della Scala and take the red-velvet stairs to the basement to pick up an audioguide (also downstairs is a bag check, WCs, and the original bank vault, which now stores racks and racks of paintings not on display).

Back upstairs, head into the main atrium of the bank, and consider the special exhibits displayed there. Then, to tackle the permanent art collection in chronological order, head to the far end of the complex and work your way back (follow signs for *Palazzo*

*Anguissola Antona Traversi* and *Palazzo Brentani*). You'll go through the café back into the Neoclassical palaces, where you'll trace the one-way route through the "Da Canova a Boccioni" exhibit, including marble reliefs by the Neoclassical sculptor Antonio Canova and Romantic paintings by Francesco Hayez. Upstairs, you'll see dramatic and thrilling scenes from the unification of Italy, as well as beautiful landscapes and cityscapes, especially of Milan. (An entire room is devoted to depictions of the now-trendy Naviglio Grande canal area in its workaday prime.)

On your way back to the bank building and the rest of the exhibit, take a moment to poke around the courtyard to find the *officina di restituzioni alle gallerie*—a lab where you can watch art restorers at work. Rejoining the permanent exhibit, you'll see paintings from the late 19th and early 20th centuries: Romantic landscapes; hyperrealistic, time-travel scenes of folk life; and Impressionism. Finally, you'll catch up to the art of the late 20th century, tucked between old bank-teller windows.

## WEST OF THE DUOMO

These sights are listed roughly in the order you'll reach them as you travel west from Piazza del Duomo. The first one is just a few short blocks from the cathedral, while the last is just over a mile away.

### ▲▲Pinacoteca Ambrosiana

This oldest museum in Milan was inaugurated in 1618 to house Cardinal Federico Borromeo's painting collection. It began as a teaching academy, which explains its many replicas of famous works of art. Highlights include original paintings by Botticelli, Caravaggio, and Titian—and, most important, a huge-scale sketch by Raphael and a rare oil painting by Leonardo da Vinci.

**Cost and Hours:** €15, Pinocoteca open Tue-Sun 10:00-18:00, closed Mon; Biblioteca open Mon-Fri 9:00-17:00, closed Sat-Sun; last entry one hour before closing, audioguide-€3, near Piazza del Duomo at Piazza Pio XI 2, Metro: Duomo or Cordusio, tel. 02-806-921, www.ambrosiana.eu.

**Visiting the Museum:** Pick up the English-language map locating the rooms and major works I highlight below, and rent the audioguide (covers both permanent and special exhibits). Then head upstairs to begin your visit.

**Raphael's Cartoon** (Room 5): Filling an entire wall, this drawing served as an outline for Raphael's famous *School of Athens* fresco at the Vatican Museums. (A cartoon—*cartone* in Italian—is a full-size sketch that's used to transfer a design to another surface.) First, watch the five-minute video introduction. While the Vatican's much-adored fresco is attributed entirely to Raphael, it was painted mostly by his students. But this *cartone* was wholly sketched by the hand of Raphael. To transfer the fresco design to the wall, his assistants riddled this cartoon with pinpricks along the outlines of the figures, stuck it to the wall of the pope's study, and then applied a colored powder. (Where the master cared more about the detail, you'll see more pinpricks.) When they removed the *cartone*, the figures' shapes were marked on the wall, and completing the fresco was a lot like filling in a coloring book.

**Jan Brueghel** (Room 7): As Cardinal Borromeo was a friend of Jan Brueghel, this entire room is filled with delightful works by the artist and other Flemish masters. Study the wonderful detail in Brueghel's *Allegory of Fire* and *Allegory of Water*. The Flemish paintings are extremely detailed—many are painted on copper to heighten the effect—and offer an insight into the psyche of the age. If the cardinal were asked why he enjoyed paintings that celebrated the secular life, he'd likely say, "Secular themes are God's book of nature."

**Leonardo Hall** (Room 24): During his productive Milan years, Leonardo painted (oil on wood) *Portrait of a Musician*—as delicate, mysterious, and thought-provoking as the *Mona Lisa*. (This is the only one of his paintings that remains in Milan.) The large fresco filling the far wall—with Christ receiving the crown of thorns—is by Bernardino Luini, one of Leonardo's disciples. But I find the big replica painting of *The Last Supper* most interesting. When the cardinal realized that Leonardo's marvelous frescoed original was fading, he commissioned Andrea Bianchi to paint on canvas a careful copy to be displayed here for posterity. Today, this copy gives a rare chance to appreciate the original colorful richness of the now-faded masterpiece.

**Biblioteca Ambrosiana:** The 17th-century library hosts a revolving display of Leonardo sketches and notes. These are from the precious Codex Atlanticus, with more than a thousand busy pages done by Leonardo for his own reference, giving us a peek into his amazing mind. On any given day 16 pages are on display with English descriptions.

### Piazza degli Affari and a Towering Middle Finger

This square and monument mark the center of Milan's financial district. The bold fascist buildings in the neighborhood were built in the 1930s under Mussolini. Italy's major stock exchange, the Borsa, faces the square. Stand in the center and appreciate the contemporary take on ancient aesthetics (you're standing atop the city's ancient Roman theater). Find the stern statues representing various labors and occupations and celebrating the nobility of workers—typical whistle-while-you-work fascist themes.

Now notice the equally bold modern statue in the center. After a 2009 contest to find the most appropriate sculpture to grace the

**MILAN**

financial district, this was the winner. With Italy's continuing financial problems, here we see how "the 99 percent" feel when they stand before symbols of corporate power. (Notice how the finger is oriented—it's the 1 percent, and not the 99 percent, who's flipping the bird.) The 36-foot-tall Carrara marble digit was made by Maurizio Cattelan, the most famous—or, at least, most controversial—Italian sculptor of our age. *L.O.V.E.*, as the statue is titled, was temporary at first. But locals liked it, and, by popular demand, it's now permanent.

### ▲Church of San Maurizio
### (San Maurizio al Monastero Maggiore)

This church, part of a ninth-century convent built into a surviving bit of Milan's ancient Roman wall, dates from around 1500. Despite its simple facade, it's a hit with art lovers for its amazing cycle of Bernardino Luini frescoes. Stepping into this church is like stepping into the Sistine Chapel of Lombardy.

**Cost and Hours:** Free; Tue-Sun 9:30-19:30, closed Mon; Corso Magenta 15 at the Monastero Maggiore, Metro: Cadorna or Cairoli, tel. 02-8844-5208.

**Visiting the Church:** Bernardino Luini (1480-1532), a follower of Leonardo, was also inspired by his contemporaries Michelangelo and Raphael. Sit in a pew and take in the art, which has the movement and force of Michelangelo and the grace and calm beauty of Leonardo.

Maurizio, the patron saint of this church, was a third-century Roman soldier who persecuted Christians, then converted, and eventually worked to stop those same persecutions. He's the guy standing on the pedestal in the upper right, wearing a bright yellow cape. The nobleman who paid for the art is to the left of the altar, kneeling and cloaked in black and white. His daughter, who joined the convent here and was treated as a queen (as nuns with noble connections were), is to the right. And all around are martyrs—identified by their palm fronds.

The adjacent **Hall of Nuns** (Aula delle Monache), a walled-off area behind the altar, is where cloistered sisters could worship apart from the general congregation. Fine Luini frescoes appear above and around the wooden crucifix. The Annunciation scene at the corners of the arch features a cute Baby Jesus zooming down from heaven (see Mary, on the right, ready to catch him). The organ dates from 1554, and the venue, with its fine acoustics, is popular

MILAN

for concerts with period instruments. Explore the pictorial Bible that lines the walls behind the wooden seats of the choir. Luini's landscapes were groundbreaking in the 16th century. Leonardo incorporated landscapes into his paintings, but Luini was among the first to make landscape the main subject of the painting.

**Nearby:** You'll exit the Hall of Nuns into the lobby of the adjacent **Archaeological Museum,** where you can pay €5 to see part of the ancient city wall and a third-century Roman tower.

## ▲▲Basilica di Sant'Ambrogio

One of Milan's top religious, artistic, and historic sights, this church was first built on top of an early Christian martyr's cemetery by St.

Ambrose around AD 380, when Milan had become the capital of the fading (and Christian) western Roman Empire.

**Cost and Hours:** Free, Mon-Sat 10:00-12:30 & 14:30-18:00, Sun 15:00-17:00, modest attire required, Piazza Sant'Ambrogio 15, Metro: Sant'Ambrogio, tel. 02-8645-0895, www.basilicasantambrogio.it.

**Visiting the Church:** Ambrose was a local bishop and one of the great fathers of the early Church. Besides his writings, he's remembered for converting and baptizing St. Augustine of Hippo, who himself became another great Church father. The original fourth-century church was later (in the 12th century) rebuilt in the Romanesque style you see today.

As you step "inside" from the street, you emerge into an arcaded **atrium**—standard in many churches back when people weren't allowed to actually enter the church until they were baptized. The unbaptized waited here during Mass. The courtyard is textbook Romanesque, with playful capitals engraved with fanciful animals. Inset into the wall (right side, above the pagan sarcophagi) are stone markers of Christian tombs—a reminder that this church, like St. Peter's at the Vatican, is built upon an ancient Roman cemetery.

From the atrium, marvel at the elegant 12th-century **facade,** or west portal. It's typical Lombard medieval style. The local bishop would bless crowds from its upper loggia. As two different monastic communities shared the church and were divided in their theology, there were also two different bell towers.

Step into the **nave** and grab a pew. The mosaic in the apse features Christ Pantocrator ("All Powerful") in the company of Milanese saints. Around you are pillars with Romanesque capitals and

MILAN

surviving fragments of the 12th-century frescoes that once covered the church.

The 12th-century **pulpit** sits atop a Christian sarcophagus dating from the year 400. Study its late Roman and early Christian iconography—on the side facing the altar, Apollo on his chariot morphs into Jesus on a chariot. You can see the moment when Jesus gave the Old Testament (the first five books, anyway) to his apostles.

The precious, ninth-century golden **altar** has four ancient porphyry columns under an elegant Romanesque 12th-century canopy. The entire ensemble was taken to the Vatican during World War II to avoid destruction. That was smart—the apse took a direct hit in 1943. A 13th-century mosaic was destroyed; today we see a reconstruction.

Step into the **crypt,** under the altar, to see the skeletal bodies of three people: Ambrose (in the middle, highest) and two earlier Christian martyrs whose tombs he visited before building the church.

**Nearby:** For a little bonus after visiting the church, consider this: The **Benedictine monastery** next to the church is now Cattolica University. With its stately colonnaded courtyards designed by Renaissance architect Donato Bramante, it's a nice place to study. It's fun to poke around and imagine being a student here.

MILAN

## ▲Leonardo da Vinci National Science and Technology Museum (Museo Nazionale della Scienza e Tecnica "Leonardo da Vinci")

The spirit of Leonardo lives here (a 10-minute walk from his *Last Supper*). Most tourists focus on the hall of Leonardo—the core of the museum—where wooden models illustrate his designs. But the rest of this immense collection of industrial cleverness is fascinating in its own right. There are exhibits on space exploration, mining, and radio and television (with some original Marconi radios); old musical instruments, computers, and telephones; chunks of the first transatlantic cable; and interactive science workshops. Out back are several more buildings containing antique locomotives and a 150-foot-long submarine from 1957. Ask for an English museum map from the ticket desk—you'll need it. On weekends, this museum is very popular with families, so come early or be prepared to wait in line.

**Cost and Hours:** €10; Tue-Fri 10:00-18:00, Sat-Sun until 19:00, shorter hours off-season, closed Mon year-round; Via San Vittore 21, Metro: Sant'Ambrogio; tel. 02-485-551, www.museoscienza.org.

## ▲▲Leonardo da Vinci's *The Last Supper* *(L'Ultima Cena/Cenacolo Vinciano)*

Decorating the former dining hall *(cenacolo)* of the Church of Santa Maria delle Grazie, this remarkable, exactingly crafted fresco by Leonardo da Vinci is one of the ultimate masterpieces of the Renaissance. Reservations are mandatory and should be booked long in advance (see options below).

**Cost:** €12, includes €2 reservation fee (9:30 and 15:30 visits cost €3.50 extra and include English tour).

**Hours:** Tue-Sun 8:00-18:45 (last entry), closed Mon. Arrive 20 minutes before your timed entry.

**Reservations:** Mandatory timed-entry reservations can be made either online or by phone (through an outfit called Vivaticket). Reservations for each calendar month go on sale about three months ahead; for example, bookings for July open in early April. Spots are snapped up quickly, so plan ahead.

To book **online,** go to www.vivaticket.it, then enter "Cenacolo Vinciano" into the search bar at the top of the page. A calendar will show available time slots for the coming months.

If you book by **phone,** you'll have a greater selection of days and time slots to choose from, since the website doesn't reflect cancellations. Note that you can't reserve same-day tickets (tel. 02-9280-0360, from the US dial 011-39-02-9280-0360, office open Mon-Sat 8:00-18:30, closed Sun; the number is often busy—once you get through, select 2 for an English-speaking operator).

**Tour Option:** If you can't get a reservation, you can book a more expensive (€60-75) walking or bus tour that includes a guided visit to *The Last Supper*. These should be reserved at least one week ahead (for details, see page 284).

**Last-Minute Tickets:** A few scattered same-day spots may be available due to cancellations. It's a low-percentage play, but you can try just showing up and asking at the desk—even if the *sold out* sign is posted (ideally when the office opens at 8:00, more likely on weekdays).

**Getting There:** The Church of Santa Maria delle Grazie is a seven-minute walk from Metro: Conciliazione. From the track, follow signs for *Cenacolo*. You'll walk four blocks. After the first bend you'll see the fine red-brick facade of the church ahead. Or take tram #16 from the Duomo (direction: San Siro or Piazzale Segesta), which drops you off in front of the church. When leaving, cross the street to catch the tram back to the Duomo.

**Getting In:** Stow your bag (free, required), pick up your ticket, and consider renting the audioguide. Your time will be called 15 minutes before, and you'll enter the waiting room. Use this time to study up. At your appointed time, the doors open and your group enters. No stress, no crowds, beautifully organized...it's a peaceful and inspiring experience. There's a fine WC at the exit.

**Audioguide:** The fine €3.50 audioguide (standard jack) is very helpful. Its spiel fills every second of the time you're in the room—a short intro (#100) and then tracks 1 through 5—for the entire 15 minutes you're inside. You can get a jump on it by listening to it in the waiting room while studying the reproduction of *The Last Supper*.

**Background:** Milan's leading family, the Sforzas, hired Leonardo to decorate the dining hall of the Dominican monastery that adjoins the church (the Dominican order traditionally placed a Last Supper on one end of their refectories, and a Crucifixion at the other). Leonardo worked on the project from about 1494 until 1498. This gift was essentially a bribe to the monks so that the Sforzas could place their family tomb in the church. Ultimately, the French drove the Sforzas out of Milan, they were never buried here, and the Dominicans got a great fresco for nothing.

Deterioration began within six years of *The Last Supper*'s completion because Leonardo painted on the wall in layers, as he would on a canvas, instead of applying pigment to wet plaster in the usual fresco technique. (Examining the extremely close-up photos in the waiting room lets you see how the paint is simply flaking off.) The church was bombed in World War II, but—miraculously, it seems—the wall holding *The Last Supper* remained standing. A 21-year restoration project (completed in 1999) peeled away 500 years of touch-ups, leaving Leonardo's masterpiece faint but vibrant.

**Visiting *The Last Supper*:** To minimize damage from humidity, only 30 tourists are allowed in every 15 minutes for exactly 15 minutes. While you wait, read the history of the masterpiece or listen to the audioguide. As your appointed time nears, you'll be herded between several rooms to dehumidify, while doors close behind you and open up slowly in front of you.

And then the last door opens, you take a step, you look right, and...there it is. In a big, vacant, whitewashed room, you'll see faded pastels and not a crisp edge. The feet under the table look like negatives. But the composition is dreamy—Leonardo captures the psychological drama as the Lord says, "One of you will betray me," and the apostles huddle in stressed-out groups of three, wondering, "Lord, is it I?" Some are scandalized. Others want more information. Simon (on the far right) gestures as if to ask a question that has no answer. In this agitated atmosphere, only Judas (fourth from left and the only one with his face in shadow)—clutching his 30 pieces of silver and looking pretty guilty—is not shocked.

The circle meant life and harmony to Leonardo. Deep into a study of how life emanates in circles—like ripples on a pool hit by a pebble—Leonardo positioned the 13 characters in a semicircle. Jesus is in the center, from whence the spiritual force of God emanates, or ripples out.

The room depicted in the painting seems like an architectural extension of the monk's dining hall. The disciples form an apse, with Jesus as the altar—in keeping with the Eucharist. Jesus anticipates his sacrifice, his face sad, all-knowing, and accepting. His feet even foreshadow his death by crucifixion. Had the door, which was cut out in 1652, not been added, you'd see how Leonardo placed Jesus' feet atop each other, ready for the nail.

The perspective is mathematically correct, with Jesus' head as the vanishing point where the converging sight lines meet. In fact, restorers found a tiny nail hole in Jesus' left eye, which anchored the strings Leonardo used to establish these lines. The table is cheated out to show the meal. Notice the exquisite lighting. The walls are lined with tapestries (as they would have been), and the one on the right is brighter in order to fit the actual lighting in the refectory (which has windows on the left). With the extremely natural effect of the light and the drama of the faces, Leonardo created a masterpiece.

The monks ate at three tables just like the one Leonardo painted, with a carefully ironed tablecloth also just like the one painted. The monks ate in silence, communicating with hand gestures (notice the ballet of hand gestures in Leonardo's composition).

Save a minute or two for the fresco of the Crucifixion on the opposite wall, which provides an instructive contrast. This is done in the traditional fresco technique—less soul and subtlety but much better preserved. It needed to be done quickly (as the plaster dried) and was finished in three months (compared to over three years for *The Last Supper*). For a good look at the contrasting styles, find the faded image of the Sforza duchess in the lower right corner. She was added to the scene by Leonardo using the same technique he used in *The Last Supper*.

Before stepping out, from the back of the room look one last time at Leonardo's masterpiece and imagine this room filled with three more tables and 60 monks immersed in devotion and with no idea that 500 years later travelers would be dropping by to appreciate the art decorating their hall.

The adjacent **Church of Santa Maria delle Grazie** survived World War II unscathed and is worth a quick look (free). Its fine Gothic arches lead to a Renaissance Bramante-designed dome. The Dominican monks frescoed in black and white on each pilaster were the first monks to eat under Leonardo's *Last Supper*.

## NORTH OF THE DUOMO
### ▲▲Brera Art Gallery (Pinacoteca di Brera)

Milan's top collection of Italian paintings (13th-20th century) is world class, but it can't top those in Rome or Florence. Established in 1809 to house Napoleon's looted art, it fills the first floor above a prestigious art college. You'll dodge scruffy starving artists...and wonder if there's a 21st-century Leonardo in your midst.

**Cost and Hours:** €12, free first Sun of month; Tue-Sun 8:30-19:15, closed Mon, last entry 45 minutes before closing; audio-guide—€5 (useful, ID required, but museum has excellent English descriptions), free lockers, Via Brera 28, Metro: Lanza or Montenapoleone, tel. 02-722-631, www.pinacotecabrera.org.

**Visiting the Museum:** Enter the grand courtyard of a former monastery, where you'll be greeted by the nude *Napoleon with Tinkerbell* (by Antonio Canova).

Climb the stairway (following signs to *Pinacoteca*), buy your ticket, and pick up an English map of the museum's masterpieces, some of which I've highlighted below. You'll follow a clockwise, chronological route through the huge collection. Take time to read the English descriptions, many of which are absolutely poetic. And, to get the most out of your visit, invest in the audioguide. Here are the highlights:

Next to the information desk peek through the window to see the 300-year-old library, then pop into the chapel (on the left) frescoed by a follower of Giotto in the 1300s. After the turnstile, enjoy the setup in the short entry hall.

Before Antonio Canova's big marble statue of naked Napoleon, head left into the dark, narrow blue hall to see Andrea Mantegna's iconic foreshortened Christ (and others by the influential early Renaissance master). Room 8 features more Mantegna, and bright and vivid paintings by the Bellini brothers from around 1500. Room 9 is for the big canvases by 16th-century Venetian masters (like Tintoretto and Paolo Veronese).

Past the towering marble statue of Napoleon, Room 15 holds four paintings by Vincenzo Campi, offering slices of local Milan life from 1591.

Then you reach the restoration lab, which offers a chance to peek in on the hard work of keeping these paintings looking so good.

Room 22 sparkles with High Gothic art. Carlo Crivelli, a contemporary of Leonardo, employed Renaissance technique while clinging to the mystique of the Gothic Age (that's why I like him so much). And Gentile da Fabriano hints at the realism of the coming Renaissance (check out the lifelike flowers and realistic, bright gold paint—he used real gold powder).

Room 26 is nicknamed "The Golden Room" for its Renaissance masterpieces from the early 16th century by Raphael *(The Marriage of the Virgin)*, Piero della Francesca *(Madonna and Child with Saints)*, and Donato Bramante.

In Room 28 don't miss gritty-yet-intimate realism of Caravaggio's *Supper at Emmaus*. Room 31 features Rubens (and other Dutch and Flemish works). And Room 35 is dedicated to "postcard" art from the 18th-century Grand Tour days (like Venicescapes by Canaletto and Francesco Guardi).

Finally, in Room 37 you come to 19th-century Romanticism, and in Room 38 three patriotic paintings, including *The Kiss* by Francesco Hayez, which evoke the spirit of Italy's fight for independence, the Risorgimento.

### ▲Risorgimento Museum

With a quick swing through this quiet one-floor museum, you'll get an idea of the interesting story of Italy's rocky road to unity: from Napoleon (1796) to the victory in Rome (1870). You'll see paintings, uniforms, monuments, a city model, and other artifacts. Thoughtful English descriptions help make this a meaningful look at this important period of Italian history.

**Cost and Hours:** Free; Tue-Sun 9:00-13:00 & 14:00-17:30, closed Mon; just around the block from Brera Art Gallery at Via Borgonuovo 23, Metro: Montenapoleone, tel. 02-8846-4176, www.museodelrisorgimento.mi.it.

### Poldi Pezzoli Museum

This classy house of art features Italian paintings of the 15th through 18th century, old weaponry, and lots of interesting decorative arts, such as a roomful of old sundials and compasses. It's all on view in a sumptuous 19th-century residence.

**Cost and Hours:** €10; Wed-Mon 10:00-18:00, closed Tue;

MILAN

audioguide–€1, Via Manzoni 12, Metro: Montenapoleone, tel. 02-794-889, www.museopoldipezzoli.it.

### Bagatti Valsecchi Museum

This unique 19th-century collection of Italian Renaissance furnishings was assembled by two aristocratic brothers who spent a wad turning their home into a Renaissance mansion.

**Cost and Hours:** €9, includes audioguide, €6 on Wed; Tue-Sun 13:00-17:45, closed Mon; Via Gesù 5, Metro: Montenapoleone, tel. 02-7600-6132, www.museobagattivalsecchi.org.

## SFORZA CASTLE AND NEARBY
### ▲▲Sforza Castle (Castello Sforzesco)

The castle of Milan tells the story of the city in brick. Today it features a vast courtyard, a sprawling museum, and—most importantly—a chance to see Michelangelo's final, unfinished pietà.

**Cost and Hours:** €10; museum open Tue-Sun 9:00-17:30, closed Mon; castle grounds open daily 7:00-19:30; WCs and free/mandatory lockers downstairs from ticket counter, Metro: Cairoli or Lanza, tel. 02-8846-3700, www.milanocastello.it.

**Background:** Built in the late 1300s as a military fortress, Sforza Castle guarded the gate to the city wall and defended Milan from enemies "within and without." It was beefed up by the Sforza duke in 1450 in anticipation of a Venetian attack. Later, the Sforza family made it their residence, building their Renaissance palace into the fortress. It was even home to their in-house genius, Leonardo. (When he applied for a position with the Sforza family, he did so as a military engineer and contributed to the design of the ramparts.) During the time of foreign rule (16th-19th century), it was a barracks for occupying Spanish, French, and Austrian soldiers. Today it houses an array of museums, but I'd concentrate on the Michelangelo pietà and the Museum of Ancient Art.

**⊙ Self-Guided Tour:** This tour begins outside the fortress, then focuses on the highlights inside.

**The Fortress:** The **gate** facing the city center stands above a ditch that was once filled with water. A relief celebrates Umberto I, the second king of Italy. Above that, a statue of St. Ambrose, the patron of Milan (and a local bishop in the fourth century), oversees the action. Notice the diagram a few steps away that shows how the city was encircled first by a crude medieval wall, and then by a state-of-the-art 16th-century wall—of which this castle was a key element. It's apparent from the enormity of these walls that Milan was a strategic prize. Today, the walls are gone, giving the city two circular boulevards.

This immense brick fortress—exhausting at first sight—can only be described as heavy. Its three huge courtyards originally functioned as military parade grounds, but today host concerts and welcome the public. (The holes in the walls were for scaffolding.)

• As you enter the main courtyard, look to your left to see the restored hospital building that houses the...

**Museo Pietà Rondanini** (Michelangelo): This is a rare opportunity to enjoy a Michelangelo statue with no crowds. Michelangelo died while still working on this piece, his fourth pietà—a representation of a dead Christ with a sorrowful Virgin Mary. While unfinished and seemingly a mishmash of corrections and reworks, it's a thought-provoking work by a genius at nearly 90 years of age, who knows he's fast approaching the end of his life. The symbolism is of life and of death: Jesus returning to his mother, as two bodies seem to become one.

Michelangelo's more famous pietà at the Vatican (carved when he was in his 20s) features a beautiful, young, and astonished Mary. Here, Mary is older and wiser. Perhaps Mary is now better able to accept death as part of life...as is Michelangelo. The pietà at the Vatican is simple and clear, showing two different people: the mother holding her dead son. Contemplating the *Pietà Rondanini*, you wonder who's supporting whom. It's confused and complex, each figure seeming to both need and support the other.

This unfinished statue shows the genius of Michelangelo midway through a major rework—Christ's head is cut out of Mary's right shoulder, and an earlier arm is still just hanging there. Above Mary's right ear, you can see the remains of a previous face (eye, brow, and hairline).

And there's a certain power to this rawness. Walk around the back to see the strain in Mary's back (and Michelangelo's rough chisel work) as she struggles to support her son. The sculpture's elongated form hints at the Mannerist style that would follow.

Facing the pietà is a bronze life-size head, based on a death mask made at the artist's passing in 1564. Imagine him working on his pietà—still vibrant and seeking.

• From the pietà, return to the big courtyard and head for the little drawbridge (on the left, directly across from where you entered the complex). Pass through to find (on the right) the entrance to the...

MILAN

**Museum of Ancient Art** (Museo d'Arte Antica): This sprawling collection fills the old Sforza family palace with interesting medieval armor, furniture, early Lombard art, and much more.

In the first room, among ancient sarcophagi (with early Christian themes), stands a fine 14th-century **equestrian statue**—a memorial to Bernabò Visconti. Of the four virtues, he selected only two (strength and justice) to stand beside his anatomically correct horse, opting out of love and patience.

Farther along, the room of **tapestries** is dominated by a big embroidery of St. Ambrose defeating the heretical Arians. While that was a fourth-century struggle, 12 centuries later, he was summoned back in spirit to deal with Protestants, in support of Archbishop Borromeo. With St. Peter's Basilica behind him, a Borromeo—like Ambrose stands tall and strong as a Counter-Reformation leader in defense of the Roman Church. The room is lined with 16th-century Flemish tapestries, which were easy to pack up quickly as the nobility traveled. These were typical of those used to warm chilly stone palaces.

Next, you'll come to the **Sala delle Asse.** The Visconti family, who grew rich making silk in the Lake Como region, had their ballroom painted by Leonardo and his followers. While plastered over for centuries, this room was restored around 1900. Not much sparkle survives, but you can appreciate the intricate canopy woven with branches and rope in complicated knots—the work of Leonardo himself, in 1498.

From here, you'll pass through rooms filled with weapons and armor from the 16th and 17th centuries.

• *At this point, you're free to go. But if you have a larger-than-average attention span, follow signs upstairs to the Decorative Arts Museum, then the Painting Gallery (Pinacoteca), and finally the Musical Instruments Museum. When you're done, consider popping out the back door of the fortress and taking a break in the lush Sempione Park.*

### Sempione Park (Parco Sempione)

This is Milan's equivalent of Central Park. With its circa-1900 English-style gardens, free Liberty Style aquarium, views of the triumphal arch, and sprawling family-friendly grounds, this park is particularly popular on weekends.

A 15-minute walk through the park, on the left, is the erector-set **Branca Tower** (Torre Branca), built for an exposition in the 1930s. For an inexpensive, commanding city view, you can ride an elevator as high as the Mary that crowns the Duomo (best in daylight, erratic hours—call or confirm at TI before making a special trip, Metro: Cadorna, www.museobranca.it, tel. 02-331-4120).

Next to the tower is the excellent **Triennale di Milano,** a design museum with changing exhibits that celebrate one of this city's fortes (www.triennale.org).

At the far end of the park is the monumental **Arco della Pace.** Originally an arch of triumph, it comes with Nike, goddess of victory, commanding a six-horse chariot. It was built facing Paris to welcome Napoleon's rule and to celebrate the ideals of the French Revolution, destined to lift Italy into the modern age. When the locals learned Napoleon was just another megalomaniac, they turned the horses around, their tails facing France.

### ▲Via Dante

This grand pedestrian boulevard and popular shopping street leads from Sforza Castle toward the town center and the Duomo. Via Dante was carved out of a medieval tangle of streets to celebrate Italian unification (c. 1870) and make Milan a worthy metropolis. Consequently, all the facades lining it are relatively new. Enjoy strolling this beautiful people zone, where you'll hear the whir of bikes and the lilting melodies of accordion players instead of traffic noise. Photo exhibits are frequently displayed up and down the street. In front of Sforza Castle, a commanding statue of Giuseppe Garibaldi, a hero of the unification movement, looks down one of Europe's longest pedestrian zones. From here you can walk to the Duomo and beyond (about 1.5 miles), appreciating Italian design both in shop windows and on smartly clothed Milanese.

## AWAY FROM THE CENTER
### ▲▲Porta Nuova: The New Milan

Milan is famous for design, including architecture and urban planning. The big news in the last decade is a sparkling forest of glassy office and condominium towers around a parklike, pedestrian-only urban-renewal district called Porta Nuova. Civic leaders have reenvisioned this once-run-down neighborhood, neglected since its WWII bombing, effectively decentralizing the city that historically has been so Duomo-centric. An hour spent wandering this happy land of sleek and successful urban Italy does more to expand your understanding of Milan (and Italy) than any other hour you could spend in the city.

**Visiting Porta Nuova:** For help orienting yourself in this district, see the "Greater Milan" map on page 273.

Ride the Metro to Garibaldi FS and exit following *Corso Como* signs. Rocketing skyward before you in a group of contemporary office towers is the tallest structure in Italy, the **UniCredit Building** (750 feet high). Follow the curved road to reach the complex upon which that building sits. As you approach some escalators, you'll see maps and signposts to keep you oriented. Head upstairs to the main square called...

**Piazza Gae Aulenti:** Enjoy the lively public hub with its delightful **pond** that transforms from shallow reflecting pool to dancing fountains throughout the day. In the center you'll see **glass "horns,"** visually echoed in a nearby corridor by brass horns that allow people to gossip from one level to the next—a reminder that piazzas have always enabled people to connect with one another.

Many locals refer to this area simply as "Garibaldi." Essentially an outdoor mall (with multinationals renting space), it's a fun place to search for views of the Alps or to sate your hunger in the fancy downstairs food court.

**The Vertical Forest:** Continue your stroll beyond the piazza toward the wooden IBM building. On your left in the Isola (Island) neighborhood, you'll see two con-dominium towers bushy with trees (800 of them plus about 20,000 other plants) called The Vertical Forest. Named the best building in Europe a couple years ago (designed by the Italian architect Stefano Boeri), these twin towers take "green" to a new level. The trees absorb the pollution created by its residents and contribute to a cooler atmosphere.

"Growing" from its base is the adjacent park called the **Library of Trees.** Laid out in a network of geometric patterns and paths, it serves as pedestrian zone, play area, and event venue. People can commune with each other and the more than 135,000 plants and trees living in this field of greens. Energy-consumption reduction, sustainability, workability, livability, and innovation are essentials of the Porta Nuova project.

**Diamond Tower:** Across the pedestrian bridge called the Passerella Gioia is the Varesine district. A cluster of jagged, balconied towers mix condominium residences with ground-floor shops and eateries. Beyond, an urban park is flanked by shorter condos and a series of commercial buildings nicknamed Diamantini (Little Diamonds), a nod to the massive, laminated glass Diamond Tower high-rise at the end of the development. Affectionately called Il Diamantone (The Big Diamond) for its irregular angles, the 31-story tower earned Gold LEED (Leadership in Environment Energy and Design) certification.

Stand in the middle of Passerella Gioia and take a 360-degree survey of this vibrant, sparkling, of-the-future neighborhood. Marvel at how this people-, business-, and environmentally friendly project has become not only an icon of the rebirth and revitalization of Milan but also a model for other cities looking ahead to smartly designed, forward-thinking urban development.

**Corso Como and Porta Garibaldi:** Back at the main square, Piazza Gae Aulenti, depart via the golden gossip horns down Via V. Capelli. Turn left on Corso Como and head to the medieval gate called Porta Garibaldi, once part of the city walls. Corso Como, while an old street, is a trendy high-end pedestrian mall popular for its *aperitivo* and cocktail bars and stylish shops. At #10 is 10 Corso Como, worth a quick look for its trendy Milanese design ware.

Immediately left of Porta Garibaldi is Eataly. **Eataly** (also in Rome, Florence, and New York) has turned the former Teatro Smeraldo into a gourmet megastore. It's overwhelming but oddly enchanting, with its overpriced Italian market goods and restaurants serving all the major food groups—pasta, meats, vegetables, chocolate, and, of course, gelato (daily 10:00-24:00, Piazza XXV Aprile 10, Metro: Moscova, tel. 02-4949-7301, www.eataly.net).

Beyond Porta Garibaldi stretches Corso Garibaldi, for more lively Milanese pedestrian and shopping action.

### ▲Naviglio Grande (Canal District)

Milan, although far from any major lake or river, has a sizable port, literally called the "Big Canal." Since 1170, boats have been able

to sail from Milan to the Mediterranean via the Ticino River (which flows into the Po River on its way to the Adriatic Sea). Five hundred years ago, Leonardo helped design a modern lock system. During the booming Industrial Age in the 19th century—and especially with the flurry of construction after Italian unification—ships used the canals to bring in the marble and stone needed to make Milan the great city it is today. In fact, one canal (filled in during the 1930s) let barges unload stone right at the building site of the great cathedral. In the 1950s, landlocked Milan was the seventh-biggest port in Italy, as its canals aided in rebuilding the bombed-out city.

Today, disused train tracks parallel the canal, old warehouse buildings recall the area's working-class heritage, and former workers' tenements—once squalid and undesirable—are being renovated. The once-rough area now dubbed Milan's "Little Venice" is trendy, traffic-free, and thriving with inviting bars and eateries. Come here for dinner or a late-afternoon drink (for recommendations, see "Eating in Milan," later).

**Getting There:** Ride the Metro (or tram #2) to Porta Genova, exit following signs to *Via Casale,* and walk the length of Via Casale one block directly to the canal. Most bars and restaurants are to the left, on both sides of the canal. (See the map on page 273).

## ▲Monumental Cemetery (Il Cimitero Monumentale)

Europe's most artistic and dreamy cemetery experience, this grand place was built just after unification to provide a suitable final rest-

ing spot for the city's "famous and well-deserving men." Any cemetery can be evocative, but this one—with its super-emotional portrayals of the deceased and their heavenly escorts (in art styles c. 1870-1930)—is in a class by itself. It's a vast garden art gallery of proud busts and grim reapers, heartbroken angels and weeping widows, too-young soldiers and countless old smiles, frozen on yellowed black-and-white photos.

**Cost and Hours:** Free, Tue-Sun 8:00-18:00, closed Mon, pick up map at the entrance gate, ride Metro purple line 5 to Monumentale, tel. 02-8846-5600.

## Leonardo's Horse

The largest equestrian monument in the world is a reconstruction of a model created in 1482 by Leonardo da Vinci for the Sforza

family. The clay prototype was destroyed in 1499 by invading French forces, who used it for target practice. In 1982, American Renaissance-art collector Charles Dent decided to build the 15-ton, 24-foot-long statue from Leonardo's design, planning to present it to the Italians in homage to Leonardo's genius. Unfortunately, Dent died before the project could be completed. In 1997, American sculptor Nina Akamu created a

new clay model that became the template for the final statue; it was unveiled in 1999.

**Getting There:** The statue (free to view) is at a horse racetrack on the western outskirts of town—ride Metro purple line 5 to San Siro Ippodromo.

# Shopping in Milan

For locations, see the map on page 324.

### High Fashion in the Quadrilateral

For world-class window shopping, visit the Quadrilateral, an elegant high-fashion shopping area around Via Montenapoleone, northeast of La Scala Opera House. This was the original Beverly Hills of Milan. In the 1920s, the top fashion shops moved in, and today it remains *the* place for designer labels. Most shops close Sunday and for much of August. On Mondays, stores open only after 16:00. In this land where fur is still prized, the people-watching is as entertaining as the window shopping. Notice also the exclusive penthouse apartments with roof gardens high above the scene. Via Montenapoleone and the pedestrianized Via della Spiga are the best streets.

Whether you're gawking or shopping, here's the best route: From Piazza della Scala, walk up Via Alessandro Manzoni to the Metro stop at Montenapoleone, browse down Via Montenapoleone, and cut left on Via Santo Spirito (lined with grand aristocratic palazzos—peek into the courtyard at #7). Across the street, step into the elegant courtyard at #10 to check out the café sitters and their poodles. Continue to the end of Via Santo Spirito, then turn right to window shop down traffic-free Via della Spiga. After a few short blocks, turn right on Via Sant'Andrea and then left, back onto Montenapoleone, which leads you through a final gauntlet of temptations to Corso Giacomo Matteotti, near the Piazza San Babila. Then (for less-expensive shopping thrills), walk back to the Duomo down the pedestrian-only Corso Vittorio Emanuele II.

### Shops near the Duomo

For a (slightly) more reasonably priced shopping excursion, step into **La Rinascente**—one of Europe's classic department stores. (It's around the left side as you face the front of the Duomo.) Simply riding the escalator up and up gives a fun overview of Italian design and marketing. The seventh floor is a top-end food circus with recommended restaurants, terrace views of the Duomo, and a public WC. The store's name translates roughly as "the place reborn" and fits its history. In an earlier life, this was a fine Art Nouveau-style building—until it burned down in 1918. Rebuilt, it was bombed in World War II and rebuilt once again (Sun-Thu 9:30-21:00, Fri-Sat until 22:00, has a VAT refund office, faces north side of the Duomo on Piazza del Duomo).

Heading away from the Duomo, stroll between the arcades on the Corso Vittorio Emanuele II, surrounded by clothing stores and other tempting material pleasures. At Via Passarella, detour to the right to check out **Excelsior,** a bold high-end concept store. Moving walkways take you from level to colorful level with pulsing music and electronic art installations. If you're looking for the perfect €1,000 shirt, you've come to the right place (daily 10:00-20:30, Galleria del Corso 4, two long blocks behind the Duomo, tel. 027-630-7301).

Double back to the Corso Vittorio Emanuele II to continue shopping all the way to the San Babila Metro station (and the ritzy Quadrilateral area described earlier).

## Nightlife in Milan

For evening action, check out the artsy Brera area in the old center, with several swanky sidewalk cafés and lots of bars that stay open late. Home to the local art university, this district has a sophisticated, lively people-watching scene. For a younger scene, try the Naviglio Grande canal district, Milan's formerly bohemian, now-gentrified "Little Venice" (Metro: Porta Genova or tram #2; for restaurant recommendations here, see "Eating in Milan," later).

There are always concerts and live music in the city—check periodicals from the TI.

## Sleeping in Milan

My recommended hotels are all within a few minutes' walk of a Metro station. With Milan's fine subway system, you can get anywhere in town in a flash.

Hotel prices in Milan rise and fall with the convention schedule. In March, April, September, and October, the city can be completely jammed by conventions, and hotel prices go sky-high (see www.fieramilano.it for convention schedule). My rankings are based on regular prices, not the much-higher convention rates.

Summer is usually wide open, with soft or discounted prices, though many hotels close in August for vacation. Hotels cater more to business travelers than to tourists, so prices and availability are a little better on Fridays and Saturdays.

There are only a few small, family-style hotels left in the center, and the good ones charge top dollar for their location. To save money, consider searching for a deal at a basic chain hotel (such as Ibis) near a Metro stop.

## NEAR THE DUOMO

The Duomo area is thick with people-watching, reasonably priced eateries, and the major sightseeing attractions, but hotel prices are high.

**$$$$ Hotel Spadari** boasts an Art Deco-inspired lobby designed by the Milanese artist Giò Pomodoro ("Joe Tomato" in English). The 40 cool-blue rooms have billowing drapes, big paintings, and designer doors. It's next to the recommended Peck Gourmet Deli, and two blocks from the Duomo (air-con, elevator, Via Spadari 11, tel. 02-7200-2371, www.spadarihotel.com, reservation@spadarihotel.com).

**$$$$ Hotel Gran Duca di York,** three blocks from the Duomo, is on a stark street of banks and public buildings. Set in a former priory-run school attended by the then-future Pope Pius X, it has comfy and spacious public areas, and the 33 rooms are modern and bright (air-con, elevator, Via Moneta 1, Metro: Cordusio or Duomo, tel. 02-874-863, www.ducadiyork.com, info@ducadiyork.com).

## BETWEEN LA SCALA AND SFORZA CASTLE

These slightly-less-central places are close to the Via Dante and Via Brera shopping and restaurant scenes.

**$$$$ Antica Locanda dei Mercanti** offers 15 rooms in an 18th-century palazzo an easy 10-minute walk from the Duomo. While each room has its own personality (some have kitchenettes, others have small terraces), all have a fresh-flower vibe that embraces old and new—a nice change for businesslike Milan (air-con, elevator, Via San Tomaso 6, reception on first floor, Metro: Cairoli or Cordusio, tel. 02-805-4080, www.locanda.it, locanda@locanda.it, Alex and Eri).

**$$$$ Hotel Cusani** prides itself on service and has 92 classy, classic, and bright rooms and ample space to lounge (air-con, elevator, family rooms, bar, pay parking; Via Cusani 13, Metro: Cairoli, tel. 028-5601, www.gruppouna.it, hotel.cusani@unahotels.it).

**$$$ Hotel Star** rents 30 rooms, most of which have been modernized and feature artsy, somewhat gaudy decor; interior rooms are quieter (air-con, elevator, Via dei Bossi 5, Metro: Cordusio, tel. 02-801-501, www.hotelstar.it, hotelstar@hotelstar.it, Vittoria).

## NEAR *THE LAST SUPPER*

These two hotels are farther from the action in a sleepy, mostly residential zone, but the prices are lower. For locations (about a 15-minute walk or quick tram or Metro ride west of the Duomo), see the map on page 279.

**$$$ Antica Locanda Leonardo,** just down the street from *The Last Supper,* has a romantic, Old World vibe, antique furnishings, and a spacious breakfast room. Each of its 17 uniquely decorated rooms faces either a courtyard (cheaper, some street noise) or a tranquil garden (some rooms with garden balcony, air-con, elevator, Corso Magenta 78, tel. 02-4801-4197, www.anticalocandaleonardo.com, info@anticalocandaleonardo.com). From the Duomo area, you can ride tram #16 or take the Metro to either Cadorna or Conciliazione and walk five minutes.

**$$ B&B Hotel Milano Sant'Ambrogio,** part of a chain of budget hotels, has 94 efficient, cookie-cutter rooms and a sizable fourth-floor terrace. Rooms come with some tram noise (request a quieter one) but are worth considering if you can get a deal (breakfast extra, air-con, elevator, Via degli Olivetani 4, Metro: S. Ambrogio, tel. 02-4810-1089, www.hotel-bb.com, mi.santambrogio@hotelbb.com). It's on a side street near the Leonardo da Vinci Science Museum, about a five-minute walk from either *The Last Supper* or Basilica Sant'Ambrogio.

## NEAR BASILICA DI SANT'AMBROGIO

These places are a 10-minute walk east of the basilica. See the map on page 279 for locations.

**$$$ Hotel Ariston,** with uniformed porters, offers 52 contemporary rooms that range from blah to fancy minimalist (some with views). It's a solid option if charm is not a prerequisite (air-con, elevator, bar, Largo del Carrobbio 2, Metro: Duomo, tel. 02-7200-0556, www.aristonhotel.com, info@aristonhotel.com).

**Hostel: ¢ Ostello Bello** sits along a skinny lane and is brimming with youthful and young-at-heart travelers. It has quirky decor and is generous, considering its value price, with complimentary food, nearly nightly activities, and a welcome drink. The multiuse entry room is the reception, dining area, bar, lounge, and entertainment venue rolled into one. Their bigger (grande) location is by Milano Centrale train station (private rooms available, air-con, elevator, game room, terraces; Via Medici 4, Metro: Duomo or Missori, tel. 02-3658-2720, mobile 334-261-0356, www.ostellobello.com, booking@ostellobello.com).

## NEAR MILANO CENTRALE TRAIN STATION

The train station neighborhood is more practical than characteristic. Its hotels are utilitarian business-class places with prices that bounce all over depending upon the convention schedule; most of the year, many have rooms in the €100-125 range. You'll find more shady characters than shady trees in the parks, and lots of ethnic restaurants and massage parlors as you head away from the immediate vicinity of the station. But it's convenient to trains, the Metro, and airport shuttles, and if you hit it outside of convention times, the prices are hard to beat.

**On Via Napo Torriani:** This street, a five-minute walk from the station, is lined with midrange hotels (exit the station, head straight across the square, then veer left onto Via Napo Torriani). **$$ Hotel Berna** feels like a classic European hotel, with an old-school lobby, uniformed bellhops, and 116 faded rooms with some nice upgrades (air-con, elevator, Via Napo Torriani 18, tel. 02-677-311, www.hotelberna.com). **$$ Hotel Garda** is cheaper and less welcoming, with 55 rooms (RS%—email first to get a promo code, then book on their website; breakfast extra, air-con, elevator, Via Napo Torriani 21, tel. 02-6698-2576, www.hotelgardamilan.com, info@hotelgardamilan.com).

**Closest to Station:** These options are in the same block of buildings just in front and to the left of the station.

**$$ Hotel Aosta** is IKEA-esque, practical, tidy, and convenient, with a gentle and helpful staff. Some of the 63 business-class rooms have views onto the piazza, as does the breakfast room (air-con, elevator, Piazza Duca d'Aosta 16, tel. 02-669-1951, www.hotelaostamilano.it, aosta@minihotel.it).

**Hostel:** **¢ Ostello Bello Grande** has converted what was a business-class hotel into a hostel with hipster flair. Worth considering even if you're not a hosteler, it comes with an inviting rooftop terrace and a shared kitchen (private rooms available, includes breakfast and *aperitivo* happy-hour snacks, air-con, elevator, laundry, Via Lepetit 33, tel. 02-670-5921, www.ostellobello.com, booking.lepetit@ostellobello.com). With the tracks to your back, leave the station to the left, cross the taxi stand, and then cross the road. The hostel is around the corner from Ristorante Giglio Rosso.

## NEAR MALPENSA AIRPORT

**$$$$ Sheraton Milan Malpensa Airport Hotel** is adjacent to Terminal 1—from the lobby, it's just a five-minute walk to airport security (tel. 02-23351, www.marriott.com). Or try **$ Best Western Cavalieri della Corona,** with big clean rooms and a good restaurant (airport shuttle–€3, 2/hour; tel. 0331-730-350, www.cavalieridellacorona.com).

# Eating in Milan

Milan's hundreds of trendy bars, delis, *rosticcerie,* and self-service cafeterias cater to people with plenty of taste and more money than time. You'll find delightful eateries all over town.

Milan's signature dishes are *risotto alla Milanese* and *ossobuco.* The risotto is flavored with saffron, which gives it an intense yellow color. The subtle flavor of the saffron pairs nicely with the veal shanks of *ossobuco* (meaning "marrow" or, literally, "hole in the bone" shank). The prized marrow, extracted with special little

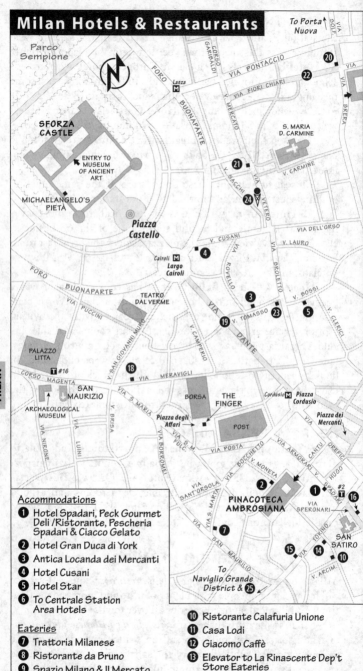

# Milan Hotels & Restaurants

To Porta Nuova

Parco Sempione

SFORZA CASTLE

ENTRY TO MUSEUM OF ANCIENT ART

MICHAELANGELO'S PIETÀ

Piazza Castello

Lanza M

S. MARIA D. CARMINE

Cairoli M
Largo Cairoli

TEATRO DAL VERME

PALAZZO LITTA

SAN MAURIZIO

ARCHAEOLOGICAL MUSEUM

BORSA

THE FINGER

Piazza degli Affari

POST

Cordusio M   Piazza Cordusio

Piazza dei Mercanti

PINACOTECA AMBROSIANA

SAN SATIRO

To Naviglio Grande District &

MILAN

### Accommodations

1. Hotel Spadari, Peck Gourmet Deli /Ristorante, Pescheria Spadari & Ciacco Gelato
2. Hotel Gran Duca di York
3. Antica Locanda dei Mercanti
4. Hotel Cusani
5. Hotel Star
6. To Centrale Station Area Hotels

### Eateries

7. Trattoria Milanese
8. Ristorante da Bruno
9. Spazio Milano & Il Mercato del Duomo

10. Ristorante Calafuria Unione
11. Casa Lodi
12. Giacomo Caffè
13. Elevator to La Rinascente Dep't Store Eateries
14. La Vecchia Latteria

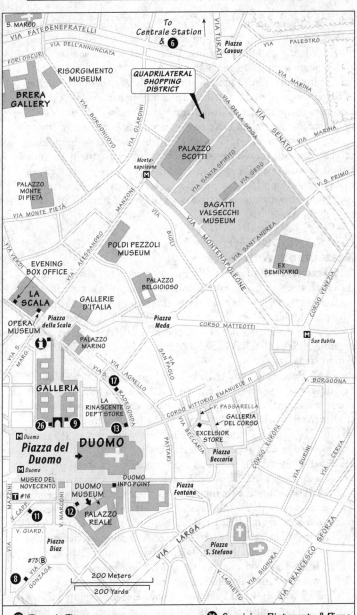

MILAN

| | |
|---|---|
| **15** Pizzeria Piz | **21** Convivium Ristorante & Pizza |
| **16** Princi & Rost. Fontana | **22** Via Fiori Chiari Eateries |
| **17** Luini Panzerotti & other takeout joints | **23** Motoplex City Lounge |
| **18** Trattoria Burla Gio | **24** Gelateria Toldo |
| **19** Via Dante Eateries | **25** To Naviglio Grande Eateries |
| **20** Bar Brera & Via Brera Eateries | **26** Bar Camparino |

forks, is considered the best part of the meal. Also popular is the *cotoletta alla Milanese,* a thin, breaded veal cutlet fried in clarified butter. Some places have supersized it and call it *orecchio di elefante,* an "elephant's ear" (large enough to share).

Many locals like to precede dinner with an *aperitivo*—a buffet of finger foods offered free with a drink during happy hour. (While Campari made its debut in Milan, a simple glass of *vino bianco* or prosecco, the Italian champagne, is just as popular.) At about 18:00, bars fill their counters with inviting baskets of munchies, served free with these drinks. A cheap drink can actually become a light meal. Locals joke you can make your *aperitivo* an *apericena* (*cena* means dinner) for the cost of a cocktail. This *aperitivo* custom is common throughout Italy but especially prized by the Milanesi—who invented it.

## NEAR THE DUOMO
### Restaurants with Class

$$$ **Trattoria Milanese,** family-run and passionately Milanese, is on a back street. It has an enthusiastic clientele and a classic energy, with a curt and professional waitstaff. Expect an old-fashioned Milanese ambience; eat early to avoid crowds (Mon-Sat 12:00-15:00 & 19:00-22:30, closed Sun and mid-July-Aug, reservations recommended, air-con, Via Santa Marta 11, behind the Pinacoteca Ambrosiana, tel. 02-8645-1991).

$$$ **Pescheria Spadari,** a beloved fish market in the Duomo neighborhood for nearly a century, has made the leap to become a fish restaurant, too. Hardworking Federico, whose menu is entirely driven by what's fresh today, offers a no-nonsense lunch special for €20 (Tue-Fri) and a fancier fish menu for dinner. It's fresh and modern-feeling (open for lunch Tue-Sun 12:30-14:30, dinner Wed-Sat 19:30-22:30, closed Mon, reservations essential for dinner, Via Spadari 4, tel. 02-878-250, www.pescheriaspadari.eu).

$$ **Ristorante da Bruno,** true to their family roots, serves Tuscan cuisine with an emphasis on fish. It's a traditional-feeling place, old-school and a bit tired, with dressy waiters, hearty food (including Milanese specialties), and a classic antipasti buffet. Eat inside or on the sidewalk under fascist-style columns (daily 12:00-23:00, reservations wise, air-con, Via M. Gonzaga 6, tel. 02-804-364, www.ristorantedabruno.biz, Graziella).

$$$$ **Ristorante al Peck** is a dressy place for a splurge above Milan's famous gourmet deli (listed next page). They cater to local professionals needing an elegant spot for lunch (two courses—€30, Tue-Sun 12:00-15:30, closed Mon) and offer a pricier and slower dinner service (Via Spadari 9, tel. 02-802-31644).

$$$ **Spazio Milano** is a dressy and romantic little place offering one of the best fine dining values in town. This is three-star

## Good *Aperitivo* Options

While lots of places pull out *aperitivo* nibbles, some do a more generous job than others with their buffet. Here are three I found particularly good (for details, see their listings): **Princi** (daily 16:30-20:00 with €8 drink), **Casa Lodi** (daily 18:00-20:00), and **Terrazza Aperol** (daily 17:30-21:30 with a €15 drink). While the first two have better food, the atmosphere is nothing special. The last has a spectacular view terrace overlooking the Duomo, with less food and a higher cost.

Michelin chef Niko Romito's cooking school, where his students get experience (daily 12:30-14:30 & 19:30-22:00, in the Il Mercato del Duomo food hall—described later, tel. 02-878-400, www.accademianikoromito.com).

## Simpler Dining

**$$ Ristorante Calafuria Unione** is a bustling, unpretentious place that attracts a sizable crowd for its pizza and traditional dishes. It feels like a well-loved neighborhood eatery (Mon-Sat 12:00-15:00 & 19:00-24:00, closed Sun, air-con, a few blocks south of Piazza del Duomo at Via dell'Unione 8, Metro: Missori, tel. 02-866-103).

**$$ Casa Lodi** brings the local farming community into the big city with an honest celebration of the area's traditions and ingredients. The menu includes salads, pastas, and the house specialty, risotto. And each evening they put out a quality *aperitivo* buffet to go with your glass of wine or *spritz*—see the sidebar (daily 12:00-22:00 except closes midday and for dinner on Mon, Via Cappellari 3, tel. 02-897-77217).

**$$ Peck Gourmet Deli** is an aristocratic deli with a pricey gourmet grocery, *rosticceria*, and pastry/gelato shop on the main level; a fancy restaurant upstairs (see Ristorante al Peck, earlier); and an expensive *enoteca* wine cellar in the basement. Even if all you can afford is the aroma, peek in. Check out the classic circa-1930 salami slicers and the assembly-line kitchen in back. The *rosticceria* serves delectable fancy food to go for a superb picnic dinner. It's sold by weight: Order by the *etto*—100-gram unit; 250 grams equals about a half-pound. Their ground-floor café, **Piccolo Peck**, serves small bites, light meals, and cocktails (Mon 15:00-20:00, Tue-Sat 9:00-20:00, Sun 10:00-17:00, Via Spadari 9, tel. 02-802-3161).

**$$ Giacomo Caffè** hides out next to the Duomo Museum entry. It's a classy fixture (whose chef is famous for his pastries) that locals and guides rely on for a pleasant lunch (salads and sandwiches, in Palazzo Reale at Piazza Duomo 12, tel. 02-890-96698).

MILAN

$$$ **Trendy Eateries with a Duomo View:** The seventh floor of **La Rinascente** department store, alongside the Duomo, has a crowded and upscale food court. **De Santis** serves great salads and top-end sandwiches. Three of its many eateries share a sunny outdoor terrace with views of the cathedral's rooftop: **Obicà** is a swanky "mozzarella bar" offering this heavenly cheese in salads, on pizzas, or on splittable €23 antipasti sampler plates, accompanied by *salumi,* tapenades, and vegetables. **Ristorante Maio** has pricey full-meal service. And **Il Bar,** living-room cozy with cushy divans and low coffee tables, serves light meals (salads, pasta), coffee, desserts, and cocktails (all three open daily until 24:00; after store hours, use the elevator on Via S. Radegonda to enter).

$$ **Il Mercato del Duomo** is a food hall facing the Duomo with four floors of noisy eateries (daily 11:00-22:00, next to Galleria Vittorio Emanuele II, above La Feltrinelli bookstore, at Piazza del Duomo 1, tel. 02-8633-1924). Ride escalators up from the bookstore past fast-food joints to the second and third floors for lots of options. **Terrazza Aperol** has a great terrace overlooking the square and serves a popular *aperitivo* (see the sidebar). On floors two and three you'll find sandwich and focaccia bars, a pasta bar, and lots of salads. The lunchtime self-serve cafeteria gets a bit more formal with sit-down service for dinner. The fourth floor features fine dining at the Spazio Milano restaurant (described earlier).

## Cheap Eats and Takeout

$ **La Vecchia Latteria,** with a 50-year history, is a homey hole-in-the-wall that serves a good vegetarian lunch. This busy joint—with tight seating in front and behind the kitchen—serves soup, salads, pastas, and imaginative veggie entrées at affordable prices. Their star offering is *il misto forno,* a delicious assortment of soufflés, quiches, and roasted and sautéed veggies (Mon-Sat 12:00-16:00, closed Sun, off Via Torino at Via dell'Unione 6, Metro: Missori, tel. 02-874-401).

$ **Pizzeria Piz** serves very basic pizzas with an evangelical fervor. Fun and down and dirty with a tiny menu, it's rustic, cheap, and memorable. They don't take reservations, but they entertain those waiting in the alley for their table (closed Tue, under Church of San Sebastian at Via Torino 34, tel. 02-864-53482).

$ **Princi** is popular for its enticing wall of fresh baked breads, focaccia, and luscious pastries. They sell rustic sandwiches all day, and at lunch they have a *tavola calda* with various €8-12 plates of the day (12:00-15:00 only). While they seem oddly strict about mixing, they will let you do two half courses for the cost of the more expensive one. They also have a good *aperitivo* buffet—see the sidebar (daily 7:00-20:00; off Via Torino, a block southwest of Piazza del Duomo at Via Speronari 6; tel. 02-874-797). If Princi is too slick and crowded for your mood, across the street at #5 is the quiet, old-fashioned **Rosticceria Fontana,** with an inviting *tavola calda* selling cooked plates by weight and stools nearby.

**$ Street Food: Luini Panzerotti,** a local institution, is a bakery that serves up €3 piping-hot mini calzones *(panzerotti)* stuffed with mozzarella, tomatoes, ham, or whatever you like. Don't overlook the *dolci* half of the menu (Mon 10:00-15:00, Tue-Sat until 20:00, closed Sun and Aug, Via S. Radegonda 16, tel. 02-8646-1917). From the back of the Duomo, head north and look for the lines out front. Order from the menus posted on the wall. Traditionally, Milanesi munch their hot little meals on the benches of nearby Piazza San Fedele (just to the north).

Panzerotti can be mobbed with tourists, and locals complain that quality has gone downhill. Several good competitors are close by, including **Antica Pizza Fritta,** which serves fried calzones (around the block directly behind Panzerotti); **Spontini,** popular for its spongy, Sicilian-style pizza by the slice (just around the corner); and **Manuelina Focacceria,** beloved for its famous focaccia (ground floor of the Annex La Rinascente department store, Via Santa Radegonda 10). And across the street is another local hit, **Cioccolati Italiani,** for chocoholics in search of something over the top.

## DINING EAST OF VIA DANTE

**$$$ Enoteca Boccondivino** is a fun-loving place with no menu. You enjoy six courses for €70, each with a different bottle of wine designed to match. A constant parade of food carts roll through the happy dining room, keeping all entertained and happily fed. Fabrizio is the master of ceremonies making sure English speakers understand what's being served: lots of quality meats and cheeses, pâté, pasta, and a token vegetable course—all "designed to maximize your cholesterol." You may share a bigger table; it's yours for the evening. The name is a play on words: a divine mouthful or a mouthful of wine (nightly from 19:30, reservations necessary, Via Carducci 17—see the map on page 280, tel. 02-866-040, www. boccondivino.com).

**$$ Trattoria Burla Gio,** homey and traditional as can be, caters to locals with €15 lunch specials and a fancier dinner menu. Paolo and Gisella carry on the 50-year family tradition with a passion for home cooking and Milanese traditions like their *cotoletta alla Milanese* (the local veal cutlet). For the best ambience, climb upstairs into a red-and-white tablecloth time-warp dining hall (just off Via San Giovanni at Via Meravigli 18, tel. 02-805-7096).

**$$ Via Dante Bars and Cafés:** Thriving and central, Via Dante is lined with hardworking eateries where you can join locals for a lively lunch. Or just swing by for a morning *caffè*, watching the parade of Milanesi heading to work.

## NEAR VIA BRERA

The Brera neighborhood, surrounding the Church of St. Carmine, is laced with narrow, inviting pedestrian streets. Make an evening of your visit by having an *aperitivo* with snacks at recommended Bar Brera or any other bar—most serve munchies with drinks from about 17:00 or 18:00 until 21:00. Afterward, stroll along restaurant row on **Via Fiori Chiari** and Via Brera, or duck into the semicircular lane of Via Madonnina to survey the sidewalk cafés as you pass fortune tellers, artists, and knockoff handbag vendors.

**$ Bar Brera** serves inexpensive sandwiches, pastas, and salads to throngs of art students and has a lively *aperitivo* happy hour (drinks and a buffet of hearty snacks starts at 18:00; open daily 7:00-late, Via Brera 23, tel. 02-877-091).

**$$$ Convivium Ristorante and Pizza** is popular for its extensive wine list, clever dishes (especially beef and fish), and tempting desserts. It's bustling and trendy, yet classy (daily 12:00-14:30 & 19:00-24:00, facing Santa Maria del Carmine church at Via Ponte Vetero 21, tel. 02-8646-3708, Claudio and Nicola).

## COFFEE AND GELATO

**Motoplex City Lounge** is more than a Vespa showroom: It's also a café that's popular with locals and the business-suit set (Mon-Fri 8:00-18:00, Sat from 12:00, closed Sun, Via Broletto 13).

For gelato, two options stand out between Sforza Castle and the Duomo: **Gelateria Toldo** has gelato and pastries (Mon-Sat 9:00-20:30, closed Sun, Via Ponte Vetero 9), while **Ciacco Gelato** is more of a purist. I like their *fior di latte* best (Mon-Sat 9:00-21:00, Sun 14:00-20:00, Via Spadari 13).

## NAVIGLIO GRANDE (CANAL DISTRICT)

Consider ending your day at the former port of Milan. This district bustles with memorable and affordable bars and restaurants and a great people scene (see listing on page 317). In addition to endless *aperitivo* spreads and traditional trattorias, there are some more creative choices, too: Greek fare, artisanal microbrews, and "Brazilian sushi."

**Getting There:** Ride the Metro or tram #2 to Porta Genova and walk down pedestrianized Via Casale, which dead-ends a block away at the canal. Walk halfway across the metal bridge and survey the scene. The street you just walked has plenty of cheap options. Most of the action—and all of my other recommendations—are to the left, on or near the canal. Do a reconnaissance stroll before settling in somewhere: Walk down the left bank of the canal to the bridge with cars, then go back on the other side.

Here are a few good options to consider, listed in the order you'll pass them.

**$$ Luca e Andrea,** one of few eateries that stays open all day long, is the place other restaurants recommend when their kitchens are closed. It's artsy-rustic, lively, and serves typical Milanese and Lombardy meals. Enjoy the conviviality indoors or people-watch as you dine outdoors (daily 12:00-22:00, Alzaia Naviglio Grande 34, near the arched bridge, tel. 02-5810-1142). If it's full, walk a few more yards to their other location **L'Altro Luca e Andrea.**

**$$$$ Ristorante Brellin** is the top romantic splurge, with a dressy crowd and fine food. The menu is international while clinging to a bit of tradition (daily 12:30-15:00 & 19:00-23:00; located where a small lane, Vicolo dei Lavandai, branches off from the canal; tel. 02-5810-1351).

**$ Pizzeria Tradizionale,** at the far end of the walk after you cross the bridge, is a local favorite (Thu-Tue 12:00-14:30 & 19:00-24:00, Wed 19:00-24:00, at the far end of canal walk, Ripa di Porta Ticinese 7, tel. 02-839-5133).

**$$ Iter** is funky and cool with clever, eclectic decor that mirrors their mishmash culinary style. Italian lunchtime dishes change weekly; a rest-of-the-day menu is influenced by another country's cuisine. Cocktails are a specialty here (daily 8:00-24:00; near the curved bridge with the zigzag design—go away from canal on Via Argelati to Via Mario Fusetti 1; tel. 02-3599-9589).

**$ Pizzeria Spaghetteria La Magolfa,** down a side street, feels like a neighborhood hangout, offering good, cheap salads, pastas, and pizzas. You can sit inside, on a veranda, or at a table on the street. For less than €20, two people could split a hearty pizza and a good bottle of wine (daily 12:00-15:00 & 18:00-24:00, go a long block past Cucina Fusetti to end of street, Via Magolfa 15, tel. 02-832-1696).

**Orso Bianco Gelateria,** on your way back to the Metro or tram, is the place for "artisanal" gelato. Their *nocciola*—or hazelnut—is *buonissimo* (Via Casale 7, on your right as you walk back to the Metro, tel. 02-9738-6848).

**MILAN**

# Milan Connections

## BY TRAIN

Unless otherwise specified, the following connections are for Trenitalia.

**From Milano Centrale to: Venice** (2/hour, most direct on high-speed ES trains, 2.5 hours), **Florence** (hourly, 2 hours; Italo: 2/hour, 2 hours), **Genoa** (hourly, 2 hours), **Rome** (1-3/hour, 3.5 hours; Italo: 11/day nonstop, 3 hours, more with stops), **Brindisi** (4 direct/day, 2 night trains, 9-15 hours), **Cinque Terre/La Spezia** (hourly, 3 hours direct or with change in Genoa; trains from La Spezia to the villages go nearly hourly), **Cinque Terre/Monterosso al Mare** (8/day direct, otherwise hourly with change in Genoa, 3 hours), **Varenna** on Lake Como (1 hour; small line direct to Lecco/Sondrio/Tirano leaves at :20 past most hours—confirm these times), **Stresa** on Lake Maggiore (about hourly; 50-minute fast train may require reservations, while 1.5-hour train doesn't), **Como** (2/hour, 45 minutes, boats go from Como to Varenna until about 19:00), **Naples** (2/hour, 4-5 hours, more with change in Rome, overnight possible; Italo: 11/day, 4-5 hours). For details see www.trenitalia.com or www.italotreno.it.

**From Milano Porta Garibaldi** (by High-Speed Train to International Destinations): **Basel,** with connections to Frankfurt (3/day, 4 hours), **Geneva** (4/day, 4 hours), **Lugano** (almost hourly, 1 hour), **Munich** (night train, 12 hours), **Nice** (3/day direct, 5 hours, operated by Thello, no rail passes; more with changes via Trenitalia), **Paris** (3/day, 7 hours; daily night train from Milano Centrale, 11 hours, operated by Thello, no rail passes), **Vienna** (night train, 12 hours), **Zürich** (4/day, 3 hours).

## BY PLANE

To get flight information for Malpensa or Linate airports or the phone number of your airline, call 02-74851 or 02-232-323 and wait for English options, or check www.milanairports.com.

Note: While the train works best for Malpensa, if you want to take a shuttle bus to any of Milan's airports, just go to Milano Centrale station and walk out the door marked *Piazza Luigi di Savoia*. There you'll find little sales kiosks aggressively selling tickets for all your options.

### Malpensa Airport

Most international flights land at Terminal 1 of the manageable Malpensa Airport (code: MXP), 28 miles northwest of Milan. Low-cost EU flights use Terminal 2 (buses connect the two). Both have ATMs and exchange offices. Terminal 1 has a pharmacy, eateries, and a hotel-reservation service disguised as a TI. To leave

the baggage-carousel area A, go right to reach services and the exit. From area B, go left. Airport info: Tel. 02-5858-0080, www. milanairports.com.

**Trains from Malpensa to Milan:** The Malpensa Express train is usually the most sensible option (not covered by rail passes, tel. 02-7249-4494, www.malpensaexpress.it). Trains leave from underground stations at Terminals 1 and 2. To reach the Terminal 2 station, exit the arrivals hall, cross the street, and follow the covered walkway to the station entrance. Both stations have ticket offices and Trenord ticket machines (credit cards accepted). A big electronic board shows the next departure times ("*bin*" = track). There are two lines: Malpensa-Milano Cadorna and Malpensa-Milano Centrale. For either, the ride costs €13 one-way (€20 round-trip). Both run from very early to late (about 5:00-23:00). Validate your ticket in the little machines, and double-check to make sure your train is going to the destination you want.

If you are headed downtown or to most other points in the city, take the **Cadorna** line, which is quicker, runs more often and later, and drops you at a convenient downtown Metro station (2/hour, 40 minutes, usually departs Terminal 2 at :20 and :50 past the hour—departs Terminal 1 about 6 minutes later; returning from

MILAN

Cadorna to the airport, the train generally departs Cadorna at :27 and :57 past the hour).

If you are heading to the area around Milano Centrale, or connecting by train to other destinations, take the **Centrale** line (2/hour, 50 minutes, usually departs Terminal 2 at :07 and :37 past the hour—departs Terminal 1 about 6 minutes later; returning from Milano Centrale to the airport, the train generally departs at :25 and :55 past the hour).

If you're **leaving Milan** to go *to* the airport, purchase your ticket before you board, either from the Trenitalia or Trenord ticket machines or, at Cadorna Station, from the staffed ticket windows. At Milano Centrale, trains usually leave from tracks 1 and 2, which are hidden behind tracks 3 and 4 and poorly signed. Cadorna is a little easier to deal with; trains usually depart from track 1.

**By Shuttle Bus:** Three bus companies run between Malpensa Airport and Milano Centrale train station, offering virtually identical, competing services. They each charge about €8 for the one-hour trip (buy ticket from driver) and depart from the same places: in front of Terminal 2 (outside exit 4) and from Piazza IV Novembre (on the west side of Milan's central train station—with your back to the tracks, exit to the right). They also pick up and drop off at Terminal 1, which, if your flight docks there, makes the bus an option. Buses leave about every 20 minutes daily, from very early until just after midnight (Malpensa Shuttle tel. 02-5858-3185, www.malpensashuttle.it; Autostradale tel. 02-30081-9000, www.autostradale.it; and Terravision, www.terravision.eu).

**By Taxi:** Taxis into Milan cost a fixed rate of €95; avoid hustlers in airport halls (catch taxis outside exit 8). Considering how far the city is from the airport and how good the train and bus services are, Milan is the last place I'd take an airport taxi.

## Linate Airport

Most European flights land at Linate (code: LIN, www.milanairports.com), five miles east of Milan. The airport has a bank with an ATM (just past customs) and a hotel-finding service disguised as a TI (daily 7:30-23:30, tel. 02-7020-0443). Eventually the Metro's new line 4 will link Linate with the city. For now, you can get to downtown Milan by bus or taxi.

**By Bus:** Public bus #73 connects Linate to the Duomo in about 50 minutes (covered by €1.50 public transit ticket, departs every 10 minutes, less frequently evenings and Sun).

If you're *leaving* Milan to go to the airport, look for the #73 bus stop near the Duomo—it's just off Piazza Armando Diaz where it meets Via Maurizio Gonzaga.

Private companies also run shuttles to Milano Centrale train station (handy only if you're catching a train; €5, 2/hour, 35 minutes, www.airportbusexpress.it).

**By Taxi:** Taxis from Linate to the Duomo cost about €30.

### Bergamo (Orio al Serio) Airport

Some budget airlines, such as Ryanair and Wizz Air, use Bergamo Airport—about 30 miles from Milan—as their Milan hub (code: BGY, tel. 035-326-323, www.milanbergamoairport.it). At least three bus companies ply the route between the east side of Milano Centrale train station (Piazza Luigi di Savoia) and Orio al Serio (€7, 5/hour, 1 hour): Autostradale (www.airportbusexpress.it), Terravision (www.terravision.eu), and the Orio Shuttle (www.orioshuttle.com).

MILAN

# THE CINQUE TERRE

*Monterosso al Mare • Vernazza • Corniglia • Manarola •
Riomaggiore*

Tucked between Genoa and Pisa, in a mountainous and seductive corner of the Italian Riviera, lies the Cinque Terre (CHINK-weh TAY-reh)—five villages carving a good life out of difficult terrain. With a traffic-free charm—a happy result of natural isolation—the Cinque Terre offers a rugged alternative to the glitzy Riviera resorts nearby.

Each village fills a ravine with a lazy hive of human activity. Calloused locals and sunburned travelers enjoy the area's unique mix of Italian culture and nature. There isn't a Fiat or museum in sight—just sun, sea, sand (well, pebbles), wine, and pure, unadulterated Italy. Choose a home base according to just how cut off you'd like to be from the outer world: resorty Monterosso, cover-girl Vernazza, hilltop Corniglia, photogenic Manarola, or amiable Riomaggiore.

This breathtakingly scenic six-mile stretch of coast was first described in medieval times as the "five lands" *(cinque terre).* Tiny communities grew up in the shadows of castles, which doubled as lookouts for pirate raids. As the threat of pirates faded, the villages prospered, catching fish and cultivating grapes. But until the advent of tourism in this generation, the towns remained isolated. Even today, each village comes with its own traditions, a distinct dialect, and a proud heritage. Other Italians think of locals here as "mountain people by the sea."

The Cinque Terre is now a national park (founded in 1999),

where all can enjoy the villages, hiking, swimming, boat rides, and evening romance of one of God's great gifts to tourism. While the region is well-discovered and can get jam-packed, I've never seen happier, more relaxed tourists.

In this chapter, I cover general tips for your visit to the Cinque Terre, then describe the five towns in order from north to south—from Monterosso to Riomaggiore.

## PLANNING YOUR TIME

The ideal stay in the Cinque Terre is two or three full days; my recommended minimum stay is two nights and an uninterrupted day.

The villages are connected by trains, boats, and trails. There's no checklist of sights or experiences—just a hike, the towns themselves, and your fondest vacation desires. Read this chapter in advance to piece together your best visit, mixing hiking, swimming, trains, and boat rides.

**Cinque Terre in Two Days:** You could spend one day hiking between towns (taking a boat or train part of the way, or as the return trip). Spend a second day visiting any towns you've yet to see, comparing main streets, beaches, and focaccia.

Here's a sample day: If you're based in Monterosso, take a morning train to Corniglia, hike to Vernazza for lunch (where you could explore the town, hike to the grand-view cemetery, or cool

## The Cinque Terre at a Glance

**▲▲Monterosso al Mare** Resorty, flat, and spread out along the coast, with a charming old town, a modern new town, and the Cinque Terre's best beaches, swimming, and nightlife. It has the most restaurants and the most comfortable hotels. See page 357.

**▲▲▲Vernazza** The region's gem—the most touristy and dramatic—crowned with a ruined castle above and a lively harborfront cradling a natural harbor below. See page 374.

**▲Corniglia** Quiet hilltop village known for its cooler temperatures (it's the only one without a harbor), fewer tourists, and a tradition of fine wines. See page 396.

**▲▲Manarola** Mellow, hiking-focused waterfront village wrapped in vineyards and dotted with a picturesque mix of shops and cliff-climbing houses. See page 401.

**▲▲Riomaggiore** The most workaday of the five villages, with nightlife, too. See page 411.

### Near the Cinque Terre

The Riviera towns north and south of the Cinque Terre make for fun, easy side trips—and some are workable home bases. See the next chapter for more on Levanto, Sestri Levante, Santa Margherita Ligure, and Portofino (all to the north), and Porto Venere and transit-hub La Spezia (to the south).

off at the beach), then catch the boat back to Monterosso to stroll the beach promenade. And that's only one day out of dozens of memorable Cinque Terre combinations you can dream up.

On any evening, linger over dinner, enjoy live music at a low-key club (or summer opera in Vernazza), try a wine tasting, or follow one of my self-guided town walks. At sunset, take a glass of your favorite beverage out to the breakwater to watch the sun slip into the Mediterranean.

**With More Time:** You may be tempted to add the nearby resort towns of Levanto, Sestri Levante, Santa Margherita Ligure, and Portofino (to the north), and Porto Venere (to the south, anchored by the major transit hub of La Spezia; all described in the next chapter). If you carve out a day and an overnight for Santa Margherita Ligure, you can fit in an afternoon side trip to Portofino. A day trip to Levanto (by train or a hike from Monterosso) with an excursion to Bonassola and Framura is fun. For double the beaches, visit Sestri Levante. South of the Cinque Terre, lovely Porto Venere merits a day trip.

**Day-Tripping to the Cinque Terre:** Speed demons could store their baggage, take a hike in the morning, have a waterfront lunch, laze on a beach in the afternoon, and leave by evening to somewhere back in the real world. But be warned: The Cinque Terre is inundated with cruise-ship groups doing the same thing. The best way to enjoy the Cinque Terre is to be here before and after the daily day-trip deluge. (Ironically, some travelers decide against an overnight because they've heard the Cinque Terre is crowded—then day-trip in, only experiencing it with those terrible crowds.) The charm of the region survives—early and late.

**When to Go:** In early spring, from mid-March through April, the Cinque Terre is typically all yours. Later spring and fall are peak season, with the best weather and the most crowds. Book rooms ahead during the busiest times: holidays (including Easter weekend and April 25—Liberation Day), May, June, all summer weekends, September, and October.

July and August are hotter and generally a bit less crowded. The winter is really dead—most hotels and some restaurants close from November to mid-March.

## Orientation to the Cinque Terre

### TOURIST AND PARK INFORMATION

Each town's train station has a Cinque Terre national park information office, which generally also serves as an all-purpose town TI and gift shop. They can answer questions about trails (including conditions and closures), shuttle bus schedules, and so on.

**Useful Websites:** The park's website is ParcoNazionale5terre. it. The "download" section of CinqueTerre.it has park info as well as boat and train timetables. A blog worth a look is CinqueTerreInsider.com, written by resident American expat Amy Inman; it's filled with up-to-date practicalities for visitors to this always-in-flux region.

### ARRIVAL IN THE CINQUE TERRE

**By Train:** The five towns of the Cinque Terre are on a milk-run line, with trains coming through about every 30 minutes; most trains connect to the Cinque Terre from La Spezia or Genoa (local train info tel. 0187-817-458, www.trenitalia.com). Big, fast trains usually speed right past the Cinque Terre, although a few IC trains connect Monterosso to Milan or Pisa.

Unless you're coming from another Cinque Terre town, you'll change trains at least once to reach Manarola, Corniglia, or Vernazza. From the south or east, you'll probably transfer at La Spe-

*CINQUE TERRE*

zia's Centrale station. From the north, you'll transfer at Genoa's Piazza Principe station, Sestri Levante, Levanto, or Monterosso.

For details on riding the train between Cinque Terre towns, see "Getting Around the Cinque Terre," later; for information on arrival in each town, see the "Arrival" section for each town. For outbound trains, see "Monterosso Connections" on page 374 and "La Spezia Connections" on page 461.

**By Train After Parking Your Car:** Don't bring a car to the Cinque Terre; you won't need it. Given the narrow roads and parking headache, the only Cinque Terre town I'd drive to is Monterosso (and then only if my hotel had parking). I could go on at great length about each town's remote and often congested little parking lot (a shuttle-bus ride up the hill from that town), but for your own good, I'll keep my advice short: Park your car in the nearest big city and take the train in—it's safer, cheaper, faster, and smarter. Parking is easy in Levanto or La Spezia (La Spezia has a fine modern underground garage at the station; for details see the next chapter).

## HELPFUL HINTS

**Pickpocket Alert:** At peak times, the Cinque Terre can be notoriously crowded, and pickpockets (often female teens in groups of three or four, frequently dressed as tourists), aggressively and expertly work the most congested areas. Be on guard, especially in train stations, on platforms, and while you're on trains, particularly when getting on or off with a crush of people. Wear a money belt, and keep your things zipped up and buttoned down.

**Money:** You'll find ATMs and banks throughout the region. Use ATMs attached to actual banks. Shops earn a commission by hosting rip-off ATMs on their premises.

**Markets:** Market days perk up the Cinque Terre and nearby towns from around 8:00 to 13:00 on Tuesday in Vernazza, Wednesday in Levanto, Thursday in Monterosso, Friday in Santa Margherita Ligure, and Saturday in Sestri Levante.

**Booking Services: Arbaspàa,** based in Manarola, sets up wine tastings, cooking classes, fishing trips, and more (www. arbaspaa.com; see page 407). **Cinque Terre Riviera,** based in Vernazza, books rooms and apartments throughout the region, Vernazza opera tickets, cooking classes, and more (www.cinqueterreriviera.com; see page 378). **BeautifuLiguria,** run by Anna Merulla, offers various excursions (www. beautifuliguria.com).

**Local Guides:** These guides are knowledgeable, a delight to be with, and charge from €125/half-day and €210/day: **Andrea Bordigoni** (mobile 393-133-9409, bordigo@inwind.it) and **Marco Brizzi** (mobile 328-694-2847, marco_brizzi@yahoo.it).

## Events in the Cinque Terre

You could use this list to find and join a festival—or to avoid crowds. For more festival information and to confirm dates, check www.lamialiguria.it. Food festivals in particular are subject to change.

| | |
|---|---|
| **Easter and Easter Monday** | Popular time to visit the Cinque Terre. As it's extremely crowded, book long in advance. |
| **April 25** | Italian Liberation Day is also very crowded (avoid this day, as locals literally shut down the trails). |
| **May 1** | Labor Day (Cinque Terre packed with day-trippers) |
| **May (3rd Sun)** | Monterosso: Lemon Festival |
| **June (3rd Sun)** | Monterosso: Anchovy Festival |
| **June 23** | Monterosso and Vernazza: Feast of Corpus Domini (procession on carpet of flowers) |
| **June 24** | Riomaggiore and Monterosso: Feast day of St. John the Baptist (procession and fireworks, floating candles on the sea; big fire on Monterosso's old-town beach the day before) |
| **June 29** | Corniglia: Feast day of Sts. Peter and Paul |
| **July 20** | Vernazza: Feast day of patron St. Margaret, with fireworks |
| **Aug (1st Sun)** | Vernazza: Feast of Nostra Signora di Reggio (hike up to Madonna di Reggio sanctuary for food and church procession) |
| **Aug 10** | Manarola: Feast day of patron St. Lawrence |
| **Aug 15** | Feast of the Assumption (Ferragosto) |
| **Sept 8** | Monterosso: Feast of Madonna di Fegina (luminarias and procession up to hilltop sanctuary) |

**Nightlife:** There's not much in this sleepy region, though Monterosso and Riomaggiore have lively late-night bars. For a little high culture, consider a Wednesday or Friday evening enjoying Vernazza's summer opera series (see the Vernazza section).

**Rainy Day Activities:** Explore the towns, taking trains to connect them; splurge for a tasty meal; or nurse a coffee or drink at a harborfront café while watching the roiling waves. If you hike, avoid the steeper trails in the rain; rocks can be slippery.

**Baggage Storage and Delivery:** You can pay to store bags at or near the train stations in Monterosso, Vernazza, and Riomaggiore. Near the Cinque Terre, you can store bags in Santa Margherita Ligure and in La Spezia. See specifics per destination.

To transfer luggage from the station to your accommodations, call ahead and arrange with **Roberto Pecunia;** he's based in Riomaggiore but works in any of the towns (mobile 370-375-7972).

**Taxi: Cinqueterre Taxi** covers all five towns (Matteo mobile 334-776-1946, Christian mobile 347-652-0837, www.cinqueterretaxi.com). The pricey **5 Terre Transfer** service is handy if you need to connect the five towns or beyond (Luciana mobile 339-130-1183, Marzio mobile 340-356-5268, www.5terretransfer.com).

## GETTING AROUND THE CINQUE TERRE

Within the Cinque Terre, you can connect towns by train, boat, or foot. Trains are the cheapest, fastest, and most frequent option. But don't get stuck in a train rut: In calm weather, **boats** connect the towns nearly as frequently—and more scenically.

### By Train

By train, the five towns are just a few minutes apart.

**Tickets:** A train ride between any two Cinque Terre towns costs €4. You must buy a new **indi-****vidual ticket** for every train ride, and tickets are valid only on the day of purchase. You can buy tickets and check schedules online (www. trenitalia.com), at train-station windows or ticket machines, or at Cinque Terre park desks. When you buy a ticket, make a note of the train number, as that's how the station monitors identify incoming and departing trains. Don't wait to buy a ticket at the last minute: Ticket machines can be broken, and there can be very long lines at the window.

The €16 **Cinque Terre Treno Card** (described later, under "Hiking the Cinque Terre") can be worthwhile even if you don't hike, as it allows you to catch trains at the last minute without ticket concerns. It pays for itself if you take four rides in one day, but its value comes more from convenience than economy (https://card.parconazionale5terre.it).

Trains are covered by the Eurail Pass, but unless you have days to waste, it doesn't make sense to use up a valuable travel day here, where train expenses are relatively low.

**Using Tickets and Cards:** Validate your ticket (or park card) before you board by stamping it in one of the green-and-white ma-

## Swimming and Kayaking in the Cinque Terre

Every coastal town has a beach—or, at least, a rocky place to **swim.** Monterosso has the Cinque Terre's biggest and sandiest beach, with umbrellas and beach-use fees (but any stretch of beach without umbrellas is free). Vernazza's main beach and

new beach are tiny—better for sunning than swimming (some people swim in the deep water off the breakwater). Manarola and Riomaggiore have the worst beaches (no sand), but Manarola offers the best deep-water swimming. Levanto, just a few minutes' train ride past Monterosso, has big and broad beaches, with even better ones an easy bike ride away, in Bonassola and Framura. And Sestri Levante, farther north, has two beautiful beaches.

Pack your swim gear. Several beaches have showers. Don't tote your white hotel towels; most hotels will provide beach towels (sometimes for a fee). Underwater sightseeing is full of fish. Sea urchins line the rocks, and sometimes jellyfish wash up

on the pebbles (water shoes and goggles sold in local shops). If no one is swimming, it's likely because of stinging jellyfish. Ask, "Medusa?"

You can rent **kayaks** or **boats** in Monterosso and Riomaggiore. While experienced boaters have a blast here, if you're not comfortable navigating a tippy kayak, this is not a good place to learn.

chines located on train platforms and in station passages. If you're not sure how to do this, ask when you buy your ticket or card. Conductors here are notorious for levying stiff fines on tourists riding with an unstamped ticket. (Note that train tickets bought online or with the Trenitalia app are prevalidated—you don't need to stamp them.)

**Station Helpers:** Red-vested track-side staff can answer your train-related questions. But be aware they are also there to keep crowds at bay as trains approach...and to nail travelers without tickets (they get a cut of the fines they levy).

**Schedules:** In peak season, trains connecting the five towns generally run two to three times hourly in each direction, but the frequency declines after about 20:00. Note that some trains do not stop at all five towns. Check schedules in advance.

Since the train is the Cinque Terre's lifeline, shops, hotels, and restaurants often post the current schedule, and many hand out paper copies. Study the key to know which departures are only for weekdays, Sundays, and so on. These schedules also tell you which towns any given train will stop in. Trains from Levanto, Monterosso, Riomaggiore, or La Spezia sometimes skip lesser stations, so confirm that the train will stop at the town you need. (Note that train numbers starting with 21 or 24 generally stop at all five towns.)

**At the Platform:** Monitors display next departure times, listed by train number and final destination (but they do not show intermediate stops). They also show if a train is late—*in ritardo*—and by how many minutes; *SOPP* means "cancelled". Trains are indicated by their final destination: Northbound trains are going to Levanto, Genova, or Sestri Levante; southbound trains are headed for La Spezia. To be sure you get on the right train, know your train's number and final destination. Northbound trains use the tracks closest to the water; southbound trains use the tracks on the mountain side.

**Getting Off:** Know your stop. As the train leaves the town previous to the one where you want to get off, go to the door and get ready to slip out before the mobs flood in. If it's crowded, you may need to be assertive. Say *"permesso"* (per-MEH-soh) and push on through. Note that stations are small and trains are long—you might have to get off deep in a tunnel, especially in Vernazza and Riomaggiore. If this happens, just head toward daylight. Also, train doors don't open automatically—you may have to open the door yourself (push the green button, twist the black handle, or lift up the red one).

## By Boat

From Easter through October, a daily boat service connects Monterosso, Vernazza, Manarola, Riomaggiore, Porto Venere, and beyond. Though they can be very crowded, these boats provide a scenic way to get from town to town (operated by 5 Terre-Golfo dei Poeti, tel. 0187-732-987, www.navigazionegolfodeipoeti.it).

Because the boats nose in and tourists have to disembark onto little more than a plank, even just a small chop can cancel some or all of the stops.

**Tickets:** The ticket price depends on the length of the boat ride (€7 for a short hop, and up to €18 for a five-town, one-way ticket with stops). An all-day Cinque Terre pass costs €27; to add Porto Venere, it's €35, plus an extra €5 for an optional 40-minute scenic ride around three small islands near Porto Venere (2/day). Buy tickets at the little stands at each town's harbor.

**Schedules:** Boat schedules are posted online and at docks, harbor bars, Cinque Terre park offices, and hotels. Boats depart Monterosso about hourly (9:45-18:00), stopping at the Cinque

## Crowd-Beating Tips

Italy's slice of traffic-free Riviera has been discovered, frustrating both locals and conscientious visitors. The most dramatic influx is created by groups—whether day-tripping tours or mobs of cruise-ship sightseers. Avoid the worst of the log-jams by following these tips:

**Time your visit carefully.** April can be ideal, with fewer crowds and cooler temperatures for hiking (although it can be too cold to swim). The busiest months are May, June, September, and October; July and August are slightly less crowded, but packed on weekends. Avoid holiday weekends (Easter and Italian Liberation Day on April 25) if you can.

**Make the most of your time early and late.** Take advantage of the cool, relaxed, and quiet morning and evening hours. Starting a hike at 8:00 or at 16:00 or 17:00 is a joy. Cruisers and day-trippers start pouring into the Cinque Terre around 10:00 and typical-

ly head out by 17:00. Those midday hours are your time to hit the beach, or find a hike away from the main trails. At midday, the main coastal trail is a hot human traffic jam. Beyond the busy coastal trail, there are plenty of hikes where you'll scarcely see another tourist.

**Sleep in the Cinque Terre—not nearby.** Levanto and La Spezia are close and well-connected by train, making them popular home bases. But it's easier to enjoy the Cinque Terre early and late—when it's quiet and cool—if you're sleeping here.

**Be careful on crowded train platforms.** At peak times, be cautious, stay well behind the yellow line, and be alert for pickpockets. Spread out to less crowded areas to wait.

**Hire your own boat.** If the regularly scheduled boats are jammed, consider hiring your own boat to zip you to the next town. Captains hang out at each town's harbor, offering one-way transfers to other towns, hour-long cruises, and more.

Terre towns (except Corniglia, the hill town) and ending up about 90 minutes later in Porto Venere. Boats from Porto Venere to Monterosso run about 8:30-17:00. In high season, three boats per day depart from Levanto to Porto Venere.

**Private Boats:** To escape the crowds—or for a scenic splurge—hire a captain to ferry you between towns. For example, at the harbor in Vernazza, you can pay around €50 to hop to any other Cinque Terre town. Split the cost among a few fellow travelers, and you have an affordable water taxi. For a memorable and relaxing time on the water, you can hire a captain for a coastal tour, swimming excursion to a hidden cove, or a fishing trip (figure €150/1 hour). Or take a sunset *aperitivo* cruise (per-person charge; you should be able to join a 2-hour sightseeing cruise with drinks for around €50). Captains offer their services at the harbors in Monterosso, Vernazza, Manarola, and Riomaggiore (see specific listings in the Monterosso and Vernazza sections).

## By Shuttle Bus

ATC shuttle buses (which locals call *pulmino*) connect each Cinque Terre town with its closest parking lot and various points in the hills (but they don't connect the five towns to each other). The one you're most likely to use runs between Corniglia's train station and its hilltop town center. Rides cost €1.50 (€2.50 from driver), and are covered by the Cinque Terre park card (described in next section). Buy tickets and get bus schedules at park info offices or TIs, or check times posted at bus stops (also online at www.atcesercizio. it). As you board, it's smart to tell the driver where you want to go. Departures often coordinate with train arrival times.

Some shuttles go beyond the parking lots and high into the hills—often terminating at the town's sanctuary church. To soak in the scenery, you can ride up and hike down. This works particularly well from Manarola and Vernazza. Or you can ride both ways (50 minutes round-trip, covered by one ticket).

# Hiking the Cinque Terre

The five Cinque Terre towns are connected by a main coastal trail and a web of trails higher up. The main coastal trail has four sections—two that are open (Monterosso to Vernazza, and Vernazza to Corniglia) and two that are closed (Corniglia to Manarola, and Manarola to Riomaggiore—the famed "Via dell'Amore"). Also closed is the alternate Riomaggiore-Manarola trail (via "La Beccara").

With only half the trails open and so many day-trippers blitzing in with the same hiking agenda, you'll want to enjoy the region's most popular hikes on the lower trail (from Vernazza to Monterosso, or from Corniglia to Vernazza) early or late. The single best high-country hike is from Manarola to Corniglia via Volastra (you can ride the ATC shuttle bus from Manarola to the high point at Volastra and hike scenically downhill to Corniglia). These hikes take roughly 1.5-2 hours and are described next.

**Cinque Terre Park Cards:** Visitors hiking on the main coastal trail must buy a park card. Cards are not needed to hike on higher trails. Cards can be purchased online, or at train stations, TIs, and trailheads, and are good for 24 or 48 hours after validation (www. parconazionale5terre.it). Some area hotels sell discounted park cards to guests—be sure to ask.

The **Cinque Terre Trekking Card** costs €7.50 for one day of hiking or €14.50 for two days (covers trails, free use of WCs, park Wi-Fi, and ATC shuttle buses, but not trains).

The **Cinque Terre Treno Card** covers what the Trekking Card does, but also includes local trains connecting all Cinque Terre towns, plus Levanto and La Spezia (€16/24 hours, €29/48 hours, validate card at train station by punching it in the machine). Even if you're not planning to hike, this card can be worth it just to save you time on buying train tickets.

**Navigation:** Trails are marked with red-and-white paint, white arrows, and some signs (*sentiero* means trail). The main coastal trail is variously indicated as "SVA," "the Blue Trail," or #592. Maps aren't necessary for the basic coastal hikes. But for the more challenging routes that leave the crowds behind, pick up a good hiking map (about €5, sold everywhere).

**Hiking Conditions:** In general, trails are narrow, steep, rocky, and come with lots of challenging steps. Don't overestimate your hiking abilities. I get many emails from readers who say the trails were tougher than they'd expected. The rocks and metal grates can be slippery in the rain. Don't venture up on these rocky cliffs without sun protection (and/or a hat), water, and proper shoes (flip-flops are not allowed). Pace yourself. While the main coastal trail is strenuous, it's doable for any fit hiker...and the scenery is worth the sweat.

Before embarking on the more difficult hikes, get advice from one of the national park offices (located at each train station), or from Cinque Terre Trekking in Manarola (see page 407).

**When to Go:** The coastal trail can be extremely crowded and very hot at midday. For the best light, coolest temperatures, and fewer crowds, start your hike early (by 8:00) or late (around 16:00 or 17:00). Before setting out for an evening hike, find out when the sun will set, and leave plenty of time to arrive at your destination before then; there's no lighting on the trails.

**Shuttle Buses:** ATC shuttle buses can make the going easier, connecting coastal villages to trailheads higher up. Locals know all the options—and shuttle bus schedules—so ask around. But be aware that shuttles heading into the high country only run in summer, and just once or twice a day. If frustrated with bus schedules, try the local taxis.

**Guided Hikes and Excursions:** Your park card includes guided hikes and other local excursions (such as town walking tours), which take place almost daily in the summer months. Even without

# Hikes at a Glance

Hikes can be done in either direction. Get local advice before you set out. I've omitted trails closed as of this printing.

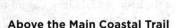

### Main Coastal Trail
▲▲▲**Vernazza-Monterosso** Challenging but dramatic 2-hour hike, including long stretches of steep steps above Monterosso.

▲▲▲**Corniglia-Vernazza** Most scenic and rewarding segment (1.5 hours) of the main coastal trail, with fine views, significant elevation changes, and moderately challenging stretches on uneven stone steps.

### Above the Main Coastal Trail
▲▲**Manarola-Corniglia via Volastra** Demanding but gorgeous 2.5-hour hike through vineyards high over the coast; made much easier and shorter if you take the shuttle bus from Manarola to Volastra. Park card not required for hike, though it covers the cheap bus ride.

▲▲**Madonna di Reggio Sanctuary Hike** Easy 30-minute downhill hike from the sanctuary above Vernazza, best reached by shuttle bus. See page 385.

a valid park ticket, these events are affordable—usually around €6. Look for schedules locally, or email visiteguidate@ati5terre.it for details.

## TOP THREE HIKES
These three hikes each give the quintessential Cinque Terre hiking experience. The first two are part of the main coastal trail (and require the national park card); the third takes you much higher (and is free).

### Main Coastal Trail
▲▲▲**Vernazza-Monterosso**
**(2 hours, 2 miles)**
The scenic up-and-down-a-lot trek from Vernazza to Monter-

CINQUE TERRE

## Extending the Coastal Trail and More

### To the North
▲**Monterosso-Levanto** Logical northward continuation of the main coastal trail, a 3.5-hour hike over Punta Mesco; a notch more challenging and longer than other coastal trail segments.

▲**Levanto-Bonassola Promenade** Level 30-minute walk that cuts through mountains (largely through tunnels) to connect Levanto to the beach town of Bonassola; fine by foot but better by bike. See page 427.

▲**Bonassola-Framura** Level 30-minute walk from Bonassola through a long line of train tunnels (better by bike) to Framura's train station; can continue to several small beaches (easy cliffside trail) or up to a cluster of little villages (via a footpath). See page 427.

### To the South
▲**Riomaggiore-Porto Venere** Very demanding, 6-hour trek high into the hills, ending at picturesque Porto Venere.

### Long, Cross-Regional Hike
▲▲**High Route between Porto Venere and Levanto** Remote, cliff-capping 22-mile trail (AV5T) high above the main coastal trail and sanctuary trails, best for well-equipped, hardy hikers.

CINQUE TERRE

osso is both challenging and rewarding. The trail is narrow, steep, and crumbly in spots, with a lot of steps but easy to follow. The views just out of Vernazza, looking back at the town, are spectacular. From there you'll gradually ascend to 550 feet, passing some scenic waterfalls populated by croaking frogs. As you approach Monterosso, you'll descend steeply through vineyards—on very deep, knee-testing stairs—and eventually follow a rivulet to the sea. The last stretch is along a pleasant, paved pathway clinging to the cliff. You'll pop out right at Monterosso's refreshing old-town beach.

### ▲▲▲Corniglia-Vernazza (1.5 hours, 2 miles)
The hike from Corniglia to Vernazza—the wildest and greenest section of the coast—is very rewarding but very hilly. From the Corniglia train station, zigzag up to the town (via the steep stairs, the longer road, or the shuttle bus). From Corniglia, you'll

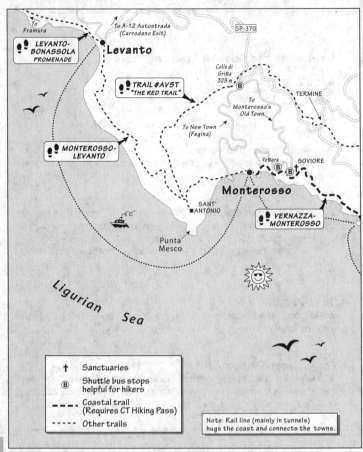

CINQUE TERRE

reach the trailhead on the main road, past Villa Cecio. You'll hike through vineyards toward Vernazza. After about 10 minutes, you'll see a faded sign to Guvano beach, far beneath you (formerly a nude beach—now closed). The scenic trail continues through lots of fragrant and flowery vegetation into Vernazza. If you need a break before reaching Vernazza, stop at Bar la Torre, with a strip of amazingly scenic and delightfully shady tables perched high above the town.

## Above the Main Coastal Trail
### ▲▲Manarola-Corniglia via Volastra (2.5 hours, 4 miles)

This challenging hike from Manarola leads up to the village of Volastra, then north through high-altitude vineyard terraces, and steeply down through a forest to Corniglia. You can shave the two steepest miles off this route by taking the ATC shuttle bus from Manarola up to Volastra (about hourly, 15-minute trip).

# Cinque Terre Hikes

SP-38

2 Kilometers

2 Miles

TRAIL #AV5T
"THE RED TRAIL"

SP-63

MADONNA
DI REGGIO
315 m

**Vernazza**

SAN
BERNARDINO
350 m    SP-51

CORNIGLIA-
VERNAZZA

MANAROLA-
CORNIGLIA
VIA VOLASTRA

TRAIL #AV5T
"THE RED TRAIL"

**Corniglia**

SALUTE

CANTINA
SOCIALE
WINE

B

**Volastra**

MANAROLA-
CORNIGLIA
(CLOSED)

**Manarola**

RIOMAGGIORE-
MANAROLA
VIA "LA BECCARA"
(CLOSED)

RIOMAGGIORE-
MANAROLA
"VIA DELL'AMORE"
(CLOSED)

RIOMAGGIORE-
PORTO VENERE

**Riomaggiore**

To
Porto Venere

To
La Spezia

MONTENERO
340 m    SP-51

**CINQUE TERRE**

If you'd rather hike to Volastra, you have two options: The national park's official route (trail #506) cuts up through the valley. Locals have cleared a more scenic but rougher alternate route that begins with the vineyard hike on my self-guided walk for Manarola (page 403); partway along this walk, where you reach

the wooden religious scenes scampering up the hillside, take a sharp right and walk uphill, following signs for *Panoramico Volastra (Corniglia)*. While steeper than the official route, this trail follows the ridge at the top of the vineyard, with wonderful sea views.

Tiny **Volastra,** perched between Manarola and Corniglia, hosts lots of Germans and Italians in the summer. Just below town, in the hamlet of Groppo, is Cantina Sociale, a cooperative winery open to the public (wine tastings, www.cantinacinqueterre.com). When you're ready to head for Corniglia, make your way to the village church (where the shuttle bus drops off) and look for *Corniglia* signs. From the front door of the church, directly across the piazza, find the trailhead (marked by an iron cross) for trail #586 to Case Pianca.

Here begins one of the region's finest hikes, tight-roping along narrow trails tucked between vineyard terraces, with spectacular bird's-eye views over the entire Cinque Terre. You'll cut up and down the terraces a bit—just keep following the red-and-white markings and arrows. After passing a little village (and following signs through someone's seaview backyard), the trail enters a forest and begins its sharp, rocky descent into Corniglia. (To skip the descent, backtrack to Volastra and return by shuttle bus to Manarola.) High above Corniglia, you'll reach a fork, where you turn left to proceed downhill on trail #587 to Corniglia.

## EXTENDING THE COASTAL TRAIL

Beyond the main coastal trail, the national park maintains a free, extensive network of trails. The Cinque Terre Park Card is not required for the following hikes.

The most challenging hikes (between Riomaggiore and Porto Venere, and the high route linking Porto Venere and Levanto) are best for very experienced hikers who are equipped with hiking boots, poles, a phone for emergencies, plenty of water, and a good map. Before attempting these hikes, get detailed local advice.

## To the North
### ▲Monterosso-Levanto (3.5 hours, 4 miles)

This strenuous, rugged-and-wild hike on the coastal trail (SVA) will take you all the way into Levanto. Wear good shoes and bring lots of water.

Starting from Monterosso, look for signs for the coastal trail at the west end of the new town, and head steeply up. You'll hike up and over Punta Mesco, the bluff that separates the two towns. The first stretch, out of Monterosso, is almost entirely big steps; the rest is mostly a gradual up-and-down.

For a short scenic detour, look for trail #591 not far out of Monterosso. This brief jog leads to the ruined chapel of Sant'Antonio.

To begin the hike in Levanto, see page 426.

**Alternate Route:** You can enjoy a higher hike by skipping the steepest stretch and riding one of Monterosso's shuttle buses to Colle di Gritta (and Hotel Monterosso Alto). From there, follow trail #591 along the ridge and down to Colle di Bagari, where several trails intersect. You can follow trail #571c from here or go a little lower to #571—both head down to trail SVA and Levanto. Or, to make your hike a loop that returns directly to Monterosso, continue from Colle di Bagari along trail #591 to trail SVA, and drop steeply into Monterosso.

### ▲Levanto-Bonassola (30 minutes)

For an easy excursion, take the train to Levanto, then stroll (or better yet, bike) the level, rails-to-trails promenade to the beach town of Bonassola (see the next chapter).

### ▲Bonassola-Framura (30 minutes)

From Bonassola (described above), the path (good for biking) continues through a series of tunnels to Framura, a cluster of small villages. You can take the scenic coastal trail to a small beach or hike up the road to the villages.

## To the South

### ▲Riomaggiore-Porto Venere (6 hours, 8 miles)

For this challenging trek, you'll hike up from Riomaggiore on trail #593 (a continuation of the coastal trail SVA) to the sanctuary at Montenero, then up to Colle del Telegrafo; and then all the way down to Porto Venere on trail AV5T. Partway along, the town of Campiglia has a little bar/restaurant (and buses to La Spezia).

## Long, Cross-Regional Hikes

### ▲▲High Route Between Porto Venere and Levanto (22 miles)

Above the coastal trails, and higher than the sanctuary trails, is the demanding 22-mile AV5T trail (*alta via 5 Terre*, also labeled trail #1 or #591/598). It connects Porto Venere to Levanto, offering sky-high views over the Cinque Terre seafront. Also called the Red Trail, it's cool, uncrowded, and at the top of the world. You could do all or part of this trail.

## OTHER CINQUE TERRE WALKS AND HIKES

For each Cinque Terre town, I include a **self-guided walk** to help you explore the town (anytime, day or night). Manarola's is the most scenic, offering an easy, rewarding stroll through vineyards with stunning views. Per town, I also list a few easy hiking options, even as simple as walking just outside town to get a lovely overview looking back (e.g., for Vernazza and Manarola).

### Sanctuary Trails (La Strada dei Santuari)

Each of the five towns has its own sanctuary (with a chapel or church dedicated to the Virgin Mary), hovering in the hills a mile or two above town, and accessible by a long, steep hike (quiet and

## Cruise Ship Travelers: Please Avoid Excursions to the Cinque Terre

There are two Cinque Terres: when the cruise groups are inundating it and when they are not.

Huge ships stop in La Spezia, Genoa, or even Livorno, and offer guided excursions to the five towns, dumping literally thousands of travelers on the Cinque Terre, which doesn't have the infrastructure for huge crowds.

When the cruise ships are in, Cinque Terre trains and platforms are dangerously overcrowded, the trails become almost impassable, and the towns' tiny main lanes are clogged. Sure, cruise travelers can cross the Cinque Terre off their "bucket list." But nobody arriving with a cruise ship horde can really experience the Cinque Terre. And locals do not like cruise groups.

Please, visit on your own. Don't try to experience the villages and fragile trails of the Cinque Terre as part of a cruise ship mob. (If you're visiting Italy by cruise, do a cruise excursion to Pisa and Lucca instead—they can handle the crowds. Or for a seaside experience, consider Porto Venere, or ride the train up to Sestri Levante or Santa Margherita Ligure—all covered in the next chapter.) I love cruising. And I love the Cinque Terre. But in my opinion, they just don't mix.

uncrowded). The sanctuaries were a place of refuge for each village in the age of pirate attacks.

Villagers feel deeply connected to these spiritual retreats, where they remember lost relatives and feel part of a timeless community. A network of "sanctuary trails" (no hiking card required) crisscrosses the hills above the main coastal route. There's no single path, but with a good map you can link up these moderately difficult trails. In most towns, the shuttle bus can take you from the town center to the sanctuary—you could ride up and hike down (described with each town's coverage next).

## Sleeping in the Cinque Terre

Accommodations in the popular Cinque Terre cost more than in other villages and are packed on holidays (especially Easter weekend and April 25); when the weather is best (May, June, Sept, and Oct); and on Fridays and Saturdays all summer (though July and

Aug can be less crowded due to sweltering heat). During these busy periods, you must reserve ahead.

**Vernazza,** the spindly and salty essence of the Cinque Terre, is my top choice for a home base. And its summer opera series has beefed up its nightlife. But if you think too many people have my book, you'll get fewer crowds and better value for your money in other towns.

**Monterosso** is a good choice for sun-worshipping beach lovers, those who prefer the ease of a real hotel, and a youthful crowd interested in nightlife.

**Manarola,** charming and not overrun, draws serious hikers and sophisticated Europeans. The town has a good range of professional-feeling small accommodations, but fewer dining and evening options.

**Riomaggiore,** one of the biggest Cinque Terre towns, has the cheapest beds and rivals Monterosso for nightlife, but it's more Italian than Rivieran.

**Corniglia,** on a hilltop (no beach), attracts hermits, anarchists, wine lovers, and mountain goats.

**Private Rooms for Rent** *(Affittacamere):* Many accommodations in the Cinque Terre (especially in Vernazza) are *affittacamere,* or private rooms for rent. These range from simple bedrooms with shared baths, to fancy bedrooms with private baths, to comfortable apartments (often with small kitchens). You get a key and come and go as you like, typically rarely seeing your landlord. Plan on paying cash. If you must cancel an *affittacamere* reservation, do it as early as possible—since people renting rooms usually don't take deposits, they lose money if you don't show up.

**Amenities:** Breakfast is not included at most *affittacamere* and other simple accommodations. (Locals take breakfast about as seriously as flossing.) The basic, very Italian choice is simply to drop by a neighborhood bar for a cappuccino and a *cornetto* (croissant) or a piece of focaccia. Some pricier places include breakfast, but this often consists of a few paltry items (packaged croissants, yogurt, instant coffee) in a minifridge in your room.

While air-conditioning is essential in the summer elsewhere in Italy, in the breezy Cinque Terre you can generally manage fine without it. Expect thin walls (pack earplugs).

## Eating in the Cinque Terre

Hanging out at a seaview restaurant while sampling local specialties could become one of your favorite Cinque Terre memories.

The key staple is anchovies *(acciughe;* ah-CHOO-gay)—ideally served the day they're caught. If you've always hated anchovies (the slimy, salty kind), try them fresh here. They're prepared in a dizzying variety of ways: marinated, salted, drenched in lemon juice, butterflied and deep-fried (sometimes with a tasty garlic/vinegar sauce called *giada*), and so on.

*Tegame alla vernazzana* is the most typical main course in Vernazza: a layered, casserole-like dish of whole anchovies, potatoes, tomatoes, white wine, oil, and herbs.

Seafood is plentiful. You'll often see *muscoli ripieni* (stuffed mussels) on menus. And, while antipasto means cheese and salami

in Tuscany, here you'll get *antipasti frutti di mare* (or simply *antipasti misti*): a plate of mixed "fruits of the sea." Many restaurants are proud of their *frutti di mare*—it's how they show off—and it's a fine way to start a meal. For two diners, splitting one of these and a pasta dish can be plenty.

This region is the birthplace of pesto. Basil, which loves the temperate Ligurian climate, is ground with cheese (half *parmigiano* and half *pecorino*), garlic, olive oil, and pine nuts, and then poured over pasta. You'll see it on gnocchi or on pasta designed specifically for pesto to cling to: *trenette* (ruffled on one side) or *trofie* (short, dense twists). Many also like pesto lasagna, made with white sauce.

*Pansotti* are ravioli with ricotta and a mixture of greens, often served with a walnut sauce *(salsa di noci)*...delightful and filling.

Focaccia—pillowy, flat, salty, olive-oily bread—also originates here in Liguria. The baker roughs up the dough with finger holes, sprinkles it with salt water, then bakes it. Focaccia comes plain or with onions, sage, or olives, and is a local favorite for a snack on the beach. Bakeries sell it in rounds or slices by weight (a portion is about 100 grams, or *un etto*).

*Farinata*, a humble flatbread snack sold at pizza and focaccia places, is made from chickpea flour, water, oil, and pepper and baked on a copper tray in a wood-burning stove. It's dense, filling, and less flavorful than focaccia.

The region also loves its locally grown lemons. The popular lemon liqueur is called *limoncino* (a.k.a. *limoncello*).

*Vino delle Cinque Terre*, while not one of Italy's top wines, flows cheap and easy throughout the region. It's white—crisp, refreshing, and great with seafood. Local wines are typically blends, predominantly using the bosco grape, found only here. As local wine has become more sophisticated and appreciated lately, there are now plenty of wine bars that offer tasting experiences.

For a sweet but potent dessert wine, *sciacchetrà* (shah-keh-TRAH) is worth a try (18 percent alcohol, often served with dunkable cookies). While 10 kilos of grapes yield 7 liters of local wine, *sciacchetrà* is made from near-raisins: 10 kilos make only 1.5 liters of the wine. The word means "push and pull"—push in lots of grapes, pull out the best wine.

# Monterosso al Mare

Monterosso al Mare—the only Cinque Terre town with some flat land—has two parts: A new town (called Fegina) with a parking lot, train station, and TI; and an old town (Centro Storico), which cradles Old World charm in its small, crooked lanes. In the old town, you'll find hole-in-the-wall shops, rustic pastel townscapes, and a new generation of creative small-businesspeople eager to keep their visitors happy. A handy pedestrian tunnel connects the old with the new.

This is a resort town with a few cars and lots of hotels, rentable beach umbrellas, and crowds. Strolling the waterfront promenade, you can pick out each of the Cinque Terre towns decorating the coast. After dark, they sparkle. Monterosso is the most enjoyable of the five for backpackers or the young-at-heart wanting to connect with others looking for a little nightlife.

## Orientation to Monterosso

### TOURIST INFORMATION

The TI, called Proloco Monterosso, is on the street below the train station (daily 9:00-18:30, longer hours in summer, shorter hours off-season, baggage storage, exit station and go left a few doors, tel. 0187-817-506, www.prolocomonterosso.it). Upstairs within the station you'll find a Cinque Terre park info desk and a ticket office near platform 1 (both usually daily 8:00-20:00, shorter hours off-season).

### ARRIVAL IN MONTEROSSO

**By Train:** Train travelers arrive in the new town. To reach most of my recommended hotels in the new town, turn right from the station. To get to the old town, turn left from the station, follow the

# Monterosso al Mare

### Accommodations
1. Hotel Villa Steno
2. Il Giardino Incantato
3. Hotel Pasquale
4. Locanda il Maestrale
5. Hotel la Colonnina
6. Albergo Marina
7. Buranco Agriturismo
8. Manuel's Guesthouse
9. L'Antica Terrazza & Gastronomia "San Martino"
10. Albergo al Carugio
11. La Villa degli Argentieri
12. To Hotel Villa Adriana
13. Hotel la Spiaggia & Bar Giò
14. A Cà du Gigante
15. Hotel Punta Mesco
16. Pensione Agavi
17. Affittacamere Rist. Il Gabbiano
18. Le Sirene/Raggi di Sole

NEW TOWN (FEGINA)

TRAIN STATION

Beach

Beach (Free)

Ligurian

Beach

To Levanto & Autostrada

VIA PADRE SEMERIA

VIA MOLINELLI

VIA PADRE SEM.

VIA FEGINA

GROCERY

To trail to Levanto

To Free Beach & Il Gigante Statue

### Eateries & Nightlife
19. Ristorante Belvedere
20. Il Casello
21. L'Ancora della Tortuga & Torre Aurora
22. Via Venti
23. L'Osteria & Emy's Way Pizzeria Friggitoria
24. Ristorante al Pozzo
25. Ciak
26. Páe Veciu
27. La Smorfia & Pasticceria Laura
28. Miky
29. La Cantina di Miky
30. Il Frantoio Focacceria

seafront promenade, then duck through the tunnel just before the point—it's a scenic, flat 10-minute stroll.

The bar at track 1 (serving salads, sandwiches, and drinks) overlooks both the tracks and the beach, and is a handy place with a cool breeze to hang out while waiting for a train to pull in. As many trains run late, this can turn a frustration into a blessing.

**Taxis** usually wait outside the train station, but if not, you can call one (€10 from station to old town, mobile 335-616-5842, 335-

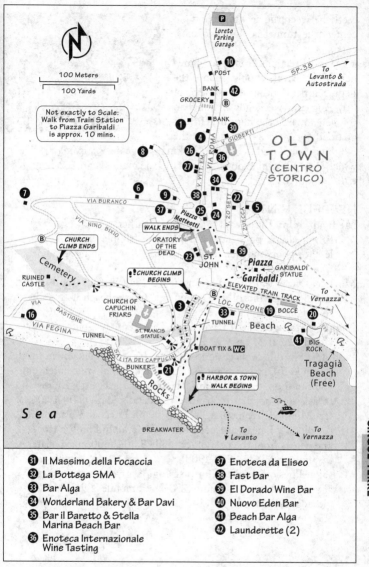

| | |
|---|---|
| ③① Il Massimo della Focaccia | ③⑦ Enoteca da Eliseo |
| ③② La Bottega SMA | ③⑧ Fast Bar |
| ③③ Bar Alga | ③⑨ El Dorado Wine Bar |
| ③④ Wonderland Bakery & Bar Davi | ④⓪ Nuovo Eden Bar |
| ③⑤ Bar il Baretto & Stella Marina Beach Bar | ④① Beach Bar Alga |
| ③⑥ Enoteca Internazionale Wine Tasting | ④② Launderette (2) |

616-5845, or 335-628-0933). ATC **shuttle buses** also go to the old town and are cheaper, but only run about once an hour.

**By Car:** Monterosso is 30 minutes off the freeway (exit: Carrodano-Levanto). About three miles above Monterosso, there's an intersection where you must choose either *Monterosso Centro Storico* (old part of town) or *Monterosso Fegina* (new town and beachfront parking). Know where you want to go, because you can't drive directly between the new town and old center (the tunnel is closed to most cars).

Get directions from your hotelier. Most drivers should choose the Fegina fork. Parking is easy (except July-Aug and weekends in June) in the new town in the huge beachfront guarded lot (€25/24 hours). In the old town, you'll find the Loreto parking garage on Via Roma, from which it's a 10-minute downhill walk to the main square (€2/hour, €20/24 hours).

## HELPFUL HINTS

**Medical Help:** The town's bike-riding, leather bag-toting, English-speaking physician is **Dr. Vitone** (simple visit—€50-100, less for poor students, mobile 338-853-0949, vitonee@yahoo. it).

**Market:** Every Thursday morning (8:00-13:00), trucks pull into the old town and fill the public area by the beach with stalls selling produce and more.

**Baggage Storage:** The **TI** will store bags (€6/day—but confirm closing time).

**Laundry:** For full-service, same-day laundry in the new town, try **Wash and Dry Lavarapido.** They'll pick up at your hotel, or you can drop it at their shop. The owners speak little English, so ask your hotelier to arrange the details (daily 9:00-19:00, Via Molinelli 17, mobile 339-484-0940, Lucia and Ivano). In the old town, head to **Luètu Lavanderia,** uphill on Via Roma and across from the post office (daily 8:00-20:00, maybe later in summer, tel. 328-286-1908).

**Massage:** Physiotherapist **Giorgio Moggia** gives good massages at your hotel or in his studio (€70/hour, mobile 339-314-6127, giomogg@tin.it).

# Monterosso Walks

These self-guided walks will introduce you to Monterosso. The first one, focusing on the mostly level town center, takes about 30 minutes. For the second one, you'll summit the adjacent hill—allow an hour or so.

## MONTEROSSO HARBOR AND TOWN WALK

• *Let's begin with an easy sweep of the sights: Hike out from the dock in the old town and stand atop the concrete breakwater. (If you're arriving by boat, you'll disembark here.)*

### Breakwater

From this point you can survey Monterosso's old town (straight ahead) and new town (stretching to the left, with train station and parking lot). Notice the bluff that separates old and new, and imagine how much harder your commute would be if the narrow road tethering these two towns were somehow cut off. It happened in the spring of 2013, when the wall below the hill-topping Capuchin church gave way in a landslide. For a time, the only way to connect the two halves of town by car was to drive six miles around; on foot, you had to hike up and over this hill. (The little fort halfway up the hill, which dates from 1550, is now a fancy restaurant, with a private home upstairs.)

Looking to the right, you can see all *cinque* of the *terre* from one spot: Vernazza, Corniglia (above the shore), Manarola, and a few buildings of Riomaggiore beyond that.

These days, the harbor hosts more paddleboats than fishing boats. Erosion is a major problem. The partial breakwater—the row of giant rocks in the middle of the harbor—is designed to save the beach from washing away. While old-timers remember a vast beach, their grandchildren truck in sand each spring to give tourists something to bask on. (The Nazis liked the Cinque Terre, too—find two of their bomb-hardened bunkers embedded in the bluff. During World War II, nearby La Spezia was an important Axis naval base, and Monterosso was bombed while the Germans were here.)

The fancy four-star Hotel Porto Roca (the pink building high on the hill, on the far right of the harbor) marks the trail to Vernazza. High above, you see an example of the costly roads built in the 1980s to connect the Cinque Terre towns with the freeway over the hills.

The two prominent capes (Punta di Montenero to the right, and Punta Mesco to the left) define the Cinque Terre region. The closer Punta Mesco is part of a protected marine sanctuary and home to a rare sea grass that provides an ideal home for fish eggs. Buoys keep fishing boats away. The cape was once a quarry, providing employment to locals who chipped out the stones used to build the local towns (the greenish stones making up part of the break-water are from there).

On the far end of the new town, marking the best free beach around, you can just see the statue named *Il Gigante* (hard to spot because it blends in with the gray rock). It's 45 feet tall and once held a trident. While it looks as if it were hewn from the rocky cliff, it's actually made of reinforced concrete and dates from the beginning of the 20th century, when it supported a dancing terrace for a *fin de siècle* villa. A violent storm left the giant holding nothing but memories of Monterosso's glamorous age.

• *From the breakwater, walk toward the old town (noticing the big drainage tunnels opening onto the beach—critical to avoid flooding during big rainstorms) and under the train tracks. Then venture right into the square and find the statue of a dandy holding what looks like a box cutter (near the big playground).*

## Piazza Garibaldi

The statue honors Giuseppe Garibaldi, the dashing firebrand revolutionary who, in the 1860s, helped unite the people of Italy into a modern nation. Facing Garibaldi, with your back to the sea, you'll see (on your right) the orange City Hall (with the European Union flag beside the Italian one). You'll also see A Ca' du Sciensa restaurant, which has historic town photos inside and upstairs; you're welcome to pop in for a look.

Just under the bell tower (with your back to the sea, it's on your left), a set of covered arcades facing the sea is where the old-timers hang out (they see all and know all). The crenellated bell tower marks the church. This was originally the tower of a fortified gate that protected the town back in the days when they hid out of view of marauding pirates.

• *Go to church.*

## Church of St. John the Baptist
## (Chiesa di San Giovanni Battista)

First, walk along the right side the church. Near the second side door, find the high-water mark *(altezza massima)* from an October 1966 flood—which also famously devastated Florence. Nearby, a second (higher) plaque commemorates the 2011 flood.

Now hook left, around the church—and appreciate its black-and-white-striped main facade. With white marble from Carrara and green marble from Punta Mesco, the church is typical of the region's Gothic style. The church's marble stripes get narrower the higher they go, creating the illusion that the church is taller than it really is. Note the lacy, stone rose window above the entrance—considered one of the finest in northern Italy. It's as delicate as crochet work, with 18 slender columns (creating the petals of the rose).

## Cinque Terre Flood and Recovery

On October 25, 2011, after a dry summer, a heavy rainstorm hit the Cinque Terre. Within four hours, 22 inches of rain fell. Flash floods rushed down the hillsides, picking up mud, rocks, trees, furniture, and even cars and buses in their raging, destructive path through the streets down to the sea. Part of Monterosso's old town and Vernazza's main drag were buried under a dozen feet of mud. Four villagers from Vernazza lost their lives. One body washed up in distant France.

Today, the Cinque Terre is back to normal. Most visitors wouldn't even notice that in the affected areas of Monterosso and Vernazza, everything is new: stoves, tables, chairs, and plates. Strolling through these towns today, you'll hear the peaceful sound of streams under most of the main streets. As you do, appreciate the resilience of the human spirit (and the importance of good drainage).

Step inside for more Ligurian Gothic: original marble columns and capitals with pointed arches to match. The octagonal baptismal font (in the back of the church) was carved from Carrara marble in 1359. Imagine the job getting that from the quarries, about 40 miles away. The fine Baroque altar was crafted with various marbles from around Italy in the 1700s. The church itself dates from 1307—the proud inscription on the left-middle column reads "MilloCCCVII."
• *Leaving the church, turn left and go to church again.*

### Oratory of the Dead (Oratorio dei Neri)

During the Counter-Reformation, the Catholic Church offset the rising influence of the Lutherans by creating brotherhoods of good works. These religious Rotary clubs were called "confraternities." Monterosso had two, nicknamed White and Black. This building is the oratory of the Black group, whose mission—as the macabre decor filling the interior indicates—was to arrange for funerals and take care of widows, orphans, the shipwrecked, and the souls of those who ignore the request for a €1 donation. It dates from the 16th century, and membership has passed from father to son for generations. Notice the fine, carved pews (c. 1700, with toothy smiling skulls reminding us that mortality is nothing to fear), just inside the door, and the haunted-house chandeliers. Look up at the ceiling to find the symbol of the confraternity: a skull-and-crossbones and an hourglass...death awaits us all.

• *On that cheery note, if you're in a lazy mood, you can end your walking tour here to enjoy strolling, shopping, gelato-licking, a day at the beach... or all of the above. But if you're up for a hike, face out to sea, look to the right and imagine the view from the top of that hill. Now...go see it.*

## CAPUCHIN CHURCH AND CEMETERY CLIMB

The hill that separates the old town from the new rewards anyone who climbs up with a peaceful church, a cemetery in the clouds, and a panoramic view.

• *From the old town's beachfront, find the brick steps squeezed between Hotel Pasquale and its restaurant, and start climbing. The lane is signed* Salita dei Cappuccini *(nicknamed* Zii di Frati*), or...*

### Switchbacks of the Friars

Follow the yellow brick road (OK, it's orange...but I couldn't help singing as I skipped skyward). Partway up, detour left to the terrace above the seaside castle at a statue of St. Francis and a wolf taking in a grand view. Enjoy an opportunity to see all five of the Cinque Terre towns. Then backtrack 20 yards to the switchback and continue uphill. (If you continue straight on from St. Francis, you'll drop down into the new town.)

• *When you reach a gate marked* Convento e Chiesa Cappuccini, *you have arrived at the...*

### Church of the Capuchin Friars

The former monastery is now manned by a single caretaker friar. (If you meet Father Renato, take a moment to speak with him—he's a joyful soul who loves to connect.) Before stepping inside, notice the church's striped Romanesque facade. It's all fake. Tap it—no marble, just cheap 18th-century stucco. Go inside and sit in the rear pew. The high altarpiece painting of St. Francis can be rolled up on special days to reveal a statue of Mary standing behind it.

The fine painting of the **Crucifixion** (on the left) recalls how, when Jesus died, the earth went dark. Notice the eclipsed sun in the painting, just to the right of the cross. Do the electric candles work? Pick one up, pray for peace, and plug it in. (Leave an offering, or unplug it and put it back.)

• *Leave and turn left through another gate to hike 100 yards uphill to the cemetery filling the ruined castle at the top of the hill. Reaching the cemetery's gate, look back and enjoy the view over the town.*

### Cemetery in the Ruined Castle

In the Dark Ages, the village huddled behind this castle. As the threat of pirates passed, it slowly expanded to the waterfront. Notice the town view from here—no sea. You're looking at the oldest part of Monterosso, tucked behind the hill, out of view of 13th-century pirates.

Respectfully explore the cemetery. Ponder the black-and-white photos of grandparents past. Read the headstones: *Q.R.P.* is *Qui Riposa in Pace* (a.k.a. R.I.P.). Rich families had their own little tomb buildings. That this is still a place treasured by the living is demonstrated by the abundance of fresh flowers.

Climb to the very summit—the castle's keep, or place of last refuge. Priests are buried in a line of graves closest to the sea, but facing inland, looking toward the town's holy sanctuary high on the hillside (above the road, with its triangular steeple just peeking above the trees). Each Cinque Terre town has a lofty sanctuary, dedicated to Mary and dear to the village hearts.

• *Your tour is over—any trail leads you back into town.*

# Experiences in Monterosso

### Hikes from Monterosso

For a relatively easy in-town hike, take a rewarding climb up to the **hilltop cemetery** between the old and the new towns (described above).

Several ambitious hikes begin in Monterosso; you can use ATC **shuttle buses** to make challenging hikes easier (for details, see page 346).

If you're hiking to **Vernazza** on the main coastal trail, you'll need a park card (sold at the trailhead). If heading north over the Punta Mesco bluff to **Levanto**, you can take the bus up to Colle di Gritta—which makes most of the rest of the hike downhill. (For more on these hikes, see "Hiking the Cinque Terre," earlier.)

You can hike to Monterosso's **Soviore sanctuary** (on trail #509) or take the shuttle bus. To hike from Soviore to Vernazza's **Madonna di Reggio sanctuary,** follow a mostly level trail (#591) to Termine, then head down to Madonna di Reggio (on #582), then steeply downhill into Vernazza (on #508). Allow 2.5 hours, if you start with the shuttle bus.

### Beaches

Monterosso's **new town** has easily the Cinque Terre's best—and most crowded—beach (immediately in front of the train station). Most of the beach is technically private, where (at Stella Marina) you'll pay €20 to rent two chairs and an umbrella for the day (prices get soft in the afternoon). Light lunches are served by beach cafés to sunbathers at their lounge chairs. Various outfits along here rent kayaks and stand-up paddleboards (look for signs at the west end of the beach—near the parking lot—or ask around). If there are no umbrellas on a stretch of beach, it's public (free), so you can spread out a towel anywhere. There's a free beach at the far west end, near the Gigante statue; others are marked on the "Monterosso al Mare" map, earlier.

The **old town** also has its own predominantly private beach; rent umbrellas, chairs, kayaks, and paddleboats from Beach Bar Alga (run by Stefano, €35 for two including showers, changing room, WC, two lounge chairs, and an umbrella), which is also a scenic spot for a drink. Tucked just beyond the private beach—under the Il Casello restaurant at the east end of town—is the free public beach called Tragagià, which is gravelly and generally less crowded (showers). The bocce ball court (next to Il Casello) is busy with older men enjoying their favorite pastime.

### Wine Tasting

**Buranco Agriturismo** is one of the largest producers of wines in the Cinque Terre, and they welcome visitors to tastings on their expansive terrace with views over the vineyards. You'll taste some of their wines plus grappa (firewater) and *limoncino*, while snacking on bruschetta, olives, and the like. It's best to call or email ahead to let them know you are coming (€20-30/person with snacks, tastings usually daily 12:00-18:00, follow Via Buranco uphill to path, 10 minutes above town, also rents recommended apartments, mobile 349-434-8046, www.burancocinqueterre.it, info@buranco.it, Mary).

**Enoteca Internazionale** is a good place in town to sample local wines. Mario is very knowledgeable and serves a selection of five wines for €20 (his bruschetta makes a fine light meal as you're sipping, open daily until late, Via Roma 62, tel. 0187-817-278).

### Boat Rides

In addition to the regularly scheduled big boats (see page 344), you can hire your own captain for transfers to other towns or for a lazy sightseeing cruise (if the water's calm).

**Stefano** has two six-person boats: the *Matilde* and the *Babaah* (about €100/hour, 90 minutes is enough for a quick spin, two hours includes time for swimming stops; longer trips to Porto Venere and offshore islands possible; mobile 333-821-2007, www.matildenavigazione.com, info@matildenavigazione.com).

**Diego** offers half-day, daylong, and sunset excursions for up to seven on his cushy boat. Longer tours can include snorkeling, village visits, and a buffet lunch onboard (group tours—€70, daily 10:30-13:30 & 17:30-20:30, best to email or call to confirm and reserve; private tours—€120/hour for up to 4 people, €150/hour for 5-7 people; mobile 339-233-9297, www.cinqueterreboat.com, 5terretourfishandchill@gmail.com).

**Sea Breeze Boat Tours** arranges day and *aperitivo* sunset tours, and will shuttle you to any of the coastal towns. They also run tours from Levanto (€85-140/person, mobile 328-824-6889 or 338-809-

9278, www.seabreezeboattours.com, info@seabreezeboattours.com, Matteo and Federica).

## Nightlife in Monterosso

Although I've listed these establishments for their nightlife, they work any time of day for a drink and spot to relax.

**Enoteca da Eliseo,** my favorite wine bar in town, comes with operatic ambience. Eliseo and his wife, Mary, love music and wine. Taste by the glass (bicchiere), or select a fine bottle from their shop shelf, then enjoy the wine, a few included nibbles, and views of the village action from their cozy tables. Eliseo stocks more than a hundred varieties of grappa (Wed-Mon 14:00-23:30, closed Tue, Piazza Matteotti 3, a block inland behind church, tel. 0187-817-308).

**Fast Bar** is super basic, but it's the best bar in town for young travelers and night owls. Customers mix travel tales with big, cold beers, and the crowd (and the rock 'n' roll) gets noisier as the night rolls on. Come here to watch Italian or American sporting events on TV all day (cheap *panini*, salads, and other light meals usually served until midnight, open 9:30-late, in the old town at Via Roma 13; Alex, Francesco, and Stefano).

**La Cantina di Miky,** in the new town just beyond the train station, is a trendy bar-restaurant with an extensive cocktail and grappa menu. The seating is in three zones: overlooking the beach, in the garden, or in the cellar. Try the fun "five villages" wine tasting. This is the best place in town for top-end Italian microbrews (Thu-Tue until late, closed Wed, Via Fegina 90, tel. 0187-802-525).

**El Dorado Wine Bar** is the local old-town nighttime hangout. Set on a small piazza, it offers music, drinks and people-watching late into the night (Piazza Garibaldi 22, daily 10:00-2:00 in the morning, tel. 331-475-9611).

**Beach Bars:** On a balmy evening, enjoy a memorable drink with a view of swimmers, sunbathers, and the languid Ligurian Sea. In the new town, try **Nuovo Eden Bar,** overlooking the beach by the big rock (drinks come with a light snack, good ice cream). In the old town, **Beach Bar Alga** has an island ambience (all outside, daily until 20:00, Stefano).

## Sleeping in Monterosso

Monterosso, the most beach-resorty of the five Cinque Terre towns, offers maximum comfort and ease. Rooms in Monterosso are a better value than similar rooms in crowded Vernazza, and the proprietors seem more genuine and welcoming.

## IN THE OLD TOWN

**$$$$ Hotel Villa Steno** is lovingly managed and features great view balconies, panoramic gardens and a roof terrace with sun beds, air-conditioning, and the friendly help of Matteo and his wife, Carla. Of their 16 rooms, 14 have view balconies (RS%, family rooms, hearty buffet breakfast, elevator, laundry service, ask about pay parking when you reserve, hike up to their panoramic terrace, closed Nov-March, Via Roma 109, tel. 0187-817-028 or 0187-818-336, www.villasteno.com, steno@pasini.com). It's a 15-minute climb (or €10 taxi ride) from the train station to the top of the old town. My readers get a free Cinque Terre info packet and a glass of local wine when they check in—ask for it.

**$$$$ Il Giardino Incantato** ("The Enchanted Garden") is a charming, comfortable four-room B&B with impressive attention to detail in a tastefully renovated 16th-century Ligurian home in the heart of the old town. It's run by kind and eager-to-please Fausto and Mariapia and their gregarious staff. Sip their homemade *limoncino* at *aperitivo* time, and have breakfast under lemon trees in their delightful hidden garden, illuminated with candles in the evening (air-con, free minibar and tea-and-coffee service, laundry service, Via Mazzini 18, tel. 0187-818-315, mobile 333-264-9252, www.ilgiardinoincantato.net, giardino_incantato@libero.it).

**$$$$ Hotel Pasquale** is modern and comfortable with 15 seaview rooms, run by the same family as Hotel Villa Steno (listed earlier). Located right on the harbor, it's just a few steps from the beach, boat dock, and tunnel entrance to the new town. While there is some train noise, the soundtrack is mostly a lullaby of waves. It has an elevator and offers easier access than most (RS%, family room, air-con, laundry service, closed Nov-March, Via Fegina 4, tel. 0187-817-550 or 0187-817-477, www.hotelpasquale. it, pasquale@pasini.com, welcoming Felicita and Marco). Felicita also rents several well-equipped apartments in the center of the old town.

**$$$ Locanda il Maestrale** rents six stylish rooms in a sophisticated and peaceful little inn. Although renovated with all the modern comforts and thoughtful details, it retains centuries-old character under frescoed ceilings. Its peaceful sun terrace overlooking the old town and Via Roma action is a delight. Guests enjoy complimentary drinks and snacks each afternoon (air-con, Via Roma 37, tel. 0187-817-013, mobile 338-4530-531, www. locandamaestrale.net, maestrale@monterossonet.com, Stefania and Giovanni).

**$$$ Hotel la Colonnina** has 22 big rooms with varying decor, generous and meticulously cared-for public spaces, a cozy garden, and an inviting shared seaview terrace with sun beds. It's buried in the town's fragrant and sleepy back streets (family rooms, all but one room has a private terrace, cash preferred but cards accepted, air-con, fridges, elevator, a block inland from main square at Via Zuecca 6, tel. 0187-817-439, www.lacolonninacinqueterre.it, info@lacolonninacinqueterre.it, Cristina).

**$$$ Albergo Marina,** run by enthusiastic husband-and-wife team Marina and Eraldo, has 23 pleasant rooms and a garden with lemon trees. They serve a filling breakfast buffet and host a happy hour most days on their terrace. With lots of little extras, they offer a fine value (RS%, family rooms, elevator, air-con, fridges, free kayak and snorkel equipment, Via Buranco 40, tel. 0187-817-613, www.hotelmarina5terre.com, marina@hotelmarina5terre.com).

**$$$ Buranco Agriturismo,** a 10-minute hike above the old town, has wonderful gardens and views over the vine-covered valley. Its primary business is wine and olive-oil production (and they host wine tastings), but they also offer three apartments. It's a rare opportunity to stay in a farmhouse but still be able to get to town on foot (air-con, tel. 0187-817-677, mobile 349-434-8046, www.burancocinqueterre.it, info@buranco.it, informally run by Loredana, Mary, and Giulietta).

**$$$ Manuel's Guesthouse,** perched high above the town among terraces, is a garden getaway run by Lorenzo and his father, Giovanni. They have six big, artfully decorated rooms and a grand view. After climbing the killer stairs from the town center, their killer terrace is hard to leave—especially after a few drinks (cash only, air-con, up about 100 steps behind church—you can ask Lorenzo to carry your bags up the hill, Via San Martino 39, mobile 333-439-0809, www.manuelsguesthouse.com, manuelsguesthouse@libero.it).

**$$ L'Antica Terrazza** rents four tight, classy rooms right in town. With a pretty terrace overlooking the pedestrian street, Raffaella and John offer a good deal (single room with private bath down the hall, air-con, Vicolo San Martino 1, mobile 347-132-6213, www.anticaterrazza.com, post@anticaterrazza.com).

**$ Albergo al Carugio** has nine practical rooms in a big apartment-style building with a small patio at the top of the old town. It's quiet, comfy, and a fine budget value; one room has a private terrace (no breakfast, air-con, fridges, Via Roma 100, tel. 0187-817-453, www.alcarugio.it, info@alcarugio.it, conscientiously run by kindly Andrea).

## IN THE NEW TOWN

**$$$$ La Villa degli Argentieri** offers 11 spacious rooms, many with balconies, from a choice position at the quiet end of the new town's beachfront street. From the front rooms you'll get a peek-a-boo look (through trees) at the water, but the inviting rooftop terrace with sunbeds has panoramic views (air-con, elevator, Via

CINQUE TERRE

Fegina 120, tel. 0187-818-963, www.lavilladegliargentieri.it, info@lavilladegliargentieri.it).

**$$$$ Hotel Villa Adriana** is big, contemporary, and bright, set on a church-owned estate with a peaceful garden, a pool, free parking, and a no-stress style. They rent 55 sterile rooms—some with terraces and/or sea views—ask for one when you reserve, but no guarantees (family rooms, air-con, elevator, free loaner bikes, fridge in every room, affordable dinners, Via IV Novembre 23, tel. 0187-818-109, www.villaadriana.info, info@villaadriana.info).

**$$$$ Hotel la Spiaggia,** facing the beach, is a venerable place with 19 rooms (half with sea views) and a quiet garden retreat (cash only, air-con, elevator, free parking—reserve in advance, Via Lungomare 96, tel. 0187-817-567, www.laspiaggiahotel5terre.com, laspiaggiahotel@gmail.com, Maria). They also rent four pricey, ultra-mod rooms in a small building on the seafront promenade.

**$$$$ A Cà du Gigante,** despite its name, is a tiny yet chic refuge with nine rooms, all on the ground floor. About 100 yards from the beach (and surrounded by blocky apartments), the interior is tastefully done with upscale comfort in mind (air-con, limited pay parking—reserve ahead, Via IV Novembre 11, tel. 0187-817-401, www.ilgigantecinqueterre.it, gigante@ilgigantecinqueterre.it, Claudia).

**$$$ Hotel Punta Mesco** is a tidy, well-run little haven renting 17 quiet, casual rooms at a good price. While none have views, 10 rooms have small terraces backed up to the building next door (family room, air-con, parking, Via Molinelli 35, tel. 0187-817-495, www.hotelpuntamesco.it, info@hotelpuntamesco.it, Roberto, Diego, and Manuel).

**$$ Pensione Agavi** has eight spartan, bright, overpriced rooms along the waterfront promenade. I'd skip it—unless you can score one of the rooms with a grand view over the beach (RS%, cheaper rooms with shared bath, expensive breakfast, refrigerators, no kids allowed, strict cancellation policy, no check-in after 18:00, turn left out of station to Via Fegina 30, tel. 0187-817-171, www. hotelagavi.com, info@hotelagavi.com, Hillary).

**$$ Affittacamere Ristorante il Gabbiano,** a touristy restaurant on the beachfront road, rents five basic, dated, but affordable rooms upstairs. Three rooms face the sea (two with small balconies); two have terraces overlooking a little garden. Check in at the Gabbiano restaurant (big family rooms, cash only, no breakfast, air-con, Via Fegina 84, tel. 0187-817-578, www.affittacamereristorante-ilgabbiano.com, lella-v71@hotmail.it, Raffaella).

**$ Le Sirene/Raggi di Sole,** with nine simple rooms in two humble buildings, is a decent budget choice in this pricey town. It's run from a hole-in-the-wall reception desk a block from the station, just off the water. I'd request the Le Sirene building, which has smaller bathrooms but no train noise, and is a bit more spacious and airy than Raggi di Sole (RS%, family rooms, fans, Via Molinelli 1A, mobile 331-788-1088 or 329-595-1063, www. sirenerooms.com, sirenerooms@gmail.com, Ermanna).

# Eating in Monterosso

## WITH A SEA VIEW

**$$ Ristorante Belvedere,** big and sprawling, serves good-value meals indoors or outdoors on the harborfront. Their huge €49 *anfora belvedere*—mixed seafood stew dumped dramatically at the table from a pottery amphora into your bowl—can easily be split among up to four diners. Their *misto mare* plate (2-person minimum, €16/person), a fishy treat, nearly makes an entire meal. Mussel fans will enjoy the *tagliolini della casa*. It's energetically run by Federico and Roberto (Wed-Mon 12:00-14:30 & 18:00-22:00, closed Tue, on the harbor in the old town, tel. 0187-817-033).

**$$ Il Casello** offers outdoor terrace seating only, on a little bluff overlooking the old town beach when the weather's nice. It's a pleasant spot for pasta, seafood, or a drink (daily 12:00-22:00, mobile 333-492-7629, Bacco).

**$$$ L'Ancora della Tortuga** is a top option in Monterosso for seaview elegance, with gorgeous outdoor seating high on a bluff and a white-tablecloth-and-candles interior fit for an admiral. While the food and service can be three-star, the setting is five-star. Drop by to choose and reserve a table for later. Consider their €40 tasting *menu* (Tue-Sun 12:30-15:30 & 18:30-21:30, closed Mon and when stormy; at the tip of the point between the old and new towns—just outside the tunnel; tel. 0187-800-065, mobile 333-240-7956, Silvia and Giamba).

**$$$$ Torre Aurora** is a top-end, fancy restaurant with no indoor seating. You'll dine outside (wrapped in a blanket if it's cold) around the medieval tower with commanding views of approaching pirates while enjoying simple yet creative dishes. Reservations are smart (daily in good weather, mobile 366-145-3702, www. torreauroracinqueterre.com, Elia). They serve cocktails outside of mealtime.

## IN THE OLD TOWN

**$$$ Via Venti** is a quiet little trattoria, hidden in an alley deep in the heart of the old town, where chef Ilaria and her husband Michele create and serve imaginative seafood dishes. Be tempted by their delicate and savory gnocchi with crab, tender ravioli stuffed with fresh fish, and pear-and-pecorino pasta. The outdoor tables are on a lane as nondescript as the humdrum interior—but you're

CINQUE TERRE

here for the food (Fri-Wed 12:00-14:30 & 18:30-22:30, closed Thu, Via XX Settembre 32, tel. 0187-818-347).

**$ Gastronomia "San Martino,"** warmly run by hard-working Moreno and Sabrina, is a tiny, humble combination of takeaway and sit-down café with surprisingly affordable, quality dishes. Belly up to the glass case and see what's cooking today, then eat at one of the few tables—inside or out on a pleasant street—or find a driftwood log for a feast-to-go. You're welcome to create your own €13 mixed plate by pointing to whatever appeals (Tue-Sun 12:00-15:00 & 18:00-22:00, closed Mon, next to recommended L'Antica Terrazza hotel at Vicolo San Martino 3, mobile 346-109-7338).

**$$ L'Osteria** is a delightful little family-run place serving "cuisine with passion" at wonderful prices. Alessandro thoughtfully explains your options and Elisa is understandably proud of her cakes. Their Possa wine, from vineyards close to the sea, is the oyster of local wines, or maybe it's just the Ligurian music the family is sure to play (Tue-Sun lunch served 12:00-14:30, evening seatings at 19:00 and 21:00, closed Mon, Via Vittorio Emanuele 5, tel. 0187-819-224). It's a cozy scene inside with a few tables outside in the shadow of the church.

**$$$ Ristorante al Pozzo** is a favorite among locals. It's family-run, with good old-fashioned quality, as Gino (with his long white beard) cooks, and his engaging English-speaking son, Manuel, serves. They have one of the best wine lists in town, serve only homemade pasta, and are known for their raw fish and wonderful seafood *antipasti misti*, which you can check out in a case near the entrance (Fri-Wed 12:00-15:00 & 18:30-22:30, closed Thu, Via Roma 24, tel. 0187-817-575).

**$$$ Ciak,** high-energy and tightly packed—inside and out—is a local institution with reliably good food, higher prices, and (sometimes) a bit of an attitude. Stroll a couple of paces past the outdoor tables up Via Roma to see what Signore Ciak (who wears his Popeye cap in the kitchen) has on the stove (Thu-Tue 12:00-15:00 & 18:00-22:30, closed Wed, Piazza Don Minzoni 6, tel. 0187-817-014, www.ristoranteciak.net).

**$$ Páe Veciu,** tucked away from the hubbub, has a short, creative menu of well-prepared seafood, pastas, and a few meat dishes. Eat inside in view of the kitchen or at one of the few streetside tables. Run by the folks from the recommended Buranco Agriturismo, it features a good selection of local wines (daily 11:30-15:00 & 18:30-22:00, Via Vittorio Emanuele 69, mobile 327-941-0430).

**$ La Smorfia**—a local favorite—cooks up good pizza in a sloppy setting that somehow seems to say, "Great pizza enjoyed here." Their large pizzas can feed three (Fri-Wed 11:00-24:00, closed Thu, Via Vittorio Emanuele 73, tel. 0187-818-395).

## IN THE NEW TOWN

**$$$$ Miky** is packed with a well-dressed clientele who know their seafood. For elegantly presented, top-quality food that celebrates local ingredients and traditions, it's worth the steep prices. It's a proud family operation—Miky (dad), Simonetta (mom), charming Sara (daughter, who greets guests)—and the attentive waitstaff all work hard. Their "pizza pasta" is served in a bowl topped with a thin pizza crust dome to contain the flavor, then flambéed at your table. Many of the wines on their fine list are available by the glass if you ask. Their mixed dessert sampler plate, *dolce misto,* serves two and is a fitting capper (Wed-Mon 12:00-15:00 & 19:00-23:00, closed Tue, reservations wise, in the new town 100 yards from train station at Via Fegina 104, tel. 0187-817-608, www.ristorantemiky. it).

**$$$ La Cantina di Miky,** a few doors down from the station, serves artfully crafted Ligurian specialties that follow in Miky's family tradition of quality. Run by son Manuel—and Christine from New Jersey—it's more youthful and informal (sit downstairs, in the garden, or on the promenade overlooking the sea). The €20 anchovy tasting plate is an education in the many ways to prepare this local specialty (creative desserts, large selection of Italian microbrews, Thu-Tue 12:00-24:00, closed Wed, Via Fegina 90, tel. 0187-802-525). This place doubles as a cocktail bar in the evenings.

## LIGHT MEALS, TAKEOUT FOOD, AND BREAKFAST

**In the Old Town:** Lots of shops and bakeries sell pizza and focaccia to eat in or take out for an easy picnic on the beach or trail. At **$ Il Frantoio Focacceria,** Simone makes tasty pizza and focaccia (Fri-Wed 9:00-14:00 & 16:30-20:00, closed Thu, just off Via Roma at Via Gioberti 1). **$ Emy's Way Pizzeria Friggitoria** offers pasta, thick-crust pizza (whole and by the slice), and deep-fried seafood in to-go cones (daily 11:00-20:00, later in summer, along the skinny street next to the church, tel. 331-788-1088, Emiliano).

**In the New Town, near the Station:** For a quick bite right at the train station (or on the beach), try **$ Il Massimo della Focaccia** for quiche-like tortes, sandwiches, focaccia pizzas, and desserts. With benches just in front, this is a good bet for a light meal with a sea view (Thu-Tue 9:00-19:00, closed Wed except June-Aug, Via Fegina 50 at the station). **La Bottega SMA** is a smart minimart with fresh produce, *antipasti*, deli items, and other picnic fare. They'll even make you a sandwich: Select a bread and filling, and pay by the weight (daily 8:00-13:00 & 16:30-19:30 except closed Sun afternoon, shorter hours off-season, near Lavarapido at Vittoria Gianni 21).

**Breakfast:** Although most hotels include breakfast in the room rate, a handful leave you to your own devices. In the **old**

**town,** for breakfast on the beach, try **Bar Alga** (from 8:00 when the weather's nice). For the freshest bakery items, follow your nose to **Pasticceria Laura,** serving coffee and pastries every morning from 7:00 (Via Vittorio Emanuele 59), or head to the **Wonderland Bakery,** offering croissants, biscotti, and savory bites to go (from 8:00, Via San Pietro 8). **Bar Davi** has the most comprehensive menu, serving bacon and eggs, yogurt, fruit, and cereal from 8:00 (pastries and coffee available from 7:00, under the arch at Via Roma 34).

In the **new town,** these places (on Via Fegina, near Hotel la Spiaggia) serve something akin to breakfast starting at 8:00: **Bar Giò** (bacon and eggs), **Bar il Baretto** (bacon and eggs), and **Stella Marina Beach Bar** (croissants and yogurt—served down on the beach). Your best bet here might be a picnic breakfast from the tiny, nearby *alimentari*/supermarket at Via Fegina 116. They open at 8:00, and have a good selection of cheeses, breads, pastries, and fruit.

## Monterosso Connections

Of the five Cinque Terre towns, Monterosso has the most direct train connections with towns outside the Cinque Terre. For more connections, check the region's southern transit hub, La Spezia.

**From Monterosso by Train to: Levanto** (3-4/hour, 4 minutes), **Sestri Levante** (hourly, 30 minutes, most trains to Genoa stop here), **Santa Margherita Ligure** (at least hourly, 45 minutes), **Genoa** (hourly, 1.5 hours; for destinations in France, you'll change trains here), **Milan** (8/day direct, otherwise hourly with change in Genoa, 3 hours), **Venice** (5/day, 6 hours, change in Milan), **La Spezia** (2-3/hour, 15-30 minutes), **Pisa** (hourly, 1-1.5 hours), **Rome** (hourly, 4.5 hours, change in La Spezia).

# Vernazza

With the closest thing to a natural harbor—overseen by a ruined castle, a stout stone church, and a pastel canyon of fisherfolk homes—Vernazza is the jewel of the Cinque Terre. Only the regular noisy slurping up of the train by the mountain reminds you of the modern world.

The action is at the harbor, where you'll find outdoor eater-

ies ringing a humble piazza, a restaurant hanging on the edge of the castle, and a breakwater with a promenade, corralled by a natural amphitheater of terraced hills.

Proud of their Vernazzan heritage, the town's 500 residents like to brag: "Vernazza is locally owned. Portofino has sold out." Fearing change, keep-Vernazza-small proponents stopped the construction of a major road into the town and region. Families are tight and go back centuries; you'll notice certain surnames (such as Basso and Moggia) everywhere. In the winter, the population shrinks, as many people return to more-comfortable big-city apartments to spend the money they earned during the tourist season.

During the day in season the tiny harborfront and one main street are clogged with gawking group excursions. But early and late Vernazza is the cool and content domain of locals...and travelers who are lucky enough to call the town home for a couple of nights.

Join (or sit on a bench and watch) the locals devoting their leisure time to taking part in the *passeggiata*—strolling lazily together up and down the main street, doing *vasche* (laps). Explore the characteristic alleys called *caruggi*. Learn—and live—the phrase *"la vita pigra di Vernazza"* (the lazy life of Vernazza).

## Orientation to Vernazza

### TOURIST INFORMATION

At the train station, you can get answers to basic questions at the gift shop/park office (daily 8:00-20:00, closed in winter, tel. 0187-812-533, WCs just down the track, see page 378 for baggage storage).

### ARRIVAL IN VERNAZZA

**By Train:** Vernazza's train station is only about three train cars long, but the trains themselves are much longer, so most cars come to a stop in a long, dimly lit tunnel. Get out anyway, and walk through the tunnel—heading for the light—to reach the station. From there the main street flows through town right down to the harbor. If you're sleeping here, many locals who rent rooms will meet you at the station and walk you to your place (call ahead to tell them which train you're on).

**By Car:** Don't drive to Vernazza. Roads to Vernazza are in terrible shape, and parking is strictly limited. If you're coming from the north, park in Levanto. If arriving from the south, park in La Spezia. From either town, hop on the train.

### HELPFUL HINTS

**Market:** Vernazza's skimpy business community is augmented Tuesday mornings (8:00-13:00), when a meager gang of cars

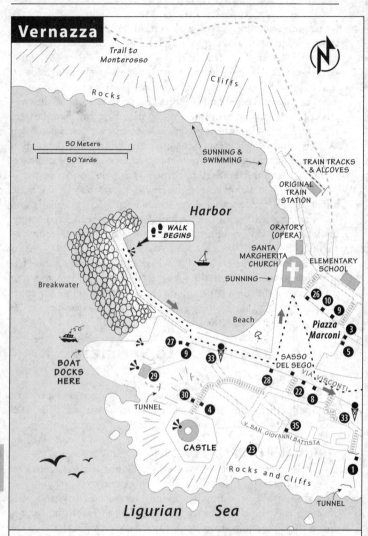

# Vernazza

CINQUE TERRE

<u>Accommodations</u>

1 La Malà & La Marina Rooms
2 Vernazza sul Mare
3 Nicolina Rooms Reception & Ristorante Pizzeria Vulnetia
4 Monica Lercari Rooms
5 Francamaria Reception & Albergo Barbara Rooms
6 Emanuela Colombo Rooms
7 Vernazza Rooms Reception
8 Rosa Vitali Rooms
9 Maria Capellini Rooms (2)
10 Martina Callo Rooms, Capitano Rooms Reception & Trattoria del Capitano
11 Rooms Francesca Reception (Enoteca Sciacchetrà)
12 Ivo's Camere
13 Memo Rooms
14 Eva's Rooms & Trattoria da Sandro
15 Rooms Elisabetta
16 Manuela Moggia Rooms
17 Casa Cato
18 Giuliano Basso Rooms

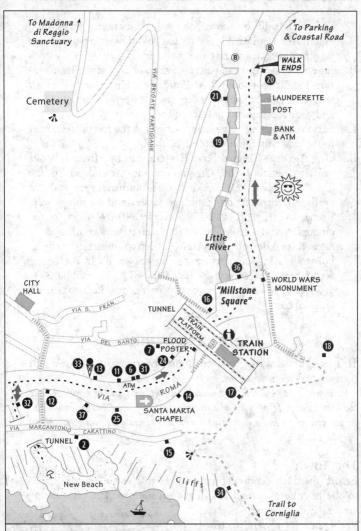

CINQUE TERRE

19 Camere Fontanavecchia
20 Tonino Basso/La Perla Rooms &
   Il Pirata delle Cinque Terre Café
21 La Rosa dei Venti
22 Gianni Franzi Reception/Ristorante
23 Gianni Franzi Rooms

Eateries & Other
24 Blue Marlin Bar
25 Lunch Box
26 Ananasso Bar
27 Pizzeria Baia Saracena

28 Gambero Rosso
29 Ristorante Belforte
30 Ristorante al Castello
31 Antica Osteria il Baretto
32 Pizzeria Ercole
33 Gelateria (3)
34 Bar la Torre
35 Vernazza Wine Experience
36 Cinque Sensi Wine Tastings
37 Cinque Terre Riviera Agency
   (Room Rental; Opera Tickets)

and trucks pulls into town for a tailgate market. Eros is often among the vendors; his family has sold flowers here for years (and he's also an amazing opera singer).

**Baggage Storage:** You can pay to leave your bags at the train station TI/gift shop (daily 9:00-19:00, closed in winter). The staff will also happily haul your luggage between the train station and your accommodations (€4/piece).

**Laundry:** A small self-serve launderette is at the top of town next to the post office (daily 9:00-22:00).

**Booking Agency: Cinque Terre Riviera,** run by Miriana, books vacation rentals in the Cinque Terre towns and La Spezia. They also sell tickets for Vernazza's summer opera and can arrange transportation, cooking classes, and weddings (Via Roma 24, tel. 0187-812-123, mobile 340-794-7358, www. cinqueterreriviera.com, info@cinqueterreriviera.com).

**Massage: Kate Allen** offers a relaxing fusion of aromatic/Swedish/holistic massage and reflexology in her studio in the center across from the pharmacy (tel. 0187-812-537, mobile 333-568-4653, www.vernazzamassage5terre.com, katarinaallen@hotmail.com).

## Vernazza Walk

This self-guided walk gives you a quick overview of the town and starts out on its breakwater.

• *From the train station, just walk downhill and all the way out onto the breakwater. (Ropes are put up to protect gawky tourists from dangerous waves.) Find a comfortable and safe place to sit and get to know Vernazza.*

### The Town

Before the 11th century, pirates made this coast uninhabitable, so the first Vernazzans lived in the hills above. The earliest references call the town "Fortress Vernazza." Its towers, fortified walls, and hillside terracing date mostly from the 12th through 15th century. That's when the threat of pirates subsided and people felt comfortable coming out of the hills. Vernazza allied itself with the Republic of Genoa, a maritime power of the day. The **big red central building** facing the harbor was once the site where Genoan warships were built (12th century).

In the Middle Ages, there was no beach or square. The water went right up to the buildings, where boats would tie up, Venetian-style. Imagine what Vernazza looked like in those days, when it was the biggest and richest of the Cinque Terre towns. Buildings had a water gate (facing today's square) and a front door on the higher inland side. There was no pastel plaster—just fine stonework (traces of which survive above Trattoria del Capitano). The town, hiding behind its little bluff, was camouflaged by its gray stonework—certainly not gaily painted to attract the eyes of marauding pirates. But apart from the added paint and plaster, the general shape and size of the town has changed little in five centuries. Survey the windows and notice inhabitants quietly gazing back. (At least they did before Airbnb changed the economic environment of touristy towns like Vernazza, driving prices up and locals away from the most charming spots.)

Vernazza has two halves. *Sciuiu* (Vernazzan dialect for "flow-ery") is the sunny side on the left, and *luvegu* (dank) is the shady side on the right. Houses below the castle were connected by an interior arcade—ideal for fleeing attacks.

The "Ligurian pastel" colors of the buildings are regulated by the regional government's commissioner of good taste. The square before you is known for some of the area's finest restaurants.

While the town has 1,500 residents in summer, only 500 stay here through the winter. Vernazza has accommodations for about that many tourists.

## Above Town

The small, **round tower** above the red building is another part of the city fortifications, reminding us of the town's importance in the Middle Ages. Back then, Genoa's enemies (rival maritime republics, especially Pisa) were Vernazza's enemies. That tower recalls a time when the town was fortified by a stone wall.

**Vineyards** fill the mountainside beyond the town. Notice the many terraces. For six centuries, the economy was based on wine and olive oil. Then came the 1980s—and the tourists. Locals turned to tourism to make a living, and stopped tending the land and vineyards.

Although many locals still maintain their small plots and proudly serve their family wines, the patchwork of vineyards is atomized and complex because of inheritance traditions. Historically, families divided their land among their children. Parents wanted each child to receive good land, though some lots were "kissed by the sun" while others were shady. Lots were split into increasingly tiny, unviable pieces, and many were eventually abandoned. The vineyards once stretched as high as you can see, but since fewer people sweat in the fields these days, the most distant terraces have gone wild again.

## Church, School, and City Hall

Vernazza's Ligurian Gothic **church,** built with black stones quarried from Punta Mesco (the distant point between Monterosso and Levanto), dates from 1318. Note the gray stone (on the left) that marks the church's 16th-century expansion. The gray-and-red house above the spire is the **elementary school** (about 25 children attend). Older students go to the "big city," La Spezia. The red building on the hill to the right of the schoolhouse, a former monastery, is now the **City Hall.** Vernazza and neighboring Corniglia function as one community. Through most of the 1990s, the local government was Communist. In 1999, residents elected a coalition of many parties working to rise above ideologies and simply make Vernazza a better place. That practical notion of government continues here today.

Finally, on the top of the hill, with the best view of all, is the **town cemetery.** It's only fair that hardworking Vernazzans—who spend their lives climbing up and down and up and down and up and down the hillsides that hem in their little town—are rewarded with a world-class view from their eternal resting place.

• *Look high on your right to the castle.*

## Castle (Castello Doria)

The castle, which is now just stones and a grassy park with super views, still guards the town (€1.50, daily 10:00-20:00, summer until 21:00, closed Nov-March; from harbor, take stairs by Trattoria Gianni and follow *Ristorante al Castello* signs, the tower is a few steps beyond). This was the town's watchtower back in pirate days.

The squat tower below the castle, overlooking the water, Ristorante Belforte, is a great spot for a glass of wine or a meal. From the breakwater, you could follow the rope to the restaurant and pop inside, past an actual submarine door. A photo of a major storm showing the entire tower under a wave (not uncommon in the winter) hangs near the bar.

## Harbor

In a moderate storm, you'd get soaked where you're sitting, as waves routinely crash over the *molo* (**breakwater,** built in 1972). Waves can rearrange the huge rocks—depositing them from the breakwater onto the piazza and its benches. Freak waves have even washed away tourists squinting excitedly into their cameras. (I've seen it happen.) In 2007, an American woman was swept away and killed by a rogue wave.

The **train line** (across the harbor) was constructed in 1874 to tie together a newly united Italy, linking Turin and Genoa with Rome. A second line (hidden in a tunnel at this point) was built in the 1920s. The yellow building alongside the tracks was Vernazza's **first train station.** Along the wall behind the tracks, you can see the four bricked-up alcoves where people once waited for trains. The wonderful concrete **sunbathing** strip (and place for late-night privacy) laid below the tracks along the rocks makes for a fun little stroll. (Buoys along the shoreline establish a boat-free swimming zone.)

Vernazza's **fishing fleet** is down to just a few boats with net spools, but Vernazzans are still more likely to own a boat than a car. Boats are moored on buoys, except in winter or when the red storm flag indicates rough seas (see the pole at the start of the breakwater). When the red flag flies, boat owners are permitted to pull them up onto the square—which is usually reserved for restaurant tables. In the 1970s, tiny Vernazza had one of Italy's top water polo teams, and the harbor was their "pool." Later, when the league required a real pool, Vernazza dropped out.

• *Stroll from the breakwater to the harbor square. Look for a small historic stone just before the narrow stairway on the right.*

## Harbor Square (Piazza Marconi)

Vernazza, with the Cinque Terre's only natural harbor, was established as the sole place boats could pick up the fine local wine. The two-foot-high square **stone** at the foot of the stairs is marked *Sasso del Sego* (stone of tallow). Workers crushed animal flesh and fat in its basin to make tallow, which drained out from the tiny hole below. The tallow was then used to waterproof boats or wine barrels.

Stonework is the soul of the region. Take some time to appreciate the medieval stonework and chestnut timbers of the restaurant interiors facing the harbor. From here steps lead to your right up to the castle.

Towns along this coast were designed as what's called a "Ligurian Palazzata"—an interlinked series of buildings intended to provide protection from seaborne attacks. Vernazza's harborfront retains its thousand-year-old "stockade" of buildings, connected with tiny and easy-to-defend staircases leading from the vulnerable harbor higher into the community.

• *Cross to the church side of the harbor, and peek into the tiny street leading away from the water with its commotion of arches. Vernazza's most characteristic **side streets** (caruggi) lead up from here. Another narrow set of stairs marks the beginning of the trail that leads up, up, up to the quintessential view of Vernazza—and, eventually, on to Monterosso (my favorite two-hour hike in the region).*

## Vernazza's Church

Vernazza's harborfront **church** sits on the tiny piazza, decorated with a river-rock mosaic. This popular hangout spot is where the town's older ladies soak up the last bit of sun, and kids enjoy a patch of level ball field. The church, nestled awkwardly into the rocks, is unusual for its east-facing (rather than the standard west-facing) entryway. With relative peace and prosperity in the 16th century, the townspeople doubled the size of their church, extending it west over what was the little piazza that faced it.

Enter under a statue of St. Margaret, patron saint of Vernazza, and climb the steps into the nave. The space was originally dark (with just the upper slit windows) before the bigger gothic window were added with the 16th-century expansion. The lighter pillars in the back mark the extension. Three historic portable crosses hanging on the walls are carried through town during religious processions. These are replicas of crosses that (locals like to believe) Vernazzan ships once carried on crusades to the Holy Land. The town priest, Don Giovanni, is popular—he stopped the church bells from ringing through the night (light sleepers rejoiced).

• *Now walk back across the harbor square and head left into town. After the lane opens up on the right, hike through the cave to the new beach.*

## "New Beach"

This is where the town's stream used to hit the sea back in the 1970s. Older locals remember frolicking on a beach here when they were kids, but the constant, churning surf eventually eroded it all the way back to the cliff. When the 2011 flood hit, it blew out the passageway and deposited landslide material here from the hills above. In the flood's aftermath, Vernazza's main drag and harbor were filled with mud and silt. Workers used the debris to fill in even more of this beach. But as time goes on, the forces of nature are once again taking it away.

• *Back on the main drag, continue uphill to...*

## Vernazza's "Main Street"

You're now strolling through Vernazza's "commercial center": souvenir shops, wine shops, the Blue Marlin Bar (a good nightspot), and so on. The small stone chapel with iron grillwork over the window (on the right) is the tiny **Chapel of Santa Marta,** where Mass is celebrated on special Sundays. You'll walk by a *gelateria*, bakery, pharmacy, grocery, and another *gelateria*. There are plenty of fun and cheap food-to-go options

here. While it's easy to get distracted by all the tourists, try to see through them to notice locals going about their business.

On the right, just before the train tracks, study the big **poster,** which shows photos of the 2011 flood (*alluvione*) and the shops it devastated. "The 25th of October" is a day that will live forever in this town's lore. Vernazza is built around one street—basically a lid over the stream in its ravine. On that fateful day, the surrounding hills acted like a funnel, directing flash-flood waters right through the middle of town. Four townspeople lost their lives. Imagine this street from here to the harbor buried under 13 feet of mud. Every shop, restaurant, and hotel on the main drag had to be rewired, replumbed, and re-equipped.

The second set of train tracks (nearer the harbor) was renovated to lessen disruptive noise. At the base of the stairs a handy monitor displays up-to-the-minute schedules for arriving and departing trains (including any running late—*ritardo*). The walls under the tracks serve as a sort of community information center. Just above the tracks (to the right), the town provides limited space for advertising for political parties (but only during the weeks leading up to an election).

• *Hike a few steps under and above the tracks to the little square.*

## "Millstone Square"

The **millstones** set on the square are a reminder that the town stream (which goes underground here and which you've been walking over ever since leaving the harbor area) once powered Vernazza's water mill. (You can still see its tiny "river" if you follow this road up a few steps.) Until the 1950s, the river ran openly through the center of town. Old-timers recall the days before the breakwater, when the river cascaded down, charming bridges spanned the ravine, and the surf sent waves rolling up Vernazza's main drag.

Corralling this stream under the modern street, and forcing it to take a hard turn here, contributed to the damage caused by the 2011 flood. After the flood, Swiss engineers redesigned the drainage system, so any future floods will be less destructive. They also installed nets above the town to protect it from landslides.

On the wall ahead at the bend in the road, notice the **World Wars Monument**—dedicated to those killed in World Wars I and II. Not a family in Vernazza was spared. Listed on the left are soldiers *morti in combattimento* who died in World War I; on the right is the WWII section. Some were deported to *Germania;* others—labeled *Part* (for *partigiani,* or partisans)—were killed while fighting against Mussolini.

The **path to Corniglia** begins from here (behind and above the monument). Even if you don't plan to hike its entire length, you don't have to go far to find fine views over Vernazza's stony peninsula.

• *To see a more workaday part of Vernazza, head a couple of minutes uphill from here to the...*

## Top of Town

First you'll pass the **ambulance barn** (on the left, at #7, with big brown garage doors and a *croce verde Vernazza* sign), where a group of volunteers is always on call for a dash to the hospital, 40 minutes away in La Spezia. Farther up, you'll come to a functional strip of modern apartment blocks facing the river. In this practical zone—the only place in town that allows cars—are a bank, the post office, a launderette, and the popular bar/café called Il Pirata delle Cinque Terre. The parking lot fills a square called **Fontana Vecchia,** named for an "old fountain" that's so old, it's long gone. Shuttle buses run from here to hamlets and sanctuaries in the hills above. (Check the schedule post if you want to enjoy the scenic shuttle bus up to the sanctuary and hike back into town—described below.)

Looming over this neighborhood is a terraced hill capped by the town cemetery (a 20-minute steep hike from here), and a 30-minute climb beyond that, the town's Madonna di Reggio sanctuary.

# Experiences in Vernazza

### Hikes from Vernazza

For a rundown of ambitious hikes from Vernazza—including the main coastal trail to Corniglia and to Monterosso—see page 346. Here are some alternatives closer to town.

From Vernazza, you can hike in either direction for classic

photo ops. Both hikes are steeply, but briefly, uphill (about 10 minutes to the best views and park ticket checkpoints).

For the best light in the morning, follow the trail **toward Corniglia;** you'll twist up through vineyards to earn great views down over the stony back side  of Vernazza's peninsula, with its round castle tower poking up and a Monterosso backdrop. The best views are from just before the national park ticket checkpoint. If you need a rewarding rest up here, Bar la Torre offers drinks with a grand view.

The trail **toward Monterosso** has the best light in the evening. From the harbor, you'll hike up through the steep and narrow alleys before popping out on the trail above town. Follow this around the bluff, enjoying better and better views of Vernazza's tidy pastel harbor. The views are fine before the ticket booth, but even better after—if you don't want to buy a Cinque Terre park card, you can hike up here in the evening, after the park officially closes (typically around 19:00).

**Hike to the Cemetery:** To hike up to Vernazza's sweet little **cemetery,** find the steep lane from the ravine at the top of town. From here, it's a 20-minute hike to the top. You'll find a peaceful world of lovingly tended family graves with stunning views over the Cinque Terre. Imagine the entire village sadly trudging up here during funerals. The cemetery is peaceful and evocative at sunset, when the fading light touches each crypt.

## ▲▲Madonna di Reggio Shuttle Bus Joyride and/or Hike

For a cheap and scenic joyride (50 minutes, €1.50), with a chance to chat about the region with friendly, English-speaking Mirco, Pietro, or Graziella, ride the ATC shuttle bus, which loops about five times a day from the top of Vernazza to sanctuaries and hamlets high in the hills—including the San Bernardino sanctuary and Madonna di Reggio sanctuary—and back again (for times, check schedule posted at the bus stop, ask at the TI, or check online at www.atcesercizio.it). Look for the bus to *Madonna di Reggio via Fornacchi.*

**Joyride:** The bus ride is absolutely stunning. It can be crowded, but most hikers get off at the first stop (San Bernardino). I prefer either to stay on for three-quarters of the loop (to Madonna di Reggio, then hike back to Vernazza from there; see below), or all the way to complete the scenic circle.

As you ride, you'll see tiny settlements that predate the Cinque

Terre villages, built back when people were afraid to live on the coast for fear of pirates. These hamlets and their terraces go back a thousand years. You'll switchback past chestnut trees, which historically provided wood for fuel and lumber, and chestnuts, which were ground to make a kind of flour in a land with no grain.

**Hiking Down from Madonna di Reggio:** For a delightful and easy (if steep) half-hour hike into Vernazza, ask the driver to let you out at the stop for *Santuario Nostra Signora di Reggio.*

First, walk two minutes below the bus stop to the sanctuary, which dates from 1248 and has a Romanesque facade. Inside the church, interesting votives (little ships and paintings of ships in angry seas given as tokens of thanks) fill the rear corner—gifts from sailors who survived storms and soldiers who survived wars. A volunteer staffs the church selling coffee, water, and snacks.

From here signs direct you to trail #508—the historic original trail down to Vernazza. You'll be walking on thousand-year-old cobbles through abandoned olive groves and past the Stations of the Cross, which have inspired generations of processions trudging up from Vernazza. You may see a parked *trenino,* one of about 40 monorail mini-trains in the area that help farmers get their grapes from distant fields to their trucks.

You'll descend through the cemetery, then either take the stairs down to the train station, or continue to the left down the lane to the square called Fontana Vecchia, where you caught the shuttle bus.

## Beaches

The harbor's sandy cove has sunning rocks and showers by the breakwater. The sunbathing lane directly under the church has a shower. A ladder on the seaside of the breakwater aids deep-water swimmers. And, while it's getting smaller and rockier each year, Vernazza's "new beach" can be accessed through a hole halfway along the town's main drag.

## Boat Rides

In addition to the regularly scheduled big boats that depart from Vernazza's harbor (see page 344), hiring your own boat can be handy for intertown transport. It's also a great way to escape the crowds and get a different angle on Cinque Terre splendor. From Vernazza, figure around €50 one-way to boat to the other towns (for up to six passengers in an outboard). Or hire a boat for a one-hour sightseeing cruise of the entire Cinque Terre (about €150); one popular stop is the tiny *acqua pendente* (waterfall) cove between Vernazza and Monterosso, which locals call their *laguna blu.*

Some boat captains offer evening *aperitivo* cruises on a per-person basis. At Vernazza's breakwater you'll find **Nord Est,** run by Vincenzo (with help from Cesare), the best-established option (mobile 338-700-0436, info@nordest-vernazza.com). **Vernazza Water Taxi,** run by Pietro, is another choice (mobile 338-911-3869, info@vernazzawatertaxi.it).

## Wine Tasting

**Vernazza Wine Experience** hides out at the top of town just under the castle. Run by Alessandro, a sommelier, it's romantic, with mellow music and a hardwood, ship-deck ambience. Tastings start at €15/person and can be matched up with meat-and-cheese small plates. While the bill can add up, the quality is excellent and the view is unforgettable (cash only, daily 17:00-20:00, hike from harborfront and turn left before castle, Via S. Giovanni Battista 31, tel. 331-343-3801). For tastings without the view or the climb, drop by his place behind the train station called **Cinque Sensi** (similar prices, Via Roma 71, daily 12:00-24:00).

## A Little Taste of Opera

A favorite Cinque Terre evening memory for many is Vernazza's summer opera. A big-name maestro from Lucca brings talented singers to town twice weekly. Performances (two singers and a piano) fill the small oratory, a medieval building with fine acoustics that was beautifully restored for this purpose (just up the steps from the church). Performances begin at 19:00 and last just over an hour—strategically timed to squeeze between a late-afternoon *aperitivo* on the harbor and a 20:30 dinner reservation (€18 in advance, €20 at the door, May-Oct Wed and Fri at 19:00, book tickets at Cinque Terre Riviera office at #24 on the main street, tel. 0187-812-123, info@cinqueterreriviera.com).

# Nightlife in Vernazza

Vernazza generally shuts down pretty early. The town's nightlife centers on the bars on its waterfront piazza, which is the place to "see and be seen." Young restaurant workers work hard throughout the tourist season, but they let loose after-hours and enjoy connecting with international visitors in the town's few nightspots (which are required to close by midnight). For a more genteel option, consider an opera performance or a wine tasting (both described above). Or in the cool, calm evening, sit on the town's breakwater with a glass of wine and watch the phosphorescence in the waves.

The **Blue Marlin Bar** dominates the late-night scene with a mix of locals and tourists, good drinks, and an open piano. If you play piano, you're welcome to join in. **Ananasso Bar** offers early-evening happy-hour fun and cocktails *(aperitivi)* that both locals and visitors enjoy. Its harborfront tables get the last sunshine of the day. For more on these bars, see their listings under "Eating in Vernazza," later.

CINQUE TERRE

# Sleeping in Vernazza

Vernazza lacks any real hotels, and almost all of my listings are *affittacamere* (private rooms for rent). I favor hosts who rent multiple rooms and have a proven track record of good communication (they speak just enough English, have email, and are reliable). Airbnb is really big in Vernazza.

Most places accept only cash, promise free Wi-Fi (often spotty), and don't include breakfast unless noted. Some have killer views, and some come with lots of stairs. Expect noise at night: Trains tearing through, church bells (after 7:00 and before 22:00), crashing waves, cars in the upper town. Come to think of it, just pack earplugs.

While a few places have all their beds in one building, most have rooms scattered all over town. Better-organized outfits have an informal reception desk (sometimes at a restaurant or other business) where you can check in. But many places have no reception at all. (The Vernazza map in this book shows only the places that have a fixed address or reception office; if I mention "reception," you'll check in there.)

If you overnight here, communicate your arrival time to your host and get clear instructions on where to meet and pick up the keys. They'll usually offer to meet you at the train station if they know when you're coming.

## ROOMS FOR RENT *(AFFITTACAMERE)*

The **Cinque Terre Riviera** agency, based in Vernazza, rents rooms here and throughout the region (www.cinqueterreriviera.com; see page 378.

### Scattered Through the Town Center
**More Expensive, with More Amenities**

**$$$$ La Malà** is the town's jet-setter pad. Four crisp, pristine white rooms boast fancy-hotel-type extras and a shared seaview terrace. It's a climb—way up to the top of town—but they'll carry your bags to and from the station. Book early; this place fills up quickly (includes breakfast at a bar, family rooms, air-con, mobile 334-287-5718, www.lamala.it, info@lamala.it, charming Giamba and his mama, Armanda). They also rent two rooms at the simpler **$ "Armanda's Room"** nearby—a great value, since you get Giamba's attention to detail and amenities without paying for a big view (includes simple breakfast, air-con).

**$$$$ Vernazza sul Mare** rents two view, luxury apartments (one- and two-bedroom, sleeping 4-6) that overlook the sea and town from private, spacious terraces. The light-filled, airy units come with sea breezes and a crashing-waves soundtrack. These are great for families and can be connected for larger groups (both with air-con, fully equipped kitchens, climb steps up to Via Carattino 12, mobile 345-363-6118, www.vernazzasulmare.com, info@vernazzasulmare.com, run by helpful American-Italian Ruth and her family).

$$$ **Nicolina Rooms** consists of seven rooms and one apartment in three different buildings. Two cheaper rooms are in the center over the pharmacy, up a few steep steps; another, pricier studio with a terrace is on a twisty lane above the harbor; and four more rooms are in a building beyond the church, with great views and church bells (all include breakfast, Piazza Marconi 29—check in at Pizzeria Vulnetia, tel. 0187-821-193, mobile 333-842-6879, www.camerenicolina.it, info@camerenicolina.it).

$$$ **La Marina Rooms** is run by hardworking Christian, who speaks English and happily meets guests at the station to carry bags. There are five well-tended, airy, and renovated units, most high above the main street: One single works as a (very) tight double, and three doubles have fine oceanview terraces; he also has two apartments—one with terrace and sea views, and the other on the harborfront square (rooms have fridges, mobile 338-476-7472, www.lamarinarooms.com, mapcri@yahoo.it).

$$$ **Monica Lercari** rents several rooms with modern comforts, perched at the top of town (more for seaview terrace, includes breakfast, air-con, tel. 0187-812-296, mobile 320-025-4515, monimarimax@gmail.com). Monica and her husband, Massimo, run the recommended Ristorante al Castello, in the old castle tower overlooking town.

### Simpler, Good-Value Places

$$ **Francamaria** and her husband Andrea rent 10 sharp, comfortable, and creatively renovated rooms. Their reception desk is on the harbor square (on the ground floor at Piazza Marconi 30), but the rooms they manage are all over town (family rooms, some with air-con, mobile 328-711-9728, www.francamaria.com, francamariareservation@gmail.com). They also rent a room in Manarola.

$$ **Emanuela Colombo** rents a spacious and classy room on the harbor square, and a molto chic split-level apartment on a quiet side street (sleeps up to four, reception at Via Roma 27, tel. 339-834-2486, www.vacanzemanuela.it, manucap64@libero.it).

$$ **Vernazza Rooms,** run by Massimo, rents 14 rooms: Four are above the Blue Marlin Bar looking down on the main street, and seven are a steep climb higher up, just under the City Hall (big family apartments, a few with air-con and others with fans, fridges in all rooms, arrange check-in time in advance and meet your host

**CINQUE TERRE**

at Via del Santo 9, mobile 351-918-3164, www.vernazzarooms. com, info@vernazzarooms.com).

**$$** Lovely **Rosa Vitali** rents a four-person apartment with a full kitchen; it's across from the pharmacy overlooking the main street—and beyond the train noise (ring bell at Via Visconti 10— just before the tobacco shop near Piazza Marconi, tel. 0187-821-181, mobile 340-267-5009, www.rosacamere.it, rosa.vitali@libero. it).

**$$ Maria Capellini** rents two simple, clean rooms that face each other across the harbor; one is at ground level just steps from the beach and with a view; the other looks over a skinny street (fridge, fans, mobile 338-436-3411, www.mariacapellini.com, mariacapellini@hotmail.it, kindly Maria and Giacomo).

**$$ Martina Callo**'s four old-fashioned, spartan rooms overlook the harbor square; they're up plenty of steps near the silent-at-night church tower. While the rooms are simple, guests pay for and appreciate the views (family rooms, cheaper nonview room, air-con, ring bell at Piazza Marconi 26, tel. 0187-812-365, mobile 329-435-5344, www.roomartina.it, roomartina@roomartina.it), Martina and her father, Giuseppe.

**$ Rooms Francesca**'s offers one tidy room with sea views and air-con, and a two-bedroom apartment with fans. Both hide out in the steep streets just below City Hall (check in at Enoteca Sciacchetrà at Via Roma 19, tel. 0187-821-112, mobile 339-101-2962, www.5terre-vernazza.it, moggia.franco@libero.it; Francesca, Franco, and Sabine).

**$ Ivo's Camere** rents two tight but well-appointed rooms several flights of stairs above the main street (air-con, Via Roma 6, mobile 333-477-5521, www.ivocamere.com, post@ivocamere. com).

**$ Albergo Barbara** rents nine tidy, Ikea-chic top-floor rooms overlooking the square with an attic communal lounge. Most have small windows and small views; view rooms are more expensive. It's a good value in a nice location, run by Alessio and Alberto (cheaper rooms with shared bathroom, lots of stairs, reserve online with credit card but pay cash, Piazza Marconi 30, tel. 0187-812-398, www.albergobarbara.it, info@albergobarbara.it).

**$ Memo Rooms** rents two clean and spacious rooms overlooking the main street, in what feels like a miniature hotel. Enrica will meet you if you call upon arrival (Via Roma 15, try Enrica's mobile first at 338-285-2385, otherwise call 0187-812-360, www. memorooms.com, info@memorooms.com).

### More Options
If my recommendations above are full, try these:

**$$ Capitano Rooms** (3 rooms and 1 apartment several flights of stairs above main drag, fans; ask for Julia, Paolo, Edoardo, or Barbara at Trattoria del Capitano restaurant on main square at Piazza Marconi 21, tel. 0187-812-201, www.tavernavernazza.com, info@tavernavernazza.com); **$ Eva's Rooms** (2 rooms on main street, air-con, train noise, 2-night minimum, call ahead to arrange meeting place, tel. 334-798-6500, www.evasrooms.it, evasrooms@yahoo.it); **$$$ Rooms Elisabetta** (2 tight, recently renovated, casually run rooms and 1 apartment at the tip-top of town with Vernazza's ultimate 360-degree roof terrace—come here for the views; fans, partway up Corniglia path at Via Carattino 62, mobile 347-451-1834, www.elisabettacarro.com, carroelisabetta@hotmail.com, Elisabetta); **$$ Manuela Moggia** (3 apartments and 2 rooms, more for kitchen or view, behind train station at Via Gavino 22 and on main square, tel. 0187-812-397, mobile 333-413-6374, www.manuela-vernazza.com, info@manuela-vernazza.com).

## In the Inland Part of Town

**Above the Train Station: $$$$ Casa Cato** offers six modern, tight but well-outfitted rooms, some with private balconies and all with access to an inviting shared terrace overlooking the sea and town (RS%, air-con, fridge, expect some train noise, mobile 334-123-8579, www.casacatocinqueterre.com, info@casacatocinqueterre.com, Lisa). They also rent an apartment in the center of town.

**$$$ Giuliano Basso**'s four carefully crafted, well-appointed rooms form a cozy little compound with a common lounge and view terrace, straddling a ravine among orange trees. Giuliano—the town's last stone-layer—proudly built the place himself. To reach this quiet retreat on the green hillside just above town and the train station, you'll climb partway up the Corniglia footpath (2 rooms have air-con, more train noise than others; follow the main road up above the station, take the ramp up toward Corniglia just before Pensione Sorriso, follow the path, and watch for a sharp left turn—or ask Giuliano to meet you at the station; mobile 333-341-4792, www.cameregiuliano.com, giuliano@cdh.it).

**In the Ravine at the Top of Town:** These practical options are a five-minute, gently uphill stroll behind the train station. While this functional zone is less atmospheric, it is easy to access (with fewer steep stairs). There's no train or church-bell noise—the constant soundtrack is Vernazza's gurgling river—but there can be traffic noise.

**$$ Camere Fontanavecchia,** run by Annamaria, is the best choice here, with eight bright and cheery rooms (three with terraces) overlooking the ravine and its rushing river (Via Gavino 15, tel. 0187-821-130, mobile 333-454-9371, www.cinqueterrecamere.com, m.annamaria@libero.it). She also rents an apartment.

**$$ Tonino Basso/La Perla,** spread over two floors, has 10 overpriced rooms in a drab, elevator-equipped, modern apartment block. La Perla's rooms feel fresher (air-con, fridge, Via Gavino 34, mobile 339-761-1651, www.toninobasso.com and www.laperladelle5terre.it, Alessandra).

$ **La Rosa dei Venti** ("The Compass Rose"), run by Giuliana Basso, houses three airy, good-value rooms in her childhood home, on the third floor of an apartment building (call to arrange meeting time, air-con, Via Gavino 19, mobile 333-762-4679, www.larosadeiventi-vernazza.it, info@larosadeiventi-vernazza.it).

## GUESTHOUSE (PENSIONE)

$$$ **Gianni Franzi,** a busy restaurant on the harbor square, runs the closest thing to a big hotel in Vernazza. There are 25 small rooms scattered across three buildings a hundred tight, winding stairs above the harbor square. Some rooms (including a few cheaper ones with shared bathrooms) are funky and decorated à la shipwreck, with tiny balconies and grand sea views. The comfy, newer rooms lack views. All guests have access to a super-scenic cliff-hanging garden and panoramic terrace (where breakfast is served in season). Steely Marisa requires check-in before 16:00 or a phone call to explain when you're coming. Emanuele, Simona, and staff speak enough English (RS%, closed Jan-Feb, Piazza Marconi 1, tel. 0187-812-228, mobile 393-9008-155, www.giannifranzi.it, info@giannifranzi.it). Pick up your keys at the restaurant, but on Wed, when the restaurant is closed, call ahead to make other arrangements.

# Eating in Vernazza

## BREAKFAST

B&Bs in Vernazza provide B but no B. That's kind of a blessing, as Vernazza has plenty of options, from full bacon and eggs (Blue Marlin and Capitano), to a Sicilian bakery of fresh pastries (Il Pirata), to coffee and a sweet roll on the harborfront (Ananasso), to any number of bakeries selling sweet and savory options to go. For a full breakfast, you'll pay €12-15. Here are your main options from the top of town to the harbor (in that order). Most of these places are also recommended in my lunch and dinner listings.

$ **Il Pirata delle Cinque Terre**, located in the workaday zone at the parking lot at the top of town, is playful, efficient, comfortable, and serves tasty breakfast bruschetta, frittatas, and an array of fresh pastries. The fun service of the dynamic duo Gianluca and Massimo (hardworking Sicilian twins, a.k.a. the Cannoli brothers) makes up for the lack of a view. They pride themselves on not serving bacon and eggs, since "this is Italy." While the atmosphere feels more like suburban Milan, it has charisma (daily 7:00-24:00, also serves lunch and dinner—see later, Via Gavino 36, tel. 0187-812-047).

**$$ Blue Marlin Bar** (midtown, just below the train station) serves a good array of clearly priced à la carte breakfast items (Italian breakfast from 7:30, eggs and bacon 8:30-11:30). If you're awaiting a train and the platform isn't crowded, it's pleasant to have a seat at Blue Marlin's outdoor seating with a prepaid drink in view of the tracks (Thu-Tue 7:30-23:00, closed Wed).

**$ Lunch Box** is the hardworking new kid on the block, with lots of hot options and a fun little perch for a couple of tables overlooking the main drag (daily 7:00-22:00, also serves lunch and dinner—see later, Via Roma 34, mobile 338-908-2841, Stefano).

**$$ Trattoria del Capitano** offers outdoor seating on the harbor, as well as cozy spots inside the restaurant and a full menu (Wed-Mon 8:00-22:00, closed Tue except in Aug, on Piazza Marconi, tel. 0187-812-201, hardworking Paolo and Barbara speak English).

**$$ Ananasso Bar** has a youthful energy, a great location right on the harbor, and a skimpy Italian breakfast menu (toasted *panini*, pastries, Muesli with yogurt, and cappuccino). You can eat a bit cheaper at the bar (you're welcome to picnic on the nearby bench or seawall rocks with a Mediterranean view) or enjoy the best-situated tables in town (Fri-Wed 8:00-late, closed Thu, on Piazza Marconi).

**Picnic Breakfast:** Drop by one of Vernazza's many little bakeries, focaccia shops, or grocery stores to assemble a breakfast to eat on the breakwater. Top it off with a coffee in a nearby bar.

## LUNCH AND DINNER

Vernazza's restaurants work hard to win your business. Wander around at about 20:00 and compare the ambience. If you dine in Vernazza but are staying in another town, check train schedules before sitting down to eat, as evening trains run less frequently, with gaps in the schedule. To get an outdoor table on summer weekends, reserve ahead. Harborside restaurants and bars are easygoing. You're welcome to grab a cup of coffee or glass of wine and disappear somewhere on the breakwater, returning your glass when you're done. You've got lots of options and prices are competitive, with €11-15 pastas and €15-25 *secondi*.

### Harborside

**$$$ Gianni Franzi** is an old standby for well-prepared seafood and pastas. Emanuele, Nicolas, and their crew provide steady, reliable, and friendly service. The outdoor seating is partially tucked under an arcade, while the indoor setting is big, open, and classy (check their *menù cucina tipica Vernazza*, Thu-Tue 12:00-15:00 & 19:00-22:00, closed Wed except in Aug, tel. 0187-812-228).

**$$$ Trattoria del Capitano** feels unpretentious and serves a short menu of straightforward local dishes, including *spaghetti allo scoglio*—pasta entangled with various types of seafood (for hours and location, see "Breakfast," earlier).

**$$$ Ristorante Pizzeria Vulnetia** has a nautical, jovial atmosphere. It serves regional specialties; but unlike the others, it also dishes up thin-crust pizzas—making this a good choice for a group with differing tastes, those on a budget, and families (Tue-Sun 12:00-22:00, closed Mon, Piazza Marconi 29, tel. 0187-821-193, Tullio and Federica).

**$$ Pizzeria Baia Saracena** ("Saracen Bay") serves forgettable pizza and pastas out on the breakwater. Eat here not for high cuisine, but for a memorable atmosphere at reasonable prices (Sat-Thu 11:30-22:00, closed Fri, tel. 0187-812-113, Luca and Andrea).

**$$$$ Gambero Rosso** rounds out the options on the harbor. Long the top restaurant in town, today it's lost its edge (it was sold to a big-city restaurateur who runs it from afar). Still, it's reliably good, and has a fine interior and great outdoor tables (Fri-Wed 12:00-15:00 & 19:00-22:00, closed Thu and Dec-Feb, Piazza Marconi 7, tel. 0187-812-265).

## Above the Harbor, by the Castle

**$$$$ Ristorante Belforte** is a cut above the rest, serving a fine blend of traditional and creative cuisine, fishy *spaghetti alla Bruno*, *trofie al pesto* (hand-rolled noodles with pesto), and classic *antipasto misto di pesce*—an assortment of fish (€24/person for 5 plates; 2-person minimum). From the breakwater, a rope leads up from the harbor to a web of tables embedded in four levels of the old castle. While their indoor seating is great, for the ultimate seaside perch, reserve a table on the *terrazza con vista* (view terrace) or request the "lovers' table" on its own little terrace. Most of Belforte's seating is outdoors—if the weather's bad, the interior can get crowded. Late in the evening, Andrea cranks up the fun (Wed-Mon 12:00-15:00 & 19:00-22:00, closed Tue and Nov-March, tel. 0187-812-222, Michela).

**$$$ Ristorante al Castello**—a bit less expensive and a bit more homey than the others—is run by gracious and English-speaking Monica, her husband Massimo, and their sometimes-gruff staff. Hike high above town to just below the castle for commanding views. Reserve one of the dozen romantic cliffside seaview tables for two—some of the tables snake around the castle, where you'll feel like you're eating all alone with the Mediterranean. Monica offers a free *sciacchetrà* or *limoncello* with biscotti with this book by request (Thu–Tue 12:00–15:00 & 19:00–22:00, closed Wed and Nov–April, tel. 0187-812-296).

## On or near the Main Street

Several of Vernazza's inland eateries manage to compete without the harbor ambience but with slightly cheaper prices.

**$$ Trattoria da Sandro,** on the main drag, mixes quality Genovese and Ligurian cuisine with friendly service and can be a peaceful alternative to the harborside scene. The family proudly maintains its cultural traditions and dishes up award-winning stuffed mussels (Wed-Mon 12:00-15:00 & 18:30-22:00, closed Tue, Via Roma 62, tel. 0187-812-223, Argentina and Alessandro).

**$$ Antica Osteria il Baretto** is another solid bet for homey, reasonably priced traditional cuisine, run by Simone and Jenny. As it's off the harbor and less glitzy than the others, it's favored by locals who prefer less noisy English while they eat great homemade fare. Sitting deep in their interior can be a tranquil escape (Tue-Sun 12:00-22:00, closed Mon, indoor and outdoor seating in summer, Via Roma 31, tel. 0187-812-381).

## Other Eating Options

**$$ Blue Marlin Bar,** on the main street, busts out of the Vernazzan cuisine rut with a short, creative menu of more casual dishes (pizzas, salads). It's a good choice if you want to grab something basic rather than dine (for more details and hours, see "Breakfast," earlier).

**$$ Il Pirata delle Cinque Terre,** a huge hit for breakfast, also attracts travelers for lunch and dinner. While you're eating at the parking lot, the food, service, and energy are great. And many are charmed by the Cannoli twins, who entertain while they serve. The menu (pastas and salads) is aimed squarely at American tourists' taste buds (lunch from 12:00, reserve ahead for dinner from 18:00, good cannoli and Sicilian slushies, at the top of town; for more details and contact info, see "Breakfast," earlier). The self-serve laundry is next door for those who like to multitask.

**$ Lunch Box** serves *panini,* salads, and fresh fruit juices from a clever and flexible menu. Assemble your own salad (or juice) from a long list of ingredients (for hours and location, see "Breakfast," earlier).

**$ Pizzeria Ercole** dishes out an array of fried and greasy gut-bombs cheap and fast with tables right in the busy center of town. More tables are in a humble little secret terrace hiding in the back (where tour guides go to escape the crowds). You're welcome to sit and munch for their takeaway prices (daily, Via Visconti 2, tel. 0187-812-545).

**Pizzerias, Sandwiches, and Groceries:** Vernazza's main-street eateries offer a fine range of quick meals. Several bakeries and creative little takeaway joints sell sandwiches and pizza by the slice. **Pino's grocery store** at #19 makes inexpensive sandwiches to order (generally Mon-Sat 8:00-13:00 & 17:00-19:30, closed Sun).

**Gelato:** The town has plenty of good gelato shops. On the harbor, the aptly named **Gelateria Il Porticciolo** ("Marina") uses fresh ingredients to create intense flavors (try their *cannella*—cinnamon, or *nocciola*—hazelnut). **Gelateria Vernazza,** near the top of the main street, takes its gelato seriously, occasionally flirting with creative ingredients (soy) and flavors (*riso*—rice, and ricotta and fig). **Gelateria Amore Mio** (midtown) used to be Gelateria Stalin, founded in 1968 by a pastry chef with that unfortunate name; now it's run by his niece Sonia and nephew Francesco, with great people-watching tables.

# Corniglia

If you think of the Cinque Terre as the Beatles, Corniglia is Ringo. This tiny, sleepy town is the only one of the five not directly on the water. According to legend, the town was originally settled by a Roman farmer who named it for his mother, Cornelia (which is how Corniglia is pronounced). Locals claim that its ancient residents produced a wine so widely exported that vases have been found at Pompeii stamped with the town name. Wine remains Corniglia's lifeblood today. Sample some when you're in town.

Less visited than the other Cinque Terre towns, Corniglia has fewer tourists, cooler temperatures, a laid-back main square, a few restaurants, a windy overlook on its promontory, and plenty of private rooms for rent. You don't go to Corniglia for the beach: Its once fine beach below the station has washed away. From the town center, signs for *al mare* or *Marina* point to where a stepped path leads steeply down to sunning rocks.

**Corniglia**

To Vernazza

Trail to Vernazza

200 Meters
200 Yards

SUNNING ROCKS

385 STEPS

LARGO TARAGIO

ORATORY

SANTA MARIA BELVEDERE

"CIAPPÀ" SQUARE & BUS STOP

To Manarola

TRAIN STATION

*Ligurian Sea*

1 Villa Cecio Rooms
2 Pan e Vin Bar (Ricci Rooms Check-In)
3 Il Carugio Rooms & Butiega Gastronomia
4 Corniglia Hostel
5 Ristorante il Buongustaio
6 Osteria Mananan & Enoteca il Pirùn
7 La Posada Ristorante
8 Gelateria

# Orientation to Corniglia

Hill-capping Corniglia is connected with its train station far below by a long set of stairs, and much easier, by a hardworking little shuttle bus. Its reliable schedule is posted both at the station and in the town. Because of the steep distance between the town and its station, and the lack of a boat dock, Corniglia is inconvenient as a home base for town-hopping.

**Tourist Information:** A TI/park information office is down at the train station (likely daily 8:00-20:00, shorter hours off-season). At busy times, there may also be a kiosk up in town on Ciappà square.

**Hiking:** From Corniglia, you can hike on the coastal trail to **Vernazza.** Also consider the challenging but rewarding "high road" to **Manarola via Volastra.** For details, see "Hiking the Cinque Terre" on page 346.

## ARRIVAL IN CORNIGLIA

**By Train:** From the station far below town, you can take a footpath zigzagging up 385 steps (and nearly that many switchbacks) to the town in about 20 minutes. If you'd rather not walk, hop on the tiny ATC shuttle that connects the station with Corniglia's main square, the starting point of my short self-guided walk (buy bus ticket at station TI, €1.50—or more from driver, 2-4/hour, gen-

*CINQUE TERRE*

erally timed to meet arriving trains, go quickly as bus departs when full).

If leaving Corniglia by train, review the shuttle schedule to plan your return to the station.

**By Car:** Only residents can park on the main road between the recommended Villa Cecio and the point where the steep switchback staircase meets the road. Beyond that area, anyone can park for a fee. All parking areas are within an easy and fairly level walk of the town center.

## Corniglia Walk

We'll explore this tiny town—population 240—and end at a scenic viewpoint. This self-guided walk might take 30 minutes or more... but only if you let yourself browse, sample the wine, or lick a gelato cone.

• *Begin near the shuttle bus stop located at a...*

### Town Square

The gateway to this community is Ciappà square, with an ATM, old wine press, bus stop, and sometimes a TI kiosk in summer. The Cinque Terre's designation as a national park sparked a revitalization of the town.

• *Look for the arrow pointing to the* centro. *Stroll along Via Fieschi, the spine of Corniglia. In the fall, the smell of grapes (on their way to becoming wine) wafts from busy cellars. Along this main street, you'll see...*

### Corniglia's Enticing Shops

As you enter Via Fieschi, a trio of neighboring gelato shops jockeys for your business. My favorite is the last one you come to (at #74, on the right), **Alberto's Gelateria** (open late). Before ordering, get a free taste of Alberto's *miele di Corniglia*, made from local honey; he and Cristina are also proud of their basil flavor. Their lemon slush *(granita)* takes pucker to new heights.

Farther along, on the left, **Enoteca il Pirùn**—named for a type of oddly shaped old-fashioned wine pitcher designed to aerate the wine and give the alcohol more kick as you squirt it into your mouth—is located in a cool cantina at Via Fieschi 115. Try some local wines (small tastes generally free, €3/glass). If you order wine to drink from the *pirùn*, Mario will give you a bib. While this is a practicality (rookies tend to dribble), it also makes a nice souvenir.

Farther along, **Butiega Gastronomia** (#142) is an old-fash-

ioned grocery store/deli where Vincenzo sells organic local specialties (daily 8:00-19:30). For picnickers, they offer €5 made-to-order
ham-and-cheese sandwiches and a fun *antipasti misti* (priced by
weight). Veronica prepares specialties such as pesto daily in the
shop's tiny kitchen. You'll find good places to picnic farther along
on this walk.
• *Following Via Fieschi, you'll end up at the mellow...*

## Main Square (Largo Taragio)

On the main square, tables from two bars and a trattoria spill
around a WWI memorial and the town's old well. It once piped
in natural spring water from the hillside to locals living without
plumbing. What looks like a church is the **Oratory of Santa Caterina.** (An oratory is a kind of spiritual clubhouse for a service
group doing social work in the name of the Catholic Church.) Up
the stairs and behind the oratory, you'll find a terrace that children
have made into a soccer field. The stone benches and viewpoint
make this a peaceful place for a picnic (less crowded than the end-
of-town viewpoint, described next).
• *Opposite the oratory, notice how steps lead steeply down (in 5 minutes)
on Via alla Marina to sunning rocks and a small deck (with a shower
and treacherous entry into the water). From the square, continue up Via
Fieschi to the...*

## End-of-Town Viewpoint

The Santa Maria Belvedere, named for a church that once stood
here, marks the scenic end of Corniglia. This is a super picnic spot.
From here, look high to the west (right), where the village and
sanctuary of San Bernardino straddle a ridge (accessible by shuttle
bus or a long uphill hike from Vernazza). Way down below are the
local swimming hole and huge sunning rocks.

# Sleeping in Corniglia

Because Corniglia has no harbor, its mostly humble accommodations are almost never full.

**$$ Villa Cecio** (pronounced "chay-choh"), sits atop the old-
time Ristorante Cecio (with great views). They offer eight freshly
decorated, well-priced, sizeable rooms on the quiet outskirts of town.
Most rooms have postcard views, and three have terraces—worth
requesting when you book. All rooms share a big rooftop view ter-
race (breakfast extra, four rooms have air-con, on main road toward
Vernazza at Via Serra 58—keep going 200 yards beyond Ciappà
square and you'll find it on the right, tel. 0187-812-043, mobile 366-
285-1178, www.cecio5terre.com, info@cecio5terre.com, Giacinto).

They also rent eight more rooms in an annex on the square where the bus stops.

**$ Cristiana Ricci** communicates well and is reliable, renting three small, clean, and peaceful rooms—one with a terrace and sweeping view—just inland from the bus stop (family rooms, check in at Pan e Vin bar at Via Fieschi 123, mobile 338-937-6547, www.corniglia-room.com, cri_affittacamere@virgilio.it). She also rents three big, modern apartments.

**$ Il Carugio** has nine modern, fresh, sunny rooms in three buildings—some in the center of the village, and most with sea views. The main building offers a communal rooftop terrace with a commanding view of the coast (2-night minimum, family rooms, air-con, no breakfast but small self-service kitchen, free parking, free self-serve laundry, tel. 0187-812-293, mobile 335-175-7946 or 339-228-3803, www.ilcarugiodicorniglia.com, info@ilcarugiodicorniglia.com, gregarious Lidia). They also have a two-bedroom apartment facing the main square.

**¢ Corniglia Hostel,** the town's former schoolhouse, rents 24 beds in a yellow municipal building up some steps from the square where the bus stops (find the entrance at the back of the building). Despite its institutional atmosphere, the hostel's prices, central location, and bright, clean rooms ensure its popularity. Its hotelesque double rooms are open to anyone (breakfast extra, office open 7:00-13:00 & 15:00-1:30 in the morning, air-con, self-serve laundry, Via alla Stazione 3, tel. 0187-812-559, www.ostellocorniglia.com, ostellocorniglia@gmail.com, Andrea, Alessandro, and Elisabetta).

## Eating in Corniglia

A typical array of pizzerias, *focaccerie*, and *alimentari* (grocery stores) line the narrow main drag. I've highlighted a few places for a quick bite on my self-guided walk, earlier.

For a full, sit-down meal, consider one of these restaurants.

**$$$ Ristorante il Buongustaio** is a good bet for dinner on the square. Daniela and the Guelfi family pride themselves in serving *cucina casalinga* (home cooking) and good seafood pasta and risotto (nice tables on the main square as well as in a big indoor dining room, daily 12:00-21:15, Via Fieschi 164, tel. 0187-821-424).

**$$ Osteria Mananan**—between the Ciappà bus stop and the main square at Via Fieschi 117—has earned a good reputation with tasty dishes and a small, stony, elegant interior (Tue-Sun 12:30-14:30 & 19:30-22:00, closed Mon, no outdoor seating, tel. 0187-821-166).

**$$ Enoteca il Pirùn,** on Via Fieschi, has a small restaurant above the wine bar, where Mario serves typical local dishes (Fri-Wed 12:00-16:00 & 19:00-23:30, closed Thu, tel. 0187-812-315).

$$ **La Posada Ristorante** offers dinner in a garden under trees, overlooking the Ligurian Sea. To get here, stroll out of town to the top of the stairs that lead down to the station (daily 12:00-16:00 & 19:00-23:00, closed Nov-March, tel. 0187-821-174, mobile 338-232-5734).

# Manarola

Mellow Manarola fills a ravine, bookended by its wild little harbor to the west and a diminutive hilltop church square inland to the east. Manarola is excep-
tional for being unexcep-
tional: While Vernazza is prettier, Monterosso glitzier, Riomaggiore big-
ger, and Corniglia more rustic, Manarola hits a fine balance, giving it the "just right" combination of Cinque Terre qualities.

Perhaps that's why it's a favorite among savvy Europeans seeking a relatively untrampled home base. The touristy zone squeezed between the cement-encased train tracks and the harbor can be stressfully congested, but head just a few steps uphill and you can breathe again.

Manarola, whose hillsides are blanketed with vineyards, also provides the easiest access to the Cinque Terre's remarkable dry-stone terraces. The trail ringing the town's cemetery peninsula, adjacent to the main harbor, provides some of the most strikingly beautiful town views anywhere in the region. For a look at all the facets of this delightful town, follow my gentle self-guided stroll from the harbor up through town to the vineyards, and a stunning Mediterranean viewpoint.

## Orientation to Manarola

### TOURIST INFORMATION

The TI/national park information office is in the train station (like-ly daily 8:00-20:00, shorter hours off-season).

### ARRIVAL IN MANAROLA

**By Train:** From the station, to reach Manarola, you'll walk through a 200-yard-long tunnel that's lined with interesting photos. (During WWII air raids, these tunnels provided refuge and a safe place

CINQUE TERRE

Manarola

To Corniglia,
(trail closed)

To Volastra
(Panoramico
trail)

SWIMMING

Punta
Bonfiglio

WC

Cemetery

Manarola
Vineyard Trail

WALK
ENDS

VIA 13 DEI GIOVANNI

BEST
VIEW

Piazza
Capellini

50 Meters

50 Yards

SWIMMING
& SHOWER

"MAIN STREET"

5

9

11

14

VIA BIROLI

10

V. BALURADO

WALK
BEGINS

7

VIA DI MEZZO

V. BELVEDERE

BOAT
DOCK

BREAKWATER

VIA
BELVEDERE

Piazza
Castello

BOAT
DOCK

Piazzetta
Eugenio Montale

Ligurian
Sea

CINQUE TERRE

for rattled villagers to sleep.) To reach the busy harbor—with touristy restaurants, boat dock, and the start of my self-guided walk, head left (downhill) when you come out of the tunnel.

The ATC **shuttle bus** runs from near the old waterwheel (halfway up Manarola's main street), stopping first at the parking lots above town, and then going all the way up to Volastra (about 2/hour except for afternoon breaks).

**By Car:** You're better off parking in La Spezia. If you're overnighting here, ask your hotelier for parking advice. Park your car in one of the two pay lots just before town, then walk down the road to the church; from there, it's an easy downhill walk to the main

Accommodations
1. La Torretta Rooms
2. B&B Da Baranin
3. Aria di Mare Rooms
4. Albergo Ca' d'Andrean
5. Marina Piccola Rooms & Restaurant
6. Da Paulin Rooms
7. 5 Terre Pelagos
8. To Hotel il Saraceno

Eateries & Other
9. Trattoria il Porticciolo & Sorbetteria 5 Terre Gelateria
10. Café il Porticciolo
11. Ristorante di Aristide & Bar Caffè Aristide
12. Trattoria dal Billy
13. Nessun Dorma Cantina
14. Grocery
15. Cinque Terre Trekking
16. Shuttle Bus to Parking Lot & Volastra

piazza, train-station tunnel, and harbor (the start of my self-guided walk), or you can wait for the shuttle bus.

# Manarola Walk

From the harbor, this 45-minute self-guided walk shows you the town and surrounding vineyards and ends at a fantastic viewpoint.
• *Start down at the waterfront. Belly up to the wooden banister overlooking the rocky harbor, between the two restaurants.*

## Harbor

Manarola is tiny and picturesque, a tumble of buildings bunny-hopping down its ravine to the fun-loving waterfront. The **breakwater**—which attempts to make this jagged harbor a bit less dangerous—was built (with reject marble from Carrara) just over a decade ago. Notice how the I-beam crane launches the boats (which must be pulled ashore when bad weather is expected, to avoid being smashed or swept away).

Facing the water, look up to the right, at the hillside Punta Bonfiglio **cemetery** and park. The trail running around the base of the point—where this walk ends—offers magnificent views back on this part of town. If you see a crowd, it's Instagram devotees who travel here from around the world (mostly Asia) to take and post their selfies.

The town's **swimming hole** is just below you. Manarola has no sand, but offers the best deep-water swimming in the area. The first "beach" has a shower, ladder, and wonderful rocks. The second has tougher access and no shower, but feels more remote and pristine (follow the paved path toward Corniglia, just around the point).

• *Go inland up the town's main drag—you'll climb a steep ramp—which is lined by classic* ***photos*** *of the noble people who eked out a living from the sea and this land before the arrival of tourists. The ramp leads to Manarola's "new" square, which covers the train tracks.*

### Piazza Capellini

Built in 2004, this square is an all-around great idea, giving the town a safe, fun zone for kids. Locals living near the tracks also enjoy a little less train noise. The mosaic in the middle of the square depicts the varieties of local fish in colorful enamel.

• *Go down the stairs at the upper end of the square. On your right, notice the tunnel that leads to Manarola's train station (and the closed Via dell'Amore trailhead). Head up...*

### Via Discovolo

Manarola's main street twists up through town, lined by modest shops and filled with pooped hikers. About 100 yards up, just before the road bends sharply right, watch (on the right) for a **waterwheel**. This recalls the origin of the town's name—local dialect for "big wheel" (one of many possible derivations). Mills like this once powered the local industry. As you continue up (all the way to the church), you'll still hear the rushing waters of Manarola's stream. Like the streams in Riomaggiore, Monterosso, and Vernazza, Manarola's rivulet was covered over after World War II. Before that time, romantic bridges arched over its ravine. You can peek below the concrete street in several places to see the stream surging below your feet.

Across the street from the waterwheel and a bit farther up, notice the **Cinque Terre Trekking** shop on your left, which outfits hikers with both information and gear (for details, see "Hikes from Manarola," later).

Around the corner is **Cantine Burasca** wine bar. With fine outdoor seating, it's a good place for a little wine tasting (closed Wed, Via Discovolo 86, mobile 339-807-1261).

• *Keep climbing until you come to the square at the...*

## Top of Manarola

The square is faced by a church, an oratory—now a religious and community meeting place—and a bell tower (with a WWI memo-

rial etched in it), which served as a watchtower when pirates raided the town (the cupola was added once the attacks ceased). To the right of the oratory, a stepped lane leads to the town's sizable tourist-free residential zone.

Check out the **church.** The Parish Church of St. Lawrence (San Lorenzo) dates from "MCCCXXXVIII" (1338). Step inside to see two altarpiece paintings from the unnamed Master of the Cinque Terre, the only painter of any note from this region (left wall and above main altar). While the style is Gothic, the work dates from the time of Michelangelo, long after Florence had entered the Renaissance. Note the humble painted stone ceiling, which replaced the wooden original in the 1800s. It features Lawrence, patron saint of the Cinque Terre, with his grill, the symbol of his martyrdom (he was roasted on it).

• *With the bell tower on your left, head about 20 yards back down the main street below the church and find a wooden railing on the right. It marks the start of a delightful stroll around the high side of town, and back to the seafront. This is the beginning of the...*

## Manarola Vineyard Trail

Don't miss this experience. Simply follow the wooden railing, enjoying lemon groves and great views. Along the path, which is primarily flat, you'll get a close-up look at the region's famous dry-stone walls and finely crafted vineyards (with dried-heather thatches to protect the grapes from southwest winds). Smell the rosemary. Study the structure of the town, and pick out the scant remains of an old fort. Notice the S-shape of the main road—once a riverbed—that flows through town. The town's roofs are traditionally made of locally quarried slate and held down by rocks during windstorms.

Halfway along the lip of the ravine, a path marked *Panorami-*

CINQUE TERRE

*co Volastra (Corniglia)* leads steeply up into the vineyards (a challenging route that leads to the tiny hamlet of Volastra and then to Corniglia—described on page 350).

Stick with your level path, passing a variety of simple wooden religious scenes, the work of local resident Mario Andreoli. Before his father died, Mario promised him he'd replace the old cross on the family's vineyard. Mario has been adding figures ever since. On religious holidays, everything's lit up: the Nativity, the Last Supper, the Crucifixion, the Resurrection, and more. Some of the scenes are left up year-round. (You can see more of his figures across the ravine, gathered together in a little open patch between buildings.) High above, notice ancient terraces that line the terrain like a topographic map.

• *Continue on the trail as it winds down to the cemetery. While the cemetery is closed to the public, you can stop by the gate for a peek inside.*

## Cemetery

Ever since Napoleon—who was king of Italy in the early 1800s—decreed that cemeteries were health risks, Cinque Terre's burial spots have been located outside the towns. The result: The dearly departed generally get first-class sea views. Each cemetery—with evocative photos and finely carved Carrara marble memorial reliefs—is worth a look. (While others are high above their towns, Manarola's—on this little low-altitude bluff—is the most easily accessible.)

In cemeteries like these, the real estate is similar to that for the living: The wealthy get their own piece of land (a **grave**), regular people get the equivalent of a condo (with their remains parked in a niche called a **loculus**), and the poor and forgotten end up tossed in a communal **ossuary.** Because of the tight space, spots are rented and a person's remains are allowed to stay only as long as their loved ones care enough to pay the rent. (No rent means you end up in the ossuary, making room for the newly dead with family willing to pay). Traditionally, locals make weekly visits to loved ones here, often bringing flowers. The rolling stepladder makes access to top-floor loculi easy.

• *From the cemetery follow the steep and narrow stairs (through the green gate immediately below the cemetery) and walk out onto the bluff.*

## Punta Bonfiglio

This point offers some of the most commanding **views** of the entire region. To find the best vantage point, walk out toward the water through a park (playground, drinking water, WC, and picnic benches). An inviting and recommended bar, **Nessun Dorma,** fills a long narrow terrace with people enjoying the vista.

Your Manarola finale is the bench at the tip of the point. (It's often congested with travelers who have taking a photo from this point on their Instagram bucket list.) Pause and take in the view.
• *From here steps go down and the path winds scenically back to the harbor, where we started.*

# Experiences in Manarola

### Hikes from Manarola

The coastal trail from Manarola—leading to **Corniglia** in one direction and to **Riomaggiore** in the other (the famous Via dell'Amore)—has been closed for years due to landslides. But you can still enjoy hiking from here.

One of my favorite easy hikes is to head up into the **vineyards above Manarola,** then drop down into the town cemetery, enjoying great views on the way. This route is outlined in my "Manarola Walk," earlier.

For a longer hike, consider taking the **high route to Corniglia via Volastra** (much easier if you ride the shuttle bus, rather than hike, up to Volastra). For details, see "Hiking the Cinque Terre" on page 346.

**Hiking Gear and Tips:** A wonderful resource for hikers, **Cinque Terre Trekking is** near the top of the main street (halfway up to the church). Christine and Nicola are generous with hiking advice, and fill their shop with all the hiking gear you may need: boots, clothes, walking sticks, maps, and more. If you're serious about hiking, stop in here to confirm your plans and to gear up (daily 11:00-13:00 & 14:00-19:00, shorter hours off-season, Via Discovolo 108, tel. 0187-920-834, www.cinqueterretrekking.com, info@cinqueterretrekking.com).

### Pesto Making

Entrepreneurial Simone at the Nessun Dorma cantina (perched next to the cemetery at the most scenic edge of Manarola) leads a pesto-making workshop for up to 30 people at 10:30, followed by lunch at noon. The setting is unforgettable, making pesto in the place of its origin is exciting, and you get to eat what you make plus a *tagliere* plate of cold cuts (€50/person, includes wine, no class on Tue, reserve ahead at www.nessundormacinqueterre.com or call mobile 340-888-4133, class cancelled in bad weather).

### Tours

**Arbaspàa** arranges vineyard wine tastings, cooking classes (6-person minimum), fishing trips, paragliding, rock climbing, and more

**CINQUE TERRE**

(see website for options and book in advance, www.arbaspaa.com; Explora office at Via Discovolo 204, tel. 0187-920-783).

### Boat Rides

To get to the dock and the boats that connect Manarola with the other Cinque Terre towns, find the steps to the left of the harbor view—they lead down to the ticket kiosk. Continue around the left side of the cliff (as you're facing the water) to catch the boats.

## Sleeping in Manarola

Manarola has some of the most appealing, well-run accommodations in the region (rivaling Monterosso's). Like the others, it also has plenty of private rooms (Airbnb has consumed the market). If you need breakfast, the recommended Bar Caffè Aristide is your best choice. Otherwise grab a coffee and croissant along the main drag.

### IN THE RESIDENTIAL ZONE ABOVE THE CHURCH

This area is a 10-minute steeply uphill hike from the train station— just huff up the main drag to the church. All are within a five-minute walk from there.

**$$$$ La Torretta** offers 14 trendy, upscale rooms (most with private deck) that cater to an elite clientele. Probably the most elegant retreat in the region, this peaceful refuge has all the comforts for those happy to pay, including a communal hot tub with a view. Guests enjoy a complimentary snack and glass of prosecco on arrival, an ample breakfast buffet, daily happy hour, and stocked minibars. Each chic room is distinct (top-end family suite, book several months in advance, closed Dec-March; on request, they'll pick you up at the station tunnel in a golf cart; on Piazza della Chiesa beside the bell tower at Vico Volto 20, tel. 0187-920-327, www.torrettas. com, torretta@cdh.it, Sonia).

**$$$ B&B Da Baranin,** with eight good rooms and one apartment, is a bit too pricey but has sleek modern style and a nice breakfast terrace (family rooms, air-con, Via Aldo Rollandi 29, tel. 0187-920-595, www.baranin.com, info@baranin.com, Sara).

**$$ Aria di Mare Rooms** rents four sunny, tidy, well-equipped rooms and two apartments a few steps beyond Trattoria dal Billy at the very top of town. While it's a steep hike up (high above the tourists), this is an excellent value. Three rooms have spacious terraces, and all can enjoy the knockout views from lounge chairs in the front yard (RS%, no breakfast but tea/coffee service in room, air-con, up the stairs at Via Aldo Rollandi 149, mobile 349-058-4155, www.ariadimare.info, info@ariadimare.info, Maurizio; ask at Billy's if no one's home).

## ON OR NEAR THE MAIN STREET

These options line up along (or near) the main street, between the harbor and the church. While in a less atmospheric area than the ones near the church, they're closer to the station—and therefore a bit handier for those packing heavy.

**$$$ Albergo Ca' d'Andrean** is quiet, comfortable, and chic. It has 10 big, sunny, tranquil rooms, with lots of tile. Public spaces artfully display family artifacts, and the cool garden oasis comes complete with lemon trees. If you don't mind stairs, consider one of their pricier top-floor rooms, with great terrace views (breakfast extra, air-con, up the hill at Via Discovolo 101, tel. 0187-920-040, www.cadandrean.it, info@cadandrean.it, Simone, Ariana, and Nicola).

**$$$ Marina Piccola,** a lesser value, offers 12 stylish rooms near the bustle of the square on the water (some with sea views). It's expensive and impersonal, but it's handy to the harbor area (air-con, Via Birolli 120, tel. 0187-920-770, www.hotelmarinapiccola. com, info@hotelmarinapiccola.com, Jessica and Micaela).

**$$ Da Paulin,** run by charming Donatella (who makes a mean *limoncello*) and Eraldo (the town's retired policeman), has three surprisingly modern, fresh, well-equipped, hotelesque rooms with a large and inviting common living room. They also rent three apartments (with fans). This fine value is at the bend in the main street, a five-minute hike above the train tracks (breakfast extra, air-con, Via Discovolo 126, mobile 334-389-4764, www.dapaulin. it, prenotazioni@dapaulin.it).

**$$ 5 Terre Pelagos** has eight pastel, shabby-chic rooms in an awkward building down a side lane. Built into the side of the mountain, the common room has a caveman ambience; some rooms come with view terraces (air-con, Via dei Mulini 26, mobile 335-122-6490, www.5terrepelagos.com, info@5terrepelagos.com, Edoardo).

## HIGH ABOVE MANAROLA, IN VOLASTRA

**$$ Hotel il Saraceno,** with seven spacious, utilitarian rooms, is a deal for drivers. Located above Manarola in the tiny town of Volastra (chock-full of vacationing Germans and Italians in summer), it's serene, clean, and right by the shuttle bus to Manarola (free parking, air-con, tel. 0187-760-081, www.thesaraceno.com, hotel@thesaraceno.com, friendly Antonella).

# Eating in Manarola

**Via Discovolo,** the main street climbing up through town from Piazza Capellini to the church, is lined with simple places and some small grocery stores where you can browse for a picnic. This strip—

CINQUE TERRE

and the short street between the elevated square and the harbor—also has several focaccia, pizza-by-the-slice, and fried-goodies carryout shops that are fine for a quick lunch. **Bar Caffè Aristide** is the busiest for breakfast. And the most enticing *gelateria* in town is **Sorbetteria 5 Terre Gelateria** (a couple of doors away).

Most of the town's (touristy) restaurants are concentrated between Piazza Capellini and the harbor. The Scorza family works hard at **$$ Trattoria il Porticciolo** (Thu-Tue 12:00-21:30, closed Wed, Via Birolli 92, tel. 0187-920-083) and at their contemporary **cafè**, cheap and fast, across the way. At the harborfront, **$$$ Marina Piccola** is famous for great views, lousy service, and overcharging naive tourists.

**$$$ Ristorante di Aristide,** right on Piazza Capellini, is run by three generations of hardworking women and offers a trendy atmosphere and a pleasant outdoor setting, with a view of budding soccer stars rather than harborfront glitz (Fri-Wed 12:00-22:30, closed Thu, Via Discovolo 290—you run right into it from the train tunnel, tel. 0187-920-000).

**$$ Bar Caffè Aristide,** next door, is a busy and modern little place. They have indoor and streetside seating, a lighter menu (see daily specials on blackboard), and breakfast options (Fri-Wed 8:00-11:30 & 12:00-16:00, closed Thu, same address and phone number; charming Elena, Mamma Monica, and Nonna Grazia). Sharing a serious kitchen with Ristorante di Aristide gives this little joint an extra dose of quality.

**$$$ Trattoria dal Billy,** the best restaurant in town, is in the residential zone high above the touristy action. Many find it's worth the climb for Edoardo and chef Enrico's homemade black pasta with seafood and squid ink, green pasta with artichokes, and homemade desserts. Their *antipasto misto di mare* comes with a dazzling array of seafood treats—each one perfectly executed. Billy's outdoor terraces offer commanding views over Manarola, while across the street an elegant, glassy dining room is carved into the rock. Either setting is perfect for a romantic candlelight meal. Reservations are a must (Fri-Wed 12:00-15:00 & 18:00-22:00, closed Thu, Via Aldo Rollandi 122, tel. 0187-920-628, www.trattoriabilly.com).

**$$ Nessun Dorma Cantina** is scenically perched under the cemetery and above the harbor. While they have no kitchen, Simone and his staff keep the masses happy with bruschetta, cold cuts, salads, and lots of drinks (Wed-Mon 12:00-21:00, closed Tue, Localita Punta Bonfiglio, mobile 340-888-4133). Simone runs a morning pesto-making class (described earlier, under "Experiences in Manarola").

# Riomaggiore

The most substantial town of the five, Riomaggiore is a disappointment from the train station. But walk through the tunnel next to the tracks, and you'll dis-
cover a more real and laid-back town than its more touristy neighbors. The main drag, while traffic-free, feels more urban than "village," and surrounding the harbor is a fascinating tangle of pastel homes leaning on each other like

drunken sailors. Despite Riomaggiore's workaday soul, the views back on its harbor from the breakwater—especially at sunset—are some of the region's prettiest.

## Orientation to Riomaggiore

### TOURIST INFORMATION
The **info point** in the station is for train info and tickets. The adjacent striped building, with a **national park shop** and info desk, is best for visitor information (both open daily 8:00-20:00, shorter hours off-season). Amy and Francesco at Riomaggiore Reservations or Ivo and Alberto at the recommended Bar Centrale are also good sources if you're in a pinch.

### ARRIVAL IN RIOMAGGIORE
**By Train:** Riomaggiore's train station is separated from the town center by a bluff. To get to the center, take the pedestrian tunnel that parallels the rail tunnel. You'll exit at the bottom of Via Colombo; most recommended accommodations are a short hike up this steep main drag. If you're staying near the top of town, you can catch the sporadic shuttle bus at the bottom of Via Colombo and ride it partway up.

For a scenic route into town (for those not carrying luggage), take my "Riomaggiore Walk," later.

**By Car:** Day-trippers park at the two-story pay-and-display lot above town (€5/hour, €35/day). If you're staying overnight, your hotel may have parking. It is easier to park at La Spezia's train station (see the next chapter) and ride the train in.

**Accommodations**
1 Edi's Rooms
2 Riomaggiore Reservations (Office) & Il Pescato Cucinato
3 Alla Marina Rooms; Enoteca & Ristorante Dau Cila
4 Casato Bapò
5 Il BoMa Rooms
6 La Dolce Vita Rooms

**Eateries & Other**
7 Rio Bistrot
8 Trattoria la Grotta
9 Bar Centrale & Gelateria
10 Primo Piatto & Vertical Lounge Bar
11 Tutti Fritti
12 Alimentari Franca
13 Bar Stazione
14 Bar & Vini A Piè de Mà
15 La Zorza Café & Bar O'Netto
16 La Conchiglia Café/Bar
17 Grocery (2)
18 Bag Storage
19 Launderette
20 Diving Center 5 Terre

## HELPFUL HINTS

**Baggage Storage:** You can check your bag at the casually run *deposito bagagli* office—it's behind the café/bar that's straight ahead as you exit the station (your fee supports the sports club, daily 9:00-12:00 & 14:00-19:00—confirm times, closed in winter).

**Services:** There are three public pay WCs in town: at the station and at the top and bottom of Via Colombo.

**Laundry:** A self-service launderette is on the main street (daily in summer 8:00-20:00, shorter hours off-season, Via Colombo 107).

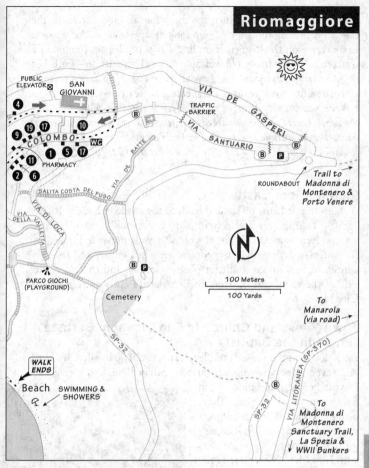

# Riomaggiore Walk

Here's an easy self-guided walk that loops up and over, taking the long and scenic way from the station into town. You'll enjoy some fine views before strolling down the main street to the harbor.

• *Start at the train station. (If you arrive by boat, cross beneath the tracks and take a left, then hike through the tunnel along the tracks to reach the station.)*

## Climb to the Top of Town

With your back to the sea and station, look left and notice the stairs climbing up just past the station building. These lead to the easy (but closed) trail to Manarola, the **Via dell'Amore.**

Hike up the main street. Listen to the paved-over creek under your feet and at the first turn see the waterfall (and turtles in the cage). Farther along is a close-up look at dry-stone rockery work. Look down on the historic train line. Soon you'll pass the top of a concrete elevator tower (an example of local ineptitude—built but never reliably functional and now abandoned). A bit farther, you'll arrive at a fine **viewpoint,** with spectacular sea views.

• *When you're ready to move on, hook left around the bluff; rounding the bend, ignore the steps marked* marina seacoast *(which lead to the harbor) and continue another five minutes along the main (level) path toward the church. Along the way, consider a steep little side trip to the castle.*

## Riomaggiore Castle

A steep stepped lane on the left leads to the castle (€2, daily 10:30-13:30). Taking this five-minute side trip, you'll find a humble art and heritage exhibit, the town's only well-preserved mural by Argentinian artist Silvio Benedetto, great sea views, and the tiny church of San Rocco (built for plague victims, and therefore outside of the town walls). More of Benedetto's murals are near the City Hall.

## Town Views and Church of San Giovanni Battista (St. John the Baptist)

Back down on the smooth and level lane, you'll go by the **City Hall** and several decaying **murals** (also by Silvio Benedetto), celebrat-

ing the heroic grape-pickers and fishermen of the region. These beautiful murals, with subjects modeled after real-life Riomaggiorians, glorify the nameless workers who constructed the nearly 300 million cubic feet of mortarless, dry-stone walls that run throughout the Cinque Terre. These walls give the region its characteristic *muri a secco* terracing for vineyards and olive groves. Unfortunately, the murals are not aging well.

Pause at the big **terrace** to enjoy the views of town and perhaps lots of local kids (the preschool is nearby). The major river of this region once ran through this valley, as implied by the name Riomaggiore (local dialect for "river" and "major"). As in the other Cinque Terre towns, the main street covers its *rio maggiore,* which carved the canyon now filled by the town's pastel high-rises. The romantic arched bridges that once connected the two sides have been replaced by a practical modern road. Other than that, the town is beautifully preserved.

The **church,** while rebuilt in 1870, was first established in 1340. It's dedicated to St. John the Baptist, the patron saint of Genoa, the maritime republic that once dominated the region.

• *Continue straight past the church and along the narrow lane leading down to the town's main street...*

## Via Colombo

Heading down the hill on Via Colombo, you'll pass several handy fast-food joints. (A hot political issue lately: too many fast-food joints and no place to sit.) Farther along, the big covered terrace on the right belongs to the recommended **Bar Centrale,** a popular hangout for international visitors day or night.

As you round the bend to the left, notice the old-timey pharmacy just above (on the right, with a good bakery underneath). On your left, at #199, peek into the **Il Pescato Cucinato** shop, where Laura fries up her husband Edoardo's fresh catch; grab a paper cone of deep-fried seafood as a snack. Where the road bends sharply right, notice the bench on your left (just before La Zorza Café)—the hangout for the town's old-timers, who keep a running commentary on the steady flow of people. Straight ahead, you can already see where this street will dead-end. The last shop on the left, **Alimentari Franca** (at #251), is a well-stocked grocery where you can gather the makings for a perfect picnic out on the harbor.

Where Via Colombo dead-ends, look right to see the tunnel leading back to the station. Look left to see two sets of stairs. Climb the "up" stairs to a parklike **square** (Piazza Vignaioli) built over the train tracks, which provides the children of the town a bit of level land on which to kick their soccer balls and to learn to ride a bike. The murals above, marking the town's middle school, celebrate the great-grandparents of these very children—the salt-of-the-earth locals who earned a humble living before the age of tourism. Riomaggiorians are proud that they are the only Cinque Terre town with their own middle school—in the other towns, kids are sent away to school much earlier.

• *Take the "down" stairs to the...*

## Harbor

This most picturesque corner of Riomaggiore features a tight cluster of buildings huddling nervously around a tiny square and harbor. Because Riomaggiore lacks the naturally protected harbor of Vernazza, when bad weather is expected, fishermen pull their boats up to the safety of the little square. This is quite an operation, so it's a team effort—the signal goes out, and anyone with a boat of their own helps move the whole fleet. Sometimes the fishermen are busy beaching their boats even on a bright, sunny day—an indication that they know something you don't.

A couple of recommended restaurants—with high prices and memorable seating—look down over the action. Head past them and up the walkway along the left side of the harbor, and enjoy the **views** back at the town's colorful pastel buildings, with the craggy coastline of the Cinque Terre just beyond. The best views are from up top, at the edge of the bluff. Below you, the breakwater (made of reject marble blocks from the famous nearby quarries of Carrara) curves out to sea, providing a bit of protection for the harbor. These rocks are popular with sunbathers by day and romantics and photographers at sunset.

For a peek at Riomaggiore's beach, continue around the bluff on this trail toward Punta di Montenero, the cape that defines the southern end of the Cinque Terre. As you walk, you'll pass the rugged boat landing and eventually run into Riomaggiore's uncomfortably rocky but still inviting beach *(spiaggia)*. Ponder how Europeans manage to look relaxed when lounging on football-sized "pebbles."

## Experiences in Riomaggiore

### Hikes from Riomaggiore

For an **easy walk** along the lip of the one-time river ravine, take **Via di Loca,** which veers off the main drag at the top of town (directly across from the stairs at the upper end of Via Colombo). This leads in just a few minutes to the town playground *(parco giochi),* benches, neighborhood pea patches, and pleasant views over town (especially at sunset). There's also a steep staircase from here up to the town cemetery; from there, an even steeper

trail runs all the way up to the town's sanctuary (or see the easier alternative—described next).

For a **scenic one-hour trail** that rises from Riomaggiore to the 14th-century **Madonna di Montenero sanctuary,** high above the town, take the main road inland until you see signs at the roundabout at the top of town; or ride the shuttle bus 12 minutes from the town center to the sanctuary trail, then walk uphill another 20 minutes (great picnic spot up top).

### Beach

Riomaggiore's rugged and tiny "beach" is rocky, but it's clean and peaceful. It's just around the bluff from the harbor, past the boat landing—to find it, see the end of my self-guided walk, above. There's a shower here in the summer, and another closer to town by the boat landing—where many enjoy sunning on and jumping from the rocks.

### Kayaks and Water Sports

**Diving Center 5 Terre** rents kayaks as well as snorkeling and scuba equipment; they also lead guided dives of the protected marine waters nearby (daily May-Sept 9:00-18:00, open only in good weather, likely weekends only in shoulder season, office down the stairs and under the tracks on Via San Giacomo, tel. 0187-920-011, www.5terrediving.it).

## Nightlife in Riomaggiore

With a youthful spirit and lively evening bustle, Riomaggiore has an enjoyable night scene. Stroll the main drag, scope out these listings (serving €6-8 cocktails), and find the one that appeals. Several of these places have full menus if you want to eat.

**Bar Centrale,** run by sociable Ivo, Alberto, and the gang, offers "nightlife" any time of day—it's a magnet for tourists. Ivo, who lived in the Bay Area, fills his bar with San Franciscan rock and a fun-loving vibe; it feels a little like the village's living room (great mojitos, daily 7:30-late, Via Colombo 144).

**Bar & Vini A Piè de Mà,** above the train station at the now closed Via dell'Amore trailhead, has piles of charm, frequent music, and stays open until midnight from June through September.

**More Bars and Cafés:** Near the bottom of Via Colombo, facing each other, are the noisy **La Zorza Café** (appealing to international tourists with thumping music and freestyle bartender) and the classier **Bar O'Netto** (geared more for young locals, with a mellower vibe and nice outdoor seating). Higher up on Via Colombo (at #76), **Vertical Lounge Bar** has a lively and loose ambience, light food (a good *aperitivo* buffet at happy-hour time), and a fine people-watching perch near the top of the promenade zone. And at sunset, you can't beat **La Conchiglia**—the simple café/bar on the bluff overlooking the harbor—a perfect location for watching the sun disappear into the Ligurian Sea and the lights of Monterosso twinkling on the horizon.

## Sleeping in Riomaggiore

Riomaggiore has few hotels worth your time; I recommend staying in one of the town's many private rooms for rent. Very few private rooms include breakfast.

## ROOM-BOOKING SERVICES

A couple of room-booking agencies—with relatively predictable office hours, English-speaking staff, and email addresses—are next to each other on Via Colombo. Each manages a corral of local rooms for rent; the quality and specific amenities can vary wildly, so get a complete picture of the room before you commit. It's smart to settle up the day before you leave in case they're closed when you need to depart. Expect lots of stairs—ask how many when you book.

**$$ Edi's Rooms** manages four double rooms and eight apartments. You pay extra for views (most rooms with air-con, office open daily in summer 9:00-13:00 & 14:00-19:30, closed Nov-Feb, reception at Via Colombo 111, tel. 0187-920-325, www.appartamenticinqueterre.net, edi-vesigna@iol.it).

**$ Riomaggiore Reservations,** run with care by American expat Amy and her Italian husband, Francesco, offers six rooms and four apartments (RS%, cash only, reception open daily 9:00-13:00 & 14:00-17:00 in season, air-con, Via Colombo 181, tel. 0187-760-575, www.riomaggiorereservations.com, info@riomaggiorereservations.com). They're a great resource for info on hiking and other activities.

## ROOMS FOR RENT *(AFFITTACAMERE)*

Another option is to book directly with someone who rents just a few rooms of their own.

**$$ Alla Marina** is Riomaggiore's best value, with five rooms—most with sea views—at the top of one of the tall, skinny buildings that rise up from the harbor. The furnishings are a combination of modern and nautical, and friendly brothers Sandro and Andrea take pride in running a tight ship. They also rent four apartments (RS%—free breakfast at nearby café, air-con, pay parking, office open 9:00-18:00, Via San Giacomo 61—ask about the easier back-door entrance, mobile 328-013-4077, www.allamarina.com, info@allamarina.com). They also rent several rooms in other parts of town.

**$$ Casato Bapò** has three airy, spacious rooms with unobstructed views at the top of town near the Church of San Giovanni. They're on the fourth floor, but accessible via the public elevator nearby (Via Pecunia 116, mobile 340-705-6723, www.casatobapo.com, casatobapo@gmail.com, Sabrina).

**$$ Il BoMa**—named for the owners, American Maddy and her Italian husband, Bombetta, has three old-fashioned rooms along the main drag (one cheaper room with private bath down the hall, air-con, up three flights at Via Colombo 99, tel. 0187-920-395, mobile 320-0748826, www.ilboma.itcom, info@ilboma.it). They also rent two nearby apartments.

**$$ La Dolce Vita** offers six modern, good-value rooms on the main drag, plus two apartments elsewhere in town (some with air-con, no breakfast, open daily 9:30-19:30—if they're closed, they're full; Via Colombo 167, tel. 0187-920-935, agonatal@libero.it, helpful Giacomo and Simone).

# Eating in Riomaggiore

## ON THE HARBOR

Harborfront dining comes with slightly higher prices, a dressy ambience, and glorious views. These two eateries share the same owner; the first one's menu is more traditionally Italian, while the second is a bit more modern.

**$$$$ Enoteca & Ristorante Dau Cila** (pronounced "dow CHEE-lah") is decked out like a black-and-white movie set in an old boat shed with extra tables outside on a rustic deck over dinghies. Try their antipasto specialty of several seafood appetizers (dinner only) and listen to the waves lapping at the harbor below (cheaper lunch menu with salads and *bruschette,* daily 12:00-24:00, Via San Giacomo 65, tel. 0187-760-032, Niccolo).

**$$$$ Rio Bistrot,** small and intimate at the top of the harbor, tries to jazz up its Ligurian cuisine with international influences. You can order à la carte from the short but well-designed menu, or try their €39 tasting *menu* (simpler and cheaper lunch menu, daily 12:00-16:00 & 18:00-22:00, Via San Giacomo 46, tel. 0187-920-616, Manuel).

## ON THE MAIN STREET, VIA COLOMBO

**$$ Trattoria la Grotta,** right in the town center (with no view), has a passion for anchovies and mussels. You'll enjoy reliably good food surrounded by historical photos and wonderful stonework in a dramatic, dressy, cave-like setting (daily 12:00-14:30 & 17:30-22:30, closed Wed in winter, Via Colombo 247, tel. 0187-920-187).

**$$ Bar Centrale** is a casual, family-friendly place for hamburgers, salads, and pesto. They also have a *gelateria* on site (long hours daily, see listing earlier, under "Nightlife in Riomaggiore").

**Light Meals:** Various handy carryout eateries along the main drag offer good lunches or snacks. **$ Primo Piatto,** at the top of town, offers takeaway handmade pastas and sauces, cooked to order on the spot. It's cheap and delicious (Wed-Mon 10:30-19:30 or later, closed Tue, Via Colombo 72, Roberta). For deep-fried seafood in a paper cone, **$ Il Pescato Cucinato** is where Edoardo fishes and his wife, Laura, fries (chalkboard out front explains what's fresh, daily 11:20-20:30, near the bottom of Via Colombo at #199). A few doors away, **$ Tutti Fritti** serves only fried nibbles, including fish (daily 10:00-21:00, Via Colombo 161, Andrea and Isabella).

**Picnics:** Groceries and delis lining Via Colombo sell food to-go for a picnic at the harbor or beach. **Co-op** grocery stores (several on the main drag) have the best prices. For a more appetizing selection and good service, head to **Alimentari Franca,** on the main street by the train-station tunnel (daily 8:00-20:00, Via Colombo 251).

**Breakfast:** Most of my recommended accommodations don't serve breakfast—and those that do often simply leave a coffee kettle and some basic continental breakfast fixings in your room. For eggs or a good croissant-and-espresso fix, drop by **Bar Centrale** (described earlier); or **Bar Stazione,** at the train station.

## NEAR THE TRAIN STATION
**$$ Bar & Vini A Piè de Mà,** at the trailhead on the Manarola end of town, is good for a scenic light bite or quiet drink at night. The

bar, with great outdoor seating, is self-service: Head into the bar to place your order, then bring it out to your preferred perch (daily 10:00-20:00, June-Sept until 24:00, closed Mon-Tue off-season, tel. 0187-921-037). Enjoy a meal on its dramatically situated terrace for an indelible Cinque Terre memory.

# RIVIERA TOWNS

*Levanto • Sestri Levante • Santa Margherita Ligure •*
*Portofino • Porto Venere • La Spezia*

The Cinque Terre is tops, but there's much more to the Italian Riviera. To the north of the Cinque Terre is a trio of beach towns: Levanto, the northern gateway to the Cinque Terre; Sestri Levante, stunningly situated on a narrow peninsula flanked by two beaches; and Santa Margherita Ligure, a thriving city with an active waterfront and easy connections to yacht-happy Portofino. At the south end of the Cinque Terre is the pretty resort of Porto Venere and the region's gritty transit hub, La Spezia.

The best of these towns—the high-end yin to the Cinque Terre's ramshackle yang—can be user-friendly home bases for day trips along the Riviera coast. But they are also worth visiting in their own right. After exploring the villages and trails of the Cinque Terre, these Riviera towns feel like a return to civilization.

Riviera hotels aren't necessarily cheaper than the Cinque Terre, but they are more likely to have space. High season here is roughly May through September, peaking in July and August. Some hotels close in winter.

**Home Bases:** Levanto, Sestri Levante, and Santa Margherita Ligure are practical home bases for drivers wanting to park at their hotel and side-trip to the Cinque Terre by train, or for those who want modern hotels with predictable resort amenities. (They're also worth a look if you find the Cinque Terre booked up.)

Levanto—just minutes north of Monterosso by train—is the handiest. Sestri Levante is a bit farther away with a little less train service. Santa Margherita Ligure is the most distant and often requires a transfer to the Cinque Terre, but the town compensates by being the most appealing—and it gives you easy access to posh

## Riviera Towns at a Glance

### North of the Cinque Terre

▲**Levanto** Town popular with surfers and families for its long beach; has speedy trains to the Cinque Terre, and offers an easy, level hike (or bike ride) to the sleepy villages of **Bonassola,** and farther on, **Framura.** See page 423.

▲**Sestri Levante** Charming town on a peninsula flanked by two crescent beaches. See page 432.

▲▲**Santa Margherita Ligure** Easygoing old-school resort town with just enough urban bustle, a handful of sights, and close proximity to Portofino. See page 437.

▲**Portofino** Yacht-harbor resort with grand scenery and easy connections (by boat, bus, or on foot) from Santa Margherita Ligure. See page 448.

### South of the Cinque Terre

▲▲**Porto Venere** Enchanting seafront village perfect for a scenic day trip (by boat or bus). See page 454.

**La Spezia** Beachless transportation hub, with trains and boats to the Cinque Terre and buses and boats to Porto Venere. See page 457.

Portofino. Porto Venere is better as a day trip, and La Spezia is more functional than appealing, although either can serve in a pinch.

If you home-base near the Cinque Terre, keep in mind that you'll be competing with other day-trippers for space on prime midday trains to and from the Cinque Terre. Turn this problem into an advantage: Enjoy your home-base town during the day, then head into the Cinque Terre in the late afternoon for untrampled charm, a romantic dinner, and a late train back.

# North of the Cinque Terre

When most people imagine the "Italian Riviera," they're thinking of the shimmering resort towns north of the Cinque Terre. Stately Old World hotels loom over crowded pebble beaches with rentable umbrellas. Fastidiously landscaped parks and promenades are jammed with more Italian visitors than American tourists. These towns are perfect for day-tripping—or even an overnight.

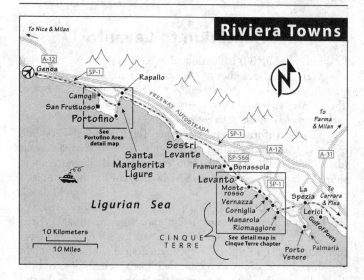

**Riviera Towns**

# Levanto

Graced with a long, sandy beach, Levanto (LEH-vahn-toh) is packed in summer and popular with families and surfers. The rest of the year, it's just a small, sleepy town with kids playing in the square and locals whizzing around on bicycles. Although not as charming as the Cinque Terre, it enjoys fewer crowds, more varied hotel and dining options, and quick connections to the Cinque Terre (4 minutes to Monterosso by train, continuing to the rest of the Cinque Terre villages on the same line).

This beach town isn't the "real" Cinque Terre, but it can be a friendly home base for budget travelers, beach bums, or families with kids who like to bike or play on the beach. (It has a high number of family rooms and large, affordable apartments with kitchenettes.) From Levanto, you can hop a train or boat to the Cinque Terre towns and beyond; take the no-wimps-allowed hike to Monterosso (3.5 hours); or bike or stroll on a delightful, level path to the nearby, uncrowded beach village of Bonassola, and farther on, smaller Framura.

**RIVIERA TOWNS**

# Orientation to Levanto

Levanto (pop. 5,400) is dominated by an uninspiring new town, a regular grid street plan of five-story apartment buildings that stretches from the train station down to the broad, curving beach. The sleepy, twisty old town—bisected by a modern street—is tucked up against the adjacent hill.

**Tourist Information:** A Cinque Terre National Park info center is at the train station. The helpful TI is on Piazza Cavour (daily 9:00-13:00 & 15:00-18:00 except closed Sun afternoon, shorter hours off-season, tel. 0187-808-125, www.visitlevanto.it).

## ARRIVAL IN LEVANTO

**By Train:** From the train station (no baggage storage), head through the parking lot and down the stairs, turn right, and cross the bridge onto Corso Roma—the main drag. The beach is straight ahead, and most of my recommended hotels, restaurants, and the TI are in the grid of streets to your left. You can walk from the station to most of my recommended places in about 10 minutes.

**By Car:** If your hotel doesn't offer parking—or if you're not sleeping here—you have a couple of good alternatives. The lots surrounding the **train station** are affordable and handy for hopping a train to the Cinque Terre towns. If you're heading for the beach, the parking lot there is handy but more expensive.

## HELPFUL HINTS

**Markets:** Levanto's modern covered *mercato*, which sells produce and fish, is on Via XXV Aprile, between the train station and the beach (daily 7:30-13:00). On Wednesday morning, an **open-air market** with clothes, shoes, and housewares fills the street in front of the *mercato*.

**Laundry:** A **self-service launderette** stuffed with snack-and-drink vending machines is at Piazza Staglieno 38, facing an inviting park (daily 24 hours, mobile 338-701-6341). Another self-service place, **Speedy Wash,** is at Via Garibaldi 32 (daily 8:00-22:00, mobile 338-701-6341).

**Bike Rental:** Relatively flat Levanto, with light traffic, is a great bike town—and the ride to nearby Bonassola and Framura is easy and delightful. Try **Cicli Raso** (€10-20/day depending on bike, daily 9:30-12:30 & 15:30-19:00, closed Sun Nov-April, Via Garibaldi 63, tel. 0187-802-511) or the **Sensafreni Bike Shop,** convenient to the beach boardwalk, with well-maintained bikes (€5/hour, €8/half-day, €15/day, more for ebikes, daily 9:00-13:00 & 16:00-19:30, Piazza del Popolo 1, tel. 0187-807-128).

**Sports Rentals:** Right on the beach, **Rosa dei Venti** rents kayaks,

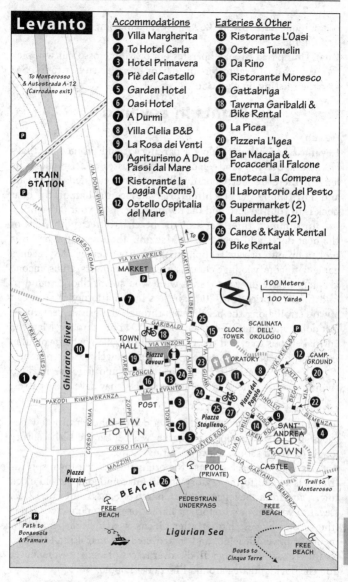

# Levanto

### Accommodations
1. Villa Margherita
2. To Hotel Carla
3. Hotel Primavera
4. Piè del Castello
5. Garden Hotel
6. Oasi Hotel
7. A Durmì
8. Villa Clelia B&B
9. La Rosa dei Venti
10. Agriturismo A Due Passi dal Mare
11. Ristorante la Loggia (Rooms)
12. Ostello Ospitalia del Mare

### Eateries & Other
13. Ristorante L'Oasi
14. Osteria Tumelin
15. Da Rino
16. Ristorante Moresco
17. Gattabriga
18. Taverna Garibaldi & Bike Rental
19. La Picea
20. Pizzeria L'Igea
21. Bar Macaja & Focacceria il Falcone
22. Enoteca La Compera
23. Il Laboratorio del Pesto
24. Supermarket (2)
25. Launderette (2)
26. Canoe & Kayak Rental
27. Bike Rental

canoes, surfboards, and windsurfing equipment (mobile 329-451-1981, www.levantorosadeiventi.it, Marco).

**Electric Bike Tours: Ebikein** offers a variety of guided tours on electric bikes—giving you a helpful boost on the hills. Options include a four-hour loop around the Bay of Levanto (€58) and a four-hour pedal up to some of the sanctuaries above the

Cinque Terre towns (€69, www.ebikein.com, mobile 334-190-0496).

**Boat Tours: Sea Breeze** operates out of Monterosso but will pick you up in Levanto for full-day or *aperitivo* sunset tours. See their listing on page 366.

# Sights in Levanto

### Beach

Levanto's beach hides below a parking lot and promenade that's elevated above the sand—look for underpasses or stairs along its length. There are pretty boardwalks up on the elevated promenade and down along the beachfront. As you face the harbor, the boat dock is to your far left, and the diving center is to your far right.

In summer, three parts of the beach are free: both sides of the boat dock, and near Piazza Mazzini. The rest of the beach is broken up into private sections that you pay to enter. Pay beaches come with comfy lounge chairs, bar service, showers, and someone keeping an eye on your things while you swim. Shop around to find the best price (€15-20/chair, less in the afternoon). You can always stroll along the beach, even through the private sections—just don't sit down. Off-season, roughly October through May, the entire beach is free, and you can lay your towel anywhere you like. Ask your hotel for towels; most have beach towels to loan or rent.

The city's seaside pool is privately run and is for serious lap swimmers only. Check with your hotel; they may have entry passes.

### Old Town

The old town clusters around Piazza del Popolo. Until a few decades ago, the town's open-air market was held at the 13th-century loggia (covered set of archways) in the square.

Explore the back streets. The original medieval town spreads from Via Guani to the oratory of San Giacomo and the old clock tower, and from the loggia to the Church of Sant'Andrea (c. 1212). Levanto was once an important harbor of the Republic of Genoa (the second biggest harbor after Genoa itself); from here, shipments of olive oil, wine, and the coveted red marble called rosso levanto set sail. You can still discover traces of ancient warehouses and the dockland area around Piazza del Popolo.

### ▲Hike to Monterosso

This 3.5-hour hike from Levanto to Monterosso is strenuous at the beginning and end but easier in the middle (for details, see page 352). To begin in Levanto, start on Piazza del Popolo, and head uphill to the striped Church of Sant'Andrea. From the church courtyard, follow the sign to the *castello* (a private residence), go under the stone arch, and continue uphill. From here, take trail

SVA (following signs toward Punta Mesco, the rugged tip of the peninsula), then drop steeply down into Monterosso. (If you have knee issues, consider starting in Monterosso instead.)

### ▲Hike or Bike to Bonassola (and Framura)

Tucked just off the main train line on a cove north of Levanto, the small beach resort of Bonassola (boh-nah-SOH-lah, pop.

950) is a peaceful little eddy. As far as Riviera beach resorts go, this is a jewel. With a low-key vibe, a tidy grid street plan that feels almost French, and a picturesque dark-sand beach hemmed in by jagged bluffs, Bonassola is a fine alternative to the region's other beaches. And the next best thing to a beach day in Bonassola is getting there: A level, easy, rails-to-trails path cuts through the mountain from Levanto—enjoyable by foot, but even better by bike.

**Levanto to Bonassola:** Local **trains** run between Levanto and Bonassola (hourly, 3 minutes, confirm your train will stop in Bonassola). But I'd rather take the **promenade.** At the northern end of Levanto's beachfront road/parking lot, you'll find a level, roughly 1.5-mile path neatly divided into bike and pedestrian lanes. Most of the route is through well-lit former train tunnels, with brief breaks overlooking the sea (and hikes down to secluded beaches). The walk takes about 30 minutes, with long stretches through cool tunnels; by bike, it's less than 10 minutes.

**Visiting Bonassola:** The town itself—with manicured promenades and piazzas—is worth exploring. **$$ Caffè delle Rose,** facing the town's elevated road (at Via Fratelli Rezzano 22), has good gelato, food, and drinks. Several *foccacerie* and other eateries cluster at the far end of town.

The beach is separated from the town center by the elevated road (shared by bicyclists, walkers, and a parking lot). The inviting **beach** has mostly private sections, with a few free public areas.

For a scenic **walk/hike,** head to the far (north) end of the beach, where a promenade snakes along the base of the cliff (with rocky perches for sunbathing and swimming). For higher views, find the stairs near the flagpole, and follow the steps up on the right side of the yellow church. Popping out at the top, turn left along the scenic, private road as it curls around the top of the bay, with great views back on the town and beach; the path ends at the blocky little Madonnina della Punta chapel.

**Bonassola to Framura** (best for bicyclists): From Bonassola, the promenade continues another 1.5 miles to the town of **Framura**—a settlement made up of five medieval hamlets that rise up from the seafront to the hilltop (pop. 750). Because this part of the route is almost entirely through tunnels, it's boring for walkers—but quick for bikers. The trail ends overlook-

ing Framura's rocky little harbor and near its train station (there's no direct access to the station—don't count on taking your bike back on the train).

**Visiting Framura:** Park your bike at the trailhead and hike down to the harbor, cross under the train tracks, and emerge near the station and the start of the scenic Via del Mare path (basic café at trailhead). This easy promenade takes you north along a cliff face in 10 minutes to two small, pristine gravel beaches that are free and uncrowded.

Hikers can walk the panoramic but steep trail that connects the five hamlets, which are sprinkled with medieval watchtowers, churches, and washhouses. To avoid the uphill climb, ride the summer shuttle to any of the five towns and walk down (shuttles run hourly, timed to the arrival of trains from the Cinque Terre). The welcoming TI at the Framura station has maps and advice (mobile 339-543-3923, www.framuraturismo.it).

## Sleeping in Levanto

**$$$ Villa Margherita,** in a 1906 Art Nouveau building, is across the river and a bit uphill (about a 10-minute walk from the town center or train station), but the shaded view gardens, 11 characteristic colorfully tiled rooms, and tranquility are worth the walk (family rooms, deluxe apartment, air-con, elevator one flight up from street level, free parking, Via Trento e Trieste 31, tel. 0187-807-212, mobile 328-842-6934, www.villamargherita.net, info@villamargherita.net, Paola).

**$$$ Hotel Carla** sits in a humdrum residential zone, about 10 minutes from the beach and the station. Its 30 rooms come with surprising contemporary style—most have balconies, and all are decorated in soothing, neutral colors (RS%, family rooms, air-con, elevator, free loaner bikes, Via Martiri della Libertà 28, tel. 0187-808-275, www.carlahotel.com, info@carlahotel.com).

**$$$ Hotel Primavera** is homey and family-run, with 17 colorful rooms—10 with balconies (but no views)—just a block from the beach (family rooms, request a quiet room off the street, includes hearty breakfast buffet, air-con, pay private parking, free loaner bikes, Via Cairoli 5, tel. 0187-808-023, www.primaverahotel.com, info@primaverahotel.com; friendly Carlo, cheerful Daniela, and daughters Giuditta and Gloria).

**$$$ Piè del Castello** is just above the campground, right on the Levanto-Monterosso trail. Andrea and his wife rent three double rooms, each with a patio and access to a sprawling garden with views of the ancient city wall and the Church of Sant'Andrea. Hikers will appreciate the location and Andrea's knowledge of area trails (air-con, fridge, ping-pong table, free parking, Via Guido Semenza 2, tel. 366-1467-7886, www.piedelcastello.com, info@piedelcastello.com).

**$$$ Garden Hotel** offers 17 functional, businesslike, modern rooms (all with balconies but no views) on the first floor of an apartment building. While it's a lesser value, you're paying for proximity to the beach—it's just across the street (a more expensive fifth-floor room has sea views and a terrace, closed Nov-mid-March, air-con, elevator, free parking but not on-site, loaner bikes, Corso Italia 6, tel. 0187-808-173, www.nuovogarden.com, info@nuovogarden.com, Davide and Damiano).

**$$ Oasi Hotel,** well-run by Silvia, has 14 rooms in a cozy small hotel behind the market hall. Some rooms have balconies, others have direct access to the garden, and a few have neither but are larger—request your choice when you reserve (RS%, air-con, elevator, parking extra, Via Ferraro, tel. 0187-807-356, www.oasihotel.eu, info@oasihotel.eu, Saverio).

**$$ A Durmì** is a happy little guesthouse owned by lovely Graziella, Gianni, and their two daughters, Elisa and Chiara. Their sunny patios, green leafy gardens, six immaculate beach bungalow-type rooms, and five sunlit apartments make this a welcoming place to stay (breakfast extra, family rooms, air-con, bar, pay parking, Via D. Viviani 12, tel. 0187-800-823, mobile 349-105-6016, www.adurmi.it, info@adurmi.it).

**$$ Villa Clelia B&B** offers five basic rooms (named for the winds—*scirocco, maestrale,* and so on) with minifridges and terraces. The rooms surround a garden courtyard just a short walk up from the sea (minimal in-room breakfast, air-con, free parking; with the old town's loggia on your left, it's straight ahead at Piazza da Passano 1; tel. 0187-808-195, mobile 329-379-4859, www.villaclelia.it, info@villaclelia.it). They also rent apartments in the center that economically sleep up to five.

**$$ La Rosa dei Venti** is an *affittacamere* just a couple of blocks from the beach, in the old town. Enthusiastic Rosanna and her son Marco rent five old-fashioned, overpriced rooms with dark hardwood floors, comfy rugs, and glittery seashore decor (air-con, pay parking, from Piazza del Popolo take the lane next to Osteria Tumelin to Via della Compera, tel. 0187-808-165, Marco's mobile 328-742-8268, www.larosadeiventilevanto.com, info@ larosadeiventilevanto.com).

**$ Agriturismo A Due Passi dal Mare** is an in-town oasis, just a five-minute walk from the beach or the train station. Friendly Francesca and husband Maurizio rent four crisp, quiet rooms—with sizable bathrooms—in the 1920s home built by her grandfather; their back garden is open to guests (free on-site parking, closed Jan-Feb, right on the main drag at Corso Roma 37, tel. 0187-809-177, mobile 338-960-1537, www.a2passidalmare.com, info@a2passidalmare.com).

**$ Ristorante la Loggia** has eight cozy, older, and cheap rooms, perched above the old loggia on Piazza del Popolo (request balcony, quieter rooms in back, two basic side-by-side apartments great for families of 4-8, lots of stairs, air-con, free parking, reception open 9:00-23:00, Piazza del Popolo 7, tel. 0187-808-107, mobile 335-641-7701, www.loggialevanto.com, laloggialaloggia@gmail.com, Alessandro). They also have a recommended restaurant.

**Hostel: ¢ Ostello Ospitalia del Mare,** a budget gem, is run by the city tourist association. It has 70 basic beds, airy rooms, an elevator, and a terrace in a well-renovated medieval palazzo a few steps from the old town (all ages, dorms with private bath, private rooms, includes breakfast, self-service laundry, no curfew or lockout; office open daily April-Oct 8:00-12:30 & 16:00-19:30, until 23:00 weekend nights; may close Nov-March, Via San Nicolò 1, tel. 0187-802-562, www.ospitalialevanto.com, info@ ospitalialevanto.com).

## Eating in Levanto

**$$$$ Ristorante L'Oasi**—spacious, bright, and with a garden feel—is the place for quality fish and seafood in Levanto. Family run, with Claudio in the kitchen and Lella supervising the dining room, this is a polished setting for enjoying fresh tuna tartare, marinated anchovies, and grilled swordfish. If you really want to treat yourself, order a whole fish baked under salt (daily 12:30-14:30 & 19:00-22:30, closed Wed Sept-June, Piazza Cavour, tel. 0187-800-856).

**$$$ Osteria Tumelin** has a dressy ambience in its elegant dining room, a casual covered terrace out front, and a wide selection of fresh seafood. Reservations are smart on weekends or to dine outside. Check out the aquarium containing giant lobster and moray eels in the first dining room on the right (daily 12:00-14:30 & 19:00-22:30, closed Thu Oct-May, Via D. Grillo 32, across the square from the loggia, tel. 0187-808-379, www.tumelin.it).

**$$ Da Rino,** a small trattoria on a quiet pedestrian lane, dishes up reasonably priced seafood, meat, and homemade Ligurian specialties. Consider the grilled *totani* (squid), *pansotti con salsa di noci* (ravioli with walnut sauce), and *trofie al pesto* (pasta with pesto sauce). Dine indoors or at one of the outdoor tables (Wed-Mon 19:00-22:00, closed Tue, Via Garibaldi 10, tel. 0187-813-475).

**$$ Ristorante la Loggia,** a Levanto standby, has been dishing up classic Ligurian cuisine for more than 50 years. Choose between the homey, wood-paneled dining room with nooks and crannies or the little terrace overlooking the square (daily 12:30-14:00 & 19:00-22:00, closed Nov-Feb, Piazza del Popolo 7, tel. 0187-808-107). They also rent rooms (see previous page).

**$$$ Ristorante Moresco** serves large portions of pasta and seafood at reasonable prices in a vaulted, candlelit room decorated with Moorish-style frescoes (daily 12:00-14:00 & 19:00-21:00, reservations appreciated, Via Jacopo 24, tel. 0187-807-253, busy Roberto and Francesca).

**$$ Gattabriga** hides out on a back lane behind Piazza del Popolo with a contemporary look; an updated and well-priced menu of pastas, seafood, and meats; and friendly service (Tue-Sun 19:00-21:30, closed Mon, Via Guani 47, tel. 366-527-3582).

**$$ Taverna Garibaldi,** a comfy good-value place on the town's most characteristic street, serves focaccia with various toppings, made-to-order *farinata* (savory chickpea crêpe), salads, and more than 30 types of pizza (Fri-Wed 19:00-22:00, closed Thu, Via Garibaldi 57, tel. 0187-808-098).

**$$ La Picea** offers wood-fired pizzas and a large selection of beers to-go, or you can dine at one of their few small tables (Tue-Sun 12:00-14:00 & 19:00-24:00 or until they use up their pizza dough, closed Mon, just off Piazza Cavour at Via della Concia 18, tel. 0187-802-063).

**$$ Pizzeria L'Igea,** usually packed with locals, is tucked just inside the Campeggio Acquadolce campground, 50 yards past the hostel. It's a favorite among locals who know you don't have to be a camper to enjoy freshly made, budget-conscious pizza and pasta in their bright dining hall. Their specialty is *gattafin*—deep-fried herb-stuffed ravioli. Come early or be prepared to wait, even for takeout (daily 12:00-14:30 & 18:45-22:30, Via Guido Semenza 5, tel. 0187-807-293).

**$-$$ Bar Macaja,** decorated in shabby chic beach-style, is a tiny place with a big happy vibe. Stop in for a continental breakfast, espresso or a drink, *panini,* and local seafood—including anchovies prepared six ways (Fri-Wed 7:00-23:00, closed Thu, just up from the beach at Via Cairoli 25, mobile 349-844-8424).

**$ Enoteca La Compera** offers a quiet respite on a hidden courtyard across the way from the campground. It's casual and friendly, serving a wide variety of *panini* that you can buy to-go, as well as plenty of wine, including affordable tastings, called *degustazione* (Tue-Sun 10:00-20:00, closed Mon, follow the red-brick road—under the stone arch—to Piazza della Compera 3, mobile 334-712-8517).

**Picnics and Bites on the Go:** *Focaccerie, rosticcerie,* and delis with takeout pasta abound on Via Dante Alighieri. **$ Focacceria il Falcone** has a great selection of focaccia with different toppings (daily 9:30-22:00, shorter hours off-season, Via Cairoli 19, tel. 0187-807-370). For more picnic options, try the *mercato* (see "Helpful Hints," earlier). It's fun to grab a crusty loaf of bread, then pair it with a pot of freshly made Genovese pesto and other gifty edibles from **$ Il Laboratorio del Pesto** (daily, Via Dante 14).

There are two **Crai supermarkets** (daily 8:00-20:00 except closed for lunch on Sun): One is just off Piazza Cavour at Via del Municipio 5; the other is nearby on Piazza Staglieno. For a shaded setting, lay out your spread on a bench in the grassy park at this piazza. Another fine picnic spot is Piazza Cristoforo Colombo, located east of the swimming pool, with benches and sea views.

## Levanto Connections

To get to the Cinque Terre from Levanto, you can take the **train** (3-4/hour, 4 minutes to Monterosso). A slower, more scenic option is the **boat,** which stops at every Cinque Terre town (except Corniglia) before heading to Porto Venere (3/day in high season, price depends on distance traveled—or get a €35 all-day hop-on, hop-off ticket; only one return boat daily from Porto Venere—departs at about 16:30; get latest boat schedule and price sheet at TI or boat dock or check website, tel. 0187-732-987, www.navigazionegolfodeipoeti.it).

# Sestri Levante

Sestri Levante (SEH-stree leh-VAHN-teh) is squeezed as skinny as a hot dog between its two beaches. The pedestrian-friendly Via XXV Aprile, which runs down the middle of the peninsula, is lined with shops that sell takeout pizza, pastries, and beach paraphernalia.

Hans Christian Andersen enjoyed his visit here in the mid-1800s, writing, "What a fabulous evening I spent in Sestri Levante!" One of the bays—Baia delle Favole—is named in his honor (*favole* means "fairy tale"). The small mermaid curled on the edge of the fountain behind the TI is another nod to the beloved Danish storyteller.

# Orientation to Sestri Levante

Sestri Levante (pop. 18,000) is dominated by its big, dull modern town in front of the train station. But don't be discouraged—the old-town peninsula, a 10-minute walk away, has charm to spare.

**Tourist Information:** It's at Corso Colombo 50, on the ground floor of Palazzo Fascie, the town's cultural center (daily 9:00-13:00 & 14:00-17:00, shorter hours off-season, tel. 0185-478-530, www.sestri-levante.net). They can tell you about the summer bike-sharing program (€8/5 hours) and direct you to the trail (south of town) for a 1.5-hour hike (each way) to the scenic Punta Manara promontory.

**Arrival in Sestri Levante:** From the train station (no baggage storage), head straight out and across the piazza to go down the arcaded Via Roma. (If you need picnic supplies, you'll pass a Carrefour Express.) To reach the enjoyable pedestrian zone, the old-town peninsula, and beaches, follow the "Stroll the Town" advice below.

**Market Day:** It's on Saturday at Piazza Aldo Moro (8:00-13:00).

**Laundry:** A self-service launderette is in the urban zone southeast of the train station (daily 8:30-20:30, Via Costantino Raffo 8, mobile 389-101-1454).

# Sights in Sestri Levante

### Stroll the Town

For a get-acquainted walk through town, head out from the train station and follow Via Roma until it dead ends at the leafy city park. Go left a few blocks to Corso Colombo (just past the Bermuda Bar). This main drag will take you to the TI before turning into the mostly pedestrianized Via XXV Aprile. This street, running the length of the peninsula, is lively with shops, eateries, and delightful pastel facades. When you reach Piazza Matteotti, dominated by a large white Renaissance-era church, you're at the narrow waist of the isthmus, with beaches to the right (pay) and left (free). If you continue up the lane to the left of the church, you'll pass a scenic amphitheater, then the evocative arches of a ruined chapel (bombed during World War II and left as a memorial). A few minutes farther on, past a stony Romanesque church, the road winds to the right to Grand Hotel dei Castelli. The rocky, forested bluff at the end of the town's peninsula is actually the huge private backyard of this fancy hotel.

**RIVIERA TOWNS**

**Sestri Levante**

To Santa Margherita Ligure

TRAIN STATION

To Rapallo & Santa Margherita Ligure

LUNGO G. DESCALPO

VIA OLIVE

Piazza Caduti

VIALE MAZZINI

VIA/ROMA

VIA V. VENETO

VIA ERALDO

To Santa Margherita Ligure & Portofino

To Cinque Terre

*Ligurian Sea*

Piazza Italia

To Levante & Cinque Terre

VIA NAZIONALE

To

Giardini Ventre

V. XX SETT.

V. TERESA C. COLOMBO

Piazza Sant' Antonio

VIA DANTE

To A-12 Freeway

*Baia delle Favole*

Piazza Repubblica

FASCIE

To A-12 Freeway

V. DANTE

Piazza Aldo Moro

PROMENADE & BIKE PATH

V. RIMEMBRANZA

Beaches

VIA XXV APRILE

VIA DELLA CHIUSA

BOAT DOCK

Piazza Matteotti

VICO CORO

VIA POZZETTO

VIA PILADE QUEIROLO

GRAND HOTEL DEI CASTELLI

(Private)

V. FENISOLA

VIA PORTO

FREE BEACH

VIA CAPPUCCINI

*Baia del Silenzio*

ROMANESQUE CHURCH

RUINED CHAPEL

N

To Punta Manara

200 Meters
200 Yards

**Accommodations**
1. Hotel Helvetia & Citta Beach Bar
2. Hotel Celeste
3. Hotel Genova
4. Albergo Marina
5. Villa Jolanda

**Eateries & Other**
6. L'Osteria Mattana
7. Polpo Mario & Ristorante La Mainolla
8. Pelagica
9. Ice Cream's Angels
10. Bacciolo Gelato
11. Tama Gelati e Molto di Più
12. Supermarket
13. To Laundrette

## Beaches

These are named after the bays *(baie)* that they border. The less scenic, bigger beach, **Baia delle Favole,** is divided up much of the year (May-Sept) into sections that you must pay to enter. Fees, up to €30 per day in August, generally include chairs, umbrellas, and fewer crowds. There are several small free sections: at the ends and in the middle (look for *libere* signs, and ask *"Gratis?"* to make sure that it's free). For less expensive sections of beach (where you can rent a chair for about €8-10), ask for *spiaggia libera attrezzata* (spee-AH-jah LEE-behr-ah ah-treh-ZAHT-tah). The usual beach-town activities are clustered along this *baia:* boat rentals, sailing lessons, and bocce courts.

The town's other beach, **Baia del Silenzio,** is picturesque, narrow, virtually all free, and jam-packed, providing a good chance to see Italian families at play. There isn't much more to do here than

unroll a beach towel and join in. Because of the bay's small size
and the currents, the water gets warmer here than at **Baia delle
Favole.** At the far end of Baia del Silenzio (under recommended
Hotel Helvetia) is the **$$ Citto Beach bar,** which offers front-row
seats with bay views (summer until very late, spring and fall until
sunset, sandwiches and salads at lunchtime only, Gilberto).

## Sleeping in Sestri Levante

**$$$$ Hotel Helvetia,** overlooking Baia del Silenzio, feels posh
and romantic, with 21 plush rooms, a large sun terrace with a
heated, cliff-hanging swimming pool, and a peaceful garden at-
mosphere. With doubles renting for €400-plus in peak season, it's
a big but enticing splurge (family rooms, air-con, elevator, shuttle
to off-site pay parking, closed Nov-March, Via Cappuccini 43,
tel. 0185-41175, www.hotelhelvetia.it, helvetia@hotelhelvetia.it,
Alex).

**$$$ Hotel Celeste,** a dream for beach lovers, rests along the
waterfront. Its 41 rooms are modern, crisp, and pricey, but you're
paying for the sea breeze (family rooms, air-con, elevator, attached beachside bar/breakfast terrace, Lungomare Descalzo 14,
tel. 0185-485-005, www.hotelceleste.com, info@hotelceleste.com,
Franco).

**$$ Hotel Genova,** well-run by the Bertoni family, is a ship-
shape hotel with 19 shiny-clean, modern, and cheery rooms (three
with sea view), a sunny lounge, rooftop sundeck, free loaner bikes,
and a good location just two blocks from Baia delle Favole (ask for
quieter room in back, family rooms, air-con, elevator, pay parking,
Viale Mazzini 126, tel. 0185-41057, www.hotelgenovasestrilevante.
com, info@hotelgenovasestrilevante.com, Stefano). They also book
apartments in a nearby palazzo (www.appartamentisestrilevante.
com).

**$$ Albergo Marina**'s friendly Magda and her brother Santo
rent 23 peaceful, clean, good-value rooms painted in sea-foam
green. Though the hotel is located on a busy boulevard in the more
urban part of town, rooms face a quiet back courtyard and it's a
short walk to the beach (family rooms, air-con, elevator, free self-
service laundry, pool table, closed Nov-Easter, Via Fascie 100, tel.
0185-41527, www.marinahotel.it, marinahotel@marinahotel.it).

**$ Villa Jolanda** is a homey, bare-bones pensione on the hilly
old town streets beyond the pedestrian zone. It has 17 dated rooms
(5 with little balconies and territorial views) and a garden court-
yard/sun terrace—perfect for families on a budget (family rooms,
pay parking, near Piazza Matteotti at Via Pozzetto 15—go up the
lane to the right of the church, tel. 0185-41354, www.villajolanda.
it, info@villajolanda.it, Mario).

## Eating in Sestri Levante

You'll find many eateries along the classic Via XXV Aprile, which also abounds with *focaccerie,* takeout pizza by the slice, and little grocery shops. Assemble a picnic or try one of the places below.

**$$ L'Osteria Mattana** has long, shared tables in two white-tiled dining rooms (one in front and the other past the wood oven and brazier). Daily specials—most featuring seafood—are listed on chalkboard menus (lunch Sat-Sun only 12:30-14.30, dinner daily 17:30-22:30, closed Mon Oct-April, cash only, Via XXV Aprile #34, tel. 0185-457-633, Marco).

**$$$ Polpo Mario** serves traditional seafood dishes and pastas from their fun people-watching location on the main drag (daily 12:00-15:00 & 19:00-23:30 except closed for lunch on Mon, Via XXV Aprile 163, tel. 0185-480-203).

**$$$ Pelagica,** a contemporary restaurant with a choice spot overlooking the Baia delle Favole, focuses on seafood—from anchovies to fried squid to traditional fish soup. Their rooftop terrace doubles as a cocktail lounge in the evening (daily 12:30-14:30 & 17:00-late, closed Wed in off-season, Via Pilade Queirolo 7, mobile 388-20255).

**$$ Ristorante La Mainolla** offers pizzas, big salads, focaccia sandwiches, and reasonably priced pastas near Piazza Matteotti (daily 12:00-16:00 & 19:00-22:00, Via XXV Aprile 187, tel. 0185-42792).

**Gelato:** Tourists flock to **Ice Cream's Angels,** at the intersection of Via XXV Aprile and Via della Chiusa, where Riccardo and Elena artfully load up your cone and top it with a dollop of Nutella chocolate-hazelnut cream (open daily until late in summer). **Bacciolo** enjoys a similar popularity (closed Thu, Via XXV Aprile 51, on the right just before the church). **Tama Gelati e Molto di Più** makes their gelato daily with fresh ingredients (near the beach at Baia delle Favole, Viale Rimembranza 34).

## Sestri Levante Connections

By **train,** Sestri Levante is 30 minutes from Monterosso (hourly connections with Monterosso; nearly hourly with other Cinque Terre towns, requiring a change in Levanto or Monterosso) and 30 minutes from Santa Margherita Ligure (2/hour).

**Boats** depart to the Cinque Terre, Porto Venere, Santa Margherita Ligure, Portofino, and San Fruttuoso from the dock *(molo)* on the peninsula (Easter-Oct, tel. 0185-284-670, www.traghettiportofino.it).

# Santa Margherita Ligure

If you need the Riviera of movie stars, park your yacht at Portofino. Or you can settle down with more elbow room in nearby and more personable Santa Margherita Ligure (SAHN-tah mar-geh-REE-tah lee-GOO-reh), one hour by train from the Cinque Terre. While Portofino's velour allure is tarnished by a nonstop traffic jam in peak season, Santa Margherita Ligure tumbles easily downhill from its train station. The town has a fun Old World resort character and a breezy harborfront with a beach promenade. With its nice big-city vitality, it feels bustling and lived-in, even off-season.

## Orientation to Santa Margherita Ligure

On a quick day trip to Santa Margherita Ligure from the Cinque Terre or Milan, walk the beach promenade and see the old town center before catching the bus or boat to Portofino to discover what all the fuss is about. With more time, Santa Margherita Ligure (pop. 10,200) makes a fine overnight stop or a home base for visiting the Portofino peninsula or a foray into the Cinque Terre.

**Tourist Information:** The TI is as central as can be, in a green kiosk at the harborside of the city traffic hub, Piazza Vittorio Veneto (daily 9:30-13:00 & 16:30-19:00, shorter hours off-season, tel. 0185-205-456, www.smlturismo. it). The ATP bus office has a ticket desk there, and bus #82 to Portofino stops at the curb in front.

### ARRIVAL IN SANTA MARGHERITA LIGURE

**By Train:** The station is a pleasant, low-stress scene. The bar/café (facing track 1) stores bags (small fee) and sells bus, train, and sightseeing-boat tickets.

To get from the station to the city center, take the stairs marked Mare (sea) down to the harbor; or turn right and head more gently down Via Roma, which leads to the town center, the TI, the start of my town walk, and recommended hotels (about 10 minutes away on foot). Bus #82 to Portofino stops a few steps below the station (4/hour, buy €3 one-way or €5 round-trip ticket at station bar/café, €1 more from driver).

**By Car:** Ask your hotelier about parking; some have free spots.

Otherwise, try a private pay lot such as the Garage Europa *autopark* next to the post office (Via Roma 38). An hourly pay-and-display lot is by the harbor, in front of the fish market. Parking is generally free where there are white lines; blue lines mean you pay.

## HELPFUL HINTS

**Market:** A market sets up on Fridays on Corso Matteotti (8:00-13:00).

**Laundry:** Self-service **Bolle Blu** is near Piazza Mazzini (daily 7:00-22:30, Via Roccatagliata 39, mobile 335-642-7203).

**Bike Rental: Ciclomania** rents city and ebikes by the day and can put together guided day trips to nearby destinations (Mon-Sat 8:30-12:00 & 15:30-19:00, closed Sun, Via Luigi Bozzo 22, tel. 0185-283-530, www.ciclomania-liguria.it, Mimmo).

**Scooter Rental: GM Rent** rents scooters and Smart Cars (daily 10:00-13:00 & 16:30-20:00, Via XXV Aprile 11, tel. 0185-284-420, www.gmrent.it, Francesco).

**Taxi:** Taxis wait outside the train station and charge €15 for a ride anywhere in town, €25 to Paraggi beach, and €35 to Portofino (tel. 0185-286-508).

**Driver:** Helpful taxi driver **Alessandro,** who has both cars and minivans, offers airport transfers to Genoa, Milan, Florence, and Nice. He is also available for local excursions, including day trips to the Cinque Terre (mobile 338-860-2349, www.alessandrotaxi.com, alessandrotaxi@yahoo.it).

# Santa Margherita Ligure Walk

Get your bearings with this self-guided walk, starting on Piazza Caprera, the square facing the exuberant Baroque facade of the Basilica of Santa Margherita.

## Basilica of Santa Margherita

The town's main church is textbook Italian Baroque (free, daily 7:30-12:00 & 15:00-18:30). Its 18th-century facade hides a 17th-century interior slathered with art and dripping with chandeliers. The altar is typical of 17th-century Ligurian altars—shaped like a boat, with lots of shelf space for candles, flowers, and relics. Its centerpiece is a much-venerated statue of Our Lady of the Rose that's adorned this altar since 1756.

Baroque is theater...and this altar is stagecraft. After the Vatican II decrees of the 1960s, priests began to face their flocks instead of the old altars. For this reason, all over the Catholic world, modern tables serving as post-Vatican II altars stand in front of earlier altars, like the one here, that are no longer the center of attention during Mass.

Wander the church and its chapels, noticing the inlaid-marble floors and sparkling glass chandeliers. As you marvel at the richness, remember that the region's aristocrats amassed wealth from trade from the 11th to the 15th century. When Constantinople fell to the Turks in 1453, free trade in the Mediterranean stopped, and Genovese traders became bankers—making even more  money. A popular saying of the day was, "Silver is born in America, lives in Spain, and dies in Genoa." Bankers here served Spain's 17th-century royalty and aristocracy, and their accrued wealth paid for the art you see here.

## Piazza Caprera

Each day this square hosts a few farmers selling their produce. On the corner of Via Cavour, just next to the basilica, visit **Seghezzo,** a venerable grocer where locals know they'll find whatever they need.

• *Now side-trip up the "via principale" (main drag) of the city, Via Palestro/Via Cavour. You'll go two blocks up to Piazza Mazzini and back.*

## "Via Principale"

The main "street" here is really two parallel streets divided by very tall, narrow buildings. As you head up Via Cavour (on the left, by Seghezzo grocery) check out the shops on the right: The buildings that separate Via Cavour from Via Palestro are so skinny you see right through to the other side. The mix of fine boutiques, wine bars, jewelers, and casual restaurants hints at the elite—but not flashy—ambience of the town.

Study the building facades as you walk. It's not unusual to see painted garlands gently hanging below a roofline or colorful ribbons over doorways and arches. Like a blank canvas, the houses are bedecked and embroidered in attractive styles. No two look just alike.

In two blocks, you'll emerge onto a square, Piazza Mazzini, with enough elbow room to study the pastel house fronts. These facades were painted and decorated in the characteristic Ligurian trompe-l'oeil style from the turn of the last century. Every building presents some sort of illusion—the decorators went so far as to add painted-on upper windows, shutters, and window frames. Ligurians were practical: It was much less expensive to hire a painter than a sculptor to add decorative detail to these houses.

Now do a U-turn onto Via Palestro to return to where we started (staying straight past the recommended **Angolo 48** restau-

# Santa Margherita Ligure

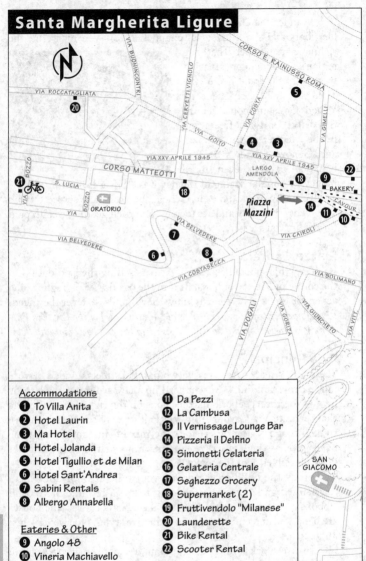

**Accommodations**
1. To Villa Anita
2. Hotel Laurin
3. Ma Hotel
4. Hotel Jolanda
5. Hotel Tigullio et de Milan
6. Hotel Sant'Andrea
7. Sabini Rentals
8. Albergo Annabella

**Eateries & Other**
9. Angolo 48
10. Vineria Machiavello
11. Da Pezzi
12. La Cambusa
13. Il Vernissage Lounge Bar
14. Pizzeria il Delfino
15. Simonetti Gelateria
16. Gelateria Centrale
17. Seghezzo Grocery
18. Supermarket (2)
19. Fruttivendolo "Milanese"
20. Launderette
21. Bike Rental
22. Scooter Rental

rant on the corner). Walking here, notice that you're surrounded by Italians doing the same *passeggiata*. At #34 (on the left), you'll pass a traditional *panificio* (bakery) where you can say, *"Vorrei un etto di focaccia"* to treat yourself to about a quarter-pound of the region's famed bread. Just beyond, on the right at #13, **Fruttivendolo "Milanese"** is just one of the many green-grocers in town selling an array of tempting produce and glass-jarred delicacies.

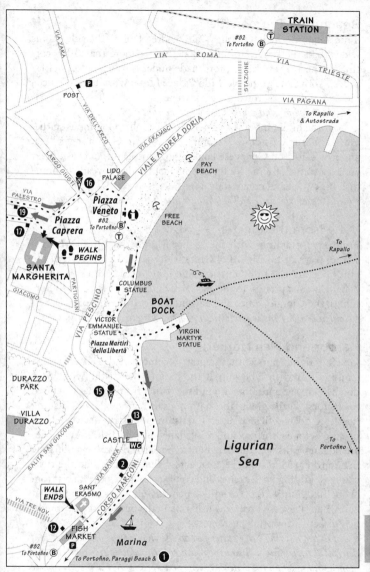

• Back on Piazza Caprera, turn left and walk away from the church one block to busy Largo Antonio Giusti. Next to the cinema (across the street), a penguin marks a recommended gelateria. Head right to Piazza Vittorio Veneto, with its busy roundabout and little park on the harbor. In the park facing the roundabout you'll find the TI, ATP bus office, and a bus stop for Portofino. Use the crosswalks to negotiate the busy intersection and reach the promenade.

RIVIERA TOWNS

## Beachfront Promenade

Take a look to the left, along Viale Andrea Doria. The sidewalk is wider than the street, an indication that for more than 100 years this has been *the* place to promenade under century-old pastel facades. Notice the grand old **Lido Palace Hotel** with its view balconies overlooking a crowded beach scene.

• *Now turn right and walk into the waterfront park.*

At the midpoint of the park is a Christopher Columbus statue. He was born "Cristoforo Colombo" in 1451 in Genoa, near here, and first sailed on Genovese boats along this Ligurian coast. Next comes a statue of King Victor Emmanuel II, always ready to brandish his sword and create Italy.

• *Head out on the little pier with the white statue facing out to sea.*

## View from the Pier

From here, standing with the "Santa Margherita Virgin Martyr" statue, you can take in all of Santa Margherita Ligure—from the villas dotting the hills, to the castle built in the 16th century to defend against pirates, to the exclusive hotels. Tourist boats to Portofino, the Cinque Terre, and beyond depart from this pier.

• *Continue along the waterfront on Corso Marconi.*

## Harbor and Fish Market

On the right, notice the trendy, recommended **Il Vernissage Lounge Bar** with tables up at the base of the castle (with WCs down below). Continuing around the corner from the castle (closed to visitors), walk along the harbor. The region's largest fishing fleet—20 boats—ties up here. The fishing industry survives, drag-netting octopus, shrimp, and miscellaneous "blue fish." (Anchovies are no longer fished from here but from nearby Sestri Levante). The **fish market** (Mercato del Pesca, across the street, inside the rust-colored building with arches and columns) wiggles weekdays from about 16:00 until 20:00 or so—depending on who's catching what and when. It's a cool scene as fishermen take bins of freshly caught fish directly to waiting customers.

• *Climb the narrow brick stairs just to the right of the fish market to a delightful little square. Find the characteristic, black-and-white pebble mosaic and relax on the benches to enjoy harbor views. Facing the square is the little...*

## Oratory of Sant'Erasmo

This pastel-hued building is named for St. Erasmus, the protector of sailors, as indicated by the stone-mosaic medallion of a ship decorating the little plaza in front. This building is an "oratory," where a brotherhood of faithful men who did anonymous good deeds congregated and worshipped. While rarely open, do check.

The interior is decorated with ships and paintings of storms that local seafarers survived—thanks to St. Erasmus. The huge crosses standing in the nave are carried through town on special religious holidays.

• *Your walk is over. For a little extra exercise to see a pleasant park, climb the long stairs from here up to the Church of San Giacomo (with an interior similar to the Basilica of Santa Margherita) and Durazzo Park.*

## Sights in Santa Margherita Ligure

### Durazzo Park (Parco di Villa Durazzo)

This park is a delight, with a breezy café, a carefully coiffed Italian garden, and an intentionally wild "English garden" below (free, daily 9:00-19:00, July-Aug until 20:00, closes earlier off-season, WC near café). The Italian garden is famous for its varied collection of palm trees and an extensive collection of camellias. It's OK to feed the large turtles in the central pond (they like bits of fish or meat).

The park is dominated by **Villa Durazzo**. It's not worth touring for most, but take the time to admire its remarkable pebble courtyard, carpeted in a fleur-de-lis pattern of white and gray stone—a Ligurian specialty (€5.50 to enter and view its Murano glass chandeliers and stucco and majolica decor, open daily, concerts held here in summer, www.villadurazzo.it).

### Beaches (Spiagge)

The handiest free beaches are just below the train station toward the boat dock (see map). But the best beaches are on the road to Portofino, including my favorite, **Giò e Rino** (just before Covo di Nord Est), which has sunbeds for rent and a fun, youthful crowd. The beach on the south side of **Grand Hotel Miramare** offers a more relaxing experience and is good for kids. Also nice is

**Minaglia,** with rentable sunbeds and kayaks. These beaches are a 20-minute walk from downtown, or you can take bus #82 from the train station or from in front of the TI at Piazza Veneto.

**Paraggi,** a small, sandy beach halfway to Portofino (and an easy stop on the bus #82 route), is better than any of the close-in Santa Margherita Ligure beaches, but it's pricey (as much as €60/day in July and Aug)—and it can be packed with sun worshippers from Portofino (where there's no beach—only rocks). There's more than one *bagni* establishment here, so choose the one that most ap-

# Rise of a Resort: The History of Santa Margherita Ligure

This town, like the entire region (from the border of France to La Spezia), was once ruled by the Republic of Genoa. In the 16th century, when Arab pirates from North Africa plagued the entire coastal area, Genoa built castles in the towns and look-out towers in the neighboring hills.

At the time, Santa Margherita Ligure was two bickering towns—each with its own bay. In 1800, Napoleon came along, took over the Republic of Genoa, and turned the rival towns into one city—naming it Porto Napoleone. When Napoleon fell in 1815, the town stayed united and took the name of the patron saint of its leading church, Santa Margherita.

In 1850, residents set to work creating a Riviera resort. They imported palm trees from North Africa and paved a fine beach promenade. Santa Margherita Ligure (and the surrounding area) was studded with fancy villas built by the aristocracy of Genoa. English, Russian, and German aristocrats discovered the town in the 19th century. Mass tourism only hit in the last generation. Even with the increased crowds, the town decided to stay chic and kept huge developments out. Its neighbor, Rapallo, chose the extreme opposite—giving the Italian language a new word for uncontrolled growth ruining a once-cute town: *rapallizzazione.*

peals. Off-season, the entire beach is all yours and free of charge. A narrow patch of sand smack-dab in the middle of Paraggi beach is free year-round.

### ▲▲Portofino Side-Trip

One of the most beautiful and famous little Mediterranean resorts, Portofino, is just a couple miles down the coast and is so easy to visit from Santa Margherita Ligure that it can be considered a sight (details on page 448).

### Fishing

To combine the art of fishing with the beauty of the Portofino promontory from the water, arrange a trip with Luca. His boat is equipped for *tonnara di Camogli:* the region's old tuna-fishing trap system (€110/2 people or €180/4 people for 4 hours, 4 people max; trip includes light snacks, snorkel masks, and stops for snorkeling and swimming; morning, afternoon, and night trips can be arranged, mobile 340-242-6483, www.portofinofishing.com, portofinofishing@gmail.com).

# Sleeping in Santa Margherita Ligure

**$$$$ Villa Anita** is an elegant-yet-homey family hotel run by Daniela and her son, Sandro. They rent 12 tidy rooms—nearly all with terraces—overlooking a peaceful residential neighborhood a five-minute uphill walk from the seaside boulevard. The in-house chef offers a varying menu of Ligurian specialties nightly (dinner extra, family rooms, playground, small gym, small heated pool and sauna, loaner bikes, air-con, free parking, closed in winter, Viale Minerva 25, tel. 0185-286-543, www.hotelvillaanita.com, info@hotelvillaanita.com).

**$$$$ Hotel Laurin,** nestled up against castle ruins, offers 44 slick, modern, and pricey rooms looking onto the sea. All double rooms face the harbor and have terraces; on the rooftop sundeck, there's a small pool and gym. Enrico and staff are helpful (RS%, double-paned windows, elevator, air-con, limited pay parking—request when you reserve, just past the castle at Corso Marconi 3, tel. 0185-289-971, www.laurinhotel.it, info@laurinhotel.it).

**$$$ Ma Hotel** is a crystal-chandelier-classy boutique hotel with a fresh, modern flair. Although it sits along a busy street, its 11 stylish and spacious rooms are at the back of the building (air-con, patio, free minibar, loaner bikes, Via XXV Aprile 18, tel. 0185-280-224, www.mahotel.it, info@mahotel.it, Annalisa).

**$$$ Pastine Hotels** is a small chain of three well-run hotels that combines solid service, sumptuous public spaces, and pleasant rooms. The two main branches are around the corner from each other, an easy walk from the station: **Hotel Jolanda** has lavish public spaces and regal colors, and its 50 pleasant rooms have a soothing decor (RS%, air-con, elevator, free use of small weight room, pay dry sauna, free loaner bikes, Via Luisito Costa 6, tel. 0185-287-512, www.hoteljolanda.it, info@hoteljolanda.it); **Hotel Tigullio et de Milan** is smaller and tidier, with updated rooms. The superior rooms are especially nice, but even most standard doubles come with a terrace—specify when you book. The rooftop sun terrace offers sunbeds, a bar, and hot tub in the summer (RS%, air-con, elevator, free loaner bikes, pay parking, Via Rainusso 3, tel. 0185-287-455, www.hoteltigullio.eu, info@hoteltigullio.eu). The newest branch, the boutique-like **Hotel Sant'Andrea,** has 11 rooms just above Piazza Mazzini, with a patio and whirlpool for guests (RS%, air-con, pay parking, Via Belvedere 10, tel. 0185-293-487, www.hotelsantandrea.net, info@hotelsantandrea.net).

**$$ Sabini Rentals,** in a dull but central residential zone, offers three straightforward rooms and one apartment with a tiny corner kitchen (RS%, family rooms, 2-night minimum, cash only, breakfast on request, laundry service, Via Belvedere 31, mobile 338-902-

**RIVIERA TOWNS**

7582, www.sabinirentals.com, info@sabinirentals.com, Cristina and Giancarlo).

**$ Albergo Annabella** is an old-style budget throwback with 11 rooms—some basic but most renovated. The more expensive rooms with bathrooms and air-conditioning are overpriced, but the cheaper rooms with shared bath and fans are a solid budget option (family rooms, no breakfast, air-con, Via Costasecca 10, tel. 0185-286-531, info@albergoannabella.it, Annabella speaks just enough English).

# Eating in Santa Margherita Ligure

### In the City Center

**$$$ Angolo 48,** run by savvy Elisa and Valentina, serves well-presented and reasonably priced Genovese and Ligurian dishes. This cozy locale is popular: Either arrive right when they open or make a reservation. There's great seating both on the square and inside. Try their handmade *pansotti* in walnut sauce (lunch Sat-Sun only 12:00-13:45, dinner Tue-Sun 18:30-22:00, closed Mon, Via Palestro 48, tel. 0185-286-650).

**$$ Vineria Machiavello** feels more urban Tuscan than seaside Ligurian. This well-stocked *enoteca* (wine shop) offers tastings and full bottles, but also serves a short menu of well-priced dishes, including beef and salmon tartare, at a few humble tables tucked between the wine racks (Wed-Mon 10:00-14:00 & 17:30-24:00, closed Tue, in the heart of the pedestrian zone at Via Cavour 17, tel. 0185-286-122).

**$$ Da Pezzi,** with a cheap cafeteria-style atmosphere, is packed with locals at midday and at night. They're standing at the bar munching *farinata* (crêpes made from chickpeas, available Oct-May 18:00-20:00), or enjoying pesto and fresh fish in the dining room. Consider the deli counter with its Genovese picnic ingredients (Sun-Fri 10:00-14:00 & 18:15-21:00, table service after 12:00 and 18:00, closed Sat, Via Cavour 21, tel. 0185-285-303, Giancarlo and Giobatta).

### On the Waterfront

All along the harbor side of Via Tommaso Bottaro, south of the marina, you'll find restaurants, pizzerias, and bars serving food with a nautical view.

**$$$ La Cambusa,** perched above the fish market, is popular for its seafood. While the food is forgettable, the view from its harborside terrace is not. In cooler weather, the terrace is covered and heated. Diners receive a free glass of *sciacchetrà* (dessert wine) and biscotti with this book (daily 12:00-15:00 & 19:00-23:00 except closed Thu Oct-June, Via Tommaso Bottaro 1, tel. 0185-287-410, www.ristorantelacambusa.net).

At **$$ Il Vernissage Lounge Bar,** you can nurse your drink with a million-dollar view appreciated by tourists and locals alike. There are 20 wines by the glass, plus cocktails and *spritzes,* which come with a nice plate of finger food (daily 18:00-late, Sun from 11:00, Salita al Castello 8, mobile 349-220-5846, Sandro).

### Budget Options

**$$ Pizzeria il Delfino,** which serves thin, big, wood-fired piz-zas, offers a rustic, fun local scene, with a few quiet tables outside and tight inside seating under nautical bric-a-brac (cash only, daily 12:00-15:00 & 18:00-23:00 except closed Tue dinner, Via Cavour 29, tel. 0185-286-488).

**Gelato:** The best *gelateria* I've found in town—with chocolate-truffle *tartufato*—is **Simonetti** (under the castle at Piazza Martiri della Libertà 48). **Gelateria Centrale,** just off Piazza Veneto near the cinema, serves up *pinguino* (penguin), a cone with your choice of gelato dipped in chocolate (Largo Antonio Giusti 14).

**Groceries:** Classy **Seghezzo** is a well-stocked grocery, deli, and wine shop, and great for a meal to go—ask them to *riscaldare* (heat up) their white *lasagne al pesto* or dish up their special *carpac-cio di polpo*—thinly sliced octopus (Thu-Tue 7:30-13:00 & 15:30-20:00, closed Wed, near the church on Via Cavour, tel. 0185-287-172). Cheaper and less romantic, the **Carrefour Express** (Largo Amendola 5) and **Co-op** grocery (Corso Giacomo Matteotti 9) are good places to stock up on well-priced Ligurian olive oil, pasta, and pesto (both generally open daily 8:00-21:00).

# Santa Margherita Ligure Connections

To reach the **Cinque Terre** towns (beyond Monterosso), you'll usu-ally have to change in Sestri Levante, Levanto, or Monterosso.

**From Santa Margherita Ligure by Train to: Sestri Levante** (2/hour, 30 minutes), **Monterosso** (hourly, 45 minutes), **La Spezia** (hourly, 1-1.5 hours), **Pisa** (1-2/hour, 2 hours, most with transfer, less frequent InterCity/IC goes direct), **Florence** (8/day, 4 hours, transfer in Pisa), **Milan** (about hourly, 2.5 hours, more with trans-fer in Genoa), **Ventimiglia**/French border (4/day, 4 hours; or hour-ly with change in Genoa), **Venice** (at least hourly, 6 hours with changes).

**By Boat to the Cinque Terre:** Tour boats make various trips to Vernazza, Porto Venere, and other ports nearly every day. Pick up a schedule of departures and excursion options from the TI, visit the ticket shack on the dock, call 0185-284-670, or check www.traghettiportofino.it.

# Portofino

Santa Margherita Ligure, with its aristocratic architecture, hints at old money. But nearby Portofino (por-toh-FEE-noh; pop. 500)—

with its sleek jewelry shops, art galleries, and haute couture boutiques filling a humble village shell—has the sheen of new money. It's the kind of place where the sailing masts are taller than the houses and church steeples. But the *piccolo* harbor, classic Italian architecture, and wooded peninsula turn glitzy Portofino into an appealing destination. Just a couple of miles down the coast, it's a fun, easy day trip from Santa Margherita Ligure.

**Planning Your Time:** In summer, my favorite Portofino plan is to visit in the late afternoon. Leave Santa Margherita Ligure by bus at about 16:30, get off at Paraggi beach, and hike 30 minutes over the bluff into Portofino. Explore the town, splurge for a drink on the harborfront, or get a takeout fruity sundae (*paciugo;* pah-CHOO-goh) and sit by the water. Then return by bus to Santa Margherita Ligure for dinner (confirm late departures). If you plan to do some hiking around Portofino, come earlier in the day.

**Tourist Information:** The Portofino TI is tucked under an arch between the harbor and the bus stop (Wed-Mon 10:00-13:00 & 14:00-18:00, closed Tue, Via Roma 35, tel. 0185-269-024, www.comune.portofino.genova.it).

## GETTING TO PORTOFINO

You can reach Portofino from Santa Margherita Ligure by bus or boat, or on foot. For a fun combination, you could go one way by bus and on foot from Paraggi, and the other way by boat. (I wouldn't suggest biking it, because of the blind corners.)

**By Bus:** Catch bus #82 from Santa Margherita Ligure's train station or at bus stops along the harbor (main stop in front of TI, €3 one-way or €5 round-trip, €1 more if bought from driver, 4/hour, 20 minutes, goes to Paraggi beach and then to Portofino). Buy tickets at the train station bar, the green ticket machine outside the TI, or any newsstand, tobacco shop, or shop that displays a *Biglietti Bus* sign. If you're at the Piazza Veneto TI kiosk, grab a bus schedule to plan your return (last bus around 24:00 in summer).

**By Boat and Bus:** If you're arriving in Portofino by boat, but will be busing back, follow the narrow lanes up from the harbor to the bus stop in Piazza della Libertà (ticket machine and tobacco store there sell tickets).

**Portofino Area**

By Taxi: A taxi ride from Santa Margherita Ligure costs around €35 to Portofino or €25 to Paraggi beach (more at night). Taxi stands in Santa Margherita Ligure are at the train station and at the curb in front of the TI.)

By Boat: The boat makes the 15-minute trip with more class and scenery, and without the traffic jams. The dock in Santa Margherita Ligure juts out from the waterfront park at Piazza Martiri della Libertà, near the TI (€7 one-way, €12 round-trip; hourly departures May-Oct daily 9:15-15:15, fewer off-season; purchase tickets at the dock or onboard, tel. 0185-284-670, www. traghettiportofino.it).

On Foot: To hike from Santa Margherita Ligure to Portofino, you have two options: You can follow the sidewalk along (and sometimes hanging over) the sea (1 hour, 2.5 miles)—although traffic can be noisy, and in places, the footpath disappears. Or, if you're hardy and ambitious, you can take a quieter two-hour hike by leaving Santa Margherita Ligure at Via Maragliano, then follow the Ligurian-symbol trail markers (keep a close eye out for red-and-white stripes). This hike takes you high into the hills. Keep left after Cappelletta delle Gave. Several blocks past a castle, you'll drop down into Paraggi beach, where you'll take the Portofino trail the rest of the way.

**Bus-and-Hike Option:** For a shorter—but rewarding—30-minute hike into Portofino, ride bus #82 from Santa Margherita Ligure only as far as Paraggi beach (tell the driver you want to get off there—you can't miss the inlet bay with a sandy beach). At the Portofino end of the beach, look for the *Parco di Portofino* sign to find the steps that begin the hilly, paved trail marked *Pedonale per Portofino* high above the road. There's a fair amount of up and down, but it's all well-paved and scenic. After Paraggi, you'll curl around another bay—with the famously top-end Hotel Splendido hovering on the hill above—before snaking your way to Portofino (you'll pop out at a yellow-and-gray church labeled *Divo Martino*).

Off-season, you can easily **reverse the bus-and-hike option**—by hiking from Portofino to Paraggi (taking the *Pedonale per Paraggi* trail near the Divo Martino church), then busing from the beach to Santa Margherita Ligure—but this works only when crowds are light; on busy days, return buses fill up in Portofino and won't stop in Paraggi.

## Sights in Portofino

### ▲▲Self-Guided Visual Tour from the Harbor

Stand or sit on the angled boat launch where Piazza Martiri dell'Olivetta meets the harbor (or nurse an overpriced cocktail at the nearby café tables), and get oriented to Portofino. It's one of the Mediterranean's most beautiful and famous little resorts.

Scanning the narrow pastel houses around the harbor, notice the painted-on details—as in Santa Margherita Ligure. You may also see laundry hanging out to dry—a surprising reminder that, while Ferragamo and Prada may reside on street level, actual villagers still live upstairs.

Now look out to the well-protected natural harbor—which has held substantial strategic value ever since the Romans first founded a town here. Since then, it has been appreciated by everyone from Napoleon to the Nazis.

A new flock of fans arrived in the 1950s, when *National Geographic* ran a beautiful article on the idyllic port. Locals claim that's when the Hollywood elite took note. Liz Taylor and Richard Burton came here annually (as did Liz Taylor and Eddie Fisher). During one famous party, Rex Harrison dropped his Oscar into the bay (it was recovered). Ava Gardner came down from her villa each evening for a drink—sporting her famous fur coat. Greta Garbo loved to swim naked in the harbor, not knowing (or caring) that half the town was watching. Truman Capote also called Portofino home. But VIPs were also here a century earlier. Friedrich Nietzsche famously wrote about philosophizing with the mythi-

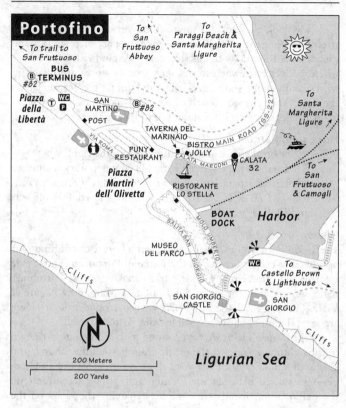

Portofino

To San Fruttuoso Abbey

To Paraggi Beach & Santa Margherita Ligure

To trail to San Fruttuoso

BUS TERMINUS ℬ #82

Piazza della Libertà Ⓣ 🅿 WC

SAN MARTINO ℬ #82

To Santa Margherita Ligure →

POST

VIA ROMA

TAVERNA DEL MARINAIO

BISTRO MAIN ROAD (SS-227) JOLLY

PUNY RESTAURANT

CALATA MARCONI CALATA 32

Piazza Martiri dell' Olivetta

RISTORANTE LO STELLA

To San Fruttuoso & Camogli

SALITA SAN GIORGIO

BOAT DOCK

MOLO UMBERTO

Harbor

MUSEO DEL PARCO

WC

To Castello Brown & Lighthouse →

Cliffs

SAN GIORGIO CASTLE

SAN GIORGIO

Cliffs

N

200 Meters

200 Yards

Ligurian Sea

cal prophet Zarathustra on the path between Portofino and Santa Margherita Ligure.

Today, the celebrity cachet lives on. When you tell locals you're going to Portofino, they say, "Maybe you'll see George and Amal Clooney!" Count the yachts and the tall-masted sailboats, and imagine who might be on them.

Now scan the panorama on the hillside in front of you. On the left is **Castello Brown,** an actual medieval castle built by the Genovese in the 16th century to protect this strategic harbor. It later became a private mansion, and today is a museum featuring lush gardens, sweeping viewpoints, and exhibits about Portofino and its history (€5, daily 10:00-18:00, June-Aug until 19:00, shorter hours off-season, tel. 0185-267-101, www.castellobrown.com).

Panning right, you'll see the **Church and Castle of San Giorgio,** with its popular two-way viewpoint terrace, looking down over the port and out over the ocean. This is an easy option for a picnic with grand views. Boats back to Portofino, or on to the San Fruttuoso Abbey, depart from the harborfront below this church. The Museo del Parco (described next) is also along this embankment.

Now look back toward town. A tidy grid of narrow cobbled streets angles gently uphill to the modern part of town, around Piazza della Libertà (with bus stop and taxi stand). These streets—where budget takeaway eateries and grocery stores are mixed in with swanky shops—are a good place to hunt for picnic fare. Up on the right is the striped church of San Martino, marking the well-manicured, enjoyable 30-minute trail to Paraggi beach.

## Museo del Parco

For an artsy break, walk around the harbor to the right, where you can stroll around a park littered with 148 contemporary sculptures by mostly Italian artists, including a few top names (€5, open Wed-Mon 10:00-13:30 & 15:00-20:00 in summer; closed Tue, off-season, and in bad weather).

## Hikes

The TIs in Portofino and Santa Margherita Ligure can outline your options. For even more detail, the **Parco di Portofino** can provide information on the many hiking trails that crisscross Portofino's regional parklands (headquartered in Santa Margherita Ligure at Viale Rainusso 1, tel. 0185 289-479, www.parcoportofino.it). Here are several options easily accessible from Portofino itself.

**Lighthouse Hike:** A paved stone path winds up and down to the lighthouse *(faro)* at the scenic point beyond the Church and Castle of San Giorgio. Start your climb on little Salita San Giorgio—it's tucked between the Delfino and Tripoli restaurants on the harborfront. Spend a few minutes enjoying the views on the church terrace (and if it's open, duck into the cemetery with a view behind the church). Rejoin the path signed *al Faro* to continue up. Walls and hedges block views at some points, but in the end, you'll be rewarded with the open sea—and a lounge/bar (open May-Sept, 25-minute walk). Consider popping into the medieval Castello Brown on the way up or down.

**Paraggi Beach Hike:** You can stroll the hilly pedestrian promenade through the trees from Portofino to Paraggi beach, and, if you're lucky, see a wild boar en route (30 minutes, path starts to the right of striped Divo Martino church just above the harborfront piazza, and ends at ritzy Paraggi beach, where bus #82 stops on its way back to Santa Margherita Ligure—though in peak season, the bus may be full and won't stop).

**San Fruttuoso Abbey Hike:** Another option is to hike out to San Fruttuoso Abbey and the nearby underwater Christ statue—see next.

## NEAR PORTOFINO
### San Fruttuoso Abbey (Abbazia di San Fruttuoso)
This Benedictine abbey, set at the water's edge, was established in the 10th century and is accessible only by foot or boat. On a visit here, you'll see the monastery and its cloister, tombs of the Doria family (longtime patrons of the abbey), and a simple church. But the abbey itself isn't the only attraction. Many are drawn here to see the statue of *Christ of the Abyss (Cristo degli Abissi)*—60 feet underwater, offshore from the abbey, in a specially protected marine area. The statue was placed there in 1954 for the divine protection of the region's divers. Boats on the beach can take you out to a spot above the statue, where you can look down to just barely see the arms of Jesus-outstretched, reaching upward. Some people bring goggles and dive in for a better view (negotiate a price, usually just a few euros).

**Cost and Hours:** Abbey entry—€7.50; daily 10:00-17:45; shorter hours off-season and closed Mon in winter; last entry 45 minutes before closing, tel. 0185-772-703, www.abbaziadisanfruttuoso. itwww.abbaziadisanfruttuoso.it.

**Getting There by Boat:** The same boats that link Santa Margherita Ligure and Portofino continue on to the San Fruttuoso Abbey (schedule at www.traghettiportofino.it). A different company's boats continue north from the abbey to Camogli (and its train station), Recco, and Punta Chiappa (€9 one-way, can return to Santa Margherita Ligure by train from Camogli or buy round-trip boat tickets, tel. 0185-772-091, schedule at www. golfoparadiso.it). For details inquire at the TI in Santa Margherita Ligure.

**Getting There by Foot:** The trail from Portofino to the abbey is steep at the beginning and end (about 2.5 hours—pick up the trailhead at the inland-most point of town, past Piazza della Libertà and the *carabinieri* station). You can also hike all the way there from Santa Margherita Ligure in about 4.5 hours via Portofino.

### Portofino Grand Tour
If you like planning and sticking to a timetable, you can make a one-day grand tour of the Portofino peninsula (confirm specifics of your plan, including trail details, with the TI in Santa Margherita Ligure before venturing out). Here's the plan: Take the boat from Santa Margherita Ligure to Portofino, have a quick look at the town, and then hike 2.5 hours to San Fruttuoso. Reserve a spot in advance at the private beach called Bagni San Fruttuoso—which gives you access to showers after your hike (€15/sunbed, towel and kayak rentals, call mobile 328-450-5521 or email bagnisanfruttuoso@gmail.it to reserve, www.

bagnisanfruttuoso.it). You'll have the rest of the afternoon to enjoy the beach, visit the abbey, and see the *Cristo* (you'll find seasonal restaurants on the beach). To finish your tour, take the 30-minute ferry to Camogli (last boat at 18:00 in June, 19:00 in July/Aug, you want the "blue line," www.golfoparadiso.it) where you can catch a train for the short ride back to Santa Margherita Ligure (2/hour, 5 minutes, station is 10 minutes on foot from the ferry port).

## EATING IN PORTOFINO

Portofino offers all kinds of harborside dining, but the quality often doesn't match the high prices. I'd rather dine in Santa Margherita Ligure. But if you do eat in Portofino, **$$$ Ristorante lo Stella,** just a few steps from the boat dock, has well-prepared dishes, friendly servers, and portholes in the bathrooms (tel. 0185-269-007). **$$$ Taverna del Marinaio,** across the harbor, has a prime location (soaking up the last of the day's sun), tables under arcades, and a small, cozy, classy interior (tel. 0185-269-103); next door, **$$$ Bistro Jolly** offers high prices at marine-varnished tables with comfy nautical cushions. And **$$$$ Puny,** at the top of the harborfront square, is a famous splurge (reserve ahead, tel. 0185-269-037).

For budget options, you'll find a variety of *foccacerie*, pizzerias, and grocery stores hiding out in the tiny grid of streets just up from the water. For dessert, opposite the boat dock, walk out to the little **Calata 32** *gelateria.*

# South of the Cinque Terre

South of the Cinque Terre is the nothing-special town of La Spezia, a handy transit hub with excellent train connections. But nearby is a gem—the resort town of Porto Venere, worthy of a day trip by boat from the Cinque Terre or by bus from La Spezia.

# Porto Venere

The perfect antidote to gritty La Spezia hides just around the bay: the enchanting resort of Porto Venere (POR-toh VEH-neh-reh). Comparably scenic to the Cinque Terre towns—but with a bit of glitz—this village clings to a rocky, fortress-crowned promontory. A rainbow of tall, skinny pastel facades rises up from an inviting harborfront promenade.

Porto Venere is light on sights, but it's a breeze to reach by boat from the Cinque Terre, and fun to explore: The higher you go, the better the views. Rather than the open sea, Porto Venere faces the beautiful Gulf of La Spezia—more romantically known as the Gulf of Poets—where Lord Byron was said to have gone for a hardy swim despite rough seas and local warnings to the

contrary. (He survived...at least, for a little while longer.) Scanning the bay, you'll see the outskirts of muscular La Spezia, the often-snow-covered peaks of the Apuan Alps, the resort town of Lerici, and—across a narrow strait—the rugged island of Palmaria.

## ORIENTATION TO PORTO VENERE

**Tourist Information:** The TI fills an old guard tower at the top of the main square (daily 10:00-12:00 & 15:00-19:00, closed Wed off-season, Piazza Bastreri 7, tel. 0187-790-691, www.prolocoportovenere.it).

**Getting There:** Porto Venere is an easy day trip from the Cinque Terre towns by **boat** (late April-mid-Oct, 1.5 hours from Monterosso, €23 one-way, €35 day pass includes hopping on and off, operated by 5 Terre-Golfo dei Poeti, tel. 0187-732-987, see schedule at www.navigazionegolfodeipoeti.it). You can also cruise between Porto Venere and Santa Margherita Ligure, with stops in Vernazza and Sestri Levante, using a different boat line (www.traghettiportofino.it). The scenic **bus** ride between La Spezia and Porto Venere curls around the Gulf of Poets (for bus details, see the end of the chapter).

For **drivers,** parking is challenging. In peak season, shuttle buses connect the parking lot just outside Porto Venere to the harborside square. Otherwise, test your luck with the pay spots on the seaside.

## VISITING PORTO VENERE

The town is essentially two streets deep: the harborfront promenade and, a block uphill, the main street (Via Capellini). A complete loop around Porto Venere includes both of these streets and a moderately steep hike up to the town's two main churches and fortress for the views. You can see everything in just a few hours; add more time for lunch or lingering.

Along the **harborfront,** seafood restaurants enjoy a Technicolor backdrop, and boat captains try to talk you into a 40-minute excursion around three nearby islands. But the real town lives on **Via Capellini** (just through the big arch from the TI—or hike

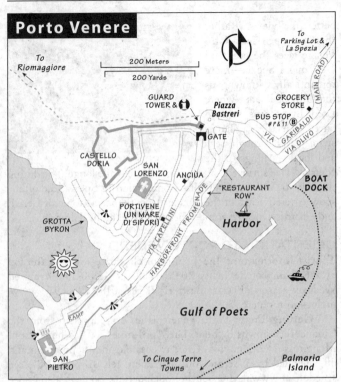

# Porto Venere

To Parking Lot &
La Spezia

To
Riomaggiore

200 Meters

200 Yards

GUARD
TOWER &

Piazza
Bastreri

GROCERY
STORE

BUS STOP
#P & 11

GATE

VIA GARIBALDI (MAIN ROAD)

VIA OLIVO

CASTELLO
DORIA

SAN
LORENZO

ANCIÙA

"RESTAURANT
ROW"

BOAT
DOCK

PORTIVENE
(UN MARE
DI SIPORI)

VIA CAPELLINI

HARBORFRONT PROMENADE

Harbor

GROTTA
BYRON

CAMP

Gulf of Poets

SAN
PIETRO

To Cinque Terre
Towns

Palmaria
Island

up any of the narrow stepped lanes from the harbor). Skinny and shaded, Via Capellini has a mix of restaurants, focaccia-and-pizza takeaway stands, several local shops, and boutiques selling gourmet gifty edibles and gaudy beachwear.

At the west end of the promenade and Via Capellini, the town comes to a point at the late-13th-century **Church of San Pietro**, with Gothic features and a black-and-white-striped interior typical of this region. Climb the stairs to the roof terrace for fine views in both directions (including the "Grotta Byron" sea cave).

More viewpoints line the walk from here up the stairs to the town's other big church, **San Lorenzo.** With a dark and brooding Romanesque interior, this church—like much of Porto Venere—was built by the Genovese to establish a strategic foothold at the entrance to the bay in the 12th century.

From in front of the church, more steps lead up to the town's fortress, **Castello Doria.** A hulking shell, it's not worth the money to go inside, but a hike up to the terrace out front is rewarded with striking panoramas.

From the castle, head back into town; to make this walk a loop, bear left to follow the very steeply stepped lane that runs just inside the crenellated wall back down to the TI.

Hardy **hikers** enjoy the five-hour (or more) hike to Riomaggiore, the nearest Cinque Terre town. Get details on this and other hikes at the TI; for more on hiking the Cinque Terre, see page 346.

## EATING IN PORTO VENERE

On the harbor, next to colorful bobbing boats, take your pick of views and menus (seafood/pizza) for a meal in a memorable setting.

For better values and more variety, stroll one block inland to Via Capellini. For a sit-down meal along here, try **$$ Portivene (Un Mare di Sipori),** serving local dishes with modern flair at reasonable prices (reservations smart, closed Mon, at #94, tel. 0187-792-722). Better yet, browse the fun selection of takeaway shops (selling pizza slices, bruschetta, focaccia, and top-notch deli items) to put together a picnic to enjoy by the port. **$ Anciùa** (at #40) assembles *panini* to order with interesting ingredients; they also have fresh fried anchovies and other Ligurian street food.

# La Spezia

While just a quick train ride south of the fanciful Cinque Terre (15-30 minutes), the working city of La Spezia (lah SPEH-tsee-ah; pop. 94,000) feels like "reality Italy." Primarily a transit point connecting to the Cinque Terre, lovely Porto Venere, or to Pisa, Lucca, and other Tuscan towns, La Spezia is slim on sights and has no beaches, but has a pleasant center filled with "Liberty"-style buildings (Italian Art Nouveau). In recent years, La Spezia has become the entry point for big cruise ships that funnel groups into the Cinque Terre. While not as inviting as its neighbors, La Spezia is a functional home base if there's no room elsewhere or if you've got a car.

## ORIENTATION TO LA SPEZIA

**Arrival in La Spezia:** The La Spezia Centrale **train** station has various services lined up along track 1. In the middle of the platform you'll find a city **TI** (daily 9:00-18:00, tel. 0187-026-152, www.myspezia.it) and a Cinque Terre **National Park information desk,** where you can buy park tickets—including the Cinque Terre Treno Card that includes both trains and trails (daily 7:30-19:30, shorter hours off-season, tel. 0187-743-500, www.parconazionale5terre.it). Don't use the La Spezia Migliarina station, where some trains terminate, which is more remote.

RIVIERA TOWNS

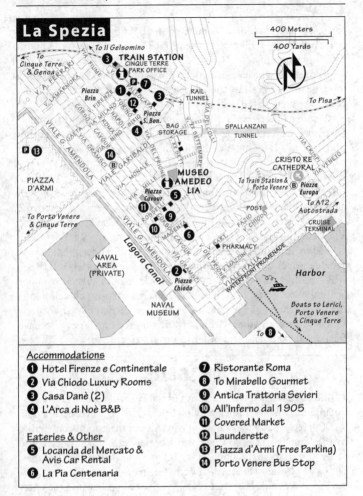

## La Spezia

400 Meters
400 Yards

To Il Gelsomino
To Cinque Terre & Genoa
**TRAIN STATION**
CINQUE TERRE PARK OFFICE
RAIL TUNNEL
To Pisa
Piazza Brin
SPALLANZANI TUNNEL
Piazza S. Bon.
BAG STORAGE
PIAZZA D'ARMI
CRISTO RE CATHEDRAL
To Train Station & Porto Venere
Piazza Europa
To A12 Autostrada
**MUSEO AMEDEO LIA**
Piazza Cavour
POST
CRUISE TERMINAL
To Porto Venere & Cinque Terre
NAVAL AREA (PRIVATE)
PHARMACY
Piazza Chiodo
Harbor
NAVAL MUSEUM
Boats to Lerici, Porto Venere & Cinque Terre
To 8

**Accommodations**
1 Hotel Firenze e Continentale
2 Via Chiodo Luxury Rooms
3 Casa Danè (2)
4 L'Arca di Noè B&B

**Eateries & Other**
5 Locanda del Mercato & Avis Car Rental
6 La Pia Centenaria
7 Ristorante Roma
8 To Mirabello Gourmet
9 Antica Trattoria Sevieri
10 All'Inferno dal 1905
11 Covered Market
12 Launderette
13 Piazza d'Armi (Free Parking)
14 Porto Venere Bus Stop

If you venture into the city, you'll find a second **TI** by the Museo Amedeo Lia (daily 10:00-13:00 & 14:00-17:00, same contact info as train station TI).

For **drivers** who want to leave a car in La Spezia, then head to the Cinque Terre by train, the easiest parking is under the train station, at the modern Park Centro Stazione (enter from Via Fiume or Via Paleocapa, €26/day, www.mobpark.eu). Free parking is at Piazza d'Armi, a 20-minute walk or short bus ride from the station (entrance at Via XV Giugno 1918).

**Baggage Storage:** Day-trippers can store bags about 350 yards from the station—a three-minute walk away—at the *deposito bagagli* at Via XX Settembre 209 (open 24/7, self-serve lockers in 3 sizes).

**Laundry:** A handy self-service **launderette** is just below the train station (daily, Via Fiume 95).

**Car Rental:** You won't need a car in the Cinque Terre region, but you may want one before or after your visit. La Spezia is the most convenient place to pick up or drop off a car near the Cinque Terre. **Avis** is closest to the train station (10 minutes on foot, closed Sat-Sun, Via Fratelli Rosselli 76, tel. 0187-770-270). Hertz and Europcar are located in Viale San Bartolomeo, a short taxi ride away.

## VISITING LA SPEZIA

If you find yourself with extra time here, and would like a meal, a museum stop, or a stroll, here's how to accomplish all three: Exit the station, turn left, and walk a long downhill block (on Via Paleocapa Pietro) to the roundabout at Piazza Saint Bon, which marks the start of a pleasant pedestrian zone—with several eateries—on **Via Fiume** (which turns into **Via del Prione).** Continuing on this street to the harborfront gardens makes a nice stroll (it's one mile from station to harbor). Along the way, you'll pass the nearly deserted **Museo Amedeo Lia,** which displays Italian paintings from the 13th to 18th century, including minor works by Venetian masters Titian, Tintoretto, and Canaletto (€10, Tue-Sun 10:00-18:00, closed Mon, tel. 0187-731-100, http://museolia.spezianet.it).

**Near La Spezia:** Without a doubt, the most appealing sight is outside La Spezia: the town of **Porto Venere.** This gorgeous Cinque Terre-esque town, overlooking a beautiful bay, is just a 30-minute bus ride away (described earlier in this chapter).

**Carrara** is an easy stop for drivers connecting La Spezia and Pisa. It's home to the world's most famous marble quarries, where Michelangelo chose the marble for his masterpieces. Carrara's Marble Museum (Museo Civico del Marmo) traces the story of marble-cutting here from pre-Roman times until today (closed Mon, Viale XX Settembre 85, tel. 0585-845-746). Sara Paolini is an excellent local guide (€100/half-day, will meet you at Carrara freeway exit or pick up from Carrara-Avenza train station, mobile 373-711-6695, sarapaolini@hotmail.com).

## SLEEPING IN LA SPEZIA

Stay in the Cinque Terre if you can, but if you're in a bind, these accommodations are within a 10-minute walk of the station. Most include breakfast: **$$$ Hotel Firenze e Continentale** is your grand, Old World splurge (68 rooms, RS%, air-con, elevator, pay parking garage, Via Paleocapa 7, tel. 0187-713-200 or 0187-713-210, www.hotelfirenzecontinentale.it, info@hotelfirenzecontinentale.it).

**$$ Via Chiodo Luxury Rooms,** with nine elegant, bright white rooms, is a soothing retreat close to the public gardens (air-con, elevator, pay parking, Via Chiodo 13, tel. 0187-22-607, www. costaestate.it, info@costaestate.it). They also rent an apartment in Porto Venere.

For *affittacamere* rooms for rent, consider the stylish **$$ Casa Danè**, offering 10 chic rooms with comfy linens and orange trees outside the door, plus 20 more rooms inside the train station, in former train conductor barracks (some rooms overlook the tracks but good windows reduce the noise, family rooms, air-con, Via Paleocapa 4, mobile 347-351-3239, www.casadane.it, reception@ casadane.it, Paolo). The homey **$ L'Arca di Noè B&B** has three bright, artsy, affordable rooms, all with private bath (air-con, comfy communal kitchen, Via Fiume 39, mobile 320-485-2434, montialessandra@email.it, Alessandra).

**$ Il Gelsomino,** best for drivers, is a homey and tranquil, three-room B&B in the hills above La Spezia overlooking the Gulf of Poets (family rooms, reconfirm arrival time in advance, Via dei Viseggi 9, tel. 0187-704-201, www.ilgelsomino.biz, ilgelsomino@ inwind.it, gracious Carla and Walter Massi).

## EATING IN LA SPEZIA

These eateries are located around the pedestrian spine of the city center, between the train station and the harbor.

**$$ Locanda del Mercato** offers Ligurian specialties that you can savor inside or out. For a food adventure, try the risotto with pumpkin cream or the roasted octopus (Tue-Sun 12:00-15:00 & 19:00-23:00, closed Mon, Via Fratelli Rosselli 88, tel. 0187-732-651).

**$ La Pia Centenaria** hosts local crowds at its counters at all hours of the day for its specialty—*farinata* (a chickpea pancake that can be eaten plain or with savory toppings). You can also get pizza here (Mon-Sat 10:00-22:00, closed Sun, Via Magenta 12, tel. 0187-739-999).

**$$$ Ristorante Roma,** next to the train station, is handy for travelers and cruisers, as they are open long hours. Their reasonable fixed-price meals even include wine, and several dishes are flavored with truffles, such as a risotto and a beef *tagliata* (daily 6:00-23:30, Via Pietro Paleocapa 18, tel. 0187-189-0177).

**$$ Mirabello Gourmet** serves light, delicious meals from a fun, informal location at the Mirabello Marina (Tue-Wed 10:00-15:00, Thu-Sun 8:00-15:00 & 18:00-23:00, closed Mon, Porto Mirabello, Viale Italia, tel. 0187-174-0168).

**$$$ Antica Trattoria Sevieri** is an elegant place close to the Piazza del Mercato, featuring fresh fish and superb seafood pastas and risotto. Alessandro, the chef/owner, will help you pick from the catch of the day and choose the cooking method (vegetarian and meat dishes too, Mon-Sat 12:00-15:00 & 19:00-24:00, closed Sun, Via della Canonica 13, tel. 0187-751-1776).

**$ All'Inferno dal 1905** is the place if you want real local food. This small, busy restaurant with a laid-back atmosphere serves traditional chickpea soup, linguine with mussels, and homemade pesto. Look for the red door in the narrow cross-street of Piazza Cavour (Mon-Sat 12:15-14:30 & 19:30-22:30, closed Sun, tel. 0187-29458, Via L. Costa 3).

## LA SPEZIA CONNECTIONS

**Trains** leave about twice hourly for the **Cinque Terre towns** (direction: Levanto). A few express trains (headed to Genoa or Milano) stop only at Monterosso. Other connections from La Spezia include **Pisa** (about hourly, 1 hour), **Florence** (5/day direct, 2.5 hours, otherwise nearly hourly with change in Pisa), **Rome** (8/day direct, more with transfers in Pisa, 3-4 hours), **Milan** (about hourly, 3 hours direct or with change in Genoa), and **Venice** (about hourly, 5-6 hours, 1-3 changes).

It's also possible to go by **boat** to the Cinque Terre, Porto Venere, and outer islands from the La Spezia dock (www.navigazionegolfodeipoeti.it).

City **buses to Porto Venere** generally depart from Viale Garibaldi; the bus stop is about a 10-minute walk from the train station (see the "La Spezia" map, earlier, for location; bus #P, 2/hour, 30 minutes, €3 each way; also bus #11 mid-June–mid-Sept, sporadically off-season; confirm schedule and buy tickets at TI; tickets also sold at tobacco shops, bars, and newsstands).

# FLORENCE

*Firenze*

Florence, the home of the Renaissance and birthplace of our modern world, has the best Renaissance art in Europe. In a single day, you could look Michelangelo's *David* in the eyes, fall under the seductive sway of Botticelli's *Birth of Venus,* and climb the modern world's first dome, which still dominates the skyline.

Get your bearings with a Renaissance walk. Florentine art goes beyond paintings and statues—enjoy the food, fashion, and street markets. You can lick Italy's best gelato while enjoying some of Europe's best people-watching.

## PLANNING YOUR TIME

Florence deserves at least one well-organized day: see the Accademia *(David),* tour the Uffizi Gallery (Renaissance art), visit the Duomo Museum (original bronze Baptistery doors) or the underrated Bargello (best statues), and do my "Renaissance Walk" (described later in this chapter; to avoid heat and crowds, do this walk in the morning or late afternoon). Art lovers will want to chisel out another day of their itinerary for the many other Florentine cultural treasures. Shoppers and ice-cream lovers may need to do the same.

Use my strategies to avoid wasting hours in long lines. This is especially true for peak season (April-Oct), holidays and weekends, and for the big attractions—the Uffizi and Accademia. Make reservations well in advance for these two sights (see "Advance Reservations for Skipping Lines," page 488).

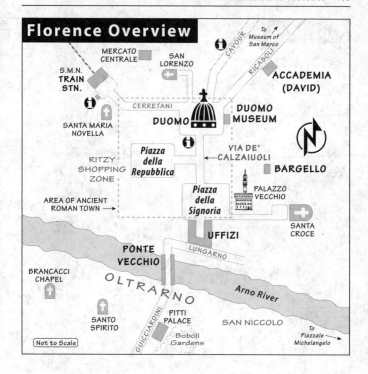

# Orientation to Florence

The best of Florence lies on the north bank of the Arno River. The main historical sights cluster around the venerable dome of the cathedral (Duomo). Everything is within a 20-minute walk of the train station, cathedral, or Ponte Vecchio (Old Bridge). The less famous but more characteristic Oltrarno area (south bank) is just over the bridge.

Though small, Florence is intense. Prepare for scorching summer heat, crowded narrow lanes and sidewalks, slick pickpockets, few WCs, steep prices, and long lines. But also prepare to celebrate the city that boldly lead Europe out of the Middle Ages and into our humanistic modern world.

## FLORENCE: A VERBAL MAP

For a big and touristy city, Florence (pop. 380,000) is remarkably compact and easy to navigate. Here's a neighborhood-by-neighborhood rundown:

**Historic Core:** The Duomo—with its iconic, towering dome—is the visual, geographical, and historical center of Florence. A 10-minute walk away is the Palazzo Vecchio (City Hall), with its skyscraping medieval spire. Connecting these two land-

# Florence

See Heart of Florence detail map

*Piazza del Crocifisso*

PORTA AL PRATO TRAIN STN.

To Airport & A-1 Autostrada (Firenze Nord exit)

V. FRATELLI ROSSELLI

V. FRATELLI ROSSELLI

V. DELLA SCALA

SAN JACOPO DI RIPOLI

EPISCOPALE AMERICANA DI ST. JAMES

VIA IL PRATO

CASA DI RIPOSO D. BEATA

V. VALFONDA

V. LUIGI ALAMANNI

PALAZZO DEGLI AFFARI

CENACOLO DI FULIGNO

*Piazza Adua*

**SANTA MARIA NOVELLA TRAIN STATION**

VIA NAZIONALE

VIA FAENZA

WC

**BUS STN.**

#12

*Piazza della Stazione*

PALAZZO DEI CARTELLONI

**SANTA MARIA NOVELLA**

*Piazza dell'Unità Italiana*

V. PANZANI

PERFUMERY

VIA DEI BANCHI

*Piazza di Santa Maria Novella*

(B)

VIA DEL SOLE

RUCELLAI PALACE

TORNABUONI

V. DE

STROZZI PALACE

TEATRO COMUNALE

CORSO ITALIA

LUNGARNO AMERIGO VESPUCCI

SAN LUCIA SUL PRATO

VIA PALAZZUOLO

OGNISSANTI

*Piazza d'Ognissanti*

BORGO OGNISSANTI

VIA PORCELLANA

VESPUCCI

**Arno River**

L. AMERIGO

**PONTE AMERIGO VESPUCCI**

LUNGARNO SANTA ROSA

PORTA SAN FREDIANO

VIA PISANA

*Piazza d. Verzaia*

VIA SANT'ONOFRIO

LUNGARNO

SODERINI

*Piazza di Cestello*

*Piazza Goldoni*

VIA VIGNA NUOVA

VIA DEL PARIONE

PALAZZO CORSINI

**PONTE ALLA CARRAIA**

L. CORSINI

SANTA TRINITA

VIA

BORGO

ACCIAIUOLI

**PONTE SANTA TRINITA**

Cimitero Israelitico

*Piazza de' Nerii*

BORGO SAN FREDIANO

L. GUICCIARDINI

*Piazza Nazaro Sauro*

VIA S. SPIRITO

*Piazza de' Frescobaldi*

VIA ALIARDI

CITY WALLS

V. CAMALDOLI

*Piazza T. Tasso*

**BRANCACCI CHAPEL**

SANTA MARIA DEL CARMINE

*Piazza del Carmine*

**OLTRARNO**

VIA MARTINO

B. SAN JACOPO

*Pza d. Passera*

*Piazza di Santa Felicità*

**SANTO SPIRITO**

VIA DELLA CHIESA

VIA DE' SERRAGLI

*Piazza di Santo Spirito*

VIA D.S.

VIA MAGGIO

D. GUICCIARDINI

GROTTO BACCHUS

VIA DEL CAMPUCCIO

PAL. DE' COSIMO RIDOLFI

Giardino Torrigiani

*Piazza di San Felice*

*Piazza de' PITTI*

**PITTI PALACE**

VIA PETRARCA

VIA ROMANA

AMPHI-THEATER

Giardino di Analena

FONTANA D. NETTUNO

GARDENS ENTRANCE

**Boboli Gardens**

PORTA ROMANA

FONTANA DELL'OCEANO

CITY WALLS

*Piazzale della Porta Romana*

## Hotels & Eateries outside the Center
1. Locanda de' Ciompi
2. Ristorante Natalino
3. Caffè del Verone

## Tour Companies
4. Artviva Tours
5. Florencetown Tours

FLORENCE

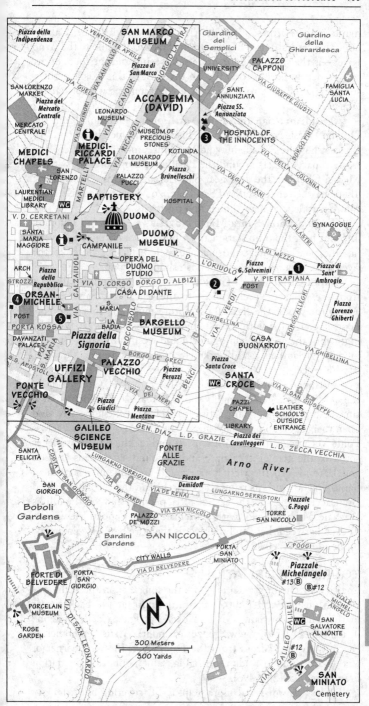

marks is the north-south pedestrian street called Via de' Calzaiuoli. This central axis—Duomo to the Palazzo Vecchio to the Arno River—is the spine for Florentine sightseeing and the route of my self-guided Renaissance Walk. To the west of this axis is a glitzy shopping zone, and to the east is a characteristic web of narrow lanes.

**Accademia/San Lorenzo** (North of the Duomo): From the Duomo, Via Cavour runs north, bisecting the neighborhood. To the east lies the Accademia and the Museum of San Marco. The western part clusters around the Basilica of San Lorenzo, with its Medici Chapels. The area near San Lorenzo teems with tourists: There are the vendor stalls of San Lorenzo Market, the lively Mercato Centrale, and many hotels and trattorias.

**Train Station/Santa Maria Novella** (West of the Duomo): The area near the train station and Church of Santa Maria Novella has inexpensive hotels and characteristic eateries. Closer to the river (near Palazzo Strozzi) is a posh shopping zone.

**Santa Croce** (East of the Duomo): A 10-minute walk east from the Palazzo Vecchio leads to the Church of Santa Croce. Along the way is the Bargello sculpture museum. This neighborhood is congested with tourists by day and students partying by night. But the area stretching north and west from Santa Croce is increasingly authentic and workaday, offering a glimpse of untouristy Florence.

**Oltrarno** (South of the River): Literally the "Other Side of the Arno River," this neighborhood reveals a Florence from a time before tourism. Many artisans still have workshops here, and open their doors to passing visitors. The Oltrarno starts just across Ponte Vecchio (jammed with tourists and tackiness) and stretches south to the giant Pitti Palace and surrounding gardens (Boboli and Bardini). To the west is the rough-but-bohemian Piazza di Santo Spirito (with its namesake church) and the lavishly frescoed Brancacci Chapel. To the east of Pitti, perched high on the hill, is Piazzale Michelangelo, with Florence's most popular viewpoint. Tucked between there and the river is the little San Niccolò neighborhood, with its lively bars and eateries.

## TOURIST INFORMATION

The city TI's main branch is across the square from the **train station** (Mon-Sat 9:00-19:00, Sun until 14:00; at the back corner of the Church of Santa Maria Novella at Piazza della Stazione 4; tel. 055-212-245, www.firenzeturismo.it). A smaller branch is centrally located **across from the Duomo,** at the west corner of Via de' Calzaiuoli (inside the Loggia, same hours as train station branch, tel. 055-288-496).

A less crowded and more helpful TI (covering both the city

and the greater province of Florence) is a couple of blocks **north of the Duomo,** just past the Medici-Riccardi Palace (Mon-Fri 9:00-13:00, closed Sat-Sun, Via Cavour 1 red, tel. 055-290-832). There's also a TI booth at the **airport.**

At any TI, you can pick up a city map and handout with the latest opening hours. For information on goings-on around town, ask for a copy of *The Florentine* newspaper, which has great articles with cultural insights (in English, published monthly and updated online every other Thu at www.theflorentine.net). *Florence Is You* (www.florenceisyou.com) is a similar online resource.

There's a handy little ticket booth at the Orsanmichele Church that often has reservations for the Uffizi and Accademia when other sources are sold out (Mon-Sat 9:00-16:15).

## ARRIVAL IN FLORENCE
### By Train

Florence's main train station is called **Santa Maria Novella** (*Firenze S.M.N.* on schedules and signs; Florence also has two suburban train stations: **Firenze Rifredi** and **Firenze Campo di Marte**).

As at any busy train station, be on guard: Don't trust "porters" who want to help you find your train or carry your bags (they're not official), and politely decline offers of help using the ticket machines by anyone other than uniformed staff.

To orient yourself to the station, stand with your back to the tracks. Look left to see the green cross of a 24-hour pharmacy *(farmacia)* and the exit to the taxi queue. Baggage storage *(deposito bagagli)* is also to the left, halfway down track 16 (long hours daily, passport required). Fast-food outlets and a bank are also along track 16. Directly ahead of you is the main hall *(salone biglietti)*, where you can buy train and bus tickets. Pay WCs are to the right, near the head of track 5.

To reach the **TI,** walk away from the tracks and exit the station; it's straight across the square, 100 yards away, by the stone church.

**Buying Tickets:** For travel within Italy, it's quick and easy to buy tickets online; with the Trenitalia app, you can even purchase them minutes before the train departs. If you decide to buy tickets at the station, take advantage of the ticket *(biglietti)* machines that display schedules, issue tickets, and even make reservations for rail-pass holders. For most international tickets, you'll need to go to a Trenitalia ticket window (in the main hall).

For Trenitalia information, use window #18 or #19 (take a number). For Italo tickets and information, use window #10 or #11, or visit their main office, opposite track 5, near the exit.

To buy ATAF city bus tickets, stop at windows #8-9 in the

FLORENCE

main hall—and ask for a transit map while you're there (TIs often do not have them).

**Eating: $ VyTA,** across from track 13, has good sandwiches, snacks, and pastries. Modern and refined **$$ Fabbricato Viaggiatori** serves drinks, salads, and other goodies and offers perhaps the best seats in the station (daily 8:00-24:00, 100 yards down track 16—enter from the street side, just beyond baggage storage). A food court is near track 16. A classy **Sapori & Dintorni Conad** supermarket in the station has lots of prepared foods (daily until 21:00).

**Services: Feltrinelli** has English language books and magazines and a café (across from track 14) while a modern **shopping gallery** with clothing stores and another café is down the escalator, across from tracks 11-12.

### Getting to the Duomo and City Center

The Duomo and town center are to your left (with your back to the tracks). Out the doorway to the left, you'll find city buses and the taxi stand. **Taxis** cost about €8 to the Duomo. **Buses** generally don't cover the center well and probably aren't the best way to reach your hotel (walking could be faster). To **walk** into town (10-15 minutes), exit the station straight ahead (with your back to the tracks) through the main hall and head straight across the square outside (toward the Church of Santa Maria Novella). On the far side of the square, keep left and head down the main Via dei Panzani, which leads directly to the Duomo.

### By Bus

The BusItalia Station is 50 yards southwest of the train station, near the T1 tram stop. To get to the city center, exit the station through the main door, and turn left along the busy street. The train station is on your left, while downtown Florence is straight ahead and a bit to the right.

### By Car

Don't even attempt driving into the city center. The autostrada has several exits for Florence. Get off at the Nord, Scandicci, Impruneta, or Sud exits and follow signs toward—but not into—the *Centro*. Park on the outskirts—see the next section—and take a bus, tram, or taxi in.

Florence has a traffic-reduction system that's complicated and confusing even to locals. Every car passing into the "limited traffic zone" (*Zona Traffico Limitato,* or *ZTL*) is photographed; those who haven't jumped through bureaucratic hoops to get a permit can expect a €100 ticket in the mail (and an "administrative" fee from the rental company). If you have a reservation at a hotel within the

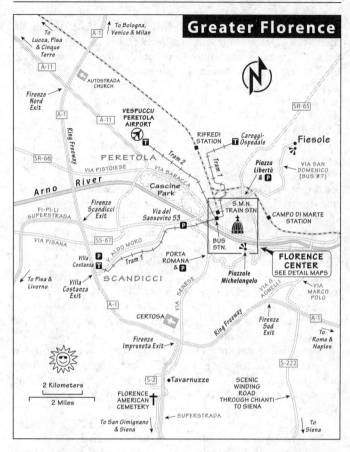

ZTL area—and it has parking—ask in advance if they can get you permission to enter town.

Another potentially expensive mistake drivers make in Florence is using the lanes designated for buses only (usually marked with yellow stripes). Driving in these lanes can also result in a ticket in the mail. Pay careful attention to signs.

**Parking in Florence:** The city center is ringed with big, efficient parking lots (signposted with a big *P*). From these, you can ride into the center (via taxi, bus, or possibly tram). Check www.firenzeparcheggi.it for details on parking lots, availability, and prices. From the freeway, follow the signs to *Centro*, then *Stadio*, then *P*.

The huge park-and-ride lot called Villa Costanza, just outside the town of Scandicci (south of Florence), has its own dedicated freeway offramp (just north of Impruneta) and is the terminus for the T1 tram line that zips smart drivers downtown (€1.50, departing every five minutes). Just look for it as you approach Florence on the autostrada (see the "Greater Florence" map in this chapter).

## By Plane

**Amerigo Vespucci Airport,** also called Peretola Airport, is about five miles northwest of the city (code: FLR, tel. 055-306-1830, www.aeroporto.firenze.it).

On the ground floor, you'll find a TI, café, and ATMs. The **T2 tram** (to the left as you exit the arrivals hall) runs every five minutes from the airport to near the train station (Alamanni Stazione, across from the station) and Piazza dell'Unità (one stop beyond the station, slightly closer to downtown) in about 20 minutes (runs 5:00-24:00, €1.50, buy ticket from machine on platform, cash or credit card, validate onboard, good for 90 minutes and transferable to bus lines, www.gestramvia.com).

**Shuttle buses** (to the far right as you exit the arrivals hall) connect the airport with Florence's train and bus stations (2/hour until 22:00, 1/hour until 00:30, 30 minutes, runs 5:00-00:30, €6 one-way—buy ticket on board, €10 round-trip—buy ticket inside airport). If you're changing to a different intercity bus in Florence (for instance, one bound for Siena), stay on the bus through the first stop (at the train station); it will continue on to the bus station nearby.

Official **taxi** companies have fixed rates for the 20- to 30-minute ride between the airport and downtown: €22 during the day (6:00-22:00), €25.30 at night, and €24 on Sunday. Be sure to use an official taxi (white, marked with *Taxi/Comune di Firenze* and a red fleur-de-lis).

The airport's **rental-car** offices share one big parking lot that's a three-minute drive away (shuttle bus departs directly outside the arrivals door).

## By Cruise Ship

If you are arriving at Florence's port, Livorno, see "Florence Connections," at the end of this chapter.

## HELPFUL HINTS

**Sightseeing Tips:** Everyone visiting Florence wants to see the same three or four sights. Consequently, these are mobbed with long lines while other worthwhile sights are quiet with no lines. While technically you can wait in line to get into these places, it's flat-out stupid to attempt a visit without a reservation. The process for making reservations online is clearly explained under "Sights in Florence," later.

One pass to consider is the **Uffizi/Pitti Palace/Boboli Gardens combo-ticket** (called "PassePartout"), which is valid for three consecutive days and offers admission to these sights at a €12 savings (€38 March-Oct, €18 Nov-Feb). Note that with this ticket, you must start your visit at the Uffizi. You can purchase the pass in advance at www.uffizi.it; look for "Intero Cumulativo 3 giorni" in the ticket options.

The 72-hour **Firenze Card** sold by the TI gets you into nearly all the sights in town for €85. While it used to be popular because it let you enter the Uffizi and Accademia without a reservation, it now requires you book a time. It's only a savings and worth buying if you'll be sightseeing like crazy for three days. And in very busy times as a last resort, you might find you can get a reservation with a Firenze Card for the Uffizi or Accademia when you otherwise can't get in.

**Summer Evening Sightseeing:** It's worth noting that Florence often keeps the Uffizi and the Accademia open until 22:00 on one or two weekday nights July through September (see "Sights in Florence" for details).

**Theft Alert:** Florence has hardworking gangs of thieves who hang out near the train station, the station's underpass (especially where the tunnel surfaces), around Mercato Centrale, and at major sights. American tourists are considered easy targets. Some thieves even dress like tourists to fool you. Any crowded bus likely holds at least one thief.

**Medical Help: Medical Service Firenze** provides 24/7 phone consults; they also do house calls in English or will see you at their walk-in clinic (clinic closed Sun—check website for hours, Via Roma 4, between the Duomo and Piazza della Repubblica, tel. 055-475-411, www.medicalservice.firenze.it). The TI has a list of English-speaking doctors.

There are 24-hour **pharmacies** at the train station and on Borgo San Lorenzo (near the Baptistery).

**Visiting Churches:** Modest dress is required in some churches, including the Duomo, Santa Maria Novella, Santa Croce, Santa Maria del Carmine/Brancacci Chapel, and the Medici Chapels. Be respectful of worshippers and the paintings; don't use a flash. Many churches, though not the biggies we mention, close from 12:00 or 12:30 until 15:00 or 16:00.

**Chill Out:** Schedule several breaks into your sightseeing when you can sit, pause, cool off, and refresh yourself with a gelato or coffee. Carry a water bottle to refill at Florence's twist-the-handle public fountains (around the corner from the "Piglet" at Mercato Nuovo, or in front of the Pitti Palace). Try the *fon-*

*tanello* (dispenser of free cold water) on Piazza della Signoria, behind the statue of Neptune (on the left side of the Palazzo Vecchio).

**Addresses:** Florence has a confusing system for street addresses, with "red" numbers for businesses and "black" numbers for residences. Street signs are indeed red or black (though usually faded and hard to read); in print, addresses are indicated with "r" (as in Via Cavour 2r) or "n" (for black—*nero,* as in Via Cavour 25n). Red and black numbers are interspersed together on the same street; each set goes in roughly consecutive order, but their numbers bear no connection with each other.

**Bookstores:** For a good selection of brand-name guidebooks (including mine), try these: **Paperback Exchange** has the widest selection of English books, new and used (Mon-Fri 9:00-19:30, Sat from 10:30, closed Sun and a couple of weeks in Aug, just south of the Duomo on Via delle Oche 4 red, www.papex.it). **RED** (stands for "Read, Eat, Dream"), a flagship store for the Feltrinelli chain (the Italian Barnes & Noble) with a café and restaurant inside, has a small selection of English books (daily 9:30-23:00, on Piazza della Repubblica).

**WCs:** Public restrooms are scarce. Use them when you can, in any café or museum you patronize. Pay public WCs are typically €1. Convenient locations include: at the Baptistery ticket office (near the Duomo); near the entrance to the Church of Santa Maria Novella; inside the train station (near track 5 and in the food court); just down the street from Piazza Santa Croce (at Borgo Santa Croce 29 red); on Piazza Santo Spirito; and up near Piazzale Michelangelo.

**Laundry:** The **Wash & Dry Lavarapido** chain offers long hours and efficient self-service launderettes at several locations (generally daily 7:30-23:00). These locations are close to recommended hotels: Via dei Servi 105 red (near *David*), Via del Sole 29 red and Via della Scala 52 red (this location is a Speed Queen, between train station and river), and Via Ghibellina 143 red (Palazzo Vecchio). On the Oltrarno side, there's one at Via dei Serragli 87 red (Santo Spirito area).

**Bike Rental: Florence by Bike** rents two-wheelers of all sizes (€12/day and up depending on type of bike, includes bike lock and helmet, child seat—€3; Mon-Sat 9:00-19:30, Sun until 18:00, closed Sun and midday Nov-March; a 15-min-

ute walk north of the Duomo at Via San Zanobi 54 red, tel.
055-488-992, www.florencebybike.it).

**Travel Agencies:** Travel agencies can be helpful for getting both
domestic and international tickets, reservations, and supplements. Convenient travel agencies in the town center are **In-
tertravel Viaggi** (also a DHL package mailing office, Mon-
Fri 9:00-18:30, Sat 9:30-12:30, closed Sun, south of Piazza
della Repubblica at Via de Lamberti 39 red, tel. 055-280-706)
and **Florentour** (Mon-Fri 9:30-16:30, closed Sat-Sun, Via dei
Servi 23 red, a block off the Duomo, tel. 055-292-237). For
locations of both, see the map on page 500.

## GETTING AROUND FLORENCE

I organize my sightseeing geographically and do it all on foot. I
think of Florence as a Renaissance treadmill—it requires a lot of
walking. You likely won't need public transit, except maybe to head
up to Piazzale Michelangelo and San Miniato Church for the view.
For major bus and tram stop locations, see the map on page 500.

### By Bus

The city's full-size buses don't cover the old center well (the whole
area around the Duomo is off-limits to motorized traffic). Pick up a
map of transit routes at the ATAF windows (#8 and #9) at the train
station; you'll also find routes online (www.ataf.net).

Buy bus tickets at tobacco shops *(tabacchi),* newsstands, or the
ATAF ticket windows (€1.50/90 minutes). Be sure to validate your
ticket in the machine on board (or risk a steep fine). You can sometimes buy a ticket on board, but you'll pay more (€2; must have
exact change). Follow general bus etiquette: Board at front or rear
doors, exit out the center.

Of the many bus lines, I find these to be of most value for seeing outlying sights:

Bus **#12** goes from the train station, over the Carraia bridge to
Porta Romana, then up to San Miniato Church and Piazzale Michelangelo (3/hour). Bus **#13** makes the return trip down the hill.

Fun little **minibuses** (many of them electric—*elettrico*) wind
through the tangled old center of town and up and down the
river—just €1.50 gets you a 1.5-hour joyride. These buses, which
run every 10 minutes from 7:00 to 21:00 (less frequent on Sun), are
popular with sore-footed sightseers and eccentric local seniors. The
minibuses also connect many major parking lots with the historic
center (buy tickets from machines at lots).

Bus **#C1** stops behind the Palazzo Vecchio and Piazza Santa
Croce, then heads north, passing near San Marco and the Accademia before heading up to Piazza Libertà. On its southbound

FLORENCE

# Florence at a Glance

▲▲▲**Accademia** Michelangelo's *David* and powerful (unfinished) *Prisoners.* Reserve ahead. **Hours:** Tue-Sun 8:15-19:00, closed Mon; July-Sept open Tue and Thu 7:00-22:00. See page 494.

▲▲▲**Uffizi Gallery** Greatest collection of Italian paintings anywhere. Reserve well in advance. **Hours:** Tue-Sun 8:15-19:00, closed Mon; July-Sept Wed-Thu until 22:00. See page 502.

▲▲▲**Bargello** Underappreciated sculpture museum (Michelangelo, Donatello, Medici treasures). **Hours:** Daily 8:15-14:00 (until 17:00 for special exhibits); closed on second and fourth Sun and first, third, and fifth Mon of each month. See page 508.

▲▲▲**Duomo Museum** Freshly renovated cathedral museum with the finest in Florentine sculpture. **Hours:** Daily 9:00-19:00, closed first Tue of each month. See page 492.

▲▲▲**Pitti Palace** Several museums in lavish palace plus sprawling Boboli and Bardini Gardens. **Hours:** Palatine Gallery, Royal Apartments, Treasury, Museum of Costume and Fashion, and Gallery of Modern Art open Tue-Sun 8:15-19:00, closed Mon; Boboli and Bardini Gardens, and Porcelain Museum open daily June-Aug 8:15-19:30, April-May and Sept until 18:30, March and Oct until 17:30, Nov-Feb until 16:30, closed first and last Mon of each month. See page 511.

▲▲**Duomo** Gothic cathedral with colorful facade and the first dome built since ancient Roman times. **Hours:** Mon-Sat 10:00-16:30, Sun 13:30-16:45. See page 490.

▲▲**Museum of San Marco** Best collection anywhere of artwork by the early Renaissance master Fra Angelico. **Hours:** Tue-Fri 8:15-14:00, Sat-Sun until 17:00; also open until 14:00 on first, third, and fifth Mon of each month. See page 496.

▲▲**Medici Chapels** Tombs of Florence's great ruling family, designed and carved by Michelangelo. **Hours:** Tue-Sat 8:15-17:00 except Oct-late May until 14:00; also open first, third, and fifth Sun and second and fourth Mon of each month. See page 497.

▲▲**Palazzo Vecchio** Fortified palace, once the home of the Medici family, wallpapered with history. **Hours:** Museum and excavations open daily 9:00-23:00 (Oct-March until 19:00), Thu until 14:00 year-round; shorter hours for tower. See page 507.

▲▲**Galileo Science Museum** Fascinating old clocks, telescopes, maps, and three of Galileo's fingers. **Hours:** Daily 9:30-18:00 except Tue until 13:00. See page 508.

▲▲**Santa Croce Church** Precious art, tombs of famous Florentines, and Brunelleschi's Pazzi Chapel in 14th-century church. **Hours:** Mon-Sat 9:30-17:00, Sun from 14:00. See page 509.

▲▲**Church of Santa Maria Novella** Thirteenth-century Dominican church with Masaccio's famous 3-D painting. **Hours:** Mon-Thu 9:00-19:00, Fri 11:00-19:00, Sat 9:00-17:30, Sun 13:00-17:30; Oct-March closes at 17:30. See page 510.

▲▲**Brancacci Chapel** Works of Masaccio, early Renaissance master who reinvented perspective. **Hours:** Wed-Mon 10:00-17:00 except Sun from 13:00, closed Tue. Reservations recommended, especially March-May. See page 514.

▲▲**San Miniato Church** Sumptuous Renaissance chapel and sacristy showing scenes of St. Benedict. **Hours:** Mon-Sat 9:30-13:00 & 15:00-19:30, until 19:00 off-season, Sun 8:15-19:30, closed sporadically for special occasions. See page 515.

▲**Climbing the Duomo's Dome** Grand view into the cathedral, close-up of dome architecture, and, after 463 steps, a glorious city vista; reservations required. **Hours:** Mon-Fri 8:30-19:00, Sat until 17:00, Sun 13:00-16:00. See page 490.

▲**Campanile** Bell tower with views similar to Duomo's, 50 fewer steps, and shorter lines. **Hours:** Daily 8:15-19:30. See page 491.

▲**Baptistery** Bronze doors fit to be the gates of paradise. **Hours:** Doors always viewable; interior open Mon-Sat 8:15-19:30, Sun until 13:30. See page 491.

▲**Piazza Santissima Annunziata** Lovely square epitomizing Renaissance harmony, with Brunelleschi's Hospital of the Innocents, considered the first Renaissance building. See page 495.

▲**Medici-Riccardi Palace** Lorenzo the Magnificent's home, with fine art, frescoed ceilings, and Gozzoli's lovely Chapel of the Magi. **Hours:** Thu-Tue 9:00-19:00, closed Wed. See page 498.

▲**Ponte Vecchio** Famous bridge lined with gold and silver shops. See page 508.

▲**Piazzale Michelangelo** Hilltop square with stunning view of Duomo and Florence, with San Miniato Church just uphill. See page 514.

route, this bus also stops near the train station, the Basilica of San Lorenzo, and the Duomo.

Bus **#C2** twists through the congested old center from the train station, passing near Piazza della Repubblica and Piazza della Signoria to Piazza Beccaria.

Bus **#C3** goes up and down the Arno River, with stops near Piazza Santa Croce, Ponte Vecchio, the Carraia bridge to the Oltrarno (including the Pitti Palace), and beyond.

Bus **#C4** goes from near the Duomo to the train station, crosses the Carraia bridge, and cruises through the Oltrarno (passing the Pitti Palace) before heading into the San Niccolò neighborhood.

## By Tram
The T1 and T2 tram lines are cheap, easy, and frequent. For travelers, they're generally useful only for service between the tram stops in town (near the train station) and either the airport (T2) or the big park-and-ride lots at Villa Costanza (T1) near the town of Scandicci (www.gestramvia.com; see "Florence Connections" at the end of this chapter for more details).

## By Taxi
The minimum cost for a taxi ride is €5 (€8.30 after 22:00, €7 on Sun); rides in the center of town should be charged as tariff #1. Taxi fares and supplements (e.g., €2 extra to call a cab rather than hail one) are clearly explained on signs in each taxi. Look for an official, regulated cab (white; marked with *Taxi/Comune di Firenze*, red fleur-de-lis, and one of the official phone numbers: 4390 or 4242). Before getting in a cab at a stand or on the street, ask for an approximate cost (*"Più o meno, quanto costa?"* pew oh MEH-noh, KWAHN-toh KOH-stah). If you can't get a straight answer or the price is outrageous, wait for the next one. It can be hard to find a cab on the street, but they stop and sometimes wait in taxi ranks near the major tourist sights (marked by orange *Taxi* signs). To call one, dial 055-4390 or 055-4242 (or ask your waiter or hotelier to call for you). Uber does not operate in Florence.

# Tours in Florence

For extra insight with a personal touch, consider the tour companies and individual Florentine guides listed here. ∩ To sightsee on your own, download my **free audio tours** that illuminate some of Florence's top sights and neighborhoods (see page 26).

Several tour companies (such as Florencetown or Artviva) offer regularly scheduled group tours that anyone can sign up for. This is usually the cheapest option for individual travelers. But families

FLORENCE

and small groups can book a private guide for a similar price (since rates are hourly for any size of group).

Some tour companies offer bus excursions that go out to smaller towns in the Tuscan countryside. The most popular day trips are Siena, San Gimignano, Pisa, and into Chianti country for wine tasting.

## Walking (and Biking) Tours
### Artviva

Artviva offers an intriguing variety of tours (guided by native English speakers, 15 people maximum). Popular choices include their overview tours (€33 "Original Florence" 3-hour town walk; €124 "Florence in One Glorious Day" combines town walk and tours of the Uffizi and Accademia, 6 hours total). They also have stand-alone Uffizi and Accademia tours, cooking classes, art classes, food tours, minibus tours around Tuscany and to the Cinque Terre, and more (RS%—10 percent discount with this book, use the password "reader"). Their office is above Odeon Cinema near Piazza della Repubblica (Mon-Sat 8:00-18:00, Sun 8:30-13:30, Via de' Sassetti 1, second floor, tel. 055-264-5033, www.artviva.com).

### Florencetown

This company runs English-language tours on foot or by bike. They offer student rates (10 percent discount) to anyone with this book. Their most popular offerings are "Walk and Talk Florence" (€29, 2.5 hours, daily at 10:00, basic stops including the Oltrarno) and "I Bike Florence" (€39; 2.5 hours on one-speed bike, 15-stop blitz of town's top sights, helmets optional; in bad weather it goes as a walking tour). Their office is at Via de Lamberti 1 (facing Orsanmichele Church; see "Florence" map earlier in this chapter); they also have a "Tourist Point" kiosk on Piazza della Repubblica, under the arches at the corner with Via Pellicceria (also offers cooking classes, tel. 055-281-103, www.florencetown.com).

### Florentia

Top-notch private walking tours—geared for thoughtful, well-heeled travelers with longer-than-average attention spans—are led by one of several Florentine scholars. The tours range from introductory city walks and museum visits to in-depth thematic walks, such as the Oltrarno, Jewish Florence, or the Medici dynasty; they also offer family-oriented tours (€275 and up, includes planning assistance by email, www.florentia.org, info@florentia.org).

### Context Florence

This scholarly group of graduate students and professors leads "walking seminars," such as a 3.5-hour study of Michelangelo's work and influence (€130/person, plus museum admission) and a

**FLORENCE**

two-hour evening orientation stroll (€79/person). See their website for other innovative offerings: Medici walk, family tours, private fresco workshop, and more (www.contexttravel.com, info@contexttravel.com).

## Walks Inside Florence

Two art historians—Paola Barubiani and Marzia Valbonesi—and their partners provide quality private tours and a discounted rate for Rick Steves readers (RS%, €190/group for three-hour introductory tour, up to 6 people). Their "Florence in a Day" tour gives you the essentials in four hours (€260/group, up to 6 people, museum admissions extra—they make the reservations so there's no waiting in line). Other offerings are described on their website (e.g. shopping tour featuring select artisans, guided evening walk, and cruise excursions from the port of Livorno; Paola's mobile 335-526-6496, www.walksinsideflorence.it, paola@walksinsideflorence.it).

## Local Guides

**Alessandra Marchetti,** a Florentine who has lived in the US, gives private walking tours of Florence and driving tours of Tuscany. Her passion is teaching about Michelangelo (€60-75/hour, mobile 347-386-9839, www.tuscanydriverguide.com, alessandramarchettitours@gmail.com).

**Paola Migliorini** and her partners offer museum tours, city walking tours, family tours, private cooking classes, wine tours, and Tuscan excursions by van—you can tailor tours as you like (€65/hour without car, €70/hour in a van for up to 8 passengers, mobile 347-657-2611, www.florencetour.com, info@florencetour.com). They also do cruise excursions from the port of Livorno (€600/up to 4 people, €680/up to 6, €780/up to 8).

**Elena Fulceri,** specializing in art, history, and secret corners, is a delightful and engaging guide. She organizes heartfelt, tailor-made private tours, has good Oltrarno artisan connections, and enjoys family tours (from €60/hour for 2 people, mobile 347-942-2054, www.florencewithflair.com, info@florencewithflair.com).

**Vanessa Garau** is an enthusiastic young guide with good connections in the Oltrarno and an infectious love of Florence (half-day private tours for €150, mobile 349-133-6894, garau.vanessa@gmail.com).

# Renaissance Walk

This great and rich city is easily covered on foot. We'll start with the soaring church dome that stands as the proud symbol of the Renaissance spirit; just opposite, you'll find the Baptistery doors that opened the Renaissance. We'll then stroll down the city's pedestrian-only main street to the Palazzo Vecchio and the Arno River. Along the way, we'll pass elegant stores, lively eateries, and the parade of people that make up Florence today.

For more details on many of the stops on this walk, see the individual listings under "Sights in Florence," later.

**Length of This Walk:** The walk is less than a mile long. Allow two hours, including visits to the interiors of the Baptistery and Orsanmichele Church.

**Tours:** ⋒ Download my free Renaissance Walk audio tour.

**Services:** Pay WCs are at the ticket office opposite the Baptistery.

**Background:** The Renaissance—the "rebirth" of Greek and Roman culture that swept across Europe—started around 1400 and lasted about 150 years. In politics, the Renaissance meant democracy; in science, a renewed interest in exploring nature. The general mood was optimistic and "humanistic," with a confidence in the power of the individual.

Renaissance art was a return to the realism and balance of Greek and Roman sculpture and architecture. Domes and round arches replaced Gothic spires and pointed arches. In painting and sculpture, Renaissance artists strove for realism. Merging art and science, they used mathematics, the laws of perspective, and direct observation of nature.

This was not an anti-Christian movement. Artists saw themselves as an extension of God's creative powers. The Church even supported the Renaissance and commissioned many of its greatest works. After 1,000 years of waiting, the embers of Europe's classical heritage burst into flames right here in Florence.

## ↴ SELF-GUIDED WALK

• *The Duomo, the cathedral with the distinctive red dome, is the center of Florence and the orientation point for this walk. If you ever get lost, home's the dome. Stroll around the piazza in front of the cathedral (the Duomo), and take in the sights. To the right of the Duomo rises its sky-scraping bell tower (the Campanile). In front of the church is the Baptistery, an octagonal, black-and-white stone building that's bigger than many churches.*

## ❶ The Duomo

Florence's massive cathedral is the city's geographical and spiritual heart. Its dome, visible from all over the city, inspired Florentines to do great things.

FLORENCE

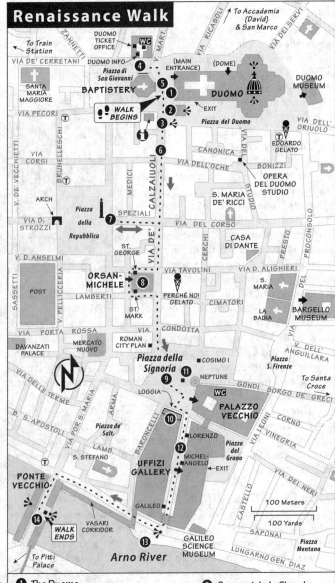

# Renaissance Walk

1. The Duomo
2. Campanile
3. View of the Dome
4. Baptistery – North Doors
5. Baptistery – East Doors (Gates of Paradise)
6. Via de' Calzaiuoli
7. Piazza della Repubblica
8. Orsanmichele Church
9. Piazza della Signoria
10. Loggia dei Lanzi
11. Savonarola Plaque
12. Uffizi Courtyard Statues
13. Arno River
14. Ponte Vecchio

The church was begun in the 1296, in the Gothic style. After generations of work, it was still unfinished. The facade was little more than bare brick, and it stood that way until it was completed in 1870 in the "Neo"-Gothic style. Its "retro" look captures

the feel of the original medieval facade, with green, white, and pink marble sheets that cover the brick construction. You'll see Gothic (pointed) arches and three stories decorated with mosaics and statues. This over-the-top facade is adored by many, while others call it "the cathedral in pajamas." The Duomo is dedicated to the Virgin Mary. Find her statue right in the center—above the main doorway but below the round window.

We won't go inside the church on this tour. It has a cavernous, bare interior with a few noteworthy sights. Entry is free, but there's often a long wait.

• *Now turn to the church's bell tower, to the right.*

## ❷ Campanile (Giotto's Tower)

The 270-foot bell tower was begun in the 1300s by the great painter Giotto. As a forerunner of the Renaissance genius, Giotto excelled in many artistic fields, just as Michelangelo would do two centuries later. In his day, Giotto was called the ugliest man to ever walk the streets of Florence, but he designed what many call the most beautiful bell tower in all of Europe.

You can climb the Campanile for great views. It doesn't require a reservation, just a Duomo combo-ticket (see page 491 for information about climbing the tower).

• *Now take in the Duomo's star attraction: the dome. The best viewing spot is just to the right of the facade, from the corner of the pedestrian-only Via de' Calzaiuoli.*

## ❸ View of Brunelleschi's Dome

Though construction of the church had begun in 1296, by the 1400s there still was no suitable roof. City fathers intended to top it with a dome, but the technology to span the 140-foot-wide hole had yet to be invented. *Non c'è problema.* The brash Florentines knew that someday someone would come along who could handle the challenge. That man was Filippo Brunelleschi.

Brunelleschi had a plan. He would cap the church's octagonal hole in the roof with a round Roman-style dome. It would be a tall, self-supporting dome as grand as that of the ancient Pantheon—which he had studied.

Brunelleschi used a dome within a dome. What you see is the outer shell, covered in terra-cotta tile. The inner dome is thicker and provides much of the structural support. The grand white skeletal ribs connect at the top, supporting each other in a way similar to a pointed arch. Hidden between them are interlocking bricks, laid in a herringbone pattern. Rather than being stacked horizontally, like traditional brickwork, the alternating vertical bricks act as "bookends." The dome grew upward like an igloo, supporting itself as it proceeded from the base. When the ribs reached the top, Brunelleschi arched them in and fixed them in place with the lantern at the top. His dome, built in only 14 years, was the largest since ancient Rome's Pantheon.

When completed in 1436, Brunelleschi's dome was the wonder of the age. It became the model for many domes to follow, from St. Peter's to the US Capitol. Michelangelo, setting out to construct the dome of St. Peter's, drew inspiration from the dome of Florence. He said, "I'll make its sister...bigger, but not more beautiful."

You can climb the dome for Florence's best views, but it requires a reservation in advance (for details, see page 489).

• *Next up, the Baptistery.*

## Baptistery and Ghiberti's Bronze Doors

Built in the 11th century, atop Roman foundations, this is Florence's oldest surviving building—a thousand years old. The Baptistery is known for its doors. The most famous ones are the East Doors, which face the cathedral, but let's start with the North Doors—around to the right, where tourists go in—which may be even more important. (Note that the original doors are in the Duomo Museum and well worth seeing.)

❹ **North Doors:** Some say that these

doors actually started the Renaissance. It was the year 1401, and Florence was holding a competition to find the best artist to make some doors for the Baptistery entrance. All the greats entered the contest, including Donatello and Brunelleschi. The winner was relatively unknown 24-year-old Lorenzo Ghiberti. For the next 25 years, he worked on these North Doors.

• *Now return to the more famous doors facing the church.*

❺ **East Doors** (Gates of Paradise): Ghiberti's bronze panels for these doors added a whole new dimension to art—depth. Michelangelo said these doors were fit to be the "Gates of Paradise." Here we see how the Renaissance masters merged art and science. Realism was in, and Renaissance artists used math, illusion, and dissection to create it. For details on these doors, see page 493.

**Inside the Baptistery:** The spacious interior, topped with an octagonal dome, features a fine example of pre-Renaissance mosaic art (1200s-1300s) in the Byzantine style. Workers from St. Mark's in Venice came here to make the remarkable ceiling mosaics (of Venetian glass) in the late 1200s.

• *Now head south, down the busy pedestrian-only street that runs from here toward the Arno River.*

## ❻ Via de' Calzaiuoli

Via de' Calzaiuoli (kahlts-ay-WOH-lee), the former "street of the stocking makers," was part of the ancient Roman grid plan that became Florence. Around the year 1400, as the Renaissance was blooming, this street connected the religious center (where we are now) with the political center (where we're heading), a five-minute walk away.

Since most vehicles were banned a few years back, this street has been transformed into a pleasant place to stroll, people-watch, window-shop, and wonder why American cities can't become more pedestrian-friendly.

• *Continue down Via de' Calzaiuoli. Two blocks down from the Baptistery, turn right on Via degli Speziali toward the triumphal arch that marks...*

## ❼ Piazza della Repubblica

This large square sits on the site of the original Roman Forum. The lone column that still stands here—nicknamed the "belly button of Florence"—once marked the intersection of the two

main Roman roads (Via Corso and Via Roma). If you look at a map of Florence today, you can make out the ghost of Rome in its streets: a grid-plan city center surrounded by a circular city wall.

In the 1860s, the square got its magnificent triumphal arch. It celebrated the unification of Italy. In fact, from 1865 to 1870, Florence became the capital of the newly united nation of Italy.

Venerable cafés and stores line the square. During the 19th century, intellectuals met in cafés here. Gilli, on the northeast corner, is a favorite for its grand atmosphere and tasty sweets (cheap if you stand at the bar, expensive to sit down).

• *Return to the main street and continue walking toward the river. A block farther, at the intersection with Via Orsanmichele, is the...*

## ❽ Orsanmichele Church

Originally, this was an open loggia (covered porch) with a huge grain warehouse upstairs. Then, as you can see, the arches of the loggia were artfully filled in (14th century) to make walls, and the building gained a new purpose—as a church.

The 14 niches in the exterior walls feature remarkable-in-their-day statues paid for by the city's rising middle class of merchants and their 21 guilds. Florence in 1400 was a republic, a government working for the interests not of a king, but of these guilds, which commissioned statues as PR gestures.

• *Circle the church exterior counterclockwise to enjoy the statues. Start on the church's right side (along Via Orsanmichele).*

In the third niche is **Nanni di Banco's** *Quattro Santi Coronati* (c. 1415-1417). These four early Christians were sculptors martyred

by the Roman emperor Diocletian because they refused to sculpt pagan gods. They seem to be contemplating the consequences of the fatal decision they're about to make.

Just to the right of Banco's saints is **Donatello's** *St. George.* He's alert, perched on the edge of his niche, scanning the horizon for dragons and announcing the new age with its new outlook. His knitted brow shows there's a drama unfolding. Sure, he's anxious, but he's also self-assured. Comparing this Renaissance-style *St. George* to *Quattro Santi Coronati*, you can psychoanalyze the heady changes underway. This is humanism.

The back side of the church is decorated by three statues worth a look. **St. Matthew,** patron of bankers, and **St. Stephen,** patron of wool merchants (both by Ghiberti), are a reminder that banking and textiles were mainstays of the Florentine economy. Nanni di Banco's *St. Eligius,* patron of metalworkers, shows workers shoeing a horse.

Around the corner, the first niche features **Donatello's *St. Mark*** (1411-1413). The evangelist cradles his gospel in his strong, veined hand and gazes out, resting his weight on the right leg while bending the left. Though subtle, St. Mark's twisting *contrapposto* pose was the first seen since antiquity. Eighty years after young Donatello carved this statue, a teenage Michelangelo Buonarroti stood here and marveled at it.

• *Backtrack to the entrance and go inside.*

Step into Florence circa 1350. The church does not have a typical nave because it was adapted from a granary. Look for the pillars (on the left wall) with rectangular **holes** in them about four feet off the ground. These were once used as chutes for delivering grain from the storage rooms upstairs.

The fanciful **tabernacle** by Andrea Orcagna was designed exactly for this space: Like the biggest Christmas tree possible, it's capped by an angel whose head touches the ceiling. The elaborate tabernacle was built to display Bernardo Daddi's *Madonna delle Grazie,* which received plague survivors' grateful prayers of thanks.

Upstairs is a free museum (open Mon and Sat only) displaying most of the originals of the statues you just saw outside.

• *Continue down the mall 50 more yards, to the huge and historic square...*

## ❾ Piazza della Signoria

What a view! This piazza—the main civic center of Florence—is dominated by the massive stone facade of the Palazzo Vecchio, with a tower that reaches for the sky. The square is dotted with statues. The stately Uffizi Gallery is nearby, and the marble greatness of old Florence litters the cobbles. Piazza della Signoria, with the

feel of an open-air museum of statuary, still vibrates with the echoes of the city's past—executions, riots, and great celebrations. There's even Roman history: Look for the **chart** showing the ancient city (in front of Chanel). Today, it's a tourist's world with pigeons, selfie sticks, horse buggies, and tired spouses. For a little pick-me-up, stop in at the recommended **$$$ Rivoire** café to enjoy its fine desserts, pudding-thick hot chocolate, and the best view seats in town.

Before you towers the **Palazzo Vecchio,** the "old palace" and palatial town hall of the Medici—a fortress designed to contain riches and survive the many riots that went with local politics. The windows are just beyond the reach of angry stones, and the tower was a handy lookout post. Justice was doled out sternly on this square. Until 1873, Michelangelo's **David** stood where you see the replica today. Step through the front door into the Palazzo Vecchio's courtyard (free). This palace was Florence's symbol of civic power. You're surrounded by art for art's sake—a cherub frivolously marks the courtyard's center, and ornate stuccoes and frescoes decorate the walls and columns. Such luxury represented a big change 500 years ago.

For more on the palazzo and climbing its tower, see page 507.
• *Back outside, check out the arcade of three arches filled with statues.*

## ⓾ Loggia dei Lanzi

The loggia, once a forum for public debate, was perfect for a city that prided itself on its democratic traditions. But later, when the Medici figured that good art was more desirable than free speech, it was turned into an outdoor sculpture gallery.

Two statues in the front deserve a closer look. At the right end of the loggia, **The Rape of the Sabine Women** (c. 1583)—with its pulse-quickening rhythm of muscles—is from the restless Mannerist period. The sculptor, Giambologna, proved his mastery of the medium by sculpting three entangled bodies from one piece of marble.

Benvenuto Cellini's **Perseus** (1545-1553), the loggia's most noteworthy piece, shows the Greek hero who decapitated the snake-headed Medusa. Cellini, a notorious braggart, placed his name prominently across the sash on the front and amazingly, included a secret self-portrait on the back of Perseus' head: his locks form the beard while the helmet frames the bushy brow and eyes.

• *Cross the square to Bartolomeo Ammanati's big **fountain of Neptune**. Near it, the guy on the horse is Cosimo I, the post-Renaissance Medici who commissioned the Uffizi. Find the round marble plaque on the ground 10 steps in front of the fountain.*

## ⓫ Savonarola Plaque

In the 1490s the Medici family was briefly thrown from power by an austere and charismatic monk named Savonarola, who made Florence a constitutional republic. He organized huge rallies lit by roaring bonfires here on the square where he preached. The devout brought their rich "vanities" (such as paintings, musical instruments, and playing cards) and threw them into the flames.

But not everyone wanted a return to the medieval past. Encouraged by the pope, the Florentines fought back and arrested Savonarola. For two days, they tortured him, and finally, on the very spot where Savonarola's followers had built bonfires of vanities, the monk was burned, ending his theocracy. Soon after, the Medici returned to power and the Renaissance picked up where it left off.

• *Stay cool, we have 200 yards to go. Follow the gaze of the fake* David *into the courtyard of the two-tone horseshoe-shaped building.*

## ⓬ Uffizi Courtyard Statues

The top floor of this building, known as the *uffizi* (offices) during Medici days, is filled with the greatest collection of Florentine painting anywhere. It's one of Europe's top four or five art galleries (see page 502 for what you'll find inside).

The courtyard is watched over by 19th-century statues of the great figures of the Renaissance: artists (Michelangelo, Giotto, Donatello, Leonardo), philosophers (Machiavelli), scientists (Galileo), poets (Dante and Petrarch), explorers (Vespucci), and the great patron of the Renaissance—Lorenzo "the Magnificent" de' Medici.

• *At the far end of the courtyard, pause at the* ⓭ **Arno River**, *with a magnificent view of the Ponte Vecchio, where we'll finish this walk.*

## ⓮ Ponte Vecchio

Since ancient times, a bridge has stood at this narrow spot in the Arno. When a flood washed away the old wooden bridge, this one

was built in 1345, and is now called the Ponte Vecchio (Old Bridge).

In times past, the bridge's shops were inhabited by butchers and hide tanners—a natural fit, because they could empty their waste into the river below. In the 1500s, the Medici booted them out and installed gold- and silversmiths who still tempt visitors to this day. Fittingly, a famous goldsmith is honored with a fine bust at the central point of the bridge—the sculptor Benvenuto *("Perseus")* Cellini.

**FLORENCE**

Look up to notice the windows running across the upper part of the buildings. This is the Vasari Corridor—a protected and elevated passageway, built by the Medici. It led from the Palazzo Vecchio through the Uffizi, across Ponte Vecchio, and up to the immense Pitti Palace, four blocks beyond the bridge.

Looking upstream and down, you have timeless views of the city. The neighborhood across the river, known as the Oltrarno, is more rustic and working-class. The other bridges are all modern replacements.

The Ponte Vecchio is a very romantic spot, especially in the evening. Street musicians play and lovers hold hands. The city of Florence—born in Roman times, flourishing in the medieval age, and blossoming in the Renaissance—remains a vibrant cultural capital.

• *From the Duomo to the Arno, we've taken in sights from Florence's medieval roots and Renaissance greats. After this introduction, several of the finest museums in Europe await your discovery—or perhaps it's time for a nice espresso or gelato. Enjoy.*

# Sights in Florence

## ADVANCE RESERVATIONS FOR SKIPPING LINES

To avoid long lines, make advance reservations for the Uffizi, Accademia, and climbing the Duomo's dome. Get reservations as soon as you know when you'll be in town. Though lines are less of a problem after 16:00, and from November through March, it's always crowded from April through October and on weekends. For peace of mind, I'd reserve a spot any time of year.

**Uffizi and Accademia Tickets:** Book your tickets in advance at the websites for these museums (see individual sight listings in this chapter)—available time-slots for full-price tickets are marked "Intero/Full." You'll receive an email with a voucher that you take to the ticket desk a few minutes before your visit to swap for an actual ticket.

If there's no availability at the official museum sites, you can try for-profit vendors such as Florence.net or Tickitaly.com, which may have time slots available, though you'll pay about €5 more per ticket.

Uffizi and Accademia tickets are also available by phone: From a US phone, dial 011-39-055-294-883, or from an Italian phone call 055-294-883 (€4/ticket reservation fee; booking office open Mon-Fri 8:30-18:30, Sat until 12:30, closed Sun).

Various companies—including those listed in this chapter—sell tours that include a reserved museum admission. If you're booking a private guide well in advance, they are often happy to obtain tickets and reservations for your tour with them.

**Climbing the Duomo's Dome:** For reservation information, see below.

## THE DUOMO AND NEARBY

Florence's most distinctive monuments—the Duomo, Baptistery, and Campanile—are gathered between the pedestrian-only Piazza San Giovanni and Piazza del Duomo. The Duomo Museum, just behind the cathedral, is the most important of these sights—and it never has long lines. But you must plan ahead for the dome climb (only possible with an advance reservation).

The Campanile and Baptistery offer no reserved tickets and come with modest lines.

**Ticketing:** While the Duomo is free to enter, several associated sights are covered by a single €18 **combo-ticket,** valid for 72 hours: the Baptistery, dome, Campanile, Duomo Museum, and Santa Reparata crypt (enter inside the Duomo). A €13 audioguide covers all of the Duomo sights.

The only way to climb the dome is with a reservation. You can buy the combo-ticket and make a **dome-climb reservation** at www.museumflorence.com. Dome-climb time slots can fill up days in advance, so reserve well ahead. If you buy your combo-ticket in Florence, you can try to reserve a time in person at the main Duomo ticket office or at a ticket machine in the Duomo Museum lobby.

The main ticket office faces the Baptistery entrance (at #7 on the square). It has a staffed counter (credit cards or cash) as well as self-service machines (credit cards only, requires PIN). There's also a ticket counter at the Duomo Museum.

**Themed Tours:** Three themed tours are organized by the Duomo (€33 each, includes combo-ticket, 1 hour, English only). These include a Duomo visit with access to the north terrace of the church (daily at 10:30); an opportunity to watch contemporary stonemasons at work in the same workshop where Michelangelo carved *David* (Mon, Wed, and Fri at 12:00); and an up-close look at the mosaics of the Baptistery (Mon, Wed, and Fri at 16:30). To book a spot, call 055-230-2885, email commerciale@operadelduomo.firenze.it, or stop by the main ticket office.

🎧 The Duomo, dome, Campanile, and Baptistery are also covered on my free Renaissance Walk audio tour.

### ▲▲Duomo (Cattedrale di Santa Maria del Fiore)

Florence's Gothic cathedral has the third-longest nave in Christendom. The church's noisy Neo-Gothic facade (from the 1870s) is covered with pink, green, and white Tuscan marble. The cathedral's claim to artistic fame is Brunelleschi's magnificent dome—the first Renaissance dome and the model for domes to follow. While viewing it from the outside is well worth ▲▲, the massive but empty-feeling interior is lucky to rate ▲—it doesn't justify the massive crowds that line up to get inside. Much of the great art is housed in the Duomo Museum behind the church.

**Cost and Hours:** Free; Mon-Sat 10:00-16:30, Sun 13:30-16:45, opening times sometimes change due to religious functions, modest dress code enforced, tel. 055-230-2885, www.museumflorence.com.

**Mass:** The church is open to all for Mass: English Mass on Sun at 17:00 and old-school Latin Mass with Gregorian chants on Sun at 10:30.

### ▲Climbing the Duomo's Dome

For a grand view into the cathedral from the base of the dome, a chance to see Brunelleschi's "dome-within-a-dome" construction,

and a glorious Florence view from the top, climb 463 steps up the dome. The claustrophobic one-way route takes you up narrow, steep staircases and walkways to the top—but it's well worth the climb.

**Cost:** Covered by Duomo combo-ticket; must reserve dome-climb time—best to buy combo-ticket and reserve a time either at the ticket office (opposite the Baptistery, at #7, open daily 8:00-19:00) or online (www.museumflorence.com).

**Hours:** Mon-Fri 8:30-19:00, Sat until 17:00, Sun 13:00-16:00; enter from the north side of the

FLORENCE

church (get in line about 15 minutes before your reservation time). The dome is closed during rain.

**Climbing the Dome:** While waiting to enter at your reserved time, spend a few minutes studying the side-entrance door, called the Porta della Mandorla ("Almond Door"). Just above the delicately carved doorframe is a colorful Annunciation mosaic by Nanni di Banco, and above that, in a sculpted almond-shaped frame, the Madonna is borne up to heaven by angels. If you look up from here you'll see an empty pedestal atop the transept. Michelangelo's *David* was originally destined to adorn one of these.

The climb is long but there are small landings where you can pull over and take a breather. Halfway up, you'll stroll on the walkway high above the altar where you can get a close-up of Vasari's *Last Judgment* ceiling (especially the ghoulish lower portion, filled with scenes of eternal torment) and a vertigo-inducing view of the nave. After a few tight, winding staircases and a steep final climb, you'll pop out of the hatch on the crowded terrace with a grand city view. If possible, visit at sunset for a romantic experience.

### ▲Campanile (Giotto's Tower)

The 270-foot bell tower has 50-some fewer steps than the Duomo's dome (but that's still 414 steps—no elevator); offers a faster, less-intense climb (with typically short lines); and has a view of that magnificent dome to boot. On the way up, there are several intermediate levels where you can catch your breath and enjoy ever-higher views. The stairs narrow as you go, creating a mosh-pit bottleneck near the very top—but the views are worth the hassle. While the viewpoints are enclosed by cage-like bars, the gaps are big enough to snap great photos.

**Cost and Hours:** Covered by Duomo combo-ticket; daily 8:15-19:30, last entry 40 minutes before closing.

### ▲Baptistery

Michelangelo said the bronze doors of this octagonal building were fit to be the gates of paradise. Check out the gleaming copies of Lorenzo Ghiberti's bronze doors facing the Duomo (the originals

are in the Duomo Museum). Making a breakthrough in perspective, Ghiberti used mathematical laws to create the illusion of receding distance on a basically flat surface.

The doors on the north side of the building (around to the right) were designed by Ghiberti when he was younger; he'd won the honor and opportunity by beating Brunelleschi in a competition (the rivals' original entries are in the Bargello).

Inside, sit and savor the medieval mosaic ceiling, where it's always Judgment Day and Jesus is giving the ultimate thumbs-up or thumbs-down.

**Cost and Hours:** Covered by Duomo combo-ticket; interior open Mon-Sat 8:15-19:30, Sun until 13:30. The (facsimile) bronze doors are on the exterior, so they are always "open" and viewable.

### ▲▲▲Duomo Museum (Museo dell'Opera del Duomo)

The often-overlooked but superbly presented cathedral museum is filled with some of the best sculpture of the Renaissance, includ-

ing a late Michelangelo pietà and statues from the original Baptistery facade. Remarkably, it's almost never crowded. It also holds Brunelleschi's models for his dome, Donatello's emaciated *Mary Magdalene* and playful choir loft, and Ghiberti's original bronze Gates of Paradise panels (the ones on the Baptistery's doors today are copies).

**Cost and Hours:** Covered by Duomo combo-ticket; daily 9:00-19:00, closed first Tue of each month, last entry one hour before closing; one of the few museums in Florence always open Mon; behind the church at Via del Proconsolo 9, tel. 055-230-2885, www.museumflorence.com.

**Visiting the Museum:** Begin with the **model of the Duomo's facade** circa 1500, the era of Michelangelo (Room 4). Notice that only the lower third is faced with marble and statues; the rest was only bare brick. Church construction began in 1296, but after an initial burst of energy, petered out. The facade was meant to be a glorious showcase of great statues set into niches.

Now enter the **Hall of Paradise** (Sala del Paradiso, Room 6). On one wall, this room re-creates that lower third of the facade we saw on the model. The opposite wall re-creates the Baptistery facade. Both buildings were a showcase of the greatest art of Florence from roughly 1300 to 1600.

Start with the Duomo wall. Peruse the various statues, done by many different artists from different eras, and consider the church's long evolution. The Duomo began life in early medieval times as a humble church overshadowed by the more prestigious Baptistery. By the 1200s, the church wasn't big enough to contain the exuberant spirit of a city growing rich from the wool trade and banking. So Florence set out to rebuild it, intending to make the finest church of the age.

Facing the facade of the church, as they did in the Middle

## Ghiberti's "Gates of Paradise"

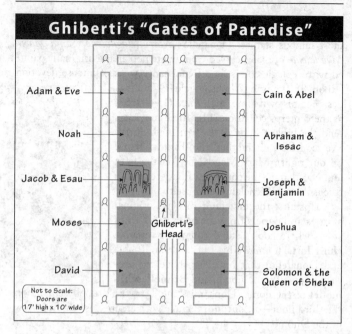

Adam & Eve

Noah

Jacob & Esau

Moses

David

Ghiberti's Head

Cain & Abel

Abraham & Issac

Joseph & Benjamin

Joshua

Solomon & the Queen of Sheba

Not to Scale: Doors are 17' high x 10' wide

Ages, are the famous doors of the Baptistery. Here's your chance to study the original panels. The oldest doors on the left are by Pisano (South Doors, c. 1330). The original competition doors on the right are the first ones done by Ghiberti (North Doors, 1403-1424). And in the center are the Gates of Paradise by Ghiberti (East Doors, 1425-1452).

These bronze "Gates of Paradise" revolutionized the way Renaissance people saw the world around them. They tell several Old Testament stories using perspective and realism as never before. Ghiberti poured his energy and creativity into these panels. That's him in the center of the door frame, atop the second row of panels—the head on the left with the shiny male-pattern baldness.

Armed with new rules of perspective, Ghiberti rendered reality with a mathematical precision revolutionary for the time. To understand how these advances made visual space feel more real than ever before, study the space created by the arches in the **Jacob and Esau panel** (left side, third from top). At the center is the so-called vanishing point on the distant horizon, where all the arches and floor tiles converge. Those closest to us, at the bottom of the panel, are big and clearly defined. Distant figures are smaller, fuzzier, and higher up. Ghiberti has placed us as part of this casual crowd of holy people—some with their backs to us—milling around an arcade. Suddenly the world has acquired a whole new dimension—depth.

Also on the ground floor are rooms dedicated to the museum's most famous statues. Donatello's **Mary Magdalene** (*Santa Maria Maddalena*, c. 1455), carved from white poplar and originally painted with realistic colors, is a Renaissance work of intense devotion (Room 8). The aging Michelangelo (1475-1564) designed his own tomb, with **Pietà** (1547-1555) as the centerpiece (Room 10). Three mourners tend the broken body of the crucified Christ. We see Mary, his mother (the shadowy figure on our right); Mary Magdalene (on the left); and Nicodemus, the converted Pharisee, whose face is that of Michelangelo himself.

Upstairs, the first floor displays original **statues and panels** from the bell tower's third story, where copies stand today, two marble **choir lofts** (*cantorie;* by Lucca della Robbia and Donatello) that once sat above the sacristy doors of the Duomo, and **Brunelleschi's model** of the dome. Don't miss the Terrazza Brunelleschiana on the third floor—an **outdoor terrace** with an up-close rooftop view of the Duomo.

## NORTH OF THE DUOMO
### ▲▲▲Accademia (Galleria dell'Accademia)

This museum houses Michelangelo's *David,* the consummate Renaissance statue of the buff, biblical shepherd boy ready to take on the giant. This six-ton, 17-foot-tall symbol of divine victory over evil represents a new century and a whole new Renaissance outlook. This is the age of Columbus and classicism, Galileo and Gutenberg, Luther and Leonardo—of Florence and the Renaissance.

The Accademia also contains some of the master's other works, including his powerful (unfinished) *Prisoners* and *St. Matthew,* as well as a pietà (possibly by one of his disciples). You'll also see some mildly interesting pre-Renaissance and Renaissance paintings, including a couple of Botticellis, the plaster model of Giambologna's *Rape of the Sabine Women,* and a musical instrument collection with an early piano.

**Cost and Hours:** €12, additional €4 for recommended reservation, free and crowded on first Sun of the month Oct-March; Tue-Sun 8:15-19:00, closed Mon; July-Sept open Tue and Thu 7:00-22:00; audioguide-€6, Via Ricasoli 60, reservation tel. 055-294-883, www.galleriaaccademiafirenze.beniculturali.it.

**Visiting the Museum:** In 1501, Michelangelo Buonarroti, a 26-year-old Florentine, was commissioned to carve a large-scale work for the Duomo. He was given a block of marble that other sculptors had rejected as too tall, shallow, and flawed to be of any value. But Michelangelo picked up his hammer and chisel, knocked a knot off what became *David*'s heart, and started to work.

The statue captures David as he's sizing up his enemy. He stands relaxed but alert, leaning on one leg in a classical pose known as *contrapposto*. In his powerful left hand, he fondles the handle of the sling, ready to fling a stone at the giant. His gaze is steady—searching with intense concentration, but also with extreme confidence. Michelangelo has caught the precise moment when David is saying to himself, "I can take this guy."

*David* is a symbol of Renaissance optimism. He's no brute. He's a civilized, thinking individual who can grapple with and overcome problems. He needs no armor, only his God-given physical strength and wits. Look at his right hand, with the raised veins and strong, relaxed fingers—many complained that it was too big and overdeveloped. But this is the hand of a man with the strength of God on his side. No mere boy could slay the giant. But David, powered by God, could...and did.

Renaissance Florentines could identify with *David*. Like him, they considered themselves God-blessed underdogs fighting their city-state rivals. In a deeper sense, they were civilized Renaissance people slaying the ugly giant of medieval superstition, pessimism, and oppression.

### ▲Piazza Santissima Annunziata

The most Renaissance square in Florence is tucked just a block behind the Accademia. It's like an urban cloister (the image of the ideal city) from the 15th century, with three fine buildings—a convent church, a hospital, and an orphanage—ringing a fine equestrian statue of Ferdinand, a Medici grand duke of the then-independent state of Tuscany. Stand in the center and slowly spin, imagining being here in 1500 as you survey the only Renaissance square in Florence, with the towering Duomo down the street.

The 15th-century **Santissima Annunziata Church** (with its Bill and Melinda Gates-type patronage attribution to the Pucci brothers: Alexander and Roberto) is worth a peek. The welcoming cloister has early-16th-

FLORENCE

century frescoes by Andrea del Sarto, and the church's interior is slathered in Baroque—rare in Florence.

Filippo Brunelleschi's **Hospital of the Innocents** (Ospedale degli Innocenti), built in the 1420s, is considered the first Renaissance building. Its graceful arches and columns, with each set of columns forming a square, embody the quintessence of Renaissance harmony and typified the new aesthetic of calm balance and symmetry. It's ornamented with terra-cotta medallions by Luca della Robbia—each showing a different way to wrap an infant (swaddled—meant to help babies grow straight, and practiced in Italy until about a century ago). Terra-cotta—made of glazed and painted clay—was a combination of painting and sculpture, durable and economic. For three generations, the Della Robbia family guarded the secret recipe and made their name by bringing this affordable art medium to Florence.

With its mission to care for the least among society (parentless or unwanted children), this hospital was also an important symbol of the increasingly humanistic and humanitarian outlook of Renaissance Florence. For four centuries (until 1875), orphans would be left at the "wheel of the innocents" (the small, barred window at the far left of the porch).

The **Museum of the Innocents** fills the hospital. A fine exhibit tells the story of these infants with artifacts that help you imagine what it was like living here. It also houses some fine art, including several iconic glazed terra-cotta medallions by the Della Robbia family (€7, daily 10:00-19:00, audioguide—€3, tel. 055-203-7301, www.museodeglinnocenti.it). **$$ Caffè del Verone,** on the museum's top terrace, offers a nice, peaceful break with rooftop views.

### ▲▲Museum of San Marco (Museo di San Marco)

One block north of the Accademia, this 15th-century monastery houses the greatest collection anywhere of frescoes and paintings by the early Renaissance master Fra Angelico. The ground floor features the monk's paintings, along with works by Fra Bartolomeo.

Upstairs are 43 cells decorated by Fra Angelico and his assistants. While the monk/painter was trained in the medieval religious style, he also learned and adopted Renaissance techniques and sensibilities, producing works that blended Christian symbols and Renaissance realism. Don't miss the cell of

Savonarola, the charismatic monk who rode in from the Christian right, threw out the Medici, turned Florence into a theocracy, sponsored "bonfires of the vanities" (burning books, paintings, and so on), and was finally burned himself when Florence decided to change channels.

**Cost and Hours:** €8, Tue-Fri 8:15-14:00, Sat-Sun until 17:00; also open until 14:00 on first, third, and fifth Mon of each month; reservations possible but unnecessary, on Piazza San Marco, tel. 055-238-8608.

### Basilica of San Lorenzo

The Basilica of San Lorenzo—on the site of the first Christian church in Florence—was built outside the Roman walls and consecrated in AD 393, then rebuilt in the early 1400s. That's when Filippo Brunelleschi was hired to replace a Romanesque church that stood here. Brunelleschi designed the building, and Donatello worked on the bronze pulpits inside (among other things). Adjacent to the church is a cloister where you can visit the crypt (with the tombs of Cosimo the Elder and Donatello) and the Laurentian Medici Library, designed by Michelangelo. (The famed Medici Chapels, with Michelangelo's tomb sculptures, are part of the church complex but have a separate ticket; see next listing.)

**Cost and Hours:** €7 for the church and crypt, buy ticket just inside cloister to the left of the facade; €9.50 combo-ticket also covers the library; €3 for library only; church and crypt open Mon-Sat 10:00-17:30, closed Sun, shorter hours off-season, library Mon-Fri 9:30-13:30, closed Sat-Sun; Piazza di San Lorenzo, tel. 055-214-042, www.operamedicealaurenziana.org.

### ▲▲Medici Chapels (Cappelle Medicee)

The burial site of the ruling Medici family in the Basilica of San Lorenzo includes the dusky crypt; the big, domed Chapel of Princes; and the magnificent New Sacristy, featuring architecture, tombs, and statues almost entirely by Michelangelo. The Medici made their money in textiles and banking, and patronized a dream team of Renaissance artists that put Florence on the cultural map. Michelangelo,

**FLORENCE**

who spent his teen years living with the Medici, was commissioned to create the family's final tribute.

**Cost and Hours:** €8, free first Sun of the month Oct-March; Tue-Sat 8:15-17:00 except Oct-late May until 14:00, last entry 45 minutes before closing; also open second and fourth Mon and first, third, and fifth Sun of each month; audioguide-€6, modest dress required, tel. 055-238-8602, www.bargellomusei.beniculturali.it.

### ▲San Lorenzo Market

Florence's vast open-air market sprawls in the streets between the Duomo and the train station, with the highest concentration in the streets ringing Mercato Centrale (daily 9:00-19:00, closed Mon in winter). More popular with tourists than locals, it's a hodgepodge of vendors selling T-shirts, scarves, cheap souvenirs, and leather goods of varying quality. At stalls or shops, prices are soft—don't be shy about bargaining.

### ▲Mercato Centrale (Central Market)

Florence's giant iron-and-glass-covered central market was constructed around 1865 as part of the city remake during the unification of Italy, when Florence was, for a few years, the capital of the newly formed country. Stand back and see it as an Industrial Age triumph...a temple of commerce and good food. Then step in and explore the fragrant and picturesque wonderland of produce.

Downstairs, you'll see parts of the cow (and bull) you'd never dream of eating (no, that's not a turkey neck), enjoy free samples, watch pasta being made, and have your pick of plenty of fun eateries sloshing out cheap and tasty pasta to locals (Mon-Fri 7:00-14:00, Sat until 17:00, closed Sun).

Upstairs, the meticulously restored glass roof and steel rafters soar over a modern and extremely touristy food court (daily 10:00-24:00). For eating ideas downstairs, upstairs, and around the market, see "Eating in Florence," later.

### ▲Medici-Riccardi Palace (Palazzo Medici-Riccardi)

Lorenzo the Magnificent's home is worth a look for its art. The tiny Chapel of the Magi contains colorful Renaissance gems such as *The Journey of the Magi* frescoes by Benozzo Gozzoli. The former library has a Baroque ceiling fresco by Luca Giordano, a prolific artist from Naples known as "Fast Luke" *(Luca fa presto)* for his speedy workmanship. While the Medici originally occupied this 1444 house, in the 1700s it became home to the Riccardi family, who added the Baroque flourishes.

**Cost and Hours:** €10, Thu-Tue 9:00-19:00, closed Wed, ticket entrance is off the central courtyard, enter from Via Cavour 1 or Via de' Ginori 1, tel. 055-276-8224, www. palazzomediciriccardi.it.

## BETWEEN THE DUOMO AND PIAZZA DELLA SIGNORIA

### ▲Orsanmichele Church

In the ninth century, this loggia (covered courtyard) was a market used for selling grain (stored upstairs). Later, it was enclosed to make a church. Outside are dynamic statue-filled niches, some with accompanying symbols from the guilds that sponsored the new Renaissance-style art. For more on the statues and the church interior (with a glorious Gothic tabernacle), see page 484.

**Cost and Hours:** Free, daily 10:00-17:00, free upstairs museum open only Mon 10:00-17:00 and Sat 10:00-12:30.

**Evening Concerts:** You can give special thanks if you're in town when the church is hosting an evening concert (tickets sold on day of concert from door facing Via de' Calzaiuoli or, on Sun, from the doorway opposite the church entrance; also books Uffizi and Accademia tickets, ticket window open Mon-Sat 9:00-16:00, closed Sun).

### ▲Mercato Nuovo (a.k.a. the Straw Market)

This market loggia is how Orsanmichele looked before it became a church. Originally a silk-and-straw market, Mercato Nuovo still functions as a rustic yet touristy market (at the intersection of Via Calimala and Via Porta Rossa; daily 9:00-18:30). Notice the circled X in the center, marking the spot where people landed after being hoisted up to the top and dropped as punishment for bankruptcy (easiest to find when the market is closed and the vendors disappear). You'll also find *Il Porcellino* (a statue of a wild boar nicknamed "The Piglet"), which people rub and give coins to ensure their return to Florence. This new copy, while only a few years old, already has a polished snout. At the back corner, a wagon sells tripe (cow innards) sandwiches—a local favorite.

### ▲Piazza della Repubblica

Located on the site of the original Roman Forum, this square holds all that survives of Roman Florence: a single column. In the 1500s, this historical square served as the center of the city's Jewish quarter (which became a ghetto after Cosimo I walled it up in 1571). The city razed the ghetto and the city walls in the 1860s to make way for Florence's transformation into the grand capital of the newly united nation of Italy. This square was to be its centerpiece,

# Heart of Florence

To Fortezza da Basso

V. VALFONDA

VIA GUELFA

PALAZZO DEGLI AFFARI

CONSERVATORIO DI FULIGNO

V. CENNINI

CENACOLO DI FULIGNO

VIA ALAMANNI

VIA PIACETO

Piazza Adua

(B) #1 & 6 (to San Marco) & 7 (to Fiesole)

VIA FIUME

VIA NAZIONALE

VIA DELL'ARIENTO

VIA TADDEA

Piazza del Mercato Centrale

MERCATO CENTRALE

SAN ZANOBI

SANTA MARIA NOVELLA TRAIN STATION

Valfonda Line T1

FAENZA

S. ANTONINO

SAN LORENZO MARKET

BORGO LA NOCE

VIA

Alamanni-Stazione Line T1 & T2

Largo Alinari

V. AMARINO

MEDICI CHAPELS

Piazza di San Lorenzo

BUS STATION (B)

#12 & 23

Piazza della Stazione

PALAZZO DEI CARTELLONI

V. DEI MELARANCIO

SAN LORENZO

S. CAT. SIENA

#C2 & C4 (B)

VIA DEGLI AVELLI

Piazza dell'Unità Italiana

LAURENTIAN MEDICI LIBRARY

ZANNETTI

VIA DE' CANACCI

SANTA MARIA NOVELLA

Unità Line T2

PEDESTRIAN UNDERPASS TO TRAIN STN.

VIA DEL GIGLIO

V. DELL'ALLORO

VIA DE' CONTI

BORGO

VIA BENEDETTA

VIA DELLA SCALA

SANTA MARIA NOVELLA PERFUMERY

VIA PALAZZUOLO

VIA D. BELLE DONNE

Piazza di Santa Maria Novella

VIA PANZANI

VIA DEI BANCHI

VIA DE' CERRETANI

Piazza di San Giovanni

TREBBIO

RONDINELLI

SANTA MARIA MAGGIORE

VIA DE PORCELLANA

OGNISSANTI

VIA D. PAOLINO

LOGGIA DI SAN PAOLO

ANTINORI

SAN GAETANO

VIA FECORI

GIAC.

VIA CORSI

PESCIONI

V. DE' VECCHIETTI

BRUNELLESCHI

ROMA

TOSINGHI

Piazza della Repubblica

Piazza d'Ognissanti

BORGO OGNISSANTI

VIA DEL SOLE

VIA DEL FOSSI

VIA DEL MORO

VIA DELLA SPADA

VIA DE' TORNABUONI

VIA D. STROZZI

PALAZZO STROZZI

LA RINASCENTE DEPT. STORE

(B) #12

LUNGARNO VESPUCCI

VIA DE' FEDERIGHI

RUCELLAI PALACE

VIA DELLA VIGNA NUOVA

INFERNO

V. D. ANSELMI

ODEON CINEMA

POST

SASSETTI

PECORIA

INTER-TRAVEL

CALIMALA

Piazza Carlo Goldoni

VIA DEL PARIONE

PURGATORIO

PALAZZO CORSINI

Piazza di Santa Trinità

Piazza de' Davanzati

VIA PORTA ROSSA

PALAZZO DAVANZATI

MERCATO NUOVO

PONTE ALLA CARRAIA

LUNGARNO CORSINI

SANTA TRINITÀ

VIA DELLE TERME

BORGO

PARIONCINO

FERRAGAMO MUSEUM

BONBARDE

S.S. APOSTOLI

VIA POR S. MARIA

MANETTO

Piazza de' Salt.

(B) #12

Arno River

LUNGARNO GUICCIARDINI

LUNGARNO ACCIAIUOLI

LAMB.

Piazza Nazaro Sauro

VIA SANTO SPIRITO

PONTE S. TRINITÀ

PONTE VECCHIO

S. Stefano

To Brancacci Chapel

VIA DE' SERRAGLI

VIA MAFFIA

VIA DEL GEPPI

VIA SANTO SPIRITO

GOVERELLI

Piazza de' Frescobaldi

SAN JACOPO

BORGO SAN JACOPO

VASARI CORRIDOR

OLTRARNO

SANTO SPIRITO

VIA S. AGOSTINO

VIA D. S. MARTINO

VIA MAGGIO

VIA D. SPRONE

V. D. RAMAGLIANTI

Piazza della Passera

To Pitti Palace

Piazza di Santa Felicità

Piazza di Santa Maria Soprarno

Piazza di Santo Spirito

FLORENCE

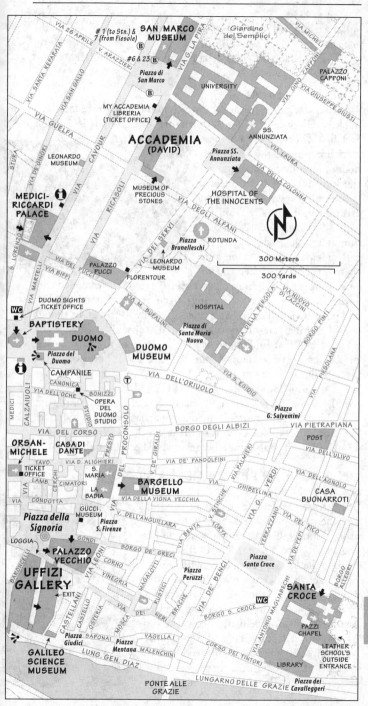

and the triumphal arch is inscribed accordingly: "The squalor of the ancient city is given a new life."

For more about Piazza della Repubblica, see the "Renaissance Walk," earlier.

### ▲Palazzo Davanzati

This five-story, late-medieval tower house offers a rare look at a noble dwelling built in the 14th century. The ground-floor loggia and first floor are always open to visitors; to see the remaining floors (more living quarters and the kitchen), you must make a timed-entry reservation for an escorted visit (usually Mon-Fri at 10:00, 11:00, and 12:00, Sat-Sun at 15:00, 16:00, and 17:00; call or email ahead to be sure there's space or ask when you ar-

rive). Like other buildings of the age, the exterior is festooned with 14th-century horse-tethering rings made from iron, torch holders, and poles upon which to hang laundry and fly flags. Inside, though the furnishings are pretty sparse, you'll see richly painted walls, a long chute that functioned as a well, plenty of fireplaces, a lace display, and even an indoor "outhouse." You can borrow English descriptions in each room.

**Cost and Hours:** €6, Mon-Fri 8:15-14:00; Sat-Sun 13:15-19:00, closed the second and fourth Sun and first, third, and fifth Mon of each month; email mn-bar.capiserviziodavanzati@beniculturali.it to book a visit to the upper floors; Via Porta Rossa 13, tel. 055-238-8610, www.bargellomusei.beniculturali.it.

## ON AND NEAR PIAZZA DELLA SIGNORIA
### ▲▲▲Uffizi Gallery

This greatest collection of Italian paintings anywhere features works by Giotto, Leonardo, Raphael, Caravaggio, Titian, and Michelangelo, and a roomful of Botticellis, including the *Birth of Venus*. Start with Giotto's early stabs at Renaissance-style realism, then move on through the 3-D experimentation of the early 1400s to the real thing rendered by the likes of Botticelli and Leonardo. Finish off with Michelangelo and Raphael. Because only 600 visitors are allowed inside the building at any one time, there's generally a very long wait. The good news: no Vatican-

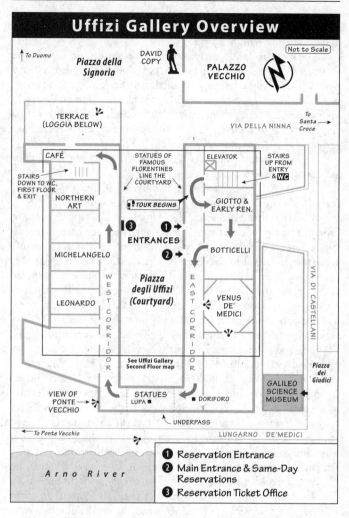

**Uffizi Gallery Overview**

To Duomo

*Piazza della Signoria*

DAVID COPY

PALAZZO VECCHIO

Not to Scale

TERRACE (LOGGIA BELOW)

VIA DELLA NINNA

To Santa Croce

CAFÉ

STATUES OF FAMOUS FLORENTINES LINE THE COURTYARD

ELEVATOR

STAIRS UP FROM ENTRY & **WC**

STAIRS DOWN TO WC, FIRST FLOOR & EXIT

NORTHERN ART

❶ TOUR BEGINS

GIOTTO & EARLY REN.

❸

❶ ➤

ENTRANCES

❷ ➤

BOTTICELLI

MICHELANGELO

WEST CORRIDOR

*Piazza degli Uffizi (Courtyard)*

EAST CORRIDOR

LEONARDO

VENUS DE' MEDICI

VIA DI CASTELLANI

See Uffizi Gallery Second Floor map

Piazza dei Giudici

VIEW OF PONTE VECCHIO

STATUES LUPA ■

■ DORIFORO

GALILEO SCIENCE MUSEUM

UNDERPASS

To Ponte Vecchio

LUNGARNO DE'MEDICI

*Arno River*

❶ Reservation Entrance
❷ Main Entrance & Same-Day Reservations
❸ Reservation Ticket Office

style mob scenes inside. The museum is nowhere near as big as it is great.

**Cost and Hours:** €20 plus €4 for recommended reservation, cheaper in winter, free and crowded on first Sun of the month Oct-March, covered by €38 Uffizi/Pitti Palace/Boboli Gardens combo-ticket; Tue-Sun 8:15-19:00, closed Mon, July-Sept Wed-Thu until 22:00 (except for two weeks in mid-Aug), last entry one hour before closing; reservation tel. 055-294-883, www.uffizi.it.

**Reservations Necessary:** To skip the notoriously long ticket-buying lines, book your Uffizi entrance in advance online or by calling the reservation number above. If you don't do that, your best bet is to arrive at the end of the day, 90 minutes before closing, and see the museum in a rush.

**Getting In:** If you arrive with a **reservation,** go first to the courtyard door #3 to pick up your ticket (labeled *Reservation Ticket Office*). There you exchange your email voucher/confirmation number for a ticket. Tickets are available for pickup 10 minutes before your appointed time. Then, with ticket in hand, walk briskly across the courtyard to door #1. Get in the queue for "individuals," not "groups."

To **buy a ticket on the spot,** line up with everyone else at door #2, marked *Main Entrance*.

**Tours:** A 1.5-hour audioguide costs €6 (€10/2 people; must leave ID). 🎧 Download my free Uffizi Gallery audio tour.

**Visiting the Museum:** The Uffizi is U-shaped, running around an exterior courtyard. The artwork we'll see is up four long flights, on the top floor. The east wing contains Florentine paintings from medieval to Renaissance times. At the far end, you pass through a short hallway filled with the kind of ancient sculpture that inspired the Renaissance. The west wing has the Renaissance biggies—Leonardo, Michelangelo, and Raphael. Downstairs there are many more rooms of art, showing how the Florentine Renaissance morphed into Mannerism (Parmigianino), spread to Venice (Titian), and inspired the Baroque (Caravaggio).

**Medieval** (1200-1400): Three similar-looking Madonna-and-Bambinos—all painted within a few decades of each other, in about the year 1300—show baby steps in the march to Renaissance realism (Room 2). **Duccio**'s piece is the most medieval and two-dimensional. There's no background, and the angels are just stacked one on top of the other, floating in the golden atmosphere. **Cimabue** mixes the iconic Byzantine style with budding Italian realism. **Giotto** creates a space and fills it. Like a set designer, he builds a three-dimensional "stage"—the canopied throne—then peoples it with real beings. The throne has angels in front, prophets behind, and a canopy over the top. But the real triumph here is Mary herself—big and monumental, like a Roman statue. Beneath her robe, she has a real live body, with knees and breasts that stick out at us. This three-dimensionality was revolutionary in its day, a taste of the Renaissance a century before it began.

**Early Renaissance** (mid-1400s): In the 1400s, painters worked out the problems of painting realistically, using mathematics to create the illusion of three-dimensionality. Paolo Uccello's colorful *Battle of San Romano* is not so much a piece of art as an exercise in perspective (Room 8). The fallen horses and soldiers are experiments in "foreshortening"—creating the illusion of distance. Some of the figures are definitely A-plus material, like the fallen gray horse in the center. But some are more like B-minus work—

the fallen soldier at the far right would be child-size if he stood up. Uccello almost literally went crazy trying to master the three dimensions (thank God he was born before Einstein discovered one more).

We don't need the wispy halo over the head of Fra Filippo Lippi's *Madonna and Child with Two Angels* to tell us she's holy—she radiates sweetness and light from her divine face (Room 8). Lippi painted idealized beauty, but his models were real flesh-and-blood human beings. You could look through all the thousands of paintings from the Middle Ages and not find anything so human as the mischievous face of one of Lippi's little angel boys.

In medieval times, only saints and angels were worthy of being painted. In the humanistic Renaissance, however, even nonreligious folk like the husband and wife *Federico da Montefeltro and Battista Sforza* had their features preserved for posterity, in this case by Piero della Francesca (Room 8). Renaissance artists discovered the beauty in ordinary people and painted them, literally, warts and all.

**The Renaissance** (1450-1500): Florence in 1450 was in a Firenz-y of activity. There was a can-do spirit of optimism in the air, led by prosperous merchants and bankers and a strong middle class. Lorenzo de' Medici, head of the powerful Medici family, epitomized this new humanistic spirit. He gathered Florence's best and brightest around him for evening wine and discussions of great ideas. One of this circle was the painter Botticelli.

The Botticelli rooms (10-14) are filled with masterpieces and classical fleshiness. Botticelli's *Spring* is the Renaissance in its first bloom, its "springtime" of innocence. Madonna is out, Venus is in. This is a return to the pre-Christian pagan world of classical Greece, where things of the flesh are not sinful. Botticelli emphasizes pristine beauty over gritty realism. The lines of the bodies have pleasing, S-like curves. The faces are idealized but have real human features. There's a look of thoughtfulness and even melancholy in the faces—as though everyone knows that the innocence of spring will not last forever.

*Birth of Venus* is a masterpiece of Western art. This is the purest expression of Renaissance beauty. Venus' naked body is not sensual, but innocent. Botticelli thought that physical beauty was a way of appreciating God.

**Classical Sculpture:** If the Renaissance was the foundation of the modern world, the foundation of the Renaissance was classical sculpture. Sculptors, painters, and poets alike turned for inspiration to these ancient Greek and Roman works as the epitome of balance, 3-D perspective, human anatomy, and beauty.

In the Tribune Room, the highlight is the **Venus de' Medici** (first century BC), a Roman copy of the lost original by the great Greek sculptor Praxiteles. Balanced, harmonious, and serene, the statue embodies the attributes of Greece's "Golden Age," when balance was admired in every aspect of life.

The **sculpture hall** has 2,000-year-old Roman copies of 2,500-year-old Greek originals. The most impressive is the male nude, *Doriforo* ("spear carrier"), a Roman copy of the Greek original by Polykleitos. The purple statue in the center of the hall—headless and limbless—is the Roman "she-wolf" (*Lupa*, c. AD 120), the animal that raised Rome's legendary founders.

**High Renaissance** (1500-1550): A scientist, architect, engineer, musician, and painter, Leonardo da Vinci (1452-1519) was a true Renaissance Man. He worked at his own pace rather than to please an employer, so he often left works unfinished.

In the *Annunciation,* the angel Gabriel has walked up to Mary, and now kneels on one knee like an ambassador, saluting her (Room 35). See how relaxed his other hand is, draped over his knee. Mary, who's been reading, looks up with a gesture of surprise and curiosity. Leonardo constructs a beautifully landscaped "stage" and puts his characters in it. He's taken a miraculous event—an angel appearing out of the blue—and presented it in a very human way.

Leonardo's human insight is even more apparent in his unfinished *Adoration of the Magi.* The poor kings are amazed at the Christ child—even afraid of him. This work is as agitated as the *Annunciation* is calm, giving us an idea of Leonardo's range.

Don't miss Michelangelo's **Holy Family** (a.k.a. *Doni Tondo,* Room 41), the only completed easel painting by the greatest sculptor in history. Florentine painters were sculptors with brushes; this shows it. Instead of a painting, it's more like three clusters of statues with some clothes painted on.

Michelangelo was a Florentine—in fact, he was like an adopted son of the Medici, who recognized his talent—but much of his greatest work was done in Rome as part of the pope's face-lift of the city. We can see here some of the techniques he used on the Sistine Chapel ceiling that revolutionized painting—monumental figures; dramatic angles (looking up Mary's nose); accentuated, rippling muscles; and bright, clashing colors.

Nearby is Raphael's *Madonna of the Goldfinch,* in which the artist brings Mary and bambino down from heaven and into the real world of trees, water, and sky. The two halves of the painting balance perfectly. Draw a line down the middle, through Mary's nose and down through her knee. John the Baptist on the left is balanced by Jesus on the right. Even the trees in the background balance each other, left and right. These things help create the subconscious feelings of balance and order that reinforce the atmosphere of maternal security in this domestic scene—pure Renaissance.

**More Art on the Lower Floor:** When you're ready to move on, go down the staircase at the end of the west wing to the first floor. On your way, you'll pass a fine café, an open-air terrace, and the WC. You'll be lead directly to an exit, if you're ready to go. But the first floor is worth a look. It features work from after the Renaissance: Mannerism (such as Parmigianino), Venetian (Titian), Baroque (Caravaggio), and finally Flemish and Dutch (Rubens and Rembrandt).

### ▲▲Palazzo Vecchio

This castle-like fortress with the 300-foot spire dominates Florence's main square. In Renaissance times, it was the Town Hall, where citizens pioneered the once-radical notion of self-rule. Its official name—Palazzo della Signoria—refers to the elected members of the city council. In 1540, the tyrant Cosimo I made the building his personal palace, redecorating the interior in lavish style. Today the building functions once again as the Town Hall.

Entry to the ground-floor Michelozzo courtyard, with its arcade of intricately carved columns, is free, so even if you don't go upstairs to the museum, you can step inside and feel the essence of the Medici. There's also a fine little exhibit of scenes from old Florence (ground level in adjacent ticketing courtyard). Paying customers can see Cosimo's (fairly) lavish royal apartments, decorated with (fairly) top-notch paintings and statues by Michelangelo and Donatello. The highlight is the Grand Hall (Salone dei Cinquecento), a 13,000-square-foot hall lined with huge frescoes and interesting statues.

**Cost and Hours:** Michelozzo courtyard-free, museum-€16.50, tower climb-€12.50 (418 steps), museum plus tower-€21.50, excavations-€4, combo-ticket for all three-€23.50. Museum and excavations open daily 9:00-23:00, Oct-March until 19:00, except

Thu until 14:00 year-round; tower keeps shorter hours (last entry one hour before closing) and closed in bad weather; last tickets for all sights sold one hour before closing; videoguide-€5, English tours available, Piazza della Signoria, tel. 055-276-8224, www.musefirenze.it.

### ▲Ponte Vecchio

Florence's most famous bridge has long been lined with shops. Originally these were butcher shops that used the river as a handy disposal system. Then, when the powerful and princely Medici built the Vasari Corridor over the bridge, the stinky meat market was replaced by more elegant gold and silver shops (some of which remain here to this day). The corridor, an elevated passageway above the bridge, was built so the Medici could commute comfortably between their Pitti Palace home and their Palazzo Vecchio offices (corridor closed until at least 2021). A statue of Benvenuto Cellini, the master goldsmith of the Renaissance, stands in the center of the bridge, ignored by the flood of tacky tourism.

### ▲▲Galileo Science Museum (Museo Galilei)

When we think of the Florentine Renaissance, we think of visual arts: painting, mosaics, architecture, and sculpture. But when the visual arts declined in the 1600s (abused and co-opted by political powers), music and science flourished in Florence. The first opera was written here. And Florence hosted many scientific breakthroughs, as you'll see in this fascinating collection of Renaissance and later clocks, telescopes, maps, and ingenious gadgets. Trace the technical innovations as modern science emerges from 1000 to 1900. Some of the most talked about bottles in Florence are  the ones here that contain Galileo's fingers. Exhibits include various tools for gauging the world, from a compass and thermometer to Galileo's telescopes. Other displays delve into clocks, pumps, medicine, and chemistry. It's friendly, comfortably cool, never crowded, and just a block east of the Uffizi on the Arno River.

**Cost and Hours:** €10, daily 9:30-18:00 except Tue until 13:00, guided tours available, Piazza dei Giudici 1, tel. 055-265-311, www.museogalileo.it.

## EAST OF PIAZZA DELLA SIGNORIA

### ▲▲▲Bargello (Museo Nazionale del Bargello)

This underappreciated sculpture museum is in a former police station-turned-prison that looks like a mini Palazzo Vecchio. The Renaissance began with sculpture, and you can see the birth of

this revolution of 3-D in the Bargello. It's a small, uncrowded museum and a pleasant break from the intensity of the rest of Florence. You'll see 150 years of great statues, spanning the history of Florence's heyday.

Highlights include Donatello's very influential, painfully beautiful *David* (the first male nude to be sculpted in a thousand years), multiple works by Michelangelo, and rooms of Medici treasures. Moody Donatello, who embraced realism with his lifelike statues, set the personal and artistic style for many Renaissance artists to follow. The best pieces are in the ground-floor room at the foot of the outdoor staircase (with fine works by Michelangelo, Cellini, and Giambologna) and in the "Donatello room" directly above (including his two different *David*s, plus Ghiberti and Brunelleschi's dueling competition entries for the Baptistery doors—and yet another *David* by Verrocchio).

**Cost and Hours:** €9, free on first Sun of the month Oct-March; daily 8:15-14:00—until 17:00 for special exhibits; closed on second and fourth Sun and first, third, and fifth Mon of each month, last entry 45 minutes before closing; reservations possible but unnecessary, audioguide-€6; Via del Proconsolo 4, tel. 055-238-8606, www.bargellomusei.beniculturali.it.

## ▲▲Santa Croce Church

This 14th-century Franciscan church, decorated with centuries of precious art, holds the tombs of great Florentines. The loud 19th-century Victorian Gothic facade faces a huge square ringed with tempting shops and littered with tired tourists. Escape into the church and admire its sheer height and spaciousness. Your ticket includes the Pazzi Chapel and a small museum; the complex also houses a leather school.

**Cost and Hours:** €8, Mon-Sat 9:30-17:00, Sun from 14:00, multimedia guide-€6, modest dress required, 10-minute walk east of the Palazzo Vecchio along Borgo de' Greci, tel. 055-246-6105, www.santacroceopera.it. The **leather school,** at the back of the church, is free and sells church tickets—handy when the church has a long line (daily 10:00-18:00, closed Sun Nov-March, has own entry behind church plus an entry within the church, www. scuoladelcuoio.com).

**Visiting the Church:** On the left wall (as you face the altar) is the tomb of **Galileo Galilei** (1564-1642), the Pisan who lived his last years under house arrest near Florence. His crime? Defying the Church by saying that the earth revolved around the sun. His heretical remains were only allowed in the church long after his death.

Directly opposite (on the right wall) is the tomb of **Michelangelo Buonarroti** (1475-1564). Santa Croce was Michelangelo's childhood church, as he grew up a block west of here. Farther up the nave is the tomb of **Niccolò Machiavelli** (1469-1527), a champion of democratic Florence and author of *The Prince*, a how-to manual on hardball politics—which later Medici rulers found instructive.

The first chapel to the right of the main altar features the famous *Death of St. Francis* fresco by Giotto. With simple but eloquent gestures, Francis' brothers bid him a sad farewell. The Sacristy has Cimabue's impressive *Crucifixion* (before 1288), a survivor of the devastating flood of 1966. Beyond that is the leather school.

Exit the church nave between the Rossini and Machiavelli tombs to enter a delightful cloister. On the left is the small Brunelleschi-designed Pazzi Chapel, whose unity and harmony of design captures the Renaissance in miniature. Straight ahead is the church museum, with several rooms of paintings, statues, and altarpieces.

### ▲Casa Buonarroti (Michelangelo's House)

A property once owned by Michelangelo, this house was built after the artist's death by his grand-nephew "Michelangelo the Younger," who turned it into a little museum honoring his famous relative. The highlights—Michelangelo's first sculptures and some sketches—are not must-sees in art-heavy Florence, but are appreciated by Michelangelovers. The place where Michelangelo actually grew up is only a few blocks from here, at 10 Via de' Bentaccordi.

**Cost and Hours:** €8, Wed-Mon 10:00-17:00, closed Tue, Via Ghibellina 70, tel. 055-241-752, www.casabuonarroti.it.

## NEAR THE TRAIN STATION
### ▲▲Church of Santa Maria Novella

This 13th-century Dominican church is rich in art. Along with crucifixes by Giotto and Brunelleschi, it contains the textbook example of the early Renaissance mastery of perspective: *The Trinity* by Masaccio. The exquisite chapels trace art in Florence from medieval times to early Baroque. The outside of the church features a dash of Romanesque (horizontal stripes), Gothic (pointed arches), Renaissance (geometric shapes), and Baroque (scrolls). Step in and look down the 330-foot nave for a 14th-century optical illusion.

Next to the church are the cloisters and the **museum,** located in the old Dominican convent of Santa Maria Novella. The museum's highlight is the breathtaking Spanish Chapel, with walls covered by a series of frescoes by Andrea di Bonaiuto.

**Cost and Hours:** Church and museum-€7.50; Mon-Thu 9:00-19:00, Fri 11:00-19:00, Sat 9:00-17:30, Sun 13:00-17:30, church closes Oct-March at 17:30, last entry 45 minutes before closing; multimedia guide-€3, modest dress required, main entrance on Piazza Santa Maria Novella, tel. 055-219-257, www.smn.it.

## THE OLTRARNO (SOUTH OF THE ARNO RIVER)
### ▲▲▲Pitti Palace

The imposing Pitti Palace, several blocks southwest of Ponte Vecchio, has many separate museums and two gardens. The main reason to visit is to see the Palatine Gallery, which houses a fine

painting collection that picks up where the Uffizi leaves off, with the High Renaissance. Lovers of Raphael's Madonnas and Titian's portraits will find some of the world's best of each. If it's a nice day, take a stroll in the Boboli Gardens, a rare and inviting patch of extensive green space within old Florence.

**Cost and Hours:** The €16 **Pitti Palace** ticket #1 covers the Palatine Gallery, Royal Apartments, Treasury of the Grand Dukes (silver museum), Museum of Costume and Fashion, and Gallery of Modern Art; open Tue-Sun 8:15-19:00, closed Mon, last entry one hour before closing. The €10 **Boboli Garden** ticket #2 covers the Boboli and Bardini Gardens as well as the Porcelain Museum located in the garden; open daily June-Aug 8:15-19:30, April-May and Sept until 18:30, March and Oct until 17:30, Nov-Feb until 16:30, closed first and last Mon of each month, last entry one hour before closing. The place is free on the first Sun of the

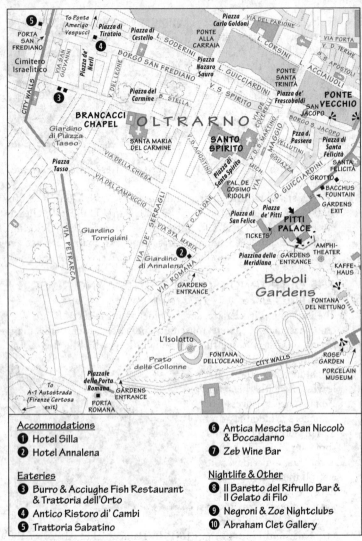

## Accommodations
1 Hotel Silla
2 Hotel Annalena

## Eateries
3 Burro & Acciughe Fish Restaurant & Trattoria dell'Orto
4 Antico Ristoro di' Cambi
5 Trattoria Sabatino

6 Antica Mescita San Niccolò & Boccadarno
7 Zeb Wine Bar

## Nightlife & Other
8 Il Baretto del Rifrullo Bar & Il Gelato di Filo
9 Negroni & Zoe Nightclubs
10 Abraham Clet Gallery

month Oct-March. The €8 audioguide explains the sprawling palace. Tel. 055-238-8614, www.uffizi.it.

**Visiting the Museum:** In the Palatine Gallery you'll walk through one palatial room after another, with walls sagging with masterpieces by 16th- and 17th-century masters, including Titian and Rembrandt. The Pitti's Raphael collection is the second-biggest anywhere—the Vatican beats it by one. Use the information folders in each room to help find the featured paintings.

The collection is all on one floor. To see the highlights, walk straight down the spine through a dozen or so rooms. After the

FLORENCE

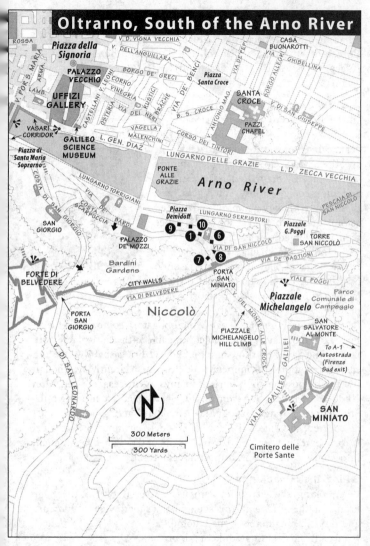

# Oltrarno, South of the Arno River

Palatine Gallery, the route flows naturally into the even more lavish rooms of the Royal Apartments. These 14 rooms (of which only
a few are open at any one time) are where the Pitti's rulers lived in
the 18th and 19th centuries. Each room features a different color
and time period. Here, you get a real feel for the splendor of the
dukes' world.

The rest of Pitti Palace is skippable, unless the various sights
match your interests: the **Gallery of Modern Art** (second floor;
Romantic, Neoclassical, and Impressionist works by 19th- and
20th-century Tuscan painters), **Treasury of the Grand Dukes**

(ground and mezzanine floors; Medici treasures from jeweled crucifixes to gilded ostrich eggs), **Museum of Costume and Fashion, Porcelain Museum,** and **Boboli and Bardini gardens** (behind the palace; enter from Pitti Palace courtyard—be prepared to climb uphill).

## ▲▲Brancacci Chapel

In the Brancacci Chapel, Masaccio created a world in paint that looks like the world we inhabit. For the first time in a thousand years, Man and Nature were frozen for inspection. Masaccio's painting techniques were copied by many Renaissance artists, and his people—sturdy, intelligent, and dignified, with expressions of understated astonishment—helped shape Renaissance men and women's own self-images.

Half of the chapel's frescoes are by Masaccio, and half by either Masolino or Filippino Lippi, who completed the chapel more than 50 years later. Although Masaccio is the star, the panels by his colleagues provide a good contrast in styles.

**Cost and Hours:** €10 Sat-Mon (obligatory combo-ticket with Fondazione Salvatore Romano, a skippable 14th-century refectory next to the Santo Spirito Church), €8 Wed-Fri, cash only; free and easy reservations recommended especially March-May, though it's usually possible to walk right in any day off-season; Wed-Mon 10:00-17:00 except Sun from 13:00, closed Tue, last entry 45 minutes before closing; videoguide—€3, knees and shoulders must be covered, in Church of Santa Maria del Carmine on Piazza del Carmine, reservations tel. 055-276-8224 or 055-276-8558 or email info@muse.comune.fi.it, http://musefirenze.it.

## ▲Piazzale Michelangelo

Overlooking the city from across the river (look for the huge bronze statue of *David*), this square has a superb view of Florence and the stunning dome of the Duomo. It's worth the 25-minute hike, taxi, or bus ride.

An inviting café (open seasonally) with great views is just below the overlook. The best photos are taken from the street immediately below the overlook. After dark, the square is packed with school kids licking ice cream and each other. About 200 yards beyond all the tour groups and teenagers is the stark, beautiful, crowd-free, Romanesque San Miniato

Church (next listing). A WC is located just off the road, halfway between the two sights.

**Getting There** (and Back): While you can catch bus #12 (from near Piazza d'Ognissanti, can be a long ride) or a taxi up to the piazza, the walk up from the Oltrarno neighborhood of San Niccolò is popular—especially in the early evening—and not that challenging (see the map on page 513).

Start at the intersection of Via San Niccolò and Via San Miniato, just below Porta San Miniato (scope out the restaurants and bars here, as you'll circle back to this spot in about an hour if you walk down). Point yourself uphill, head through the old gate, and continue until you reach a broad, terraced hill-climb to the left. Up top, Piazzale Michelangelo will be to your left, and San Miniato Church to your right.

When you're ready to leave, the hike down is quick and enjoyable (or take bus #13). You can retrace your steps, or you can turn this walk into a loop: From the parking lot, take the ramp leading down toward Ponte Vecchio (near the replica *David*). At the bottom of the ramp, cross the street and continue down the pathway. You'll cross one more street, then zigzag downhill toward the river. You are descending on the so-called Poggi ramps, developed in the late 19th century as a string of staircases, fountains, and grottos that embellishes (and stabilizes) the hillside. When you draw even with the big tower (Porta San Niccolò), turn left onto Via San Niccolò and make your way back to the passel of lively cafés and restaurants where you started (for recommendations, see page 547).

## ▲▲San Miniato Church

According to legend, the martyred St. Minias—this church's namesake—was beheaded on the banks of the Arno in AD 250.

He picked up his head and walked here (this was before the #12 bus), where he died and was buried in what became the first Christian cemetery in Florence. In the 11th century, this church was built to house Minias' remains.

The church's green-and-white marble facade (12th century) is classic Florentine Romanesque, one of the oldest in town. Inside you'll find some wonderful 3-D paintings, a plush ceiling of glazed terracotta panels by Luca della Robbia, and an exquisite Renaissance chapel (on the left side of the nave). The highlight for me is the brilliantly preserved art in the sacristy (upstairs to right of altar, in the room on right) showing scenes from the life of St. Benedict (circa 1350, by a follower of Giotto). Drop €2 into the electronic panel in the corner to light the room for five minutes. The evening vesper service with the monks chanting in Latin offers a meditative worship experience—a peaceful way to end your visit.

**Cost and Hours:** Free, Mon-Sat 9:30-13:00 & 15:00-19:30, until 19:00 off-season, Sun 8:15-19:30, closed sporadically for special occasions, tel. 055-234-2731, www.sanminiatoalmonte.it.

**Getting There:** It's about 200 yards above Piazzale Michelangelo. Follow the walking directions in the Piazzale Michelangelo listing above, or take bus #12 to the San Miniato al Monte stop (hop off and hike up the grand staircase); bus #13 takes you back down the hill.

**Gregorian Chants:** These are held Mon-Fri at 7:15 and 17:45, and Sun at 17:30—but as the schedule is subject to change, double-check with any TI, the church's website, or call ahead.

# Shopping in Florence

Florence may be one of Europe's best shopping towns—it's been known for its sense of style since the Medici days. Smaller stores are generally open about 9:00-13:00 and 15:30-19:30, usually closed on Sunday, often closed on Monday (or at least Monday morning), and sometimes closed for a couple of weeks around August 15. Bigger stores have similar hours, without the afternoon break.

For authentic, locally produced wares, look for shops displaying the *Esercizi Storici Fiorentini* seal, with a picture of the Palazzo Vecchio's tower. At these city-endorsed "Historical Florentine Ventures," you may pay a premium, but quality is assured (for a list of shops, see www.esercizistoricifiorentini.it).

### Department Stores

Department store chains include **Coin,** the Italian equivalent of Macy's (Mon-Sat 10:00-20:00, Sun from 10:30, on Via de' Calzaiuoli, near Orsanmichele Church); the upscale **La Rinascente** (Mon-Sat 9:00-22:00, Sun 10:30-20:30, on Piazza della Repubblica); and **OVS,** a discount clothing chain (Mon-Sat 9:00-19:30, Sun from 10:00, near train station at intersection of Via Panzani and Via del Giglio).

### Best Shopping Areas

**San Lorenzo Market:** The market stalls between the Basilica of San Lorenzo and Mercato Centrale are no secret—this is ground zero for tourists seeking cheap, cut-rate souvenirs, lower-end leather, clothing, T-shirts, and handbags. It's a fun area to browse and bargain (just hang onto your wallet—this is pickpocket central). You'll find many of the stalls in the narrow streets around Mercato Centrale (daily 9:00-19:00, closed Mon in winter).

**Upscale Boutique Streets:** The entire area between the river and the cathedral is busy with inviting boutiques that show off ritzy Italian fashions. The highest concentration of shops is along Via dei Calzaiuoli, Via de' Tornabuoni, and the streets in between (particularly around Piazza della Repubblica). For a fun and productive shopping stroll, trace a triangle from Via del Parione, Via della Vigna Nuova, and Via de' Tornabuoni. You'll get a good look at high fashion, one-of-a-kind boutiques, craft workshops, and collectibles.

**Borgo Santi Apostoli:** This narrow street, just one short block up from Ponte Vecchio, hosts boutiques, designer handbag shops, antique and art stores, and jewelers.

**Via Romana:** Running southwest in the Oltrarno from the Pitti Palace into a sleepy residential quarter, this workaday street features an eclectic mix of art galleries, antique shops, and creative boutiques.

**Via di Santo Spirito:** Running parallel to the Arno through the heart of the Oltrarno, this street contains a number of old *palazzi* once owned by wealthy Florentine families such as the Machiavellis (#5) and the winemaking Frescobaldis (#11). Today, the ground floors of those buildings are filled with fine local shops, with some real artisans mixed in. The furniture, antique, and home-decor shops on this street make for satisfying window-shopping, and there's also a smattering of clothing boutiques.

# Sleeping in Florence

Most of my recommended hotels are grouped in central Florence. If arriving by train, you can either walk (usually around 10-20 minutes) or take a taxi (roughly €6-8) to reach most of my recommended accommodations.

**Hotel Tips:** I rank accommodations from $ budget to $$$$ splurge. For the best deal, contact my family-run accommodations directly by phone or email. When you book direct, the owner avoids a commission and may be able to offer a discount. Book well in advance for peak season or if your trip coincides with a major holiday or festival (see the appendix). Note, though, that Florence can be busy any time of year. For some travelers, short-term, Airbnb-type rentals can be a good alternative; search for places in my recommended hotel neighborhoods.

For more details on reservations, short-term rentals, and more, see the "Sleeping" section in the Practicalities chapter.

**Beware of Bugs:** Florence is notorious for its mosquitoes. If your hotel lacks air-conditioning, request a fan and don't open your windows, especially at night. Many hotels furnish a small plug-in bulb *(zanzariere)*—usually set in the ashtray—that helps keep the bloodsuckers at bay. If not, you can purchase one cheaply at any pharmacy *(farmacia)*.

## AROUND THE DUOMO

**$$$$ Palazzo Niccolini al Duomo,** one of five elite Historic Residence Hotels in Florence, is run by the Niccolini di Camugliano family. The lounge (where tea and pastries are offered every afternoon) is palatial, but the six rooms and seven suites, while splendid, vary in size and quality (some have Duomo views). If you have the money and want a Florentine palace to call home, this can be a good bet (RS%, elevator, air-con, pay parking—reserve ahead, Via dei Servi 2, tel. 055-282-412, www.niccolinidomepalace.com, info@niccolinidomepalace.com).

**$$$$ Hotel Duomo**'s 24 rooms are modern and comfortable enough, but you're paying for the location and the views—the Duomo looms like a monster outside the hotel's windows. If staying here, you might as well spring the extra €20 or so for a "classic" room with a view (RS%, air-con, historic elevator, Piazza del Duomo 1, fourth floor, tel. 055-219-922, www.hotelduomofirenze.it, info@hotelduomofirenze.it; Paolo, Gilvaneide, and Federico).

**$$$ Soggiorno Battistero** rents seven simple yet pristine rooms, most with great views, overlooking the Baptistery and the Duomo square. Request a view or a quieter room in the back when you book, but keep in mind there's always some noise in the city center. It's a minimalist place with no public spaces or full-time reception, but the location is great (RS%, air-con, elevator, Piazza San Giovanni 1, third floor, tel. 055-295-143, www.soggiornobattistero.it, info@soggiornobattistero.it, Francesco).

**$$$ Residenza Giotto B&B** offers a well-priced chance to stay on Florence's upscale shopping drag, Via Roma. Occupying the top floor of a 19th-century building, this place has six bright rooms (three with Duomo views) and a terrace with knockout views of the Duomo's tower. Reception is generally open Mon-Sat 9:00-17:00 and Sun 9:00-13:00; let them know your arrival time in advance (RS%, air-con, elevator, Via Roma 6, tel. 055-214-593, www.residenzagiotto.it, info@residenzagiotto.it, helpful Giorgio).

**$$ La Residenza del Proconsolo B&B** has six older-feeling rooms a minute from the Duomo (three rooms have Duomo views). The place lacks public spaces, but the rooms are quite large and nice—perfect for eating breakfast, which is served in your room (extra cost for slightly larger "deluxe" with view, air-con, no elevator, Via del Proconsolo 18 black, tel. 055-264-5657, www.proconsolo.com, info@proconsolo.com, Susie).

## NORTH OF THE DUOMO
### Near the Accademia

**$$$$ Hotel dei Macchiaioli** offers 15 fresh and spacious rooms on one high-ceilinged, noble floor in a restored palazzo owned for generations by a well-to-do Florentine family. You'll eat breakfast under original frescoed ceilings while enjoying modern comforts (RS%, air-con, Via Cavour 21, tel. 055-213-154, www. hoteldeimacchiaioli.com, info@hoteldeimacchiaioli.com, helpful Francesca and Paolo).

**$$$$ Hotel Loggiato dei Serviti,** at a prestigious address on the most Renaissance-y square in town, gives you Old World romance with hair dryers. Stone stairways lead you under open-beam ceilings through this 16th-century monastery's monumental public rooms. The 32 well-worn rooms are both rickety and characteristic. The hotel staff is professional yet warm (RS%, family rooms, elevator, pay valet parking, Piazza Santissima Annun-

ziata 3, tel. 055-289-592, www.loggiatodeiservitihotel.it, info@ loggiatodeiservitihotel.it; Chiara B., Chiara V., and Alex). When full, they rent five spacious and sophisticated rooms in a 17th-century annex a block away.

**$$$$ Hotel Morandi alla Crocetta,** a former convent, envelops you in a 16th-century cocoon. Located on a quiet street with 12 rooms, its period furnishings, squeaky clean parquet floors, and original frescoes take you back a few centuries and up a few social classes. A few rooms come with lovely patios (family rooms, air-con, elevator, pay parking, a block off Piazza Santissima Annunziata at Via Laura 50, tel. 055-234-4748, www.hotelmorandi. it, welcome@hotelmorandi.it, well-run by Maurizio, Rolando, and Cristiano).

**$$$ Residenza dei Pucci** rents 13 pleasant rooms (each one different) spread over three floors (with no elevator). The appealing decor, a mix of traditional fabrics and aristocratic furniture, makes this place feel upscale for the price range (RS%—use code "RICK," family rooms, air-con, reception open 9:00-20:00, shorter hours off-season—let them know if you'll arrive late, Via dei Pucci 9, tel. 055-281-886, www.residenzadeipucci.com, info@ residenzadeipucci.com, friendly Rossella and Marina).

## North of Mercato Centrale

After dark, this neighborhood can feel a little deserted, but I've never heard of anyone running into harm here. It's a short walk from the train station and a stroll to all the sightseeing action. While workaday, it's practical, with plenty of good budget restaurants and markets nearby.

**$$$ Relais & Maison Grand Tour** has six cozy, eclectic, and

# Florence Hotels

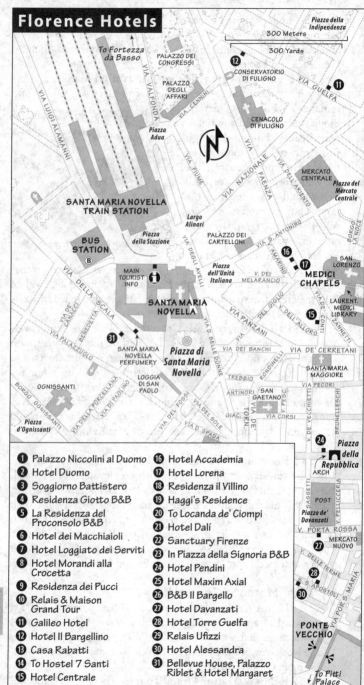

To Fortezza da Basso

Piazza della Indipendenza

300 Meters
300 Yards

PALAZZO DEI CONGRESSI

PALAZZO DEGLI AFFARI

CONSERVATORIO DI FULIGNO

CENACOLO DI FULIGNO

VIA GUELFA

Piazza Adua

VIA VALFONDA

VIA LUIGI ALAMANNI

VIA CENNINI

VIA FIUME

VIA NAZIONALE

VIA FAENZA

VIA DELL'ARIENTO

MERCATO CENTRALE

Piazza del Mercato Centrale

BORGO LA NOCE

SANTA MARIA NOVELLA TRAIN STATION

Largo Alinari

PALAZZO DEI CARTELLONI

VIA S. ANTONINO

SAN LORENZO

BUS STATION

Piazza della Stazione

VIA DEGLI AVELLI

Piazza dell'Unità Italiana

V. DEI MELARANCIO

MEDICI CHAPELS

VIA DE' CONTI

VIA FAENZA

VIA DE' PANZANI

VIA DE' CANACCI

VIA DELLA SCALA

BENEDETTA

MAIN TOURIST INFO

SANTA MARIA NOVELLA

VIA DEL GIGLIO

V. DELL'ORO

LAURENT. MEDICI LIBRARY

VIA ZANNETTI

VIA DE' CERRETANI

SANTA MARIA NOVELLA PERFUMERY

Piazza di Santa Maria Novella

VIA DEI BANCHI

RONDINELLI

TREBBIO

SANTA MARIA MAGGIORE

VIA PECORI

VIA PALAZZUOLO

BORGO OGNISSANTI

OGNISSANTI

VIA DELLA PORCELLANA

VIA DI PARIONE

LOGGIA DI SAN PAOLO

VIA DELLE BELLE DONNE

ANTINORI

SAN GAETANO

VIA DE' VECCHIETTI

BRUNELLESCHI

Piazza d'Ognissanti

VIA DEL FOSSI

VIA DEL SOLE

VIA DE' TORN.

VIA CORSI

GIAC.

VIA D. SPADA

V. DE' VECCHIETTI

Piazza della Repubblica

ARCH

SASSETTI

POST

V. PESC.

Piazza de' Davanzati

V. PORTA ROSSA

V. PELLICCERIA

MERCATO NUOVO

V. DELLE TERME

S. S. APOSTOLI

VIA POR S. MARIA

PONTE VECCHIO

To Pitti Palace

1. Palazzo Niccolini al Duomo
2. Hotel Duomo
3. Soggiorno Battistero
4. Residenza Giotto B&B
5. La Residenza del Proconsolo B&B
6. Hotel dei Macchiaioli
7. Hotel Loggiato dei Serviti
8. Hotel Morandi alla Crocetta
9. Residenza dei Pucci
10. Relais & Maison Grand Tour
11. Galileo Hotel
12. Hotel Il Bargellino
13. Casa Rabatti
14. To Hostel 7 Santi
15. Hotel Centrale
16. Hotel Accademia
17. Hotel Lorena
18. Residenza il Villino
19. Haggi's Residence
20. To Locanda de' Ciompi
21. Hotel Dalí
22. Sanctuary Firenze
23. In Piazza della Signoria B&B
24. Hotel Pendini
25. Hotel Maxim Axial
26. B&B Il Bargello
27. Hotel Davanzati
28. Hotel Torre Guelfa
29. Relais Ufizzi
30. Hotel Alessandra
31. Bellevue House, Palazzo Riblet & Hotel Margaret

FLORENCE

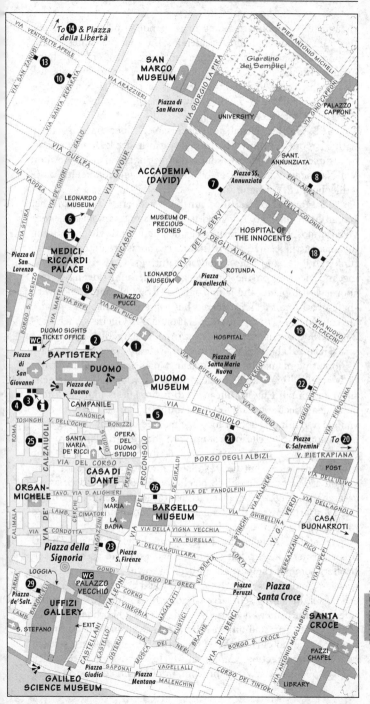

thoughtfully appointed rooms on a nondescript street between the train station and the Accademia. The spacious suites on the ground floor come with a garden ambience (RS%, family suites; includes breakfast voucher for the corner bar, for "green" rate, ask to skip breakfast and daily cleaning; air-con, Via Santa Reparata 21, tel. 055-399-5223, www.florencegrandtour.com, info@florencegrandtour.com, Ulrike).

**$$$ Galileo Hotel,** a comfortable, older business hotel with 31 rooms, is run with familial warmth (RS%, family rooms, quadruple-paned windows shut out street noise, air-con, elevator, Via Nazionale 22a, tel. 055-496-645, www.galileohotel.it, info@galileohotel.it, Vicenzo).

**$$ Hotel Il Bargellino,** run by Bostonian Carmel and her Italian husband Pino, is a good-value place with an old-time convivial atmosphere. In a residential neighborhood within walking distance of the center, the 10 summery rooms are decorated with funky antiques and Pino's modern paintings. Guests enjoy relaxing and chatting on the big, breezy, momentum-slowing terrace adorned with plants and lemon shrubs (RS%, cheaper rooms with shared bath, no breakfast served but espresso available in rooms, air-con extra, north of the train station at Via Guelfa 87, tel. 055-238-2658, www.ilbargellino.com, carmel@ilbargellino.com).

**$ Casa Rabatti** is the ultimate if you always wanted to have a Florentine mama. Its simple, clean rooms are run with warmth by Marcella. This is a great place to practice your Italian: Marcella speaks minimal English but loves to invite guests into her kitchen to chat. Seeing decades of my family Christmas cards on their walls, I'm reminded of how long she has been keeping budget travelers happy (RS%, cheaper rooms with shared bath, family rooms, cash only but secure reservation with credit card, no breakfast, one room with air-con but fans available for the rest, 5 blocks from station at Via San Zanobi 48 black, mobile 338-153-4159, www.casarabatti.it, info@casarabatti.it). Marcella also rents three modern **$$ apartments** with kitchenettes, air-conditioning, and access to a tranquil garden—ideal for longer stays.

**Hostel:** Calling itself a "hostel-meets-hotel," **¢ Hostel 7 Santi** fills a former convent, but you'll feel like you're in an old school. It offers some of the best cheap beds in town, is friendly to older travelers, and comes with the services you'd expect in a big, modern hostel, including self-serve laundry. It's about a 10-minute bus ride from the center, in a largely residential neighborhood near the Campo di Marte stadium (private rooms available, breakfast and dinner extra, no curfew; Viale dei Mille 11—from train station, take bus #17, direction: Campo di Marte, to bus stop Sette Santi; tel. 055-504-8452, www.7santi.com, info@7santi.com).

## Near the Medici Chapels

The mostly pedestrianized Via Faenza is the spine of this neighborhood, with lots of tourist services.

**$$$$ Hotel Centrale** is indeed central, just a short walk from the Duomo. The 35 spacious but overpriced rooms—with a tasteful mix of old and new decor—are over a businesslike conference center (RS%, air-con, elevator, Via dei Conti 3, check in at big front desk on ground floor, tel. 055-215-761, www.hotelcentralefirenze. it, info@hotelcentralefirenze.it, Roberto).

**$$$$ Hotel Accademia** has 18 quiet rooms on a pedestrianized street in a convenient location. The modern, sizeable rooms cluster around a sunny courtyard (RS%, air-con, no elevator, Via Faenza 7, tel. 055-290-993, www.hotelaccademiafirenze.com, info@hotelaccademiafirenze.com, Tea and Francesca).

**$ Hotel Lorena,** just across from the Medici Chapels, has 19 simple, well-worn rooms (six with shared bathrooms) and a tiny lobby. Though it feels a little like a youth hostel, it's well located, inexpensive, and run with care by the Galli family (air-con, elevator from first floor, Via Faenza 1, tel. 055-282-785, www.hotellorena. com, info@hotellorena.com).

## EAST OF THE DUOMO

While convenient to the sights and offering a good value, these places are mostly along nondescript urban streets, lacking the grit, charm, or glitz of some of my other recommended neighborhoods.

**$$$ Residenza il Villino** has 10 charming rooms and a picturesque, peaceful little courtyard. The owner, Neri, has turned part of the breakfast room into a museum-like tribute to his grandfather, a pioneer of early Italian fashion. As it's in a "little villa" (as the name implies) set back from the street, this is a quiet refuge from the bustle of Florence (RS%, family rooms, air-con, parking available, just north of Via degli Alfani at Via della Pergola 53, tel. 055-200-1116, www.ilvillino.it, info@ilvillino.it, Giovanni).

**$$$ Haggi's Residence,** once a convent and today part of the owner's extensive home, is a classy B&B, with five chic, romantic, and ample rooms, antique furnishings, and historic architectural touches (RS%, family room, air-con, Via della Pergola 42, mobile 351-818-7488, www.pergola42.com, info@pergola42.com, suave Alex).

**$$ Locanda de' Ciompi,** overlooking the inviting Piazza dei Ciompi in a lively neighborhood, is just right for travelers who want to feel like a part of the town. Alessio and daughter Lisa have five attractive rooms that are tidy, lovingly maintained, and a good value (RS%, cheaper room with private bath across the hall, includes breakfast at nearby bar, air-con, 8 blocks behind the Duomo

**FLORENCE**

at Via Pietrapiana 28 black—see map on page 464, tel. 055-263-8034, www.bbflorencefirenze.com, info@bbflorencefirenze.com).

**$$ Hotel Dalí** has 10 cheery, worn rooms in a nice location for a great price. Samanta and Marco, who run this guesthouse with a charming passion and idealism, are a delight to know (request one of the quiet and spacious rooms facing the courtyard when you book, cheaper rooms with shared bath available, nearby apartments sleep 2-6 people, no breakfast, fans but no air-con, elevator, free parking, 2 blocks behind the Duomo at Via dell'Oriuolo 17 on the second floor, tel. 055-234-0706, www.hoteldali.com, hoteldali@tin.it).

**$$ Sanctuary Firenze,** run by the Oblate Sisters of the Assumption, is an institutional 35-room hotel in a Renaissance building with a dreamy garden, great public spaces, appropriately simple rooms, and a quiet, prayerful ambience (family rooms, single beds only, air-con, elevator, 23:30 curfew, limited pay parking—request when you book, Borgo Pinti 15, tel. 055-248-0582, www.sanctuarybbfirenze.com, info@sanctuarybbfirenze.com). As there's no night porter, it's best to time your arrival and departure to occur during typical business hours.

## SOUTH OF THE DUOMO
### Between the Duomo and Piazza della Signoria

Buried in the narrow, characteristic lanes in the very heart of town, these are the most central of my accommodation recommendations (and therefore a little overpriced). While this location is worth the extra cost for many, nearly every hotel in this chapter can be considered central given Florence's walkable, essentially traffic-free core.

**$$$$ In Piazza della Signoria B&B,** in a stellar location overlooking Piazza della Signoria, is peaceful, refined, and homey. The service is friendly and efficient. The nine rooms are beautifully decorated; the priciest ones have genuine views of the square (from other rooms, views are peekaboo). Guests enjoy socializing at the big, shared breakfast table (RS%, 2 family apartments, air-con, tiny elevator, Via dei Magazzini 2, tel. 055-239-9546, mobile 348-321-0565, www.inpiazzadellasignoria.com, info@inpiazzadellasignoria.com, Sonia and Alessandro).

**$$$$ Hotel Pendini,** with three stars and 44 plush, flowery rooms, fills the top floor of a grand building overlooking Piazza della Repubblica. This place just feels classy; walking into the lobby is like stepping back in time. While pricey, this level of elegance makes it a good value for those looking to indulge (RS%, "deluxe" rooms come with square view and after-hours liveliness, family rooms, air-con, elevator, Via Strozzi 2, tel. 055-211-170, www.hotelpendini.it, info@hotelpendini.it).

**$$$ Hotel Maxim Axial,** run by the Maoli family since 1981, has 42 straightforward rooms spread over three floors in a good location on the main pedestrian drag. Its painting-lined halls and cozy lounge have old Florentine charm. More expensive "comfort" and "deluxe" superior rooms are renovated and fresh, but budget travelers can choose an "economy" room on the fourth floor—which is a walk-up from the third floor (RS%—use code "RICK," family rooms, reception on third floor, air-con, elevator, Via de' Calzaiuoli 11, tel. 055-217-474, www.hotelmaximaxial.com, info@ hotelmaximaxial.com, Chiara).

**$$ B&B Il Bargello** is a home away from home, run by friendly and helpful Canadian expat Gabriella. Hike up three long flights (no elevator) to reach six smart, relaxing rooms. Gabriella offers a cozy living room, a communal kitchenette, and an inviting rooftop terrace with close-up views of Florence's towers (RS%, fully equipped apartment across the hall sleeps up to six with one shared bathroom; air-con, 20 yards off Via Proconsolo at Via de' Pandolfini 33 black, tel. 055-215-330, mobile 339-175-3110, www. firenze-bedandbreakfast.it, info@firenze-bedandbreakfast.it).

## Near Ponte Vecchio

This sleepy zone is handy to several sights and some fine shopping streets, though it's accordingly pricey and lacks a neighborhood feel of its own.

**$$$$ Hotel Davanzati,** bright and shiny with artistic touches, has 25 cheerful rooms with all the comforts. The place is a family affair, thoughtfully run by friendly Tommaso and father Fabrizio, who offer drinks and snacks each evening at their candlelit happy hour, plus lots of other extras (RS%, family rooms, free mini iPads equipped with mobile data in every room, free on-demand videos—including my travel shows about Italy—on your room TV, air-con, 20 steep steps to the elevator, handy room fridges, next to Piazza Davanzati at Via Porta Rossa 5—easy to miss so watch for low-profile sign above the door, tel. 055-286-666, www.hoteldavanzati. it, info@hoteldavanzati.it).

**$$$$ Hotel Torre Guelfa** has grand public spaces and is topped by a fun medieval tower with a panoramic rooftop terrace (72 stairs take you up—and back 720 years). Its 31 pricey rooms vary wildly in size and furnishings, but most come with the noise of the city center. Room 315, with a private terrace, is worth reserving several months in advance (RS%, family rooms, air-con, elevator, a couple of blocks northwest of Ponte Vecchio, Borgo SS. Apostoli 8, tel. 055-239-6338, www.hoteltorreguelfa.com, info@ hoteltorreguelfa.com, Niccolo).

**$$$$ Relais Uffizi** is a peaceful little gem, offering a friendly welcome and tight maze of 15 classy rooms tucked away down a tiny alley off Piazza della Signoria. The lounge has a huge window overlooking the action in the piazza—a unique view (RS%, family rooms, air-con, elevator; official address is Chiasso del Buco 16—from the square, go down tiny Chiasso de Baroncelli lane—right of the loggia—and after 50 yards turn right through the arch and look for entrance on your right; tel. 055-267-6239, www.relaisuffizi.it, info@relaisuffizi.it, charming Alessandro and Elizabetta).

$$$ **Hotel Alessandra** is a tranquil and sprawling place, occupying part of a 16th-century building with 27 big, old-school rooms with frescoes and a tiny Arno-view terrace (family rooms, air-con, 30 steps to the elevator, Borgo SS. Apostoli 17, tel. 055-283-438, www.hotelalessandra.com, info@hotelalessandra.com; Anna, son Andrea, and spunky Monti).

## NEAR SANTA MARIA NOVELLA

These fine, charming little budget options are around the corner from Santa Maria Novella, near the train station.

$$ **Bellevue House** is a third-floor oasis of tranquility, with six spacious, old-fashioned rooms flanking a long, mellow-yellow lobby. It's a peaceful home away from home, thoughtfully run by the Michel family (RS%, family rooms, no breakfast, air-con, elevator, Via della Scala 21, tel. 055-260-8932, www.bellevuehouse.it, info@bellevuehouse.it; Luciano, Susan, and Alessandro). On a lower floor, their other property, $$ **Palazzo Riblet,** offers three upscale rooms (one with a private terrace) with frescoes and elegant furnishings (tel. 055-260-8932, www.palazzoriblet.it, info@palazzoriblet.it).

$$ **Hotel Margaret,** homey yet minimalist, offers seven tidy, simple rooms but no public lounge or breakfast (RS%, some cheaper rooms with shower but toilet down the hall, apartment, air-con in most rooms, Via della Scala 25, tel. 055-210-138, www.hotel-margaret.it, info@hotel-margaret.it; Francesco and Graziano).

## THE OLTRARNO

$$$$ **Hotel Palazzo Guadagni,** perched high above Piazza Santo Spirito, is a romantic, Grand Tour retreat from modern Florence. The 15 refined rooms are spacious, with antique furnishings and frescoes. While the ample, chandeliered public spaces are pleasant, the highlight is the panoramic wraparound loggia/terrace with comfy, stay-awhile seating and lovely views (RS%, air-con, elevator, Piazza Santo Spirito 9, tel. 055-265-8376, www.palazzoguadagni.com, info@palazzoguadagni.com).

**$$$$ Hotel la Scaletta** has 36 pricey, sleek rooms hiding in a convoluted floor plan. Their fabulous rooftop terrace overlooks the Boboli Gardens (RS%, family suites, breakfast extra, air-con, elevator, Via de' Guicciardini 13, tel. 055-283-028, www.hotellascaletta.it, info@hotellascaletta.it, Sara).

**$$$ Hotel Silla** is a classic three-star hotel with 36 cheery, spacious rooms. Across the river from Santa Croce Church, it has a breezy terrace and faces the river, overlooking a small park and near the San Niccolò neighborhood. There's free coffee and tea for guests in the late afternoon. The surroundings can be a bit noisy (RS%—use promo code "RICK," air-con, elevator, pricey self-service washing machine, pay parking, Via dei Renai 5, for location see map on page 512, tel. 055-234-2888, www.hotelsilla.it, hotelsilla@hotelsilla.it; Laura, Chiara, Massimo, Ravin, and Stefano).

**$$ Hotel Annalena,** on the third floor of a faded palazzo, is a bit tatty but it's in a quiet location near the Pitti Palace. Many of its 20 tidy rooms (some with terraces) overlook a private park next door (family rooms, bar/lounge, air-con, no elevator, laundry service, pay parking, opposite the side entrance to the Boboli Gardens at Via Romana 34, for location see map on page 512, tel. 055-222-402, www.annalenahotel.com, reception@annalenahotel.com).

**$$ Casa Santo Nome di Gesù** is a grand convent whose sisters—Franciscan Missionaries of Mary—are thankful to rent 23 simple but spacious rooms to tourists. Staying in this 15th-century palace, you'll be immersed in the tranquil atmosphere created by a huge, peaceful garden, generous and prayerful public spaces, and smiling nuns. It's best to reserve a couple of months in advance (family rooms, no air-con but rooms have fans, elevator, memorable breakfast room, 1:00 in the morning curfew, pay parking, Piazza del Carmine 21, tel. 055-213-856, www.fmmfirenze.it, info@fmmfirenze.it).

**$ Soggiorno Alessandra** has four bright and comfy rooms, all with en suite bathrooms. Because of its double-paned windows, you'll hardly notice the traffic noise (family rooms, includes basic breakfast in room, air-con, no elevator; there's no formal reception, so let them know what time you'll arrive; just past the Carraia Bridge at Via Borgo San Frediano 6, tel. 055-290-424, www.soggiornoalessandra.it, info@soggiornoalessandra.it, Alessandra).

**$ Foresteria Valdese di Firenze,** with 40 clean and functional rooms, is located in a 17th-century palace overlooking a beautiful garden courtyard. The complex also houses the Instituto Gould, which helps socially disadvantaged kids, and proceeds raised from renting rooms help fund that important work (extra for quieter garden rooms, air-con, elevator reaches most rooms, family rooms, breakfast extra, Via dei Serragli 49, tel. 055-212-576, www.firenzeforesteria.it, info@firenzeforesteria.it). The reception desk

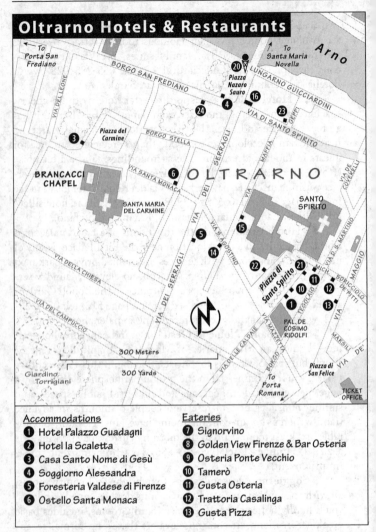

# Oltrarno Hotels & Restaurants

**Accommodations**
1 Hotel Palazzo Guadagni
2 Hotel la Scaletta
3 Casa Santo Nome di Gesù
4 Soggiorno Alessandra
5 Foresteria Valdese di Firenze
6 Ostello Santa Monaca

**Eateries**
7 Signorvino
8 Golden View Firenze & Bar Osteria
9 Osteria Ponte Vecchio
10 Tamerò
11 Gusta Osteria
12 Trattoria Casalinga
13 Gusta Pizza

closes at lunchtime—confirm hours before you arrive. After-hours check-in is possible with advance notice.

**Hostel:** ¢ **Ostello Santa Monaca** is a well-run, institutional-feeling hostel a long block east of the Brancacci Chapel. As clean as its guests, it attracts a young backpacking crowd (2:00 in the morning curfew, air-con, bike rental, pay laundry, Via Santa Monaca 6, tel. 055-268-338, www.ostellosantamonaca.com, info@ostellosantamonaca.com).

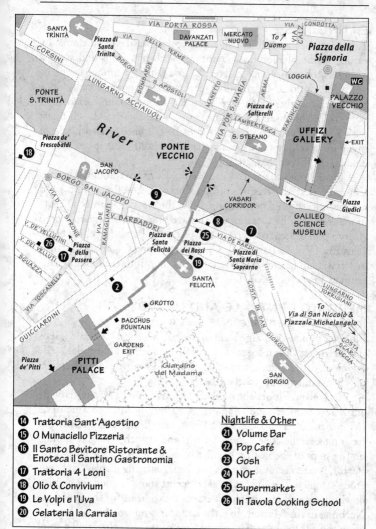

⑭ Trattoria Sant'Agostino
⑮ O Munaciello Pizzeria
⑯ Il Santo Bevitore Ristorante &
   Enoteca il Santino Gastronomia
⑰ Trattoria 4 Leoni
⑱ Olio & Convivium
⑲ Le Volpi e l'Uva
⑳ Gelateria la Carraia

<u>Nightlife & Other</u>
㉑ Volume Bar
㉒ Pop Café
㉓ Gosh
㉔ NOF
㉕ Supermarket
㉖ In Tavola Cooking School

# Eating in Florence

The old center of Florence is dominated by tourism. Locals still keep restaurants busy at lunch, but with the city's many Airbnb guests and city-center traffic restrictions, the hometown clientele retreats away from downtown in the evening. This makes it tough to find a "nontouristy" place for dinner. Still, the competition is fierce, and you'll find plenty of fine options and good values even in the tourist zone. For the best experience and better quality meals, hike to places further out and across the river in the Oltrarno.

FLORENCE

## EATING TIPS

To save money and time, you can keep lunches fast and simple by eating at one of Florence's countless sandwich shops and stands, pizzerias, or self-service cafeterias. You'll find a unique range of sandwich options. In addition to the basic *panino* (usually on a baguette), crostini (open-faced, toasted baguette), and *semel* (big, puffy roll), you'll see places advertising *schiaccata* (sandwich made with a "squashed," focaccia-like bread). Florence is also home to many carts selling tripe sandwiches—a prized local specialty; for details, see the sidebar.

Picnicking is easy. You can picnic your way through Mercato Centrale, near the Basilica of San Lorenzo. You'll also find good *supermercati* throughout the city. I like the classy Sapori & Dintorni markets (run by Conad), which have branches near the Duomo (Borgo San Lorenzo 15 red) and just over Ponte Vecchio in the Oltrarno (Via de Bardi 45). Carrefour Express is another handy grocery chain (there's one around the corner from the Duomo Museum at Via dell'Oriuolo 66).

## MERCATO CENTRALE AND NEARBY
### In Mercato Centrale

Florence's Industrial Age steel-and-glass Mercato Centrale (Central Market) is a fun-to-explore edible wonderland of vendors selling meat, fish, produce, and other staples to a mostly local clientele, plus some lunch-only food counters.

**$ Ground Floor:** The market zone, with lots of raw ingredients and a few humble food counters, is open only through lunchtime (Mon-Fri 7:00-14:00, Sat until 17:00, closed Sun). Buy a picnic of fresh mozzarella cheese, olives, fruit, and crunchy bread to munch on the steps of the nearby Basilica of San Lorenzo. The fancy deli, **Perini,** is famous for its quality products, enticing display, and generous samples. The adjacent **Pasta Perini** stand is good for a quick bowl of pasta. For a simple sit-down meal, head for the venerable **Nerbone in the Market.** Join the shoppers and workers who crowd up to the bar to grab their inexpensive plates, and then find a stool at the cramped shared tables nearby. Of the several cheap market diners, this feels the most authentic (lunch menu served Mon-Sat 12:00-14:00, cash only, on the side closest to the Basilica of San Lorenzo). Its less-famous sisters, nearby, have better seating and fewer crowds.

**$$ Upstairs:** The upper floor is a touristy, overcrowded and overpriced food court (daily 10:00-24:00) with counters selling pizza, pasta, fish, meat, *salumi*, *lampredotto*, wine, and so on.

## Near Mercato Centrale

A huge array of eateries is within a couple of blocks of the market. Each has its own distinct vibe, so scout around to find your favorite.

**$ Casa del Vino,** Florence's oldest operating wine shop, is a crowded little bar offering an unforgettable stand-up lunch experience with a selection of wine by the glass from 25 different bottles (notice the prices chalked onto each bottle). Owner Gianni, whose family has owned the Casa for more than 70 years, is a class act. The sandwiches, crostini, and his €7 "Tuscany appetizer plate" of meat and cheese are perfect. During busy times, it's a mob scene—you'll munch and sip standing outside amongst workers on a quick lunch break. But come early or late, and you can actually connect with Gianni (Mon-Thu 9:30-15:30, Fri-Sat 9:30-20:30; closed Sun year-round, Sat in summer, and Aug; Via dell'Ariento 16 red, tel. 055-215-609).

**$$ Pepò,** a colorful and charmingly unpretentious space, is tucked just around the corner from the touristy glitz on Piazza del Mercato Centrale. The short menu offers simple but well-prepared Florentine classics such as *ribollita* and *pollo alla cacciatora*—chicken cacciatore (daily 12:00-14:30 & 19:00-22:30, Via Rosina 4 red, tel. 055-283-259).

**$$ Trattoria Sergio Gozzi** is your classic neighborhood lunch-only place, serving hearty, traditional Florentine fare to market-goers since 1915—long before the tourist crush of today. The handwritten menu is limited and changes daily, and the service can be hectic, but it remains a local favorite (Mon-Sat 12:00-15:00, closed Sun, reservations smart, Piazza di San Lorenzo 8, tel. 055-281-941).

**$$ Trattoria la Burrasca** is a rustic gem with a time-warp atmosphere, where a dozen rickety tables cluster under a single vault. Elio and his hard-working staff offer a traditional menu featuring fine steak and good-value seasonal specials of Tuscan home cooking (Tue-Sat 12:00-15:00 & 19:00-22:30, closed Sun-Mon, reservations smart, Via Panicale 6, north corner of Mercato Centrale, tel. 055-215-827).

**$ Simbiosi Organic Pizza and Lovely Food** is a happy little pizzeria under a medieval vault with a young crew, open fire, and healthy energy (good salads, daily 12:00-23:00, organic and gluten-free, craft beer, Via de' Ginori 56 red, tel. 055-064-0115). Their similarly named pasta sister is next door at #58.

**$$$ La Ménagère Bistro and Restaurant** is a youthful place serving nicely presented, modern Italian dishes to a smart crowd in a spacious and dressy atmosphere. Their creative dishes are a nice alternative to traditional Florentine fare. In front, their more casual bistro, with a trendy flower-shop feel, serves salads, sandwiches, and simple plates. The fancier restaurant hides out in the

# Florence Restaurants

Piazza della Indipendenza

300 Meters
300 Yards

To Fortezza da Basso

PALAZZO DEI CONGRESSI

**32** CONSERVATORIO DI FULIGNO

VIA VALFONDA

PALAZZO DEGLI AFFARI

VIA GUELFA

VIA SAN ZANOBI

VIA GENNINI

CENACOLO DI FULIGNO

Piazza Adua

VIA FIUME

VIA NAZIONALE

VIA PANICALE

VIA TADDEA

VIA DELL'ARIENTO

VIA LUIGI ALAMANNI

**5**

MERCATO CENTRALE

Piazza del Mercato Centrale

**1**

**3**

**SANTA MARIA NOVELLA TRAIN STATION**

Largo Alinari

PALAZZO DEI CARTELLONI

VIA FAENZA

VIA S. ANTONINO

**2**

BORGO LA NOCE

VIA STURA

**4**

Piazza della Stazione

Piazza di San Lorenzo

**BUS STATION B**

Piazza dell'Unità Italiana

V. DEI MELARANCIO

V. S. AMARINO

**MEDICI CHAPELS**

SAN LORENZO

VIA DEGLI AVELLI

VIA DE' CONTI

**8**

LAURENTIAN MEDICI LIBRARY

VIA DELLA SCALA

MAIN TOURIST INFO

**SANTA MARIA NOVELLA**

VIA DEL GIGLIO

V. DELL'ALLORO

B. SAN LORENZO

**42**

**WC**

VIA DE' CERACIOL

BENEDETTA SCALA

**26**

VIA DE' BELLE DONNE

VIA DE' ZANNETTI

VIA PALAZZUOLO

**39**

SANTA MARIA NOVELLA PERFUMERY

Piazza di Santa Maria Novella

VIA PANZANI

VIA DEI BANCHI

VIA DE' CERRETANI

Santa Maria Maggiore

Piazza di San Giovanni

**38**

TREBBIO

RONDINELLI

VIA PECORI

OGNISSANTI

**36**

LOGGIA DI SAN PAOLO

ANTINORI

SAN GAETANO

VIA CORSI

**10**

LOGGIA DI BIGALLO

VIA DEL PORCELLANA

VIA DI PAOLINO

VIA DEL SOLE

GIAC.

V. DE' VECCHIETTI

BRUNELLESCHI

TOSINGHI

VIA DEL MORO

VIA DELLA SPADA

**13**

PESCIONI

ARCH

**11**

MEDICI

ROMA

BORGO OGNISSANTI

**41**

VIA DE' FOSSI

VIA DE' FEDERIGHI

RUCELLAI PALACE

**37**

VIA D. STROZZI

STROZZI PALACE

Piazza della Repubblica

**40**

LUNGARNO VESPUCCI

VIA DELLA VIGNA NUOVA

VIA DEL TORNABUONI

V. D. ANSELMI

**ORSAN-MICHELE**

Piazza Carlo Goldoni

PALAZZO CORSINI

VIA DEL PARIONE

PURGATORIO

INFERNO

MONALDA

SASSETTI

POST

V. PELLICCERIA

CALIMALA

**PONTE ALLA CARRAIA**

FARINCINO

Santa Trinità

LUNGARNO CORSINI

Piazza di Santa Trinita

Piazza de' Davanzati

VIA PORTA ROSSA

VIA CALIMALA

VIA

Piazza Nazaro Sauro

LUNGARNO GUICCIARDINI

**Arno River**

BOMBARDE

VIA DELLE TERME

DAVANZATI PALACE

**18**

MERCATO NUOVO

Piazza de' Salt.

**16**

BORGO

S. S. APOSTOLI

LAMBERTESCA

ARM

**17**

PONTE S. TRINITÀ

LUNGARNO ACCIAIUOLI

VIA POR S. MARIA

S. Stefano

Piazza de' Frescobaldi

**PONTE VECCHIO**

**22**

SANTO SPIRITO

SAN JACOPO

BORGO SAN JACOPO

V. D. RAMAGLI-ANTI

To Pitti Palace

**OLTRARNO**

Piazza della Passera

VIA MAGGIO

## Gelaterie

**43** Gelateria Carabè
**44** Edoardo
**45** Perchè No!
**46** Gelateria de' Neri

FLORENCE

1. Mercato Centrale Eateries
2. Casa del Vino
3. Pepò
4. Trattoria Sergio Gozzi
5. Trattoria la Burrasca
6. Simbiosi Organic Pizza & Lovely Food
7. La Ménagère Bistro & Restaurant
8. Trattoria lo Stracotto
9. Enoteca Coquinarius
10. Self-Service Ristorante Leonardo
11. Caffè Paszkowski
12. Eataly
13. Procacci
14. Rosalia Salad Gourmet
15. Caffetteria delle Oblate
16. Rivoire Café
17. Ristorante Toto
18. Osteria del Porcellino
19. Osteria Vini e Vecchi Sapori
20. Cantinetta dei Verrazzano
21. I Fratellini
22. 'Ino Sandwich Shop/Wine Bar
23. L'Antico Trippaio, Pizzeria Totò & Grocery
24. Da' Vinattieri
25. Il Cernacchino
26. Shake Café (3)
27. Ará è Sicilia
28. La Mescita Fiaschetteria
29. Pasticceria Robiglio
30. To Antica Trattoria da Tito
31. Ristorante Cafaggi
32. Trattoria la Gratella
33. Ristorante del Fagioli
34. Trattoria Anita
35. All'Antico Vinaio
36. Trattoria Sostanza-Troia
37. Trattoria Marione
38. Trattoria al Trebbio
39. Trattoria "da Giorgio"
40. Caffè Tosca & Nino
41. Sesto Bar
42. Groceries (4)

**FLORENCE**

back where you can choose between small tables or bigger shared ones (daily 12:00-23:00, dinner from 19:30—reservations smart, Via de' Ginori 8 red, tel. 055-075-0600, www.lamenagere.it).

**$$ Trattoria lo Stracotto** is an inviting eatery with a modern interior and good outdoor seating, where you'll enjoy good-value, standard Tuscan dishes in the shadow of the Medici Chapels (daily 12:00-15:00 & 18:00-22:30, Piazza di Madonna degli Aldobrandini 17, tel. 055-230-2062, Francesco and Tomasso).

## AROUND THE DUOMO

**$$ Enoteca Coquinarius** feels as welcoming as someone's cool and spacious living room or library. It's an unstressful, hip place with a slow-food ethic and lots of tasty salads and pastas, and a nice selection of wines by the glass (daily 12:30-15:30 & 18:30-22:30, a few steps from the Duomo workshop at Via delle Oche 11 red, tel. 055-230-2153, Nicola and Luca).

**$$ Ristorante Natalino** is worth the short walk for a memorable dinner. It's a family-run fixture in its neighborhood with outdoor seating on a characteristic corner. The place is known for its homemade pasta, *bistecca alla fiorentina*, and classic Tuscan dishes (daily 12:00-14:30 & 18:30-22:30, Borgo degli Albizi 17 red, for location see map on page 464, tel. 055-289-404).

**$ Self-Service Ristorante Leonardo** is a quick, cheap, air-conditioned, and handy cafeteria just a block from the Duomo. While it's no-frills and stuck in the 1970s, the food is better than many table-service eateries in this part of town. Stefano and Luciano run the place with enthusiasm and free pitchers of tap water (lots of vegetables, daily 11:45-14:45 & 18:45-21:45, upstairs at Via Pecori 11, tel. 055-284-446).

**$$ Caffè Paszkowski** is a venerable place on Piazza della Repubblica. While famously expensive as a restaurant, it serves inexpensive, quick lunches. At the display case, order a salad or plate of pasta or cooked veggies (or half-and-half), pay the cashier, and find a seat upstairs. To get this deal, you'll need to sit where the staff designates (lunch served 12:00-15:00, Piazza della Repubblica 35 red—northwest corner, tel. 055-210-236).

**$$ Eataly,** a slick, modern space a half-block from the Duomo, is an outpost of a chain of foodie mini malls located in big Italian cities (as well as in a few major US cities). Along with a grocery store for top-end Italian ingredients, plenty of edible gifts, and kitchen gadgets, it has a bright, modern dining area in the back serving pastas, pizzas, salads, and *secondi* (daily 10:00-22:30, Via de' Martelli 22 red, tel. 055-015-3601).

**$$$ Procacci,** right on Florence's most genteel boutique-browsing street, is upscale yet affordable. This wine bar, with a swanky, 1885 atmosphere, specializes in pungent truffle-scented ingredients: cheap mini *panini* and €20 sampler plates of *salumi* and cheeses. The sandwiches may be Florence's cheapest way to dine on truffles. Paired with a €8 glass of wine, it makes an elegant light meal (daily 10:00-21:00, Via Tornabuoni 64 red, tel. 055-211-656).

**$ Rosalia Salad Gourmet** is a quick, build-your-own-salad spot behind the Duomo. Eat in or take out a salad bowl, veggie wrap, smoothie, or fresh fruit juice. They also serve American-style eggs at breakfast (daily 8:00-20:00, Via dei Servi 37, mobile 320-706-9331).

**$ Caffetteria delle Oblate** is a laid-back budget eatery just a block from the Duomo located within a cultural center and library. You'll eat well-priced pastas with students in the top-floor cafeteria, either on an outdoor terrace or in the bright interior—with unobstructed views of the Duomo's dome (Mon 14:00-17:00, Tue-Sat 9:00-23:00, closed Sun, enter through the courtyard at Via dell'Oriuolo 26 and take the elevator to the top floor, tel. 055-263-9685).

## NEAR PIAZZA DELLA SIGNORIA

Piazza della Signoria, the scenic square facing the Palazzo Vecchio, is ringed by beautifully situated yet touristy eateries serving over-priced, forgettable food with an unforgettable view. If you're deter-mined to eat on the square, go for pizza at the touristy Ristorante il Cavallino, bar food at the adjacent Irish pub, or a bite at Rivoire.

**$$$ Rivoire** café is famous for its fancy desserts and thick hot chocolate (€7). A bowl of pasta or a salad—when enjoyed at the best view tables on the square—can be a worthwhile experience. Their delightful bar is perfectly affordable, and drinks often come with fine *aperitivo* munchies (daily 8:00-24:00, tel. 055-214-412).

**$$ Ristorante Toto** is a simple, fun, traditional eatery with a spacious dining hall serving classic Tuscan plates at decent prices. The focus is on steak and pizza (Thu-Tue 12:00-15:00 & 19:00-22:00, closed Wed, two blocks from the Ponte Vecchio at Borgo SS. Apostoli 6 red, tel. 055-212-096).

**$$$ Osteria del Porcellino** is a classic place deep in the center with a romantic ambience inside and quiet seating outside. Enzo—whose family has owned this restaurant since 1969—serves Tuscan classics. At dinner, he offers a complementary glass of bubbly when you sit down, and a vin santo with *contucci* after your meal (good €15 lunch special, daily 12:00-23:00, Via Val di Lamona 7 red, tel. 055-264-148).

**$$ Osteria Vini e Vecchi Sapori** is a colorful eatery—tight, tiny, and with attitude. They serve Tuscan food—like *pappardelle* with duck—from a fun, accessible menu of delicious pastas and *secondi* (Mon-Sat 12:30-14:30 & 19:30-22:30, closed Sun, res-ervations necessary—call ahead, Via dei Magazzini 3 red, tel.

# Florentine and Tuscan Cuisine

In general, Tuscan cuisine is hearty, simple food: grilled meats, high-quality seasonal vegetables, fresh herbs, prized olive oil, and rustic bread. If a dish ends with *"alla toscana"* or *"alla fiorentina,"* it's cooked in the Tuscan or Florentine style—usually a preparation highlighting local products. In addition to specialty dishes, most restaurants also serve pasta and pizza, veal cutlets, and salad (for more on Italian cuisine, see page 1165).

There's nothing wrong with your Tuscan bread—it's supposed to taste like that. *Pane alla toscana* is unsalted and nearly flavorless (from the days when salt's preservative powers made it more valuable than gold). Italians drench it in olive oil and sprinkle it with salt, or use it to scoop up sauce.

## *Antipasti* (Appetizers)

**Bruschetta:** Toasted bread brushed with olive oil and rubbed with garlic, topped with chopped tomato, mushrooms, or whatever else sounds good.

**Crostini:** Toasted bread rounds topped with meat or vegetable pastes. *Alla toscana* generally means with chicken liver pâté.

**Panzanella:** A simple summer salad, made of day-old bread, chopped tomatoes, onion, and basil, tossed in a light vinaigrette.

**Pecorino cheese:** Fresh *(fresco)* or aged *(stagionato)*, from ewe's milk.

**Porcini mushrooms:** Harvested in fall; used in pasta and soups, as a topping on meats and bruschetta, and sometimes deep-fried.

**Salumi:** Cold cuts, usually air- or salt-dried pork. Popular kinds include prosciutto (air-cured ham hock), pancetta (cured pork belly), *lardo* (cured pork lard), and *finocchiona* (fennel salami). For a list of other *salumi,* see page 1175.

**Tagliere:** A wooden platter with cold cuts and/or cheeses.

## *Primo Piatto* (First Course)

**Carabaccia:** Onion soup.

**Pappa al pomodoro:** Thick stew of tomatoes, olive oil, and bread.

**Pappardelle al sugo di lepre:** A rich sauce with wild hare over long, broad noodles.

**Pici al ragù:** A fat, spaghetti-like, hand-rolled pasta served with a meat-tomato sauce.

**Ribollita:** "Reboiled" soup, traditionally made with leftovers including white beans *(fagioli)*, seasonal vegetables, and olive oil, with layers of day-old Tuscan bread.

**Zuppa alla volterrana:** Volterra-style soup, similar to *ribollita* but with fresh bread.

## *Secondo Piatto* (Second Course)

**Arrosto misto:** An assortment of roasted meats, sometimes served on a skewer *(spiedino)*.

**Bistecca alla fiorentina:** A thick T-bone steak, generally grilled very rare and lightly seasoned (often sold by weight—per *etto*, or 100 grams). The best—and most expensive—is from the white Chianina breed of cattle you'll see grazing throughout Tuscany.

**Cinghiale:** Wild boar, served grilled or in soups, stews, and pasta. It is also made into many varieties of sausage and salami.

**Fegatelli:** Liver meatballs.

**Game birds:** Squab *(piccione)*, pheasant *(fagiano)*, and guinea hen *(faraona)* are popular.

**Trippa alla fiorentina:** Tripe (intestines) and vegetables sautéed in tomato sauce, sometimes baked with parmesan. *Trippa* (and the similar *lampredotto*) are popular in sandwiches.

## Dolci (Desserts)

**Cantucci:** Florentines love to end a meal by dipping this crunchy almond cookie in vin santo wine (described below). These are commonly misnamed "biscotti" by Americans.

**Gelato:** The Florentines claim they invented Italian-style ice cream. Rather than order dessert in a restaurant, I like to stroll with a gelato. For more on gelato, see page 1176; for tips on enjoying it here, see page 543.

**Panforte:** Dense, clove-and-cinnamon-spiced cake from Siena.

## Local Wines

Many Tuscan wines are made with sangiovese ("blood of Jupiter") grapes. But the characteristics of the soil, temperature, and exposure make each wine unique to its area.

**Brunello di Montalcino:** One of Italy's best reds, this full-bodied wine comes from the slopes of Montalcino, south of Siena. Smooth and dry, it pairs well with hearty, meaty food.

**Chianti:** This red hails from the Chianti region (20 miles south of Florence). Varieties range from cheap, acidic basket-bottles of table wine (called *fiaschi*) to the hearty Chianti Classico.

**Rosso di Montalcino:** This cheaper, younger "baby Brunello," also made in Montalcino, lacks Brunello's depth of flavor and complexity—but it's still a great wine at a bargain price.

**Super Tuscans:** This newer wine blends traditional grapes with locally grown non-Italian grapes (such as cabernet or merlot).

**Vernaccia di San Gimignano:** This medium-dry white goes well with pasta and salad. Trebbiano and vermentino are two other local white grapes.

**Vin Santo:** Sweet and syrupy, this "holy" dessert wine is often served with a cookie for dipping.

**Vino Nobile di Montepulciano:** This high-quality, ruby red, dry wine pairs well with meat, especially chicken.

055-293-045, run by Mario while wife Rosanna cooks and son Tommaso serves).

## Favorite Sandwiches Near Piazza della Signoria

**$$ Cantinetta dei Verrazzano** is an elegant wine bar serving delightful sandwich plates. Their *selezione Verrazzano* is a plate of four little crostini featuring breads, cheeses, and meats from the Chianti region. The *tagliere di focacce,* a sampler of mini focaccia sandwiches, is also fun. Add a glass of Chianti to either of these dishes to make a fine, light meal. Office workers pop in for a quick lunch, and it's traditional to share tables. They also have a long bench with tiny tables for eating at takeout prices. Simply step to the back and point to a hot *focacce* sandwich, order a drink at the bar, and take away your food or sit with Florentines and watch the action while you munch (daily 8:00-16:30, no reservations taken, off Via de' Calzaiuoli, at Via dei Tavolini 18 red, tel. 055-268-590).

**$ I Fratellini** is a hole-in-the-wall stand-up joint where the "little brothers" have served peasants more than 30 kinds of sandwiches and a fine selection of wine at great prices (see list on wall) since 1875. Join the local crowd to order, then sit on a nearby curb to eat, placing your glass on the wall rack before you leave. Be adventurous with the menu (order by number). Consider *finocchiona e caprino* (#15, a Tuscan salami and soft goat cheese), *lardo di Colonnata* (#22, cured lard aged in Carrara marble), and *cinghiale* (#19, spicy boar salami) sandwiches. It's worth ordering the most expensive wine they're selling by the glass (daily 9:00-19:30 or until the bread runs out, 20 yards in front of Orsanmichele Church on Via dei Cimatori, tel. 055-239-6096).

**$ 'Ino Sandwich Shop/Wine Bar** is a mod little spot (on a back alley between the Uffizi and Ponte Vecchio) where Alessandro and his staff serve creative sandwiches and glasses of wine. You'll munch your meal while perched on a tiny, uncomfortable stool— and be glad you did. The sandwiches—arguably the best in town— are easily splittable (daily 12:00-16:00, immediately behind Uffizi Gallery courtyard on Ponte Vecchio side, near the potted olive tree at Via dei Georgofili 7 red, tel. 055-214-154).

**$ Cheap Takeout on Via Dante Alighieri:** Three handy places for those traveling on a hobo's budget line up between Piazza della Signoria and the Duomo. **L'Antico Trippaio,** a food cart, is a fixture in the town center. Cheap and authentic as can be, this is where locals come for *panini* stuffed with specialties like *trippa* (tripe), *lampredotto* (stomach), and a list of more appetizing options, including *bollito.* They offer a free plastic glass of rotgut Chianti with each sandwich for travelers with this book (daily 9:00-19:00, on Via Dante Alighieri). Next to the tripe stand is a pizza-by-the-slice place (**Pizzeria Totò,** Via Dante Alighieri 28 red) and a handy little **grocery store.** The best place to enjoy your sandwich while people-watching is nearby on Piazza della Signoria.

**More Sandwich Shops:** Two well-regarded places to grab a cheap sandwich are **Da' Vinattieri** (*schiacciata* sandwiches plus *trippa* and *lampredotto,* daily 11:30-19:00, next to Casa di Dante at Via Santa Margherita 4 red); and **Il Cernacchino** (closed Sun, just north of the Palazzo Vecchio at Via della Condotta 38 red).

## NEAR THE ACCADEMIA

There aren't many appealing sit-down restaurants in the boring streets near the Accademia. But hungry tourists looking for a quick lunch between sightseeing stops find plenty of options. There are a couple of basic cafeterias a block away facing Piazza di San Marco.

**Picnic on Piazza Santissima Annunziata:** You can grab a takeout bite at one of several places along Via degli Alfani or at the **Carrefour Express Supermarket,** which has a sandwich counter and picnic provisions (daily 8:00-20:00, across from the Accademia entrance at Via Ricasoli 109 red). Then hike around the block and join the bums on the traffic-free Piazza Santissima Annunziata, the first Renaissance square in Florence. There's a fountain for washing fruit on the square. Grab a stony seat anywhere you like.

**$ Shake Café,** great for a quick and healthy lunch, is a modern salad bar on busy Via Cavour with spacious and inviting courtyard seating. Along with tasty salads, the menu includes veggie bowls, wraps, smoothies, and fancy juices (daily 7:00-20:00, Via Cavour 67 red). Another Shake location, recommended later, is near the Church of Santa Maria Novella, and a third can be found between the Duomo and Bargello, at Via del Corso 28.

**$ Ará è Sicilia,** just around the corner from *David,* is tiny, bright, and packed with Italians ordering up chef Carmelo's take on Sicilian street food: *arancini* (filled risotto balls) and *pizzole* (stuffed pizza) in fresh, inventive flavors, chased by homemade sorbet, cannoli, or pistachio biscotti. Order to take away or perch on one of the few stools (daily 10:00-22:00, Via degli Alfani 127 red, mobile 333-198-3927).

**$ La Mescita Fiaschetteria** is a characteristic hole-in-the-wall where, since 1919, locals have been enjoying a simple menu of pastas, traditional Tuscan soups, and the daily *secondi* with tasty, cheap house wine. The place can either be mobbed by students or a peaceful time warp, depending on when you stop by. Mirco and Alessio are gregarious to the point of being a bit pushy...order carefully and check your bill (daily 11:30-15:30, Via degli Alfani 70 red, mobile 338-992-2640).

**Sit-Down Lunch in a Classy Café:** A smart little café with friendly service, **$$ Pasticceria Robiglio,** has a stately and calm dining area and a few shaded tables on the sidewalk. They have a small lunch-only menu of salads and daily pasta and *secondi* specials. It's good any time for a coffee and one of their pretty pastries—famous among Florentines (café open daily 7:30-20:00, lunch served 12:00-16:00, a block toward the Duomo off Piazza Santissima Annunziata at Via dei Servi 112 red, tel. 055-212-784).

## Memorable Restaurants a Bit Farther from the Accademia

These places—within a short walk of the Accademia—are worth going out of your way for.

**$$$ Antica Trattoria da Tito,** a 10-minute hike from the Accademia along Via San Gallo, is great for a memorable meal with a local crowd and smart-aleck service. The boss, Bobo, serves (theatrically) quality traditional food and lots of wine. The food is good, and there's no pretense—it's a noisy playground of Tuscan cuisine. To gorge on a feast of antipasti (cold cuts, cheeses, a few veggies, and bruschetta), consider ordering *fermami* (literally "stop me")—for €18, Bobo brings you food until you say, *"Fermami!"* A couple can get *fermami* for two, desserts, and a nice bottle of wine for around €60 total. Dinner is served in two seatings: 19:30 (more sanity) and 21:30 (less sanity)—reservations are smart (€18 *gran tagliere*—big plate of cheese and meat, show this book for a free after-dinner drink, Mon-Sat 12:30-15:00 & 19:00-23:00, closed Sun, Via San Gallo 112 red, tel. 055-472-475, www.trattoriadatito.it).

**$$$ Ristorante Cafaggi** fills a bright yet low-energy space on a drab street between the Accademia and Mercato Centrale. With a vaguely 1950s vibe, the place emphasizes their generations-old passion for Florentine food, serving up *ribollita* (a hearty Tuscan soup), *ossobuco,* and tripe. It's been family-run since 1922 (Mon-Sat 12:30-15:00 & 19:00-22:00, closed Sun and several weeks in Aug, Via Guelfa 35 red, tel. 055-294-989).

**$$$ Trattoria la Gratella,** near my recommended hotels north of the center, serves solid Tuscan cuisine to a mostly local crowd. The crowded front room gives way to a sprawling interior and an outdoor courtyard, full of diners grilling their own *bistecca alla fiorentina* on mini barbeques at the table (daily 12:00-15:00 & 19:00-23:00, Via Guelfa 81 red, tel. 055-211-292).

## BETWEEN THE PALAZZO VECCHIO AND SANTA CROCE CHURCH

**$$ Ristorante del Fagioli** is an enthusiastically run eatery where you can sense the heritage, from the wood-paneled dining room to the daily specials chalked on a board. Maurizio commands the kitchen while family members Antonio and Simone keep the throngs of loyal customers returning. The cuisine: home-style bread soups, hearty steaks, and other Florentine classics. Don't worry—while *fagioli* means "beans," that's the family name, not the extent of the menu (Mon-Fri 12:30-14:30 & 19:30-22:30, closed Sat-Sun, cash only, reserve for dinner, a block north of the Alle Grazie bridge at Corso dei Tintori 47 red, tel. 055-244-285).

**$$ Trattoria Anita,** midway between the Uffizi and Santa Croce, feels old-school, with wood paneling decorated by dusty rows of wine bottles. Brothers Nicola, Gianni, and Maurizio offer good value—both for their weekday lunch special featuring three hearty Tuscan courses for €12 and their à la carte dinner (Mon-Sat 12:00-14:30 & 19:00-22:15, closed Sun, on the corner of Via Vinegia and Via del Parlagio at 2 red, tel. 055-218-698).

**$ All'Antico Vinaio** (and the Sandwich Mosh Pit): Via dei Neri has become a human traffic jam of people munching hearty and cheap sandwiches in the street. All over town, these low-end sandwich shops are the trend, and the storm seems to have originated here (at #65). At All'Antico Vinaio, you have two options: stand in the street with a crusty sandwich and pour your own wine, or head across the street to their more comfortable and expensive osteria (sandwiches available at both shops, Mon-Sat 10:30-22:30, Sun 12:00-16:00, Via dei Neri 65 red, tel. 055-238-2723).

## NEAR THE CHURCH OF SANTA MARIA NOVELLA

**$$$ Trattoria Sostanza-Troia,** characteristic and well established, is famous for its steaks and its *pollo al burro* (chicken in butter). Whirling ceiling fans and walls strewn with old photos evoke earlier times, while the artichoke pie *(tortino di carciofi)* reminds locals of Grandma's cooking. Crowded, with just eight shared tables, a small menu, and grumpy service, the place feels like a simple bistro. Reservations are essential for their two dinner seatings: 19:30 and 21:00 (cash only, open Mon-Sat, closed Sun year-round and Sat off-season, lunch served 12:30-14:00, Via del Porcellana 25 red, tel. 055-212-691).

**$$ Trattoria Marione** serves home-style meals to a mixed group of tourists and Florentines crowding very tight tables beneath hanging ham hocks. The ambience is happy and a bit frantic—no reservations, so arrive early. You come here for the character...not for fine cuisine (daily 12:00-16:00 & 19:00-23:00, Via della Spada 27 red, tel. 055-214-756).

**$$ Trattoria al Trebbio** features all the traditional Tuscan classics at average prices in an eclectic, modern setting. Dine inside, surrounded by old movie posters and framed prosciutto legs, or grab one of the few tables outside (daily 12:00-15:00 & 19:00-23:00, half a block off Piazza Santa Maria Novella at Via delle Belle Donne 47 red, tel. 055-287-089, Giulia).

**$$ Trattoria "da Giorgio"** is a rustic family-style diner on a sketchy street serving up simple home cooking to happy locals and tourists alike. Their €14 three-course fixed-price meal, including a drink, is a great value. This place is completely without pretense— head here for a taste of working-class Florence (no reservations, Mon-Sat 12:00-14:30 & 19:00-22:00, closed Sun, Via Palazzuolo 100 red, tel. 055-284-302, Silvano).

$ **Shake Café**, another outpost of the chain listed earlier, is a trendy and healthy salad bar with seating on Piazza Santa Maria Novella, across from the church. This is a great spot for a quick lunch, with a menu of veggie bowls, wraps, smoothies, and juices (daily 7:00-20:00, two blocks in front of the train station at Via degli Avelli 2 red).

## HIDDEN ROOFTOP CAFÉ TERRACES

If you're willing to pay extra to enjoy a drink surrounded by splendid Florentine views, head to one of these rooftop terraces:

$$ **Caffè Tosca & Nino** is on the rooftop of La Rinascente department store overlooking Piazza della Repubblica. While fairly plain, it comes with commanding views of the Duomo, which looms gloriously on the horizon (€3 coffee drinks, light bites, daily 9:00-24:00).

$$$$ **Sesto** is a dressy bar on a partially covered terrace atop the luxurious Westin Hotel. While cocktails here are pricey, they come with amazing city views. To turn your spendy drink into a light dinner, come during their *aperitivo* happy hour (19:00-21:00) when, for €25, your drink includes access to a little buffet, giving you something to nibble as you enjoy the sunset (daily 12:00-24:00, Piazza Ognissanti 3, tel. 055-27151, www.sestoonarno.com).

$$ **Caffè del Verone** is perched on the rooftop terrace of the Hospital of the Innocents on Piazza Santissima Annunziata. It offers a nice, peaceful atmosphere for a coffee break with rooftop view (no ticket required, just catch the elevator by the museum entrance, daily until 19:00, later on weekends, Piazza Santissima Annunziata 13, for location see map on page 464, mobile 392-498-2559).

## THE OLTRARNO

In general, dining in the Oltrarno, south of the Arno River, offers a more authentic experience. While it's just a few minutes' walk beyond Ponte Vecchio, this area sees far fewer tourists than the other side of the river. You may even find that Florentines outnumber tourists. Unless otherwise noted, see the map on page 528 for locations.

### Dining or Drinking with a Ponte Vecchio View

$$$ **Signorvino** is a bright and modern *enoteca* (wine shop) with a simple restaurant that has a rare terrace literally over the Arno

# Gelato

Italy's best ice cream is in Florence—many think they serve some of the world's best. But beware of scams at touristy joints on busy streets that turn a simple request for a cone into a €10 "tourist special" rip-off. To avoid this, survey the size options and specify what you want—for example, *un cono da tre euro* (a €3 cone). A rule of thumb: Stay away from places with heaping mounds of brightly (artificially) colored gelato. For

more gelato tips, see the "Eating" section of the Practicalities chapter. All of these places, which are a cut above the norm, are open daily for long hours.

**Near the Accademia:** A Sicilian choice on a tourist thoroughfare, **Gelateria Carabè** is particularly famous for its pistachio and its luscious *granite*—Italian ices made with fresh fruit. A *cremolata* is a *granita* with a dollop of gelato (almond and pistachio work well together). If you'd like a real Sicilian cannoli, get it here (from the Accademia, it's a block toward the Duomo at Via Ricasoli 60 red—Simone clearly loves his work).

**Near the Duomo:** A favorite, **Edoardo** features organic ingredients and tasty handmade cones (facing the southwest corner of the Duomo at Piazza del Duomo 45 red).

**Near Orsanmichele Church:** This shop's name, **Perchè No!,** translates to "Why not!"—good advice when it comes to gelato. It feels touristy but serves one of the widest range of flavors around, and the quality's top notch (just off the busy main pedestrian drag, Via de' Calzaiuoli, at Via dei Tavolini 19).

**Near the Church of Santa Croce:** Florentines flock to **Gelateria de' Neri,** with an enticingly wide array of flavors (Via dei Neri 9 red).

**Just Across the Carraia Bridge:** On the Oltrarno side of the bridge, **Gelateria la Carraia** is a hit with locals (Piazza Nazario Sauro 25 red—see the map on page 528).

River, with Ponte Vecchio views. Though it lacks historic charm with its stark-white IKEA vibe, it's a fun-loving place with no pretense and a passion for quality Italian ingredients. They serve regional dishes and plates of fine meats and cheeses to pair with a wonderful array of wines by the glass, allowing you to drink and eat your way merrily across Italy (food served 11:30-23:00, call to reserve, especially for terrace seating, Via dei Bardi 46 red, tel. 055-286-258, www.signorvino.com).

**$$$ Golden View Firenze** is two-in-one: a classy restaurant and the simpler **Bar Osteria,** both overlooking the Ponte Vecchio and Arno River. The white, minimalist interior is a dramatic contrast to atmospheric old Florence. Reservations for window tables are essential. Mixing their fine wine, river views, and live jazz makes for a wonderful evening (daily 12:00-24:00, jazz usually Mon, Fri, and Sat nights in the restaurant at 21:00; 50 yards east of Ponte Vecchio at Via dei Bardi 58, tel. 055-214-502, www.goldenviewopenbar.com, run by Paolo).

**$ Osteria Ponte Vecchio** is a tiny place—little more than a bar—serving basic drinks, *panini*, and microwaved snacks with a couple of amazing tables on the river (daily 10:00-23:00, off-season until 20:00, a block downstream from Ponte Vecchio at Via Borgo San Jacopo 16 red, Giacomo).

## On or near Piazza di Santo Spirito

Piazza di Santo Spirito is a thriving neighborhood square in the heart of the Oltrarno, with a collection of fun **$$** eateries and rustic bars. Several bars offer *aperitivo* buffets with their drinks during happy hour (generally 18:00-20:00). Later in the evening, the area becomes a club scene, filled with foreign students and young locals.

**$$ Tamerò** is an arty pasta bar in an old auto mechanic's shop serving Sardinian-Tuscan dishes. Sit in the funky interior with local hipsters or outside on the square (daily 12:00-late, Piazza Santo Spirito 11 red).

**$$ Gusta Osteria,** just around the corner from the piazza, serves big salads and predictable Tuscan fare at fun, cozy indoor seating or at outdoor tables (Tue-Sun 12:00-23:00, closed Mon, Via de' Michelozzi 13 red, tel. 055-285-033).

**$$ Trattoria Casalinga,** an inexpensive standby, comes with bustling aproned waiters. Florentines (who enjoy the tripe and tongue) and tourists (who opt for *ribollita* and easier to swallow Tuscan favorites) both pack the place and leave full and happy (Mon-Sat 12:00-14:30 & 19:00-22:00, after 20:00 call to reserve, closed Sun and Aug, just off Piazza di Santo Spirito, near the church at Via de' Michelozzi 9 red, tel. 055-218-624, www.trattorialacasalinga.it, Andrea and Paolo).

**$ Gusta Pizza** is a jam-packed, touristy, cheap, sloppy, and fun neighborhood pizzeria (Tue-Sun 11:30-15:30 & 19:00-23:30, closed Mon, two blocks off Piazza di Santo Spirito at Via Maggio 46 red, tel. 055-285-068).

**$$ Trattoria Sant'Agostino,** a block away from the Piazza di Santo Spirito action, is charming and more relaxed with comfortable seating and a good place for traditional local cuisine (daily 12:00-23:00, Via Sant'Agostino 23 red, tel. 055-281-995).

**$ O Munaciello Pizzeria,** named after a ghost of Neapolitan folklore, is a kitschy, sprawling, family-friendly festival of happy eating. The menu is fun, there's a youthful energy, and the Naples-style pizza is a hit with locals (daily 12:30-15:00 & 19:00-24:00, Via Maffia 31 red, tel. 055-287-198).

**Night Spots:** Piazza di Santo Spirito is lined with popular bars and restaurants. **Volume** caters to a younger crowd with a living-room atmosphere in an old woodshop (daily, Piazza di Santo Spirito 5 red). On the opposite side of the square, **Pop Café** feels trendy, though it's plastic-plate simple (daily, Piazza di Santo Spirito 18). A bit farther from the square, **Gosh** bar, wallpapered in pink flamingoes, mixes up craft cocktails and herb-infused drinks with flair (daily, Via Santo Spirito 46 red). **NOF** is a late-night hangout with drinks and live music (Mon-Sat 18:30-late, Borgo San Frediano 17 red).

## Beyond Piazza del Carmine, away from Tourists

While Piazza di Santo Spirito is well known by tourists, a short walk beyond it gets you completely away from the tourist scene. These two restaurants (side by side on Via dell'Orto) are worth the five-minute walk beyond Piazza del Carmine. For locations, see the map on page 512.

**$$$ Burro & Acciughe Fish Restaurant** ("butter and anchovies") is a minimalist place packed with locals enjoying fresh seafood. With just 35 seats in a long, narrow setting, it oozes quality (Tue-Sun 19:40-24:00, closed Mon, Via dell'Orto 35 red, tel. 055-045-7286).

**$$ Trattoria dell'Orto** is a classic Florentine trattoria filled with Florentines enjoying steaks, grilled dishes, and quintessential local fare. It has a fun vibe, almost no tourists, and an inviting covered outdoor terrace in back (Wed-Mon 12:00-15:00 & 19:30-23:30, closed Tue, Via dell'Orto 35a, tel. 055-224-148).

## Dining Well in the Oltrarno

Of the many good and colorful restaurants in the Oltrarno, these are my favorites. Reservations are a good idea in the evening.

**$$$ Il Santo Bevitore Ristorante,** lit like a Rembrandt painting and unusually spacious, serves creative, modern Tuscan cuisine at dressy tables. They're enthusiastic about matching quality produce from the area with the right wine (good wine list by the glass or bottle, daily 12:30-14:30 & 19:30-23:00, reservations smart, three tables on the sidewalk, acoustics can make it noisy inside, Via di Santo Spirito 64 red, tel. 055-211-264, www.ilsantobevitore.com).

**$$ Enoteca il Santino Gastronomia,** Il Santo Bevitore's tiny wine bar next door, feels like the perfect after-work hangout for foodies who'd like a glass of wine and a light bite. Tight, cozy, and atmospheric, the place can be intimidating if you're shy. It has a prominent bar, where you can assemble an €8-12 *tagliere* of local cheeses and *salumi.* They also have a few affordable hot dishes. Their food and the wine are locally sourced from small producers (daily 12:30-23:00, Via di Santo Spirito 60 red, no reservations, tel. 055-230-2820).

**$$$ Trattoria 4 Leoni** creates the quintessential Oltrarno dinner scene, and is understandably popular with tourists. The Tuscan-style food is made with an innovative twist and an appreciation for vegetables. Their steak and *fiocchetti* pasta are big hits. You'll enjoy the fun energy and characteristic seating, both outside on the colorful square and inside (daily 12:00-24:00, dinner reservations smart; midway between Ponte Vecchio and Piazza di Santo Spirito, on Piazza della Passera at Via de' Vellutini 1; tel. 055-218-562, www.4leoni.com).

**$$$ Antico Ristoro di' Cambi** is thick with Tuscan traditions, rustic touches, T-bone steaks, and a bustling beer-hall energy. The glass case filled with red chunks of Chianina beef makes clear the house specialty (for the famous *bistecca alla fiorentina* it's €45/kilo—figure a quarter-kilo per person). Before you order, they'll show you the cut and tell you the weight. Unless you insist otherwise, the steak comes nearly uncooked (as it's air-dried for 21 days, it's not really raw, just very tasty and tender). Sit inside the convivial woody interior or outside on the square (Mon-Sat 12:00-14:30 & 18:00-22:30, closed Sun, reserve on weekends and to sit outside, Via Sant'Onofrio 1 red, one block south of Ponte Amerigo Vespucci, see map on page 513, tel. 055-217-134, www. anticoristorodicambi.it, run by Stefano).

**$$$$ Olio & Convivium** is primarily a catering company for top-end events, and this is where they showcase their artful, slow-food cooking. Their three dressy and intimate rooms are surrounded by fine *prosciutti,* cheeses, and wine shelves. It can seem a little formal, but well-dressed foodies will appreciate this place for its romantic, exclusive atmosphere. Their list of €14-25 *gastronomia* plates offers an array of taste treats and fine wines by the glass. They also have €35-49 tasting menus and stylish €22 lunches with wine (Tue-Sun 12:00-14:30 & 19:00-22:30, closed Mon, Via di Santo Spirito 4, tel. 055-265-8198, www.oliorestaurant.it, Tommaso is the chef and owner).

## Casual Oltrarno Neighborhood Eateries

**$$ Le Volpi e l'Uva,** a wine bar just steps from Ponte Vecchio, has a limited menu of *affettati* (cold cuts), cheese, and *crostone* (hearty

## Cooking Classes

The options listed below represent only a few of your many choices. As this is a fast-changing scene, it's worth doing some homework online and booking well ahead.

**In Tavola:** A dedicated cooking school in the heart of the Oltrarno, In Tavola features trained, English-speaking Italian chefs who quickly demonstrate each step before setting you loose. You'll work in a functional kitchen, then sit down to eat in the cozy wine cellar (classes range from €57-129/person, ideally book well ahead but you can try calling last-minute, between the Pitti Palace and Brancacci Chapel at Via dei Velluti 18 red, tel. 055-217-672, www.intavola.org, info@intavola.org, Fabrizio).

**Artviva:** The Artviva walking-tour company offers a range of hands-on cooking, pasta, and pastry classes (€59-73/person, see their listing on page 477).

**Florencetown:** This walking-tour company offers a five-hour experience that starts with a trip to Mercato Centrale, then settles into their kitchen for a cooking lesson (from €79/person, also 3-hour pizza- and gelato-making class for €59/person, see listing on page 477).

bruschetta)—a nice spot for a light lunch (daily 11:00-21:00, 65 yards south of Ponte Vecchio—walk through Piazza Santa Felicità to Piazza dei Rossi 1, tel. 055-239-8132).

**$ Trattoria Sabatino,** the farthest away of my Oltrarno listings (and not touristy), is a spacious, brightly lit mess hall. It's changed little since it opened in 1956. It's disturbingly cheap, with family character and a simple menu—a super place to watch locals munch, especially since you'll likely be sharing a table. It's a 15-minute walk from Ponte Vecchio (Mon-Fri 12:00-14:30 & 19:15-22:00, closed Sat-Sun, just outside Porta San Frediano, Via Pisana 2 red, see map on page 513, tel. 055-225-955, little English spoken).

### Via di San Niccolò and Nearby

This charming little street—just over Ponte alle Grazie, behind Hotel Silla—is the heart of the San Niccolò neighborhood and is a fun place to get away from the tourist mobs (see the map on page 512). There's a convivial neighborhood pizzeria, an *enoteca*, a good *gelateria* (**Il Gelato di Filo,** at Via San Miniato 5 red), and a rollicking bar (**Il Baretto del Rifrullo,** at Via San Niccolò 55 red), which serves a generous buffet during happy hour. Street-art lovers enjoy popping into the gallery of **Abraham Clet,** the artist who stealthily alters street signs around town (daily, but closed Mon morning, Via dell'Olmo 8 red).

For those looking to dine, three good eateries anchor the square:

**$$ Antica Mescita San Niccolò,** with traditional decor but a modern approach, feels like the grandkids took over Nonno's trattoria. Technically a wine bar, they also serve up Tuscan standbys (like soups and stews). There's delightful seating outside in good weather; their cellar is less cozy (daily 12:00-24:00, Via San Niccolò 60 red, tel. 055-234-2836).

**$$ Boccadarno,** next door at #56 red, is family-run by brother-and-sister team Gerardo and Carlotta. The service is friendly, and the menu is strong in grilled fish. Eat in the light, bright interior or at an outdoor table (Tue-Sat 11:30-23:30, closed Sun dinner and all day Mon, tel. 055-386-0860).

**$$$ Zeb** is a tight, mod, minimalist wine-bar/deli with one long counter (just two dozen seats). Although the name stands for *zuppe e bolliti* ("soup and boiled meats"), they dish up all types of well-executed and elegantly presented Florentine food. Portions are large and fun to share, served up by charming Mama Guiseppina and her son Alberto. Dinner reservations are smart (Thu-Tue 12:00-15:30 & 19:30-22:30, closed Wed, Via San Miniato 2 red, tel. 055-234-2864, www.zebgastronomia.com).

**Nightlife:** To rub elbows with the locals, head toward tiny Piazza Demidoff (cross the bridge east of Ponte Vecchio and turn left, about a 10-minute walk). These places have outdoor seating: **Negroni** (opens Mon-Fri at 8:30, Sat-Sun at 19:00, Via dei Renai 17 red, tel. 055-247-8853) and **Zoe** (opens Mon-Sat at 9:00, Sun at 18:00, Via dei Renai 13 red, tel. 055-243-111).

# Florence Connections

Florence is Tuscany's transportation hub, with fine train, bus, and plane connections to virtually anywhere in Italy. The city has several train stations, a bus station (next to the main train station), and an airport (and Pisa's airport is nearby). Livorno, on the coast west of Florence, is a major cruise-ship port.

## BY TRAIN

For general information on train travel in Italy—including ticket-buying options—see the Practicalities chapter. The following connections are for Trenitalia; Italo options are specifically noted.

**From Florence by Train to: Pisa** (2/hour, 45-75 minutes), **Lucca** (2/hour, 1.5 hours), **Siena** (direct trains hourly, 1.5 hours; bus is better because Siena's train station is far from the center), **Camucia-Cortona** (hourly, 1.5 hours), **Livorno** (hourly, 1.5 hours, some change in Pisa), **La Spezia** (for the Cinque Terre, 5/day direct, 2.5 hours, otherwise nearly hourly with change in Pisa), **Milan** (hourly, 2 hours; Italo: 2/hour, 2 hours), **Venice** (hourly, 2-3 hours, may transfer in Bologna, often crowded—reserve ahead; Italo: 4/day, 2 hours, reservations required), **Assisi** (7/day direct, 2-3 hours), **Orvieto** (hourly, 2 hours, some with change in Campo di Marte or Rifredi Station), **Rome** (2-3/hour, 1.5 hours, most require seat reservations; Italo: 2/hour, 1.5 hours), **Naples** (at least hourly, 3 hours; Italo: hourly, 3 hours).

## BY BUS

The BusItalia Station is 50 yards southwest of the train station, near the T1 tram stop. Schedules for regional trips are posted, and monitors show imminent departures. Bus service drops dramatically on Sunday. Generally it's best to buy tickets in the station, as you'll pay 30 percent more to buy tickets onboard. Bus info: Tel. 800-373-760 (Mon-Fri 9:00-15:00, closed Sat-Sun), www.fsbusitalia.it.

**From Florence by Bus to: San Gimignano** (hourly, fewer on Sun, 1.5-2 hours, change in Poggibonsi), **Siena** (roughly 2/hour—fewer off-season, 1.5-hour *rapida/via superstrada* buses are fastest, avoid the slower *ordinaria* buses, in Siena get off at Piazza Gramsci or Via Tozzi, www.tiemmespa.it), **Volterra** (4/day Mon-Sat, 1/day Sun, 2 hours, change in Colle di Val d'Elsa to CTT bus #770, www.pisa.cttnord.it; or faster train to Pontedera-Casciana Terme and then CTT bus #500 to Volterra, 7/day, fewer on Sun, 1.5 hours, www.pisa.cttnord.it), **Montepulciano** (1-2/day, 2 hours, LFI bus, www.lfi.it; or train to Chiusi, then Tiemme/Siena Mobilità bus to Montepulciano, www.tiemmespa.it).

## BY PRIVATE CAR

For small groups with more money than time, zipping to nearby towns by private car service can be a comfortable option. Florence-based **Transfer Chauffeur Service** has a fleet of modern vehicles with drivers who can whisk you between cities throughout Italy, to and from the cruise ship port at Livorno, and through the Tuscan countryside for around the same price as a cab (mobile 338-862-3129, www.transfercs.com, welcome@transfercs.com, Marco). **Prestige Rent** also has friendly, English-speaking drivers and offers similar services (office at Via della Saggina 98, tel. 055-286-059, www.prestigerent.com, usa@prestigerent.com, Saverio).

## BY PLANE

For information on Florence's **Amerigo Vespucci Airport**, see page 470.

**FLORENCE**

## BY CRUISE SHIP

Cruise ships dock in the coastal town of Livorno, about 60 miles west of Florence. The most seamless transfer from the port to Florence (or Pisa/Lucca) is via TuscanyBus.com; they guarantee you'll make it back to your ship in plenty of time (tel. 058-6188-8623, www.tuscanybus.com). On your own, you can take a train to Florence (hourly, 1.5 hours). Taxis are pricey, but sharing a minibus taxi with other cruisers can bring the round-trip cost down. For more details, see my *Rick Steves Mediterranean Cruise Ports* guidebook.

**Local Guide: Karin Kibby,** an Oregonian living in Livorno who leads Rick Steves tours, offers a morning "slice of Italian life" walk through Livorno, focusing on local culture (includes its fantastic food market), as well as day trips throughout Tuscany (2-10 people, mobile 333-108-6348, klkibby@yahoo.com).

# PISA & LUCCA

The two Tuscan towns of Pisa and Lucca, near Florence and each other, make for easy daytrips. But both cities deserve more than a touristy quickie. If you can, take the time to savor Pisa's rich architectural heritage and to bask in Lucca's genuine charm.

The Leaning Tower of Pisa is one of the most iconic images in the world. It's touristy but worth a visit. Many travelers are surprised to see that the famous tower is only a small part of a gleaming white architectural complex—featuring a massive cathedral and baptistery—that dominates the grand green square called the Field of Miracles. The rest of the city is virtually tourist-free and merits a wander for its rich history, architecture, and student vibe.

Lucca, contained within its fine Renaissance wall, lacks any blockbuster sights, but has a charm that causes many connoisseurs of Italy to claim it as a favorite stop. The town's garden-topped city wall is perfect for a laid-back bike ride—the single must-do activity in this pleasant getaway.

The two towns are about 25 minutes apart by train and 50 minutes by bus (for side-tripping between Pisa and Lucca, see the "Connections" sections later). Each is about 1.5 hours (or less) by train from Florence and well-served by excellent highways.

Using public transportation, you could day-trip from Florence to both cities. But with more time, stay overnight in Lucca. Take the train to Pisa in the morning, do your sightseeing, catch the bus or train to Lucca late in the afternoon, enjoy the evening scene, and stay the night. Sightsee Lucca the next day, then move on to your next destination by train.

# Pisa

Famous for its tipsy Tower, Pisa ("PEE-zah") is much more than its iconic landmark. This thriving midsize city has a wealth of history and architectural treasures, an unexpectedly fun-to-explore arcaded core, and a prestigious university. The Tower and its companion buildings at the Field of Miracles are undoubtedly a must-see. But beyond that tourist-clogged zone, Pisa feels like a real-world antidote to all that Tuscan cutesiness...a humbler version of Florence.

Centuries ago, Pisa was a major power—rivaling Venice and Genoa for control of the seas. City leaders erected an ensemble of Pisan Romanesque landmarks—the Duomo, Baptistery, and Tower—that float regally on the best lawn in Italy. Even as the church was being built, Piazza del Duomo was nicknamed the "Campo dei Miracoli," or Field of Miracles, for the grandness of the undertaking.

After its port silted up, Pisa was left high and dry, and eventually entered a period of steady decline...leaving those grand landmarks as reminders of its past glory.

## PLANNING YOUR TIME

For most visitors, Pisa is a touristy quickie—seeing the Tower, visiting the square, and wandering through the Duomo are 90 percent of their Pisan thrills. But it's a shame to skip the rest of the city. Considering Pisa's historic importance and the ambience created by its rich architectural heritage and vibrant student population, the city deserves at least a half-day visit.

To ascend the Tower, it's smartest to book a time in advance online at OPAPisa.it. Otherwise, go straight to the ticket office upon arrival to snag an appointment—usually for a couple of hours later, especially in summer. If you'll be seeing both the town and the Field of Miracles, plan on a six-hour stop. If just blitzing the Field of Miracles, three hours is the minimum.

# Orientation to Pisa

Pisa is manageable, with just 100,000 people. The city is framed on the north by the Field of Miracles (with the Leaning Tower) and on the south by Pisa Centrale train station. The Arno River flows east to west, bisecting the city. The two main streets for tourists and shoppers are Via Santa Maria (running south from the Tower) and Corso Italia/Borgo Stretto (running north from the station). A thousand years ago the city was a fortified burg on the north side of the river between those two main streets.

## TOURIST INFORMATION
The main TI is located on the Field of Miracles, next to the Duomo's ticket office at the Museum of the Sinopias (daily 9:30-17:30, Piazza Duomo 7, tel. 050-550-100, www.turismo.pisa.it). It sells bus tickets and offers videoguide walking tours of the main sights and the city center (€5-8). For those doing Pisa as a stopover, the TI offers baggage storage.

## ARRIVAL IN PISA
### By Train
Most trains (and visitors) arrive at Pisa Centrale station, about a mile south of the Tower and Field of Miracles. A few trains, particularly those from Lucca or La Spezia, stop at the smaller Pisa San Rossore Station, an easy five-minute walk from the Tower.

**Pisa Centrale Station:** This station has a baggage-check desk—look for *deposito bagagli* (daily 7:00-21:00). It's at the far end of platform 1.

To get to the Field of Miracles, you can **walk** (30 minutes direct, one hour if you follow my self-guided walk), take a **taxi** (€10, tel. 050-541-600, taxi stand at station), or go by **bus** (which can be plagued by pickpockets).

Bus **LAM Rossa** (also marked *L/R*) stops in front of the station (to the right when you exit; bus stop at the corner). Buy a €1.50 bus ticket from ticket machines at the bus stop, the tobacco/magazine kiosk in the train station's main hall, or at a nearby tobacco shop (€2.50 on board; bus usually departs every 10 minutes, less-frequent off-season, runs until 20:45, 15-minute trip). The bus lets you off at Piazza Manin, in front of the gate to the Field of Miracles (stop: Torre).

To return to the train station from the Tower, catch bus LAM Rossa across from the BNL bank, on the opposite side of the street from where you got off. Buy your ticket at the ticket machine at the bus stop (tobacco shops are scarce in the area). You'll find a taxi stand 30 yards from the Tower or in front of the BNL bank on Piazza Manin.

**Pisa San Rossore Station:** This little suburban train station is just a four-block (5-minute) walk to the Tower. Exit the underpass at platform 2L, and follow the exit signs to *Torre Pendente*. Once out of the station area, turn left and follow brown *Torre Pendente* signs on Via Andrea Pisano, heading for the Baptistery's dome. You'll see the Tower soon, straight ahead.

## By Car

Pisa has several restricted driving areas that are monitored by camera and marked by "*ZTL*" signs (you could get a ticket by mail). For a quick visit, try the **Parcheggio di Piazza dei Miracoli** lot, just west of the Tower (€2/hour, enter from Via Giovanni Battista Niccolini). Or leave your car at the big **Pietrasantina parking lot,** designed for tour buses and tourists with cars (who park for free). From there, you can walk to the Field of Miracles or hop on a bus. To reach this parking lot, exit the autostrada at *Pisa Nord* and follow signs to *Pisa* (on the left), then *Bus Parking*.

At the center of the lot is a high-roofed bus stop where you can catch the LAM Rossa **bus** to Piazza Manin at the gate of the Field of Miracles (€1.50 at the parking lot's cafeteria, €2.50 on board). Or, for an in-depth visit, stay on bus LAM Rossa as it continues to Pisa Centrale train station, then follow my self-guided walk through Pisa back to the Field of Miracles.

The **walk to the Tower** takes about 15 minutes: From the newspaper/souvenir kiosk at the east end of the lot, turn right onto the curving road. Follow the blue signs indicating a pedestrian path and brown signs pointing to the Leaning Tower. You'll cross train tracks on the left, then continue to the right.

## By Plane

For details on Pisa's Galileo Galilei Airport, see "Pisa Connections," later.

## HELPFUL HINTS

**Markets:** An open-air produce market attracts picnickers to Piazza delle Vettovaglie, one block north of the Arno River near Ponte di Mezzo, and nearby Piazza Sant'Uomobuono (Mon-Sat 8:00-13:00, closed Sun). A street market—with more practical goods than food—bustles on Wednesday and Saturday mornings between Via del Brennero and Via Paparrelli (8:00-13:00, just outside of wall, about 6 blocks east of the Tower). A small flea market pops up in Via San Martino every Wednesday and Saturday morning.

**Supermarket:** Just to the northwest of the Field of Miracles entrance, **Carrefour Express** has everything you need. It sells quick lunch items, has a coffee bar and picnic area, Wi-Fi, and a clean WC free to customers (daily 8:00-20:00, Largo Cocco Griffi).

**Local Guides:** One option is **Dottore Vincenzo Riolo,** who guides tours of the Field of Miracles, the city center, and other Tuscan destinations (€150/3 hours, mobile 338-211-2939, www.pisatour.it, info@pisatour.it). **Martina Manfredi** happily guides visitors through the Field of Miracles, but her real passion is helping them discover Pisa's other charms (€140/3 hours, mobile 328-898-2927, www.tuscanyatheart.it, artemarty@libero.it).

# Pisa Walk

A leisurely one-hour self-guided stroll from Pisa Centrale train station to the Tower is a great way to get acquainted with the more subtle virtues of this fine city. Because the hordes who descend daily on the Tower rarely bother with the rest of the town, you'll find most of Pisa to be delightfully untouristy—a student-filled, classy, Old World town with an Arno-scape much like its upstream rival, Florence.

• *From Pisa Centrale, walk north (under the fascist marble arcade) up Viale Antonio Gramsci to the circular square called...*

## Piazza Vittorio Emanuele II

The Allies considered Pisa to be strategically important in World War II, and both the train station and its main bridge were targeted for bombing. Forty percent of this district was destroyed. The piazza has been rebuilt, and now this generous public space with grass and benches is actually a lid for an underground parking lot.

PISA & LUCCA

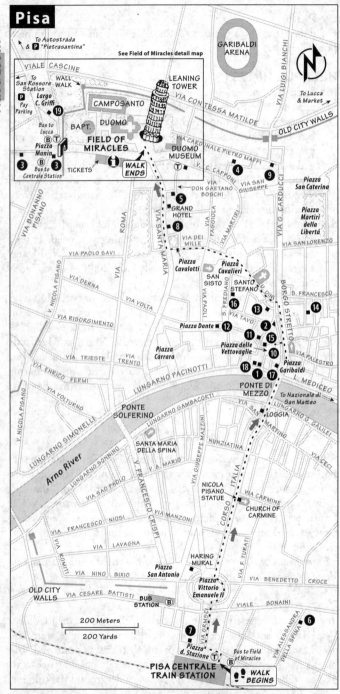

# Pisa

To Autostrada
& P "Pietrasantina"

GARIBALDI
ARENA

See Field of Miracles detail map

VIALE CASCINE

WALL
WALK

To
San Rossore
Station

P
Pay Parking

Largo
C. Griffi
19

BAPT.

CAMPOSANTO

DUOMO

FIELD OF
MIRACLES

LEANING
TOWER

VIA CONTESSA MATILDE

VIA LUIGI BIANCHI

OLD CITY WALLS

To Lucca
& Market

VIA CARDINALE PIETRO MAFFI

Piazza
Mania

B  T
Bus to
Lucca

3

B
Bus to
Centrale Station

3

TICKETS

WALK
ENDS

DUOMO
MUSEUM

T

V. C. Capponi

4

9

Piazza
San Caterina

VIA SAN
GIUSEPPE

VIA
DON GAETANO
BOSCHI

5

GRAND
HOTEL

8

VIA BONANNO PISANO

VIA
FAGGIOLA

VIA
MARTIRI

ROMA

VIA SANTA MARIA

VIA DEI
MILLE

VIA G. CARDUCCI

Piazza
Martiri
della
Libertà

VIA SAN LORENZO

VIA PAOLO SAVI

Piazza
Cavalotti

Piazza
Cavalieri

V. NICOLA PISANO

VIA DERNA

SAN
SISTO

SANTO
STEFANO

BORGO STRETTO

S. FRANCESCO

VIA VOLTA

S. FREDIANO

VIA P. DINI

14

VIA RISORGIMENTO

VIA TAVOLI

16

13

2

VIA PAOLI

Piazza Dante

12

11

15

VIA TRIESTE

VIA
TRENTO

Piazza
Carrara

Piazza delle
Vettovaglie

10

VIA S. PALESTRO

VIA ENRICO
FERMI

18

1

17

Piazza
Garibaldi

L. MEDICEO

V. NICOLA PISANO

VIA VOLTURNO

LUNGARNO PACINOTTI

PONTE DI
MEZZO

To Nazionale di
San Matteo

PONTE
SOLFERINO

LUNGARNO GAMBACORTI

VIA SAN
MARTINO

LOGGIA

LUNGARNO G. GALILEI

LUNGARNO SIMONELLI

LUNGARNO SONNINO

VIA GIUSEPPE MAZZINI

NUNZIATINA

VIA CECI

Arno River

SANTA MARIA
DELLA SPINA

V. A. MARIO

CORSO ITALIA

VIA SAO PAOLO

VIA FRANCESCO CRISPI

NICOLA
PISANO
STATUE

VIA CARMINE

CHURCH OF
CARMINE

VIA FRANCESCO NIOSI

VIA MANZONI

VIA F. TURATI

VIA LAVAGNA

HARING
MURAL

VIA NINO BIXIO

V. KOMITI

Piazza
San Antonio

Piazza
Vittorio
Emanuele II

VIA BENEDETTO
CROCE

VIALE BONAINI

OLD CITY
WALLS

VIA CESARE BATTISTI

BUS
STATION
B

VIA ALESSANDRA
DELLA SPINA

6

200 Meters

200 Yards

7

Piazza
d. Stazione
T

Bus to
Field of
Miracles
B

PISA CENTRALE
TRAIN STATION

WALK
BEGINS

## Pisa Key

**Accommodations**

**1** Hotel Royal Victoria
**2** Relais dei Mercanti
**3** Hotel Pisa Tower & Annex (2)
**4** Casa San Tommaso
**5** Hotel Helvetia
**6** Hotel Alessandro della Spina
**7** Stazione22

**Eateries & Other**

**8** Ristorante-Pizzeria La Torre
**9** Pizzeria al Bagno di Nerone

**10** La Vineria di Piazza & Produce Market
**11** Antica Trattoria il Campano
**12** Caffetteria BetsaBea
**13** Il Montino Pizzeria
**14** Orzo Bruno Brewpub
**15** La Mescita
**16** Osteria Lo Scioglipepe
**17** La Bottega del Gelato
**18** De' Coltelli Gelato & Caffè dell'Ussero
**19** Supermarket

The circular pink building in the middle of the square, on the right, is La Bottega del Parco, a shop that sells Tuscan products and offers light meals.

At the top of the square, on the left (by the Credito Artigiano bank), find the little piazza with a colorful bar/café that faces a

mural, called *Tuttomondo (Whole Wide World)*, painted by American artist **Keith Haring**. The mural, which decorates the back of a church that was bombed and rebuilt in the 1950s, is worth studying. It's a celebration of diversity, chaos, and the liveliness of our world, vibrating with energy. Enjoy the symbolism: the cross of people, three races connected like nesting dolls holding a heart. The message of tolerance is as timely today as it was when this mural was completed in 1989. Haring (who died of AIDS in 1990) brought New York City graffiti into the mainstream.

• *Head back to the middle of the big square and take the first left. This is Pisa's main drag.*

### Corso Italia

As you leave Piazza Vittorio Emanuele II, look to the right (on the wall of the bar on the corner, under the gallery) and orient yourself with the circa-1960 wall map of Pisa with a steam train. Then follow the pedestrianized Corso Italia straight north for several blocks, toward the river. This is Pisa's main shopping street for locals, not tourists. Students hang out and stroll here—you'll see plenty of cheap department stores and youthful fashions.

A few blocks up, in front of the Church of Santa Maria del

Carmine (#88), meet **Nicola Pisano.** He and his son, Giovanni (who worked in the 13th century) represented the pinnacle of Gothic art and inspired Michelangelo. Although they were from the south, their work in their adopted town earned them the name "Pisano" (from Pisa).

Continuing on Corso Italia, just before the river, you run into a stately **loggia.** Like much of the city, this was built under Medici (Florentine) rule—and it resembles the markets you'll still find in Florence. But remember that before Florence ruled Pisa, this city was an independent and strong maritime republic.

• *At the Arno River, cross to the middle of the bridge.*

## Ponte di Mezzo

This modern bridge, the site of Pisa's first bridge and therefore its birthplace, marks the center of Pisa. In the Middle Ages, Ponte di Mezzo (like Florence's Ponte Vecchio) was lined with shops. It's been destroyed several times by floods...and in 1943 by British and American bombers. Enjoy the view from the center of the bridge of the elegant mansions that line the riverbank, recalling Pisa's days of trading glory—the cityscape feels a bit like Venice's Grand Canal.

Looking downstream on the right, notice the red-brick building (the former silk merchants' quarters) that looks like it's about to slide into the river. Pisa sits on shifting delta sand, making construction tricky. The entire town leans.

• *Cross the bridge to...*

## Piazza Garibaldi

This square is named for the charismatic leader of the Risorgimento, the unification movement that led to Italian independence in 1860. Knowing Pisa was strongly nationalist (and gave many of its sons to the national struggle), a wounded Garibaldi came here to be nursed back to health. Find his statue and study the left side of the bronze relief at the base of the statue to see him docking in Pisa and receiving a warm and caring welcome.

For a gelato break, stop by **La Bottega del Gelato,** right on this square and most Pisans' sentimental favorite. Or, for a fresh take on the same old gelato, head about 100 yards downstream (to the left on Lungarno Pacinotti as you come off the bridge) to **De' Coltelli** (at #23), which scoops up organic, artisanal gelato with unusual and vibrant flavors. Just beyond that, in the slouching red building (at #28), step into **Caffè dell'Ussero.** This venerable café has long been a hangout of both politicians...and the students bent on overthrowing them.

• *Back on Piazza Garibaldi, continue north up the elegantly arcaded street called...*

## Borgo Stretto

Welcome to Pisa's other main shopping street—this one higher-end. On the right, the Church of St. Michael, with its fine Pisan Romanesque facade, was likely built upon a Roman temple.

From here, look farther up the street and notice how it undulates like a flowing river. In the sixth century BC, Pisa was born when two parallel rivers were connected by canals. This street echoes the flow of one of those canals.

• *Just past the church, pause to appreciate the Renaissance arcades (loggias) in every direction. Then detour left onto Via delle Colonne, and walk one block down to...*

## Piazza delle Vettovaglie

Pisa's historic market square, Piazza delle Vettovaglie, is lively by day and sketchy by night. Its Renaissance loggia has hosted the fish-and-vegetable market for generations. Stalls are set up in this piazza in the morning and stay open later in the neighboring piazza to the west (Piazza Sant'Uomobuono). You could cobble together a picnic from the sandwich shops and fruit-and-veggie stalls ringing these squares, or enjoy lunch at the recommended **La Vineria di Piazza** trattoria (under the arcades of Piazza delle Vettovaglie).

• *Return to Borgo Stretto and continue north another 100 yards, passing a modern apartment development at Largo Ciro Menotti, an example of 1960s city design that followed WWII bombings. You'll pass Pasticceria Salza—an elegant place for a coffee and a central perch from which to observe the scene since 1898.*

*Take the second left on nondescript Via Ulisse Dini (immediately at the arcade's end, just before the pharmacy). This leads to Pisa's historic core, the square called...*

## Piazza dei Cavalieri (Knights' Square)

For Pisans, this square is a reminder of past and lost glory. It feels sad, nostalgic...the only square I've seen in Italy without a bar or café. The square (site of the market or forum in ancient Roman times) long hosted the head of a proud and independent Pisan government. A Palazzo Vecchio-like capitol stood here during Pisa's glory days when the city was a big maritime power in a league with Genoa and Amalfi.

Then came a couple of centuries of Florentine rule. The statue of Cosimo I, a Medici who ruled the Grand Duchy of Tuscany (and

Pisa), is a reminder of those dark times. Cosimo asserted Florentine rule by turning this square into a Florentine military base. The Pisan palace became the late Renaissance Florentine military school you see here today.

From here, take Via Corsica (to the left of the clock tower). The humble 11th-century **Church of San Sisto,** ahead on the left, is worth a quick look. This was the standard Romanesque style that predated the more lavish Pisan Romanesque style of the Field of Miracles structures: simple bricks, assorted reused columns—some of them ancient Roman—a delightful assortment of capitals, heavy walls, and tiny windows. Its 11th-century facade was once covered with plaster and colorfully painted. You can see the remains of the Eastern-flavored ceramic bowls across the top that once shined in the sun like gems.

• *Follow Via Corsica as it turns into Via dei Mille, then turn right on Via Santa Maria, which leads north, becoming a touristy can-can of eateries, and finally ends at the Field of Miracles and the Tower. (Consider the Grand Hotel Duomo the border between tolerable touristy restaurants and terrible touristy restaurants nearer the Leaning Tower.)*

## Sights in Pisa

### THE BEST OF THE FIELD OF MIRACLES

Imagine arriving in Pisa as a sailor in the 12th century, when the river came to just outside the walls surrounding this square, the church here was one of the biggest in the world, and this ensemble in gleaming white marble was the most impressive space in Christendom. Calling it the Field of Miracles (Campo dei Miracoli) would not have been hyperbole.

Scattered across a golf-course green lawn are five grand buildings: the cathedral (or Duomo), its bell tower (the Leaning Tower), the Baptistery, the hospital (today's Museum of the Sinopias), and the Camposanto Cemetery. Each building has a simple ground floor and rows of delicate columns and arches that form open-air arcades, giving the Campo a pleasant visual unity.

The style is called Pisan Romanesque. Unlike traditional Romanesque, with its heavy fortress-like feel, Pisan Romanesque is light and elegant. At ground level, most of the structures have simple half-columns and arches. On the upper levels, you'll see a little of everything—tight rows of thin columns; pointed Gothic gables and prickly spires; Byzantine mosaics and horseshoe arches; and

**Pisa's Field of Miracles**

- ❶ Ticket Offices (2)
- ❷ Baggage Check
- ❸ Bus to Centrale Station
- ❹ Bus to Lucca

geometric designs (such as diamonds) and striped, colored marbles inspired by mosques in Muslim lands.

Architecturally, the Campo is unique and exotic. Traditionally, its buildings marked the main events of every Pisan's life: christened in the Baptistery, married in the Duomo, called to celebrate by the bells in the tower, healed in the hospital, and buried in the Camposanto Cemetery.

Lining this field of artistic pearls are dozens of people who have simultaneously had the same bright idea: posing for a photo as though they're propping up the Leaning Tower. Although the smooth green carpet looks like the ideal picnic spot—and many people are doing just that—officially, lounging on this lawn can result in a €25 fine.

### ▲▲▲Leaning Tower

A 15-foot lean from the vertical makes the Leaning Tower one of Europe's most recognizable images. You can see it for free—it's always viewable—or you can pay to climb nearly 300 stairs to the top.

The off-kilter Tower parallels Pisa's history. It was started in the late 12th century, when Pisa was at its peak: one of the world's richest, most powerful, and most sophisticated cities. Pisans had built their huge cathedral to reflect their city's superpower status, and the cathedral's bell tower—the Leaning Tower—was the per-

## Field of Miracles Tickets

Pisa's combo-ticket scheme is designed to get you into its neglected secondary sights: the Baptistery, Camposanto Cemetery, Duomo Museum, and Museum of the Sinopias (fresco patterns). For €5, you get your choice of one of these sights; for two sights, the cost is €7; for the works, you pay €8 (credit cards accepted). It's free to enter the Duomo, but you either need a voucher with an appointed time, or you can get in anytime with any combo-ticket. With any ticket,  you'll pay an additional €18 for a timed-entry ticket to climb the Tower.

You can get the Duomo voucher and any of these tickets from either ticket office on the Field of Miracles: One is behind the Leaning Tower and the other is at the Museum of the Sinopias (near the TI, less crowded). It's also possible to buy tickets in advance online at OPAPisa.it (no sooner than 20 days but at least one day ahead of your visit; Duomo voucher not available online).

And what about entering the Tower? Is it worth that hefty price tag—and a likely wait to enter? It's a minor thrill to clomp up those twisty stairs, and the view from the top is enjoyable. But Pisa isn't particularly scenic, and it's a lot of expense and hassle for a view. Unless climbing the Tower is what you came to do, I'd say the real thrill comes from seeing it from the outside.

fect complement. But as Pisa's power declined, the Tower reclined, and both have required a great deal of effort to prop up. Modern engineering has stabilized the Tower, so you can admire it in all its cockeyed glory and even climb up for a commanding view.

**Cost and Hours:** €18, kids under age 8 not allowed, daily April-Sept 8:00-20:00 (until 22:00 mid-June-Aug), Oct 9:00-19:00, Nov-Feb 10:00-17:00, March 9:00-18:00, ticket office opens 30 minutes early, reservations necessary if you value your time, OPAPisa.it.

**Getting In:** Entry to the Tower is by a timed ticket good for a 30-minute visit. Every 15 minutes, 50 people can clamber up the 294 tilting steps to the top. Children ages 8-18 must be accompanied by—and stay at all times with—an adult.

**Reservations: Online bookings** are accepted no earlier than 20 days and no later than one day in advance. Choose your entry

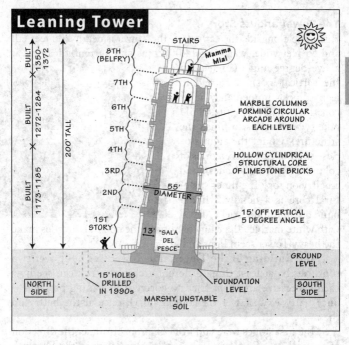

**Leaning Tower**

STAIRS

BUILT 1350-1372

8TH (BELFRY)

Mamma Mia!

7TH

6TH

MARBLE COLUMNS FORMING CIRCULAR ARCADE AROUND EACH LEVEL

BUILT 1272-1284

200' TALL

5TH

4TH

HOLLOW CYLINDRICAL STRUCTURAL CORE OF LIMESTONE BRICKS

3RD

2ND

55' DIAMETER

BUILT 1173-1185

15' OFF VERTICAL 5 DEGREE ANGLE

1ST STORY

13' "SALA DEL PESCE"

GROUND LEVEL

NORTH SIDE

15' HOLES DRILLED IN 1990s

FOUNDATION LEVEL

MARSHY, UNSTABLE SOIL

SOUTH SIDE

time and buy your ticket at OPAPisa.it. Print out the voucher and bring it to the Tower 15 minutes before your entry time.

To reserve in person, go to either **ticket office:** behind the Tower on the left (in the yellow building) or (less crowded) at the Museum of the Sinopias.

**Planning Your Time:** In summer, for same-day entry, you'll likely wait 2-3 hours before going up (see the rest of the monuments and grab lunch while waiting). With a reservation, arrive at least 15 minutes ahead of your entry time or you may not be allowed in.

It's busiest between 12:00 and 15:00. If you come after 18:00 there's generally no line at all...on my last visit, I was the only one climbing the Tower at 19:00.

**Baggage Check:** You can't take anything up the Tower other than your phone or camera. Day-bag-size lockers are available at the ticket office next to the Tower—show your ticket to check your bag. You may check your bag 15 minutes before your reservation time and must pick it up immediately after your Tower visit.

**Caution:** The railings are skinny, the steps are slanted, there are no handrails, and rain makes the marble slippery—all in all, it's more dizzying than you might expect. Anyone with balance issues of any sort should think twice before ascending.

## The Tower and Its Story

Rising up alongside the cathedral, the Tower is nearly 200 feet tall and 55 feet wide, weighing 14,000 tons and currently leaning at a five-degree angle (15 feet off the vertical axis). It started to lean almost immediately after construction began (it would take two centuries to finish the structure). Count the eight stories—a simple base, six stories of columns (forming arcades), and a belfry on top. The inner structural core is a hollow cylinder built of limestone bricks, faced

with white marble. The thin columns of the open-air arcades make the heavy Tower seem light and graceful.

**The Building of the Tower:** The Tower was built over two centuries by at least three different architects. You can see how each successive architect tried to correct the leaning problem—once halfway up (after the fourth story), once at the belfry on the top.

The first stones were laid in 1173, probably under the direction of the architect Bonanno Pisano (who also designed the Duomo's bronze back door). Five years later, just as the base and the first arcade were finished, someone said, "Is it just me, or does that look crooked?" The heavy Tower—resting on a very shallow 13-foot foundation—was sinking on the south side into the marshy, multilayered, unstable soil. (Actually, all of the Campo's buildings tilt somewhat.) The builders carried on anyway, until they'd finished four stories (the base, plus three arcade floors). Then, construction suddenly halted—no one knows why—and for a century the Tower sat half-finished and visibly leaning.

Around 1272, the next architect continued, trying to correct the problem by angling the next three stories backward, in the opposite direction of the lean. The project then again sat mysteriously idle for nearly another century. Finally, Tommaso Pisano put the belfry on the top (c. 1350-1372), also kinking it to overcome the leaning.

**Man Versus Gravity:** After the Tower's completion, several attempts were made to stop its slow-motion fall. The architect/artist/writer Giorgio Vasari reinforced the base in 1550, and it actually worked. But in 1838, well-intentioned engineers pumped out groundwater, destabilizing the Tower and causing it to increase its lean at a rate of a millimeter per year.

As well as gravity, erosion threatens the Tower. Since its construction, 135 of the Tower's 180 marble columns have had to be replaced. Stone decay, deposits of lime and calcium phosphate, accumulations of dirt and moss, cracking from the stress of the lean—all of these are factors in its decline.

It got so bad that in 1990 the Tower was closed for repairs, and $30 million was spent cleaning it and trying to stabilize it. Engineers dried the soil with pipes containing liquid nitrogen, anchored the Tower to the ground with steel cables, and buried 600 tons of lead on the north side as a counterweight (not visible)—all with little success. The breakthrough came when they drilled 15-foot-deep holes in the ground on the north side and sucked out 60 tons of soil, allowing the Tower to sink on the north side and straighten out its lean by about six inches.

All the work to shore up, straighten, and clean the Tower has probably turned the clock back a few centuries. In fact, art historians figure the Tower leans today as much as it did when Galileo reputedly conducted his gravity experiment here 400 years ago.

## ▲▲Duomo (Cathedral)

The huge Pisan Romanesque cathedral, with its carved pulpit by Giovanni Pisano, is artistically more important than its more famous bell tower. Budget some sight-seeing time for the church's artistic and historic treasures.

**Cost and Hours:** Free. If you have any combo-ticket you can walk right in; otherwise, pick up a voucher with an entry time at either ticket office (every 30 minutes, voucher not available in advance online, see the "Field of Miracles Tickets" sidebar earlier); daily April-Sept 10:00-20:00, Oct until 19:00, Nov-Feb 10:00-13:00 & 14:00-17:00, March 10:00-18:00.

**Dress Code:** Shorts are OK as long as they're not too short, and shoulders should be covered (although it's not really enforced).

### ➔ Self-Guided Tour

The Duomo is the centerpiece of the Field of Miracles' complex of religious buildings. Begun in 1063, it was financed by a galley-load of booty ransacked that year from the Muslim-held capital of Palermo, Sicily. The architect Buschetto created the frilly Pisan Romanesque style that set the tone for the Baptistery and Tower that followed. In the 1150s, the architect Rainaldo added the impressive main-entrance facade.

**Exterior View:** The lower half of the church is simple Roman-

esque, with blind arches. The upper half has four rows of columns that form arcades. Stripes of black-and-white marble, mosaics, stone inlay, and even recycled Roman tombstones complete the decoration.

• *Enter the church at the west facade, opposite the Baptistery.*

**Nave:** The 320-foot nave was designed to be the longest in Christendom when it was built. It's modeled on a traditional Roman basilica, with 68 Corinthian columns of granite (most shipped from Elba and Corsica in 1063) dividing the space into five aisles. But the striped marble and arches-on-columns give the nave an exotic, almost mosque-like feel.

• *Hanging from the ceiling of the central nave is...*

**Galileo's Lamp:** The bronze incense burner is said to be the one (actually, this is a replacement of the original) that caught the teenage Galileo's attention one day in church. According to legend, someone left a church door open, and a gust of wind set the lamp swinging. Galileo timed the swings and realized that the burner swung back and forth in the same amount of time regardless of the width of the arc. This pendulum motion was a constant that allowed Galileo to measure our ever-changing universe.

• *High up in the apse (behind the altar) is the...*

**Apse Mosaic:** The mosaic (c. 1300, partly done by the great artist Cimabue) shows Christ Pantocrator ("All Powerful") between Mary and St. John the Evangelist. The Pantocrator image of Christ is standard fare among Eastern Orthodox Christians—that is, the "Byzantine" people who were Pisa's partners in trade.

**Dome:** Look up into the dome. Because this church is dedicated to Mary—the patron and protector of the city—you'll see the Assumption of Mary. As the heavens open, and rings of saints and angels spiral upward, a hazy God greets Mary (in red). Beneath the dome is an inlaid-marble, Cosmati-style mosaic floor. The modern (and therefore controversial) marble altar and pulpit were carved by a Florentine artist in 2002.

• *Next to Galileo's Lamp, you'll find...*

**Giovanni Pisano's Pulpit** (1301-1311): The 15-foot-tall, octagonal pulpit by Giovanni Pisano (c. 1240-1319) is the last, biggest, and most complex of the four pulpits created by the Pisano father-and-son team. Four hundred intricately sculpted figures smother the pulpit. The creamy-white Carrara marble has the look and feel of carved French ivories, which the Pisanos loved. At the base, lions roar and crouch over their prey, symbolizing how Christ (the lion) triumphs over Satan (the horse, as in the Four Horsemen of the Apocalypse).

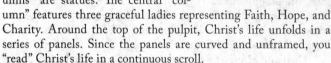

Four of the pulpit's support "columns" are statues. The central "column" features three graceful ladies representing Faith, Hope, and Charity. Around the top of the pulpit, Christ's life unfolds in a series of panels. Since the panels are curved and unframed, you "read" Christ's life in a continuous scroll.

• *Find the following two sights in the right (south) transept.*

**St. Ranieri's Body:** In a glass-lined casket on the altar, the skeleton of Pisa's patron saint lies, encased in silver at his head with his hair shirt covering his body.

• *Look on the wall to the left to find...*

**Emperor Henry VII's Tomb:** Pause at the tomb of Holy Roman Emperor Henry VII, whose untimely death plunged Pisa into its centuries-long decline. Henry lies sleeping, arms folded, his head turned to the side, resting on a soft pillow. This German king (c. 1275-1313) invaded Italy and was welcomed by Pisans as a nonpartisan leader who could bring peace to Italy's warring Guelphs and Ghibellines. In 1312, he was crowned emperor by the pope in Rome. He was preparing to polish off the last opposition when he caught a fever and died.

• *Exit the church, turn left, and walk around to its back end (facing the Tower), where you'll find (under a canopy) the...*

**Bronze Doors of St. Ranieri** (Porta San Ranieri): Designed by Bonanno Pisano (c. 1186)—who is thought by some historians to have been the Tower's first architect—the doors have 24 different panels that show Christ's story using the same simple, skinny figures found in Byzantine icons. (The originals are housed in the Duomo Museum.)

## THE REST OF THE FIELD OF MIRACLES

The Leaning Tower nearly steals the show from the massive cathedral, which muscles out the other sights. But don't neglect

the rest of the Field of Miracles: the Baptistery, Camposanto Cemetery, Museum of the Sinopias, and Duomo Museum. To do all of these sights takes about two hours. Start with the Baptistery, located in front of the Duomo's facade, and then head for Camposanto Cemetery, behind the church on the north side of the Field of Miracles. Next visit the Museum of the Sinopias, across the street from the Baptistery entrance. End your visit at the Duomo Museum, behind the Tower.

**Cost and Hours:** €5 for one sight, €7 for two sights, €8 covers everything. All four sights share the same schedule: daily April-Sept 8:00-20:00, Oct 9:00-19:00, Nov-Feb 10:00-17:00, March 9:00-18:00.

### Baptistery

Pisa's Baptistery is Italy's biggest. It's interesting for its pulpit and interior ambience, and especially great for its acoustics (which are demonstrated twice an hour).

**Visiting the Baptistery:** The building is 180 feet tall—John the Baptist on top is almost eye-to-eye with the tourists looking out from the nearly 200-foot Leaning Tower. Notice that the Baptistery leans nearly six feet to the north (the Tower leans 15 feet to the south). The building (begun in 1153) is modeled on the circular-domed Church of the Holy Sepulchre in Jerusalem, seen by Pisan Crusaders who occupied Jerusalem in 1099.

From the **outside,** you see three distinct sections, which reflect the changing tastes of the years spent building it: simple Romanesque blind arches at the base (1153) and ornate Gothic spires and pointed arches in the middle (1250). The roofing looks mismatched, but was intentionally designed with red clay tiles on the seaward side and lead tiles (more prestigious but prone to corrosion) on the sheltered east side. The statues of the midsection are by Nicola Pisano (c. 1220-1278, Giovanni's father), who sculpted the pulpit inside.

**Inside,** it's simple, spacious, and baptized with light. Tall arches atop thin columns once again echo the Campo's architectural theme of arches above blank spaces. The columns encircle just a few pieces of religious furniture.

In the center sits the beautiful marble **octagonal font** (1246). A statue of the first Baptist, John the Baptist, stretches out his hand and says, "Welcome to my Baptistery." The font contains plenty of space for baptizing adults by immersion (the medieval custom), plus four wells for dunking babies.

Baptismal fonts—where sinners symbolically die and are re-born—are traditionally octagons. The shape suggests a cross (sym-bolizing Christ's death), and the eight sides represent the eighth day of Christ's ordeal, when he was resurrected. The font's sides, carved with inlaid multicolored marble, feature circle-in-a-square patterns, indicating the interlocking of heaven and earth. The cir-cles are studded with interesting faces, both human and animal. Behind the font, the altar features similar inlaid-marble work.

On your left is the **pulpit** created by Nicola Pisano. Is this the world's first Renaissance sculpture? It's the first authenticated (signed) work by the "Giotto of sculpture," working in what came to be called the Renaissance style. The freestanding sculpture has classical columns, realistic people and animals, and 3-D effects in the carved panels.

The 15-foot-tall, hexagonal pulpit is the earliest (1260) and simplest of the four pulpits by the Pisano father-and-son team. Nic-ola, born in southern Italy, settled in Pisa, where he found steady work. Ten-year-old Giovanni learned the art of pulpit-making here at the feet of his father.

The speaker's platform stands on columns that rest on the backs of animals, representing Christianity's triumph over pagan-ism. The white Carrara-marble panels are framed by dark rose-colored marble, making a pleasant contrast.

Make a sound in here and it echoes for a good 10 seconds. A priest standing at the baptismal font could sing three tones with-in those 10 seconds—"Ave Maria"—and make a chord, singing haunting harmonies with himself. Today, a security guard sings every 30 minutes (on the hour and half-hour), starting when the doors open in the morning.

You can climb 75 steps to the interior **gallery** (midway up) for an impressive view back down on the baptismal font. Try to be here when the guard sings.

### Camposanto Cemetery

Until people started getting excited about the Leaning Tower around 1900, the big attraction in Pisa was its dreamy and ex-quisite cemetery, the Camposanto (built from 1278-1465). High-lights are the building's cloistered interior courtyard, some an-cient sarcophagi, and the large 14th-century fresco, *The Triumph of Death*.

PISA & LUCCA

**Visiting the Cemetery:**
The delightful open-air **court-yard** is surrounded by an arcade with intricately carved tracery in the arches. The courtyard's grass grows on special dirt shipped here by returning 12th-century Crusaders from Jerusalem's Mount Calvary, where Christ was

crucified. If you couldn't be buried in the Holy Land, you could be buried in dirt from the Holy Land.

Displayed in the arcade are dozens of ancient Roman **sarcophagi.** These coffins, which originally held dead Romans, were reused by medieval big shots. In anticipation of death, a wealthy Pisan would shop around, choose a good sarcophagus, and chip his message into it. When he died, his marble box was placed with the others around the exterior of the cathedral. Great sculptors such as Nicola and Giovanni Pisano passed them daily, gaining inspiration.

After decorating these corridors for 600 years, the **frescoes** of Camposanto Cemetery were badly damaged in World War II. They've been under restoration ever since. Along these walls, you'll see the ones that have been returned to their original position, including the masterpiece *Triumph of Death.* This 1,000-square-foot fresco (c. 1340, by a 14th-century master) captures late-medieval Europe's concern with death in a fascinating composition.

In the lower left, a parade of wealthy (finely dressed) and powerful (some with crowns) hedonists are riding gaily through the countryside when they come across a hermit-monk who blocks their path and shows them three corpses in coffins. Confronted with death, they each react differently—a woman puts her hand thoughtfully to her chin, a man holds his nose against the stench, while a horse leans in for a better whiff. Above them, a monk scours the Bible for the meaning of death. Elsewhere, young people gather in a garden to play music (symbolizing earthly pleasure), oblivious to the death around them.

This is just one of four big frescoes: Next to *The Triumph of Death* are *The Last Judgment,* the extremely graphic *Hell,* and *The Pious Life* (a handbook for avoiding hell). A posted information plaque near each fresco describes the intense scenes.

Stepping back outside into the **piazza,** consider how this richly artistic but utilitarian square fit into the big picture of life. The ensemble around you includes the Baptistery, the cathedral, the bell tower, the hospital (present-day Museum of the Sinopias), and the cemetery you just visited.

## Museum of the Sinopias (Museo delle Sinopie)

Housed in a 13th-century hospital, this museum features the original preliminary sketches (sinopias) for the Camposanto's frescoes. If you loved *The Triumph of Death* and others in the Camposanto, or if you're interested in fresco technique, this museum is worthwhile. If not, you'll wonder why you're here.

Whether or not you pay to go in, you can watch two free videos in the entry lobby that serve to orient you to the square: a 15-minute story of the Tower, its tilt, and its fix.

Once inside the turnstile, the stars of this museum are the sinopias: sketches made in red paint directly on the wall, designed to guide the making of the final colored fresco. The master always did the sinopia himself. It was a way for him (and for those who paid for the work) to see exactly how the scene would look in its designated spot. If it wasn't quite right, the master changed a detail here and there. Next, assistants made a "cartoon" by tracing the sinopia onto large sheets of paper *(cartone)*. Then the sinopia was plastered over. To put the drawing back on the wall, assistants perforated the drawing on the cartoon, hung the cartoon over the wall, and dabbed it with a powdered bag of charcoal. This process printed dotted lines onto the newly plastered wall, re-creating the cartoon. While the plaster was still wet, the master and his team quickly filled in the color and details, producing the final frescoes (now on display at the Camposanto). These sinopias—never meant to be seen—were uncovered by the bombing and restoration of the Camposanto and brought here.

## Duomo Museum (Museo dell'Opera del Duomo)

Near the Tower is the entrance to the Duomo Museum, which houses many of the original statues and much of the artwork that once adorned the Campo's buildings (where copies stand today), notably the statues by Nicola and Giovanni Pisano. It's big on Pisan art, displaying treasures of the cathedral, paintings, silverware, and sculptures (from the 12th to 14th century), as well as ancient Egyptian, Etruscan, and Roman artifacts. You'll see several large-scale wooden models of the Duomo, Baptistery, and Tower, as well as the Duomo's original 12th-century bronze doors of St. Ranieri, with scenes from the life of Jesus, done by Bonanno Pisano.

# Sleeping in Pisa

## NORTH OF THE RIVER, NEAR THE TOWER

**$$ Hotel Royal Victoria** is like sleeping in a museum. Overlooking the Arno River, it's been run by the Piegaja family since 1837 (though it was a hotel long before that). Its tiled hallways and 38 creaky, antique-filled rooms with bygone plumbing and chipped plaster may not be for everybody. But with the elegant ambience of a long-gone era, it's ideal for romantics who missed out on the Grand Tour. The location—midway between the Tower and Pisa Centrale train station—is the most atmospheric of my listings (RS%, family rooms, air-con in most rooms, elevator, tight pay parking garage, lush communal terrace, Lungarno Pacinotti 12, tel. 050-940-111, www.royalvictoria.it, post@royalvictoria.it).

**$$ Relais dei Mercanti** is tucked away in the historic core of the city, on a lively square that throbs on Friday and Saturday. The six rooms are bright, modern, and well-appointed, with shiny marble floors and bathrooms (air-con, Piazza Sant'Omobono 16, tel. 050-520-2135, www.relaisdeimercanti.it, relaisdeimercanti@gmail.com).

**$$ Hotel Pisa Tower** provides a yesteryear elegance in a stately mansion with 14 rooms thoughtfully decorated with clean lines and graceful warmth. In good weather, enjoy the garden for breakfast or an *aperitivo*. The annex, with 12 similar rooms, overlooks the noisy, tacky-souvenir-stand square just outside the gate to the Field of Miracles, along a busy street. Four more budget rooms are in a nondescript apartment block across the street from the main building (family rooms, air-con, pay parking; a long block west of Piazza Manin at Via Andrea Pisano 23, tel. 050-520-0700, www.hotelpisatower.com, info@hotelpisatower.com, Lotta).

**$ Casa San Tommaso** has 22 classic-feeling, homey rooms on a quiet back lane about a five-minute walk from the Tower (air-con, Via San Tommaso 13, tel. 050-830-782, www.casasantommaso.it, santommaso@paimturismo.it, Giuliano).

**$ Hotel Helvetia,** a friendly, no-frills, clean, and quiet inn just 100 yards from the Tower, rents 29 economical rooms over four floors. Ask them to show you the "biggest cactus in Tuscany" in their garden courtyard...it really is (cheaper rooms with shared bath, family suites, no breakfast, ceiling fans, no elevator, Via Don G. Boschi 31, tel. 050-553-084, www.pensionehelvetiapisa.com, helvetiapisatower@gmail.com, Micaele and Sandra).

## SOUTH OF THE RIVER, NEAR THE TRAIN STATION

This zone is far less atmospheric than the zone near the Tower—with a lot of concrete, congestion, and loitering.

**$$ Hotel Alessandro della Spina,** run by Pio and family, has 16 elegant and colorful rooms, each named after a flower (RS%, air-con, elevator, pay parking; leaving the station, go right on Via Filippo Corridoni, take the third left on Via Alessandro della Spina, then find #5; tel. 050-502-777, www.hoteldellaspina.it, info@hoteldellaspina.it, Louisa).

**$ Stazione22** is a tidy B&B just across the piazza from the train station, perfect for a quick overnight or if your luggage is heavy. Friendly Alessandra tends her five budget rooms with a youthful warmth (air-con, elevator, Piazza della Stazione 22, tel. 327-857-5259, stazione22@gmail.com).

# Eating in Pisa

## A QUICK LUNCH CLOSE TO THE TOWER

The Via Santa Maria tourist strip is pedestrianized and lined with touristy eateries. From the Tower, walk past Grand Hotel Duomo to avoid the worst of the tourist traps. Beyond the hotel you can find a decent quick sandwich, pizza, or salad at any number of places. Of these, **$$ Ristorante-Pizzeria La Torre** (Via Santa Maria 86) has a good reputation.

**$$ Pizzeria al Bagno di Nerone,** a five-minute walk from the Tower, is particularly popular with students. Belly up to the bar and grab a slice to go, or sit in their small dining room for a whole pie. Try the *cecina,* a crêpe-like garbanzo-bean flatbread (Wed-Mon 12:00-14:30 & 17:45-22:30, closed Tue, Largo Carlo Fedeli 26, tel. 050-551-085).

## REAL MEALS DEEPER IN THE TOWN CENTER

These places are within about a 10- to 15-minute walk from the Tower, near the river, and several are within a few steps of the old Renaissance-style market loggia, Piazza delle Vettovaglie.

**$$ La Vineria di Piazza** is a quintessential little Tuscan trattoria tucked under the arcades of Piazza delle Vettovaglie. The menu changes with the seasons. Their wine selection is high quality. Sit in the elegantly simple interior or out at tables facing the market (lunch daily 12:00-15:00, dinner Wed-Sat 20:00-23:00, Piazza delle Vettovaglie 14, tel. 050-520-7846).

**$$ Antica Trattoria il Campano,** just off the market square, has a typically Tuscan menu and a candlelit, stay-awhile atmosphere. The ground floor, surrounded by wine bottles, is cozier, while the upstairs—with high wood-beam ceilings—is classier (nightly 19:30-22:45, open Sat-Sun for lunch in high season, Via Cavalca 19, tel. 050-580-585, Giovanna).

**$ Caffetteria BetsaBea** is handy for takeaway meals, has good seating on the square, whips up hearty and creative salads—which you design with their interactive menu—and is popular for its *aperitivo* happy hour (Mon-Sat 8:00-18:30, closed Sun, Piazza San Frediano 6).

**$ Il Montino** is a rambunctious favorite for tasty, no-frills pizza. Tucked behind a church in a grubby corner deep in the old center, it has a loyal following among students. Enjoy full pies in the *nuovo rustico* interior or out on the alley (Mon-Sat 11:30-15:00 & 17:30-22:30, closed Sun, Vicolo del Monte 1, tel. 050-598-695).

**$$ Orzo Bruno**—*il birrificio artigiano* ("the artisan brew-pub")—is a lively, rollicking brew hall filled with Pisans of all ages enjoying rock, jazz, and blues, with seven different microbrews (including a rotating tap) and a simple menu of sandwiches and cold cuts (nightly 19:00-late, a block off Borgo Stretto at Via Case Dipinte 6, tel. 050-578-802).

**$$ La Mescita,** just off the market square, serves up pasta and meat dishes in a jazz-inspired, artsy interior (daily 12:30-14:30 & 19:30-23:00, Via Domenico Cavalca 2, tel. 050-314-4680).

**$$ Osteria Lo Scioglipepe** is a good spot for an upscale, modern Tuscan meal at reasonable prices. Their menu takes typical dishes up a notch and includes vegetarian and seafood options (Thu-Tue 19:30-22:30, lunch Fri-Sun 12:30-14:30, closed Wed, Via San Frediano 10, tel. 050-969-052).

## Pisa Connections

Pisa has good connections by train, bus, or car. The busy airport (popular with discount airlines) is practically downtown. Note that the Pisa Centrale train station area is a maze of tunnels; leave yourself enough time to find the ticket machines and make it to the platform.

**Side-Tripping to Lucca:** Pisa and Lucca are well-connected by train and by bus (both options are about €3), making a half-day side trip from one town to the other particularly easy. The **train** takes about half as long as the bus—but getting to the Centrale train station is more time-consuming. Perhaps the best option: If you're heading to Lucca from the Leaning Tower, you can catch the train at Pisa San Rossore Station, about a five-minute walk from the Field of Miracles: From the tacky souvenir zone just outside the gate, cross the busy street and continue straight ahead along Via Andrea Pisano. After two blocks, you'll see the gray gateway to the train station on your right.

A handy **bus** connects the Field of Miracles with Lucca's Piazzale Giuseppe Verdi in about 50 minutes (€3.50, Mon-Sat hourly, fewer on Sun, buy ticket on bus; in Pisa, wait at the Vaibus signpost off of Piazza Manin, immediately outside the wall behind the Baptistery on the right). You can also catch this bus at Pisa's airport, or at Pisa Centrale train station.

**From Pisa Centrale Station by Train to: Florence** (2/hour, 45-75 minutes), **Livorno** (2/hour, 20 minutes), **Rome** (1-2/hour, 3 hours, some change in Florence), **La Spezia** (about hourly, 1.5 hours), **Monterosso** (hourly, 1-1.5 hours), **Siena** (2/hour, 1.5 hours, some change at Empoli), **Lucca** (1-2/hour, 30 minutes, also stops at Pisa San Rossore Station).

**By Car:** The drive between Pisa and Florence is that rare case where the regular highway (free, more direct, and at least as fast) is a better deal than the autostrada.

**By Plane:** Pisa's handy **Galileo Galilei Airport**—just two miles from the train station—handles both international and domestic flights (code: PSA, tel. 050-849-300, www.pisa-airport. com). The Pisa Mover train offers an easy connection to Pisa Centrale train station where you can catch the LAM Rossa bus—see "Arrival in Pisa," earlier—to the Leaning Tower (€2.70, daily 4:30-very late, every 5 minutes, 5-minute trip, www.pisa-mover.com). You can taxi into town for about €10.

Pisa's airport is handy for other towns as well: The bus to **Lucca** (described above) originates at the airport. To reach **Florence,** the **Cinque Terre,** or other destinations in Italy, take the Pisa Mover to Pisa Centrale train station and connect from there (allow about 1.5 hours total). Two companies also run buses from the airport directly to Florence's Santa Maria Novella train station in about 1.5 hours (about €5 for either one): Terravision (about hourly, www.terravision.eu) and Autostradale (typically coordinated with Ryanair flights, www.autostradale.it).

# Lucca

Surrounded by well-preserved ramparts, layered with history, alternately quaint and urbane, Lucca charms its visitors. The city is a paradox. Though it hasn't been involved in a war since 1430, it is Italy's most impressive fortress city, encircled by a perfectly intact wall. Most cities tear down their walls to make way for modern traffic, but Lucca's effectively keeps out both traffic and, it seems, the stress of the modern world. Locals are very protective of their wall, which they enjoy like a community roof garden.

Lucca has no single monumental sight to attract tourists—it's simply a uniquely human and undamaged, never-bombed city.

Romanesque churches and shady piazzas filled with soccer-playing children seem to be around every corner. Even its touristic center—the mostly traffic-free old town—feels more local than touristy (aside from a few cruise excursions from nearby Livorno that pass through each day). The city is big enough to have its own heritage and pride, yet small enough that it seems like the

Lucchesi (loo-KAY-zee) all went to school together. Simply put, Lucca has elegance and plenty of reasons to be proud.

## PLANNING YOUR TIME

Lucca is easy to enjoy. With a day in town, start with my self-guided Lucca Walk and spend the afternoon biking (or strolling) atop the wall, popping in on whatever other sights interest you, and browsing. Music lovers enjoy the evening Puccini concert. The busy sightseer can consider visiting Pisa's Field of Miracles (with the Leaning Tower), an easy half-day side trip away by train (to Pisa San Rossore Station in 30 minutes) or bus (from downtown Lucca to the Leaning Tower in 50 minutes).

# Orientation to Lucca

Lucca (population 87,000, with roughly 10,000 living within the town walls) is big enough to be engaging but small enough to be manageable. Everything of interest to a visitor is within the 2.5-mile-long city wall; it takes just 20 minutes to walk from one end of the old town to the other. The train station sits south of the wall (just beyond the cathedral), and the bus to and from Pisa stops just inside the western tip. My self-guided walk traces the main thoroughfares through town; venturing beyond these streets, you realize Lucca is bigger than it first seems, but its back streets are very sleepy. While the core of the town is based on an old Roman grid street plan, the surrounding areas—especially near the circular footprint of the amphitheater—are more confusing. This, combined with tall houses and a lack of consistent signage, makes Lucca easy to get lost in. Pick up the town map at your hotel and use it.

## TOURIST INFORMATION

Lucca's helpful TI is on Piazzale Giuseppe Verdi (daily 9:30-18:30, Oct-March until 16:30, WC, baggage storage—€1.50/hour for 2 bags, tel. 0583-583-150, www.turismo.lucca.it).

## ARRIVAL IN LUCCA

**By Train:** See "Helpful Hints" for specifics on checking your bags. To reach the city center from the train station, walk toward the walls and head left, to the entry at Porta San Pietro. Or, if you don't mind steps, go straight ahead and follow the path through the moat-like park to go up and over the wall. Taxis wait out front; otherwise, try calling 025-353 (ignore any recorded message—just wait for a live operator); a ride from the station to Piazza dell'Anfiteatro costs about €8.

**By Bus:** Buses from Pisa, Viareggio, and nearby villages arrive inside the walls at Piazzale Giuseppe Verdi (near the TI).

**By Car:** Don't drive within the walls: Much of the center of Lucca is a limited traffic zone (€90 fine). You'll know when you're about to enter it when you see the letters "ZTL" painted on the road.

The old town is ringed by convenient parking lots. Parking is always free in **Piazzale Don Franco Baroni,** a five-minute walk north of the city walls. **Parking Carducci** is the first lot you hit after leaving the autostrada (€8/day). Or park outside the gates near the train station or on the boulevard surrounding the city (about €2/hour). Overnight parking (20:00-8:00) on city streets and in city lots outside the walls is usually free. Check with your hotelier to be sure.

## HELPFUL HINTS

**Markets:** Lucca's atmospheric markets are worth visiting. On the third weekend of the month, one of the largest **antique markets** in Italy sprawls in the blocks between Piazza Antelminelli and Piazza San Giovanni (8:00-19:00). The last weekend of the month, local artisans sell **arts and crafts** around town, mainly near the cathedral (8:00-19:00). At the **general market,** held Wednesdays and Saturdays on Piazza Don Franco Baroni, you'll find produce and household goods (8:30-13:00).

**Shops and Museums Alert:** City-run museums are closed Sunday and Monday. Most shops close Sunday and Monday mornings.

**Puccini Concerts:** Each night San Giovanni Church hosts a themed one-hour concert featuring a pianist and singers performing works by hometown composer Giacomo Puccini (€25 at the door, €20 in advance—buy tickets at the venue, the TI, or possibly your hotel; daily at 19:00, Thu-Sat off-season, www.puccinielasualucca.com).

**Festivals:** The Lucca Classica festival offers lots of free concerts (four days in early May, www.luccaclassica.it). On September 13 and 14, the city celebrates Volto Santo ("Holy Face"), with

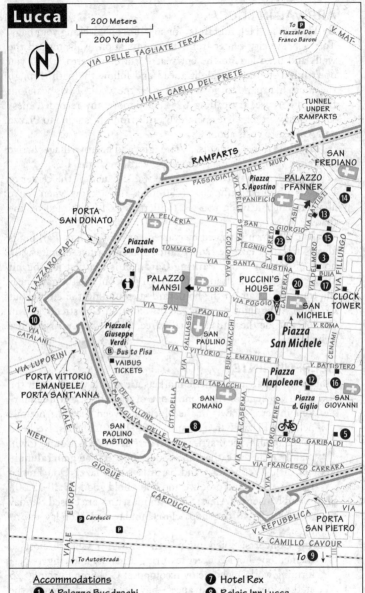

# Lucca

200 Meters
200 Yards

V. MAT.

To P
Piazzale Don
Franco Baroni

VIA DELLE TAGLIATE TERZA

VIALE CARLO DEL PRETE

TUNNEL
UNDER
RAMPARTS

RAMPARTS

PASSAGGIATA DELLE MURA

SAN
FREDIANO

Piazza
S. Agostino

PALAZZO
PFANNER

PORTA
SAN DONATO

VIA PELLERIA

PANIFICIO

14

VIA

V. DELLE STUFA

SAN

ASILI

13

V. BATTISTI

VIA GIORGIO

Piazzale
San Donato

TOMMASO

VIA COLOMBAIA

TEGNINI

V. LORETO

23

15

VIA SANTA GIUSTINA

18

VIA DEL MORO

3

BUIA

VIA FILLUNGO

PALAZZO
MANSI

V. TORO

PUCCINI'S
HOUSE

17

VIA SAN

PAOLINO

VIA POGGIO

20

CLOCK
TOWER

To
10

V. CATALANI

Piazzale
Giuseppe
Verdi

21

SAN
MICHELE

V. ROMA

VIA LUPORINI

B Bus to Pisa
VAIBUS
TICKETS

VIA GALLIASSI

SAN
PAULINO

VIA BURLAMACCHI

CALDERIA

Piazza
San Michele

V. CENAMI

PORTA VITTORIO
EMANUELE/
PORTA SANT'ANNA

VIA VITTORIO EMANUELE II

V. BATTISTERO

V. NIERI

SAN
PAOLINO
BASTION

CITTADELLA

VIA DEL TABACCHI

Piazza
Napoleone

12

16

VIA DELLA CASERMA

SAN
ROMANO

Piazza
d. Giglio

SAN
GIOVANNI

VIA DEI PALLONE

8

VITTORIO VENETO

5

PASSAGGIATA DELLE MURA

CORSO GARIBALDI

V. EUROPA

GIOSUÈ

VIA FRANCESCO CARRARA

VIALE

CARDUCCI

VIA
REPUBBLICA

PORTA
SAN PIETRO

P Carducci

P

V. CAMILLO CAVOUR

To Autostrada

To 9

V. LAZZARO PAPI

PORTA
SAN DONATO

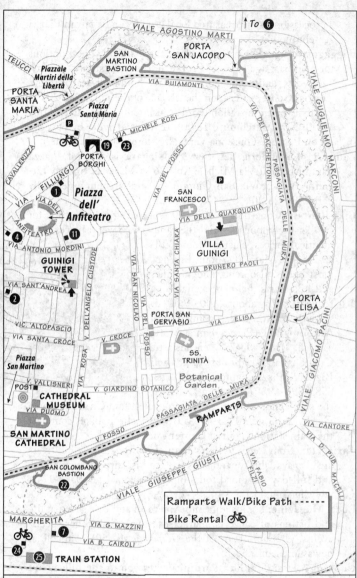

**13** Osteria dal Manzo

**14** La Bottega di Anna & Leo

**15** Osteria Via San Giorgio

**16** Il Cuore Enogastronomia

**17** Pizzeria da Felice

**18** Trattoria da Leo

**19** Porta dei Borghi Bars

**20** Caffè del Mercato

**21** De' Coltelli Gelateria, Alice Pizza & Grocery

**22** Caffetteria San Colombano

**23** Launderette (2)

**24** Tourist Center Lucca (Bag Storage, Bikes)

**25** Profer (Bag Storage)

a procession of the treasured local crucifix and a fair in Piazza Antelminelli.

**Baggage Storage:** For train travelers, there are two good options for paid baggage storage: **Profer,** in the train station at track 1 (€5/day, daily 8:00-20:00, shorter hours off-season), and **Tourist Center Lucca,** on the left side of the square at #203 as you exit the train station (€5/day, also rents bikes, daily 9:00-19:00, Nov-March until 18:00). If you're arriving by bus, the **TI** on Piazzale Giuseppe Verdi also stores bags (see earlier).

**Laundry: Lavanderia Self-Service Niagara** is just off Piazza Santa Maria at Via Michele Rosi 26 and **Easy & Speedy Lavanderia** is at Via San Giorgio 45 (similar hours, generally daily 7:00-23:00).

**Bike Rental:** A one-hour rental (ID required) gives you time for two leisurely loops around the ramparts. Several places with identical prices cluster around Piazza Santa Maria (€4/hour, €16/day,  most shops also rent tandem bikes and bike carts, helmets available on request, daily about 9:00-19:00 or sunset). Try these easygoing shops: **Antonio Poli** (Piazza Santa Maria 42, tel. 0583-493-787, enthusiastic Cristiana) and, right next to it, **Cicli Bizzarri** (Piazza Santa Maria 32, tel. 0583-496-682, Australian Dely). At the south end, at Porta San Pietro, you'll find **Chronò** (Corso Garibaldi 93, tel. 0583-490-591, www.chronobikes.com). At the train station, **Tourist Center Lucca** is good.

**Taxi:** A taxi from Lucca to Pisa's Leaning Tower costs €45. Drivers are also available for transfers (€80 to Pisa airport) or for half- and full-day unguided tours (up to 8 people, tel. 0583-1745, www.luccataxi.it).

**Local Magazine:** For insights into American and British expat life and listings of concerts, markets, festivals, and other special events, pick up a copy of the *Grapevine* (€2.50), available at newsstands and the TI.

**Cooking Class: Gianluca Pardini** invites you to the hills above Lucca to learn to prepare and then eat a four-course Tuscan meal. Depending on how many others attend, the price ranges from €50-70. This is great for groups of four or more (€14 taxi ride from town, 3-hour lesson plus time to dine, includes wine, reserve at least 2 days in advance, Via di San Viticchio 414, mobile 347-678-7447, www.italiancuisine.it, info@italiancuisine.it).

# Tours in Lucca

## Walking Tours

The **TI** offers two-hour guided city walks in English and Italian, departing from the office on Piazzale Giuseppe Verdi (€10, pay at TI, daily April-Oct at 14:00, weekends only in winter, tel. 0583-583-150).

The **Andante...ma con Brio Music tour** celebrates Lucca's musical heritage with a music-loving local guide, visits to the Teatro del Giglio and the Puccini Museum, and musical clips along the way (€15 includes theater and museum entry, pay guide, daily mid-April-Oct at 11:00, 2.5 hours, in Italian and English, meet at Teatro del Giglio, turislucca@turislucca.com, tel. 0583-342-404).

**Lucca Urban Adventures** offers almost-daily three-hour, casual, youthful, stream-of-conscious rambles through town with three stops in small bars or delis. These small-group tours are English-only and led by a proud local who loves sharing Luccan culture—past and present (basic food tour—€65, at 10:00; bike and food tour—€96, at 14:00; *aperitivo* walk—€71, at 17:30; RS%—20 percent discount if you book direct by email, www.luccaurbanadventures.com, info@luccaurbanadventures.com, Chiara and Luca).

## Local Guide

**Gabriele Calabrese** knows and shares his hometown well. He was a big help in creating the Lucca Walk in this chapter, and with his guidance you'll go even deeper into the city (€130/3 hours, by foot or bike, tel. 0583-342-404, mobile 347-788-0667, www.turislucca.com, turislucca@turislucca.com).

# Lucca Walk

This hour-long self-guided walk (not counting time at the sights) connects Lucca's main points of interest by way of its most entertaining streets.

• *Start right in the heart of things, at Lucca's main square. For the classic view of the circular square, stand at the east end of the oval at #29.*

## ❶ Piazza dell'Anfiteatro

The architectural ghost of a Roman amphitheater can be felt in the delightful Piazza dell'Anfiteatro. With the fall of Rome, the theater (which seated 10,000 and sat just outside the original rectangular city walls) was gradually cannibalized for its stones and inhabited by people living in a mishmash of huts. The huts were cleared away at the end of the 19th century to better show off the town's illustrious past and make one purely secular square (every

PISA & LUCCA

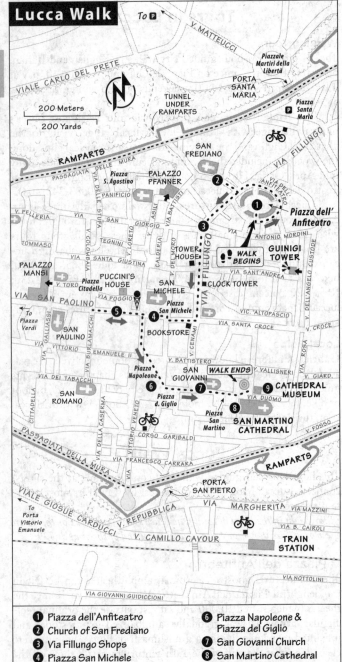

# Lucca Walk

To P

V. MATTEUCCI

Piazzale Martiri della Libertà

PORTA SANTA MARIA

Piazza Santa Maria

VIALE CARLO DEL PRETE

TUNNEL UNDER RAMPARTS

200 Meters
200 Yards

RAMPARTS

PASSAGIATA DELLE MURA

SAN FREDIANO

VIA FILLUNGO

VIA DELL'ANFITEATRO

Piazza S. Agostino

PALAZZO PFANNER

❷

❸

❶ Piazza dell' Anfiteatro

PANIFICIO

VIA DELLE SIGNE

VIA BATTISTI

VIA

ANTONIO MORDINI

GUINIGI TOWER

V. PELLERIA

VIA

SAN GIORGIO

CALDERIA

VIA DEL MORO

WALK BEGINS

TOMMASO

TEGNINI

VIA SANTA GIUSTINA

TOWER HOUSE

SAN MICHELE

VIA SANT'ANDREA

CLOCK TOWER

VIA DELL'ANGELO CUSTODE

PALAZZO MANSI

V. TORO

Piazza Citadella

PUCCINI'S HOUSE

VIA POGGIO

Piazza San Michele

VIC. ALTOPASCIO

VIA SAN PAOLINO

V. GALLIASSO

❺

BOOKSTORE

VIA SANTA CROCE

V. CROCE

To Piazza Verdi

SAN PAULINO

VIA BURLAMACCHI

❹

V. CENAMI

V. ROSA

VIA VITTORIO EMANUELE II

V. BATTISTERO

WALK ENDS

V. VALLISNERI

V. GIARD.

VIA DEI TABACCHI

Piazza Napoleone

SAN GIOVANNI

❼

❾

CATHEDRAL MUSEUM

CITADELLA

SAN ROMANO

VIA DELLA CASERMA

❻

Piazza d. Giglio

VIA DUOMO

❽

SAN MARTINO CATHEDRAL

V. FOSSO

Piazza San Martino

VITTORIO VENETO

CORSO GARIBALDI

PASSAGIATA DELLA MURA

VIA FRANCESCO CARRARA

RAMPARTS

VIALE GIOSUE CARDUCCI

PORTA SAN PIETRO

To Porta Vittorio Emanuele

V. REPUBBLICA

VIA MARGHERITA

VIA MAZZINI

VIA B. CAIROLI

V. CAMILLO CAVOUR

TRAIN STATION

VIA NOTTOLINI

VIA GIOVANNI GUIDICCIONI

❶ Piazza dell'Anfiteatro
❷ Church of San Frediano
❸ Via Fillungo Shops
❹ Piazza San Michele
❺ Via San Paolino

❻ Piazza Napoleone & Piazza del Giglio
❼ San Giovanni Church
❽ San Martino Cathedral
❾ Cathedral Museum

other square is dominated by a church) for the town market. The modern street level is nine feet above the original arena floor.

Today, the square is a circle of touristy shops, galleries, mediocre restaurants, and inviting al fresco cafés.

Leave the amphitheater through the arch at #42, turn left, and begin circling it counterclockwise along Via Anfiteatro. At #89-95—right where you enter the street—is the butcher's shop (Carni Val Serchio) where Felicino prepares meat and special dishes for appreciative locals. Farther along, on the right at #75, "The Loom of Penelope" is an innovative and caring place that helps young people address mental health problems through weaving therapy.

Across from #61, look up and study the exterior of the Roman amphitheater and notice how medieval scavengers transformed it. Barbarians didn't know how to make bricks. But they could recycle building material and stack stones in order to camp out in Roman ruins. As you circle for the next 100 yards or so, study the stonework and see how medieval buildings filled the ancient arches.

Next you'll pass the tempting Pizzicheria la Grotta *salumi* shop (on the left at #2) with lots of gifty edibles—worth popping into for a peek at local specialties (like hay-covered pecorino from mountain farms). Then you reach the busy shopping street, Via Fillungo.

• *Turn left and walk a block down Via Fillungo. Check out Zizzi at #126 (with a busy loom, weaving totally Italian scarves), then go right and cross a little square to the big church with a fine mosaic facade.*

## ❷ Church of San Frediano

This impressive church was built in 1112 by the pope to one-up Lucca's bishop and his spiffy cathedral (which we'll see later on this

walk). Lucca was the first Mediterranean stop on the pilgrim route from northern Europe, and the pope wanted to remind pilgrims that the action, the glory, and the papacy awaited them in Rome. Therefore, he had the church made "Roman-esque." The pure marble facade frames an early Christian Roman-style mosaic of Christ with his 12 apostles. Inside (€3, daily 9:00-18:00), there's a notable piece of art in each corner: a 12th-century baptistery showing the story of Moses; St. Zita's body, put there in 1278; a particularly serene Virgin Mary, depicted at the moment she gets the news that she'll bring the Messiah into the world; and a painting on wood of the *Assumption of the Virgin* (c. 1510), with Doubting Thomas receiving Mary's red belt as she ascends so he'll doubt no more.

• *Leaving the church, head straight back through the little square, and turn right to peruse the many...*

## ❸ Via Fillungo Shops

Lucca's best street to stroll and main pedestrian drag connects the town's two busiest squares: Piazza dell'Anfiteatro (which we just left) and Piazza San Michele. Along the way, you'll get a taste of Lucca's rich past, including several elegant, century-old storefronts.

Head down the street. On the left, you'll pass Piazza degli Scapellini, with market stalls and another entrance into Piazza dell'Anfiteatro.

As you stroll, notice how many of the original storefront paintings, reliefs, and mosaics survive—even if today's shopkeeper sells something entirely different. Observe the warm and convivial small-town vibe on the street. Notice also the powerful heritage of shops named for the families that have run them for many generations, the creative new energy brought by small entrepreneurs, and the aggressive inroads big chain stores are making in this tender urban econo-system.

At #92 (left) a shop sells an array of beers from nearby microbreweries. Since 2007, vino-centric Italy has enjoyed a trendy and youthful microbrew industry. There are four breweries just in Lucca.

At #97 (right) is the classic old **Carli Jewelry Store.** Signore Carli is the 12th generation of jewelers from his family to work on this spot. (He still has a once-state-of-the-art 17th-century safe in the back.) The Carli storefront has kept its T-shaped arrangement, which lets it close up tight as a canned ham. After hours, all you see from the street is a wooden T in the wall, and during opening hours it unfolds with a fine old-time display. This design dates from when the merchant sold his goods in front, did his work in the back, and lived upstairs.

Judging from its historic sign, **"Intimo"** (#56, on the left) was once an underwear shop. It now sells truffles and generally offers samples of little treats with truffle oil. Across the street at #83, a former perfume shop sells chocolate, and has a funky old café in the back.

At #67 is a surviving five-story **tower house** (at the corner with

Via Buia). At one time, nearly every corner in Lucca sported its own tower. The stubby stones that still stick out once supported wooden staircases (there were no interior connections between floors). So many towers cast shadows over this part of town that this cross street is called "Dark Street" (Via Buia). Look left down Via Sant'Andrea for a peek at the town's tallest tower, Guinigi, in the distance—capped by its characteristic mini oak-tree forest. You can pay to climb up for the view (see "More Sights in Lucca," later).

The shop at #65 (right) sports a beautiful, Liberty-style *Profumaria Venus* sign. For over a century, its sexy reliefs (dating from the time of Puccini) have stirred Lucchesi menfolk to buy their women a fragrant gift. Today the storefront is protected as a historic landmark—and, fittingly, a new perfume shop recently took up residence here.

At #45, you'll see two more good examples of tower houses. On the left is the 14th-century **Clock Tower** (Torre delle Ore, #26), which has a hand-wound Swiss clock that clanged four times an hour since 1754...until it died for good a few years back (€4 to climb the 207 wooden steps for the view and to see the non-functioning mechanism, €9 combo-ticket includes Guinigi Tower, daily 9:30-18:30, Oct and March until 17:30, closed Nov-Feb, corner of Via Fillungo and Via del'Arancio).

A bit farther along, on the left, is the striking 13th-century facade of a **Pisan Romanesque church.**

The intersection of Via Fillungo and Via Roma/Via Santa Croce marks the center of town, where the two original Roman roads crossed. The big old palace

you're facing (on the right)—with the heavy grates on the windows and the benches built into its stony facade—is the **In Mondadori bookstore.** While the interior is worth a peek (for its speckled mosaic floors, columns, and stained-glass skylight), the benches out front are even more interesting: They're the town hangout, where old-timers sit to swap gossip.

• *Turn right down Via Roma, studying the people warming those stone benches along the way. You'll pop out at...*

## ❹ Piazza San Michele

This square has been the center of town since Roman times, when it was the forum. It's dominated by the **Church of San Michele.** Circle around to the church's main door. Towering above the fancy Pisan Romanesque facade, the archangel Michael stands ready to flap his wings (which he actually did on special occasions with the help of crude but awe-inspiring-in-its-day mechanical assistance from behind). Perched above many of the columns are the faces of a dozen or so heroes in the Italian independence and unification movement: Victor Emmanuel II (with a crown, above the short red column on the right, second level up), the Count of Cavour (next to Victor, above the column with black zigzags), and—hey, look—there's Giuseppe Mazzini (on the far left, fourth from the end).

The square is surrounded by an architectural hodgepodge. The circa-1495 loggia (to the right as you face the church) was the first Renaissance building in town. There's a late-19th-century interior in Buccellato Taddeucci, a 130-year-old pastry shop (#34, behind the church, next to its tower). The left section of the BNL bank (#5, facing the church facade) sports an Art Nouveau facade that celebrates both Amerigo Vespucci and Cristoforo Colombo. This was the original facade of the Bertolli shipping company—famed among Italian-Americans as the shipping company their grandparents sailed with to reach America.

If the church is open, pop in. A fine 12th-century wooden crucifix hangs above the high altar, which shows off the body of St. Davino, sporting the scallop shells that identify him as a pilgrim. Nearby is an exquisite painting, *The Four Saints,* by Filippino Lippi (a student of the Florentine master Sandro Botticelli). You may notice curious little doodles on the pillars, scratched into the marble back in the 12th century.

• *From here, continue out of the square (opposite from where you entered) to take a little detour down...*

## ❺ Via San Paolino

This bustling street—which eventually goes all the way to Piazzale Giuseppe Verdi (with the TI and bus to Pisa)—is another fine shopping drag. Along here, a wide variety of storefronts cater not just to tourists but also to locals. You'll also pass—after just a half-block, on the right—my vote for the best gelato in town (De' Coltelli, Sicilian-style gelato, at #10; described under "Eating in Lucca").

One block down this street, in the little square called **Piazza Citadella** (on the right), a statue of Giacomo Puccini (1858-1924) sits genteelly on a chair, holding court. The great composer of operas was born in the house down the little alley over his left shoulder (now the well-presented Puccini's House museum, worth a visit for music lovers—see "More Sights in Lucca," later). (If you'd like to hear some Puccini while you're in town, Lucca's San Giovanni Church hosts nightly concerts of his music—see "Helpful Hints," earlier, for details).

• *Feel free to browse your way as far down this street as you like, but eventually return to Piazza San Michele to continue the walk to Lucca's cathedral. Facing the church facade, turn right and go down Via Vittorio Veneto (with the loggia on your left) to the vast, café-lined pair of squares...*

## ❻ Piazza Napoleone and Piazza del Giglio

The first of these two squares is named for the French despot who was the first outsider to take over Lucca. The dominant building on the right was the seat of government for the independent Republic of Lucca from 1369 to 1799—the year Napoleon came and messed everything up. Caffé Ninci, on the left (with some nice tables for people-watching), has been caffeinating locals since 1925 and serves what's considered to be the best coffee in town.

Cross diagonally through this square into the smaller **Piazza del Giglio,** dominated by the Giglio Theater. Like a mini La Scala, this has long been the number-one theater (of seven) in the highly cultured city of Puccini.

• *Continue to the left, along the big orange building, up Via del Duomo. After a block, you'll see...*

## ❼ San Giovanni Church

This first cathedral of Lucca is interesting only for its archaeological finds. The entire floor of the 12th-century church has been excavated in recent decades, revealing layers of Roman houses, ancient hot tubs that date back to the time of Christ, early churches, and theological graffiti. Sporadic English translations help you understand what you're looking at. As you climb under the church's present-day floor and wander the lanes of Roman Lucca, remember that the entire city sits on similar ruins. Ascend the 190 steps of the church's campanile (bell tower) for a panoramic view (but not quite as good as the one from the Guinigi Tower).

**Cost and Hours:** €4, €9 combo-ticket includes cathedral and Cathedral Museum, admission includes tower climb; daily 10:00-18:00; Nov-March Mon-Fri until 14:00, Sat-Sun until 18:00; audioguide—€2. For info on nightly Puccini concerts held at the church, see Helpful Hints, earlier.

• *Continuing past San Giovanni, you'll be face-to-face with...*

## ❽ San Martino Cathedral

This cathedral—the main church of the Republic of Lucca and worth ▲—begun in the 11th century, is an entertaining mix of architectural and artistic styles. It's also home to the exquisite 15th-century tomb of Ilaria del Carretto, who married into the wealthy Guinigi family.

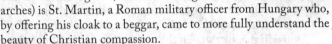

**Cost and Hours:** €3, €9 combo-ticket includes Cathedral Museum and San Giovanni Church, tower climb-€3; Mon-Fri 9:30-18:00, Sat until 19:00, Sun from 12:00; Nov-March daily 9:30-17:00; Piazza San Martino, www.cattedralelucca.it. There's a WC under the bell tower.

**Visiting the Cathedral:** The cathedral's elaborate Pisan Romanesque **facade** features Christian teaching scenes, animals, and candy-cane-striped columns. The horseback figure (over the two right arches) is St. Martin, a Roman military officer from Hungary who, by offering his cloak to a beggar, came to more fully understand the beauty of Christian compassion.

The **interior**—bigger than it seems from outside—features brightly frescoed Gothic arches, Renaissance paintings, and stained glass from the 19th century. On the left side of the nave, a small, elaborate, birdcage-like temple contains the wooden crucifix—much revered by locals—called **Volto Santo**. It's said to have been sculpted by Nicodemus in Jerusalem and set afloat in an unmanned boat that landed on the coast of Tuscany, from where wild oxen miraculously carried it to Lucca in 782.

On the right side of the nave, the sacristy houses the enchanting **memorial tomb** of Ilaria del Carretto by Jacopo della Quercia (1407). This young bride of silk baron Paolo Guinigi is so realistically realized that the statue was nicknamed "Sleeping Beauty." Her nose is partially worn off because of a long-standing tradition of lonely young ladies rubbing it for luck in finding a boyfriend.

As you head for the church's exit, stop by the third painting from the end (on the left)—*The Last Supper* by Jacopo Tintoretto. This is a typical Baroque spectacle, with the drama of the event emphasized as if it's theater. Notice the actors on the stage and how the mother, giving her child his "first supper" in the foreground, connects with us, inviting us to be present.

• *There's one more sight to consider, but it's extra credit. As you face the cathedral facade, on the little square to the left is the entrance to the...*

## ❾ Cathedral Museum (Museo della Cattedrale)

This beautifully presented museum houses original paintings, sculptures, and vestments from the cathedral and other Lucca churches. Pass through a room with illuminated manuscripts on your way to the ticket desk, then follow the one-way route up and down through the collection. You'll see church paintings and sculptures, silver ecclesiastical gear, and a big cutaway model of the cathedral (€4, €9 combo-ticket includes cathedral and San Giovanni Church; daily 10:00-18:00; Nov-March Mon-Fri 10:00-14:00, Sat-Sun until 18:00; audioguide—€2, left of the cathedral on Piazza Antelminelli).

• *Our walk is finished. From here, it's just a short stroll south to the city wall—and a bike-rental office, if you want to take a spin. Otherwise, simply explore the city...lose yourself in Lucca.*

## More Sights in Lucca

### Lucca Ramparts (and Bike Ride)

Lucca's most remarkable feature, its Renaissance wall, is also its most enjoyable attraction, worth ▲▲—especially when circled on a rental bike. Stretching for 2.5 miles, this is an ideal place to come for an overview of the city by foot or bike.

Lucca has had a protective wall for 2,000 years. You can read three walls into today's map: the first rectangular Roman wall, the later medieval wall (nearly the size of today's), and the 16th-century Renaissance ramparts that still survive.

With the advent of cannons, thin medieval walls were suddenly vulnerable. A new design—the same one that stands today—was state-of-the-art when it was built (1550-1650). Much of the old medieval wall (look for the old stones) was incorporated into the Renaissance wall (with uniform bricks). The new wall was squat: a 100-foot-wide mound of dirt faced with bricks, engineered to absorb a cannonball pummeling. The townspeople cleared a wide no-man's-land around the town, exposing any attackers from a distance. Eleven heart-shaped bastions (now inviting picnic areas) were designed to minimize exposure to cannonballs and to maximize defense capabilities. The ramparts were armed with 130 cannons.

The town invested a third of its income for more than a century to construct the wall, and—since it kept away the Florentines and nasty Pisans—it was considered a fine investment. In fact, nobody ever bothered to try to attack the wall. Locals say that the only time it actually defended the city was during an 1812 flood of the Serchio River, when the gates were sandbagged and the ramparts kept out the high water.

If exploring the wall, you can venture into its tunnels and interior at either San Paolino Bastion or San Martino Bastion.

Today, the ramparts seem made to order for a leisurely bike ride (a wonderfully smooth 20-30-minute pedal, depending on how fast you go and how crowded the wall-top park is). You can rent bikes cheaply and easily from one of several bike-rental places in town (listed earlier, under "Helpful Hints"). There are also several handy places to get up on the wall. Note that the best people-watching—and slowest pedaling—is during *passeggiata* time, just before dinner, when it seems that all of Lucca is doing slow laps around its beloved wall.

### Guinigi Tower (Torre Guinigi)

Many Tuscan towns have towers, but none is quite like the Guinigi family's. Up 227 steps is a small garden with fragrant trees, sur-

rounded by fine views over the city's rooftops. You'll head up wide stone stairs, then huff up twisty metal ones through the hollow brick tower. From the top, orient yourself to the town. Lucca sits in a flat valley ringed by protective hills, so it's easy to see how the town managed to stay independent through so much of its history, despite its lack of a strategic hilltop position. From up here, pick out landmarks: the circular form of Piazza dell'Anfiteatro to the north, with the mosaic facade of the Church of San Frediano nearby; to the left (east), the open top of the Clock Tower, marking the Roman grid-planned streets of the oldest part of town; and to the south, the big, marble facade of San Martino Cathedral.

**Cost and Hours:** €4, €6 combo-ticket includes Clock Tower, erratic hours but likely daily 9:30-18:30—possibly later in summer, shorter hours Nov-March, Via Sant'Andrea 41.

### Puccini's House

This modern, well-presented museum fills the home where Giacomo Puccini grew up. It's well-worth a visit for opera enthusiasts... but mostly lost on anybody else. Buy your ticket at the shop/office on the square, then buzz to be let in. You'll tour the composer's birthplace—including the room where he was born—and see lots of artifacts (including the Steinway piano where he did much of his composing, his personal belongings, and pullout drawers with original compositions and manuscripts). An elaborate costume from one of his works is on display, and if you ask, the attendant can accompany you for a peek in the garret (storage room up above the house), where a stage set from *La Bohème* evokes the composer's greatest work.

**Cost and Hours:** €7; daily 9:30-19:30; April and Oct Wed-Mon until 18:30, closed Tue; Nov-March shorter hours and closed Tue; Corte San Lorenzo 9, tel. 0583-584-028, www.puccinimuseum.it.

# Sleeping in Lucca

### FANCY BOUTIQUE B&BS WITHIN THE WALLS

**$$$$ A Palazzo Busdraghi** has eight comfortable, pastel-colored rooms with modern baths (some with whirlpool tubs) in a tastefully converted 13th-century palace tucked inside a creaky old court-yard. Sweet Marta hustles to keep guests happy, and bakes tasty cakes for breakfast. It's conveniently located on busy Via Fillungo, but can be noisy on weekends (family room, air-con, pay parking, Via Fillungo 170, tel. 0583-950-856, www.apalazzobusdraghi.it, info@apalazzobusdraghi.it).

**$$ La Romea B&B,** in an air-conditioned, restored 14th-century palazzo near Guinigi Tower, feels like a royal splurge. Its five rooms are lavishly decorated in handsome colors and surround a big, plush lounge with stately Venetian-style mosaic-linoleum floors (RS%, family rooms, Vicolo delle Ventaglie 2, tel. 0583-464-175, www.laromea.com, info@laromea.com, Giulio and wife Gaia).

**$$ La Bohème B&B** has a cozy yet elegant ambience, offering six large rooms, each named for a Puccini opera. Chandeliers, 1920s-vintage tile floors, and tasteful antiques add to the charm (RS%, air-con, pay parking, Via del Moro 2, tel. 0583-462-404, www.boheme.it, info@boheme.it, Laura).

### SLEEPING MORE FORGETTABLY WITHIN THE WALLS

**$$$ Hotel la Luna** has 29 rooms in a great location in the heart of the city. Rooms are split between two adjacent buildings just off the main shopping street. Rooms in the main, historical building are larger and classier, with old wood-beam ceilings (and, in some, original frescoes), while the modern building feels newer and has an elevator but less personality (RS%, family rooms, air-con, pay parking, Via Fillungo at Corte Compagni 12, tel. 0583-493-634, www.hotellaluna.it, info@hotellaluna.it).

**$$ Albergo San Martino** is friendly and conveniently lo-cated for train travelers, with rooms in three buildings. The 12 art-adorned rooms in the main hotel—with a nice lounge and curbside breakfast terrace—are cozy, while the six rooms in the **annex** are newer and slightly cheaper. And the nine rooms in their sister **$ Hotel Diana** are fresh, with a colorful Italian-modern design flair at an affordable price (breakfast extra at Hotel Diana; family rooms, air-con, tight pay parking, reception at Via della Dogana 9, tel. 0583-469-181, www.albergosanmartino.it, info@ albergosanmartino.it, Andrea).

## OUTSIDE THE WALLS

**$$$ Hotel San Marco,** a 10-minute walk outside the Porta Santa Maria or Porta San Jacopo, is a postmodern place with a peaceful garden and pool. Its 42 rooms are sleek, with all the comforts, and its easy location makes it a good choice for drivers (air-con, elevator, pool, bike rental, free parking, taxi from station-€13, Via San Marco 368, tel. 0583-495-010, www.hotelsanmarcolucca.it, info@ hotelsanmarcolucca.it, proud Francesco).

**$$ Hotel Rex,** run by Maurizia and family, rents 25 rooms in a practical contemporary building on the train station square. While in the modern world, you're just 200 yards away from the old town and get more space for your money. Ask for a slightly quieter room at the back (family rooms, children's play area and toys, air-con, elevator, free loaner bikes, free parking, a few steps from the train station at Piazza Ricasoli 19, tel. 0583-955-443, www. hotelrexlucca.com, info@hotelrexlucca.com, Elisabetta).

**$$ Relais Inn Lucca** takes up a stately palazzo near Piazza Napoleone. Their nine rooms are chic and modern, and run with youthful enthusiasm by Alessandra (air-con, elevator, pay parking, Corso Garibaldi 19, tel. 0583-464-218, www.relaisinnlucca. it, info@relaisinnlucca.it).

**$ Hotel Moderno** is indeed modern, with 12 rooms tastefully decorated. Although it's in a strange location, backing up to the train tracks, the rooms are quiet, and it offers class unusual for this price range (RS%, air-con, Via Vincenzo Civitali 38— turn left out of train station and go over stair-heavy bridge across tracks, tel. 0583-55-840, www.albergomodernolucca.com, info@ albergomodernolucca.com).

**$ La Mimosa B&B** has five cozy, if musty, rooms a 10-minute walk west of Porta Sant'Anna. Practical if you're arriving or leaving Lucca by bus, it's on a main road, but double-paned windows reduce traffic noise (air-con, free loaner bikes, free street parking nearby, Via Pisana 66; leave Piazzale Giuseppe Verdi through Porta Sant'Anna, swing right, then cross road, walk straight down Via Catalani, and take second road on the left; tel. 0583-583-121, www.bblamimosa.it, info@bblamimosa.it).

# Eating in Lucca

## FINE AND ROMANTIC DINING

**$$ Canuleia Trattoria** is run by enthusiastic Matteo (the chef) and Eleonora (head waiter), who make everything fresh in their small kitchen. You can eat tasty Tuscan cuisine in a tight, dressy, and romantic little dining room or outside on the garden courtyard. As this place is justifiably popular, reserve for dinner (Tue-Sun 12:30-14:00 & 19:30-22:00, closed Mon, Via Canuleia 14, tel. 0583-467-470, www.canuleiatrattoria.it).

**$$$ Ristorante Giglio** is a venerable old dining hall where waiters are formal but not stuffy, and the spirit of Puccini lives on. This is where local families enjoy special occasions under a big chandelier. The short but thoughtful menu features a fusion of traditional Tuscan and creative international gastronomy concocted by three young chefs. Though pricier than most of my listings, this is a big step up in dining experience. Consider their tasting menus to best appreciate how they've earned a Michelin star (reservations smart, impressive wine list, Wed-Mon 12:15-14:30 & 19:15-22:15, closed Tue, Piazza del Giglio 2, tel. 0583-494-058, www.ristorantegiglio.com).

**$$$ Osteria dal Manzo** is a classy restaurant run by classy Antonio (who speaks English and warmly welcomes diners), with an elegantly simple dining room and elegantly simple, seasonal cuisine. The menu is easy and enticing—five items for each of three courses—always two meat, two fish, and one vegetarian (Mon-Sat from 19:30, closed Sun, Via Cesare Battisti 28, tel. 0583-490-649).

## CHARMING AND RUSTIC DINING

**$$ La Bottega di Anna & Leo,** run by Claudio and Lidia (and named for their children), is a pastel and lovable little eatery with a simple menu and a passion for quality. They have tight seating inside and a few charming tables facing the side of the Church of San Frediano (Tue-Sat 12:00-14:30 & 19:00-22:30, closed Sun and Mon, reservations smart, Via San Frediano 16, mobile 393-577-9910 or 393-530-2512, www.labottegadiannaeleo.it).

**$$ Osteria Via San Giorgio,** where Daniela cooks and her brother Piero serves, is a cheery family eatery that satisfies both fish and meat lovers. The indoor seating is tight and convivial, the outdoor courtyard is cheery in summer, and the house wine is high quality (daily 12:00-16:00 & 18:30-23:00, Via San Giorgio 26, tel. 0583-953-233).

**$$ Il Cuore Enogastronomia** is a cozy blend of restaurant and deli—if you like your meal you can buy more to take home. Browse their cases of prepared dishes and order some to take away, or sit in the dining room for homemade pasta, big salads, pizza, meats,

## Specialties in Lucca

Lucca has some tasty specialties worth seeking out. *Ceci* (CHEH-chee), also called *cecina* (cheh-CHEE-nah), makes an ideal cheap snack any time of day. This crepe-like garbanzo-bean flatbread is sold in pizza shops and is best accompanied by a nip of red wine. *Farro,* a grain (spelt) dating back to ancient Roman cuisine, shows up in restaurants in soups or as a creamy rice-like dish *(risotto di farro). Tordelli,* the Lucchesi version of *tortelli,* is homemade ravioli. It's traditionally stuffed with meat and served with more meat sauce, but chefs creatively pair cheeses and vegetables, too. *Lardo di Colonnata* is *salumi* made with cured lard and rosemary, sliced thin, and served as an antipasto.

Meat, not fish, is the star at most restaurants, especially steak, which is listed on menus as *filetto di manzo* (filet), *tagliata di manzo* (thin slices of grilled tenderloin), or the king of steaks, *bistecca alla fiorentina.* Order *al sangue* (rare), *medio* (medium rare), *cotto* (medium), or *ben cotto* (well). Anything more than *al sangue* is considered a travesty for steak connoisseurs. *Ravellino* is a thin cut of beef that's deep-fried, then pan-fried again later to heat it up.

Note that steaks (as well as fish) are often sold by weight, noted on menus as *s.q.* (according to quantity ordered) or *l'etto* (cost per 100 grams—250 grams is about an 8-ounce steak).

For something sweet, bakeries sell *buccellato,* bread dotted with raisins, lightly flavored with anise, and often shaped like a wreath. It's sold only in large quantities, but luckily it stays good for a few days (and it also pairs well with vin santo—fortified Tuscan dessert wine). An old proverb says, "Coming to Lucca without eating the *buccellato* is like not having come at all." *Buon appetito!*

and desserts (daily 10:00-22:00, closed Jan-Feb, Via del Battistero 4, tel. 0583-493-196, enthusiastic Anna takes good care of diners).

**$ Pizzeria da Felice** is a mom-and-pop hole-in-the-wall take-out pizza joint. Grab an *etto* of *cecina* (garbanzo-bean crepes) or a slice of freshly baked pizza and a short glass of wine. From September through April, they're known for their *castagnaccio,* a cake made with roasted chestnuts and ricotta (daily 10:00-20:30 except closed Sun Jan-Aug and closed 2 weeks in Aug, Via Buia 12, tel. 0583-494-986).

**$$ Trattoria da Leo** packs in chatty locals for characteristic home cooking in a high-energy, diner-type atmosphere. Sit in the rollicking interior, or out on a tight, atmospheric lane (daily 12:00-15:30 & 19:30-22:30, Via Tegrimi 1, tel. 0583-492-236).

## SNACKS, GELATO, AND HAPPY-HOUR *APERITIVO* BARS

*Aperitivi* near **Porta dei Borghi:** This gate at the end of Via Fillungo (and the little square just beyond it) is a great area for characteristic bars serving free and tasty buffets with any drink during their *aperitivo* time. These places are popular with young locals and are a perfect spot to relax after cycling the wall (near Piazza Santa Maria bike rentals).

**Vinarkia,** a characteristic wine bar, is popular for its *aperitivo* buffet from 18:30 to 20:00 (closed Tue, Via Fillungo 188, tel. 0583-152-5357, Alekos).

**De Cervesia** is a craft beer pub with three microbrews on rotating taps (and one English-style pull) and dozens by the bottle (Tue-Sun 17:00-22:00, closed Mon, Via Michele Rosi 20, tel. 0583-492-620, Matteo).

**Ciclo DiVino,** across the street, is a wine bar with a bike-shop theme and enticing snacks (Mon-Fri 16:00-22:00, Sat-Sun 11:00-22:00, Via Michele Rosi 7, tel. 0583-471-869).

*Aperitivi* on **Piazza San Michele: Caffè del Mercato,** on the other side of the old town and catering to an older clientele, has a good *aperitivo* buffet nightly from 18:00 to 20:00 (facing church at Piazza San Michele 17, tel. 0583-494-127).

**Gelato:** Just off Piazza San Michele, **De' Coltelli** has some of my favorite gelato in Italy. It's proudly Sicilian-style (with Arab roots) and many of their flavors rotate with the season. Sample with a spirit of adventure and then have fun ordering: The salted caramel is a standout, and their *granita* takes the slushy to new heights (Sun-Thu 11:00-20:00, Fri-Sat until 21:00, Via San Paolino 10, Valentina).

**Pizza:** Two doors away from De' Coltelli, **Alice Pizza** offers good pizza by the slice (Tue-Sun 10:00-20:30, closed Mon, Via San Paolino 22, tel. 0583-572-712).

**Refreshments on the Wall: Caffetteria San Colombano** is a handy pit stop for bikers and walkers on the city wall. This place is slick with bite-sized snacks and cappuccinos, perfect for a takeaway meal on top of the wall (overpriced at the table). If you're not feeling too wobbly already from biking, try a *caffè corretto* (espresso with your choice of Sambuca, rum, or grappa) or a *Biadina,* a bittersweet liqueur served with pine nuts. The fancier sit-down restaurant serves pasta and big salads with a view (daily 9:00-late, near the top of ramp at the San Colombano Bastion, tel. 0583-464-641).

**Groceries: Pam** is a small, central market just off Piazza San Michele (daily 8:00-22:00, Via San Paolino 16).

# Lucca Connections

Even if you have a car, I'd opt for the much faster and cheaper train or bus to reach the Leaning Tower. For more on day-tripping to Pisa, see page 574.

**From Lucca by Train to: Florence** (2/hour, 1.5 hours), **Pisa** (1-2/hour, 30 minutes; if going directly to Leaning Tower, hop off at Pisa San Rossore Station), **Livorno** (about hourly, 1-1.5 hours, transfer at Pisa Centrale), **Milan** (2/hour except Sun, 4-5 hours, transfer in Florence), **Rome** (1/hour except Sun, 3-4 hours, change in Florence), **Cinque Terre** (hourly, about 2 hours, transfer in Viareggio and La Spezia).

**From Lucca by Bus:** Vaibus has handy direct routes from Lucca's Piazzale Giuseppe Verdi to **Florence** (your bus ticket gets you on the connect tram to the city center) and its **airport** (bus #DD, Mon-Sat nearly hourly, less on Sun, 1.25 hours to airport, 1.5 hours total to downtown Florence), and to **Pisa** and its **airport** (€3.50, drops you right at the Leaning Tower or at the station, airport is last stop, Mon-Sat hourly, fewer on Sun, 50 minutes). Before boarding, buy tickets at the bus ticket office on Piazzale Giuseppe Verdi (Mon-Sat 6:00-20:00, Sun 8:00-19:30)—or buy them from the driver for a small surcharge.

# SIENA

Siena was medieval Florence's archrival. And while Florence ultimately won the battle for political and economic superiority, Siena still competes for the tourists. Sure, Florence has the heavyweight sights. But Siena seems to be every Italy connoisseur's favorite town.

Situated atop three hills, Siena qualifies as Italy's ultimate "hill town." Its thriving historic center, with movie-set lanes cascading every which way, offers Italy's best medieval city experience. Most people visit Siena, just 35 miles south of Florence, as a day trip, but it's best experienced at twilight. While Florence has the blockbuster museums, Siena has an easy-to-enjoy soul: Courtyards sport flower-decked wells, alleys dead-end at rooftop views, and today, even with all the tourists, a strong local spirit pervades.

For those who dream of a Fiat-free Italy, Siena is a haven. Pedestrians rule in the old center of town, as the only drivers allowed are residents and cabbies. Nurse a drink on the main square. Wander narrow streets, tether an imaginary horse to the old metal rings, be stirred by colorful flags. Take time to savor the first European city to eliminate automobile traffic from its main square (1966) and then, just to be silly, wonder what would happen if they did it in your hometown.

## PLANNING YOUR TIME
On a quick trip, consider spending two nights in Siena (or three nights with a whole-day side trip into Florence). Whatever you do, be sure to enjoy a sleepy medieval evening in Siena. The next morning, you can see the city's major sights in half a day.

# Orientation to Siena

Siena lounges atop a hill, stretching its three legs out from Il Campo. This pedestrianized main square is the historic meeting point of Siena's neighborhoods.

Just about everything mentioned in this chapter is within a 10-minute walk of the square. Navigate by three major landmarks (Il Campo, Duomo, and Basilica of San Domenico), following the excellent system of street-corner signs. The typical visitor sticks to the Il Campo-San Domenico axis. Stray from this main artery. Sienese streets go in anything but a straight line, so it's easy to get lost—but equally easy to get found. Explore.

Siena itself is one big sight. Its individual attractions come in two clusters: the square (Civic Museum and City Tower) and the cathedral (Baptistery and Duomo Museum, with its surprise viewpoint), plus the Pinacoteca for art lovers. Check off these sights, and then you're free to wander.

**Tourist Information:** The TI, just across from the cathedral, is next to worthless (daily 10:00-18:00; Piazza del Duomo 2, tel. 0577-280-551, www.terresiena.it). The bookshop next to the information desk sells detailed Siena maps.

## ARRIVAL IN SIENA
### By Train

Siena's small train station is at the base of the hill, on the edge of town. It has a bar/tobacco shop, an intercity bus office (daily 9:00-12:15 & 14:30-18:30), and a newsstand (which sells city bus tickets). Stow bags at Piazza Gramsci where the city bus drops you—see "By Florence-Siena Bus," later. A shopping mall with a supermarket is across the plaza facing the station. WCs are on track 1, past the pharmacy.

**Getting from the Train Station to the City Center:** To reach central Siena, you can hop a city bus, ride a long series of escalators, or take a taxi. For two or more traveling together, the **taxi** is your best value (€8 to the center, taxi stand just outside station, tel. 0577-49222).

*By Escalator or City Bus:* To reach either the bus or the escalators, head for the shopping mall across the square (far left corner as you leave). The first of a series of **escalators** climbs through the mall up into the town. From the top of the escalators, it's a 20-minute walk to the town center.

To ride the **city bus,** head to the dreary, concrete, cave-like bus

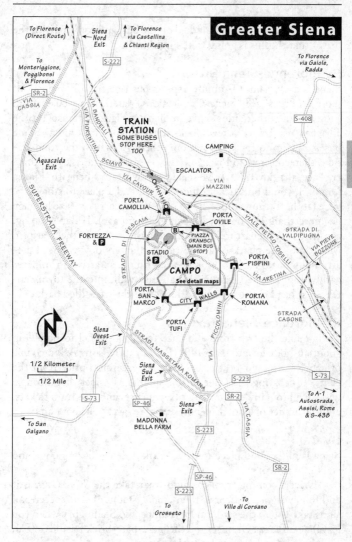

stop below the mall (catch the down elevator from inside the mall's first glass door on immediate right). All buses (big and small) go to Piazza Sale or Piazza Gramsci (both at the edge of the action and within a block of each other). Buy your bus ticket from the train station newsstand, and before boarding, confirm that the bus is going to the center (ask "*Centro?*").

**Returning to the Train Station from the City Center:** Catch a small shuttle bus directly to the station from Piazza del Sale, or take a big city bus from Piazza Gramsci. Look for *Ferrovia* or

*Stazione* on schedules and marked on the bus, and confirm with the driver that the bus is going to the *stazione*.

## By Florence-Siena Bus

Siena is a pleasant 90-minute express bus ride from Florence (for more on buses, see "Siena Connections," later). Most buses from Florence and other cities arrive in Siena at Piazza Gramsci (or the adjacent Via Tozzi), a few blocks north of the city center. (Some buses only go to the train station; others go first to the train station, then continue to Piazza Gramsci—to confirm, ask your driver, "pee-aht-sah GRAHM-shee?") Downstairs, beneath Piazza Gramsci, you'll find ticket offices, WCs, and a place to store baggage (at the Tiemme office, daily 7:00-19:00, carry-on-size luggage no more than 33 pounds, no overnight storage). If day-tripping, confirm your departure from timetables posted at the platform where you disembark or at the ticket counters downstairs. Late-afternoon buses back to Florence can fill up, so arrive 15 minutes early. From Piazza Gramsci, it's an easy walk into the town center—just head in the opposite direction of the tree-filled park.

## By Florence-Siena Taxi

Taxis make the trip from Florence to Siena—hotel to hotel—in about an hour for around €140. (Prices can be soft. Ask a couple of cabbies for their best price. Clearly agree on a price from the start.) If debating the value of this splurge, consider that a couple will spend roughly €40 for two taxi transfers and two train tickets, and the luxury of a hotel-to-hotel cab ride saves you about an hour.

## By Car

Siena is not a good place to drive. Park in a big lot or garage and walk into town.

Drivers coming from the autostrada take the *Siena Ovest* exit and follow signs for *Centro*, then *Stadio* (stadium). The soccer-ball signs take you to the stadium lot (Parcheggio Stadio, pay when you leave) near Piazza Gramsci and the huge, bare-brick Basilica of San Domenico. The Fortezza lot is also nearby.

Another good option is the underground Santa Caterina garage (you'll see signs on the way to the stadium lot). From the garage, hike 150 yards uphill through a gate to an escalator on the right, which carries you up into the city. Take a left at the top onto Siena's main street.

If you're staying in the south end of town, try the Il Campo lot, near Porta Tufi.

On parking spots, blue stripes mean pay and display; white stripes mean free parking, but watch for signs that say *solo per gli residenti* (residents only). Signs showing a street cleaner and a day of the week indicate when the street is closed to cars for cleaning. You can park for free in the lot west of the Fortezza; in white-striped spots south of the Fortezza; and overnight in most city lots (20:00-8:00).

Driving within Siena's city center is restricted to local cars and is policed by automatic cameras. If you drive or park anywhere marked *Zona Traffico Limitato (ZTL),* you'll likely have a hefty ticket waiting for you in the mail back home (if you rented a car, they know how to find you). Check with your hotel in advance if you plan to drop off your bags before parking.

## HELPFUL HINTS

**Combo-Tickets:** Siena often experiments with different combo-tickets, but in general, only three are worth considering: the Opa Si Pass for the Duomo and its related sights; the combo-ticket covering the Civic Museum and Santa Maria della Scala; and the combo-ticket covering the Civic Museum, Santa Maria della Scala, and City Tower. See the "Sights in Siena" section, later, for ticket details.

**Markets:** Every Wednesday morning a market of clothes, knick-knacks, and food sprawls between the Fortezza and Piazza Gramsci along Viale Cesare Maccari and the adjacent Viale XXV Aprile. Friday mornings see an organic food market in the same location.

**Bookstores:** For books and magazines in English, try **Libreria Senese** (daily, Via di Città 62) and the **Feltrinelli** bookstore (closed Sun, Via Banchi di Sopra 52).

**Cooking Classes:** At **Fonte Giusta Cooking School,** you'll prepare a meal (pasta, pizza, meats, dessert) under the instruction of a local chef—and then eat it. Lessons last two hours and cost €50-85, depending upon what you cook (Via Camollia 78, call 0577-40506 or email info@trattoriafontegiusta.com for schedule and details, www.fontegiusta.it).

**Laundry:** Try **Lavanderia San Pietro** (daily 8:00-22:00, not far from the Duomo at Via San Pietro 70, and **Lavanderia Waterland** (daily 7:00-22:00, north of Il Campo near Porta San Francesco at Via dei Rossi 94).

# Tours in Siena

🎧 To sightsee on your own, download my free Siena City Walk audio tour (see sidebar on page 26).

## LOCAL GUIDES

**Federica Olla,** who leads walking tours of Siena, is a smart, friendly guide with a knack for creative teaching (€55/hour, mini-

# Visiting Tuscany

It's a joy to downshift to the more peaceful pace of Italy's small cities...and even smaller hill towns. I've covered my favorites in this book.

Siena, Pisa, and Lucca are in a category of their own, with more artistic and historic sights. **Siena** is the ultimate (and biggest) hill town, with an unrivaled spirit any visitor can enjoy. Like a medieval stage set, its pedestrian-friendly old town is surrounded by its fortified wall. Siena's stunning main square—the gently tilted red-brick Campo—is the city's proud centerpiece. As Tuscany's hub, Siena is well-connected by bus to Florence (also handy by train) and the surrounding hill towns.

**Pisa**'s iconic Leaning Tower draws flocks of tourists, but this midsize city also offers plenty of history and beautiful architecture, along with a thriving student scene. Lesser-known and smaller, charming **Lucca** is a "flat hill town" with winding streets ringed by a well-preserved Renaissance wall, perfect for circling on a bike. Both lie an hour or so west of Florence and are easily reached by train or bus.

But how in Dante's name does one choose from among Tuscany's hundreds of small hill towns? The one(s) you visit will depend on your interests, time, and mode of transportation.

**Volterra**—with its rustic vitality—is a beautifully preserved jewel. Its out-of-the-way location keeps this town from being trampled by tourist crowds, and its Etruscan history makes for compelling sightseeing. With 14 surviving medieval towers, walled **San Gimignano** is a classic. Because it's easy to visit from Florence—about 1.5 hours by bus—midday crowds can overwhelm its charms (it's an evocative delight early and late). Both Volterra and San Gimignano work best for drivers, but can be reached by public transportation.

South of Siena, in the region I call the "Heart of Tuscany," drivers have their pick of hill towns. Ridge-hugging **Montepulciano**'s medieval cityscape resembles a miniature Florence. With several historic wine cellars and easy access to wine country, it attracts wine aficionados, as does **Montalcino,** itself a happy gauntlet of wine shops and art galleries. Fans of architecture and urban design appreciate little **Pienza**'s well-planned streets and squares. All three towns are covered in the Heart of Tuscany chapter.

## Getting Around Tuscany

**By Bus or Train:** Buses are often the only public-transportation choice to get between small hill towns. Train stations are likely to be in the valley below the town center, connected by a local bus.

**By Car:** Exploring Tuscany and its hill towns by car can be a great experience. Wait to pick up your car until the last sizable town you visit (or at the nearest airport to avoid big-city traffic), and carry a good, detailed road map in addition to any digital navigation systems. Freeways (such as the toll autostrada and the

free *superstrada*) are the fastest way to connect two points, but smaller roads, including the super-scenic S-222, connecting Florence and Siena, are more rewarding.

Some towns don't allow visitors to drive or park in the city center. Be alert for "ZTL" *(Zona Traffico Limitato)* signs, indicating no cars allowed. Leave your car outside the walls and walk into town. Lots are usually free and plentiful outside city walls (and sometimes linked to the town center by elevators or escalators). For more driving and parking tips, see the Practicalities chapter.

## Sleeping in Rural Tuscany and Beyond

For a relaxing break from big-city Italy, settle down in an *agriturismi*—a farmhouse that rents out rooms to travelers (usually for a minimum of a week in high season). These rural B&Bs—almost by definition in the middle of nowhere—provide a good home base from which to find the magic of Italy's hill towns. Many provide memorable meals from locally sourced ingredients. I've listed several good options in the following four chapters. For more information, see *"Agriturismi"* in the Practicalities chapter.

## Siena at a Glance

▲▲▲**Il Campo** Best square in Italy. See page 608.

▲▲▲**Duomo** Art-packed cathedral with mosaic floors and statues by Michelangelo and Bernini. **Hours:** Mon-Sat 10:30-19:00, Sun 13:30-18:00, Nov-Feb closes daily at 17:30. See page 619.

▲▲**Civic Museum** City museum in City Hall with Sienese frescoes, the *Effects of Good and Bad Government*. **Hours:** Daily 10:00-19:00, Nov-mid-March until 18:00. See page 616.

▲▲**Duomo Museum** Siena's best museum, with cathedral art (Duccio's *Maestà*) and sweeping Tuscan views. **Hours:** Daily 10:00-19:00, Nov-Feb 10:30-17:30. See page 623.

▲**City Tower** Siena's 330-foot tower climb. **Hours:** Daily 10:00-19:00, mid-Oct-Feb until 16:00. See page 617.

▲**Pinacoteca** Fine Sienese paintings. **Hours:** Tue-Sat 8:15-19:15, Sun-Mon 9:00-13:00. See page 618.

▲**Baptistery of San Giovanni** Cave-like building with baptismal font decorated by Ghiberti and Donatello. **Hours:** Daily 10:30-19:00, Nov-Feb until 17:30. See page 625.

▲**Santa Maria della Scala** Museum with much of the original Fountain of Joy, Byzantine reliquaries, and vibrant frescoes depicting day-to-day life in a medieval hospital. **Hours:** Daily 10:00-19:00, Thu until 22:00; closes earlier mid-Oct-mid-March. See page 626.

mum 2 hours, mobile 338-133-9525, www.ollaeventi.com, info@ollaeventi.com).

**Anna Piperato,** fiercely proud of her adopted hometown of Siena and an expert on Palio culture, leads walking tours in Siena—including a visit to her *contrada*, Lupa—and environs (RS%—10 percent discount, €55/hour, minimum 2 hours, mobile 333-6829-336, www.sienaitalytours.com, anna@sienaitalytours.com).

**GSO Guides Co-op** is a group of young professionals who offer good tours covering Siena and all of Tuscany and Umbria (€158/half-day, €315/full day, RS%—10 percent discount, they don't drive but can join you in your car, www.guidesienaeoltre.com). Among them, **Stefania Fabrizi** stands out (mobile 338-640-7796, stefaniafabriziguide@gmail.com).

## ON FOOT
### Walking Tours from the TI

The TI offers walking tours of the old town, including the Duomo. Guides usually conduct their walks (unfortunately) in both English and Italian (€20—pay guide directly, daily April-Oct at 11:00, 2 hours, depart from TI, Piazza del Duomo 2, tel. 0577-280-551).

### Siena Info Point Walking Tour

These basic one-hour town walks depart from Siena Info Point's tiny office on Il Campo and end at the Duomo (€15, daily at 11:15, 13:00, and 18:00, just show up). For €5 extra you can extend the tour to the Duomo interior (office open daily 9:30-19:30, mobile 331-742-2646, www.sienainfopoint.com, left of City Hall at Piazza del Campo 72).

### Siena City Walks by Roberto

Roberto and his guides offer private three-hour Siena walking tours (€180 for up to 8 people, admissions extra) or joinable group tours (€45/person, admissions extra, minimum 4 people; book online or call 320-147-6590, www.toursbyroberto.com, toursbyroberto@gmail.com).

## OTHER TOURS
### Tuscany Minibus Tours by Roberto

Roberto Bechi and his guides lead off-the-beaten-path, full-day minibus tours of the countryside surrounding Siena (€100/person, up to eight passengers, pickup at hotel). The first participants to book choose one of seven itineraries—then others join until the van fills. Roberto and his team share the same passion for Sienese culture, Tuscan history, and local cuisine (see website for tour options, RS%—10 percent discount, entry fees extra; also offers multiday tours, booking mobile 320-147-6590, Roberto's mobile 328-425-5648, www.toursbyroberto.com, toursbyroberto@gmail.com). See above and below for Roberto's walking and farm tours; he also provides private van connections to Volterra—see the Volterra & San Gimignano chapter.

### Wine Tasting

The Tuscan Wine School offers two foodie experiences in English. The midday food tour (12:00 Mon, Wed, and Sat) focuses on local food culture with tastings (focaccia, cured meats, truffles, gelato) at vendors around town. The afternoon wine-appreciation classes (Mon-Sat at 16:00), held in their classroom, let you taste six Tuscan wines paired with small bites (€45 for either tour, RS%—20 percent discount, Via di Stalloreggi 26, 30 yards from Hotel Duomo, tel. 0577-221-704, mobile 333-722-9716, www.tuscanwineschool.com, tuscanwineschool@gmail.com, Georgia and Milo). They also

SIENA

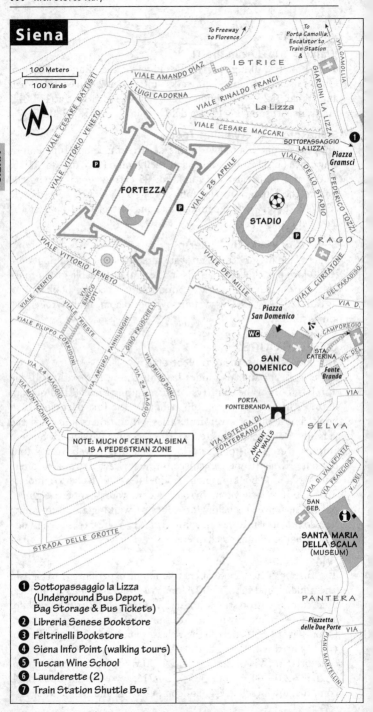

# Siena

100 Meters
100 Yards

To Freeway to Florence

To Porta Camollia, Escalator to Train Station &

ISTRICE

La Lizza

VIALE AMANDO DIAZ
V. LUIGI CADORNA
VIALE RINALDO FRANCI
VIALE CESARE MACCARI
VIALE CESARE BATTISTI
VIALE VITTORIO VENETO

VIA GAMOLLIA
GIARDINI LA LIZZA

SOTTOPASSAGGIO LA LIZZA

Piazza Gramsci

❶

V. FEDERICO TOZZI

VIALE DELLO STADIO

FORTEZZA

P

P

VIALE 25 APRILE

STADIO

P

DRAGO

VIALE VITTORIO VENETO

VIALE DEI MILLE

VIALE CURTATONE

V. DEI PARADISO

VIA D.

VIALE TRENTO
VIA ENRICO TOTI
VIALE TRIESTE
VIALE FILIPPO CORRIDONI
V. GINO FRUSCHELLI
VIA ARTURO PANILUNGHI
VIA BRUNO BONCI
VIA 24 MAGGIO
VIA 24 MAGGIO
VIA MONTICCHELLO

Piazza San Domenico

WC

SAN DOMENICO

STA. CATERINA

V. CAMPOREGIO

VIC. DEL

Fonte Branda

VIA

PORTA FONTEBRANDA

SELVA

VIA ESTERNA DI FONTEBRANDA

ANCIENT CITY WALLS

VIA DI VALLEPIATTA
VIA FRANCIOSA
V. DEL

NOTE: MUCH OF CENTRAL SIENA IS A PEDESTRIAN ZONE

SAN SEB.

SANTA MARIA DELLA SCALA (MUSEUM)

STRADA DELLE GROTTE

PANTERA

Piazzetta delle Due Porte

VIA

PIANO MANTELLINI

❶ Sottopassaggio la Lizza (Underground Bus Depot, Bag Storage & Bus Tickets)
❷ Libreria Senese Bookstore
❸ Feltrinelli Bookstore
❹ Siena Info Point (walking tours)
❺ Tuscan Wine School
❻ Launderette (2)
❼ Train Station Shuttle Bus

**SIENA**

**SIENA'S "CONTRADE"(NEIGHBORHOODS)**

AQUILA (Eagle)

BRUCO (Caterpillar)

CIVETTA (Owl)

DRAGO (Dragon)

GIRAFFA (Giraffe)

ISTRICE (Porcupine)

LEOCORNO (Unicorn)

LUPA (Wolf)

OCA (Goose)

ONDA (Wave)

PANTERA (Panther)

SELVA (Forest)

TARTUGA (Tortoise)

TORRE (Tower)

NOTE: MORE *CONTRADE*
LIE BEYOND THE MAP
BOUNDARIES.

offer countryside food- and wine-oriented tours, convenient for those without their own wheels (www.siena-wine-tour.com).

**Farm Visit**

Madonna Bella, a farm co-owned by local guide Roberto Bechi, sits just a few minutes outside Siena. Paola welcomes visitors to stop in, enjoy the views, visit the farm, take part in wine and olive-oil tastings, and learn how olive oil and pasta are made. It's best to book ahead if you want to enjoy a food/wine pairing that anyone would consider an abundant lunch (Strada del Tesoro 25—just outside Siena on road SP-46, mobile 393-858-2981, www.madonnabella.com).

# Siena City Walk

This short self-guided walk laces together Siena's most important sights. If you do the walk without entering the sights, it works great at night when the city is peaceful.

🎧 This walk is also available as a free Rick Steves audio tour.

• *Start in the center of the main square, Il Campo, standing just below the fountain.*

## ❶ Il Campo

This square is the heart of Siena, both geographically and metaphorically—and it's worth ▲▲▲. First laid out in the 12th century, today Il Campo (officially the Piazza del Campo) is the only town square I've seen where people stretch out as if at the beach. At the flat end of its clamshell shape is City Hall, where you can tour the Civic Museum and climb the City Tower. From there the square fans out as if to create an amphitheater. All eyes are on Il Campo twice each summer, when it hosts the famous Palio horse races (see sidebar on page 612).

Originally, this area was just a field *(campo)* outside the city walls (which encircled the cathedral). Bits of those original walls, which curved against today's square, can be seen above the pharmacy (the black-and-white stones, third story up, to the right as you face City Hall). In the 1200s, with the advent of the Sienese republic, the city expanded. Il Campo became its marketplace and the historic junction of Siena's various competing *contrade* (neighborhood districts). The square and its build-

ings are the color of the soil upon which they stand—a color known to artists and Crayola users as "burnt sienna."

**City Hall** (Palazzo Pubblico), with its looming tower, dominates the square. In medieval Siena, this was the center of the city, and the whole focus of Il Campo still flows down to it.

The **City Tower** was built around 1340. At 330 feet, it's one of Italy's tallest secular towers. Medieval Siena was a proud republic, and this tower stands like an exclamation point—an architectural declaration of independence from papacy and empire. The tower's Italian nickname, Torre del Mangia, comes from a hedonistic bell-ringer who consumed his earnings like a glutton consumes food. (His chewed-up statue is just inside City Hall's courtyard, to the left as you enter.)

The open **chapel** located at the base of the tower was built as thanks to God for ending the Black Death of 1348 (after it killed more than a third of the population). These days, the chapel is where Palio contestants are blessed (and where EMTs stand by during the race).

You can visit the Civic Museum inside City Hall and climb the tower (see page 616).

• *Now turn around and take a closer look at the fountain in the top center of the square.*

## ❷ Fountain of Joy (Fonte Gaia)

This fountain—a copy of an early-15th-century work by Jacopo della Quercia—marks the square's high point. The joy is all about

how the Sienese republic blessed its people with water. Find Lady Justice with her scales and sword (right of center), overseeing the free distribution of water to all. The Fountain of Joy still reminds locals that life in Siena is good. The relief panel on the left shows God creating Adam by helping him to his feet. It's said that this reclining Adam (carved a century before Michelangelo's day) influenced Michelangelo when he painted his Sistine Chapel ceiling. The fountain's original statuary is exhibited at Santa Maria della Scala (see page 626).

• *Leave Il Campo uphill on the widest ramp. With your back to the tower, it's at 10 o'clock. After a few steps you reach Via di Città. Turn left and walk 100 yards uphill toward the imposing white palace with brick crenellations on top.*

Halfway to the palace, at the first corner, notice small plaques on the first level of the building facades—these mark the neighborhood, or ***contrada***. If the flags are flying, they reinforce the point.

SIENA

SIENA

# Siena Walk

1. Il Campo
2. Fountain of Joy
3. Chigi-Saracini Palace
4. Quattro Cantoni
5. Piazza del Duomo & Duomo
6. The Unfinished Church
7. Supporting an Oversized Church
8. Piazza Indipendenza
9. Loggia della Mercanzia
10. Banchi di Sopra & Banchi di Sotto
11. Piazza Salimbeni

You are stepping from the *contrada* of the Forest (Selva) into the *contrada* of the Eagle (Aquila). Notice also the once mighty and foreboding medieval **tower house.** Towers once soared all around town, but they're now truncated and no longer add to the skyline—look for their bases as you walk the city.

• *On the left, you reach the big curving facade of the...*

## ❸ Chigi-Saracini Palace (Palazzo Chigi-Saracini)

This old fortified noble palace is today home to a prestigious music academy, the Accademia Musicale Chigiana. If open, step into the courtyard with its photogenic well (powerful medieval families enjoyed direct connections to the city aqueduct). The walls of the loggia are decorated with the busts of Chigi-Saracini patriarchs, and the vaults are painted in the "grotesque" style popular during the Renaissance. What look like pigeonholes in the other walls are actually for scaffolding, for both construction and ongoing maintenance. The palace hosts a music festival each July and August with popular concerts almost nightly, international talent, and affordable tickets (box office just off courtyard). They offer €7 one-hour tours of the palace's library, art, and musical instruments (Mon-Fri at 11:30 plus Thu-Fri at 16:00, closed Sun, call to request English tour; Via di Città 89, tel. 0577-22091, www.chigiana.it).

• *Walk uphill to the next major intersection...*

## ❹ Quattro Cantoni

The intersection known as Quattro Cantoni (Four Corners) offers a delightful perch from which to study the city. The modern column (from 1996) with a Carrara marble she-wolf marks one of the three original hills upon which the city was built. You are still in the Eagle district (see the fountain and the corner plaque)—but beware. Just one block up the street, a ready-to-pounce panther—from the rival neighboring district—awaits.

Only the very rich could afford stone residences. The fancy facades here hide their economical brick construction behind a stucco veneer. The stone tower on this corner had only one door—30 feet above street level and reached by ladder, which could be pulled up as necessary. Within a few doors, you'll find a classy bar, an elegant grocery store, and a *gelateria.*

Take a little side trip, venturing up Via di San Pietro. Interesting stops include the window with Palio video clips playing (at #1), Simon and Paula's art shop with delightful Palio and *contrada* knickknacks (#5), a weaver's shop (#7), the recommended La Vecchia Latteria *gelateria* (#10), an art gallery (#11), and four enticing little osterias. At the end of the block you'll reach the best art museum in town, the **Pinacoteca** (for a self-guided tour of its interior, see page 618).

## Siena's *Contrade* and the Palio

Siena's 17 historic neighborhoods, or *contrade*—each with a parish church, well or fountain, and square—still play an active role in the life of the city. Each is represented by a mascot (porcupine, unicorn, wolf, etc.) and unique colors worn proudly by residents.

*Contrada* pride is evident year-round in Siena's parades and colorful banners, lamps, and wall plaques. If you hear the thunder of distant drumming, run to it for some medieval action—there's a good chance it'll feature flag throwers. Buy a scarf in *contrada* colors, and join in the merriment of these lively neighborhood festivals.

*Contrada* rivalries are most visible twice a year—on July 2 and August 16—during the city's world-famous horse race, the **Palio di Siena.** Ten of the 17 neighborhoods compete (chosen by rotation and lot), hurling themselves with medieval abandon into several days of trial races and traditional revelry. Jockeys—usually from out of town—are considered hired guns, no better than paid mercenaries. Bets are placed on which *contrada* will win...and lose. Despite the shady behind-the-scenes dealing, on the big day the horses are taken into their *contrada*'s church to be blessed. ("Go and return victorious," says the priest.) It's considered a sign of luck if a horse leaves droppings in the church.

On the evening of the race, Il Campo is stuffed to the brim with locals and tourists. Dirt is brought in and packed down to create the track's surface, while mattresses pad the walls of surrounding buildings. The most treacherous spots are the sharp

---

• *Back at the Four Corners, head up Via del Capitano, passing another massive Chigi family palace (at #1). Up next, at the end of the street, is the...*

## ❺ Piazza del Duomo and the Duomo

The pair of she-wolves atop columns flanking the cathedral's facade says it all: The church was built and paid for not by the pope but by the people and the republic of Siena.

This 13th-century Gothic cathedral, with its striped bell tower—Siena's ultimate tribute to the Virgin Mary—is heaped with statues, plastered with frescoes, and paved with art.

The current structure dates back to 1215, with the major decoration done during Siena's heyday (1250-1350). The lower story, by Giovanni Pisano (who worked from 1284 to 1297), features remnants of the fading Romanesque style (round arches over the doors),

corners, where many a rider has bitten the dust.

Picture the scene: Ten snorting horses and their nervous riders line up near the pharmacy (on the west side of the square) to await the starting signal. Then they race like crazy while spectators wave the scarves of their neighborhoods.

Every possible vantage point and perch is packed with people straining to see the action. One lap around the course is about a quarter of a mile; three laps make a full circuit. In this no-holds-barred race—which lasts just over a minute—a horse can win even without its rider (jockeys ride precariously without saddles and often fall off the horses' sweaty backs).

When the winner crosses the line, 1/17th of Siena—the prevailing neighborhood—goes berserk. Winners receive a *palio* (banner), typically painted by a local artist and always featuring the Virgin Mary (the race is dedicated to her). But the true prizes are proving that your *contrada* is *numero uno,* and mocking your losing rivals.

All over town, sketches and posters depict the Palio. This is not some folkloric event—it's a real medieval moment. If you're packed onto the square with 15,000 people, all hungry for victory, you may not see much, but you'll feel it. Bleacher and balcony seats are expensive, but it's free to join the masses in the square. Go with an empty bladder as there are no WCs, and be prepared to surrender any sense of personal space.

While the actual Palio packs the city, you can more easily see the horse-race trials—called *prove*—on any of the three days before the main event (usually at 9:00 and after 19:00, bleacher seats may be available). Good sources for more information include IlPalio.org and ComitatoAmiciDelPalio.it.

topped with the pointed arches of the new Gothic style that was seeping in from France. The upper half, in full-blown frilly Gothic, was designed and built a century later.

The six-story bell tower (c. 1315) looks even taller, thanks to an optical illusion: The white marble stripes get narrower toward the top, making the upper part seem farther away.

The interior is a Renaissance riot of striped columns, remarkably intricate inlaid-marble floors, a Michelangelo statue, evocative Bernini sculptures, and the amazing Piccolomini Library. (If you want to enter now, you'll need a ticket from the office in the piazza corner, to the right; for a self-guided tour of the interior, see page 620.)

Facing the cathedral is Santa Maria della Scala, a huge building that housed pilgrims and, until the 1990s, was used as a hospital. Its labyrinthine 12th-century cellars—carved from sandstone and finished with brick—go down several floors and, during medieval times, stored supplies for the hospital upstairs. Today, the exhibit-filled hospital and cellars can be a welcome refuge from the hot streets (for a self-guided tour, see page 626).

• *Walk along the right side of the church toward its rear end. This is part of what was once intended to be an extension of the Duomo.*

## ❻ The Unfinished Church

Grand as Siena's cathedral is, it's actually the rump of a failed vision. After rival republic Florence began its grand cathedral (1296), proud Siena planned to build an even bigger one, the biggest in all Christendom.

To the right, find the unfinished wall with see-through windows (circa 1330). From here you can envision the audacity of this vision.

Picture it: Today's cathedral would have been just a transept. Worshippers would have entered the church from the far end of the piazza through the unfinished wall. (Look way up at the highest part of the wall. That viewpoint is accessible from inside the Duomo Museum.) Some of the nave's green-and-white-striped columns were built, but the space between them is now partially filled in with brick. White stones in the pavement mark where a row of pillars would have been.

But this grand vision underestimated the complexity of constructing such a building without enough land. That, coupled with the devastating effects of the 1348 plague, killed the city's ability and will to finish the project. Many Sienese saw the Black Death as a sign from God, punishing them for their pride. They canceled their plans and humbly faded into the background of Tuscan history.

• *Take note of the Duomo Museum, housing the church's art (see page 623). To continue our walk, exit the piazza through the doorway in a wall, heading to the back end of the church. After a few steps, pause at the top of the marble stairs leading down.*

## ❼ Supporting an Oversized Church

From here you can see how the church sticks out, high above the lower street level. Because there wasn't enough flat ground, builders propped up the overhanging edge with the church's subterranean features—the Crypt and Baptistery. (Both the Baptistery and the Crypt are worth entering; see page 625.)

• *Descend the stairs, nicknamed "The Steps of St. Catherine," as she would have climbed them each day on her walk from home to the hospital where she worked (Santa Maria della Scala). Below the Baptistery, jog right, then left, through a tunnel down Via di Diacceto. Just ahead, pause on the bridge (originally a drawbridge) to enjoy a beautiful view (to the left) of the towering brick Dominican church in the distance. Then continue straight up the lane until you reach the next big square.*

SIENA

## ❽ Piazza Indipendenza

This square celebrates the creation of a unified Italy (1860) with a 19th-century loggia sporting busts of the first two Italian kings. Stacking history on history, the neo-Renaissance loggia is backed by a Gothic palace and an older medieval tower.

• *Head right downhill one block (on Via delle Terme), back to the grand Via di Città, and take a few steps to the left to see another, fancier loggia.*

## ❾ Loggia della Mercanzia

This Gothic-Renaissance loggia was built about 1420 as a kind of headquarters for the union of merchants. Siena's nobility purchased the loggia, and eventually it be-came the clubhouse of the local elites. To this day, it's a private, ritzy, and notoriously out-of-step-with-the-times men's club. The "Gli Uniti" above the door is a "let's stick together" declaration.

• *Next to the loggia, steep steps lead down to Il Campo, but we'll go left and uphill on Via Banchi di Sopra. Pause at the intersection of...*

## ❿ Banchi di Sopra and Banchi di Sotto

These main drags are named "upper row of banks" and "lower row of banks." They were once lined with market tables *(banchi)*, and vendors paid rent to the city for a table's position along the street. If the owner of a *banco* neglected to pay up, thugs came along and literally broke *(rotto)* his table. It is from this practice—*banco rotto*, broken table—that we get the English word "bankrupt."

In medieval times, these streets were part of the Via Francigena, the main thoroughfare (busy with pilgrims, merchants, and crusaders) linking Rome with northern Europe. Today, strollers—out each evening for their *passeggiata*—fill Via Banchi di Sopra. Join the crowd, strolling past Siena's finest shops.

A block or so farther up the street, Piazza Tolomei faces the imposing Tolomei family palace (now an imposing bank). This is a center for the Owl *contrada*. The column in the square, topped by the she-wolf, marks another of Siena's three hills.

• *Continue on Banchi di Sopra to Piazza Salimbeni; this gets my vote for Siena's finest stretch of palaces.*

### ⓫ Piazza Salimbeni

The next square, Piazza Salimbeni, is dominated by Monte dei Paschi, the head office of a bank founded in 1472. It's amazing to think this bank has been in business on this square for over 500 years. Originally Monte dei Paschi was a kind of community bank for common people. The statue in the center of the square honors Sallustio Antonio Bandini, a reformer who helped develop a system that let people secure firm title to their land.

Directly across from Piazza Salimbeni, the steep little lane called Costa dell'Incrociata leads straight (down and then up) to the Basilica of San Domenico (it's worth the hike; see page 627). Also nearby (behind the cute green newsstand) is the most elegant grocery store in town, Consorzio Agrario di Siena (see page 637).

• *With this walk under your belt, you've got the lay of the land. The city is ready for further exploration—the sights associated with City Hall and the Duomo are all just a few minutes away. Enjoy delving deeper into Siena.*

## Sights in Siena

### IL CAMPO AND NEARBY

The gorgeous red-brick square known as Il Campo—worth ▲▲▲—is the best in Italy (for more on the square itself, see page 608). It's also home to City Hall (with the Civic Museum and City Tower) and other sights.

### ▲▲City Hall (Palazzo Pubblico) and Civic Museum (Museo Civico)

Siena's fine Gothic City Hall is still the seat of city government. With its proud tower, this building symbolizes a republic independent from the pope and the Holy Roman Emperor. It also represents a rising secular society, one that appeared first in Tuscany in late medieval times, then spread throughout Europe as humanism took hold during the Renaissance.

City Hall has a fine and manageable museum on its top floor. You'll see the large assembly hall where democracy was forged, adorned with some of Siena's most historic frescoes. There's memorabilia from the birth of the nation of Italy.

The highlight is a room of medieval-era frescoes depicting fascinating examples of governance—good and bad. Strolling the halls, you'll get a glimpse into the city-as-utopia, when this proud town understandably considered itself the vanguard of Western civilization.

**Cost and Hours:** Museum-€10, €14 combo-ticket with Santa Maria della Scala, €15 combo-ticket with City Tower, €20 combo-ticket includes City Tower and Santa Maria della Scala, ticket office is straight ahead as you enter City Hall courtyard; open daily 10:00-19:00, Nov-mid-March until 18:00, last entry 45 minutes before closing; videoguide-€5 in bookshop, tel. 0577-292-232, www.comune.siena.it.

**Visiting the Museum:** Start in the Sala del Risorgimento, with dramatic scenes of the 19th-century unification of Italy. Make your way to the chapel, where the city's governors and bureaucrats prayed, then enter the Sala del Mappamondo.

On one end of the room is the beautiful *Maestà* (*Enthroned Virgin,* 1315), by Siena's great Simone Martini (c. 1280-1344). This is a groundbreaking work. It's Siena's first fresco showing a Madonna not in a faraway, gold-leaf heaven, but under the blue sky of a real space that we inhabit.

On the opposite end of the room is the famous *Equestrian Portrait of Guidoriccio da Fogliano* (1330; traditionally attributed to Simone Martini), which depicts a mercenary commander surveying the siege fort, with the catapult that helped Siena win.

Next is the Sala della Pace, where the Council of Nine, who ruled Siena from 1287 to 1355, met. To remind them of their responsibility to rule wisely, they were surrounded by a fascinating fresco series showing the *Effects of Good and Bad Government,* by Ambrogio Lorenzetti (1337-1340).

Notice the better-preserved fresco (on the long wall to the right) depicting the beneficial effects of good government. Compare the whistle-while-you-work happiness against the crime, devastation, and societal mayhem of a community ruled by politicians with more typical values.

You can cap your visit by climbing the **stairs to a grand view** of the city and its surroundings. (For a less impressive view, you could skip the stairs and simply peek behind the curtains in the Sala della Pace.)

## ▲City Tower (Torre del Mangia)

The tower's nearly 400 steps get pretty skinny at the top, but the reward is one of Italy's best views. For more on the tower, see page 609.

**Cost and Hours:** €10, €15 combo-ticket with Civic Mu-

seum, €20 combo-ticket with Civic Museum and Santa Maria della Scala, daily 10:00-19:00, mid-Oct-Feb until 16:00, last entry 45 minutes before closing, closed in rain, free and mandatory bag check.

**Crowd Alert:** Admission is limited to 50 people at a time. Wait at the bottom of the stairs for the green *Avanti* light. Try to avoid midday crowds (up to an hour wait at peak times).

## ▲Pinacoteca

If you're into medieval art, you'll likely find this quiet, uncrowded, colorful museum delightful. The museum (officially the Pinacoteca Nazionale di Siena) walks you through Siena's art chronologically, from the 12th through the 16th century, when a revolution in realism was percolating in Tuscany.

**Cost and Hours:** €4, Tue-Sat 8:15-19:15, Sun-Mon 9:00-13:00. From Il Campo, walk out Via di Città and go left on Via San Pietro to #29; tel. 0577-281-161, www.pinacotecanazionale.siena.it.

**Visiting the Museum:** In general, the collection lets you follow the evolution of painting styles from Byzantine to Gothic, then to International Gothic, and finally to Renaissance.

Long after Florentine art went realistic, the Sienese embraced a timeless, otherworldly style glittering with lots of gold. But Sienese art features more than just paintings. In this city of proud craftsmen, the gilding and carpentry of the frames almost compete with the actual paintings. The exquisite attention to detail gives a glimpse into the wealth of the 13th and 14th centuries, Siena's Golden Age. The woven silk and gold clothing you'll see was worn by the very people who once walked these halls, when this was a private mansion (appreciate the colonnaded courtyard).

The core of the collection is on the second floor, in Rooms 1-19. Works by Duccio di Buoninsegna (who created the *Maestà* in the Duomo Museum) feature groundbreaking innovations that are subtle: less gold-leaf background, fewer gold creases in robes, translucent garments, inlaid-marble thrones, and a more human Mary and Jesus. Notice that the Madonna-and-Bambino pose is eerily identical in each version.

Works by Duccio's one-time assistant, Simone Martini, including his *St. Augustine of Siena,* show the saint's life in realistic Sienese streets, buildings, and landscapes. In each panel, the saint pops out at the oddest (difficult to draw) angles to save the day.

(Simone Martini also did the *Maestà* and possibly the Guidoriccio frescoes in the Civic Museum.)

Also look for religious works by the hometown Lorenzetti brothers (Ambrogio is best known for the secular masterpiece, the *Effects of Good and Bad Government,* in the Civic Museum). Two famous small wooden panels, *Città sul Mare (City by the Sea)* and *Castello in Riva al Lago (Castle on the Lakeshore),* feature a strange, medieval-landscape Cubism. Notice the weird, melancholy light that captures the sense of the Dark Ages.

Several colorful rooms on the first floor are dedicated to Domenico Beccafumi (1486-1551), who designed many of the Duomo's inlaid pavement panels (including *Slaughter of the Innocents*). With strong bodies, twisting poses, and dramatic gestures, Beccafumi's works epitomize the Mannerist style.

## DUOMO AND RELATED SIGHTS

Siena's monumental cathedral complex encompasses the Duomo, Duomo Museum (and its panoramic terrace), Baptistery, and Crypt. While it's possible to enter the Duomo itself with an individual ticket, admission to the related sights is possible only with a combo-ticket, the **Opa Si Pass** (valid for 72 hours, includes Duomo admission). The price varies with the time of year: March-mid-Aug-€13, mid-Aug-Oct-€15, Nov-Feb-€8 (admission to the Duomo itself is free in winter).

The **Porta del Cielo** (Heaven's Gate) Pass covers everything in the Opa Si Pass but adds an escorted visit up into the cathedral dome and onto the cathedral's rooftop (€20, available March-Dec). To include Santa Maria della Scala as well, buy the **Acropoli Pass** (€13-20, depending on time of year).

**Buying Passes and Tickets:** Individual Duomo tickets and the Opa Si Pass can be bought online (www.operaduomo.siena.it) or from the on-site ticket office (facing the cathedral entry, the ticket office, with a fine bookstore, is behind you to the right). The Porta del Cielo and Acropoli passes are sold at the ticket office (not available online), but because of space limitations for the cathedral roof visit, it's smart to reserve these in advance by phone (tel. 0577-286-300) or email (opasiena@operalaboratori.com).

Note that Santa Maria della Scala, directly opposite the Duomo, has its own ticketing scheme (see details later) but shares its ticket office with that for the Duomo (in the corner of Piazza del Duomo).

### ▲▲▲Duomo (Duomo di Siena)

Siena's 13th-century cathedral and striped bell tower are one of the most illustrious examples of Romanesque-Gothic style in Italy. This ornate but surprisingly secular shrine to the Virgin Mary is

slathered with colorful art inside and out, from inlaid-marble floors to stained-glass windows. The cathedral's interior showcases the work of the greatest sculptors of successive eras—Pisano, Donatello, Michelangelo, and Bernini—and the Piccolomini Library features a series of 15th-century frescoes chronicling the adventures of Siena's philanderer-turned-pope, Aeneas Piccolomini.

**Cost:** €6, €9 mid-Aug-Oct and on Sundays when marble floors are on display, includes cathedral and Piccolomini Library, covered by Duomo combo-ticket; admission to the Duomo is free Nov-Feb.

**Hours:** Mon-Sat 10:30-19:00, Sun 13:30-18:00, Nov-Feb closes daily at 17:30. Tel. 0577-286-300, www.operaduomo.siena.it.

**Avoiding Lines:** If there's a long line to get into the cathedral (or even to buy a ticket for it), use ticket office desk 1 or 2 to pay €1 extra for a reserved ticket that lets you use the short "fast entry" line at the church. Another good alternative is to purchase tickets online in advance.

**Tours:** The commentary on the available **videoguide** (€6 church only, €8 for all combo-ticket sights) is informative but dry; I'd stick with this chapter.

**Going to Church:** Worshippers attending Mass can enter the church free; use the entrance to the right of the main one (Mon-Sat at 9:00 and 10:00, Sun at 8:00, 11:00, 12:15, and 18:30, no Mass mid-Aug-Oct).

**Dress Code:** Modest dress is required, but stylish paper ponchos are provided for the inappropriately clothed.

**Cathedral Roof Visit:** To make a 30-minute escorted (but not guided) visit to the dome's cupola and roof, buy the Porto del Cielo (Heaven's Gate) combo-ticket (reservation recommended; see "Buying Passes and Tickets," earlier; escorted visits go each half-hour, March-Dec Mon-Sat from 10:30-19:00, Sun 13:30-17:30—but from 9:30 on some Sun).

**❷ Self-Guided Tour:** Grab a spot on a stone bench opposite the entry to take in this architectural festival of green, white, pink, and gold. The Duomo sits atop Siena's highest point, with one of the most extravagant facades in all of Europe. Like a medieval altarpiece, the facade is divided into sections, each frame filled with patriarchs and prophets, studded with roaring gargoyles, and topped with prickly pinnacles (for more about the facade, see page 612).

• *Step inside, putting yourself in the mindset of a pilgrim as you take in this trove of religious art.*

**Nave:** The heads of 171 popes—who reigned from the time of St. Peter to the 12th century—peer down from above, looking over the fine inlaid art on the floor. With a forest of striped columns, a coffered dome, a large stained-glass window at the far end (it's a copy—the original is viewable up close in the Duomo Museum), and an art gallery's worth of early Renaissance art, this is one busy interior. If you look closely at the popes, you'll see the same four faces repeated over and over.

For almost two centuries (1373-1547), 40 artists paved the marble floor with scenes from the Old Testament, allegories, and intricate patterns. The series starts near the entrance with historical allegories; the larger, more elaborate scenes surrounding the altar are mostly stories from the Old Testament. Many of the floor panels are roped off and covered to prevent further wear and tear. But from mid-August through October, the cathedral uncovers them and holds Mass in another church. The second pavement panel from the entrance depicts Siena as a she-wolf. The proud city of Siena is the center of the Italian universe, orbited by such lesser lights as Roma, Florentia (Florence), and Pisa.

The fourth pavement panel from the entrance is the Fortune Panel, with Lady Luck (lower right) arriving on earth, where she teeters back and forth on a ball and a tipsy boat. The lesson? Fortune is an unstable foundation for life. On the right wall hangs a dim **painting of St. Catherine** (fourth from entrance). Siena's homegrown saint had a vision in which she mystically married Christ.

• *On the opposite wall is a marble altarpiece decorated with statues.*

**Piccolomini Altar:** This was commissioned by the Sienese-born Pope Pius III (born Francesco Piccolomini) but was never used. The altar is most interesting for its statues: one by Michelangelo and three by his students. Michelangelo was originally contracted to do 15 statues, but another sculptor had started the marble blocks, and Michelangelo's heart was never in the project. He personally finished the figure of St. Paul (lower right, clearly more interesting than the bland, bored saints above him).

• *Now grab a seat under the dome. The dome sits on a 12-sided base, but its "coffered" ceiling is a painted illusion.*

**Duccio's Stained-Glass Rose Window:** At the far end of the church, high up above the altar, is the rose window. Made in 1288 and dedicated to the Virgin Mary, it's a kaleidoscope of colors and intricate designs. This is a copy of the original window (described on page 624).

• *Closer to you is a stone podium sitting atop columns. This is...*

**Pisano's Pulpit:** The octagonal Carrara marble pulpit (1268) rests on the backs of lions, symbols of Christianity triumphant. Like the lions, the Church eats its catch (devouring paganism) and nurses its cubs. The seven relief panels tell the life of Christ in rich detail. The pulpit is the work of Nicola Pisano (c. 1220-1278), the "Giotto of sculpture," whose revival of classical forms (columns, sarcophagus-like relief panels) signaled the coming Renaissance. His son Giovanni (c. 1240-1319) carved many of the panels, mixing his dad's classicism and realism with the decorative detail and curvy lines of French Gothic.

• *A few steps to the left of the pulpit (in the left transept), find a panel in the floor, the...*

**Slaughter of the Innocents Pavement Panel:** Herod (left), sitting enthroned amid Renaissance arches, orders the massacre of all babies to prevent the coming of the promised Messiah. It's a chaotic scene of angry soldiers, grieving mothers, and dead babies, reminding locals that a republic ruled by a tyrant will always experience misery.

• *Nearby in the left transept is a small chapel with a well-known statue.*

**Donatello's St. John the Baptist:** The rugged saint in his famous rags stands in a quiet chapel. Donatello, the aging Florentine sculptor whose style was now considered passé in Florence, came here to build bronze doors for the church (similar to Ghiberti's in Florence). Donatello didn't complete the door project, but he did finish this bronze statue (1457).

• *Cross the church. Directly opposite find the Chigi Chapel (with its iron-work entrance), also known as the...*

**Chapel of the *Madonna del Voto:*** To understand why Bernini is considered the greatest Baroque sculptor, step into this sumptuous chapel (designed in the early 1660s for Fabio Chigi, a.k.a. Pope Alexander VII). Move up to the altar and look back at the **two Bernini statues:** Mary Magdalene in a state of spiritual ecstasy and St. Jerome playing the crucifix like a violinist lost in heavenly music.

The painting over the altar is the *Madonna del Voto,* a Madonna and Child adorned with a real crown of gold and jewels (painted by a Sienese master in the mid-13th century). In typical medieval fashion, the scene is set in the golden light of heaven. Mary has the almond eyes, long fingers, and golden folds in her robe that are found in orthodox icons of the time. Still, this Mary tilts her head and looks out sympathetically, ready to listen to the prayers of the faithful. This is the Mary to whom the Palio is dedicated, dear to the hearts of the Sienese.

In thanks, they give **offerings** of silver hearts and medallions, many of which now hang on the walls to the right and left as you exit the chapel.

• *Cross back to the other side of the church. Next to the altar, look for the door to the...*

**Piccolomini Library:** Brilliantly frescoed, the library captures the exuberant, optimistic spirit of the 1400s, when humanism and the Renaissance were born. The never-restored frescoes look nearly as vivid now as the day they were finished 550 years ago. The painter Pinturicchio (c. 1454-1513) was hired to celebrate the life of one of Siena's hometown boys—a man many call "the first humanist," Aeneas Piccolomini (1405-1464), who became Pope Pius II. Each of the 10 scenes is framed with an arch, as if Pinturicchio were opening a window onto the spacious 3-D world we inhabit.

SIENA

The library also contains intricately decorated, illuminated music scores and a statue (a Roman copy of a Greek original) of the Three Graces, who almost seem to dance to the beat. The oddly huge sheepskin sheets of music are from the days before individual hymnals—they had to be big so that many singers could read the music from a distance. Appreciate the fine painted decorations on the music—the gold-leaf highlights, the blue tones from expensive ultramarine (made from precious lapis lazuli), and the miniature figures. All of this exquisite detail was lovingly crafted by Benedictine monks for the glory of God.

• *Our tour is finished. But to truly appreciate the grandeur of the Duomo, exit the church and make a U-turn to the left, walking alongside the church to Piazza Jacopo della Quercia. Had the massive church Siena envisioned been built, the nave would be where the piazza is today. Look through the unfinished entrance facade, note blue sky where the stained-glass windows would have been, and ponder the struggles, triumphs, and failures of the human spirit. (For more on the unfinished church, see page 614.)*

## ▲▲Duomo Museum
### (Museo dell'Opera e Panorama)

Siena's most enjoyable museum, housing the cathedral's art, is located in a corner of the Duomo's grand but unfinished extension (to the right as you face the main facade). Stand eye-to-eye with the saints and angels who once languished, unknown, in the church's upper reaches (where copies are found today).

**Cost and Hours:** Covered by Duomo combo-ticket, daily 10:00-19:00, Nov-Feb 10:30-17:30, videoguide-€4 (€6/2 people) but you'll do fine with just the commentary in this listing, tel. 0577-286-300, www.operaduomo.siena.it.

**SIENA**

**⊙ Self-Guided Tour:** Start on the ground floor, which houses the church's original statues, mainly from the facade and exterior. After descending a few steps, turn your back on the hall of statues and wrought-iron gate. You're now face-to-face with **Donatello's Madonna and Child** (c. 1458). In this round, carved relief, a slender and tender Mary gazes down at her chubby-cheeked baby. Her sad eyes say that she knows the eventual fate of her son.

At the opposite end of the room is **Duccio's Stained-Glass Window** (c. 1287-1290). This splendid original window was installed for centuries above and behind the Duomo's altar. Now the church has a copy, and art lovers can enjoy a close-up look at this masterpiece. The rose window—20 feet across—is dedicated (like the church and the city itself) to the Virgin Mary.

The work is by Siena's most famous artist, Duccio di Buoninsegna (c. 1255-1319). Duccio combined elements from rigid Byzantine icons (Mary's almond-shaped bubble, called a *mandorla*, and the full-frontal saints that flank her) with a budding sense of 3-D realism (the throne turned at a three-quarter angle to simulate depth, with angels behind).

Upstairs awaits a private audience with **Duccio's *Maestà*** (*Enthroned Virgin*, 1311). The panels in this room were once part of the Duomo's main altarpiece. Grab a seat and study one of the great pieces of medieval art. Although the former altarpiece was disassembled (and the frame was lost), most of the pieces are displayed here, with the front side (*Maestà*, with Mary and saints; pronounced my-STAH) at one end of the room and the back side (26 Passion panels) at the other.

The painting was revolutionary for the time in its sheer size and opulence, and in Duccio's budding realism, which broke standard conventions. Duccio, at the height of his powers, used every innovative arrow in his quiver. He replaced the standard gold-leaf background (symbolizing heaven) with a gold, intricately patterned curtain draped over the throne. Mary's blue robe opens to reveal her body, and the curve of her knee suggests real anatomy beneath the robe. Baby Jesus wears a delicately transparent garment. Their faces are modeled with light—a patchwork of bright flesh and shadowy valleys, as if lit from the left (a technique Duccio likely learned from his contemporary, Giotto, during a visit to Florence).

**The Passion of Christ:** The flip side of the altarpiece featured these 26 smaller panels showing colorful scenes from the Passion of Christ.

• *Our museum tour is done, but the finale of your visit is yet to come.*

*Eventually you'll climb down the steps and then up about 40 tight and claustrophobic spiral stairs to the first viewpoint. You can continue up another 100 steps of a similar spiral staircase to reach the very top.*

**Panorama del Facciatone:** Standing on the wall from this high point in the city, you're rewarded with a stunning view of Siena...and an interesting

perspective. Look toward the Duomo and remember this: To outdo Florence, Siena had planned to enlarge this cathedral by turning it into a transept and constructing an enormous nave. You're standing on top of what would have been the new entrance facade. Columns would have stood where you see the rows of white stones in the pavement below. Had the church been completed, you'd be looking straight down the nave toward the altar.

## ▲Baptistery of San Giovanni (Battistero di San Giovanni)

This richly adorned and quietly tucked-away cave of art is worth a look for its cool tranquility and exquisite art, including an ornately painted vaulted ceiling. The highlight is the baptismal font created in the 1420s by a host of early Renaissance all-stars. Made of marble, bronze, and enamel, the overall design was by Jacopo ("Fountain of Joy") della Quercia. On the base, the first bronze panel you encounter was done by Lorenzo ("Gates of Paradise") Ghiberti. To the right, the tiny bronze statues of Lady Faith and (farther right) the Angel of Hope, were done by the great Donatello. Also on the right side, Donatello made the bronze panel depicting John the Baptist's severed head being brought in on a platter, set in a 3-D banquet hall of receding arches. With this font, we're witnessing the start of the Renaissance.

**Cost and Hours:** Covered by Duomo combo-ticket, daily 10:30-19:00, Nov-Feb until 17:30, located on the back end of the Duomo.

## Crypt (Cripta)

The cathedral "crypt" is archaeologically important. The site of a small 12th-century Romanesque church, it was filled in with dirt a century after its creation to provide a foundation for the huge church that sits atop it today. Recently excavated (with modern metal supports from the 1990s), the several rediscovered rooms show off what are likely the oldest frescoes in town (well-described in English).

**Cost and Hours:** Covered by Duomo combo-ticket, daily

10:30-19:00, Nov-Feb until 17:30, located on the back end of the Duomo.

## Other Cathedral-Area Sights
### ▲Santa Maria della Scala

This museum, opposite the Duomo, operated for centuries as a hospital, foundling home (orphanage), and pilgrim lodging. Many of those activities are visible in the 15th-century frescoes of its main hall, the Pellegrinaio. Today, the hospital and its cellars are filled with fascinating exhibits (well-described in English).

**Cost and Hours:** €9, €14 combo-ticket with Civic Museum, €20 combo-ticket includes Civic Museum and City Tower, also covered by Acropoli Pass; daily 10:00-19:00, Thu until 22:00; closes earlier mid-Oct-mid-March; on Piazza del Duomo opposite the cathedral, ticket office at corner, tel. 0577-534-571, www.santamariadellascala.com.

**Visiting the Museum:** It's easy to get lost in this gigantic complex, so stay focused on the main attractions—the fancily frescoed Pellegrinaio Hall (ground floor) and the Fountain of Joy statues (one floor down). Then explore the lower floors.

From the entrance, turn right to enter what was, until the 1970s, Siena's main hospital. Enter the first room on your right, the **Sacristy,** which displays some powerful relics preserved in golden and silver reliquaries. You may see a drop of Jesus' blood in a vial *(sangue di Christo)*, a nail from Jesus' cross *(sacro chiodo)*, a piece of the Virgin's robe *(beata Vergine)*, and lots of saints' bones. They're encased in reliquaries that befit the preciousness of these sacred bits and saintly pieces. Some of the oldest are Byzantine reliquaries made of gold, silver, and precious stones.

Continue down the hallway (browsing exhibits in side rooms) until you reach the sumptuously frescoed **Pellegrinaio Hall.** This was a reception hall for visiting pilgrims before being converted into a hospital room, lined with beds for the sick. The frescoes (mostly by Domenico di Bartolo, c. 1440) show medieval Siena's innovative healthcare and social welfare system in action.

Now head downstairs, following signs to *Fonte Gaia*. These are the original statues from the Fountain of Joy (Fonte Gaia), Siena's landmark fountain on Il Campo. Jacopo della Quercia's early-15th-century masterpiece began crumbling, so in the 19th century, it was dismantled and plaster casts were made. (These casts formed the replica that graces Il Campo today.) Here you'll see the badly eroded original statues and relief panels, paired alongside their casts (labeled "calco").

In the second basement, under the groin vaults of the **Archaeological Museum** (Museo Archeologico), you're alone with piles of ancient stuff, from Bronze Age axes to Roman pottery. The highlight is a group of Etruscan artifacts excavated from tombs dating from the seventh to second century before Christ—the Etruscan heyday. You'll see their coins, figurines, and terra-cotta funeral urns for ashes (often designed with a standard body but a personalized head). The sarcophagi show the deceased reclining atop the lid, a reminder of their lofty social status.

## SAN DOMENICO AREA

### Basilica of San Domenico (Basilica di San Domenico)

This huge brick church is worth a quick look. Spacious and plain (except for the colorful flags of the city's 17 *contrade*), the Gothic interior fits the austere philosophy of the Domin-icans and invites medita-tion on the thoughts and deeds of St. Catherine. Halfway up the nave on the right, find a copper bust of St. Catherine (for four centuries it contained her skull), a small case housing her thumb, and her little flagellation whip. In the chapel, surrounded

by candles, you'll see Catherine's head (a clay mask around her skull with her actual teeth showing through) atop the altar.

**Cost and Hours:** Free, daily 7:00-18:30, shorter hours off-season, www.basilicacateriniana.com.

### Sanctuary of St. Catherine (Santuario di Santa Caterina)

Step into the cool and peaceful site of Catherine's home. Siena re-members its favorite hometown gal, a simple, unschooled but mystically devout soul who helped convince the pope to return from France to Rome. Pilgrims have visited this place since 1464, and architects and artists have greatly embellished what was probably once a humble home (her family worked as wool dyers). You'll see paintings throughout showing scenes from her life.

**Cost and Hours:** Free, daily 9:00-18:00 but chapel closes 12:30-15:00, a few downhill blocks toward the center from San Domenico—follow signs to *Santuario di Santa Caterina*—at Costa di Sant'Antonio 6, tel. 0577-288-175.

# Sleeping in Siena

Finding a room in Siena is tough during Easter or the Palio (July 2 and Aug 16). Many hotels won't take reservations until the end of May for the Palio, and even then they might require a four-night stay. If tranquility is important to you, ask for a room that's off the street, or consider staying outside the center.

**SIENA**

## BIGGER HOTELS NEAR IL CAMPO

**$$$$ Pensione Palazzo Ravizza** is elegant, friendly, and well-run, with 40 rooms and an aristocratic feel—fitting for what was once a noble's residence. Guests enjoy a peaceful garden set on a dramatic bluff, along with a Steinway in the upper lounge (RS%, family rooms, rooms in back overlook countryside, air-con, elevator, free parking makes this a good value for drivers, Via Piano dei Mantellini 34, tel. 0577-280-462, www.palazzoravizza.it, bureau@palazzoravizza.it).

**$$$ Hotel Duomo** is dated but well-located, with 20 spacious but overpriced rooms (many with Duomo views—request when booking), a picnic-friendly roof terrace, and a bizarre floor plan (family rooms, air-con, elevator with some stairs, expensive pay parking; Via di Stalloreggi 38, tel. 0577-289-088, www.hotelduomo.it, booking@hotelduomo.it, Alessandro).

## SIMPLE PLACES NEAR IL CAMPO

**$$ Piccolo Hotel Etruria,** with 20 simple rooms, is well-located, restful, and a fine value (RS%—use code "RSITA," family rooms, breakfast extra, air-con May-Oct only, elevator, at Via delle Donzelle 3, tel. 0577-288-088, www.hoteletruria.com, info@hoteletruria.com, friendly Leopoldo and Lucrezia). They also rent apartments nearby.

**$ Albergo Tre Donzelle,** run by the same family as Piccolo Hotel Etruria, has 20 homey rooms that may be the best value in the center. Il Campo, a block away, is your terrace (RS%—use code "RSITA," cheaper rooms with shared bath, family rooms, breakfast extra, fans, no elevator; with your back to the tower, head away from Il Campo toward 2 o'clock to Via delle Donzelle 5; tel. 0577-270-390, www.tredonzelle.com, info@tredonzelle.com, Leopoldo and Lucrezia).

**$ Hotel Cannon d'Oro,** a few blocks up Banchi di Sopra, is a bland, labyrinthine slumbermill renting 30 institutional, overpriced rooms (RS%, family rooms, fans, elevator with some stairs, Via dei Montanini 28, tel. 0577-44321, www.cannondoro.com, info@cannondoro.com; Maurizio, Tommaso, and Rodrigo).

## B&BS IN THE OLD CENTER

**$$ Antica Residenza Cicogna** is a seven-room guesthouse with a homey elegance and an ideal location. It's warmly run by the young and charming Elisa and her friend Ilaria, who set out biscotti, vin santo, and tea for their guests in the afternoon. With artfully frescoed walls and ceilings, this is remarkably genteel for the price (air-con, no elevator, Via delle Terme 76, tel. 0577-285-613, mobile 347-007-2888, www.anticaresidenzacicogna.it, info@anticaresidenzacicogna.it).

SIENA

**$$ Palazzo Masi B&B,** run by friendly Alizzardo and Daniela, is just below Il Campo. They rent six pleasant, spacious, antique-furnished rooms with shared common areas on the second and third floors of a restored 13th-century building (RS%—use code "RICK," cheaper rooms with shared bath, no elevator; breakfast provided on Il Campo; from City Hall, walk 50 yards down Casato di Sotto to #29; mobile 349-600-9155, www.palazzomasi.com, info@palazzomasi.it). The place is sometimes unstaffed, so confirm your arrival time in advance.

**$$ B&B Alle Due Porte** is a charming little establishment renting three big rooms with sweet furniture under medieval beams. The shared breakfast room is delightful. Manager Egisto is a phone call and 10-minute scooter ride away (air-con, Via di Stalloreggi 51, mobile 368-352-3530, www.sienatur.it, soldatini@interfree.it).

**$$ Siena Gallery B&B,** run by kindhearted Elisabetta and Fabio, is tucked onto the fourth floor of a relatively modern building, offering four contemporary yet simple rooms (air-con, elevator, Via Banchi di Sopra 31, enter at Galleria Odeon—look for green pharmacy sign, mobile 334-3997-8694, www.sienagallery.it, info@sienagallery.it).

**$$ I Terzi di Siena,** run by the same family as Siena Gallery B&B, houses nine rooms in an 11th-century building. It's absent an elevator but full of humble charm and noteworthy views (air-con, cheaper rooms with shared bath, apartments available; Via dei Termini 13, mobile 339-6699-143, www.terzidisiena.it, info@terzidisiena.it).

**$$ B&B Siena in Centro** is a clearinghouse managing 15 rooms and 5 apartments. Their handy office functions as a reception area for picking up keys. The rooms are generally spacious, quiet, and comfortable (RS%, some with air-con and others with fans, family rooms, reception open 9:00-13:30 & 15:00-22:00, Via di Stalloreggi 16, tel. 0577-48111, mobile 331-281-0136 or 347-465-9753, www.bbsienaincentro.com, info@bbsienaincentro.com, Gioia or Michela).

**$ Le Camerine di Silvia,** a romantic hideaway perched near a sweeping, grassy olive grove, rents five simple rooms in a converted

16th-century building. A small terrace with fruit trees and a private hedged garden lends itself to contemplation (cash only, view room on request, no breakfast, fans, free parking nearby, Via Ettore Bastianini 1, just below recommended Pensione Palazzo Ravizza, mobile 338-761-5052 or 339-123-7687, www.lecamerinedisilvia.com, info@lecamerinedisilvia.com, Conti family).

**SIENA**

## NEAR BASILICA OF SAN DOMENICO

**$$$ Hotel Chiusarelli,** with mix of 48 classic and modern rooms in a beautiful, frescoed Neoclassical villa, is just outside the medieval town center on a busy street—ask for a quieter room in back when you reserve (RS%, family rooms, air-con, limited free parking, across from San Domenico at Viale Curtatone 15, tel. 0577-280-562, www.chiusarelli.com, info@chiusarelli.com).

**$$$ Hotel Villa Elda** rents 11 bright and light rooms in a recently renovated villa. It's classy, stately, and run with a stylish charm (view rooms extra, air-con, no elevator, garden and view terrace, closed Nov-March, Viale Ventiquattro Maggio 10, tel. 0577-247-927, www.villaeldasiena.it, info@villaeldasiena.it).

**$$ Albergo Bernini** makes you part of a Sienese family in a modest, clean home with 10 traditional rooms. Giovanni, charming wife Daniela, and their daughters welcome you to their spectacular view terrace—a great spot for a glass of wine or a picnic (cheaper rooms with shared bath, family rooms, breakfast extra, fans, on the main Il Campo-San Domenico drag at Via della Sapienza 15, tel. 0577-289-047, www.albergobernini.com, info@albergobernini.com).

**$ Alma Domus** is a church-run hotel and a great value, featuring 28 tidy, streamlined rooms with quaint balconies, some fantastic views (ask for a room *con vista*), stately public rooms, and a pleasant atmosphere (but nearby church bells can be a drawback). Consider upgrading to a snazzy superior room for slightly more (family rooms, air-con, elevator; from San Domenico, walk downhill toward the view with the church on your right, turn left down Via Camporegio, make a U-turn down the brick steps to Via Camporegio 37; tel. 0577-44177, www.hotelalmadomus.it, info@hotelalmadomus.it, Louis).

## FARTHER FROM THE CENTER

**$$ Hotel Minerva** is your big, impersonal, plain, efficient option. It's got zero personality and mediocre views, but offers predictable business-class comfort in its 56 rooms. It works best for those with cars—its pay parking is reasonable, and it's only a 15-minute walk from the action (RS%, view rooms extra, air-con, elevator, just inside Porta Ovile at the north end of town at Via Garibaldi 72, tel. 0577-284-474, www.albergominerva.it, info@albergominerva.it).

# Eating in Siena

Sienese restaurants are a great value by Florentine and Venetian standards. For pasta, a good option is *pici* (PEE-chee), a thick Sienese spaghetti that seems to be at the top of every menu. Reservations are generally wise for dinner.

## IN THE OLD TOWN
### Fine Dining

**$$$$ Osteria le Logge** caters to a fancy crowd and offers pricey Tuscan favorites with a gourmet twist, made with seasonal local ingredients. Inside you'll enjoy a gorgeous living-room setting (books, wood, and wine bottles), and outside there's fine seating on a pedestrian street. I find dining inside on the ground floor most romantic (Mon-Sat 12:00-15:00 & 19:00-23:00, closed Sun, two blocks off Il Campo at Via del Porrione 33, tel. 0577-48013, www. osterialelogge.it, Mirko).

**$$$$ Ristorante Tar-Tufo** offers a spacious setting, a gourmet presentation, a twist of pretense, and contemporary and innovative Tuscan cuisine—much of it garnished with truffles. While you could eat on their terrace with a view of the countryside, I prefer dining inside under dramatic arches (Thu-Tue 12:00-14:30 & 19:00-22:30, closed Wed, a 10-minute walk behind Il Campo at Via del Sole 6, tel. 0577-284-031, www.tar-tufo.com, chef Pino).

**$$$ Compagnia dei Vinattieri,** a good bet for wine lovers, serves Tuscan dishes with a creative touch. In this elegant space, you can enjoy a romantic meal under graceful brick arches. The menu is small and accessible. Owner Marco is happy to take you down to the marvelous wine cellar (beef is big here, leave this book on the table for a complimentary *aperitivo* or *digestivo*, daily 12:30-15:00 & 19:30-23:00, Via delle Terme 79, tel. 0577-236-568, www. vinattieri.net).

**$$ Osteria la Sosta di Violante,** beyond the tourist zone, is the best fine-dining value of my listings. You'll share this dreamy little spot with smart locals. For 20 years chefs Duccio and Enrico have offered gourmet food with no pretense—they make sure diners feel right at home. Order with a sense of adventure. Diners with this book cap their meal with complimentary vin santo and *cantucci* (great indoor and outdoor seating, Mon-Sat 12:30-15:00 & 19:00-23:00, closed Sun, walk down Via Banchi di Sotto to Via Pantaneto 115, tel. 0577-43774).

## Traditional and Rustic Places

**$$ Trattoria Papei** is a sprawling place with festive outdoor seating under a big tent and a high-energy interior. It has a casual, rollicking family atmosphere and friendly servers dishing out gen-

**SIENA**

# Siena Hotels & Restaurants

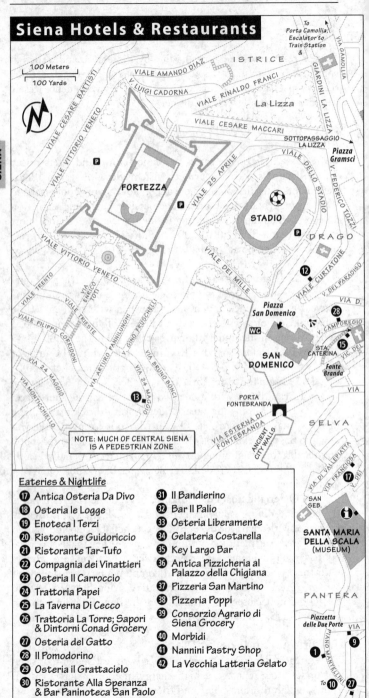

100 Meters
100 Yards

NOTE: MUCH OF CENTRAL SIENA IS A PEDESTRIAN ZONE

## Eateries & Nightlife

17 Antica Osteria Da Divo
18 Osteria le Logge
19 Enoteca I Terzi
20 Ristorante Guidoriccio
21 Ristorante Tar-Tufo
22 Compagnia dei Vinattieri
23 Osteria Il Carroccio
24 Trattoria Papei
25 La Taverna Di Cecco
26 Trattoria La Torre; Sapori & Dintorni Conad Grocery
27 Osteria del Gatto
28 Il Pomodorino
29 Osteria il Grattacielo
30 Ristorante Alla Speranza & Bar Paninoteca San Paolo

31 Il Bandierino
32 Bar Il Palio
33 Osteria Liberamente
34 Gelateria Costarella
35 Key Largo Bar
36 Antica Pizzicheria al Palazzo della Chigiana
37 Pizzeria San Martino
38 Pizzeria Poppi
39 Consorzio Agrario di Siena Grocery
40 Morbidi
41 Nannini Pastry Shop
42 La Vecchia Latteria Gelato

### Accommodations

1. Pensione Palazzo Ravizza
2. Hotel Duomo
3. Piccolo Hotel Etruria
4. Albergo Tre Donzelle
5. Hotel Cannon d'Oro
6. To Casa Laura
7. Antica Residenza Cicogna
8. Palazzo Masi B&B
9. B&B Alle Due Porte
10. To Le Camerine di Silvia
11. B&B Siena in Centro
12. Hotel Chiusarelli
13. Hotel Villa Elda
14. Albergo Bernini
15. Alma Domus
16. Hotel Minerva

SIENA

erous portions of rib-stickin' Tuscan specialties and grilled meats (daily 12:00-15:00 & 19:00-22:30, on the market square behind City Hall at Piazza del Mercato 6, tel. 0577-280-894; Amedeo and Eduardo).

**$$ Osteria il Carroccio,** artsy and convivial, seats guests in a characteristic but tight dining room. They serve traditional "slow food" with innovative flair at affordable prices. To maintain their quality, they have only 35 seats and don't turn the tables—reserve ahead (€30 tasting *menu*—minimum two people, Thu-Tue 12:15-15:00 & 19:15-22:00, closed Wed, Casato di Sotto 32, tel. 0577-41165). They give complimentary vin santo and *cantucci* with this book.

**$$ La Taverna di Cecco** is a cozy, comfortable little eatery on a quiet back lane where grandma Olga cooks, and earnest Luca and Gianni serve. The elegant place settings feel like nana's finest, and the few tables outside are inviting as well. They offer a simple menu of traditional Sienese favorites along with hearty salads (daily 12:00-16:00 & 19:00-23:00, Via Cecco Angiolieri 19, tel. 0577-288-518).

**$$ Trattoria la Torre** is an unfussy family-run *casalinga* (home-cooking) place, popular for its homemade pasta. Its open kitchen and 10 tables are packed under one medieval brick arch. Service is brisk and casual—the only menu is posted outside because they like to explain your options individually. Even though located just under the City Tower, it feels more like a local hangout than a tourist trap (Fri-Wed 12:00-15:00 & 19:00-22:00, closed Thu, steps below Il Campo at Via di Salicotto 7, tel. 0577-287-548, Marco).

**$ Osteria del Gatto** is a classic neighborhood fixture thriving with townspeople and powered by a passion for good Sienese cuisine. Friendly Marco Coradeschi and his staff cook and serve daily specials with attitude. As it's so small and popular, it can get loud (Mon-Sat 12:30-15:00 & 19:30-22:00, closed Sun, 10-minute walk from Il Campo at Via San Marco 8, look for *La Vecchia Osteria* sign, tel. 0577-287-133).

**$ Osteria il Grattacielo** is a funky hole-in-the-wall with a tight and homey interior and three tables under a tunnel-like arch outside, perfect for a cheap, hearty, memorable yet no-frills meal. Luca, who's clearly found his niche in life, has no menu and just one solid house wine. You'll eat what he's cooking. Lunch is a mixed plate from the bar (be bold and point) or pasta (€10, includes wine). Dinner is three courses—antipasto bar, pasta, and a *secondi*—€15 for Rick Steves readers; €3 extra adds a vin santo and cookies finale (daily 12:00-15:00 & 19:30-21:30, Via dei Pontani 8, mobile 331-742-2835).

# Gelato, Tea, and Cocktails in Siena

Evenings are a wonderful time to be out and about in Siena, after the tour groups have left for the day. Join the evening *passeggiata* (peak strolling time is 19:00) along Banchi di Sopra with gelato in hand.

**Gelato:** There's always a good gelato place nearby (all open daily, generally until late): The gourmet chain Venchi is reliably tasty (across from the Loggia della Mercanzia at Via di Città 28). A good locally owned option is La Vecchia Latteria (a 5-minute walk from Il Campo at Via di San Pietro 10). And, for gelato on Il Campo, drop by the *bar gelateria* Il Camerlengo (at #6, just to the right of City Hall, with a handy WC).

**Tea:** The Tea Room is an artful ensemble of stone vaults, cozy furniture, romantic lighting, lovingly presented pastries, and a long list of fine teas. Hiding out behind City Hall, it offers a tranquil and relaxing escape (Tue-Sun 17:00-24:00, closed Mon, 200 yards below Il Campo, from the car park banister at the far end of Piazza del Mercato, look down and to the left, at Porta Giustizia 11, tel. 0577-222-753).

***Aperitivo* Happy Hour:** As elsewhere in Italy, you'll find bars all over town attracting an early evening crowd by offering an *aperitivo*—a free buffet of food that's included with the purchase of a drink. For many, this happy-hour special (usually nightly from 18:00-20:00) can make a light dinner. Some good ones to consider are: Morbidi, a trendy and youthful cocktail bar (closed Sun, Via Banchi di Sopra 75); the classic *caffè/pasticceria* Nannini (Via Banchi di Sopra 24, also a branch at Piazza Matteotti 15); and Bar il Palio and Osteria Liberamente, for cocktails and light bites on Il Campo (both described below). A great way to cap any meal or day in Siena is with a drink or dessert on Il Campo.

## ON IL CAMPO

If you choose to dine on perhaps the finest town square in Italy, you'll pay a premium, meet waiters who don't need to hustle, and eat mediocre food. And yet I highly recommend it. Consider surveying the scene during your sightseeing day and reserving a table of your choice at the place that feels best to you. (All places listed are open daily for long hours.)

### Dining and Drinks on the Square

**$$$ Ristorante alla Speranza** has primo views and is a decent option for dining on the square (Piazza del Campo 32, tel. 0577-280-190, www.allasperanza.it).

**$$$ Il Bandierino** is another option for drinks or pizza, with an angled view of City Hall (no cover but a 20 percent service charge, Piazza del Campo 64, tel. 0577-275-894).

**$$$ Bar il Palio** is the best bar on Il Campo for a before- or after-dinner drink: It has straightforward prices, no cover, and a fine view (Piazza del Campo 47, tel. 0577-282-055).

**$$$ Osteria Liberamente,** a dynamic little bar with a trendy vibe, is popular with young locals. Consider a drink at *aperitivo* time, from 17:00 on, when drinks come with a small plate of snacks (fine wines by the glass and €7 cocktails, Piazza del Campo 27, tel. 0577-274-733, Pino).

## Drinks or Snacks Overlooking Il Campo

These places (all open daily until late) have skinny balconies with benches overlooking the main square for their customers.

**$ Gelateria Costarella,** on the corner of Via di Città and Costarella dei Barbieri, is a modern cocktail/gelato bar with a great little balcony over Il Campo—which is open to anyone ordering off their pricier menu (Via di Città 33).

**$ Bar Paninoteca San Paolo** has a youthful English-pub ambience and a row of stools overlooking the square. They have dozens of hearty sandwiches, big salads, and several beers on tap—it's not traditional Italian, but it's quick, filling, and available all day (order and pay at the counter, under the arch on Vicolo di San Paolo, tel. 0577-226-622).

**$ Key Largo Bar** has a nondescript interior, but two long, upper-story benches in the corner offer a wonderful secret perch. Buy your drink or snack at the bar, climb upstairs, and open the ancient door (no cover and no extra charge to sit on the balcony). Enjoy stretching out, and try to imagine how, during the Palio, three layers of spectators cram into this space—notice the iron railing used to plaster the top row of sardines up against the wall. Suddenly you're picturing Palio ponies zipping wildly around the square's notoriously dangerous corner (on the corner at Via Rinaldini 17, tel. 0577-236-339).

**$ Salumeria il Cencio** is a simple rustic sandwich shop with a tiny balcony upstairs (enter through back), where, for the take-out price, you can munch your humble meal (daily, near Key Largo Bar at the corner of Il Campo and Via del Porrione, tel. 0577-283-007).

## DINING WITH LOCALS, AWAY FROM THE CENTER

A pleasant 10-minute stroll north of Il Campo, Via Camollia—a continuation of the chic Via Banchi di Sopra and Via dei Montanini shopping streets—offers good eating options. **$$ Trattoria Fonte Giusta,** at #102, is a big family-friendly eatery known for its pizza and meat dishes (plenty of streetside tables, daily 12:00-23:00, tel. 0577-40506). My favorite in this area is farther on, at #167—**$$ Osteria il Vinaio.** Festooned with neighborhood memorabilia on the walls, it's an informal place—bright and fun—offering simple dishes at good prices from an inviting menu (Mon-Sat 19:00-22:00, closed Sun, tel. 0577-49615, run by Bobbe and Davide). Beyond that, at #193, is **$$ Osteria Titti,** where friendly Duccio creates a quieter atmosphere, serving Sienese classics in an eclectic and funky setting (Mon-Sat 12:00-15:00 & 19:00-23:00, closed Sun, tel. 0577-285-813).

## EATING CHEAPLY IN THE CENTER
**Consorzio Agrario di Siena** gourmet market is a great place to assemble a cheap yet top-quality meal (salad and smoothie bar at the front, bakery/pizzeria at the back). Take a stool at the excellent pizzeria in the rear, or find a spot on the big comfy stone bench across the way on Piazza Salimbeni (Mon-Sat 8:00-20:30, Sun 9:30-20:00, just off Piazza Matteotti, facing Piazza Salimbeni at Via Pianigiani 9).

**Sapori & Dintorni Conad,** at the bottom of Il Campo next to the City Tower, is a classy bakery/supermarket/*rosticceria* serving fresh food to go or to eat at one of their tiny tables (daily 8:30-20:00, Piazza Il Campo 80).

## DESSERTS AND TREATS
Siena's claim to caloric fame is its panforte, a rich, chewy concoction of nuts, honey, and candied fruits that impresses even fruitcake haters. There are a few varieties: *Margherita,* dusted in powdered sugar, is fruitier, while *panpepato* has a spicy, peppery crust. Locals prefer a chewy, white macaroon-and-almond cookie called *ricciarelli*.

**Nannini** is the top end, classic café and pastry shop every grandmother has fond memories of. It's ideally located in the center of the evening strolling scene a few blocks off the Campo. For a special dessert or a sweet treat any time of day, stop by. The local specialties are around back at the far end of the bar (Mon-Fri 7:30-21:30, Sat-Sun 8:00-23:00, *aperitivo* happy hour 18:00 until closing, Banchi di Sopra 24). There's also a branch at Piazza Matteotti 15.

# Siena Connections

Siena has sparse train connections but is a handy hub for buses to the hill towns. For most, Florence is the gateway to Siena. The bus and train take about the same amount of time, but Siena's bus station is more convenient and central than its train station.

## BY TRAIN
Siena's train station is at the edge of town. For details on getting between the town center and the station, see page 598.

**From Siena by Train to: Florence** (direct trains hourly, 1.5 hours), **Pisa** (2/hour, 1.5 hours, some change at Empoli), **Assisi** (10/day, about 4 hours, most involve 2 changes, bus is faster), **Rome** (1-2/hour, 3-4 hours, 1 change), **Orvieto** (12/day, 2.5 hours, change in Chiusi). Train info: Trenitalia.com.

## BY BUS

The main bus companies are **Tiemme/Siena Mobilità** (mostly regional destinations, tel. 0577-204-111, www.tiemmespa.it) and **Flixbus** (for long-distance connections, https://global.flixbus.com). On schedules, the fastest buses are marked *rapida*. Many buses depart Siena from Piazza Gramsci (sometimes labeled *Via Tozzi* on schedules); others leave from the train station or right behind it (confirm when you buy your ticket).

**Tickets and Information:** You can buy tickets in the underground passageway (called Sottopassaggio la Lizza) beneath Piazza Gramsci—look for stairwells in front of NH Excelsior Hotel. You can also get bus tickets from a kiosk at the train station as well as on online. If necessary, you can buy tickets from the driver, but it costs extra.

**Tiemme/Siena Mobilità Buses to: Florence** (roughly 2/hour—fewer off-season, take the 1.5-hour *rapida/via superstrada* bus—*ordinaria* buses take longer; tickets available at tobacco shops/*tabacchi;* generally leaves from Piazza Gramsci as well as train station), **San Gimignano** (8/day direct, on Sun must change in Poggibonsi, 1.5 hours, from Piazza Gramsci), **Volterra** (4/day Mon-Sat, no buses on Sun, 2 hours, change in Colle di Val d'Elsa, leaves from Piazza Gramsci), **Montepulciano** (6-7/day, none on Sun, 1.5 hours, from train station), **Pienza** (6/day, none on Sun, 1.5 hours, from train station), **Montalcino** (6/day Mon-Sat, 4/day Sun, 1.5 hours, from train station or Piazza del Sale), **Pisa's Galileo Galilei Airport** (3/day, 2 hours, one direct, two via Poggibonsi), **Rome's Fiumicino Airport** (3/day, 3.5 hours, from Piazza Gramsci).

**Flixbus Buses to: Rome** (13/day, 3 hours, from Piazza Gramsci or the train station, arrives at Rome's Tiburtina station on Metro line B with easy connections to the central Termini train station), **Naples** (6/day direct, 5.5 hours, one overnight bus that departs at 00:20), **Milan** (6-8/day direct, 5-7 hours, arrives at Milan's Lampugnano Metro station for the red line 1), **Assisi** (3/day direct, 2 hours, departs from Siena train station. To reach the town center of **Pisa,** the train is better (described earlier).

# VOLTERRA & SAN GIMIGNANO

This fine duo of hill towns—perhaps Italy's most underrated and most overrated, respectively—sits just a half-hour drive apart in the middle of the triangle formed by Florence, Siena, and Pisa. San Gimignano is the region's glamour girl, getting all the fawning attention from passing tour buses. And a quick stroll through its core, in the shadows of its 14 surviving medieval towers, is a delight. But once you've seen it, you've seen it...and that's when you head for Volterra. Volterra isn't as eye-catching as San Gimignano, but it has unmistakable authenticity and surprising depth, richly rewarding travelers adventurous enough to break out of the San Gimignano rut. With its many engaging museums, Volterra offers the best sightseeing of all of Italy's small hill towns.

## GETTING THERE

These towns work best for drivers, who can easily reach both in one go. Volterra is farther off the main Florence-Siena road, but it's near the main coastal highway connecting the north (Pisa, Lucca, and Cinque Terre) and south (Montalcino/Montepulciano and Rome). It's a little more than an hour's drive from Pisa or Florence.

If you're relying on public transportation, both towns are reachable—to a point. Visiting either one by bus from Florence or Siena requires a longer-than-it-should-be trek, often with a change (in Colle di Val d'Elsa for Volterra, in Poggibonsi for San Gimignano). Volterra can also be reached by a train-and-bus combination from La Spezia, Pisa, or Florence (transfer to a bus in Pontedera). See each town's "Connections" section for details.

San Gimignano is better connected, but Volterra merits the additional effort. Note that while these towns are only about a

## Volterra & San Gimignano Area

30-minute drive apart, they're poorly connected to each other by public transit.

## PLANNING YOUR TIME

Volterra and San Gimignano are a handy yin-and-yang pair. Ideally, you'll overnight in one town and visit the other either as a side trip or en route. Sleeping in Volterra lets you really settle into a charming burg with good restaurants, but it forces you to visit San Gimignano during the day, when it's busiest. Sleeping in San Gimignano lets you enjoy that gorgeous town when it's relatively quiet, but some visitors find it *too* quiet. Ultimately I'd aim to sleep in Volterra, and try to visit San Gimignano as early or late in the day as is practical to avoid crowds. Those with a car may choose to stay in the countryside between the two, visiting Volterra during the day and dining in San Gimignano at night.

# Volterra

Encircled by impressive walls and topped with a grand fortress, Volterra perches high above the rich farmland surrounding it. More than 2,000 years ago, Volterra was an important Etruscan city, and much larger than we see today. Greek-trained Etruscan artists worked here, leaving a significant stash of art, particularly cinerary urns. Eventually Volterra was absorbed into the Roman Empire, and for centuries it was an independent city-state. Volterra fought bitterly against the Florentines, but like many Tuscan towns, it lost in the end and was given a Medici fortress atop the city to "protect" its citizens.

Unlike other famous towns in Tuscany, Volterra feels neither cutesy nor touristy...but real, vibrant, and almost oblivious to the allure of the tourist dollar. Millennia past its prime, Volterra seems to have settled into a well-worn groove; locals are resistant to change. At a town meeting about whether to run a high-speed internet cable to the town, a local grumbled, "The Etruscans didn't need it—why do we?" This stubbornness helps make Volterra a refreshing change of pace from its more aggressively commercial neighbors. Volterra also boasts some interesting sights for a small town, from an ancient Roman theater, to a finely decorated Pisan Romanesque cathedral, to an excellent museum of Etruscan artifacts. And most evenings, charming Annie and Claudia give a delightful, one-hour guided town walk sure to help you appreciate their city (see "Tours in Volterra," later). All in all, Volterra is my favorite small town in Tuscany.

# Orientation to Volterra

Compact and walkable, Volterra (pop. 11,000—6,000 inside the old wall) stretches out from the pleasant Piazza dei Priori to the old city gates and beyond. Be ready for some steep walking: While the spine of the city from the main square to the Etruscan Museum is fairly level, nearly everything else involves a climb.

**Tourist Information:** The helpful TI is on the main square, at Piazza dei Priori 20 (daily 9:30-13:00 & 14:00-18:00, tel. 0588-87257, www.volterratur.it). The TI's excellent €5 audioguide narrates 20 stops (2-for-1 discount with this book). They have bus schedules, and their free *Handicraft in Volterra* booklet is useful for understanding the town's traditional artisans. Check the TI website for details on frequent summer festivals and concerts.

## ARRIVAL IN VOLTERRA

**By Public Transport:** Buses stop at Piazza Martiri della Libertà in the town center. Train travelers can reach the town with a short bus ride from Poggibonsi, which has the nearest train station.

**By Car:** Don't drive into the town center; it's prohibited except for locals (and you'll get a huge fine). It's easiest to simply wind to the top where the road ends at Piazza Martiri della Libertà. (Halfway up the hill, there's a confusing hard right—don't take it; keep going straight uphill under the wall.) Immediately before the Piazza Martiri bus roundabout is the entry to an **underground garage** (€2/hour, €15/day, keep ticket and pay as you leave) that's within a few blocks of nearly all my recommended hotels and sights.

If the main garage is full, the police may direct you to other pay **lots** that ring the town walls (try the handy-but-small lot facing the Roman Theater and Porta Fiorentina gate). You can also pay to park outside the walls in any street spot marked with blue lines. Behind town, a lot named Docciola is free, but it requires a steep climb from the Porta di Docciola gate up into town.

If you're staying in town, check with your hotel about the best parking options.

## HELPFUL HINTS

**Volterra Card:** This €16 card covers all the main sights—except for the Palazzo Viti (valid 72 hours, buy at any covered sight). If traveling with kids, ask about the family card, an especially good deal (€24 for 1-2 adults and kids under 16).

**Market Day:** The market is on Saturday morning near the Roman Theater (8:00-13:00, Nov-March it moves to Piazza dei Priori). The TI hands out a list of other market days in the area.

**Laundry:** The handy self-service **Lavanderia Splash** is just off the main square (daily 7:00-23:00, Via Roma 7, tel. 0588-80030). Their next-door dry-cleaning shop also provides wash-and-dry services that usually take about 24 hours (closed Sun).

# Tours in Volterra

### ▲▲Guided Volterra Walk

Annie Adair and her colleague Claudia Meucci offer a great one-hour, English-only introductory walking tour of Volterra for €10. The walk touches on Volterra's Etruscan, Roman, and medieval history, as well as the contemporary cultural scene (daily April-Oct, rain or shine Mon, Wed, and Fri at 12:30, other days at 18:00; meet in front of alabaster shop on Piazza Martiri della Libertà, no need to reserve, tours run with a minimum of 3 people or €30; www.volterrawalkingtour.com or www.tuscantour.com, info@volterrawalkingtour.com). There's no better way to spend €10 and one hour in this city. I mean it. Don't miss this beautiful experience.

### Local Guides

American **Annie Adair** is an excellent guide for private, in-depth tours of Volterra (€60/hour, minimum 2 hours). Her husband **Francesco,** an easygoing sommelier and wine critic, leads a Wine Tasting 101 crash course in sampling Tuscan wines (€60/hour per group, plus cost of wine). Annie and Francesco also offer excursions to a honey farm, alabaster quarry, and winery, or a more wine-focused trip to Montalcino or the heart of Chianti (about €450/day for 2-4 people, larger groups possible, mobile 347-143-5004, www. tuscantour.com, info@tuscantour.com).

## Sights in Volterra

I've linked these sights with handy walking directions.
• *Begin at the Etruscan Arch at the bottom of Via Porta all'Arco (about 4 blocks below the main square, Piazza dei Priori).*

### ▲Etruscan Arch (Porta all'Arco)

Volterra's renowned Etruscan arch was built of massive stones in the fourth century BC. The original city wall was four miles around—twice the size of today's wall. Imagine: This city had 20,000 people four centuries before Christ. Volterra was a key trading center and one of 12 leading towns in the confederation of Etruria. The three seriously eroded heads, dating from the first century BC, show what happens when you leave something outside for 2,000 years. The newer stones are part of the 13th-century city wall, which incorporated parts of the much older Etruscan wall.

A plaque just outside remembers June 30, 1944. That night, Nazi forces were planning to blow up the arch to slow the Allied advance. To save their treasured landmark, Volterrans ripped up the stones that pave Via Porta all'Arco, plugged up the gate, and managed to convince the Nazi commander that there was no need to blow up the arch. Today, all the paving stones are back in their places, and like silent heroes, they welcome you through the oldest standing gate into Volterra. Locals claim this as the oldest surviving rounded arch of the Etruscan age; some experts believe this is where the Romans got the idea for using a keystone in their arches.
• *Go through the arch and head up Via Porta all'Arco, which I like to call...*

### "Artisan Lane" (Via Porta all'Arco)

This steep and atmospheric lane is lined with interesting shops featuring the work of artisans and producers. Because of its alabaster heritage, Volterra developed a tradition of craftsmanship and

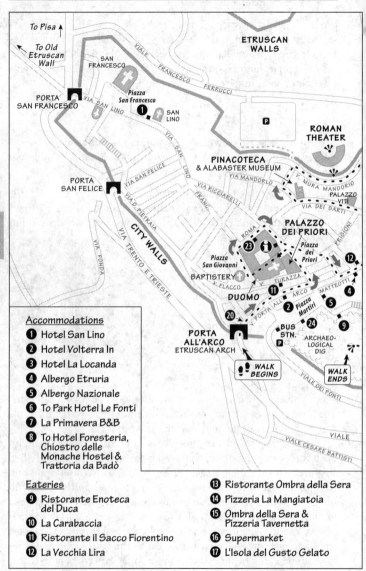

VOLTERRA & SAN GIMIGNANO

**Accommodations**
1. Hotel San Lino
2. Hotel Volterra In
3. Hotel La Locanda
4. Albergo Etruria
5. Albergo Nazionale
6. To Park Hotel Le Fonti
7. La Primavera B&B
8. To Hotel Foresteria, Chiostro delle Monache Hostel & Trattoria da Badò

**Eateries**
9. Ristorante Enoteca del Duca
10. La Carabaccia
11. Ristorante il Sacco Fiorentino
12. La Vecchia Lira
13. Ristorante Ombra della Sera
14. Pizzeria La Mangiatoia
15. Ombra della Sera & Pizzeria Tavernetta
16. Supermarket
17. L'Isola del Gusto Gelato

artistry, and today you'll find a rich variety of handiwork (shops generally open Mon-Sat 10:00-13:00 & 16:00-19:00, closed Sun).

From the Etruscan Arch, browse your way up the hill, checking out these shops and items (listed from bottom to top): alabaster shops (#57 and #45); book bindery and papery (#26); jewelry (#25); etchings (#23); and bronze work (#6).

• Reaching the top of Via Porta all'Arco, turn left and walk a few steps into Volterra's main square, Piazza dei Priori. It's dominated by the...

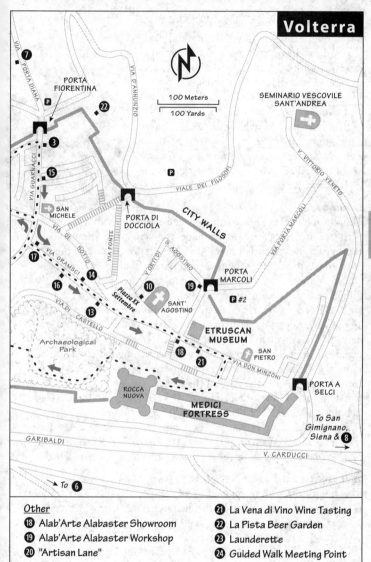

# Volterra

SEMINARIO VESCOVILE
SANT'ANDREA

PORTA
FIORENTINA

100 Meters
100 Yards

PORTA DIANA

VIA D'ANNUNZIO

VIALE DEI FILOSOFI

CITY WALLS

SAN
MICHELE

PORTA DI
DOCCIOLA

VIA FONTE

VIA GUARNACCI

VIA DI SOTTO

VIA GRAMSCI

V. ORTI DI S. AGOSTINO

PORTA
MARCOLI

V. VITTORIO VENETO

VIA PORTA MARCOLI

Piazza IX
Settembre

SANT'
AGOSTINO

ETRUSCAN
MUSEUM

SAN
PIETRO

VIA DI CASTELLO

Archaeological
Park

VIA DON MINZONI

PORTA A
SELCI

ROCCA
NUOVA

MEDICI
FORTRESS

To San
Gimignano,
Siena & ⑧

GARIBALDI

V. CARDUCCI

→ To ⑥

**VOLTERRA & SAN GIMIGNANO**

### Other
⑱ Alab'Arte Alabaster Showroom
⑲ Alab'Arte Alabaster Workshop
⑳ "Artisan Lane"
㉑ La Vena di Vino Wine Tasting
㉒ La Pista Beer Garden
㉓ Launderette
㉔ Guided Walk Meeting Point

## Palazzo dei Priori

Volterra's City Hall, built about 1200, claims to be the oldest of any Tuscan city-state. It clearly inspired the more famous Palazzo Vecchio in Florence. Town halls like this are emblematic of the era of powerful city-states. They were architectural exclamation points declaring that, around here, no pope or emperor called the shots. Towns such as Volterra were truly city-states—proudly independent and relatively democratic. They had their own armies, taxes, and even weights and measures. Notice the horizontal "cane" cut into the City Hall wall (10 yards to the right of the door). For a thousand years, this square hosted a market, and the "cane" was the local yardstick.

**Cost and Hours:** €6, includes council chambers and tower climb, daily 10:30-17:30, Nov-mid-March until 16:30, tower closed in bad weather.

• *As you face the City Hall, find the little back door in the black-and-white striped wall (to the right), which leads into Volterra's cathedral.*

## Duomo

This church is not as elaborate as its cousin in Pisa, but it is a beautiful example of the Pisan Romanesque style. The simple 13th-century facade conceals a more intricate interior (rebuilt in the late 16th and 19th centuries), with a central nave flanked by monolithic stucco columns, painted to imitate pink granite, and topped by a gilded, coffered ceiling. Just past the pulpit midway down the nave (at the Rosary Chapel), check out the *Annunciation,* painted in 1497 by Mariotto Albertinelli and Fra Bartolomeo (both were students of Fra Angelico). The two, friends since childhood, delicately give worshippers a way to see Mary "conceived by the Holy Spirit." Note the vibrant colors, exaggerated perspective, and Mary's *contrapposto* pose—all attributes of the Renaissance.

**Cost and Hours:** Free, daily 8:00-12:30 & 15:00-18:00, Nov-Feb until 17:00, closed Fri 12:30-16:00 for cleaning.

• *Exit the cathedral through its "front" door and go right, circling all the way around the block to return to Piazza dei Priori. Exit the far end of the square; after one short block, you're standing at the head (on the left) of…*

## ▲Via Matteotti

The town's main drag, named after the popular Socialist leader Giacomo Matteotti (killed by the fascists in 1924), provides a good cultural scavenger hunt.

At #1, on the left, is a typical **Italian bank security door.** (Step in and say, "Beam me up, Scotty.") Back outside, stand at the corner and look up and all around. Find the medieval griffin torch-holder—symbol of Volterra, looking down Via Matteotti—and imagine it holding a flaming torch. The pharmacy sports the symbol of its medieval guild. Across the street from the bank, #2 is the base of what was a San Gimignano-style **fortified Tuscan tower.** Look up and imagine heavy beams cantilevered out, supporting extra wooden rooms and balconies crowding out over the street. Throughout Tuscany, today's stark and stony old building fronts once supported a tangle of wooden extensions.

As you head down Via Matteotti, notice how the doors show centuries of refitting work. Doors that once led to these extra rooms are now partially bricked up to make windows. Contemplate urban density in the 14th century, before the plague thinned out the population. Be careful: A **wild boar** (a local delicacy) awaits you at #10.

At #12, on the right, notice the line of doorbells: This typical **palace,** once the home of a single rich family, is now occupied by many middle-class families. After the social revolution in the 18th century and the rise of the middle class, former palaces were condominium-ized. Even so, the original family still lives here—apartment #1 is the home of Count Guidi.

On the right at #16, pop in to the **alabaster showroom.** Alabaster, quarried nearby, has long been a big industry here. Volterra alabaster—softer and more translucent than marble—was sliced thin to serve as windows for Italy's medieval churches.

At #19, the recommended **La Vecchia Lira** is a lively cafeteria and restaurant. The **Bar L'Incontro** across the street is a favorite for breakfast and pastries; in the summer, they sell homemade gelato, while in the winter they make chocolates. In the evening, it's a bustling local spot for a drink.

Across the way, side-trip 10 steps up Vicolo delle Prigioni to the fun **Panificio Rosetti** bakery. They're happy to sell small quantities if you want to try the local *cantuccini* (almond biscotti) or another treat.

Continue on Via Matteotti to the end of the block. Notice the bit of **Etruscan wall** artfully used to display more alabaster art (at #51). Nearby is the alabaster **art gallery** of Paolo Sabatini, who specializes in unique, contemporary sculptures (#56A).

Locals gather early each evening at **Osteria dei Poeti** (#57) for some of the best cocktails in town (served with free munchies). The cinema is across the street. Movies in Italy are rarely in *versione originale;* Italians are used to getting their movies dubbed into Italian. To bring some culture to this little town, they also show live broadcasts of operas and concerts (advertised in the window).

Another **Tuscan tower** on the corner (#66) marks the end of the street. This noble house had a ground floor with no interior access to the safe upper floors. Rope ladders were used to get upstairs. The tiny door was wide enough to let in your skinny friends...but definitely not anyone wearing armor and carrying big weapons.

Across the little square stands the ancient **Church of St. Michael.** After long years of barbarian chaos, the Germanic Langobards moved in from the north in the sixth century and asserted law and order in places like Volterra. That generally included building a Christian church over the old Roman forum to symbolically claim and tame the center of town. The church standing here today is Romanesque, dating from the 12th century.

Around the right side, find the crude little guy and the smiling octopus under its eaves—they've been making faces at the passing crowds for 800 years.

• *When you reach the little* piazzetta *with a Romanesque church, turn left down Via dei Sarti. Our next stop—Palazzo Viti—is halfway down the block. But if you want to linger on the square for a bit, drop in for a glass of wine at* **Enoteca Scali** *(at Via Guarnacci 3), where friendly Massimo and Patrizia sell a vast selection of wines and local delicacies in an inviting atmosphere.*

## ▲Palazzo Viti

Palazzo Viti takes you behind the rustic, heavy stone walls of the city to see how the wealthy lived—in this case, rich from the 19th-century alabaster trade. This time warp is popular with Italian movie directors. With 12 rooms on one floor open to the public, Palazzo Viti feels remarkably lived in—because it is. Behind the ropes you'll see intimate family photos. You'll often find Signora Viti herself selling admission tickets. In high season, your visit may end in the cellar with a short wine tasting.

**Cost and Hours:** €5, daily 10:00-17:30, by appointment only Nov-March, Via dei Sarti 41, tel. 0588-84047, www.palazzoviti.it, info@palazzoviti.it.

**Visiting the Palazzo:** The elegant interior is compact and well-described. You'll climb up a stately staircase, buy your ticket, and head into the grand ballroom. From here, you'll tour the blue-hued dining room (with slice-of-life Chinese scenes painted on rice paper); the salon of battles (with warfare paintings on the walls); and the long hall of temporary exhibits. Looping back, you'll see the porcelain hall (decorated with priceless plates) and the inviting library (notice the delicate lamp with a finely carved alabaster lampshade).

The Brachettone Salon is named for the local artist responsible for the small sketch of near-nudes hanging just left of the door into the next room. Brachettone (from *brache,* "pants") is the nickname for the hometown 16th-century artist Daniele da Volterra, who owns the dubious distinction of having painted all those wispy loincloths over the genitalia of Michelangelo's figures in the *Last Judgment* at the Sistine Chapel. (In this drawing, notice a similar aversion to showing the full monty...though everything-but is fair game.) On the table, notice the family wedding photo with Pope John Paul II presiding. In the red room, a portrait of Giuseppe Viti (looking like Pavarotti) hangs next to the exit door. He's the man who purchased the place in 1850. Your visit ends with bedrooms and a dressing room.

Your Palazzo Viti ticket sometimes gets you a fine little cheese, salami, and wine tasting, typically in high season. As you leave the palace, climb down into the cool cellar (used as a disco on some weekends), where you can pop into a Roman cistern, marvel at an Etruscan well, and enjoy a friendly sit-down snack.

• *A block past Palazzo Viti, also on Via dei Sarti, is the...*

### Pinacoteca and Alabaster Museum
### (Pinacoteca e Ecomuseo dell'Alabastro)

The Pinacoteca fills a 15th-century palace with fine paintings that feel more Florentine than Sienese—a reminder of whose domain this town was in. You'll see a stunning altarpiece by Taddeo di Bartolo, once displayed in the original residence. You'll also find roomfuls of gilded altarpieces and saintly statues, as well as a trio of striking High Renaissance altar paintings by Signorelli, Fiorentino, and Ghirlandaio.

The adjoining Alabaster Museum gives a fascinating overview of the local alabaster industry, past and present.

**Cost and Hours:** €8, daily 9:00-19:00, off-season 10:00-16:30, Via dei Sarti 1, tel. 0588-87580.

• *Exiting the building, circle right along the side of the museum into the tunnel-like Passo del Gualduccio passage; then turn right and walk along the wall, with fine views of the...*

### Roman Theater (Teatro Romano)

With this fine aerial view from the city wall promenade, there's no reason to pay to enter this well-preserved, first-century theater

(although it is covered by the Volterra Card). The 13th-century wall that you're standing on divided the theater from the town center...so, naturally, the theater became the town dump. Over time, the theater was forgotten—covered in the garbage of Volterra. It was rediscovered in the 1950s and excavated.

The stage wall (immediately in front of the theater seats) was standard Roman design—with three levels from which actors would appear: one level for mortals, one for heroes, and the top one for gods. Parts of two levels still stand. Gods leaped out onto the third level for the last time around the third century AD, which is when the town began to use the theater stones to build fancy baths instead. You can see the scant remains of the baths behind the theater, including the little round sauna in the far corner with brick supports that raise the heated floor.

From this vantage point, you can trace Volterra's vast Etruscan wall. Find the church in the distance, on the left, and notice the stones just below. They are from the Etruscan wall that followed the ridge into the valley and defined Volterra in the fourth century BC.

• *From the theater viewpoint, continue along the wall downhill to the T-intersection (the old gate, Porta Fiorentina, with fine wooden medieval doors, is on your left). Turn right, making your way uphill on Via Guarnacci back to Via Matteotti. A block up Via Matteotti, you can't miss the wide, pedestrianized shopping street called Via Gramsci. Follow this up to Piazza XX Settembre, walk through that leafy square, and continue uphill on Via Don Minzoni. Watch on your left for the...*

## ▲▲Etruscan Museum (Museo Etrusco Guarnacci)

Filled top to bottom with rare Etruscan artifacts, this museum—even with few English explanations and its dusty, old-school style—makes it easy to appreciate how advanced this pre-Roman culture was.

**Cost and Hours:** €8, daily 9:00-19:00, Nov-mid-March 10:00-16:30, audioguide-€3, Via Don Minzoni 15, tel. 0588-86347, www.comune.volterra.pi.it/english.

**Visiting the Museum:** The museum's three floors feel dusty and disorganized. As there are scarcely any English explanations, consider the serious but interesting audioguide; the information below hits the highlights. There's an inviting public garden out back.

The collection starts on the **ground floor** with a small gathering of pre-Etruscan Villanovian artifacts (c. 1500 BC), with the oldest items to the left as you enter. To the right are an impressive warrior's hat and a remarkable, richly decorated, double-spouted military flask for wine and water. Look down to see Etruscan foundations and a road (the discovery of which foiled the museum's attempt to build an elevator here). It's mind-boggling to think that 20,000 people lived within the town's Etruscan walls in 400 BC.

Filling the rest of the ground floor is a vast collection of stone Etruscan **cinerary urns** (seventh-first century BC). Etruscan urns have two parts: The box on the bottom contained the cremated remains (with elaborately carved panels), while the lid was decorated with a sculpture of the departed. The carved bas-relief scenes and motifs decorating the urns are a prized catalog of Etruscan life and activities.

First pay attention to the people on top. While contemporaries of the Greeks, the Etruscans were more libertine. Their religion was less demanding, and their women were a respected part of both the social and public spheres. Women and men alike are depicted lounging on Etruscan urns. While they seem to be just hanging out, the lounging dead were actually offering the gods a banquet—in order to gain the Etruscan equivalent of salvation. Etruscans really did lounge like this in front of a table, but this banquet had eternal consequences. The dearly departed are often depicted holding blank wax tablets (symbolizing blank new lives in the next world). Men hold containers that would generally be used at banquets, including libation cups for offering wine to the gods. The women are finely dressed, sometimes holding a pomegranate (symbolizing fertility) or a mirror. Look at the faces, and imagine the lives they lived.

Now tune into the reliefs carved into the fronts of the boxes. The motifs vary widely, from floral patterns to mystical animals (such as a Starbucks-like mermaid) to parades of magistrates. Some show journeys on horseback—appropriate for someone leaving this world and entering the next. Some show the fabled horseback-and-carriage ride to the underworld, where the dead are greeted by Charun, an underworld demon, with his hammer and pointy ears.

While the finer urns are carved of alabaster, most are made of limestone. Originally they were colorfully painted. Many lids are mismatched—casualties of reckless 18th- and 19th-century archaeological digs.

Head upstairs to the **first floor.** You'll enter a room with a circular mosaic in the floor (a Roman original, found in Volterra and transplanted here). Explore more treasures in a series of urn-filled rooms.

Fans of Alberto Giacometti will be amazed at how the tall, skinny figure called *The Evening Shadow* (*L'Ombra della Sera*, third century BC) looks just like the modern Swiss sculptor's work—but 2,500 years older. This is an example of the ex-voto bronze statues that the Etruscans created in thanks to the gods. With his supremely lanky frame, distinctive wavy hairdo, and inscrutable smirk, this Etruscan lad captures the illusion of a shadow stretching long, late in the day. Admire the sheer artistry and modernity of the statue.

The museum's other top piece is the **Urn of the Spouses** (*Urna degli Sposi*, first century BC). It's unique for various reasons, including its material (it's in terra-cotta—relatively rare for these urns) and its depiction of two people rather than one. Looking at this elderly couple, it's easy to imagine the long life they spent together and their desire to pass eternity lounging with each other at a banquet for the gods.

Other highlights include alabaster urns with more Greek myths, ex-voto water-bearer statues, kraters (vases with handles used for mixing water and wine), bronze hand mirrors, exquisite golden jewelry that would still be fashionable today, a battle helmet ominously dented at the left temple, black glazed pottery, and hundreds of ancient coins.

The **top floor** features a re-created gravesite, with several neatly aligned urns and artifacts that would have been buried with the deceased. Some of these were funeral dowries that the dead would pack along—including mirrors, coins, hardware for vases, votive statues, pots, pans, and jewelry.

• *After your visit, duck across the street to the...*

## ▲Alabaster Showroom and Workshop

For a fun peek into the art of alabaster, visit the Alab'Arte showroom, directly across from the Etruscan Museum, and their powdery workshop, a block

down the narrow lane (Via Porta Marcoli) next to the museum. Here you can watch Roberto Chiti and Giorgio Finazzo at work. (Everything—including Roberto and Giorgio—is covered in a fine white dust.) Lighting shows off the translucent quality of the stone and the expertise of these artists, who are delighted to share their art with visitors. This is not a touristy guided visit, but something far more special: the chance to see busy artisans practicing their craft.

**Cost and Hours:** Free, showroom—daily 10:00-13:00 & 15:00-19:00, closes at 17:30 in off-season, closed Nov-Feb, Via Don Minzoni 18; workshop—Mon-Sat 10:00-12:30 & 15:00-19:00, closed Sun, Via Orti Sant'Agostino 28, www.alabarte.com.

## ▲La Vena di Vino Wine Tasting

La Vena di Vino, just across from the Etruscan Museum, is a fun *enoteca* where Bruno and Lucio have devoted themselves to the wonders of wine and share it with a fun-loving passion. Each day they open six or eight bottles, serve your choice by the glass, pair it with characteristic munchies, and offer

fine music (guitars available for patrons) and an unusual decor (the place is strewn with bras). Hang out here with the local characters. According to Bruno, a Brunello is just right with wild boar, and a Super Tuscan is perfect for meditation. Although Volterra is famously quiet late at night, this place is full of action (Wed-Mon 11:30-24:00, closed Tue, Nov-Feb open Fri-Sat only, Via Don Minzoni 30, tel. 0588-81491, www.lavenadivino.com).

• *Volterra's final sight is perched atop the hill just above the wine bar. Climb up one of the lanes nearby, then walk (to the right) along the formidable wall to find the park.*

## Medici Fortress and Archaeological Park (Fortezza Medicea and Parco Archeologico)

The archaeological park marks what was the acropolis of Volterra from 1500 BC until AD 1472, when Florence conquered the pesky city. The Florentines burned Volterra's political and historic center, turning it into a grassy commons and building the adjacent Medici Fortress. The old fortress—a symbol of Florentine dominance—now keeps people in rather than out. It's a maximum-security prison housing only about 150 special prisoners.

The park sprawling next to the fortress (toward the town center) is a rare, grassy meadow at the top of a rustic hill town—a favorite place for locals to relax and picnic on a sunny day. Nearby are the scant remains of the acropolis, which can be viewed through the fence for free, or entered for a fee. Of more interest to antiquities enthusiasts is the acropolis' first-century Roman cistern. You can descend 40 tight spiral steps to stand in a chamber that once held about 250,000 gallons of water, enough to provide for more than a thousand people. While not huge, it provides a good look at Roman engineering and reminds you just how important a supply of water was to the survival of a hill town.

**Cost and Hours:** Park—free, open until 20:00 in peak of summer, shorter hours off-season; acropolis and cistern—€5, daily 10:30-17:30, closes at 16:30 off-season.

## Evening Scene

**La Pista:** Volterra is pretty quiet at night. For a little action during summer evenings you can venture just outside the wall to La Pista, a Tuscan family-friendly neighborhood beer-garden kind of hangout (DJ on weekends, snacks and drinks sold, playground, closed off-season). It's outside the Porta Fiorentina (100 yards to the right in the shadow of the wall).

*Passeggiata:* As they have for generations, Volterrans young and old stroll during the cool of the early evening. The main cruising is along Via Gramsci and Via Matteotti to the main square, Piazza dei Priori.

*Aperitivo:* Each evening several bars put out little buffet

# Under the Etruscan Sun
## (c. 900 BC-AD 1)

Around 550 BC—just before the Golden Age of Greece—the Etruscan people of central Italy had their own Golden Age. Though their origins are unclear, their mix of Greek-style art with Roman-style customs helped lay a civilized foundation for the rise of the Roman Empire. As you travel through Italy—particularly in Tuscany (from "Etruscan")—you'll find traces of this long-lost people. Etruscan tombs and artifacts are still being discovered, often by farmers in the countryside.

The Etruscans were established in central Italy by the early seventh century BC, when a number of settlements sprouted up in sparsely populated Tuscany and Umbria, including today's hill towns of Cortona, Chiusi, and Volterra. Possibly immigrants from Turkey, but more likely local farmers who moved to the city, they became sailors, traders, and craftsmen, and welcomed new ideas from Greece.

More technologically advanced than their neighbors, the Etruscans mined iron ore, smelting and exporting it around the Mediterranean. They drained and irrigated large tracts of land, creating the fertile farmland of central Italy's breadbasket. With their disciplined army, warships, merchant vessels, and (from the Greek perspective) pirate galleys, they ruled central Italy and the major ports along the Tyrrhenian Sea. For nearly two centuries (c. 700-500 BC), much of Italy lived in peace and prosperity under the Etruscan sun.

Judging from the frescoes and many luxury items that have survived, the Etruscans enjoyed the good life: They look healthy and vibrant as they play flutes, dance with birds, or play party games. Etruscan artists celebrated individual people, showing their wrinkles, crooked noses, silly smiles, and funny haircuts.

Scholars today have deciphered the Etruscans' Greek-style alphabet and some individual words, but they have yet to fully understand their language, which is unlike any other in Europe. Much of what we know of the Etruscans comes from their tombs. The tomb was a home in the hereafter, complete with the deceased's belongings. The urn might have a statue on the lid of the deceased at a banquet—lying across a dining couch, spooning with his wife, smiles on their faces, living the good life for all eternity.

Seven decades of wars with the Greeks (545-474 BC) disrupted their trade routes and drained the Etruscan League, just as a new Mediterranean power was emerging: Rome. In 509 BC, the Romans overthrew their Etruscan king, and Rome expanded, capturing Etruscan cities one by one (the last in 264 BC). Etruscan resisters were killed, the survivors intermarried with Romans, and their kids grew up speaking Latin. By Julius Caesar's time, the only remnants of Etruscan culture were its priests, who became Rome's professional soothsayers. Interestingly, the Etrus-

**VOLTERRA & SAN GIMIGNANO**

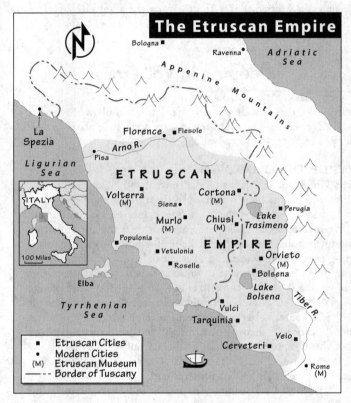

### The Etruscan Empire

*Etruscan Cities* (■), *Modern Cities* (•), (M) *Etruscan Museum*, *Border of Tuscany* (— - —)

can prophets had foreseen their own demise, having predicted that Etruscan civilization would last 10 centuries.

But Etruscan culture lived on in Roman religion (pantheon of gods, household gods, and divination rituals), art (realism), lifestyle (the banquet), and in a taste for Greek styles—the mix that became our "Western civilization."

## Etruscan Sights in Italy

**Rome:** Traces of original Etruscan engineering projects (e.g., Circus Maximus), Vatican Museum artifacts, and Villa Giulia Museum, with the famous "husband and wife sarcophagus."

**Orvieto:** Archaeological Museum (coins, dinnerware, and a sarcophagus), necropolis, and underground tunnels and caves.

**Volterra:** Etruscan gate (Porta all'Arco, from fourth century BC) and Etruscan Museum (urns, pottery, and devotional figures).

spreads free with a drink to attract a crowd. Bars popular for their *aperitivo* include VolaTerra (Via Turazza 5, next to City Hall), L'Incontro (Via Matteotti 19), and Bar dei Poeti (across from the cinema, Via Matteotti 57). And the gang at La Vena di Vino (described under "Sights in Volterra") always seems ready for a good time.

# Sleeping in Volterra

Volterra has plenty of places offering a good night's sleep at a fair price. Lodgings outside the old town are generally a bit cheaper (and easier for drivers). But keep in mind that these places involve not just walking, but steep walking.

## INSIDE THE OLD TOWN

**$$$ Hotel San Lino** fills a former convent with 42 modern rooms, all named for the nuns who lived in them. It's at the sleepy lower end of town—close to the Porta San Francesco gate, and about a five-minute uphill walk to the main drag. Although it's within the town walls, it doesn't feel like it: The hotel has a fine swimming pool and view terrace and is the only in-town option that's convenient for drivers, who can reserve pay parking at the on-site garage (RS%, air-con, elevator, closed Nov-Feb, Via San Lino 26, tel. 0588-85250, www.hotelsanlino.com, info@hotelsanlino.com).

**$$$ Hotel Volterra In** is fresh, tasteful, and in a central yet quiet location. Marco rents 10 bright and spacious rooms with thoughtful, upscale touches and a hearty buffet breakfast (RS%, air-con, elevator, Via Porta all'Arco 41, tel. 0588-86820, www.hotelvolterrain.it, info@hotelvolterrain.it).

**$$ Hotel La Locanda** feels stately and old-fashioned. This well-located place (just inside Porta Fiorentina, near the Roman Theater and parking lot) rents 18 rooms with flowery decor and modern comforts (RS%, family rooms, air-con, elevator, Via Guarnacci 24, tel. 0588-81547, www.hotel-lalocanda.com, staff@hotel-lalocanda.com, Irina).

**$ Albergo Etruria** is on Volterra's main drag. They offer a good location, a peaceful rooftop garden, and 19 frilly rooms (RS%, family rooms, some air-con, Via Matteotti 32, tel. 0588-87377, www.albergoetruria.it, info@albergoetruria.it, Paola, Daniele, and Sveva).

**$ Albergo Nazionale,** with 38 big and aging rooms, is simple, a little musty, popular with school groups, and steps from the bus stop. It's a nicely located last resort if you have your heart set on sleeping in the old town (RS%, family rooms, elevator, Via dei Marchesi 11, tel. 0588-86284, www.hotelnazionale-volterra.it, info@hotelnazionale-volterra.it).

## JUST OUTSIDE THE OLD TOWN

These accommodations are within a 5- to 20-minute walk of the city walls.

**$$$ Park Hotel Le Fonti,** a dull and steep 10-minute walk downhill from Porta all'Arco, can't decide whether it's a business hotel or a resort. The spacious, imposing building, old and stately, has 64 modern, comfortable rooms, half with views. While generally overpriced, it can be a good value if you manage to snag a deal. In addition to the swimming pool, guests can use its small spa (pay more for a view or a balcony, air-con, elevator, on-site restaurant, wine bar, free parking, Via di Fontecorrenti 2, tel. 0588-85219, www.parkhotellefonti.com, info@parkhotellefonti.com).

**$ La Primavera B&B** feels like a British B&B transplanted to Tuscany. It's a great value just a few minutes' walk outside Porta Fiorentina (near the Roman Theater). Silvia rents five charming, neat-as-a-pin rooms that share a cutesy-country lounge. The house is set back from the road in a pleasant courtyard and with a garden to lounge in. With free parking and a short walk to the old town, this is a handy option for drivers (RS%, fans but no air-con, Via Porta Diana 15, tel. 0588-87295, mobile 328-865-0390, www.affittacamere-laprimavera.com, info@affittacamere-laprimavera.com).

**$ Hotel Foresteria,** near the Chiostro delle Monache hostel and run by the same organization, has 35 big, utilitarian, new-feeling rooms with decent prices but the same location woes as the hostel described below; it's worth considering for a family with a car and a tight budget (family rooms, air-con, elevator, restaurant, free parking, Borgo San Lazzaro, tel. 0588-80050, www.foresteriavolterra.it, info@foresteriavolterra.it).

**¢ Chiostro delle Monache,** Volterra's youth hostel, fills a wing of the restored Convent of San Girolamo. It's modern, spacious, and very institutional, with lots of services and a tranquil cloister. Unfortunately, it's about a 20-minute hike from town, in a boring area near deserted hospital buildings (private rooms available and include breakfast, family rooms, reception closed 13:00-15:00 and after 19:00, elevator, free parking, kids' playroom; Via dell'Teatro 4, look for hospital sign from main Volterra-San Gimignano road; tel. 0588-86613, www.chiostrodellemonache.com, info@chiostrodellemonache.it).

## IN THE COUNTRYSIDE NEAR VOLTERRA

Charming farmhouse accommodations dot the countryside surrounding Volterra, and for drivers, these can be a good value and a fun experience. Some properties offer swimming pools, cooking classes, and more. For locations, see the map on page 640.

**$$ Podere Marcampo** is an *agriturismo* set in the dramatic landscape surrounding Volterra. Run by Genuino (owner of the recommended Ristorante Enoteca del Duca), his wife Ivana, and their English-speaking daughter Claudia, this peaceful spot has three dark but well-appointed rooms and three apartments, plus a swimming pool with panoramic views. Genuino produces his sangiovese and award-winning merlot on site; you can tour where the wine is made and then sample it in their view tasting room. Cooking classes at their restaurant in town are also available (breakfast included for Rick Steves readers, air-con, free self-service laundry, free parking, about two miles north of Volterra on the road to Pisa, tel. 0588-85393, Claudia's mobile 328-174-4605, www.agriturismo-marcampo.com, info@agriturismo-marcampo.com).

**$$ Agriturismo Podere San Lorenzo** is a short drive from the walls of Volterra but feels a world away. Mariella rents eight apartments and three rooms in an old farmhouse, clustered around a small church that is now the breakfast room. The grounds are scenic, with a natural swimming pool that looks like an artistic pond. She offers a fixed-price dinner (€30, on request) and cooking classes (breakfast extra, air-con, free self-service laundry, free parking, Via degli Alloi 80, tel. 0588-39080, www.agriturismo-volterra.it, info@agriturismosanlorenzo.it).

**$$ Agriturismo il Mulinaccio** is a welcoming, family-friendly farm about a 15-minute drive down a dirt road outside Volterra. Alessio and his family rent four apartments and four bed-and-breakfast rooms, all with a cozy style. They also offer dinner, truffle hunts, and a spa/wellness center (air-con, pool, Via Vicinale di Pretenzano 49, mobile 338-149-8432, www.agriturismoilmulinaccio.it, info@agriturismoilmulinaccio.it).

**$$ Agriturismo Santa Vittoria** sits on the top of a hill, with commanding views into the Volterra countryside. Their four bright apartments, decorated with funky art, have access to a cliffside pool. Their popular restaurant serves up hearty dishes from their farm, served at view tables (breakfast extra, air-con, Localita Molino d'Era, tel. 0588-33071, www.agriturismosantavittoria.com, info@agriturismosantavittoria.com, Katuscia).

## Eating in Volterra

Menus feature a Volterran take on regional dishes. *Zuppa alla Volterrana* is a fresh vegetable-and-bread soup, similar to *ribollita*. *Torta di ceci*, also known as *cecina*, is a savory crêpe-like garbanzo-bean flatbread that's served at *pizzerie*. Those with more adventurous palates dive into *trippa* (tripe stew, the traditional breakfast of the alabaster carvers). *Fegatelli* are meatballs made with liver.

**$$$$ Ristorante Enoteca del Duca,** serving well-presented and creative Tuscan cuisine, offers the best elegant meal in town.

You can dine under a medieval arch with walls lined with wine bottles, in a sedate, high-ceilinged dining room (with an Etruscan statuette at each table), in their little *enoteca* (wine cellar), or in their terraced garden in summer. Chef Genuino, daughter Claudia, and the friendly staff take good care of diners. The fine wine list includes Genuino's own highly regarded merlot and sangiovese. The spacious seating, dressy clientele, and calm atmosphere make this a good choice for a romantic splurge. Their €55 food-sampler fixed-price meal comes with a free glass of wine for diners with this book (Wed-Mon 12:30-15:00 & 19:30-22:00, closed Tue, near City Hall at Via di Castello 2, tel. 0588-81510).

**$$ La Carabaccia** is unique: It feels like a local family invited you over for a dinner of classic Tuscan comfort food that's rarely seen on restaurant menus. They serve only two pastas and two *secondi* on any given day (listed on the chalkboard by the door), in addition to quality cheese and cold-cut plates. Committed to tradition, on Fridays they serve only fish. They also have fun, family-friendly outdoor seating on a traffic-free piazza (Tue-Sat 12:30-14:30 & 19:30-22:00, Sun 12:30-14:30, closed Mon, reservations smart, Piazza XX Settembre 4, tel. 0588-86239, https://lacarabacciavolterra.it, Patrizia and daughters Sara and Ilaria).

**$$ Ristorante il Sacco Fiorentino** is a family-run local favorite for traditional cuisine and seasonal specials. While mostly indoors, the restaurant has a few nice tables on a peaceful street (Thu-Tue 12:00-15:00 & 19:00-22:00, closed Wed, Via Giusto Turazza 13, tel. 0588-88537, Cristina).

**$$ Trattoria da Badò,** a 10-minute hike out of town, is popular with a local crowd for its *cucina tipica Volterrana*. Giacomo and family offer a rustic atmosphere and serve food with no pretense—"the way you wish your mamma cooks." Reserve before you go, as it's often full, especially on weekends (Thu-Tue 12:30-14:30 & 19:30-22:00, closed Wed, Borgo San Lazzero 9—along the main road toward San Gimignano, near the turnoff for the old hospital, tel. 0588-80402, www.trattoriadabado.com).

**$$ La Vecchia Lira,** bright and cheery, is a classy self-serve eatery that's a hit with locals as a quick and cheap lunch spot by day and a mediocre sit-down restaurant at night (Fri-Wed 11:30-14:30 & 19:00-22:30, closed Thu, Via Matteotti 19, tel. 0588-86180, Lamberto and Massimo).

**$$ Ristorante Ombra della Sera** is another good fine-dining option for elegant Tuscan cuisine and truffle dishes. While they have a dressy interior, I'd eat here to be on the street and part of the *passeggiata* action (Tue-Sun 12:00-15:00 & 19:00-22:00, closed Mon and mid-Nov-mid-March, Via Gramsci 70, tel. 0588-86663, Massimo and Cinzia).

**$$ Pizzeria La Mangiatoia** is a fun and convivial place with a Tuscan-cowboy interior and picnic tables outside amid a family-friendly street scene. Enjoy pizzas, huge salads, and kebabs at a table or to go (Thu-Tue 12:00-23:00, closed Wed, Via Gramsci 35, tel. 0588-85695).

**Side-by-Side Pizzerias: $ Ombra della Sera** dishes out what local kids consider the best pizza in town (Tue-Sun 12:00-15:00 & 19:00-22:00, closed Mon and mid-Nov-mid-March, Via Guarnacci 16, tel. 0588-85274). **$ Pizzeria Tavernetta,** next door, has a romantically frescoed dining room upstairs for classier pizza eating (Wed-Mon 12:00-15:00 & 18:30-22:30, closed Tue, Via Guarnacci 14, tel. 0588-88155).

**Picnic:** You can assemble a picnic at the few *alimentari* around town and eat in the breezy archaeological park. The most convenient supermarket is **Punto Simply** at Via Gramsci 12 (Mon-Sat 7:30-13:00 & 16:00-20:00, Sun 8:30-13:00).

**Gelato:** Of the many ice-cream shops in the center, I've found **L'Isola del Gusto** to be reliably high quality, with flavors limited to what's in season (daily, closed Nov-Feb, Via Gramsci 3, cheery Giorgia will make you feel happy).

## Volterra Connections

**By Bus:** In Volterra, buses come and go from Piazza Martiri della Libertà (buy tickets at the tobacco shop right on the piazza or on board). Most connections are with the C.T.T. bus company (www.pisa.cttnord.it) through Colle di Val d'Elsa ("koh-leh" for short), a workaday town in the valley (4/day Mon-Sat, 1/day Sun, 50 minutes); for Pisa, you'll change in Pontedera or Saline di Volterra. Ask at the TI for schedules.

From Volterra, you can ride the bus to these destinations: **Florence** (4/day Mon-Sat, 1/day Sun, 2 hours, change in Colle di Val d'Elsa), **Siena** (4/day Mon-Sat, no buses on Sun, 2 hours, change in Colle di Val d'Elsa), **San Gimignano** (4/day Mon-Sat, 1/day Sun, 2 hours, change in Colle di Val d'Elsa, one connection also requires change in Poggibonsi), **Pisa** (9/day, fewer on Sun, 2 hours, change in Pontedera).

**By Train:** The nearest train station is in Saline di Volterra, a 15-minute bus ride away (7/day, 2/day Sun); however, trains from Saline run only to the coast, not to the major bus destinations listed here. It's better to take a bus from Volterra to Pontedera (CTT bus

#500, 8/day, 1 on Sun, 1.5 hours), where you can catch a train to **Florence, Pisa,** or **La Spezia** (convenient for the Cinque Terre).

**By Car:** From Pisa, take the highway known as FI-PI-LI (for "Firenze-Pisa-Livorno") in the direction of Florence, exiting at Pontedera to follow the scenic country road SR-439 toward Ponsacco and on to Volterra. From Florence, leave the city to the south to reach SR-2 toward Siena. Exit just past Poggibonsi onto SR-68 toward Colle di Val d'Elsa, passing San Gimignano on the way to Volterra.

**By Private Transfer:** For those with more money than time, or for travel on tricky Sundays and holidays, a private transfer to or from Volterra is the most efficient option. **Roberto Bechi** and his drivers can take up to eight people in their comfortable vans (€165 to Siena, €185 to Florence, for reservations call mobile 320-147-6590, Roberto's mobile 328-425-5648, www.toursbyroberto.com, toursbyroberto@gmail.com).

# San Gimignano

The epitome of a Tuscan hill town, with 14 medieval towers still standing (out of an original 72), San Gimignano (sahn jee-meen-YAH-noh) is a perfectly preserved tourist trap. There are no important interiors to sightsee, and the town feels greedy and packed with crass commercialism. The locals seem spoiled by the easy money of tourism, and  most of the rustic is faux. But San Gimignano is so easy to reach and so visually striking that it remains a good stop, especially if you can sidestep some of the hordes. The town is an ideal place to go against the touristic flow—arrive late in the day, enjoy it at twilight, then take off in the morning before the deluge begins. (Or day-trip here from Volterra—a 30-minute drive away—and visit early or late.)

In the 13th century—back in the days of Romeo and Juliet—feuding noble families ran the hill towns. They'd periodically battle things out from the protection of their respective family towers. Pointy skylines like San Gimignano's were the norm in medieval Tuscany.

San Gimignano's cuisine is mostly what you might find in Siena—typical Tuscan home cooking. *Cinghiale* (cheen-gee-AH-lay, boar) is served in almost every way: stews, soups, cutlets, and, my favorite, salami. The area is well-known for producing some of the best saffron in Italy; you'll find the spice for sale in shops and as a flavoring in meals at finer restaurants. Although Tuscany is normally a red-wine region, the most famous Tuscan white wine comes from here: the inexpensive, light, and fruity Vernaccia di San Gimignano.

# Orientation to San Gimignano

While the basic ▲▲▲ sight here is the town of San Gimignano itself (pop. 7,800, just 2,000 of whom live within the walls), there are a few worthwhile stops. The wall circles an amazingly preserved stony town, once on the Via Francigena pilgrimage route to Rome. The road, which cuts through the middle of San Gimignano, is named for St. Matthew in the north of town (Via San Matteo) and St. John in the south (Via San Giovanni). The town is centered on two delightful squares—Piazza del Duomo and Piazza della Cisterna—where you find the town well, City Hall, and cathedral (along with most of the tourists).

**Tourist Information:** The helpful TI is in the old center on Piazza del Duomo (daily March-Oct 10:00-13:00 & 15:00-19:00, Nov-Feb 10:00-13:00 & 14:00-18:00, sells bus tickets to Siena and Florence, tel. 0577-940-008, www.sangimignano.com). They offer occasional countryside tours and a guided city tour (€15, April-Oct Mon, Wed, Fri-Sat at 11:00 and 16:00, Sun at 11:00).

## ARRIVAL IN SAN GIMIGNANO

The **bus** stops at the main town gate, Porta San Giovanni. There's no baggage storage in town.

You can't **drive** within the walled town; drive past the "*ZTL*" red circle and you'll get socked with a big fine. Three numbered pay lots are a short walk outside the walls (and connected to town by a shuttle bus in summer; see later): The handiest is Parcheggio Montemaggio (P2), at the bottom of town near the bus stop, just outside Porta San Giovanni (€2/hour, €15/day). Least expensive but a steeper walk into town is the lot below the roundabout and Co-op supermarket, Parcheggio Giubileo (P1; €1.50/hour, €6/day). And at the north end of town, by Porta San Jacopo, is Parcheggio Bagnaia (P3/P4, €2/hour, €15/day). Note that some lots—including the one directly in front of Co-op and the one just outside Porta San Matteo—are designated for locals and have a one-hour limit for tourists.

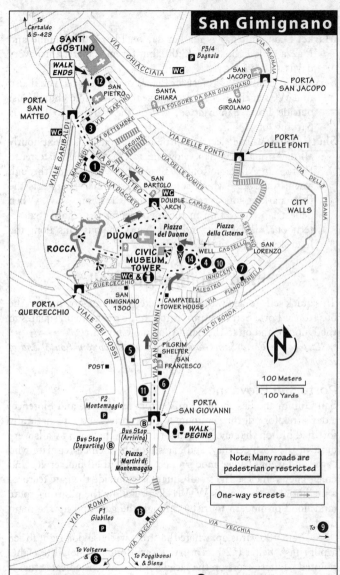

## San Gimignano

**Accommodations**
1. Hotel l'Antico Pozzo
2. Le Undici Lune
3. Locanda il Pino
4. Hotel la Cisterna
5. Palazzo al Torrione
6. Hotel Belsoggiorno (Torrione Check-in)
7. Le Vecchie Mura Camere & Rist.
8. To Locanda dei Logi
9. To Podere Ponte a Nappo

**Eateries & Other**
10. Dulcis in Fundo Ristorante
11. Trattoria Chiribiri
12. Locanda di Sant'Agostino
13. Supermarket
14. Gelateria Dondoli

VOLTERRA & SAN GIMIGNANO

## HELPFUL HINTS

**Market Day:** Thursday is market day on Piazza del Duomo and Piazza delle Erbe (8:00-13:00), but for local merchants, every day is a sales frenzy.

**Services:** A public WC is just off Piazza della Cisterna; you'll also find WCs at the Rocca fortress, near San Bartolo church, just outside Porta San Matteo, and at the Parcheggio Bagnaia parking lot.

**Shuttle Bus:** A little electric shuttle bus does its laps about hourly all day from Porta San Giovanni to Piazza della Cisterna to Porta San Matteo. Route #1 runs back and forth through town; route #2—which runs only in summer—connects the three parking lots to the town center (€1.20 one-way). When pedestrian congestion in the town center is greatest (Sat afternoons, all day Sun, and May-Sept), the bus runs along the road skirting the outside of town.

# San Gimignano Walk

This quick self-guided walking tour takes you across town, from the bus stop at Porta San Giovanni through the town's main squares to the Duomo, and on to the Sant'Agostino Church.

• *Start at the Porta San Giovanni gate at the bottom (south) end of town.*

## Porta San Giovanni

San Gimignano lies about 25 miles from both Siena and Florence, a day's trek for pilgrims en route to those cities, and on a naturally fortified hilltop that encouraged settlement. The town's walls were built in the 13th century, and gates like this helped regulate who came and went. Today, modern posts keep out all but service and emergency vehicles. The small square just outside the gate features a memorial to the town's WWII dead. Follow the pilgrims' route (and flood of modern tourists) through the gate and up the main drag.

About 100 yards up, where the street widens, look right to see a pilgrims' shelter (12th century, Pisan Romanesque). The eight-pointed Maltese cross on the facade of the church indicates that it was built by the Knights of Malta, whose early mission (before they became Crusaders) was to provide care for sick and poor pilgrims. It was one of 11 such shelters in town. Today, only the wall of the shelter remains, and the surviving interior of the church houses yet one more shop selling gifty edibles.

• *Carry on past all manner of shops, up to the top of Via San Giovanni. Look up at the formidable inner wall, built 200 years before today's outer wall. Just beyond that is the central Piazza della Cisterna. Sit on the steps of the well.*

## Piazza della Cisterna

The piazza is named for the cistern that is served by the old well standing in the center of this square. A clever system of pipes drained rainwater from the nearby rooftops into the underground cistern. This square has been the center of the town since the ninth century. Turn in a slow circle and observe the commotion of rustic-yet-proud facades crowding in a tight huddle around the well. Imagine this square in pilgrimage times, lined by inns and taverns for the town's guests. Now finger the grooves in the lip of the well and imagine generations of women and children fetching water. Each Thursday morning, the square fills with a market—as it has for more than a thousand years.

• *Notice San Gimignano's famous towers.*

## The Towers

Of the original 72 towers, only 14 survive (and one can be climbed—at the City Hall). Some of the original towers were just empty, chimney-like structures built to boost noble egos, while others were actually the forts of wealthy families.

Before effective city walls were developed, rich people needed to fortify and protect their homes themselves. These towers provided a handy refuge when ruffians and rival city-states were sacking the town. If under attack, tower owners would set fire to the external wooden staircase, leaving the sole entrance unreachable a story up; inside, fleeing nobles pulled up behind them the ladders that connected each level, leaving invaders no way to reach the stronghold at the tower's top. These towers became a standard part of medieval skylines. Even after town walls were built, the towers continued to rise—now to fortify noble families feuding within a town (Montague and Capulet-style).

In the 14th century, San Gimignano's good times turned very bad. At the start of that century, about 13,000 people lived within the walls. But in 1348, a six-month plague decimated the population, leaving the once-mighty town with barely 4,000 survivors. Once fiercely independent, now crushed and demoralized, San Gimignano came under Florence's control and was forced to tear down most of its towers. (The Banca CR Firenze building occupies the remains of one such toppled tower.) And, to add insult to injury, Florence redirected the vital trade route away from San Gimignano. The town never recovered, and poverty left it in an architectural time warp. That well-preserved 14th-century cityscape, ironically, is responsible for the town's prosperity today.

• *From the well, walk 30 yards uphill to the adjoining square with the cathedral.*

## Piazza del Duomo

Stand at the base of the stairs in front of the church. Since before there was gelato, people have lounged on these steps. Take a

360-degree spin clockwise: The cathedral's 12th-century facade is plain-Jane Romanesque—finished even though it doesn't look it. To the right, the two Salvucci Towers date from the 13th century. (Locals claim that the architect who designed New York City's Twin Towers was inspired by these). The towers are empty shells, built by the wealthy Salvucci family simply to show off. At that time, no one was allowed a vanity tower higher than the City Hall's 170 feet. So the Salvuccis built two 130-foot towers—totaling 260 feet of stony ego trip.

The stubby tower next to the Salvucci Towers is the Merchant's Tower. Imagine this in use: ground-floor shop, warehouse upstairs (see the functional shipping door), living quarters, and finally the kitchen on the top (for fire-safety reasons). The holes in the walls held beams that supported wooden balconies and exterior staircases. The tower has heavy stone on the first floor, then cheaper and lighter brick for the upper stories.

Opposite the church stands the first City Hall, with its 170-foot tower, nicknamed "the bad news tower." While the church got to ring its bells in good times, these bells were for battles and fires. The tower's arched public space hosted a textile market back when cloth was the foundation of San Gimignano's booming economy.

Next is the supersize "new" City Hall with its 200-foot tower (the only one in town open to the public; for visiting info, see the Civic Museum and Tower listing, later). The climbing lion is the symbol of the city. The coats of arms of the city's leading families have been ripped down or disfigured. In medieval times locals would have blamed witches or ghosts. For the last two centuries, they've blamed Napoleon instead.

Between the City Hall and the cathedral, a statue of St. Gimignano presides over all the hubbub. The fourth-century bishop protected the village from rampaging barbarians—and is now the city's patron saint. (To enter the cathedral, walk under that statue.)

• *You'll also see the...*

## Duomo (Duomo di San Gimignano/La Collegiata)

The nave of San Gimignano's Romanesque cathedral is lined with frescoes that tell the stories of the Bible—Old Testament on the left and New Testament on the right. Painted by masters of the 14th-century Sienese school, the frescoes are a classic use of teaching through art, with parallel themes aligned: Creation faces the Annunciation, the birth of Adam is opposite the Nativity, and—farther forward—the suffering of Job faces the agony of Jesus. Many scenes are portrayed with a 14th-century "slice of life" setting to help lay townspeople relate to Jesus.

To the right of the altar, the St. Fina Chapel honors the devout, 13th-century local girl who brought forth many miracles on her death. Her tomb is beautifully frescoed with scenes from her life by Domenico Ghirlandaio (famed as Michelangelo's teacher). The altar sits atop Fina's skeleton, and its centerpiece is a reliquary that contains her skull (€4, includes dry audioguide; April-Oct Mon-Fri 10:00-19:30, Sat until 17:30, Sun 12:30-19:30; shorter hours off-season; buy ticket and enter from courtyard around left side, www.duomosangimignano.it).

• *From the church, hike uphill (passing the church on your left) following signs to* Rocca e Parco di Montestaffoli. *Keep walking until you enter a peaceful hilltop park and olive grove, set within the shell of a 14th-century fortress the Medici of Florence built to protect this town from Siena.*

## Hilltop Views at the Rocca

On the far side, 33 steps take you to the top of a little tower (free) for the best views of San Gimignano's skyline; the far end of town and the Sant'Agostino Church (where this walk ends); and a commanding 360-degree view of the Tuscan countryside. San Gimignano is surrounded by olives, grapes, cypress trees, and—in the Middle Ages—lots of wild dangers. Back then, farmers lived inside the walls and were thankful for the protection.

• *Return to the bottom of Piazza del Duomo, turn left, and continue your walk, cutting under the double arch (from the town's first wall).*

In around 1200, this wall defined the end of town. The **Church of San Bartolo** stood just outside the wall (on the right). The Maltese cross over the door indicates that it likely served as a hostel for pilgrims. As you continue down Via San Matteo, notice that the crowds have dropped by at least half. Enjoy the breathing room as you pass a fascinating array of stone facades from the 13th and 14th centuries—now a happy cancan of wine shops and galleries.

• *Reaching the gateway at the end of town, follow signs to the right to reach...*

## Sant'Agostino Church

This tranquil church, at the far end of town (built by the Augustinians who arrived in 1260), has fewer crowds and more soul. Behind the altar, a lovely fresco cycle by Benozzo Gozzoli (who painted the exquisite Chapel of the Magi in the Medici-Riccardi Palace in Florence) tells of the life of St. Augustine, a North African monk who preached simplicity (pay a few coins for light). The kind, English-speaking friars (often from Britain and the US) are happy to tell you about the frescoes and their way of life. Pace the peaceful cloister before heading back into the tourist mobs (free, April-Oct daily 9:00-12:00 & 15:00-19:00, shorter hours off-season; Sunday Mass in English at 11:00).

# Sights in San Gimignano

### ▲Civic Museum and Tower (Musei Civici and Torre Grossa)

This small, entertaining museum, consisting of three unfurnished rooms, is inside the City Hall (Palazzo Comunale). The main reason to visit is to scale the tower, which offers sweeping views over San Gimignano and the countryside.

**Cost and Hours:** €9 includes museum and tower; daily 10:00-19:30, Oct-March 11:00-17:30, audioguide-€2, Piazza del Duomo, tel. 0577-990-312, www.sangimignanomusei.it.

**Visiting the Museum:** You'll enter the complex through a delightful stony courtyard (to the left as you face the Duomo). Climb up to the loggia to buy your ticket.

The main room (across from the ticket desk), called the **Sala del Consiglio** (a.k.a. Dante Hall, recalling his visit in 1300), is covered in festive frescoes, including the *Maestà* by Lippo Memmi (from 1317). This virtual copy of Simone Martini's *Maestà* in Siena proves that Memmi didn't have quite the same talent as his famous brother-in-law. The art gives you a peek at how people dressed, lived, worked, and warred back in the 14th century.

Upstairs, the **Pinacoteca** displays a classy little painting collection of mostly altarpieces. The highlight is a 1422 altarpiece by Taddeo di Bartolo honoring St. Gimignano (far end of last room). You can see the saint, with the town—bristling with towers—in his hands, surrounded by events from his life.

Before going back downstairs, be sure to stop by the **Mayor's Room** (Camera del Podestà, across the stairwell from the Pinacoteca). Frescoed in 1310, it offers an intimate and candid peek into the 14th century. As you enter, look right up in the corner to find a young man ready to experience the world. He hits his parents up for a bag of money and is on his way. Suddenly (above the window), he's in trouble, entrapped by two prostitutes, who lead him into a tent where he loses his money, is turned out, and is beaten. Above the door, from left to right, you see a parade of better choices: marriage, the cradle of love, the bride led to the groom's house, and newlyweds bathing together and retiring happily to their bed.

The highlight for most visitors is a chance to climb the **Tower** (entrance halfway down the stairs from the Pinacoteca). The city's tallest tower, 200 feet and 218 steps up, rewards those who climb it with a commanding view. See if you can count the town's 14 towers. It's a sturdy, modern staircase most of the way, but the last stretch is a steep, ladder-like climb.

### ▲Campatelli Tower House (Torre e Casa Campatelli)

The Campatelli family, wealthy landowners from Florence, bought an age-old tower and adjacent properties in the 19th century and turned them into a palatial residence. They lived here until 2005, when the last of the family donated it to a nonprofit organization that protects historic buildings and gardens, which then opened it to the public. The house contains family belongings and tells the story of upper-class life in Tuscany, but the highlights are an audiovisual presentation on the history of the city and the chance to peer up through the tower, with a cutaway staircase and floor, to see how the towers in San Gimignano were built.

**Cost and Hours:** €7, Thu-Tue 10:30-17:30, closed Wed, weekends only off-season, Via San Giovanni 15, tel. 0577-941-419, www.fondoambiente.it/luoghi/beni-fai.

### San Gimignano 1300

Artists and brothers Michelangelo and Raffaello Rubino share an interesting attraction in their workshop: a painstakingly rendered 1:100 scale clay model of San Gimignano at the turn of the 14th century. Step through a shop selling their art to enjoy the model. You can see the 72 original "tower houses," and marvel at how unchanged the street plan remains today. You'll peek into cross-sections of buildings, view scenes of medieval life both within and outside the city walls, and watch a video about the making of the model.

**Cost and Hours:** Free, daily 10:00-18:00, Dec-April until 17:00, on a quiet street a block over from the main square at Via Costarella 3, mobile 327-439-5165, www.sangimignano1300.com.

# Sleeping in San Gimignano

Although the town is a zoo during the daytime, locals outnumber tourists when evening comes, and San Gimignano becomes mellow and enjoyable.

## NEAR PORTA SAN MATTEO, AT THE QUIET END OF TOWN

If arriving by bus, save yourself a crosstown walk to these accommodations by asking for the Porta San Matteo stop. Drivers can park at the less-crowded Bagnaia lots (P3 and P4), and walk around to Porta San Matteo.

**$$$ Hotel l'Antico Pozzo** is an elegantly restored, 15th-century townhouse with 18 comfortable rooms, a peaceful interior courtyard terrace, and an elite air (air-con, elevator, Via San Matteo 87, tel. 0577-942-014, www.anticopozzo.com, info@anticopozzo.com; Emanuele, Elisabetta, and Mariangela).

**$$ Le Undici Lune** ("The 11 Moons") is situated in a tight but characteristic circa-1300 townhouse with steep stairs at the tranquil end of town. Its three rooms and one apartment are colorfully decorated (air-con, Via Mainardi 9, mobile 392-450-5221, le11lune@libero.it, Vincenzo).

**$ Locanda il Pino** has just seven rooms and a big living room. It's plain but clean and quiet. Run by English-speaking Elena and her family, it sits above their elegant restaurant just inside Porta San Matteo (fans, Via Cellolese 4, tel. 0577-907-003, www.locandailpino.it, locandailpino@gmail.com).

## NEAR THE MAIN SQUARE, AT THE BUSY END OF TOWN

**$$ Hotel la Cisterna,** right on Piazza della Cisterna, feels old and stately. Its 48 rooms range from old-fashioned to contemporary, and some have panoramic view terraces (RS%, air-con, elevator, good restaurant with great view, closed Jan-Feb, Piazza della Cisterna 23, tel. 0577-940-328, www.hotelcisterna.it, info@hotelcisterna.it, Alessio and Paola).

**$$ Palazzo al Torrione,** on an untrampled side street just inside Porta San Giovanni, is quiet and handy. Their 10 modern rooms, some with countryside views and terraces, are spacious and tastefully appointed (RS%, family rooms, breakfast extra, air-con, pay parking, inside and left of gate at Via Berignano 76; check-in at Hotel Belsoggiorno, 2 blocks away, on the main drag at Via

San Giovanni 91; tel. 0577-940-375, www.palazzoaltorrione.com, info@palazzoaltorrione.com, Vanna).

$ **Le Vecchie Mura Camere** offers three good rooms above their recommended restaurant along a rustic lane, clinging just below the main square (no breakfast, air-con, Via Piandornella 15, tel. 0577-940-270, www.vecchiemura.it, info@vecchiemura.it, Bagnai family).

## IN THE COUNTRYSIDE

$$$$ **Locanda dei Logi,** in the tiny *borgo* of San Donato—eight minutes from San Gimignano—houses six ultramodern, luxury rooms within a cluster of medieval buildings. Each room is elegantly designed, and all look out over the property's vineyard. Wine lovers can combine an overnight and a tasting of their top-notch wines in their cantina (wine tastings available by appointment, dinner on request, air-con, Localita San Donato 1, mobile 392-506-8229, www.locandadeilogi.it, info@locandadeilogi.it).

$$ **Podere Ponte a Nappo,** run by enterprising Carla Rossi and her English-speaking sons Francesco and Andrea, has six basic rooms and two apartments in a kid-friendly farmhouse boasting fine San Gimignano views. Located a mile below town, it can be reached by foot in about 20 minutes if you don't have a car. A picnic dinner lounging on their comfy garden furniture next to the big swimming pool as the sun sets is good Tuscan living (RS%—use code "RickSteves," air-con, free parking, tel. 0577-907-282, mobile 349-882-1565, www.accommodation-sangimignano.com, info@rossicarla.it). About 100 yards below the monument square at Porta San Giovanni, find tiny Via Baccanella/Via Vecchia and drive downhill. They also rent a dozen rooms and apartments in town.

# Eating in San Gimignano

My first two listings cling to quiet, rustic lanes overlooking the Tuscan hills; the rest are buried deep in the old center.

$$$ **Dulcis in Fundo Ristorante,** small and family-run, proudly serves modest portions of "revisited" Tuscan cuisine (with a modern twist and gourmet presentation) in a jazzy ambience. This enlightened place uses top-quality ingredients, many of which come from their own farm (Thu-Tue 12:30-14:30 & 19:15-21:45, closed Wed and Nov-Feb, Vicolo degli Innocenti 21, tel. 0577-941-919, Roberto and Cristina).

$$ **Le Vecchie Mura Ristorante** is welcoming, with good service, great prices, tasty if unexceptional home cooking, and the ultimate view. It's romantic indoors or out. They have a dressy, modern interior where you can dine with a view of the busy stainless-steel kitchen under rustic vaults, but the main reason to come

is for the incredible cliffside garden terrace. To reserve a cliffside table, call or drop by: Ask for "front view" (surcharge for outdoor tables, open only for dinner 18:00-22:00, closed Tue, Via Piandornella 15, tel. 0577-940-270, Bagnai family).

**$ Trattoria Chiribiri,** just inside Porta San Giovanni, serves homemade pastas and desserts at good prices. While its petite size and tight seating make it hot in the summer, it's a good budget option—and as such, it's in all the guidebooks (daily 11:00-23:00, Piazza della Madonna 1, tel. 0577-941-948, Roberto and Maurizio).

**$$ Locanda di Sant'Agostino** spills out onto the peaceful square, facing Sant'Agostino Church. It's homey and cheerful, serving lunch and dinner daily—big portions of basic food in a restful setting. Dripping with wheat stalks and atmosphere on the inside, it has shady on-the-square seating outside (Thu-Tue 11:00-16:00 & 18:30-23:00, closed Wed, closed Jan-Feb, Piazza Sant'Agostino 15, tel. 0577-943-141, Genziana and sons).

**Near Porta San Matteo:** Just inside Porta San Matteo is a variety of handy and inviting good-value restaurants, bars, cafés, and *gelaterie.*

**Picnics:** The big, modern **Co-op supermarket** sells all you need for a nice spread (Mon-Sat 8:30-20:00, closed Sun, at parking lot below Porta San Giovanni). Or browse the little shops guarded by boar heads within the town walls; they sell pricey boar meat *(cinghiale).* Pick up 100 grams (about a quarter pound) of boar, cheese, bread, and wine and enjoy a picnic in the garden at the Rocca or the park outside Porta San Giovanni.

**Gelato:** To cap the evening and sweeten your late-night city stroll, stop by **Gelateria Dondoli** on Piazza della Cisterna (at #4, tel. 0577-942-244, www.gelateriadondoli.com, sergio@ gelateriadondoli.com, Dondoli family). Charismatic Sergio also offers hands-on gelato-making classes in his kitchen down the street.

## San Gimignano Connections

Bus tickets are sold at the bar just inside the town gate or at the TI. Many connections require a change at Poggibonsi (poh-jee-BOHN-see), which has the nearest train station. Note that the bus connection to Volterra is four times as long as the drive; if you're desperate to get there faster, you can pay about €70 for a taxi.

**From San Gimignano by Bus to: Florence** (hourly, fewer on Sun, 1.5-2 hours, change in Poggibonsi), **Siena** (8/day direct, on Sun must change in Poggibonsi, 1.5 hours), **Volterra** (4/day Mon-Sat; 1/day Sun—in the late afternoon and usually crowded—with no return to San Gimignano; 2 hours, change in Colle di Val d'Elsa, one connection also requires change in Poggibonsi).

**By Car:** San Gimignano is an easy 45-minute drive from Florence (take the A-1 exit marked *Firenze Imprugneta,* then a right past tollbooth following *Siena per 4 corsie* sign; exit the freeway at *Poggibonsi Nord*). From San Gimignano, it's a scenic and windy half-hour drive to Volterra.

# THE HEART OF TUSCANY

*Montepulciano • Pienza • Montalcino • Heart of Tuscany Drive*

If your Tuscan dreams feature vibrant neon-green fields rolling to infinity, punctuated by snaking, cypress-lined driveways; humble but beautiful (and steep) hill towns; and world-class wines to make a connoisseur weep, set your sights on the heart of this region.

An hour south of Siena, this slice of splendor—which specializes in views and wine—is a highlight, particularly for drivers. With an astonishing diversity of towns, villages, abbeys, wineries, countryside restaurants, and accommodations—all set within jaw-dropping scenery—this subregion of Tuscany is a fine place to abandon your itinerary and just slow down.

Even though the area's towns sometimes seem little more than a rack upon which to hang the vine-draped hills, each one has its own endearing personality. The biggest and most interesting, Montepulciano, boasts a medieval cityscape wearing a Renaissance coat, wine cellars that plunge deep into the cliffs it sits upon, and a classic town square. Pienza is a sure-of-itself, planned Renaissance town that gave the world a pope. And mellow Montalcino is (even more than most towns around here) all about its wine: the famous Brunello di Montalcino.

## PLANNING YOUR TIME

As this compact region is hemmed in by Italy's two main north-south thoroughfares—the A-1 expressway and SR-2 highway—even those with a few hours to spare can get an enticing taste. But ideally, spend two nights and three full days. Many travelers enjoy home-basing here, appreciating not only the area's many attractions, but also its strategic position for day trips to Siena (less than an hour away), or Volterra, San Gimignano, Florence, and Orvieto (each about 1.5 hours away).

Montepulciano is the most all-around engaging town; it's the best choice for those without a car (though connections can still be tricky). With easy access to the vineyards, Montalcino makes sense for wine pilgrims. For drivers who'd like to home-base in the countryside, I've listed several *agriturismi* and other rural accommodations.

## The Heart of Tuscany in Three Days

Here's a smart plan, assuming you're coming from Siena. (If coming from the south, do it in reverse.)

**Day One:** On your way south from Siena, make a winery stop north of Montalcino before settling into Montepulciano (or your countryside accommodation).

**Day Two:** Follow my Heart of Tuscany Drive, including a sightseeing-and-gelato stop in Pienza. Have dinner back in Montepulciano, or in the nearby countryside.

**Day Three:** Your day is free to enjoy and sightsee Montepulciano, or drive to countryside attractions (confirm tour availability at La Foce Gardens in advance). You could head to your next destination this afternoon, or spend a third night.

## GETTING AROUND THE HEART OF TUSCANY

**By Car:** This area is ideal by car. Distances are short, and it's easy to mix-and-match sights.

Navigate by town names and use a good map or—better yet—a mapping app to keep you on track. Some sights and wineries are on tiny back lanes, marked only with easy-to-miss, low-profile signs. In small hill towns, make it a habit to park at the lot just outside town and walk in. White lines indicate free parking; blue lines indicate paid parking (pay at the station, then display the ticket on your windshield); and yellow lines are only for locals.

**By Public Transportation:** While you can reach many of this chapter's sights by public buses, connections are slow, infrequent, and often require a transfer. Taxis can help connect the dots more efficiently. Montepulciano is the best home base for those without a car (though it's still not entirely convenient).

**HEART OF TUSCANY**

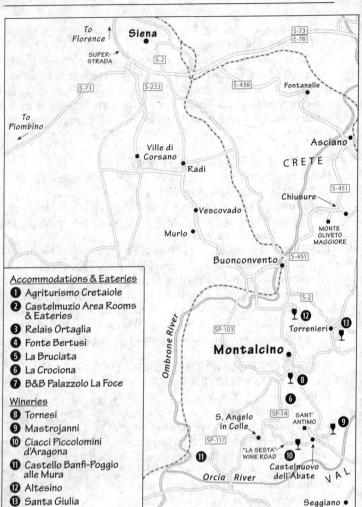

Accommodations & Eateries
1. Agriturismo Cretaiole
2. Castelmuzio Area Rooms & Eateries
3. Relais Ortaglia
4. Fonte Bertusi
5. La Bruciata
6. La Crociona
7. B&B Palazzolo La Foce

Wineries
8. Tornesi
9. Mastrojanni
10. Ciacci Piccolomini d'Aragona
11. Castello Banfi-Poggio alle Mura
12. Altesino
13. Santa Giulia

## TOURS IN TUSCANY

A good local guide can help you take full advantage of everything this area has to offer. One with a car can save you lots of time and stress.

**Antonella Piredda** is smart, well organized, and enjoyably opinionated (€60/hour, 3-hour minimum, €350/all day, she can join you in your car or hire a driver for extra, mobile 347-456-5150, www.antonellapiredda.com, antonella.piredda@live.it).

**Roberto Bechi** runs all-day minibus tours with a passion for local culture, hands-on experiences, and offbeat sights. The price is reasonable, since he assembles groups of up to eight people to

share the experience...and the cost (see website for tour options, RS%—10 percent discount, full-day minibus tours—€100/person, mobile 320-147-6590, www.toursbyroberto.com, toursbyroberto@ gmail.com). For more on Roberto's tours, see page 605.

## COUNTRYSIDE ACCOMMODATIONS

A beautiful way to more fully experience this area is to sleep in a farmhouse B&B. For locations, see the "Heart of Tuscany" map. Many of these are working farms (a prerequisite to be officially called an *agriturismo*) and give a great sense of rural family life. Others are just lovely homes in the countryside. The common denominator is the wonderful people you'll meet as your hosts.

## Near Pienza

**The Isabella Experience:** A variety of accommodations and culturally rich experiences in the countryside near Pienza are warmly run by Isabella, her farmer husband Carlo, and their team. Compare options on the website (www.theisabellaexperience.com) or call Isabella (mobile 338-740-9245)—she's happy to answer questions. Here's a rundown:

**$$$ Agriturismo Cretaiole** is perfect for fully experiencing Tuscany with a group of other travelers. A one-week stay is required (Sat to Sat), which facilitates guests becoming a community of about 20 people—guided by Carlotta—who take part in farm tours, olive oil tastings, pasta-making classes, and more (no air-con or swimming pool, shorter stays may be possible off-season, Carlotta's mobile 338-835-1614).

**$$$$ La Moscadella,** on the outskirts of Castelmuzio (five miles north of Pienza), provides a more elevated country-hotel experience—with 12 impeccably decorated rooms and a two-bedroom cottage, plus a gourmet-quality restaurant. Run by Isabella and Doriana, La Moscadella also offers à la carte cultural experiences (weeklong stays preferred but may be flexible, air-con, swimming pool; tel. 0577-665-516, Doriana mobile 338-256-6043).

In the village of Castelmuzio, they rent two other properties: **$$$ Le Casine di Castello,** a townhouse with two units; and **$$$$ Casa Moricciani,** a swanky villa with dreamy views and a garden terrace.

**More Accommodations Near Pienza: $$$$ Relais Ortaglia,** run by Americans Sandy and Phil, rents five pricey rooms in a converted 17th-century farmhouse with modern amenities such as an infinity pool, activities (cooking classes), and a free bottle of prosecco for my readers. Leaving Montepulciano on the main road toward Pienza, watch for the easy-to-miss brown *Ortaglia* sign on the left, just a half-mile past the San Biagio church turnoff (includes breakfast, 2-night minimum, air-con, mobile 391-163-9887, www.relaisortaglia.com, tuscany@ortaglia.it).

**$$$ Fonte Bertusi,** a classy and artistic guesthouse between Pienza and Cretaiole, is nicely run by young couple Manuela and Andrea, Andrea's artist-father Edoardo, and their attention-starved cats. The eight apartments mix rustic decor with avant-garde creations. The setting is sublime, with a grand sunset-view terrace, a communal barbecue and outdoor kitchen, and a swimming pool (laundry service, just outside Pienza toward San Quirico d'Orcia

## Heart of Tuscany at a Glance

▲▲▲**Montepulciano** Hill town with grand vistas, wonderful wine cellars, and a medieval soul that corrals the essence of Tuscany within its walls. See page 680.

▲▲▲**Heart of Tuscany Drive** An unforgettable day lacing together the views, villages, and rural attractions of this region (including both Montepulciano and Pienza). See page 712.

▲▲**Pienza** Unique, pint-sized planned Renaissance town that's amazingly well-preserved, very touristy, and relatively unhilly. See page 695.

▲▲**Montalcino** Touristy "Brunello-ville" wine capital that still exudes a stony charm; aside from the wine, it feels like a second-rate repeat of Montepulciano. See page 703.

▲▲**Sleeping at an *Agriturismo* or Countryside B&B** The best way to experience rural Tuscany: rustic, rural accommodations ranging from fragrant working farms to luxurious retreats. Most are run by families dedicated to making sure their cows and their guests are both well fed. See page 677.

▲**La Foce Gardens** Delightful, unique gardens with gorgeous plantings, engaging history, and fine panoramas. **Hours:** Visit by 45-minute tour only; April-Oct Wed at 15:00, 16:00, 17:00, and 18:00; Sat-Sun at 11:30, 15:00, and 16:30; no tours in winter. See page 716.

▲**Bagno Vignoni** Quirky little spa town that's simply fun to check out, whether you take a dip or not. See page 717.

on the right—just after the turnoff for "Il Fonte," tel. 0578-748-077, Manuela's mobile 339-655-5648, www.fontebertusi.it, info@fontebertusi.it).

**$$ La Bruciata** is a family-friendly *agriturismo* charmingly tucked in the countryside a five-minute drive outside Montepulciano (on the way to Pienza). Can-do Laura and several generations of her family produce wine and olive oil and rent several tasteful, modern rooms that share a peaceful yard with a swimming pool. From April through October, they prefer one-week stays (pay air-con, farm-fresh meals, cooking classes, Via del Termine 9, tel. 0578-757-704, mobile 339-781-5106, www.agriturismolabruciata.it, info@agriturismolabruciata.it). Leaving Montepulciano toward Pienza, turn off on the left for *Poggiano*, then carefully track brown *La Bruciata* signs (on gravel roads).

## Near Montalcino

**$$ La Crociona,** an *agriturismo* farm and working vineyard, rents seven fully equipped apartments with dated furnishings. Fiorella Vannoni and Roberto and Barbara Nannetti offer cooking classes and tastes of the Brunello wine grown and bottled on the premises (reception open 9:00-13:00 & 14:30-19:30, laundry service, covered pool, hot tub, fitness room, La Croce 15, tel. 0577-847-133, www.lacrociona.com, info@lacrociona.com). The farm is about two miles south of Montalcino on the road to the Sant'Antimo Abbey; don't turn off at the first entrance to the village of La Croce—wait for the second one, following signs to *Tenuta Crocedimezzo e Crociona*. A good restaurant is next door.

## At La Foce Gardens, near Montepulciano

**$$$ B&B Palazzolo La Foce** lets you sleep aristocratically in a small villa just below La Foce Gardens. Its seven colorful rooms share a welcoming lounge and breakfast area with a giant fireplace, and an outdoor swimming pool with glorious Tuscan views. All the rooms bask in fine panoramas (no air-con but breezy, Strada della Vittoria 61—check in at gardens' main entrance to get specific directions to your room, villas also available, tel. 0578-69101, www.lafoce.com, info@lafoce.com, Origo family).

# Montepulciano

Curving its way along a ridge, Montepulciano (mohn-teh-puhl-CHAH-noh) delights visitors with *vino*, views, and—perhaps more than any other large town in this area—a sense of being a real, bustling community rather than just a tourist depot.

Alternately under Sienese and Florentine rule, the city still retains its medieval *contrade* (districts), each with a mascot and flag. The neighborhoods compete the last Sunday of August in the Bravio delle Botti, where teams of men push large wine casks uphill from Piazza Marzocco to Piazza Grande, all hoping to win a banner and bragging rights. The entire last week of August is a festival: Each *contrada* arranges musical entertainment and serves food at outdoor eateries, along with generous tastings of the local *vino*.

The city is a collage of architectural styles, but the elegant San Biagio Church, just outside the city walls at the base of the hill, is its best Renaissance building. Most visitors ignore the architecture and focus more on the city's other creative accomplishment, the tasty Vino Nobile di Montepulciano red wine.

Montepulciano is a great starting and ending point for my scenic loop drive through the Heart of Tuscany, described later in this chapter.

# Orientation to Montepulciano

Commercial action in Montepulciano centers in the lower town, mostly along Via di Gracciano nel Corso (nicknamed "Corso"). This stretch begins at the town gate called Porta al Prato (near the TI, bus station, and some parking) and winds slowly up, up, up through town—narrated by my self-guided walk. Strolling here, you'll find eateries, gift shops, and tourist traps. The back streets are worth exploring. The main square, at the top of town (up a steep switchback lane from the Corso), is Piazza Grande. Standing proudly above all the touristy sales energy, the square has a noble, Florentine feel.

## TOURIST INFORMATION

The helpful TI is just outside the Porta al Prato city gate, in the small P1 parking lot (Mon-Sat 9:00-13:00 & 15:00-19:00, Sun 9:00-13:00, daily until 20:00 in July-Aug, sells bus and train tickets, Piazza Don Minzoni, tel. 0578-757-341, www.prolocomontepulciano.it).

The office on the main square that looks like a TI is actually the privately run Valdichiana Living agency. They provide wine-road maps, wine tours in the city, minibus winery tours farther afield, and cooking classes and other culinary experiences (Mon-Fri 10:00-13:30 & 14:30-18:00, shorter Sat hours, Sun 10:00-13:00, Piazza Grande 7, tel. 0578-717-484, www.valdichianaliving.it).

## ARRIVAL IN MONTEPULCIANO

Whether you arrive by car or bus, ease your climb to the top of town by riding up on the shuttle bus. For details, see "Helpful Hints," later.

**By Car:** Well-signed pay-and-display parking lots ring the city center (marked with blue lines). Some free spaces are mixed in (marked with white lines)—look around before you park, and keep an eye out for time limits.

To start your visit by following my self-guided walk (up the length of the Corso to the main square), park at the north end of town, near the Porta al Prato gate. Around here, the handiest lots are P1 (in front of the TI, with some free spaces) and the unnumbered lot just above, directly in front of the stone gate. If these are full, try lots P2 or P4, or lot P5 near the bus station.

For quicker access to the main square up top, use one of the parking lots at the top end of town: Approaching Montepulciano, follow signs for *centro storico, duomo,* and *Piazza Grande,* and use the Fortezza or San Donato lots (flanking the fortress).

Avoid the "ZTL" no-traffic zone (signs marked with a red circle). If you're sleeping in town, your hotelier can give you a permit to park within the walls; be sure to get very specific instructions before you arrive.

**By Bus:** Buses leave passengers at the bus station on Piazza Nenni, downhill from the Porta al Prato gate. From the station, cross the street and head inside the modern orange-brick structure burrowed into the hillside, where there's an elevator. Ride to level 1, walk straight down the corridor (following signs for *centro storico*), and ride a second elevator (to a different level 1 and the Poggiofanti Gardens); walk to the end of this park and hook left to find the Porta al Prato gate.

## HELPFUL HINTS

**Market Day:** It's on Thursday morning (8:00-13:00), near the bus station.

**Services:** There's no official **baggage storage,** but the TI might let you leave bags with them if they have space. Public **WCs** are located at the TI, to the left of Palazzo Comunale, and at the Sant'Agostino Church.

**Shuttle Bus to the Top of Town:** To avoid the hike up through town to Piazza Grande, hop on the orange shuttle bus. It departs about every 15 minutes from the parking lot near the bus station and from the lane leading to the Porta al Prato gate, just above the TI (€1.20, buy tickets at bars, tobacco shops, or the TI).

**Laundry:** An elegant self-service launderette is at the top of town at Via del Paolino 2, just around the corner from the recommended Camere Bellavista (daily 8:00-22:00, tel. 0578-717-544).

**Taxis:** Two taxi drivers operate in Montepulciano. Call 330-732-723 for short trips within town (€10 for rides up or down hill); to reach other towns, call 348-733-5343.

# Montepulciano Walk

This two-part self-guided walk traces the spine of the town from its main entrance up to its hilltop seat of power. Part 1 begins at the big gate at the bottom of town, Porta al Prato (near the TI and several parking lots); Part 2 focuses on the square at the very top of

# Montepulciano

## Accommodations

1. La Locanda di San Francesco & E Lucevan le Stelle Wine Bar
2. Mueblè il Riccio
3. Albergo Duomo
4. Vicolo dell'Oste B&B
5. Camere Bellavista

## Eateries

6. Ost. dell'Acquacheta
7. Osteria del Conte
8. Le Pentolaccia
9. Ai Quattro Venti
10. Sgarbi Gelato Natura
11. To La Grotta

## Other

12. Copper Shop
13. Copper Workshop
14. Contucci Cantina
15. De' Ricci Cantine
16. Cantina della Talosa
17. Launderette

Ⓑ Local Shuttle Bus

**HEART OF TUSCANY**

To Siena via Sinalunga & A-1 Autostrada Freeway
To Chiusi

VIA E. PEENABEI

SANT' AGNESE

VIA CAL

P #3

P #4

Piazza Don Minzoni

Poggio-fanti Gardens

BUS STN.

VIALE DELLE LETERE

Ⓑ

P #1

VIA SANGALLO

Porta al Prato

ELEVATOR

Ⓑ

Piazza Nenni

P

ⓘ

Porta al Prato

PORTA AL PRATO

VIALE 1 MAGGIO

P #5

WC

P #2

**WALK BEGINS**

PALAZZO BUCELLI

COLONA DEL MARZOCCO

SANT' AGOSTINO

WC

10

SANTA LUCIA

VIA GRACCIANO NEL CORSO

CLOCK TOWER

POST

PORTA DI GOZZANO

VIA FIANA

ARCHI

V. COSTE

VIA POGGIOLO

LOGGIA

VIA DI VOLTAIA NEL CORSO

SAN FRANCESCO

UBI

CAFFÈ POLIZIANO

200 Meters
200 Yards

Piazza San Francesco

1

4

VICOLO SDRUCC.

VIA DI VOLTAIA NEL CORSO

**WALK ENDS**

17

5

GESÙ

8

PORTA DI GRASSI

15

VIA RICCI

TALOSA

16

2

14

VIA D. ORIOLO

PALAZZO COMUNALE

Piazza Grande

WC

9

Ⓑ

13

VIA TEATRO

VIA CAGNANO

12

VIA DELL'OPIO NEL CORSO

P #7

VIA DI SAN BIAGIO

DUOMO

VIA FIORENZUOLA VECCHIA

VIA DI SPAGGE

COPPER SHOP

PORTA DI FARINE

VIA D. CIRCONVALLAZIONE

3

6

To San Biagio Church & 11

7

Fortezza

P San Donato

VIA SAN DONATO

VIA COLLAZZI

FORTEZZA

V. POLIZIANO

P #8

VIA DI SAN PIETRO

To Pienza, Montalcino

SANTA MARIA

VIA DEL FILOSOFI

Ⓑ Local Shuttle Bus

town and the nearby streets. Part 1 is steeply uphill; to skip straight to the more level part of town (and Part 2), ride the shuttle bus up, or park at one of the lots near the Fortezza. (When you're done there, you can still do Part 1—backwards—on the way back down.)

## PART 1: UP THE CORSO

This guided stroll takes you up through Montepulciano's commercial (and touristy) gamut from the bottom of town to the top. While the street is lined mostly with gift shops, you'll pass a few relics of an earlier age.

Begin in front of the imposing Porta al Prato, one of the many stout city gates that once fortified this highly strategic town. Facing the gate, find the sign for the Porta di Bacco *"passaggio segreto"* on the left. While Montepulciano did have secret passages tunneled through the rock beneath it (handy during times of siege), this particular passage—right next to the city's front door—was probably no *segreto*...though it works great for selling salami.

Walk directly through the **Porta al Prato,** looking up to see the slot where the portcullis (heavily fortified gate) could slide down to seal things off. Notice that there are two gates, enabling defenders to trap would-be invaders in a no-man's-land where they could be doused with hot tar. Besides having a drop-down portcullis, each gate also had a hinged door—effectively putting four barriers between the town and its enemies.

Pass through the gate and head a block uphill to reach the **Colonna del Marzocco.** This column, topped with a lion holding the Medici shield, is a reminder that Montepulciano existed under the auspices of Florence—but only for part of its history.

The column is also the starting point for Montepulciano's masochistic tradition, the **Bravio delle Botti,** held on the last Sunday of August, in which each local *contrada* (neighborhood) selects its two stoutest young men to roll a 180-pound barrel up the hill through town. If the vertical climb through town wears you out, be glad you're only toting a daypack. Do you see colorful flags lining the street? If so, you'll notice you're in the Gracciano *contrada*, symbolized by the green, black, and yellow lion. Notice how the flags change with the neighborhood as you continue through town.

A few steps up, on the right (at #91, with stylized lion heads), is one of the many fine noble palaces that front Montepulciano's main strip. The town is fortunate to be graced with so many bold and noble *palazzi*—Florentine nobility favored Montepulciano as a breezy and relaxed place for a secondary residence. The higher you go in Montepulciano, the closer you are to the town center...and the fancier the mansions.

Farther up on the right, at #73 (Palazzo Bucelli), take a moment to examine the **Etruscan and Roman fragments** embedded

in the wall, left here by a 19th-century antiques dealer. You can quickly distinguish which pieces came from the Romans and those belonging to the earlier Etruscans by their alphabets: The "backwards" Etruscan letters (they read from right to left) resemble Greek. Many of the fragments show a circle flanked by a pair of inward-facing semicircular designs. This symbol represents the libation cup used for drinking at an Etruscan banquet.

At the top of the block on the right is the **Church of Sant'Agostino.** Its late-Gothic facade features a terra-cotta sculpture group by the architect Michelozzo, a favorite of the Medicis in Florence. The interior is a clean, serene, white-and-beige space.

Hike up a few more steps, then take a breather to look back and see the **clock tower** in the middle of the street. The bell ringer at the top takes the form of the character Pulcinella, one of the wild and carefree revelers familiar from Italy's commedia dell'arte theatrical tradition.

Continuing up, at the *alimentari* on the right (at #23), notice the classic old sign advertising milk, butter, margarine, and olive and canola oil. Keep on going (imagine pushing a barrel now), and bear right with the street under another sturdy **gateway**—indicating that this city grew in concentric circles. Passing through the gate, you'll run into a loggia (with the Florentine Medici seal—a shield with balls).

Facing the loggia, veer left and keep on going. As you huff and puff, notice (on your right, and later on both sides) the steep, narrow, often-covered lanes called *vicolo* ("little street"). You're getting a peek at the higgledy-piggledy medieval Montepulciano. Only when the rationality of Renaissance aesthetics took hold was the main street realigned, becoming symmetrical and pretty. Beneath its fancy suit, though, Montepulciano remains a rugged Gothic city.

Again, notice the fine and ever-bulkier palaces. On the left, a tiny courtyard makes it easier to appreciate the grandiosity of the next palace, now home to **UBI Banca.** By the way, the stone scrolls under the window are a design element called a "kneeling window"—created by Michelangelo and a popular decorative element in High Renaissance and Mannerist architecture. You'll see kneeling windows all over town.

Just after is a fine spot for a coffee break (on the left, at #27): **Caffè Poliziano,** the town's most venerable watering hole (from 1868). Step inside to soak in the genteel atmosphere, with a busy espresso machine, loaner newspapers on long sticks, and a little terrace with spectacular views.

A bit farther up, on the right, notice the precipitous **Vicolo dello Sdrucciolo**—literally "slippery lane." Any *vicolo* on the right can be used as a steep shortcut to the upper part of town, while those on the left generally lead to fine vistas. Many of these side lanes are spanned by brick arches, allowing centuries-old buildings to lean on each other for support rather than toppling over—a fitting metaphor for the tight-knit communities that vitalize small Italian towns.

Continuing up, notice more kneeling windows. The next church on the left, the Jesuit **Church of Gesù,** is worth a look. Its interior is elliptical in shape and full of 3-D illusions (the side chapels and the cupola are all painted on flat surfaces). Soon the street levels out—enjoy this nice, lazy, easy stretch, with interesting shops and artisan workshops (such as the mosaics studio at #14, on the right). A few short blocks farther, across from #64, a lane leads to a charming terrace with a commanding view of the Tuscan countryside.

The **Mazzetti** copper shop (#64) is crammed full of decorative and practical items. The production of hand-hammered copper vessels like these is a dying art; in this shop, you can see works by Cesare, who makes them in his workshop just up the street.

Continuing steeply uphill will take you to the main square. At the bend just before the square, Cesare's buddy Adamo loves to introduce travelers to Montepulciano's fine wines at the **Contucci Cantina** (described later). Visit Cesare and Adamo now, or head up to the square for Part 2 of this walk.

Either way, Montepulciano's main square is just ahead. You made it!

## PART 2: PIAZZA GRANDE AND NEARBY

This pleasant, lively piazza is surrounded by a grab bag of architectural sights. The medieval **Palazzo Comunale,** or town hall, resembles Florence's Palazzo Vecchio—yet another reminder that Florence dominated Montepulciano in the 15th and 16th centuries. The crenellations along the roof were never intended to hide soldiers—they just symbolize power. The big, square central tower makes it clear that the city is keeping an eye out in all directions.

Take a moment to survey the square, where the town's four great powers stare each other down. Face

the Palazzo Comunale, and keep turning to the right. You'll see the one-time building of the courts, behind the well (Palazzo del Capitano); the noble Palazzo Tarugi, a Renaissance-arcaded confection (with a public loggia at ground level and a private loggia—now enclosed—directly above); and the aristocratic Palazzo Contucci, with its 16th-century Renaissance facade. (The Contucci family still lives in their palace, producing and selling their own wine.) Continuing your spin, you see the unfinished Duomo looking glumly on, wishing the city hadn't run out of money for its facade.

A cistern system fed by rainwater draining from the roofs of surrounding palaces supplied the fine **well** in the corner. Check out its 19th-century pulleys, the grilles to keep animals from contaminating the water supply, and its decorative top: the Medici coat of arms flanked by lions (representing Florence) dwarfing griffins (representing Montepulciano).

Climbing the town hall's **tower** rewards you with a windblown but commanding panorama from the terrace below the clock. Go into the Palazzo Comunale, head up the stairs to your left, and pay on the second floor. You can pay to go just as far as the terrace, at the base of the tower (€2.50, 71 stairs, or ride the elevator halfway up); or pay more to go all the way to the top, twisting up extremely narrow brick steps past the antiquated bell-ringing mechanism (€5, 76 additional stairs). If you don't mind the claustrophobic climb, it's worth paying extra to reach the very top, from where you can see all the way to Pienza (look just to the right of San Biagio Church; tower open daily May-Oct 10:00-18:00, closed in winter). The street to the left as you face the tower leads to the **Fortezza.**

**To the Church of San Francesco and Views:** From the main square, a short, mostly level walk leads to a fine viewpoint. You could head 200 yards straight down the wide street to the right as you face the tower. But for a more interesting look at Montepulciano behind its pretty Renaissance facades, go down **Via Talosa,** the narrow lane between the two palaces in the corner of the square. Pause at the recommended Mueblè il Riccio B&B (with a fine courtyard—peek inside) and look high up across the street to see how centuries of structures have been stitched together, sometimes gracelessly. Across the street is the recommended Cantina della Talosa wine cellar—imagine the wine caves below your feet.

Follow this lane as it bends left, and eventually you'll pop out just below the main square, a few doors from the recommended De' Ricci Cantine wine cellar. Turn right and head down toward the church. Just before #21 (on the left), look for a red-and-gold **shield** over a door with the name *Talosa.* This marks the home of one of Montepulciano's *contrade,* or neighborhoods; birth and death an-

## The Beauty of Tuscany's Geology (and Vice Versa)

While tourists have romanticized notions of the "Tuscan" landscape, there is a surprisingly wide variety of landforms in the region. Never having been crushed by a glacier, Tuscany is anything but flat. Its hills and mountains are made up of different substances, each suited to very different types of cultivation.

The Chianti region (between Florence and Siena) is rough and rocky, with an inhospitable soil that challenges grape vines to survive while coaxing them to produce excellent wine grapes.

South of Siena, the soil switches from rock to clay, silt, and sand. The region called the Crete Senesi is the perfectly described "Sienese Clay Hills." Looking out from a breezy viewpoint, you can easily visualize how these clay hills were once at the bottom of the sea floor. The soil here is perfect for truffles and for vast fields of wheat, sun-yellow rapeseed (for canola oil), and periodically fava beans (to add nitrogen to the soil). In the spring and summer, the Crete Senesi is blanketed with brightly colorful crops and flowers in spring and summer, but by the fall, after the harvest, it's brown, dusty, and desolate. Within the Crete Senesi, you can distinguish two types of hills shaped by erosion: smooth, rounded *biancane* and pointy, jagged *calanchi*.

nouncements for the *contrada* are posted on the board next to the door.

Across the street and a few steps farther (on the right), you hit a **viewpoint.** From here, it's easy to appreciate Montepulciano's highly strategic position. The ancient town sitting on this high ridge was surrounded by powerful forces—everything you see in this direction was part of the Papal States, ruled from Rome. In the distance is Lake Trasimeno, once a notorious swampland that made it even harder to invade this town.

Continue a few steps downhill, then uphill, into the big parking lot in front of the **Church of San Francesco.** Head out to the overlook for a totally different view: the rolling hills that belonged to Siena. And keep in mind that Montepulciano itself belonged to Florence. For the first half of the 16th century, those three formidable powers—Florence, Siena, and Rome (the papacy)—vied to control this small area. You can also see Montepulciano's most impressive church, San Biagio—well-worth a visit for drivers or hikers.

From here, you can head back up to the main square, or drop into one of my recommended cantinas to spelunk their wine cellars.

The area around Montepulciano and Montalcino is more varied, with rocky protuberances that break up the undulating clay hills and provide a suitable home for wine grapes. Even farther south is the Val d'Orcia. This valley of the Orcia River is similar to the Crete Senesi, but has fewer rocks and jagged *calanchi*. Montepulciano sits in a unique position between the Val d'Orcia and the much flatter Val di Chiana (through which Italy's main north-south expressway runs).

You'll see many hot springs in this part of Tuscany, as well as town names with the word Terme (for "spa" or "hot spring") or Bagno ("bath"). These generally occur where clay meets rock: Water moving through the clay encounters a barrier and gets trapped. A byproduct of these mineral springs is the limestone called travertine, explaining the quarries you may see around spa towns.

# Sights and Experiences in Montepulciano

For me, Montepulciano's best "experiences" are personal: dropping in on Adamo, the winemaker at Contucci Cantina, and Cesare, the coppersmith at Ramaio Cesare. Both will greet you with a torrent of cheerful Italian; just smile and nod, pick up what you can from gestures, and appreciate this rare opportunity to meet a true local character.

### ▲▲Contucci Cantina

Montepulciano's most popular attraction isn't made of stone—it's the famous wine, Vino Nobile. This robust red can be tasted in any of the cantinas lining Via Ricci and Via di Gracciano nel Corso, but the cantina in the basement of Palazzo Contucci is both historic and fun. Skip the palace's formal wine-tasting showroom facing the square, and instead head down the lane on the right to the actual cellars, where you'll meet lively Adamo (ah-DAH-moh), who has been making wine here since 1961 and welcomes tourists into the cellar. While at the palace, you may meet Andrea or Ginevra Contucci, who love to share their family's products with the public. Adamo and the Contuccis usually have a half-dozen bottles open, and at busy times, other members of their staff are likely to speak English.

After sipping a little wine with Adamo, explore the palace basement, with its 13th-century vaults. Originally part of the town's wall, these chambers have been filled since the 1500s with huge barrels of wine.

**Cost and Hours:** Free drop-in tasting, free cellar tour upon request, daily 10:00-18:30, shorter hours off-season, Piazza Grande 13, tel. 0578-757-006, www.contucci.it.

### ▲Ramaio Cesare

Cesare the coppersmith is an institution in Montepulciano, carrying on his father's and grandfather's trade by hammering into existence an immense selection of copper objects in his cavernous workshop. Though his English is limited, Cesare (CHEH-zah-ray) is happy to show you photos of his work—including the copper top of the Duomo in Siena and the piece he designed and personally delivered to Pope Benedict. Peruse his tools: a giant Road Runner-style anvil, wooden hammers, and stencils dating from 1857 that have been passed down from his grandfather and father. Next door, he has assembled a fine museum with items he and his relatives have made, as well as pieces from his personal collection. Cesare's justifiable pride in his vocation evokes the hardworking, highly skilled craft guilds that once dominated small-town Italy.

**Cost and Hours:** Demonstration and museum are free, Cesare is generally in his workshop Mon-Sat 9:00-12:30 & 14:30-18:30, closed Sun, 50 yards steeply downhill from the Contucci Cantina at Via del Teatro 4, tel. 0578-758-753, www.rameria.com. Cesare's delightful shop is on the main drag, a block below, at Corso #64—look for *Rameria Mazzetti,* open long hours daily.

### Duomo

This church's unfinished facade—rough stonework left waiting for the final marble veneer—is not that unusual. Many Tuscan churches were built just to the point where they had a functional interior, and then, for various practical reasons, the facades were left unfinished. But step inside, where, amid the fairly austere interior, you'll be rewarded with some fine art. A beautiful blue-and-white, glazed terra-cotta *Altar of the Lilies* by Andrea della Robbia is behind the baptismal font (on the left as you enter). The high altar, with a top like a pine forest, features a luminous, late-Gothic Assumption triptych by the Sienese artist Taddeo di Bartolo. Showing Mary in her dreamy eternal sleep as she ascends to be crowned by Jesus, it illustrates how Siena clung to the Gothic aesthetic—elaborate gold leaf and lacy pointed arches—to show heavenly grandeur.

**Cost and Hours:** Free, daily 8:30-18:30.

### ▲De' Ricci Cantine

The most impressive wine cellars in Montepulciano sit below the Palazzo Ricci, just a few steps off the main square (toward the Church of San Francesco). Enter through the unassuming door and find your way down, down, down a spiral staircase—with rounded steps designed to go easy on fragile noble feet, and lined with rings held in place by tiny, finely crafted wrought-iron goat heads. You'll wind up in the dramatic cellars, with gigantic barrels under even more gigantic vaults—several stories high. As you go deeper into the cellars, natural stone seems to take over the brick. At the deepest point, you can peer into the atmospheric Etruscan cave, where a warren of corridors spins off from a filled-in well. Finally you wind up in the shop, where you're welcome to taste a few wines (with some local cheese). Don't miss their delightful dessert wine, vin santo.

**Cost and Hours:** First three tastings-free, two additional premium tastes-€5, €12-35 bottles, affordable shipping, daily 10:30-18:30, enter Palazzo Ricci at Via Ricci 11—look for signs for *Cantine de' Ricci*, tel. 0578-757-166, www.cantinadericci.it, Enrico.

### Cantina della Talosa

This historic cellar, which goes down and down to an Etruscan tomb at the bottom, ages a well-respected wine. With a passion and love of their craft, Andrea and Cristian Pepi give enthusiastic tours and tastings. While you can drop by for a free sample, it's also possible to call ahead to book a complete tour and tasting (€20, including five wines to taste and light food).

**Cost and Hours:** Free tasting, daily March-Oct 10:30-19:00, shorter hours off-season, a block off Piazza Grande at Via Talosa 8, tel. 0578-757-929, www.talosa.it.

## ON THE OUTSKIRTS
### ▲San Biagio Church (Chiesa de San Biagio)

The church is just west of town, at the base of Montepulciano's hill, down a picturesque cypress-lined driveway. Often called the "Temple of San Biagio" because of its Greek-cross style, this church—designed by Antonio da Sangallo the Elder and built of locally quarried travertine—feels like Renaissance perfection. If the church is empty, experiment worshipfully with the marvelous acoustics. Consider a picnic or snooze on the grass in back, with fine vistas over the Chiana Valley. The recommended La Grotta restaurant is across the street from the church.

**Cost and Hours:** €3.50, includes 20-minute audioguide; daily 10:00-18:00, longer hours in summer, shorter hours in winter.

## Sleeping in Montepulciano

**$$$$ La Locanda di San Francesco** is overpriced but luxurious, with four stylish view rooms over a classy wine bar on a quiet square at Montepulciano's summit (closed Nov-Easter, air-con, free parking nearby, Piazza San Francesco 5, tel. 0578-758-725, www.locandasanfrancesco.it, info@locandasanfrancesco.it, Luca).

**$$ Mueblè il Riccio** ("The Hedgehog") is medieval-elegant, with 10 modern and spotless rooms, an awesome roof terrace, and friendly owners. Five are newer "superior" rooms with grand views across the Tuscan valleys (family rooms, breakfast extra, air-con, limited free parking—request when you reserve, a block below the main square at Via Talosa 21, tel. 0578-757-713, www.ilriccio.net, info@ilriccio.net, Gió and Ivana speak English). Charming Gió and his son Iacopo give tours of the countryside (€50/hour) in one of their classic Italian cars.

**$$ Albergo Duomo** is big, modern, and nondescript, with 13 simple but dignified rooms (with small bathrooms) and a comfortable lounge downstairs. With a handy location just a few steps from the main square, it's at the very top of town, with free private parking nearby (RS%—use code "Steves," family rooms, elevator, air-con in some rooms—extra charge, Via di San Donato 14, tel. 0578-757-473, www.albergoduomo.it, albergoduomo@libero.it, Simone).

**$$ Vicolo dell'Oste B&B,** just off the main drag halfway up through town, has five family-friendly modern rooms. Some are like tiny apartments (RS%, includes breakfast at nearby café, on Via dell'Oste 1—an alley leading right off the main drag just after Caffè Poliziano and opposite the *farmacia* at #47, tel. 0578-758-393, www.vicolodelloste.it, info@vicolodelloste.it, Luisa and Giuseppe).

**$ Camere Bellavista** has 10 tidy rooms. True to its name, the rooms have fine views—though some are better than others. Room 6 has a view terrace worth reserving; there's also one economy room without a view (cash only, no breakfast, lots of stairs with no elevator, reception not always staffed—call before arriving or ring bell, Via Ricci 25, mobile 347-823-2314, www.camerebellavista.it, info@camerebellavista.it, Gabriella and Alessio speak just enough English).

# Eating in Montepulciano

Unless otherwise noted, these places are all open for lunch (about 12:30-14:30) and again for dinner (about 19:30-22:00).

**$$$ Osteria dell'Acquacheta** is a carnivore's dream come true, beloved among locals for its beef steaks. Its long, narrow

room is jammed with shared tables and tight, family-style seating, with an open fire in back and a big hunk of red beef lying on the counter like a corpse on a gurney. Giulio and his wife, Chiara, run a fun-loving but tight ship—posing with slabs of red meat yet embracing decades of trattoria tradition (you'll get one glass to use alternately for wine and water). Steaks are sold by weight (€32/kilo). Typically, two people split a 1.6-kilo steak (that's 3.5 pounds; the smallest they'll cook is 1.2 kilos). They also serve hearty pastas and salads and a fine house wine (or bring your own wine for a tiny corkage fee, reservations required; seatings generally at 12:30, 14:30, 19:30, and 21:30 only; closed Tue and unpredictably on other days; Via del Teatro 22, tel. 0578-717-086, www.acquacheta.eu).

**$$ Osteria del Conte,** an attractive but humble family-run bistro, offers cooking like your Italian mom's. While the interior is very simple, they also have outdoor tables on a stony street at the top of the historic center (closed Mon, Via San Donato 19, tel. 0578-756-062).

**$$ Le Pentolaccia** is a small, family-run restaurant about two-thirds of the way up the main drag. With both indoor and outdoor seating, they make tasty traditional Tuscan dishes as well as daily fish specials. Cristiana serves, and husband-and-wife team Jacobo and Alessia stir up a storm in the kitchen (closed Thu, Corso 86, tel. 0578-757-582).

**$$ Ai Quattro Venti** is right on Piazza Grande, with a simple dining room and outdoor tables on the square. It offers reasonable portions of unfussy Tuscan food in an unpretentious setting. Try their own organic olive oil and wine (closed Thu, next to City Hall on Piazza Grande, tel. 0578-717-231, Chiara).

**Wine Bar/Bistro:** With a terrace on a tranquil square in front of the Church of San Francesco, **$ E Lucevan le Stelle** (part of La Locanda di San Francesco) is a fine place to nurse a glass of local wine (also pastas, salads, and soups; daily 12:00-24:00, closed Nov-Easter, Piazza San Francesco 5, tel. 0578-758-725, Luca).

**Gelato:** For the best gelato in town, look for **Sgarbi Gelato Natura,** near the bottom of the main drag. Owner Nicola makes his gelato fresh every morning, using locally sourced ingredients from producers he knows personally. The gelato is ready around 13:00—and when it's gone, it's gone (daily 11:00-20:00, Corso 50; also runs Buon Gusto in Pienza).

**Just Outside Montepulciano:** Facing San Biagio Church (at the base of Montepulciano's hill, and described earlier), **$$$ La Grotta** has an excellent reputation for elevated Tuscan cuisine in a sophisticated, dressy setting. Reservations are recommended (Thu-Tue 12:30-14:15 & 19:30-22:00, closed Wed, Via di San Biagio 15, tel. 0578-757-479, www.lagrottamontepulciano.it).

**Near Montepulciano:** Skim this chapter for recommendations, and consider combining dinner with a scenic joyride. Good choices include **Ristorante Daria** in Monticchiello (page 719) and **The Isabella Experience**'s dinners near Castelmuzio (page 702).

## Montepulciano Connections

Get bus schedules at the TI or the bus station on Piazza Pietro Nenni, which seems to double as the town hangout, with a lively bar and locals chatting inside. In fact, there's no real ticket window—buy your tickets at the bar. Check www.tiemmespa.it for schedules.

**By Bus to: Florence** (1/day departs in the wee hours, 2/week additional departures a bit later in the morning, 2 hours, LFI bus, www.lfi.it; or take a bus to Chiusi to catch a train—see below), **Siena** (6-7/day, none on Sun, 1.5 hours, also possible to change here for Florence express bus), **Pienza** (8/day, 30 minutes), **Montalcino** (3-4/day, none Sun, change in Torrenieri, 1 hour; or consider a taxi—see below).

**By Train:** Trains are impractical here; the Montepulciano train station, five miles from town and connected by a 15-minute bus ride, has only milk-run trains (but could be useful for reaching Siena on a Sunday, when buses are scarce—get details at the TI). More convenient, consider riding the hourly bus 50 minutes to the town of **Chiusi,** which is on the main Florence-Rome rail line.

**Taxi Alternatives:** As the **Montalcino** bus connection is infrequent and complicated, consider hiring a taxi (about €70; see contact info under "Helpful Hints," earlier).

# Pienza

Set on a crest and surrounded by green, rolling hills, the small town of Pienza packs a lot of Renaissance punch. In the 1400s, locally born Pope Pius II of the Piccolomini family decided to remodel his birthplace into a city fit for a pope, in the style that was all the rage: Renaissance. Propelled by papal clout, the town of Corsignano was transformed—in only five years' time—into a jewel of Renaissance architecture. It was renamed Pienza, after Pope Pius.

Pienza's architectural focal point is its main square, Piazza Pio II, surrounded by the Duomo and the pope's family residence, Palazzo Piccolomini. While Piazza Pio II is Pienza's pride and joy, the entire town—a mix of old stonework, potted plants, and grand views—is fun to explore, especially with a camera or sketchpad in hand. You can walk every lane in the tiny town in well under an hour. Pienza is situated on a relatively flat plateau rather than the steep pinnacle of more dramatic towns like Montepulciano and Montalcino. (This is a plus for visitors with limited mobility, who find basically level Pienza easy to explore.)

Tourists flood Pienza on weekends and in peak season, and authentic local shops are outnumbered by boutiques selling gifty packages of pecorino cheese and local wine. Restaurants here tend to be more expensive and less reliable than alternatives in the nearby countryside. For these reasons, Pienza is made to order as a stretch-your-legs break to enjoy the townscape and panoramas, but it's not ideal for lingering overnight (though some excellent options exist just outside town; see "Countryside Accommodations," earlier). For the best experience, visit late in the day, after the day-trippers have dispersed.

Nearly every shop sells the town's specialty: pecorino, a pungent sheep's cheese (you'll smell it before you see it) that's sometimes infused with other ingredients, such as truffles or cayenne pepper. Look on menus for warm pecorino (*al forno* or *alla griglia*), often topped with honey and pine nuts or pears and served with bread. Along with a glass of local wine, this just might lead you to a new understanding of *la dolce vita*.

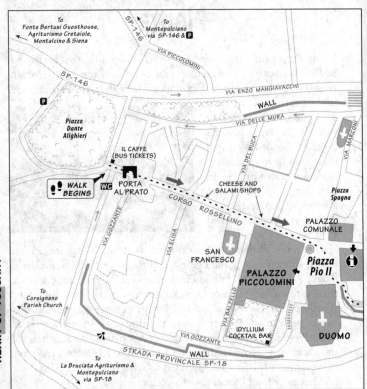

# Orientation to Pienza

**Tourist Information:** The TI is 10 yards up the street from Piazza Pio II, inside the skippable Diocesan Museum (Wed-Mon 10:30-18:30 except Sat-Sun 10:00-16:00 off-season, closed Tue year-round, Corso il Rossellino 30, tel. 0578-749-905). Ignore the *Informaturista* kiosk just outside the gate—it's a private travel agency.

**Arrival in Pienza:** If **driving**, read signs carefully—some parking spots are reserved for locals, others require the use of a cardboard clock, and others are pay-and-display. Parking is tight, so if you don't see anything quickly, head for the large pay lot at Piazza del Mercato near Largo Roma outside the old town: As you approach town and reach the "ZTL" cul-de-sac (marked with a red circle) in front of the town gate, head up the left side of town and look for the parking turnoff on the left (closed Fri morning during market). **Buses** drop you just a couple of blocks from the town's main entrance.

**Helpful Hints:** On Friday mornings, a **market** fills Piazza del

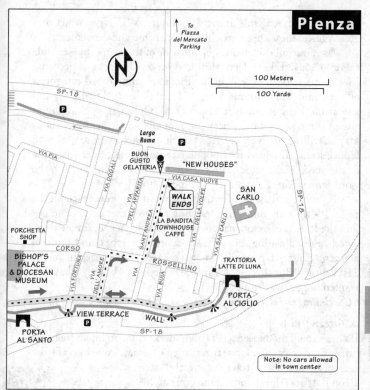

Mercato, the main parking lot just outside the town walls. A public **WC,** marked *gabinetti pubblici,* is on the right as you face the town gate from outside on Piazza Dante Alighieri (down the lane next to the faux TI).

# Sights in Pienza

I've connected Pienza's main sights with walking directions, which can serve as a handy little orientation to the town. You could do this stroll in 30 minutes, but entering some of the sights could extend your visit to a few hours.

• *Begin in the little park just in front of the town (near the main round-about and bus stop), called Piazza Dante Alighieri. Facing the town, go through the big, ornamental gateway on the right (which was destroyed in World War II, and rebuilt in 1955) and head up the main street...*

## Corso il Rossellino

This main drag—named for Bernardo Rossellino (1409-1464), the Renaissance architect who redesigned Pienza according to Pius' orders—is jammed with touristy boutiques. While you won't find great values, these shops are (like Pienza) cute and convenient.

As you stroll this street, step into one of the many **cheese-and-salami shops.** Take a deep whiff and survey the racks of pecorino cheese, made from sheep's milk. There are three broad categories of pecorino: *fresco* (young, soft, and mild), *medio* (medium), and *stagionato* (hard, crumbly, and pungent). Consider stocking up at one of these shops for a pricey but memorable picnic; some shops may be willing to give you a free sample. *Finocchiona* is salami with fennel seeds. This was first popularized by wine traders, because fennel seeds make wine taste better. To this day, Italians use the word *infinocchiare* ("fennel-ize") to mean "to trick."

Farther along, watch for the **Church of San Francesco** on the right. It's the only important building in town that dates from before the Pius II extreme makeover. Its humble facade, simple nave, wood-beamed ceiling, bits of 14th-century frescoes, and tranquil adjacent cloister have a charm that's particularly peaceful in the 21st century. But this gloomy medieval style was exactly what Pius wanted to get away from.

• *Continuing one more block, you'll pop out at Pienza's showcase square...*

### ▲Piazza Pio II

Pienza's small main piazza gets high marks from architecture highbrows for its elegance and artistic unity. One day, Pope Pius II (who

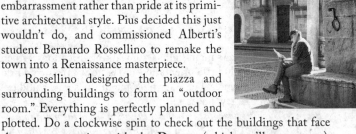

was born here) was traveling nearby with Leon Battista Alberti, one of the great architectural pioneers of the Renaissance. Proud to show off his hometown, Pius brought Alberti here...but, seeing it through the eyes of his esteemed companion, he was filled with embarrassment rather than pride at its primitive architectural style. Pius decided this just wouldn't do, and commissioned Alberti's student Bernardo Rossellino to remake the town into a Renaissance masterpiece.

Rossellino designed the piazza and surrounding buildings to form an "outdoor room." Everything is perfectly planned and plotted. Do a clockwise spin to check out the buildings that face the square, starting with the **Duomo** (which we'll enter soon). High up on the facade is one of many examples you'll spot around town of the Piccolomini family crest: five half-moons, advertising the number of crusades that his family funded.

To the right of the Duomo is the **Piccolomini family palace,** now a tourable museum. Notice that the grid lines in the square's pavement continue all the way up the sides of this building, creat-

## Pope Pius II

Pope Pius II (Enea Silvio Bartolomeo Piccolomini, 1405-1464) was born into one of the most powerful families in Siena. He had an illustrious career as a diplomat, traveled far and wide (fathering two illegitimate children, in Switzerland and Scotland), and gained a reputation for his erotic writings *(The Tale of Two Lovers)*. Upon donning the frock, Piccolomini went from ordination to the papacy in just 11 years—a stunning pace spurred, no doubt, by his esteemed lineage. Owing to his educated and worldly upbringing, upon ascending to the papacy Piccolomini chose a name that was not religious, but literary: the ancient poet Virgil first used the term "pious" to describe his hero, Aeneus. One of the most enlightened popes of his time, Pius embraced the burgeoning Renaissance and set out to remake his hometown in pure Renaissance style. Pius was also the first prominent figure known to have suggested the notion of a united Europe, with a common heritage and shared goals (at that time, facing off against the invading Ottomans).

ing a Renaissance cube. Upon closer inspection, you can see that the windows at the far end of the building are a bit narrower—creating an optical illusion that the palace is longer than it actually is.

Looking farther right, you'll see **City Hall** (Palazzo Comunale), with a Renaissance facade and a fine loggia (to match the square) but a 13th-century bell tower that's shorter than the church's tower. That's unusual here in civic-minded Tuscany, where municipal towers usually trumpet the importance of town over Church.

Looking up the lane to the left of City Hall, notice the cantilevered upper floors of the characteristic old houses—a reminder that, while Pienza appears Renaissance on the surface, much of that sheen was added later to fit Pius' vision. Turning right again, see the **Bishop's Palace,** also called the Borgia Palace (now housing the TI and the skippable Diocesan Museum). Pius envisioned his remade hometown as a sort of "summer Vatican," where an entourage of VIPs would spend time—and each one needed their own palace. The Borgia clan, who built this palace, produced one of the most controversial popes of that age, Alexander VI, who ascended to the papacy a few decades after Pius II.

Finally, between the Bishop's Palace and the Duomo, a lane leads to the best **view terrace** in town.

• *Before going there, take the time to tour whichever of the square's sights interest you:*

## Duomo

The cathedral's classic, symmetrical Renaissance facade (1462) dominates Piazza Pio II. The interior, bathed in light, is an illuminating encapsulation of Pius II's architectural philosophy (free, generally daily 7:00-13:00 & 14:30-19:00). Pius envisioned this church as an antidote to dark, claustrophobic medieval churches, like the Church of San Francesco we saw earlier. Instead, this was to be a "house of glass," representing the cultural enlightenment that came with the Renaissance. As you walk to the end of the church, notice the cracks in the apse walls and floor, and get seasick behind the main altar. The church's cliff-hanging position bathes the interior in light, but the building also feels as though it could break in half if you jumped up and down.

## ▲Palazzo Piccolomini

This palace, the home of Pius II and the Piccolomini family (until 1962), is not quite the interesting slice of 15th-century aristocratic life that it could be (I'd like to know more about the pope's toilet). But this is still the best small-town palace experience I've found in Tuscany. (It famously starred as the Capulets' home in Franco Zeffirelli's 1968 Academy Award-winning *Romeo and Juliet*.) You can peek inside the door for free to check out the well-preserved courtyard. In Renaissance times, most buildings were covered with elaborate paintings like those you'll see here.

**Cost and Hours:** €7, includes dry audioguide, Wed-Mon 10:00-18:30, until 16:00 off-season, closed Tue, Piazza Pio II 2, tel. 0578-748-392, www.palazzopiccolominipienza.it.

• *When you're done sightseeing, head up the little lane to the left of the church facade. This takes you out to a grand pedestrian-only...*

## View Terrace

Stroll this panoramic promenade to the end, taking in views over the Tuscan countryside and, in the distance, Monte Amiata, the largest mountain in southern Tuscany. Retrace your steps and exit the viewpoint down the first alley, Via del'Amore—the original Lover's Lane—which leads back to the main drag, Corso il Rossellino.

• *Turn right and stroll along this street one block, then turn left up Via Sant'Andrea. Soon you'll run into* **Via delle Case Nuove,** *a charming row of homes with staggered doorways. These "new houses" (as the street's name means) were built by the pope to house the poor. Just to the left (as you face these houses) is Pienza's "destination" gelateria, the recommended* **Buon Gusto.**

## JUST OUTSIDE PIENZA
### Corsignano Parish Church (Pieve di Corsignano)
This classic Romanesque parish church *(pieve)*, hugging the slope just below Pienza, is a reminder of a much earlier, rougher, simpler time (before Pope Pius II). This was one of the medieval pilgrimage stops on the Via Francigena.

The round, eighth-century watchtower guards the squat, 11th-century church, whose unusual exterior iconography is from an age when the pagan roots of early Christianity were vivid and unmistakable—especially here, deep in the countryside. The church is decorated not with saints and angels, but with geometric and flowery motifs as well as mysterious creatures. Inside, near the entrance on the right, look for the font that was used to baptize the infant who would grow up to be Pope Pius II.

**Getting There:** On foot from Pienza, it's a steep 10-minute downhill walk (as you exit Pienza into the main park, look to your left for *pieve di Corsignano* signs). Drivers loop around the far end of town (as described on my Heart of Tuscany drive, later); just before the road bends sharply left and twists downhill, watch for the *pieve di Corsignano* signs on the right (free parking).

# Eating in and near Pienza

## IN PIENZA
**$$$ La Bandita Townhouse Caffè** offers a break from Tuscan rusticity, focusing instead on tempting modern Italian cuisine (such as spring pea soup or spicy Chianina beef tartare). Diners watch the chef work in his open kitchen (dinner nightly 19:30-22:00, lunch Tue-Sun 12:30-15:00, indoor/outdoor seating, Corso il Rossellino 111, easier to enter around the corner on Via Sant'Andrea, tel. 0578-749-005).

**$$ Trattoria Latte di Luna,** with outdoor tables filling a delightful little square, is the more traditional choice. While the food can be hit-or-miss, locals swear by their specialty, roast suckling pig *(maialino da latte arrosto)*. Run by friendly Roberto with Delfina in the kitchen, the dining room features an ancient well and sits on top of Etruscan tunnels (Wed-Mon 12:10-15:30 & 19:10-22:00, closed Tue, at the far end of town at Via San Carlo 2, tel. 0578-748-606).

**Quick Lunch:** For something cheap, characteristic, and fast, just grab a tasty **$ *porchetta* sandwich** at the little no-name shop 30 yards off the main square (at Corso il Rossellino 81) and munch it under the loggia or at the viewpoint (daily 8:00-20:00).

**Top-Quality Gelato:** Small batches and quality ingredients are on the menu at **Buon Gusto.** Nicola creates fun original flavors, which can include carrot-ginger, creamy basil, or kiwi-spinach. The gelato is typically ready by around 13:30—just in time for after lunch. They also do fresh-pressed juices and smoothies (daily 11:00-20:00, until 22:00 in summer, closed off-season, Via delle Case Nuove 26, mobile 335-704-9165). Nicola also runs Sgarbi Gelato Natura in Montepulciano.

**Cocktails with Nibbles:** Pienza isn't much for nightlife, but for a cocktail in a somewhat local-feeling setting, drop in at **Idyllium**—a hip cocktail bar serving creative herb-infused drinks, light food, and outdoor seating facing grand Tuscan splendor (daily 11:00-late, from the main square, go down the little lane to the right of the church to Via Gozzante 67, tel. 0578-748-176).

## NEAR PIENZA

Despite having more than its share of tourists, Pienza suffers from a lack of quality restaurants. These options are all within about a 15-minute drive and offer a more memorable meal than places in town. To locate Castelmuzio, see the "Heart of Tuscany" map on page 676.

**Just Outside Castelmuzio:** For an excellent meal and a memorable activity, consider dinner at the fine **$$$$** restaurant at **La Moscadella,** run by The Isabella Experience (recommended in "Countryside Accommodations," earlier in this chapter). A limited number of tables are available to nonguests who book ahead. One evening there may be a truffle hunt through the woods followed by a truffle dinner; the next, an olive oil tasting session may be followed by a meal with olive oil pairings. Expect to pay around €60 per person, including the premeal experience, a four-course meal, *aperitivo,* and wine; the truffle hunt/meal is €120/person (reservations required, usually offered Fri-Tue, veggie alternatives available, tel. 0577-665-516, info@theisabellaexperience.com).

**In Castelmuzio:** To escape Pienza's tourist crowds, drive about 15 minutes to the remote village of Castelmuzio. The hamlet's lone restaurant, **$$ Locanda di Casalmustia,** is a cozy and typically uncrowded spot serving good local cuisine. Choose between sitting out on the stony lane or in a cute fresco-ceilinged dining room. While not quite a destination restaurant, it's a good excuse to explore an untrampled hill town and enjoy sweeping views of the countryside (Tue-Sun 8:00-22:00, closed Mon, in the heart of the town at Piazza della Pieve 3, tel. 0577-665-166).

**In Monticchiello:** In the opposite direction, but about the same distance away is the excellent **Ristorante Daria** (see "Eating in Monticchiello," later in this chapter; for location see the "Heart of Tuscany" drive map on page 713).

## Pienza Connections

Bus tickets are sold at the bar/café (marked *Il Caffè*, closed Tue) just outside Pienza's town gate (or pay a little extra and buy tickets from the driver). Buses leave from a few blocks up the street, directly in front of the town entrance. Montepulciano is the nearest transportation hub.

**From Pienza by Bus to: Siena** (6/day, none on Sun, 1.5 hours), **Montepulciano** (8/day, 30 minutes), **Montalcino** (3-4/day, none Sun, change in Torrenieri, 60 minutes). Bus info: www.tiemmespa.it.

# Montalcino

On a hill overlooking vineyards and valleys, Montalcino is famous for its delicious and pricey Brunello di Montalcino red wines. It's a pleasant, low-impact town crawling with wine-loving tourists and a smattering of classy shops, but little sightseeing. Everyone touring this area seems to be relaxed and in an easy groove...as if enjoying a little wine buzz.

While today it's all about the wine, Montalcino (mohn-tahl-CHEE-noh) has an incredibly long history—human settlement here dates back some 200,000 years. That's because Montalcino has a unique setting, with protective caves and a freshwater spring high atop a rocky pinnacle—a highly desirable position for Neolithic humans. For much of its long history, Montalcino was a veritable fortress, perched high overlooking the valley below and its Via Francigena pilgrim route.

Flash forward to the Middle Ages, when Montalcino was considered Siena's biggest ally. Originally aligned with Florence, the town switched sides after the Sienese beat up Florence in the Battle of Montaperti in 1260. The Sienese persuaded the Montalcinesi to join their side by forcing them to collect corpses and sleep one night in the bloody, Florentine-strewn battlefield. Later, the Montalcinesi took in Sienese refugees. To this day, in gratitude for their support, the Sienese invite the Montalcinesi to lead the parade that kicks off Siena's Palio celebrations.

Montalcino prospered under Siena, but like its ally, it waned after the Medici family took control of the region. The village became a humble place. Then, in the late 19th century, the Biondi Santi family created a fine, dark red wine, calling it "the brunette" (Brunello). Today's affluence is due to the town's much-sought-after wine. (For more on this wine, see the "Wines in the Region" sidebar later in this chapter). Montalcino provides a handy springboard for exploring the surrounding wine region.

# Orientation to Montalcino

Sitting atop a hill amidst a sea of vineyards, Montalcino is surrounded by walls and dominated by the Fortezza (a.k.a. "La Rocca"). From here, roads lead down into the two main squares: Piazza Garibaldi and Piazza del Popolo.

**Tourist Information:** The helpful TI, just off Piazza Garibaldi in City Hall, sells bus tickets; can call ahead to book a visit at a countryside winery (small fee); and has information on taxis to nearby towns, abbeys, and monasteries (daily 10:00-13:00 & 14:00-17:50, tel. 0577-849-331, www.prolocomontalcino.com).

**Arrival in Montalcino:** For a short visit here by **car,** drivers should head to the pay lot in Piazzale Fortezza. Skirt around the fortress, take the first right (just past a little park), and follow signs to *parking* and *Fortezza* (€1.60/hour, free 20:00-8:00). Or, if you don't mind a short climb, park for free below the fortress: At the roundabout with the ugly statue, take the small downhill lane into the big lower parking lot (blue lines mean that you have to pay, but the lower-level unmarked spots are always free). If these lots are full, follow the town's western wall toward the Madonna del Soccorso church and a long pay lot.

The **bus** stop is on Piazza Cavour, a little park about 300 yards from the town center. From here, simply follow the main drag, Via Mazzini, straight up into town. While Montalcino has no official baggage storage, a few shops are willing to hold on to one or two bags on a short-term basis; ask at the TI.

**Helpful Hints:** Friday is **market** day (7:00-13:00) on Viale della Libertà, near the Fortezza.

# Sights in Montalcino

### Piazza del Popolo

All roads in tiny Montalcino lead to the main square, Piazza del Popolo ("People's Square").

**City Hall** was the fortified seat of government. It's decorated with the coats of arms of judges who, in the interest of fairness, were from outside of town. Like Siena, Montalcino was a republic in the Middle Ages. When Florentines took Siena in 1555, Siena's ruling class retreated here and held out for four more years. The Medici coat of arms (with the six balls, or pills) dominates the others. The one-handed **clock** was the norm until 200 years ago.

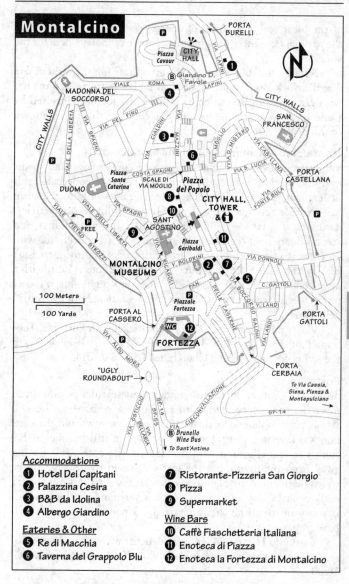

## Montalcino

**Accommodations**
1. Hotel Dei Capitani
2. Palazzina Cesira
3. B&B da Idolina
4. Albergo Giardino

**Eateries & Other**
5. Re di Macchia
6. Taverna del Grappolo Blu
7. Ristorante-Pizzeria San Giorgio
8. Pizza
9. Supermarket

**Wine Bars**
10. Caffè Fiaschetteria Italiana
11. Enoteca di Piazza
12. Enoteca la Fortezza di Montalcino

For five centuries, the large arcaded **loggia** (on your left as you face the clock tower) hosted the town market.

For some wine-centric whimsy, go up around the right side of the City Hall and find a series of **plaques** (each designed by a different artist), which show off the annual rating of the Brunello harvest from two to five stars—important, as wine is the lifeblood of the local economy. And, of course, it's fun to simply observe the *passeggiata*—these days mostly a parade of tourists here for the wine.

Back on the square, notice the grand café (on the right as you face the clock tower). Since 1888, **Caffè Fiaschetteria Italiana** has been *the* elegant place to enjoy a drink. Its founder, inspired by Caffè Florian in Venice, brought fine coffee to this humble town of woodcutters.

### Montalcino Museums (Musei di Montalcino)

While technically two museums in one (archaeology and medieval and modern art), and surprisingly big and modern for this little town, Montalcino's lone museum ranks only as a decent bad-weather activity. The cellar is filled with interesting artifacts dating back as far as—gulp—200,000 BC. The ground, first, and second floors hold the medieval and modern art collections, with an emphasis on Gothic sacred art (with works from Montalcino's heyday, the 13th to 16th century). The ground floor is best, with a large collection of crucifixes and the museum's highlights, a glazed terra-cotta altarpiece and a statue of St. Sebastian, both by Andrea della Robbia.

**Cost and Hours:** €4.50, €6 combo-ticket with Fortezza, Tue-Sun 10:00-13:00 & 14:00-17:30, closed Mon, Via Ricasoli 31, to the right of Sant'Agostino Church, tel. 0577-846-014.

### Fortezza

This 14th-century fort, built under Sienese rule, is now little more than an empty shell (with a popular wine bar—see below). It was built to defend against catapults and arrows, but the cannon was invented shortly thereafter. You can still see pockmarks from cannonballs fired here in 1553 on the outer wall (facing away from the town), but the fort withstood the attack. You're welcome to enter the big, open courtyard (with WCs out the far end), or just enjoy a picnic in the park surrounding the fort, but if you want to climb the ramparts for a panoramic view, you'll have to pay.

**Cost and Hours:** €4, €6 combo-ticket with Montalcino Museums, enter though wine bar, daily 9:00-20:00, off-season 10:00-18:00.

### Wine Bars in Town

If you won't make it to the wineries outside Montalcino, simply visit a wine bar in town, where you can comfortably taste a variety of vintages before stumbling safely back to your hotel. This is also a great strategy for Sundays, when many countryside wineries are closed.

**Caffè Fiaschetteria Italiana,** a classic café/wine bar, was founded by Ferruccio Biondi Santi, the creator of the famous Brunello wine. The wine library in the back of the café boasts many local choices. A meeting place since 1888, this grand café also serves light lunches. But if you're not seeking venerable ambience and sidewalk seating, you can taste wine more affordably elsewhere (Brunellos by the glass, light snacks and plates; same prices inside, outside, or in back room; daily 7:30-23:00, Piazza del Popolo 6, tel. 0577-849-043).

**Enoteca di Piazza**—part of a chain of wine shops with mechanical dispensers—is a fun way to efficiently taste a variety of different wines in a forget-table setting. Here's how it works: A "drink card" (like a debit card) keeps track of the samples you take, for which you'll pay from €1 to €9 apiece. They stock 100 different wines, including some whites— rare in this town. This is a

good spot to assemble a box of wine from different local producers to ship home. Their small restaurant lets you enjoy your drink card with local dishes (daily 9:00-20:00, near Piazza del Popolo at Via Matteotti 43, tel. 0577-848-104, www.enotecadipiazza.com).

**Enoteca la Fortezza di Montalcino** offers a chance to taste top-end wines by the glass, each with an English explanation. While the prices are a bit higher than other *enoteche* in town, the medieval setting inside Montalcino's fort is popular with tourists. Spoil yourself with Brunello in the cozy *enoteca* or at an outdoor table in the fortress courtyard (tastings start at €15 for 3 wines and go up from there; pricey full meals and sampler plates of cheeses, *salumi*, honeys, and olive oil available; daily 9:00-20:00, until 18:00 Nov-March, inside the Fortezza, tel. 0577-849-211).

## Wineries near Montalcino

The countryside around Montalcino is littered with wineries, some of which offer tastings. As Brunello is the poshest of Italian wines, these wineries feel a bit upscale, and most require an advance reservation. It's a simple process (just call and arrange a time), and they'll delight in showing you around. Tours generally last 45-60 minutes, cost €10-15 per person, and conclude with a tasting of three or four wines. The Montalcino TI can give you a list of more than 150 regional wineries and will call ahead for you. Or check with the vintners' consortium (tel. 0577-848-246, www. consorziobrunellodimontalcino.it). Many wineries are closed on

## Wines in the Region

This region has two well-respected red wines, each centered on a specific town: Montepulciano is known for its Vino Nobile, while Montalcino is famous for its Brunello. In each wine, the predominant grape is a clone of sangiovese (Tuscany's main red wine grape).

**Vino Nobile di Montepulciano** ("noble wine of Montepulciano") is a high-quality, dry ruby red, made mostly with the Prugno-lo Gentile variety of sangiovese (70 percent), plus other varieties including Mammolo (30 percent). Aged two years (or three for a *riserva*)—one year of which must be in oak casks—it pairs well with meat, especially roasted lamb with rosemary, rabbit or boar ragù over pasta, grilled portobello mushrooms, and local cheeses like pecorino. Several large wineries produce and age their Vino Nobile in the sprawling cellars beneath the town of  Montepulciano. Three of these are fun and easy to tour (see "Sights and Experiences in Montepulciano" on page 689). The oldest red wine in Tuscany, Vino Nobile has been produced since the late 1500s.

Sunday, so check before heading out. For locations of the wineries listed below, see the "Heart of Tuscany" map, near the beginning of the chapter.

If you lack a car (or don't want to drive), you can take a tour on the **Brunello Wine Bus,** which laces together visits to four wineries, with a lunch break in the middle, either on your own in Montalcino or at a farmhouse for an extra fee (€140; tours run March-Nov Tue and Thu only; departs at 10:00, returns at 19:00; tours leave from their office, or they will pick you up within 3 miles—5 km—of Montalcino; half-day tours available Tue and Thu-Sat for €75; Via Circonvallazione 3, tel. 0577-846-021, www.winetravelsforyou.com, info@winetravelsforyou.com).

If you're paying for a wine tasting, you aren't obligated to buy. But if a winery is doing a small tasting just for you, they're hoping you'll buy a bottle or two.

## South of Montalcino

### Tornesi

This charmingly low-key, family-run winery is a short drive outside of Montalcino, perched on a grand view terrace overlooking the famous Biondi Santi winery (where Brunello was invented).

**Brunello di Montalcino** ("the little brown one of Montalcino"—named for the color of the grapes before harvest) is even more highly regarded and ranks among Italy's finest and most expensive wines. Made from 100 percent Sangiovese Grosso (a.k.a. Brunello) grapes, it's smooth, dry, and aged for a minimum of two years in wood casks, plus an additional four months in the bottle. *Riserva* wines are aged an additional year. Brunello is designed to cellar for 10 years or longer—but who can wait? It pairs well with the local cuisine, but the perfect match is the fine Chianina beef.

Today, there are around 240 mostly small producers of Brunello in the Montalcino region; I've recommended just a few, which I find fun and accessible. A simpler option is to sample a few different wines at one of the good wine bars in Montalcino (see page 706).

You'll also see Rosso di Montalcino (a younger version of Brunello), which is aged for one year. This "poor man's Brunello" is very good, at half the price.

Maurizio, Elisa, and Valentina offer tours and tastings in this scenic setting. They enjoy explaining how their logo—the cuckoo *(kukula)* bird—was inspired by their chatty grandfather (reserve ahead, €13 for 3 tastes plus tour, €20 includes tasting and lunch, €20-40 bottles, closed Sun, mobile 349-093-2167, www.brunellotornesi.it). Leaving Montalcino, at the main roundabout, go uphill toward *Grosetto*, then watch for the brown *Benducce* sign on the left (just before the road bends right). Tornesi is a short drive down this gravel road, on the left.

**Mastrojanni**

Perched high above the Romanesque Sant'Antimo Abbey, overlooking sprawling vineyards, this winery (owned by the Illy coffee company) is big and glitzy—yet doesn't feel as corporate or soulless as some of the bigger players (€17-36 bottles, reserve ahead, Podere Loreto e San Pio, tel. 0577-835-681, www.mastrojanni.com). To reach it, head up into the town of Castelnuovo dell'Abate (just above Sant'Antimo Abbey), bear left at the Bassomondo restaurant, and continue up along the gravel road (enjoying vineyard and abbey views).

### Ciacci Piccolomini d'Aragona

This well-respected, family-run vineyard has a classy tasting room/*enoteca* and an outdoor view terrace. If you're just dropping in, belly up to the wine bar for two or three free tastes. Or reserve ahead for a more formal tasting of top-quality wines for €10-25, which includes a tour of the cellar (April-Oct Mon-Fri 9:00-19:00, Sat 10:30-18:30, closed Sun; down a back lane near Sant'Antimo Abbey—head toward Castelnuovo dell'Abate but go right before entering that town, following signs toward *Sant'Angelo in Colle*, tel. 0577-835-616, www.ciaccipiccolomini.com, visite@ciaccipiccolomini.com).

### Castello Banfi-Poggio alle Mura

Much bigger and glossier than the other recommended wineries, Banfi is one of the largest producers in the area. Despite its size, the estate is charming, set in a castle located in a picturesque corner southwest of Sant'Antimo. This is a good option for Sundays, when other places are closed, or for a spontaneous drop-in tasting at the winery's *enoteca* (tastings start at €12, daily 10:00-19:30, until 18:00 Nov-March, tours available on request, tel. 055-877-500, www.castellobanfiilborgo.com, enoteca@banfi.it). You'll find Banfi about 20 minutes south of Montalcino; follow SP-14 to Borgo Santa Rita and cut back north, following signs to *Poggio alle Mura*.

## North of Montalcino

### Altesino

Elegant and stately, Altesino owns perhaps the most stunning location of all, just off the back road connecting Montalcino north to Buonconvento. You'll twist up on cypress-lined gravel lanes to this perch, which looks out over an expanse of vineyards with Montalcino hovering on the horizon (€15 for tour and basic tasting, daily, reserve ahead, Loc. Altesino 54, tel. 0577-806-208, www.altesino.it, info@altesino.it). You'll find the turnoff for Altesino along the back road (SP-45) between Montalcino and Buonconvento.

### Santa Giulia

On the outskirts of Torrenieri, this is a quintessential family-run winery, with an emphasis on quality over quantity (only 20,000 bottles a year). They also produce excellent olive oil, prosciutto, and salami. Less picturesque and much more rustic than the other wineries listed here, a tour at Santa Giulia is a Back Door experience. Call to find a time that fits their schedule; around lunchtime, you can arrange a "Zero Kilometer" tasting, with farm-fresh cold cuts, cheese, and bruschetta for €20; add pasta and dessert for €15 more (€20 for 3 tastes and tour, 2-person minimum, €15-32 bottles, Loc. Santa Giulia 48, closed Sun, tel. 0577-834-270, www.

santagiuliamontalcino.it, info@santagiuliamontalcino.it). From Torrenieri's main intersection, follow the brown *Via Francigena* signs. After crossing the train tracks and a bridge, watch on the left to follow signs for *Sasso di Sole*, then *Sta. Giulia;* you'll take gravel roads through farm fields to the winery.

## Sleeping in Montalcino

**$$$ Hotel Dei Capitani,** at the end of town near the bus station, has plush public spaces, an inviting summertime pool, and a cliff-side terrace offering plenty of reasons for lounging. About half the 29 rooms come with vast Tuscan views and are worth paying a bit extra for (request a view room when you reserve); the nonview rooms are bigger but face a somewhat noisy street (RS%, air-con, elevator, limited free parking—first come, first served, Via Lapini 6, tel. 0577-847-227, www.deicapitani.it, info@deicapitani.it).

**$$ Palazzina Cesira** (cheh-SHEE-rah), right in the heart of the old town, is a gem, renting five spacious and tastefully decorated rooms in a fine 13th-century residence with a palatial lounge and a pleasant garden. You'll enjoy a refined and tranquil ambience, a nice breakfast (with eggs), and the chance to get to know Lucilla and her American husband Roberto, who are generous with local advice (2-night minimum, air-con, free off-street parking, Via Soccorso Saloni 2, tel. 0577-846-055, www.montalcinoitaly.com, info@montalcinoitaly.com).

**$ B&B da Idolina** has four good rooms above a wine shop on the main street (includes basic breakfast in shared kitchen, check-in 15:00-19:00—call if arriving later, parking available, Via Mazzini 65, check in at the wine shop next door, tel. 0577-849-212, www.idolina1946.com, fulvia.soda@gmail.com, Fulvia).

**$ Albergo Giardino,** a great value, has nine big rooms done in a modern-minimalist style, no public spaces, and a convenient location near the bus stop (RS%, no breakfast, Piazza Cavour 4, tel. 0577-848-257, mobile 320-404-4655, www.albergoilgiardino.it, info@albergoilgiardino.it, Roberto and dad Mario).

## Eating in Montalcino

**$$$ Re di Macchia** is an invitingly intimate restaurant where Antonio serves up the big, hearty portions of Tuscan fare that Roberta cooks. Look for their seasonal menu and a fine Montalcino wine list (Fri-Wed 12:00-14:00 & 19:00-21:00, closed Thu, reservations strongly recommended, Via Soccorso Saloni 21, tel. 0577-846-116).

**$$ Taverna del Grappolo Blu,** tucked in a cellar down a picturesque staircase off the main drag, is serious about its wine, game, homemade pasta, and vegetarian options (reservations smart, daily

**HEART OF TUSCANY**

12:00-15:00 & 19:00-22:00, a few steps off Via Mazzini at Scale di Via Moglio 1, tel. 0577-847-150, www.grappoloblu.it, Luciano).

**$$ Ristorante-Pizzeria San Giorgio** is a homey trattoria/pizzeria with traditional decor and reasonable prices. It's great for families and a reliable choice for a simple meal (daily 12:00-15:00 & 19:00-22:30, closed Tue off-season, Via Soccorso Saloni 10, tel. 0577-848-507, Mara).

**Quick Bite:** The **$** *pizza al taglio* shop, right on Piazza del Popolo at #11, has both pizza slices and sandwiches that they can heat up for you—ask for *scalda* (daily 10:30-21:30).

**Picnic:** Gather ingredients at the **Co-op supermarket** on Via Sant'Agostino (Mon-Sat 8:30-13:00 & 16:00-20:00, closed Sun, just off Via Ricasoli in front of Sant'Agostino Church), then enjoy your feast up at the Madonna del Soccorso Church, with vast territorial views.

## Montalcino Connections

Montalcino is well connected to Siena; other bus connections are inconvenient but generally workable. Montalcino's bus stop is on Piazza Cavour, within the town walls. Bus tickets are sold at the bar on Piazza Cavour, at the TI, and at some tobacco shops, but not on board. Check schedules at the TI, at the bus station, or online (at www.tiemmespa.it). The nearest train station is a 30-minute bus ride away, in Buonconvento.

**From Montalcino by Bus:** For long-distance journeys, you'll always start out on bus #114, which goes to **Siena** (6/day Mon-Sat, 4/day Sun, 1.5 hours). En route, this bus goes through Torrenieri (change for **Pienza** or **Montepulciano,** 3-4/day, none on Sun); from Torrenieri it's 25 minutes to Pienza, 45 minutes to Montepulciano, then **Buonconvento** (where you can catch a train to **Florence**). You can also reach Florence by riding the bus to Siena, then taking the train from there. Since the Montepulciano bus connection is sporadic, consider hiring a taxi (about €70 one-way).

# Heart of Tuscany Drive

## VAL D'ORCIA LOOP

If you have just one day to connect the ultimate Tuscan towns and views, this is the loop I'd stitch together with a driving tour. In addition to larger towns (Montepulciano, Pienza) and smaller ones (Bagno Vignoni, Rocca d'Orcia), this loop drive, worth ▲▲▲, gives you a good look at the area called the Val d'Orcia (val DOR-chah), boasting some of the best scenery in Italy. Most of this jour-

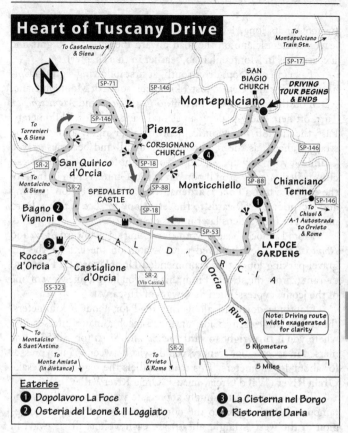

**Heart of Tuscany Drive**

To Montepulciano Train Stn.
To Castelmuzio & Siena
SP-17
SAN BIAGIO CHURCH
**DRIVING TOUR BEGINS & ENDS**
SP-71
SP-146
**Montepulciano**
SP-146
**Pienza**
To Torrenieri & Siena
SP-146
CORSIGNANO CHURCH
SP-146
SP-18
④
SR-2
**San Quirico d'Orcia**
SP-88
**Monticchiello**
SP-88
**Chianciano Terme**
To Montalcino & Siena
SR-2
SPEDALETTO CASTLE
SP-18
SP-146
To Chiusi & A-1 Autostrada to Orvieto & Rome
**Bagno** ② **Vignoni**
SP-18
①
③
SP-53
**LA FOCE GARDENS**
**Rocca d'Orcia**
**Castiglione d'Orcia**
V A L   D '   O R C I A
SR-2 (Via Cassia)
Orcia River
SS-323
To Montalcino & Sant'Antimo
To Monte Amiata (in distance)
To Orvieto & Rome
SR-2
Note: Driving route width exaggerated for clarity
5 Kilometers
5 Miles

**Eateries**
❶ Dopolavoro La Foce
❷ Osteria del Leone & Il Loggiato
❸ La Cisterna nel Borgo
❹ Ristorante Daria

ney is through velvety, gentle, rolling hillsides generously draped with vivid-green crops in the springtime, and a parched moonscape in the late summer and fall. This almost otherworldly smoothness constitutes many travelers' notions of Tuscan perfection.

**Planning Your Drive:** If you're in a rush and don't linger in any of the towns, you could do this drive in a couple of hours. To hit the sights, explore the towns, and linger over a meal or a glass of wine, spread it out over an entire day. (You could even splice in a side trip to a Brunello winery for a tasting.) I've started and ended the clockwise loop in Montepulciano, but you could just as easily start and end in Pienza. If gardens are your thing, do this loop when La Foce Gardens are open.

## From Montepulciano to Bagno Vignoni (via La Foce)

Before leaving Montepulciano, consider dropping by the showpiece Renaissance **San Biagio Church,** which sits at the base of the town (watch for its long, level, tree-lined driveway exactly where you leave Montepulciano on the road toward Pienza—see "Sights and Experiences in Montepulciano," earlier in this chapter).

To begin our loop, drive south, at first following signs to *Chianciano Terme* and *Chiusi*. Just 1 kilometer south of Montepulciano, watch on the right for the turnoff to *Castelluccio* and *Monticchiello*. Turn off here and zip along a pastoral back road for 5 kilometers. Pass the turnoff for Monticchiello on your right, and carry on straight ahead, as the road continues uphill and becomes gravel. Grinding your way up, watch on your right for the jagged Tuscan cliffs called *calanchi*. You'll pop out at the T-intersection in front of the entrance to **La Foce Gardens** (from this intersection, parking and reception are 50 yards to the left—look for *Loc. La Foce*; learn more about the gardens later in this chapter).

From La Foce, head downhill tracking signs toward *Siena* and *Roma*. After a few hundred yards, watch on the left for the big gravel parking lot of the recommended **Dopolavoro La Foce** restaurant (across the street). From this lot, you have a fine view of one of the iconic cypress-lined driveways of Tuscany.

Continue downhill along this road for about 5 kilometers, through pristine farm fields, until you reach a major intersection, where you'll turn right toward *Pienza* and *Siena* (on SP-53). Immersed in spectacular scenery, you'll twist between giant cypresses for about 10 kilometers. This road parallels the region's namesake **Orcia River** ("Val d'Orcia" means "Orcia River Valley").

Take a moment to simply appreciate your surroundings. The famous Chianti region to the north (right) and the Brunello region to the west (straight ahead) are each a short drive away; in those places, the rocky soil is perfect for grapes. But here, instead of rocks, you're surrounded by clay hills—once the floor of a prehistoric sea—that are ideal for cereal crops. Grains alternate every few years with a crop of fava beans, which help reintroduce nitrogen to the soil. It seems that every grassy hilltop is capped with a family farmhouse. Partway along this road, you'll pass a turnoff (on the right) offering a speedy shortcut to Pienza, just 8 stunning kilometers away. But there's so much more to see; I'd rather carry on with our loop.

The tower looming on the hill ahead of you is Rocca d'Orcia's Tentennano Castle (described later). Nearing the end of the road, you'll pass (on the left) the front door of an old farmhouse with oddly formidable crenellated towers, like a little castle in the field. This is **Spedaletto Castle,** built during the 12th century as a hospice for pilgrims walking the Via Francigena to Rome. Today it serves a similar purpose, as an *agriturismo* called La Grancia ("The Granary"), housing wayfarers like you.

When you reach a T-intersection with the main SR-2 highway,

turn left (toward *Roma*), then immediately take the exit for **Bagno Vignoni.** To explore this fascinating medieval spa town—with its main square filled with a thermal-spring-fed pool—see "Heart of Tuscany Sights," in the next section. To see the empty fortress at **Rocca d'Orcia,** stay on the SR-2 highway just 1 kilometer past Bagno Vignoni, then watch for the next turnoff.

## From Bagno Vignoni to Pienza (with Detours to Brunello Wineries and Tuscan Views)

From Bagno Vignoni, head north on SR-2 (toward *San Quirico d'Orcia* and *Siena*). After just 4 kilometers, in San Quirico d'Orcia, turn off onto the SP-146 road to Pienza, also marked for *Chiusi, Chianciano Terme,* and *Montepulciano.*

But before heading down that road, consider a few potential detours: First, if you won't have time to delve deeply into Brunello wine country, now is a good time to side-trip to your choice of **Brunello wineries;** those I've recommended on page 707 are all within about a 20- to 25-minute drive of San Quirico. Read the descriptions, take your pick, and ideally call ahead to reserve a tour and tasting. Another option is to zip into the town of **Montalcino** itself—an easy and well-signed 15-minute drive from San Quirico—and taste some local vintages at a wine bar there.

Back on the SP-146 road from San Quirico to Pienza, you enjoy one of the region's most postcard-worthy stretches—with grand panoramas in both directions, including two more quintessential Tuscan scenes: the **Chapel of Madonna di Vitaleta** (after 2 kilometers, on the right); and a classic **farmhouse with trees,** just before Pienza (about 9 kilometers after San Quirico, on the left).

Finally, you'll pull into **Pienza,** where you can park and tour the town using the information earlier in this chapter.

## From Pienza to Montepulciano (via Monticchiello)

If you're in a hurry or losing sunlight, just hop back on the main SP-146 road for the 12-kilometer straight shot back to Montepulciano (enjoying some pullouts on the left with fine views of the town). But I prefer this longer, even more dramatic route, via the fortified village of Monticchiello.

From the traffic circle at the entry to Pienza's town center, instead of heading for Montepulciano, follow the road that runs along the left side of town (marked *Amiata* and *Monticchiello*—as you face Pienza, you'll continue straight when the main road bends left). This road loops around behind and below the far end of the village, where you can consider a brief detour to see Pienza's oldest church: Turn off on the right at the brown sign for *Pieve di*

*Corsigiano* and drive a few hundred yards to **Corsignano Parish Church** (described on page 701).

Continuing on the main road past that turnoff, you'll drop steeply down into the valley, feeling as if you're sinking into a lavish painting. Dead ahead is **Monte Amiata,** the tallest mountain in Tuscany. This looming behemoth blocks bad weather, creating a mild microclimate that makes the Val d'Orcia a particularly pleasant place to farm...or to vacation. Meanwhile, don't forget to savor the similarly stellar views of Pienza in your rearview mirror. After 5 kilometers, look on the left for the turnoff to Monticchiello (brown sign). From here, carry on for 4 kilometers—watching on the left for fine vistas of Pienza and for another classic twisty cypress-lined road—to the pleasant town of **Monticchiello.** This town, with an excellent recommended restaurant (Daria) and a compact, fortified townscape worth exploring, is a good place to stretch your legs; see more in the next section.

From Monticchiello, there are two routes back to Montepulciano: For the shorter route (6 kilometers), partly on gravel roads, drive all the way to the base of the Monticchiello old town, then turn right. For the longer route (10 kilometers), which stays on paved roads but circles back the way our loop started, turn off for Montepulciano at the main intersection, in the flat part of town that's lower down.

## HEART OF TUSCANY SIGHTS

Below are the main sights you'll pass on my Heart of Tuscany driving route. Two of the main stops—the towns of Montepulciano and Pienza—are covered earlier in this chapter.

### ▲La Foce Gardens

One of the finest gardens in Tuscany, La Foce (lah FOH-cheh) caps a hill with geometrical Italian gardens and rugged English gardens that flow seamlessly into the Tuscan countryside. The gardens were a labor of love for Iris Origo, an English-born, Italian-bred aristocrat who left her mark on this area and wrote evocatively about her time here. The gardens—which are worth a pilgrimage for garden lovers—can be visited only with a  guided tour, and only three days a week (Wed, Sat, Sun) and some holidays.

**Cost and Hours:** €10; 45-minute tours offered April-Oct Wed at 15:00, 16:00, 17:00, and 18:00, Sat-Sun and holidays at

11:30, 15:00, and 16:30—but can be closed for private events, so check online in advance; private tours available, no tours in winter, ticket office opens 15 minutes before tour time, tel. 0578-69101, www.lafoce.com.

**Getting There:** La Foce sits in the hills above the busy town of Chianciano Terme. You can avoid SP-146 from Montepulciano through Chianciano (heavy traffic, poor signage) by following a more scenic route through the countryside (described at the start of my Heart of Tuscany Drive).

**Eating and Sleeping near La Foce:** Near the gardens, the Origo family runs a memorably charming roadside restaurant, **$$ Dopolavoro La Foce** ("After Work"). Once the quitting-time hangout for local farmers, today its interior is country-chic. The menu offers basic sandwiches or pasta and meat (featuring elegant hamburgers). The garden terrace out back is a chirpy delight, and the parking lot across the busy road offers one of the best vantage points on that perfect Tuscan road (Tue-Sun 9:00-22:00, closed Mon and Nov-March, Strada della Vittoria 90, tel. 0578-754-025, run with flair by Asia). Also nearby is their remote, restful B&B (described on page 680).

## ▲Bagno Vignoni

Thanks to the unique geology of this part of Tuscany (see sidebar, page 688), several natural hot springs bubble up between the

wineries and hill towns. And the town of Bagno Vignoni (BAHN-yoh veen-YOH-nee)—with a quirky history, a pleasant-to-stroll street plan punctuated with steamy canals, and various places to take a dip—is the most accessible and enjoyable to explore. If you'd like to recuperate from your sightseeing and wine tasting by soaking in the thermal baths, bring your swimsuit.

**Getting There:** Bagno Vignoni is well signed, just off the main SR-2 highway linking Siena to Rome (5 kilometers south of San Quirico d'Orcia). Park in the pay lot (coins only) by the big roundabout and walk into town, taking the left fork (in front of Hotel Le Terme).

**Bagno Vignoni Town Walk:** Emerging into the main square, walk under the covered loggia and look out over the aptly named **Piazza delle Sorgenti** ("Square of the Sources"), filled with a vast pool. Natural spring water bubbles up at the far end at temperatures around 125 degrees Fahrenheit. Known since Roman times, these hot springs were harnessed for their medicinal properties in the Middle Ages.

You're not allowed to wade or swim in this main pool today, but an easy stroll through town shows you other facets of these healing waters. Facing the pool, turn left, walk to the end of the loggia, then turn left again down Via delle Sorgenti. Listen for the water that gushes under your feet, as it leaves the pool and heads for its big plunge over the cliff. You'll emerge at an open zone with the cliff-capping **ruins** of medieval mills and cisterns that once made full use of Bagno Vignoni's main resource. Here you'll have a chance to dip your toes or fingers into streams of now-tepid water. At the canals' end, the water plunges down into the gorge carved by the Orcia River.

**Taking the Waters:** The modern **Piscina Val di Sole** bath complex, inside Hotel Posta Marcucci, is simple but sophisticated. It's a serene spot to soak (in water ranging from 80 to 105 degrees Fahrenheit) while taking in soaring views of Rocca d'Orcia across the valley (€20-27, €5 towel rental with €10 deposit, Fri-Wed 9:30-18:00, Wed and Sat also 21:00-24:00, closed Thu, tel. 0577-887-112, www.postamarcucci.it).

**Eating in Bagno Vignoni:** The town's class act is **$$$ Osteria del Leone,** on the cheery little *piazzetta* just behind the loggia, with charming tables out on the square. Inside it's dull and modern, with a fine interior garden (closed Mon, Via dei Mulini 3, tel. 0577-887-300, www.osteriadelleone.it). For something a bit more affordable and casual, drop by the nearby **$$ Il Loggiato,** with stony indoor seating or outdoor tables (closed Thu, Via delle Sorgenti 36, tel. 0577-888-973).

## Rocca d'Orcia

The fortress looming over Rocca d'Orcia (ROH-kah DOR-chah) perches high above the main SR-2 highway. Likely inhabited and fortified since Etruscan times, this strategic hilltop was a seat of great regional power in the 12th century. During this time, Rocca d'Orcia was one of a chain of forts that watched over pilgrims walking the Via Francigena to Rome.

Today the **Rocca di Tentennano** fortress—an empty shell of a castle with modern steel stairs and a grand 360-degree panorama at its top—looks stark and abandoned. It seems to dare you to pay €3 to take the very steep hike up from the parking lots below (May-Sept daily 10:30-13:30 & 16:30-18:30; shorter hours off-season, mobile 392-003-3028 or 333-986-0788).

**Eating in Rocca d'Orcia:** On Rocca's main square, **$$ La Cisterna nel Borgo** faces the town's namesake cistern. Marta and Fede serve up deliciously executed dishes in a classic setting (Mon-

Fri 12:00-14:00 & 19:00-22:00, Sat-Sun 19:00-22:00 only, Borgo Mestro 37, tel. 0577-887-280).

### ▲Monticchiello

This 200-person fortified village clings to the high ground in the countryside just south of Pienza and Montepulciano. While not quite "undiscovered," Monticchiello is relatively untrampled, and feels like a real place where you can get in touch with authentic Tuscan village life.

**Eating in Monticchiello:** At the warm and classy **$$$ Ristorante Daria,** owner Daria pleases diners with seasonal, traditional Tuscan dishes presented with flair in a modern setting. It's in the heart of the stony hill town amid sumptuous scenery. Reservations are wise (Thu-Tue 12:15-14:30 & 19:15-22:00, closed Wed, Via San Luigi 3, tel. 0578-755-170, www.ristorantedaria.it). Arriving in Monticchiello, walk through the town's gate, head about 50 yards straight up the hill, and bear right.

# ASSISI

Assisi is famous for its hometown boy, St. Francis, who made very, very good. While Francis the saint is interesting, Francesco Bernardone the man is even more so, and mementos of his days in Assisi are everywhere—where he was baptized, a shirt he wore, a hill he prayed on, and a church where a vision changed his life.

Around the year 1200, this simple friar from Assisi countered the decadence of Church government and society in general with a powerful message of nonmaterialism and a "slow down and smell God's roses" lifestyle. Like Jesus, Francis taught by example, living without worldly goods and aiming to love all creation. A huge monastic order grew out of his teachings, which were gradually embraced (some would say co-opted) by the Church. Christianity's most popular saint and its purest example of simplicity is now glorified in beautiful churches, along with his female counterpart, St. Clare. In 1939, Italy made Francis one of its patron saints; in 2013, the newly elected pope took his name.

Francis' message of love, simplicity, and sensitivity to the environment has a broad and timeless appeal. But every pilgrimage site inevitably gets commercialized, and Francis' legacy is now Assisi's basic industry. In summer, this Umbrian town bursts with flash-in-the-pan Francis fans and Franciscan knickknacks. Those able to see past the glow-in-the-dark rosaries and bobble-head friars can have a "travel on purpose" experience. Even a block or two off the congested main drag, you'll find pockets of serenity that, it's easy to imagine, must have made Francis feel at peace.

## PLANNING YOUR TIME

Assisi is worth a day and a night. Its walled old town has a half-day of sightseeing and another half-day of wonder. The essential sight is the Basilica of St. Francis. For a good visit, take my self-guided Assisi Walk, going from the top of town to the basilica at the bottom, and my Basilica of St. Francis Tour. With more time, wander the back streets and linger on the main square, Piazza del Comune.

Most visitors are day-trippers. While the town's a zoo by day, it's a delight at night. Assisi after dark is closer to a place Francis could call home. But for most visitors, two nights is more than you really need.

# Orientation to Assisi

Crowned by a ruined castle, Assisi spills downhill to its famous Basilica of St. Francis. The town is beautifully preserved and rich in history. A 5.5-magnitude earthquake in 1997 did more damage to the tourist industry than to the town's buildings. Fortunately, tourists—whether art lovers, pilgrims, or both—have returned, drawn by Assisi's special allure.

The city stretches across a ridge that rises from a flat plain. The Basilica of St. Francis sits at the low end of town; Piazza Mat-

teotti (bus stop and parking lot) is at the high end; and the main square, Piazza del Comune, lies in between. The main drag (called Via San Francesco for most of its course) runs from Piazza del Comune to the basilica. Capping the hill above the town is the ruined castle, called the Rocca Maggiore, and rising above that is Mount Subasio. The town is smaller than its fame might lead you to think: Walking uphill from the basilica to Piazza Matteotti takes 30 minutes, while the downhill journey takes about 15 minutes. Some Francis sights lie outside the city walls, in the flat area beneath the ridge (the modern part of town, called Santa Maria degli Angeli) and in the hills above.

## TOURIST INFORMATION

The TI is in the center of the old town on Piazza del Comune (daily 9:00-19:00, tel. 075-813-8680, www.visit-assisi.it). From April to October, there's also a branch (with shorter hours) down in the valley, across the street from the big piazza in front of the Basilica of Santa Maria degli Angeli.

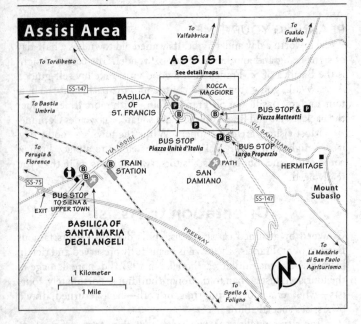

**ASSISI**

## ARRIVAL IN ASSISI

**By Train:** The train station is about two miles below Assisi, in Santa Maria degli Angeli. There is no official baggage storage, but the bar on the main floor will hold bags for a small charge (look for *ristorante* sign on the platform). There's no baggage storage in the old town.

Gray-and-blue Busitalia city **buses** (line #C) connect the station with the hilltop old town, stopping just outside the wall at three convenient places. Buses usually leave twice hourly from the bus stop immediately to your left as you exit the station (daily 5:30-23:00, schedule posted at stop, 15-minute ride; buy tickets at the newsstand inside the train station for €1.30, or on board the bus for €2—exact change only, validate ticket at yellow box as you board). The bus may be awaiting the arrival of your train. If so, don't dawdle or you may miss it.

Be sure you're on a bus going toward the center (ask *"Centro?"*—it should be marked *Matteotti/S. Francesco*). On the way up into town, the bus makes three stops: **Piazza Unità d'Italia** (near Porta San Pietro, below the Basilica of St. Francis), **Largo Properzio** (just outside Porta Nuova), and finally up top at **Piazza Matteotti**. The middle stop, Largo Properzio, is best for hotels in the center—just walk through the gateway and take the straight, mostly level street (past the Basilica of St. Clare) about 10 minutes to the main square.

Returning from the old town to the train station, buses reverse the route, leaving Piazza Matteotti twice hourly, driving down through town to the train station (then proceeding one more stop to the Basilica of Santa Maria degli Angeli).

**Taxis** from the train station to the old town cost about €15, with extra charges for luggage, night service, additional people (four is customary)...and sometimes just for being a tourist. When departing the old town, you'll find taxi stands at Piazza Giovanni Paolo II, the Basilica of St. Francis, the Basilica of St. Clare, and Piazza del Comune (or have your hotel call for you, tel. 075-813-100). Expect to pay a minimum of €10 for any ride.

**By Bus:** Buses from Siena generally arrive at the stop next to the Basilica of Santa Maria degli Angeli, near the train station (see earlier for directions from the station into town). Most other intercity buses arrive at the base of the old town.

**By Car:** Drivers coming in for the day can follow the signs to several handy parking lots *(parcheggi)*. Piazza Matteotti's wonderful underground parking garage is at the top of the town and comes with bits of ancient Rome in the walls. Another big lot, Parcheggio Giovanni Paolo II, is at the bottom end of town, 200 yards below the Basilica of St. Francis (next to the Piazza Unità d'Italia bus stop). At Parcheggio Porta Nuova, at the south end of town, an escalator delivers you to Porta Nuova near St. Clare's. The lots vary in price (about €1.50/hour, most €20/day). For day-trippers, the best plan is to park at Piazza Matteotti, follow my self-guided town walk, tour the Basilica of St. Francis, and then either catch a bus back to Piazza Matteotti or simply wander back up through town to your car.

## HELPFUL HINTS

**Best Shopping:** Tacky knickknacks line the streets leading to the Basilica of St. Francis. For better shops (with local handicrafts), head to Via San Rufino and Corso Mazzini (both just off Piazza del Comune; some shops described on page 734). A Saturday-morning market fills Via Borgo San Pietro (along the bottom edge of town).

**Festivals:** Assisi hosts several annual festivals commemorating St. Francis and life in the Middle Ages. The springtime medieval **Festa di Calendimaggio** features costume parades, concerts, and competitions among Assisi's rival neighborhoods (www.calendimaggiodiassisi.it). The **Settimana Francescana** commemorates the beginning of the end of Francis' life, when he made his way for the last time to the Porziuncola Chapel (Sept 28). This week-long celebration culminates on October 4 in the **Festa di San Francesco,** which marks his death with religious processions, special church services, and an arts, crafts, and folklore fair.

ASSISI

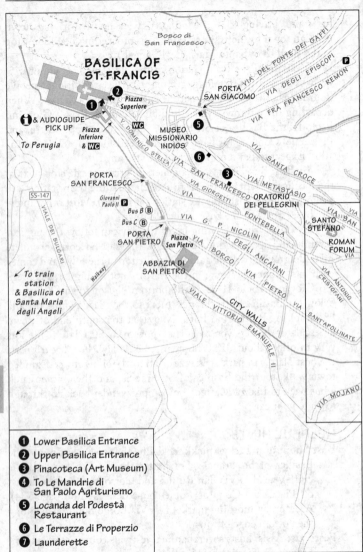

ASSISI

1 Lower Basilica Entrance
2 Upper Basilica Entrance
3 Pinacoteca (Art Museum)
4 To Le Mandrie di
   San Paolo Agriturismo
5 Locanda del Podestà
   Restaurant
6 Le Terrazze di Properzio
7 Launderette

**Laundry:** If they're not too busy, **3 Elle Blu' Lavanderia** can do
same-day laundry for you at a reasonable price (Mon-Fri 9:00-
18:00, Sat until 13:00, closed Sun, Via Borgo Aretino 6a, tel.
075-816-084).

**Travel Agencies:** You can purchase train, bus, and plane tickets
at **Agenzia Viaggi Stoppini,** centrally located between Piazza del Comune and the Basilica of St. Clare. Manager Fabrizio is patient with tourists' needs (Mon-Fri 9:00-12:30 &
15:30-19:00, Sat 9:00-12:30, closed Sun, also offers day trips

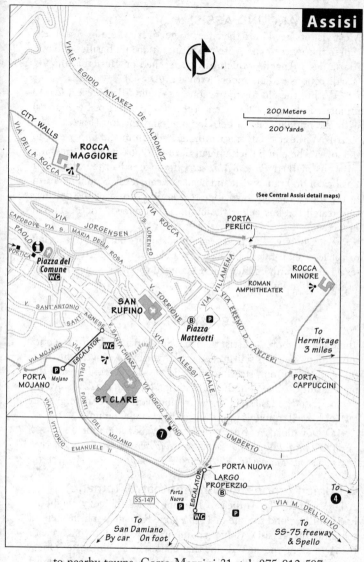

to nearby towns, Corso Mazzini 31, tel. 075-812-597, www. viaggistoppiniassisi.it).

**Local Guides: Giuseppe Karabotis** is a good licensed guide (€130/3 hours, €260/6 hours, mobile 328-867-0567, iokarabot@libero.it). **Daniela Moretti** is a hardworking young guide from Perugia who knows Assisi and all of Umbria (€120/half-day, €240/day, mobile 335-829-9984, www. danyguide.com, danyguide@hotmail.com). If they're busy, they can recommend other guides.

## GETTING AROUND ASSISI

Most visitors need only their feet to get everywhere in Assisi, except to the lower town—with the train station and Basilica of Santa Maria degli Angeli—which can be reached on Busitalia line #C (see directions earlier, under "Arrival in Assisi").

Within the old town, minibuses #A and #B run every 20-40 minutes, linking the lower end (near the Basilica of St. Francis) with the middle (Piazza del Comune) and the top (Piazza Matteotti). While it's only a 15-minute stroll from the upper end to the lower, the climb back up can have you looking for a lift. Hop on a bus marked *Piazza Matteotti* if you're exhausted after your Basilica of St. Francis visit and need a sweat-free five-minute return to the top of the old town. Before boarding, confirm the destination (catch the bus below the basilica, just outside the Porta San Francesco).

You can buy a bus ticket (good on any city bus) at a newsstand or tobacco shop for €1.30, or get a ticket from the driver for €2 (exact change only). After you've stamped your ticket on board, it's valid for 90 minutes.

# Assisi Walk

There's much more to Assisi than just St. Francis and what the blitz tour groups see. This self-guided walk, worth ▲▲, covers the town from top to bottom, starting near Piazza Matteotti. To reach the piazza, ride the bus from the train station (or from Piazza Giovanni Paolo II) to the last stop; drive up (and park in the underground lot); or hike 10 minutes uphill from Piazza del Comune.

🎧 Download my free Assisi Town Walk audio tour.

• *Start 50 yards beyond Piazza Matteotti (down the small lane between two stone houses, away from city center—see map).*

### ❶ Roman Amphitheater (Anfiteatro Romano)

A lane named Via Anfiteatro Romano skirts the cozy neighborhood built around the site of a long-gone Roman amphitheater—a reminder that Assisi was once an important Roman town. Circle to the right along the curved lane that marks the amphitheater's footprint. Imagine how colorful the town laundry basin (on the right) must have been in previous generations, when the women of Assisi gathered here to do their wash. Just beyond, above another small rectangular basin, are the coats of arms of Assisi's leading families. A few steps farther, leave the amphitheater, hiking up the stairs on the right to the top of the hill, for an overhead view of the ancient oval. The Roman stones have long been absorbed into the medieval architecture. It was Roman tradition to locate the amphitheater outside of town, which this used to be. While the amphitheater dates from the first century AD, the buildings filling it today were built in the 13th and 14th centuries. Notice the town's carefully maintained complexion: When redoing a roof, locals will mix old and new tiles.

• *Continue on, enjoying the grand view of the fortress in the distance. Take the gravel lane that branches off to the right, leading down to a city gate (on the right). Step through the gate for an...*

## ❷ Umbrian View

Outside of Assisi's Porta Perlici stretches a commanding view. Umbria, called the "green heart of Italy," is the country's geographical center and only landlocked region. Enjoy the various shades of green: silver green on the valley floor (olives), emerald green (grapevines), and deep green on the hillsides (evergreen oak trees). The valleys are dotted by small family farms, many of which rent rooms as *agriturismi*. Also notice Rocca Maggiore ("big fortress"), which provided townsfolk a refuge in times of attack. In the opposite direction, Rocca Minore ("little fortress")—which you saw a moment ago—gives the town's young lovers a little privacy. A quarry under the Rocca Maggiore was a handy source for Assisi's characteristic pink limestone.

• *Go back through the gate and follow Via Porta Perlici—it's immediately on your right—downhill into town (toward Hotel la Rocca). Enjoy the higgledy-piggledy architecture (this neighborhood has some of the most photogenic back lanes in town). Fifty yards down, to the left of the arched gate, find the wall containing an* **aqueduct** *that dates from Roman times. It still brings water from a mountain spring into the city (push the brass tap for a taste). After another 50 yards, turn left through a medieval town gate (with Hotel la Rocca on your right). Just after the hotel, you'll pass a second gate dating from Roman times. Follow Via Porta Perlici a few atmospheric blocks downhill until you hit a fine square facing a big church.*

## ❸ Cathedral of San Rufino (Cattedrale San Rufino)

Trick question: Who's Assisi's patron saint? While Francis is one of Italy's patron saints, Rufino (the town's first bishop, martyred and buried here in the third century) is Assisi's. This cathedral (seat of the local bishop)—worth ▲▲—is 11th-century Romanesque with a Neoclassical interior, and dedicated to Rufino. Although it has what is considered to be one of the best and purest Romanesque facades in all of Umbria, the big triangular top (just a decorative wall) was added in Gothic times.

**Cost and Hours:** Cathedral—free, daily 7:00-19:00, Nov-mid-March closed Mon-Fri 12:30-14:30, tel. 075-812-283;

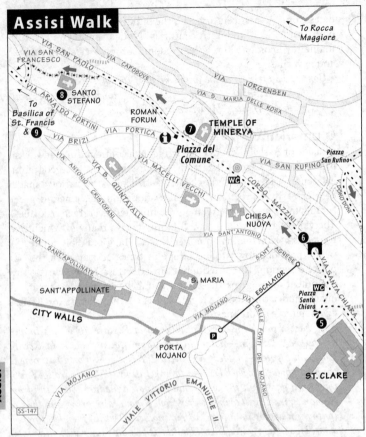

**Assisi Walk**

museum—€3.50, Thu-Tue 10:00-13:00 & 15:00-18:00, closed Wed, shorter hours off-season and Sun, www.assisimuseodiocesano.it.

**Visiting the Church:** Before going in, study the facade—a jungle of beasts emphasizing how the church was a refuge and sanctuary in a scary world. Notice the lions at the base of the facade, flanking each door. One is eating a Christian martyr, reminding worshippers of the courage of early Christians. Here, as in other medieval Assisi churches, worshippers absorbed pre-Christian themes and symbols into their world.

Enter the church. While the front of the church is an unremarkable mix of 17th- and 18th-century Baroque and Neoclassical,

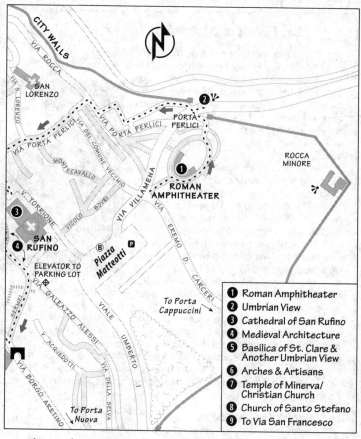

the rear (near where you enter) has several points of interest. Notice the two fine statues at the bases of the first pillars: *St. Francis* and *St. Clare* (by Giovanni Dupré, 1888).

In the church's back-right corner is an old baptismal font (surrounded by a semicircular black iron grate). In about 1181, a baby boy was baptized in this font. His parents were upwardly mobile Francophiles who called him Francesco ("Frenchy"). In 1194, a nobleman baptized his daughter Clare here. Eighteen years later, their paths crossed in this same church, when Clare attended a class and became mesmerized by the teacher—Francis. Traditionally, the children of Assisi are still baptized here.

In the nave, the striking glass panels in the floor reveal foundations preserved from the ninth-century church that once stood here. You're walking on history. After the 1997 earthquake, structural inspectors checked the church from ceiling to floor. When they looked under the paving stones, they discovered graves (until Napoleon decreed otherwise, it was common practice to bury peo-

# St. Francis of Assisi (1181-1226)

In 1202, young Francesco Bernardone donned armor and rode out to battle the Perugians (residents of Umbria's capital city). The battle went badly, and Francis was captured and imprisoned for a year. He returned a changed man. He avoided friends and his father's lucrative business and spent more and more time outside the city walls fasting, praying, and searching for something.

In 1206, a vision changed his life, culminating in a dramatic confrontation. He stripped naked before the town leaders, threw his clothes at his father—turning his back on the comfortable material life—and declared his loyalty to God alone.

Idealistic young men flocked to Francis, and they wandered Italy like troubadours, spreading the joy of the Gospel to rich and poor. Francis became a cult figure, attracting huge crowds. They'd never seen anything like it—sermons preached outdoors, in the local language (not Church Latin), making God accessible to all. Francis' new order of monks was also extremely unmaterialistic, extolling poverty and simplicity. Despite their radicalism, the order eventually gained the pope's approval and spread through the world. Francis, who died in Assisi at the age of 44, left a legacy of humanism, equality, and love of nature that would eventually flower in the Renaissance.

## In Francis' Sandal Steps
1. Baptized in Assisi's **Cathedral of San Rufino.**
2. Raised in the family home just off Piazza del Comune (now the **Chiesa Nuova**).
3. Heard call to "rebuild church" in **San Damiano.** (The crucifix of the church is now in the **Basilica of St. Clare.**)
4. Settled and established his order of monks at the **Porziuncola Chapel** (inside today's Basilica of Santa Maria degli Angeli).
5. Met Clare. (Her tomb and possessions are at the **Basilica of St. Clare.**)
6. Received the pope's blessing for his order (1223 document in the reliquary chapel at the **Basilica of St. Francis**).
7. Had many visions and was associated with miracles during his life (depicted in **Giotto's frescoes** in the Basilica of St. Francis' upper level).
8. Died at the **Porziuncola,** his body later interred beneath the **Basilica of St. Francis.**

ple in churches). Underneath that level, they found Roman foundations and some animal bones (suggesting the possibility of animal sacrifice). There might have been a Roman temple here; churches were often built upon temple ruins. Stand at the back of the church facing the altar, and look left to the Roman cistern that collected rainwater (just beyond the great stone archway, next to where you entered). Take the three steps down (to trigger the light) and marvel at the fine stonework and Roman engineering. In the Middle Ages, this was the town's emergency water source when under attack.

**Diocesan Museum:** Underneath the church, incorporated into the Roman ruins and columns, are the foundations of an earlier Church of San Rufino, now the crypt and a fine little museum. When it's open, you can go below to see the saint's sarcophagus (third century) and the cathedral's art from centuries past (down the stairs, near the baptismal font, well-described in English).

• *Leaving the church, walk to the end of the square and take a sharp left (at the pizza-by-the-slice joint, on Via Dono Doni). After 20 yards, take a right and go all the way down the stairway to see some...*

## ❹ Medieval Architecture

At the bottom of the stairs, notice the pink limestone pavement, part of the surviving medieval town. The arches built over doorways indicate that the buildings date from the 12th through the 14th century, when Assisi was booming. Italian cities such as Assisi—thriving on the north-south trade between northern Europe and Rome—were in the process of inventing free-market capitalism, dabbling in democratic self-rule, and creating the modern urban lifestyle. The vaults you see that turn lanes into tunnels are reminders of medieval urban expansion—creating more living space (mostly 15th century). While the population grew, people wanted to live within the town's protective walls. Medieval Assisi had several times the population density of modern Assisi.

Notice the blooming balconies; Assisi holds a flower competition each June.

• *From the bottom of the stairs, head to the left and continue downhill. When you arrive at a street, turn left, going slightly uphill for a long block, then take the low road (right) at the Y, and head down Via Sermei. Continue down to the big church. Walk right, under the three massive buttresses, to Piazza Santa Chiara and the front of the church.*

## ❺ Basilica of St. Clare (Basilica di Santa Chiara)

Dedicated to the founder of the Order of the Poor Clares, this Umbrian Gothic church—worth ▲▲—is simple, in keeping with the nuns' dedication to a life of contemplation. In Clare's lifetime, the order was located in the humble Church of San Damiano, in the valley below, but after Clare's death, they needed a bigger and more glorious building. The church was built in 1265, and the huge buttresses were added in the next century.

**Cost and Hours:** Free, daily 6:30-12:00 & 14:00-19:00, until 18:00 in winter, crypt opens Mon-Fri at 9:00, tel. 075-812-282.

**Visiting the Basilica:** The interior's fine frescoes were whitewashed in Baroque times. The battered remains of one on the left show how the fresco surface was hacked up so whitewash would stick. Imagine all the pristine frescoes hiding behind the whitewash (here and all over Europe).

On the right is the door to the Chapel of the Crucifix of San Damiano, with the simple wooden crucifix that changed Francis' life. In 1206, an emaciated, soul-searching, stark-raving Francis knelt before this crucifix of a living Christ (then located in the Church of San Damiano) and asked for guidance. According to legend, the crucifix spoke: "Go and rebuild my Church, which you can see has fallen into ruin." Francis followed the call.

Stairs lead from the nave down to the tomb of St. Clare. Her tomb—discovered in about 1850—is at the far right end of the richly ornamented neo-Gothic crypt (the image is fiberglass; her actual bones lie underneath). As you circulate with the crowd of pilgrims, notice the paintings on the walls depicting spiritual lessons from Clare's life and death. At the opposite end of the crypt (back between the stairs, in a large glassed-in area, well-described on the wall) are important relics: the saint's robes, hair (in a silver box), and an enormous tunic she made—along with relics of St. Francis (including a bloodstained stocking he wore after receiving the stigmata). The attached cloistered community of the Poor Clares has flourished for 700 years.

• *Leave the church and belly up to the viewpoint at the edge of the square for...*

**Another Umbrian View:** On the left is the convent of St. Clare (global headquarters of all the Poor Clares). Below you lies the olive grove of the Poor Clares, which has been there since the 13th century. In the distance is a grand Umbrian view. Assisi overlooks the richest and biggest valley in otherwise hilly and mountainous Umbria. Across the valley to the far right (and over the Tiber River), the rival town Perugia, where Francis was imprisoned, sits on its own hill.

The lower town, called Santa Maria degli Angeli, grew up

## St. Clare (1194-1253)

The 18-year-old rich girl of Assisi fell in love with Francis' message, and made secret arrangements to meet him. The night of Palm Sunday, 1212, she slipped out of her father's mansion in town and escaped to the valley below. A procession of friars with torches met her and took her to (what is today) the Basilica of Santa Maria degli Angeli. There, Francis cut her hair, clothed her in a simple brown tunic, and welcomed her into a life of voluntary poverty. Clare's father begged, ordered, and physically threatened her to return, but she would not budge.

Clare was joined by other women who banded together as the Poor Clares. She spent the next 40 years of her life within the confines of the convent of San Damiano: barefoot, vegetarian, and largely silent. Her regimen of prayer, meditation, and simple manual labor—especially knitting—impressed commoners and popes, leading to her canonization almost immediately after her death. St. Clare is often depicted carrying a monstrance (a little temple holding the Eucharist wafer).

with the coming of the railway in the 19th century. In the haze, the church with the grayish-blue dome is the Basilica of Santa Maria degli Angeli (described later), the cradle of the Franciscan order. A popular pilgrimage site today, it marks the place where St. Francis lived, worked, and died.

By the way, many Spanish-speaking Franciscans settled in California. Three of their missions grew into major cities: Los Angeles (named after this church), San Francisco (named after St. Francis), and Santa Clara (named after St. Clare).

• *From the church square, step out into Via Santa Chiara.*

## ❻ Arches and Artisans

Look left and right to find three old town gates, which illustrate how the city has grown (in concentric circles) since antiquity. First, look to the left, uphill on Via Santa Chiara, the high road. This first arch marks the site of the original Roman wall. In Roman days, this was the extent of Assisi. Now look right, beyond the church. This old gate over the road dates from 1265, as the town expanded during the boom years and the city wall was pushed outward. Farther on, you can just make out the crenellations of the third gate:

the Porta Nuova. Built in 1316, this "New Gate" marks the final expansion of Assisi, before its centuries of slow decline.

Walk uphill along Via Santa Chiara (which becomes Corso Mazzini) to the city's main square. As you pass under the arch you enter what was Roman Assisi—the city that Francis knew. The street is lined with interesting shops selling traditional embroidery, religious souvenirs, and gifty edibles. The shops on Corso Mazzini, on the stretch between the gate and Piazza del Comune, show off many local crafts. As you browse, watch for the following shops:

Galleria d'Arte Perna (on the left, #20b) sells the medieval fantasy townscapes of Paolo Grimaldi, a local painter who runs this shop with his brother, Alessandro.

A helpful travel agency is across the street and a few steps up (at #31, Agenzia Viaggi Stoppini; see "Helpful Hints," earlier).

Next, the aptly named Assisi Olive Wood (on the left at #14E) sells olive-wood carvings, as does d'Olivo, across the street at #23. It's said that St. Francis made the first Nativity scene to help humanize and, therefore, teach the Christmas message. That's why you'll see so many crèches in Assisi. (Even today, nearby villages are enthusiastic about their "living" manger scenes, and Italians everywhere enjoy setting up elaborate crèches in churches for Christmas.)

At #14A (also on the left) is a bakery, Bar Sensi, selling the traditional raisin-and-apple strudel called *rocciata* (roh-CHAH-tah, big enough to share).

Farther along on the left (on the corner at #2A) is Antichita il Duomo, selling religious art, manger scenes, Christmas ornaments, and Crucifixion figurines. Across the street at #5A is Galleria del Corso, selling finely embroidered linens and baby clothes.

And on the square (at #34, on the right), the recommended La Bottega dei Sapori is worth a visit for edible and drinkable souvenirs.

You've walked up what was, in ancient times, the main drag into town. Ahead of you, the six fluted Corinthian columns of the Temple of Minerva marked the forum (today's Piazza del Comune). Sit at the fountain on the piazza for a few minutes of people-watching—don't you just love Italy? Within a few hundred yards of this square, on either side, were the medieval walls. Imagine the commotion of 5,000 people confined within these walls. No wonder St. Francis needed an escape for some peace and quiet.

Today, while the municipality of Assisi has a population of 25,000, only 3,500 people live in the old town: Many who left damaged homes after the 1997 earthquake decided to stay in the modern city below. This is one reason for the old town's plethora of tourist shops (and few services for residents like supermarkets or hardware stores).

• *Now, head over to the temple on the square.*

## ❼ Temple of Minerva/Christian Church

Assisi has always been a spiritual center. The Romans went to great lengths to make this first-century BC Temple of Minerva a centerpiece of their city. Notice the col-
umns that cut into the stairway. It
was a tight fit here on the hilltop.
In ancient times, the stairs went
down—about twice as far as they do
now—to the main drag, which has
gradually been filled in over time.
The Church of Santa Maria sopra
("over") Minerva was added in the
9th century. The bell tower is from
the 13th century.

Pop inside the temple/church
(free, daily 7:15-19:30, in winter
closes at sunset and midday). To-
day's interior is 17th-century Baroque. Walk to the front. Flanking
the altar to the back are the original Roman temple floor stones.
You can even see the drains for the bloody sacrifices that took place
here. Behind the statues of Peter and Paul, the original Roman
embankment peeks through.

As you exit the church, look to the right, next to the door of
the bell tower. The shapes set into the wall are the medieval city
standards for the market that used to take place here. The large
shapes are building materials, bricks, and roof tiles. The metal bars
were the official measuring sticks for goods sold by length, a mea-
surement that could change from city to city.

• *Across the square next to #11, step into the 16th-century frescoed vaults
of the...*

**Loggia of the Palazzo del Comune:** Notice the Italian flair
for fine design. Even this little loggia features decorative art (in
the Grotesque style—named for the fanciful paintings of bizarre
creatures found on unfinished lower-level walls at Nero's Golden
House in Rome). This scene was indisputably painted after 1492.
How do they know? Because it features turkeys—first seen in Europe after Columbus returned from the Americas with his ship full
of exotic souvenirs. The turkeys painted here may have been that
bird's European debut.

• *From the main square, hike left past the temple up the high road, Via
San Paolo. After 150 yards (across from #24), a sign on the left directs
you down a stepped lane to the...*

## ❽ Church of Santo Stefano (Chiesa di Santo Stefano)

Surrounded by cypress, fig, and walnut trees, Santo Stefano—which used to be outside the town walls in the days of St. Francis—is a delightful bit of offbeat Assisi (free, daily 8:30-20:00, shorter hours off-season). Legend has it that Santo Stefano's bells miraculously rang on October 3, 1226, the day St. Francis died. Step inside. This is the typical rural Italian Romanesque church—no architect, just built by simple stonemasons who put together the most basic design. Hundreds of years later, it still stands.

• *The lane zigzags down to Via San Francesco. When you reach the narrow lane, go left (downhill). Then, emerging at the wider street, turn right and walk under the arch toward the Basilica of St. Francis. To trace the rest of our route, see the "Assisi" map on page 724.*

## ❾ Via San Francesco

This main drag leads from the town to the basilica holding the body of St. Francis. Francis was a big deal even in his own day. He was made a saint in 1228—the same year that the basilica's foundations were laid—and his body was moved here by 1230. Assisi was a big-time pilgrimage center, and this street was its booming hub. The arch marks the end of what was Assisi in St. Francis' day. Notice the fine medieval balcony immediately past the arch (on the left).

About 30 yards farther down (on the left), find the **fountain** where medieval pilgrims might have cooled themselves. The hospice next door was built in 1237 to house pilgrims. Notice the three surviving faces of its fresco: Jesus, Francis, and Clare.

Farther down on the left, across from #12A, is the **Oratorio dei Pellegrini,** dating from the 1450s. A brotherhood ran a hostel here for travelers passing through to pay homage to St. Francis. The chapel offers a richly frescoed 14th-century space designed to inspire pilgrims—perfect for any traveler to pause and contemplate the saint's message (Mon-Fri 9:00-12:00 & 16:00-18:00, Sat afternoon only, closed Sun).

From here, the road continues a few more short blocks downhill to the Basilica of St. Francis. Just before the basilica is a three-floor museum about Capuchin missionaries' work in the Amazon region since 1909 (**Museo Missionario Indios,** on the left at #19, closed Mon). Depending on your feelings about missionaries in the developing world, this may be of interest—with exhibits on ethnography, flora and fauna, and Franciscan theology.

• *Continuing on, you'll reach Assisi's main sight, the Basilica of St. Francis. For the start of my self-guided tour, walk downhill to the basilica's lower courtyard.*

# Basilica of St. Francis Tour

The Basilica of St. Francis (Basilica di San Francesco), worth
▲▲▲, is one of the artistic and religious highlights of Europe.

It stands where, in 1226,
St. Francis was buried
(with the outcasts he had
stood by) outside of his
town on the "Hill of the
Damned"—now called the
"Hill of Paradise." The basilica is frescoed from top
to bottom with scenes by
the leading artists of the
day: Cimabue, Giotto, Simone Martini, and Pietro Lorenzetti. A
13th-century historian wrote, "No more exquisite monument to
the Lord has been built."

From a distance, you see the huge arcades "supporting" the
basilica. These were 15th-century quarters for the monks. The arcades that line the square and lead to the church housed medieval
pilgrims.

## ORIENTATION

**Cost and Hours:** The complex is free to enter, with different hours
for various parts. The **lower basilica** and **tomb** are open to
tourists daily 6:00-17:30, Nov-March until 16:30—but in
practice, the space remains open for worship (and discreet
sightseers) more than an hour later. Within the lower basilica,
the **reliquary chapel** opens at 9:00 but is often closed Sat-
Sun (and occasionally at other times for religious services).
The **upper basilica** is open daily 8:30-18:50, Nov-March until
18:00. And the skippable **treasury/museum** is open Mon-Tue
and Thu-Sat 9:30-18:00, Sun 11:00-17:00, closed Wed, shorter hours off-season, closed Jan-Feb.

**Dress Code:** Modest dress is required to enter the church—no
above-the-knee skirts or shorts and no sleeveless tops for men,
women, or children.

**Information:** Tel. 075-819-0170, www.sanfrancescoassisi.org.
Call or check the website to find out about upcoming events at
the basilica. A handy information office is in the arcade of the
lower courtyard—on the right as you face the church (Mon-
Sat 9:00-18:00, closed Sun, shorter hours off-season).

**Tours:** Videoguides loaded with a one-hour tour are available at
the information office under the arcade in the courtyard of the
lower basilica (€6, €10/2 people).

🎧 Download my free Basilica of St. Francis audio tour.

ASSISI

**Bookstore:** The church bookshop is in the inner courtyard behind the upper and lower basilica. It sells an excellent guidebook, *The Basilica of Saint Francis: A Spiritual Pilgrimage* (€3, by Goulet, McInally, and Wood); I used this book, and a tour with Brother Michael, as sources for this self-guided tour.

**Church Services:** To worship in the basilica, consider joining the Franciscan brothers for Mass in *Italiano* (Mon-Sat at 7:15, 11:00, and 18:00—or 17:00 off-season; Sun at 7:30, 9:00, 10:30, 12:00, 17:00, and 18:30), or experience a Mass sung by the basilica choir many Sundays at 10:30. On Sundays in summer (Easter-Oct), there's an English Mass in the upper basilica at 9:00. Additional English and sung Masses don't follow a set schedule. Call the basilica to find out when English-speaking pilgrimage groups or choirs have reserved Masses, and attend with them (tel. 075-819-0170).

## OVERVIEW

The Basilica of St. Francis, a theological work of genius, can be difficult for the 21st-century tourist/pilgrim to appreciate.

Since the basilica is the reason that most people visit Assisi, and the message of St. Francis has even the least devout sightseers blessing the town Vespas, I've designed this self-guided tour with an emphasis on the place's theology (rather than art history).

A disclaimer before we start: Just as Francis used many biblical legends to help teach the Christian message, legends from the life of Francis were told in later ages to teach the same message. Are they true? In general, probably not. Are they in keeping with Francis' message? Yes. Do I share legends here as if they are historic? Sure.

The church has three parts: the upper basilica, the lower basilica, and the saint's tomb (below the lower basilica). We'll tour the complex from the bottom up. To get oriented, head down the ramp from the grassy lawn and stand in the big plaza that stretches in front of the lower entrance. While empty today, centuries ago this main piazza was cluttered with pilgrim services and the medieval equivalent of souvenir shops. As you face the church, the information office is under the arcade to your right, and the WCs are just behind that. (Go before you enter, as there aren't any WCs inside the basilica.)

ASSISI

## ➋ SELF-GUIDED TOUR

Enter through the grand doorway of the lower basilica. Just inside, decorating the top of the first arch, look up and see St. Francis, who greets you with a Latin inscription. Sounding a bit like John Wayne, he says the equivalent of, "Slow down and be joyful, pilgrim. You've reached the Hill of Paradise. And, if you're observant and thoughtful, this church will knock your spiritual socks off."

• *Start with the tomb. To get there, turn left into the nave. Midway down, follow the signs and go right, to the tomb downstairs.*

### The Tomb

The saint's remains are above the altar in the stone box with the iron ties. In medieval times, pilgrims came to Assisi because St. Francis was buried here. Holy relics were the "ruby slippers" of medieval Europe. Relics gave you power—they answered your prayers and won your wars—and ultimately helped you get back to your eternal Kansas. Assisi made no bones about promoting the saint's relics, but hid his tomb for obvious reasons of security. His body was buried secretly while the basilica was under construction, and over the next 600 years, the exact location was forgotten. When the tomb was to be opened to the public in 1818, it took more than a month to find his actual remains.

Francis' four closest friends and first followers are memorialized in the corners of the room. Opposite the altar, up four steps between the entrance and exit, notice the small copper box behind the metal grille. This contains the remains of Francis' rich Roman patron, Jacopa dei Settesoli. She traveled to see him on his deathbed but was turned away because she was female. Francis waived the rule and welcomed "Brother Jacopa" to his side. These five tombs—in the Franciscan spirit of being with your friends—were added in the 19th century.

The candles you see are the only real candles in the church (others are electric). Pilgrims pay a coin, pick up a candle, and place it in the small box on the side. The friars will light it later.

• *Climb back up to the lower nave.*

### Lower Basilica

Appropriately Franciscan—subdued and Romanesque—this nave is frescoed with parallel scenes from the lives of Christ (right) and Francis (left), connected by a ceiling of stars. The Passion of Christ and the Compassion of Francis lead to the altar built over Francis' tomb. After the church was built and decorated, side chapels were erected to provide mausoleums for the rich families that patronized the work of the order. Unfortunately, in the process, huge arches were cut out of some frescoed scenes, but others survive.

In the fresco directly above the entry to the tomb, Christ is

# Basilica of St. Francis—Lower Level

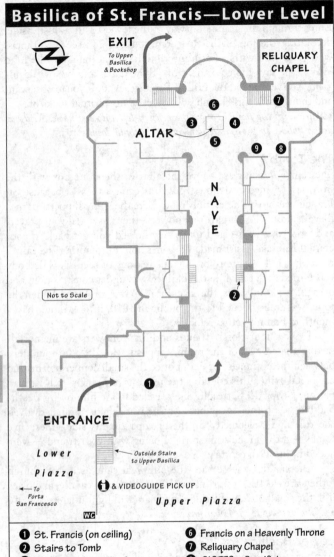

**EXIT**
To Upper
Basilica
& Bookshop

**RELIQUARY
CHAPEL**

**6**

**3** **4**

**ALTAR**

**5**

**9** **8**

**N
A
V
E**

Not to Scale

**2**

ASSISI

**1**

**ENTRANCE**

*Lower*

*Piazza*

← To
Porta
San Francesco

Outside Stairs
to Upper Basilica

🛈 & VIDEOGUIDE PICK UP

*Upper Piazza*

**WC**

**1** St. Francis *(on ceiling)*
**2** Stairs to Tomb
**3** Obedience *(on ceiling)*
**4** Chastity *(on ceiling)*
**5** Poverty *(on ceiling)*

**6** Francis on a Heavenly Throne
**7** Reliquary Chapel
**8** GIOTTO – Crucifixion
**9** CIMABUE – St. Francis

being taken down from the cross (just the bottom half of his body can be seen, on the left), and it looks like the story is over. Defeat. But in the opposite fresco (above the tomb's exit), we see Francis preaching to the birds, reminding the faithful that the message of the Gospel survives.

These stories directed the attention of the medieval pilgrim to the altar, where he could meet God through the sacraments. The church was thought of as a community of believers sailing toward God. The prayers coming out of the nave (*navis*, or ship) fill the triangular sections of the ceiling—called *vele*, or sails—with spiritual wind. With a priest for a navigator and the altar for a helm, faith propels the ship.

Walk around the altar, stand behind it (toes to the bottom step, facing the entrance), and look up. The three scenes above you represent the creed of the Franciscans: Directly above the tomb of St. Francis, to the right, **Obedience** (Francis appears twice, wearing a rope harness and kneeling in front of Lady Obedience); to the left, **Chastity** (in her tower of purity held up by two angels); and straight ahead, **Poverty**. Here Jesus blesses the marriage as Francis slips a ring on Lady Poverty. In the foreground, two "self-sufficient" yet pint-size merchants (the new rich of a thriving northern Italy) are throwing sticks and stones at the bride. But Poverty, in her patched wedding dress, is fertile and strong, and even bare brambles blossom into a rosebush crown.

St. Francis called money the "devil's dung." The jeweled belt of a rich person was all about material wealth. A bag of coins hung from it, as did a weapon to protect that wealth. The simple rope Franciscan monks use to tie their tunics has three knots that symbolize—and serve as constant reminders of—their vows of obedience, chastity, and poverty.

Now turn around and put your heels to the altar and—bending back like a drum major—look up for a peek at the reward for a life of obedience, chastity, and poverty: **Francis on a heavenly throne** in a rich, golden robe. He traded a life of earthly simplicity for glory in heaven.

• *Turn to the right and march to the corner, where steps lead down into the...*

## Reliquary Chapel

This chapel is filled with fascinating relics (which a €0.50 flier explains in detailed English; often closed Sat-Sun). Step in and circle the room clockwise. You'll see the silver chalice and plate that Francis used for the bread and wine of the Eucharist (in a small, dark, windowed case set into the wall, marked *Calice e Patena*). Francis believed that his personal possessions should be simple, but the items used for worship should be made of the finest materials.

ASSISI

## The Franciscan Message

Francis' message caused a stir. Not only did he follow Christ's teachings, he also followed Christ's lifestyle, living as a poor, wandering preacher. He traded a life of power and riches for one of obedience, poverty, and chastity. He was never ordained as a priest, but his influence on Christianity was monumental.

The Franciscan realm (Brother Sun, Sister Moon, and so on) is a space where God, man, and the natural world frolic harmoniously. Francis treated every creature—animal, peasant, pope—with equal respect. He and his "brothers" (*fratelli*, or friars) slept in fields, begged for food, and exuded the joy of nonmaterialism. Franciscan friars were known as the "Jugglers of God," modeling themselves on French troubadours who roved the countryside singing, telling stories, and cracking jokes.

In an Italy torn by rival political factions, Francis promoted peace and the restoration of order. (He set an example by reconstructing the crumbled San Damiano chapel.) While the Church was waging bloody Crusades, Francis pushed ecumenism and understanding. And the Franciscan message had an impact. In 1288, just 62 years after Francis died, a Franciscan became pope (Nicholas IV). Francis' message also led to Church reforms that

Next, the Veli di Lino is a cloth Jacopa wiped her friend's brow with on his deathbed. In the corner display case is a small section of the itchy haircloth *(cilizio)*—not sheep's wool, but cloth made from scratchy horse or goat hair—worn by Francis as penance (the cloth he chose was the opposite of the fine fabric his father sold). In the next corner are the tunic and slippers that Francis donned during his last days. Next, find a prayer (in a fancy silver stand) that St. Francis wrote for Brother Leo and signed with a T-shaped character—his tau cross. The last letter in the Hebrew alphabet, tav ("tau" in Greek) is symbolic of faithfulness to the end, and Francis adopted it for his signature. Next is a papal document (1223) legitimizing the Franciscan order and assuring his followers that they were not risking a (deadly) heresy charge. Finally, just past the altar, see the tunic that was lovingly patched and stitched by followers of the five-foot, four-inch-tall St. Francis.

Before leaving the chapel, notice the modern paintings done recently by local artists. Over the entrance, Francis is shown being

many believe delayed the Protestant Reformation by a century.

The richly decorated Assisi basilica seems to contradict the teachings of the poor monk it honors, but it was built as an act of religious and civic pride to remember the hometown saint. It was also designed—and still functions—as a pilgrimage center and a splendid classroom. Though monks in robes may not give off an "easy-to-approach" vibe, the Franciscans of today are still God's jugglers (and many of them speak English).

Here is Francis' message, in his own words:

### *The Canticle of the Sun*

Good Lord, all your creations bring praise to you!

Praise for Brother Sun, who brings the day. His radiance reminds us of you!

Praise for Sister Moon and the stars, precious and beautiful.

Praise for Brother Wind, and for clouds and storms and rain that sustain us.

Praise for Sister Water. She is useful and humble, precious and pure.

Praise for Brother Fire who cheers us at night.

Praise for our sister, Mother Earth, who feeds us and rules us.

Praise for all those who forgive because you have forgiven them.

Praise for our sister, Bodily Death, from whose embrace none can escape.

Praise and bless the Lord, and give thanks, and, with humility, serve him.

ASSISI

born in a stable like Jesus (by Capitini). Scenes from the life of Clare and Padre Pio (a Capuchin priest, very popular in Italy, who was sainted in 2002) were painted by Stefanelli and Antonio.

• *Return up the stairs, stepping into the...*

## Lower Basilica's Transept

The decoration of this church brought together the greatest Sienese (Lorenzetti and Simone Martini) and Florentine (Cimabue and Giotto) artists of the day.

Look around at the painted scenes. In 1300, this was radical art—believable homespun scenes, landscapes, trees, real people. Directly opposite the reliquary chapel, study **Giotto's painting of the Crucifixion,** with the eight sparrow-like angels. For the first time, holy people are expressing emotion: One angel turns her head sadly at the sight of Jesus, and another scratches her hands down her cheeks, drawing blood. Mary (lower left), previously in control, has fainted in despair. The Franciscans, with their goal of bringing

God to the people, found a natural partner in Europe's first naturalist (and therefore modern) painter, Giotto.

To grasp Giotto's artistic leap, compare his work with the painting to the right, by Cimabue. It's Gothic, without the 3-D architecture, natural backdrop, and slice-of-life reality of Giotto's work. **Cimabue's St. Francis** (far right) shows the saint with the stigmata—Christ's marks of the Crucifixion. Contemporaries described Francis as being short, with a graceful build, dark hair, and sparse beard. (This is considered the most accurate portrait of Francis—done according to the description of one who knew him.) The sunroof haircut (tonsure) was standard

for monks of the day. According to legend, the brown robe and rope belt were inventions of necessity. When Francis stripped naked and ran away from Assisi, he grabbed the first clothes he could, a rough wool peasant's tunic and a piece of rope, which became the uniform of the Franciscan order.

To the left, at eye level under the sparrow-like angels, are paintings of **saints** and their exquisite halos (by Simone Martini or his school). To the right of the door at the same level, see five of Francis' closest **followers**—clearly just simple folk.

Francis' friend, **"Sister Bodily Death,"** was really not all that terrible. In fact, Francis would like to introduce you to her now (above and to the right of the door leading into the reliquary chapel). Go ahead, block the light from the door with this book and meet her. Before his death, Francis added a line to *The Canticle of the Sun:* "Praise for our sister, Bodily Death, from whose embrace none can escape."

• *Now, cross the transept to the other side of the altar (enjoying some of the oldest surviving bits of the inlaid local-limestone flooring—c. 13th century) and find the staircase going up. Immediately above the stairs is Lorenzetti's Francis Receiving the Stigmata. (Francis is considered the first person ever to earn the marks of the cross through his great faith and love of the Church.) Make your way up the stairs to the...*

## Courtyard

The courtyard overlooks the 15th-century cloister, the heart of this monastic complex. Pope Sixtus IV (of Sistine Chapel fame) had it built as a secure retreat for himself. Balanced and peaceful by design, the courtyard also functioned as a cistern to collect rainwater, supplying enough for 200 monks (today, there are about 40). The Franciscan order emphasizes teaching. This place functioned as a kind of theological center of higher learning, which rotated monks in for a six-month stint, then sent them back home more prepared and better inspired to preach effectively. That explains the complex narrative of the frescoes wallpapering the walls and halls here.

The **treasury** *(Museo del Tesoro)* to the left of the bookstore features ornately decorated chalices, reliquaries, vestments, and altarpieces.

• *From the courtyard, climb the stairs (next to the bookshop) to the...*

## Upper Basilica

Built later than its counterpart below, the brighter upper basilica is considered the first Gothic church in Italy (started in 1228). You've  followed the intended pilgrims' route, entering the lower church and finishing here. Notice how the pulpit (embedded in the corner pillar) can be seen and heard from every spot in the packed church. The spirit of the order was to fill the church and preach. See also the design in the round window in the west end (high above the entry). The tiny centerpiece reads "IHS" (the first three letters of Jesus' name in Greek). And, as you can see, this trippy kaleidoscope seems to declare that all light radiates from Jesus.

The windows here are treasures from the 13th and 14th centuries. Those behind the altar are among the oldest and most precious in Italy. Imagine illiterate medieval peasants entranced by these windows, so full of meaning that they were nicknamed "Bibles of the Poor."

But for art lovers, the basilica's draw is that Giotto and his assistants practically wallpapered it circa 1297-1300. Or perhaps the job was subcontracted to other artists—scholars debate it (for more on Giotto, see page 138). Whatever the case, the anatomy, architectural depth, and drama of these frescoes helped to kick off the Renaissance. The gallery of frescoes shows 28 scenes from the life of St. Francis. The events are a mix of documented history and folk legend.

• *Take a walk through Francis' life, via these glorious illustrations. As you stand in front of the altar, facing the front of the church, begin with the first fresco on the right. From here, you'll work clockwise (moving to the right) along the north wall. Follow along with the help of the num-*

**ASSISI**

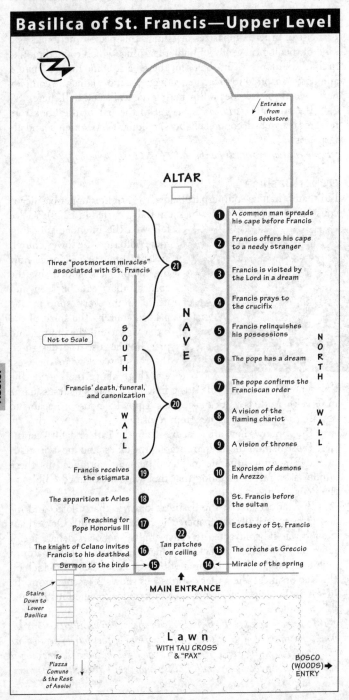

# Basilica of St. Francis—Upper Level

ALTAR

Three "postmortem miracles" associated with St. Francis — 21

Not to Scale

Francis' death, funeral, and canonization — 20

Francis receives the stigmata — 19

The apparition at Arles — 18

Preaching for Pope Honorius III — 17

The knight of Celano invites Francis to his deathbed — 16

Sermon to the birds → 15

SOUTH WALL

NAVE

NORTH WALL

1 A common man spreads his cape before Francis

2 Francis offers his cape to a needy stranger

3 Francis is visited by the Lord in a dream

4 Francis prays to the crucifix

5 Francis relinquishes his possessions

6 The pope has a dream

7 The pope confirms the Franciscan order

8 A vision of the flaming chariot

9 A vision of thrones

10 Exorcism of demons in Arezzo

11 St. Francis before the sultan

12 Ecstasy of St. Francis

13 The crèche at Greccio

14 ← Miracle of the spring

22 Tan patches on ceiling

MAIN ENTRANCE

Stairs Down to Lower Basilica

To Piazza Comune & the Rest of Assisi

Lawn
WITH TAU CROSS & "PAX"

BOSCO (WOODS) ENTRY

ASSISI

*bered map key. The subtitles in the faded black strip below the frescoes describe each scene in clear Latin—and affirm my interpretation.*

**❶ A common man spreads his cape before Francis** in front of the Temple of Minerva on Piazza del Comune. Before his conversion, young Francis was the model of Assisian manhood—handsome, intelligent, and well-dressed, befitting the son of a wealthy cloth dealer. Above all, he was liked by everyone, a natural charmer who led his fellow teens in nights of wine, women, and song. Medieval pilgrims understood the deeper meaning of this scene: The "eye" of God (symbolized by the rose window in the Temple of Minerva) looks over the young Francis, a dandy "imprisoned" in his own selfishness (the Temple—with barred windows—was once a prison).

**❷ Francis offers his cape to a needy stranger.** Francis was always generous of spirit. He became more so after being captured in battle and held for a year as a prisoner of war, then suffering from illness. Charity was a Franciscan forte.

**❸ Francis is visited by the Lord in a dream.** Still unsure of his calling, Francis rode off to the Crusades. One night, he dreams of a palace filled with armor marked with crosses. Christ tells him to leave the army—to become what you might consider the first "conscientious objector"—and go home to wait for a nonmilitary assignment in a new kind of knighthood. He returned to Assisi and, though reviled as a coward, would end up fighting for spiritual wealth, not earthly power and riches.

**❹ Francis prays to the crucifix** in the Church of San Damiano. After months of living in a cave, fasting, and meditating, Francis kneels in the run-down church and prays. The crucifix speaks, telling him: "Go and rebuild my Church, which you can see has fallen into ruin." Francis hurried home and sold his father's cloth to pay for God's work. His furious father dragged him before the bishop.

**❺ Francis relinquishes his possessions.** In front of the bishop and the whole town, Francis strips naked and gives his dad his clothes, credit cards, and a time-share on Capri. Francis raises his hand and says, "Until now, I called you father. From now on, my only father is my Father in Heaven." Notice God's hand blessing the action from above. Francis then ran off into the hills, naked and singing. In this version, Francis is covered by the bishop, symbolizing his transition from a man of the world to a man of the Church. Notice the disbelief and concern on the bishop's advisors' faces; subtle expressions like these wouldn't have made it into other medieval frescoes of the day.

**❻ The pope has a dream.** Francis headed to Rome, seeking the pope's blessing on his fledgling movement. Initially rebuffing

ASSISI

Francis, the pope then dreams of a simple, barefooted man propping up his teetering Church, and then...

**❼ The pope confirms the Franciscan order,** handing Francis and his gang the 1223 document now displayed in the reliquary chapel.

Francis' life was peppered with visions and miracles, shown in three panels in a row: **❽ vision of the flaming chariot, ❾ vision of thrones,** and **❿ exorcism of demons in Arezzo.**

• *Next see...*

**⓫ St. Francis before the sultan.** Francis' wandering ministry took him to Egypt during the Crusades (1219). He walked unarmed into the Muslim army camp. They captured him, but the sultan was impressed with Francis' manner and let him go, reportedly whispering, "I'd convert to your faith, but they'd kill us both." Here the sultan gestures from his throne.

**⓬ Ecstasy of St. Francis.** This oft-painted scene shows the mystic communing with Christ.

**⓭ The crèche at Greccio.** A creative teacher, Francis invents the tradition of manger scenes.

• *Around the corner, see the...*

**⓮ Miracle of the spring.** Shown here getting water out of a rock to quench a stranger's thirst, Francis felt closest to God when in the hills around Assisi, seeing the Creator in the creation.

• *Cross over to the far side of the entrance door.*

**⓯ Sermon to the birds.** In his best-known miracle, Francis is surrounded by birds as they listen to him teach. Francis embraces all levels of creation. One interpretation of this scene is that the birds, which are of different species, represent the diverse flock of humanity and nature, all created and beloved by God and worthy of one another's love.

This image of well-fed birds is an appropriate one to take with you. It's designed to remind pilgrims that, like the birds, God gave us life, plenty of food, feathers, wings, and a world to fly around in. Francis, patron saint of the environment and animals, taught his followers to see God in nature and to count their blessings. A monk here reminded me that even a student backpacker today eats as well as the wealthiest nobleman in the days of Francis.

• *Continue to the south wall for the rest of the panels.*

Despite the hierarchical society of his day, Francis was welcomed by all classes, shown in these three panels: **⓰ the knight of Celano invites Francis to his deathbed; ⓱ preaching for Pope Honorius III,** who listens intently; and **⓲ the apparition at Arles,** which illustrates how Francis could be in two places at once (something only Jesus and saints can pull off). The proponents of Francis, who believed he was destined for sainthood, show him performing the necessary miracles.

❶ **Francis receives the stigmata.** It's September 17, 1224, and Francis is fasting and praying on nearby Mount Alverna when a six-winged angel (called a seraph) appears with holy laser-like powers to burn in the marks of the Crucifixion, the stigmata. For the strength of his faith, Francis is given the marks of his master, the "battle scars of love." These five wounds suffered by Christ (nails in palms and feet, lance in side) marked Francis' body for the rest of his life.

The next panels deal with ❷ **Francis' death, funeral, and canonization.** The last panels show ❸ **miracles** associated with the saint after his death, proving that he's in heaven and bolstering his eligibility for sainthood.

Francis died thanking God and singing his *Canticle of the Sun*, in which he refers to the sun as his brother and the moon as his sister. Francis also called his body "Brother Ass" (because of the heavy burdens he asked it to carry)—and conceded on his deathbed that he'd been a bit tough on Brother Ass. Ravaged by an asceticism extreme enough to earn him the stigmata, Francis died in 1226.

Before leaving through the front entrance, look up at the ceiling and the walls near the rose window to see ❹ **large tan patches.** In 1997, when a 5.5-magnitude quake hit Assisi, it shattered the upper basilica's frescoes into 300,000 fragments. An aftershock then shook the ceiling frescoes down, killing two monks and two art scholars who were standing here. Later, the fragments were meticulously picked up and pieced back together.

Outside, on the lawn, the Latin word *pax* (peace) and the Franciscan tau cross are sculpted from shrubbery. For a drink or snack, the Bar San Francesco (facing the upper basilica) is handy. For *pax*, take the high lane back to town, up to the castle, or into the countryside.

# More Sights in Assisi

## IN THE OLD TOWN

These sights are in the upper town, near the main square or basilica.

### ▲Roman Forum (Foro Romano)

For a look at Assisi's Roman roots, check out the Roman Forum from the town of "Asisum"—beneath today's Piazza del Comune. You'll enter through a nondescript doorway (just a few steps off the main square) into a room filled with carved stone capitals, tombstones, sarcophagi, and sculpture fragments. From there, you'll follow tunnels back under the square itself, seeing various landmarks that once lined the streets of Asisum: a tribunal for speeches, a fountain, columns, the original Roman road, and much more, all displayed in situ (where it was discovered). A helpful five-minute

ASSISI

video (subtitled in English) helps resurrect the rubble.

**Cost and Hours:** €5, €9 combo-ticket with the next two sights, daily 10:00-18:00, June-Sept until 19:00, enter at Via Portica 2, tel. 075-815-5077.

### Pinacoteca

This small, unexciting museum attractively displays its 13th- to 17th-century art (mainly frescoes). There's a damaged Giotto Madonna and a rare secular fresco (to the right of the Giotto art), but it's mainly a peaceful walk through a pastel world—best for art lovers.

**Cost and Hours:** €3, €9 combo-ticket includes Forum and Rocca Maggiore, April-Oct daily 10:00-18:00, closed Nov-March except by appointment, on the main drag between Piazza del Comune and Basilica of St. Francis at Via San Francesco 12—look for banner above entryway, tel. 075-867-4341.

### ▲Rocca Maggiore

The "big castle" offers a few restored medieval rooms, a good look at a 14th-century fortification, and a fine view of Assisi and the Umbrian countryside. If you're pinching your euros, skip it—the view is just as good from outside the castle.

**Cost and Hours:** €6, €9 combo-ticket includes Forum and Pinacoteca, daily June-Aug 9:00-20:00, Sept from 10:00, April-May and Oct 10:00-18:30, shorter hours off-season, last entry 45 minutes before closing, Via della Rocca, tel. 075-815-5077.

## IN THE LOWER TOWN
### ▲▲Basilica of Santa Maria degli Angeli
### (Basilica of St. Mary of the Angels)

This huge basilica, towering above the buildings of Santa Maria degli Angeli—the modern part of Assisi in the flat valley below the hill town—marks the spot where Francis lived, worked, and died. It's a grandiose church built around a humble chapel—reflecting the monumental impact of this simple saint on his town and the world.

**Cost and Hours:** Free, Mon-Sat 6:15-12:40 & 14:30-19:30, Sun from 6:45, tel. 075-805-11.

**Dress Code:** Modest dress is required (no shorts or tank tops).

**Visitor Services:** A little TI is across the street from the souvenir stands, under the arches (generally Tue-Sun 10:00-12:30 & 15:30-18:00, closed Mon, tel. 075-804-4554). As you face the church, there are big pay WCs behind the bushes on your right.

**Getting There:** Whether you're traveling by car or by train, it's most practical to visit this sight on the way into or out of town. From Assisi's train station, it's a five-minute walk (exit station left, after 50 yards take the underground pedestrian walkway—*sotto-passaggio*—on your left, then walk straight ahead, passing several handy eateries). There's ample well-marked parking next to the train station, and some free (time-limited) spaces tucked behind the basilica.

From the old town, you can reach the basilica on the same Busitalia (line #C) that runs down to the train station (stay on one more stop to reach the basilica; confirm with driver). In the opposite direction, buses from the basilica up to the old town run twice hourly. Leaving the church, the stop is on your right, by the side of the building. For more bus details, see "Getting Around Assisi," earlier.

**Visiting the Basilica:** This grand church was built in the 16th century around the tiny but historic **Porziuncola Chapel** (now directly under the dome) after the chapel became too small to accommodate the many pilgrims wanting to pay homage to St. Francis. Some local monks had given Francis this *porziuncola,* or "small portion," after his conversion—a little land with a fixer-upper chapel. Francis lived here after he founded the Franciscan order, and this was where he consecrated St. Clare as a Bride of Christ. What would humble Francis think of the huge church—Christianity's 10th largest—built over his tiny chapel?

Behind the Porziuncola Chapel on the right, find the **Cappella del Transito,** which marks the site of Francis' death on October 3, 1226. Only 44 years old, Francis died as he'd lived—simply, in a small hut located here. On his last night on earth, he invited some friars to join him in a Last Supper-style breaking of bread. Then he undressed, lay down on the bare ground, and began to recite Psalm

141: "Lord, I cry unto thee." He spoke the last line, "Let the wicked fall into their own traps, while I escape"…and he passed on.

From the right transept, follow *Roseto* signs to the rose garden. You'll walk down a passage with gardens on either side (viewable through the windows)—on the left, a tranquil park with a statue of Francis petting a sheep, and on the right, the **rose garden.** Francis, fighting a temptation that he never named, once threw himself onto the roses. As the story goes, the thorns immediately dropped off. Thornless roses have grown here ever since.

Exiting the passage, turn right to find the **Rose Chapel** (Cappella delle Rose), built over the place where Francis lived.

The next hallway has exhibits that change occasionally, but you'll likely see a giant **Nativity scene**—a reminder to pilgrims that Francis first established the tradition of manger scenes as a teaching aid. The bookshop has some works in English and an "old pharmacy" selling herbal cures.

**Porziuncola Museum:** Continuing on, you'll pass this small museum featuring early depictions of St. Francis by 13th-century artists, a model of Assisi during Francis' lifetime, and religious art and objects from the basilica. On the museum's upper floor are some monks' cells, which provide intriguing insight into the spartan lifestyles of the pious and tonsured (€3, ask for English brochure, Thu-Tue 9:00-13:00 & 14:30-17:00, closed Wed, tel. 075-805-1419, www.porziuncola.org).

## ON THE OUTSKIRTS
### Church of San Damiano (Chiesa di San Damiano)

Located on the slope steeply below the Basilica of St. Clare, this modest church and convent was where Francis received his call and where Clare spent her days as mother superior of the Poor Clares. As you enter, signs point you through a series of simple rooms—including the dining hall where Clare ate with her flock and the room where she died—to a peaceful, flowery courtyard. Drivers can zip right there (watch for the turnoff on the road up to Piazza Matteotti), while walkers descend pleasantly from Assisi for 15 minutes through an olive grove.

In 1206, Francis was inside when he heard the wooden crucifix order him to rebuild the church. (The crucifix in San Damiano is a copy; the original is now displayed in the Basilica of St. Clare.) Francis initially interpreted these miraculous words as a call to rebuild crumbling San Damiano. He sold his father's cloth for money to fix the church. (The church we see today, however, was rebuilt later by others.) Eventually, Francis realized his charge was to revitalize the Christian Church at large.

As he approached the end of his life, Francis came to San Damiano to visit his old friend Clare. She set him up in a simple reed

ASSISI

hut in the olive grove, where he was inspired to write his poem *The Canticle of the Sun* (see page 743).

**Cost and Hours:** Free, daily, convent open 10:00-12:00 & 14:00-18:00, until 16:30 in winter, church opens at 6:15; start walking from the Porta Nuova parking lot at the south end of Assisi and follow the signs; tel. 075-812-273, www.assisiofm.it.

## Commune with Nature

For a picnic with the same birdsong and views that inspired St. Francis, leave the tourists behind and **hike to the Rocca Minore** (small private castle, not tourable) above Piazza Matteotti.

For a more organized nature experience, try the 160-acre **San Francesco Woods** (Bosco di San Francesco), where you can follow three routes through forest, monastery ruins, and a land-art installation (€5 suggested donation, picnic area; daily 10:00-19:00, Oct-March until 16:00 and closed Mon Sept-June, last entry one hour before closing, off the piazza in front of the upper basilica, tel. 075-813-157).

## ▲Hermitage (Eremo delle Carceri)

If you want to follow further in St. Francis' footsteps, take a trip up the rugged slopes of nearby Mount Subasio to the humble, peaceful hermitage where Francis and his followers retreated for solitude. Today the spot is marked by a 14th-century friary that's still occupied by Franciscan monks. You'll twist through the head-thumping doorframes and steep stairways of the medieval structure, the highlight of which is the tiny, dank cave where Francis would retire for private prayer. Emerging at the far side, near a stone bridge, you'll see a tree (held together with braces) dating from Francis' time. This is said to be where Francis preached to the birds. From here, rustic paths lead to open-air "chapels" in the surrounding forest. Be a Franciscan for a little while. Sit peacefully and listen. Pick out the different sounds of nature: wind blowing through the trees, chirping birds, gravel crunching underfoot. And listen for the spaces *between* the sounds. That's where Francis found God.

**Cost and Hours:** Free, daily 8:30-19:00, until 18:00 in winter, tel. 075-812-301.

**Getting There:** Drive, take a taxi, or hike—there is no public transportation. Drivers can follow signs out of Assisi toward Mount Subasio, then park on the switchback just above the entrance. For hikers starting from Assisi's Porta Cappuccino gate, it's a stiff 3-mile, 1.5-hour hike with an elevation gain of about 1,000 feet. You'll walk along a narrow, paved road (with no shoulders) enjoying brisk air and sporadic views. A souvenir kiosk at the entrance sells drinks and sandwiches, and there are WCs just uphill from the friary.

ASSISI

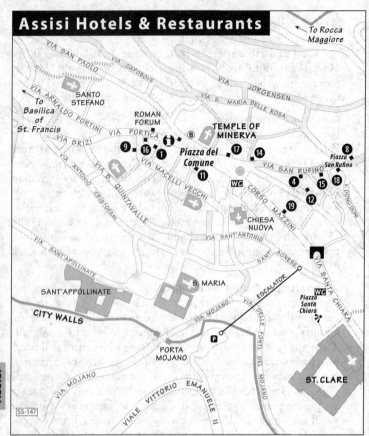

# Sleeping in Assisi

Assisi accommodates large numbers of pilgrims on religious holidays (see list on page 1208). Finding a room at any other time should be easy. My price rankings are based on rates in spring (April-mid-June) and fall (mid-Aug-Oct). Few hotels are air-conditioned.

## HOTELS AND ROOMS

**$$ Hotel Umbra,** a peaceful villa in the middle of town, has 24 spacious, antique-furnished rooms with great view terraces. It's a bit old-fashioned, but well-run, well-maintained, friendly, and beautifully located. Stepping into the breakfast room is like entering a time warp (RS%, family rooms, air-con, elevator, garden, and view sun terrace, most rooms have views, closed Dec-March, just off Piazza del Comune under the arch at Via degli Archi 6, tel.

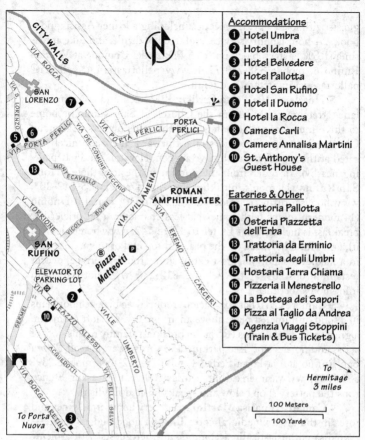

**Accommodations**
1. Hotel Umbra
2. Hotel Ideale
3. Hotel Belvedere
4. Hotel Pallotta
5. Hotel San Rufino
6. Hotel il Duomo
7. Hotel la Rocca
8. Camere Carli
9. Camere Annalisa Martini
10. St. Anthony's Guest House

**Eateries & Other**
11. Trattoria Pallotta
12. Osteria Piazzetta dell'Erba
13. Trattoria da Erminio
14. Trattoria degli Umbri
15. Hostaria Terra Chiama
16. Pizzeria il Menestrello
17. La Bottega dei Sapori
18. Pizza al Taglio da Andrea
19. Agenzia Viaggi Stoppini (Train & Bus Tickets)

075-812-240, www.hotelumbra.it, info@hotelumbra.it, Laudenzi family).

**\$\$ Hotel Ideale,** on a ridge overlooking the valley, offers 13 bright and airy rooms (all with views and balconies), a tranquil garden setting, and free (but tight) private parking. As it's just off the main road into town, it's a handy pick for timid drivers—but it means a longer walk to the sights (RS%, two apartments with kitchens available, air-con, Piazza Matteotti 1, tel. 075-813-570, www.hotelideale.it, info@hotelideale.it, sisters Lara and Ilaria).

**\$ Hotel Belvedere,** along the road into town from Porta Nuova, has 12 dated rooms—eight with sweeping views (breakfast extra, elevator, large communal view terrace, 2 blocks past Basilica of St. Clare at Via Borgo Aretino 13, tel. 075-812-460, www.assisihotelbelvedere.com, hotelbelvedereassisi@yahoo.it, thoughtful Enrico speaks fluent New Jerseyan).

**\$ Hotel Pallotta** offers seven tight rooms and a beautiful top-floor lounge with rooftop views. The conscientious hosts provide guests with loads of extra niceties including a loaner Assisi guide-book, 24-hour laundry service, and free hot drinks and cake at tea-time (RS%, a steep block up from Piazza del Comune at Via San Rufino 6, mobile 338-740-7574, www.pallottaassisi.it, pallotta@pallottaassisi.it; Stefano and Jenni).

**$ Hotels on Via Porta Perlici:** This steep and characteristic lane, stretching uphill from the Church of San Rufino, is home to three interchangeable hotels with the same owners (Carlo and Christian). Inexpensive and straightforward, these are nicely lo-cated at the top of town (all have air-con, elevators, and pay park-ing nearby). In order from the bottom to the top, there's **Hotel San Rufino** (11 rooms, breakfast extra, at #7a; tel. 075-812-803, www.hotelsanrufino.it, info@hotelsanrufino.it); **Hotel il Duomo** (14 modern rooms with somewhat less character, a bit pricier but breakfast is included, at #13, tel. 075-812-742, www.hotelilduomo. it); and **Hotel la Rocca** (at the peaceful top end of town, 32 rooms in a medieval shell, breakfast extra, sunny rooftop terrace, decent restaurant upstairs, at #27, tel. 075-812-284, www.hotelarocca.it, info@hotelarocca.it).

**$ Camere Carli** has six spacious rooms with bizarre floor plans in a solid, minimalist place above an art gallery. The loft rooms are a great value for families (RS%, no breakfast, family rooms, lots of stairs and no elevator, free parking 150 yards away, just off Piazza San Rufino at Via Porta Perlici 1, tel. 075-812-490, mobile 339-531-1366, www.camerecarli.it, carliarte@live.it, pleasant Franco runs the pottery shop below and speaks limited English).

**¢ Camere Annalisa Martini** is a cheery home amid vines and roses in the town's medieval core. This is a good budget choice—Annalisa enthusiastically accommodates her guests with a picnic garden, communal refrigerator, and six homey rooms with cheerful peeling wallpaper and flea market furniture (cash only, 3 rooms share 2 bathrooms, laundry service, no breakfast; one block from Piazza del Comune—go downhill toward the Basilica of St. Francis, turn left on Via San Gregorio to #6; tel. 075-813-536, cameremartini@libero.it). Mamma Rosignoli doesn't speak Eng-lish, but Annalisa does.

## SWEET DREAMS IN A CONVENT

Assisi is filled with convents, most of which rent rooms to pilgrims and travelers. While you don't need to be a pilgrim or even a Chris-tian to be welcome, it's just common sense to stay in a convent *only* if you're approaching Assisi with a contemplative mindset. Con-vents feel institutional, house many groups, and are not particu-larly cheap—but they come with all the facilities you might need to enjoy a spirit-filled visit to Assisi.

**$ St. Anthony's Guest House** is where the Franciscan Sisters of the Atonement offer a very warm and tranquil welcome. Their oasis of peace is just above the Basilica of St. Clare. They have 35 beds in 19 sparkling-clean rooms, some with great views—request when you reserve (family rooms available, 2-night minimum, no problem if couples want to share a bed, elevator, no air-con but fans, 23:00 curfew, closed mid-Nov-Feb, library, views, picnic garden, parking by donation; from the parking cashier in Piazza Matteotti, take the stairs down to the *"tunnel romano,"* walk around the little park, then continue down on the elevator—it's just to the left at Via Galeazzo Alessi 10; tel. 075-812-542, atoneassisi@tiscali.it).

### *AGRITURISMO* NEAR ASSISI

**$$ Le Mandrie di San Paolo** ("The Herd of St. Paul") is a meticulously restored 1,000-year-old stone house renting 13 rustic but comfortable rooms on a hillside high above the valley. Soulful Alex, his brother Andrew, and their team are justifiably proud of their passion for hospitality and connection to the land. They have an olive grove, lots of animals, a beautiful swimming pool, a sauna, a fine restaurant, and spectacular views over Assisi and the valleys of Umbria (apartments and family rooms, mobile 349-821-7867, tel. 075-806-4070, www.agriturismomandriesanpaolo.it, mandrie10@gmail.com). It's about a 10-minute drive from Assisi, above the village of Viole (a.k.a. San Vitale). Just head southeast of Assisi following signs for *Viole;* when you enter town, turn left before you reach the arch and follow signs up the hill. Their recommended **$$$$** restaurant is a great choice: They produce their own olive oil, cheese, salami, and flour, and fire their ovens with their own wood.

**ASSISI**

# Eating in Assisi

I've listed decent, central, good-value restaurants. Assisi's food is heavy and rustic. Locals brag about their sausage and love to grate truffles on pasta.

To bump up any meal, consider a glass or bottle of the favorite homegrown red wine, Sagrantino de Montefalco. Sagrantino is Umbria's answer to Brunello (although many wine lovers around here would say that it's vice versa). Before or after dinner, enjoy a drink on the main square facing the Roman temple...or hang out with the local teens with a takeaway beer under the temple's columns.

### IN THE TOWN CENTER

**$$$ Trattoria Pallotta** is a local favorite with white tablecloths and a living-room ambience. It's run by a friendly and hardworking family—with Margarita in charge of the kitchen—and offers delicious, well-presented regional specialties, such as *piccione* (squab, a.k.a. pigeon) and *coniglio* (rabbit). And they enjoy serving split courses *(bis)* featuring the two local pastas. They have various fixed-price choices, including an €18 tourist meal, a blowout €35 tasting *menu* showcasing local specialties, and a vegetarian option. Reservations are smart (Wed-Mon 12:00-14:30 & 19:00-21:30, closed Tue, a few steps off Piazza del Comune across from temple/church at Vicolo della Volta Pinta 2, tel. 075-815-5273, www.pallottaassisi.it).

**$$$ Osteria Piazzetta dell'Erba** is an inviting, trendy, youthful-feeling restaurant under medieval vaulted ceilings. Dishes are beautifully presented and inspired by local cuisine (Tue-Sun 12:30-14:30 & 19:30-22:30, closed Mon, seating indoors and on a peaceful square, reservations smart, just off the main piazza toward the Cathedral of San Rufino at Via S. Gabriele dell'Addolorata 15a, tel. 075-815-352, www.osterialapiazzetta.it, chef Matteo).

**$$ Trattoria da Erminio** has peaceful tables on a tiny square and indoor seating under a big, medieval (but air-conditioned) brick vault. Run by Federico and his family for three generations, it specializes in local meat cooked on an open-fire grill. They have good Umbrian wines—before you order, ask for a taste of their specialties (Fri-Wed 12:00-14:30 & 19:00-21:00, closed Thu; from Piazza San Rufino, go a block up Via Porta Perlici and turn right to Via Montecavallo 19a; tel. 075-812-506).

**$$ Trattoria degli Umbri** has a few nice tables just above the fountain overlooking Assisi's main square (the main reason to come here). They serve delightful Umbrian dishes and quality wines by the glass (Fri-Wed 12:00-15:00 & 19:00-22:00, closed Thu, Piazza del Comune 40, tel. 075-812-455).

**$$ Hostaria Terra Chiama** is a bright, modern little place run by Diego and his family, who serve traditional Umbrian dishes with seasonal specials (daily, lunch from 12:30, dinner from 19:00, Via San Rufino 16, tel. 075-819-9051).

**$ Pizzeria il Menestrello** serves huge, inexpensive Umbrian-style pizzas (wood-fired, thin, and crisp) in an elegant medieval vaulted setting that makes your beer and pizza feel like something King Arthur would eat for dinner (daily 12:00-14:30 & 19:00-22:30, Via San Gregorio 1a, tel. 075-812-746).

## PICNIC ON THE MAIN SQUARE

There are a few little grocery stores *(alimentari)* near Piazza del Comune (one is a block uphill from the main square, at Via San Rufino 19), plus bakeries selling pizza by the slice.

**La Bottega dei Sapori** is handy for assembling a picnic of Umbrian treats: good *porchetta* sandwiches and specialty items, including truffle paste and olive oil. Sandwich chef Saverio also makes a nice *taglieri misti* (meat and cheese plate) starting at €18 for two people. They like expensive ingredients, so it can get pricey here—be sure you're clear on the cost when you order (daily 9:30-21:00, shorter hours off-season, Piazza del Comune 34, tel. 075-812-294, Fabrizio). You can eat your sandwich on any of the benches surrounding the piazza.

**Pizza al Taglio da Andrea,** facing the Church of San Rufino on Piazza San Rufino, has perhaps the best pizza-by-the-slice in town. Locals also like their *torta al testo,* the Umbrian flatbread sandwich (daily 8:00-21:30, Via San Rufino 26, tel. 075-815-325).

## ABOVE THE BASILICA OF ST. FRANCIS

For locations, see the "Assisi" map near the beginning of this chapter.

**$$ Locanda del Podestà,** tucked inside a medieval gate just above the basilica, is a cozy spot with a traditional menu of tasty grilled Umbrian sausages, *gnocchi della locanda* (with gorgonzola and truffles), and tasty *scottadito* ("scorch your fingers") lamb chops (Thu-Tue 12:00-14:30 & 19:00-21:30, closed Wed and Feb, 5-minute walk uphill along Via Cardinale Merry del Val from basilica, Via San Giacomo 6C—see map on page 725, tel. 075-816-553).

**$$$ Le Terrazze di Properzio,** just up the street from Podestà, is the place to go to dine with a big view on a lovely terrace. The traditional menu includes seasonal specials. While the interior has a nice atmosphere, I'd skip this restaurant unless you're seated outside—you're paying a premium for the terrace (daily 12:00-14:30 & 19:00-21:30, terrace closed in bad weather, Via Metastasio 9, tel. 075-816-868).

## COUNTRYSIDE FARM-TO-TABLE DINNER

**$$$$ Le Mandrie di San Paolo,** in a 1,000-year-old farmhouse a 10-minute drive outside Assisi, makes many of its own ingredients and serves an exquisite dinner to guests and nonguests alike. This is a good example of a "zero-kilometer meal"—all the ingredients are sourced on the property (€30-35 four-course meal, daily 19:45-22:00, in winter on request, reservations preferred, see "Sleeping in Assisi" for location, www.agriturismomandriesanpaolo.it).

# Assisi Connections

If the train station's ticket office is closed, you'll find a ticket machine on the platform. Up in Assisi's old town, you can get train information and tickets from Agenzia Viaggi Stoppini (see listing under "Helpful Hints," earlier). That's also the best place to buy bus tickets—except for the FlixBus connection to Siena, which can easily be booked online.

**From Assisi by Train to: Rome** (6/day direct, 2 hours, more options with a change in Foligno), **Florence** (7/day direct, 2-3 hours), **Orvieto** (roughly hourly, 2-3 hours, with transfer in Terontola or Orte), **Siena** (10/day, about 4 hours, most involve 2 changes; bus is faster). Italian train timetables change frequently—double-check details at www.trenitalia.com.

**By Bus:** Service to **Rome** is operated by the Sulga bus company (2/day, 3 hours, pay driver, departs from Piazza San Pietro below the Basilica of St. Francis, arrives at Rome's Tiburtina station, one departure continues on weekdays to Fiumicino airport, tel. 800-099-661, www.sulga.it). FlixBus runs buses to **Siena** (2 hours, better than the long train ride, https://global.flixbus.com). Be clear on the departure point for your bus: Sometimes it leaves from Santa Maria degli Angeli, in the valley below Assisi (you'll find the stop at the far end of the big, long park in front of the Basilica of Santa Maria degli Angeli); other departures are from Piazza Unità d'Italia, below the Basilica of St. Francis. Don't take the bus to **Florence;** the train is better.

**By Plane:** Perugia/Assisi Airport is about 10 miles from Assisi (code: PEG, tel. 075-592-141, www.airport.umbria.it). Bus service between Assisi and the airport is so sporadic (just a few times a day—see www.umbriamobilita.it) that most travelers wind up taking a taxi (about €30).

# ORVIETO & CIVITA

While Tuscany is justifiably famous for its many fine hill towns, Umbria, just to the south, has some stellar offerings of its own. Assisi (covered in its own chapter) is a must for nature lovers and Franciscan pilgrims. But if you're after views, wine, and charming villages, you'll find Umbria's best in Orvieto and in Civita di Bagnoregio (which is technically just across the border in Lazio, the same region as Rome).

About a 30-minute drive apart, these hill towns—one big, one small—perch high above scenic plains. Pleasant Orvieto is best known for its colorful-inside-and-out cathedral and its fine Orvieto Classico wine. Tiny Civita di Bagnoregio is a "dead city": It's effectively one big open-air museum with a smattering of accommodations and eateries, perched precariously on a hill pinnacle that you pay to enter. Taken together, Orvieto and Civita make a perfect duet for experiencing what all the hill-town fuss is about.

## PLANNING YOUR TIME

Orvieto and Civita deserve at least an overnight, although even a few hours in each is enough to sample what they have to offer. Both are also great places to slow down and relax. Stay in one and side-trip to the other (Orvieto has more restaurants and other amenities and is easier to reach, while Civita really lets you get away from it all). The two are connected by a 30-minute drive or a one-hour bus ride. Orvieto is conveniently close to Rome (about an hour away by train or expressway).

# Orvieto & Civita Area

1. Alta Rocca Wine Resort
2. Agriturismo Locanda Rosati
3. Agriturismo Poggio della Volara
4. Tenuta Le Velette Winery & Accommodations
5. Agriturismo Cioccoleta & Neri Winery
6. Agriturismo Fattoria di Vibio
7. Custodi Winery

# Orvieto

Just off the freeway and the main train line, Umbria's grand hill town entices those zipping between Florence and Rome. The town sits majestically on its *tufo* throne a thousand feet above the valley floor. The city's stony streets are a delight to explore. With its brown stone cityscape, atmospheric covered alleys, and well-tended flowerpots, Orvieto is a photographer's dream. Every side street is a still life. The cathedral provides a great sightseeing experience: detailed scenes carved into its outer columns and a priceless chapel slathered in colorful art by Renaissance big shots Luca Signorelli and Fra Angelico.

Orvieto also provides perhaps the easiest introduction to Umbria—that pastoral region that all too often gets overshadowed by

## Orvieto's (Very Long) History

For a little town, Orvieto has a very big history. A few centuries before Christ, Orvieto—then called Velzna—was one of a dozen major Etruscan cities. Some historians believe it may have been a religious center—a kind of Etruscan Mecca (they're still looking for archaeological proof—the town and surrounding countryside are dotted with Etruscan ruins).

Imagine the history: From 900 BC to 264 BC, the town was Etruscan Velzna. After a two-year Roman siege, it was destroyed and the ruins left abandoned for six centuries. Rome fell in AD 476, and in the chaos of that power vacuum, with invaders from the north terrorizing the peninsula, people in the valley headed back into the hills in search of safety. They rebuilt over the old Etruscan foundations, and named the settlement Urbs Vetus, meaning "old town" in Latin. Over time, Urbs Vetus became Orvieto.

Orvieto flourished as a Middle Ages regional power. During Orvieto's glory days—from the 11th to 13th century—it was a city-state of about 30,000 people (like Perugia, Assisi, and Siena) and an occasional home to the pope. Today, with only 5,000 people living in less than a square mile atop its hill, and only half of its 50 churches still active, Orvieto is again a small town.

neighboring Tuscany. Orvieto's many excellent restaurants serve up toothsome pastas, flavorful game, and pungent truffles.

Orvieto has three claims to fame: cathedral, Classico wine, and ceramics. Drinking a shot of the local white wine in a ceramic cup as you gaze up at the cathedral lets you experience Orvieto's three C's all at once. (Is the cathedral best in the afternoon, when the facade basks in golden light, or early in the morning, when it rises above the hilltop mist? You decide.) Though loaded with tourists by day, Orvieto is quiet by night, and a visit here comes with a wonderful bonus: close proximity to the unforgettable Civita di Bagnoregio.

# Orientation to Orvieto

Orvieto has two distinct parts: the old-town hilltop and the dreary modern town below (called Orvieto Scalo). Whether coming by train or car, you first arrive in the nondescript lower part of town. From there you can drive or take the funicular to the medieval upper town, an atmospheric labyrinth of streets and squares where all the sightseeing action is.

ORVIETO & CIVITA

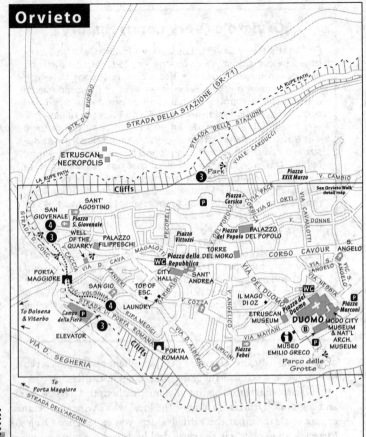

## TOURIST INFORMATION

The well-organized TI is on the cathedral square at Piazza del Duomo 24 (Mon-Thu 8:15-13:50 & 16:00-19:00, Fri-Sun 9:00-19:00, tel. 0763-341-772, www.liveorvieto.com). The TI has several excellent maps: a general city map with current hours for sights, the *Anello della Rupe* map for a hike around the base of the city, and maps for longer hikes into the countryside. The ticket office next door sells combo-tickets and books reservations for Orvieto Underground Tours (tel. 0763-340-688).

**Combo-Tickets:** Orvieto's sights are covered by a constantly changing array of combo-tickets.

The full-meal deal is the €20 **Carta Unica** combo-ticket, which covers virtually every sight recommended here (including the underground tours) and one round-trip on the bus and funicular. This is a good value only if you plan to do everything covered.

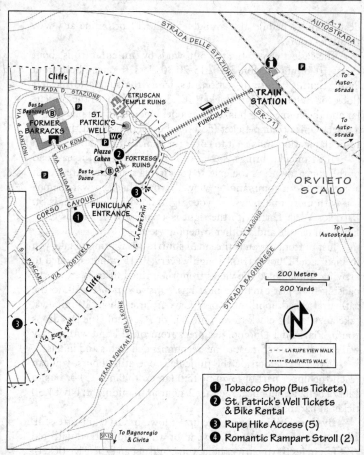

① Tobacco Shop (Bus Tickets)
② St. Patrick's Well Tickets & Bike Rental
③ Rupe Hike Access (5)
④ Romantic Rampart Stroll (2)

To use the combo-ticket for your funicular ride, buy it on arrival at the lower funicular station (also available at the bar inside the train station). It's also sold at the ticket office next to the TI on Piazza del Duomo and at most covered sights.

For a quicker, more targeted visit—just to the sights around the cathedral, but not the underground tour or the funicular—consider the €10 **La Piazza dei Musei** combo-ticket, which covers the cathedral, MoDo City Museum, Etruscan Museum, and National Archaeological Museum (sold at covered sights).

## ARRIVAL IN ORVIETO

**By Train:** The train station is at the foot of the hill the old town sits on. There's a convenient baggage-check service below and behind the station at the bus parking lot (described later, under "Helpful Hints"). Check at the station for the train schedule to your next destination (schedule also available at the TI or online at www. trenitalia.com).

The easiest way to the top of town is by **funicular** (runs about every 10 minutes Mon-Sat 7:15-20:30, less frequent Sun from 8:00). Exiting the train station, it's across the square to the left (look for *Funicolare* sign). Tickets (€1.30) include both the funicular and the connecting bus to Piazza del Duomo. If you plan to get a Carta Unica combo-ticket (described earlier), buy it at the lower funicular station and use it to cover the funicular ride.

The funicular brings you up to Piazza Cahen, at the east end of the upper town. As you exit, to your left is a ruined fortress with a garden and a commanding view. Beyond that is a war memorial with more fine views. To your right, down a steep path, is St. Patrick's Well. Farther to the right is a park with the ruins of an Etruscan temple and another sweeping view.

Just in front of you is the small **shuttle bus** waiting to take you to Piazza del Duomo (runs roughly every 10-15 minutes, timed to arriving funiculars). The views from the ruined fortress are worth pausing for—just catch the next bus. Or you can just walk to the cathedral (head uphill on Corso Cavour; after about 10 minutes, take a left at the clock tower onto Via del Duomo). The bus drops you in Piazza del Duomo, just steps from the TI and within easy walking distance of most of my recommended sights and hotels.

If you arrive outside the funicular's operating hours, you can reach the upper part of town by **taxi** (an exorbitant €15) or **bus** to Piazza della Repubblica (roughly 2/hour until midnight; buy €1.30 ticket at bar inside station).

**By Car:** Driving inside the upper town of Orvieto is stressful. It's a maze of narrow lanes, several of which are marked with red "ZTL" circles (if you drive there, you could get an expensive ticket). Consider using one of two parking lots outside the old center. The free option is the big lot **below the train station** (turn right immediately after the autostrada underpass and follow *Tour Bus Parking* signs). From the parking lot, walk through the station and ride the funicular up the hill (see "By Train," earlier). The other stress-free option is the **Campo della Fiera** garage, which is tucked behind Orvieto's hill (as you approach town, follow signs with a *P*, a little bullseye, and elevator and escalator icons—you'll curl around the left side of Orvieto's ridge, then switchback up to the lot). While you'll pay to use this lot (€1.50/hour), it's an easier ascent into town—using either an elevator or the series of escalators, which whisk you up to the west end of the old center.

Those comfortable driving in Italian cities (and careful to avoid ZTL zones) can enter Orvieto's old center by driving up Via Postierla and Via Roma, then take your pick of short-term, pay-and-display parking areas (€1.50/hour): blue-lined spots on Piazza

Cahen; a parking lot on Via Roma northwest of Piazza Cahen; blue-lined spots on Piazza Marconi, behind the cathedral; and the private, tree-lined lot with an attendant next to the cathedral (a central choice for overnight stays in the center—€17/day).

## HELPFUL HINTS

**Bike Rental and Bag Check:** The bright and helpful **Info Point,** run by Valerio, welcomes visitors just below and behind the train station at the tour bus depot/big free parking lot. They offer pay WCs and rent electric bikes (€20/day), and have a secure bag check—the only one in town (daily 9:00-18:00). In the upper town, you can rent bikes at the **St. Patrick's Well** ticket office, next to the upper funicular station (details under "Sights in Orvieto," later).

**Market Days and Festivals:** On Thursday and Saturday mornings, Piazza del Popolo becomes a busy **farmers market.**

The city's biggest event is **Corpus Domini** (June 14 in 2020), a medieval procession and festival celebrating a miraculous relic (described in the Duomo tour later in this chapter). Corpus Domini events include flag tossing, concerts, and a giant chess game with costumed people as pieces.

**Laundry:** The central **Lavagettone** self-service launderette is handy for travelers (daily 7:00-22:00, Via Garibaldi 30, www.lavagettone.it).

**After Dark:** In the evening, there's little going on other than strolling and eating. The big *passeggiata* scene is down Via del Duomo and Corso Cavour. The recommended **Bar Duomo,** filling a little square along Via del Duomo with outdoor tables, is lively late.

# Tours in Orvieto

## Walking Tours

Guided walks of about 1.5 hours are the specialty of **David Tordi** and his colleagues (€12, 3/week, April-Oct only, schedule at www.teseotur.com/en/shared-tours; buy ticket from guide, meet at Underground Orvieto ticket office at Piazza Duomo 23). They also offer €10, one-hour cathedral tours (3/week, does not include entrance ticket).

## Local Guide

A good choice is **Manuela del Turco** (€130/2.5-hour tour, mobile 333-221-9879, manueladel@virgilio.it). **David Tordi** (listed above) also organizes custom tours focused on food and culture (€250/half-day, €350/day, tel. 0763-300-491, www.teseotur.com, info@teseotur.com).

## Taxi Excursions

For excursions to Civita, **Giuliotaxi,** run by English-speaking Giulio and his sister, Maria Serena, offers two options from Orvieto for Rick Steves readers: to and from Civita with a one-hour wait (€100/car for up to 4 people, €130/minibus for up to 8), or a two-hour visit to Civita and Lake Bolsena (5 hours total, €160/car, €200/minibus, mobile 349-690-6547, giuliotaxi@libero.it). **Taxis** hang around the Orvieto train station ready to negotiate a little excursion to Civita, likely for a better price than Giuliotaxi.

# Orvieto Walk

This quickie L-shaped self-guided walk takes you from the Duomo through Orvieto's historic center to the ramparts above the original Etruscan part of town, with vast Umbrian views. Each evening, this route is the scene of the local *passeggiata*.

**❶ Piazza del Duomo:** Start at the cathedral and admire its attention-grabbing facade (see the "Duomo" listing under "Sights in Orvieto" for a full explanation). Imagine how, as World War II raged around Orvieto, the fine reliefs gracing the front of the cathedral were encased in protective *tufa* walls. (Orvieto and its cathedral were spared destruction, perhaps thanks to a "safe cities" designation by a Nazi general who appreciated the town—or one of its women.)

As you face the cathedral, the papal palace (now hosting various museums) is to your right, and the TI and shuttle bus to the funicular are over your right shoulder. A nice gelato shop is around the church to the left.

• *Head left a few steps to the...*

**❷ Clock Tower** and **Via del Duomo:** Also known as the Maurizio Tower, this was built in the 14th century and equipped with an early mechanized clock, originally used to keep track of workers' time while building the cathedral.

The tower marks the start of Via del Duomo, lined with shops selling ceramics. The tradition of fine ceramics in Orvieto goes way back—the clay from the banks of the nearby Tiber is ideal for pottery. During the Renaissance, the town's pottery was brightly painted and highly prized.

• *Stroll down Via del Duomo.*

At the second left, The Wizard of Oz (Il Mago di Oz) shop awaits a few steps down Via dei Magoni (at #3). This shop is a wondrous toy land created by eccentric Giuseppe Rosella. Have Giuseppe push a few buttons, and you're far from Kansas.

Back on Via del Duomo, about 30 yards before the next tower is Emilio's meat-and-cheese shop (on the right, at #11). Pop in for a fragrant reminder that wild boar is an Umbrian specialty—and they love their other meats and cheeses, too.

• *Follow Via del Duomo to Orvieto's main intersection, where it meets Corso Cavour. Here you'll find the tall, stark, 11th-century...*

❸ **Tower of the Moor** (Torre del Moro): Eighty such towers, each the pride and security of a powerful noble family, once

decorated the town's skyline. Today only a few survive. This tower marks the center of town, serves as a handy orientation tool, and is decorated by the coats of arms of past governors. An elevator leaves you with 173 steps still to go to earn a commanding view (€2.80, daily March-Oct 10:00-19:00, May-Aug until 20:00, shorter hours off-season).

This crossroads divides the town into four quarters (notice the *Quartiere* signs on the corners). In the past, residents of the four districts competed in a lively equestrian competition, parading all over town during the annual Corpus Domini celebration. Historically, the four streets led from here to four landmarks: Piazza del Popolo with its market and fine palazzo, St. Patrick's Well, the Duomo, and the City Hall.

• *Before heading left down Corso Cavour, side-trip a block farther ahead, behind the tower, for a look at the striking...*

❹ **Palazzo del Popolo:** Built of local *tufo*, this is a textbook example of a fortified medieval public palace: a fortress designed to house the city's leadership and military (built atop an Etruscan temple), with a market at its base, fancy meeting rooms upstairs, and aristocratic living quarters on the top level. A lively market still bustles here Thursday and Saturday mornings, selling food, clothes, and household goods.

• *Return to the tower, turn right, and head down Corso Cavour past classic storefronts to...*

❺ **Piazza della Repubblica** and the **Church of Sant'Andrea:** The original vision—though it never came to fruition—was for the City Hall to have five arches flanking the central arch (marked by the flags today). The Church of Sant'Andrea (left of City Hall) sits atop the Etruscan forum that was likely the birthplace of Orvieto, centuries before Christ. Inside is an interesting architectural progression: 11th-century Romanesque (with few frescoes surviving), Gothic (the pointy vaults over the altar), and a Renaissance barrel vault in the apse (behind the altar)—all dimly lit by alabaster windows.

On this spot, visitors can track a layer cake of history: Under the Christian church lie the remains of the Etruscan city, destroyed

**ORVIETO & CIVITA**

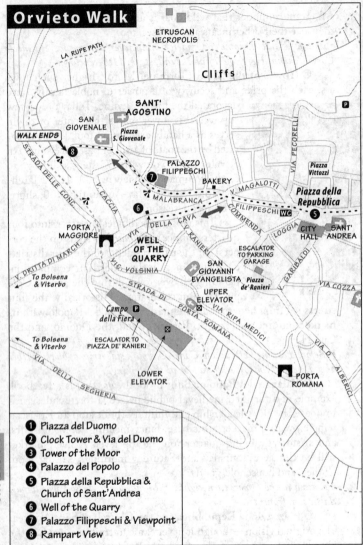

# Orvieto Walk

1. Piazza del Duomo
2. Clock Tower & Via del Duomo
3. Tower of the Moor
4. Palazzo del Popolo
5. Piazza della Repubblica &
   Church of Sant'Andrea
6. Well of the Quarry
7. Palazzo Filippeschi & Viewpoint
8. Rampart View

by the Romans. The ruins, currently accessible only with a tour, give you a sense of the history stacked beneath your feet throughout Orvieto (€5/person, call archaeologist Francesco Pacelli to book, tel. 328-191-1316).

• From Piazza della Repubblica, continue straight downhill on Via Filippeschi—passing a public WC on the left—for 100 yards until you reach a fork. Check out the friendly, traditional Galleria del Pane **bakery** on the right (at Via Malabranca 6; we'll return to this intersec-

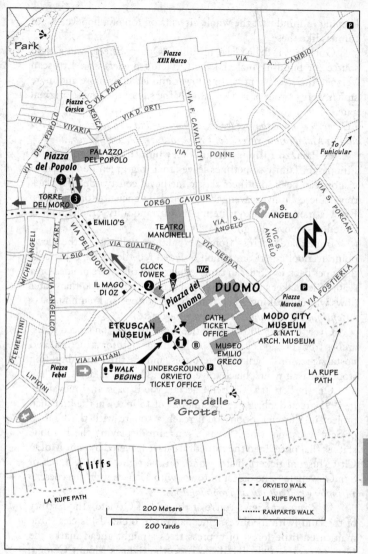

*tion after a short detour). Walk downhill along Via della Cava about 70 yards to a restaurant with a green sign (at #26, on the right) to find the...*

❻ **Well of the Quarry** (Pozzo della Cava): While renovating their trattoria here in the oldest part of town, an Orvieto family discovered a vast underground network of Etruscan-era caves, wells, and tunnels. The excavation started in 1984 and continues to this day. A visit to the well makes for a fun subterranean wander (see more details in "Underground Orvieto," later in this chapter),

**ORVIETO & CIVITA**

keeping in mind that the whole city sits on top of a honeycomb of tunnels like these.

Outside, Via della Cava, meaning "Quarry Street," was a main source for building material for Orvieto's predecessor, Etruscan Velzna. The street kept getting lower and lower as more and more stones were cut out of it. Downhill is the site of the town's original gate.

• *Climb back up to the fork (with the bakery) and do a sharp U-turn left up Via Malabranca. After about 70 yards, at #22, you'll reach...*

❼ **Palazzo Filippeschi and Viewpoint:** The friendly, noble Filippeschi family sometimes leaves their big green door open so visitors can peek into their classic medieval courtyard, with black travertine columns scavenged from nearby ancient Roman villas. Enjoy a moment of exquisite medieval tranquility. (If the door is closed, just move along.)

Immediately across from the palazzo, belly up to the viewpoint overlooking a commotion of faded red-tile roofs. This tradition goes back to Etruscan times, when such tiles were molded on a seated tile-maker's thigh—wide to narrow. They nest so that water flows without leaking—handy for both rooftops and plumbing.

• *Continue on, downhill now, as the street crests.*

Over the next 200 yards notice faded frescoes on stucco walls, arches from previous iterations of buildings (left for structural and nostalgic reasons), built-in letterboxes, and the three local building stones—basalt white, black travertine, and brown tufa.

On the left (at Via del Caccia), you'll pass an innovative-in-1991 green defibrillator station (one of 15 in town, the first such project in Europe). Soon you'll reach a square with the Church of Sant'Agostino, which hosts a museum displaying the Baroque statues that once lined the cathedral's nave (covered by your MoDo City Museum ticket). Just beyond, on the right, is the Church of San Giovenale—the oldest in town, with 11th-century frescoes.

• *Finally you'll pop out at a commanding...*

❽ **Rampart View:** You're at the end of Orvieto. The fertility of the land (with its olives, vines, and fruit orchards) is clear. The manicured little forest of cypress trees straight ahead marks the Orvieto cemetery. In the distance to the right is Mount Cetona, guarding the south end of Tuscany.

Go 50 yards along the rampart to the left for the best view of the natural fortification that made this town the choice of Etruscans before the rise of ancient Rome, of stability-starved peasants after the fall of Rome, and of several popes in the high Middle Ages. From this perch you can understand why the city was never taken by force.

• *The walk is over. From here, you can retrace your steps or follow the rampart farther left, down and up, over the original Etruscan town gate and circle back to the center from there.*

# Sights in Orvieto

### ▲▲▲Duomo

Orvieto's cathedral has Italy's liveliest facade. This colorful, prickly Gothic facade, divided by four pillars, has been compared to a medieval altarpiece. The optical-illusion interior features some fine art, including Luca Signorelli's lavishly frescoed Chapel of San Brizio.

**Cost and Hours:** €4, €5 combo-ticket with MoDo City Museum; buy ticket in building to the right as you face the facade (also covered by various combo-tickets described under "Tourist Information," earlier); April-Sept Mon-Sat 9:30-19:00, Sun 13:00-17:30; closes one hour earlier March and Oct; shorter hours Nov-Feb; sometimes closes for religious services, www.opsm.it.

### ◑ Self-Guided Tour

• *After buying your ticket, return to the front of the church. Begin by viewing the…*

**Exterior Facade:** Study this gleaming mass of mosaics, stained glass, and sculpture (c. 1300, by Lorenzo Maitani and others). Note how it's literally just a facade, ornamenting an otherwise very plain, mostly Romanesque exterior.

At the base of the cathedral, the four broad **marble pillars** carved with biblical scenes tell the history of the world in four acts, from left to right. The relief on the far left shows the ❶ **Creation** (see God creating Eve from Adam's rib, Cain clubbing Abel, the snake tempting Eve, and a dramatic expulsion). Next is the ❷ **Tree of Jesse** (Jesus' family tree—with Jesus on top, and Mary just below, flanked by Old Testament stories). Look up at the roaring lion of St. Mark and the grand facade filling your view—awe-inspiring as intended. In the third panel, with scenes from the ❸ **New Testament,** look for the unique manger scene, and other events from the life of Christ. On the far right is the ❹ **Last Judgment;** see Christ judging on top, with a commotion of sarcophagi popping open and all hell breaking loose at the bottom.

Each pillar is topped with a bronze symbol of one of the Evangelists (left to right): angel (Matthew), lion (Mark), eagle (John),

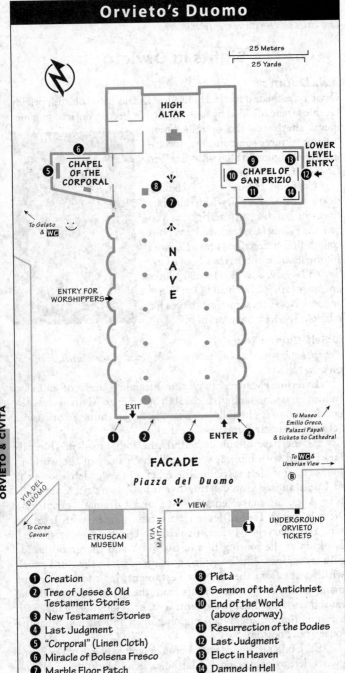

# Orvieto's Duomo

1. Creation
2. Tree of Jesse & Old Testament Stories
3. New Testament Stories
4. Last Judgment
5. "Corporal" (Linen Cloth)
6. Miracle of Bolsena Fresco
7. Marble Floor Patch
8. Pietà
9. Sermon of the Antichrist
10. End of the World (above doorway)
11. Resurrection of the Bodies
12. Last Judgment
13. Elect in Heaven
14. Damned in Hell

and ox (Luke). The bronze doors are modern, by the Sicilian sculptor Emilio Greco. (A gallery devoted to Greco's work is to the immediate right of the church; see "Museums Near the Duomo," later.)

Stand back and survey the facade, looking for the central theme—it's clear the church is dedicated to the ascension of Mary. In the mosaic below the rose window, Mary is transported to heaven. In the uppermost mosaic, Mary is crowned.

• *Ticket in hand, step inside.*

**Nave:** The nave feels spacious and less cluttered than most Italian churches. Until 1877, it was much busier, with statues of the apostles at each column and fancy chapels. Then the people decided they wanted to "un-Baroque" their church. (The original statues are now on display in the Church of Sant'Agostino, at the west end of town.) Bits of medieval fresco survive in the niches—once covered by altars and confessionals. From the back of the nave you can appreciate the fine stained glass above

the altar—it's original from the 14th century and some of the oldest in Italy. The stripes of the church are purely decorative, made of locally quarried basalt and black travertine.

The interior is warmly lit by **alabaster windows,** highlighting the black-and-white striped stonework. Why such a big and impressive church in such a little town? First of all, it's not as big as it looks. By lining the nave with striped columns and opening up the side aisles with arcaded chapels, the architect made the space seem longer and bigger than it is. Still, it's a big and rich cathedral—the seat of a bishop.

The cathedral's historic importance and wealth is thanks to a miracle that happened nearby in 1263. According to the story, a skeptical priest named Peter of Prague passed through the town of Bolsena (12 miles from Orvieto) while on a pilgrimage to Rome. He had doubts that the bread used in communion could really be transformed into the body of Christ. But during Mass, as he held the host aloft and blessed it, the bread began to bleed, running down his arms and dripping onto a linen cloth (a "corporal") on the altar. That miraculously bloodstained cloth is now kept here, in the Chapel of the Corporal.

• *We'll tour the church's interior. First, find the chapel in the north transept, left of the altar.*

**Chapel of the Corporal:** The ❺ **bloody cloth** from the mir-

## Italy Is Made of Tuff Stuff

Tuff (*tufo* in Italian) is a light-colored volcanic rock that is common in Italy. A part of Tuscany is even called the "Tuff Area."

The seven hills of Rome are made of tuff, and quarried blocks of this stone can be seen in the Colosseum, Pantheon, and Castel Sant'Angelo. Just outside of Rome, the catacombs were carved from tuff. Sorrento rises above the sea on a tuff outcrop. Orvieto, Civita di Bagnoregio (pictured), and many other hill towns perch on bluffs of tuff.

Italy's early inhabitants, including the Etruscans and Romans, carved caves, tunnels, burial niches, and even roads out of tuff. Blocks of this rock were quarried to make houses and walls. Tuff is soft and easy to carve when it's first exposed to air, but hardens later, which makes it a good building stone.

Italy's tuff-producing volcanoes resulted from a lot of tectonic-plate bumping and grinding. This violent geologic history is reflected in Italy's volcanoes, like Vesuvius and Etna, and earthquakes such as the 2009 quake in the L'Aquila area northeast of Rome.

Tuff is actually just a big hardened pile of old volcanic ash. When volcanoes hold magma that contains a lot of water, they erupt explosively (think heat + water = steam = POW!). The exploded rock material gets blasted out as hot volcanic ash, which settles on the surrounding landscape, piles up, and over time welds together into the rock called tuff.

So when you're visiting an area in Italy of ancient caves or catacombs built out of this material, you'll know that at least once (and maybe more) upon a time, it was a site of a lot of volcanic activity.

acle is displayed in the turquoise frame atop the chapel's altar. It was brought from Bolsena to Orvieto, where Pope Urban IV happened to be visiting. The amazed pope proclaimed a new holiday, Corpus Domini (Body of Christ), and the Orvieto cathedral was built (begun in 1290) to display the miraculous relic. For centuries, the precious linen was paraded through the streets of Orvieto in an ornate reliquary (now in the MoDo City Museum).

The room was frescoed in the 14th century with scenes attesting to Christ's presence in the communion wafer and offering a vivid peek at life here at that time. The ❻ **miracle of Bolsena** (here set in 13th-century Orvieto) is depicted on the chapel's right wall.

• *Now walk to the middle front of the church, where (just before the two steps) you'll see a decorative area in the floor the size of a Turkish carpet.*

❼ **Marble Floor Patch:** This patch in the marble floor marks where the altar stood before the Counter-Reformation. It's a re-minder that as the Roman Catholic Church countered the Refor-mation, it made reforms of its own. For instance, altars were moved back so that the congregation could sit closer to the spectacular frescoes and stained glass. (These decorations were designed to impress commoners by illustrating the glory of heaven—and the Catholic Church needed that propaganda more than ever during the Counter-Reformation.)

Enjoy the richness that surrounds you. This cathedral put Or-vieto on the map, and with lots of pilgrims came lots of wealth. The town—perched on its easy-to-defend hilltop—was used off and on for a couple centuries as a papal refuge, whenever the current pope's enemies forced him to flee Rome. Over the altar, the bril-liant stained glass is the painstakingly restored original, from the 14th century. The fine organ, high on the left, has more than 5,000 pipes. Look high up in the right transept at the alabaster rose win-dow. Then turn and face down the nave, the way you came in. Note how the architect's trick—making the church look bigger from the rear—works in reverse from here. From this angle, the church ap-pears stubbier than it actually is.

• *A few steps to your left as you face the altar, near the first pillar, is a beautiful white-marble statue.*

❽ *Pietà:* The marble pietà (statue of Mary holding Jesus' just-crucified body) was carved in 1579 by local artist Ippolito Scalza. Clearly inspired by Michelangelo's *Pietà*, this exceptional work, with four figures, was sculpted from one piece of marble. Walk around it to notice the texture that Scalza achieved, and how the light plays on the sculpture from every angle.

• *Now face the main altar. To the right is Orvieto's one must-see artistic sight, the...*

**Chapel of San Brizio:** This chapel features Luca Signorelli's brilliantly lit frescoes of the Day of Judgment and Life after Death (painted 1499-1504). Step into the chapel and you're surrounded by vivid scenes crammed with figures. Al-though the frescoes refer to themes of resurrection and salvation, they also re-flect the turbulent political and religious atmosphere of late-15th-century Italy.

The chapel is decorated

ORVIETO & CIVITA

in one big and cohesive story. Start with the panel on your left as you enter, and do a quick counterclockwise spin to get oriented to the basic plot: Antichrist (a false prophet), end of the world (above the arch leading to the nave), Resurrection of the Bodies, hell, Judgment Day (Fra Angelico—who worked on the chapel 50 years before Signorelli—painted Jesus above the window), and finally heaven.

Now do a slower turn to take in the full story: In the ❾ **Sermon of the Antichrist** (left wall), a crowd gathers around a man preaching from a pedestal. It's the Antichrist, who comes posing as Jesus to mislead the faithful. This befuddled Antichrist forgets his lines midspeech, but the Devil is on hand to whisper what to say next. Notice how the arm in front of the Antichrist is attached to both figures, suggesting they are joined as one. His words sow wickedness through the world, including executions (upper right). The worried woman in red and light blue (foreground, left of pedestal) gets money from a man for something she's not proud of (perhaps receiving funds from a Jewish moneylender—notice the Stars of David on his purse). Many of the faces in the crowd are probably actual portraits.

Most likely, the Antichrist himself is a veiled reference to Savonarola (1452-1498), the charismatic Florentine monk who defied the pope, drove the Medici family from power, and riled the populace with apocalyptic sermons. Many Italians—including the painter Signorelli—viewed Savonarola as a tyrant and heretic, the Antichrist who was ushering in the Last Days.

In the upper left, notice the hardworking angel. He looks as if he's at batting practice, hitting followers of the Antichrist back to earth as they try to get through the pearly gates. In the bottom left is a self-portrait of the artist, **Luca Signorelli** (c. 1450-1523), well-dressed in black with long golden hair. Signorelli, from nearby Cortona, was at the peak of his powers, and this chapel was his masterpiece. He looks out proudly as if to say, "I did all this in just a few years, on time and on budget," confirming his reputation as a speedy, businesslike painter. Next to him (also in black) is the artist Fra Angelico, who started the chapel decoration five decades earlier but completed only a small part of it: the Last Judgment over the window and the angels around it.

Compare the style of painting between these two masters—Angelico's angels stacked like little wooden dolls next to Signorelli's intertwined naked bodies. You can clearly see the huge effect the Renaissance had on painting in just a few decades.

Around the arch opposite the windows are signs of the ❿ **end of the world:** eclipse, tsunami, falling stars, earthquakes, violence in the streets, and a laser-wielding gray angel.

On the right wall (opposite the Antichrist) is the ⓫ **Resurrec-**

**tion of the Bodies.** Trumpeting angels blow a wake-up call, and the dead climb dreamily out of the earth to be clothed with new bodies, some of the randy skeletons finding time for flirting. On the same wall (below the action, at eye level) is a gripping pietà. Also by Signorelli, this pietà gives insight into the artist's genius and personality. Look at the emotion in the faces of the two Marys and consider that Signorelli's son had just died. The small black-and-white Deposition scene (behind Jesus' leg) seems inspired by ancient Greek scenes of a pre-Christian hero's death. In the confident spirit of the Renaissance, the artist incorporates a pagan scene to support a Christian story. This 3-D realism in a 2-D sketch shows the work of a talented master.

The altar wall (with the windows) features the ⓬ **Last Judgment.** To the left of the altar (and continuing around the corner,

filling half the left wall) are the ⓭ **Elect in Heaven.** They spend eternity posing like bodybuilders while listening to celestial Muzak. To the right (and continuing around the corner on the right wall) are the ⓮ **Damned in Hell,** in the scariest mosh pit ever. Devils torment sinners in graphic detail, while winged demons control the airspace overhead. In the center, one lusty demon turns to tell the frightened woman on his back exactly what he's got planned for their date. (According to legend, this was Signorelli's lover, who betrayed him...and ended up here.) Signorelli's ability to tell a story through human actions and gestures, rather than symbols, inspired his younger contemporary, Michelangelo, who meticulously studied the elder artist's nudes.

In this chapel, Christian theology sits physically and figuratively upon a foundation of lassical logic. Below everything are Greek and Latin philosophers, plus Dante, struggling to reconcile Classical truth with Church doctrine. You can see the intellectual challenge on their faces as they ponder the puzzle of theology that survives the test of reason.

The figures are immersed in fanciful Grotesque (that is, grotto-esque) decor. Dating from 1499, this is one of the first uses of the frilly, nubile, and even sexy "wallpaper pattern" so popular in the Renaissance. (It was inspired by the decorations found in Nero's Golden House in Rome, which had been discovered under street level just a few years earlier and was mistaken for an underground grotto.)

ORVIETO & CIVITA

During the Renaissance, nakedness symbolized purity. When attitudes changed during the Counter-Reformation, the male figures in Signorelli's frescoes were given penis-covering sashes. In a 1982 restoration, most—but not all—of the sashes were removed. A little of that prudishness survives to this day, as those in heaven were left with their sashes modestly in place.

• *Our tour is finished. As you step outside the church, you're surrounded by great sights. Across the square is the Etruscan Museum, the TI, and the ticket office for Underground Orvieto tours. Around the side of the church (near the cathedral ticket office) are the MoDo City Museum and the National Archaeological Museum. And just beyond that, you can keep going (passing a small parking lot and WC) to reach a park that affords a fine Umbrian view.*

## MUSEUMS NEAR THE DUOMO

### ▲▲MoDo City Museum (Museo dell'Opera del Duomo)

This museum is an ensemble of three different sights scattered around town: the Emilio Greco collection (in Palazzo Soliano, next to the cathedral); the Cathedral Art Collections, immediately behind the cathedral (enter through the lower level of the right transept); and, at the far end of town, the Church of Sant'Agostino.

**Cost and Hours:** €4 MoDo ticket covers all MoDo sights, €5 combo-ticket includes the Duomo; also covered by La Piazza dei Musei and Carta Unica combo-tickets; April-Sept daily 9:30-19:00; March and Oct daily 10:00-18:00; Nov-Feb until 17:00 and closed Mon; Piazza Duomo, tel. 0763-343-592, www.opsm.it.

**Visiting the MoDo City Museum Branches:** You'll buy your ticket for the MoDo (and for the cathedral) inside Palazzo Soliano. It's the building marked *MUSEO*, to the right as you face the cathedral. This building also houses the Museo Emilio Greco. A good plan is to buy a ticket, visit the Greco collection while you're there, then tour the cathedral interior (described earlier). Afterward, enter the Cathedral Art Collections. If you want to also see the National Archaeological Museum, its entrance hides between the Cathedral Art Collections and the Museo Emilio Greco.

**Museo Emilio Greco:** This fresh little collection—filling a space behind the MoDo and cathedral ticket desk—shows off the work of Emilio Greco (1913-1995), a Sicilian artist who designed the modern doors of Orvieto's cathedral. His sketches and about 30 of his bronze statues are on display here, showing his absorption with gently twisting and turning nudes. Greco's sketchy outlines of women are simply beautiful. The artful installation of his work in this palazzo, with walkways and a spiral staircase up to the ceiling, is designed to let you view his sculptures from different angles.

• *To find the Cathedral Art Collections, enter the lower level of the right transept—around the right side as you face the cathedral's main facade.*

**Cathedral Art Collections:** Behind the Duomo, a complex of medieval palaces called the Palazzi Papali (Papal Palaces) shows off the city's best devotional art. This is the main attraction of the MoDo City Museum and well worth a visit.

Entering through the cathedral's right transept, you'll walk through the striped cellars. Under the vaults is equipment used for working on the cathedral (giant pulley mechanisms) and neatly stacked fragments of sculptures and tiles.

Follow signs right (to *Museum* and *Popes Palace*) to reach the main part of the museum. The ground floor features a skippable exhibit of frescoes. But from here, you can head outside, then go up the metal staircase to a delightful collection.

The highlight is just inside the upstairs entrance: a marble Mary and Child who sit beneath a bronze canopy, attended by exquisite angels. This proto-Renaissance ensemble, dating from around 1300, once filled the niche in the center of the cathedral's facade (where a replica sits today).

Now proceed through several art-filled rooms on this floor. Entering the first large room, look left to see an exquisite *Madonna and Child* from 1322 by the Sienese great Simone Martini, who worked in Orvieto. Nearby are saintly wooden statues and fine inlaid woodwork from the original choir. Farther along, you'll find Luca Signorelli's *Mary Magdalene* (1504), then a large room of Baroque paintings from the late 1500s that decorated the side chapels with a harsh Counter-Reformation message. (Think about how dramatically church art evolved in the 200 years from Martini's almost 2-D medieval style, to Signorelli's Renaissance humanism, to the bombast of Baroque.)

In the hall with the Baroque paintings, step into the smaller side-room. This is the Albèri Library, with delicate black-and-white frescoes done by Signorelli's workshop while he was in town working on the cathedral's Chapel of San Brizio. This hall displays items from the cathedral treasury, including the reliquary used to parade a holy bloodstained cloth on Corpus Domini.

Continuing through the main collection, go back past the entry to one more large hall, with statues of St. Michael and the dragon, more altarpieces and statues, and sinopias (preliminary drawings for the frescoes decorating the cathedral's Chapel of the Corporal, with a roughed-up surface so the wet plaster would stick).

**Church of Sant'Agostino:** At the west end of town (a 15-minute walk), this church has statues of the 12 apostles that were added to the Duomo in the Baroque Age (c. 1700) and removed in the late 1800s. It's skippable for most visitors, but those taking my "Orvieto Walk" can drop in with their MoDo ticket.

### National Archaeological Museum of Orvieto (Museo Archeologico Nazionale di Orvieto)

This small five-room collection, immediately behind the cathedral in the ground floor of Palazzi Papali (under MoDo), beautifully shows off a trove of well-preserved Etruscan bronzes, terra-cotta objects, and ceramics—many from the necropolis at the base of Orvieto, and some with painted colors surviving from 500 BC. To see the treasure of this museum, ask an attendant for the Golini tombs (named after the man who discovered them in 1836). You'll be escorted to the reconstructed, fourth-century BC tombs, frescoed with scenes from an Etruscan banquet in the afterlife.

**Cost and Hours:** €4, €5 combo-ticket with Etruscan Necropolis, also covered by La Piazza dei Musei and Carta Unica combo-tickets, daily 8:30-19:30, tel. 0763-341-039, www.archeopg.arti. beniculturali.it. For background on the Etruscans, see page 654.

### ▲Etruscan Museum (Museo Claudio Faina e Museo Civico)

This 19th-century, Neoclassical nobleman's palace stands on the main square facing the cathedral. Its elegantly frescoed rooms hold an impressive Etruscan collection. The ground floor features the "Museo Civico," with fragments of Etruscan sculpture. On the first floor is the "Collezione Conti Faina," with Etruscan jewelry and an extensive array of Roman coins (push the brass buttons and the coins rotate so you can see both sides). The top floor features the best of the Etruscan and proto-Etruscan (from the ninth century BC) vases and bronzes, lots of votives found buried in nearby tombs, and fine views of the Duomo.

**Cost and Hours:** €4.50, also covered by La Piazza dei Musei and Carta Unica combo-tickets; April-Sept daily 9:30-18:00, Oct-March Tue-Sun 10:00-17:00, closed Mon Nov-Feb; tel. 0763-341-511, www.museofaina.it.

### Teatro Mancinelli

A short walk from the cathedral, on the main drag, Teatro Mancinelli is a fine 19th-century Italian theater (from 1866) with 500 seats, elegant boxes, and frilly Romantic ceiling paintings—all well-described in English. Visitors are welcome to climb upstairs to the foyer for a chance to peek into a private box. The theater hosts the recommended Café del Teatro—buy a drink and you can wander the theater without paying the €2 entry fee (typically open Mon-Sat 8:00-14:00, closed Sun, Corso Cavour 122, www.teatromancinelli.com).

## UNDERGROUND ORVIETO

These sights—showing off the remarkable bounty of history beneath your feet—are scattered around (and outside) the old center. For locations, see the main "Orvieto" map at the start of this chapter.

## ▲▲St. Patrick's Well (Pozzo di San Patrizio)

Modern engineers are impressed by this deep well—175 feet deep and 45 feet wide—designed in the 16th century with a double-helix pattern. The two spiral stairways allow an efficient one-way traffic flow: intriguing now, but critical then. Imagine if donkeys and people, balancing jugs of water, had to go up and down the same stairway. At the bottom is a bridge that people could walk on to scoop up water. Touring the well requires hiking 248 (awkwardly spaced) steps down, then back up. That's lots of exercise (allow 20-30 minutes round-trip) and not much to see...other than some mesmerizing 16th-century engineering.

The well was built because a pope got nervous. After Rome was sacked in 1527 by renegade troops of the Holy Roman Empire, the pope fled to Orvieto. He feared that even this little town (with no water source on top) would be besieged. He commissioned a well, which was started in 1527 and finished 10 years later. It was a huge project. (As it turns out, the town was never besieged, but supporters believe that the well was worth the cost and labor because of its deterrence value—attackers would think twice about besieging a town with a reliable water source.) Even today, when a local is faced with a difficult task, people say, "It's like digging St. Patrick's Well."

**Cost and Hours:** €5, interesting €2 audioguide, daily May-Aug 9:00-20:00, shorter hours off-season, ticket office immediately to your right as you exit the funicular, you'll walk a few minutes down the path to enter the well, Viale Sangallo, tel. 0763-343-768.

## ▲Well of the Quarry (Pozzo della Cava)

A five-minute walk west of Piazza della Repubblica, this complex of Etruscan-era caves, wells, and tunnels leads down to a fat, cylindrical, beautifully carved 2,500-year-old well. Go ahead, spit (or drop a coin 100 feet down—coins are collected each Christmas for a local charity). Your visit is capped with a review of local pottery-making.

**Cost and Hours:** €4, RS%—€2.50 with this book, Tue-Sun 9:00-20:00, closed Mon, enter through restaurant at Via della Cava 26, tel. 0763-342-373, www.pozzodellacava.it.

### Orvieto Underground Tours (Parco delle Grotte)

Beginning from a ticket office next to the TI, guides weave archaeological history into a good look at about 100 yards of Etruscan and medieval caves. You'll see the remains of an old olive press, an impressive 130-foot-deep Etruscan well shaft, what's left of a primitive cement quarry, and an extensive dovecote (pigeon coop) where the birds were reared for roasting (pigeon dishes are still featured on many Orvieto menus; look for—or avoid—*piccione*).

**Cost and Hours:** €7; one-hour English tours depart daily at 11:15, 12:30, 16:15, and 17:30; book in advance and confirm schedule for English guide, book tour and depart from ticket office facing the cathedral at Piazza Duomo 23, tel. 0763-340-688, www.orvietounderground.it.

### Etruscan Necropolis
### (Necropoli Etrusca di Crocifisso del Tufo)

Below town, at the base of the cliff, is a remarkable "city of the dead" that dates back to the sixth to third century BC. The tombs,

which are laid out in a kind of street grid, are empty, and there's precious little to see here other than the basic stony construction. But it is both eerie and fascinating to wander the streets of an Etruscan cemetery.

**Cost and Hours:** €3, €5 combo-ticket with National Archaeological Museum; Wed-Sat 10:00-19:00, Oct-March until 18:00, also open the first two Sun of the month, closed Mon-Tue year-round; drivers will find it on the ring road below town, hikers can reach it via the Rupe path (see next); tel. 0763-343-611, www.archeopg.arti.beniculturali.it.

## VIEW WALKS
### ▲Hike Around the City on the Rupe

Orvieto's Rupe is a peaceful path that completely circles the town at the base of the cliff upon which it sits. With the help of the TI's

*Anello della Rupe* map, you'll see there are five access points from the town for the three-mile walk, which includes a series of sightseeing stops along the way (allow about two hours round-trip). From the access points, you'll walk or take stairs down, down, down to the trail that hugs the

cliff. The easy-to-follow path is wide and partially paved, though it has some steep, gravelly descents—wear good shoes and be prepared for a climb. On one side you have the cliff, with the town high above. On the other side you have Umbrian views stretching into the distance. The path is peaceful, with few other people and only the sound of the wind and birds to accompany you. It makes for a delightful evening walk (not lit after dark).

I'd leave Orvieto at Piazza Marconi and walk left (counterclockwise) three-quarters of the way around the town (there's a fine view down onto the Etruscan Necropolis midway), and ride the escalator and elevator back up to the town from the big Campo della Fiera parking lot. If you're ever confused about the path, follow signs for *Anello della Rupe*.

### ▲Shorter Romantic Rampart Stroll

Thanks to its dramatic hilltop setting, several fine little walks wind around the edges of Orvieto. My favorite after dark, when it's lamp-lit and romantic, is along the ramparts at the far west end of town. Start at the Church of Sant'Agostino (near the end of my self-guided Orvieto Walk). With your back to the church, go a block to the right to the end of town. Then head left along the ramparts, with cypress-dotted Umbria to your right, and follow Vicolo Volsinia to the Church of San Giovanni Evangelista, where you can reenter the old-town center near several recommended restaurants.

## NEAR ORVIETO
### Wine Tasting

Orvieto Classico wine is justly famous. Two inviting wineries sit just outside Orvieto on the scenic Canale route to Bagnoregio; if you're side-tripping to Civita, it's easy to stop at either or both for a tasting (call ahead for a reservation). Two more wineries lie to the north where the soil changes from *tufo* to clay, which changes the character of the wines. For locations, see the "Orvieto and Civita Area" map near the beginning of this chapter.

**Between Orvieto and Bagnoregio:** For a tour of a historic winery with Etruscan cellars, make an appointment to visit **Tenuta Le Velette,** where English-speaking Corrado, Cecilia (cheh-CHEEL-yah), and Teresa Bottai offer a warm welcome. Their wines are considered to be some of the best in the region (€8-25 for tour and tasting, price varies depending on wines, number of people, and food requested; Mon-Fri 8:30-12:00 & 14:00-17:00, Sat 8:30-12:00, closed Sun; also has accommodations—see listing later in this chapter, tel. 0763-29090, mobile 348-300-2002, www.levelette.it). From their sign (5-minute drive past Orvieto at top of switchbacks just before Canale, on road to Bagnoregio), cruise

ORVIETO & CIVITA

down a long tree-lined drive, then park at the striped gate (must call ahead; no drop-ins).

**Custodi** is another respected family-run winery that produces Orvieto Classico, grappa, and olive oil on a modern 140-acre estate. Helpful Chiara and Laura Custodi speak English. Reserve ahead for a tour of their cantina, an explanation of the winemaking process, and a tasting of four wines. An assortment of *salumi* and local cheeses to go with your wine tasting is available on request (€13/person for wines only, €23/person with light lunch, daily 8:30-12:30 & 15:30-18:30 except closed Sun afternoon, Viale Venere S.N.C. Loc. Canale; on the road from Orvieto to Civita, a half-mile after Le Velette, it's the first building before Canale; tel. 0763-29053, mobile 338-316-0405, www.cantinacustodi.com).

**To the North:** In the rolling hills just north of Orvieto, **Neri** rests amid postcard-pretty estate grounds, with an ancient manor house and grand views of Orvieto and the countryside. Their wines are simple and traditional (tour and tastings from €10, reservations preferred, daily 9:30-17:00; just down the road from recommended Agriturismo Cioccoleta at Località Bardano 28—head north from Orvieto following signs to *Sferracavallo* and *Bardano;* tel. 0763-316-196, mobile 393-331-3844, www.neri-vini.it, visite@neri-vini.it, Enrico).

# Sleeping in Orvieto

Orvieto's high season (with higher hotel prices) is roughly May to early July, September, and October. You'll save a little money off-season.

## IN THE TOWN CENTER

**$$$ Grand Hotel Italia** is businesslike, with a stay-awhile lobby and terrace. While not as "grand" as it once was, it brings predictable modern amenities to this small town. The 46 overpriced rooms are well located in the heart of Orvieto, a block off the main drag and near the market square (RS%, air-con, elevator, off-site pay parking—reserve ahead, Via di Piazza del Popolo 13, tel. 0763-342-065, www.grandhotelitalia.it, hotelita@libero.it).

**$$$ Hotel Virgilio** is small, cheery, modern, and a bit pricey, renting 13 rooms facing the side of the cathedral (air-con, elevator, Piazza Duomo 5, tel. 0763-394-937, www.orvietohotelvirgilio.com, booking@orvietohotelvirgilio.com).

**$$ Hotel Duomo** is centrally located and modern, with splashy art in 17 rooms and a friendly welcome. It's tucked a few steps off the cathedral square, but double-paned windows keep the sound of the church bells well-muffled (RS%, family rooms, air-con, elevator, private pay parking, sunny terrace, a block from the Duomo at

Vicolo di Maurizio 7, tel. 0763-341-887, www.orvietohotelduomo. com, orvietohotelduomo@gmail.com; Gianni and Maura Massaccesi don't speak English, daughter Elisa and son-in-law Diego do). They also run a three-room B&B 50 yards from the hotel (lower prices, breakfast at the main hotel).

**$$ Hotel Corso** is friendly, with 18 frilly and flowery rooms—a few with balconies and views. Their sunlit little terrace is enjoyable, but the location—halfway between the center of town and the funicular—is less convenient than others (RS%, family rooms, ask for quieter room off street, air-con, elevator, reserved pay parking, Corso Cavour 339, tel. 0763-342-020, www.hotelcorso.net, info@hotelcorso.net, Carla).

**$ La Magnolia B&B** has lots of fancy terra-cotta tiles, a couple of rooms with frescoed ceilings, terraces, and other welcoming touches. Its seven unique rooms—some of them mini-apartments with kitchens—are cheerfully decorated and on the town's main drag. The three units facing the busy street are air-conditioned and have double-paned windows (RS%, family rooms, no elevator, washing machine, Via del Duomo 29, tel. 0763-342-808, mobile 349-462-0733, www.bblamagnolia.it, info@bblamagnolia.it, Serena).

**$ B&B Michelangeli** offers two comfortable and well-appointed apartments hiding along a residential lane a few blocks from the tourist scene. It's run by eager-to-please Francesca, who speaks limited English but provides homey touches and free tea, coffee, and breakfast supplies. From the Corso, follow Via Michelangeli, a street full of wood sculptures made by her famous artistic family (family rooms, fully equipped kitchen, washing machine, private pay parking, Via dei Saracinelli 20—ring bell labeled *M. Michelangeli*, tel. 0763-393-862, mobile 347-089-0349, www. bbmichelangeli.com).

**$ Affittacamere Valentina** rents six clean, airy, well-appointed rooms, all with big beds and antique furniture. It's in the heart of Orvieto, on a quiet street behind the palace on Piazza del Popolo (RS%, no breakfast, family rooms, air-con, pay parking, Via Vivaria 7, tel. 0763-341-607, mobile 393-970-5868, www.bandbvalentina. com, camerevalentina@gmail.com). Welcoming Valentina also rents four apartments in the center.

**$ Hotel Posta** is a centrally located, long-ago-elegant palazzo renting 20 quirky, clean, cheap rooms with dark wood floors and vintage furniture. It feels a little institutional, but it's well-run, and the rooms without private bath are among the cheapest in town (breakfast extra, elevator, Via Luca Signorelli 18, tel. 0763-341-909, www.hotelpostaorvieto.it, hotelposta@orvietohotels.it, Alessia).

**$ Villa Mercede,** a good value and excellent location, is owned

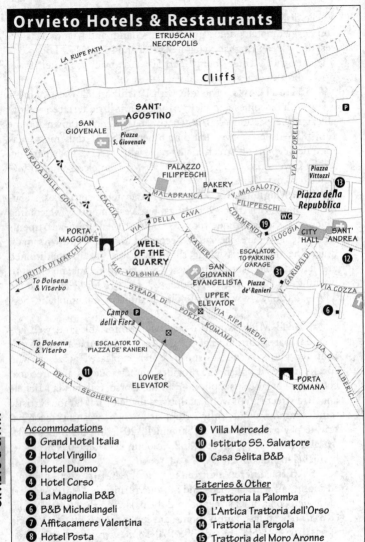

# Orvieto Hotels & Restaurants

**Accommodations**
1. Grand Hotel Italia
2. Hotel Virgilio
3. Hotel Duomo
4. Hotel Corso
5. La Magnolia B&B
6. B&B Michelangeli
7. Affittacamere Valentina
8. Hotel Posta
9. Villa Mercede
10. Istituto SS. Salvatore
11. Casa Sèlita B&B

**Eateries & Other**
12. Trattoria la Palomba
13. L'Antica Trattoria dell'Orso
14. Trattoria la Pergola
15. Trattoria del Moro Aronne

by a religious institution and offers 26 cheap, simple, mostly twin-bedded rooms, each with a big modern bathroom and many with glorious Umbrian views (elevator, free parking, a half-block from Duomo at Via Soliana 2, reception upstairs, tel. 0763-341-766, www.villamercede.it, info@villamercede.it).

**$ Istituto SS. Salvatore** rents nine spotless twin rooms and five singles in their convent, which comes with a peaceful terrace and garden, great views, and a 24:00 curfew. Though the nuns don't speak English, they have mastered Google Translate, and will hap-

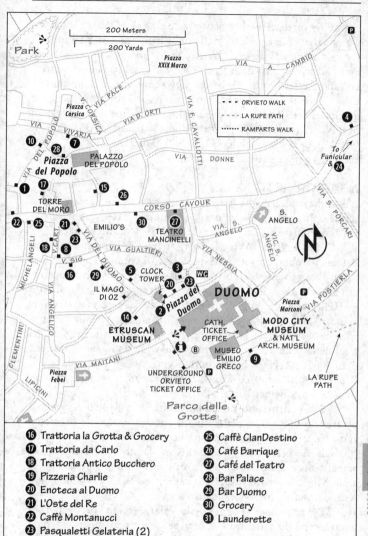

| | |
|---|---|
| ⑯ Trattoria la Grotta & Grocery | ㉕ Caffè ClanDestino |
| ⑰ Trattoria da Carlo | ㉖ Café Barrique |
| ⑱ Trattoria Antico Bucchero | ㉗ Café del Teatro |
| ⑲ Pizzeria Charlie | ㉘ Bar Palace |
| ⑳ Enoteca al Duomo | ㉙ Bar Duomo |
| ㉑ L'Oste del Re | ㉚ Grocery |
| ㉒ Caffè Montanucci | ㉛ Launderette |
| ㉓ Pasqualetti Gelateria (2) | |
| ㉔ To La Musa Gelateria | |

pily use it to answer your questions (cash only, no breakfast, elevator, Wi-Fi in common areas only, free parking, just off Piazza del Popolo at Via del Popolo 1, tel. 0763-342-910, istitutosansalvatore@tiscali.it).

**Just Outside the Town Center:** A peaceful country house, **$ Casa Sèlita B&B** offers easy access to Orvieto (best for drivers, but workable for adventurous train travelers who want an *agriturismo*-style experience). It's nestled in an orchard just below the town cliffs; to get to town, you'll climb an uphill path through their olive orchard (with a view terrace along the way) to reach the Campo della Fiera parking lot, with its handy escalator taking you the rest of the way up into Orvieto. Its five rooms with terraces are airy and fresh, with dark hardwood floors, fluffy down comforters, and modern baths. Enjoy the views from the relaxing garden. Conscientious Sèlita, her husband, Ennio, and daughter Elena are gracious hosts (RS%, cash preferred, air-con, free parking, closed mid-Nov-Easter, Strada di Porta Romana 8, ask for directions—GPS can be tricky, mobile 339-225-4000 or 328-611-2052, www.casaselita.com, info@casaselita.com).

## NEAR ORVIETO

All of these (except the last one) are within a 20-minute drive of Orvieto, in different directions, and require a car—see the "Orvieto and Civita Area" map, near the beginning of this chapter.

**$$$ Alta Rocca Wine Resort,** run by Emiliano and Sabrina, is a fancy "country resort" and spa, located 15 minutes north of Orvieto. They produce their own olive oil and wine, and rent 30 modern and air-conditioned rooms and a few apartments. Popular on weekends as a wedding location, this place has *luna di miele* (honeymoon) written all over it (2 pools, panoramic view restaurant, wellness center with Jacuzzi and steam room, massages and spa treatments available, visit to winery and wine tasting upon request, gym, mountain bikes, bocce court, hiking paths to private lake, tel. 0763-344-210 or 0763-393-437, www.altaroccawineresort.com, info@altaroccawineresort.com).

**$$$ Agriturismo Locanda Rosati,** where you'll be greeted by friendly host Giampiero Rosati, rents 10 tastefully decorated rooms in a pleasant, homey atmosphere. The peaceful, flower-lined grounds are perfect for a retreat (RS%, family rooms, full traditional dinners for €40 on request, air-con, swimming pool, 5 miles from Orvieto on the road to Viterbo, tel. 0763-217-314, www.locandarosati.it, info@locandarosati.it).

**$$ Agriturismo Poggio della Volara,** located between Todi and Orvieto (12 miles from either), has seven apartments (sleeping from two to five people) and five rooms in two buildings overlooking a swimming pool. Along with keeping rabbits, geese, dogs, and ducks, Marco produces wine, olive oil, and salami made from wild boar that he hunts. If you're looking for a real farmhouse experience far out in the countryside, this is it (air-con, €30-35 dinners on request, mobile 347-335-2523, www.poggiodellavolara.it, info@poggiodellavolara.it).

**$$ Tenuta Le Velette** is a sprawling, historic, family-run estate and winery. Cecilia and Corrado Bottai rent six fully furnished apartments and villas scattered over their family's expansive and scenic grounds. Rooms range wildly in size—accommodating from

2 to 14 people—but they all nestle in perfect Umbrian rural peace and tranquility. See the website for details on their various villas (2-night minimum, discount for weekly stay, pool, bocce court, 10 minutes from Orvieto—drive toward Bagnoregio-Canale and follow *Tenuta Le Velette* signs, tel. 0763-29090, mobile 348-300-2002, www.levelette.it, cecilialevelette@libero.it). They also offer wine tastings (see description under "Near Orvieto," earlier in this chapter).

**$$ Agriturismo Cioccoleta** ("Little Stone") has eight rooms with cozy country decor, each named after one of the grapes grown in the *agriturismo's* vineyards. It's family run and offers sweeping views of Orvieto and the pastoral countryside (RS%, fans, 3 miles north of Orvieto at Località Bardano 34 in Bardano, tel. 0763-316-011, mobile 349-860-9780, www.cioccoleta.it, info@cioccoleta.it, Angela Zucconi).

**Farther Out:** Northeast of Orvieto, **$$$ Agriturismo Fattoria di Vibio** produces olive oil and honey, sells organic products, and offers classes and spa services. In August, its 14 rooms rent at peak prices and have a minimum-stay requirement. The rest of the year, no minimum stay is required, although rates drop dramatically for longer visits. Its two cottages sleep from four to six people and rent only by the week (panoramic pool, expensive restaurant, farthest cottage is 20 miles from Orvieto, www.fattoriadivibio.com, info@fattoriadivibio.com).

# Eating in Orvieto

## TRATTORIAS IN THE CENTER

**$$$ Trattoria la Palomba** features excellent game and truffle specialties in a wood-paneled dining room. Giampiero, Enrica, and the Cinti family enthusiastically take care of their diners, offering a fine value, high quality, and classy conviviality. Truffles are shaved right at your table—try the *umbricelli al tartufo* (homemade pasta with truffles) or *spaghetti dell'Ascaro* (with truffles). Their *filetto alla cardinale* and mixed-cheese plates are popular. As slow-foodies, they use organic and locally sourced ingredients (Thu-Tue 12:30-14:15 & 19:30-22:00, closed Wed and July, reservations smart, off Piazza della Repubblica at Via Cipriano Manente 16, tel. 0763-343-395).

**$$$ L'Antica Trattoria dell'Orso** offers well-prepared Umbrian cuisine paired with fine wines in a homey, bohemian-chic, peaceful atmosphere. Owner Stefano and chef Hania offer a good deal for my readers: €30 for two people—my vote for the best dining value in town (Wed-Mon 12:00-14:30 & 19:30-22:00, closed Tue and Feb, just off Piazza della Repubblica at Via della Misericordia 18, tel. 0763-341-642).

**$$$ Trattoria la Pergola,** run by chef Enrico and family, with a serious kitchen in back next to a covered patio, offers a small, accessible menu of seasonal Umbrian specialties. Closer to the center, this spot is touristy, but the food is tasty and lovingly presented (reservations smart, air-con, Thu-Tue 12:15-15:00 & 19:15-22:00, closed Wed, Via dei Magoni 9, tel. 0763-343-065).

**$$ Trattoria del Moro Aronne** is a long-established family bistro run by Cristian and his mother, Rolanda, who lovingly prepare homemade pasta and market-fresh Umbrian specialties. Consider their *nidi*—folds of fresh pasta enveloping warm, gooey pecorino cheese sweetened with honey. Three small and separate dining areas make the interior feel intimate. While touristy and not particularly atmospheric, this place is known locally as an excellent value (Wed-Mon 12:30-14:30 & 19:30-22:00, closed Tue, Via San Leonardo 7, tel. 0763-342-763).

**$$ Trattoria la Grotta** prides itself on serving only the freshest food and finest wine. The decor is Signorelli-mod, and the ambience is quiet, with courteous service. They've been at it for more than 50 years, and promise diners a free coffee, grappa, *limoncello*, or vin santo with this book (Wed-Mon opens at 12:00 for lunch and at 19:00 for dinner, closed Tue, Via Luca Signorelli 5, tel. 0763-341-348).

**$$ Trattoria da Carlo,** hiding on its own little *piazzetta* between Via Corso Cavour and Piazza del Popolo, is a cozy spot with a bright, white-tiled interior and inviting tables outside. Animated and opinionated Carlo—a young, likeable loudmouth—holds court, chatting up his diners as much as he cooks, while his mama scuttles about taking orders, busing dishes, and lovingly rolling her eyes at her son's big personality. Carlo likes big flavors and putting a modern twist on traditional dishes (daily 12:00-15:00 & 19:00-24:00, often closed Sun dinner, Vicolo del Popolo 1, tel. 0763-343-916).

**$$ Trattoria Antico Bucchero,** elegant under a big, white vault, makes for a nice memory with its delicious food—especially game and wild boar (daily 12:00-15:00 & 19:00-23:00 except closed Wed Nov-March, seating indoors and on a peaceful square in summer, air-con, a half-block south of Corso Cavour, between Torre del Moro and Piazza della Repubblica at Via de Cartari 4, tel. 0763-341-725; Piero and Silvana, plus sons Fabio and Pericle).

**$$ Pizzeria Charlie** is a local favorite. Its noisy dining room and stony courtyard are reminiscent of a beer hall, and popular with families and students for casual dinners of wood-fired gourmet pizzas. In a quiet courtyard guarded by a medieval tower, it's a block southwest of Piazza della Repubblica (Wed-Mon 19:00-23:00, closed Tue, Via Loggia dei Mercanti 14, tel. 0763-344-766).

**$$$ Enoteca al Duomo** is to the left of the Duomo and has pleasant outdoor seating with a cathedral view. They serve wines by the glass and a vast selection of Italian wines by the bottle, and a full menu of local dishes in a contemporary wine-bar atmosphere (daily 10:00-22:00, closed Feb, Piazza del Duomo 13, tel. 0763-344-607).

## FAST AND CHEAP EATS

**$ L'Oste del Re** is a simple osteria on Corso Cavour, where Maria Grazia and Claudio offer pasta, bruschetta, enticing meat-and-cheese plates, and hearty, made-to-order sandwiches to eat in or take out (good gluten-free options, daily 11:00-15:30 & 19:00-22:00—but usually closed for dinner Nov-May, Corso Cavour 58, tel. 0763-343-846).

**$ Caffè Montanucci,** the dominant hangout on the main street—for good reason—lays out an appetizing display of pastas and main courses behind the counter. Choose one (or two—called a *bis*), find a seat in the modern interior or sunny courtyard, and they'll bring it out on a tray. You'll eat among locals on lunch break. They also have good *caffè*, simple sandwiches, and tasty sweets all day (daily 7:00-24:00, meals for lunch only—though they may be open for dinner in summer, Corso Cavour 21, tel. 0763-341-261).

**Panini and a Picnic:** Scattered around town you'll find many *alimentari* (grocers) selling cured meats, cheese, and other staples. If you're feeling gamey, order prosciutto or salami made from *cinghiale* (cheen-gee-AH-lay; wild boar), a surprisingly mild-tasting local favorite. They're usually willing to make you a simple sandwich of bread, cold cuts, and/or cheese for a few euros.

Elsewhere along the Corso Cavour, you'll find places selling fruit, vegetables, and other picnic items. The fortress/garden, to the right as you face the funicular, is a great spot to enjoy your meal.

**Groceries:** While a small *alimentari* might have what you need for a picnic, two slightly larger **Pam Local** markets are tucked away two minutes from the Duomo (both Mon-Sat 8:00-20:00, Sun from 9:00, one at Corso Cavour 100 and the other just past recommended Trattoria la Grotta at Via Luca Signorelli 23).

**Gelato:** For dessert, *gelateria* **Pasqualetti,** next to the cathedral, is a favorite (daily, may close in cold weather, closed Dec-Feb; one location is next to left transept of church, Piazza del Duomo 14; another branch is a few steps off the main drag at Via del Duomo 10). Closer to the funicular, **La Musa** has a nice variety of creative flavors (daily, Corso Cavour 351).

## CAFÉ SCENE ON CORSO CAVOUR AND NEARBY

Orvieto has a charming, traffic-free, pedestrian-friendly vibe. To enjoy it, be sure to spend a little time savoring *la dolce far niente*—the art of doing nothing—while sitting at a café. There are

ORVIETO & CIVITA

inviting places all over town, but these are either on or very near Corso Cavour, the main strolling drag, and offer the best people-watching.

**Caffè Montanucci** is the town's venerable place for a coffee and pastry, but has no on-street seating (Corso Cavour 21, described earlier for lunch). **Caffè ClanDestino** is well-located, with plenty of streetside seating and endless little bites served with your drink (Corso Cavour 40). **Café Barrique** is less crowded, less trendy, and quieter, with nice outdoor tables and good free snacks with your drink (Corso Cavour 111).

**Café del Teatro,** at Teatro Mancinelli (described earlier), can be a fun experience. While entry to the historic theater is normally €2, if you buy a drink, you're free to wander around on your own. Drink streetside, at the bar, or in the theater lobby (Mon-Sat 8:00-14:00, closed Sun, may be open later when there's a show, Corso Cavour 122, tel. 0763-531-502).

**On Piazza del Popolo:** A sunny, relaxed perch, **Bar Palace** faces a big square that's generally quiet (except on market day), with quality coffee and pastries.

**Cafés Facing the Cathedral:** Several cafés on Piazza del Duomo invite you to linger over a drink with a view of Orvieto's amazing cathedral.

## Orvieto Connections

**From Orvieto by Train to: Rome** (every 1-2 hours, 1-1.5 hours), **Florence** (6/day, 2.5 hours, use Firenze S.M.N. train station), **Siena** (12/day, 2.5 hours, change in Chiusi), **Assisi** (roughly hourly, 2-3 hours, 1 or 2 transfers), **Milan** (2/day direct, 5.5 hours; otherwise about hourly with a transfer in Florence, Bologna, or Rome, 4.5-5 hours). The train station's Buffet della Stazione is surprisingly good if you need a quick focaccia sandwich or pizza picnic for the train ride.

**Tip for Drivers:** If you're thinking of driving to Rome, consider stashing your car in Orvieto instead. You can easily park the car, safe and free, in the big lot below the Orvieto train station (for up to a week or more), and zip effortlessly into Rome by train (roughly hourly, 1-1.5 hours).

# Civita di Bagnoregio

Perched on a pinnacle in a grand canyon, the 2,500-year-old, traffic-free village of Civita di Bagnoregio is Italy's ultimate hill town. Civita's only connection to the town of Bagnoregio (ban-yoh-REH-joh)—and the world—is a long pedestrian bridge. In the last decade, the old, self-sufficient Civita (chee-VEE-tah) has died—the last of its lifelong residents have passed on, and the only employment here is in serving gawking sightseers. But Civita remains an amazing place to visit. And it remains popular as a backdrop for movies, soap operas, and advertising campaigns.

Civita's history goes back to Etruscan and ancient Roman times. In the early Middle Ages, Bagnoregio was a suburb of Civita, which had a population of about 4,000. Later, Bagnoregio surpassed Civita in size—especially following a 1695 earthquake, after which many residents fled Civita to live in Bagnoregio, fearing their houses would be shaken off the edge into the valley below. Bagnoregio is dominated by Renaissance-style buildings, while architecturally, Civita remains stuck in the Middle Ages.

Despite being a "dead city," Civita can be very crowded—especially on the weekends and at lunchtime. The best way to enjoy Civita is early or late in the day, when you have the village to yourself. While Bagnoregio lacks the pinnacle-town romance of Civita, it's a healthy, vibrant community. In Bagnoregio, get a haircut, sip a coffee on the square, and walk down to the old laundry (ask, *"Dov'è la lavanderia vecchia?"*).

**Planning Your Time:** In high season—and especially on weekends—little Civita can be uncomfortably jammed; for a better experience, treat it like a major museum and visit either early or late in the day. If side-tripping by bus from Orvieto, it works well to get up early, take the 7:50 bus, and see Civita in the cool morning calm. The next bus after 7:50 is at 12:45. If you take this later one, you can make the last bus back (around 17:20), but your time in Civita may feel a little rushed. Note that the buses connecting Orvieto to Bagnoregio (and Civita) do not run on Sundays or holidays.

## GETTING THERE

To reach Civita from Orvieto, you'll first head for the adjacent town of Bagnoregio. From there, it's a 30-minute walk or 5-minute drive to the base of Civita's pedestrian bridge, followed by a steep 10-minute hike up to the town's main square.

**By Bus to Bagnoregio:** The blue Cotral bus runs to Bagnoregio about 10 times each day, including some very early departures and a long break mid-morning; get the detailed schedule at the TI or at www.cotralspa.it (Italian only; no bus on Sundays or holidays). The

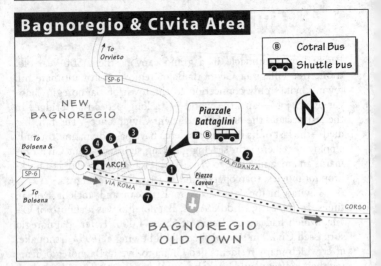

## Bagnoregio & Civita Area

trip takes about 45 minutes, and tickets are €2.20 one-way if bought in advance at a bar or tobacco shop, or €7 one-way if purchased from driver. In Orvieto's upper town, buy your ticket from Silvia at the tobacco shop at Corso Cavour 306, a block up from the funicular (daily 7:00-13:00 & 16:00-20:00)—otherwise you'll pay the premium ticket price on board the bus. If you'll be returning to Orvieto by bus, buy two tickets now (they're harder to get in Bagnoregio).

Buses depart from a courtyard within the former military barracks, a short walk from the upper funicular station at the east end of Orvieto. It's tricky to find: With your back to the funicular, walk to the right, bear left (uphill) with the street, then go right under the arch marked *Caserma Piave*. Angle left through the parking lot to find the blue Cotral bus, under and behind the tall trees. (Note: Lots of buses marked *Umbria Mobilità* stop in front of the funicular, but Civita is served by a different bus company, Cotral.)

Buses departing the barracks stop five minutes later at Orvieto's train station—to catch the bus there, wait to the left of the funicular station (as you're facing it); schedule and tickets are available in the tobacco shop/bar in the train station.

For information on buses returning to Orvieto, see "Bagnoregio Connections," later.

**Getting from Bagnoregio Bus Stop to Civita:** By Cotral bus from Orvieto, you'll arrive in Bagnoregio at Piazzale Battaglini, at the opposite

Accommodations
1 Romantica Pucci B&B
2 Hotel Divino Amore

4 Il Ripi&Go
5 L'Arte del Pane
6 Edicola 76 (Bus Tickets)
7 Tobacco Shop
(Cotral Bus Tickets)

Eateries & Other
3 Il Peperoncino

CIVITA DI
BAGNOREGIO

400 Meters
400 Yards

CIVITA
TICKET
OFFICE

BELVEDERE

FOOTBRIDGE

MAZZINI

STREET
PARKING

PARKING
(BIGGEST)

STAIRS

DEAD-END
STAIRS

end of the old center from Civita. To get to Civita's bridge, it's a 20- to 30-minute, mostly downhill **walk** through the middle of Bagnoregio. The walk itself is enjoyable, as it offers a delightful look at a workaday Italian town. To walk, take the road going uphill, Via Garibaldi (overlooking the big parking lot), then jog a block over to the main drag, Via Roma, which changes names a few times as it takes you all the way to Civita.

If you'd rather not walk, you can take a **shuttle.** It runs to Civita from near the Piazzale Battaglini bus stop—look for white minibuses labeled *EPF Tours.* The shuttle is especially handy for the uphill return—it drops you right at the Orvieto-bound bus stop (usually 1-2/hour, 5 minutes, 7:30-18:15 but few buses 13:15-15:00 or on Sun Oct-March, €0.70 one-way, €1 round-trip, pay driver).

**By Taxi or Shared Taxi to Civita:** If you can share the cost with other travelers, a 30-minute taxi ride from Orvieto to Civita is a reasonable value (basic rate: €50 one-way, €80 round-trip with an hour wait). Giuliotaxi can take groups by car or minibus (see "Tours of Orvieto," earlier in this chapter).

**By Car to Bagnoregio and Civita:** Driving from Orvieto to Civita takes about 30 minutes. Orvieto overlooks the autostrada (and has its own exit). From the Orvieto exit, the shortest way to Civita is to turn left (below Orvieto), and then simply follow the signs to *Lubriano* and *Bagnoregio.*

A more winding and scenic route takes a few minutes longer: From the Orvieto exit on the autostrada, go right (toward *Orvieto*), then at the first big roundabout, follow signs to *Bolsena* (passing under hill-capping Orvieto on your right). Take the first left (direction: Bagnoregio), winding up past great Orvieto views and the recommended Tenuta Le Velette and Custodi wineries (reserva-

ORVIETO & CIVITA

tions required) en route to Canale, and through farms and fields of giant shredded wheat to Bagnoregio.

Whichever route you take, for a breathtaking view of Civita, just before Bagnoregio follow signs left to *Lubriano*, head into that village, turn right as you enter town, and pull into the first little square by the yellow church (on the left). You'll find an even better view farther into the town, from the tiny square at the next church (San Giovanni Battista). Then return to the Bagnoregio road.

Once in Bagnoregio, you'll drive right up the main street—which seems pedestrian-only, but isn't (follow yellow *Civita* signs). As you approach Civita, you'll begin to see pay-and-display parking lots and blue-painted lines along the side of the road (all charge €2/hour). The closest you can get is the lot at the end of the tree-lined stretch of road, right in front of the belvedere—but this is often full, in which case the larger lot farther back likely has space.

**Walking Across the Bridge to Civita:** Whether arriving by foot, shuttle bus, or car, first head out to the belvedere at the very end of Bagnoregio for a superb viewpoint (through the little garden). From there, backtrack a few steps (the staircase next to the viewpoint is a dead end) and take the stairs down to the road leading to the bridge. You'll first head downhill, then pay the admission fee and hike up the narrow bridge into town.

# Orientation to Civita

Civita charges a €5 **admission fee** to enter the old town (waived for overnight guests). The revenue helps with its extensive maintenance expenses. Buy your ticket from the brown kiosk, just before the bridge, on the left.

## HELPFUL HINTS
**Market Day:** A lively market fills the Bagnoregio bus-station parking lot each Monday.

**Orvieto Bus Tickets:** Because the Orvieto-Bagnoregio bus ticket is much cheaper purchased in advance (€2.20 one-way) than from the driver (€7), ideally you'll buy both tickets in Orvieto. But if you wind up in Bagnoregio needing a ticket, only two places sell them—and both are closed for several hours in the afternoon. Buy one on arrival so you have it when you need it later. One option is the newsstand (named Edicola 76) across from the gas station near the Bagnoregio bus stop (look for the white awning at #47; daily 7:00-13:00 & 17:00-20:00 except closed Sun and Thu afternoons). The other option is the tobacco shop up along the main drag of Bagnoregio, directly uphill from the big parking lot, next to the GemminOro shop (Mon-Sat 8:00-13:00 & 17:00-20:00, closed Sun, Larga Fidenza 6).

## Civita di Bagnoregio

Note: Map not to scale; a walk across Civita takes approx. 5 minutes—but don't rush it!

To Lubriano Town

To Bagnoregio

Cliffs

Cliffs

Cliffs

OSTERIA AL FORNO DI AGNESE

ANTICO FORNO TRATTORIA & CIVITA B&B

LOCANDA DELLA BUONA VENTURA

L'ARCO DEL GUSTO

WC

OLD LAUNDRY

*Piazza*

CAMPANILE (BELL TOWER)

CHURCH

ETRUSCAN COLUMNS

ANTICO FRANTOIO OLIVE PRESS & BRUSCHETTERIA

ALMA CIVITA

ARCH

MAIN STRADA

FOOTBRIDGE

BAR LA PIAZZETTA

WINE BAR D'ANDREA

TRATTORIA LA CANTINA DE ARIANNA

ANTICA CIVITA MUSEUM

WINE BAR DA PEPPONE & GEOLOGICAL MUSEUM

PALACE (PRIVATE)

CAVES & CHAPEL CARVED IN ROCK

Cliffs

RUINS OF HOUSE OF ST. BONAVENTURE

Trail to Etruscan tunnel under Civita

## Civita Walk

Civita was once connected to Bagnoregio, before the saddle between the separate towns eroded away. Photographs around town show the old donkey path—the original bridge. It was bombed in World War II and replaced in 1966 with the footbridge that you're climbing today.

• *Entering the town, you'll pass through* **Porta Santa Maria**, *a 12th-century Romanesque arch. This stone passageway was cut by the Etruscans 2,500 years ago, when this town was a stop on an ancient trading route. Inside the archway, you enter a garden of stones. Stand in the little square—the town's antechamber—facing the Bar La Piazzetta. Over your right shoulder are the remains of a...*

### Renaissance Palace

The wooden door and windows (above the door) lead only to thin air. They were part of the facade of one of five palaces that once graced Civita. Much of the palace fell into the valley, riding a chunk of the ever-eroding rock pinnacle. Today, the door leads to a remaining section of the palace—complete with Civita's first hot

**ORVIETO & CIVITA**

tub. It was once owned by the "Marchesa," a countess who married into Italy's biggest industrialist family.

• *A few steps uphill, farther into town (on your left, beyond the Bottega souvenir store), notice the two shed-like buildings.*

## Old WC and Laundry (Vecchio Lavatoio)

In the nearer building (covered with ivy), you'll see the town's old laundry, which dates from just after World War II, when water was finally piped into the town. Until a few years ago, this was a lively village gossip center. Now, locals park their mopeds here. Just behind that is another stone shed, which houses a poorly marked and less-than-pristine WC.

• *The main square is just a few steps farther along, but we'll take the scenic circular route to get there, detouring around to the right. Walk past the ruined palace and belly up to the...*

## Canyon Viewpoint

Lean over the banister and listen to the sounds of the birds and the bees. Survey old family farms, noticing how evenly they're spaced. Historically, each one owned just enough land to stay in business. Turn left along the belvedere and walk a few steps to the site of the long-gone home of Civita's one famous son, St. Bonaventure, known as the "second founder of the Franciscans" (look for the small plaque on the wall).

• *From here, a lane leads past delightful old homes and gardens, and then to...*

## Civita's Main Square

The town church faces Civita's main piazza. Grab a stone seat along the biggest building fronting the square (or a drink at Peppone's bar) and observe the scene. They say that in a big city you can see a lot, but in a small town like this you can feel a lot. The generous bench is built into the long side of the square, reminding me of how, when I first discovered Civita back in the 1970s and 1980s, the town's old folks would gather here every night.

The piazza has been integral to Italian culture since ancient Roman times. While Civita is humble today, imagine the town's former wealth, when mansions of the leading families faced this square, along with the former City Hall (opposite the church, to your left). The town's history includes a devastating earthquake in 1695. Notice how stone walls were reinforced with thick bases, and how old stones and marble slabs were recycled and built into walls.

Here in the town square, you'll find **Bar Da Peppone** (open daily, local wines and microbrews, inviting fire in the winter) and two restaurants. There are wild donkey races on the first Sunday of June and the second Sunday of September. At Christmastime, a living Nativity scene is enacted in this square, and if you're visiting at the end of July or beginning of August, you might catch a play here. The pillars that stand like giants' bar stools are ancient Etruscan. The church, with its campanile (bell tower), marks the spot where an Etruscan temple, and then a Roman temple, once stood. Across from Peppone's, on the side of the former City Hall, is a small, square stone counter. Old-timers remember when this was a meat shop, and how one day a week the counter was stacked with fish for sale.

The humble **Geological Museum**, next to Peppone's, tells the story of how erosion is constantly shaping the surrounding "Bad Lands" valley, how landslides have shaped (and continue to threaten) Civita, and how the town plans to stabilize things (€3; June-Aug Tue-Sun 9:30-13:30 & 14:00-18:30, closed Mon; Sept-May Fri-Sun 10:00-13:30 & 14:00-19:30, closed Mon-Thu; www.museogeologicoedellefrane.it, mobile 328-665-7205).

• *Now step inside...*

## Civita's Church

A cathedral until 1699, the church houses records of about 60 bishops that date back to the seventh century (church open daily 10:00-13:00 & 15:00-17:00, often closed Feb). Inside you'll see Romanesque columns and arches with faint Renaissance frescoes peeking through Baroque-era whitewash. The central altar is built upon the relics of the Roman martyr St. Victoria, who once was the patron saint of the town. St. Marlonbrando served as a bishop here in the ninth century; an altar dedicated to him is on the right. The fine crucifix over this altar, carved out of pear wood in the 15th century, is from the school of Donatello. It's remarkably expressive and greatly venerated by locals. Jesus' gaze is almost haunting. Some say his appearance changes based on what angle you view him from: looking alive from the front, in agony from the left, and dead from the right. Regardless, his eyes follow you from side to side. On Good Friday, this crucifix goes out and is the focus of the midnight procession.

On the left side, midway up the nave above an altar, is an intimate fresco known as *Madonna of the Earthquake*, given this name because—in the great shake of 1695—the whitewash fell off and revealed this tender fresco of Mary and her child. (During the Baroque era, a white-and-bright interior was in vogue, and

ORVIETO & CIVITA

churches such as these—which were covered with precious and historic frescoes—were simply whitewashed over. Look around to see examples.) On the same wall—just toward the front from the *Madonna*—find the faded portrait of Santa Apollonia, the patron saint of your teeth; notice the scary-looking pincers.

• *From the square, you can follow...*

## The Main Street

A short walk takes you from the church to the end of the town. Along the way, you'll pass a couple little eateries (described later, under "Eating in Civita"), olive presses, gardens, a rustic town museum, and valley views. The rock below Civita is honeycombed with ancient tunnels, caverns (housing olive presses), cellars (for keeping wine at a constant temperature all year), and cisterns (for collecting rainwater, since there was no well in town). Many date from Etruscan times.

Wherever you choose to eat (or just grab a bruschetta snack), be sure to take advantage of the opportunity to poke around—every place has a historic cellar. At the trendy **Alma Civita,** notice the damaged house facing the main street—broken since the 1695 earthquake and scarred to this day. Just beyond, the rustic **Antico Frantoio Bruschetteria** serves bruschetta in an amazing old space. Whether or not you buy food, venture into their back room to see

an interesting collection of old olive presses (if you're not eating here, a €1 donation is requested). The huge olive press in the entry is about 1,500 years old. Until the 1960s, blindfolded donkeys trudged in the circle here, crushing olives and creating paste that filled the circular filters and was put into a second press. Notice the 2,500-year-old sarcophagus niche. The hole in the floor (with the glass top) was a garbage hole. In ancient times, residents would toss their jewels down when under attack; excavations uncovered a windfall of treasures.

In front is the wellhead of an ancient cistern—designed to collect rainwater from neighboring rooftops—carved out of *tufo* and covered with clay to be waterproof.

• *Across the street and down a tiny lane, find...*

## Antica Civita

This is the closest thing the town has to a history museum. The humble collection is the brainchild of Felice, the old farmer who hung black-and-white photos, farm tools, olive presses, and local artifacts in a series of old caves. Climb down to the "warm blood machine" (another donkey-powered grinding wheel) and a viewpoint. You'll see rooms where a mill worker lived until the 1930s. Felice wants to give visitors a feeling for life in Civita when its traditional economy was strong (€1, daily 10:00-19:00, until 17:00 in winter, some English explanations, tel. 320-110-4279).

• *Another few steps along the main street take you to...*

## The End of Civita

Here the road is literally cut out of the stone, with a dramatic view of the Bad Lands opening up. To savor the scene, consider popping into the cute **"Garden of Poets"** (immediately on the left just outside town; they'll ask for a donation, or you can purchase something at their little local-products shop). Then, look back up at the end of town and ponder the precarious future of Civita. There's a certain stillness here, far from the modern world and high above the valley.

Continue along the path a few steps toward the valley below the town, and you come to some shallow caves used as stables until a few years ago. The third cave, cut deeper into the rock, with a barred door, is the **Chapel of the Incarcerated** (Cappella del Carcere). In Etruscan times, the chapel—with a painted tile depicting the Madonna and child—may have been a tomb, and in medieval times, it was used as a jail (which collapsed in 1695).

Although it's closed to the public now, an Etruscan tunnel just beyond the Chapel of the Incarcerated cuts completely through the hill. Tall enough for a woman with a jug on her head to pass through, it may have served as a shortcut to the river below. It was widened in the 1930s so that farmers could get between their scattered fields more easily. Later, it served as a refuge for frightened villagers who huddled here during WWII bombing raids.

• *Hike back into town, taking some time to explore the peaceful back lanes before returning to the modern world.*

# Sleeping in Civita or Bagnoregio

Civita has nine B&B rooms up for grabs. Bagnoregio has larger lodgings, and there are plenty of *agriturismi* nearby; otherwise, there's always Orvieto. Off-season, when Civita and Bagnoregio are deadly quiet—and cold—I'd side-trip in from Orvieto rather than spend the night here.

## IN CIVITA

**$$ Alma Civita** is a classic old stone house that has been renovated by a sister-and-brother team, Alessandra and Maurizio (hence the name: Al-Ma). These are Civita's two most comfortable, modern,

ORVIETO & CIVITA

and warmly run rooms and they also have a recommended restaurant (tel. 0761-792-415, mobile 347-449-8892, www.almacivita.com, prenotazione@almacivita.com).

**$$ Locanda della Buona Ventura** rents four overpriced rooms, up narrow stairs, decorated in medieval rustic-chic, and overlooking Civita's piazza. You're not likely to see the owner—the Dallaiti shop across the square functions as the reception (tiny bathrooms, skimpy breakfast, tel. 0761-792-025, mobile 347-627-5628, www.locandabuonaventura.com, info@locandabuonaventura.com).

**$ Civita B&B,** run by gregarious Franco Sala, has three little rooms above Trattoria Antico Forno, each overlooking Civita's main square. Two are doubles with private bath. The third is a triple (with one double and one kid-size bed), which has its own bathroom across the hall (RS%, family rooms, continental breakfast, Piazza del Duomo Vecchio, tel. 076-176-0016, mobile 347-611-5426, www.civitadibagnoregio.it, fsala@pelagus.it). Franco also rents a few apartments in Civita, Bagnoregio, and nearby.

### IN BAGNOREGIO

**$ Romantica Pucci B&B** is a haven for city-weary travelers. Its five spacious rooms are indeed romantic, with canopied beds and flowing veils (air-con, free parking, along the main drag at Piazza Cavour 1, tel. 0761-792-121, www.hotelromanticapucci.it, info@hotelromanticapucci.it).

**$ Hotel Divino Amore** has 23 bright, modern rooms, four with perfect views of a miniature Civita. These view rooms, and the seven rooms with air-conditioning, don't cost extra—but they book up first (closed Jan-March, a block below the main drag at Via Fidanza 25-27, tel. 076-178-0882, mobile 329-344-8950, www.hoteldivinoamore.com, info@hoteldivinoamore.com, Silvia).

# Eating in Civita or Bagnoregio

### IN CIVITA

Note that opening hours are highly unpredictable in this little town—when it's quiet, places can close unexpectedly. Take the hours listed here as rough estimates.

**$$ Osteria Al Forno di Agnese** is a delightful spot where Manuela and her friends serve visitors simple yet delicious meals and a good selection of local wines on a covered patio just off Civita's main square or in a little dining room in gloomy weather (daily at 12:00 for lunch, June-Sept also at 19:00 for dinner, closed sometimes in bad weather, tel. 0761-792-571, mobile 340-1259-721).

**$$ Trattoria Antico Forno** serves up rustic dishes, homemade pasta, and salads at affordable prices. Try their homemade pasta with truffles (daily 12:30-15:30 & 19:00-22:00—but not always open for dinner, on main square, also rents rooms—see Civita B&B listing earlier, tel. 076-176-0016, Franco, daughter Elisabetta, and assistants Nina and Daniela).

**$$ Trattoria La Cantina de Arianna** is a family affair, with a busy open fire specializing in grilled meat and wonderful bruschetta. It's run by Arianna, her sister, Antonella, and their parents, Rossana and Antonio. After eating, wander down to their cellar, where you'll see traditional winemaking gear and provisions for rolling huge kegs up the stairs. Tap on the kegs in the bottom level to see which are full (daily 12:00-16:30, Sat also dinner from 19:30, tel. 0761-793-270).

**$$ Alma Civita** feels like a fresh, new take on old Civita, owned by a sister-and-brother team of longtime residents: Alessandra (an architect) and Maurizio (who runs the restaurant). Choose from one of three seating areas: outside on a stony lane, in the modern and trendy-feeling main-floor dining room, or in the equally modern but atmospheric cellar. Even deeper is an old Etruscan tomb that's now a wine cellar (April-Oct lunch Wed-Mon 12:00-15:15, dinner Fri-Sat only 19:00-21:30, closed Tue; Nov-March Thu-Sun only for lunch plus Sat for dinner; they also rent recommended rooms, tel. 0761-792-415).

**$ Antico Frantoio Bruschetteria,** the last place in town, is a rustic, super-atmospheric spot for a bite to eat. The specialty here: delicious bruschetta toasted over hot coals. Peruse the menu, choose your toppings (chopped tomato is super), and get a glass of wine for a fun, affordable snack or meal (roughly 10:00-18:00—sometimes later in summer, mobile 328-689-9375, Fabrizio).

**Sandwich Shop:** If you just want a quick bite, **$ L'Arco del Gusto** can make you a sandwich using local products (daily 10:30-16:30, tucked in an archway near the start of town).

## IN BAGNOREGIO

The recommended **$$ Romantica Pucci B&B** offers a small restaurant with tables in its private garden (closed Mon, see contact details earlier). For good gelato, on your walk to Civita you'll go right past a branch of Orvieto's **Pasqualetti**, on the main drag at Mazzini 32.

**Near the Bagnoregio Bus Stop:** Several basic eateries are along Via Giacomo Matteotti just below the bus stop in Bagnoregio, including **$ Il Peperoncino,** selling pizza by the slice (closed Wed, #49); **$$ Il Ripi&Go,** a sit-down eatery serving traditional food (closed Wed, #35); and—a half-block past Il Ripi&Go—fresh pastries at **$ L'Arte del Pane** (#5).

**ORVIETO & CIVITA**

## Bagnoregio Connections

**From Bagnoregio to Orvieto:** Cotral buses connect Bagnoregio to Orvieto (about 10/day Mon-Sat only—no buses Sun or holidays, 45 minutes, €2.20 one-way if purchased in advance, €7 one-way from driver). For information, call 06-7205-7205 or 800-174-471 (press 7 for English), or see www.cotralspa.it (click "Orari," then fill in "Bagnoregio" and "Orvieto" in the trip planner—Italian only). For info on coming from Orvieto, see "Getting There" near the start of this section.

**From Bagnoregio to Points South:** Cotral buses also run to **Viterbo,** which has good train connections to Rome (about 10/day Mon-Fri, fewer Sat, no buses Sun, 35 minutes).

# ROME

*Roma*

Two thousand years ago the word "Rome" meant civilization itself. Everything was either civilized (part of the Roman world) or barbarian. Today, Rome is Italy's political capital, the spiritual capital of a billion Roman Catholics, and an open-air museum of the evocative remains of the capital of what was the greatest empire in the history of humanity.

As you peel through Rome's fascinating and jumbled layers, you'll find the marble ruins of ancient times, tangled streets of the medieval world, early Christian churches, grand Renaissance buildings and statues, Baroque fountains and church facades, 19th-century apartments, 21st-century traffic, and nearly three million people. And then, of course, there are Rome's stupendous sights.

Visit St. Peter's, the greatest church on earth, and scale Michelangelo's 448-foot-tall dome. Learn something about eternity at the huge Vatican Museums, where the story of creation is as bright as when Michelangelo first painted it in the restored Sistine Chapel. Ramble among the rabble and rubble, doing the "Caesar Shuffle" through ancient Rome's Colosseum and Forum, mentally resurrecting those tumble-down stones. Peer into the eyes of Roman busts at the National Museum of Rome, and savor Bernini's lifelike sculptures at the sumptuous Borghese Gallery. Wander through the surrounding Villa Borghese Gardens, Rome's biggest public park.

When the museums close and the crowds thin, Rome relaxes. The city, so monumental by day, becomes intimate and approachable. Its neighborhoods feel more like villages, and its famous squares become places to simply hang out. Do as the Romans do. Early in the evening, join the promenade—called the *passeggiata*—

up and down the main streets. After a sociable stroll, take a break for an *aperitivo*—a before-dinner drink.

Rome can be romantic...but hard on the unprepared. If you're careless, you could get pickpocketed. And if you have the wrong attitude, you'll be frustrated by the kind of chaos that only an Italian can understand. On a recent visit, my cabbie struggled with the traffic and said, *"Roma chaos."* I responded, *"Bella chaos."* He agreed.

Make it easy on yourself. If you choose a comfortable hotel for a refuge, pace yourself, enjoy a siesta during midday heat, organize your sightseeing, and take sensible precautions to protect your valuables, you'll love Rome. Soon you'll be the one at the Trevi Fountain throwing in a coin to ensure your return.

## PLANNING YOUR TIME

Rome is wonderful, but it's huge and exhausting. On a first-time visit, many travelers find that Rome is best done quickly—Italy is more charming elsewhere. But whether you're here for a day or a week, you won't be able to see everything, so don't try—you'll keep coming back to Rome.

**Rome in a Day:** Some people actually "do" Rome in a day. Crazy as that sounds, if all you have is a day, it's one of the most exciting days Europe has to offer. Start at 8:30 at the Colosseum. Then explore the Forum (skip the Palatine Hill), hike over Capitoline Hill, and cap your "Caesar Shuffle" with a Pantheon visit. After a quick lunch, taxi to the Vatican Museums, then head to St. Peter's Basilica (open until 19:00 April-Sept). Taxi to Campo de' Fiori for dinner, then finish your day lacing together the famous floodlit spots (following my "Heart of Rome Walk"). Note: This busy plan is possible only if you reserve entry times for the Vatican Museums and the Colosseum in advance.

**Rome in Two to Three Days:** On the first day, do the "Caesar Shuffle" from the Colosseum (book ahead) to the Forum, then over Capitoline Hill (visiting the Capitoline Museums), and on to the Pantheon. After a siesta, add some sightseeing to suit your interest. In the evening enjoy a sound-and-light show at the Forum and/or a colorful stroll in Trastevere or the Monti district. On the second day, see Vatican City (St. Peter's, dome climb, Vatican Museums—book ahead). Have dinner near the atmospheric Campo de' Fiori, and then walk to the Trevi Fountain and Spanish Steps (following my "Heart of Rome Walk"). With a third day, add the Borghese Gallery (reservations required) and more sights.

ROME

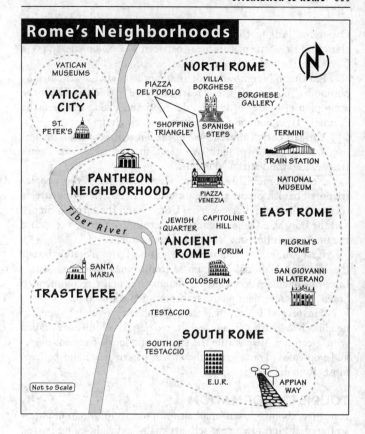

# Rome's Neighborhoods

VATICAN MUSEUMS

**VATICAN CITY**

ST. PETER'S

**NORTH ROME**

PIAZZA DEL POPOLO

VILLA BORGHESE

BORGHESE GALLERY

"SHOPPING TRIANGLE"

SPANISH STEPS

TERMINI TRAIN STATION

NATIONAL MUSEUM

**PANTHEON NEIGHBORHOOD**

*Tiber River*

PIAZZA VENEZIA

JEWISH QUARTER

CAPITOLINE HILL

**ANCIENT ROME**

FORUM

COLOSSEUM

**EAST ROME**

PILGRIM'S ROME

SAN GIOVANNI IN LATERANO

SANTA MARIA

**TRASTEVERE**

TESTACCIO

**SOUTH ROME**

SOUTH OF TESTACCIO

E.U.R.

APPIAN WAY

Not to Scale

# Orientation to Rome

Today's Rome sprawls over about 500 square miles, but the city center within the ancient Aurelian Wall is all you need to know— and that's only four square miles. The old core, with most of the tourist sights, sits inside a diamond formed by Termini train station (in the east), the Vatican (west), Villa Borghese Gardens (north), and the Colosseum (south). The Tiber River snakes through the diamond from north to south. At the center of the diamond is Piazza Venezia, a busy square and traffic hub.

## ROME BY NEIGHBORHOOD

Think of Rome as a collection of neighborhoods, huddling around major landmarks, and it becomes manageable.

**Ancient Rome:** In ancient times, this was home to the grandest buildings of a city of a million people. Today, the best of the classical sights stand in a line from the Colosseum (huge stadium) to the ruined Roman Forum (main square and marketplace) over

ROME

Capitoline Hill to the Pantheon (Roman temple turned into a church). Just north of this area, between Via Nazionale and Via Cavour, is the trendy Monti district.

**Pantheon Neighborhood:** The Pantheon anchors the neighborhood I like to call the "Heart of Rome," which includes the atmospheric squares of Campo de' Fiori and Piazza Navona, the dramatic Trevi Fountain, and several historic churches.

**Vatican City:** Located west of the Tiber River, this is a compact world of its own, with two great, massive sights: St. Peter's Basilica and the Vatican Museums.

**North Rome:** This modern, classy area hosts the people-friendly Spanish Steps, an elegant grid of trendy shopping streets (between the main drag—Via del Corso—and the Spanish Steps), and the Borghese Gallery (gorgeous Bernini sculptures) set within the fun-on-a-sunny-day Villa Borghese Gardens.

**East Rome:** This neighborhood around Termini Station boasts the stunning National Museum of Rome (ancient Roman sculpture) and includes Piazza della Repubblica, many recommended hotels, and convenient public-transportation connections.

**Trastevere:** Trastevere is the colorful, wrong-side-of-the-river neighborhood with a village feel. Its red pastel buildings are draped with green ivy, Vespas rule the streets, and locals frequent mom-and-pop cafés. Trastevere is the city at its crustiest...and perhaps most "Roman."

## TOURIST INFORMATION

Rome has about a dozen small city-run tourist information offices scattered around town that sell city maps and sightseeing passes. The largest TIs are at Fiumicino Airport (Terminal 3, daily 8:00-21:00) and Termini train station (daily 8:00-18:45, exit by track 24 and walk 100 yards down along Via Giovanni Giolitti). Little kiosks (most open daily 9:30-19:00) are on Via Nazionale (at Palazzo delle Esposizioni), between the Trevi Fountain and Pantheon (at the corner of Via del Corso and Via Minghetti), near Piazza Navona (at Piazza delle Cinque Lune), and in Trastevere (at Piazza Sidney Sonnino). A larger information center is directly across from the Forum entrance, on Via dei Fori Imperiali (see page 871). There are also offices at Tiburtina train station and Ciampino Airport.

The TI's website is www.turismoroma.it, but a better site for practical information is www.060608.it. That's also the number for Rome's **call center**—the best source of up-to-date tourist information, with English speakers on staff (answered daily 9:00-19:00, tel. 06-0608, press 2 for English).

Your hotel will have a freebie map and may also have a booklet with up-to-date listings of the city's sights and hours. To find the city's many small streets and alleys, map apps work better than

ROME

paper maps. If you do want a paper map, you'll find better quality ones at bookstores than at newsstands. See "Getting Around
Rome" later in this chapter for recommended public transport
maps.

## ARRIVAL IN ROME
### By Train at Termini Station

Termini, Rome's main train station (www.romatermini.com), is a
buffet of tourist services. At the head of the tracks are two atriums.

The inner atrium, open at
both ends, houses shops
and eateries. The outer
atrium, with glass walls,
houses ticket windows
and ticket machines plus
a good-sized bookstore.
(Note that ticket win-
dows can be jammed with
travelers—find the small

red kiosk, take a number, and wait.) Outside the station is a large
square where city buses depart. A basement shopping area extends
beneath both atriums.

For security, entry to the train platforms themselves is restricted to ticketholders. Entrances are from the inner atrium and from
the halls to the sides of the tracks. You may need to show your ticket, but there are no metal detectors and lines are generally short.

**Eating:** In general, the best places in the station to sit are in its
eateries (open long hours daily). A snack bar and a good self-service
cafeteria (Ciao) are perched one floor above the ticket windows in
the outer atrium, accessible from the side closest to track 24. For
good-quality sandwiches to go, try VyTA in the inner atrium across
from track 1. The large Sapori & Dintori supermarket is on the
basement shopping level, below the inner atrium (go down the escalators on the Via Marsala side).

For something more substantial, try the Terrazza Termini food
court near track 15 (good, clean WCs), or the Mercato Centrale
food counters near track 24 (see listings on pages 946 and 947).

**Services:** In the hall along Via Giovanni Giolitti, on the
southwest side of the station (near track 24), you'll find the TI
(daily 8:00-18:45), a travel agency, a car-rental desk, a medical
center, and baggage storage (*deposito bagagli;* paying €12 daily rate
rather than hourly allows you to skip the line; daily 6:00-23:00).
The Leonardo Express train to Fiumicino Airport runs from track
23 or 24 on this side of the station (see page 953).

In the hall along Via Marsala, on the northeast side of the station (near track 1), you'll find a pharmacy. Pay WCs are down the

escalators from the inner atrium and inside the Mercato Centrale (near track 24).

The station has some sleazy sharks with official-looking business cards; avoid anybody selling anything unless they're in a legitimate shop at the station. Other shady characters linger around the ticket machines—offers to help usually come with the expectation of a "tip." There are no official porters; if someone wants to carry your bags or help you find your platform, they are simply angling for some cash.

**Getting Between Termini and Rome Hotels:** From Termini, many of my recommended hotels are easily accessible by foot or by Metro (for those in the Colosseum and Vatican neighborhoods). The Termini Metro station, where Metro lines A and B intersect, is beneath the station. City buses leave from the square directly in front of the outer atrium. Buses to the airport leave from the streets on both sides of the station. Taxis queue in front and outside exits on both the north and south sides; if there's a long taxi line in front, try a side exit instead. Avoid con men hawking "express taxi" services in unmarked cars (only use official white taxis with the maroon *Roma Capitale* logo).

## By Train or Bus at Tiburtina Station

Tiburtina, Rome's second-largest train station (www.stazioneromatiburtina.it), sits next to the Tiburtina Metro station in the city's northeast corner, and across the road from Rome's bus station. It's a pass-through station: Fast trains along the Milan-Naples line stop here and continue on quickly. A few of these fast trains now stop only at Tiburtina, but most stop at both Tiburtina and Termini. Use the station that's most convenient for you.

**Getting Between Tiburtina and Downtown Rome:** Tiburtina is on Metro line B, four stops from Termini. Note that when going to Tiburtina, Metro line B splits—you want a train signed *Rebibbia*, not *Jonio*. Bus #492 runs conveniently between Tiburtina, several city-center stops (including Piazza Barberini, Piazza Venezia, and Piazza Navona), and the Vatican neighborhood (as you emerge from the train station's front door, the city bus stop is just to the left).

## By Car

A car is a worthless headache in Rome. If you're visiting Rome as part of a longer trip, avoid a pile of stress and save money by parking at the huge, easy, free, and relatively safe lot behind the train station in the hill town of Orvieto (follow *P* signs from the autostrada) and catching a cheap *regionale* train to Rome (every 1-2 hours, 1.5 hours).

Or, if Rome is the first stop of your trip and you plan to rent

ROME

a car for the rest of Italy, you could sightsee Rome, then take the train to Orvieto and rent a car there (Hertz has an office down the street from the train station). If you absolutely must drive and park a car in Rome, there's a large underground garage at the Villa Borghese Gardens near the Spagna Metro station, just outside the restricted downtown zone (€18/day, Viale del Galoppatoio 33, www. sabait.it).

Alternatively, use one of the more than two dozen park-and-ride lots at Rome's outlying Metro stations (€5/24 hours). These vary in size and convenience; one of the largest is at the Anagnina Metro station, just inside Rome's ring expressway along the Via Tuscolana (southeast of downtown). For details, search for "park and ride" *(parcheggi di scambio)* at www.atac.roma.it.

## By Plane or Cruise Ship

For information on Rome's airports and Civitavecchia's cruise ship terminal, see the end of this chapter.

## HELPFUL HINTS

**Sightseeing Tips:** Despite the huge crowds inundating Rome, you'll only find lines a problem at **St. Peter's Basilica** (go early or late to minimize), **Vatican Museums** (easy to avoid by booking in advance online), the **Colosseum** (book online and go early morning or late afternoon), and the exquisite **Borghese Gallery** (requires a ticket with timed entry purchased in advance).

Even with a reservation, these sights can be very crowded. If that's not for you, remember that Rome has many historical treasures, such as the **Capitoline Museums** and the **Baths of Caracalla,** with no crowds at all.

The **Roma Pass** is only worthwhile if you want a public transit pass (covers 2 or 3 days of transit, entry to 2 sights, and discounts at others—but you'll still need a Colosseum reservation).

**Closed Days:** If you're in Rome on a Sunday, note that the **Vatican Museums** are closed (except for last Sun of the month, when it's free and even more crowded). The **Borghese Gallery** is closed on Mondays, and **St. Peter's Basilica** may be closed on Wednesday mornings for a papal audience.

**Bookstores:** It's easy to find stores selling English-language books (open daily unless noted otherwise). There are two large chains: **Bòrri Books** at Termini Station, and **Feltrinelli International,** with a large English section, just off Piazza della Repubblica at Via Vittorio Emanuele Orlando 86 (see map on page 902, tel. 06-487-0171). A few small, independent bookstores have a more personal touch: The **Anglo-American**

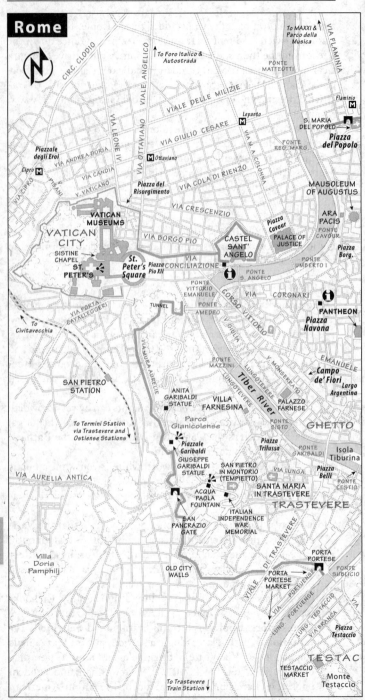

# Rome

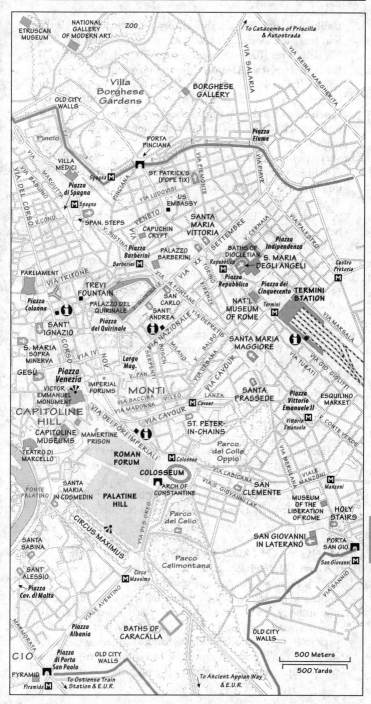

**Bookshop** has great art and history sections (closed all day Sun and Mon morning, a few blocks south of Spanish Steps at Via della Vite 102—see map on page 832, tel. 06-679-5222). In Trastevere, the **Almost Corner Bookshop** stocks an extensive Italian-interest section (Via del Moro 45—see map on page 927, tel. 06-583-6942, Dermot from Ireland), and the **Open Door Bookshop** carries the only used books in English in town (closed Sun, Via della Lungaretta 23—see map on page 927, tel. 06-589-6478).

**Laundry:** Coin launderettes are common in Rome. Your hotelier can direct you to the closest one. The **Wash & Dry Lavarapido** chain has a branch near Piazza Barberini (Mon-Sat 9:00-21:00, closed Sun, Via degli Avignonesi 17—see map on page 922, tel. 06-4201-3158). The Funny Palace Hostel's **Splashnet,** two blocks from Termini, offers full-service laundry for about the same price (see page 922).

**Travel Agencies:** Instead of making a trip to a train station or purchasing online, you can get train tickets and rail pass-related reservations and supplements at travel agencies (at little or no additional cost). Your hotelier will know of a convenient agency.

**Best Views:** You have good choices: From the rooftop of the Victor Emmanuel Monument (take the Rome from the Sky elevator to the top); from the top of the dome of St. Peter's Basilica; and from the top of Castel Sant'Angelo. One of the best views of the Roman Forum is from the Farnese Gardens viewpoint on Palatine Hill. Another is on Capitoline Hill—from two free overlooks plus the Tabularium (underground galleries) that is part of the Capitoline Museums.

**Best Hangouts:** The city's most atmospheric squares are Campo de' Fiori and Piazza Navona, interesting day and night. For monuments, it's the Trevi Fountain. The Monti neighborhood, near the Roman Forum, is a popular gathering spot in the evening (particularly Piazza della Madonna dei Monti) and a delight to explore any time of day.

## DEALING WITH (AND AVOIDING) PROBLEMS

**Theft Alert:** While violent crime is rare in the city center, petty theft is rampant. Always use your money belt. If you carry a backpack, never leave it unattended and try to keep it attached to your body in some way (even when you're seated for a meal).

Be particularly on guard in crowds and wear your daypack in front, especially when boarding and leaving buses and subways. You'll find less crowding and commotion—and less risk—waiting for the end cars of a subway rather than the middle cars. Thieves are particularly thick on the Metro and the crowded and made-for-tourists buses #40 and #64.

Thieves strike when you're distracted. Don't trust kind strangers or be deceived by appearance: Sneaky thieves may pose as businessmen or tourists, moms with babies, or gangs of children.

Scams abound: Always be clear about what paper money you're giving someone, demand clear and itemized bills, and count your change. Don't give your wallet to self-proclaimed "police" who stop you on the street, warn you about counterfeit (or drug) money, and ask to see your cash.

**Reporting Losses:** To report lost or stolen items, file a police report (at Termini Station, with *polizia* at track 11 or with Carabinieri at track 20; offices are also at Piazza Venezia and at the corner of Via Nazionale and Via Genova). For information on how to replace a passport or report lost or stolen credit cards, see page 1144.

**Pedestrian Safety:** Your main safety concern in Rome is crossing streets without incident. Use caution. Some streets have pedestrian-crossing signals (red means stop—or jaywalk carefully; green means go...also carefully; and yellow means go... extremely carefully, as cars may be whipping around the corner). But just as often, multilane streets have crosswalks with no signals at all. And even when there are traffic lights, they are provisional: Scooters don't need to stop at red lights, and even cars exercise what drivers call the "logical option" of not stopping if they see no oncoming traffic.

Follow locals like a shadow when you cross a street (or spend a good part of your visit stranded on curbs). When you do cross alone, find a gap in the traffic and walk with confidence while making eye contact with approaching drivers— they won't hit you if they can tell where you intend to go.

**Staying/Getting Healthy:** The siesta is a key to survival in summertime Rome. Lie down and contemplate the extraordinary power of gravity in the Eternal City. I drink lots of cold, refreshing water from Rome's many drinking fountains (the Forum has three) which are handy for refilling your bottle and staying hydrated.

Every neighborhood has a **pharmacy** (marked by a green cross). The 24-hour Farmacia Piram is several blocks down from Piazza della Repubblica at Via Nazionale 228 (tel. 06-488-4437). Pharmacies stay open late in Termini Station (daily 7:30-22:00, along northeast side of station, enter from Via Marsala), at Piazza dei Cinquecento 51 (Mon-Fri 7:00-23:30, Sat-Sun 8:00-23:00, next to Termini Station on the corner of Via Cavour—see map on page 902, tel. 06-488-0019), and in

ROME

# Rome Sightseeing Tips

Rome is doing its best to cope with an ever-increasing number of visitors, but especially in peak season you'll encounter lines, crowds, and exasperating changes to ticketing and tour procedures. These tips will help you use your time and money efficiently, making the Eternal City seem less eternal and more entertaining.

**Skipping the Colosseum:** While it sounds like a sacrilege, a visit to the interior of the Colosseum may not be worth suffering through the mob scene. Half the thrill of the Colosseum is seeing it from outside (free and easy at any time).

**Advance Tickets and Reservations:** You should buy tickets online to avoid long lines at the Vatican Museums, Colosseum, and Roman Forum. The Borghese Gallery requires reservations in advance (for specifics, see the individual listings for these sights).

**Forum/Palatine Hill:** These two sights share an admission ticket. You must see them to-gether on a single visit (don't exit the Forum and try to reenter at Palatine Hill).

**Roma Pass:** Until recently, this pass was an exciting option for tourists, as it let you go directly into the Colosseum. As that's no longer the case, the Roma Pass is little more than a glorified two- or three-day transit pass that includes entrance to two sights and discounts to others.

**Avoiding Crowds:** Can't get reservations to the main sights (or you just can't stand crowds)? Keep in mind that Rome has many magnificent attractions without the hordes. Try the Palatine Hill, Baths of Caracalla, National Museum of Rome, or Capitoline

the Pantheon neighborhood (Farmacia Senato, between Piazza Navona and the Pantheon, Mon-Fri 7:30-24:30, Sat from 8:30, Sun 12:00-23:00, Corso del Rinascimento 50—see map on page 936).

Embassies and hotels can recommend English-speaking **doctors.** Consider MEDline, a 24-hour private home-medical service; doctors speak English and make calls at hotels for about €150 (tel. 06-808-0995, www.soccorso-medico.com). Another private clinic is International Medical Services, Via Firenze 47, tel. 06-488-2371. Anyone is entitled to emergency treatment at public hospitals. The hospital closest to Termini Station is Policlinico Umberto I (entrance for emergency treatment on Via Lancisi, translators available, Metro: Policlinico).

Museums. Even in peak season, you'll often be all alone with the wonders of ancient world, wondering, "Where is everyone?"

**Opening Hours:** Rome's sights have notoriously variable hours from season to season. It's smart to check each sight's website in advance. On holidays, expect shorter hours or closures.

**Churches:** Many churches, which have divine art and free entry, open early (around 7:00-7:30), close for lunch (roughly 12:00-15:30), and close late (about 19:00). Kamikaze tourists maximize their sightseeing hours by visiting churches before 9:00 or late in the day; during the siesta, they see major sights that stay open all day (St. Peter's, Colosseum, Forum, Capitoline Museums, Pantheon, and National Museum of Rome). Dress modestly for churches.

**Picnic Discreetly:** Public drinking and eating is not allowed at major sights, though the ban has proven difficult to enforce. To avoid the small risk of a fine, choose an empty piazza for your picnic, or keep a low profile as you munch discreetly.

**Morning Magic:** When I want to reconnect with the city, I walk through the historical center before Rome wakes up. In the early morning, I've never met more than six people at the Trevi Fountain, and Rome shows its calm, majestic face. It's a great way to get energized for the day ahead.

**Miscellaneous Tips:** I carry a water bottle and refill it at Rome's many public drinking spouts. Because public restrooms are scarce, use WCs at museums, restaurants, and bars.

## GETTING AROUND ROME

You can see a lot of Rome on foot, and I've grouped your sightseeing into walkable neighborhoods. Make it a point to visit sights in a logical order. Needless backtracking wastes precious time.

To connect sights beyond walking distance, you can ride the Metro or a city bus, or take a taxi. As Rome is a great taxi town (most rides cost €7-12), especially for couples and families, I'd rely more on taxis than public transit.

## Public Transportation

Rome's public transportation system is cheap and efficient, but also confusing and crowded. The three Metro lines are relatively sane and straightforward, but serve a limited area. Buses are more chaotic—there are no posted timetables or maps, and stop names are announced only in the newest vehicles. But they run frequently and go everywhere. If you're in town for more than a day or two, mastering a couple key bus routes serving your neighborhood is worth the effort and will make you feel like a Rome pro.

The website www.atac.roma.it has a **journey planner** in English that will help you sort through the thicket of routes, as well as downloadable network maps. If you have a smartphone and an international data plan, consider downloading the free apps "Moov-it" (by ATAC), "Roma Bus" (by Movenda), or "Muoversi a Roma."

There's no official paper map of the system, but Edizioni Lozzi produces a frequently updated "Roma Metro Bus" map (at bookstores), which includes a booklet with details on all bus routes. For information by phone, call ATAC at 06-57003.

### Buying Tickets

All public transportation uses the same ticket. It costs €1.50 and is valid for one Metro ride—including transfers underground—plus unlimited city buses and trams during a 100-minute period. Passes good on buses and the Metro are sold in increments of 24 hours (€7), 48 hours (€12.50), 72 hours (€18), one week (€24—about the cost of three taxi rides), and one month (€35, valid for a calendar month).

You can purchase tickets and passes from machines at Metro stations and a few major bus stops (cash/coins only), and from some newsstands and tobacco shops (*tabacchi*, marked by a black-and-white *T* sign). Tickets are not sold on board. It's smart to stock up on tickets early—that way you don't have to run around searching for an open tobacco shop when you spot your bus approaching.

Validate your ticket by sticking it in the Metro turnstile (magnetic strip-side up, arrow-side first) or in the machine when you board the bus (magnetic strip-side down, arrow-side first)—watch others and imitate. It'll return your ticket with your expiration time printed. To get through a Metro turnstile with a transit pass, press the card to the turnstile's electronic sensor pad. On buses and trams, you need to validate your pass only your first time using it.

If you need help from a real person, ATAC runs a small ticket office at Termini Station. Follow signs for *Metro Linea B*, then *ATAC ticket office* (Mon-Sat 7:00-20:00, Sun 8:00-20:00).

ROME

### By Metro

The Roman subway system (Metropolitana, or "Metro") is simple, clean, cheap, and fast. The two lines you need to know—A and B—intersect at Termini Station. Line A serves the Vatican area, Piazza del Popolo, Spanish Steps/ Villa Borghese, Baths of Diocletian, Termini Station, and San Giovanni in Laterano. Line B connects the Tiburtina train and bus stations with Termini,  the Colosseum and Forum/Palatine Hill, Testaccio, and EUR. The Metro runs from 5:30 to 23:30 (Fri-Sat until 1:30 in the morning). The subway's first and last compartments are generally the least crowded, and the least likely to harbor pickpockets.

### By Bus

The Metro is handy, but it won't get you everywhere—you often have to take the bus (or tram). Bus routes are listed at each stop.

Route and system maps aren't posted, but with some knowledge of major stops, you can wing it without one. (The ATAC website has a PDF bus map that you can download, bookstores sell paper transport maps, and the ATAC journey planner is helpful.) Rome's few tram lines function for all intents and purposes identically to buses.

Buses—especially the touristy #40 and #64—are havens for thieves and pickpockets. These two lines in particular can be nose-to-armpit crowded during peak times...and while you're sniffing that guy's pit, his other hand could be busily rifling through your pockets. Assume any commotion is a thief-created distraction. If one bus is packed, there's likely a second one on its tail with far fewer crowds and thieves. Or read the signs posted at stops to see if a different, less crowded bus route can get you to or near your destination.

On buses, tickets must be inserted in the yellow box with the digital readout (magnetic strip-side down, arrow-side first; be sure to retrieve your ticket after it's spit out). Do this as you board, otherwise you're cheating. Inspectors fine even innocent-looking tourists €50. You don't need to validate a transit pass on

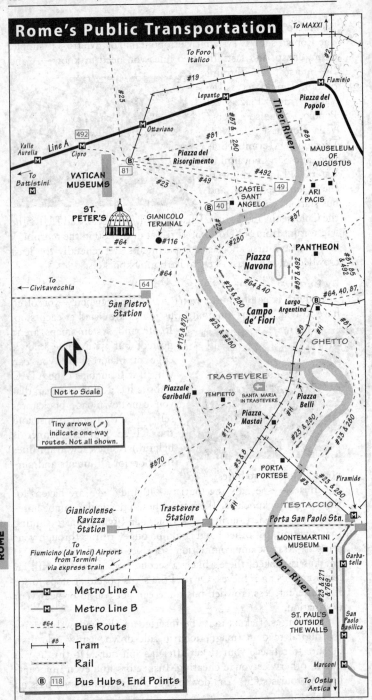

# Rome's Public Transportation

To MAXXI ↑

To Foro Italico

#19

#25

Lepanto M

To #2

Flaminio M

Piazza del Popolo

Tiber River

Valle Aurelia M

Line A 492

Ottaviano

Cipro M

#81

#87 & 280

#81

To Battistini M

VATICAN MUSEUMS

B 81

Piazza del Risorgimento

#23

#49

#492

49

MAUSEUM OF AUGUSTUS

ARA PACIS

ST. PETER'S

#64

GIANICOLO TERMINAL

●#116

CASTEL SANT' ANGELO

B 40

#23

#280

#87

PANTHEON

#81, 85 & 492

Piazza Navona

#64 & 40

#87 & 492

To ← Civitavecchia

64

#64

San Pietro Station

#115 & 870

#23 & #280

#23 & 280

Campo de' Fiori

Largo Argentina

B #64, 40, 87

#8

#H

#81

GHETTO

TRASTEVERE

Not to Scale

Tiny arrows (↗) indicate one-way routes. Not all shown.

Piazzale Garibaldi

TEMPIETTO

SANTA MARIA IN TRASTEVERE

#H

Piazza Belli

Piazza Mastai

#115

#23 & 280

#23 & 280

#5 & 8

#870

PORTA PORTESE

#5

#23 & 280

Piramide

Gianicolense-Ravizza Station

Trastevere Station

#H

Porta San Paolo Stn.

TESTACCIO

M

To Fiumicino (da Vinci) Airport from Termini via express train

MONTEMARTINI MUSEUM

Tiber River

Garbatella

#23 & 271 & 160

ST. PAUL'S OUTSIDE THE WALLS

San Paolo Basilica M

Marconi M

To Ostia Antica ↓

## Legend

| | |
|---|---|
| M — | Metro Line A |
| M ⋯ | Metro Line B |
| #64 – – – | Bus Route |
| #8 ⊢⊢⊢ | Tram |
| ⋯⋯⋯ | Rail |
| Ⓑ 118 | Bus Hubs, End Points |

ROME

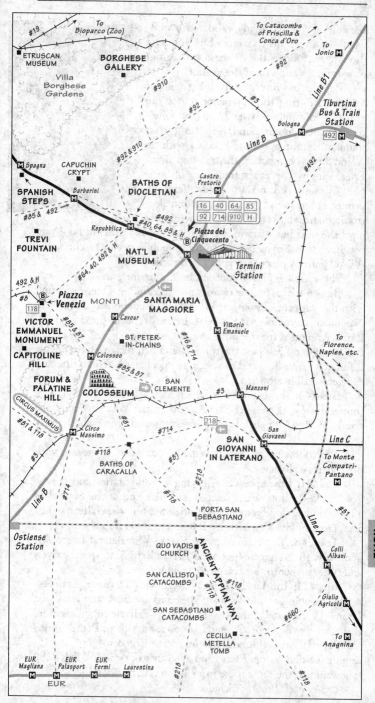

**ROME**

the bus if you've already validated it else-where in the transit system. Bus etiquette (not always followed) is to board at the front or rear doors and exit at the middle.

Regular bus lines start running at about 5:30, and during the day major routes run every 10-15 minutes. After 23:30 (and some-times earlier) and on Sundays, buses are less frequent. Night buses are marked with an *N* and an owl symbol on the bus-stop signs. Frustratingly, the exact frequency of vari-ous bus routes is difficult to predict (and not printed at bus stops). At major stops, an elec-tronic board shows the number of minutes until the next buses arrive, but at most stops to find out how long you have to wait you'll need to use a mobile device to check the ATAC journey planner or apps listed earlier.

These are the most important bus routes for tourists:

**Bus #64:** This bus cuts across the city, linking Termini Station with the Vatican, stopping at Piazza della Repubblica (sights), Via Nazionale (recommended hotels), Piazza Venezia (near Forum), Largo Argentina (near Pantheon and Campo de' Fiori), St. Peter's Basilica (get off just past the tunnel), and San Pietro Station. Ride it for a city overview and to watch pickpockets in action. The #64 can get horribly crowded.

**Bus #40:** This express bus, which mostly follows the #64 route (but ends near the Castel Sant'Angelo on the Vatican side of the river), is especially helpful—fewer stops and (somewhat) fewer crowds.

The following routes conveniently connect Trastevere with other parts of Rome:

**Bus #H:** This express bus, linking Termini Station and Traste-vere, makes a stop near Piazza Repubblica and at the bottom of Via Nazionale (for Trastevere, get off at Sonnino/S. Gallicano, just after crossing the Tiber River). It doesn't run on Sundays.

**Tram #8:** This tram connects Piazza Venezia and Largo Ar-gentina with Trastevere (get off at Piazza Belli, just over the river) and runs further to the Trastevere train station.

**Bus #23:** This bus links the Vatican with Trastevere and Tes-taccio, stopping at the Vatican Museums (nearest stop is on Via Leone IV), Castel Sant'Angelo (Sforza Pallavicini), Trastevere (Lungotevere de Cenci/Arenula, on opposite side of Ponte Garib-aldi), Porta Portese (Sunday flea market at Emporio stop), and Pi-ramide (Ostiense stop; Metro and gateway to Testaccio). **Bus #280** follows much the same route from Trastevere to Piramide.

Other useful routes include:

ROME

**Bus #49:** Piazza Cavour/Castel Sant'Angelo, Piazza Risorgimento (Vatican), and Vatican Museums.

**Bus #81:** San Giovanni in Laterano, Largo Argentina, and Piazza Risorgimento (Vatican).

**Buses #85 and #87:** Piazza Navona (#87 only), Pantheon, Via del Corso (#85 only), Piazza Venezia, Forum, Colosseum, San Clemente, and San Giovanni in Laterano.

**Bus #492:** Travels east-west across the city, connecting Tiburtina (train and bus stations), Largo Santa Susanna (near Piazza della Repubblica), Piazza Barberini, Piazza Venezia, Largo Argentina (near Pantheon and Campo de' Fiori), Piazza Cavour (Castel Sant'Angelo), and Piazza Risorgimento (St. Peter's Basilica and Vatican).

**Tram #3:** Zips from the Colosseum to San Giovanni in Laterano (and onward to Valle Giulia) in one direction, and to Piramide/Testaccio (and onward to Trastevere, though a 15-minute walk from the touristic heart) in the other.

## By Taxi

I use taxis in Rome more often than in other cities. They're reasonable and useful for efficient sightseeing in this big, hot metropolis.

Three or four companions with more money than time should taxi almost everywhere. Taxis start at €3, then charge about €1.50 per kilometer (surcharges: €1.50 on Sun, €3.50 for nighttime hours of 22:00-6:00, one regular suitcase or bag rides free, tip by rounding up—€1 or so). Sample fares: Termini area to Vatican—€15; Termini area to Colosseum—€7; Termini area to the Borghese Gallery—€9; Colosseum to Trastevere—€12 (or look up your route at www.worldtaximeter.com).

**Calling a Cab:** You can always just hail a cab on the street. But Romans generally walk to the nearest taxi stand (many are marked on this book's maps) or ask a passerby or a clerk in a shop, *"Dov'è una fermata dei taxi?"* (doh-VEH OO-nah fehr-MAH-tah DEH-ee TAHK-see). Easiest of all, have your hotel or restaurant call a taxi for you. (It's routine for Romans to ask the restaurant to call a taxi when they're ready to go.) The meter starts when the call is received. To call a cab on your own, dial 06-3570, 06-4994, or 06-6645, or use the official city taxi line, 06-0609; they'll likely ask you for an Italian phone number (give them your mobile number or your hotel's).

You can also use the Free Now app, which orders an official white taxi at regular taxi rates, with the convenience of paying via the app.

**Avoid Scams:** Beware of corrupt taxis. First, only use official Rome taxis. They're white, with a taxi sign on the roof and a maroon logo on the door that reads *Roma Capitale.*

When you get in, make sure the meter *(tassametro)* is turned on (you'll see the meter either on the dashboard or up by the rearview mirror). If the meter isn't on, get out and find another cab. Check that the meter is reset to the basic drop charge (should be around €3, or around €5 if you phoned for the taxi). You'll rarely pay more than €12 for a ride in town. Keep an eye on the fare on the meter as you near your destination; some cabbies turn the meter off instantly when they stop and tell you a higher price.

By law, every cab must display a multilingual official price chart—usually on the back of the seat in front of you. If the fare doesn't seem right, point to the chart and ask the cabbie to explain it.

At the train station or airport, avoid hustlers conning naive visitors into unmarked, rip-off "express taxis" (for tips on taking a taxi from the airport, see page 954). If you encounter any problems with a taxi, making a show of writing down the taxi number (to file a complaint) can motivate a driver to quickly settle the matter.

**Taxi Alternative:** Uber works in Rome as it does in the US, but only at the more expensive Uber Black level.

## Tours in Rome

🎧 To sightsee on your own, download my free audio tours, including my Heart of Rome, Jewish Ghetto, and Trastevere neighborhood walks, and my tours of the Pantheon, Colosseum, Roman Forum, St. Peter's Basilica, Vatican Museums, and Sistine Chapel (see sidebar on page 26 for details).

### ON FOOT

You can either hire a local to serve as your personal guide, or sign up for a group tour with a tour company, joining up to 50 fellow travelers. Private guides are good but pricey (around €180 for a three-hour tour). Tour companies are cheaper (€30/person), but quality and organization are unreliable. If you do hire a private Italian guide, consider inviting others from your hotel to join you and split the cost. This ends up costing about the same per person as going on a scheduled tour from one of the walking-tour companies listed next—and you'll likely get a better guide.

## Local Guides

I've worked with and enjoyed each of these licensed independent local guides. They're native Italians, speak excellent English, and enjoy tailoring tours to your interests. Prices (roughly €60/hour) flex with the day, season, and demand. Arrange your date and price by email. **Carla Zaia** (carlaromeguide@gmail.com); **Cristina Giannicchi** (mobile 338-111-4573, www.crisromanguide.com, crisgiannicchi@gmail.com); **Sara Magister** (a.magister@iol.it); **Giovanna Terzulli** (gioterzulli@gmail.com); **Alessandra Mazzoccoli** (www.romeandabout.com, alemazzoccoli@gmail.com); and **Massimiliano Canneto** (a Catholic guide with a Vatican forte, but does all of Rome, massicanneto@gmail.com).

**Francesca Caruso,** who works almost full time with my tours when in Rome, has contributed generously to this book (www.francescacaruso.com, francescainroma@gmail.com); she offers private tours for €300/half-day. Popular with my readers, Francesca understandably books up quickly; if she's busy, she'll recommend one of her colleagues (at the standard €60/hour listed for guides above). At her website you can listen to the many interviews I've enjoyed with Francesca on my public radio program.

## Walking-Tour Companies

Rome has many highly competitive tour companies, each offering a series of themed walks through various slices of the city. Three-hour guided walks generally cost €25-30 per person. Guides are usually native English speakers, often American expats. Before your trip, spend some time on these companies' websites to get to know your options, as each company has a particular teaching and guiding personality. Some are highbrow and more expensive. Others are less scholarly. It's sometimes required, and always smart, to book a spot in advance (easy online).

These companies are each well-established, creative, and competitive. Each offers a 10 percent discount with most online bookings for Rick Steves travelers.

**Walks of Italy** (RS%—enter "RICKWALKSROME," US tel. 888/683-8670, tel. 06-9480-4888, www.walksofitaly.com).

**Europe Odyssey** (RS%, tel. 06-8854-2416, mobile 328-912-3720, www.europeodyssey.com, Rahul).

**Through Eternity** (RS%—look for "Group Tours Rome" and enter "RICKSTEVES," tel. 06-700-9336, www.througheternity.com, office@througheternity.com, Rob).

**The Roman Guy** (RS%—enter "ricksteves," ask about electric-assist bike tours, theromanguy.com, Sean Finelli).

**Miles & Miles Private Tours,** described under "Car & Minibus Tours," later, also offers walking tours (www.milesandmiles.net). They are a great value, especially if a car is used.

ROME

# Rome at a Glance

▲▲▲**Colosseum** Huge stadium where gladiators fought. **Hours:** Daily 8:30 until one hour before sunset: April-Aug until 19:15, Sept until 19:00, Oct until 18:30, off-season closes as early as 16:30. See page 845.

▲▲▲**Roman Forum** Ancient Rome's main square, with ruins and grand arches. **Hours:** Same as Colosseum. See page 851.

▲▲▲**Capitoline Museums** Ancient statues, mosaics, and expansive view of Forum. **Hours:** Daily 9:30-19:30. See page 864.

▲▲▲**Pantheon** The defining domed temple. **Hours:** Mon-Sat 8:30-19:30, Sun 9:00-18:00, holidays 9:00-13:00, closed for Mass Sat at 17:00 and Sun at 10:30. See page 873.

▲▲▲**St. Peter's Basilica** Most impressive church on earth, with Michelangelo's *Pietà* and dome. **Hours:** Church—daily April-Sept 7:00-19:00, Oct-March 7:00-18:30, often closed Wed mornings; dome—daily April-Sept 7:30-19:00, Oct-March 7:30-18:00. See page 878.

▲▲▲**Vatican Museums** Four miles of the finest art of Western civilization, culminating in Michelangelo's glorious Sistine Chapel. **Hours:** Mon-Sat 9:00-18:00. Closed on religious holidays and Sun, except last Sun of the month (open 9:00-14:00). Open Fri nights mid-April-Oct by online reservation only. See page 885.

▲▲▲**Borghese Gallery** Bernini sculptures and paintings by Caravaggio, Raphael, and Titian in a Baroque palazzo. Reservations mandatory. **Hours:** Tue-Sun 9:00-19:00, Thu until 21:00, closed Mon. See page 898.

▲▲▲**National Museum of Rome** Greatest collection of Roman sculpture anywhere. **Hours:** Tue-Sun 9:00-19:45, closed Mon. See page 903.

▲▲**Palatine Hill** Ruins of emperors' palaces, Circus Maximus view, and museum. **Hours:** Same as Colosseum. See page 861.

▲▲**Trajan's Column, Market, and Forum** Tall column with narrative relief, forum ruins, and museum with entry to Trajan's Market. **Hours:** Forum and column always viewable; museum open daily 9:30-19:30. See page 868.

▲▲**Museo dell'Ara Pacis** Shrine marking the beginning of Rome's Golden Age. **Hours:** Daily 9:30-19:30. See page 833.

---

▲▲**Dolce Vita Stroll** Evening *passeggiata* where Romans strut their stuff. **Hours:** Roughly Mon-Sat 17:00-19:00 and Sun afternoons. See page 831.

---

▲▲**Catacombs of Priscilla** Underground tomb just outside city walls. **Hours:** Tue-Sun 9:00-12:00 & 14:00-17:00, closed Mon, closed one random month a year. See page 901.

---

▲**Mamertine Prison** Ancient prison where Saints Peter and Paul were held. **Hours:** Same as Colosseum. See page 866.

---

▲**Arch of Constantine** Honors the emperor who legalized Christianity. **Hours:** Always viewable. See page 850.

---

▲**The Roman House at Palazzo Valentini** Remains of an ancient house and bath. **Hours:** Wed-Mon 9:30-18:30, closed Tue. See page 871.

---

▲**St. Peter-in-Chains** Church with Michelangelo's *Moses*. **Hours:** Daily 8:00-12:30 & 15:00-19:00, Oct-March until 18:00. See page 871.

---

▲**Piazza del Campidoglio** Square atop Capitoline Hill, designed by Michelangelo, with a museum, grand stairway, and Forum overlooks. **Hours:** Always open. See page 863.

---

▲**Victor Emmanuel Monument** Gigantic edifice celebrating Italian unity, with Rome from the Sky elevator ride up to 360-degree city view. **Hours:** Monument open daily 9:30-18:45 (shorter in winter), elevator until 19:00. See page 867.

---

▲**Trevi Fountain** Baroque hot spot into which tourists throw coins to ensure a return trip to Rome. **Hours:** Always flowing. See page 875.

---

▲**Castel Sant'Angelo** Hadrian's Tomb turned castle, prison, papal refuge, now museum. **Hours:** Daily 9:00-19:30. See page 895.

---

▲**Baths of Diocletian/Basilica S. Maria degli Angeli** Once ancient Rome's immense public baths, now a Michelangelo church. **Hours:** Daily 7:30-18:30, closes later May-Sept and Sun year-round. See page 905.

**ROME**

**Tom Rankin,** an American architect, offers thought-provoking architectural walks and educational tours around Italy. They're not cheap, but the small-group seminars are worth it to some for the authentic engagement in local culture (RS%, half-day: €100/person or €400/group, info@tomrankinarchitect.com, www.tomrankinarchitect.com).

## Car and Minibus Tours

**Miles & Miles Private Tours** offers tours with good English-speaking Italian driver/guides and fine air-conditioned cars and minibuses. Their basic line-up for groups of up to eight people includes a five-hour "History and Fun" tour (a fine first day by car with a broad overview and a chance to get out when you like, €350), "Squares and Fountains" (three-hour walking tour starting at Piazza Farnese, €250) and day trips from Rome into Umbria including Civita di Bagnoregio (9 hours with hotel pickup, €600). They also provide walking tours, shore excursions (from Civitavecchia and other ports), and unguided long-distance transportation; if traveling with a small group or a family from Rome to Florence, the Amalfi Coast, or elsewhere, consider paying extra for this convenience (RS%—mention Rick Steves when booking direct, then show this book; mobile 331-466-4900, www.milesandmiles.net, info@milesandmiles.net).

## ON WHEELS
### Hop-On, Hop-Off Bus Tours

Several different agencies run hop-on, hop-off, double-decker bus tours around Rome. These tours make the same 90-minute, eight-stop loop through the traffic-congested town center with about four pickups at each stop per hour. Buses provide an easy way to see the city from above the traffic (choose open or with canopy), but you'll likely feel trapped rather than entertained. The lazy recorded narration does little more than identify the

sightseeing icons you drive by and misses the opportunity to fill the time with worthwhile information. You can join one (and pay as you board; usually around €20) at any stop; Termini Station and Piazza Venezia are handy hubs.

## Car and Driver Service

**Autoservizi Monti Concezio,** run by gentle, capable, and English-speaking Ezio (pronounced Etz-io), offers private cars or minibuses with driver/guides (car—€40/hour, minibus—€45/hour, 3-hour minimum for city sightseeing, transfers between cities are more expensive, mobile 335-636-5907 or 349-674-5643, info@tourservicemonti.it).

# Walks in Rome

Take a refreshing early evening walk (Dolce Vita Stroll) and enjoy the thriving local scene, best at night (Heart of Rome Walk).

## DOLCE VITA STROLL

All over the Mediterranean world, people are out strolling in the early evening in a ritual known in Italy as the *passeggiata*, worth ▲▲ (see the sidebar on page 908). Rome's *passeggiata* is both elegant (with chic people enjoying fancy window shopping in the grid of streets around the Spanish Steps) and a little crude (with young people on the prowl). The major sights along this walk are covered later in this section.

Romans' favorite place for a chic evening stroll is along Via del Corso. Join in as you walk from Piazza del Popolo (Metro: Flaminio) down a wonderfully traffic-free section of Via del Corso, and up Via Condotti to the Spanish Steps. Historians can continue to Capitoline Hill. Although busy at any hour, this area really attracts crowds from around 17:00 to 19:00 each evening (Fri and Sat are best), except on Sunday, when it occurs earlier in the afternoon. Leave before 18:00 if you plan to visit the Ara Pacis (Altar of Peace), which closes at 19:30.

As you stroll, you'll see shoppers, flirts, and people-watchers filling this neighborhood of some of Rome's most fashionable stores (mostly open until 20:00). The most elegance survives in the grid of streets between Via del Corso and the Spanish Steps. If you get hungry during your stroll, see page 944 for listings of neighborhood wine bars and restaurants.

❶ **Self-Guided Walk:** To reach **Piazza del Popolo,** where the stroll starts, take Metro line A to Flaminio and walk south to the square. Delightfully car-free, Piazza del Popolo is marked by an obelisk that was brought to Rome by Augustus after he conquered Egypt. (It used to stand in the Circus Maximus.) In medieval times, this area was just inside Rome's main entry.

If starting your stroll early enough, the Baroque church of **Santa Maria del Popolo** is worth popping into (next to gate in old wall on north side of square). Inside, look for Raphael's Chigi Chapel (second on left as you face the main altar) and two paintings by Caravaggio (in the Cerasi Chapel, left of altar).

From Piazza del Popolo, stroll down **Via del Corso.** While many Italians shop online or at the mall these days, and the el-

ROME

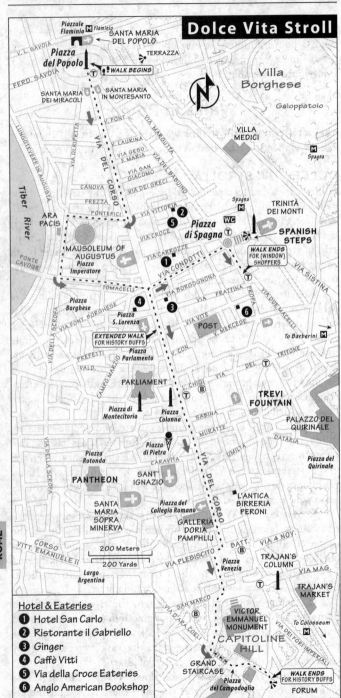

# Dolce Vita Stroll

Piazzale Flaminio — Flaminio
SANTA MARIA DEL POPOLO
Piazza del Popolo
TERRAZZA
WALK BEGINS
V. L. SAVOIA
FERD. SAVOIA
SANTA MARIA DEI MIRACOLI
SANTA MARIA IN MONTESANTO
Villa Borghese
Galoppatoio
VILLA MEDICI
Spagna
VIA DI RIPETTA
V. FONT.
V. LAURINA
VIA GESU E MARIA
VIA SAN GIACOMO
VIA DEL BABUINO
VIA MARGUTTA
VIA DEL CORSO
CANOVA
FREZZA
VIA DEI GRECI
PONTEFICI
VIA VITTORIA
Piazza di Spagna
Spagna
WC
TRINITÀ DEI MONTI
SPANISH STEPS
Tiber River
LUNGOTEVERE IN AUGUSTA
ARA PACIS
PONTE CAVOUR
MAUSOLEUM OF AUGUSTUS
Piazza Imperatore
VIA CROCE
VIA CARROZZE
VIA CONDOTTI
WALK ENDS FOR (WINDOW) SHOPPERS
VIA SISTINA
TOMACELLI
Piazza Borghese
VIA FONT. BORGHESE
Piazza S. Lorenza
VIA DELLA SCROFA
VIA BORGOGNONA
VIA FRATTINA
PROPA
VIA DUE MACELLI
VIA VITE
POST
V. MERCEDE
To Barberini
EXTENDED WALK FOR HISTORY BUFFS
Piazza Parlamento
PREFETTI
VALD.
CAMPO MARZIO
V. CON.
V. CHIGI
B
TRITONE
VIA DEL
T
PARLIAMENT
Piazza di Montecitorio
Piazza Colonna
SABINA
MURATTE
DATARIA
UMILTÀ
TREVI FOUNTAIN
PALAZZO DEL QUIRINALE
Piazza del Quirinale
Piazza Rotonda
Piazza di Pietra
CARAVITA
VIA DEL CORSO
PANTHEON
SANT' IGNAZIO
Piazza del Collegio Romano
SANTA MARIA SOPRA MINERVA
GALLERIA DORIA PAMPHILIJ
L'ANTICA BIRRERIA PERONI
BATT.
B
VIA 4 NOV.
VIA MAG.
TRAJAN'S COLUMN
TRAJAN'S MARKET
CORSO VITT. EMANUELE II
Largo Argentina
VIA PLEBISCITO
Piazza Venezia
VICTOR EMMANUEL MONUMENT
CAPITOLINE HILL
To Colosseum
VIA DEI FORI IMPERIALI
SAN MARCO
VIA D'ARA COELI
B
GRAND STAIRCASE
Piazza del Campidoglio
WALK ENDS FOR HISTORY BUFFS
FORUM
200 Meters
200 Yards

ROME

## Hotel & Eateries

1. Hotel San Carlo
2. Ristorante il Gabriello
3. Ginger
4. Caffè Vitti
5. Via della Croce Eateries
6. Anglo American Bookshop

egance of this street has been replaced by international chains targeting local teens, this remains a fine place to feel the pulse of Rome at twilight.

Historians can side-trip right down Via Pontefici past the fascist architecture to see the massive, round-brick **Mausoleum of Augustus,** topped with overgrown cypress trees. This long-neglected sight, honoring Rome's first emperor, is slated for restoration and redevelopment. Beyond it, next to the river, is the **Ara Pacis,** consecrated by Augustus in 9 BC and today enclosed within a protective glass-walled museum worth ▲▲ (€10.50, or look in through huge windows for free, daily 9:30-19:30). From the mausoleum, walk down Via Tomacelli to return to Via del Corso and the 21st century.

From Via del Corso, window shoppers should take a left down **Via Condotti** to join the parade to the **Spanish Steps** (described in more detail next, under "Heart of Rome Walk"), passing big-name boutiques. The streets that parallel Via Condotti to the south (Borgognona and Frattina) are also elegant and filled with high-end shops. A few streets to the north hides the narrow Via Margutta. This is where Gregory Peck's *Roman Holiday* character lived (at #51); today it has a leafy tranquility and is filled with pricey artisan and antique shops.

**History Buffs:** Another option is to ignore Via Condotti and forget the Spanish Steps. Stay on Via del Corso, which has been straight since Roman times, and walk a half-mile down to the Victor Emmanuel Monument. Climb Michelangelo's stairway to his glorious (especially when floodlit) square atop Capitoline Hill. Stand on the balcony (just past the mayor's palace on the right), which overlooks the Forum. As the horizon reddens and cats prowl the unclaimed rubble of ancient Rome, it's one of the finest views in the city.

## HEART OF ROME WALK

Rome's most colorful neighborhood features narrow lanes, intimate piazzas, fanciful fountains, and some of Europe's best people-watching. During the day, this walk—worth ▲▲▲—shows off the colorful Campo de' Fiori market and trendy fashion boutiques as it meanders past major monuments such as the Pantheon and the Spanish Steps.

But the sunset brings unexpected magic. A stroll in the cool of the evening is made memorable by the romance of the Eternal City at its best. Sit so close to a bubbling fountain that traffic noise evaporates. Jostle with kids to see the gelato flavors. Watch lovers straddling more than the bench. Jaywalk past *polizia* in bulletproof vests. And marvel at the ramshackle elegance that softens this brutal city for those who were born here and can't imagine

ROME

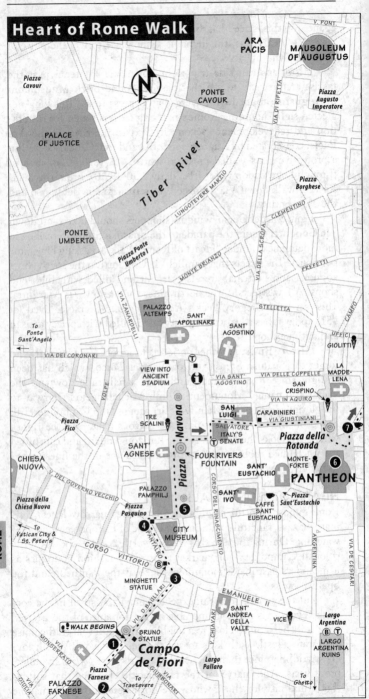

# Heart of Rome Walk

ARA PACIS

MAUSOLEUM OF AUGUSTUS

Piazza Cavour

V. PONT.

PONTE CAVOUR

V. DI RIPETTA

Piazza Augusto Imperatore

PALACE OF JUSTICE

Tiber River

Piazza Borghese

LUNGOTEVEKE MARZIO

PONTE UMBERTO

CLEMENTINO

Piazza Ponte Umberto I

MONTE BRIANZO

VIA DELLA SCROFA

PREFETTI

VIA ZANARDELLI

To Ponte Sant'Angelo

VIA DEI CORONARI

PALAZZO ALTEMPS

SANT' APOLLINARE

STELLETTA

CAMPO

UFFICI GIOLITTI

VOLPE

VIEW INTO ANCIENT STADIUM

SANT' AGOSTINO

VIA SANT' AGOSTINO

VIA DELLE COPPELLE

LA MADDE-LENA

Piazza Fico

TRE SCALINI

Piazza Navona

SAN LUIGI

CARABINIERI

VIA IN AQUIRO

SAN CRISPINO

CHIESA NUOVA

SANT' AGNESE

SALVATORE ITALY'S SENATE

VIA GIUSTINIANI

Piazza della Rotonda

7

Piazza della Chiesa Nuova

V. DEL GOVERNO VECCHIO

PALAZZO PAMPHILJ

FOUR RIVERS FOUNTAIN

SANT' EUSTACHIO

MONTE-FORTE

6

PANTHEON

Piazza Pasquino

SANT' IVO

CORSO DEL RINASCIMENTO

Piazza Sant'Eustachio

To Vatican City & St. Peter's

4

CITY MUSEUM

5

CAFFÈ SANT' EUSTACHIO

SANT' EUSTACHIO

ARGENTINA

VIA DE CESTARI

CORSO VITTORIO

PANTALEO

MINGHETTI STATUE

3

EMANUELE II

SANT' ANDREA DELLA VALLE

VICE

B T

Largo Argentina

WALK BEGINS

1

BRUNO STATUE

Campo de' Fiori

VIA D. BAULLARI

V. CHIAVARI

V. GIUBBONARI

LARGO ARGENTINA RUINS

MONSERRATO

Piazza Farnese

2

Largo Pallaro

To Ghetto

VIA GIULIA

PALAZZO FARNESE

To Trastevere

ROME

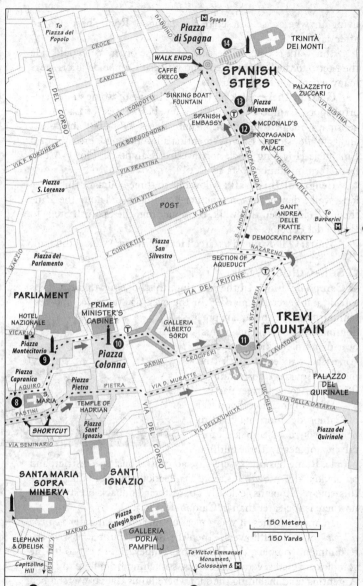

1. Campo de' Fiori
2. Piazza Farnese
3. Via dei Baullari to Corso Vittorio Emanuele II
4. Pasquino Statue
5. Piazza Navona
6. Pantheon
7. Caffè Tazza d'Oro
8. Piazza Capranica
9. Piazza di Montecitorio
10. Piazza Colonna & Via del Corso
11. Trevi Fountain
12. Palazzo di Propaganda Fide
13. Column of the Immaculate Conception
14. Spanish Steps

ROME

living anywhere else. These are the flavors of Rome, best enjoyed after dark.

This walk is equally pleasant in reverse order. You could ride the Metro to the Spanish Steps and finish at Campo de' Fiori, near many recommended restaurants.

**Getting There:** Kick off this walk in one of Rome's most colorful spots, Campo de' Fiori. It's a few blocks west of Largo Argentina, a major transportation hub. Buses #40, #64, and #492, and tram #8, stop at Largo Argentina and/or along Corso Vittorio Emanuele II (a long block northwest of Campo de' Fiori). A taxi from Termini station costs about €14.

**Length of This Walk:** Allow one to three hours for this mile-long walk, depending on whether you linger and tour the Pantheon. To lengthen this walk, continue from the Spanish Steps to Piazza del Popolo.

**Tours:** ∩ Download my free Heart of Rome Walk audio tour.

## ◑ Self-Guided Walk

**❶ Campo de' Fiori:** In the morning, this bohemian piazza hosts a fruit-and-vegetable market. In the evening, the cafés and res-

taurants that line the square pre-
dominate. On weekend nights,
beer-drinking kids (mostly
American students) pack the
medieval square, transforming it
into a vast Roman street party.

With the neighborhood feel
of Campo de' Fiori, it's hard to
believe you're in a major capital city of nearly three million

people. Rome has no skyscrapers, no central business district, and no obvious downtown. It's more a collection of urban villages, like this square. Romans jealously guard their laidback lifestyle, and nowhere is it clearer than in Campo de' Fiori.

In ancient times, it was a pleasant meadow—literally a *campo de' fiori*, or "field of flowers." Then the Romans built a massive entertainment complex, the Theater of Pompey, right next to it. The complex covered several city blocks, stretching from here to Largo Argentina (and including the spot where Julius Caesar was stabbed to death).

In medieval times, Christian pilgrims passed through the *campo* on their way to the Vatican, and a thriving market developed. As popes modernized the city in Renaissance and Baroque times, this square kept its local flavor.

Today's Romans live amid the eclectic heritage of their ancestors. For example, at the east end of the square (behind the statue of the heretic Bruno), see how the ramshackle apartments are built right into the older parts. Find the pinkish-beige brick building, midway up, and the two white columns incorporated into it. Those ancient columns were once part of that Theater of Pompey.

Lording over the center of the square is the statue of **Giordano Bruno,** an intellectual who was burned on this spot in 1600. The pedestal shows scenes from Bruno's trial and execution, and an inscription translates, "And the flames rose up." The statue, facing a Vatican administration building, was erected in 1889, a time when the new state of Italy and the Vatican were feuding. Vatican officials protested the heretic in their midst, but they were overruled by angry neighborhood locals. This district is still known for its free spirit and antiauthoritarian demonstrations.

The square is surrounded by fun eateries, and is great for people-watching. Bruno faces the bustling **Forno** (in the left corner of the square), where takeout *pizza bianca* is sold hot from the oven.

• *If Bruno did a hop, step, and jump forward, then turned left, in a block he'd reach...*

❷ **Piazza Farnese:** While the higgledy-piggledy Campo de' Fiori feels free and easy, the 16th-century Renaissance Piazza Farnese, named for the family whose palace dominates it, seems to stress order. The Farnese family was nouveau riche and needed to make a statement. They hired Michelangelo to help design their palace. He created the jutting roofline (the cornice), and made the window in the very center a little wider than the others. This gave the whole facade a pleasant symmetry and focused attention on the balcony, from where Farnese nobles gave speeches.

Note the flags over the entrance and the security presence. The palazzo now houses the French embassy.

The twin fountains decorating the square date from the third century and were made with repurposed stone tubs from the ancient Baths of Caracalla. Rome is famous for its fountains. In times past, they were functional, providing neighborhoods with a water supply. These particular fountains are fed by an ancient aqueduct, the Acqua Vergine. It's the same source that feeds the Trevi Fountain and others that we'll see along this walk. After 2,000 years, the aqueduct is still bringing the water of life into the city.

• *Walk back to Campo de' Fiori, cross the square, and continue a couple of blocks down...*

❸ **Via dei Baullari to Corso Vittorio Emanuele II:** As you slalom through the crowds, notice the crush of cheap cafés, bars, and restaurants—the center of medieval Rome is morphing into a playground for tourists, students, and locals visiting from the suburbs. High rents are driving families out and changing the character of this district. That's why the Campo de' Fiori market increasingly sells more gifty edibles than basic fruits and vegetables.

**ROME**

After a couple of blocks, you reach the busy boulevard, Corso Vittorio Emanuele II. In Rome, any road big enough to have city buses like this is post-unification: constructed after 1870. Look left and right down the street—the facades are mostly 19th-century neo-Renaissance, built after this main thoroughfare sliced through the city. Traffic in much of central Rome is limited to city buses, taxis, motorbikes, "dark cars" (limos and town cars of VIPs), delivery vans, residents, and disabled people with permits (a.k.a. friends of politicians). This is one of the increasingly rare streets where any vehicle is welcome.

• *Cross Corso Vittorio Emanuele II, and enter a square with a statue of Marco Minghetti, an early Italian prime minister. Angle left at the statue, walking along the left side of the skippable City Museum of Rome, down Via di San Pantaleo. A block down, at the corner, you'll find a beat-up old statue.*

❹ **Pasquino:** Pasquino—a third-century-BC statue that was discovered near here—is one of Rome's "talking statues." For 500 years, this statue has served as a kind of community billboard, allowing people to complain anonymously when it might be dangerous to speak up. And, to this day, you'll see old Pasquino strewn with political posters, strike announcements, and grumbling graffiti. The statue looks worn down by centuries of bitching.

• *Facing Pasquino, veer to the left and head up Via di Pasquino. You'll soon emerge into a place where all the layers of Rome are on display: ancient, medieval, Baroque, and contemporary.*

❺ **Piazza Navona:** This long, oblong square is dotted with fountains, busy with outdoor cafés, lined with palazzos and churches, and thronged with happy visitors. By its shape you might guess that this square started out as a racetrack, part of the training grounds built here by Emperor Domitian around AD 80. That was the same year the Colosseum opened: Rome was at its peak.

But much of what we see today came in the 1600s, when the whole place got a major renovation. At the time, the popes were trying to put some big scandals behind them, and beautification projects like this were a peace offering to the public.

Three Baroque fountains decorate the piazza. The first fountain, at the southern end, features a Moor wrestling with a dolphin. In 17th-century Rome, Moors (North Africans) represented all that was exotic and mysterious. In the fountain at the northern end, Neptune slays a giant octopus.

The most famous fountain, though, is in the center: the **Four Rivers Fountain** by Gian Lorenzo Bernini, the man who in the mid-1600s remade Rome in the Baroque style. It's topped with an Egyptian-style obelisk—another of the themes we'll see along this walk. Obelisks were popular with Roman emperors because Egyptian society saw its rulers as divine—an idea Roman rulers liked to promote.

Get close to admire Bernini's four enormous statues at the base. As the water of the world gushes everywhere, these four burly river gods represent the four quarters of the world.

Piazza Navona is Rome's most interesting night scene, with street music, artists, fire-eaters, local Casanovas, ice cream, and outdoor cafés that are worthy of a splurge if you've got time to sit and enjoy Italy's human river.

• *Leave Piazza Navona directly across from* **Tre Scalini** *(famous for its* tartufo, *a rich, chocolate gelato concoction), and go east down Corsia Agonale, past rose peddlers and palm readers. Ahead of you (across the busy street) stands the stately Palazzo Madama, where the* **Italian Senate** *meets. (Hence, security is high.) Jog left around this building, and follow the brown* Pantheon *sign straight down Via del Salvatore.*

*After a block, you'll pass (on your left) the* **Church of San Luigi dei Francesi,** *with its* très *French decor and precious Caravaggio paintings. If it's open, pop in. Otherwise, continue along, following the crowd to...*

❻ **The Pantheon:** Perhaps the most magnificent building surviving from ancient Rome is this temple to the "pantheon" (literally, all the gods).

The 40-foot, single-piece granite columns of the Pantheon's entrance show the scale the ancient Romans built on. The columns support a triangular Greek-style roof with an inscription that proclaims, "M. Agrippa built this." In fact, the present structure was built *(fecit)* by Emperor Hadrian (AD 120), who gave credit to the builder of an earlier temple. This impressive entranceway gives no clue that the greatest wonder of the build-

ing is inside—a domed room that inspired later domes, including Michelangelo's St. Peter's and Brunelleschi's Duomo in Florence.

If the Pantheon is open, pop in and take a look around (for details on the interior, see page 873). Afterward, consider detouring to several interesting churches nearby (see page 874). If the Pantheon is closed, just stand for a while under the portico, which is romantically floodlit and moonlit at night.

· *To continue this walk, with your back to the Pantheon, veer to the right, uphill toward the yellow sign on Via Orfani that reads* Casa del Caffè—*you've reached the...*

**❼ Caffè Tazza d'Oro:** This is one of Rome's top coffee shops, dating back to the days when this area was licensed to roast coffee beans. Locals come here for a shot of espresso or, when it's hot, a refreshing *granita di caffè con panna* (coffee and crushed ice with whipped cream).

· *From here, our walk continues past some interesting landmarks to the Trevi Fountain. To get there more directly, take a* **shortcut** *by bearing right at the coffee shop onto Via de' Pastini, which leads through Piazza di Pietra (with some surviving chunks of the Temple of Hadrian), then across busy Via del Corso, where it becomes the touristy, pedestrianized Via delle Muratte and heads straight for the fountain.*

*To stick with me for the slightly longer version, bear left at the coffee shop and continue up Via degli Orfani to the next square...*

**❽ Piazza Capranica:** This square is home to the big, plain Florentine-Renaissance-style Palazzo Capranica (directly opposite as you enter the square). Its stubby tower was once much taller, but when a stronger government arrived, the nobles were all ordered to shorten their towers. Like so many of Rome's churches, the church on the square—Santa Maria in Aquiro—is older than its Baroque-era facade. Notice the circular little shrine on the street corner (between the palace and the apartment building). For centuries, worshipful spots like this have made pilgrims (and, today, tourists) feel welcome.

· *Leave the piazza to the right of the palace, heading down Via in Aquiro. The street jogs to the left and into a square called...*

**❾ Piazza di Montecitorio:** This square, home to Italy's Parliament, is marked by an **Egyptian obelisk** from the sixth century BC. It adorned a temple in Egypt for half a millennium before Emperor Augustus brought it to Rome as a trophy proclaiming his victory over Mark Antony and Cleopatra. Made of red granite, the obelisk stands 70 feet tall—or well over 100 feet when you include the base.

In Augustus' day, the obelisk acted as a sundial and calendar, aligned to cast a shadow across the solarium altar on the emperor's birthday. Today, the obelisk still functions as a sundial. Follow the zodiac markings in the pavement to the square's next big sight—the **Italian Parliament.** This impressive building is where the legislature's lower chamber (the equivalent of the US House of Representatives) attempts to govern the nation.

• *One block to your right is Piazza Colonna, where we're heading next—unless you like gelato. A one-block detour to the left (past Hotel Nazionale) brings you to a famous Roman gelateria,* ***Giolitti.***

**❿ Piazza Colonna and Via del Corso:** The square features a massive **column** that has stood here since the second century AD.

The column's shaft is 12 feet across, almost 100 feet tall, and stands on a 30-foot base, which rests on a platform. It's a particularly imposing-looking column because it doesn't taper at the top. The whole thing is carved from the finest white marble in the world, from Carrara—the favorite quarry of the ancient Romans and of Michelangelo.

This isn't a single piece of marble. It's 28 cylindrical blocks stacked atop each other like a pile of 10-ton checkers. A carved frieze winds from the bottom to the top, telling the story of Emperor Marcus Aurelius heroically battling barbarians about AD 170.

Beyond Piazza Colonna runs noisy **Via del Corso,** Rome's main north-south boulevard. In ancient times, this was the Via Flaminia, the highway that stretched from the Roman Forum to the Adriatic coast. For 2,000 years, all travelers from northern Europe first entered Rome and headed downtown on this street. In the Middle Ages, the street brought pilgrims to the Vatican.

The street was renamed "corso" for a famous medieval horse race that took place here during the crazy Carnevale season leading up to Lent. In 1854, Via del Corso became one of Rome's first gas-lit streets. It still hosts some of the city's most chic stores. Every evening, the pedestrian-only stretch of the Corso is packed with people on parade, taking to the streets for their *passeggiata.*

Before crossing the street, look left (to the obelisk marking Piazza del Popolo—the ancient north gate of the city) and right (to the Victor Emmanuel Monument).

• *Cross Via del Corso to enter a big palatial building with columns, the* ***Galleria Alberto Sordi*** *shopping mall. To the left are convenient WCs* *and ahead is **Feltrinelli,** the biggest Italian bookstore chain.*

*Go to the right and exit out the back. (If you're here after 21:00, when the mall is closed, circle around the right side of the Galleria on Via dei Sabini.) At any time, be on guard for pickpockets, who thrive in the nearby Trevi Fountain crowds. Once out the back, the tourist kitsch builds as you head up Via de Crociferi to the roar of the water, lights, and people at the...*

⑪ **Trevi Fountain:** The Trevi Fountain is the ultimate showcase for Rome's love affair with water.

Architect Nicola Salvi conceived this liquid Baroque avalanche in 1762, cleverly incorporating the palace behind the fountain as a theatrical backdrop. Centerstage is the enormous figure known simply as the "Ocean." He symbolizes water in every form. The statue stands in his shell-shaped chariot, surfing through his wet dream. Water gushes from 24 spouts and tumbles over 30 different kinds of plants. Winged horses represent cresting waves. They're led by Tritons who blow on their conch shells. *Drammatico!*

The square that faces the fountain has a lively atmosphere. The magic is enhanced by the fact that no streets directly approach it. You can hear the excitement as you draw near, and then—*bam!*—you're there. Enjoy the scene. Romantics toss a coin over their shoulder into the fountain. Legend says it will assure your return to Rome. Every year I go through this tourist ritual...and so far it's working.

• *Facing the Trevi Fountain, walk along its right side up Via della Stamperia. Cross busy Via del Tritone. Angle left as you continue about 30 yards up Via del Nazareno to #9, where you'll pass a fence on the left, with an exposed bit of that ancient Acqua Vergine aqueduct. At the T-intersection ahead, turn right on Via Sant'Andrea delle Fratte. The street becomes Via di Propaganda. You'll pass alongside the...*

⑫ **Palazzo di Propaganda Fide:** At #1, on the right, the white-and-yellow entrance marks the palace from which the Catholic Church "propagated," or spread, its message to the world. Back in the 1600s, this "Propaganda Palace" was the headquarters of the Catholic Church's P.R. department—a priority after the Reformation. The building was designed by that dynamic Baroque duo, Bernini and Borromini (with his concave lines). It flies the yellow-and-white flag signifying that it is still owned by the Vatican.

• *The street opens up into a long piazza. You're approaching the Spanish Steps. But first, pause at the...*

**⓭ Column of the Immaculate Conception:** Atop a tall column stands a bronze statue of Mary. She wears a diadem of stars for a halo, and stands on a crescent moon atop a globe of the earth, which is crushing a satanic serpent.

Picture the festive scene here every December 8, the feast day of the Immaculate Conception. The pope attends, the fire department brings out a ladder truck, and fresh flowers are placed high on Mary's statue. (You may see wilted remains of a flower wreath in Mary's hand.) This is the traditional event that kicks off Rome's Christmas season—the locals all go home and decorate their trees on this December day.

To Mary's immediate left stands the Spanish embassy to the Vatican. Rome has double the embassies of a normal capital because here countries need two: one to Italy and one to the Vatican. And because of this 300-year-old embassy, the square and its famous steps are called "Spanish."

• *Just 100 yards past Mary, you reach the climax of our walk, the...*

**⓮ Spanish Steps:** The wide, curving staircase is one of Rome's iconic sights. Its 138 steps lead sharply up from Piazza di Spagna.

Partway up, the steps fan out around a central terrace, forming a butterfly shape. The design culminates at the top in an obelisk framed between two Baroque church towers.

For decades the steps were a favorite Roman hangout, but recently the city banned anyone from sitting on them. You can walk up and down the steps, but if you sit, you'll face a €250 fine.

At the foot of the steps is the aptly named Sinking Boat Fountain. It was built by Gian Lorenzo Bernini's father, Pietro. This fountain is powered by that same Acqua Vergine aqueduct. Because the water pressure here is low, the water can't shoot high in the air.

ROME

So Bernini designed the fountain to be low key—a sinking boat filled with water.

The piazza is a thriving scene both day and night. From here you can window-shop along Via Condotti, which stretches away from the steps. But before you head off, take a final 360-degree spin of the piazza. It features many of the themes we've enjoyed on this walk—fountains, obelisks, public spaces, statues, and gelato. Most of all, it's a glimpse at today's Rome—a city where friends and families live much the same kind of life as their ancient cousins.

• Our walk is finished. To reach the top of the steps sweat-free, take the free elevator just inside the Spagna Metro stop (to the left, as you face the steps; elevator closes at 23:30). The nearby McDonald's (as you face the Spanish Steps, go right one block) is big and lavish, with a salad bar and WC. When you're ready to leave, you can zip home on the Metro (usually open until 23:30) or grab a taxi at the north or south ends of the piazza.

# Sights in Rome

I've clustered Rome's sights into walkable neighborhoods. Save transit time by grouping your sightseeing according to location. For example, in one great day you can start at the Colosseum, then go to the Forum, then Capitoline Hill, and from there either to the Pantheon or back to the Colosseum (by way of additional ruins along Via dei Fori Imperiali).

When you see a 🎧 in a listing, it means the sight is also covered in a free audio tour (via my Rick Steves Audio Europe app—see page 26).

For general tips on sightseeing, see page 1152. Rome's good city-run information website, www.060608.it, lists current opening hours.

**Avoiding Free-Entry Crowds:** State museums in Italy are free to enter once or twice a month. Free days are actually bad news—they attract crowds. In peak season, I'd check state museum websites in advance and make a point to avoid their free days. For Rome, that means the Colosseum, Roman Forum, Palatine Hill, Borghese Gallery, National Museum of Rome, Castel Sant'Angelo, Etruscan Museum, and Baths of Caracalla.

## ANCIENT ROME

The core of ancient Rome, where the grandest monuments were built, is between the Colosseum and Capitoline Hill. Among the ancient forums, a few modern sights have popped up. I've listed these sights generally from south to north, starting with the biggies—the Colosseum and Forum—and continuing up to Capito-

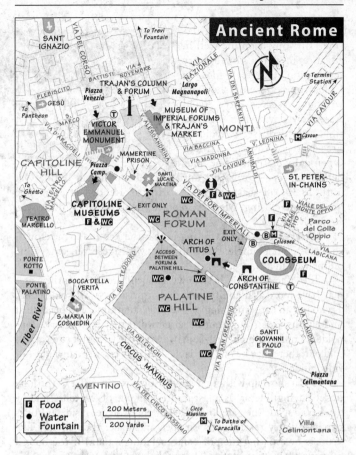

Ancient Rome

line Hill and Piazza Venezia. Between the Capitoline and the river is the former Jewish Ghetto. As a pleasant conclusion to your busy day, consider my relaxing self-guided walk back south along the broad, parklike main drag—Via dei Fori Imperiali—with some enticing detours to nearby sights (described in the "Imperial Forums" listing, later).

## Ancient Core
### ▲▲▲Colosseum (Colosseo)
This 2,000-year-old building is the classic example of Roman engineering. Used as a venue for entertaining the masses, this colossal, functional stadium is one of Europe's most recognizable landmarks. Whether you're playing gladiator or simply marveling at the remarkable ancient design and construction, the Colosseum gets a unanimous thumbs-up.

**Cost and Hours:** €16 combo-ticket covers the Colosseum

and the Roman Forum/Pala-
tine Hill. Buy it online well in
advance to get a timed-entry
reservation (€2 fee) for the
Colosseum. Do not show up
without a reserved entry. Avoid
free-entry days when it's horribly crowded (see "Avoiding
Free-Entry Crowds," earlier).
Open daily 8:30 until one hour

before sunset—April-Aug until 19:15, Sept until 19:00, Oct
until 18:30, off-season closes as early as 16:30; last entry one
hour before closing, Metro: Colosseo, tel. 06-3996-7700, www.
coopculture.it.

**Reservations and Avoiding Lines:** The solution to the crowded Colosseum is simple: Buy your ticket with a reserved-entry time
online well in advance.

The official site is best (www.coopculture.it) but other sites
may have more availability for a higher price (www.il-colosseo.it).
Try to get an early-morning or late-afternoon time slot, because at
midday the Colosseum can be so crowded that even reservation-
holders can face ridiculously long waits. If the time slot you want is
sold out, there may be one available if you pay extra for an audio- or
videoguide.

If you show up without a reservation you can suffer in the long
ticket-buying line or, as a last resort, join one of the tours sold by
hawkers outside the gate, then ditch it once you get inside. (Guides
purchase entry reservations on spec and make their money like
scalpers by inflating the price and including a tour.) If you book a
private tour in advance (see "Tours," below), the guide may be able
to book your ticket and reservation.

Generally, crowds are thinner (and lines shorter) in the afternoon (especially after 16:00 in summer); this is also true at the
Forum. A line typically has already formed at 8:30 when the Colosseum opens.

**Getting There:** The Colosseo Metro stop on line B is just
across the street from the monument. Buses #51, #75, #85, #87,
and #118 stop along Via dei Fori Imperiali near the Colosseum entrance (buses don't run on this street on Sun but still stop nearby),
one of the Forum/Palatine Hill entrances, and Piazza Venezia.
Tram #3 stops behind the Colosseum.

**Getting In:** The single entry point has two lines: one for those
with reservations and another for the sorry lot without reservations.

**Tours:** A fact-filled **audioguide** is available just past the turnstiles (€5.50/1 hour). A handheld **videoguide** senses where you are

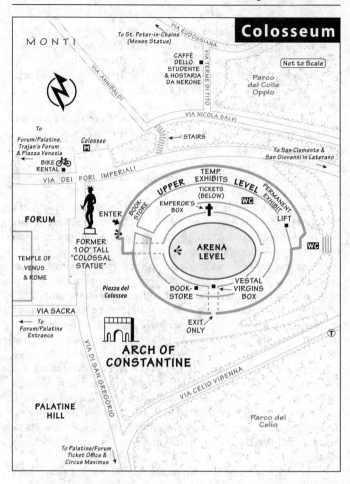

Colosseum

MONTI

To St. Peter-in-Chains
(Moses Statue)

VIA EUDOSSIANA

Not to Scale

CAFFÈ
DELLO
STUDENTE
& HOSTARIA
DA NERONE

VIA ANNIBALDI

VIA TERME DI TITO

Parco
del Colle
Oppio

VIA NICOLA SALVI

To
Forum/Palatine,
Trajan's Forum
& Piazza Venezia

Colosseo
M

STAIRS

To San Clemente &
San Giovanni in Laterano

BIKE
RENTAL

VIA DEI FORI IMPERIALI

TEMP.
EXHIBITS

UPPER LEVEL

TICKETS
(BELOW)

ENTER

BOOK-STORE

EMPEROR'S
BOX

WC

PERMANENT
EXHIBIT

FORUM

FORMER
100' TALL
"COLOSSAL
STATUE"

LIFT

ARENA
LEVEL

WC

TEMPLE OF
VENUS
& ROME

Piazza del
Colosseo

BOOK-
STORE

VESTAL
VIRGINS
BOX

VIA SACRA

To
Forum/Palatine
Entrance

EXIT
ONLY

T

ARCH OF
CONSTANTINE

VIA DI SAN GREGORIO

VIA CELIO VIBENNA

PALATINE
HILL

Parco del
Celio

To Palatine/Forum
Ticket Office &
Circus Maximus

in the site and plays related clips (€6/50 minutes) but can be hard to see in bright sunlight.

⋒ Download my free Colosseum **audio tour.**

Official **guided tours** in English depart roughly hourly between 9:45 and 15:00 (€5 plus Colosseum ticket, 45-60 minutes, purchase inside Colosseum near ticket booth marked *Visite didattiche*).

A longer, interesting, but not essential 1.5-hour guided "Underground and Belvedere" tour takes you through areas that are otherwise off-limits, including the top floor and underground passageways. Advance reservations are required, either by phone or online.

**Private guides** stand outside the Colosseum looking for business (€25-30/2-hour tour of the Colosseum, Forum, and Palatine

Hill). If booking a private guide on the spot, make sure that your tour will start right away and that the ticket you receive covers all three sights: the Colosseum, Forum, and Palatine Hill.

**Baggage:** Small bags are no problem. Larger bags and backpacks are not allowed, and there is no bag check. Spray cans and glass bottles are prohibited.

**Restoration:** The arena is being cleaned from top to bottom, given permanent lighting, and outfitted with new shops and services. These ongoing renovations, scheduled to last several years, may affect your visit.

**Visitor Services:** A WC (often crowded) is inside the Colosseum, and there are also water fountains.

**Background:** Built when the Roman Empire was at its peak in AD 80, the Colosseum represents Rome at its grandest. The Flavian Amphitheater (the Colosseum's real name) was an arena for gladiator contests and public spectacles. When killing became a spectator sport, the Romans wanted to share the fun with as many people as possible, so they stuck two semicircular theaters together to create a freestanding amphitheater, the largest in the empire.

The sheer size of the Colosseum is impressive, even in our era of mega-stadiums. With four oversized stories, it's 160 feet high, nearly a third of a mile around, and makes an oval-shaped footprint that covers six acres.

Imagine the Colosseum in its glory days. The whole thing was a brilliant white, highlighted with brightly painted trim. Monumental statues of Greek and Roman gods (Zeus, Venus, Hercules), also in bright colors, stood in the arches of the middle two stories. The top of the structure was studded with wooden beams sticking straight up, to hold a canvas awning that shaded the spectators inside.

The stadium could accommodate 50,000 roaring fans (that's 100,000 thumbs). As Romans arrived for the games, they'd be greeted outside by a huge bronze statue of the emperor Nero—100 feet tall, gleaming in the sunlight—standing where the cypress trees stand today, between the Colosseum and the Metro stop.

**Visiting the Colosseum:** Here's how I would structure my visit: After the turnstiles, walk directly to the arena and view it from ground level—near the Christian cross (see the "Colosseum" map in your book). The cross is a good reference point, and I'd consider using the WC near here if it's not jammed. Then, climb the stairs to the permanent exhibit on the upper level. Tour the exhibit. Then step out to view the arena from that upper level. Circle the arena clockwise three-quarters of the way around. From there, enjoy a viewpoint overlooking the Arch of Constantine and Roman Forum, check out the fine bookstore, then take the stairs down to ground level and head for the exit.

ROME

As you pass into the interior, imagine being an ancient spectator arriving for the games. Fans could pour in through ground-floor entrances; there were 76 numbered ones in addition to the emperor's private entrance on the north side. Your ticket (likely a pottery shard) was marked with your entrance, section, row, and seat number. You'd pass by concession stands selling fast food and souvenirs such as wine glasses with the names of famous gladiators. A hallway leading to the seats was called a *vomitorium*. At exit time, the Colosseum would "vomit" out its contents, giving us the English word. It's estimated that a capacity crowd could enter and exit in just 15 minutes.

The games took place in this oval-shaped **arena,** 280 feet long by 165 feet wide. When you look down into the arena, you're seeing the underground passages beneath the playing surface (which can be visited only on a private tour). The arena was originally covered with a wooden floor, then sprinkled with sand (*arena* in Latin). The bit of reconstructed floor gives you an accurate sense of

the original arena level and the subterranean warren where animals and prisoners were held. As in modern stadiums, the spectators ringed the playing area in bleacher seats that slanted up from the arena floor. Around you are the big brick masses that supported the tiers of seats.

The **games** pitted men against men, men against beasts, and beasts against beasts. The program began in the morning with a few warm-up acts. First came the animals, things like watching dogs bloody themselves attacking porcupines. At lunchtime came Act Two. This was when criminals and POWs were executed, often in creative ways. They might've been thrown to the lions—naked and unarmed. Or they were dressed up like classical heroes and forced to star in a play featuring their own death. Finally, in the afternoon, came the main event: the gladiators. Trumpets would blare, drums would pound, and the gladiators would enter the arena from the west end, parade around to the music, and pause at the south side. There, they'd acknowledge the Vestal Virgins sitting in their special box seats on the 50-yard line. (They got season tickets as a reward for their unique contribution to Roman society—chastity.) After a nod to the Virgins, the gladiators continued on to the emperor's box. There, they'd raise their weapons, salute, and shout *"Ave, Caesar!"*—"Hail Caesar! We who are about to die salute you!" (Though some scholars doubt they actually said that.)

ROME

In an age without a hint of a newsreel, it was hard for local Romans to visualize and appreciate the faraway conquests of their empire. The Colosseum spectacles were a way to bring home the environments, animals, and people of these conquered lands, parade them before the public, and make them

real. Imagine never having seen an actual lion, and suddenly one jumps out to chase a prisoner in the arena. Seeing the king of beasts slain by a gladiator reminded the masses of man's triumph over nature.

Don't miss the **permanent exhibit,** with lots of ancient artifacts and fascinating reconstruction models (all well-described in English); it helps bring to life both the ancient and medieval scene. It features intimate details, including pullies, pastimes, and seating hierarchy, and gives a close-up look at architectural details.

### ▲Arch of Constantine

This well-preserved arch, which stands between the Colosseum and the Forum, commemorates a military coup and, more important,

the acceptance of Christianity by the Roman Empire. When the ambitious Emperor Constantine (who had a vision that he'd win under the sign of the cross) defeated his rival Maxentius in AD 312, Constantine became sole emperor of the Roman Empire and legalized Christianity. The arch is free to see—always open and viewable.

## Roman Forum and Palatine Hill

Though I've covered them separately, the Forum and Palatine Hill are organized as a single sight with one admission. You'll need to see both sights in a single visit.

**Cost and Hours:** €16 combo-ticket includes the Colosseum

(buy online in advance to secure an entry time for the Colosseum). If you plan to skip the Colosseum, you can buy the combo-ticket at the gate (usually no entry lines). A "SUPER" combo-ticket (from €18) adds minor sights—the Palatine's museum, House of Augustus, and House of Livia—but doesn't cover the Colosseum. Avoid sporadic free days when the Forum is crowded. Same hours and free days as Colosseum, Metro: Colosseo, tel. 06-3996-7700, www.coopculture.it.

### ▲▲▲Roman Forum (Foro Romano)

This is ancient Rome's birthplace and civic center, and the common ground between Rome's famous seven hills. As just about anything important that happened in ancient Rome happened here, it's arguably the most important piece of real estate in Western civilization. While only a few fragments of that glorious past remain, history seekers find plenty to ignite their imaginations amid the half-broken columns and arches.

**Avoiding Lines:** Save time by buying your ticket in advance online. Generally, crowds are smaller in the afternoon, especially after 16:00 in summer.

**Getting There:** The closest Metro stop is Colosseo. Buses #51, #75, #85, #87, and #118 stop along Via dei Fori Imperiali near the Colosseum, the Forum, and Piazza Venezia (buses don't run on this street on Sun but still stop nearby).

**Getting In:** There are three main entrances to the Forum/Palatine Hill sight: 1) from the Colosseum (the most crowded entry)—nearest the Arch of Titus, where this chapter's guided walk starts; 2) from Via dei Fori Imperiali; and 3) from Via di San Gregorio—at south end of Palatine Hill, which is least crowded. Study your map for more details.

**Tours:** An unexciting yet informative **audioguide** helps decipher the rubble (€5/2 hours, €7 version includes Palatine Hill and lasts 3 hours, must leave ID). You must return it to where you rented it.

🎧 Download my free Roman Forum **audio tour.**

**Visitor Services:** A free information center, located across from the Via dei Fori Imperiali entrance, has a bookshop, small café, food stand, and WCs (daily 9:30-19:00). Bookstalls sell a variety of colorful books with plastic overlays that restore the ruins.

WCs are at the Palatine Hill and Via dei Fori Imperiali ticket

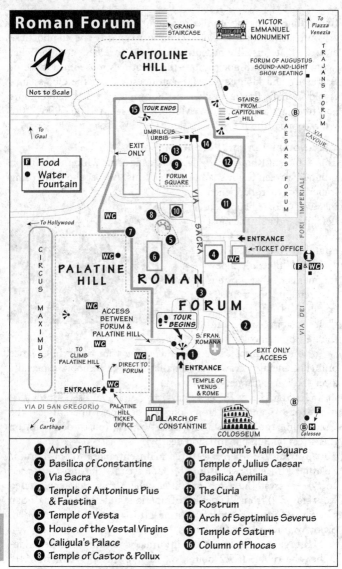

## Roman Forum

GRAND STAIRCASE

VICTOR EMMANUEL MONUMENT

To Piazza Venezia

CAPITOLINE HILL

FORUM OF AUGUSTUS SOUND-AND-LIGHT SHOW SEATING

Not to Scale

TRAJANS FORUM

To Gaul

15 TOUR ENDS

STAIRS FROM CAPITOLINE HILL

B

VIA CAVOUR

CAESARS FORUM

UMBILICUS URBIS

EXIT ONLY

14

13

16

F Food

• Water Fountain

9

FORUM SQUARE

12

FORI IMPERIALI

To Hollywood

WC

11

8

10

7

ENTRANCE

TICKET OFFICE

i

(F & WC)

VIA SACRA

5

PALATINE HILL

WC •

ROMAN

6

4

WC

VIA DEI

CIRCUS MAXIMUS

FORUM

3

WC

ACCESS BETWEEN FORUM & PALATINE HILL

WC

TO CLIMB PALATINE HILL

TOUR BEGINS

S. FRAN. ROMANA

2

WC

DIRECT TO FORUM

1

EXIT ONLY ACCESS

ENTRANCE

ENTRANCE WC

PALATINE HILL TICKET OFFICE

TEMPLE OF VENUS & ROME

B

VIA DI SAN GREGORIO

To Carthage

ARCH OF CONSTANTINE

COLOSSEUM

F

B M Colosseo

| ❶ Arch of Titus | ❾ The Forum's Main Square |
| ❷ Basilica of Constantine | ❿ Temple of Julius Caesar |
| ❸ Via Sacra | ⓫ Basilica Aemilia |
| ❹ Temple of Antoninus Pius & Faustina | ⓬ The Curia |
| ❺ Temple of Vesta | ⓭ Rostrum |
| ❻ House of the Vestal Virgins | ⓮ Arch of Septimius Severus |
| ❼ Caligula's Palace | ⓯ Temple of Saturn |
| ❽ Temple of Castor & Pollux | ⓰ Column of Phocas |

ROME

entrances. Within the Forum itself, there's one near #7 on the map. Others are at the base of Palatine Hill.

○ **Self-Guided Tour:** As you begin this Forum tour, see things with "period eyes." We imagine the structures in ancient Rome as mostly white, but ornate buildings and monuments like the Arch of Titus were originally more colorful. Through the ages, builders scavenged stone from the Forum, and the finest stone—

the colored marble—was cannibalized first. If any was left, it was generally the white stone. Statues that filled the niches were vividly painted, but the organic paint rotted away as statues lay buried for centuries. Lettering was inset bronze and eyes were inset ivory. Even seemingly intact structures, like the Arch of Titus, have been reassembled. Notice the columns are half smooth and half fluted. The fluted halves are original; the smooth parts are reconstructions—intentionally not trying to fake the original.

• *Start at the Arch of Titus, which rises above the rubble on the Colosseum end of the Forum.*

**❶ Arch of Titus** (Arco di Tito): The Arch of Titus commemorated the Roman victory over the province of Judaea (Israel) in AD

70. The Romans had a reputation as benevolent conquerors who tolerated local customs and rulers. All they required was allegiance to the empire, shown by worshipping the emperor as a god. No problem for most conquered people, who already had half a dozen gods on their prayer lists anyway. But Israelites believed in only one god, and it wasn't the emperor. Israel revolted. After a short but bitter war, the Romans defeated the rebels, took Jerusalem, destroyed their temple (leaving only a fragment of one wall's foundation—today's revered "Wailing Wall"), and brought home 50,000 Jewish slaves...who were forced to build this arch (and the Colosseum).

• *Walk down Via Sacra into the Forum. Imagine Roman sandals on these original basalt stones—the oldest street you'll ever walk. Many of the stones under your feet were walked on by Caesar Augustus 2,000 years ago. After about 50 yards, turn right and follow a path uphill to the three huge arches of the...*

**❷ Basilica of Constantine** (Basilica Maxentius): Yes, these are big arches. But they represent only one-third of the original Basilica of Constantine, a mammoth hall of justice. The arches

## Rome: Republic and Empire
### (500 BC-AD 500)

Ancient Rome lasted for a thousand years, from about 500 BC to AD 500. During that time, Rome expanded from a small tribe of barbarians to a vast empire, then dwindled slowly to city size again. For the first 500 years, when Rome's armies made her ruler of the Italian peninsula and beyond, Rome was a republic governed by elected senators. Over the next 500 years, a time of world conquest and eventual decline, Rome was an empire ruled by a military-backed dictator.

Julius Caesar bridged the gap between republic and empire. This ambitious general and politician, popular with the people because of his military victories and charisma, suspended the Roman constitution and assumed dictatorial powers in about 50 BC. A few years later, he was assassinated by a conspiracy of senators. His adopted son, Augustus, succeeded him, and soon "Caesar" was not just a name but a title.

Emperor Augustus ushered in the Pax Romana, or Roman peace (AD 1-200), a time when Rome reached her peak and controlled an empire that stretched even beyond Eurail—from England to Egypt, Turkey to Morocco.

were matched by a similar set along the Via Sacra side (only a few squat brick piers remain). Between them ran the central hall, which was spanned by a roof 130 feet high—about 55 feet higher than the side arches you see. (The stub of brick you see sticking up began an arch that once spanned the central hall.) The hall itself was as long as a football field, lavishly furnished (with colorful inlaid marble, a gilded bronze ceiling, and statues), and filled with strolling Romans. At the far (west) end was an enormous marble statue of Emperor Constantine on a throne. (Pieces of this statue, including a hand the size of a man, are on display in Rome's Capitoline Museums.)

This "basilica" was not a church but a Roman hall of justice. In a society that was as legal-minded as America is today, you needed a lot of lawyers—and a big place to put them. Citizens came here to work out matters like inheritances and building permits, or to sue somebody.

• *Now backtrack downhill and stroll deeper into the Forum, turning right along the...*

**❸ Via Sacra:** Stroll through the trees, down this main drag of the ancient city. Imagine being an out-of-town visitor during Rome's heyday—maybe from Gaul (modern France) or Londinium (modern London). You know a little Latin, but nothing would have prepared you for the bustle of Rome—a city of a million people— by far the biggest city in Europe. This street would be swarming with tribunes, slaves, and courtesans. Chariots whizzed by. Wooden stalls lined the roads, where merchants peddled their goods.

On your right, you'll pass a building with a green door still swinging on its 17th-century hinges—the original bronze door to a temple that survived because it became a church shortly after the fall of Rome. This ancient temple is still in use, sometimes hosting modern exhibits. No wonder they call Rome the Eternal City.

• *Just past the ancient temple, 10 huge columns stand in front of a much newer-looking church. This colonnade was part of the...*

❹ **Temple of Antoninus Pius and Faustina:** The Senate built this temple to honor Emperor Antoninus Pius (AD 138-161) and his deified wife, Faustina. (The lintel's inscription calls them *"divo"* and *"divae."*) The 50-foot-tall Corinthian (leafy) columns must have been awe-inspiring to out-of-towners who grew up in thatched huts. Although the temple has been inhabited by a church, you can still see the basic layout—a staircase led to a shaded porch (the columns), which admitted you to the main building (now a church), where the statue of the god sat.

Picture a Roman priest climbing these steps to make an offering to the god inside. And imagine these columns with gilded capitals, supporting brightly painted statues in a triangular pediment, and the whole building capped with a gleaming bronze roof. The stately gray rubble of today's Forum is a faded black-and-white photograph of a 3-D Technicolor era.

The building is a microcosm of many changes that occurred after Rome fell. In medieval times, the temple was pillaged. Note the diagonal cuts high on the marble columns—a failed attempt by scavengers to cut through the pillars to pull them down for their precious stone. (They tried using vinegar and rope to cut the marble...but because vinegar also eats through rope, they abandoned the attempt.) In 1550, a church was housed inside the ancient temple. The green door shows the street level at the time of Michelangelo. The long staircase was underground until excavated in the 1800s.

• *With your back to the colonnade, walk straight ahead—jogging a bit to the right to stay on the path. The dirt path leads to two sights associated with Rome's Vestal Virgins. Head for the three short columns, all that's left of the...*

❺ **Temple of Vesta:** This is perhaps Rome's most sacred spot. Notice that the temple remains are curved. Originally, this temple was circular, like a glorified farmer's hut—the kind Rome's first families lived in. Although we think of the Romans as decadent, in fact they prided themselves on their family values. People venerated their parents, grandparents, and ancestors, even keeping small statues of them in sacred shrines in their homes. This temple represented those family values on a large scale; its fire symbolized the "hearth" of the extended family that was Rome. As long as the sacred flame burned, Rome would stand. The flame was tended by six priestesses known as the Vestal Virgins.

• *Backtrack a few steps up the path, behind the Temple of Vesta. You'll find a few stairs that lead up to a big, enclosed field with two rectangular brick pools (just below the hill). This was the courtyard of the...*

❻ **House of the Vestal Virgins:** The Vestal Virgins lived in a two-story building surrounding a long central courtyard with two pools at one end. Rows of statues depicting leading Vestal Virgins flanked the courtyard. This place was the model—both architecturally and sexually—for medieval convents and monasteries.

Chosen from noble families before they reached the age of 10, the six Vestal Virgins each served a 30-year term. Honored and revered by the Romans, the Vestals even had their own box seats opposite the emperor in the Colosseum. The statues that line the courtyard honor dutiful Vestals.

Their sacred duty was to be ceremonial homemakers, tending the temple-home of the goddess Vesta. They brought water from a sacred spring, cooked sacred food, polished the ritual silverware, and—most importantly—made sure the hearth fire never went out.

As the name implies, a Vestal took a vow of chastity. If she served her term faithfully—abstaining for 30 years—she was given a huge dowry and allowed to marry. But if they found any Virgin who wasn't, she was strapped to a funeral car, paraded through the streets of the Forum, taken to a crypt, given a loaf of bread and a lamp...and buried alive. Many Vestals suffered the latter fate.

• *Looming just beyond this field is Palatine Hill—the corner of which may have been...*

❼ **Caligula's Palace** (Palace of Tiberius): Emperor Caligula (ruled AD 37-41) had a huge palace on Palatine Hill overlooking the Forum. It actually sprawled down the hill into the Forum (some supporting arches remain in the hillside).

Caligula was not a nice person. He tortured enemies, stole senators' wives, and parked his chariot in handicap spaces. But Rome's luxury-loving emperors only added to the glory of the Forum, with each one trying to make his mark on history.

• *Continue downhill, passing the three short columns of the Temple of Vesta, where you'll get a view of three very tall columns just beyond.*

❽ **Temple of Castor and Pollux:** These three columns—all that remain of a once-prestigious temple—have become the most photographed sight in the Forum. The temple was one of the city's oldest, built in the fifth century BC. It commemorated the Roman victory over the Tarquin, the notorious Etruscan king who once oppressed them. After the battle, the legendary twin brothers Castor and Pollux watered their horses here, at the Sacred Spring of Juturna (which has been excavated nearby). As a symbol of Rome's self-governing republic, the temple was often used as a meeting place of senators, and its front steps served as a podium for free speech.

• *The path spills into a flat, open area that stretches before you. This was the center of the ancient Forum.*

❾ **The Forum's Main Square:** The original Forum, or main square, was this flat patch about the size of a football field, stretching to the foot of Capitoline Hill. Surrounding it were temples, law courts, government buildings, and triumphal arches.

Rome was born right here. According to legend, twin brothers Romulus (Rome) and Remus were orphaned in infancy and raised by a she-wolf on top of Palatine Hill. Growing up, they found it hard to get dates. So they and their cohorts attacked the nearby Sabine tribe and kidnapped their women. After they made peace, this marshy valley became the meeting place and then the trading center for the scattered tribes on the surrounding hillsides.

Ancient Rome's population exceeded one million, more than any city until London and Paris in the 19th century. All those Roman masses lived in tiny apartments as we would live in tents at a campsite, basically just to sleep. The public space—their Forum, today's piazza—is where they did their living. Consider how, to this day, the piazza is still such an important part of any Italian town. Since Roman times, the piazza has reflected and accommodated the gregarious and outgoing nature of the Italian people.

The Forum is now rubble, but imagine it in its prime: blindingly brilliant marble buildings with 40-foot-high columns and shining metal roofs; rows of statues painted in realistic colors;

**ROME**

processional chariots rattling down Via Sacra. Mentally replace tourists in T-shirts with tribunes in togas. Imagine the buildings towering and the people buzzing around you while an orator gives a rabble-rousing speech from the Rostrum. If things still look like just a pile of rocks, at least tell yourself, "But Julius Caesar once leaned against these rocks."

• *And speaking of Julius Caesar, at the near end of the main square (the end closest to the Colosseum) find the foundations of a temple now sheltered by a peaked wood-and-metal roof.*

**⓾ Temple of Julius Caesar** (Tempio del Divo Giulio, or Ara di Cesare): On March 15, in 44 BC, Julius Caesar (100-44 BC) was stabbed 23 times by political conspirators. After his assassination, Caesar's body was cremated on this spot (under the metal roof). Afterward, this temple was built to honor him. Peek behind the wall into the small apse area, where a mound of dirt usually has fresh flowers—given to remember the man who, more than any other, personified the greatness of Rome.

Although he was popular with the masses, not everyone liked Caesar's urban design or his politics. When he assumed dictatorial powers, he was ambushed and stabbed to death by a conspiracy of senators, including his adopted son, Brutus *("Et tu, Brute?")*.

The funeral was held here, facing the main square. The citizens gathered, and speeches were made. Mark Antony stood up to say (in Shakespeare's words), "Friends, Romans, countrymen, lend me your ears. I come to bury Caesar, not to praise him." When Caesar's body was burned, his adoring fans threw anything at hand on the fire, requiring the fire department to come put it out. Later, Emperor Augustus dedicated this temple in his name, making Caesar the first Roman to become a god.

• *Continue past the Temple of Julius Caesar, to the open area between the columns of the Temple of Antoninus Pius and Faustina (which we passed earlier) and the boxy brick building (the Curia). You can view the ruins of the Basilica Aemilia from a ramp next to the Temple of Antoninus Pius and Faustina, or (if the path is open) walk among them.*

**⓫ Basilica Aemilia:** Notice the layout. This was a long, rectangular building. The stubby columns all in a row form one long, central hall flanked by two side aisles. Medieval Christians required a larger meeting hall for their worship services than Roman temples provided, so they used the spacious Roman basilica as the model for their churches. Cathedrals from France to Spain to England, from Romanesque to Gothic to Renaissance, all have the same basic floor plan as a Roman basilica.

• *Now head for the big, well-preserved brick building with the triangular roof—the Curia. It's just to the right of the big triumphal arch at the foot of Capitoline Hill. While often closed, the building is impressive even from outside.*

## Rome Falls

Remember that Rome lasted 1,000 years—500 years of growth, 200 years of peak power, and 300 years of gradual decay.  The fall had many causes, among them the barbarians who pecked away at Rome's borders. Christians blamed the fall on moral decay. Pagans blamed it on Christians. Socialists blamed it on a shallow economy based on the spoils of war. (Republicans blamed it on Democrats.)

Whatever the reasons, the far-flung empire could no longer keep its grip on conquered lands, and it pulled back. Barbarian tribes from Germany and Asia attacked the Italian peninsula and even looted Rome itself in AD 410, leveling many of the buildings in the Forum. In 476, when the last emperor checked out and switched off the lights, Europe plunged into centuries of ignorance, poverty, and weak government—the Dark Ages.

But Rome lived on in the Catholic Church. Christianity was the state religion of Rome's last generations. Emperors became popes (both called themselves "Pontifex Maximus"), senators became bishops, orators became priests, and basilicas became churches. The glory of Rome remains eternal.

**⓬ The Curia** (Senate House): The Curia was the most important political building in the Forum. Since the birth of the republic, this was the site of Rome's official center of government. Three hundred senators, elected by the citizens of Rome, donned their togas, tucked their scrolls under their arms, and climbed the steps into this great hall. Inside, they gave speeches, debated  policy, and created the laws of the land. They sat with their backs to the walls, surrounding the big hall on three sides, in three rows of seats. At the far end sat the Senate president—and later, the emperor—on his podium. The vast room still echoes with stirring speeches and passionate debates.

The present Curia building dates from AD 283, when it replaced an earlier Senate building. It's so well-preserved because it was used as a church since early Christian times. In the 1930s, it was restored as a historic site.

• *Go back down the Senate steps and find the 10-foot-high wall just to the left of the big arch, marked...*

**⓭ Rostrum:** Nowhere was Roman freedom of speech more apparent than at this "Speaker's Corner." The Rostrum was a raised platform, 10 feet high and 80 feet long, decorated with statues, columns, and the prows of ships.

On a stage like this, Rome's orators, great and small, tried to draw a crowd and sway public opinion. Picture the backdrop these speakers would have had—a mountain of marble buildings piling up on Capitoline Hill. Mark Antony rose to offer Caesar the laurel-leaf crown of kingship, which Caesar publicly (and hypocritically) refused—while privately becoming a dictator. Men such as Cicero—a contemporary of Julius Caesar—railed against the corruption and decadence that came with the city's newfound wealth. (Cicero paid the price: he was executed, and his head and hands were nailed to the Rostrum.)

In later years, when emperors ruled, it took real daring to speak out against the powers that be. Rome's democratic spirit was increasingly squelched. Eventually, the emperor and the army—not the Senate and the citizens—held ultimate power, and Rome's vast empire began to rot from within.

• *In front of the Rostrum are **trees** bearing fruits that were sacred to the ancient Romans: olives (provided food, oil for light, and preservatives), figs (tasty), and wine grapes (made a popular export product). Now turn your attention to the big arch to the right of the Rostrum, the...*

**⓮ Arch of Septimius Severus:** In imperial times, the Rostrum's voices of democracy would have been dwarfed by images of the empire, such as the huge six-story-high Arch of Septimius Severus (AD 203). The reliefs commemorate the African-born emperor's battles in Mesopotamia. Near ground level, see soldiers marching captured barbarians back to Rome for the victory parade. More and more, Rome's economy was based on slave power and foreign booty rather than on domestic production. And despite efficient rule by emperors like Severus, Rome's empire began to crumble under the weight of its own corruption, disease, and decaying infrastructure.

• *As we near the end of Rome's history, we're also nearing the end of our tour. Our next stop is the Temple of Saturn. You can see it from here—it's the eight big columns just up the slope of Capitol Hill. Or you could make your way to it for a closer look.*

**⓯ Temple of Saturn:** These columns framed the entrance to the Forum's oldest temple (497 BC). Inside was a humble, very old wooden statue of the god Saturn. The statue's claim to fame was its pedestal, which held the gold bars, coins, and jewels of Rome's state treasury, the booty collected by conquering generals.

Even older than the Temple of Saturn is the **Umbilicus Urbis,** which stands nearby (next to the Arch of Septimius Severus). A humble brick ruin marks this historic "Navel of the City." The spot was considered the center of the cosmos, and all distances in the empire were measured from here.

• *Now turn your attention from the Temple of Saturn, one of the Forum's first buildings, to one of its last monuments. Find a lone, tall column standing in the Forum in front of the Rostrum. It's fluted and topped with a leafy Corinthian capital. This is the...*

🟦 **Column of Phocas:** This is the Forum's last monument (AD 608), a gift from the powerful Byzantine Empire to a fallen empire—Rome. Given to commemorate

the pagan Pantheon's becoming a Christian church, it was a symbolic last nail in ancient Rome's coffin. After Rome's 1,000-year reign, the city was looted by Vandals, the population of a million-plus shrank to about 10,000, and the once-grand city center—the Forum—was abandoned, slowly covered up by centuries of silt and dirt. In the 1700s, an English historian named Edward Gibbon overlooked this spot from Capitoline Hill. Hearing Christian monks singing at these pagan ruins, he looked out at the few columns poking up from the ground, pondered the decline and fall of the Roman Empire, and thought, "Hmm, that's a catchy title..."

• *Your tour is over. If you want to see Palatine Hill, don't leave the Forum complex; you won't be allowed back in without a new ticket. Instead, return to the Arch of Titus.*

*If you'd rather exit the Forum, be aware that the exact ways in and out change from year to year. Refer to your map for possible exit locations. If heading for Capitoline Hill, your best escape is likely on the west side (behind #16 on the map in this chapter).*

### ▲▲Palatine Hill (Monte Palatino)

While nearly empty of tourists, Palatine Hill is jam-packed with history—"the huts of Romulus," the huge Imperial Palace, a view of the Circus Maximus—but only the barest skeleton of rubble is left to tell the story.

We get our word "palace" from this hill, where the emperors chose to live. It was once so filled with palaces that later emperors had to build out. (Looking up at it from the Forum, you see the substructure that supported these long-gone palaces.) The

Palatine Museum contains statues and frescoes that help you
imagine the luxury of the imperial Palatine. From the pleasant
garden, you'll get an overview of
the Forum. On the far side, unless excavations are blocking the
viewpoint, look down into an
emperor's private stadium and
then beyond at the grassy Circus

Maximus, once a chariot course. Imagine the cheers, jeers, and furious betting.

While many tourists consider Palatine Hill just extra credit
after the Forum, it offers insight into the greatness of Rome that's
well worth the effort. (And, if you're visiting the Colosseum or
Forum, you've got a ticket whether you like it or not.)

**Cost and Hours:** Covered by same tickets and open same
hours as Roman Forum, listed earlier.

**Getting There:** The nearest Metro stop is Colosseo. Buses
#51, #75, #85, #87, and #118 stop along Via dei Fori Imperiali near
the Colosseum, the Forum, and Piazza Venezia (buses don't run on
this street on Sun but still stop nearby).

**Getting In:** There are three entrances to the combined Pala-
tine/Forum sight; see the map on page 852. The easiest is the entrance on Via di San Gregorio, 150 yards from the Colosseum.
Upon entering, follow the path to the left as it winds to the top.
Alternatively, if you sightsee the Forum first, to get to Palatine Hill
you must walk up from the Arch of Titus.

**Visitor Services:** You'll find WCs at the ticket office when you
enter, on top of the hill near the stadium, at the museum, near the
access point to the Forum, and hiding among the orange trees in
the Farnese Gardens.

## South of the Ancient Core
### Baths of Caracalla (Terme di Caracalla)

Inaugurated by Emperor Caracalla in AD 216, this massive bath
complex—supplied by its own branch of an aqueduct—could ac-

commodate 1,600 visitors
at a time. Today it's just a
shell—a huge shell—with
all of its sculptures and
most of its mosaics moved
to museums.

This sight is dramatic
in part because nothing
was built around or on top

of it. It's stood here, in ruins, for 1,500 years. You'll see a two-story roofless brick building surrounded by a garden, bordered by ruined walls. The two large rooms at either end of the building were used for exercise. In between the exercise rooms was a pool flanked by two small mosaic-floored dressing rooms.

**Cost and Hours:** €8; free and crowded once or twice a month, specific day varies in peak season (in low season, it's the first Sun); open Mon 9:00-14:00, Tue-Sun 9:00 until one hour before sunset: April-Aug until 19:15, Sept until 19:00, Oct until 18:30, off-season closes as early as 16:30; last entry one hour before closing, audioguide-€5, good €8 guidebook, Metro: Circo Massimo, then a 5-minute walk south along Via delle Terme di Caracalla; tel. 06-3996-7700, www.coopculture.it.

## Capitoline Hill

Of Rome's famous seven hills, this is the smallest, tallest, and most famous—home of the ancient Temple of Jupiter and the center of city government for 2,500 years. There are several ways to get to the top of Capitoline Hill. If you're coming from the north (from Piazza Venezia), take Michelangelo's impressive stairway to the right of the big, white Victor Emmanuel Monument.

Coming from the southeast (the Roman Forum), take the steep staircase near the Arch of Septimius Severus. From near Trajan's Forum along Via dei Fori Imperiali, take the winding road. All three converge at the top, in the square called Campidoglio (kahm-pee-DOHL-yoh).

### ▲Piazza del Campidoglio

This square atop the hill, once the religious and political center of ancient Rome, is still the home of the city's government. In the 1530s, the pope called on Michelangelo to reestablish this square as a grand center. Michelangelo placed the ancient equestrian statue of Marcus Aurelius as its focal point—very effective. (The original statue is now in the adjacent museum.) The twin buildings on either side are the Capitoline Museums. Behind the replica of the statue is the mayoral palace (Palazzo Senatorio).

Michelangelo intended that people approach the square from his grand stairway off Piazza Venezia. From the top of the stairway, you see the new Renaissance face of Rome, with its back to the Forum. Michelangelo gave the buildings the "giant order"—huge pilasters make the existing two-story build-ings feel one-storied and more harmonious with the new square. Notice how the statues atop these buildings welcome you and then draw you in.

The terraces just downhill (past either side of the mayor's palace) offer grand views of the Forum. To the left of the mayor's pal-ace is a copy of the famous she-wolf statue on a column. Farther down is *il nasone* ("the big nose"), a refreshing water fountain (see photo). Block the spout with your fingers, and water spurts up for drinking. Romans joke that a cheap Roman boy takes his date out for a drink at *il nasone*.

### ▲▲▲Capitoline Museums (Musei Capitolini)

Some of ancient Rome's most famous statues and art are housed in the two palaces (Palazzo dei Conservatori and Palazzo Nuovo) that flank the equestrian statue in the Campidoglio. They're con-nected by an underground passage that leads to the Tabularium, an ancient building with a panoramic overlook of the Forum.

**Cost and Hours:** €15, daily 9:30-19:30, last entry one hour before closing, videoguide-€6, good children's audioguide-€4, tel. 06-0608, www.museicapitolini.org.

**Visiting the Museum:** You'll enter at the **Palazzo dei Con-servatori** (on your right as you face the equestrian statue), cross underneath the square (beneath the Palazzo Senatorio, the may-oral palace, not open to public), and exit from the Palazzo Nuovo (on your left). This enjoyable museum complex claims to be the world's oldest, founded in 1471 when a pope gave ancient statues to the citizens of Rome. Many of the museum's statues have gone on to become instantly recognizable cultural icons, including the 13th-century *Capitoline She-Wolf* (the little statues of Romulus and Remus were added in the Renaissance). Don't miss the *Boy Ex-tracting a Thorn* and the enchanting *Commodus as Hercules.* Behind Commodus is a statue of his dad, Marcus Aurelius, on a horse. The greatest surviving equestrian statue of antiquity, this was the origi-nal centerpiece of the square (where a copy stands today). Chris-tians in the Dark Ages thought that the statue's hand was raised in blessing, which probably led to their misidentifying him as Con-stantine, the first Christian emperor. While most pagan statues were destroyed by Christians, "Constantine" was spared.

The museum's second-floor café, **Caffè Capitolino,** has a splendid patio offering city views. It's lovely at sunset (public en-

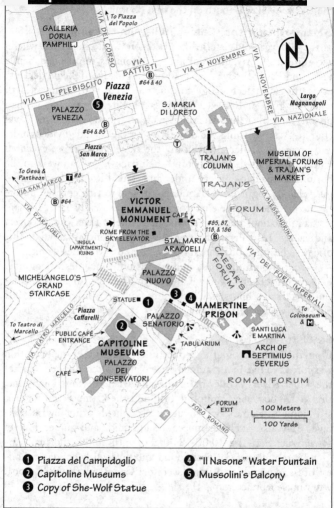

## Capitoline Hill & Piazza Venezia

1 Piazza del Campidoglio
2 Capitoline Museums
3 Copy of She-Wolf Statue
4 "Il Nasone" Water Fountain
5 Mussolini's Balcony

trance for those without a museum ticket off Piazzale Caffarelli and through door #4).

The **Tabularium,** built in the first century BC, once held the archives of ancient Rome. (The word Tabularium comes from "tablet," on which Romans wrote their laws.) You won't see any tablets, but you will see a stunning head-on view of the Forum from the windows.

The **Palazzo Nuovo** houses mostly portrait busts of forgotten emperors. But it also has two must-see statues: the *Dying Gaul* and the *Capitoline Venus* (both on the first floor up).

### ▲Mamertine Prison (Carcer Tullianum Museum)

This 2,500-year-old cistern-like prison on Capitoline Hill is where, according to Christian tradition, the Romans imprisoned Saints Peter and Paul. Today it's a small but impressive archeological site using the latest technology to illustrate what you might unearth when digging in Rome: a pagan sacred site, an ancient Roman prison, an early Christian pilgrimage destination, or a medieval church. After learning the context using the included videoguide, and browsing artifacts (including the skeletons of those executed with their hands still tied behind their backs), you can walk to the bottom of this dank cistern under an original Roman stone roof—marvel at its engineering. Amid fat rats and rotting corpses, unfortunate prisoners of the emperor awaited slow deaths here. It's said that a miraculous fountain sprang up inside so Peter could convert and baptize his jailers, who were also subsequently martyred. This pricey sight is a good value for pilgrims and antiquities wonks.

**Cost and Hours:** €10, credit cards only, includes videoguide, €20 combo-ticket includes Colosseum and Roman Forum/Palatine Hill, same hours as Colosseum, Clivo Argentario 1, tel. 06-698-961, www.tullianum.org.

## Jewish Quarter

From the 16th through the 19th century, Rome's Jewish population was forced to live in a cramped ghetto at an often-flooded bend of the Tiber River. While the medieval Jewish ghetto is long gone, this area—between Capitoline Hill and the Campo de' Fiori—is still home to Rome's synagogue and fragments of its Jewish heritage (€11 ticket includes museum audioguide and guided tour of synagogue; Sun-Thu 10:00-18:00, Fri until 16:00; shorter hours Oct-March, closed Sat year-round and on Jewish holidays; modest dress required, on Lungotevere dei Cenci, tel. 06-6840-0661, www.museoebraico.roma.it).

## Piazza Venezia

This vast square, dominated by the big, white Victor Emmanuel Monument, is a major transportation hub and the focal point of modern Rome. With your back to the monument (you'll get the best views from the terrace by the guards and eternal flame), look down Via del Corso, the city's axis, surrounded by Rome's classiest shopping district. In the 1930s, Benito Mussolini whipped up Italy's nationalistic fervor from a balcony above the square (it's the less-grand building on the left). Mussolini lied to his people, mixing fear and patriotism to push his country to the right and embroil

ROME

the Italians in expensive and regrettable wars. In 1945, they shot Mussolini and hung him from a meat hook in Milan.

With your back still to the monument, circle around the left side to reach two staircases leading up Capitoline Hill. One is Michelangelo's grand staircase up to the Campidoglio. The steeper of the two leads to **Santa Maria in Aracoeli,** a good example of the earliest style of Christian church. The contrast between this climb-on-your-knees ramp to God's house and Michelangelo's elegant stairs illustrates the changes Renaissance humanism brought civilization.

### ▲Victor Emmanuel Monument

This oversized monument to Italy's first king, built to celebrate the 50th anniversary of the country's unification in 1861, was part of

Italy's push to overcome the new country's strong regionalism and create a national identity. Today, the monument houses museums, a café with a view, and a €10 elevator to an even better view. See the map on page 845.

The scale of the monument is over the top: 200 feet high, 500 feet wide. The 43-foot-tall statue of the king on his high horse is one of the biggest equestrian statues in the world. The king's moustache forms an arc five feet long, and a person could sit within the horse's hoof. At the base of this statue, Italy's Tomb of the Unknown Soldier (flanked by Italian flags and armed guards) is watched over by the goddess Roma (with the gold mosaic background).

With its gleaming white sheen (from a recent scrubbing) and enormous scale, the monument provides a vivid sense of what Ancient Rome looked like at its peak—imagine the Forum filled with shiny, grandiose buildings like this one.

**Cost and Hours:** Monument—free, daily 9:30-18:45, a few WCs scattered throughout; Rome from the Sky elevator—€10, daily until 19:00; ticket office closes 15 minutes earlier, tel. 06-0608; follow *ascensori panoramici* signs inside the Victor Emmanuel Monument (no elevator access from street level).

**ROME**

### The Imperial Forums

Though the original Roman Forum is the main attraction for today's tourists, there are several more ancient forums nearby, known collectively as "The Imperial Forums." The forums stretch in a line along Via dei Fori Imperiali, from Piazza Venezia to the Colosseum. The boulevard was built by the dictator Benito Mussolini

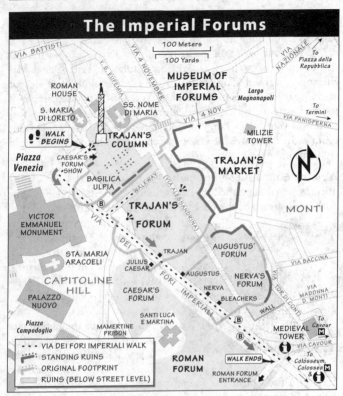

# The Imperial Forums

VIA BATTISTI

V. S. EUFEMIA

VIA 4 NOVEMBRE

100 Meters
100 Yards

VIA NAZIONALE

To
Piazza della
Repubblica

ROMAN
HOUSE

S. MARIA
DI LORETO

SS. NOME
DI MARIA

MUSEUM OF
IMPERIAL
FORUMS

Largo
Magnanapoli

To
Termini

VIA 4 NOV.

VIA PANISPERNA

WALK
BEGINS

TRAJAN'S
COLUMN

MILIZIE
TOWER

Piazza
Venezia

CAESAR'S
FORUM
-SHOW

TRAJAN'S
MARKET

BASILICA
ULPIA

Ⓑ

WALKWAY (VIA ALESANDRINA)

TRAJAN'S

FORUM

MONTI

VICTOR
EMMANUEL
MONUMENT

VIA

DEI

TRAJAN

AUGUSTUS'
FORUM

VIA BACCINA

STA. MARIA
ARACOELI

JULIUS
CAESAR

AUGUSTUS

NERVA'S
FORUM

VIA
MADONNA
D. MONTI

CAPITOLINE
HILL

CAESAR'S
FORUM

FORI

NERVA

IMPERIALI

BLEACHERS

VIA TOR DI CONTI

WALL

PALAZZO
NUOVO

SANTI LUCA
E MARTINA

Ⓑ

Ⓑ

MEDIEVAL
TOWER

To
Cavour
Ⓜ

Piazza
Campodoglio

MAMERTINE
PRISON

VIA CAVOUR

- - - VIA DEI FORI IMPERIALI WALK

STANDING RUINS

ORIGINAL FOOTPRINT

RUINS (BELOW STREET LEVEL)

ROMAN
FORUM

WALK ENDS

To
Colosseo,
Colosseo Ⓜ
& ℹ

ROMAN FORUM
ENTRANCE

ROME

in the 1930s—supposedly so he could look out his office window on Piazza Venezia and see the Colosseum, creating a military parade ground and a visual link between the glories of the imperial past with what he thought would be Italy's glorious imperial future. Today, the once-noisy boulevard is a pleasant walk, since it is closed to private vehicles—and, on Sundays, to all traffic.

The ruins are out in the open, never crowded, and free to look down on from street level at any time, any day. For an overview of the archaeological area, take this walk from Piazza Venezia down Via dei Fori Imperiali to the end of the Imperial Forums.

○ **Self-Guided Walk:** Start at Trajan's Column, the colossal pillar that stands alongside Piazza Venezia.

**Trajan's Column:** The world's grandest column from antiquity (rated ▲▲) anchors the first of the forums we'll see—Trajan's Forum. The 140-foot column is decorated with a spiral relief of 2,500 figures trumpeting the emperor's exploits. It has stood for centuries as a symbol of a truly cosmopolitan civilization. At one point, the ashes of Trajan and his wife were held in the base, and the sun glinted off a polished bronze statue of Trajan at the top. Since the 1500s, St. Peter has been on top. (Where's the original bronze statue of Trajan? Spaghetti pots.) Built as a stack of 17 marble doughnuts, the column is hollow (note the small window slots) with a spiral staircase inside, leading up to the balcony.

The **relief** unfolds like a scroll, telling the story of Rome's last and greatest foreign conquest, Trajan's defeat of Dacia (modern-day Romania). Originally, the entire story was painted in bright colors. If you were to unwind the scroll, it would stretch over two football fields—it's far longer than the frieze around the Parthenon in Athens.

• *Now, start heading toward the Colosseum, walking along the left side of Via dei Fori Imperiali. You're walking alongside...*

**Trajan's Forum:** The dozen-plus gray columns mark one of the grandest structures in Trajan's Forum, the Basilica Ulpia, the largest law court of its day. Nearby stood two libraries that contained the world's knowledge in Greek and Latin. (The internet of the day, contained in two big buildings.)

Rome peaked under Emperor Trajan (ruled AD 98-117), when the empire stretched from England to the Sahara, from Spain to the Fertile Crescent. A triumphant Trajan returned to Rome with his booty and shook it all over the city. Most was spent on this forum, complete with temples, law courts, and the monumental column trumpeting his exploits. To build his forum, Trajan cut away a ridge that once connected the Quirinal and Capitoline hills, creating this valley. This was the largest forum ever, and its opulence astounded even jaded Romans. Looking at this, you can only think that for every grand monument here, there was untold hardship and suffering in the Barbarian world.

• *Most astounding of all was Trajan's Market. That's the big, semicircular brick structure nestled into the cutaway curve of Quirinal Hill. If you want a closer look, a pedestrian pathway leads you close to it.*

**Trajan's Market:** This structure was part shopping mall, part warehouse, and part administration building and/ or government offices. For now the conventional wisdom holds that at ground level, the 13 tall (shallow) arches housed shops selling fresh fruit, vegetables, and flowers to people who

passed by on the street. The 26 arched windows (above) lit a covered walkway lined with shops that sold wine and olive oil. On the roof (now lined with a metal railing) ran a street that likely held still more shops and offices, making about 150 in all. Shoppers could browse through goods from every corner of Rome's vast empire—exotic fruits from Africa, spices from Asia, and fish-and-chips from Londinium.

Above the semicircle, the upper floors of the complex housed bureaucrats in charge of a crucial element of city life: doling out free grain to unemployed citizens, who lived off the wealth plundered from distant lands. Better to pacify them than risk a riot. Above the offices, at the very top, rises a (leaning) tower added in the Middle Ages.

To walk around the market complex and see some excavated statues, you can visit the **Museum of the Imperial Forums,** which features discoveries from the forums built by the different emperors. It's well-displayed and helps put all these ruins in context (€11.50, daily 9:30-19:30, last entry one hour before closing).

• *Return to the main street and continue toward the Colosseum for about 100 more yards.*

You're still walking alongside Trajan's Forum, but the ruins you see in this section are from the medieval era. These are the foundations of the old neighborhood that was built atop the ancient city. In modern times, that neighborhood was cleared out to build the new boulevard.

You'll soon reach a bronze **statue of Trajan** himself. Though the likeness is ancient, this bronze statue is not. It was erected by the dictator Benito Mussolini when he had the modern boulevard built. Notice the date on the pedestal—Anno XI. That would be "the 11th year of the Fascist Renovation of Italy"—i.e., 1933. Across the street is a similar statue of **Julius Caesar.** That marks the first of these imperial forums, **Caesar's Forum,** built by Julius in 46 BC as an extension of the Roman Forum. Near Julius stand the three remaining columns of his forum's Temple of Venus—the patron goddess of the Julian family.

• *Continue along (down the left side). As Trajan's Forum narrows to an end, you reach a statue of Emperor Augustus that indicates...*

**The Forums of Augustus and Nerva:** The statue captures **Emperor Augustus** in his famous hailing-a-cab pose (a copy of the original, which you can see at the Vatican Museums). This is his "commander talking to his people" pose. Behind him was the Forum of Augustus. It separated fancy "downtown Rome" from the workaday world beyond.

Farther along is a statue of **Emperor Nerva,** trying but failing to have the commanding presence of Augustus. Behind Nerva, you can get a closer look at his forum.

• *You've reached the end of the Imperial Forums at the intersection of Via dei Fori Imperiali and busy Via Cavour. Nearby is the colorful neighborhood of Monti, home to a slew of fun little eateries. Two blocks up busy Via Cavour is the Cavour Metro stop. From there, you could turn right to find St. Peter-in-Chains Church. Across Via dei Fori Imperiali is an entrance to the Roman Forum; 100 yards farther down Via dei Fori Imperiali (on the left) is a tourist information center with a handy café, info desk, and WC.*

## Near the Imperial Forums

Several worthwhile sights sit north of Via dei Fori Imperiali from the Roman Forum—and offer a break from the crowds. If you'll be here in the evening, consider taking in a sound-and-light show (see page 908).

### ▲The Roman House at Palazzo Valentini (Le Domus Romane di Palazzo Valentini)

For a quality (air-conditioned) experience, duck into this underground series of ancient spaces at the base of Trajan's Column. The 1.5-hour tour with good English narration and evocative lighting features scant remains of an elegant ancient Roman house and bath. The highlight is a small theater where you'll learn the entire story depicted by the 2,600 figures who parade around the 650-foot relief carved onto Trajan's Column.

**Cost and Hours:** €12, Wed-Mon 9:30-18:30, closed Tue, entrance is on the half-hour, 15 people per departure—reservations smart (€1.50 fee), tel. 06-2276-1280, www.palazzovalentini.it.

### ▲St. Peter-in-Chains Church (San Pietro in Vincoli)

A church was first built on this spot in the fifth century, to house the chains that once restrained St. Peter. Today's church, restored in the 15th century, is famous for its Michelangelo statue of Moses, intended for the (unfinished) tomb of Pope Julius II. Check out the chains under the high altar, then focus on mighty Moses. (Note this isn't the famous St. Peter's—that's in Vatican City.)

Pope Julius II commissioned Michelangelo to build a massive tomb, with 48 huge statues, topped with a grand statue of this egomaniacal pope. The pope had planned to have his tomb placed in the center of St. Peter's Basilica. When Julius died, the work had barely begun, and no one had the money or necessary commitment to Julius to finish the project.

In 1542, some of the remnants of the tomb project were brought to St. Peter-in-Chains and pieced together by Michelangelo's assistants. Some of the best statues ended up elsewhere, such as the *Prisoners* in Florence and the *Slaves* in the Louvre. *Moses* and the Louvre's *Slaves* are the only statues Michelangelo personally completed for the project. Flanking *Moses* are the Old Testament

ROME

# Pantheon Neighborhood

sister-wives of Jacob, Leah (to our right) and Rachel, both begun by Michelangelo but probably finished by pupils.

The powerful statue of Moses—mature Michelangelo—is worth studying. Moses has received the Ten Commandments. As he holds the stone tablets, his eyes show a man determined to stop his tribe from worshipping the golden calf and idols...a man determined to win salvation for the people of Israel. Why the horns? Centuries ago, the Hebrew word for "rays" was mistranslated as "horns."

**Cost and Hours:** Free, daily 8:00-12:30 & 15:00-19:00, Oct-March until 18:00, modest dress required; the church is a 10-minute uphill walk from the Colosseum, or a shorter, simpler walk (but with more steps) from the Cavour Metro stop; tel. 06-9784-4950.

## PANTHEON NEIGHBORHOOD

Besides being home to ancient sites and historic churches, the area around the Pantheon is another part of Rome with an urban village feel. Wander narrow streets, sample the many shops and eateries, and gather with the locals in squares marked by bubbling fountains. Just south of the Pantheon is the Jewish quarter, with remnants of Rome's Jewish history and culture.

Exploring this area is especially nice in the evening, when restaurants bustle and streets are jammed with foot traffic. For a self-guided walk in this neighborhood, from Campo de' Fiori to the Trevi Fountain (and ending at the Spanish Steps), see my "Heart of Rome Walk," earlier.

### ▲▲▲Pantheon

For the greatest look at the splendor of Rome, antiquity's best-preserved interior is a must. Built two millennia ago, this influential domed temple served as the model for Michelangelo's dome of St. Peter's and many others.

**Cost and Hours:** Free, Mon-Sat 8:30-19:30, Sun 9:00-18:00, holidays 9:00-13:00, tel. 06-6830-0230, www.pantheonroma.com.

**When to Go:** Don't go at midday, when the Pantheon is packed. If you visit before 9:00, you'll have it all to yourself.

**Dress Code:** No visitors with skimpy shorts or bare shoulders allowed inside the Pantheon.

**Tours:** The Pantheon has a €6, 30-minute audioguide (€10/2 people). ∩ Download my free Pantheon audio tour.

**Visiting the Pantheon:** The Pantheon was a Roman temple dedicated to all *(pan)* of the gods *(theos)*. The original temple was built in 27 BC by Emperor Augustus' son-in-law, Marcus Agrippa. In fact, the inscription below the triangular **pediment** proclaims (in Latin), "Marcus Agrippa, son of Lucio, three times consul made this." But after a couple of fires, the structure we see today was completely rebuilt by Emperor Hadrian around AD 120. After the fall of Rome, the Pantheon became a Christian church (from "all the gods" to "all the martyrs"), which saved it from architectural cannibalism and ensured its upkeep through the Dark Ages.

The dome is what makes this building unique—and perhaps the most influential architectural design in art history. The Pantheon's dome was the model for the Florence cathedral dome, which launched the Renaissance, and for Michelangelo's dome of St. Peter's, which capped it all off. Even the US Capitol in Washington, DC, was inspired by this dome.

Wander into the **portico** with its forest of 16 enormous **columns**. They're 40 feet tall and 15 feet around, made of red-and-gray granite. Whereas many ancient columns are a stack of cylindrical

**ROME**

drums, these columns are each a single piece of stone. Imagine how impressive this portico was in its heyday, when the ceiling was covered with shiny bronze plating. Check out the giant doorway—it's considered original. The **doors** are 23 feet tall and made of bronze. The magnificent, soaring **dome,** the largest made until the Renaissance, is set on a circular base. The mathematical perfection of this dome-on-a-base design is a testament to Roman engineering; it's as high as it is wide—142 feet. To picture it, imagine a basketball wedged inside a wastebasket so that it just touches bottom.

The dome is made from concrete, a Roman invention. It gets lighter and thinner as it reaches the top. The base of the dome is 23 feet thick and made from heavy concrete mixed with travertine, while near the top, it's less than five feet thick and made with a lighter volcanic rock (pumice) mixed in. Note the square indentations in the surface of the dome. This **coffered ceiling** reduces the weight of the dome without compromising strength. The walls are strengthened by brick relieving arches ("blind" arches)—visible in the exposed brickwork in a few of the interior niches and easy to see from outside.

Both Brunelleschi and Michelangelo studied this dome before building their own, in Florence and the Vatican, respectively. (The grandiose vision for St. Peter's Basilica was to place the dome of the Pantheon atop the Forum's Basilica of Constantine.)

At the top, the **oculus** is the building's only light source. It's completely open and almost 30 feet across. The 1,800-year-old **floor**—with 80 percent of its original stones surviving—has holes in it and slants toward the edges to let rainwater drain. Although some of the floor's marble has been replaced, the design—alternating circles and squares—is original.

While its ancient statuary is long gone, today the Pantheon's interior holds decorative sculptures and the tombs of important people from more recent centuries. The artist **Raphael** (1483-1520) lies in a stone coffin to the left of the main altar, in a lighted glass niche. Facing each other across the rotunda are the tombs of modern Italy's first two kings, members of the House of Savoy: **Victor Emmanuel II** and **Umberto I.** Beneath Umberto's tomb lies that of his queen (and first cousin), Margherita.

### ▲▲Churches near the Pantheon

The following churches are free to visit; modest dress is recommended.

The **Church of San Luigi dei Francesi** has a magnificent chapel painted by Caravaggio (free, daily 9:30-12:30 & 14:30-18:30 except closed Sun morning, between Pantheon and north end of Piazza Navona, www.saintlouis-rome.net). The only Gothic church in Rome is the **Church of Santa Maria sopra Mi-**

ROME

**nerva,** with a little-known Michelangelo statue, *Christ Bearing the Cross* (free, Mon-Fri 7:00-19:00, Sat from 10:00, Sun from 8:10; closes midday Sat-Sun; on a little square behind the Pantheon, to the east, www.santamariasopraminerva.it). The **Church of Sant'Ignazio,** several blocks east of the Pantheon, is a riot of Baroque illusions with a false dome (free, Mon-Sat 7:30-19:00, Sun from 9:00, www.chiesasantignazio.it). A few blocks away, across Corso Vittorio Emanuele, is the rich and Baroque **Gesù Church,** headquarters of the Jesuits in Rome (free, daily 7:00-12:30 & 16:00-19:45, interesting daily ceremony at 17:30, www.chiesadelgesu.org).

### ▲Trevi Fountain

The bubbly Baroque fountain, worth ▲▲ by night, is a minor sight to art scholars...but a major nighttime gathering spot for teens on the make and tourists tossing coins. Those coins are collected daily to feed Rome's poor. For more on the fountain, see page 842.

## VATICAN CITY

Vatican City, the world's smallest country, contains St. Peter's Basilica (with Michelangelo's exquisite *Pietà*) and the Vatican Museums (with Michelangelo's Sistine Chapel). A helpful **TI** is just to the left of St. Peter's Basilica as you're facing it (Mon-Sat 8:30-18:15, closed Sun, tel. 06-6988-2019, www.vaticanstate.va). The entrances to St. Peter's and the Vatican Museums are a 15-minute walk apart (follow the outside of the Vatican wall,

which links the two sights). The nearest Metro stop—Ottaviano— still involves a 10-minute walk to either sight.

**Dress Code:** Modest dress is technically required of men, women, and children throughout Vatican City, even outdoors. The policy is strictly enforced in the Sistine Chapel and at St. Peter's Basilica but is more relaxed elsewhere (though always at the discretion of guards). To avoid problems, cover your shoulders; bring a light jacket or cover-up if you're wearing a tank top. Wear long pants or capris instead of shorts. Skirts or dresses should extend below your knee.

ROME

# Vatican City & Nearby

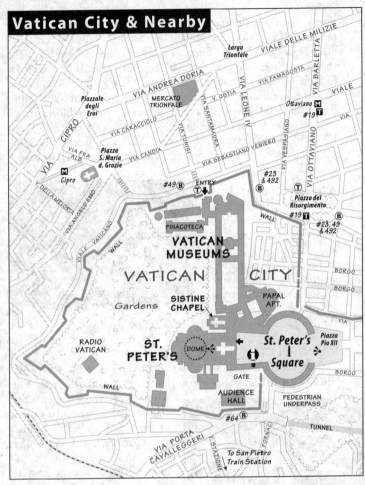

**ROME**

## St. Peter's Square

St. Peter's Square, with its ring of columns, symbolizes the arms of the church welcoming everyone—believers and nonbelievers—in its motherly embrace. It was designed a century after Michelangelo by the Baroque architect Gian Lorenzo Bernini, who did much of the work that we'll see inside. Numbers first: 284 columns, 56 feet high, in stern Doric style. Topping them are Bernini's 140 favorite saints, each 10 feet tall. The "square" itself is actually elliptical, 660 by 500 feet (roughly the same dimensions as the Colosseum). Though large, it's designed like a saucer, a little higher around the edges, so that even when full of crowds (as it often is), it allows those on the periphery to see above the throngs.

The **obelisk** in the center is 90 feet of solid granite weighing

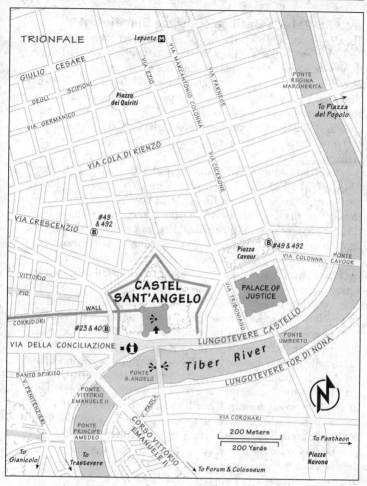

more than 300 tons. It once stood about 100 yards from its current location, in the center of the circus course (to the left of where St. Peter's is today). Think for a second about how much history this monument has seen. Originally erected in Egypt more than 2,000 years ago, it witnessed the fall of the pharaohs to the Greeks and then to the Romans. Then the emperor Caligula moved it to imperial Rome, where it stood impassively watching the slaughter of Christians at the racecourse and the torture of Protestants by the Inquisition (in the yellow-and-rust building just outside the square, to the left of the church). Today, it watches over the church, a reminder that each civilization builds on the previous ones. The puny cross on top reminds us that Christian culture has cast but a thin veneer over our pagan origins.

ROME

### ▲▲▲St. Peter's Basilica (Basilica San Pietro)

There is no doubt: This is the richest and grandest church on earth. To call it vast is like calling Einstein smart. Plaques on the floor show you where other, smaller churches would end if they were placed inside. The ornamental cherubs would dwarf a large man. Birds roost inside, and thousands of people wander about, heads craned heavenward, hardly noticing each other. Don't miss Michelangelo's *Pietà* (behind bulletproof glass) to the right of the entrance. Bernini's altar work and twisting, towering canopy are brilliant.

**Cost and Hours:** Free, daily April-Sept 7:00-19:00, Oct-March 7:00-18:30. The church closes on Wednesday mornings during papal audiences (until roughly 13:00). Masses occur daily throughout the day. The view from the dome is worth the climb (€10 for elevator to roof, then take stairs; €8 to climb stairs all the way, cash only, allow an hour to go up and down, daily April-Sept 7:30-19:00, Oct-March 7:30-18:00, last entry one hour before closing if you take the stairs the whole way). Tel. 06-6988-2019, www.vaticanstate.va.

**Avoiding Lines:** There's often a bottleneck at the security check. The checkpoint is typically on the north side of the square, but is sometimes closer to the church or tucked under the south colonnade. If you're visiting the Vatican Museums first, a shortcut usually—but not always—lets you exit from the Sistine Chapel directly into St. Peter's, thereby avoiding the security line at the church (for details, see page 895). You can visit before 10:00 to avoid the worst crowds. Crowds are also thinner after 16:00—just as sunbeams begin working their magic on the altar. But after 16:00, the crypt is closed, and the altar area is often roped off.

**Dress Code:** No shorts, above-the-knee skirts, or bare shoulders (applies to men, women, and children). Attendants enforce this dress code, so carry a cover-up if necessary.

**Getting There:** Take the Metro to Ottaviano, then walk 10 minutes south on Via Ottaviano. The #40 express bus drops off at Piazza Pio, next to Castel Sant'Angelo—a 10-minute walk from St. Peter's. The more crowded bus #64, beloved by pickpockets, stops just outside St. Peter's Square to the south (get off the bus after it crosses the Tiber, at the first stop past the tunnel; backtrack toward the tunnel and turn left when you see the rows of columns; the return bus stop is adjacent to the tunnel). Bus #492 heads through the center of town, stopping at Largo Argentina, and gets you near Piazza Risorgimento (get off when you see the Vatican walls). A few other handy buses (see page 824) get you to the general Vatican area. A taxi from Termini train station costs about €15.

**Church Services:** Mass, generally in Italian, is said varyingly

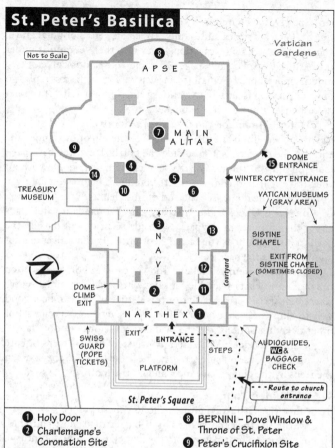

# St. Peter's Basilica

Not to Scale

APSE

Vatican Gardens

MAIN ALTAR

DOME ENTRANCE

WINTER CRYPT ENTRANCE

VATICAN MUSEUMS (GRAY AREA)

TREASURY MUSEUM

SISTINE CHAPEL

EXIT FROM SISTINE CHAPEL (SOMETIMES CLOSED)

NAVE

Courtyard

DOME CLIMB EXIT

NARTHEX

SWISS GUARD (POPE TICKETS)

EXIT

**ENTRANCE**

STEPS

AUDIOGUIDES, **WC** & BAGGAGE CHECK

PLATFORM

- - - Route to church entrance

**St. Peter's Square**

1. Holy Door
2. Charlemagne's Coronation Site
3. Michelangelo's Greek-Cross Church
4. St. Andrew Statue; View of Dome; Crypt Entrance
5. St. Peter Statue (with Kissable Toe)
6. Pope John XXIII
7. Main Altar (under Bernini's Canopy & over Peter's Tomb)
8. BERNINI – Dove Window & Throne of St. Peter
9. Peter's Crucifixion Site
10. RAPHAEL – Mosaic Copy of The Transfiguration
11. MICHELANGELO – Pietà
12. Tomb of Pope John Paul II
13. Blessed Sacrament Chapel
14. Treasury Museum
15. Dome Entrance

**ROME**

in the south (left) transept, the Blessed Sacrament Chapel (on right side of nave), or at the main altar. Confirm times on the signboard as you enter. Typical schedule: Mon-Sat at 8:30, 9:00, 10:00, 11:00, 12:00, and at 17:00 (in Latin, at the main altar); Sun and holidays at 9:00, 10:30 (in Latin), 11:30, 12:15, 13:00, 16:00, 16:45 (vespers), and 17:30.

**Tours: Audioguides** can be rented near the baggage check

(€5 plus ID, for church only, daily 8:30-17:00). ∩ Download my free St. Peter's Basilica **audio tour.** To see St. Peter's original grave, you can take a *Scavi* (excavations) tour into the **Necropolis** under the basilica (€13, 1.5 hours, ages 15 and up only). Book at least two months in advance by email (scavi@fsp.va) for the fastest reply; go to www.scavi.va (select "Excavations Office") for details. If you get no response, it means they're booked.

**Dome Climb:** You can take an elevator or climb 231 stairs to the roof, then climb another 323 steps to the top of the dome. The entry to the elevator is just outside the north side of the basilica—look for signs to the *cupola.* If you're climbing the dome without your travel partner, confirm where you'll exit before you split up. For more on the dome, see the end of this chapter.

**Baggage Check:** The free bag check (mandatory for bags larger than a purse or daypack) is inside security, but outside the basilica (to the right as you face the entrance). Pocketknives are not allowed inside the basilica.

**Vatican Museums Tickets:** The Vatican TI at St. Peter's often has museum tickets available for sale (with same-day, timed-entry reservations; see listing earlier in this section). This can be a good way to skip the ticket-buying line at the Vatican Museums (for other ticketing options, see the "Vatican Museums" section, later).

**Visitor Services:** WCs are on both sides of St. Peter's Square (by the TI and just outside security), near the baggage check down the steps by the church entrance, and on the roof.

### ◗ Self-Guided Tour

To sample the basilica's highlights, follow these points:

❶ The **narthex** (portico) is itself bigger than most churches. Its huge white columns date from the first church (fourth century). Five famous bronze doors lead into the church. Made from the melted-down bronze of the original door of Old St. Peter's, the central door was the first Renaissance work in Rome (c. 1450). It's only opened on special occasions.

The far-right entrance is the **Holy Door,** opened only during Holy Years (and special "Jubilee" years designated by the pope). On Christmas Eve every 25 years, the pope knocks three times with a silver hammer and the door opens, welcoming pilgrims to pass through.

Looking down the nave, we get a sense of the splendor of ancient Rome that was carried on by the Catholic Church. The floor plan, with a central

ROME

aisle (nave) flanked by two side aisles, is based on that of ancient Roman basilicas—large halls built to accommodate business and legal meetings. In fact, many of the stones used to build St. Peter's were scavenged from the ruined law courts of ancient Rome.

**❷** On the floor near the central doorway is a round slab of porphyry stone in the maroon color of ancient Roman officialdom. This is the spot where, on Christmas night in AD 800, the king of the Franks **Charlemagne was crowned** Holy Roman Emperor. Look down the main hall—this church is huge. Stand at the very back of the nave and survey the heavenly expanse. It's a riot of marble, gold, stucco, mosaics, columns of stone, and pillars of light. As the symbol of global Catholicism, this church is appropriately big. Size before beauty: The golden window at the far end is two football fields away. The dove in the golden window has the wingspan of a 747 (OK, maybe not quite, but it *is* big). The church covers six acres. The babies at the base of the pillars along the main hall (the nave) are adult-size. The lettering in the gold band along the top of the pillars is seven feet high. Really. The church has a capacity of 60,000 standing worshippers (or 1,200 tour groups).

• *Now, walk straight up the center of the nave toward the altar.*

**❸** Michelangelo was 71 when the pope persuaded him to take over the church project and cap it with a dome. He agreed, intending to put the dome over Donato Bramante's original **Greek-cross floor plan.** In optimistic Renaissance times, this symmetrical arrangement symbolized perfection—the orderliness of the created world and the goodness of man (who was created in God's image). But Michelangelo was a Renaissance Man in Counter-Reformation times. The Church, struggling against Protestants and its own corruption, opted for a plan designed to impress the world with its grandeur—the Latin cross of the Crucifixion, with its nave extended to accommodate the grand religious spectacles of the Baroque period.

**❹** Park yourself in front of the **statue of St. Andrew** to the left of the altar, the guy holding an X-shaped cross. (Note that the **entrance to the crypt** is usually here; in winter it's by the dome entrance.) Like Andrew, gaze up into the dome, and also like him, gasp.

The **dome** soars higher than a football field on end, 448 feet from the floor of the cathedral to the top of the lantern. It glows with light from its windows, the blue-and-gold mosaics creating a cool, solemn atmosphere.

In this majestic vision of heaven (not painted by Michelangelo), we see (above the windows) Jesus, Mary, and a ring of saints, rings of more angels above them, and, way up in the ozone, God the Father (a blur of blue and red, unless you have binoculars).

**❺** Back in the nave sits a bronze **statue of St. Peter** under a canopy. This is one of a handful of pieces of art that were in the earlier church. In one hand he holds keys, the symbol of the authority given him by Christ, while with the other hand he blesses us. His big right toe has been worn smooth by the lips of pilgrims and foot fetishists. Stand in line and kiss it, or, to avoid foot-and-mouth disease, touch your hand to your lips, then rub the toe. This is simply an act of reverence with no legend attached, though you can make one up if you like.

• Circle to the right around the statue of Peter to find the lighted glass niche.

**❻** The red-robed body is **Pope John XXIII,** whose papacy lasted from 1958 to 1963. Nicknamed "the good pope," he is best known for initiating the landmark Vatican II Council (1962-1965) that instituted major reforms, bringing the Church into the modern age. In 2000, during the beatification process (a stop on the way to sainthood), Church authorities checked his body, and it was surprisingly fresh. So they moved it upstairs, put it behind glass, and now old Catholics who remember him fondly enjoy another stop on their St. Peter's visit. Pope John was canonized in 2014.

**❼** Sitting over St. Peter's tomb, the **main altar** (the white marble slab with cross and candlesticks) beneath the dome and canopy is used only when the pope himself says Mass. He sometimes conducts the Sunday morning service when he's in town, a sight worth seeing.

The tiny altar would be lost in this enormous church if it weren't for Gian Lorenzo Bernini's seven-story bronze canopy (God's "four-poster bed"), which "extends" the altar upward and reduces the perceived distance between floor and ceiling. The corkscrew columns echo the marble ones that surrounded the altar/tomb in Old St. Peter's. Some of the bronze used here was taken and melted down from the ancient Pantheon.

**❽** Bernini (1598-1680), the Michelangelo of the Baroque era, is the man most responsible for the interior decoration of the church.

His **dove window** shines above the smaller front altar used for everyday services. The Holy Spirit, in the form of a six-foot-high dove, pours sunlight onto the faithful through the alabaster windows, turning into artificial rays of gold and reflecting off swirling gold clouds, angels, and winged babies. During a service, real sunlight passes through real clouds of incense, mingling with Bernini's sculpture. Beneath the dove is the centerpiece

of this structure, the so-called **Throne of St. Peter,** an oak chair built in medieval times for a king. Subsequently, it was encrusted with tradition and encased in bronze by Bernini as a symbol of papal authority. In the apse, Mass is said daily for pilgrims, tourists, and Roman citizens alike.

• *To the left of the main altar is the* **south transept.** *It may be roped off for worship, but anyone can step past the guard if you say you're there "for prayer." At the far end, left side, find the dark "painting" of St. Peter crucified upside down.*

❾ This marks the exact spot (according to tradition) of **Peter's crucifixion.** Peter had come to the world's greatest city to preach Jesus' message of love to the pagan, often hostile Romans. During the reign of Emperor Nero, he was arrested and brought to Nero's Circus so all of Rome could witness his execution. When the authorities told Peter he was to be crucified just like his Lord, Peter said, essentially, "I'm not worthy" and insisted they nail him on the cross upside down.

❿ Around the corner on the right (heading back toward the central nave), pause at the mosaic copy of Raphael's epic painting of *The Transfiguration.* The original is now beautifully displayed in the Pinacoteca of the Vatican Museums. This and all the other "paintings" in the church are actually mosaic copies made from thousands of colored chips the size of your little fingernail. Because smoke and humidity would damage real paintings, since about 1600 church officials have replaced the paintings with mosaics (a.k.a. the "art of eternity") produced by the Vatican Mosaic Studio.

• *Back near the entrance of the church, in the far corner behind bulletproof glass, is the sculpture everyone has come to see, the* Pietà.

⓫ Michelangelo was 24 years old when he completed this **pietà**—a representation of Mary with the body of Christ taken from the cross. It was his first major commission, done for Holy Year 1500.

Michelangelo, with his total mastery of the real world, captures the sadness of the moment. Mary cradles her crucified son in her lap. Christ's lifeless right arm drooping down lets us know how heavy this corpse is. Mary looks at her dead son with sad tenderness. Her left hand turns upward, asking, "How could they do this to you?"

• In the chapel to the left is the Tomb of Pope John Paul II.

🄬 John Paul II (1920-2005) was one of the most beloved popes of recent times. During his papacy (1978-2005), he was the highly visible face of the Catholic Church as it labored to stay relevant in an increasingly secular world. The first non-Italian pope in four centuries, he oversaw the fall of communism in his native Poland. He survived an assassination attempt, and he publicly endured his slow decline from Parkinson's disease with great stoicism.

When John Paul II died in 2005, hundreds of thousands lined up outside the church, waiting up to 24 hours to pay their respects. He was sainted in April 2014, just nine years after his death. St. John Paul II lies beneath a painting of the steadfast St. Sebastian, his favorite saint.

🄭 You're welcome to step through the metalwork gates into the **Blessed Sacrament Chapel** (Capella di Santissimo Sacramento), an oasis of peace reserved for prayer and meditation (on right side of church, about midway to the altar). Mass is sometimes said here.

🄮 The **Treasury Museum** (Museo-Tesoro), on the left side of the nave near the altar, contains the room-size tomb of Sixtus IV by Antonio Pollaiuolo, a big pair of Roman pincers used to torture Christians, an original corkscrew column from Old St. Peter's, and assorted jewels, papal robes, and golden reliquaries—a marked contrast to the poverty of early Christians.

The foundations of Old St. Peter's, the **Crypt** (Grotte/Tombe), contains tombs of popes and memorial chapels. In summer, the crypt entrance is usually beside the statue of St. Andrew, to the left of the main altar (near #4 on the map); in winter, it's by the dome entrance. Stairs lead you down to the floor level of the previous church, where you'll pass the sepulcher of Peter. This lighted niche with an icon is not Peter's actual tomb, but part of a shrine that stands atop Peter's tomb. Nearby is the chapel where Pope John Paul II was buried before being moved upstairs in 2011. Continue your one-way visit until it spills you out, usually near the checkroom.

🄯 For one of the best views of Rome, go up to the **dome.** The entrance is along the right (north) side of the church, but the line begins to form out front, at the church's right door (as you face the church). Look for *cupola* signs.

There are two levels: the rooftop of the church and the very top of the dome. Climb or take an elevator to the first level, on the church roof just above the facade. From the roof, you can also go inside the gallery ringing the interior of the dome and look down inside the church.

To go all the way up to the top of the dome, you'll take a staircase that actually winds between the outer shell and the inner one. It's a sweaty, crowded, claustrophobic 15-minute, 323-step climb, but worth it. The view from the summit is great, the fresh air even better. Admire the arms of Bernini's colonnade encircling St. Peter's Square. Find the big, white Victor Emmanuel Monument, with the two statues on top; and the Pantheon, with its large, light, shallow dome. The large rectangular building to the left of the obelisk is the Vatican Museums complex, stuffed with art. Look down into the square at the tiny pilgrims buzzing like electrons around the nucleus of Catholicism.

## ▲▲▲Vatican Museums (Musei Vaticani)

The four miles of displays in this immense museum complex—from ancient statues to Christian frescoes to modern paintings—culminate in the Raphael Rooms and Michelangelo's glorious Sistine Chapel. This is one of Europe's top three or four houses of art. It can be exhausting, so plan your visit carefully, focusing on a few themes. Allow two hours for a quick visit, three or four hours to really enjoy it.

**Cost and Hours:** €17, €4 online reservation fee, Mon-Sat 9:00-18:00, last entry at 16:00 (though the official closing time is 18:00, the staff starts ushering you out at 17:30), closed on religious holidays and Sun except last Sun of the month (when it's free, more crowded, and open 9:00-14:00, last entry at 12:30); open Fri nights mid-April-Oct 19:00-23:00 (last entry at 21:30) by online reservation only—check the website. Hours are subject to frequent change and holidays; look online for current times.

**Closed Days:** The museum is closed on many holidays (mainly religious ones), including Jan 1 (New Year's), Jan 6 (Epiphany), Feb 11 (Vatican City established), March 19 (St. Joseph's Day), Easter Sunday and the following Monday, May 1 (Labor Day), June 29 (Sts. Peter and Paul), Aug 15 (Assumption of the Virgin), Nov 1

# Vatican City

The tiny independent country of Vatican City is contained entirely within Rome. (Its 100 acres could fit eight times over in New York's Central Park.) The Vatican has its own postal system, armed guards, beautiful gardens, helipad, mini train station, and radio station (KPOP). It also has two huge sights: St. Peter's Basilica and the Vatican Museums. Politically powerful, the Vatican is the religious capital of 1.2 billion Roman Catholics. If you're not a Catholic, become one for your visit.

The pope is both the religious and secular leader of Vatican City. For centuries, the Vatican was the capital of the Papal States, and locals referred to the pontiff as "King Pope." Because of the Vatican's territorial ambitions, it didn't always have good relations with Italy. Even though modern Italy was created in 1870, the Holy See didn't recognize it as a country until 1929.

**Vatican Gardens:** To walk through the manicured Vatican Gardens (with views over Rome and a good look at St. Peter's dome), book a guided tour several days in advance at www.museivaticani.va (€33, 2 hours, daily except Wed and Sun, includes entry to Vatican Museums; tours usually start at 9:30 or 11:00 at Vatican Museums tour desk). On rare occasions, same-day tickets are available at the Vatican TI. A 45-minute open-bus tour through the gardens is offered in good weather (€37, includes audioguide and entry to Vatican Museums).

**General Audience Tickets:** For the Wednesday audience at 10:00, a (free) ticket gets you closer to the papal action. Reserve tickets (available a month or two in advance) by sending a request by mail or fax (access the form at www.vatican.va—select "Prefecture of the Papal Household" at the bottom of the page). You'll then pick up the tickets at St. Peter's Square before the audience (available Tue 15:00-19:00 and Wed 7:00-9:00; usually

(All Saints' Day), Dec 8 (Immaculate Conception), and Dec 25 and 26 (Christmas). Always check the current hours and calendar on the museum website.

Individual rooms may close at odd hours, especially in the afternoon. The rooms described here are usually open.

**Information:** Tel. 06-6988-4676, www.museivaticani.va.

**Reservations:** You're crazy to come without a reservation: The Vatican Museums can be extremely crowded, with waits of up to two hours just to buy tickets. Bypass these long lines by reserving an entry time online for €21 (€17 ticket plus €4 booking fee). It's easy—and it

under Bernini's colonnade, to the left of the church).

You can also book tickets online through the American Catholic Church in Rome, headquartered at St. Patrick's Church (details at www.stpatricksamericanrome.org; free, but donations appreciated). Pick up your tickets or check for last-minute availability at the church office the Tuesday before the audience between 16:30 and 18:15 (just south of Villa Borghese Gardens on Via Boncompagni 31, Metro: Barberini, office tel. 06-8881-8727).

Finally, starting the Monday before the audience, Swiss Guards hand out tickets from their station near the basilica exit (see the "St. Peter's Square" map). Don't go through security—just march up, ask nicely, and say *"danke."* While this is perhaps easiest, I'd reserve in advance to guarantee a ticket.

**General Audience Tips:** On Wednesday morning, you'll need to be dressed modestly (shoulders covered, no short shorts or tank tops—long pants or knee-length skirts are safest) and clear security (no big bags; lines tend to move more quickly on the side of the square farthest from the Metro stop). To get a seat (much less a good one), it's smart to be there a couple of hours early—there are far fewer seats than ticketholders. If you just want to see the pope, get a good photo, and don't mind standing, you can show up later (though still at least 30 minutes early) and take your place in the standing-room section in the back half of the square. The service gets underway around 9:30. Shortly thereafter, the Popemobile appears, winding through the adoring crowd (the best places—seated or standing—are near the cloth-covered wooden fences that line the Popemobile route). Around 10:00, the Pope's multilingual message begins and lasts for about an hour (you can leave at any time).

can change your day. For sights covered by my self-guided tour, select the ticket called "Vatican Museums and Sistine Chapel." Print the emailed voucher to present at the museum (see "Getting In," later). You can also receive your reservation on your mobile phone.

**When to Go:** The museum is generally crowded, with shoulder-to-shoulder sightseeing through much of it. The best time to visit is a weekday after 14:00—the later the better. Another good time is during the papal audience on Wednesday morning, when many tourists are at St. Peter's Square (the drawback is that St. Peter's Basilica is closed until roughly 13:00, as is the exit to it from the Sistine Chapel). The worst days are Saturdays, the last Sunday of the month (when the museum is free), Mondays, rainy days, and any day before or after a holiday closure.

**More Line-Beating Tips:** Booking a **guided tour** (described later, under "Tours") gets you right in—just show the guard your

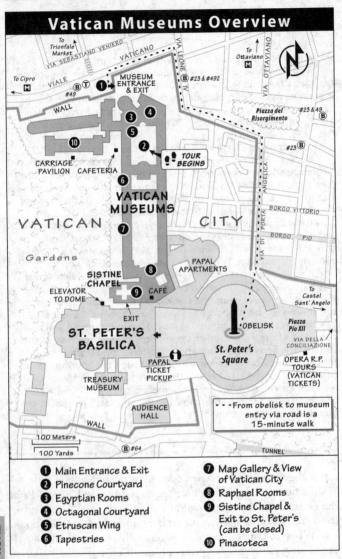

## Vatican Museums Overview

1. Main Entrance & Exit
2. Pinecone Courtyard
3. Egyptian Rooms
4. Octagonal Courtyard
5. Etruscan Wing
6. Tapestries
7. Map Gallery & View of Vatican City
8. Raphael Rooms
9. Sistine Chapel & Exit to St. Peter's (can be closed)
10. Pinacoteca

voucher. You can often buy **same-day timed-entry reservations** without a ticket-buying line at the Vatican TI in St. Peter's Square (to the left as you face the basilica—see details under "Vatican City," earlier). The Opera Romana Pellegrinaggi (a.k.a., Roma Cristiana), a private pilgrimage tour company, also sells same-day tickets (€30, entrances almost hourly, office in front of St. Peter's Square, Piazza Pio XII 9, tel. 06-698-961, www.operaromanapellegrinaggi.org). **Hawkers** peddling skip-the-line access swarm the Vatican area, offering guided tours—but museum staff advise against accepting their offers (while legitimate, the tour caliber is often low—use them only as a last resort).

**Dress Code:** While modest dress (no shorts, above-knee skirts, or bare shoulders) is technically required throughout the Vatican Museums, this dress code is most strictly enforced inside the Sistine Chapel.

**Getting There:** The Ottaviano Metro stop is a 10-minute walk from the entrance. Bus #49 from Piazza Cavour/Castel Sant'Angelo stops at Piazza Risorgimento and continues right to the entrance. Bus #23 from Trastevere hugs the west bank of the Tiber and stops on Via Leone IV, just downhill from the entrance. Bus #492 heads from the city center past Piazza Risorgimento and the Vatican walls, and stops on Via Leone IV. Bus #64 stops on the other side of St. Peter's Square, a 15- to 20-minute walk (facing the church from the obelisk, take a right through the colonnade and follow the Vatican Wall). Or take a taxi from the city center—they are reasonable (hop in and say, "moo-ZAY-ee vah-tee-KAH-nee").

**Getting In:** Approaching the exterior entrance (the big white door), you'll see three lines: individuals without reservations (far left), individuals with reservations (usually shorter and faster), and groups (on the right). Make sure you get in the correct entry line. All visitors must pass through a metal detector (no pocketknives allowed).

**With a reservation,** show your voucher to the guard and enter via the reserved ticket-holder line. Inside, after the security check, go to any window on the left to show your voucher and pick up your ticket, then go up the steps and enter the museum. (Or, you can skip the ticket-window line by going upstairs and processing your voucher on a machine.)

**Without a reservation,** enter via the far left line. Once you clear security, go upstairs to buy your ticket.

**Tours:** An €8 **audioguide** is available at the top of the spiral ramp/escalator, and can be prepaid when you book tickets online. No ID is required to rent an audioguide, and you can drop it off either where you rented it or after leaving the Sistine Chapel if taking the shortcut to St. Peter's (described later, under "Museum Strategies"). Confirm the drop-off location when renting. ∩ Download my free Vatican Museums and Sistine Chapel **audio tours.** The Vatican offers **guided tours** in English that are easy to book on their website (€33, includes admission). Present your confirmation voucher to a guard to the right of the entrance; then, once inside, go to the Guided Tours desk (in the lobby, up a few stairs).

For a list of **private tour** companies and guides, see page 827.

**Visitor Services:** The museum's "checkroom" (to the right after security) takes only bigger bags, not day bags. (Note: If you use the checkroom, you can't take advantage of the shortcut directly from the Sistine Chapel to St. Peter's.) The post office, with stamps that make collectors drool, is upstairs. WCs are mainly at the entrance/exit, plus a few scattered within the collection.

**Museum Strategies:** The museum has two exits. The **main exit** is near the entrance. Use this if you need to return an audioguide, retrieve bags from the checkroom, or if you plan on visiting the Pinacoteca (featuring paintings by Raphael, Leonardo, Caravaggio, and others) at the end.

The other exit is a handy (but sometimes closed) **shortcut** that leads from the Sistine Chapel directly to St. Peter's Basilica (spilling out alongside the church; see map on page 879). The shortcut saves you a 30-minute walk to the basilica's main entrance and lets you avoid the often-long security line for others entering the basilica. Officially, this exit is for Vatican guides and their groups only. However, it's often open to anyone (depending on how crowded the chapel is and how the guards feel). It's worth a shot (try blending in with a group that's leaving), but be prepared for the possibility that you won't get through.

### ❍ Self-Guided Tour

Our tour starts in the large open-air "Pinecone Courtyard." This vast space sums up the Vatican's vast collection: Pinecone—ancient, a 2,000 year-old offering to Isis. Bronze sphere—modern, created in 1990. And the courtyard around it—Renaissance, designed by Bramante.

We'll begin our museum visit as civilization did, in **Egypt and Mesopotamia.** Backtrack inside and up the stairs to the right to find linen-wrapped mummies, stiff statues, and early writing on clay tablets.

After a stop at a view balcony, make your way to the Octagonal Courtyard, decorated with some of the best **Greek and Roman statues** in captivity. The *Apollo Belvedere* is a Roman copy (4th century BC) of a Hellenistic original that followed the style of the great Greek sculptor Praxiteles. It fully captures the beauty of the human form. The anatomy is perfect, his pose is natural. Instead of standing at attention, face-forward with his arms at his sides (Egyptian-style), Apollo is on the move, coming to rest with his weight on one leg.

*Laocoön* was sculpted some four centuries after the Golden Age (5th-4th century BC), after the scales of "balance" had been tipped. Whereas *Apollo* is a balance between stillness and motion, this is unbridled motion. *Apollo* is serene, graceful, and godlike, while *Laocoön* is powerful, emotional, and gritty. The figures (carved from four blocks of marble pieced together seamlessly) are powerful, not light and graceful. The poses are as twisted as possible, accentuating every rippling muscle and bulging vein.

The centerpiece of the next hall is the *Belvedere Torso* (just a 2,000-year-old torso, but one that had a great impact on the art of Michelangelo). Finishing off the classical statuary are two fine fourth-century porphyry sarcophagi. These royal purple tombs were made (though not used) for the Roman emperor Constantine's mother (Helena, on left) and daughter (Constanza, on right).

After long halls of tapestries, old maps, broken penises, and fig leaves, you'll come to what most people are looking for: the Raphael Rooms and Michelangelo's Sistine Chapel.

**Raphael Rooms:** The highlight of the Raphael Rooms, frescoed by Raphael and his assistants, is the restored *School of Athens*. It is remarkable for its blatant pre-Christian classical orientation, especially considering it originally wallpapered the apartments of Pope Julius II. Raphael honors the great pre-Christian thinkers—Aristotle, Plato, and company—who are portrayed as the leading artists of Raphael's day. There's Leonardo da Vinci, whom Raphael worshipped, in the role of Plato. Michelangelo broods in the foreground, added later. When Raphael snuck a peek at the Sistine Chapel, he decided that his arch-competitor was so good that he had to put their personal differences aside and include him in this tribute to the artists of his generation. Today's St. Peter's was under construction as Raphael was working. In the *School of Athens*, he gives us a sneak preview of the unfinished church.

**Sistine Chapel:** Next is the brilliantly restored Sistine Chapel. This is the pope's personal chapel and also the place where, upon the death of the ruling pope, a new pope is elected.

The Sistine Chapel is famous for Michelangelo's pictorial culmination of the Renaissance, showing the story of creation, with a powerful God weaving in and out of each scene through that busy first week. This is an optimistic and positive expression of the High Renaissance and a stirring example of the artistic and theological maturity of the 33-year-old Michelangelo, who spent four years on this work.

The ceiling shows the history of the world before the birth of Jesus. We see God creating the world, creating man and woman, destroying the earth by flood, and so on. God himself, in his

# The Sistine Ceiling

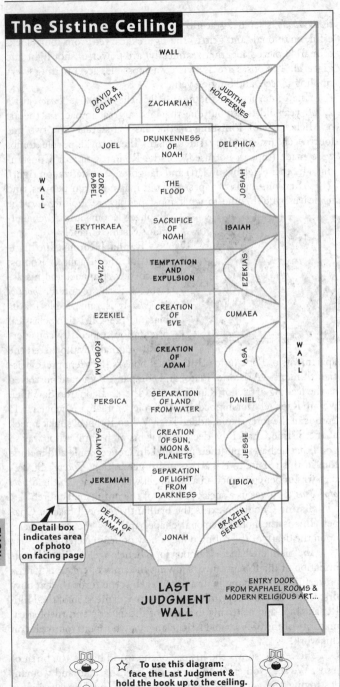

WALL

DAVID & GOLIATH

ZACHARIAH

JUDITH & HOLOFERNES

WALL

| | | |
|---|---|---|
| JOEL | DRUNKENNESS OF NOAH | DELPHICA |
| ZORO-BABEL | THE FLOOD | JOSIAH |
| ERYTHRAEA | SACRIFICE OF NOAH | ISAIAH |
| OZIAS | TEMPTATION AND EXPULSION | EZEKIAS |
| EZEKIEL | CREATION OF EVE | CUMAEA |
| ROBOAM | CREATION OF ADAM | ASA |
| PERSICA | SEPARATION OF LAND FROM WATER | DANIEL |
| SALMON | CREATION OF SUN, MOON & PLANETS | JESSE |
| JEREMIAH | SEPARATION OF LIGHT FROM DARKNESS | LIBICA |

WALL

Detail box indicates area of photo on facing page

DEATH OF HAMAN

JONAH

BRAZEN SERPENT

ROME

LAST JUDGMENT WALL

ENTRY DOOR FROM RAPHAEL ROOMS & MODERN RELIGIOUS ART...

☆ To use this diagram: face the Last Judgment & hold the book up to the ceiling.

purple robe, actually appears in the first five scenes. Along the sides (where the ceiling starts to curve), we see the Old Testament prophets and pagan Greek prophetesses who foretold the coming of Christ. Dividing these scenes and figures are fake niches (a painted 3-D illusion) decorated with nude statue-like figures with symbolic meaning.

In the central panel of the *Creation of Adam,* God and man take center stage in this Renaissance version of creation. Adam, newly formed in the image of God, lounges dreamily in perfect naked innocence. God, with his entourage, swoops in with a swirl of activity (which—with a little imagination—looks like a cross-section of a human brain... quite a strong humanist statement). Their reaching hands are the center of this work. Adam's

is limp and passive; God's is strong and forceful, his finger twitching upward with energy. Here is the very moment of creation, as God passes the spark of life to man, the crowning work of his creation.

This is the spirit of the Renaissance. God is not a terrifying giant reaching down to puny and helpless man from way on high. Here they are on an equal plane, divided only by the diagonal bit of sky. God's billowing robe and the patch of green upon which Adam is lying balance each other. They are like two pieces of a jigsaw puzzle, or two long-separated continents, or like the yin and yang symbols finally coming together—uniting, complementing each other, creating wholeness. God and man work together in the divine process of Creation.

When the ceiling was finished and revealed to the public, it simply blew 'em away. It both caps the Renaissance and turns it in a new direction. In perfect Renaissance spirit, it mixes Old Testament prophets with classical figures. But the style is more dramatic, shocking, and emotional than the balanced Renaissance works before it. This is a very personal work—the Gospel according to Michelangelo—but its themes and subject matter are universal. Many art scholars contend that the Sistine ceiling is the single greatest work of art by any one human being.

Later, after the Reformation wars had begun and after the Catholic army of Spain had sacked the Vatican, the reeling Church began to fight back. As part of its Counter-Reformation, a much older Michelangelo was commissioned to paint the *Last Judgment* (behind the altar).

It's Judgment Day, and Christ—the powerful figure in the center, raising his arm to spank the wicked—has come to find out who's naughty and who's nice. Beneath him, a band of angels blows its trumpets Dizzy Gillespie-style, giving a wake-up call to the sleeping dead. The dead at lower left leave their graves and prepare to be judged. The righteous, on Christ's right hand (the left side of the picture), are carried up to the glories of heaven. The wicked on the other side are hurled down to hell, where demons wait to torture them. Charon, from the underworld of Greek mythology, waits below to ferry the souls of the damned to hell.

When *The Last Judgment* was unveiled to the public in 1541, it caused a sensation. The pope is said to have dropped to his knees and cried, "Lord, charge me not with my sins when thou shalt come on the Day of Judgment."

And it changed the course of art. The complex composition, with more than 300 figures swirling around the figure of Christ, went far beyond traditional Renaissance balance. The twisted figures shown from every imaginable angle challenged other painters to try and top this master of 3-D illusion. And the sheer terror and drama of the scene was a striking contrast to the placid optimism of, say, Raphael's *School of Athens*. Michelangelo had Baroque-en all the rules of the Renaissance, signaling a new era of art.

**Exiting the Vatican Museums:** To go **directly to St. Peter's Basilica** (see "Museum Strategies," earlier), take the shortcut exit at the far-right corner of the chapel (with your back to the altar—once through this door, you've left the Vatican Museums). Though this corner door is likely labeled "Exit for authorized guides and tour groups only," you can probably slide through with the crowds (or protest that your group has left you behind). If this exit is closed (which can happen without notice), hang out in the Sistine Chapel for a few more minutes—it'll likely reopen shortly.

If you skip the shortcut and take the long march back, you'll find, along with the Pinacoteca, a cafeteria (long lines, uninspired food), the underrated early Christian art section, and the exit via the souvenir shop.

## ▲Castel Sant'Angelo

Built as a tomb for the emperor, used through the Middle Ages as a castle, prison, and place of last refuge for popes under attack, and today a museum, this giant pile of ancient bricks is packed with history. The structure itself is striking, the opulent papal rooms are dramatic (and cool inside during the summer), and the views up top are some of the best in Rome.

**Cost and Hours:** €10, more with special exhibits, daily 9:00-19:30, last entry one hour before closing, near Vatican City, 10-minute walk from St. Peter's Square at Lungotevere Castello 50, Metro: Lepanto or bus #40 or #64, café, tel. 06-681-9111, www.castelsantangelo.beniculturali.it.

**Visiting the Castle:** Ancient Rome allowed no tombs within its walls, so Emperor Hadrian grabbed the most commanding po-

sition across the river and built this towering tomb. In the year 590, the archangel Michael appeared above the mausoleum to signal the end of a plague. The tomb became a fortified palace, renamed for the "holy angel." Castel Sant'Angelo spent the Dark Ages as a fortress and prison, but was connected to the Vatican via an elevated corridor in the 13th century (since Rome was repeatedly plundered by invaders, Castel Sant'Angelo was a handy place of last refuge for popes). In anticipation of long sieges, rooms were decorated with papal splendor.

A one-way route circulates visitors through the medieval and then the ancient parts of the monument. After the ticket booth, head upstairs to the rampart with its four bastions (named for the evangelists: Matthew, Mark, Luke, and John). Then climb a ramp and cross a bridge that traverses the sacred chamber in the center. Next, you reach a sunny courtyard with a 16th-century statue of St. Michael. Climbing to another rampart, you then pass the little 19th-century military museum and later enter medieval rooms built for the pope. The papal library was painted by followers of Raphael. Eventually you reach the rooftop terrace with the statue of the Archangel Michael sheathing his sword—and one of the best views anywhere of Rome and St. Peter's Basilica.

## NORTH ROME
### ▲Villa Borghese Gardens

Rome's somewhat scruffy three-square-mile "Central Park" is

great for its quiet shaded paths and for people-watching plenty of modern-day Romeos and Juliets. The best entrance is at the head of Via Veneto (Metro: Barberini, then 10-minute walk up Via Veneto and through the old Roman wall at Porta Pinciana, or catch a cab to Via Vene-

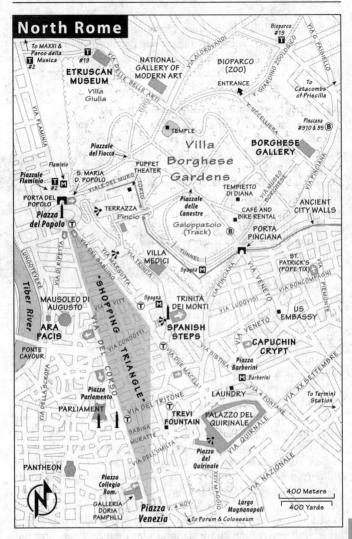

# North Rome

To MAXXI & Parco della Musica #2

ETRUSCAN MUSEUM
Villa Giulia

NATIONAL GALLERY OF MODERN ART

VIA DELLE BELLE ARTI

VIA ALDROVANDI

Bioparco #19

BIOPARCO (ZOO)
ENTRANCE

V. GIARDINO ZOOLOGICO

To Catacombs of Priscilla

VIA FLAMINIA

Flaminio

Piazzale del Fiocco

TEMPLE

Villa Borghese Gardens

Piazzale Flaminio #2

S. MARIA D. POPOLO

PUPPET THEATER

PORTA DEL POPOLO

VIALE DEL MURO TORTO

VIA UCCELLIERA

Pinciana #910 & 95

BORGHESE GALLERY

VIA MUSEO BORGHESE

TEMPIETTO DI DIANA

VIA PINCIANA

Piazza del Popolo

TERRAZZA Pincio

Piazzale delle Canestre

CAFÉ AND BIKE RENTAL

ANCIENT CITY WALLS

Galoppatoio (Track)

PORTA PINCIANA

Tiber River

MAUSOLEO DI AUGUSTO

VIA DI RIPETTA

VIA DEL BABUINO

VIA MARGUTTA

VILLA MEDICI

TUNNEL

Spagna M

ST. PATRICK'S (POPE TIX)

VIA VENETO

VIA BONCOMPAGNI

VIA PINCIANA

VIA LUDOVISI

US EMBASSY

VIA PIEMONTE

VIA VITT.

Spagna

TRINITÀ DEI MONTI

SHOPPING TRIANGLE

VIA DEL CORSO

VIA CONDOTTI

SPANISH STEPS

CAPUCHIN CRYPT

VIA VENETO

ARA PACIS

PONTE CAVOUR

VIA DELLA SCROFA

Piazza Parlamento

PARLIAMENT

VIA DUE MACELLI

VIA SISTINA

Piazza Barberini

M Barberini

VIA XX SETTEMBRE

To Termini Station

VIA DEL TRITONE

SABINA MURATTE

TREVI FOUNTAIN

LAUNDRY

VIA 4 FONTANE

PANTHEON

VIA DELL'UMILTÀ

PALAZZO DEL QUIRINALE

Piazza del Quirinale

VIA QUIRINALE

VIA NAZIONALE

Piazza Collegio Rom.

GALLERIA DORIA PAMPHILJ

V. NOV.

Piazza Venezia

XXIV MAGGIO

Largo Magnanapoli

400 Meters
400 Yards

To Forum & Coliseum

N

ROME

to—Porta Pinciana). There you'll find a cluster of buildings with a café, a kiddie arcade, and bike rental (€4/hour). Rent a bike or, for romantics, a pedaled rickshaw (*riscio*, €12/hour). Bikes come with locks to allow you to make sightseeing stops. Follow signs to discover the park's cafés, fountains, statues, lake, and prime picnic spots. Some sights require paid admission, including the Borghese Gallery, Rome's zoo, and the National Gallery of Modern Art (which holds 19th-century art).

You can also enter the gardens from the top of the Spanish Steps (facing the church, turn left and walk down the road 200 yards beyond Villa Medici, then angle right on the small pathway into the gardens), and from Piazza del Popolo (in the northeast corner of the piazza, stairs lead to the gardens via a terrace with grand views out to St. Peter's Basilica—bikes and Segways can be rented nearby).

### ▲▲▲Borghese Gallery (Galleria Borghese)

This plush museum, filling a cardinal's mansion in the park, offers one of Europe's most sumptuous art experiences. You'll enjoy a col-

lection of world-class Baroque sculpture, including Bernini's *David* and his excited statue of Apollo chasing Daphne, as well as paintings by Caravaggio, Raphael, Titian, and Rubens. The museum's mandatory reservation system keeps crowds to a manageable size.

**Cost and Hours:** €15, Tue-Sun 9:00-19:00, Thu until 21:00, closed Mon; free and very crowded once or twice a month when no reservations are taken, specific day varies in peak season (in low season, it's the first Sun). The 1.5-hour audioguide is excellent.

**Information:** Tel. 06-32810 (tickets and information), www.galleriaborghese.it.

**Advance Reservations Required:** Reservations are mandatory and simple to get. Entry times are 9:00, 11:00, 13:00, 15:00, and 17:00 plus 19:00 on Thu. You'll get exactly two hours for your visit. The sooner you reserve, the better. It's easiest to book online at www.tosc.it (€2/person booking fee; choose to pick up tickets at venue). You can also reserve with a real person over the telephone (€2/person booking fee, tel. 06-32810, press 2 for English, phones answered Mon-Fri 9:00-18:00, Sat 9:00-13:00, closed Sat in Aug and Sun year-round). Arrive 30 minutes before your appointed time to pick up your ticket in the lobby on the lower level (remember to bring your reservation confirmation). Don't cut it close—arriving late can mean forfeiting your reservation.

**Getting There:** The museum, at Piazzale del Museo Borghese 5, is set idyllically but inconveniently in the vast Villa Borghese Gardens. A taxi drops you 100 yards from the museum. Your destination is the Galleria Borghese, near Via Pinciana. Don't tell the cabbie "Villa Borghese," which is the park, not the museum. To go by public transit, take bus #910 from Termini train station/Piazza della Repubblica to the Via Pinciana stop, 100 yards from the museum (but note that #910 runs back to Termini by a different, less convenient route). Bus #53 runs to the same Via Pinciana stop from

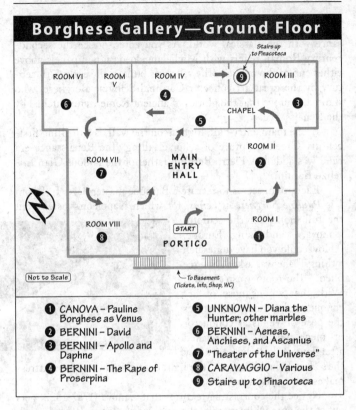

# Borghese Gallery—Ground Floor

Stairs up to Pinacoteca

ROOM VI | ROOM V | ROOM IV | **9** | ROOM III

**6** — **4** — **3**

CHAPEL

ROOM II

**5** — **2**

ROOM VII

**7**

MAIN ENTRY HALL

ROOM VIII

**8**

START

PORTICO

ROOM I

**1**

Not to Scale

To Basement (Tickets, Info, Shop, WC)

**1** CANOVA – Pauline Borghese as Venus
**2** BERNINI – David
**3** BERNINI – Apollo and Daphne
**4** BERNINI – The Rape of Proserpina
**5** UNKNOWN – Diana the Hunter; other marbles
**6** BERNINI – Aeneas, Anchises, and Ascanius
**7** "Theater of the Universe"
**8** CARAVAGGIO – Various
**9** Stairs up to Pinacoteca

Largo Chigi (not far from the Trevi Fountain) and the Barberini Metro station. You can also go by foot (20 minutes) from the Barberini Metro stop: Walk 10 minutes up Via Veneto, enter the park, and turn right, following signs another 10 minutes to the Borghese Gallery.

**Tours:** Guided English tours are offered every day at 9:00 and 11:00 (€6.50; reserve online or by phone). Or consider the museum's excellent 1.5-hour audioguide (€5), which covers more than this chapter.

**Baggage Check:** Baggage check is free, mandatory, and strictly enforced. Even small purses must be checked.

**Visiting the Museum:** Two hours is all you get...and you'll want every minute. Budget most of your time for the more interesting ground floor, but set aside 30 minutes for the paintings of the Pinacoteca upstairs (highlights are marked by the audioguide icons). It's hard to believe that a family of cardinals and popes would display so many works with secular and sensual—even erotic—themes. But the Borgheses felt that all forms of human expression, including pagan myths and physical passion, glorified God.

The essence of the collection is the connection of the Renaissance with the classical world. As you enter, notice the second-century Roman reliefs with Michelangelo-designed panels above either end of the portico. The villa was built in the early 17th century by the great art collector Cardinal Scipione Borghese, who wanted to prove that the glories of ancient Rome were matched by the Renaissance.

In the main entry hall, high up on the wall, is a thrilling first-century Greek sculpture of a horse falling. The Renaissance-era rider was added by Pietro Bernini, father of the famous Gian Lorenzo Bernini.

Each room seems to feature a Baroque masterpiece. In Room I is *Pauline Borghese as Venus,* for which Napoleon's sister went the full monty for the sculptor Canova, scandalizing Europe. ("How could you have done such a thing?!" she was asked. She replied, "The room wasn't cold.") With the famous nose of her conqueror brother, she strikes the pose of Venus as conqueror of men's hearts. Her relaxed afterglow and slight smirk say

she's already had her man. The light dent she puts in the mattress makes this goddess human.

Notice the contrasting textures that Canova (1757-1822) gets out of the pure white marble: the rumpled sheet versus her smooth skin, the satiny-smooth pillows and mattress versus the creases in them, her porcelain skin versus the hint of a love handle. Canova polished and waxed the marble until it looked as soft and pliable as cloth.

The mythological pose, the Roman couch, the ancient hairdo, and the calm harmony make Pauline the epitome of the Neoclassical style.

In Room II, Gian Lorenzo Bernini's **David** twists around to put a big rock in his sling. He purses his lips, knits his brow, and winds his body like a spring as his eyes lock onto the target: Goliath, who's somewhere behind us, putting us right in the line of fire. Compared with Michelangelo's *David,* this is unvarnished realism—an unbalanced pose, bulging veins, unflattering face, and armpit hair. Michelangelo's *David* thinks, whereas Bernini's acts. Bernini slays the pretty-boy *David*s of the Renaissance and prepares to invent Baroque.

The best one of all is in Room III: Bernini's *Apollo and Daphne.* It's the perfect Baroque subject—capturing a thrilling, action-filled moment. In the mythological story, Apollo—made stupid by

Cupid's arrow of love—chases after Daphne, who has been turned off by the "arrow of disgust." Just as he's about to catch her, she calls to her father to save her. Magically, her fingers begin to sprout leaves, her toes become roots, her skin turns to bark, and she transforms into a tree. Frustrated Apollo will end up with a handful of leaves. Walk slowly around the statue. It's more air than stone.

But don't stop here. In Room IV, admire Bernini's *The Rape of Proserpina,* proof that even at the age of 24 the sculptor was the master of marble. Over in Room VI, Bernini's first major work for Cardinal Borghese—*Aeneas, Anchises, and Ascanius*—reveals the then-20-year-old sculptor's astonishing aptitude for portraying human flesh, though the statue lacks the Baroque energy of his more mature work. And in Room VIII is a fabulous collection of paintings by **Caravaggio,** who brought Christian saints down to earth with gritty realism.

Upstairs, in the Pinacoteca (Painting Gallery), are busts and paintings by Bernini, as well as paintings by Raphael, Titian, Correggio, and Domenichino.

### ▲▲Catacombs of Priscilla (Catacombe di Priscilla)

While most tourists head out to the Appian Way to see the famous catacombs of San Sebastiano and San Callisto (7.5 miles south of downtown, easiest by taxi), the Catacombs of Priscilla are more central, less commercialized, and less crowded—they just feel more intimate, as catacombs should. You enter from a convent and explore the result of 250 years of tunneling that occurred from the second to the fifth centuries. Visits are by 30-minute guided tour only (English-language tours go whenever a small group gathers—generally every 20 minutes or so). You'll see a few thousand of the 40,000 niches carved here, along with some beautiful frescoes, including what is considered the first depiction of Mary nursing the Baby Jesus.

**Cost and Hours:** €8, €5 for kids 7-15, free for kids 6 and under, Tue-Sun 9:00-12:00 & 14:00-17:00, closed Mon, closed one random month a year—check website or call first, Via Salaria 430, tel. 06-8620-6272, www.catacombepriscilla.com.

**Getting There:** The catacombs are on the northeast edge of the city but well-served by direct buses (30 minutes from Termini or 40 minutes from Piazza Venezia) or a €15 taxi ride. From Termini, take bus #92 or #310 from Piazza Cinquecento or Metro B1

ROME

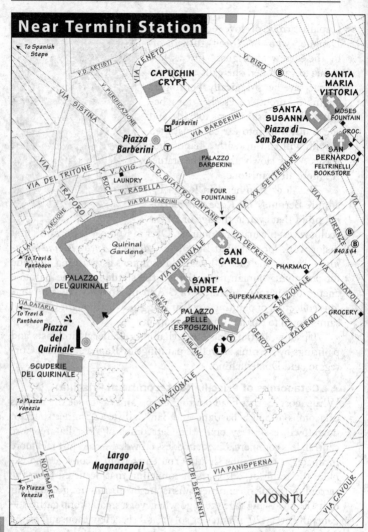

**Near Termini Station**

(direction: Jonio) to Libia or Sant'Agnese/Annibaliano stop. From Piazza Venezia, along Via del Corso or Via Barberini, take bus #63 or #83. Tell the driver "Piazza Crati" and "kah-tah-KOHM-bay" and you'll be let off near Piazza Crati (at the Nemorense/Crati stop). From there, walk through the little market in Piazza Crati, then down Via di Priscilla (about 5 minutes). The entrance is in the orange building on the left at the top of the hill.

## EAST ROME
## Near Termini Train Station
Most of these sights are within a 10-minute walk of the station.

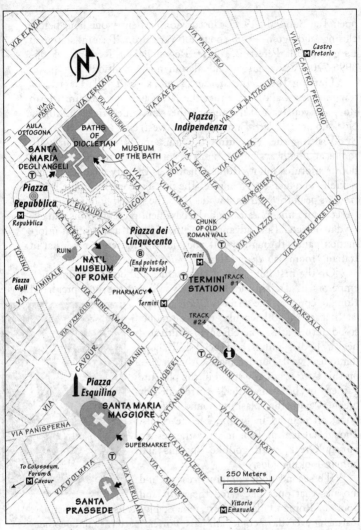

### ▲▲▲National Museum of Rome
### (Museo Nazionale Romano Palazzo Massimo alle Terme)

The National Museum's main branch, at Palazzo Massimo, houses the greatest collection of ancient Roman art anywhere. Think of this museum as a walk back in time. As you gaze at the same statues that the Romans swooned over, the history of Rome comes alive—from Julius Caesar's murder to Caligula's incest to Vespasian's Colosseum to the coming of Christianity.

**Cost and Hours:** €10, €12 combo-ticket covers three other branches—all skippable; free and crowded once or twice a month, specific day varies in peak season (in low season, it's the first Sun);

open Tue-Sun 9:00-19:45, closed Mon, last entry one hour before closing; audioguide—€5, about 100 yards from Termini station at Largo di Villa Peretti 2, Metro: Repubblica or Termini, tel. 06-3996-7700, www.museonazionaleromano.beniculturali.it.

**Getting There:** The museum is at Largo di Villa Peretti 2, a few minutes' walk from either the Repubblica or Termini Metro stop. As you leave Termini, it's the sandstone-brick building a block up on your left. Enter at the far (west) end.

**Visiting the Museum:** The museum is rectangular, with rooms and hallways built around a central courtyard. The ground-floor sculptures follow Rome's history as the city changes from a republic to a dictatorial empire. The first-floor exhibits take Rome from its peak through its slow decline. The second floor houses rare frescoes and fine mosaics, and the basement presents coins and everyday objects. Take advantage of the thoughtfully written information panels throughout. As you tour this museum, note that in Italian, "room" is *sala* and "hall" is *galleria*.

On the first floor, along with statues and busts showing such emperors as Trajan and Hadrian, you'll see the best-preserved Roman copy of the Greek *Discus Thrower*.

Statues of athletes like this commonly stood in the baths, where Romans cultivated healthy bodies, minds, and social skills, hoping to lead well-rounded lives. Other statues on this floor originally stood in the pleasure gardens of the Roman rich—surrounded by greenery with the splashing sound of fountains, all painted in bright, lifelike colors. Though created by Romans, the themes are mostly Greek, with godlike humans and human-looking gods.

The second floor contains frescoes and mosaics that once decorated the walls and floors of Roman villas. They're remarkably realistic and unstuffy, featuring everyday people, animals, flowery patterns, and geometrical designs. The Villa Farnesina frescoes—in black, red, yellow, and blue—are mostly architectural designs, with fake columns, friezes, and garlands. The Villa di Livia frescoes, owned by the wily wife of Augustus, immerse you in a leafy green garden full of birds and fruit trees, symbolizing the gods.

Finally, descend into the basement to see fine gold jewelry, the mummified body of an eight-year-old girl, and vault doors leading into the best coin collection in Europe, with fancy magnifying glasses maneuvering you through cases of coins from ancient Rome to modern times.

### ▲Baths of Diocletian/Church of Santa Maria degli Angeli (Terme di Diocleziano/Basilica S. Maria degli Angeli)

Of all the marvelous structures built by the Romans, their public baths were arguably the grandest, and the Baths of Diocletian were the granddaddy of them all. Built by Emperor Diocletian around AD 300 and sprawling over 30 acres—roughly five times the size of the Colosseum—these baths could cleanse 3,000 Romans at once. They functioned until AD 537, when barbarians attacked and the city's aqueducts fell into disuse, plunging Rome into a thousand years of poverty, darkness, and BO. Today, tourists can visit one grand section of the baths, the former main hall. This impressive remnant of the ancient complex was later transformed (with help from Michelangelo) into the Church of Santa Maria degli Angeli.

**Cost and Hours:** Free, daily 7:30-18:30, closes slightly later May-Sept and Sun year-round, entrance on Piazza della Repubblica (Metro: Repubblica), www.santamariadegliangeliroma.it.

### ▲Church of Santa Maria della Vittoria

This church, originally a poor Carmelite church, was slathered with Baroque richness in the 17th century. It houses Bernini's best-known statue, the swooning *St. Teresa in Ecstasy*.

**Cost and Hours:** Free (anyone collecting money at the door is not affiliated with the church), pay €0.50 for light, Mon-Sat 8:30-12:00 & 15:30-18:00, Sun 15:30-18:00, about 5 blocks northwest of Termini train station at Via XX Settembre 17, Metro: Repubblica.

**Visiting the Church:** Inside the church, you'll find St. Teresa to the left of the altar. Teresa has just been stabbed with God's arrow of fire. Now, the angel pulls it out and watches her reaction. Teresa swoons, her eyes roll up, her hand goes limp, she parts her lips...and moans. The smiling, cherubic angel understands just how she feels. Teresa, a 16th-century Spanish nun, later talked of the "sweetness" of "this intense pain," describing her oneness with God in ecstatic, even erotic, terms.

Bernini, the master of multimedia, pulls out all the stops to make this mystical vision real. Actual sunlight pours through the alabaster windows, and bronze sunbeams shine on a marble angel holding a golden arrow. Teresa leans back on a cloud and her robe ripples from within, charged with her spiritual arousal. Bernini has created a little stage-setting of heaven. And watching from the

ROME

"theater boxes" on either side are members of the family who commissioned the work.

# Shopping in Rome

Rome is a wonderful city to shop in. Even if you're not aiming to buy anything, exploring popular shopping areas provides a break from stressful, clogged tourist sights and an excuse to lose yourself on a charming street. Sometimes window-shopping, rather than museum-going, is the best way to connect with the contemporary life of a city. And that's certainly true in Rome.

## Department Stores

The shopping complex under Termini train station is a convenient place to peruse clothes, bags, shoes, and perfume at several major Italian chain stores (most open daily 8:00-22:00).

A good upscale department store is **La Rinascente** (Via del Tritone 61). Besides deluxe brands, it has a fine design section with great and often affordable ideas for gifts, a magnificent rooftop terrace for a romantic *aperitivo,* good restaurants, free bathrooms, and a section of an ancient aqueduct in the basement (worth a quick visit). You'll find another branch on Piazza Fiume (east of the Borghese Gallery).

The **Galleria Alberto Sordi** is an elegant 19th-century "mall" (across from Piazza Colonna). **UPIM** is a popular midrange department store (many branches, including inside Termini train station, Via Nazionale 111, and Piazza Santa Maria Maggiore). **Oviesse/OVS,** a cheap clothing outlet, is near the Vatican Museums (on the corner of Via Candia and Via Mocenigo, Metro: Cipro) and also near Piazza Barberini (Via del Tritone 172, Metro: Barberini).

## Affordable Shopping

The shopping area all along **Via del Corso** features moderately priced goods, with prices increasing as you head toward Piazza di Spagna (by the Spanish Steps). **Via Nazionale** also features a range of reasonably priced shops, especially for clothes and shoes. Near the bottom of Via Nazionale, in the **Monti** neighborhood near the Roman Forum, Via del Boschetto and Via dei Serpenti are more unique, with a mix of clothing shops and designer bric-a-brac. **Via Cola di Rienzo,** near the Vatican, is good for midrange clothes. Cheapskates scrounge through the junky but dirt-cheap shops in the gritty area around **Piazza Vittorio.**

## Boutique Shopping: Rome's "Shopping Triangle"

The triangular-shaped area between the Spanish Steps, Piazza Venezia, and Piazza del Popolo (along Via del Corso, see map on page 814) contains Rome's highest concentration of upscale boutiques and fashion stores. For top fashion, stroll the streets around the Spanish Steps, including **Via Condotti, Via Borgognona** (for the big-name shops), and **Via del Babuino** (more big names and a few galleries). For antiques and vintage items, wander **Via dei Coronari** (between Piazza Navona and the bend in the river), **Via Giulia** (between Campo de' Fiori and the river), **Via dei Banchi Vecchi** (parallel to Via Giulia), and the super-chic **Via Margutta,** with art galleries, too (hidden parallel to Via del Babuino and running from the Spanish Steps to Piazza del Popolo). For dozens of stores selling affordable apparel aimed mainly at a younger crowd, try **Via Giubbonari** near Campo de' Fiori.

### Flea Markets

For antiques and fleas, the granddaddy of markets is the **Porta Portese** *mercato delle pulci* (flea market). This Sunday-morning market

is long and spindly, running between the actual Porta Portese (a gate in the old town wall) and the Trastevere train station. While the shopping gets old (and the vendor food shouldn't be consumed), the people-watching is endlessly entertaining (6:30-13:00 Sun only, on Via Portuense and Via Ippolito Nievo; to get to the market, catch bus #75 from Termini train station or tram #8 from Piazza Venezia, get off on Viale di Trastevere, and walk toward the river—and the noise).

At the **Via Sannio** market, you'll find new and used clothing and leather goods, some handicrafts, and random items that were probably stolen. You won't find antiques (Mon-Sat 9:00-13:30, closed Sun, behind Coin department store, just outside the walls of San Giovanni in Laterano, Metro: San Giovanni).

For something a bit hipper, visit the weekend **Mercato Monti.** This Monti district flea market has an emphasis on vintage clothes and housewares and up-and-coming designers (Sat-Sun 10:00-20:00, closed July-Aug, Hotel Palatino, Via Leonina 46, Metro: Cavour, www.mercatomonti.com).

### Open-Air Produce Markets

For a fun and colorfully authentic experience, wander through the easygoing neighborhood produce markets that clog certain streets and squares every morning (7:00-13:30) except Sunday. Consider the huge **Mercato Trionfale** (three blocks north of Vatican Museums at Via Andrea Doria). Another great food market is the **Mercato Esquilino** (near Termini Station at Via Filippo Turati, Metro:

## The *Passeggiata*

Throughout Italy, early evening is time to stroll. While elsewhere in Italy this is called the *passeggiata,* in Rome it's a cruder, big-city version called the *struscio* (meaning "to rub").

Many of Italy's youth live with their parents even into their 30s. They spend a lot of time being trendy and hanging out. Like American kids once gathered at the mall, working-class suburban youth *(coatto)* converge on the old center, as there's little to keep them occupied in Rome's dreary outskirts (which lack public spaces). The hot *vroom-vroom* motor scooter is their symbol; haircuts and fashion are follow-the-leader.

In a more genteel small town, the *passeggiata* comes with sweet whispers of *"bella"* and *"bello"* ("pretty" and "handsome"). In Rome, the admiration is a little cruder and oriented toward consumption—they say *"buona"* and *"buono"*—roughly meaning "tasty."

You can be a spectator, sipping a drink at a sidewalk table, but it's more fun to stroll along with everyone else.

Vittorio Emanuele). The covered **Mercato di Testaccio** sells produce and housewares and is a hit with photographers and people-watchers (Metro: Piramide). Smaller but equally charming slices of everyday Roman life are at markets on these streets and squares: **Piazza delle Coppelle** (near the Pantheon), **Via Balbo** (near Termini train station), and **Via della Pace** (near Piazza Navona). And **Campo de' Fiori,** despite having become quite touristy, is still a fun scene.

# Nightlife in Rome

For most visitors, the best after-dark activity is simply to grab a gelato and join in the *passeggiata,* the evening stroll through the medieval lanes that connect Rome's romantic, floodlit squares and fountains. Head for Piazza Navona, the Pantheon, Campo de' Fiori, Trevi Fountain, the Spanish Steps, Via del Corso, Trastevere (around the Santa Maria in Trastevere Church), or Monte Testaccio.

### Sound-and-Light Shows

The Imperial Forums area hosts two atmospheric and inspirational sound-and-light shows that give you a chance to fantasize about the world of the Caesars. During each of these "nighttime journeys through ancient Rome" you spend about an hour with a headphone dialed to English, listening to an artfully crafted narration synced with projections on ancient walls, columns, and porticos. The final effect is worth the price tag (€15, both for €25, nightly mid-April-mid-Nov—bring your warmest coat, tickets sold online and at the gate, shows can sell out on busy weekends, tel. 06-0608, www.viaggioneifori.it).

**Caesar's Forum Stroll:** Starting at Trajan's Column, this tour leads you to eight stops along a wooden sidewalk of a few hundred yards, while an hour's narration tells the dramatic story of Julius Caesar.

**Forum of Augustus Show:** From your perch on wooden bleachers overlooking the remains of a vast forum, you'll learn the story of Augustus through images projected on an ancient firewall that survives to provide a fine screen for modern-day spectacles.

## Museums

Some museums have later opening hours (especially on Sat in summer), offering a good chance to see art in a cooler, less-crowded environment. See the "Rome at a Glance" sidebar on page 828 for suggestions.

## Performances and Film

Check out the current listings of concerts, operas, dance, and films. Posters around town also advertise upcoming events. For the most up-to-date events calendar, check these English-language websites: www.inromenow.com, www.wantedinrome.com, and www.angloinfo.com.

## Contemporary Music

Music lovers will seek out the mega-music complex of the Rome **Auditorium** (Auditorium Parco della Musica), designed by contemporary architect Renzo Piano and hosting concerts by both Italian and international artists (€20-60 tickets, check availability in advance—concerts often sell out, Viale Pietro de Coubertin 30, take Metro to Flaminio and then catch tram #2 to Apollodoro, from there it's a 5-minute walk east, just beyond the elevated road, tram/metro runs until 23:30, box office tel. 02-6006-0900, www.auditorium.com). Also called the "Park of Music," it's a place where many Romans go just for the scene—music store, restaurants, cafés, and fresh modern architecture with three state-of-the-art auditoriums (known as "the beetles" for their appearance). If you want to see today's Romans enjoying the modern culture of their city, an evening here is the best you'll do.

## Classical Music and Opera

The **Teatro dell'Opera** has an active schedule of opera and classical concerts. In the summer, the productions move to the Baths of Caracalla, where ancient ruins make an evocative backdrop. You'll brush shoulders with locals in all their finery, so pull your fanciest outfit from your backpack (tickets from €25, online reservations encouraged, box office takes phone reservations beginning five days prior at tel. 06-4816-0255; Via Firenze 72, a block off Via Nazionale, Metro: Repubblica; www.operaroma.it).

**Opera da Camera di Roma** is a cute, greatest-hits-for-tourists opera performance in the theater of the Palazzo Santa Chiara. While their advertising makes the show seem grander than it is, it's still a charming hour of music. In a plain little theater with a string quartet and two singers (a soprano and a tenor), you'll enjoy a touristy revue of the most popular Italian arias and Neapolitan songs in a casual and fun-loving atmosphere. The theater is so tiny (140 seats) that—unless you have money to burn—there's no reason to pay for more than the cheapest seats (€30). Book direct: Buying the cheapest tickets and request the Rick Steves upgrade (RS%, performances Tue-Sun at 19:30, none on Mon, a block behind the Pantheon at Piazza di Santa Chiara 14; drop by any time to pick up a ticket, or call to check availability and then just show up, mobile 320-530-7112, www.operadacameradiroma.com).

Tourist-oriented musical events take place at the Episcopal **Church of St. Paul's Within the Walls.** The music ranges from orchestral concerts (usually Tue and Fri at 20:30) to full operatic performances (usually Sat at 20:30). Some Sunday evenings at 18:30, the church hosts hour-long candlelit "Luminaria" concerts. Check the church website (under "Music") to see what's on (€10-30, same-day tickets usually available, arrive 30-45 minutes early for best seat, Via Napoli 58 at corner of Via Nazionale, Metro: Repubblica, tel. 06-482-6296, www.stpaulsrome.it).

## Jazz

Rome has a small but vibrant jazz scene. **Alexanderplatz** is the venerable club in town, with performances most evenings (Sun-Thu concerts at 21:45, Fri-Sat at 22:30, closed in summer, Via Ostia 9, Metro: Ottaviano, tel. 06-3972-1867, alexanderplatzjazzclub.com).

**Il Pentagrappolo** is a recommended *enoteca* (see listing on page 935) that hosts live music (usually jazz) many Friday and Saturday evenings starting at 22:00 from September to June—check under "Eventi musicali" on their website to confirm (best to reserve on weekends, three blocks east of the Colosseum at Via Celimontana 21, www.ilpentagrappolo.com, tel. 06-709-6301).

**TramJazz,** a creative venture by the public transit company, combines dinner, music, and a journey through the city in a vintage cable car for a mostly local crowd (€65, daily at 21:00, 3 hours, leaves from Piazza di Porta Maggiore—reached by tram #5 or #14 from Termini Station, book at least a week in advance, www.tramjazz.com).

## Movies

Movies in their original language are scarce in Rome, but not impossible to come by (look for v.o.—*versione originale*). For a list of

what's showing in English, check www.inromenow.com and www.
romereview.com. The most reliable theater for English-language
films is the **Nuovo Olimpia** (3 blocks north of Piazza Colonna,
just off Via del Corso at Via in Lucina 16, tel. 06-686-1068). **Mul-
tisala Barberini** occasionally has v.o. screenings as well (Piazza
Barberini, barberini.18tickets.it).

### Bars and Nightspots

I've listed some fun neighborhoods worth exploring after dark,
along with a few bars and *enoteche* (wine bars) in each. All of these
places are recommended in the "Eating in Rome" section, where
you'll find more details on each.

    **Heart of Rome, near the Pantheon:** The scene here is tour-
isty but delightful. The monuments—especially the Pantheon and
Trevi Fountain—are magically floodlit at night. Not far from the
Trevi Fountain, **L'Antica Birreria Peroni** is a big, boisterous beer
hall. Farther south, Campo de' Fiori and the surrounding streets
become one big, rude street party around 22:00. One good place
to sample the youthful energy, as well as some craft beers, is the
rollicking **Open Baladin** pub. (For more on these places, see their
listings under "Pantheon Neighborhood" on page 935.)

    **North Rome, near the Spanish Steps and Via del Corso:** A
babel of international tourists, this glitzy zone is bustling after dark.
For many, just hanging out around the Spanish Steps is enough to
fill an evening. For nearby dining options, see page 944.

    **Near the Colosseum and Forum, in Monti:** The best plan in
this lively village-Rome zone is to pop the top off a brew and hang
out at the fountain on Piazza della Madonna dei Monti. To join the
after-dark scene, buy a drink at the shop on the uphill side of the
square (cheap bottles of wine with plastic glasses, beer, fruit, and
munchies) and be part of what becomes the hottest bar in the area.
There are plenty of makeshift benches around the fountain. For
more details, see the "Monti" section of "Eating in Rome."

## Sleeping in Rome

Choosing the right neighborhood in Rome is as important as
choosing the right hotel. All of my recommended accommodations
are in safe areas convenient to sightseeing. Most central, hotels
near **ancient Rome** are close to the Colosseum and Roman Forum.
The most romantic ambience is in neighborhoods near the **Pantheon,** which encompass the **Campo de' Fiori** and the **Jewish Ghetto.**
Hotels near **Vatican City** put St. Peter's and the Vatican Museums
at your doorstep. The **Termini train station** neighborhood is handy
for public transit and services, although not particularly charming.

**ROME**

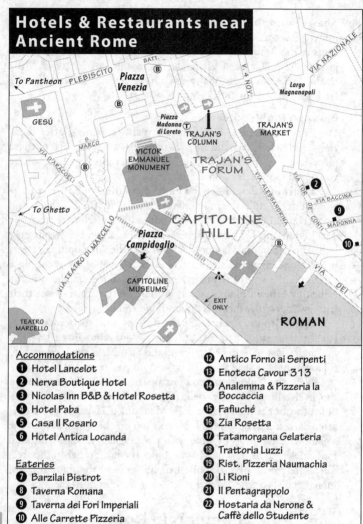

# Hotels & Restaurants near Ancient Rome

**Accommodations**
1. Hotel Lancelot
2. Nerva Boutique Hotel
3. Nicolas Inn B&B & Hotel Rosetta
4. Hotel Paba
5. Casa Il Rosario
6. Hotel Antica Locanda

**Eateries**
7. Barzilai Bistrot
8. Taverna Romana
9. Taverna dei Fori Imperiali
10. Alle Carrette Pizzeria
11. Trattoria da Valentino

12. Antico Forno ai Serpenti
13. Enoteca Cavour 313
14. Analemma & Pizzeria la Boccaccia
15. Fafiuché
16. Zia Rosetta
17. Fatamorgana Gelateria
18. Trattoria Luzzi
19. Rist. Pizzeria Naumachia
20. Li Rioni
21. Il Pentagrappolo
22. Hostaria da Nerone & Caffè dello Studente

Finally, the bohemian Trastevere neighborhood is a good choice for living like a Roman when in Rome for a few days.

**Hotel Tips:** I rank accommodations from $ budget to $$$$ splurge. For the best deal, contact my family-run accommodations directly by phone or email. When you book direct, the owner avoids a commission and may be able to offer a discount. Book well in advance for peak season or if your trip coincides with a major holiday or festival (see the appendix).

It's common for hotels in Rome to lower their prices in the off-

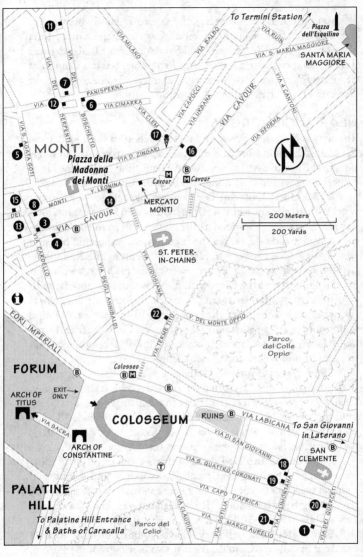

season, although prices at hostels and cheaper hotels won't fluctuate much. Room rates are lowest in sweltering August. For some travelers, short-term, Airbnb-type rentals can be a good alternative; search for places in my recommended hotel neighborhoods.

For more details on reservations, short-term rentals, and more, see the "Sleeping" section in the Practicalities chapter.

**Sleeping at Convents:** Rome has many convents that rent out rooms. At convents, the beds are twins and English is often in short supply, but the price is right. I've listed four nun-run places: Casa

Il Rosario (near Piazza Venezia), the expensive but divine Casa di Santa Brigida (near Campo de' Fiori), Casa per Ferie Santa Maria alle Fornaci (near the Vatican), and Suore di Santa Elisabetta (near Termini Station). For a longer list of convents, see the Church of St. Patrick's website (www.stpatricksamericanrome.org)—select "Resources" and then "Convent Accommodations."

## NEAR ANCIENT ROME

This area is central, so you'll find these hotels are a short walk from the Colosseum and Roman Forum, as well as restaurants and shopping in the Monti district (see pages 911 and 930). All except Hotel Lancelot are within a 10-minute walk of the Cavour Metro stop.

**$$$$ Hotel Lancelot** is a comfortable refuge—a 60-room hotel with an elegant feel at a fair price. Located in a pleasant, low-key residential neighborhood a 10-minute stroll from the Colosseum, it's quiet and safe, with a shady courtyard, restaurant, bar, and tiny communal sixth-floor terrace. It's well-run by the Khan family, who serve a good €25 dinner—a tasty way to connect with your hotel neighbors and the friendly staff. No wonder it's popular with returning guests (family rooms, some view rooms, air-con, elevator, wheelchair-accessible, cheap parking, 10-minute walk behind Colosseum near San Clemente Church at Via Capo d'Africa 47, tel. 06-7045-0615, www.lancelothotel.com, info@lancelothotel.com). Faris and Lubna speak the Queen's English.

**$$$$ Nerva Boutique Hotel** is a snazzy slice of tranquility with 20 small, stylish, and often discounted rooms. It sits on a quiet, ideally located side street that faces the Roman Forum and backs onto the enjoyable Monti neighborhood (RS%—use code "RICK-STEVES," air-con, elevator, Via Tor de' Conti 3, tel. 06-678-1835, www.hotelnerva.com, info@hotelnerva.com, Antonio and Paolo).

**$$$ Nicolas Inn Bed & Breakfast,** a delightful little four-room place with thoughtful touches, is spacious and bright, and right on busy Via Cavour. Staying here can make you feel like you have caring friends in Rome (RS%, cash only, air-con, Via Cavour 295, mobile 328-555-3004, www.nicolasinn.it, info@nicolasinn.it).

**$$$ Hotel Paba** is homey, chocolate-box tidy, and lovingly cared for by Alberta Castelli. It's just two blocks from the Forum. You'll take a vintage elevator to reach the seven rooms. Although some overlook busy Via Cavour, it's quiet enough (RS%, email reservations preferred, big beds, breakfast served in room, air-con, elevator, Via Cavour 266, second floor, tel. 06-4782-4497, www.hotelpaba.com, info@hotelpaba.com).

**$$$ Casa Il Rosario** is a peaceful, well-run Dominican convent renting 40 rooms with monastic simplicity to both pilgrims and tourists in a steep but pleasant corner of the Monti neighborhood. Doubles have two single beds which can be pushed together (cheaper single rooms with shared bath, reserve several months in advance, some rooms with air-con and others with fans, elevator, small garden and rooftop terrace, midnight curfew, near bottom of Via Nazionale at Via Sant'Agata dei Goti 10, bus #40 or #170 from Termini, tel. 06-679-2346, www.casailrosarioroma.it, info@casailrosarioroma.it).

**$$ Hotel Antica Locanda** is a gem on a small street in the heart of the Monti neighborhood. While there are four floors and no elevator, the 15 rooms—each named for a composer or an artist—come with romantically rustic, stylish furnishings. The rooftop terrace is great for sunbathing or relaxing with a sunset drink (air-con, no elevator, Via del Boschetto 84, tel. 06-484-894, www.anticalocandaroma.it, anticalocandaroma@gmail.com).

**$ Hotel Rosetta,** a homey and family-run *pensione* in the same building as Nicolas Inn, rents 15 simple rooms. It's pretty minimal, with no lounge and no breakfast, but its great location makes it a fine budget option (air-con, up one flight of stairs, Via Cavour 295, tel. 06-4782-3069, www.rosettahotel.com, info@rosettahotel.com, Antonietta and Francesca).

## PANTHEON NEIGHBORHOOD

Winding, narrow lanes filled with foot traffic and lined with small shops and tiny trattorias...this part of Rome still feels like a village. As in a real village, buses and taxis are the only practical way to connect with other destinations. The atmosphere doesn't come cheap, but this is a great place to be—especially at night, when Romans and tourists gather in the floodlit piazzas.

This neighborhood has two main transportation hubs: Piazza delle Cinque Lune (just north of Piazza Navona) has a TI, a taxi stand, and (just around the corner) handy buses #81 and #87. Largo Argentina has buses to almost everywhere, a taxi stand, and the tram to Trastevere (#8). Peruse my recommended buses on page 824, and you'll likely find a few (#81, #87, #492, and others) that stop near your hotel.

There are two **Co-op supermarkets** in the neighborhood. One is a half-block from the Pantheon toward Piazza Navona (daily until 22:00, Via Giustiniani 18b). A larger Co-op, with a good bakery and sandwich section, is three blocks from the Pantheon, near Largo Argentina (daily until 21:00, Corso Vittorio Emanuele II 42; for Co-op locations see the map on page 936).

### Near Largo Argentina and Campo de' Fiori

Each of these places is romantically set deep in the tangled back streets near the idyllic Campo de' Fiori and, for many, worth the extra money. This area is connected to Termini Station by bus along Via Nazionale (#40 or #64). From the airport, consider taking the

**ROME**

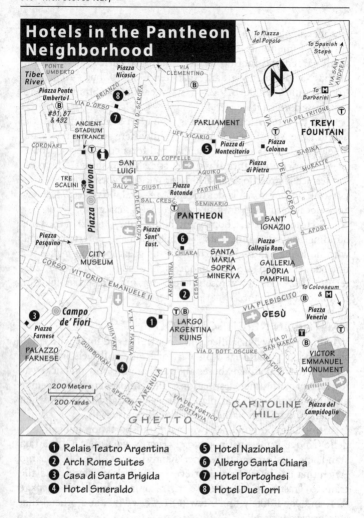

# Hotels in the Pantheon Neighborhood

To Piazza del Popolo
To Spanish Steps
VIA SANT' ANDREA
PONTE UMBERTO
Tiber River
Piazza Nicosia
VIA CLEMENTINO
N
To M Barberini
VIA DEL TRITONE
TREVI FOUNTAIN
Piazza Ponte Umberto I
(B) #81, 87 & 492
BRIANZO
VIA D. ORSO
VIA D. SCROFA
ANCIENT STADIUM ENTRANCE
UFF. VICARIO
PARLIAMENT
Piazza Colonna
SABINA
CORONARI
VIA D. COPPELLE
Piazza di Montecitorio
MURATTE
SAN LUIGI
AQUIRO
Piazza di Pietra
DEL
TRE SCALINI
SALV. GIUST. VIA DELLA SCROFA
SAL. CRESC.
Piazza Rotonda
PASTINI
SEMINARIO
CORSO
Piazza Navona
PANTHEON
SANT' IGNAZIO
S.-APOST.
Piazza Pasquino
Piazza Sant' Eust.
S. CHIARA
Piazza Collegio Rom.
GALLERIA DORIA PAMPHILJ
CITY MUSEUM
CORSO VITTORIO EMANUELE II
SANTA MARIA SOPRA MINERVA
To Colosseum & M
ARGENTINA
CESTARI
VIA PLEBISCITO
Piazza Venezia
Campo de' Fiori
Y. M. D. FARINA
LARGO ARGENTINA RUINS
GESÙ
Piazza Farnese
CHIAVARI
VIA DI SAN MARCO
ARACOELI
PALAZZO FARNESE
Y. GIUBBONARI
VIA D. BOTT. OSCURE
VICTOR EMMANUEL MONUMENT
200 Meters
200 Yards
SPECCHI
VIA ARENULA
VIA DEL PORTICO D'OTTAVIA
CAPITOLINE HILL
Piazza del Campidoglio
GHETTO

1 Relais Teatro Argentina
2 Arch Rome Suites
3 Casa di Santa Brigida
4 Hotel Smeraldo
5 Hotel Nazionale
6 Albergo Santa Chiara
7 Hotel Portoghesi
8 Hotel Due Torri

regional train to Trastevere Station and then the #8 tram to Largo Argentina.

**$$$$ Relais Teatro Argentina,** a six-room gem, is steeped in tasteful old-Rome elegance, but has all the modern comforts. It's cozy and quiet like a B&B and couldn't be more centrally located (air-con, 3 flights of stairs, breakfast in room or on balcony, Via del Sudario 35, tel. 06-9893-1617, www.relaisteatroargentina.com, info@relaisteatroargentina.com, kind Paolo).

**$$$ Arch Rome Suites,** in a tranquil palace on the site of the former Baths of Agrippa, is just a few steps from the Pantheon and near the Jewish Ghetto. It rents 12 spacious, modern, and cozy rooms—some with balconies and views (family rooms, air-con, elevator, Via dell'Arco della Ciambella 19, tel. 06-4549-8947, www.archromesuites.it, info@archromesuites.com, friendly Marika and Omar).

**$$$ Casa di Santa Brigida** overlooks the elegant Piazza Farnese. With soft-spoken sisters gliding down polished hallways and pearly gates instead of doors, this lavish 20-room convent makes exhaust-stained Roman tourists feel like they've died and gone to heaven. You won't have a double bed or a TV in your room, but you can luxuriate in the inn's public spaces or on its lovely roof terrace (book well in advance, air-con, elevator, tasty €25 dinners—reserve ahead, roof garden, plush library, Via di Monserrato 54, tel. 06-6889-2596, www.brigidine.org, piazzafarnese@brigidine.org, many of the sisters are from India and speak English—pray you get to work with wonderful sister Gertrude).

**$$$ Hotel Smeraldo,** with 66 rooms, is clean and a reasonable deal in a good location. Sixteen of the rooms are in an annex across the street, but everyone has breakfast in the main building (air-con, elevator, roof terrace, midway between Campo de' Fiori and Largo Argentina at Via dei Chiavari 20, tel. 06-687-5929, www.smeraldoroma.com, info@smeraldoroma.com, Massimo and Walter).

## Close to the Pantheon

These places are buried in the pedestrian-friendly heart of ancient Rome, each within about a five-minute walk of the Pantheon. They're an easy walk from many sights, but are a bit distant from the major public transportation arteries (though buses do run nearby). To get close, arrive and depart by taxi.

**$$$$ Hotel Nazionale,** a four-star landmark, is a 16th-century palace that shares a well-policed square with the Italian Parliament building. Its 100 rooms are accentuated by lush public spaces, fancy bars, a uniformed staff, and a marble-floored breakfast room. It's a big, stuffy hotel, but it's a worthy splurge if you want security, comfort, and the heart of Rome at your doorstep (RS%—use code "RICK," family rooms, air-con, elevator, Piazza Montecitorio 131, tel. 06-695-001, www.hotelnazionale.it, info@hotelnazionale.it).

**$$$$ Albergo Santa Chiara,** in the old center, is big, solid, and hotelesque. Flavia, Silvio, and their fine staff offer marbled elegance (but basic furniture) and all the hotel services. Its ample public lounges are dressy and professional, and its 96 rooms are quiet and spacious (RS%—use code "RICK," family rooms, air-con, elevator, behind the Pantheon at Via di Santa Chiara 21, tel. 06-687-2979, www.albergosantachiara.com, info@albergosantachiara.com).

**$$$$ Hotel Portoghesi** is a classic hotel with 27 colorful rooms in the medieval heart of Rome. It's peaceful, quiet, and comes with a delightful roof terrace—though you pay for the location (family rooms, breakfast on roof, air-con, elevator, Via dei Por-

**ROME**

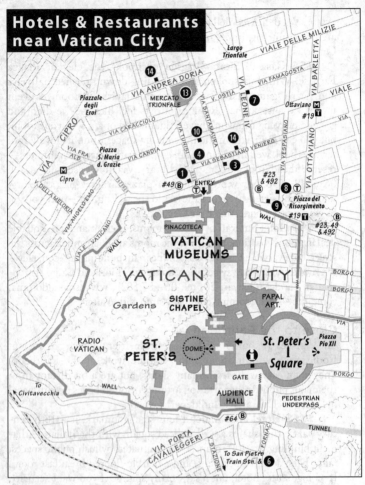

# Hotels & Restaurants near Vatican City

toghesi 1, tel. 06-686-4231, www.hotelportoghesiroma.it, info@ hotelportoghesiroma.it).

$$$ **Hotel Due Torri**, hiding out on a tiny quiet street, is beautifully located. It feels professional yet homey, with an ac-commodating staff, generous public spaces, and 26 rooms (the ones on upper floors are smaller but have views). While the lo-cation and lounge are great, the rooms are overpriced unless you score a discount (family rooms, air-con, elevator, a block off Via della Scrofa at Vicolo del Leonetto 23, tel. 06-6880-6956, www. hotelduetorriroma.com, info@hotelduetorriroma.com, Cinzia and her daughter Giorgia).

## Near the Spanish Steps

$$$$ **Hotel San Carlo** is buried in the thick of Rome's bustling

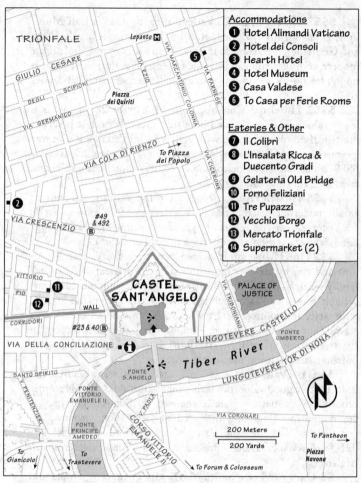

**Accommodations**
1. Hotel Alimandi Vaticano
2. Hotel dei Consoli
3. Hearth Hotel
4. Hotel Museum
5. Casa Valdese
6. To Casa per Ferie Rooms

**Eateries & Other**
7. Il Colibrì
8. L'Insalata Ricca & Duecento Gradi
9. Gelateria Old Bridge
10. Forno Feliziani
11. Tre Pupazzi
12. Vecchio Borgo
13. Mercato Trionfale
14. Supermarket (2)

pedestrian-friendly "shopping triangle," close to the Spagna Metro stop. It has 47 rooms connected by a treehouse floor plan (RS%, air-con, elevator, Via delle Carrozze 92—see the "Dolce Vita Stroll" map on page 832, tel. 06-678-4548, www.hotelsancarloroma.com, info@hotelsancarloroma.com).

ROME

## NEAR VATICAN CITY

Sleeping near the Vatican costs a little more, but some enjoy calling this relaxed, residential neighborhood home. The tree-lined streets are wider than in the historical center, so it feels less claustrophobic. Although it's handy to the Vatican, everything else is a long way away. Fortunately, it's well-served by public transit, especially the Metro (line A). Most of these listings are within a 10-minute walk of either the Cipro or Ottaviano Metro stops.

$$$$ **Hotel Alimandi Vaticano,** facing the Vatican Museums, is beautifully designed. Run by the Alimandi family (Nico and Germano), it features four stars, 24 spacious rooms, and all the modern comforts you can imagine (air-con, elevator, Viale Vaticano 99, tel. 06-3974-5562, www.alimandi.com, alimandivaticano@alimandi.com).

$$$$ **Hotel dei Consoli,** family-run with 28 rooms, is a lesser value pleasantly located on a side street. Breakfast is served on its leafy rooftop terrace, with a view to St. Peter's—a nice way to start the day (RS%, air-con, elevator, Via Varrone 2D, tel. 06-6889-2972, www.hoteldeiconsoli.com, info@hoteldeiconsoli.com, friendly Laura and mom Amalia).

$$$$ **Hearth Hotel,** a block from the Vatican wall, has 22 small, modern, efficient, and characterless rooms (RS%—use code "rick steves," air-con, elevator, Via Santamaura 2, tel. 06-3903-8383, www.hearthhotel.com, info@hearthhotel.com).

$$$ **Hotel Museum** is located steps from the Vatican Museums and run by another branch of the entrepreneurial Alimandi family—Luca, Irene, and Barbara. It has 31 modest but comfortable rooms and large public spaces, including a piano lounge, pool table, and rooftop terrace where the grand buffet breakfast is served (family rooms, air-con, elevator, down the stairs directly in front of Vatican Museums, Via Tunisi 8, tel. 06-3972-3941, www.hotelmuseum.it, info@hotelmuseum.it).

$$ **Casa Valdese** is a well-managed, Protestant Church-run hotel that's a good value and feels a bit institutional. Its 33 recently renovated—but basic—rooms come with the bonus of two breezy, communal roof terraces with incredible views (family rooms, air-con, elevator, Via Alessandro Farnese 18, Metro: Lepanto, tel. 06-321-5362, www.casavaldeseroma.it, reception@casavaldeseroma.it, Matteo).

$$ **Casa per Ferie Santa Maria alle Fornaci** is simple and efficient, housing pilgrims and secular tourists just a five-minute walk south of the Vatican in a dull, high-rise residential zone. Its 54 utilitarian rooms are mostly twin-bedded. Reserve at least three months in advance (air-con, elevator; take bus #64 from Termini train station to San Pietro train station, then walk 100 yards north along Via della Stazione di San Pietro to Piazza Santa Maria alle Fornaci 27; or from the airport, take the train to Trastevere Station, then transfer to San Pietro Station; tel. 06-3936-7632, www.santamariafornaci.com, Carmine).

## NEAR TERMINI STATION

While this neighborhood is not as atmospheric as other areas of Rome, the hotels near Termini train station are less expensive, and the Metro and buses link you easily to the rest of the city. My recommendations are within a 10-minute walk of the station (some are actually closer to the Repubblica Metro stop).

## West of the Station

Most of these hotels are on or near Via Firenze, a safe, handy, central, and relatively quiet street that's a 10-minute walk from Termini and the airport train, and two blocks beyond Piazza della Repubblica. The Defense Ministry is nearby, so you've got heavily armed guards watching over you all night.

The neighborhood is served by two Metro stops: Repubblica (line A), and Termini (intersection of lines A and B). Virtually all the city buses that rumble down Via Nazionale (#60, #64, #70, and the #40 express) take you to Piazza Venezia (near the Forum).

These neighborhood supermarkets are all open daily until late (for locations see the map on page 946): **Co-op** (Via Nazionale 213, at the corner of Via Venezia), **Simply** (behind Santa Maria Maggiore Church at Piazza Santa Maria Maggiore 5B, in the basement), and **Sapori & Dintori** (downstairs from the inner atrium at Termini Station). There are many smaller grocery stores as well.

**$$$$ Residenza Cellini** feels like the guest wing of a gorgeous Neoclassical palace. It offers 13 rooms, "ortho/anti-allergy beds," four-star comforts and service, and a small, breezy terrace (RS%, breakfast extra, air-con, elevator, Via Modena 5, third floor, tel. 06-4782-5204, www.residenzacellini.it, info@residenzacellini. it; Barbara, Gaetano, and Donato).

**$$$$ Hotel Modigliani,** a delightful 23-room place, is energetically run in a clean, bright, minimalist yet in-love-with-life style that its artist namesake would appreciate. It has a vast and plush lounge, a garden, and a newsletter introducing you to each of the staff (RS%, air-con, elevator; from Tritone Fountain on Piazza Barberini, go 2 blocks up Via della Purificazione to #42; tel. 06-4281-5226, www.hotelmodigliani.com, info@hotelmodigliani. com, Giulia and Marco).

**$$$$ IQ Hotel,** in a modern blue building facing the Opera House, feels almost Scandinavian in its efficiency, without a hint of the Old World. It lacks charm, but more than compensates with modern amenities. Its 90 rooms are fresh and spacious, the roof garden comes with a play area and foosball, and vending machines dispense bottles of wine (RS%, family rooms, breakfast extra, air-con, elevator, cheap self-service laundry, gym, Via Firenze 8, tel. 06-488-0465, www.iqhotelroma.it, info@iqhotelroma.it, Diego).

**$$$$ Hotel Aberdeen,** which combines quality and friendliness, is warmly run by Annamaria, with support from sister Laura, cousin Cinzia, and staff member Costel. The 37 comfy rooms, on the ground floor and one floor up, are a fine value (RS%—use "Rick Steves reader reservations" link, family rooms, air-con, Via Firenze

**ROME**

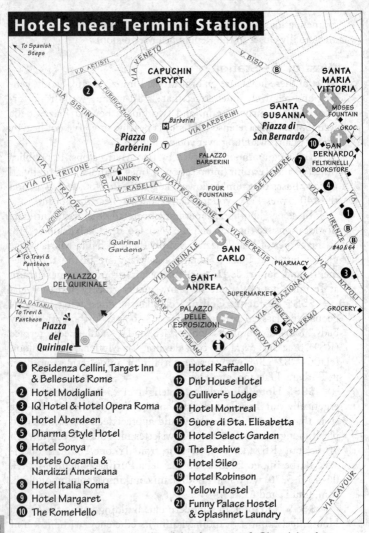

# Hotels near Termini Station

1. Residenza Cellini, Target Inn & Bellesuite Rome
2. Hotel Modigliani
3. IQ Hotel & Hotel Opera Roma
4. Hotel Aberdeen
5. Dharma Style Hotel
6. Hotel Sonya
7. Hotels Oceania & Nardizzi Americana
8. Hotel Italia Roma
9. Hotel Margaret
10. The RomeHello
11. Hotel Raffaello
12. Dnb House Hotel
13. Gulliver's Lodge
14. Hotel Montreal
15. Suore di Sta. Elisabetta
16. Hotel Select Garden
17. The Beehive
18. Hotel Sileo
19. Hotel Robinson
20. Yellow Hostel
21. Funny Palace Hostel & Splashnet Laundry

48, tel. 06-482-3920, www.hotelaberdeen.it, info@hotelaberdeen. it).

**$$$ Dharma Style Hotel** spreads its 40 stylish rooms and suites across a few floors of a big palazzo, with elegant furnishings and room to breathe (RS%, family rooms, air-con, elevator, Via del Viminale 8, reception at #10, tel. 06-482-4460, www. dharmastylehotel.it, booking@dharmastylehotel.it).

**$$$ Hotel Opera Roma,** with contemporary furnishings and marble accents, boasts 15 spacious, modern, and thoughtfully appointed rooms. It's quiet and just a stone's throw from the Opera House (air-con, elevator, Via Firenze 11, tel. 06-487-1787, www.

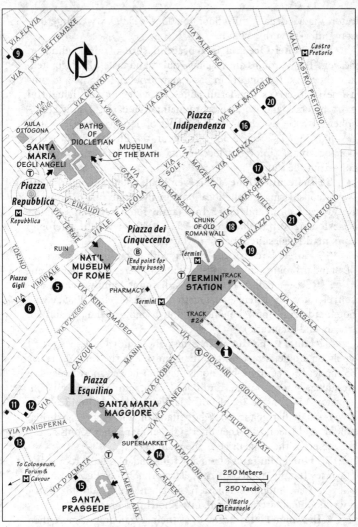

hoteloperaroma.com, info@hoteloperaroma.com; Reza, Litu, and Federica).

**$$$ Hotel Sonya** offers 40 well-equipped rooms in varied sizes, a hearty breakfast, and decent prices (RS%—see the "Special Offers" page, family rooms, air-con, elevator, some rooms face the Opera House at Via Viminale 58, tel. 06-481-9911, www. hotelsonya.it, info@hotelsonya.it, Francesca and Simone).

**$$$ Target Inn** is a sleek, practical seven-room place next to Residenza Cellini (listed earlier). It's owned by the same people who run the recommended Target Restaurant nearby (air-con, elevator, Via Modena 5, third floor, tel. 06-474-5399, www.targetinn. com, info@targetinn.com).

**$$$ Hotel Oceania** is a peaceful slice of air-conditioned heaven. The 24 rooms are spacious, quiet, and tastefully decorated, and the elegant sitting room has a manor-house feel. Stefano runs a fine staff, serves wonderful coffee, provides lots of thoughtful extra touches, and works hard to maintain a caring family atmosphere (RS%—use code "RICKSTEVES," family rooms, elevator, TV lounge, Via Firenze 38, third floor, tel. 06-482-4696, www. hoteloceania.it, info@hoteloceania.it; Anna, Kira, and Roberto round out the staff).

**$$ Bellesuite Rome** offers seven small but nice rooms that are worth considering for the location—in the same fine building as Residenza Cellini and Target Inn (family rooms, air-con, elevator, Via Modena 5, third floor, tel. 06-9521-3049, www.bellesuiterome. com, mail@bellesuiterome.com, Martina).

**$$ Hotel Nardizzi Americana,** with a small rooftop terrace, 40 standard rooms, and a laid-back atmosphere, is another decent value (RS%—email reservation for discount, family rooms, air-con, elevator, Via Firenze 38, fourth floor, tel. 06-488-0035, www. hotelnardizzi.it, info@hotelnardizzi.it; friendly Stefano, Fabrizio, Mario, and Giancarlo).

**$$ Hotel Italia Roma,** in a busy and handy locale, is located safely on a quiet street next to the Ministry of the Interior. It has 35 modest but comfortable rooms plus four newer, more expensive "residenza" rooms on the third floor (RS%, family rooms, air-con, elevator, Via Venezia 18, just off Via Nazionale, tel. 06-482-8355, www.hotelitaliaroma.it, info@hotelitaliaroma.it; Andrea, Sabrina, Abdul, and Eleonora). They offer eight similar annex rooms across the street for the same price as the main hotel.

**$$ Hotel Margaret** offers few frills and 11 simple rooms at a fair price (family rooms, air-con, elevator, north of Piazza Repubblica at Via Antonio Salandra 6, fourth floor, tel. 06-482-4285, www.hotelmargaretrome.com, info@hotelmargaret.net).

**¢ The RomeHello** hostel is, as their slogan brags, "more than just a bed." Recently opened, it's a modern, quiet, and friendly hostel run with a mission to employ locals and provide a comfortable home for travelers, with about 200 beds in doubles, triples, and dorms. The public areas and guest kitchen feel like a computer-generated image of a hostel utopia (Via Torino 45, tel. 06-9686-0070, www.theromehello.com, ciao@theromehello.com).

## Southwest of the Station

These good-value places cluster around the basilica of Santa Maria Maggiore. Most are a five-minute walk from the Cavour Metro stop.

**$$$ Hotel Raffaello,** with its courteous and professional staff, offers 41 rooms in a grand 19th-century building on the edge of the Monti district. This formal hotel comes with generous public spaces and a breakfast room fit for aristocrats (family rooms, air-con, elevator, Via Urbana 3, tel. 06-488-4342, www.hotelraffaello.it, info@hotelraffaello.it).

**$$ Dnb House Hotel,** owned by the Oblate Sisters of Baby Jesus, is a spacious, pristine, and institutional-feeling hotel. The 38 high-ceilinged rooms are modest yet classy, and guests have access to a peaceful and leafy courtyard garden (RS%, air-con, elevator, expensive pay parking, Via Cavour 85A, tel. 06-4782-4414, www.dnbhotel.com, info@dnbhotel.com).

**$$ Gulliver's Lodge** has four colorful rooms on the ground floor of a large, secure building. Although it's on a busy street, the rooms are quiet. The public spaces are few, but in-room extras like Netflix make it a fine home base (RS%, price includes breakfast at nearby bar, cash only, air-con, Via Cavour 101, tel. 06-9727-3787, www.gulliverslodge.com, info@gulliverslodge.com, Stella and Gianluca).

**$$ Hotel Montreal** is a basic, three-star place with 27 rooms on a big, noisy street a block southeast of Santa Maria Maggiore (RS%, family rooms, air-con, elevator, small garden terrace; Via Carlo Alberto 4, 1 block from Metro: Vittorio Emanuele, 3 blocks from Termini train station, tel. 06-445-7797, www.hotelmontrealroma.it, info@hotelmontrealroma.it, Fabrizio).

**$ Suore di Santa Elisabetta** is a heavenly Polish-run convent with a serene garden, roof terrace with grand views, and 37 rooms. All doubles have twin beds. Often booked long in advance, with such tranquility it's a super value (family rooms, cheaper rooms with shared bath, fans but no air-con, elevator for top floors, guest kitchen, Wi-Fi in lounge only, 23:00 curfew; a block southwest of Santa Maria Maggiore at Via dell'Olmata 9, Metro: Termini or Vittorio Emanuele; tel. 06-488-8271, www.csse-roma.com, select "Casa per ferie" for English, ist.it.s.elisabetta@libero.it).

## Sleeping Cheaply, Northeast of the Station

The cheapest beds in town are beyond Termini train station, to the northeast: Standing so that the tracks dead-end into your back, this neighborhood is to your right (Metro: Termini). The streets quiet down a block or so away from the station, and these hotels feel plenty safe. The **Splashnet** launderette offers full-service laundry (daily 8:30-23:00, just off Via Milazzo at Via Varese 33, tel. 06-4470-3523).

**$$ Hotel Select Garden,** a modern and comfortable 21-room hotel run by the cheery Picca family, is a welcoming refuge (air-

**ROME**

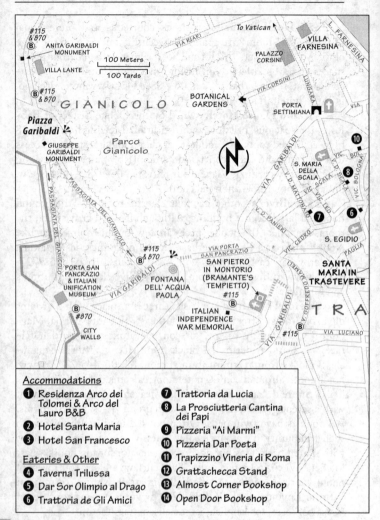

**Accommodations**

1. Residenza Arco dei Tolomei & Arco del Lauro B&B
2. Hotel Santa Maria
3. Hotel San Francesco

**Eateries & Other**

4. Taverna Trilussa
5. Dar Sor Olimpio al Drago
6. Trattoria de Gli Amici
7. Trattoria da Lucia
8. La Prosciutteria Cantina dei Papi
9. Pizzeria "Ai Marmi"
10. Pizzeria Dar Poeta
11. Trapizzino Vineria di Roma
12. Grattachecca Stand
13. Almost Corner Bookshop
14. Open Door Bookshop

ROME

con, Via V. Bachelet 6, tel. 06-445-6383, www.hotelselectgarden. com, info@hotelselectgarden.com, Cristina and Maurizia).

**$ The Beehive** gives vagabonds—old and young—a cheap, clean, and comfy home in Rome (air-con in some rooms, breakfast extra, 2 blocks from Termini train station at Via Marghera 8, tel. 06-4470-4553, www.the-beehive.com, info@the-beehive.com).

**$ Hotel Sileo** is a homey little place renting 10 basic rooms. It's worn, but run with warmth (RS%, air-con, elevator, Via Magenta 39, fourth floor, tel. 06-445-0246, www.hotelsileo.com, info@hotelsileo.com).

**$ Hotel Robinson** is tucked away from the commotion. Set on an interior courtyard, it has 20 small and simple rooms

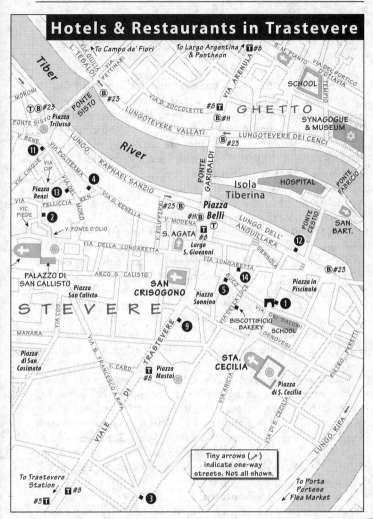

## Hotels & Restaurants in Trastevere

(Map labels, reading roughly top to bottom, left to right:)

To Campo de' Fiori — To Largo Argentina & Pantheon — S. M. PIANTO — VIA DEL PORTICO D'OTTAVIA — TEMPIO

Tiber — L. TEBALDI — VIA GIULIA — PETTINARI — VIA ARENULA — SCHOOL — GHETTO — SYNAGOGUE & MUSEUM

MORONI — PONTE SISTO — Piazza Trillusa — VIA D. ZOCCOLETTE — LUNGOTEVERE VALLATI — LUNGOTEVERE DEI CENCI — HOSPITAL — PONTE FABRICIO

V. BENE — LUNGO RAPHAEL SANZIO — River — PONTE GARIBALDI — Isola Tiberina — SAN BART.

VIA CINQUE — VIA CIP — VIA POLITEAMA — VIA DEL MORO — VIA D. RENELLA — Piazza Belli — LUNGO. DELL' ANGUILLARA — PONTE CESTIO

Piazza Renzi — PELLICCIA — VIC. PIEDE — V. FONTE D'OLIO — V. FILIPPERI — V. MODENA — S. AGATA — GENSOLA

PALAZZO DI SAN CALLISTO — VIA DELLA LUNGARETTA — Largo S. Giovanni — VIA LUNGARETTA — Piazza in Piscinula

Piazza San Calisto — ARCO S. CALISTO — SAN CRISOGONO — Piazza Sonnino — VIA DEI SALUMI

S T E V E R E — VIA COS. — VIA TRASTEVERE — BUCO — VIA DELLA LUCE — BISCOTTIFICIO BAKERY — SCHOOL — GENOVESI

MANARA — VIA S. FRANCESCO A RIPA — STA. CECILIA — PIETRO PERETI

Piazza di San Cosimato — V. CARD. — Piazza Mastai — Piazza di S. Cecilia — LUNGO. RIPA

VIALE DI — VIA ANICIA — VIA DI S. CECILIA — VIA PORTESE

To Trastevere Station — #3 — To Porta Portese Flea Market

Tiny arrows ( ⤴ ) indicate one-way streets. Not all shown.

---

(RS%—includes breakfast and air-con when you pay in cash, apartment also available, Via Milazzo 3, tel. 06-491-423, www.hotelrobinsonrome.com, info@hotelrobinsonrome.com).

¢ **Yellow Hostel** rents 220 beds to 18- through 45-year-olds only. Hip yet sane, it's well-run with fine facilities, including a café/late-night bar (reserve online, breakfast extra, elevator, no curfew, just past Via Vicenza at Via Palestro 44, tel. 06-446-3554, www.yellowhostel.com, questions@the-yellow.com).

¢ **Funny Palace Hostel**—adjacent to Splashnet and run by the same entrepreneurial owner, Mabri—is less convivial than Yellow Hostel, but good for introverts (cash only, includes breakfast at café, elevator, guest kitchen, reception at Splashnet, Via Varese

33, tel. 06-4470-3523, www.funnyhostel.com, funnypalace031@ gmail.com).

## TRASTEVERE

Colorful and genuine, with uneven cobbles and remnants of its tumbledown past, Trastevere is a treat for travelers looking for a more residential, bohemian atmosphere. (∩ Download my free Trastevere Walk **audio tour** to explore the neighborhood.) The heart of Rome and its ancient ruins are just across the river, and tram #8 makes getting there and back a snap. Convenient bus #23 runs to the Vatican area, bus #H runs direct to Termini (none on Sun), and tram #3 goes to the Colosseum. From the airport, you can reach these listings by taking the regional train to Trastevere train station, and the #8 tram downhill from there.

$$$$ **Residenza Arco dei Tolomei** is your most poetic Trastevere experience imaginable, with six small, unique, antique-filled rooms, some boasting fragrant balconies. In this quiet and elegant setting, you can pretend you're visiting aristocratic relatives (reserve well in advance, from Piazza Piscinula a block up Via dell'Arco de' Tolomei at #27, tel. 06-5832-0819, www.bbarcodeitolomei.com, info@bbarcodeitolomei.com, Marco and Gianna Paola).

$$$$ **Hotel Santa Maria** sits like a lazy hacienda in the middle of Trastevere. Surrounded by a medieval skyline, you'll feel as if you're on some romantic stage set. Its 20 small but well-equipped, air-conditioned rooms—former cells in a cloister—are mostly on the ground floor, as are a few suites for up to six people. The rooms circle a gravelly courtyard of orange trees and stay-awhile patio furniture (RS%, family rooms, email reservations preferred, free loaner bikes, face church on Piazza Maria Trastevere and go right down Via della Fonte d'Olio 50 yards to Vicolo del Piede 2, tel. 06-589-4626, www.hotelsantamariatrastevere.it, info@ hotelsantamaria.info).

$$$ **Hotel San Francesco,** big and blocky yet welcoming, stands practically and efficiently at the far end of all the Trastevere action. It rents 24 trim rooms and comes with an inviting roof terrace. It's fine, but a bit more distant than the others listed here (email reservations preferred, air-con, elevator, Via Jacopa de' Settesoli 7, tel. 06-5830-0051, www.hotelsanfrancesco.net, hotelsanfrancesco@gmail.com).

$$$ **Arco del Lauro B&B** rents six tight, whitewashed, straightforward rooms around a dim, quiet back courtyard. Consider it the less expensive version of the Residenza Arco dei Tolomei, which is upstairs. The lower prices make up for the lack of public spaces and mostly offsite management (one family room, includes small breakfast at nearby café, air-con, from Piazza Piscinu-

ROME

la a block up Via dell'Arco de' Tolomei at #29, tel. 06-9784-0350, www.arcodellauro.it, info@arcodellauro.it, Lorenza and Daniela).

# Eating in Rome

Romans take great pleasure in dining well. Embrace this passion over a multicourse meal at an outdoor table, watching a parade of passersby while you sip wine with loved ones.

Roman meals are still lengthy social occasions. Simple, fresh, seasonal ingredients dominate the dishes. The *cucina* is robust, strongly flavored, and unpretentious—much like the people who've created it over the centuries. It is said that Roman cooking didn't come out of emperors' or popes' kitchens, but from the *cucina povera*—the home cooking of the common people. This may explain the Romans' fondness for meats known as the *quinto quarto* ("fifth quarter"), such as tripe, tail, brain, and pigs' feet, as well as their interest in natural preservatives like chili peppers and garlic.

Rome belongs to the warm, southern region of Lazio, which produces a rich variety of flavorful vegetables and fruit that are the envy of American supermarkets. Rome's proximity to the Mediterranean also allows for a great variety of seafood.

## EATING TIPS

Kitchens close at most restaurants between lunch and dinner; if it's a quality restaurant, it won't reopen before 19:00. If a smaller restaurant is booked up later in the evening (from 20:30 or so), they may accommodate walk-ins if you're willing to eat quickly.

**Choosing Restaurants:** I've listed restaurants that I enjoy. Many are in characteristic and touristy (and therefore pricey) areas such as Piazza Navona, Campo de' Fiori, and Trastevere. Others are tucked away from the tourist crush.

I'm impressed by how small the price difference can be between a mediocre Roman restaurant and a fine one. You can pay about 20 percent more for double the quality. If I had $100 for three meals in Rome, I'd spend $50 for one and $25 each for the other two, rather than $33 on all three. For splurge meals, I'd consider (in this order): Gabriello (near the Spanish Steps), Fortunato (near the Pantheon), and Taverna Trilussa (in Trastevere; all described later).

Rome's fabled squares—most notably Piazza Navona, near the Pantheon, and Campo de' Fiori—are lined with the outdoor tables of touristy restaurants with enticing menus and formal-vested waiters. The atmosphere is super romantic. I, too, like the idea of dining under floodlit monuments, amid a constantly flowing parade of people. But restaurants in these areas are notorious for surprise charges, forgettable food, microwaved ravioli, and bad service.

ROME

I enjoy the view by savoring just a drink or dessert on a famous square, but I dine with locals on nearby low-rent streets, where the proprietor needs to serve a good-value meal and nurture a local following to stay in business.

If you're set on eating—or just drinking and snacking—on a famous piazza, you don't need a guidebook listing to choose a spot; enjoy the ritual of slowly circling the square, observing both the food and the people eating it, and sit where the view and menu appeal to you.

**The *Aperitivo* Tradition:** For a light, budget meal, consider partaking in an *aperitivo* buffet. Bars all over town serve up a buffet of small dishes, from about 18:00 to 21:00, and anyone buying a drink (generally €8-12) gets to eat "for free."

**Picnicking:** Another cheap way to eat is to assemble a picnic and dine with Rome as your backdrop. Buy ingredients for your picnic at one of Rome's open-air produce markets (mornings only; see page 907), an *alimentari* (corner grocery store), a *rosticerie* (cheap food to go), or a *supermercato,* such as Conad or Co-op. You'll find handy late-night supermarkets near the Pantheon (Via Giustiniani), Spanish Steps (Via Vittoria), Trevi Fountain (Via del Bufalo), and Campo de' Fiori (Via di Monte della Farina). Note that Rome discourages people from picnicking or drinking at historic monuments in the old center. Technically violators can be fined, although it rarely happens. You'll be OK if you eat *with* a view rather than *in* the view.

## ANCIENT ROME: NEAR THE COLOSSEUM AND FORUM

Within a block of the Colosseum and Forum, you'll find convenient eateries catering to weary sightseers, most offering neither memorable food nor good value. To get your money's worth, stick with one of my recommendations, even if it means a 10-minute walk from the ruins. For locations, see the map on page 912.

### Monti

Behind the Imperial Forums, nestled in the tight and cobbled lanes between Via Nazionale and Via Cavour, is the characteristic (and recently trendy) Monti neighborhood. It's just a few steps farther from the ancient sites than the battery of forgettable touristy restaurants, but that extra effort opens up a world of characteristic dining experiences. From the Forum, head up Via Cavour and then left on Via dei Serpenti; the action centers on Piazza della Madonna dei Monti and nearby lanes.

**$$ Barzilai Bistrot,** a wine bar with a kitchen under stout timbers, feels like the neighborhood hangout. The bar is inviting if you just want a nice glass of wine with a plate of meat and cheese.

It's family-run, with a fun menu ranging from pastas to burgers. Granny's meatloaf is a hit (daily, no reservations, Via Panisperna 44, tel. 06-487-4979).

**$$ Taverna Romana** is small, simple, and a bit chaotic—with an open kitchen and hams and garlic hanging from the ceiling. This family-run eatery's *cacio e pepe* (cheese-and-pepper pasta) is a favorite. Arrive early, as they take no reservations (daily 12:30-14:45 & 19:00-22:45, Via della Madonna dei Monti 79, tel. 06-474-5325).

**$$ Taverna dei Fori Imperiali** serves typical, slightly higher-priced Roman cuisine in a snug interior that bustles with energy (Wed-Mon 12:30-15:00 & 19:30-22:30, closed Tue, reserve for dinner, Via della Madonna dei Monti 9, tel. 06-679-8643, www.latavernadeiforiimperiali.com).

**$$ Alle Carrette Pizzeria**—simple, rustic, and family-friendly—serves great wood-fired pizza just 200 yards from the Forum. It's cheap and fast (daily 12:00-15:30 & 19:00-24:00, Vicolo delle Carrette 14, tel. 06-679-2770).

**$ Trattoria da Valentino** is a classic time warp hiding under its historic (and therefore protected) *Birra Peroni* sign. They specialize in *scamorza* (grilled cheese with various toppings; about €10), list the day's pastas on a chalkboard, and serve a variety of meat dishes (Mon-Sat 13:00-14:45 & 19:30-23:00, closed Sun, Via del Boschetto 37, tel. 06-488-0643).

**$ Antico Forno ai Serpenti,** a hip bakery with a few simple tables, puts out a small selection of *panini,* baked potatoes, and lasagna. They also bake good bread and pastries and do breakfasts (order at the counter, daily 8:00-23:00, closes at 22:00 on Sun, Via dei Serpenti 122, tel. 06-4542-7920).

**$$ Enoteca Cavour 313** is a quality wine bar with a menu ranging from Lazio specialties and salads to high-quality *affettati* (cold cuts) and cheese. You'll be served with a mellow ambience under lofts of wine bottles, enjoying spacious-for-Rome seating (Mon-Sat 12:30-14:45 & 18:00-23:30, closed Sun, 100 yards off Via dei Fori Imperiali at Via Cavour 313, tel. 06-678-5496, Angelo).

**Monti** *Aperitivo:* Look for bars hosting the *aperitivo*—happy hours where, for the cost of a drink (€8-12), you get access to a buffet of simple dishes. It's a basic dinner (the Italian equivalent of macaroni and cheese, Spam, and Jello) in a fun scene with a drink. A good example, just a block off Monti's main square, is **Analemma,** which has a casual, youthful scene and a nightly buffet with a drink for €10 (18:30-22:00, Via Leonina 77).

### Monti Food Crawl

The streets of Monti are crowded with fun and creative places offering inexpensive quality snacks and light meals to eat on tiny in-

# Roman Cuisine

Here are some of the specialties worth seeking out on the menu. For more on Italian food, including *salumi*, cheeses, pizza, and pasta, see the "Eating" section of the Practicalities chapter.

## Antipasti (Appetizers)

**Antipasto misto:** A plate of marinated or grilled vegetables (eggplant, artichokes, peppers, mushrooms), cured meats, cheeses, or seafood (anchovies, octopus).

**Bruschetta:** Toasted bread brushed with olive oil and garlic, topped with chopped tomatoes, mushrooms, or other tidbits.

**Fritti:** Fried snacks that have been either battered or breaded—often olives stuffed with meat, potato croquettes, and mozzarella cheese. Other classic *fritti* are *supplí* (rice balls with tomato sauce and mozzarella) and *fiori di zucca* (squash blossoms filled with mozzarella and anchovies).

**Prosciutto e melone:** Cantaloupe wrapped in thin-sliced ham.

## Primo Piatto (First Course)

**Bucatini all'amatriciana:** Thin pasta tubes with a sauce of tomatoes, onion, pancetta, and pecorino cheese.

**Gnocchi alla romana:** Small, flattened dumplings made from semolina (not potatoes) and baked with butter and cheese.

**Penne all'arrabbiata:** Spicy tomato sauce with chili peppers (*peperoncini*) and garlic over penne.

**Rigatoni con la pajata:** Pasta topped with a stew of calf intestines.

**Spaghetti alla carbonara:** Eggs, pancetta or *guaniciale* (cured pork cheek), cheese (*pecorino romano* or *parmigiano reggiano*), and black pepper over pasta.

**Spaghetti alle vongole veraci:** Pasta served with small clams in the shell sautéed with white wine and herbs.

**Stracciatella alla romana:** Meat broth with whipped eggs, topped with parmesan.

## Secondo Piatto (Second Course)

**Abbacchio alla scottadito:** Baby lamb chops grilled and eaten as finger food.

**Anguillette in umido:** Stewed baby eels from Lake Bracciano.

**Coda alla vaccinara:** Oxtail braised with garlic, wine, tomato, and celery.

**Filetti di baccalà:** Fried salt cod (like fish-and-chips minus the chips).

**Involtini di vitello al sugo:** Veal cutlets rolled with prosciutto, celery, and cheese in a tomato sauce.

**Saltimbocca alla romana:** "Jump-in-the-mouth"—thinly sliced veal layered with prosciutto and sage, then lightly fried.

**Trippa alla romana:** Tripe braised with onions, carrots, and mint.

## Contorni (Side Dishes)

You may want to order a side dish if your second course is not served with a vegetable. Note that if you order a salad, olive oil and wine vinegar are the only dressings.

**Carciofi:** Artichokes served either *alla romana* (simmered with garlic and mint) or *alla giudia* (flattened and fried).

**Fave al guanciale:** Fava beans simmered with cured pork cheek and onion.

**Misticanza:** Mixed green salad of arugula *(rucola)* and curly endive *(puntarelle)* with anchovies.

## Dolci (Desserts)

Dessert can be a seasonal fruit, such as *fragole* (strawberries) or *pesche* (peaches), or even cheese, such as *pecorino romano* (made from ewe's milk) or *caciotta romana* (combination of ewe's and cow's milk).

**Bignè:** Cream-puff-like pastries filled with *zabaione* (egg yolks, sugar, and Marsala wine).

**Crostata di ricotta:** A cheesecake-like dessert with ricotta, sweet Marsala wine, cinnamon, and bits of chocolate.

**Grattachecca:** Sweetened shaved ice. Vendors at little booths scrape shavings off ice blocks, then flavor them with syrups, such as *limoncocco* (lemon and coconut with fresh chunks of coconut).

**Tartufo:** Rich dark-chocolate gelato ball with a cherry inside, sometimes served *con panna* (with whipped cream).

### Roman Pizza

Roman-style pizza is made with a very thin and crispy dough called *scrocchiarella* (thinner and less chewy than Neapolitan-style pizza). In Rome, *pizza bianca* (white pizza) can mean a pizza

made without tomato sauce, but can also simply mean a chunk of flat, crispy bread, or a sandwich made with that bread (similar to what's called a *panino* in other parts of Italy).

### Local Wines

Rome is located in the region of Lazio, which produces several pleasant white wines and a few reds. Frascati, probably the best-known wine of the region, is an inexpensive dry white made from trebbiano (from the hills just south of Rome) and malvasia grapes. Castelli Romani, light and fairly dry, is made from trebbiano grapes and is similar to Marino, Colli Albani, and Velletri wines. Torre Ercolana is a dense, balanced, medium-bodied red made from the regional cesanese grape, as well as cabernet and merlot (known as Lazio's best-quality red, aged at least five years).

formal tables or to take away. For a fun movable feast, drop in for a bite to whatever casual places you see that appeal. Here are some ideas:

**Wine with *Aperitivo*** (dinner only): **$$ Fafiuché** is an intimate yet vibrant family-run wine bar with a fun-loving vibe and no pretense. They serve a broad selection of wines and beers inside or at tables on the cobblestones outside. Andrea, Maria, and their son Gianmarco offer serious dishes from Apulia and Piedmont. And, if you're assembling a mobile dinner, they put out an inviting buffet for your choice of €3 tapas plates (Mon-Sat 18:30-21:00, closed Sun, Via della Madonna dei Monti 28).

**Pizza by the Slice on the Square:** The hole-in-the-wall **$ Pizzeria la Boccaccia** is good for a takeaway slice. Point at what you like and mime how big of a rectangle you want (pricing by the *etto*, or 100 grams, daily, Via Leonina 73). Take it a block away to the main square (Piazza della Madonna dei Monti), buy a beer at the convenience store (top of the square), and make the piazza scene.

**Gourmet Sandwich and Veggie Juice:** Gourmet *rosette*, sandwiches on rose-shaped buns, are the specialty at **$ Zia Rosetta.** At €3-4 for the tiny ones or €6-7 for the standard size, they're perfect for a light bite—either to take away or eat in. A fun, healthy, and creative menu includes salads and €4 *centrifughe*—fresh-squeezed, vitamin-bomb fruit and veggie juices (Mon-Thu 11:00-16:00, Fri-Sun until 22:00, Via Urbana 54).

**Gelato:** Hiding on the welcoming little square just above Zia Rosetta, **Fatamorgana** features the most creative gelato combinations I've seen in Italy, along with more conventional flavors. Portions are small but good quality—everything is organic and gluten-free (long hours daily, Piazza degli Zingari 5).

## Behind the Colosseum

A pleasant little residential zone just up the street from the back of the Colosseum (the opposite direction from the Forum) features a real neighborhood feel and a variety of restaurants that capably serve tired and hungry sightseers.

**$ Trattoria Luzzi** is a well-worn, no-frills eatery serving simple food in a high-energy—sometimes chaotic—environment (as they've done since 1945). With good prices, big portions, and proximity to the Colosseum, it draws a crowd, so reserve ahead or expect a short wait at lunch and after 19:30 (Thu-Tue 12:00-24:00, closed Wed, Via Celimontana 1, tel. 06-709-6332).

**$$ Ristorante Pizzeria Naumachia** is a good second bet if Trattoria Luzzi next door is jammed up. It's a bit more upscale and serves good-quality pizza and pastas at decent prices (Via Celimontana 7, tel. 06-700-2764).

**$$ Li Rioni,** a pizzeria, is open only for dinner, when its over-the-rooftops interior and terrace out front are jammed with Romans watching the busy chef plunge dough into its wood-fired oven, then pull out crispy-crust Roman-style pizzas (Wed-Mon 19:30-24:00, closed Tue, Via dei SS. Quattro 24, tel. 06-7045-0605).

**$$ Il Pentagrappolo** is an intimate *enoteca* serving light meals (proudly, no pasta) to go with their selection of quality wines, many organic. Their €12 lunches include water, and on some nights there's live music (see "Jazz" in the "Nightlife in Rome" section, earlier). The location is convenient to the Forum and Colosseum (food served Mon-Fri 12:00-15:00, also Tue-Sun 18:00-24:00, best to reserve on weekends, three blocks east of the Colosseum at Via Celimontana 21, www.ilpentagrappolo.com, tel. 06-709-6301).

### Between the Colosseum and St. Peter-in-Chains Church

You'll find these places across the street and up the hill from the Colosseum. They're more convenient than high cuisine, though they work fine in a pinch.

**$$ Hostaria da Nerone** is a traditional place serving hearty classics, including tasty homemade pasta dishes. Their antipasti plate—with a variety of veggies, fish, and meat—is a good value for a quick lunch. While the antipasti menu indicates specifics, you can have a plate of whatever's out—just direct the waiter to assemble the €10 antipasti plate of your lunchtime dreams (Mon-Sat 12:00-15:00 & 19:00-23:00, closed Sun, indoor/outdoor seating, Via delle Terme di Tito 96, tel. 06-481-7952).

**$ Caffè dello Studente,** a normal neighborhood bar popular with tourists and students attending the nearby Sapienza University, is run by Pina, her cheerful daughter Simona, and son-in-law Emiliano. I'd skip the microwaved pasta and stick to toasted sandwiches and salad. If it's not busy, show this book when you order at the bar and sit at a table without paying extra (daily 7:30-20:00, closed Sun Nov-March, Via delle Terme di Tito 95, mobile 320-854-0333).

### PANTHEON NEIGHBORHOOD

I've listed the restaurants in this central area based on which landmark they're closest to: Campo de' Fiori, Piazza Navona, the Trevi Fountain, or the Pantheon itself.

### On and near Campo de' Fiori

By day, Campo de' Fiori hosts a colorful fruit-and-veggies market (with an increasing number of tourist knickknacks; Mon-Sat until around 13:30, closed Sun). Combined with a sandwich and a sweet

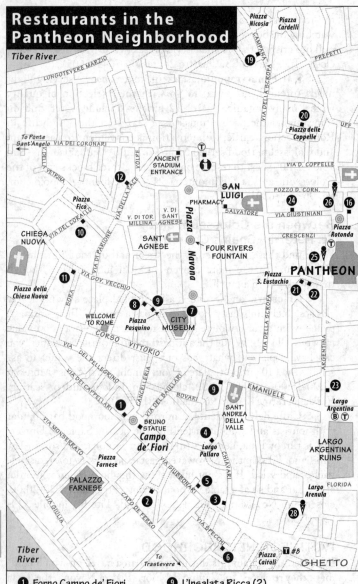

# Restaurants in the Pantheon Neighborhood

1. Forno Campo de' Fiori
2. Enoteca L'Angolo Divino
3. Antico Forno Roscioli
4. Trattoria der Pallaro
5. Filetti di Baccalà
6. Open Baladin Pub
7. Vivi Bistrot
8. Cul de Sac
9. L'Insalata Ricca (2)
10. Rist. Pizzeria "da Francesco"
11. Pizzeria da Baffetto
12. Chiostro del Bramante
13. To Hostaria Romana
14. Origano
15. L'Antica Birreria Peroni
16. Ristorante da Fortunato & Wine Bar

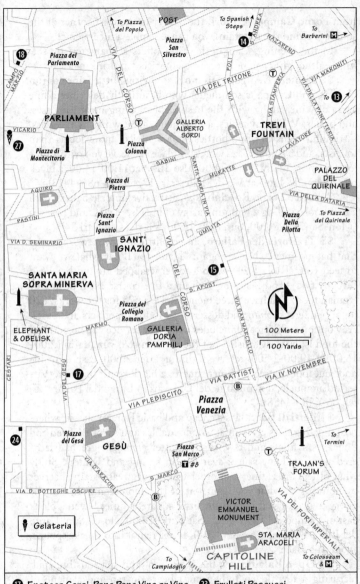

**17** Enoteca Corsi, Pane Pane Vino ar Vino & L'Antico Caffee della Pigna

**18** Trattoria dal Cavalier Gino

**19** Ristorante la Campana

**20** Osteria delle Coppelle & Osteria da Mario

**21** Ginger

**22** Miscellanea

**23** Frullati Pascucci

**24** Supermarket (2)

**25** Crèmeria Monteforte

**26** San Crispino Gelateria

**27** Giolitti Gelateria

**28** Gelateria Artigianale Corona

from **Forno Campo de' Fiori,** the bakery in the west corner of the square (behind the fountain), you can assemble a nice picnic.

In the evening, Campo de' Fiori offers a characteristic setting—although it can be overrun by tourists out drinking.

**$$ Enoteca L'Angolo Divino** is an inviting little wine bar run by Massimo Crippa, a sommelier who beautifully describes a fine array of wines along with the best accompanying meats, cheeses, and pastas. With tiny tables, a tiny menu, great wines by the glass, intriguing walls of wine bottles, smart advice, more locals than tourists, and a smooth jazz vibe, this place can leave you with a life-long memory (daily 17:00-24:00, also Tue-Sat 11:00-14:00, a block off Campo de' Fiori at Via dei Balestrari 12, tel. 06-686-4413).

**$ Antico Forno Roscioli** is an attractive upscale bakery with a few stools, selling a tempting array of breads, pizzas, and pastries (Mon-Sat 7:00-20:00, Sun 8:00-19:00, Via dei Chiavari 34).

**$$ Trattoria der Pallaro,** an eccentric and well-worn eatery that has no menu, has a slogan: "Here, you'll eat what we want to feed you." Paola Fazi—with a towel wrapped around her head turban-style—and her gang dish up a five-course meal of homey Roman food. You have three menu choices: €25 for the works; €20 for appetizers, *secondi,* and dessert; or €16 for appetizers and pasta. Any option is filling and includes wine. The service can be odd and the food is, let's say...rustic, but the experience is fun (daily 12:00-16:00 & 19:00-24:00, reserve if dining after 20:00, cash only, indoor/outdoor seating on quiet square, a block south of Corso Vittorio Emanuele, down Largo del Chiavari to Largo del Pallaro 15, tel. 06-6880-1488).

**$ Filetti di Baccalà** is a cheap and basic Roman classic, where nostalgic regulars cram in at wooden tables and savor €6 fried cod finger-food fillets and raw, slightly bitter *puntarelle* greens (slathered with anchovy sauce, available in spring and winter). Study what others are eating, and order from your grease-stained server by pointing at what you want. Sit in the fluorescently lit interior or try to grab a seat out on the little square, a quiet haven a block east of Campo de' Fiori (Mon-Sat 17:00-23:00, closed Sun, Largo dei Librari 88, tel. 06-686-4018). If you're not into greasy spoons, avoid this place.

**$$ Open Baladin** is a busy, modern, and spacious brewpub featuring a few dozen Italian craft beers on tap and a menu of burgers, salads, and freshly cooked potato chips. As burger bars are trendy in Italy, prices are somewhat high. It's a nice break if you're parched and ready for pub grub (daily 12:00-24:00, Via degli Specchi 5, tel. 06-683-8989).

## Near Piazza Navona

Piazza Navona and the streets just to the west are jammed with an amazing array of restaurants. The places lining the piazza itself are traditional and touristy. Instead, survey the scene on the two streets heading west from the square. Here are my favorites in that zone:

**$$ Vivi Bistrot** is in the Museum of Rome building at the south end of Piazza Navona, with two window tables overlooking the square. This cheery and modern little restaurant serves salads, pastas, and burger plates with a focus on organic ingredients (Tue-Sun 10:00-24:00, closed Mon, Piazza Navona 2, tel. 06-683-3779).

**$$ Cul de Sac,** a long and skinny trattoria lined with wine bottles, is packed with an enthusiastic crowd enjoying a wide-ranging menu, from pasta to homemade pâté. They have fun sampler plates of *salumi* and cheese, good wines by the glass, and fine outdoor seating. It's jammed with regulars, and they don't take reservations—come early to avoid a wait (daily 12:00-24:00, a block off Piazza Navona on Piazza Pasquino 73, tel. 06-6880-1094).

**$$ L'Insalata Ricca,** a popular local chain, specializes in filling salads and also serves pasta and €12 meal deals. A small branch is at Piazza Pasquino 72 (tel. 06-6830-7881), and a more spacious and enjoyable location is a couple of blocks toward Largo Argentina, just across busy Corso Vittorio Emanuele (Largo dei Chiavari 85, tel. 06-6880-3656). Both are open daily 12:00-24:00.

**$$$ Ristorante Pizzeria "da Francesco,"** bustling and authentic, has a 50-year-old tradition, a hardworking young waitstaff, great indoor seating, and a few tables stretching along the quiet street. Their blackboard explains the daily specials (daily 12:00-15:30 & 19:00-24:00, Piazza del Fico 29, tel. 06-686-4009, www.dafrancesco.it). While a bit overpriced, it's very popular. Reservations are required for evening seatings at 19:00, 20:30, or 22:00.

**$ Pizzeria da Baffetto** is famous among visiting Italians and therefore generally comes with a ridiculous line. The pizzas are great, the service is surly, and the tables are tightly arranged amid the mishmash of sketches littering the walls. The pizza-assembly kitchen keeps things energetic, and the pizza oven keeps the main room warm. Streetside tables are less congested and sweaty, but also less memorable (daily 12:00-15:30 & 18:30-late, cash only, order "M" or "D"—medium or large, Via del Governo Vecchio 114, tel. 06-686-1617).

**$$ Chiostro del Bramante** ("Bramante's Cloister") is a museum café serving light lunches in a unique setting—overlooking the tranquil open-air *chiostro*. Gaze out as the Renaissance master Bramante brings symmetry to your meal. With not a hint of tourism, it's a refined and elegant place, and fine for a predinner drink, too. Enter just to the left of the church entrance and tell the ticket-window staff that you're just going to the café (daily 10:00-20:00, meals served 12:00-15:00, Arco della Pace 5, tel. 06-6880-9035).

## Near the Trevi Fountain

The streets surrounding the Trevi Fountain are littered with mediocre restaurants catering exclusively to tourists. Skip them and walk a few blocks away to one of these. Also consider nearby **Hostaria Romana,** behind the fountain near the Palazzo del Quirinale (walk along Via Rasella to reach the restaurant; see the listing on page 949).

**$$$ Origano** is a bustling, modern bistro (and café) located three blocks away from the Trevi Fountain. It serves well-priced traditional Roman specialties and wood-fired pizza in an often chaotic setting (daily 12:00-24:00, Via di Sant'Andrea delle Fratte 25/26, tel. 06-699-20907, Germana).

**$$ L'Antica Birreria Peroni** is Rome's answer to a German beer hall. Serving hearty mugs of the local Peroni beer and lots of just plain fun beer-hall food and Italian classics, the place is a hit with Romans for a cheap night out (Mon-Sat 12:00-24:00, closed Sun, midway between Trevi Fountain and Capitoline Hill, a block off Via del Corso at Via di San Marcello 19, tel. 06-679-5310).

## Close to the Pantheon

Eating on the square facing the Pantheon is a temptation, and I'd consider it for breakfast or just to relax and enjoy the Roman scene over a drink. But if you walk a block or two away, you'll get less view and better value. Here are some suggestions:

**$$$$ Ristorante da Fortunato** is an Italian classic, with white-coated, black-tie career waiters politely serving good meat and fish to politicians, foreign dignitaries, and well-heeled tourists. Peruse the photos of their famous visitors—everyone from Prince Charles to Bill Clinton is pictured with the late Signore Fortunato, who started this restaurant in 1975 and was a master of simple edible elegance. (His son Jason now runs the show.) The outdoor seating is fine for people-watching, but the elegance is inside (figure €50/person, daily 12:30-16:00 & 18:30-23:30, in front of Pantheon at Via del Pantheon 55, tel. 06-679-2788, www.ristorantefortunato. it). The **Fortunato Wine Bar** is a classy place for a glass of fine wine with a plate of properly paired cold meats and cheeses. For a fun wine option, you can run up a tab from the bar's tasting machine while dining next door.

**$$ Enoteca Corsi,** a wine shop that grew into a thriving restaurant, is a charming local scene with the family table in back, where the kids do their homework. The Paiella family serves straightforward, traditional cuisine to an appreciative crowd of office workers. The board lists daily specials (gnocchi on Thursday, fish on Friday, and so on). Friendly Manuela and her staff offer fine wine at a third of the price you'd pay in normal restaurants—buy from their shop and pay a corking fee. Show this book for a free

ROME

## Resources for Foodies

For those looking to take their Roman culinary endeavors seriously, there's no shortage of in-depth advice. Here is a sampling:

**KatieParla.com:** Food author Katie Parla's website has all the latest on the Roman food scene. She also offers private tours and top-notch tastings and has an easy-to-use app, Katie Parla's Rome (works without Internet connection).

**Eat Italy:** Food writer Elizabeth Minchilli's excellent app lists a wide range of good eateries and food-oriented shops. It covers many cities—including Rome (and works without Internet connection). Her website also features recipes and private food tours (www.elizabethminchilliinrome.com).

**Eating Italy Food Tours:** This tour company leads fun and insightful walks almost daily through Rome's colorful Testaccio neighborhood, interspersing history, tradition, and local food culture while giving you a glimpse into daily life in less-seen parts of the city. Each group of around a dozen people makes about 10 tasty stops (€79-99, RS%—10 percent discount with promo code "ricksteves," 3-4 hours, several morning and evening departures Mon-Sat, www.eatingitalyfoodtours.com). They also offer cooking classes.

**Vino Roma:** This small wine "school" is run by several sommeliers who offer evening tasting classes (€50/person), designed to help you understand and enjoy Italian wine. They also lead several neighborhood walks (www.vinoroma.com).

**Local Aromas:** Giuliana and her daughters Benedetta and Valeria offer excellent food and market tours (€55/person), wine and craft beer tours (€65), and cooking classes (€86) from a view penthouse two blocks from the Vatican Museums (www.localaromas.com).

glass of homemade *limoncello* for dessert (Mon-Sat 12:00-15:30, Wed-Fri also 19:00-22:30, closed Sun, a block toward the Pantheon from the Gesù Church at Via del Gesù 87, tel. 06-679-0821).

**$$** Next to Enoteca Corsi are two other good lunch-only options popular with local office workers: **Pane Pane Vino ar Vino** is a creative little sandwich bar with a delightful menu (Via del Gesù 84) and **L'Antico Caffee della Pigna** is a timeless old café serving pastas, salads, and sandwiches (Piazza della Pigna 57).

**$$ Trattoria dal Cavalier Gino,** tucked away on a tiny street behind the Parliament, has been a favorite since 1963. Photos on the wall recall the days when it was the haunt of big-time politicians. English-speaking siblings Carla and Fabrizio serve up traditional Roman favorites. They offer four seatings a day: 13:00, 14:30, 20:00, and 22:00. Reserve ahead, even for lunch, as you'll be packed in with savvy locals (Mon-Sat, closed Sun, behind Piazza del Parlamento and just off Via di Campo Marzio at Vicolo Rosini 4, tel. 06-687-3434).

**$$$ Ristorante la Campana** is a classic—an authentic slice of old Rome appreciated by well-dressed locals. Claiming a history dating to 1518, this place feels unchanged over the years. It serves typical Roman dishes and daily specials, plus it has a self-service *antipasti* buffet, which makes a nice €12 lunch (Tue-Sun 12:30-15:00 & 19:30-23:00, closed Mon, inside seating only, just off Via della Scrofa and Piazza Nicosia at Vicolo della Campana 18, tel. 06-687-5273, www.ristorantelacampana.com).

**$$ Osteria delle Coppelle,** a slapdash, trendy place, serves traditional dishes to a local crowd and a fun selection of €3 *cicchetti* (small plates) that lets you enjoy a variety of Roman dishes as tapas. It has a rustic interior and jumbled exterior seating, with a much classier dining section in the back (daily 12:30-15:30 & 19:00-late, Piazza delle Coppelle 54, tel. 06-4550-2826). They run a fun "speakeasy" bar which opens nightly at 22:00—but don't tell anyone. On the same charming square, the more old-school **Osteria da Mario,** with classic tables inside or out, is also worth considering.

**$$ Ginger** is a crisp, modern restaurant one block from the Pantheon, with a spacious and bright interior and seating on a delightful square. The menu selection—pastas, *panini*, salads, and smoothies—is healthy, organic, and a bit pricey (daily 8:00-23:00, Piazza di S. Eustachio 54, tel. 06-6830-8559). A second location is four blocks in front of the Spanish Steps (see listing later, under "North Rome").

**$$ Miscellanea** is run by much-loved Miki, who's on a mission to keep foreign students well-fed. He offers €4 sandwiches, pizza-like bruschetta, and a long list of hearty salads, along with pasta and other staples—it's a good value for a cheap and filling dinner in a convenient location. Miki (and his son Romeo) often tosses in a fun little extra (like their "sexy wine") if you have this book on the table (daily 9:00-24:00, just behind the Pantheon at Via della Palombella 37, tel. 06-6813-5318).

### Picnicking Close to the Pantheon

It's fun to picnic with a view of the Pantheon. (Remember to be discreet.) Here are some options:

**$ Frullati Pascucci,** a hole-in-the-wall convenient for take-away, has been making refreshing €4-5 fruit *frullati* and frappés (like smoothies and shakes), plus fruit salads, for more than 80 years. Add a €4 sandwich to make a healthy light meal (Mon-Sat 6:00-23:00, closed Sun, north of Largo Argentina at Via di Torre Argentina 20, tel. 06-686-4816).

For picnic goodies, try the **Co-op** supermarket. There's one a half block from the Pantheon (daily 8:30-22:00, Via Giustiniani 18b) and another one three blocks away (daily until 21:00, Corso Vittorio Emanuele II 42).

### Gelato Close to the Pantheon

Several fine *gelaterie* are within three or four blocks of the Pantheon.

**Crèmeria Monteforte** is known for its traditional gelato and super-creamy sorbets *(cremolati)*. The fruit flavors are especially refreshing—think gourmet slushies (closed Mon, faces the west side of the Pantheon at Via della Rotonda 22).

**San Crispino** serves small portions of tasty gourmet gelato. Because of their commitment to natural ingredients, the colors are muted; ice cream purists know that bright colors are artificial and used to attract children (a block in front of the Pantheon at Piazza della Maddalena 3).

**Giolitti** is Rome's most famous and venerable ice-cream establishment (although few would say it has the best gelato). Takeaway prices are reasonable, and it has elegant Old World seating (just off Piazza Colonna and Piazza Montecitorio at Via Uffici del Vicario 40).

**Gelateria Artigianale Corona** feels like a time warp and is nothing fancy, but it's got some of the finest homemade gelato in town, with an array of creative flavors (just south of Largo Argentina at Largo Arenula 27).

## NEAR VATICAN CITY

As in the Colosseum area, some eateries near the Vatican prey on exhausted tourists. Avoid the restaurant pushers handing out fliers: They're usually hawking places with bad food and expensive menu tricks. Instead, tide yourself over with a slice of pizza or at any of these eateries (see map on page 918), and save your euros for a better meal elsewhere.

### Handy Lunch Places near Piazza Risorgimento

These listings are a stone's throw from the Vatican wall. They're mostly fast and cheap, with a good *gelateria* nearby.

**$$ Il Colibrì,** run by the Ricci brothers, has noisy streetside seating and a quiet interior (daily 10:30-15:30 & 17:00-24:00, at corner of Via Leone IV and Via Famagosta 69, tel. 06-3751-4767).

**$ L'Insalata Ricca** is another branch of the popular chain that serves hearty salads and pastas (daily 12:00-23:30, across from the Vatican walls at Piazza Risorgimento 5, tel. 06-3973-0387).

**$ Duecento Gradi** is a good bet for fresh and creative sandwiches—though at €5-8 they're expensive by Roman standards.

Munch your lunch sitting down (€1 extra) or take it away (daily 11:00-24:00, Piazza Risorgimento 3, tel. 06-3975-4239).

**Gelateria Old Bridge** scoops up hearty portions of fresh gelato for tourists and nuns alike—join the line (just off Piazza Risorgimento across from the Vatican walls at Viale dei Bastioni di Michelangelo 3).

## Other Options in the Vatican Area

Most of these listings are near the Vatican Museums and Cipro Metro stop. The Borgo Pio eateries are near St. Peter's Basilica.

**Viale Giulio Cesare** and **Via Candia:** These streets are lined with cheap *pizza rustica* shops and self-serve places. **$ Forno Feliziani** (closed Sun, Via Candia 61) is a fancy version with nicely presented pizza by the slice and simple cafeteria-style dishes that you can eat in or take out.

**Covered Market:** Turn your nose loose in the wonderful **Mercato Trionfale,** one of the city's best market halls. It's more of a sight than a place to eat. Almost completely untouristy (with lots of vendors, but no real prepared-food stands aside from a bakery and a sandwich counter), it's located just three blocks north of the Vatican Museums (Mon-Sat roughly 7:00-14:00, Tue and Fri some stalls stay open until 19:00, closed Sun, corner of Via Tunisi and Via Andrea Doria). If the market is closed, try one of these grocery stores (both open daily until 20:30): **Co-op,** with a big bakery section and tables where you can eat pizza by the slice (to the northwest at Via Andrea Doria 46), or the smaller **Carrefour Express** (closer to the Vatican at Via Sebastiano Veniero 16).

**Eating Close to St. Peter's:** The pedestrian-only Borgo Pio—a block from Piazza San Pietro—has restaurants worth a look, such as the traditional **$$ Tre Pupazzi** (Mon-Sat 12:00-15:00 & 19:00-23:00, closed Sun, at corner of Via Tre Pupazzi and Borgo Pio, tel. 06-6880-3220). At **$ Vecchio Borgo,** across the street, you can get pasta, pizza by weight, and veggies to go or to eat at simple tables (daily 9:30-22:30, Borgo Pio 27a).

## NORTH ROME: NEAR THE SPANISH STEPS AND ARA PACIS

To locate these restaurants, see the map on page 832.

**$$$$ Ristorante il Gabriello** is inviting and small—modern under medieval arches—and provides a peaceful and local-feeling respite from all the top-end fashion shops in the area. Claudio serves with charisma, while his brother Gabriello cooks creative Roman cuisine using fresh, organic products from his wife's farm. Italians normally just trust their waiter and say, "Bring it on." Tourists are understandably more cautious, but you can be trusting here. Invest €55—not including wine—in "Claudio's Extravaganza," created especially for my readers (not on the menu). Specify whether you'd prefer fish, meat, or both. (Be warned: Romans think raw shellfish is the ultimate in fine dining. If you don't, make that clear.) While you're likely to dine surrounded by my readers here (especially if eating before 21:00), the atmosphere is fun and convivial (dinner only, Mon-Sat 19:00-23:00, closed Sun, reservations smart, air-con, dress respectfully—no shorts, 3 blocks from Spanish Steps at Via Vittoria 51, tel. 06-6994-0810, www.ilgabriello.com).

**$$ Ginger,** four blocks in front of the Spanish Steps, is modern and bright, with an emphasis on sustainable and healthy ingredients (daily 8:00-23:00, Via Borgognona 43, tel. 06-9603-6390). A sister location near the Pantheon is described earlier.

**$$$ Caffè Vitti,** delightfully set on a fine traffic-free square, has been serving its neighborhood for over a century. The food won't win any awards—and you pay for the location—but it offers a delightful chance to enjoy a meal (good salads, pizza) or a cocktail on a quiet and characteristic square. Sit outside and people-watch amidst a professional Roman crowd. The cocktails come with a little tray of munchies (daily 6:30-24:00, Piazza San Lorenzo in Lucina 33, tel. 06-687-6304).

### Via della Croce Stand-Up Food Crawl

Two blocks north of the Spanish Steps, touristy Via della Croce is a fun street to graze for a light meal or snack. As you peruse this street from Via del Corso, you'll pass these enticing stops for a bite:

**Grano Frutta e Farina** (#49) sells hard-to-resist pizza by weight. Consider a tasting plate with a tiny bit of each pizza.

**Focacci Deli** (#43) makes sandwiches on request. Choose from their long, enticing counter of meats and cheeses.

**Antica Enoteca** (#76) is an inviting bar for a glass of wine in wonderful surroundings.

**Salsamenteria F.lli Fabbi** (#28) is a classic *alimentari* (corner grocery/deli). They'll make a sandwich to your specs and price it by weight.

**Venchi** (#25) can make your gelato and chocolate dreams come true.

**Pompi** (#82), the self-proclaimed "kingdom of tiramisù," features several flavors (classic, strawberry, pistachio, chocolate-banana, and more) in €4 portions.

**Pastificio** (#8), with a history going back to World War I, serves up two fresh €4 pasta dishes each day; a glass of water or wine is included when you eat at the stools along the wall.

### NEAR TERMINI STATION

With a constant swarm of hungry, well-worn travelers, Rome's train station and the streets on either side of it are a nightmare

ROME

# Restaurants near Termini Station

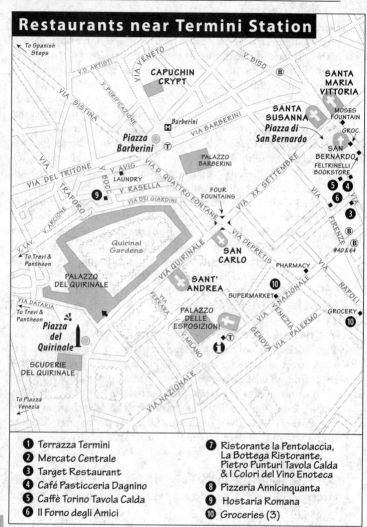

1. Terrazza Termini
2. Mercato Centrale
3. Target Restaurant
4. Café Pasticceria Dagnino
5. Caffè Torino Tavola Calda
6. Il Forno degli Amici
7. Ristorante la Pentolaccia, La Bottega Ristorante, Pietro Punturi Tavola Calda & I Colori del Vino Enoteca
8. Pizzeria Annicinquanta
9. Hostaria Romana
10. Groceries (3)

ROME

of mostly low-end eateries. A few places stand out as options to consider:

## At the Station

From near track 15, ride the escalator up to a food court called **$ Terrazza Termini.** It's bright, spacious, and safe-feeling, with several decent mall-type eateries, free Wi-Fi and charging stations, and plenty of places to sit. You'll notice competing *aperitivo* deals (17:00-20:00, €7 for a drink and access to buffet, **Eccellenze della Costiera** is best). There are also large self-service **cafeterias** on the ground floor.

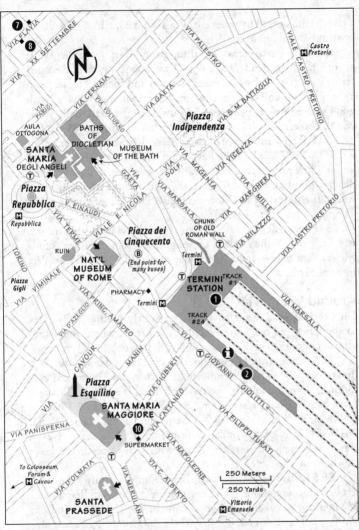

The upscale **Mercato Centrale** (about 200 yards up track 24 facing Via Giovanni Giolitti) is a thriving and slick food market hall with a great vibe and plenty of **$$** foodie options (daily 8:00-24:00).

## Around Recommended Via Firenze Area Hotels

**$$$ Target Restaurant** seems to be the favorite recommendation of every hotel receptionist on Via Firenze. It has a sleek and dressy ambience, capable service, and food that's reliably good, but pricey (free *aperitivo* with this book, daily 12:00-15:30 & 19:00-24:00, closed Sun at lunch, reserve to specify seating outside or inside—

avoid getting seated in basement, Via Torino 33, tel. 06-474-0066, www.targetrestaurant.it).

**$$ Café Pasticceria Dagnino,** a time-warp from the 1960s set in a tired old arcade, has a big selection at its *tavola calda* counter. It's known for its fine pastry section and Sicilian treats from *arancini* to cannoli. It's fast, reasonably priced, and reliable, with good seating inside, upstairs, and outside in the mall (daily 7:00-23:00, Galleria Esedra, enter at Via Torino 95, tel. 06-481-8660).

**$ Caffè Torino Tavola Calda** is another workers' favorite for a quick, cheap lunch. They have good, fresh, hot dishes ready to go for a fine price. Head back past the bar to peruse their enticing display, point at what you want, then grab a seat and the young waitstaff will serve you (Mon-Fri 6:00-18:00, closed Sat-Sun, Via Torino 40, tel. 06-487-0000).

**$ Il Forno degli Amici,** handy if your hotel is on Via Firenze, is a little dive selling salads by weight, pizza by the slice, sandwiches, and bakery items (Mon-Sat until 21:00, closed Sun, Via Firenze 51).

## Around Via Flavia

For a serious meal near the station, it's worth walking 10 minutes to the quiet and residential-feeling Via Flavia, where you'll find almost no tourism and a cluster of fine dining options.

**$$$ Ristorante la Pentolaccia,** upscale and romantic, is a dressy but still tourist-friendly place with tight seating and traditional Roman cooking—consider their daily specials. This is a local hangout, and reservations are smart (daily 12:00-15:00 & 18:00-23:00, a block off Via XX Settembre at Via Flavia 38, tel. 06-483-477, www.lapentolaccia-restaurant.it, Vincenzo gives a warm welcome). To start things off with a free bruschetta, leave this book on the table.

**$$$ La Bottega Ristorante,** in the Punturi family since 1919, is a bright, contemporary, and easygoing place serving Roman and Mediterranean cuisine, and good wine by the glass (nightly from 17:00, Via Flavia 46, tel. 06-487-0391). They run the adjacent pizzeria.

**$ Pietro Punturi Tavola Calda** is a *rosticceria* cooking up super casual dishes sold by weight and eaten on plastic at its fast-food-type seating (Mon-Sat 8:30-20:30, closed Sun, Via Flavia 46).

**$$ Pizzeria Annicinquanta,** big and modern, is a neighborhood fixture serving Neapolitan-style pizzas in a calm ambience with outdoor seating (daily 12:00-15:30 & 19:30-24:00, Via Flavia 3, tel. 06-4201-0460).

**$$$ I Colori del Vino Enoteca** is a classy wine bar that feels like a laboratory of wine appreciation. It has a creative menu of *af-*

ROME

*fettati* (cold cuts) and cheeses, and a great list of fine wines by the glass. Helpful, English-speaking Marco carries on a long family tradition of celebrating the fundamentals of good nutrition: fine wine, cheese, meat, and bread (Mon-Sat 12:00-15:00 & 18:00-23:00, closed Sun, Via Aureliana 15 at corner of Via Flavia, tel. 06-474-1745). This is a great stop after dinner for a dessert wine (which comes with a plate of cookies).

### Between Piazza Barberini and Trevi Fountain

**$$$ Hostaria Romana,** near the Quirinale, is a busy bistro with a hustling and fun-loving gang of waiters and makes a good choice on your way to or from Trevi Fountain. The upstairs is a tight, tidy, glassed-in terrace, while the cellar has noisy walls graffitied by happy eaters. As its menu specializes in traditional Roman dishes, it's a good place to try *saltimbocca alla romana* or *bucatini all'amatriciana.* Their €12 *antipasti della casa* plate, with a variety of vegetables and cheeses, makes a hearty start to your meal (Mon-Sat 12:30-15:00 & 19:15-23:00, closed Sun and Aug, reservations smart, midway between Piazza Barberini and Trevi Fountain at Via del Boccaccio 1, tel. 06-474-5284, www.hostariaromana.it).

### TRASTEVERE

Restaurants line the streets of colorful Trastevere. It's a favorite dining neighborhood for both Romans and tourists—more rustic than the downtown zone, but just a short walk across the river. (∩ Download my free Trastevere Walk **audio tour** to combine sightseeing with dinner.) While it's become extremely touristy, if you venture away from the central square (Piazza di Santa Maria in Trastevere) into the back streets you'll find places that serve with sincerity and charm. For locations, see the map on page 927.

**$$$$ Taverna Trilussa** is your best bet for dining well in Trastevere. Brothers Massimo and Maurizio offer quality without pretense. With a proud 100-year-old tradition, this place has the right mix of style and informality. The service is fun-loving (they're happy to let you split plates into smaller portions to enjoy a family-style meal), yet professional. The menu celebrates local classics and seasonal specials—as well as their award-winning *pasta amatriciana*—and comes with a big wine selection. The spacious dining hall is strewn with eclectic Roman souvenirs. Outdoors, Trilussa has an actual hedged-in terrace rather than just tables jumbled together on the sidewalk (dinner only, Mon-Sat from 19:30, closed Sun, reservations smart, Via del Politeama 23, tel. 06-581-8918, www.tavernatrilussa.it).

**$$$ Dar Sor Olimpio al Drago,** with a small, romantic dining room (no outdoor seating), has a friendly staff and an enticing menu—both typical Roman and modern Italian. The chef enjoys

ROME

exercising a little creative license (Mon-Sat from 18:00, Sun from 12:00, Piazza del Drago 2, mobile 339-885-7574).

**$$ Trattoria de Gli Amici** employs people with mental disabilities (who are helped and mentored by volunteers) to offer delightful meals in a charming atmosphere. Be a part of that community service mission and enjoy traditional Roman cuisine with a modern twist while surrounded by contemporary art in a medieval building or on a romantic square (daily 12:00-23:00, Piazza Sant'Egidio 6, tel. 06-580-6033).

**$$ Trattoria da Lucia** is your basic old-school Trastevere dining experience, family-run since before World War II. The specialty is *spaghetti alla Gricia,* with pancetta (Tue-Sun 12:30-15:30 & 19:30-23:00, closed Mon and much of Aug, cash only, evocative outdoor or comfy indoor seating—but avoid back room, just off Via del Mattonato at Vicolo del Mattonato 2, tel. 06-580-3601; sisters Livia, Zoe, and Elisa).

**$$ La Prosciutteria Cantina dei Papi** is a cozy and friendly place celebrating the wine, cheese, and meats of Lazio and Tuscany. They serve hearty *taglieri* (easily splittable boards) of regional delights (€5-15) and fine wine by the big or little bottle. If you're in the mood for *porchetta* and *mortadella,* look no further. Nothing's hot and you order at the counter (daily 12:00-24:00, Via della Scala 71, tel. 06-6456-2839).

## Classic Pizzerias in Trastevere

**$$ Pizzeria "Ai Marmi"** is a noisy festival of pizza. Tight marble-slab tables (hence the nickname "the Morgue") fill the seating area in front of the oven and pizza-assembly line. It's a classic Roman scene whether you enjoy the chaos inside, sit at a sidewalk table, or take the famously good, thin, and crispy €8-9 pizza home. They also serve fried cod, rice balls with mozzarella *(supplì),* and bean dishes. Expect brusque service and a long line between 20:00 and 22:00 (Thu-Tue 18:30 until very late, closed Wed, cash only, tram #8 from Piazza Venezia to first stop over bridge, just beyond Piazza Sonnino at Viale di Trastevere 53, tel. 06-580-0919).

**$$ Pizzeria Dar Poeta,** tucked in a back alley and a hit with local students, cranks out €9 wood-fired pizzas and calzones. These pizzas are easily splittable and, if you're extra hungry, pay an extra euro for *pizza alta* (thicker crust). Choose between their sloppy, cramped interior or the lively tables outside on the cobblestones (daily 12:00-24:00, call to reserve, arrive before 19:00, or expect a wait, 50 yards directly in front of Santa Maria della Scala Church at Vicolo del Bologna 45, tel. 06-588-0516).

**$ Trapizzino Vineria di Roma** is a modern cousin to these classic pizzerias. It's a bar with just two items on the menu: a variety of €4 *trapizzini* (pizza-like wraps with delicious freshly toasted crusts) and €2 *suppli* (the Roman answer to *arancini*—Sicily's fried rice balls). They serve a good variety of Lazio wine and play classic American pop music (daily 10:00 until late, Piazza Trilussa 46, tel. 06-581-7312). It's a fast and cheap option if you're in the mood for something like pizza—but a bit different.

# Rome Connections

## BY TRAIN

Rome's primary train station, centrally located **Termini,** has high-speed connections to other Italian cities and fast trains to the airport. Rome's other major station is called **Tiburtina.** Most trains you encounter depart from Termini. But it's always smart to confirm whether your train departs from Termini or Tiburtina (or one of Rome's even smaller stations). For in-depth descriptions of Termini and Tiburtina stations, see page 811.

Rome also has about a dozen small train stations that are usually only useful if you're staying nearby. The ones you're most likely to use are **San Pietro** (south of Vatican City; bus #64 connects it to Piazza Venezia and Termini; if you're staying near the Vatican and taking a regional train, get off here); **Trastevere** (a few minutes' ride on tram #8 from Trastevere and Piazza Venezia); and **Ostiense** (5 minutes from the Piramide Metro stop via an underground walkway).

Italy has two train companies: Trenitalia, with most connections (tel. 06-6847-5475, www.trenitalia.it), and Italo, with high-speed routes between larger cities (no rail passes accepted, tel. 06-8937-1892, www.italotreno.it). For general information on train travel in Italy—including ticket-buying options—see page 1187.

## Train Connections

Unless otherwise specified, the following connections are for Trenitalia.

**From Termini by Train to: Fiumicino Airport** (Leonardo Express; 2/hour, 32 minutes—see details under "By Plane," later), **Venice** (hourly, 4 hours, 1 direct night train, 7 hours; Italo: 4/day, 3.5 hours), **Florence** (2-3/hour, 1.5 hours; Italo: 2/hour, 1.5 hours), **Siena** (1-2/hour, 1 change, 3-4 hours), **Orvieto** (every 1-2 hours, 1.5 hours; regional trains are half the price and only slightly slower than Intercity trains), **Assisi** (4/day direct, 2 hours; more with change in Foligno), **Pisa** (1-2/hour, 3 hours, some change in Florence), **La Spezia** (7/day direct, 3-4 hours), **Milan** (1-3/hour, 3.5 hours; Italo: 11/day nonstop, 3 hours, more with stops), **Naples** (1-4/hour, 1 hour on Frecciarossa, 2 hours on Intercity, 2.5 hours and much cheaper on regional trains; Italo: hourly, 70 minutes), **Sorrento** (Italo train/bus combination, 2/day, 3.5 hours),

**ROME**

**Civitavecchia** cruise-ship port (regional trains roughly hourly, 80 minutes; faster but pricier trains every 2 hours, 40-50 minutes), **Brindisi** (3/day, 5 hours), **Bern** (3/day, 6.5 hours, change in Milan), **Munich** (4/day, 10 hours, change in Verona or Padua; 1 direct night train, 11.5 hours), **Nice** (2/day, 9 hours, change in Milan), **Paris** (2/day, 11.5 hours, change in Turin; 1 night train, 13.5 hours, change in Milan), **Vienna** (3/day, 12 hours, 1-2 changes; 1 direct night train, 14 hours).

## BY BUS

Long-distance buses use Autostazione Tiburtina, 200 yards from the Tiburtina train and Metro station. Buses are slower than trains, but fares are cheap (as little as €5 to Naples or Florence). Buses are also handy for destinations poorly served by rail. To reach the bus station from Tiburtina station, don't follow the *Bus* signs, which lead to the city bus stop. Instead, exit the station, cross the street under the elevated freeway, and look for the fenced-in area with bus platforms. The station is chaotic and crowded, with nowhere to sit. Ticket-window lines can be slow, so buy your ticket online in advance if possible. If your bus departure platform isn't listed on the digital board, ask one of the drivers for help.

**From Rome by Bus to: Siena** (9/day, 3 hours, https://global.flixbus.com), **Sorrento** (1-2/day, 4 hours; this is a cheap and easy way to go straight to Sorrento, buy tickets at www.marozzivt.it—in Italian only, at the Tiburtina ticket office, travel agencies, or on board for a €3.50 surcharge; tel. 080-579-0111), **Naples** (every 1-2 hours, 3 hours, https://global.flixbus.com or www.megabus.com), **Florence** (every 1-2 hours, 4 hours, https://global.flixbus.comor www.megabus.com), **Assisi** (2/day, 3 hours, www.sulga.it—the train makes much more sense).

## BY PLANE

Rome's two airports—**Fiumicino** (a.k.a. Leonardo da Vinci, airport code: FCO) and the small **Ciampino** (airport code: CIA)—share the same website (www.adr.it).

### Fiumicino Airport

Rome's major airport is manageable. Terminals T1, T2, and T3 are all under one roof—walkable end to end in 20 minutes. T5 is a separate building requiring a short shuttle trip. (T4 is still being built.) The T1-2-3 complex has ground transport, a TI (in T3, daily 9:00-17:30, longer in summer), ATMs, banks, luggage storage, shops, and bars. For airport information, call 06-65951.

## Getting Between Fiumicino Airport and Downtown Rome

In either direction, give yourself lots of time to allow for traffic delays, travel between your hotel and the train/bus station, finding your train or bus, and walking to the terminal.

**By Train:** Trenitalia's slick, direct, first-class-only Leonardo Express train connects the airport train station (called Fiumicino Aeroporto) and Rome's central Termini Station in 32 minutes for €14. At either station, buy your ticket from a Trenitalia machine, a ticket office *(biglietteria),* or a newsstand near the platform. Machines sell open tickets that can be used on any train. (You know you're in Italy when the machine makes you choose a departure time—even though you're allowed to take any train.) You must validate your ticket before boarding by stamping it in a green-and-gray machine near the track. Trains run at least twice hourly in both directions from roughly 6:00 to 23:00 (up to 4/hour in busy times).

From the airport's arrival gate, follow signs to the train icon or *Stazione/Railway Station.* Make sure the train you board is going to the central "Roma Termini" station, as trains from the airport serve other destinations, too.

Returning from Termini train station *to* the airport, trains usually depart from track 23 or 24. Check the departure boards for "Fiumicino Aeroporto" and confirm with an official or a local on the platform that the train is indeed going to the airport.

You can access most of the airport's terminals from the airport train station. If your flight leaves from terminal T5 (where most American air carriers flying direct to the US depart), catch the T5 shuttle bus *(navetta)* on the sidewalk in front of T3—it's too far to walk with luggage.

Cheaper (€8) local trains also run between the airport and some of Rome's smaller train stations (including Trastevere, Ostiense, and Tiburtina). If you're staying in Trastevere or the Pantheon area, it can be simpler and cheaper to take the local train to Trastevere station, then walk out to the street and take the #8 tram downhill to your hotel. The train to Tiburtina is useful if you have a long-distance bus to catch.

Only a couple of long-distance trains per day serve the airport. To connect to other Italian cities, you'll usually have to change at Termini or Tiburtina.

**By Bus:** Four bus companies—Terravision (www.terravision. eu), SIT (www.sitbusshuttle.com), T.A.M. (www.tambus.it), and Schiaffini (www.romeairportbus.com)—connect Fiumicino and Termini train station. The SIT bus also stops near the Vatican. I'd just hop on whichever one is departing first (every 10-15 minutes at peak times). While cheaper than the train (about €7 one-way), buses take twice as long (about an hour, depending on traffic) and can fill up (allow plenty of extra time). At the airport, the bus station is at the far end of terminal T3. At Termini, T.A.M. and Schiaffini depart from the south side of the station; Terravision and SIT from the north side.

**By Airport Shuttle:** Shared shuttle van services can be economical for one or two people. Consider Rome Airport Shuttle (€25 for one person, extra people-€6 each, by reservation only, tel. 06-4201-4507 or 06-4201-3469, www.airportshuttle.it).

**By Taxi:** A taxi between Fiumicino and downtown Rome takes 45 minutes in normal traffic (for taxi tips, see page 825) and costs exactly €48. (Add a €2-5 tip for good service.) From the airport, be sure to catch an official taxi at the taxi stand. Avoid unmarked, unmetered taxis; these guys will try to tempt you away from the taxi-stand lineup by offering an immediate (rip-off) ride. Rome's official taxis are white, with a "taxi" sign on the roof and a maroon *Roma Capitale* logo on the door. By law, taxi drivers can only charge €48 for the ride to anywhere in the historic center (within the old city walls, where my recommended hotels are located). The fare covers up to four people with normal-size bags (to save money, try teaming up with any tourist also just arriving—most are heading for hotels near yours). An official taxi will have the fare amount clearly posted on its door.

Cabs based in Fiumicino (the town near the airport) charge €60 for the ride to downtown Rome. Signs stating the Rome and Fiumicino price caps are posted next to the taxi stand. It's best to use the Rome city cabs and establish the price before you get in. If your driver tries to point to the price for Fiumicino-based cabs or otherwise charge you more than the official rate, say, *"Quarant'otto euro—è la legge"* (kwah-RAHNTOH-toe AY-oo-roh—ay lah LEJ-jay; which means, "Forty-eight euros—it's the law"), and they should back off.

When departing Rome, your hotel can arrange a taxi to the airport at any hour. Alternatively, they sometimes work with comparably priced private car services, which are usually just fine (if not nicer than a regular cab).

## Ciampino Airport

Rome's smaller airport (tel. 06-6595-9515) handles charter flights and some budget airlines (including most Ryanair flights).

**Getting Between Ciampino Airport and Downtown Rome:** Bus companies Terravision, Schiaffini, and SIT will take you to Rome's Termini train station (about €5, 2/hour, 45 minutes). Atral runs a quicker route (25 minutes, www.atral-lazio.com) to the Anagnina Metro stop, where you can connect to the stop nearest your hotel (departs every 40 minutes). City bus #520 runs from Ciampino to the Subaugusta Metro stop for a single transit ticket.

The fixed price for any official **taxi** (with the maroon *Roma Capitale* logo on the door) is €30 to downtown (within the old city walls, including most of my recommended hotels).

**Rome Airport Shuttle** also offers shared van rides to and from Ciampino (€25 for one person, listed earlier).

## BY CRUISE SHIP

Hundreds of cruise ships dock each year at the small, manageable port city of Civitavecchia (chee-vee-tah-VEH-kyah), about 45 miles northwest of Rome. For more details, see my *Rick Steves Mediterranean Cruise Ports* guidebook.

**Getting to Rome:** As road traffic between Civitavecchia and Rome is terrible, generally the fastest (and most economical) way to day-trip into Rome is to take the **train.** Trains connect Civitavecchia with several stations in Rome, including Ostiense (two Metro stops from the Colosseum), San Pietro (a short walk from Vatican City), or Termini (the main transit hub, but farther from key sights). Trains depart frequently for Rome and take 40-80 minutes. You can buy train tickets at Civitavecchia's station, or the "Tourist Information" travel agency at the station, which also sells other transportation tickets. To reach Civitavecchia's train station, take a free shuttle bus from your ship to the Largo della Pace transit hub. City bus service from the hub to the train station is fast and reliable (€2, 6/hour, 10 minutes, buy tickets from kiosk before boarding). Or you can walk (about 25 minutes) or take a taxi to the station (€15-20, triple the fair metered rate).

Other options for getting into Rome include a cruise-ship excursion package, a taxi, organized tours run by private tour companies, or a private bus. A **taxi** into Rome takes about 1.5 hours and costs around €150-200 one-way, though many cabbies inflate their prices (avoid unlicensed taxis offering a huge price break; you can be fined for taking one). **Organized tours** into Rome are offered by Can't Be Missed Tours (RS%, mobile 329-129-8182, www.cantbemissedtours.com) and Miles & Miles Private Tours (see page 830). Several private companies offer cheap **bus transfers** from the transit hub to Rome or Rome's airports (try Civita Tours, mobile 346-217-7803, www.civitatours.com).

ROME

# NAPLES

*Napoli*

If you like Italy as far south as Rome, go farther south—it gets better. If Italy is getting on your nerves, stop at Rome. Italy intensifies as you plunge deeper. Naples is Italy in the extreme—its best (birthplace of pizza) and its worst (home of the Camorra, Naples' "family" of organized crime).

Before Italy unified in the late 1800s, Naples was the country's richest city. But Naples' fortunes nosedived when the capital of modern Italy was established in Rome. Things got so bad that many of its residents emigrated. The Italy America knows—pizza, spaghetti, and "O Sole Mio"/"Santa Lucia"—came from 19th-century Naples, as brought to the US by all those immigrants.

Today, Naples impresses visitors with one of Europe's top archaeological museums (showcasing the artistic treasures of Pompeii), fascinating churches that convey the city's unique personality and powerful devotion, an underground warren of Greek and Roman ruins, fine works of art (including pieces by Caravaggio, who lived here for a time), and evocative Nativity scenes (called *presepi*). Of course, Neapolitans make great pizza and tasty pastries (try the crispy, ricotta-stuffed *sfogliatella*). But more than anything, Naples has a brash and vibrant street life—"Italy in your face" in ways both good and bad. Walking through its colorful old town is one of my favorite experiences anywhere in Europe. For a grand overlook, head to the hilltop viewpoint (San Martino) for sweeping views of the city and its bay.

Naples is southern Italy's leading city, the third-largest city in Italy, and Europe's most densely populated city, with more than one million people and few open spaces or parks. While in many ways it feels like an urban jungle, Naples surprises the observant traveler with its impressive knack for living, eating, and raising children with good humor and decency. Overcome your fear of being run down or ripped off long enough to talk with people. Enjoy a few smiles and jokes with the man running the neighborhood tripe shop, or the woman taking her daycare class on a walk through the traffic.

The pulse of Italy throbs in Naples. Like Cairo or Mumbai, it's shocking and captivating at the same time, the closest thing to "reality travel" that you'll find in Western Europe. But this tangled mess still somehow manages to breathe, laugh, and sing—with a joyful Italian accent. Thanks to its reputation as a dangerous place, Naples doesn't get nearly as many tourists as  it deserves. While the city has its problems, it has improved a lot in recent years. And even though it remains a bit edgy, I feel comfortable here. Naples richly rewards those who venture in.

Naples is also the springboard to an array of nearby sightseeing treats (covered in the next three chapters): Just beyond Naples are the remarkable ruins of Pompeii and Herculaneum, and the brooding volcano that did them both in, Mount Vesuvius. A few more miles down the road is the pleasant resort town of Sorrento and the offshore escape isle of Capri. Next comes the dramatic scenery of the Amalfi Coast. Plunging even farther south, you'll reach the Greek temples of Paestum.

## PLANNING YOUR TIME

Naples is an ideal day trip either from Rome or from the comfortable home base of Sorrento, each just over an hour away. Or you can stow your bag at the station and see Naples in a few hours while you change trains here on the way between Rome and Sorrento. For some, a little Naples goes a long way. If you're not comfortable in chaotic and congested cities, think twice before spending the night here. But those who are intrigued by the city's sights and street life enjoy overnighting in Naples.

On a quick visit, start with the Archaeological Museum (closed Tue), follow my self-guided Naples Walk, and celebrate your survival with pizza. With more time, dip into more churches, go underground to see Greek and Roman ruins, trek to Capodimonte to see art treasures, or ascend San Martino for the view. Spend an early evening strolling Naples' romantic Lungomare harborside promenade.

# Planning Your Time in the Region

Give the entire area—including Sorrento and Naples—a mini-mum of three days. If you use Sorrento as your sunny spring-board, you can spend a day in Naples, a day exploring the Amalfi Coast, and a day split between Pompeii and the town of Sorrento. While Paestum (Greek temples), Mount Vesuvius, Herculaneum (an ancient Roman site like Pompeii), and the island of Capri are fine destinations, they are worthwhile only if you have more time. For a map of the region, see page 1015.

The **Campania ArteCard** regional pass may save you a few euros if you're here for two or three days, use public transportation, and visit multiple major sights (such as Pompeii, Herculaneum, Paestum, Naples' Archaeological Museum, and several other museums in Naples). The **three-day Campania** version (€32) is good if you'll be visiting both Naples and Sorrento; it includes free entry to two sights, a 50 percent discount off others, and transportation within Naples, on the Circumvesuviana train (but not the Campania Express), and on Amalfi Coast buses. The **seven-day Campania** version (€34) covers five sights and discounts on others, but no transporta-tion. If you're focusing on Naples, the **three-day Napoli** ver-sion (€21) covers transportation within Naples and three city sights, plus discounts on others, but doesn't cover outlying ancient sites. The card is sold at participating sights and some Naples TIs (cards activate on first use, expire 3 or 7 days later at midnight, www.campaniartecard.it).

For a blitz tour from Rome, you could have breakfast on an early Rome-Naples express train (usually daily 7:35-8:45), zip to Pompeii by bus or train, return to Naples and hit the Archaeologi-cal Museum, and be back in Rome before you turn into a zucchini. That's exhausting, but more memorable than a fourth day in Rome.

Yes, Naples is huge. But if you stick to my suggestions and grab a cab when you're lost or tired, it's fun. Treat yourself well in Naples; the city is cheap by Italian standards. Splurging on a sane and comfortable hotel is a worthwhile investment.

On summer afternoons, Naples' street life slows and many churches, museums, and shops close as the temperature soars. The city comes back to life in the early evening.

# Orientation to Naples

Naples is set deep inside the large, curving Bay of Naples, with Mount Vesuvius looming just five miles away. Although Naples is a sprawling city, its fairly compact core contains the most interest-ing sights. The tourist's Naples is a triangle, with its points at the Centrale train station in the east, the Archaeological Museum to the west, and Piazza del Plebiscito (with the Royal Palace) and the port to the south. Steep hills rise above this historic core, including San Martino, capped with a mighty fortress.

## TOURIST INFORMATION

Central Naples has multiple small TIs, none of them particularly helpful—just grab a map and browse the brochures. The handiest one is in **Centrale train station** (daily 8:30-19:30, near the La Feltrinelli bookstore, tel. 081-268-779). Two others are by the entrance to the **Galleria Umberto I** shopping mall, across from Teatro di San Carlo (Mon-Sat 9:00-17:00, Sun until 13:00, tel. 081-402-394), and on Spaccanapoli, across from the **Church of Gesù Nuovo** (same hours as Galleria Umberto I TI, tel. 081-551-2701). For information online, the best overall website is www.inaples.it.

## ARRIVAL IN NAPLES

Whether arriving by train, boat, or airplane, expect some chaos. Instead of getting frustrated, consider it part of the charm of Naples—as most locals do. If you're connecting to another destination from Naples, see the "Getting Around the Region" sidebar on page 1014.

### By Train

Naples has several train stations, but all trains coming into town stop at either Napoli Centrale Station or Garibaldi Station—which are essentially the same place, with Centrale on top of Garibaldi. Stretching in front of this station complex is the vast Piazza Garibaldi, with an underground shopping mall and Metro entrance.

**Centrale Station,** on the ground floor, is the slick, modern main station. It has a small TI (near track 24), a travel agency (on the left of the main lobby), a bookstore (La Feltrinelli, near track 24—beyond the pharmacy), and baggage check (*deposito bagagli*, run by Kipoint, near track 2). Pay WCs are down the stairs across from track 13. Shops and eateries are concentrated in the underground level. A good supermarket (Sapori & Dintorni) is out the front door and to the left.

**Garibaldi Station,** on the lower level, is used exclusively by the narrow-gauge Circumvesuviana commuter train and the Campania Express (options you can use to connect to Sorrento or Pompeii; for details, see page 1014). Note that this is not the terminus for the Circumvesuviana; that's one stop farther downtown, at the station called Porta Nolana.

**Getting Downtown from the Station:** Arriving at either station, the best bet for reaching most sights and hotels is either the Metro or a taxi. **Metro** lines 1 and 2 are signposted throughout Centrale and Garibaldi. Line 1 is handy for city-center stops, in-

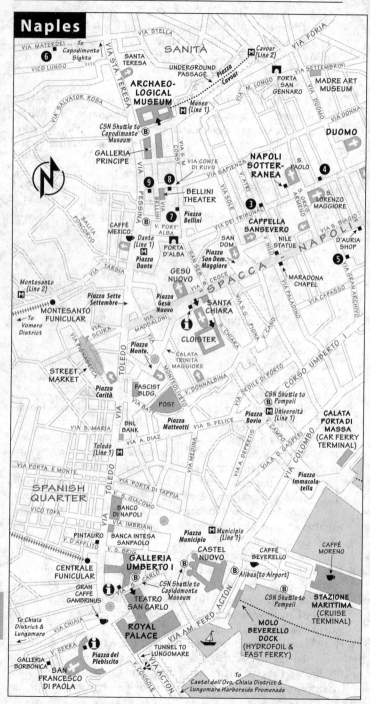

# Naples

SANITÀ

VIA STELLA

VIA MATERDEI
VICO LUNGO
To Capodimonte Sights

VIA STA. TERESA

SANTA TERESA

VIA SALVATOR ROSA

**6**

UNDERGROUND PASSAGE

Piazza Cavour

Cavour (Line 2)

VIA FORIA

VIA SETTEMBRINI

VIA M. LONGO

PORTA SAN GENNARO

VIA DUOMO

MADRE ART MUSEUM

VIA DONNA...

**ARCHAEO-LOGICAL MUSEUM**

Museo (Line 1)

DUOMO

CSN Shuttle to Capodimonte Museum

**B**

GALLERIA PRINCIPE

VIA PESSINA

VIA S.M. CONST.

VIA CONTE DI RUVO

VIA SAPIENZA

**NAPOLI SOTTER-RANEA**

S. PAOLO

**4**

S. LORENZO MAGGIORE

VIA S. GREG. ARMENO

**9** **8**

**BELLINI THEATER**

**7**

Piazza Bellini

V. PORT'ALBA

**B**

CAFFÈ MEXICO

Dante (Line 1)

PORTA D'ALBA

Piazza Dante

VIA BELLINI

VIA SOLE

**3**

VIA DEI TRIBUNALI

**CAPPELLA SANSEVERO**

SAN DOM.

NILE STATUE

NAPOLI

D'AURIA SHOP

Piazza San Dom. Maggiore

**5**

MARADONA CHAPEL

VIA S. BIAGIO

VIA GRAN ARCHIO

Montesanto (Line 2)

To Vomero District

**MONTESANTO FUNICULAR**

Piazza Sette Settembre

VIA TARSIA

VIA PISANISECCA

VIA P. SCURA

VIA TOLEDO

**GESÙ NUOVO**

Piazza Gesù Nuovo

VIA B. CROCE

SPACCA

VIA S.G. PIGNA

VIA CAPASSO

VIA FALADINO

VIA S. CAND.

**STREET MARKET**

Piazza Carità

Piazza Monte.

CALATA TRINITÀ MAGGIORE

VIA MADDALONI

SANTA CHIARA

S. CHIARA

i

**CLOISTER**

CORSO UMBERTO I

VIA BATT.

FASCIST BLDG.

POST

VIA MONTEOLIVETO

V. DONNALBINA

VIA SEDILE DI PORTO

CSN Shuttle to Pompeii

**B**

**M** Università (Line 1)

CALATA PORTA DI MASSA (CAR FERRY TERMINAL)

BNL BANK

Piazza Matteotti

VIA S. FELICE

VIA A. DIAZ

Piazza Bovio

VIA A. DEPRETIS

VIA A. P. GASPERI

VIA COLOMBO

Piazza Immacola-tella

Toledo (Line 1) **M**

VIA MEDINA

VIA PORTA E. MONTE

**SPANISH QUARTER**

VICO TOFA

VIA PORTA DI TAPPIA

VIA TOLEDO

V. S. GIACOMO

BANCO DI NAPOLI

VIA IMBRIANI

BANCA INTESA SANPAOLO

V. S. BRIG.

VIA S. MARIA

Piazza Municipio

**M** Municipio (Line 1)

PINTAURO

V. D'AFFLITO

**CENTRALE FUNICULAR**

GRAN CAFFÈ GAMBRINUS

**GALLERIA UMBERTO I**

VIA S. CARLO

**B**

CSN Shuttle to Capidomonte Museum

**B**

**CASTEL NUOVO**

CAFFÈ BEVERELLO

**B** Alibus (to Airport)

CAFFÈ MORENO

CSN Shuttle to Pompeii

**B**

**STAZIONE MARITTIMA (CRUISE TERMINAL)**

i

**TEATRO SAN CARLO**

VIA AM. FERD. ACTON

To Chiaia District & Lungomare

V. CHIAIA

**ROYAL PALACE**

V. SERRA

i

Piazza del Plebiscito

**GALLERIA BORBONICA**

**SAN FRANCESCO DI PAOLA**

TUNNEL TO LUNGOMARE

V. CONSOLE

VIA ACTON

**MOLO BEVERELLO DOCK (HYDROFOIL & FAST FERRY)**

To Castel dell'Ovo, Chiaia District & Lungomare Harborside Promenade

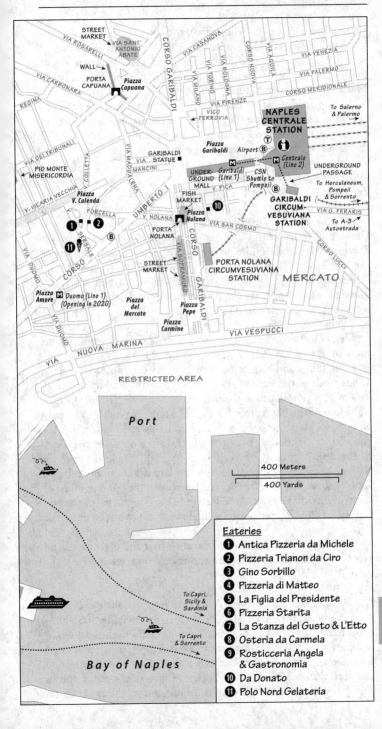

STREET MARKET
VIA ROSARELLI
VIA SANT' ANTONIO ABATE
WALL
PORTA CAPUANA
Piazza Capuana
VIA CARBONARA
REGINA
VIA DEI TRIBUNALI
PIO MONTE MISERICORDIA
V. VICARIA VECCHIA
Piazza V. Calenda
FORCELLA
VIA DUOMO
CORSO
SPESALE
Piazza Amore
Duomo (Line 1) (Opening in 2020)
Piazza del Mercato
Piazza Pepe
Piazza Carmine
VIA DUOMO
VIA NUOVA MARINA
VIA

CORSO GARIBALDI
VIA CASANOVA
CORSO NUOVA
VIA AQUILA
VIA VENEZIA
VIA PALERMO
CORSO MERIDIONALE
VIA MILANO
VIA TORINO
VIA BOLOGNA
VIA FIRENZE
VICO FERROVIA
VIA COLLETTI
VIA MADDALENA
VIA MANCINI
UMBERTO
GARIBALDI STATUE
Piazza Garibaldi
UNDER-GROUND MALL
Garibaldi (Line 1)
VIA PICA
FISH MARKET
Piazza Nolana
PORTA NOLANA
VIA NOLANA
CORSO GARIBALDI
VIA SOPRAMURO
STREET MARKET
VIA SAN COSMO
PORTA NOLANA CIRCUMVESUVIANA STATION
MERCATO
CORSO LUCCI

NAPLES CENTRALE STATION
Airport
Piazza Garibaldi
Centrale (Line 2)
UNDERGROUND PASSAGE
To Salerno & Palermo
To Herculaneum, Pompeii & Sorrento
VIA G. FERARIS
To A-3 Autostrada
GARIBALDI CIRCUM-VESUVIANA STATION
CSN Shuttle to Pompeii
CORSO GARIBALDI

**10**
**1** **2**
**11**

VIA VESPUCCI

RESTRICTED AREA

*Port*

400 Meters
400 Yards

To Capri, Sicily & Sardinia

To Capri & Sorrento

*Bay of Naples*

**Eateries**
**1** Antica Pizzeria da Michele
**2** Pizzeria Trianon da Ciro
**3** Gino Sorbillo
**4** Pizzeria di Matteo
**5** La Figlia del Presidente
**6** Pizzeria Starita
**7** La Stanza del Gusto & L'Etto
**8** Osteria da Carmela
**9** Rosticceria Angela & Gastronomia
**10** Da Donato
**11** Polo Nord Gelateria

**NAPLES**

cluding the cruise port (Municipio), the main shopping drag (Toledo and Dante), and the Archaeological Museum (Museo). Line 2 is slightly quicker for reaching the Archaeological Museum (ride it to the Cavour stop and walk 5 minutes). For tips on navigating the Metro, see "Getting Around Naples," later.

Long rows of white **taxis** line up out front. Ask the driver to charge you the fixed rate *(tariffa predeterminata)*, which varies from €9 for the old center to €15 for the most distant hotel I list. The TI in the station can tell you the going rate.

## By Ferry or Cruise Ship

Ferries and cruise ships dock next to each other in the shadow of the old fortress (Castel Nuovo), a short walk from the old town sightseeing action. Naples has great ferry connections to Sorrento, Capri, and other nearby destinations. Cruise ships use the giant Stazione Marittima cruise terminal, hydrofoils and faster ferries use the Molo Beverello dock (to the west of the terminal), and slower car ferries leave from Calata Porta di Massa, east of the terminal. The entire port area is currently a big construction zone with work scheduled to be complete by 2022.

Whether arriving by ferry or cruise ship, you can get to the city center by taxi, Metro, or on foot; the Alibus shuttle bus runs to the airport (see "By Plane," next).

The **taxi** stand is in front of the port area. Expect to pay €12-15 for a ride to the train station or the Archaeological Museum.

Straight ahead across the road from the cruise terminal (on the right side of the big fortress) is Piazza Municipio, with the handy Municipio **Metro** stop. From here, line 1 zips you right to the Archaeological Museum (Museo stop) or, in the opposite direction, to the train station (Garibaldi stop). A €1.10 single ticket *(corsa singola)* covers rides on line 1. You can buy tickets at any tobacco shop or some cafés: Caffè Moreno is between the two buildings of the cruise terminal, and Caffè Beverello is along the busy street on the waterfront. Remember to validate your ticket as you enter the Metro station.

On foot, it's a seven-minute **walk**—past the gigantic Castel Nuovo—to Piazza del Plebiscito and the old city center.

## By Plane

Naples International Airport (Aeroporto Internazionale di Napoli, a.k.a. Capodichino, code: NAP) is close to town (tel. 081-789-6767, handy info desk just outside baggage claim to the left, www. aeroportodinapoli.it). Alibus **shuttle buses** zip you in 10 minutes from the airport to Naples' Centrale train station, and then head to the port/Piazza Municipio for boats to Capri and Sorrento (buses run daily 6:00-23:00, 4/hour, 20-30 minutes to the port, €5 on board only—ticket machines inside airport do not function, stops at train station and port only). The shuttle bus departs from a stop located straight out the airport exit, past the rental car lots. If you take a **taxi** to or from the airport, ask the driver for the fixed price (€18 to the train station, €21 to the port, €25 to the Chiaia district near the waterfront).

To reach **Sorrento** from Naples Airport, take the direct Curreri bus (see page 1065). A taxi to Sorrento costs about €110.

## HELPFUL HINTS

**Theft Alert:** While most travelers visit Naples safely, err on the side of caution. Be aware that thieves and con artists hang out close to where travelers tumble into Naples: the train station and the port. Although the train station itself has been nicely spruced up, its glow doesn't extend far. The areas nearby are frequented by some of Italy's most downtrodden people, but remember that poor and chaotic do not necessarily mean dangerous. Don't let your first impression of the station area get in your way of enjoying Naples—the city changes drastically as you move further away. Touristy Spaccanapoli, Capodimonte, and the posh Via Toledo shopping boulevard are more upscale, but you may still see panhandlers.

Stick to busy streets and beware the odd gang of hoodlums. A third of the city is unemployed, and past local governments have set an example of corruption that the Mafia would be proud of. As in most big cities, consider any jostle or commotion a possible thief-team smokescreen. Keep a low profile, carry only the bare minimum, and leave heavy bags at your hotel or at the left-luggage office in Centrale Station.

Walk with confidence, as if you know where you're going and what you're doing. Use the sidewalk (even if the locals don't) and carry your belongings on the side away from the street—thieves on scooters have been known to snatch bags as they swoop by. Keep valuables buttoned up (or secure them at your hotel).

Perhaps your biggest risk of theft is while catching or riding the Circumvesuviana commuter train. While I ride the Circumvesuviana comfortably and safely, each year I hear of travelers who get ripped off on this ride. You won't be mugged—but you may be conned or pickpocketed. At the train station, carry your own bags—there are no official porters. If you're connecting from a long-distance express, you'll be going from a relatively secure compartment into an often-crowded and dingy train, where disoriented tourists with luggage delicately mix with Naples' down-and-out. Be ready for this very common trick: A team of thieves blocks the door at

**NAPLES**

# Still Naples After All These Years

For three centuries (1500-1800), Naples was one of the world's richest and most sophisticated cities. The remnants we see today are an elegant reminder of that golden age, and a fascinating case study in what went wrong.

**500 BC-AD 500—Greek-Speaking Romans:** Naples got its start as Neapolis ("new city"), a thriving Greek colony. Even when conquered by the Romans, the city never fully adopted the Latin language and Roman ways. Actually, those sophisticated Hellenist traditions were exactly what the Romans admired about Naples and made them want to vacation there. For the next 2,000 years, this pattern would repeat itself: The city, living under foreign rule, would evolve independently from the rest of the Italian peninsula.

**500-1500—Independence Despite Foreign Rule:** The city powered on relatively unchanged after the fall of Rome, ruled as the independent Duchy of Naples under Ostrogoths, Byzantines, and Lombards. Next, in late-medieval times, it was the Germans and French (or "Angevins") who possessed it as the Kingdom of Naples. As sea trade became more important to the European economy, Naples was suddenly smack-dab in the geographical heart of commerce—the Mediterranean.

**1500-1800—Golden Age:** In 1502, Spain conquered Naples, and their combined wealth made Naples one of the great cities on Earth. With a population of 300,000, only Paris was larger. Deputies of the Spanish king called viceroys presided over the city, and proceeded to use Spain's New World wealth to beautify Naples.

When Spain's monarchy passed to the Austrian Habsburgs and Spanish Bourbons, the cosmopolitan nature of Naples was only enhanced. Naples was home to nobles and royalty from across Europe. Baroque culture thrived, with artists like Caravaggio and Bernini, thinkers like Giordano Bruno, composers like Scarlatti, and a new art form called opera. Naples took on the

---

a stop, pretending it's stuck. While everyone rushes to try to open it, an accomplice picks their pockets. Wear your money belt, and avoid the Circumvesuviana train late at night when it's plagued by intimidating ruffians. For peace of mind, sit in the front car, where there is a driver who may be able to monitor activity.

**Traffic Safety:** In Naples, red lights are timed short, and pedestrians need to be wary, particularly of motor scooters that zip among the cars. Even on "pedestrian" streets, stay alert to avoid being sideswiped by scooters that nudge their way through the crowds. Smart tourists jaywalk in the shadow of bold locals, who generally ignore crosswalks. Wait for a break in traffic, cross with confidence, and make eye contact with

"look" it retains today, with palatial Neoclassical buildings in pastel colors and lavishly ornamented churches.

Despite its veneer of sophistication, trouble was brewing. In 1656, a vicious bubonic plague (Europe's last) killed off half the population. Trade routes shifted west as Europe industrialized, but Naples languished, remaining feudal and agricultural, with the church owning much of the land. The gap between rich foreign elites and homegrown poor grew.

**1800-2000:** Napoleon conquered the city. Then the monarchy was restored under a medieval-era political arrangement called the Kingdom of the Two Sicilies (uniting Naples and Sicily). The city was still rich, thanks to its Spanish Bourbon rulers, but it was increasingly backward, left behind by a more industrialized and democratic Europe.

Meanwhile, sweeping down from the north, there was a movement for Italian nationhood. Naples—with its legacy of independence from the rest of the peninsula—resisted. But in 1860, Naples was forcefully united with the new nation-state of Italy. Its vast wealth was confiscated and taken to the capital in Rome.

This began a century-plus of decline. There was no foreign wealth and no local economy. An estimated four million southern Italians fled, emigrating to northern Italy and the US. During World War II, Naples suffered Italy's worst bombings. The postwar economic recovery in northern Italy never trickled south, which remained under the thumb of the feudal-style Camorra (the Naples-based Mafia).

**Today:** The lack of a postwar economic recovery is a boon to tourists. It preserved an independent way of life that dates back centuries. Visitors today enjoy a rare sight—a city that has been continuously inhabited, independent-minded, and self-sustaining for 2,500 years.

approaching drivers and motor scooters. The traffic will slow to let you pass.

**Bookstore: La Feltrinelli,** conveniently located in Centrale Station, carries a small selection of English-language books (daily 7:00-21:00, near track 24).

**Laundry: Lavasciuga,** a block from the Università Metro stop, is convenient but has just three washing machines (Mon-Sat 9:00-19:00, closed Sun, Via Sedile di Porto 54, mobile 327-754-6639).

## GETTING AROUND NAPLES

Sightsee Naples with help from its subway (Metro), funiculars, and taxis. (There are also public buses but these generally aren't useful

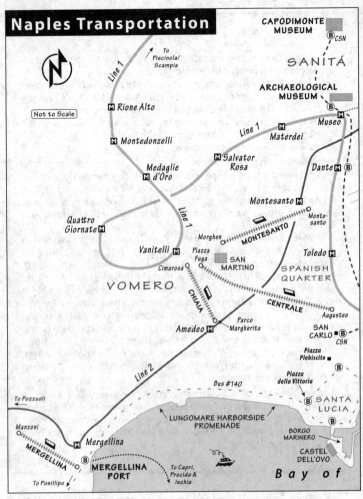

# Naples Transportation

Not to Scale

To Piscinola/Scampia

CAPODIMONTE MUSEUM

SANITÁ

ARCHAEOLOGICAL MUSEUM

Line 1

Rione Alto

Montedonzelli

Medaglie d'Oro

Salvator Rosa

Materdei

Museo

Dante

Line 1

Montesanto

Quattro Giornate

Vanitelli

Line 1

Morghen

MONTESANTO

Montesanto

Piazza Fuga

SAN MARTINO

Toledo

SPANISH QUARTER

VOMERO

Cimarosa

CHIAIA

CENTRALE

Augusteo

Amedeo

Parco Margherita

SAN CARLO
CSN

Piazza Plebiscito

Line 2

Bus #140

Piazza della Vittoria

SANTA LUCIA

To Pozzuoli

LUNGOMARE HARBORSIDE PROMENADE

BORGO MARINERO

Manzoni

Mergellina

CASTEL DELL'OVO

MERGELLINA

Mergellina

MERGELLINA PORT

To Capri, Procida & Ischia

Bay of

To Posillipo

for travelers.) For general transit information, maps, and fares in English, visit www.unicocampania.it. The TI hands out a good free map showing Metro, funicular, and bus routes. For schedules, your only option is the Italian-only site www.anm.it. For journey planning, use maps.google.com.

**Tickets and Passes:** Most of Naples' public transportation system—Metro, funiculars, and buses—use the same ticket, which must be stamped as you enter (in yellow or blue machines). Tickets are sold at tobacco stores, some newsstands, clunky machines at Metro stations (coins and small bills only), and occasionally at station windows. Basically, anywhere you see a queue near the station, people are buying tickets.

A €1.10 single ticket *(corsa singola)* covers any ride on bus, fu-

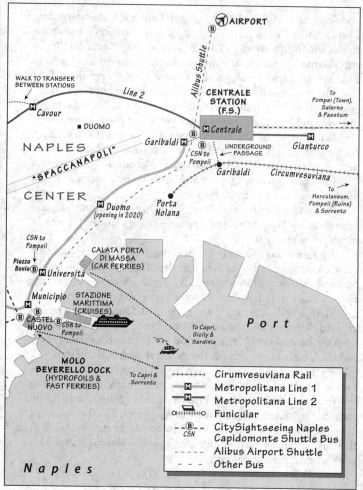

nicular, or Metro line 1, with no transfers; for Metro line 2 you need the €1.30 version. (This ticket is a long, printed receipt with a QR code that needs to be punched at the machine—fold your ticket in half and insert.) A *giornaliero* day pass costs €3.50 (or €4.50 including Metro line 2), and pays for itself quickly, but can be hard to find; many tobacco stores don't sell them. A weekly ticket (Mon-Sun) costs €12.50, or €16 including Metro line 2. Several versions of the Campania ArteCard (see sidebar on page 958) include free public transport in Naples.

**By Metro** *(Metropolitana):* Naples' subway has three main lines *(linea).* Station entrances and signs to the Metro are marked by a red square with a white *M.*

**Line 1** is very useful for tourists. Starting from the train station (stop name: Garibaldi), it heads to Università (the university), Municipio (at Piazza Municipio, just above the harbor and cruise terminal), Toledo (south end of Via Toledo, near Piazza del Plebiscito), Dante (Piazza Dante), and Museo (Archaeological Museum). Four stops beyond Museo is the Vanvitelli stop, near the hilltop San Martino sights. Many of line 1's stations are huge and elaborate, designed by prominent artists and architects; Naples is proud of them, and locals are excited to tell you about their favorite.

**Line 2** (part of the Italian national rail system) is most useful for getting quickly from the train station to Piazza Cavour (a 5-minute walk from the Archaeological Museum) or Montesanto (the top of the Spanish Quarter and Spaccanapoli street, and base of one funicular up to San Martino).

The under-construction **line 6** will begin at Municipio and head west to Mergellina and beyond—but it's unlikely to be of much use to tourists.

**By Funicular:** Central Naples' three funiculars *(funicolare)* carry commuters and sightseers into the hilly San Martino neighborhood just west of downtown. All three converge near Piazza Fuga, a short walk from the hilltop fortress and monastery/museum. The Centrale line runs from the Spanish Quarter, just near Piazza del Plebiscito and the Toledo Metro stop; the Montesanto line from the Montesanto Metro stop and Via Pignasecca market zone; and the Chiaia line from near the Piazza Amadeo Metro stop.

**By Taxi:** A short ride in town should cost €10-15. Always ask for the *tariffa predeterminata* (a fixed rate). Your hotel or a TI can tell you the going rate for a given ride. For metered rides there are some legitimate extra charges (baggage fees, €2.50 supplement after 22:00 or all day Sun and holidays) but destinations covered in this chapter are covered by the *tariffa predeterminata*. Radio Taxi 8888 is one reputable company (tel. 081-8888).

# Tours in Naples

🎧 To sightsee on your own, download my free Rick Steves audio tours of the Naples Archaeological Museum and my Naples Walk.

### Local Guides

**Pina Esposito** has a Ph.D. in ancient archaeology and art and does fine private walking and driving tours of Naples and the region (Pompeii, Capri, the Amalfi Coast, etc.), including Naples' Archaeological Museum (€60/hour, 2-hour minimum, 10 percent off with this book, additional discounts for full-day tours, mobile 338-763-4224, annamariaesposito1@virgilio.it).

The team at **Mondo Guide** offers private tours of the Archaeological Museum (€120/2 hours) and city (€240/4 hours), and can provide guides or drivers throughout the region (tel. 081-751-3290, www.mondoguide.com, info@mondoguide.com).

### Walking Tours

**Mondo Guide** offers my readers special shared tours of Naples and of Pompeii, as well as other trips in the region. For details, see the sidebar.

### Hop-On, Hop-Off Bus Tours

**CitySightseeing Napoli** tour buses make two different hop-on, hop-off loops through the city. Only the red line, which loops around the historical center and stops at the Archaeological Museum and Capodimonte, is particularly helpful. The bus route will give you a sense of greater Naples that this chapter largely ignores (€23, ticket valid 24 hours, 2/hour, buy from driver or from kiosk at Piazza Municipio in front of Castel Nuovo near the port, scant recorded narration, tel. 081-551-7279, www.napoli.city-sightseeing.it).

The same company offers a shorter, more frequent route around the old center in an open-top minibus, a handy shuttle from the city center to the Capodimonte Museum (see details in the museum listing, later), and shuttles to Pompeii (see the "Getting Around the Region" sidebar on page 1014).

### Cruise-Ship Excursions

**Mondo Guide** offers shared shore excursions for my readers (see sidebar).

Convenient for cruise-ship passengers, the **Can't Be Missed** tour company takes you from the port of Naples on an all-day, big-bus trip along the Amalfi Coast that includes a stop in Sorrento and a guided tour of Pompeii (€69, meet at 8:00 in front of port, bus leaves at 8:30, returns at 17:15, Pompeii ticket extra, mobile 329-129-8182, www.cantbemissedtours.com, RS%—10 percent off when you use promo code "RICKSTEVES" on their website).

# Archaeological Museum Tour

Naples' Archaeological Museum (Museo Archeologico), worth ▲▲▲, is one of the world's great museums of ancient art. It boasts supersized statues as well as art and decorations from Pompeii and Herculaneum, the two ancient burgs that were buried in ash by the eruption of Mount Vesuvius in AD 79. For lovers of antiquity, this museum alone makes

# Mondo Guide Tours of Pompeii, Naples, the Amalfi Coast, and Capri for My Readers

Mondo Guide, a big Naples-based company, offers "shared tours" for Rick Steves readers. These allow you the luxury of a private, professional guide at a fraction of the usual cost, because you'll be sharing the expense with other travelers using this book. Their tours, which run from April through October, include **Pompeii,** a walking tour of **Naples,** and two longer-distance trips from Sorrento: an **Amalfi Coast** van tour and a private boat to the **isle of Capri.** The Pompeii and Naples tours are designed to work together—they are timed so you can do both on the same day. Mondo also offers shore excursions for cruise passengers arriving in Naples or Salerno. I don't receive a cut from the tours; I set this up with Mondo Guide to help my readers have the most economical experience in this region.

Reservations are required. For specifics and to sign up, go to www.sharedtours.com (Mondo tel. 081-751-3290, mobile 340-460-5254, www.mondoguide.com, info@mondoguide.com). On the website, use your credit-card number to reserve a spot. You'll then pay cash for the tour. If you must cancel, email more than three days in advance or you'll be billed.

Each tour requires a minimum of six participants. You'll be sent an email confirmation as soon as they're sure your tour will run. If there's not enough demand to justify the trip, they'll notify you three days before the departure date (giving you time to come up with an alternative plan). Confirmed departures are continually updated on the website.

**Pompeii Tour:** This two-hour guided walk brings to life the ruins of the excavated city (€15, Pompeii entry extra—your guide will collect money and buy tickets, daily at 11:00; meet in Pompeii at Hotel/Ristorante Suisse, a 5-minute walk from the train station—exiting the station, turn right, pass the Porta Marina entrance, and continue down the hill to the restaurant, on the right).

**Historic Naples Walk:** Naples is a challenge to enjoy and understand; on this three-hour walk, a local Neapolitan guide helps you uncover the true character of the city (€25; daily at 15:00; meet at the steps of the Naples Archaeological Museum—you can

Naples a worthwhile stop. When Pompeii was excavated in the late 1700s, Naples' Bourbon king bellowed, "Bring me the best of what you find!" The finest art and artifacts ended up here, leaving the ancient sites themselves barren (though still impressive). It's here at the Archaeological Museum that you can get up close and personal with the ancient world.

do the museum on your own before joining your guide).

**Full-Day Amalfi Coast Minibus Tour from Sorrento:** The Amalfi Coast can be complicated and time-consuming to visit on your own, making a shared minibus the simplest and most affordable way to enjoy the sights. (Small groups use an eight-seat minibus with only a driver; larger groups use a 19-seat minibus with a driver and a guide.) This nine-hour trip saves time and money and maximizes your experience. It begins in Sorrento and heads south for the breathtaking (and lightly narrated) drive, several photo stops, and an hour or two on your own in each of the three main towns—Positano, Amalfi, and Ravello—before returning to Sorrento. Lunch isn't included; to save time for exploring, grab a quick lunch in one of the towns (€55, daily at 9:00; meet in Sorrento in front of Hotel Antiche Mura, at Via Fuorimura 7, a block inland from Piazza Tasso).

**Full-Day Capri Boat Trip from Sorrento:** To sidestep the hassles of taking public boats from Sorrento for a Capri side trip, Mondo offers a trip to the island on a small private boat (12 people maximum), which includes an early visit to the Blue Grotto sea cave when conditions allow (€13, optional) and about four hours of free time to explore the island on your own. After your time on land, the boat takes you on a lightly narrated trip around the island with drinks, snacks, and a chance to swim if the weather cooperates (€100, daily at 8:00, pickup at Sorrento hotel, may be cancelled in bad weather).

**Shore Excursions from Naples or Salerno:** If you arrive by cruise ship at the port of Naples or the port of Salerno, Mondo Guide offers an all-day itinerary that combines three big sights in the region and the scenic Amalfi Coast. From Naples, a guided visit to Pompeii with an hour of free time each in Sorrento and Positano; from Salerno, a guided visit to Pompeii with an hour of free time each in Sorrento and Amalfi town (€70/person, departing daily at 8:00-8:30 from the main exit of the Naples cruise terminal building or from your ship in Salerno).

## ORIENTATION

**Cost and Hours:** €15, sometimes more for temporary exhibits; Wed-Mon 9:00-19:30, closed Tue. Avoid lines by purchasing your ticket online. Early and temporary closures are noted on a board near the ticket office: Expect some rooms to be closed in July and August.

**Free Entry:** The museum is free and very crowded once or twice a month—the specific day varies in peak season (in low season, it's the first Sun).

**Information:** Tel. 081-442-2149, www.museoarcheologiconapoli.it.

**Getting There:** From Centrale Station, you can reach the museum by Metro or taxi. **Metro** line 2 is quickest: At the station, buy a single transit ticket at a newsstand or tobacco shop—specify you want line 2 since the price and ticket are different from line 1. Follow signs for *Metro Linea 2,* then fold and punch your ticket in the small blue boxes near the escalator going down to the tracks. You're looking for trains heading in the direction of Pozzuoli (attendants will ask and confirm which direction you're going). Ride one stop to Piazza Cavour. Follow *Museo* signs through the underground passage or exit and walk five minutes uphill through the park. Look for a grand old red building located up a flight of stairs at the top of the block.

You can also take the Metro's cheaper line 1 five stops from Centrale Station to Museo—it's only a little slower. Figure about €13 for a **taxi** from the train station to the museum.

**Visitor Information:** The shop sells a worthwhile *National Archaeological Museum of Naples* guidebook for €12.

**Tours:** The self-guided tour in this chapter covers all the basics. For more detail, the decent **audioguide** (€5, leave ID at ticket desk) focuses largely on the provenance of the artifacts and how they ended up here. For a **guided tour,** book Pina Esposito (see "Tours in Naples," earlier).

∩ Download my free Archaeological Museum **audio tour.**

**Baggage Check:** Bag check is obligatory and free.

**Eating:** The museum has no café, but vending machines sell drinks and snacks. There are several good places to grab a meal within a few blocks; see page 1008.

## ❷ SELF-GUIDED TOUR

Entering the museum, cross the atrium, and stand at the base of the grand staircase. To your right, on the ground floor, are the larger-than-life statues of the Farnese Collection, starring the *Toro Farnese* and the *Farnese Hercules.* Up the stairs on the mezzanine level are mosaics and frescoes from Pompeii, including the Secret Room of erotic art. On the top floor are more artifacts from Pompeii, a scale model of the doomed city, and bronze statues from Herculaneum. WCs are behind the staircase.

• *From the base of the* ❶ *grand staircase, turn right through the door marked* Collezione Farnese *and head for the far end, walking through a rich collection of ancient portrait* ❷ *busts.*

# Naples Archaeological Museum

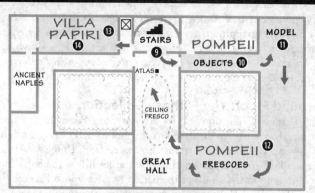

## Second Floor (2)

VILLA PAPIRI ⑬ ⑭

STAIRS ⑨

POMPEII

MODEL ⑪

OBJECTS ⑩

ANCIENT NAPLES

ATLAS

CEILING FRESCO

POMPEII ⑫

GREAT HALL

FRESCOES

*Not to Scale*

⊠ Elevator

## Mezzanine (1)

SECRET ROOM ⑦

⑥

⑧ MOSAICS

STAIRS

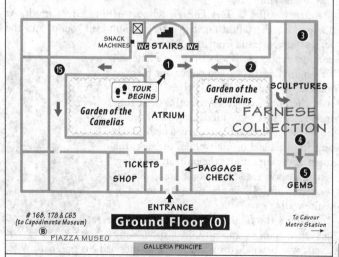

## Ground Floor (0)

SNACK MACHINES

WC STAIRS WC

❸

❶ TOUR BEGINS

⓯

❷

SCULPTURES

Garden of the Camelias

ATRIUM

Garden of the Fountains

FARNESE COLLECTION

❹

❺ GEMS

TICKETS SHOP

BAGGAGE CHECK

ENTRANCE

# 168, 178 & C63 (to Capodimonte Museum)

Ⓑ PIAZZA MUSEO

To Cavour Metro Station →

GALLERIA PRINCIPE

**NAPLES**

❶ Grand Staircase
❷ Hall of the Busts
❸ Toro Farnese
❹ Farnese Hercules
❺ Farnese Cup
❻ Various Mosaics
❼ Dancing Faun & Battle of Alexander
❽ Secret Room
❾ Great Hall
❿ Metal, Ivory & Glass Objects
⓫ Model of Pompeii
⓬ Frescoes
⓭ Papyrus Scrolls
⓮ Bronze Statues
⓯ Doriforo

*Pause at the busts of **Caracalla** (a third of the way down, on the left), and marvel at how he evolved from idealistic youth to cruel tyrant (and nemesis of Russell Crowe in the movie* Gladiator). *Admire the **Seated Agrippina** (two-thirds of the way down) with her typical hairstyle, realistic face, and pensive look. Nearby, look in **Vespasian**'s right ear and see how the huge head was hollowed out in medieval times. Now, continue to the end and jog right, then left, entering Room 13.*

## Ground Floor: The Farnese Collection

The Farnese Collection statues are not from Pompeii, but from Rome. Today they're displayed in this grand hall of huge, bright, and wonderfully restored statues excavated from Rome's Baths of Caracalla. Peruse the larger-than-life statues filling the hall. They were dug up in the 1540s at the behest of Alessandro Farnese (by then Pope Paul III) while he was building the family palace on the Campo de' Fiori in Rome. His main purpose in excavating the baths was to scavenge quality building stone. The sculptures were a nice extra and helped the palace come in under budget on decorations. In the 1700s, the collection ended up in the hands of Charles, the Bourbon king of Naples (whose mother was a Farnese). His son, the next king, had it brought to Naples.

• *Quick—look down to the left end of the hall. There's a woman being tied to a snorting bull.*

The tangled ❸ **Toro Farnese** tells a thrilling Greek myth. At 13 feet, it's the tallest ancient marble group ever found, and the largest intact statue from antiquity. A third-century AD copy of a lost bronze Hellenistic original, it was carved out of one piece of marble. Michelangelo and others "restored" it at the pope's request—meaning that they integrated surviving bits into a new work. Some pieces were actually carved by Michelangelo: the head of the woman in back, the torso of the aunt under the bull, and the dog. (Imagine how the statue would stand out if it were thoughtfully lit and not surrounded by white walls.)

Here's the tragic story behind the statue: Once upon an ancient Greek time, King Lycus was bewitched by Dirce. He abandoned his pregnant wife, Antiope (standing regally in the background). The single mom gave birth to twin boys. When they grew up, they killed their deadbeat dad and tied Dirce to the horns of a bull to be bashed against a mountain. Captured in marble, the action is thrilling: cape flailing, dog snarling, hooves in the air. You can almost hear the bull snorting. And in the back, Antiope oversees this harsh ancient justice with satisfaction.

At the opposite end of the hall stands the ❹ *Farnese Hercules.* The great Greek hero is exhausted. He leans wearily on his club (draped with his lion skin) and bows his head. He's just finished the daunting Eleventh Labor, having traveled the world, fought men and gods, freed Prometheus from his rock, and carried Atlas' weight of the world on his shoulders. Now he's returned with the prize: the golden apples of the gods, which he cups behind his back. But, after all that, he's just been told he has to return the apples and do one final labor: descend into hell itself. Oh, man.

The 10-foot colossus is a third-century AD Roman marble copy (signed by "Glykon") of a fourth-century BC Greek bronze original (probably by Lysippos). The statue was enormously famous in its day. Dozens of copies—some marble, some bronze—have been found in Roman villas and baths. This version was unearthed in Rome's Baths of Caracalla in 1546, along with the *Toro Farnese.*

The *Farnese Hercules* was equally famous in the 16th-18th centuries. Tourists flocked to Rome to admire it, art students studied it from afar in prints, Louis XIV made a copy for Versailles, and petty nobles everywhere put small-scale knock-offs in their gardens. This curly-haired version of Hercules became the modern world's image of the Greek hero.

• *Behind Hercules is a doorway into the impressive Farnese gem collection (Rooms 9 and 10). You'll see cameos and the ancient cereal bowl-shaped* ❺ *Farnese Cup, which features a portrait thought to be of Cleopatra. When you're ready to move on, backtrack to the main entry hall with its grand staircase—perhaps stopping briefly to admire the magnificent sarcophagi in adjacent rooms, then head up to the mezzanine level (turn left at the lion and go under the* Mosaici *sign), and enter Room 57.*

## Mezzanine: Pompeiian Mosaics and the Secret Room

These ❻ **mosaics**—mostly of animals, battle scenes, and geometric designs—were excavated from the walls and floors of Pompeii's ritzy villas. The *Chained Dog* once graced a home's entryway. The colorful mosaic columns (to your right in adjoining Room 58) shaded a courtyard, part of an ensemble of wall mosaics and bubbling fountains. In Room 59, admire the realism of the tambourine-playing musicians, the drinking doves, and the skull—a reminder of impending death.

Continue a few steps into Room 60, with objects taken from one of Pompeii's greatest villas, the House of the Faun. The 20-inch-high statue was the house's delightful centerpiece, the ❼ *Dancing Faun*. This rare surviving Greek bronze statue (from the fourth century BC) is surrounded by some of the best mosaics of that age. (Find the little cat, who's caught a bird.)

A museum highlight, just beyond the statue, is the grand *Battle of Alexander*, a second-century BC copy of the now-lost original

Greek fresco, done a century earlier. It decorated a floor in the House of the Faun and was found intact. (The damage you see occurred as this treasure was moved from Pompeii to the king's collection here.) Alexander (left side of the scene, with curly hair and sideburns) is about to defeat the Persians under Darius (central figure, in chariot with turban and beard). This pivotal victory allowed Alexander to quickly overrun much of Asia (331 BC). Alexander is the only one without a helmet...a confident master of the battlefield while everyone else is fighting for their lives, eyes bulging with fear. Notice how the horses, already in retreat, add to the scene's propaganda value. Notice also the shading and perspective, which Renaissance artists would later work so hard to accomplish. (A modern reproduction of the mosaic is now back in Pompeii, at the House of the Faun.)

Farther on, the ❽ **Secret Room** (Gabinetto Segreto, Room 65) contains a sizable assortment of erotic frescoes, well-hung pottery, and perky statues that once decorated bedrooms, meeting rooms, brothels, and even shops at Pompeii and Herculaneum. These bawdy statues and frescoes—many of them once displayed in Pompeii's grandest houses—were entertainment for guests. (By the time they made it to this museum, in 1819, the frescoes could be viewed only with permission from the king—see the letters in the glass case just outside the door.) The Roman nobles commissioned the wildest scenes imaginable. Think of them as ancient dirty jokes.

At the entrance, you're enthusiastically greeted by big stone penises that once projected over Pompeii's doorways. A massive phallus was not necessarily a sexual symbol, but a magical amulet used against the "evil eye." It symbolized fertility, happiness, good luck, riches, straight A's, and general wellbeing.

Circulating counterclockwise through this section, look for the following: the fresco—high up—of a faun playfully pulling the sheet off a beautiful woman (#12), only to be surprised by both male and female plumbing (perhaps the original *"Mamma mia!"*). A few steps farther, see horny pygmies from Africa in action (#27). There's a toga with an embarrassing bulge (#34). A particularly high-quality statue depicts a goat and a satyr engaging in a sex act (#36). And, watching over it all with remarkable aplomb, is Venus, the patron goddess of Pompeii (#39).

The back room is furnished and decorated the way an ancient brothel might have been. The 10 frescoes on the wall functioned as both a menu of services offered and as a kind of *Kama Sutra* of sex positions. The glass cases contain more phallic art, including dangling mobiles used as party favors at rowdy banquets.

• *So, now that your travel buddy is finally showing a little interest in art...finish up your visit by climbing the stairs to the top floor.*

*At the top of the stairs, pause and get oriented to our final sights. Directly ahead is a doorway (marked* Salone Meridiana*) that leads into a big, empty hall. To the left of this grand hall is a series of rooms with more artifacts from Pompeii. To the right are rooms of statues from Herculaneum. Keep this general layout in mind, because occasionally doorways and routes are altered, and you may have to improvise a bit to find your way.*

## Top Floor: Frescoes, Statues, Artifacts, and a Model of Pompeii

First, step into the Salone Meridiana. This was the ❾ **great hall** of the university (17th and 18th centuries) until the building became the royal museum in 1777. Walk to the center. The sundial (from 1791) still works. Look up to the far-right corner of the hall and find the tiny pinhole. At noon (13:00 in summer), a ray of sun enters the hall and strikes the sundial, showing the time of the year... if you know your zodiac.

Now enter the series of rooms to the left of the grand hall, with ❿ **Metal, Ivory, and Glass Objects** found in Pompeii. You enter through a doorway marked *Vetri e Avori,* which leads into Room 89. Browse your way to the far end, with the stunning *Blue Vase* (Room 85), decorated with cameo Bacchuses harvesting grapes. Turn left, then right, to find the huge, room-filling ⓫ **model of Pompeii,** a 1:100 scale model of the ruins (Room 96). Face the model from the side labeled *plastico di Pompeii.* This is how tourists enter today, up the street, and spilling into the large rectangular forum with the Temple of Jupiter at one end. Farther up in the model are the city's two amphitheater-shaped theaters. This was all that had been excavated when the model was made in 1879. Another model (displayed on the wall) shows the site in 2004, after more excavations, when they'd dug up as far as the huge oval-shaped arena. Video screens capture images from the 1879 model and reconstruct buildings in 3D as they would have appeared before the eruption.

Continue on (through Rooms 83-80) and enter Room 75 (marked *affreschi*) to see the museum's impressive collection of (nonerotic) ⓬ **frescoes** taken from the walls of Pompeii villas. Pompeiians loved to decorate their homes with scenes from mythology (Hercules' labors, Venus and Mars in love), landscapes, everyday market scenes, and faux architecture. To the left (in Room 78), find the famous dual portrait of baker Terentius Neo and his wife—possibly two of the 2,000 victims when Vesuvius erupted.

• *Browse through more frescoes and objects from Pompeii in this labyrinth of rooms until, eventually, you end up back near the great hall. From here (facing the hall entrance), turn right and find the entrance to the wing labeled* La Villa dei Papiri.

These artifacts came from the Herculaneum holiday home of Julius Caesar's father-in-law. ⓭ In Room 114, find the glass cases holding two blackened examples of the 2,000 **papyrus scrolls** that gave the villa its name. The half-burned scrolls were unrolled and (with luck) read after excavation in the 1750s. Apparently Caesar's father-in-law was an educated man who appreciated everything from Greek philosophy to Latin history.

Continuing into Room 116, enjoy some of the villa's ⓮ **bronze statues.** Look into the lifelike blue eyes of the intense *Corridore* (runners), bent on doing their best. The *Five Dancers,* with their inlaid-ivory eyes and graceful poses, decorated a portico. The next room (117) has more fine works: *Resting Hermes* (with his tired little heel wings) is taking a break. Nearby, the *Drunken Faun* (singing and snapping his fingers to the beat, a wineskin at

his side) is clearly living for today. This statue epitomizes the *carpe diem* lifestyle of the Epicurean philosophy followed by Caesar's father-in-law and so many other Romans living in Herculaneum and Pompeii on that fateful morning of August 24, AD 79, when Vesuvius changed everything.

• *Ka-pow. The artistic explosion you've just experienced in this mighty museum is now over. To exit, return to the ground floor. To reach the exit, circle around the museum courtyard to the gift shop. But for extra credit, stop at one more sight on your way out.*

### Doriforo

As you circle the courtyard toward the exit, find ⓕ **Doriforo.** (If he's been moved, ask a guard, *"Dov'è il* Doriforo?") This seven-foot-tall "spear-carrier" (the literal transla-  tion of *doriforo*) just stands there, as if holding a spear. What's the big deal about this statue, which looks like so many others? It's a marble replica made by the Romans of one of the most-cop- ied statues of antiquity, a fifth-century BC bronze Greek original by Polycli- tus. This copy once stood in a Pompeii gym, where it inspired ancient athletes by showing the ideal proportions of Greek beauty. So full of motion, and so realistic in its *contrapposto* pose (weight on one foot), the *Doriforo* would later inspire Donatello and Michelangelo, helping to trigger the Renais- sance. And so the glories of ancient Pompeii, once buried and for- gotten, live on today.

# Naples Walk

Naples, a living medieval city, is its own best sight. Couples artfully make love on Vespas surrounded by more smiles per cobblestone than anywhere else in Italy. Sure, Naples has its important sights. But to capture its essence, take this walk through the core of the city.

## A SLICE OF NEAPOLITAN LIFE

This self-guided walk, worth ▲▲▲, takes you from the Archaeo- logical Museum through the heart of town and back to Centrale Station. Allow at least two hours for the full two-part walk, plus time for pizza and sightseeing stops. If your time is short, you can end the walk at Piazza Carità and take the Metro back to the sta- tion. If you're overnighting in Naples, you could split the walk over two days.

🎧 You can also download my free Naples City Walk audio tour.

## Part 1: Archaeological Museum to Piazza Carità

Start at the Archaeological Museum, at the top of Piazza Cavour (Metro: Cavour or Museo; for directions on getting here, see page 972). From here, we'll ramble down a fine boulevard before cutting into the medieval heart of the city.

**NAPLES**

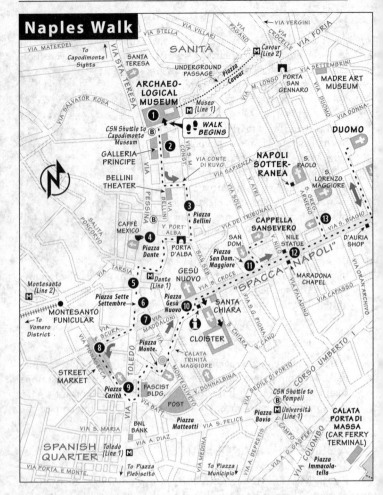

**Naples Walk**

- VIA VERGINI →
- ← VIA VILLARI
- ← VIA PAGANO
- VIA STELLA
- VIA MATERDEI
- VIA FORIA
- SANITÀ
- VIA CROCELLE
- Cavour (Line 2)
- VIA SETTEMBRINI
- To Capodimonte Sights
- SANTA TERESA
- UNDERGROUND PASSAGE
- Piazza Cavour
- VIA M. LONGO
- PORTA SAN GENNARO
- MADRE ART MUSEUM
- VIA SALVATOR ROSA
- ARCHAEO-LOGICAL MUSEUM
- Museo (Line 1)
- ❶
- WALK BEGINS
- VIA DUOMO
- VIA DONNA
- DUOMO
- CSN Shuttle to Capodimonte Museum
- ❷
- GALLERIA PRINCIPE
- VIA CONTE DI RUVO
- VIA SAPIENZA
- NAPOLI SOTTER-RANEA
- S. PAOLO
- S. LORENZO MAGGIORE
- BELLINI THEATER
- ❸
- Piazza Bellini
- VIA DEI TRIBUNALI
- CAPPELLA SANSEVERO
- ❶❸
- VIA S. BIAGIO
- D'AURIA SHOP
- CAFFÈ MEXICO
- ❹
- Piazza Dante
- PORTA D'ALBA
- SAN DOM
- Piazza San Dom. Maggiore
- NILE STATUE
- ❶❶
- ❶❷
- "SPACCA-NAPOLI"
- MARADONA CHAPEL
- Montesanto (Line 2)
- Piazza Sette Settembre
- ❺
- Dante (Line 1)
- GESÙ NUOVO
- VIA B. CROCE
- MONTESANTO FUNICULAR
- ❻
- Piazza Gesù Nuovo
- ❶❶
- SANTA CHIARA
- To Vomero District
- ❼
- VIA MADDALONI
- CLOISTER
- ❽
- Piazza Monte.
- CALATA TRINITÀ MAGGIORE
- STREET MARKET
- ❾
- Piazza Carità
- FASCIST BLDG
- POST
- CSN Shuttle to Pompeii
- Università (Line 1)
- CALATA PORTA DI MASSA (CAR FERRY TERMINAL)
- BNL BANK
- Piazza Matteotti
- Piazza Bovio
- SPANISH QUARTER
- Toledo (Line 1)
- To Piazza Plebiscito
- To Piazza Municipio
- Piazza Immacola-tella

❶ **Archaeological Museum:** The palatial building, built in the mid-1700s, captures the glory of Naples at its peak, and is a great introduction to the Naples we'll see. Back then, the city was rich from sea trade and home to erudite nobles from abroad. They built a magnificent capital of buildings like this one. On this walk we'll see that grand city they built...and its remnants following centuries of decline.

• *From the door of the Archaeological Museum, cross the street, veer right, and enter the arched doorway of the beige-colored Galleria Principe di Napoli mall. (If the entrance is blocked, simply loop around the block to another entrance or pick up our walk behind the Galleria.)*

❷ **Galleria Principe di Napoli:** There's no better example of Naples' grandeur—and decline—than this elegant 19th-century

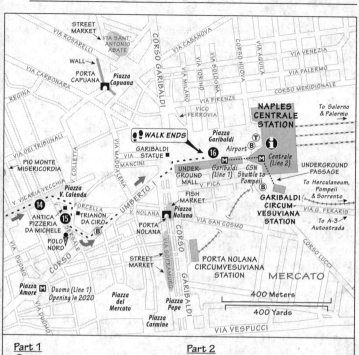

### Part 1

1. Archaeological Museum
2. Galleria Principe di Napoli
3. Piazza Bellini
4. Piazza Dante
5. Via Toledo
6. Piazza Sette Settembre
7. Spaccanapoli
8. Via Pignasecca
9. Piazza Carità

### Part 2

10. Piazza Gesù Nuovo
11. Piazza San Domenico Maggiore
12. Statue of the Nile
13. Via San Gregorio Armeno
14. Via Vicaria Vecchia
15. Eateries
16. Piazza Garibaldi

shopping mall. You'll enjoy a soaring skylight, carved woodwork, ironwork lanterns, playful cupids, an elegant atmosphere...and

empty shops. Built with great expectations, the galleria was named for the first male child of the royal Savoy family, the Prince of Naples. Malls like these were popular in Paris and London. In the US, we call this decorative style Art Nouveau; in Italy it's "Liberty Style," named for a British department store that was in vogue at a time when Naples was nicknamed the "Paris of the South." (Parisian artist Edgar Degas even left Paris to adopt Naples—which he actually considered more cosmopolitan and sophisticated—as his hometown.) Despite its grandeur,

NAPLES

the mall never took off. Ambitious renovations in recent years have failed to attract much business, leaving the mall in a state of disrepair. Falling debris occasionally closes the entire structure.

• *Leaving the gallery through the opposite end, walk one block downhill on a pedestrian street. You'll pass alongside the palatial golden facade of the Academy of Fine Arts, fronted by tropical plants and (usually) busy with students at its outdoor cafés. At Via Conte di Ruvo, turn left, passing the fine* **Bellini Theater** *(also in Liberty Style). All along our walk, be sure to enjoy the architecture of the late 19th century, when Naples was the last stop on Romantic Age travelers' Grand Tour of Europe. After one block, turn right on Via Santa Maria di Costantinopoli. Walking between two grand churches, continue directly downhill to a small park with a statue in the center called...*

❸ **Piazza Bellini:** Suddenly you're in neighborhood Napoli. The statue honors the opera composer Vincenzo Bellini, whose career was launched in Naples in the early 1800s, when opera itself was being born. Just past the statue, peer down into the sunken area to see Naples' ancient origins as a fifth-century BC Greek colony called Neapolis—literally, "the new city." These tuff blocks without mortar were part of a tower in the city wall. (And you're standing on land that, back then, was outside of the town.) You can see how the street level has risen from the rubble of centuries.

Now look around at the city of today. Survey the many balconies—and the people who use them as a "backyard" in this densely packed city. The apartment blocks were originally the palaces of noble families, as indicated by the stately family crests above grand doorways. For 2,500 years, laundry has blown in the breeze right here.

• *Walk 30 yards downhill on the right side. Stop at the horseshoe-shaped* **Port'Alba gate.** *Spin slowly 360 degrees and take in the scene. The proud tile across the street (upstairs, between the two balconies) shows Piazza Bellini circa 1890. Don't ignore the graffiti; try to figure out the issues that artists are calling attention to. Pass through the gate, down Via Port'Alba, and stroll through this pleasant passage lined with book stalls. You emerge into a big square called...*

❹ **Piazza Dante:** This square is marked by a statue of Dante, the medieval poet. Fittingly, half the square is devoted to bookstores. Old Dante looks out over an urban area that was once grand, then chaotic, and is now slowly becoming grand again.

Along one side is a grandiose, orange-and-gray **pseudo-facade** of columns and statues designed by Luigi Vanvitelli, an architect who made his mark on the city in the late 1700s. Vanvitelli remade an existing Jesuit monastery into this new school, representing the power of the Bourbon monarchy when Naples was at its peak. Originally, a statue of the king stood in the square. But in 1799, the Bourbon monarchy was toppled when Napoleon invaded. The king's statue was removed and replaced with the generic figure of Dante. And note the name that was later added to the big facade—Victor Emmanuel. These suggest the next phase of Naples' history—its decline—which we'll see in just a bit.

The Neapolitan people are survivors. A long history of corrupt and greedy colonial overlords (German, Norman, French, Austrian, Spanish, Napoleon, etc.) has taught Neapolitans to deal creatively with authority. Many credit this aspect of Naples' past for the strength of organized crime here.

• *Before moving on, note the red "M" that Dante seems to be gesturing to. This marks the* **Dante Metro station,** *the best of Napoli's art-splashed Metro stations. (To take a look, go down three flights of escalators and then back up; you'll need a ticket, unless you can sweet-talk a guard.) Then, exit Piazza Dante at the far end, walking downhill on...*

❺ **Via Toledo:** The long, straight street heading downhill from Piazza Dante is Naples' principal shopping drag. It originated as a military road built by the Spanish viceroys (hence the name) who made Naples great in the 16th century. Back then, Via Toledo skirted the old town wall to connect the Spanish military headquarters (now the museum where you started this walk) with the Royal Palace (down by the bay). As you stroll, peek into the many lovely atriums, which provide a break from the big street.

After a couple hundred yards, you'll reach the triangular ❻ **Piazza Sette Settembre.** This public space recalls the event that precipitated Naples' swift decline. On September 7, 1860, from the white marble balcony of the Neoclassical building overlooking the square, the famous revolutionary Giuseppe Garibaldi celebrated his conquest of Naples. He declared Italy united and Victor Emmanuel II its first king. And a decade later, that declaration became reality when Rome also fell to unification forces. It was the start of a glorious new era for Italy, Rome, and the Italian people. But not for Naples.

Naples' treasury was confiscated to subsidize the industrial expansion of the north, and its bureaucrats were transferred to the new capital in Rome. Within a few decades, Naples went from being a thriving cultural and political capital to a provincial town, with its economy in shambles and its dialect considered backward.

• *Continue straight on Via Toledo. A block past Piazza Sette Settembre you'll come to Via Maddaloni, which marks the start of the long, straight, narrow street nicknamed...*

**NAPLES**

**❼ Spaccanapoli:** Via Maddaloni is the modern name for the beginning of this thin street that, since ancient times, has bisected the city. The name

Spaccanapoli translates as "split Naples." Look left down the street (toward the train station), and right (toward San Martino hill), and you get a sense of how Spaccanapoli divides this urban jungle of buildings.

• *At this point in our walk, take a moment to plan your next move. From here, our walk loops to the right, through the edge of the intense residential Spanish Quarter neighborhood to Piazza Carità before cutting over to the Spaccanapoli district. (If you were to side-trip to the Royal Palace and Piazza del Plebiscito-area sights—described later in "Sights in Naples"—you'd do that from here...but that makes this walk very long.)*

*At the Spaccanapoli intersection, go right (toward the church facade on the hill), heading up Via Pasquale Scura. After about 100 yards, you hit a busy intersection. Stop. You're on one of Naples' most colorful open-air market streets...*

**❽ Via Pignasecca:** Take in the colorful scene at the intersection. Then, turn left down Via Pignasecca and stroll this colorful market strip. You'll pass fish stalls, tripe vendors, butchers, produce stands, cheap clothes stores, street-food vendors, and much more. There's more activity during the morning, but afternoon offers better light for photography.

This is a taste of Naples' famous **Spanish Quarter** (its center is farther down Via Toledo but this area provides a good sampling).

The Spanish Quarter is a classic world of *basso* (low) living. The streets—which were laid out in the 16th century for the Spanish military barracks outside the city walls—are

unbelievably narrow (and cool in summer), and the buildings rise five stories high. In such tight quarters, life—flirting, fighting, playing, and loving—happens in the road. This is *the* cliché of life in Naples, as shown in so many movies. The Spanish Quarter is Naples at its most characteristic. The shop-keepers are friendly, and the mopeds are bold (watch out). Concerned locals will tug on their lower eyelids, warning you to be wary. Hungry? Pop into a grocery shop and ask the clerk to make you his best prosciutto-and-mozzarella sandwich (it should cost you about €4).

NAPLES

• *Turn left and follow Via Pignasecca as it leads back to Via Toledo at the square called...*

**❾ Piazza Carità:** This square, built for an official visit by Hitler to Mussolini in 1938, is full of stern, straight, obedient lines. The big building belonged to an insur-

ance company. (For the best example of fascist architecture in town, take a slight detour from here: With your back to Via Toledo, leave Piazza Carità downhill on the right-hand corner and walk a block to the Poste e Telegrafi building. There you'll see several government buildings with stirring reliefs singing the praises of lobotomized workers and a totalitarian society.)

In Naples—long a poor and rough city—rather than being heroic, people learn from the cradle the art of survival. The modern memorial statue in the center of this square celebrates Salvo d'Acquisto, a rare hometown hero. In 1943, he was executed after falsely confessing to sabotage...saving 22 fellow Italian soldiers from a Nazi revenge massacre.

• *We're at the midpoint of this walk. Need a WC? Pop into the Burger King. Running out of time and energy? If you end the walk here, you'll find many cafés and wine bars nearby, and it's a short stroll down Via Toledo to the Toledo Metro station.*

*To continue, from Piazza Carità veer northwest (past more fascist-style architecture) on Via Morgantini through Piazza Monteoliveto. Cross the busy street, then angle up Calata Trinità Maggiore to the fancy column in the piazza at the top of the hill.*

## Part 2: Piazza Gesù Nuovo to Centrale Station

• *You're back on the straight-as-a-Greek-arrow Spaccanapoli, formerly the main thoroughfare of the Greek city of Neapolis. (Spaccanapoli changes names several times: Via Maddaloni, Via B. Croce, Via S. Biagio dei Librai, and Via Vicaria Vecchia.) Linger for a moment on...*

**❿ Piazza Gesù Nuovo:** This square is marked by a tower-

ing 18th-century Baroque monument to the Counter-Reformation. Although the Jesuit order was powerful in Naples because of its Spanish heritage, locals never attacked Protestants here with the full fury of the Spanish Inquisition.

**NAPLES**

If you'd like, you can visit two bulky old churches, starting with the dark, fortress-like, 17th-century **Church of Gesù Nuovo,** followed by the simpler **Church of Santa Chiara** (in the courtyard across the street; both described under "Sights in Naples"). There's also a **TI** on this square.

• *Continue along the main drag for another 200 yards. Since this is a university district, you may see students and bookstores. As this neighborhood is also famously superstitious, look for incense-burning women with carts full of good-luck charms for sale.*

*Passing Palazzo Venezia—the embassy of Venice to Naples when both were independent powers—you'll emerge into the next square...*

**⓫ Piazza San Domenico Maggiore:** This square is marked by another ornate 17th-century monument built to thank God for ending the plague. From this square, you can detour left along the right side of the castle-like church, then follow yellow signs, taking the first right and walking one short block to the remarkable Baroque **Cappella Sansevero** (described later, under "Sights in Naples").

• *After touring the chapel, return to Via B. Croce (a.k.a. Spaccanapoli), turn left, and continue your cultural scavenger hunt. At the intersection of Via Nilo, find the...*

**⓬ Statue of the Nile** (on the left): A reminder of the multi-ethnic makeup of Greek Neapolis, this statue is in what was the Egyptian quarter. Locals like to call this statue *The Body of Naples,* with the overflowing cornucopia symbolizing the abundance of their fine city. (I once asked a Neapolitan man to describe the local women, who are famous for their beauty, in one word. He replied, simply, "Abundant.") This intersection is considered the center of old Naples.

• *Directly opposite the statue, inside of Bar Nilo, is the...*

**"Chapel of Maradona":** The small "chapel" on the right wall is dedicated to Diego Maradona, a soccer star who played for Naples in the 1980s. Locals consider soccer almost a religion, and this guy was practically a deity. You can even see a "hair of Diego" and a teardrop from the city when he went to another team for more money. Unfortunately, his reputation has since been sullied by problems he's had with organized crime, drugs, and police. Perhaps inspired by Maradona's example, the coffee bar has posted a quadrilingual sign (though, strangely, not in English) threatening that those who take a picture without buying a cup of coffee may find their camera damaged...*Capisce?*

• *Continue on another 100 yards. You may pass*

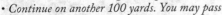

*gold and silver shops. Some say stolen jewelry ends up here, is melted down immediately, and gets resold in some other form as soon as it cools. Look for* compro oro *("I buy gold") signs—a sign of Naples' continuing tough economic times after the 2008 economic crisis. Continue to a tiny square at the intersection with Via San Gregorio Armeno.*

**⓭ Via San Gregorio Armeno:** Stroll up this tiny lane toward the fanciful tower that arches over the street. The street is lined

with stalls selling lots of souvenir kitsch, as well as some of Naples' most distinctive local crafts. Among the many figurines on sale, find items relating to *presepi* (Nativity scenes). Just as many Americans keep an eye out year-round for Christmas-tree ornaments, Italians regularly add pieces to the family *prese-pe*, the centerpiece of their holiday decorations. You'll see elaborate manger scenes made of bark and moss, with niches to hold baby Jesus or mother Mary. You'll also see lots of jokey figurines caricaturing local politicians, soccer stars, and other celebrities. (Some of the highest-quality *presepi* pieces are sold at the D'Auria shop, a little farther down Spaccanapoli, on the right at #87. Expressive figures are made from terra-cotta, wood, and cloth, often fetching over €250. They even sell the classy *campane* version, under a glass bell.)

Another popular Naples souvenir sold here—and all over—is the *corno,* a skinny, twisted, red horn that resembles a chili pepper. The *corno* comes with a double symbolism for fertility: It's a horn of plenty, and it's also a phallic symbol turned upside-down. Neapolitans explain that fertility isn't sexual; it provides the greatest gift a person can give—life—and it ensures that one's soul will live on through the next generation. In today's Naples, just as in yesterday's Pompeii (where bulging erections greeted visitors at the entrance to a home), fertility is equated with good luck.

(By the way, a bit farther up Via San Gregorio Armeno, you'll find the underground **Napoli Sotterranea archaeological site,** along Via dei Tribunali, which also has some of the city's best **pizzerias**—both are described later.)

• *Continue down Spaccanapoli another 100 yards until you hit busy Via Duomo. Consider detouring five minutes north (left) up Via Duomo to visit Naples'* **Duomo***; just around the corner from that is the* **Pio Monte della Misericordia Church***, with a fine Caravaggio painting (both described later, under "Sights in Naples"). But for now, continue straight, crossing Via Duomo. Here, Spaccanapoli is named...*

**⓮ Via Vicaria Vecchia:** Here along Via Vicaria Vecchia, the main "sight" is the vibrant street life. It's grittier and less touristy, but just as atmospheric as what we've been seeing. The street and side-street scenes intensify. The area is said to be a center of the Camorra (the Naples-based version of the Sicilian Mafia), but as a tourist, you won't notice. Paint a picture with these thoughts: Naples has the most intact street plan of any surviving ancient Greek or Roman city. Imagine this city during those times (and retain these images as you visit Pompeii), with streetside shop fronts that close up after dark, and private homes on upper floors. What you see today is just one more page in a 2,000-year-old story of a city: all kinds of meetings, beatings, and cheatings; kisses, near misses, and little-boy pisses.

You name it, it occurs right on the streets today, as it has since ancient times. People ooze from crusty corners. Black-and-white death announcements add to the clutter on the walls. Widows sell cigarettes from buckets. For a peek behind the scenes in the shade of wet laundry, venture down a few side streets. Buy two carrots as a gift for the woman on the fifth floor, if she'll lower her bucket to pick them up. The neighborhood action seems best at about 18:00.

At the tiny fenced-in triangle of greenery, hang out for a few minutes to just observe the crazy motorbike action and teen scene.

• *From here, veer right onto Via Forcella. You emerge into Piazza Vincenzo Calenda, where there's a round fence protecting another chunk of that ancient **Greek wall** of Neapolis. Hungry? Turn right here, on Via Pietro Colletta, and close out the walk with three typical Neapolitan...*

🕒 **Eateries:** Step into the North Pole at the recommended **Polo Nord Gelateria** (at #41). The oldest *gelateria* in Naples has had four generations of family working here since 1931. Before you order, sample a few flavors, including their *bacio*, or "kiss," flavor (named after the national chocolate-and-praline candy)—all are made fresh daily.

Two of Napoli's most competitive **pizzerias** are nearby. **Trianon da Ciro** (across the street from Polo Nord) has been serving them up hot and fast for almost a century. A half-block farther, on the right, is the place where some say pizza was born—at **Antica Pizzeria da Michele**. (For more on both, see "Eating in Naples," later.)

• *Our walk is over. It's easy to return to Centrale Station. Continue straight ahead, downhill, until you hit the grand boulevard, Corso Umberto I. Turn left here, and it's a straight 15-minute walk to Centrale*

*Station. (Or cross the street and hop on a bus; they all go to the station.) You'll pass a gauntlet of purse/CD/sunglasses salesmen and shady characters hawking stolen mobile phones. You'll soon reach the vast* **⑯** *Piazza Garibaldi, with a modern canopy in the middle. On the far side is the station. You made it.*

# Sights in Naples

Naples' best sights are the Archaeological Museum and my self-guided Naples Walk, both covered earlier. For extra credit, consider these sights.

## CHURCHES ON OR NEAR SPACCANAPOLI

These churches are linked—in this order—on the second half of my Naples Walk.

### ▲Church of Gesù Nuovo

This church's unique pyramid-grill facade survives from a fortified 15th-century noble palace. Step inside for a brilliant Neapolitan Baroque interior. The second chapel on the right features a much-adored **statue of St. Giuseppe Moscati** (1880-1927), a Christian doctor famous for helping the poor. In 1987, Moscati became the first modern doctor to be canonized. Sit and watch a steady stream of Neapolitans taking turns to kiss and touch the altar, then hold the good doctor's highly polished hand.

Continue on to the third chapel (past his vertical tombstone) and enter the **Sale Moscati.** Look high on the walls of this long room to see hundreds of ex-votos—tiny red-and-silver plaques of thanksgiving for prayers answered with the help of St. Moscati (each has a symbol of the ailment cured). Naples' practice of using ex-votos, while incorporated into its Catholic  rituals, goes back to its pagan Greek roots. Rooms from Moscati's nearby apartment are on display, and a glass case shows possessions and photos of the great doctor. As you leave the Sale Moscati, notice the big bomb casing that hangs high in the left corner. It fell through the church's dome in 1943, but caused almost no damage... yet another miracle.

**Cost and Hours:** Free, daily 6:45-13:00 & 16:00-19:30, Piazza del Gesù Nuovo, www.gesunuovo.it.

## Church of Santa Chiara

Dating from the 14th century, this church is from a period of French royal rule under the Angevin dynasty. Consider the stark contrast between this church (Gothic) and the Gesù Nuovo (Baroque), across the street. Inside, look for the faded Trinity on the back wall (on the right as you face the door, under the stone canopy), which shows a dove representing the Holy Spirit between the heads of God the Father and Christ (c. 1414). This is an example of the fine frescoes that once covered the walls. Most were stuccoed over during Baroque times or destroyed in 1943 by Allied bombs. Continuing down the main aisle, you'll step over a huge inlaid-marble Angevin coat of arms on the floor. The altar is adorned with four finely carved Gothic tombs of Angevin kings. A chapel stacked with Bourbon royalty is just to the right.

**Cost and Hours:** Free, daily 7:30-13:00 & 16:30-20:00, Piazza del Gesù Nuovo, www.monasterodisantachiara.it. Its tranquil cloistered courtyard, around back, is not worth its €6 entry fee.

## ▲▲Cappella Sansevero

This small chapel is a Baroque explosion mourning the body of Christ, who lies on a soft pillow under an incredibly realistic veil.

It's also the personal chapel of Raimondo de Sangro, an eccentric Freemason, containing his tomb and the tombs of his family. Like other 18th-century Enlightenment figures, Raimondo was a wealthy man of letters, scientist and inventor, and patron of the arts—and he was also a grand master of the Freemasons of the Kingdom of Naples. His chapel—filled with Masonic symbolism—is a complex ensemble, with statues representing virtues such as self-control, religious zeal, and the Masonic philosophy of freedom through enlightenment. Though it's a pricey private enterprise, the chapel is worth a visit.

**Cost and Hours:** €7, buy tickets at office at the corner—or skip the long ticket-buying line by reserving ahead online (€2 fee); open Wed-Mon 9:30-18:30, closed Tue; Via de Sanctis 19, tel. 081-551-8470, www.museosansevero.it. The least crowded time to visit is after 16:00—the later the better. Pick up the free floor plan, which identifies each of the statues lining the nave.

**Visiting the Chapel:** Study the incredible *Veiled Christ* in the center. Carved out of marble, it's like no other statue I've seen (by Giuseppe "Howdeedoodat" Sammartino, 1753). The Christian message (Jesus died for our salvation) is accompanied by a Masonic message (the veil represents how the body and ego are obstacles to real spiritual freedom). As you walk from Christ's feet to his head, notice how the expression on Jesus' face goes from suffering to peace.

Raimondo's mom and dad are buried on either side of the **main altar.** To the right of the altar, marking his father's tomb, a statue representing *Despair* or *Disillusion* struggles with a marble rope net (carved out of a single piece of stone), symbolic of a troubled mind. The flames on the head of the winged boy represent human intellect—more Masonic symbolism, showing how knowledge frees the human mind. To the left of the main altar is a statue of *Modesty*, marking the tomb of Raimondo's mother (who died after his birth, and was only 20). The veiled woman fingers a broken tablet, symbolizing an interrupted life.

Raimondo de Sangro himself lies buried in a side altar (on the right). Among his inventions was the deep-green pigment used on the ceiling fresco. The inlaid M. C. Escher-esque maze on the floor around de Sangro's tomb is another Masonic reminder of how the quest for knowledge gets you out of the maze of life. This tilework once covered the floor of the entire chapel.

Your Sansevero finale is downstairs: two mysterious...**skeletons.** Perhaps another of the mad inventor's fancies: Inject a corpse with a fluid to fossilize the veins so that they'll survive the body's decomposition. While that's the legend, investigations have shown that the veins were artificial, and the models were created to illustrate how the circulatory system works.

## ▲Duomo

Naples' historic cathedral, built by imported French Anjou kings in the 14th century, boasts a breathtaking Neo-Gothic facade. Step into the vast interior to see the mix of styles along the side chapels—from pointy Gothic arches to rounded Renaissance ones to gilded Baroque decor.

**Cost and Hours:** Free, Mon-Sat 8:30-13:30 & 14:30-20:00, Sun 8:30-13:30 & 16:30-19:30, Via Duomo.

**Visiting the Church:** Explore the two largest side-chapels (flanking the nave, about halfway to the transept). Each is practically a church in its own right. On the right is the **Chapel of San Gennaro**—dedicated to the beloved patron saint of Naples—decorated with silver busts of centuries of bishops, and six paintings done on bronze (skip the €3 chapel audioguide). On the left, the **Chapel of Santa Restituta** stands on the site of the original, early Christian church that predated the cathedral (at the far end, you can pay a small fee to see its sixth-century baptismal font under mosaics and go downstairs to see its even earlier foundations; shorter hours than cathedral).

The cathedral's **main altar** at the front is ringed by carved wooden seats, filled three times a year by clergy to witness the Miracle of the Blood. Thousands of Neapolitans cram into this church for a peek at two tiny vials with the dried blood of St. Gennaro. As the clergy roots—or even jeers—for the miracle to occur, the blood temporarily liquefies. Neapolitans take this ritual with deadly seriousness, and believe that if the blood remains solid, it's terrible luck for the city. Sure enough, on the rare occasion that the miracle fails, locals can point to a terrible event soon after—such as an earthquake, an eruption of Mount Vesuvius, or an especially disappointing soccer loss.

The stairs beneath the altar take you to a **crypt** with the relics of St. Gennaro and a statue of the bishop who rescued the relics from a rival town and returned them to Naples. These relics are said to have stopped the lava from a 1631 Vesuvius eruption from destroying the city.

### Pio Monte della Misericordia

This small church (near the Duomo, and run by a charitable foundation) displays one of the best works by Caravaggio, *The Seven Works of Mercy*. Upstairs is a ho-hum art gallery. The price is steep, but it may be worth it for Caravaggio fans.

**Cost and Hours:** €7 (ticket booth across the street), includes audioguide, Thu-Tue 9:00-14:30, closed Wed, Via dei Tribunali 253, tel. 081-446-944, www.piomontedellamisericordia.it.

**Visiting the Church:** Caravaggio's *The Seven Works of Mercy* hangs over the main altar in a darkened gray chapel. The painting is well-lit, allowing Caravaggio's characteristically dark canvas to really pop. In one crowded canvas, the great early-Baroque artist illustrates seven virtues: burying the dead (the man carrying a corpse by the ankles); visiting the imprisoned and feeding the hungry (Pero breastfeeding her starving father—a scene from a famous Roman story); sheltering the homeless (a pilgrim on the Camino de Santiago, with his floppy hat, negotiates with an innkeeper); caring for the sick and clothing the naked (St. Martin offers part of his cloak to the injured man in the foreground); and giving drink to the thirsty (Samson chugs from a jawbone in the background)—all of them set in a dark Neapolitan alley and watched over by Mary, Jesus, and a pair of angels.

Caravaggio painted this work in Naples in 1607 while in exile from Rome, where he had been sentenced to death for killing a man in a duel. Three years later Caravaggio died from an unknown illness on his way back to Rome to receive a pardon from the Pope.

## NEAR THE PORT

This cluster of important sights can be found between the big ceremonial square, Piazza del Plebiscito, and the cruise ship terminal. If touring the entire neighborhood, I'd see it in the order described here. For locations, see the map on page 1010.

### ▲Piazza del Plebiscito

This square celebrates the 1861 vote (*plebiscito*, plebiscite) in which Naples chose to join Italy. Dominating the top of the square is the Church of San Francesco di Paola, with its Pantheon-inspired dome and broad, arcing colonnades. If it's open, step inside to ogle the vast interior—a Neoclassical re-creation of one of ancient Rome's finest buildings.

• *Opposite is the...*

### Royal Palace (Palazzo Reale)

Having housed Spanish, French, and even Italian royalty, this building displays statues of all those who stayed here. From the

square in front of the palace, look for eight kings in the niches, each from a different dynasty (left to right): Norman, German, French, Spanish, Spanish, Spanish, French (Napoleon's brother-in-law), and, finally, Italian—Victor Emmanuel II, King of Savoy. The statues were done at the request of V. E. II's son, so his dad is the most dashing of the group. As far as palaces go, the interior is relatively unimpressive.

**Cost and Hours:** €6, skip the painfully dry €3 audioguide (each room has excellent panel descriptions in English; Thu-Tue 9:00-20:00, closed Wed, last entry one hour before closing; tel. 848-082-408, www.coopculture.it).

**Visiting the Palace:** The palace's grand Neoclassical staircase leads up to a floor with 30 plush rooms. You'll follow a one-way route featuring the palace theater, paintings by "the Caravaggio Imitators," Neapolitan tapestries, fine inlaid-stone tabletops, chandeliers, gilded woodwork, and more. The rooms do feel quite grand, even if they lack the personality and sense of importance of Europe's better palaces. As a less-visited sight, wandering through the rooms at leisure makes you feel like royalty yourself. Don't miss the huge, tapestry-laden Hercules Hall or the chance to dance on the wooden floor of the wide-open ballroom. Ask a guard (nicely) to open the terrace garden balcony door to enjoy sweeping views of the Bay of Naples. On the way out, step into the royal chapel, with an altar made entirely of precious stones and a fantastic Nativity scene—a commotion of 18th-century ceramic figurines.

• *Continue 50 yards past the Royal Palace (toward the trees) to enjoy a...*

### Fine Harbor View

While boats busily serve Capri and Sorrento, Mount Vesuvius smolders ominously in the distance. Look back to see the vast "Bourbon red" palace—its color inspired by Pompeii. The hilltop above Piazza del Plebiscito is San Martino, with its Carthusian monastery-turned-museum and Castle of St. Elmo (remember, the Centrale funicular to the top is just across the square and up Via Toledo). The promenade you're on continues to Naples' romantic harborfront—the fishermen's quarter (Borgo Marinaro)—a fortified island connected to the mainland by a stout causeway, with its fanciful, ancient Castel dell'Ovo (Egg Castle) and trendy harborside restaurants. From there, the Lungomare harborside promenade—described later—continues past the Santa Lucia district, stretching out along the Bay of Naples. This long promenade, running along Via Francesco Caracciolo to the Mergellina district and beyond, is a delightful people-watching scene on balmy nights.

• *Head back through the piazza and pop into...*

### Gran Caffè Gambrinus

This coffeehouse, facing the piazza, takes you back to the elegance of 1860. It's a classic place to sample a crispy *sfogliatella* pastry, or perhaps the mushroom-shaped, rum-soaked bread-like cakes called *babà*, which come in a huge variety. Stand at the bar *(banco)*, pay double to sit *(tavola)*, or just wander around as you imagine the café buzzing with the ritzy intellectuals, journalists, and artsy bohemian types who munched on *babà* here during Naples' 19th-century heyday (daily 7:00-24:00, Piazza del Plebiscito 1, tel. 081-417-582).

• *A block away, tucked behind the palace, you can peek inside the Neoclassical...*

### Teatro di San Carlo

Built in 1737, 41 years before Milan's La Scala, this is Europe's oldest opera house and Italy's second-most-respected (after La Scala).

The original theater burned down in 1816, and was rebuilt within the year. Guided 35-minute visits in English basically just show you the fine auditorium with its 184 boxes—each with a big mirror to reflect the candlelight (€6; tours Mon-Sat at 10:30, 11:30, 12:30, 14:30, 15:30, and 16:30; Sun at 10:30, 11:30, and 12:30; tel. 081-797-2331, www.teatrosancarlo.it).

• *Beyond Teatro di San Carlo and the Royal Palace is the huge, harbor-front...*

## Castel Nuovo

This imposing castle now houses government bureaucrats and the **Civic Museum.** It feels like a mostly empty shell, with a couple of dusty halls of Neapolitan art, but the views over the bay from the upper terraces are impressive (€6, Mon-Sat 8:30-19:00, closed Sun, last entry one hour before closing, tel. 081-795-7722, www.comune.napoli.it).

• *Head back to Teatro di San Carlo, cross the street, and go through the tall yellow arch into...*

## ▲Galleria Umberto I

This Victorian iron-and-glass shopping mall opened in 1890 to reinvigorate the district after a devastating cholera epidemic occurred here. Gawk up, then walk left to bring you back out on Via Toledo.

• *Just up the street and behind Piazza del Plebiscito is an interesting subterranean experience.*

## ▲Galleria Borbonica

Beneath Naples' Royal Palace was a vast underground network of caves, aqueducts, and cisterns that originated as a quarry in the 15th century. In the mid-1800s, when popular revolutions were threatening royalty across Europe, the understandably nervous king of Naples, Ferdinand II, had this underground world expanded to create an escape tunnel from the palace to his military barracks nearby. In World War II, it was used as an air-raid shelter; after the war, the police used it to store impounded cars and motorcycles. Today, enthusiastic guides take the curious on a fascinating 70-minute, 500-yard-long guided walk through this many-layered world littered with disintegrating 60-year-old vehicles upon which Naples sits.

**Cost and Hours:** €10 English-language tours leave Fri-Sun at 10:00, 12:00, 15:00, and 17:00; tel. 081-764-5808, www.galleriaborbonica.com. The most convenient entry is just behind Piazza del Plebiscito—up Via Gennaro Serra and down Vico del

Grottone to #4 (to avoid that entrance's 90 steep steps, enter at Via Morelli 61).

## NORTH OF SPACCANAPOLI
### ▲Napoli Sotterranea

This archaeological site, a manmade underground maze of passageways and ruins from Greek and Roman times, can only be toured with a guide. You'll descend 121 steps under the modern city to explore two underground areas. One is the old Greek tuff quarry used to build the city of Neapolis, which was later converted into an immense cistern by the Romans. The other is an excavated portion of the Greco-Roman theater that once seated 6,000 people. The space has been encroached upon by modern development—some current residents' windows literally look down into the theater ruins. The tour involves a lot of stairs, as well as a long, narrow 20-inch-wide walkway—lit only by candlelight—that uses an ancient water channel (a heavyset person could not comfortably fit through this, and claustrophobes will be miserable). Although there's not much to see, the experience is fascinating and includes a little history from World War II—when the quarry/cistern was turned into a shelter to protect locals from American bombs.

**Cost and Hours:** €10, includes 1.5-hour tour, tours in English offered daily every two hours from 10:00 to 18:00. If the ticket-buying line is long, talk to an attendant: They *might* be able to move you into the next English-language tour. Bring a light sweater. Tel. 081-296-944, www.napolisotterranea.org.

**Getting There:** The site is at Piazza San Gaetano 68, along Via dei Tribunali. It's a 15-minute walk from the Archaeological Museum, and just a couple of blocks uphill from Spaccanapoli's statue of the Nile. The entrance is immediately to the left of the Church of San Paolo Maggiore (look for the *Sotterranea* signs).

### MADRE

MADRE, a museum of contemporary art, displays works by Jeff Koons, Anish Kapoor, Francesco Clemente, and other big names in the art world. Aficionados of modern art consider it one of the better collections in the country. Some descriptions are in English—you'll need them.

**Cost and Hours:** €7, free on Mon; Wed-Mon 10:00-19:30—Sun until 20:00, closed Tue, last entry one hour before closing; Via Settembrini 79, tel. 081-1973-7254, www.madrenapoli.it.

### ▲▲Sanità District

While the characteristic Spaccanapoli and Spanish Quarter are being tamed, today's clear winner for wild-and-crazy Neapolitan life in the streets is the gritty Sanità District, north of the Archaeological Museum.

A big part of the attraction of Naples is its *basso* living (life in the streets). Many locals with enough money to move to the sanity of the suburbs choose instead to keep living where the action is—in a cauldron of flapping laundry, police sirens, broken cobblestone lanes, singing merchants, sidewalks clogged with makeshift markets, and walls crusted with ancient posters and graffiti.

One of Naples' most historic and colorful zones, Sanità is sometimes called "the living *presepe*" for the way people live stacked on top of each other in rustic conditions, as if in an elaborate manger scene. (Because organized crime is still strong in this quarter, development is slow.) Literally "the healthy place" (named for the freshness of the air, originally so high above the dense city), this is *the* place for a photo safari.

While the reason to visit Sanità is simply to swim through its amazing river of life, there are two remarkable burial sites in the district: the Catacombs of San Gaudioso, at the Basilica Santa Maria della Sanità, and the Cemetery of the Fountains (described later, under "On Capodimonte").

**Visiting the Sanità District:** Check to be sure your valuables are zipped or buttoned safely away. From near the Porta San Gennaro gate (just west of Via Duomo, two blocks east of Metro: Cavour, six blocks east of Archaeological Museum), leave Via Foria and head up Via Crocelle. Venture a block up Via Crocelle and then three blocks up Via dei Vergini through a thriving daily market scene. Pop into the courtyard of the Palazzo dello Spagnuolo (#19 on the left) to peek at an extravagant 18th-century staircase.

Then dog-leg left on Via Arena della Sanità and continue uphill (past another massive staircase in the courtyard at #6) to Piazza Sanità, at the base of Capodimonte, where you'll stand before the Basilica Santa Maria della Sanità, which sits atop the Catacombs of San Gaudioso (entrance inside the church, €9 combo-ticket covers Catacombs of San Gennaro, hourly English tours run daily 10:00-13:00). Because this area was just outside the old city walls, the dead were buried here—for details, see www.catacombedinapoli.it.

From here you have three options: Browse your way back down the way you just came; continue 10 minutes up Via Sanità and Via Fontanelle to the Cemetery of the Fountains; or ride a free elevator (just past the church, under the high viaduct) up to the modern world.

## ON CAPODIMONTE

### ▲▲Capodimonte Museum (Museo di Capodimonte)

This hilltop, about a mile due north from the Archaeological Museum, is home to Naples' top art museum. This pleasant collection has lesser-known (but still masterful) works by Michelangelo, Raphael, Titian, Caravaggio, and other huge names. It fills the Bourbons' cavernous summer palace, set in the midst of a sprawling hilltop park overlooking Naples, and part of the museum showcases the palace's history and furnishings. While most visitors to Naples prefer to focus on the city's vibrant street life, characteristic churches, and ancient artifacts, art lovers and royalty buffs enjoy a visit to Capodimonte.

**Cost and Hours:** €12, Thu-Tue 8:30-19:30, closed Wed, last entry one hour before closing, avoid lines by purchasing your ticket online (€2 fee), fine audioguide-€5 (bring earbuds for better sound), café, Via Miano 2, tel. 081-749-9111, www.museocapodimonte. beniculturali.it.

**Free Entry:** The museum is free and busier once or twice a month—the specific day varies in peak season (in low season, it's the first Sun).

**Getting There:** It's easiest by taxi (figure €15 from the city center). You can also catch the CitySightseeing shuttle bus that runs from Teatro San Carlo and Piazza Municipio directly to the museum (€8 round-trip, tel. 081-551-7279, www.napoli.city-sightseeing.it).

**Visiting the Museum:** After buying your ticket, pick up the free map and head up several flights of stairs (or ride the elevator) to the "first" floor and the Galleria Farnese. Engraved room numbers above doors can be difficult to read, so expect to backtrack occasionally.

**Room 2:** At the far end of the first big hall is Titian's *Portrait of Paul III.* It depicts Alessandro Farnese, the local bigwig whose family married into Bourbon royalty; later, as Pope Paul III, he was responsible for bringing great art to Naples. Four paintings to the right, you'll see a Raphael: a portrait of the same red-attired pope as a much younger cardinal.

**Room 3:** In the next, smaller room, the section of an altarpiece (1426) by the early Renaissance pioneer Masaccio shows a primitive attempt at 3-D: Masaccio has left out Jesus' neck to create the illusion that he's looking down on us.

**Room 4:** If it's open, don't miss the adjoining room (look to the left, lights go on as you enter), with large charcoal drawings by Raphael (Moses shields his eyes from the burning bush, 1514) and Michelangelo (a group of soldiers, 1546; and *Venus and Love,* 1534).

**Room 8:** Continuing into the Borgia Collection, look for works by Mantegna (including the medallion-like *Portrait of Ludovico Gonzaga,* c. 1461, a very small but finely executed profile portrait) and Giovanni Bellini's *Circumcision of Christ.* (Bellini was Titian's master.) Rooms 9 and 10 feature Mannerism paintings.

**Room 11:** Here you see one of many versions of Titian's *Danaë,* where—as told in the Greek myth—the sensuous central character looks up at a cloud containing the essence of Zeus (a shower of coins), about to impregnate her. Enjoy the cupid's surprised look at the action as the courtesan awaits her union. Nearby, Titian's poignant portrait of a penitent Mary Magdalene has finely detailed tears running down her cheeks (1565).

**Room 12:** Parmigianino's *Antea* (1531-1535), another of the collection's highlights, addresses us with an unblinking, dilated gaze. She wears a mink stole (astonishingly lifelike, with disgusting little teeth), gold chain, and hair brooch—items commonly presented by a lover. By wearing the gifts, Antea signals her acceptance of her suitor's advances.

**Room 14:** The small, dim adjoining room shows off the kings' "collection of wonders." Don't miss the *Farnese Box* (*Cassetta Farnese*, 1563), a masterwork of gold decoration with engraved rock crystal, which held a prayer book.

**Room 17:** Down the main hall is a remarkable work by Pieter Bruegel the Elder. *The Misanthrope* (1568) suggests the pointlessness of giving up on life and becoming a hermit; cut off from the world and lost in thought, the title figure doesn't even notice that he's about to step on a trail of thorns. Behind him, a wild-eyed young man is stealing the misanthrope's money pouch (Hey! I saw that guy on the Circumvesuviana!).

**Room 20:** Looking at you from the end of the corridor, Annibale Carracci's *Hercules at the Crossroads* (1596) presents the hero with a choice: virtue (on the left, nature and letters, but a steep uphill climb) or vice (on the right, scantily clad women, music, theater masks, and an easy, flat path). While his foot points one way, he looks the other...his mind not yet made up.

**Royal Apartments:** It's easy to forget that this museum is set in a royal palace. Originally a simple hunting lodge, in the 18th century the king decided it could be a grand palace. Several dynasties enjoyed its regal ballrooms and imposing reception rooms while amassing their impressive collections of art. From here on out, you'll pass through some of the opulent apartments of this building, decorated with stunning period details and furniture.

The first room is slathered with frescoes, in the style of those excavated at Pompeii. The grand hall in the corner comes with a massive bronze chandelier hanging over an ancient Roman inlaid-marble floor, which originally decorated the palace of Roman Emperor Tiberius on Capri (installed here in 1877). The following rooms tell stories of three Bourbon kings with portraits and objects from their reign. Just off Room 34 is a room filled with royal porcelain—considered white gold—from all corners of Europe: Naples, Vienna, Paris (Sèvres), and Berlin. Imagine attending a regal ball in the grand *Salone delle Feste* (Room 42). Later, you come upon a small living room decorated entirely with porcelain and mirrors (c. 1750). This is a masterwork of *chinoiserie*—a style reflecting Europe's fascination with Chinese culture.

**Room 54:** You now find yourself face-to-face with Napoleon. From here are several rooms decorated in the Napoleon-pleasing Neoclassical style—a reminder that Napoleon's older brother once ruled the Kingdom of Napoli. Look for the stunning circular table with a Roman mosaic centerpiece, surrounded with newer mosaics containing Napoleon's favorite honey-bee symbol.

**Second Floor:** Circling back to where you started, head up four flights of stairs (or take the elevator) to the second floor where you'll find art from private collections and paintings mostly from local churches. You'll see a cycle of Flemish tapestries, then halls of Gothic altarpieces.

**Room 65:** Heading down the first corridor, enjoy the fine altarpiece from Nottingham, England. Carved out of alabaster in the 15th century, it shows expressive scenes from the Passion of Christ.

**Room 66:** At the end of the first corridor, you'll see Simone Martini's lavish and delicate portrait from 1317 of San Ludovico di Tolosa crowning Roberto king of Naples.

**Room 67:** Find Colantonio's painting *San Girolamo nello Studio* (c. 1445), in which the astonishing level of detail—from the words on the page of the open book, to the balled-up pages tucked away at the bottom of the frame—drives home the message: Only through complete devotion and meticulous dedication can you hope to accomplish great things...like pulling a thorn out of a lion's paw.

**Room 78:** Farther along on this floor, shining at the end of the long corridor, you'll reach another of the museum's top pieces, Caravaggio's *The Flagellation*. Typical of his *chiaroscuro* (light/dark) style, Caravaggio uses a ribbon of light to show us only what he wants us to see: A broken Christ about to be whipped, and the manic fury of the man (on his left) who will do the whipping. This scene could be set in a Naples alley. Compare this with most of the paintings we've seen so far—of popes, saints, and aristocrats. Caravaggio was given refuge in Naples while fleeing a murder trial in Rome. (They put him to work painting. Of the eight canvases he painted during this period, three remain in Naples.) Caravaggio was revolutionary in showing real life rather than idealized scenes—helping common people to better relate to these stories.

**The Rest of the Museum:** Continue through the maze of rooms to find pieces by Spanish master José de Ribera, his Italian contemporary Luca Giordano, and a exhibit of works from the museum's collection, on display here for the first time. (As in all great collections, more works of art are in storage than can be displayed at any given moment.) The museum wants to surprise visitors, encourage dialogue about lesser-known artists, and get you thinking about what might be hiding in other museum storerooms.

**Nearby:** While people visiting the Capodimonte Museum are understandably focused on its paintings, don't overlook the expansive **Capodimonte Park** surrounding it. Once a hunting ground for royalty, the park is now a pleasure garden—beloved by Neapolitans—with elegant paths and lovely gardens sprouting trees and exotic plants from around the world. If you've planned ahead, this is a lovely spot for a picnic.

### ▲▲Catacombs of San Gennaro

Behind the towering modern church of Madre del Buon Consiglio (Mother of Good Counsel) are tucked the most impressive ancient catacombs south of Rome. It started as a pagan tomb of little consequence, but then St. Agrippino, the local bishop, was buried here in the third century. Later, in the fifth century, the bones of St. Gennaro (patron of Naples) were moved here. Suddenly a site of special reverence—complete with miracles—it became a place where Neapolitans wanted to be buried as well. Today, the catacombs are run by a nonprofit organization of earnest young people who conduct walking tours. These half-mile walks survey more than a thousand burial niches on two levels that date from the second to sixth centuries (many with frescoes surviving...barely).

**Cost and Hours:** €9 combo-ticket with Catacombs of San Gaudioso; included English-language tours depart on the hour Mon-Sat 10:00-17:00, Sun 10:00-14:00; Via di Capodimonte 13, tel. 081-744-3714.

### ▲Cemetery of the Fountains (Cimitero delle Fontanelle)

A thousand years ago, cut into the hills at the high end of Napoli was a quarry. Then, in the 16th century, churches with crowded cemeteries began moving the bones of their long dead here to make room for the newly dead. Later these caves housed the bones of plague victims and the city's paupers. In the 19th century, many churches again emptied their cemeteries and added even more skulls to this vast ossuary. Then a cult of people appeared whose members adopted the skulls. They named the skulls, put them in little houses, brought them flowers, and asked them to intervene with God for favors from the next life. Today, the quirky caves—stacked with human bones and dotted with chapels—are open to the public.

**Cost and Hours:** Tips accepted, daily 10:00-17:00, Via Fontanelle 77, tel. 081-795-6160.

**Getting There:** Located in a sketchy-feeling neighborhood at the top end of Sanità, you can get here by hopping in a taxi, riding the Metro to the Materdei stop and following the brown signs for 10 minutes, or by hiking 10 minutes from the Basilica Santa Maria della Sanità up Via Sanità and Via Fontanelle (see "Sanità District" listing, earlier).

## SOUTH OF SPACCANAPOLI
### Porta Nolana Open-Air Fish Market

Naples' fish market squirts and stinks as it has for centuries under the darkened Porta Nolana (gate in the city wall), four long blocks down from Centrale Station. Of the town's many boisterous out-door markets, this will net you the most photos and memories. From Piazza Nolana, wander under the medieval gate and take your first left down Via So-pramuro, enjoying this wild and entirely edible cultural scaven-ger hunt (Tue-Sun 8:00-14:00, closed Mon). Stalls display the best catch of the day as water jets caress mounds of mussels and clams.

Two other markets with more clothing and fewer fish are at Piazza Capuana (several blocks northwest of Centrale Station and tumbling down Via Sant'Antonio Abate, Mon-Sat 8:00-18:00, Sun 9:00-13:00) and a similar cobbled shopping zone along Via Pignasecca (just off Via Toledo, west of Piazza Carità, described on page 984).

### ▲▲Harborside Promenade: The Lungomare *Passeggiata*

Each evening, relaxed and romantic Neapolitans in the mood for a scenic harborside stroll do their *vasche* (laps) along the in-viting Lungomare harborside promenade and beyond. To join in this elegant people-watching scene (best after 19:00), stroll down to the waterfront from Piazza del Plebiscito and then along Via Nazario Sauro to the beginning of a delightful series of harborside promenades that stretch romantically all the way out of the city. Along the way, you'll enjoy views of Mount Vesuvius and the Bay of Naples. The entire route is crowded on weekends and lively any evening of the week with families, amorous couples, and friends hanging out. Here's a brief rundown of its three sections:

**Santa Lucia and Borgo Marinaro**: Via Nazario Sauro passes the Santa Lucia district, so called because this is where the song "Santa Lucia" was first performed. (The song is probably so famous in America because immigrants from Naples sang it to remember the old country.) At the fortified causeway, make a short detour out to Borgo Marinaro ("Fisherman's Quarter"), and poke around this fabled island neighborhood. With its striking Castel dell'Ovo and a trendy restaurant scene, you can dine here amid yachts with a view of Vesuvius. From here, follow Via Partenope to Piazza Vittoria.

**Piazza Vittoria and Via Francesco Caracciolo:** From Piazza Vittoria the strolling action stretches along the Lungomare on Via Francesco Caracciolo all the way to the Mergellina district. The convenient bus #140 starts at Piazza Vittoria, making stops all along the promenade to Posillipo (at the end of the nice strolling stretch). Walk as far as you like away from the city center and, when you're ready to return, just hop on the bus or grab a cab. (From Piazza Vittoria you can shortcut scenically directly back to Piazza del Plebiscito by heading inland through Piazza dei Martiri and down Via Chiaia.)

**Mergellina and Via Posillipo:** The promenade continues past yacht harbors and rocks popular for swimming and sunbathing, under lavish Liberty Style villas, to tiny coves and inviting fish restaurants. Perched on the hillside at Posillipo (the end of the nice stretch) awaits a delightful $$$ restaurant with majestic views (Ristorante Reginella, Via Posillipo 45a, tel. 081-240-3220) and the bus #140 stop for your quick return.

## ON SAN MARTINO

The ultimate view overlooking Naples, its bay, and the volcano is from San Martino hill, just above (and west of) the city center.

Up top you'll find a mighty fortress (which charges for entry but offers the best views from its ramparts) and the adjacent Baroque monastery-turned-museum. The surrounding neighborhood (especially Piazza Fuga) has a classy "uptown" vibe compared to the gritty city-center streets below. Cheapskates can enjoy the views for free from the benches on the square in front of the monastery.

**Getting There:** From Via Toledo, the Spanish Quarter gradually climbs up San Martino's lower slopes, before steep paths take you up the rest of the way. But the easiest way to ascend San Martino is by **funicular.** Three different funicular lines with departures every 10 minutes lead from lower Naples to the hilltop: the Centrale line from near the bottom of Via Toledo; the Montesanto line from the Metro stop of the same name (near the top end of Via Toledo); and the Chiaia line from farther out, near Piazza Amadeo. All three are covered by any regular local transit ticket. Ride any of these three up to the end of the line. All lines converge within a few blocks at the top of the hill—Centrale and Chiaia wind up at opposite ends of the charming Piazza Fuga, while Montesanto terminates a bit closer to the fortress and museum.

Leaving any of the funiculars, head uphill, carefully seeking out the brown signs for *Castel S. Elmo* and *Museo di San Martino* (a few strategically placed escalators make the climb easier). Regardless of where you come up, you'll pass the Montesanto funicular station—angle left (as you face the station) past the municipal police station, and then continue following the signs. You'll reach the castle with its bronze plaque first, and then the monastery/museum (both about a 10-minute walk from Piazza Fuga).

Another convenient—if less scenic—approach is via the Metro's line 1 to the Vanvitelli stop, which is near the upper funicular terminals.

### Castel Sant'Elmo

While it's little more than an empty husk with a decent modern art museum, this 16th-century, Spanish-built, star-shaped fortress boasts commanding views over the city and the entire Bay of Naples. Buy your ticket at the booth, then ride the elevator up to the upper courtyard and climb up to the ramparts for a slow circle to enjoy the 360-degree views. In the middle of the yard is the likeable little Museo del Novecento, a gallery of works by 20th-century Neapolitan artists (covered by same ticket); the castle also hosts temporary exhibits.

**Cost and Hours:** €5, half-price after 16:15, open Wed-Mon 9:00-19:00, closed Tue, last entry one hour before closing, Via Tito Angelini 22, tel. 081-229-4401, www.polomusealecampania.beniculturali.it.

### ▲▲San Martino Carthusian Monastery and Museum (Certosa e Museo di San Martino)

The monastery, founded in 1325 and dissolved in the early 1800s, is now a sprawling museum with several parts. The square out front has city views nearly as good as the ones you'll pay to see from inside, and a few cafés angling for your business.

**Cost and Hours:** €6, Thu-Tue 8:30-19:30, closed Wed, last entry one hour before closing, some rooms (such as the Naval Museum) open at 9:30—don't arrive too early, audioguide—€5, Largo San Martino 5, tel. 081-229-4502.

**Visiting the Monastery and Museum:** After purchasing your ticket, step into the **church** across the courtyard. First built in the mid-1300s, this church (as well as the entire complex) received a makeover by master Baroque architect Cosimo Fanzago—responsible for most of the big Baroque you've already seen in the city center. To protect the inlaid marble floor, you're not allowed into the nave; instead you can enjoy this Baroque explosion with beautifully decorated **chapels** from its main entryway. (The space behind the altar is accessible later in your visit.)

A variety of museum exhibits, art, and sculpture are housed in the rest of the complex. The **Naval Museum** has nautical paintings, model boats, and giant ceremonial gondolas that were used by various royalty. In a series of rooms opposite the Naval Museum is an excellent collection of *presepi* (Nativity scenes), both life-size and miniature, including a spectacular one by Michele Cucinello—the best I've seen in this *presepi*-crazy city. Beyond the *presepi* is the larger **garden cloister,** where monks would eventually rest in peace (look for the carved skulls).

Follow *chiesa* signs to access the back of the church and the the the **sacristy.** Cherub-covered ceilings painted by Naples favorite Luca Giordano and intricate, inlaid wood cabinets compete for your attention. Return to the cloister and find the terra-cotta-tiled floor to enter a **painting gallery** (with lots of antique maps and artifacts of old Naples). Finally, step into the massive **Prior's Quarters** with its private corner terrace and privileged views of the bay. Another view terrace is just outside, but the prior had the power view.

# Sleeping in Naples

As an alternative to intense Naples, most travelers prefer to sleep in mellow Sorrento, just over an hour away (see the Sorrento chapter). But, if needed, here are a few good options. High season in Naples is spring and late fall. Prices are soft during the hot, slow summer months (July-Sept) and plunge during the pleasantly cool winters.

## ON AND AROUND VIA TOLEDO

To see the city's best face, stay in the area that stretches between the Archaeological Museum and the port.

**$$$$ Decumani Hotel de Charme** is a classy oasis tucked away on a residential lane in the very heart of the city, just off Spaccanapoli. While the street is Naples-dingy, the hotel is an inviting retreat, filling an elegant 17th-century palace with 42 rooms and a gorgeous breakfast room (air-con, elevator, Via San Giovanni Maggiore Pignatelli 15, Metro: Università; if coming from Spaccanapoli, this lane is one street toward the train station from Via Santa Chiara, tel. 081-551-8188, www.decumani.com, info@decumani.com).

**$$$ Hotel Piazza Bellini** is an artistically decorated hotel with 48 stripped-down, minimalist but comfy rooms surrounding a peaceful and inviting courtyard. Two blocks below the Archaeological Museum and just off the lively Piazza Bellini, it offers modern sanity in the city center (air-con, elevator, Via Santa Maria di Constantinopoli 101, Metro: Dante, tel. 081-451-732, www. hotelpiazzabellini.com, info@hotelpiazzabellini.com).

**$$$ Art Resort Galleria Umberto** has 17 rooms in two different buildings inside the Umberto I shopping gallery at the bottom of Via Toledo, just off Piazza del Plebiscito. This genteel-feeling place gilds the lily, with an aristocratic setting and decor but older bathrooms. Consider paying about €20 extra for a room overlooking the gallery (air-con, elevator, Galleria Umberto 83, fourth floor—ask at booth for coin to operate elevator if needed, Metro: Toledo, tel. 081-497-6224, www.artresortgalleriaumberto. com, booking@hotelgalleriaumberto.com).

**$$$ Hotel Il Convento,** with 14 small but comfortable rooms with balconies, is a good choice for those who want to sleep in the tight tangle of lanes called the Spanish Quarter—quintessential Naples. You're only a couple of short blocks off the main Via Toledo drag, and heavy-duty windows help block out some—but not all—of the scooter noise and church bells. A rare haven in this characteristic corner of town, it's in all the guidebooks (family rooms, top-floor rooms with private garden terrace, air-con, elevator; Via Speranzella 137A, Metro: Toledo—from just below Banco di Napoli entrance, walk two blocks up Vico Tre Re a Toledo; tel. 081-403-977, www.hotelilconvento.com, info@hotelilconvento.com).

**$$ Chiaja Hotel de Charme,** with the same owner as the Decumani (listed earlier), rents 33 rooms on the Via Chiaia pedestrian shopping drag near Piazza del Plebiscito. The building has a fascinating history: Part of it was the residence of a marquis, and the rest was one of Naples' most famous brothels (some view rooms, air-con, elevator, Via Chiaia 216, first floor, Metro: Toledo, tel. 081-415-555, www.hotelchiaia.it, info@hotelchiaia.it).

## AT THE TRAIN STATION

These hotels are less convenient for sightseeing and dining, and the neighborhood gets dodgy as you move away from the station. But they're handy for train travelers, practical for a quick stay, and less expensive.

**$$ Hotel Stelle** has 38 sterile, identical, newly remodeled rooms with modern furnishings. It feels sane compared to its hectic surroundings, and a back entrance leads directly into the train station (air-con, elevator, Corso Meridionale 60, exit station near track 5, tel. 081-1889-3090, www.stellehotel.com, info@stellehotel.com).

**$$ Ibis Styles Napoli Garibaldi,** with 88 rooms, offers chain predictability and a bright, youthful color scheme a three-minute walk from the station (air-con, elevator, pay parking; Via Giuseppe

Ricciardi 33, exit station onto Piazza Garibaldi, then take second left onto Via G. Ricciardi; tel. 081-690-8111, www.ibis.com, h3243@accor.com).

**$ Grand Hotel Europa,** across the seedy street right next to the station, has 89 decent rooms and hallways whimsically decorated with not-quite-right reproductions of famous paintings. The hotel is a decent value, and its 1970s-era vibe (including the Kool-Aid and canned fruit at breakfast) makes for fun memories (RS%, family rooms, air-con, elevator, restaurant, Corso Meridionale 14, across street from station's north exit near track 5, tel. 081-267-511, www.grandhoteleuropa.com, info@grandhoteleuropa.com).

# Eating in Naples

## FANTASTIC, FAMOUS PIZZA

Naples is the birthplace of pizza. Its pizzerias bake just the right combination of fresh dough (soft and chewy, as opposed to Roman-

style, which is thin and crispy), mozzarella, and tomatoes in traditional wood-burning ovens. You can head for the famous, venerable places, but these can have long lines stretching out the door, and half-hour waits for a table. If you want to skip the hassle, just ask your hotel for directions to the neighborhood pizzeria. An average one-person pie (usually the only size available) costs €6-9; most places offer both takeout and eat-in, and pizza is often the only thing on the menu.

### Near the Station

These two pizzerias—the most famous—are both a few long blocks from the train station, and near the end of my self-guided Naples Walk.

**$ Antica Pizzeria da Michele** is for pizza purists. Filled with locals (and tourists), it serves just two varieties: *margherita* (tomato sauce and mozzarella) and *marinara* (tomato sauce, oregano, and garlic, no cheese). Come early to sit and watch the pizza artists in action. A pizza with beer costs around €8. As this place is often jammed with a long line, arrive early or late to get a seat. If there's a mob, head inside to get a number. If it's just too crowded to wait, the less-exceptional Pizzeria Trianon (described next) often has room (Mon-Sat 10:30-24:00, closed Sun; look for the vertical red *Antica Pizzeria* sign at the intersection of Via Pietro Colletta and Via Cesare Sersale at #1; tel. 081-553-9204).

**$ Pizzeria Trianon da Ciro,** across the street and left a few doors, has been da Michele's archrival since 1923. It offers more choices, higher prices, air-conditioning, and a cozier atmosphere. For less chaos, head upstairs. While waiting for your meal, you can survey the transformation of a humble wad of dough into a smoldering, bubbly feast in their entryway pizza kitchen (daily 11:00-15:30 & 19:00-23:00, Via Pietro Colletta 42, tel. 081-553-9426).

## On and near Via dei Tribunali

This street, which runs a couple of blocks north of Spaccanapoli, is legendary for its pizzerias and fun eateries. It's packed with hungry strollers and long lines marking the most popular places.

**$ Gino Sorbillo** is a local favorite and is on all the "best pizza in Naples" lists...as you'll learn the hard way if you show up at peak mealtimes, when huge mobs crowd outside the front door waiting for a table (Mon-Sat 12:00-15:30 & 19:00-24:00, closed Sun, Via dei Tribunali 32, tel. 081-446-643). Relatives run similarly named places on the same street at #35 (a good option for its specialty: fried pizza) and #37.

**$ Pizzeria di Matteo** is popular for its fried takeout treats. People waiting out front line up at the little window to snack on deep-fried goodies—*arancini* (with rice, gooey cheese, peas, and sausage), *melanzane* (eggplant), *frittatine* (balls of mac and cheese plus sausage), and *crocché* (croquettes)—for €1 apiece or less (sometimes closed Sun, Via dei Tribunali 94, tel. 081-455-262).

**$ La Figlia del Presidente** sits a block and a half south of the two legendary joints listed above and is quickly establishing its own loyal clientele. Push your way through the locals gathered around the door to get a number, then patiently wait for a slice of heaven. With abundant and innovative toppings, this small pizzeria updates the Neapolitan classics (Tue-Sat 12:00-15:30 & 19:00-23:30, Mon 12:00-15:30, closed Sun, Via Grande Archivio 24, tel. 081-286-738).

## Near the Archaeological Museum

If you've had enough of crowds at the museum, head a few blocks north for world-class pizza without the throngs of people.

**$ Pizzeria Starita** has been in business for over 100 years, first as a cantina (featured in a Sophia Loren flick) then offering pizza since the 1950s. The fourth generation currently runs this bustling, friendly eatery just off the normal tourist circuit. Neapolitans think less is more with regard to pizza, but Starita offers both modern and traditional toppings (Tue-Sun 12:00-15:30 & 19:00 until late, closed Mon, no reservations—just show up and add your name to the wait list, from the museum walk 10 minutes up Via Santa Teresa degli Scalzi to the intersection with Via Materdei—the pizzeria is a few steps down on the left at #27, Metro: Museo, tel. 081-557-3682).

## RESTAURANTS

If you want a full meal rather than a pizza, consider these options.

### Between Spaccanapoli and Via Toledo

**$$$ Ecomesarà** serves up quality Neapolitan and *meridionale* (southern Italian) dishes, abiding by the Slow Food ethic, in a modern setting just below the Santa Chiara cloister, a long block south of Spaccanapoli. The atmosphere is mellow, modern, and international. Cristiano and his staff are happy to explain the menu (Tue-Sun 13:00-15:00 & 20:00-23:30, closed Mon, Via Santa Chiara 49, tel. 081-1925-9353).

**$$ Tandem Ragù Restaurant,** tiny with a few charming tables inside and out, features a fun menu specializing in Neapolitan *ragù* (beef, pork, or vegetarian options). The *scarpetta* (little shoe) dishes are simply various *ragùs* with baskets of bread for dunking (daily from 12:30 and 19:00, Via Giovanni Paladino 51, 50 yards off Spaccanapoli, below the statue of the Nile, tel. 081-1900-2468).

**$$ Taverna a Santa Chiara** is your classic little eatery buried deep in the old center of Naples. It's convivial, warmly run, and simple. Just 100 yards from the tourist commotion of Spaccanapoli, it provides a fun and easygoing break (daily from 13:00 and 20:00, closed Sun at dinner, Via Santa Chiara 6, tel. 081-048-4908).

**$$ Trattoria Campagnola** is a classic family place with a daily home cooking-style chalkboard menu on the back wall, mama busy cooking in the back, and wine on tap. Here you can venture away from pastas, be experimental with a series of local dishes, and not go wrong (daily 12:30-16:00 & 19:30-23:00, opposite the famous pizzerias at Via Tribunali 47, tel. 081-459-034 but no reservations).

**$$ Osteria il Garum** is great if you'd like to eat on a classic Neapolitan square. It's named for the ancient fish sauce that was widely used in Roman cooking. These days, mild-mannered Luigi and his staff inject their pricey local cuisine with centuries of tradition, served in a cozy split-level cellar or outside on a covered terrace facing a neighborhood church. It's just between Via Toledo and Spaccanapoli, a short walk from the Church of Gesù Nuovo (daily 12:00-15:30 & 19:00-23:30, Piazza Monteoliveto 2A, tel. 081-542-3228).

**$$ Trattoria da Nennella** is fun-loving chaos buried in the Spanish Quarter, with red-shirted waiters barking orders, a small festival anytime someone puts a tip in the bucket, and the fruit course served in plastic bidets. There's one price—€15 per person—and you choose three courses plus a fruit. House wine and water is served in tiny plastic cups, the crowd is ready for fun, and the food's

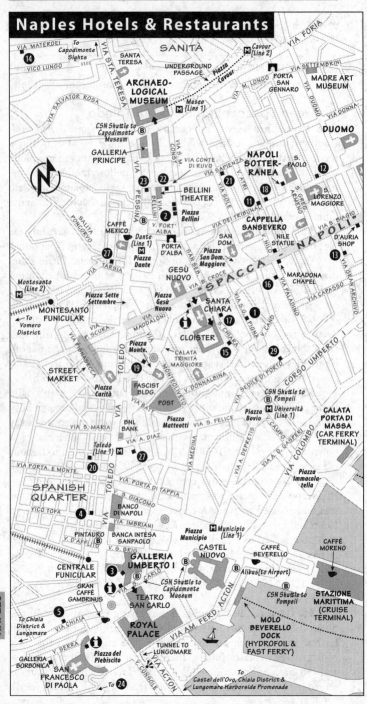

# Naples Hotels & Restaurants

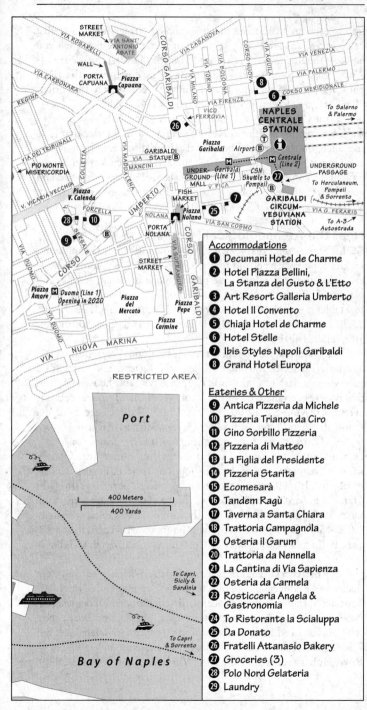

**Accommodations**

1. Decumani Hotel de Charme
2. Hotel Piazza Bellini, La Stanza del Gusto & L'Etto
3. Art Resort Galleria Umberto
4. Hotel Il Convento
5. Chiaja Hotel de Charme
6. Hotel Stelle
7. Ibis Styles Napoli Garibaldi
8. Grand Hotel Europa

**Eateries & Other**

9. Antica Pizzeria da Michele
10. Pizzeria Trianon da Ciro
11. Gino Sorbillo Pizzeria
12. Pizzeria di Matteo
13. La Figlia del Presidente
14. Pizzeria Starita
15. Ecomesarà
16. Tandem Ragù
17. Taverna a Santa Chiara
18. Trattoria Campagnola
19. Osteria il Garum
20. Trattoria da Nennella
21. La Cantina di Via Sapienza
22. Osteria da Carmela
23. Rosticceria Angela & Gastronomia
24. To Ristorante la Scialuppa
25. Da Donato
26. Fratelli Attanasio Bakery
27. Groceries (3)
28. Polo Nord Gelateria
29. Laundry

NAPLES

good. You can sit indoors or on a cobbled terrace under a trellis. No reservations are taken, so put your name on the list when you arrive—the line moves pretty fast (Mon-Sat 12:00-15:00 & 19:00-23:00, closed Sun, leave Via Toledo a block down from the BNL bank and walk up Vico del Teatro Nuovo three blocks to the corner, Vico Lungo del Teatro Nuovo 103, tel. 081-414-338).

$ **La Cantina di Via Sapienza** is a lunch-only hole-in-the-wall, serving up traditional Neapolitan fare in an interior that feels like a neighborhood joint (but has also been discovered by tourists). It's a block north of the congested, pizzeria-packed Via dei Tribunali, and a good alternative if those places are just too crowded and your heart isn't set on pizza (Mon-Sat for lunch only, closed Sun, Via Sapienza 40, tel. 081-459-078).

## Near the Archaeological Museum

$$ **La Stanza del Gusto,** two blocks downhill from the museum, tackles food creatively and injects crusty Naples with a little modern color and irreverence. The ground floor is casual, trendy, and playful, while the upstairs is more refined yet still polka-dotted. A few tables are on the sidewalk (weekday lunch specials, daily 12:00-23:30 except Sun until 17:30, Via Santa Maria di Constantinopoli 100, tel. 081-401-578).

$$ **Osteria da Carmela** serves up traditional Neapolitan classics only mama could make—like *ragù, polpetti,* and tasty fried fish—with a dash of Old World charm. Affordable house wine and fine cheeses complete the meal. Tables are limited, so reservations are smart (Mon-Sat 12:00-15:00 & 19:00-24:00, closed Sun, Via Conte di Ruvo 11, tel. 081-549-9738, www.osteriadacarmela.it).

$ **L'Etto** is fast, fun, and cheap, with tasty dishes constantly coming out of the kitchen to fill an inviting buffet line. Choose from 20 vegetable, meat, and fish options (perfect for vegetarians or vegans). It's self-serve—weigh and pay €2.50 per 100 grams (100 grams is an *etto,* hence the name). Bread and water are free at the table. It's bright, mod, and friendly with outdoor tables, too (daily 12:30-15:30 & 19:30-22:30, longer hours on weekends, facing Piazza Bellini at Via S. Maria di Costantinopoli 102, tel. 081-1932-0967).

$ **Rosticceria Angela** is a *tavola calda* with hot ready-to-eat dishes and a coffee bar, run by a team of older gentlemen. Pricing is honest and there's simple, peaceful, air-conditioned indoor seating. Next door is **Gastronomia,** a tiny meat, cheese, and bread shop with all you need for a cheap meal to go (*rosticceria* open Mon-Sat 7:30-21:00, closed Sun, 3 blocks below museum at Via Conte di Ruvo 21, between Via Pessina and Via Bellini, tel. 081-033-2928).

## A Romantic Splurge on the Harbor

**$$$ Ristorante la Scialuppa** ("The Rowboat") is a great bet for a fine local meal on the harbor. Located in the romantic Santa Lucia district, you'll walk across the causeway to the Castel dell'Ovo in the fisherman's quarter (the castle on the island) just off Via Partenope. They boast fine indoor and outdoor seating, attentive waitstaff, a wonderful assortment of *antipasti*, great seafood, and predictably high prices. Reservations are smart (Tue-Sun 12:30-15:00 & 19:30-24:00, closed Mon, Piazzetta Marinari 5, tel. 081-764-5333, www.ristorantelascialuppa.net).

## Near the Station

**$$ Da Donato,** an excellent, traditional, family-run trattoria on a glum street near the station, serves delicious food in an unpretentious atmosphere. The best approach is for two people to share the astonishing *antipasti* sampler—*degustazione "fantasia" della Casa Terra e Mare*—for €25. You'll get more than a dozen small portions, each more delicious than the last. A version without seafood is €15 (Tue-Sun 12:30-14:30 & 19:30-22:00, closed Mon, two blocks from Piazza Garibaldi—turn down Via Silvio Spaventa to #39, tel. 081-287-828).

## PASTRY

To get the full overview of Neapolitan pastries at good prices, visit the bakery outlet of **Fratelli Attanasio** on a small alley near the train station—with your back to the station building, it's off the far-right corner of the big square. Come early for the best selection (Tue-Sun 6:30-19:30, closed Mon, Vico Ferrovia 1, tel. 081-285-675).

## PICNICS

A good supermarket for picnic supplies is **Sapori & Dintorni,** in the train-station complex (Mon-Sat 8:00-20:30, Sun 8:00-15:00, enter from outside, right of bookstore). By Piazza Dante is a small **Superò** that's convenient to hotels near this stretch of Via Toledo (Mon-Sat 8:30-20:30, Sun 8:30-14:00, at corner of Via Tarsia and Vico San Domenico Soriano). By the Toledo Metro stop a small **Conad** is handy to hotels near Galleria Umberto I and the Spanish Quarter (daily 8:00-21:00, Via Roberto Bracco 4).

# Getting Around the Region

To connect Naples, Sorrento, and the Amalfi Coast, you can travel by train, bus, and taxi, but consider taking a boat—it's faster, cooler, and more scenic, and you can take coastline photos that you can't get from land. For specifics, check the "Connections" sections of each chapter. Confirm times and prices locally.

**By Bus:** CitySightseeing's fleet of bright red buses with audio commentary offer easy trips from Naples to Pompeii (see page 1018), along the popular Amalfi Coast (see page 1084), and even up to the town of Ravello (see page 1110). Crowded SITA buses also traverse the Amalfi Coast; see page 1083.

**By Train:** The dingy, crowded **Circumvesuviana** commuter train—popular with locals, tourists, and pickpockets—links Naples, Herculaneum, Pompeii, and Sorrento. The most important Circumvesuviana station in Naples (called "Garibaldi") is underneath Naples' Centrale Station. To find it, follow the signs downstairs to *Statione Garibaldi* and then *Circumvesuviana* signs down the corridor to the Circumvesuviana ticket windows and turnstiles (stand in line or get your ticket at a newsstand). Buy your ticket, confirm time and track, insert your ticket at the turnstiles, and head down another level to the platforms.

The Circumvesuviana is covered by the Campania ArteCard (see page 958), but not by rail passes. If you're heading to Pompeii or Herculaneum, take any Circumvesuviana train marked *Sorrento*—they all stop at both (usually depart from platform 3). Sorrento-bound trains depart twice hourly, and take about 15 minutes to reach Ercolano Scavi (for the Herculaneum ruins, €2.20 one-way), 35 minutes to reach Pompei Scavi-Villa dei Misteri (for the Pompeii ruins, €2.90 one-way), and 60 minutes to reach Sorrento, the end of the line (€3.60 one-way). Express trains to Sorrento marked *DD* (6/day) reach Sorrento 15 minutes sooner (and also stop at Herculaneum and Pompeii). You may save a little with a "TIC" ticket, which covers the Circumvesuviana plus public transport to and from the train station in Naples (for example, Pompeii to Napoli Centrale, then by Metro to your hotel). For schedules, see the Italian-only website www.eavsrl.it.

On the platform, double-check with a local that the train goes to Sorrento (avoid lines that branch out to other destinations). When returning to Naples on the Circumvesuviana, validate your ticket before boarding and get off at the next-to-the-last station, Garibaldi (Centrale Station is just up the escalator). For more tips about riding the Circumvesuviana, see page 963.

Pricier **Campania Express trains,** operated by Circumvesuviana, use the same tracks and stops. They run only four times a day, but staff check tickets as you enter, so trains are much less crowded—and they have air-conditioning (€4 one-way to Herculaneum, 10 minutes; €6 one-way to Pompeii, 30 minutes; €8 one-way to Sorrento, 1 hour; mid-March-Oct only, not covered by Campania ArteCard or TIC ticket, online sales at http://ots.eavsrl.it or buy at the station).

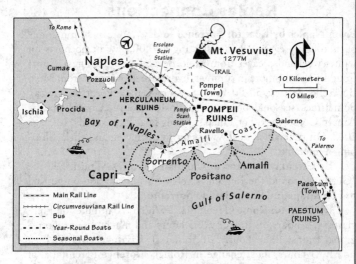

The **national rail network** is useful only if you need to get to Salerno (for boats and buses to Amalfi) or Paestum—direct trains run to both from Naples.

**By Taxi:** For €110, you can take a 30-mile taxi ride from Naples directly to your Sorrento hotel (ask the driver for the non-metered *tariffa predeterminata*). You can hire a cab on Capri for about €70/hour. Taxis on the Amalfi Coast are generally expensive, and more than willing to overcharge you, but they can be convenient, especially with a larger group. See "Getting Around the Amalfi Coast—By Taxi" on page 1085.

**By Boat:** Major companies include Caremar (www.caremar. it), SNAV (www.snav.it), Gescab (a.k.a. NLG Jet, www.gescab. it), Navigazione Libera del Golfo (www.navlib.it), Alilauro (www. alilauro.it), Travelmar (www.travelmar.it), and Alicost (www. alicost.it). Each company has different destinations and prices; some compete for the same trips. Some lines (like Sorrento-Capri) run all year; others (on the Amalfi Coast, for example) only in summer. Trips can be cancelled in bad weather. Faster watercraft cost a little more than slow car ferries. A hydrofoil, sometimes called a "jet boat," skims between Naples and Sorrento—it's swifter, safer from pickpockets, more scenic, and more expensive than the Circumvesuviana train.

For schedules, check online (www.capritourism.com; click "Shipping Timetable"), or ask at any TI or at Naples' Molo Beverello boat dock. (The handy departure board on the rooftop of the Molo Beverello terminal shows all the upcoming departures.) Most boats charge €2 or so for luggage. When you arrive, note the return times—the last boat usually leaves before 19:00. The preset price for a taxi between Naples' Centrale train station and its port (Molo Beverello) is €11, or you can take Metro line 1 to the Municipio stop and walk to the port.

# Naples Connections

**From Naples by Boat to: Sorrento** (6/day, more in summer, departs roughly every 2 hours starting at 9:00, few or no boats on winter weekends, leaves from Molo Beverello, 40 minutes), **Capri** (roughly hourly, more in summer, hydrofoil: 45 minutes from Molo Beverello; ferries: 50-80 minutes from Calata Porta di Massa). Sometimes seasonal boats go to **Positano** and **Amalfi,** on the Amalfi Coast—ask. For a map showing boat connections, see page 1043. For timetables, visit www.capritourism.com and click "Shipping Timetable."

**By Circumvesuviana or Campania Express Train:** See the "Getting Around the Region" sidebar for information on getting to **Herculaneum, Pompeii,** and **Sorrento.**

**By Train to: Rome** (Trenitalia: 1-5/hour, 70 minutes on Frecciarossa, 2 hours on Intercity, 2.5 hours and much cheaper on regional trains; Italo: hourly, 70 minutes), **Civitavecchia** (at least hourly, 3 hours, most change in Rome), **Florence** (Trenitalia: at least hourly, 3 hours, most change in Pisa or Rome; Italo: hourly, 3 hours), **Salerno** (Trenitalia: at least hourly, 35-45 minutes, change in Salerno for bus or boat to Amalfi; *"regionale"* trains are cheaper but Intercity and Freccia express trains have a first class section for a little extra; avoid slower "Metropolitana" trains that leave from the same platforms as Metro's line 2; Italo: 4/day, 45 minutes), **Paestum** (12/day, 1 hour, direction: Sapri or Reggio), **Brindisi** (4/day, 5-6 hours, change in Caserta; from Brindisi, ferries sail to Greece), **Milan** (Trenitalia: 2/hour, 4-5 hours; Italo: 11/day, 4-5 hours), **Venice** (Trenitalia: almost hourly, 5.5 hours, some change in Bologna or Rome; Italo: 3/day, 5.5 hours, reservations required), **Palermo** (2/day direct, 9.5 hours, also an overnight train). Any train listed on the schedule as leaving Napoli PG or Napoli-Garibaldi departs not from Napoli Centrale, but from the adjacent Garibaldi Station.

# POMPEII & NEARBY

*Pompeii • Herculaneum • Vesuvius*

Stopped in their tracks by the eruption of Mount Vesuvius in AD 79, Pompeii and Herculaneum offer the best look anywhere at what life in Rome must have been like around 2,000 years ago. These two cities of well-preserved ruins are yours to explore. Of the two sites, Pompeii is grander, while Herculaneum is smaller, more intimate, and more intact. Pompeii is easily reached from Naples on the CitySightseeing bus or the Circumvesuviana commuter (or Campania Express) train; Herculaneum is best reached by train. Vesuvius, still smoldering ominously, rises up on the horizon. It last erupted in 1944, and is still an active volcano. Buses from the train stations at Herculaneum or Pompeii drop you a half-hour hike below its crater rim.

# Pompeii

A once-thriving commercial port of 20,000, Pompeii (worth ▲▲▲) grew from Greek and Etruscan roots to become an important Roman city. Then, on August 24, AD 79, everything changed. Vesuvius erupted and began to bury the city under 30 feet of hot volcanic ash. For the archaeologists who excavated it centuries later, this was a shake-and-bake

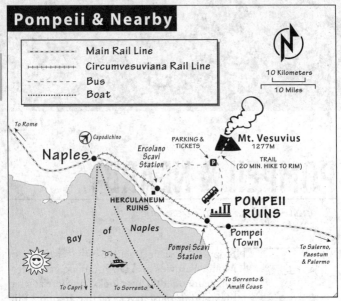

windfall, teaching them volumes about daily Roman life. Pompeii was accidentally rediscovered in 1599; excavations began in 1748.

## GETTING TO POMPEII

**By Train or Train-and-Bus Combo from Rome:** It's possible to day-trip to Pompeii from Rome, if you start early and plan on a long day. For tips, see the "Planning Your Time" section in the Naples chapter.

**By Shuttle Bus from Naples:** CitySightseeing Italy offers a convenient, clean, and stress-free shuttle bus from Naples to Pompeii. The bus also allows you to experience Naples' insane traffic without actually having to drive in it (a spectacle almost worth ▲). Three pick-up points are handy to all my recommended Naples hotels: the Molo Beverello boat dock, Piazza Bovio near the Università Metro stop, and Centrale Station (stop located across the street and left when exiting, near the Hotel D'Anna).

Tickets can be purchased online, but be aware that each bus has a specific return time about four hours after arrival; no return-trip changes are allowed. Early morning departures beat the heat at Pompeii, but traffic congestion can delay your arrival and cut into your sightseeing time. Departures from Centrale Station in summer are at 9:30, 10:15, and 11:15, with corresponding return trips at 13:20, 14:40, and 16:00; fewer departures off-season; 30-minute ride from the train station if traffic is light (€8 one-way, €15 round-trip, tel. 081-551-7279, www.city-sightseeing.it). Skip the option to purchase your Pompeii entrance ticket through CitySightseeing—you'll pay more than buying it yourself online (details later).

**By Train from Naples or Sorrento:** Pompeii is roughly midway between Naples and Sorrento on the crowded, run-down **Circumvesuviana commuter train** line (2/hour, 35 minutes from Naples, 30 minutes from Sorrento, either trip costs €2.90 one-way, not covered by rail passes, no air-con, Italian-only website: www.eavsrl.it). Get off at the Pompei Scavi-Villa dei Misteri stop; from Naples, it's the stop after Villa Regina. DD express trains (6/day) bypass several stations but do stop at Pompei Scavi, shaving 10 minutes off the trip from Naples. Less-frequent **Campania Express trains** use the same tracks and stops, but are less crowded and have air-conditioning (4/day, 30 minutes from Naples, 25 minutes from Sorrento, either trip costs €6 one-way, mid-March-Oct only, http://ots.eavsrl.it). For train details, see page 1014.

From the Pompei Scavi train station, it's just a two-minute walk to the Porta Marina entrance: Leaving the station, turn right and walk down the road about a block to the entrance (on your left).

*Pompei vs. Pompei Scavi:* Make sure you're taking the Circumvesuviana commuter train or Campania Express to Pompei Scavi (*scavi* means "excavations"), the station right next to the ancient site. Pompei is the name of a separate train station on the main national rail line that's a long, dull walk from the ruins. It serves the ugly modern city of Pompei (always with one "i"). When coming from Rome, it's better to transfer at Naples' Centrale Station to the CitySightseeing shuttle bus or the Circumvesuviana/Campania Express for Pompei Scavi than to take the national rail straight to the Pompei city station and walk from there.

**By Car:** Parking is available at Camping Zeus, next to the Pompei Scavi train station (€2.50/hour, €10/12 hours); several other campgrounds/parking lots are nearby.

## ORIENTATION TO POMPEII

**Cost:** €15, includes special exhibits. If you plan to eat or sightsee outside of the archaeological site, ask for an entrance/exit bracelet that allows you to reenter the site up to three times on the same day. Consider the Campania ArteCard (see page 958) if visiting other sights in the region.

**Hours:** Mon-Fri 9:00-19:30, Sat-Sun 8:30-19:30, Nov-March daily until 17:00, last entry 1.5 hours before closing.

**Free Entry:** Pompeii is free to enter (and very crowded) once or twice a month; the specific day varies in peak season (in low season, it's the first Sun). Up to 15,000 visitors are allowed on free days—it's packed. I'd avoid Pompeii on those days. Free days in peak season are listed on the Italian "Orari e tariffe"

POMPEII & NEARBY

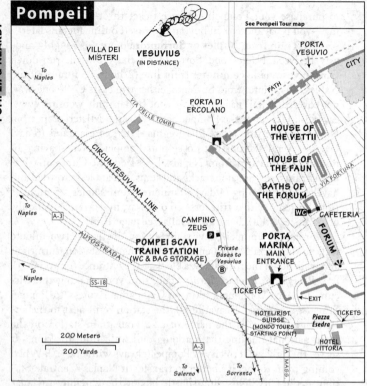

page of the Pompeii website; use Google Translate or email pompei.info@beniculturali.it.

**Information:** Tel. 081-857-5347, general info at www.pompeiisites. org, tickets at www.ticketone.it.

**Crowd-Beating Tips:** To skip ahead of everyone, purchase your ticket online at www.ticketone.it (€2 surcharge). If you're buying onsite and there's a very long ticket line at the Porta Marina entrance, continue walking three minutes to the ticket booth near Hotel Vittoria (rarely a line). Buy your ticket, return to Porta Marina, and walk right in.

**Closures:** Some buildings and streets are bound to be closed for restoration when you visit. Make a point to use your map and numbers to find your way. Street names and building numbers are very clearly marked throughout the site.

**Visitor Information:** Admission includes a wonderful English guidebooklet and map (be sure to get and use this). Ask for it when you buy your ticket, or check at the info window to the left of the WCs—the maps aren't available within the walls of Pompeii. The bookshop sells a couple of books with plastic overlays that allow you to re-create Pompeii from the ruins

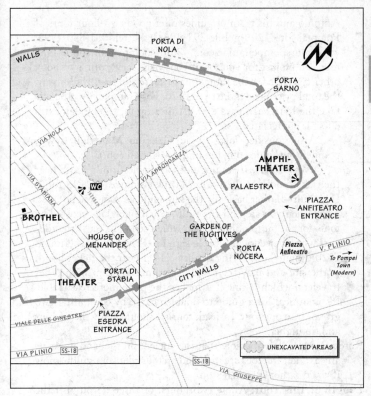

(€16; if you buy from a street vendor, pay no more than that). Another good book is the €6 *Pompeii (Brief) Guide,* with excellent photos and additional walking routes.

Ignore the "info point" kiosk at the train station, which is a private agency selling tours.

**Tours:** Here are several ways to enjoy an organized and educational visit to Pompeii.

Simply follow the **self-guided** tour in this chapter (or, better, enjoy the audio version with my free 🎧 Rick Steves Audio Europe app). Both cover the basics and provide a good framework for exploring the site on your own. Combined with the fine booklet and map included with your entry fee, these provide plenty of information for do-it-yourselfers.

Join a **Mondo Guide shared tour** for Rick Steves readers. This is your best budget bet for a tour with an actual guide (€15, doesn't include €15 Pompeii entry, daily at 11:00, reservations required; meet at Hotel/Ristorante Suisse, just down the hill from the Porta Marina entrance; for details, see page 970).

Hire guide **Antonio Somma** for a private or shared tour.

Antonio and his team of guides offer good two-hour tours of Pompeii for €120 (mobile 393-406-3824, tel. 081-850-1992, www.tourspompeiiguide.com, info@pompeitour.com). The tour can be just for you, or, if you wish, they can try to book other travelers for the same tour to share the cost. Either way, the total price is no more than €120. For example, if six people take the tour, each pays €20. (A nice tip for the guide's extra effort is appreciated.)

Also consider local guide **Gaetano Manfredi** (www. pompeiitourguide.com, gmguide63@gmail.com).

*Other Options:* Audioguides available from a kiosk near the ticket booth at the Porta Marina entrance (€8, €13 for 2, ID required) offer basically the same info as your free booklet.

When you step off the train, you'll likely be accosted by touts for the "info point" kiosk, which sells €15 tours that depart whenever enough people sign up. Private guides (around €120/2 hours) of varying quality cluster near the ticket booth at the site and may try to herd you into a group with other travelers, which is fine if it makes the price more reasonable. It's unethical for a guide to double charge by combining two groups into one tour. Instead, tourists should enjoy the savings and tip higher.

**Rated Risqué:** Parents, note that the ancient brothel and its sexually explicit frescoes are included on tours; let your guide know if you'd rather skip that stop.

**Length of This Tour:** Allow two hours, or three if you visit the theater and amphitheater. With less time, focus on the Forum, Baths of the Forum, House of the Vettii, House of the Faun, and brothel.

**Baggage Check:** Use the free baggage check near the turnstiles at the site entrance (just yards from the station). The train station also offers pay luggage storage (downstairs, by the WC).

**Services:** There's a pay WC at the train station. The Pompeii site has three WCs—one near the entrance, one in the cafeteria, and another near the end of this tour, uphill from the theaters.

**Eating:** These **$** eateries offer reasonably priced meals (though your cheapest bet may be to bring your own food for a discreet picnic). The **Ciao cafeteria,** within the site, serves good sandwiches, pizza, and pasta. You're welcome to picnic here if you buy a drink. **Bar Sgambati,** the café/restaurant at the train station, has air-conditioning, Wi-Fi, sandwiches to go, and pastas and pizzas. **Marius Juice Shop** (run by local guide Antonio Somma's family) sells sandwiches to go, and is located between Bar Sgambati and the Porta Marina entrance. A second cluster of eateries around the ticket booth near Hotel Vittoria dishes out handy slices of pizza, salads, and pasta.

**Starring:** Roofless (collapsed) but otherwise intact Roman buildings, plaster casts of hapless victims, some erotic frescoes, and the dawning realization that these ancient people were not that different from us.

## BACKGROUND

Pompeii, founded in 600 BC, eventually became a booming Roman trading city. Not rich, not poor, it was middle class—a perfect ex-

ample of typical Roman life. Most streets would have been lined with stalls and jammed with customers from sunup to sundown. Chariots vied with shoppers for street space. Two thousand years ago, Rome controlled the entire Mediterranean—making it a kind of free-trade zone—and Pompeii was a central and bustling port.

There were no posh neighborhoods in Pompeii. Rich and poor mixed it up as elegant houses existed side by side with simple homes. While nearby Herculaneum would have been a classier place to live (traffic-free streets, fancier houses, far better drainage), Pompeii was the place for action and shopping. It served an estimated 20,000 residents with more than 40 bakeries, 130 bars, restaurants and hotels, and 30 brothels. With most of its buildings covered by brilliant white ground-marble stucco, Pompeii in AD 79 was an impressive town.

As you tour Pompeii, remember that its best art is safeguarded in the Archaeological Museum in Naples (described in the Naples chapter). Visiting the museum before or after going to Pompeii will help put this fascinating sight into context.

## ⊙ SELF-GUIDED TOUR

• *Just past the ticket-taker, start your approach up to the...*

### ❶ Porta Marina

The city of Pompeii was born on the hill ahead of you. This was the original town gate. Before Vesuvius blew and filled in the harbor, the sea came nearly to here. Notice the two openings in the gate (ahead, up the ramp). Both

were left open by day to admit major traffic. At night, the larger one was closed for better security.

• *Pass through the Porta Marina and continue up to the top of the street, pausing at the three large stepping-stones in the middle.*

## ❷ Pompeii's Streets

Every day, Pompeiians flooded the streets with gushing water to clean them. These stepping-stones let pedestrians cross with-

out getting their sandals wet. Chariots traveling in either direction could straddle the stones (all had standard-size axles). A single stepping-stone in a road means it was a one-way street, a pair indicates an ordinary two-way, and three (like this) signifies a major thoroughfare. The basalt stones are the original Roman pavement. The sidewalks (elevated to hide the plumbing—you'll see ancient plumbing revealed throughout the site) were paved with bits of broken pots (an ancient form of recycling) and studded with reflective bits of white marble. These "cats' eyes" helped people get around after dark, either by moonlight or with the help of lamps.

• *Continue straight ahead, don your mental toga, and enter the city as the Romans once did. The road opens up into the spacious main square: the Forum. Stand at the right end of this rectangular space and look toward Mount Vesuvius.*

## ❸ The Forum (Foro)

Pompeii's commercial, religious, and political center stands at the intersection of the city's two main streets. While it's the most ru-

ined part of Pompeii, it's grand nonetheless. Picture the piazza surrounded by two-story buildings on all sides. The pedestals that line the square once held statues of VIPs and various gods (now safely displayed in the museum in Naples). In Pompeii's heyday, its citizens gathered here in the main square to shop, talk

politics, and socialize. Business took place in the important buildings that lined the piazza.

The Forum was dominated by the **Temple of Jupiter,** at the far end (marked by a half-dozen ruined columns atop a stair-step base).

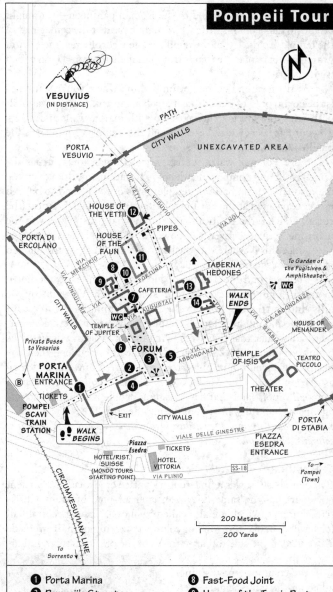

# Pompeii Tour

VESUVIUS (IN DISTANCE)

PATH

CITY WALLS

UNEXCAVATED AREA

PORTA VESUVIO

VIA VETTI

VIA VESUVIO

VIA NOLA

HOUSE OF THE VETTII ⑫

PIPES

PORTA DI ERCOLANO

HOUSE OF THE FAUN

⑪

To Garden of the Fugitives & Amphitheater

VIA MERCURIO

VIA FORTUNA

TABERNA HEDONES

WC

VIA CONSOLARE

CITY WALLS

⑧

⑩

⑬

VIA

⑨

CAFETERIA

VIA NOLA

WALK ENDS

VIA ABBONDANZA

⑦

VIA AUGUSTALI

⑭

VIA TEATRI

VIA STABIANA

HOUSE OF MENANDER

WC

TEMPLE OF JUPITER

⑥ FORUM

VIA ABBONDANZA

TEMPLE OF ISIS

TEATRO PICCOLO

Private Buses to Vesuvius

⑫

⑤

THEATER

PORTA MARINA ENTRANCE

①

②

③

⑤

B

④

TICKETS

POMPEI SCAVI TRAIN STATION

WALK BEGINS

EXIT

CITY WALLS

PORTA DI STABIA

Viale delle Ginestre

Piazza Esedra

TICKETS

PIAZZA ESEDRA ENTRANCE

HOTEL/RIST. SUISSE (MONDO TOURS STARTING POINT)

HOTEL VITTORIA

SS-18

To Pompei (Town)

VIA PLINIO

CIRCUMVESUVIANA LINE

To Sorrento

200 Meters

200 Yards

| ❶ Porta Marina | ❽ Fast-Food Joint |
|---|---|
| ❷ Pompeii's Streets | ❾ House of the Tragic Poet |
| ❸ Forum | ❿ Aqueduct Arch |
| ❹ Basilica | ⓫ House of the Faun |
| ❺ Via Abbondanza | ⓬ House of the Vettii |
| ❻ Forum Granary; Plaster Casts of Victims | ⓭ Bakery & Mill |
| ❼ Baths of the Forum | ⓮ Brothel |

Jupiter was the supreme god of the Roman pantheon—you might be able to make out his little white marble head at the center-rear of the temple. To the left of the temple is a fenced-off area, the **Forum granary,** where many artifacts from Pompeii are stored (and which we'll visit later).

At the near end of the Forum (behind where you're standing) is the **curia,** or City Hall. Like many Roman buildings, it was built with brick and mortar, then covered with marble walls and floors. To your left (as you face Vesuvius and the Temple of Jupiter) is the **basilica,** or courthouse.

Since Pompeii was a pretty typical Roman town, it has the same layout and components that you'll find in any Roman city—main square, curia, basilica, temples, axis of roads, and so on. All power converged at the Forum: religious (the temple), political (the curia), judicial (the basilica), and commercial (this piazza was the main marketplace). Even the power of the people was expressed here, since this is where they gathered to vote. Imagine the hubbub of this town square in its heyday.

Look beyond the Temple of Jupiter. Five miles to the north looms the ominous backstory to this site: **Mount Vesuvius.** Mentally draw a triangle up from the two remaining peaks to reconstruct the mountain before the eruption. When it blew, Pompeiians had no idea that they were living under a volcano, as Vesuvius hadn't erupted for 1,200 years. Imagine the wonder—then the horror—as a column of pulverized rock roared upward, and then ash began to fall. The weight of the ash and small rocks collapsed Pompeii's roofs later that day, crushing people who had taken refuge inside buildings instead of fleeing the city.

• *As you face Vesuvius, the basilica is to your left, lined with stumps of columns. Step inside.*

## ❹ Basilica

Pompeii's basilica was a first-century palace of justice. This ancient law court has the same floor plan later adopted by many Christian churches (which are also called basilicas). The big central hall (or nave) is flanked by rows of columns marking off narrower side aisles. Along the side walls are traces of the original stucco imitating marble.

The columns—now stumps all about the same height—were not ruined by the volcano. Rather, they were left unfinished when Vesuvius blew. Pompeii had been devastated by an earthquake in AD 62, and was just in the process of rebuilding the basilica when Vesuvius erupted, 17 years later. The half-built columns show off the technology of the day. Uniform bricks were stacked around a cylindrical core. Once finished, they would have been coated with marble-dust stucco to simulate marble columns—an economical construction method found throughout Pompeii (and the Roman Empire).

Besides the earthquake and the eruption, Pompeii's buildings have suffered other ravages over the years, including Spanish plunderers (c. 1800), 19th-century souvenir hunters, WWII bombs, creeping and destructive vegetation, another earthquake in 1980, and modern neglect. The fact that the entire city was covered by the eruption of AD 79 actually helped preserve it, saving it from the sixth-century barbarians who plundered many other towns into oblivion.

• *Exit the basilica and cross the short side of the square to where the city's main street hits the Forum. Stop at the three white stones that stick up from the cobbles.*

### ❺ Via Abbondanza

Glance down Via Abbondanza, Pompeii's main street. Lined with shops, bars, and restaurants, it was a lively, pedestrian-only zone.

The three "beaver-teeth" stones are traffic barriers that kept chariots out. On the corner at the start of the street (just to the left), take a close look at the dark travertine column standing next to the white one. Notice that the marble drums of the white column are not chiseled entirely round—another construction project left unfinished when Vesuvius erupted.

• *Our tour will eventually end a few blocks down Via Abbondanza after making a big loop. But now, head toward Vesuvius, cutting across the Forum. To the left of the Temple of Jupiter is the...*

### ❻ Forum Granary

A substantial stretch of the west side of the Forum was the granary and ancient produce market. Today, it houses thousands of artifacts excavated from Pompeii. You'll see lots of crockery, pots, pans, jugs, and containers used for transporting oil and wine. You'll also see casts of a couple of victims (and a dog) of the eruption. These casts show Pompeiians eerily captured in their last moments, hands covering their mouths as they gasped for air. They were quickly suffocated by a superheated avalanche of gas and ash, and their bodies were encased in volcanic debris. While excavating, mod-

## The Eruption of Vesuvius

At about 1:00 in the afternoon on August 24, AD 79, Mount Vesuvius erupted, sending a mushroom cloud of ash, dust, and rocks 12 miles into the air. It spewed for 18 hours straight, as winds blew the cloud southward. The white-gray ash settled like a heavy snow on Pompeii, its weight eventually collapsing roofs and floors, but leaving the walls intact. And though most of Pompeii's 20,000 residents fled that day, about 2,000 stayed behind.

Although the city of Herculaneum was closer to the volcano—about four miles away—at first it largely escaped the rain of ash, due to the direction of the wind. However, 12 hours after Vesuvius awoke, the type of eruption suddenly changed. The mountain let loose a superheated avalanche of ash, pumice, and gas. This red-hot "pyroclastic flow" sped down the side of the mountain at nearly 100 miles per hour, engulfing Herculaneum and cooking its residents alive. Several more flows over the next few hours further entombed Herculaneum, burying it in nearly 60 feet of hot material that later cooled into rock, freezing the city in time. Then, at around 7:30 in the morning, another pyroclastic flow headed south and struck Pompeii, dealing a fatal blow to those who'd remained behind.

ern archaeologists detected hollow spaces underfoot, created when the victims' bodies decomposed. By gently filling the holes with plaster, the archaeologists created molds of the Pompeiians who were caught in the disaster.

A few steps to the left of the granary is a tiny alcove that contained the Mensa Ponderaria, a counter where standard units (such as today's liter or gallon) were used to measure the quantities of liquid and solid food that were sold. And just to the right of the granary is the remains of a public toilet. You can imagine the many seats, lack of privacy, and constantly flushing stream running through the room.

• *Exit the Forum by crossing it again in front of the Temple of Jupiter and turning left. Go under the arch. In the road are more "beaver-teeth" traffic blocks. On the pillar to the right, look for the pedestrian-only road sign (two guys carrying an amphora, or ancient jug; it's above the* REG VII INS IV *sign). The modern cafeteria (on the left) is the only eatery inside the archaeological site. Twenty yards past the cafeteria, on the left-hand side at #24, is the entrance to the...*

## ❼ Baths of the Forum (Terme del Foro)

Pompeii had six public baths, each with a men's and a women's section. You're in the men's zone. The leafy courtyard at the entrance was the gymnasium. After working out, clients could relax with a hot bath *(caldarium)*, warm bath *(tepidarium)*, or cold plunge *(frigidarium)*.

The first big, plain room you enter served as the **dressing room.** Holes on the walls were for pegs to hang clothing. High up, the window (with a faded Neptune underneath) was originally covered with a less-translucent Roman glass. Walk over the nonslip mosaics into the next room.

The *tepidarium* is ringed by mini statues or *telamones* (male caryatids, figures used as supporting pillars), which divided the lockers. Clients would undress and warm up here, perhaps relaxing on one of the bronze cow-footed benches near the bronze heater while waiting for a massage. Look at the ceiling—half crushed by the eruption and half intact, with its fine blue-and-white stucco work.

Next, admire the engineering in the steam-bath room, or *caldarium.* The double floor was heated from below—so it was nice for bare feet (look into the grate across from where you entered to see the brick support towers). The double walls with brown terracotta tiles held the heat. Romans soaked in the big tub, which was filled with hot water. Opposite the big tub is a fountain, which spouted water onto the hot floor, creating steam. The lettering on the fountain reminded those enjoying the room which two politicians paid for it...and how much it cost them. (On the far right, the Roman numerals indicate they paid 5,250 *sestertii*). To keep condensation from dripping annoyingly from the ceiling, fluting (ribbing) was added to carry water down the walls.

• *Today's visitors exit the baths through the original entry (at the far end of the dressing room). Hungry? Immediately across the street is an ancient...*

## ❽ Fast-Food Joint

After a bath, it was only natural to want a little snack. So, just across the street is a fast-food joint, marked by a series of rectangular marble counters. Most ancient Romans didn't cook for themselves in their tiny apartments, so to-go places like this were commonplace. The holes in the counters held the pots for food. Each container was like a thermos, with a wooden lid to keep the soup hot, the wine cool, and so on. You could dine in the back or get your food to go. Notice the groove in the front doorstep and the holes out on the curb. The holes likely accommodated cords for stretching awnings over the sidewalk to shield the clientele from the hot

sun, while the grooves were for the shop's folding accordion doors. Look at the wheel grooves in the pavement, worn down through centuries of use. Nearby are more stepping-stones for pedestrians to cross the flooded streets.

• *Just a few steps uphill from the fast-food joint, at #5 (with a locked gate), is the...*

## ❾ House of the Tragic Poet (Casa del Poeta Tragico)

This house is typical Roman style. The entry is flanked by two family-owned shops (each with a track for a collapsing accordion door). The home is like a train running straight away from the street: atrium (with skylight and pool to catch the rain), den (where deals were made by the shopkeeper), and garden (with rooms facing it and a shrine to remember both the gods and family ancestors). In the entryway is the famous "Beware of Dog" *(Cave Canem)* mosaic.

When it's open, today's visitors enter the home by the back door (circle around to the left). On your way there, look for the modern exposed pipe on the left side of the lane; this is the same as ones used in the ancient plumbing system, hidden beneath the raised sidewalk. The richly frescoed dining room is off the garden. Diners lounged on their couches (the Roman custom) and enjoyed frescoes with fake "windows," giving the illusion of a bigger and airier room. Next to the dining room is a humble BBQ-style kitchen with a little closet for the toilet (the kitchen and bathroom shared the same plumbing).

• *Return to the fast-food place and continue about 10 yards downhill to the big intersection. From the center of the intersection, look left to see a giant arch, framing a nice view of Mount Vesuvius.*

## ❿ Aqueduct Arch—Running Water

Water was critical for this city of 20,000 people, and this arch was part of Pompeii's water-delivery system. A 100-mile-long aqueduct carried fresh water down from the hillsides to a big reservoir perched at the highest point of the city wall. Since overall water pressure was disappointing, Pompeiians built arches like the brick one you see here (originally covered in marble) with hidden water tanks at the top. Located just below the altitude of the main tank, these smaller tanks were filled by gravity and provided each neighborhood with reliable pressure. Look closely at the arch and you'll see 2,000-year-old pipes (made of lead imported all the way from Cornwall in Britannia) embedded deep in the brick.

If there was a water shortage, democratic priorities prevailed: First the baths were cut off, then the private homes. The last to go were the public fountains, where all citizens could get drinking and cooking water.

• *If you're thirsty, fill your water bottle from the modern fountain. Then continue straight downhill one block (50 yards) to #2 on the left.*

## ❶ House of the Faun (Casa del Fauno)

Stand across the street and marvel at the grand entry with *"HAVE"* (hail to you) as a welcome mat. Go in. Notice the two shrines above the entryway—one dedicated to the gods, the other to this wealthy family's ancestors. (Contemporary Neapolitans still carry on this practice; you'll notice little shrines embedded in walls all over Naples.)

You are standing in Pompeii's largest home, where you're greeted by the delightful small bronze statue of the *Dancing Faun,* famed for its realistic movement and fine proportion. (The original, described on page 976, is in Naples' Archaeological Museum.) With 40 rooms and 27,000 square feet, the House of the Faun covers an entire city block. The next floor mosaic, with an intricate diamond-like design, decorates the homeowner's office. Note the pieces of multicolored stone that remain embedded in the floor, and think of how vibrant and luxurious this house would have seemed before the eruption. Beyond that, at the far end of the first garden, is the famous floor mosaic of the *Battle of Alexander.* (The original is also at the museum in Naples.) In 333 BC, Alexander the Great beat Darius and the Persians. Romans had much respect for Alexander, the first great emperor before Rome's. While most of Pompeii's nouveau riche had notoriously bad taste and stuffed their palaces with over-the-top, mismatched decor, this guy had class. Both the faun (an ancient copy of a famous Greek statue) and the Alexander mosaic show an appreciation for history.

The house's back courtyard is lined with pillars rebuilt after the AD 62 earthquake. Take a close look at the brick, mortar, and fake-marble stucco veneer.

• *Leave the House of the Faun through its back door in the far-right corner, past a tiny guard's station. (If closed, exit out the front and walk around to the back.) Turn right and walk about a block until you see metal cages over the sidewalk protecting exposed stretches of ancient lead water pipes. Continue east and take your first left, walking about 20 yards to the entrance (on your left) to the...*

## ⑫ House of the Vettii

This is Pompeii's best-preserved home, retaining many of its mosaics and frescoes. The House of the Vettii was the bachelor pad of two wealthy merchant brothers. In the entryway, it's hard to miss the huge erection. This was not pornography. This was a symbol of success: The penis and sack of money balance each other on the goldsmith scale above a fine bowl of fruit. Translation? Only with a balance of fertility and money can you enjoy true abundance.

Step into the atrium with its replica wooden ceiling open to the sky and a lead pipe to collect water for the house cistern. The pool was flanked by two large moneyboxes (one survives, the footprint of the other shows how it was secured to the ground). The brothers wanted all who entered to know how successful they were. A variety of rooms give an intimate peek at elegant Pompeiian life. The dark room to the right of the entrance (as you face out) is filled with exquisite frescoes. Notice more white "cat's eye" stones embedded in the floor. Imagine these glinting like little eyes as the brothers and their friends wandered around by oil lamp late at night, with their sacks of gold, bowls of fruit, and enormous...egos.

• *Our next stop, the Bakery, is located about 150 yards south (downhill) from here. To get there, return to the street in front of the House of the Vettii. Walk downhill along Vicolo dei Vetti. Go one block, to where you dead-end at a T-intersection with Via della Fortuna. Go a few steps left and then right at the first corner. Continue down this gently curving road to #22.*

## ⑬ Bakery and Mill

The stubby stone towers are flour grinders. Grain was poured into the top and donkeys or slaves, treading in a circle, pushed wooden bars that turned the stones that ground the grain. The powdered grain dropped out the bottom as flour—flavored with tiny bits of rock. Nearby, the thing that looks like a modern-day pizza oven was...a brick oven. Each neighborhood had a bakery just like this.

• *Continue down the curvy road to the next intersection. As you walk consider the destructive power of all the plants and vines that you see around. Also, notice the chariot grooves worn into the pavement. When the curvy road reaches the intersection with Via degli Augustali, turn left. Ahead, in 50 yards, at #44, is the Taberna Hedones, an ancient tavern with an original floor mosaic still intact. A few steps past that, turn right and walk downhill to #18—one of many Pompeii brothels.*

## ⑭ Brothel (Lupanare)

You'll find the biggest crowds in Pompeii at a place that was likely also quite popular 2,000 years ago—the brothel. Prostitutes were nicknamed *lupe* (she-wolves), alluding to the call they made when attracting business. The brothel was a simple place, with beds and pillows made of stone and then covered with mattresses. The ancient graffiti includes tallies and exotic names of the women, indicating the prostitutes came from all corners of the Mediterranean (it also served as feedback from satisfied customers). The faded frescoes above the cells may have been a kind of menu for services offered. Note the idealized women (white, which was considered beautiful; one wears an early bra) and the rougher men (dark, considered horny). The bed legs came with little disk-like barriers to keep critters from crawling up, the tiny rooms had curtains for doors, and the prostitutes provided sheepskin condoms.

• *Leaving the brothel, go right, then take the first left, and continue going downhill two blocks to return to Via Abbondanza. This walk is over. The Forum—and exit—are to the right. If you exit now, you'll be routed through the exhibition rooms—where you'll find a scale model of the city, an interesting video, some artifacts—and the gift shop.*

  *But before you leave, consider these extra stops—all worth the time and energy (if you have any left). To locate them, refer to your map.*

## Temple of Isis

This temple served Pompeii's Egyptian community. The little white stucco shrine with the modern plastic roof housed holy water from the Nile. Isis, from Egyptian myth, was one of many foreign gods adopted by the eclectic Romans. Pompeii must have had a synagogue, too, but it has yet to be excavated.

## Theater

Originally a Greek theater (Greeks built theirs with the help of a hillside), this was the birthplace of the Greek port here in 470 BC. During Roman times, the theater sat 5,000 people in three sets of seats, all with different prices: the five marble terraces up close (filled with romantic wooden seats for two), the main section, and the cheap nosebleed section (surviving only on the high end, near the trees). The square stones above the cheap seats once supported a canvas rooftop. The high-profile boxes, flanking the stage, were for guests of honor. From this perch, you can see the gladiator barracks—the colonnaded courtyard beyond the theater. They lived in tiny rooms, trained in the courtyard, and fought in the nearby amphitheater. Check out the adjacent and well-preserved smaller Teatro Piccolo.

## House of Menander (Casa di Menandro)

Once owned by a wealthy Pompeiian, this house takes its current name from a fresco of the Greek playwright Menander on one of the walls. Admire the grand atrium (with frescoes depicting scenes from Homer's *Iliad* and *Odyssey,* and an altar to the family gods), the wall frescoes, and the mosaics. The cloister-like back courtyard leads to a room with skeletons (not plaster casts) of eruption victims from this house. Farther back, a passage leads to the servants' quarters.

## Viewpoint

You're at ground level—post eruption. To the right (inland), the farmland shows how locals lived on top of the ruins for centuries without knowing what was underneath. To the left, you can see the entire ancient city of Pompeii spread out in front of you and appreciate the magnitude of the excavations.

## Garden of the Fugitives

There's no better reminder in Pompeii of the horror caused by a volcanic eruption (and how we all might act given the same circumstances) than this "garden." Archaeologists identified this house as belonging to a middle-class merchant family. Plaster casts of this fleeing ("fugitive") family are placed exactly as the bodies were found after the eruption: lined up in single file as they attempted to escape several cubic feet of already fallen ash. Their exit was stopped by a sudden wave of hot gas and volcanic material, likely traveling over 100 miles per hour. Frozen in time, servants cannot be distinguished from their masters.

## Amphitheater

If you can, climb to the upper level of the amphitheater (though the stairs are often blocked). With Vesuvius looming in the background, mentally replace the tourists below with gladiators and wild animals locked in combat. Walk along the top of the amphitheater and

look down into the grassy rectangular area surrounded by columns. This is the **Palaestra,** an area once used for athletic training. (If you can't get to the top of the amphitheater, you can see the Palaestra from outside—in fact, you can't miss it, as it's right next door.) Facing the other way, look for the bell tower that tops the roofline of the modern city of Pompei, where locals go about their daily lives in the shadow of the volcano, just as their ancestors did 2,000 years ago.

• *If it's too crowded to bear hiking back along uneven lanes to the entrance, you can slip out the site's "back door," which is next to the amphitheater. Exiting, turn right and follow the site's wall all the way back to the entrance.*

# Herculaneum

Smaller, less crowded, and not as ruined as its famous big sister, Herculaneum (worth ▲▲, Ercolano in Italian) offers a closer, more intimate peek into ancient Roman life but lacks the grandeur of Pompeii (there's barely a colonnade).

## GETTING TO HERCULANEUM

Ercolano Scavi, the nearest train station to Herculaneum, is about 20 minutes from Naples and 50 minutes from Sorrento on the same

Circumvesuviana train that goes to Pompeii (for details on the Circumvesuviana, see page 1014). Walking from the Ercolano Scavi train station to the ruins takes 10 minutes: Leave the station and turn right, then left down the main drag; continue straight, eight blocks gradually downhill to the end of the road, where you'll run right into the grand arch that marks the entrance to the ruins. (Skip Museo MAV.) Pass through the arch and continue 200 yards down the path—taking in the bird's-eye first impression of the site to your right—to the ticket office in the modern building.

## ORIENTATION TO HERCULANEUM

**Cost:** €12, free (and crowded) once or twice a month; the specific day varies in peak season (in low season, it's the first Sun); covered by the Campania ArteCard (see page 958).

**Hours:** Daily April-Oct 8:30-19:30, Nov-March until 17:00, ticket office closes 1.5 hours earlier.

**Information:** Tel. 081-777-7008, http://ercolano.beniculturali.it.

**Closures:** Like Pompeii, various sections of Herculaneum can be closed unexpectedly.

**Visitor Information:** Pick up a free, detailed map and excellent booklet at the info desk next to the ticket window. The booklet gives you a quick explanation of each building. There's a bookstore inside the site, next to the audioguide stand.

**Tours:** The audioguide basically recites the text in the free booklet (€8, €13 for 2, ID required, rent at kiosk near site entry).

**Length of This Tour:** Allow one hour.

**Baggage Storage:** Herculaneum is harder than Pompeii for those with luggage, but not impossible. Herculaneum's train station has lots of stairs and no baggage storage, but you can roll wheeled luggage down to the ruins and store it for free in a locked area in the ticket office building (pick up bags at least 30 minutes prior to site closing). To get back to the station, consider splurging on a €5 taxi (ask the staff to call one for you).

**Services:** There's a free WC in the ticket office building, and another near the site entry.

**Eating:** Vending machines and café tables are near the entry to the site. There are also several eateries on the way from the train station.

## ⊙ SELF-GUIDED TOUR

Caked and baked by the same AD 79 eruption that pummeled Pompeii (see sidebar on page 1028), Herculaneum is a small community of intact buildings with plenty of surviving detail. While Pompeii was initially smothered in ash, Herculaneum was spared at first—due to the direction of the wind—but got slammed about 12 hours after the eruption started by a superheated avalanche of ash and hot gases roaring off the volcano. The city  was eventually buried under nearly 60 feet of ash, which hardened into tuff, perfectly preserving the city until excavations began in 1748.

After leaving the ticket building, go through the turnstiles and walk the path below the site to the entrance. Look seaward and note where the shoreline is today; before the eruption, it was where you are standing, a quarter-mile inland. This gives you a

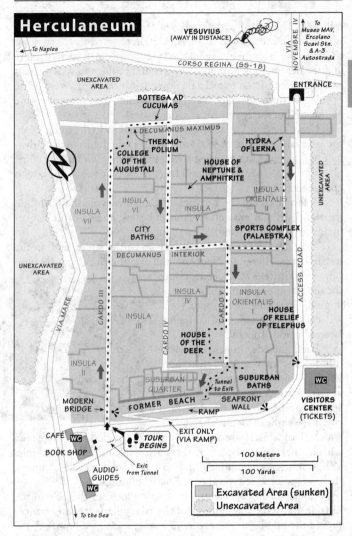

Herculaneum

VESUVIUS (AWAY IN DISTANCE)

← To Naples

CORSO REGINA (SS-18)

VIA NOVEMBRE IV

To Museo MAV, Ercolano Scavi Stn. & A-3 Autostrada

ENTRANCE

UNEXCAVATED AREA

BOTTEGA AD CUCUMAS

DECUMANUS MAXIMUS

THERMO-POLIUM

COLLEGE OF THE AUGUSTALI

HYDRA OF LERNA

HOUSE OF NEPTUNE & AMPHITRITE

INSULA VI

INSULA V

INSULA ORIENTALIS II

INSULA VII

CITY BATHS

SPORTS COMPLEX (PALAESTRA)

DECUMANUS INTERIOR

UNEXCAVATED AREA

CARDO III

INSULA IV

INSULA ORIENTALIS I

INSULA III

CARDO IV

CARDO V

HOUSE OF RELIEF OF TELEPHUS

VIA MARE

HOUSE OF THE DEER

INSULA II

SUBURBAN QUARTER

Tunnel to Exit

SUBURBAN BATHS

MODERN BRIDGE →

FORMER BEACH

← RAMP

SEAFRONT WALL

WC

VISITORS CENTER (TICKETS)

CAFÉ WC

BOOK SHOP

TOUR BEGINS

EXIT ONLY (VIA RAMP)

AUDIO-GUIDES

Exit from Tunnel

WC

↓ To the Sea

100 Meters

100 Yards

Excavated Area (sunken)
Unexcavated Area

sense of how much volcanic material piled up. The present-day city of Ercolano looms just above the ruins. The modern buildings don't look much different from their ancient counterparts.

As you cross the modern bridge into the excavation site, look down into the moat-like **ditch**. On one side, you see Herculaneum's seafront wall. On the other is the wall that you just walked on, a solidified ash layer from the volcano that shows how deeply the town was buried.

After crossing the bridge, stroll straight to the end of the street and find the **College of the Augustali** (Sede degli Augustali, #24). Decorated with frescoes of Hercules (for whom this city was named), it belonged to an association of freed slaves working together to climb their way up the ladder of Roman society. Here and farther on, look around doorways and ceilings to spot ancient wood charred by the pyroclastic flows. Most buildings were made of stone, with wooden floors and beams (which were preserved here by the ash but rarely survive at ancient sites).

Leave the building through the back and go to the right, down the lane. The adjacent *thermopolium* (#19) was the Roman equivalent of a lunch counter or fast-food joint, with giant jars for wine, oil, and snacks. Most of the buildings along here were shops, with apartments above.

A few steps on, the **Bottega ad Cucumas** wine shop (#14, on the right) still has charred remains of beams, and its drink list remains frescoed on the outside wall (under glass).

Take the next right, go halfway down the street, and on the left find the **House of Neptune and Amphitrite** (Casa di Nettuno e Anfitrite, #7). Outside, notice the intact upper floor and imagine it going even higher. Inside, you'll see colorful mosaics and a unique "frame" made of shells.

Back outside, continue downhill to the intersection, then head left for a block and proceed straight across the street into the don't-miss-it **sports complex** (*palaestra*; #4). First you'll see a row of "marble" columns, which (look closer) are actually made of rounded bricks covered with a thick layer of plaster, shaped to look like carved marble. While important buildings in Rome had solid marble columns, these imitations are typical of ordinary buildings.

Continuing deeper into the complex, look for the hole in the hillside and walk through one of the triangular-shaped entrances to find the highlight: the Hydra of Lerna, a sculpted bronze fountain that features the seven-headed monster defeated by Hercules as one of his 12 labors. If this cavernous space is unlit, go to the second doorway on the left wall and press the light switch.

Return through the sports complex and turn downhill to the **House of the Deer** (Casa dei Cervi, #21). It's named for the statues of deer being attacked by dogs in the garden courtyard (these are copies; the originals are in the Archaeological Museum in Naples). As you wander through the rooms, notice the colorfully frescoed walls. Ancient Herculaneum, like all Roman cities of that age, was filled with color, rather than the stark white we often imagine (even the statues were painted).

You can see more of these colors, this time bright orange, across the street in the **House of Relief of Telephus** (Casa del Rilievo del Telefo, #2).

Continue downhill through the archway. The **Suburban Baths** illustrate the city's devastation (Terme Suburbane, #3; enter near the side of the statue on the terrace, sometimes closed). After you descend into the baths, look back at the steps. You'll see the original wood charred in the disaster, protected by the wooden planks you just walked on. At the bottom of the stairs, in the waiting room to the right, notice where the floor collapsed under the sheer weight of the volcanic debris. (The sunken pavement reveals the baths' heating system: hot air generated by wood-burning furnaces and circulated between the different levels of the floor.) A doorway in front of the stairs is still filled with solidified ash. Despite the damage, elements of refinement remain intact, such as the delicate stuccoes in the *caldarium* (hot bath).

Back outside, make your way down the steps to the sunken area just below. As you descend, you're walking across what was formerly Herculaneum's beach. Looking back, you'll see **arches** that were part of boat storage areas. Archaeologists used to wonder why so few victims were found in Herculaneum. But during excavations in 1981, hundreds of skeletons were discovered here, between the wall of volcanic stone behind you and the city in front of you. Some of Herculaneum's 4,000 citizens tried to escape by sea, but were overtaken by the pyroclastic flows.

Thankfully, your escape is easier. Either follow the sound of water and continue through the tunnel (you'll climb up and pop out near the site entry), or, more scenically, backtrack and exit the same way you entered.

# Vesuvius

The 4,000-foot-high Vesuvius, mainland Europe's only active volcano, has been sleeping restlessly since 1944. While Europe has other dangerous volcanoes, only Vesuvius sits in the middle of a three-million-person metropolitan area that would be impossible to evacuate quickly.

Many tourists don't know that you can easily visit the summit. Up top, it's desolate and lunar-like, and the rocks are newly born. Walk the entire accessible part of the crater lip for the most interesting views; the far end overlooks Pompeii. Be still. Listen to the wind and the occasional cascades of rocks tumbling into the crater. Any steam? Vesuvius could blow again. (Don't worry—there'd likely be at least a few hours or days of warning.)

## GETTING TO VESUVIUS

**By Car or Taxi:** Drivers take the exit *Torre del Greco* and follow the signs to *Vesuvio*. Just drive to the end of the road and pay to park. A taxi costs €90 round-trip from Naples, including a 2-hour wait; it's about €70 from Pompeii.

**By Private Bus from Pompeii:** From near the Pompei Scavi train station on the Circumvesuviana line (just outside the main entrance to the Pompeii ruins), you have two bus services to choose from, each taking about three hours (40 minutes up, 40 minutes down, and about 1.5 hours at the summit).

The old-fashioned **Vesuvius Trolley Tram** (Tramvia del Vesuvio) uses the main road up (€25 round-trip plus €10 summit admission, 6/day, tickets sold at and tram departs from Pompei Scavi train station, tel. 081-777-6750, www.tramvianapoli.com).

**Busvia del Vesuvio** winds you up a bumpy back road to the crater rim (Via Boscotrecase) in a cross between a shuttle bus and a monster truck. The walk up to the rim at the end is about the same, but you approach it from the other direction. It's a fun, more scenic way to go, but not for the easily queasy (€22 includes summit admission, hourly April-Oct Mon-Sat 9:00-15:00, until later June-Aug, buy tickets at "info point" at Pompei Scavi train station, tel. 0126-426-1213, www.busviadelvesuvio.com).

**By Private Bus from Herculaneum:** The quickest trip up is on the **Vesuvio Express.** These small buses leave from the Ercolano Scavi train station (on the Circumvesuviana line, where you get off for the Herculaneum ruins; €10 round-trip plus €10 summit admission, daily from 9:30, runs every 45 minutes based on demand, 20 minutes each way—about 2.5 hours total, office on square in front of train station, tel. 0414-525-1213, www.vesuvioexpress.it).

## ORIENTATION TO VESUVIUS

**Cost and Hours:** €10 covers national park entry and the park guide's orientation; ticket office open daily July-Aug 9:00-18:00, April-June and Sept until 17:00, closes earlier off-season. Bad weather can occasionally close the trail.

**Information:** The ticket office is 200 yards downhill from the parking lot. Tel. 081-865-3911, www.vesuviopark.it (official site) or www.guidevesuvio.it (more helpful site run by guides).

**When to Go:** Early-morning visitors enjoy the freshest air and snare the best parking spots. The mountain is open all year, but spring and fall are the most comfortable times to visit. Yellow broom flowers blossom in May and June.

## VISITING VESUVIUS

Bring sunscreen, water, a light jacket in summer, and a hat and warm coat in winter. By bus, taxi, or private car, you'll reach the volcano crater up a good but windy road from Torre del Greco (between Herculaneum and Pompeii). As you drive up, you'll pass the remnants of the pre-AD 79 mountain (on your left, now called Monte Somma) and lava flows from the most recent 1944 eruption. No matter how you travel up, you'll land at the parking lot.

Backtrack 200 yards downhill to buy your ticket at the office. Use the pay WC, as there's none at the summit. From the parking lot, it's a moderately steep half-mile, 20-minute hike (with a 600-foot elevation gain) up a dirt access road to the top. Say "no thank you" to the gentleman passing out walking sticks in return for a tip—you don't need one.

At the rim, a sweeping view of the Bay of Naples is on your right; on your left, fenced off, there's a fearsome drop into the crater. Mountain guides orient you and then set you free.

# SORRENTO & CAPRI

Just an hour south of Naples, serene Sorrento makes an ideal home base for exploring this fascinating region. From this easy-to-enjoy town, you can take day trips to Naples, Pompeii, the Amalfi Coast, the Greek temples at Paestum, and the romantic island of Capri. And every night you can return "home" to Sorrento, to enjoy its elegant strolling scene and sort through its many fine restaurant options.

## Sorrento

Wedged on a ledge under the mountains and over the Mediterranean, spritzed by lemon and olive groves, Sorrento is an attractive resort of 20,000 residents and, in summer, just as many tourists. It's as well-located for regional sightseeing as it is a fine place to stay and stroll. The Sorrentines have gone out of their way to create a relaxed place for tourists to come and spend money. As 90 percent of the town's economy is tourism, everyone seems to speak fluent English and work for the Chamber of Commerce. This gateway to the Amalfi Coast has a pedestrianized old quarter, lively shopping streets, and a spectacular cliffside setting. Residents are proud of the many world-class romantics who've vacationed here, such as famed tenor Enrico Caruso, who chose Sorrento as the place to spend his last months.

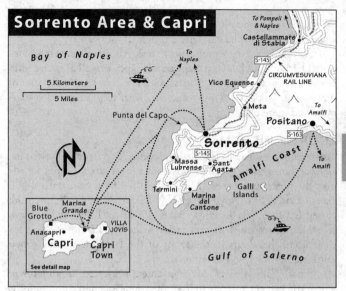

**Sorrento Area & Capri**

Bay of Naples

To Pompeii & Naples

Castellammare di Stabia

S-145

To Naples

CIRCUMVESUVIANA RAIL LINE

5 Kilometers

5 Miles

Vico Equense

Meta

To Amalfi

Punta del Capo

**Sorrento**

S-145

**Positano**

S-163

To Amalfi

Massa Lubrense

Sant' Agata

Termini

Marina del Cantone

Galli Islands

Amalfi Coast

Marina Grande

Blue Grotto

Anacapri

**Capri**

VILLA JOVIS

Capri Town

See detail map

Gulf of Salerno

SORRENTO & CAPRI

## PLANNING YOUR TIME

Sorrento itself has no world-class sights, but it can easily give you a few pleasant hours. More importantly, Sorrento is a fine base for visiting nearby destinations, all reachable within an hour or so: Naples (by boat or train); Pompeii, Herculaneum, and Mount Vesuvius (by train, plus a bus for Vesuvius); the Amalfi Coast (by bus or boat); and the island of Capri (just 30 minutes by boat).

Sorrento hibernates in winter. Many places close down in November—others after the New Year—and stay closed until the town reawakens in March.

# Orientation to Sorrento

Downtown Sorrento is long and narrow. Piazza Tasso marks the town's center. The main drag, Corso Italia, runs parallel to the sea through Piazza Tasso and then out toward the cape, where the road's name becomes Via Capo. Nearly everything mentioned here (except Marina Grande and the hotels on Via Capo) is within a 10-minute walk of the station. The town is perched

on a cliff (some hotels have elevators down to sundecks on the water); the best real beaches are a couple of miles away.

Sorrento has two separate port areas. Marina Piccola is a functional harbor with boats to Naples and Capri, as well as cruise-ship tenders. Despite its name, Marina Grande, below the other end of downtown, is a little fishing enclave, with recommended restaurants and more charm.

## TOURIST INFORMATION

The helpful regional TI (labeled *Azienda di Soggiorno*)—located inside the **Foreigners' Club**—hands out a great city map and schedules for boats and buses (Mon-Sat 9:00-19:00, Sun until 18:00 except closed Sun April-May; Nov-March Mon-Fri 8:30-16:00, closed Sat-Sun; Via Luigi de Maio 35, tel. 081-807-4033, www.sorrentotourism.com). If you arrive after the TI closes, look for their useful handouts in the lobby of the Foreigners' Club (open until midnight, closed in winter).

Small "Info Points" are conveniently located around town, where you can get answers to basic questions (open in warm months only). Find them just outside the **train station** in the green caboose; near **Piazza Tasso** at the corner of Via Correale (under the yellow church); at **Marina Piccola,** where cruise-ship tenders and boats from Naples arrive; and at the Achille Lauro **parking garage.**

## ARRIVAL IN SORRENTO

**By Train or Bus:** Sorrento is the last stop on the Circumvesuviana train line from Naples. In front of the train station is the town's main bus stop, as well as taxis waiting to overcharge you (€15 minimum). All recommended hotels—except those on Via Capo—are within a 10-minute walk. (For details on taking the bus to Via Capo, see "Sleeping in Sorrento," later in this chapter.)

**By Boat:** Passenger boats and cruise-ship tenders dock at Marina Piccola. As you walk toward town from the marina, go up the big staircase where the pier bends. Standing on the promenade and facing town, you'll see the bus stop directly ahead; a TI kiosk and ticket windows for boats to Capri and Naples in the lower area to your left; and the elevator up to town to the right, about a five-minute walk along the base of the cliff (follow *lift/acensore* signs).

The elevator (€1, www.sorrentolift.it; faster, cheaper, and more predictable than a bus) takes you to the Villa Comunale city park. From there, exit through the park's iron gate and bear left; Piazza Tasso is about four blocks away. A less-reliable option, buses from the port can take you to Piazza Tasso (city bus #B or #C, buy €1.20 ticket at newsstand or tobacco shop); for more on buses, see "Getting Around Sorrento," later.

**By Car:** The Achille Lauro underground parking garage is

centrally located, just a couple of blocks in front of the train station (€2/hour, €24/12 hours, €40 overnight, on Via Correale).

## HELPFUL HINTS

**Church Services:** The **cathedral** hosts an English-language Anglican service at 17:00 most Sundays from April to October (but not in August). At **Santa Maria delle Grazie** (perhaps the most beautiful Baroque church in town), cloistered nuns sing from above and out of sight during a Mass each morning at 7:30 (on Via delle Grazie).

**Bookstore:** For a decent selection of books in English (including this one), head to **Libreria Tasso** (daily 9:30-22:00, closed in winter, Via San Cesareo 96, one block north of cathedral, near Sorrento Men's Club, tel. 081-807-1639).

**Baggage Storage:** The underground parking lot Parcheggio de Curtis, downhill from the train station, moonlights as a convenient place to store luggage (daily 7:30-23:30, Via E. de Curtis 5, just before Corsa Italia). Another option, especially for longer-term storage with pick-up and drop-off service, is **Sorrento Luggage** (mobile 338-431-7323, www.sorrentoluggage. com).

**Laundry:** A handy 24-hour self-service launderette, **Rosy Laundry,** is a couple of blocks past the station (daily, Corso Italia 321, mobile 331-912-1122).

**Haircuts:** A fun hair salon for men, **Satisfhair,** is run by hairless Luca and Tony and makes for a happy memory (€18 for a good cut, closed Sun-Mon, Via S. Maria della Pieta 17, tel. 081-878-3476).

**Guided Tours of Pompeii, Naples, the Amalfi Coast, and Capri:** Naples-based **Mondo Guide** offers affordable tours of these destinations, including an Amalfi Coast drive that starts from Sorrento (meet in front of the Hotel Antiche Mura; kindly do not use hotel facilities if you are not a guest). You'll sign up in advance and team up with fellow Rick Steves readers to split the cost. For details, see page 970.

**Local Guides:** For excursions to Sorrento and Amalfi, **Giovanna Donadio** is a good tour guide (€100/half-day, €180/day, same price for any size group, mobile 338-466-0114, giovanna_ dona@hotmail.com) who can also escort six to eight people from Sorrento on a well-organized full day of fun on Capri (€180 plus public transportation expenses and admissions). **Giovanni Visetti** is a high-energy nature lover, mapmaker, and orienteer who organizes hikes and has a fine website with the best description of all local trails. His online map collection covers Capri and the Path of the Gods (mobile 339-694-2911, www.giovis.com, giovis@giovis.com).

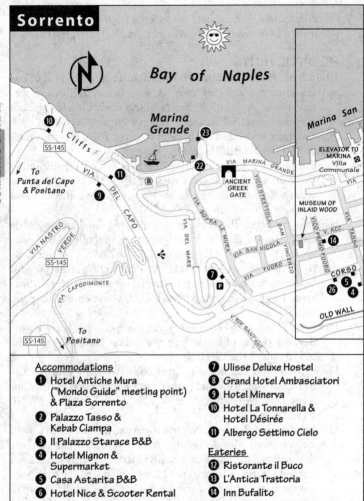

**Sorrento**

Bay of Naples

Marina Grande

Marina San

To Punta del Capo & Positano

To Positano

ELEVATOR TO MARINA Villa Communale

ANCIENT GREEK GATE

MUSEUM OF INLAID WOOD

OLD WALL

**Accommodations**

**1** Hotel Antiche Mura ("Mondo Guide" meeting point) & Plaza Sorrento

**2** Palazzo Tasso & Kebab Ciampa

**3** Il Palazzo Starace B&B

**4** Hotel Mignon & Supermarket

**5** Casa Astarita B&B

**6** Hotel Nice & Scooter Rental

**7** Ulisse Deluxe Hostel

**8** Grand Hotel Ambasciatori

**9** Hotel Minerva

**10** Hotel La Tonnarella & Hotel Désirée

**11** Albergo Settimo Cielo

**Eateries**

**12** Ristorante il Buco

**13** L'Antica Trattoria

**14** Inn Bufalito

## GETTING AROUND SORRENTO

Distances are short in Sorrento. If taking a bus seems too complicated, use the elevator, stairs, and your feet.

**By Bus:** City buses all stop near the main square, Piazza Tasso, and run until at least 20:00 (3/hour, www.eavsrl.it). Bus #A takes a long route parallel to the coast, heading east to Meta beach or west to the hotels on Via Capo before continuing to Massa Lubrense; buses #B and #C loop up and down, connecting the port (Marina Piccola) to the town center; and minibus #D heads to the fishing village (Marina Grande). The trip between Piazza Tasso and Marina Piccola (or Marina Grande) costs €1.30 (buy tickets at

SORRENTO & CAPRI

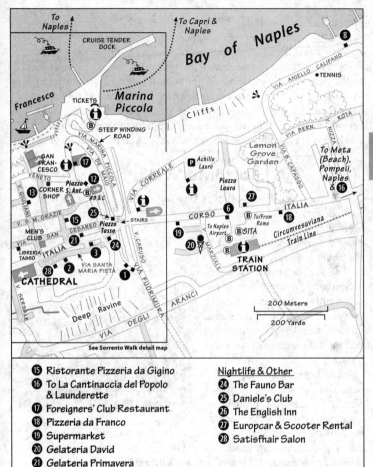

- **15** Ristorante Pizzeria da Gigino
- **16** To La Cantinaccia del Popolo & Launderette
- **17** Foreigners' Club Restaurant
- **18** Pizzeria da Franco
- **19** Supermarket
- **20** Gelateria David
- **21** Gelateria Primavera
- **22** Trattoria da Emilia
- **23** Porta Marina

<u>Nightlife & Other</u>
- **24** The Fauno Bar
- **25** Daniele's Club
- **26** The English Inn
- **27** Europcar & Scooter Rental
- **28** Satisfhair Salon

tobacco shops and newsstands). Stamp your ticket upon entering the bus. The €10, 24-hour Costiera SITA Sud pass, good for the entire Amalfi Coast, also covers Sorrento city buses.

Bus stops are often unmarked; if you're lucky you'll see an EAV sign with the word *fermata*. Buses #A and #D generally stop near where Corso Italia passes through Piazza Tasso, but no stop is indicated—drivers tend to stop wherever they can in this busy square. Buses #B and #C stop at the corner of Piazza Sant'Antonino, just down the hill toward the water.

**By Scooter:** Several places near the station rent motor scooters for about €35 per day, including **Europcar** (Corso Italia 210p, tel. 081-878-1386, www.sorrento.it) and **Autoservizi De Martino,** in

Hotel Nice (Corso Italia 259, tel. 081-878-2801, www.admitaly.com). Don't rent a vehicle in summer unless you enjoy traffic jams.

**By Taxi:** Taxis charge an outrageous €15 for the short ride from the station to most hotels (more for Via Capo). Thanks to traffic and one-way roads, you'll get to most central locations faster by walking. If you do use a taxi, agree to a set price and be sure it has a meter (all official taxis have one). I think taxis here are a huge rip-off, since city officials don't have the nerve to regulate them, and hotels are afraid to alienate them. Walk or take the bus instead.

## Sorrento Walk

Get to know Sorrento with this lazy self-guided town stroll that ends down by the waterside at the small-boat harbor, Marina Grande.

• *Begin on the main square. Stand under the flags between the sea and the town's main square...*

❶ **Piazza Tasso:** As in any southern Italian town, this piazza is Sorrento's living room. It may be noisy and congested, but lo-cals want to be where the ac-tion is...and be part of the scene. The most expensive apartments and top cafés are on or near this square.

Look out at the Bay of Na-ples. You can see the city of Na-ples in the distance. From here, it's a five-minute walk—includ-ing 130 stairs— to Marina Piccola, the harbor for cruise-ship ten-ders and boats to Capri and Naples. On the right side of the gorge, overlooking the bay, is Hotel Excelsior Vittoria. This elegant, 19th-century Grand Tour hotel is where tenor Enrico Caruso (who died in 1921) spent his last months.

Turn to face the square. A statue of St. Anthony the Abbot, patron of Sorrento, is surrounded by traffic. He faces north as if greeting those coming from Naples (on festival days, he's equipped with an armload of fresh lemons and oranges).

This square bridges the gorge that divides downtown Sorren-to. The newer section (to your left) was farm country just two cen-turies ago. The older part (to your right) retains its ancient Greek gridded street plan. (Like much of southern Italy, Sorrento was Greek-speaking for centuries before it was Romanized.)

For a better glimpse of the city's gorge-gouged landscape, con-sider this quick detour: With the water to your back, cross through the square and walk straight ahead a block inland, under a canopy of trees and past a long taxi queue. Belly up to the green railing in

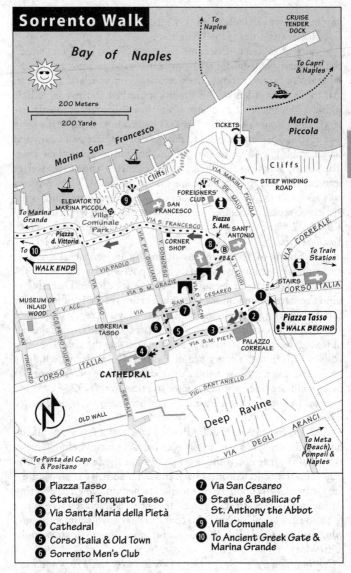

# Sorrento Walk

Bay of Naples

200 Meters
200 Yards

To Naples

CRUISE TENDER DOCK

To Capri & Naples

Marina Piccola

TICKETS

Cliffs

STEEP WINDING ROAD

Marina San Francesco

Cliffs

ELEVATOR TO MARINA PICCOLA

To Marina Grande

Villa Comunale Park

FOREIGNERS' CLUB

SAN FRANCESCO

VIA S. FRANCESCO

VIA DE MAIO

VIA MARINA PICCOLA

Piazza S. Ant.

SANT' ANTONIO

VIA CORREALE

Piazza d. Vittoria

To 10

WALK ENDS

VIA PAOLO

CORNER SHOP

VIA PR. GIULIANI

VIA DOMORSO

VIA S. M. GRAZIE

VIA S. M. PIETA

VIA D'ARCHI

VIA CESAREO

SAN

#B & C.V. LUIGI

STAIRS
CORSO ITALIA

To Train Station

MUSEUM OF INLAID WOOD

V. ACC.

VIA TASSO

LIBRERIA TASSO

VICO PRIMO FUORO

CORSO ITALIA

SAN VINCENZO

VIA

Piazza Tasso
WALK BEGINS

PALAZZO CORREALE

CATHEDRAL

V. BERSALE

V. SANT'ANIELLO

OLD WALL

Deep Ravine

VIA DEGLI ARANCI

To Punta del Capo & Positano

To Meta (Beach), Pompeii & Naples

N

① Piazza Tasso
② Statue of Torquato Tasso
③ Via Santa Maria della Pietà
④ Cathedral
⑤ Corso Italia & Old Town
⑥ Sorrento Men's Club
⑦ Via San Cesareo
⑧ Statue & Basilica of St. Anthony the Abbot
⑨ Villa Comunale
⑩ To Ancient Greek Gate & Marina Grande

front of Hotel Antiche Mura and look down to see steps that were carved centuries before Christ. Later, this was called the "Valley of the Mills" and was busy with river-powered saw- and flour mills, along with a public laundry, until well into the 19th century.

The combination of the gorge and the seaside cliffs made Sorrento easy to defend. A small section of wall closed the landward gap in the city's defenses (you can still see a surviving piece of it a few blocks away, near Hotel Mignon).

Sorrento's name may come from the Greek word for "siren," the legendary half-bird, half-woman that sang an intoxicating lullaby. According to Homer, the sirens lived on an island near here. All those who sailed by the sirens succumbed to their incredible musical charms...and to death when they shipwrecked on the island. But Homer's hero Ulysses was determined to hear the song and restrain his manhood. He put wax in his oarsmen's ears and had himself lashed to the mast of his ship and survived their song. The sirens, thinking they had lost their powers, threw themselves into the sea, and the place became safe to inhabit. Ulysses' odyssey was all about the westward expansion of Greek culture, and to the ancient Greeks, places like Sorrento were the wild, wild west.

• *Back at Piazza Tasso, head to the far-left inland corner of the square. You'll find a...*

❷ **Statue of Torquato Tasso:** The square's namesake, a Sorrento native, was a lively Renaissance poet—but today he seems only to wonder which restaurant to choose for dinner. Directly behind the statue, pop into the **Fattoria Terranova** shop, one of many fun, family-run, and touristy boutiques. They sell regional goodies and offer free biscuits and tastes of liqueurs, and the shop makes all of its organic products on an *agriturismo* outside the city. The gifty edibles spill into the courtyard of **Palazzo Correale,** which gives you a feel for an 18th-century aristocratic palace's courtyard. Its patio walls are lined with characteristic tiles from 1772.

• *As you're leaving the courtyard, on your immediate left you'll see the narrow...*

❸ **Via Santa Maria della Pietà:** Here, just a few yards off the noisy main drag, is a street that goes back centuries before Christ. About 100 yards down the lane, at #24 (on the left), find a 13th-century palace (no balconies back then...for security reasons), now an elementary school. A few steps farther on, you'll see a tiny shrine across the street. Typical of southern Italy, it's where the faithful pray to their saint, who contacts Mary, who contacts Jesus, who contacts God. This shrine is a bit more direct—it starts right with Mary.

• *Continue down the lane (passing a recommended kebab shop and trattoria) to reach the delightful...*

❹ **Cathedral:** Walk through the wrought-iron gate, which leads to the church patio. The church is free to enter (daily 8:00-12:30 & 16:30-21:00). Step inside the main door and examine the impressive *intarsio* (inlaid-wood) interior doors. They show religious scenes and depict this very church. Take a cool stroll down the right-hand side of the nave, checking out the intricate inlaid Stations of the Cross. You'll find even more inlaid wood on the side entrance doors. They show scenes of the town and its industry, as well as an old-town map (find Piazza Tasso, trace the fortified walls, and notice the Greek grid street plan). These doors were made to celebrate Pope John Paul II's visit in 1992. Notice the fine inlaid-marble seat of the bishop nearby and how the church's elegance matches that of the town. Before exiting, on the right find the *presepe* (manger scene) with its lovingly painted terra-cotta figures, each with an expressive face. This takes Bethlehem on that first Christmas and sets it in Sorrento—with pasta, mozzarella, salami, local lemons, the gorge with the Valley of the Mills, and even Mount Vesuvius in the background.

• *Cross the open plaza—where the end of the narrow street you just walked down meets the main drag.*

❺ **Corso Italia and the Old Town:** In the summer, this stretch of road is closed to traffic each evening, when it hosts a wonderful *passeggiata*. Look at the bell tower, with the scavenged ancient Roman columns at its base. Now go left down Via P. Reginaldo Giuliani, following the old Greek street plan. Locals claim the ancient Greeks laid out the streets east-west for the most sunlight and north-south for the prevailing and cooling breeze. Pause at the poster board on your right to see who's died lately.

• *One block ahead, on your right, the 14th-century loggia (called Sedil Dominova) is home to the...*

❻ **Sorrento Men's Club:** Once the meeting place of the town's nobles, for generations now the Sedil Dominova has been a retreat for retired working-class men. Strictly no women—and no phones.

Italian men venerate their mothers. (Italians joke that Jesus must have been a southern Italian because his mother believed her son was God, he believed his mom was a virgin, and he lived at home with her until he was 30.) But Italian men have also built into their culture ways to be on their own. Here,  men play cards and gossip under an historic emblem of the city and a finely frescoed 16th-century dome, with its marvelous 3-D scenes.

• *Turn right for a better view of the Men's Club and a historical marker describing the building. Then continue along...*

❼ **Via San Cesareo:** This touristy pedestrian-only shopping street eventually leads back to Piazza Tasso. It's lined with competitive little shops where you can peruse (and sample) lemon products. Notice the huge ancient doorways with their tiny doors—to let the right people in, carefully, during a more dangerous age.

• *After a block, take a left onto Via degli Archi, go under the arch, and then hang a right (under another arch) to the square with the...*

❽ **Statue and Basilica of St. Anthony** (San Antonino): Sorrento's town saint humbly looms among the palms, facing the Basilica of St. Anthony the Abbot, a.k.a. St. Anthony the Great (free to enter). Step inside and descend into the crypt (stairs beside main altar) where you'll find a chapel and reliquary containing a few of Anthony's bones surrounded by lots of votives. Locals have long turned to St. Anthony when faced with challenges and hard times. Exploring the room, you'll find count-

less tokens of appreciation to the saint for his help. Before tourism, fishing was the big employer. The back walls feature paintings of storms with Anthony coming to the rescue. Circle behind the altar with Anthony's relics and study the shiny ex-votos (religious offerings) thanking the saint for healthy babies, good employment, surviving heart attacks and lung problems, and lots of strong legs.

• *Back outside, follow the road that skirts the piazza with St. Anthony's statue (don't go down the street with the line of trees and Porto signs). Watch on the left for The Corner Shop, where Giovanni sells a wide variety of wines, limoncello, pastas, and other foods, specializing in edibles from the Campania region. Soon after, on the right you'll see the trees in front of the Imperial Hotel Tramontano, and to their right a path leading to the...*

❾ **Villa Comunale:** This fine public park overlooks the harbor. Belly up to the banister to enjoy the view of Marina Piccola and the Bay of Naples. Notice Naples' skyline and the boats that commute from here to there in 35 minutes. Imagine the view in AD 79 when Vesuvius blew its top and molten mud flowed down the mountain, burying Pompeii. From here, steps zigzag down to the harbor, where lounge chairs, filled by vacation-

ers working on tans, line the sundecks (there's also the elevator to the harbor). The Franciscan church fronting this square faces a fine modern statue of Francis across the street.

Next to the church is a dreamy little **cloister.** Pop inside to see local Gothic—a 13th-century mix of Norman, Gothic, and Arabic styles, all around the old pepper tree. This is an understandably popular spot for weddings and concerts.

At the far side of the cloister, stairs lead to a **photo exhibit:** *The Italians* shows off the work of local photographer Raffaele Celentano, who artfully captures classic Italian scenes from 1990 to 2016 in black and white (€2.50, daily 10:00-22:00, great prints for sale, fun photo-op through the grand tree on their deck, adjacent music box exhibit is free).

• *From here, you can quit the walk and stay in the town center, or continue another few minutes downhill to the waterfront at Marina Grande. If you take the elevator down, the road to the right leads to Marina Piccola, where boats depart to Capri and other nearby towns. Piers and beaches to the left do not connect to the next stop on this walk.*

❿ To continue to **Marina Grande,** return to the road and keep going downhill. At the next square (Piazza della Vittoria, with a dramatic WWI memorial and another grand view), cut over to the road closest to the water. After winding steeply down for a few minutes, it turns into a wide stairway, then makes a sharp and steep switchback (take the right fork to continue downhill). Farther down, just before reaching the waterfront, you pass under an...

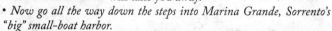

**Ancient Greek Gate:** This gate fortified the city of Sorrento. Beyond it was Marina Grande, technically a separate town with its own proud residents—it's said that even their cats look different. Because Marina Grande dwellers lived outside the wall and were more susceptible to rape, pillage, and plunder, Sorrentines believe that they come from Saracen (pirate) stock. Sorrentines still scare their children by saying, "Behave—or the pirates will take you away."

• *Now go all the way down the steps into Marina Grande, Sorrento's "big" small-boat harbor.*

**Marina Grande:** Until recently, this little community was famously traditional, with its economy based on its fishing fleet.

To this day, fathers pass their houses and fishing-boat stalls down to their sons. Locals recall when women wore black when a relative died (1 year for an uncle, aunt, or sibling; 2-3 years for a husband or parent). Men got off easy, just wearing a black memorial button.

Two recommended restaurants are on the harbor. **Trattoria da Emilia** has an old newspaper clipping, tacked near the door, about Sophia Loren filming here. At the far-right end of the harbor, **Porta Marina** is smaller, less fancy, and more local but with food every bit as tasty as that of its competition.

• *From here, where the road hits the beach, minibus #D returns to the center at Piazza Tasso every hour (pay the driver). Or you can walk back up.*

# Sights in Sorrento

### ▲▲Strolling

Each balmy evening Sorrento offers one of Italy's most enchanting *passeggiata* scenes. Take time to explore the surprisingly pleasant old city between Corso Italia and the sea. The views from Villa Comunale, the public park next to Imperial Hotel Tramontano, are worth the detour. Each night in summer (May-Oct at 19:30; Nov-April weekends only), the police close off Corso Italia to traffic, and Sorrento's main drag becomes a thriving people scene.

The *passeggiata* peaks at about 22:00 in the warmest months.

### Lemon Products Galore

Via San Cesareo is lined with hardworking rival shops selling a mind-boggling array of lemon products and offering samples of lots of sour goodies. You'll find *limoncello*, lemon biscuits, lemon pasta, lemon drops, lemon chocolate, lemon perfume, lemon soap, and on and on. Poke around for a pungent experience (and read the "Lemons" sidebar, later). A few produce stands are also mixed in.

### ▲Lemon Grove Garden (Agruminato)

This lemon-and-orange grove, lined with shady, welcoming paths, was rescued from development by the city of Sorrento and turned into a park. The family that manages it has seasoned green thumbs and descends from the family that started working here decades ago, when the grove was still in private hands. The garden is dotted with benches, tables, and an inviting little tasting (and buying) stand. You'll get a chance to sniff and taste the varieties of lemons and enjoy free samples of *limoncello* along with other homemade liqueurs made from mandarins, licorice, or fennel. Check out how they've grafted orange-tree branches onto a lemon tree so that both fruits grow on the same tree.

**Cost and Hours:** Free, daily April-Sept 10:00-21:00, shorter hours off-season, closed in rainy weather, tel. 081-878-1888, www.igiardinidicataldo.it. Enter the garden on Corso Italia (100 yards north of the train station—where painted tiles show lemon fantasies) or at the intersection of Via Capasso and Via Rota (next to Hotel La Meridiana).

**Eating:** For a cheap and relaxing meal, get a big-enough-to-split *saltimbocca* sandwich to go from the recommended **Pizzeria da Franco** (across the street on Corso Italia) and enjoy it in the lemon grove.

**Nearby:** The entrepreneurial family's small "factory"—where you can see how they use the lemons, and buy a tasty gelato, *granita,* or lemonade—is just past the parking garage along the road below the garden (Via Correale 27). They also have a small shop across from the Corso Italia entrance (at #267).

## Museum of Inlaid Wood
## (Museobottega della Tarsialignea)

Sorrento doesn't have much in the way of museums, but if you want to get out of the heat and crowds, this is a good place to do it. It's not only a collection of inlaid wood, but also a painting gallery featuring scenes of 19th-century Sorrento, antique maps, and portraits, and a fine decorative arts collection. The basement displays modern examples of inlaid wood. While pricey, it's serious, thoughtfully presented, and bursting with local pride.

**Cost and Hours:** €8, daily 10:00-18:30, Nov-March until 17:30, Via San Nicola 28, tel. 081-877-1942, www.museomuta.it.

## ▲Swimming and Sunbathing

If you require immediate tanning, you can rent a chair on a pier by the port. There are no great beaches in Sorrento—the gravelly, jam-packed private beaches of **Marina Piccola** are more for partying than pampering, and there's just a tiny spot for public use. The elevator in Villa Comunale city park (next to the Church of San Francesco) gets you down for €1. There's another humble beach at **Marina Grande.**

The classic, sandy Italian beach two miles away at **Meta** is generally overrun with teenagers from Naples. Bus #A goes from Piazza Tasso to Meta beach (last stop, schedule posted for hourly returns; you can also get there on the Circumvesuviana but the Meta stop is a very long walk from the beach). At Meta, you'll find pizzerias, snack bars, and a little free section of beach, but the place is mostly dominated by several sprawling private-beach complexes—if you go, pay for a spot in one of these, such as Lido Metamare (lockable changing cabins, lounge chairs, tel. 081-532-

SORRENTO & CAPRI

---

## Lemons

Around here, *limoni* are ubiquitous: screaming yellow painted on ceramics, dainty bottles of *limoncello,* and lemons the size of softballs at the fruit stand.

The Amalfi Coast and Sorrento area produce several different kinds of lemons. The gigantic, bumpy "lemons" are actually citrons, called *cedri,* and are more for show—they're pulpier than they are juicy, and make a good marmalade. The juicy *sfusato sorrentino,* grown only in Sorrento, is shaped like an American football, while the *sfusato amalfitano,* with knobby points on both ends, is less juicy but equally aromatic. These two kinds of luscious lemons are used in sweets such as *granita* (shaved ice doused in lemonade), *limoncello* (a candy-like liqueur with a big kick, called *limoncino* on the Cinque Terre), *delizia al limone* (a dome of fluffy cake filled and slathered with a thick whipped lemon cream), *spremuta di limone* (fresh-squeezed lemon juice), and, of course, gelato or *sorbetto al limone.*

---

2505). It's a very Italian scene—locals complain that it's "too local" (that is, inundated with riffraff)—with light lunches, a playground, a manicured beach, loud pop music...and no international tourists.

More relaxing beaches are west of Sorrento. Tarzan might take Jane to the wild and stony beach at **Punta del Capo,** a 15-minute bus ride from Piazza Tasso (the same bus #A explained earlier, but in the opposite direction from Meta; 2/hour, get off at stop on Via Capo just after the Maxim Gorky house, then walk 10 minutes down Calata Punta del Capo, past ruined Roman Villa di Pollio).

Another good choice is **Marina di Puolo,** a tiny fishing town popular in the summer for its sandy beach, surfside restaurants, and beachfront disco (to get here, stay on bus #A a bit farther beyond the Punta del Capo stop above—ask driver to let you off at Marina di Puolo—then follow signs and hike down about 15 minutes).

### More Activities

**Sorrento Food Tours:** Run by a US expat with long experience doing food and wine tours throughout Italy, this outfit offers an information-filled, fast-paced food tour. Tamara and colleagues dish up a parade of local edibles interspersed with lots of food history, stopping at eight places in three hours (€75, 15 percent discount for Rick Steves readers, use code "ricksteves"; departures at 10:30 and 16:00 with demand, maximum 12 people; mobile 331-304-5666, www.sorrentofoodtours.com).

**Tennis:** The Sorrento Sport Snack Bar has two tennis courts open to the public (long hours daily, pay to use the court and rent equipment, call to reserve, across from recommended Grand Hotel Ambasciatori at Via Califano 5, tel. 081-807-1616).

**Snorkeling and Scuba Diving:** To snorkel or scuba dive in the Mediterranean, contact Futuro Mare for details on a one-hour boat ride to the protected marine zone between Sorrento and Capri (options for snorkelers, beginners, and experienced certified divers; about 3 hours round-trip, call 1-2 days in advance to reserve, mobile 349-653-6323, www.sorrentodiving.it, info@futuromare.it).

**Motorboat Rental:** You can rent motorboats big enough for four people (with your back to the ferry-ticket offices, it's to the left around the corner at Via Marina Piccola 43; tel. 081-807-2283, www.nauticasicsic.com).

# Nightlife in Sorrento

## PUBS AND CLUBS

Sorrento is a fun place to enjoy a drink or some dancing after dinner. The crowd is older, and the many local English expats seem to have paved the way for you.

**The Fauno Bar,** which dominates Piazza Tasso with tables spilling onto the square, is a fine place to make the scene over a drink any time of day.

**Daniele's Club** is run by DJ Daniele, who tailors music to the audience (including karaoke, if you ask nicely). The scene, while sloppy, is generally comfortable for the 30- to 60-year-old crowd. If you're alone, there's a pole you can dance with (no cover charge, try their signature cocktail, "Come Back to Sorrento," a mojito made with *limoncello;* no food, nightly from 21:30, down the steps from the flags at Piazza Tasso 10).

**The English Inn** offers both a streetside sports pub and a more refined-feeling garden out back—at least until the evening, when the music starts blaring. English vacationers come to Sorrento in droves (many have holidayed here annually for decades). The menu includes fish-and-chips, all-day English breakfast, baked beans on toast, and draft beer (daily, Corso Italia 55, tel. 081-878-2570).

**The Foreigners' Club** (known in Italian as the **Terrazza delle Sirene**) offers live Neapolitan songs, Sinatra-style classics, and jazzy elevator music nightly at 20:00 throughout the summer. It's just right for old-timers feeling frisky (Via Luigi de Maio 35, entrance just past the TI).

## THEATER SHOW

At **Armida Theater Cinema,** a hardworking troupe puts on *The Sorrento Musical,* a folk-music show that treats visitors to a schmaltzy dose of Neapolitan Tarantella music and dance—complete with "Funiculì Funiculà" and "Santa Loo-chee-yee-yah." The 75-minute Italian-language extravaganza features a cast playing guitar, mandolin, saxophone, and tambourines, and singing operatically from Neapolitan balconies...complete with Vesuvius erupting in the background. Your €25 ticket includes a drink before the show (€50 with 4-course dinner at Basilico Italia restaurant; RS%—Maurizio promises my readers a €5 discount if you buy directly at the box office and show this book, 2 tickets/book; shows run 3-5 nights/week mid-April-Oct at 21:00, bar opens 30 minutes before show, dinner starts at 20:00 and must be reserved in advance—in person or by email; box office open long hours daily, theater seats 500, about halfway between Piazza Tasso and the train station at Corsa Italia 219, tel. 081-878-1470, www.cinemateatroarmida.it, booking@cinemateatroarmida.it).

# Sleeping in Sorrento

Given the location, hotels here often have beautiful views, and many offer balconies. At hotels that offer sea views, ask for a room *"con balcone, con vista sul mare"* (with a balcony, with a sea view). *"Tranquillo"* is taken as a request for a quieter room off the street.

Hotels listed are either near the train station and city center (where balconies overlook city streets) or on cliffside Via Capo (with sea-view balconies). Via Capo is a 20-minute walk—or short bus ride—from the station.

You should have no trouble finding a room any time except in August, when the town is jammed with Italians and prices often rise above the regular high-season rates.

The spindly, more exotic, and more vertical Amalfi Coast town of Positano (see next chapter) is also a good place to spend the night.

## IN THE TOWN CENTER

**$$$$ Hotel Antiche Mura,** with 50 rooms and four stars, is sophisticated, elegant, and plush. It offers all the amenities, including an impressive breakfast buffet. Surrounded by lemon trees, the pool and sundeck are a peaceful oasis. Just a block off the main square, it's quieter than some central hotels because it's perched on the ledge of a dramatic ravine (RS%, some rooms with balconies, family rooms, air-con, elevator, pay parking, closed Jan-Feb, a block inland from Piazza Tasso at Via Fuorimura 7, tel. 081-807-3523, www.hotelantichemura.com, info@hotelantichemura.com, Michele).

**$$$$ Palazzo Tasso,** nicely located near the center, has 11 small, sleek, fashionably designed modern rooms; there's no public space except for the breakfast room (some rooms with balconies, air-con, elevator, Via Santa Maria della Pietà 33, tel. 081-878-3579, www.palazzotasso.com, info@palazzotasso.com, Elena).

**$$$$ Plaza Sorrento** is a contemporary-feeling, upscale refuge in the very center of town (next door to Antiche Mura but not as elegant). Its 65 rooms mix mod decor with wood grain, and the rooftop swimming pool is inviting (RS%, some rooms with balconies, air-con, elevator, closed Jan-Feb, Via Fuorimura 3, tel. 081-878-2831, www.plazasorrento.com, info@plazasorrento.com).

**$$$ Il Palazzo Starace B&B,** conscientiously run by Massimo, offers seven tidy, modern rooms in a little alley off Corso Italia, one block from Piazza Tasso (RS%—use code "RSWEL", some rooms with balconies, family room, air-con, lots of stairs, luggage dumbwaiter and no elevator, ring bell around corner from Via Santa Maria della Pietà 9, tel. 081-807-2633, mobile 366-950-5377, www.palazzostarace.com, info@palazzostarace.com).

**$$$ Hotel Mignon** rents 22 soothing blue rooms with beautiful, tiled public spaces, a rooftop sundeck, and a small garden surrounded by a lemon grove (RS% with code "2020RSE" when booked on their website, most rooms have balconies but no views, air-con, closed in Jan-Feb; from the cathedral, walk a block farther up Corso Italia and look for the hotel up a small gated lane to your left; Via Sersale 9, tel. 081-807-3824, www.sorrentohotelmignon.com, info@sorrentohotelmignon.com, Paolo).

**$$$ Casa Astarita B&B,** hiding upstairs in a big building facing the busy main street, has a crazy-quilt-tiled entryway and eight bright, tranquil, creatively decorated rooms (three with little balconies). Thin doors, echoey tile, and a buzzing location can result in noise...bring earplugs (air-con, open year-round, 50 yards past the cathedral on Corso Italia at #67, tel. 081-877-4906, www.casastarita.com, info@casastarita.com, Annamaria and Alfonso). If there's no one at reception, ask at Hotel Mignon (described above)—the same family runs both hotels.

**$$ Hotel Nice** rents 27 simple, cheap rooms with high ceilings 100 yards in front of the train station on the main drag. This last resort is worth considering only for its very handy-to-the-train-station location. Alfonso promises a quiet room—double-paned windows help dim the hum of its busy location—if you request it when you book by email (RS%, air-con, elevator, sundeck terrace, closed Nov-March, Corso Italia 257, tel. 081-878-1650, www.hotelnice.it, info@hotelnice.it).

**$ Ulisse Deluxe Hostel** is the best budget deal in town. This "hostel" is actually a hotel, with 56 well-equipped, marble-tiled rooms and elegant public areas, but it also has two single-sex dorm rooms with bunks (RS%, family rooms, breakfast buffet extra, air-con, elevator, spa and pool use extra, pay parking, closed Jan-mid-

Feb, Via del Mare 22, tel. 081-877-4753, www.ulissedeluxe.com, info@ulissedeluxe.com, Chiara). It's a five-minute walk from the old-town action: From Corso Italia, walk down the stairs just beyond the hospital (ospedale) to Via del Mare. Go downhill along the right side of the big parking lot to find the entrance.

## AT THE EAST END OF TOWN

$$$$ **Grand Hotel Ambasciatori** is a sumptuous five-star hotel with 100 rooms, a cliffside setting, a sprawling garden, and a pool. This is Humphrey Bogart land, with plush public spaces, a relaxing stay-awhile ambience, and a free elevator to its "private beach"—actually a sundeck built out over the water (RS%, some view rooms, balconies in all rooms, air-con in summer, elevator, pay parking, closed Nov-March, Via Califano 18, tel. 081-878-2025, www.ambasciatorisorrento.com, ambasciatori@manniellohotels.com). It's a short walk from the town center (10-15 minutes from the train station or Piazza Tasso).

## WITH A VIEW, ON VIA CAPO

These cliffside hotels are outside of town, toward the cape of the peninsula (from the train station, go straight out Corso Italia, which turns into Via Capo). Once you're set up, commuting into town by bus or on foot is easy. Hotel Minerva is my favorite Sorrento splurge, while Hotel Désirée is a super budget bet with comparable views. If you're in Sorrento to stay put and luxuriate, especially with a car, these accommodations are perfect (although I'd rather luxuriate in Positano—see next chapter).

**Getting to Via Capo:** From the city center, it's a gradually uphill 15-minute walk (20 minutes from train station, last part is a bit steeper), a €20 taxi ride, or a cheap bus ride. If you're arriving with luggage, you can wait at the train station for one of the long-distance SITA buses that stop on Via Capo on their way to Massa Lubrense (about every 40 minutes; some buses heading for Positano/Amalfi also work—check with the driver). Frequent Sorrento city buses leave from near Piazza Tasso in the city center (go down a block and turn left on Corso Italia; from far side of the piazza, look for bus #A, about 2-3/hour). Get off at the Hotel Belair stop for the hotels listed here.

**Getting from Via Capo into Town:** Buses work great once you get the hang of them (and it's particularly gratifying to avoid the taxi racket). To reach downtown Sorrento from Via Capo, catch any bus heading downhill from Hotel Belair (2-3/hour, buses run all day and evening). Or ask your hotel to call a taxi.

$$$$ **Hotel Minerva** is a sun-worshipper's temple. The road-level entrance (on a busy street) leads to an elevator that takes you to the fifth-floor reception. Getting off, you'll step onto a spec-

tacular terrace with outrageous Mediterranean views. Bright common areas, a small rooftop swimming pool, and a cold-water Jacuzzi complement 60 large, tiled, colorful rooms with views, some with balconies (3-night peak-season minimum, air-con, pay parking, closed Nov-March, Via Capo 30, tel. 081-878-1011, www.minervasorrento.com, info@minervasorrento.com).

**$$$$ Hotel La Tonnarella** is an old-time Sorrentine villa-turned-boutique-hotel, with several terraces, stylish tiles, and indifferent service. Eighteen of its 24 rooms have views of the sea, and you can pay extra for a terrace (air-con, pay parking, small beach with private elevator access, closed Nov-March, Via Capo 31, tel. 081-878-1153, www.latonnarella.it, info@latonnarella.it).

**$$$ Albergo Settimo Cielo** ("Seventh Heaven") is an old-fashioned, family-run cliffhanger sitting 300 steps above Marina Grande. The reception is just off the waterfront side of the road, and the elevator passes down through four floors with 50 clean but spartan rooms—all with grand views, and many with balconies. The rooms feel dated for the price—you're paying for the views (family rooms, air-con in summer, parking, inviting pool, sun terrace, closed Nov-March, Via Capo 27, tel. 081-878-1012, www.hotelsettimocielo.com, info@hotelsettimocielo.com; Giuseppe, sons Stefano and Massimo, and daughter Serena).

**$ Hotel Désirée** is a modest affair, with reasonable rates, humbler vistas, and no traffic noise. The 22 basic rooms have high, ravine-facing or partial-sea views, and half come with balconies (all the same price). There's a fine rooftop sunning terrace and a lovable cat, Tia. Owner Corinna (a committed environmentalist), daughter Cassandra, and receptionist Antonio serve an organic breakfast and are helpful with tips on exploring the peninsula (family rooms, most rooms have fans, lots of stairs and no elevator, laundry services, free parking, shares driveway and beach elevator with La Tonnarella, closed early Nov-Feb except open at Christmas—rare for this area, Via Capo 31, tel. 081-878-1563, www.desireehotelsorrento.com, info@desireehotelsorrento.com).

## Eating in Sorrento

### GOURMET SPLURGES

In a town proud to have no McDonald's, consider eating well for a few extra bucks. Both of these places are worthwhile splurges run by a hands-on boss with a passion for good food and exacting service. The first is gourmet and playful. The second is classic. Both are romantic. Be prepared to relax and stay awhile.

**$$$$ Ristorante il Buco,** once the cellar of an old monastery, is now a small, dressy restaurant—with spacious seating—that serves delightfully presented and creative modern Mediterranean dishes under a grand, rustic arch. Peppe holds a Michelin star, and he and his staff love to explain exactly what's on the plate—often sophisticated dishes with an emphasis on seafood, but a good vegetarian selection as well. They offer lots of fine wines by the glass. Reserve ahead (extravagant-tasting €75-100 fixed-price meal, 10 percent discount when you show this book, Thu-Tue 12:30-14:30 & 19:30-22:30, closed Wed and Jan; just off Piazza Sant'Antonino—facing the basilica, go under the grand arch on the left and immediately enter the restaurant at II Rampa Marina Piccola 5; tel. 081-878-2354, www.ilbucoristorante.it).

$$$$ L'Antica Trattoria enjoys a sedate, *romantico*, candlelit ambience, tucked away in its own little world. The cuisine is traditional but with modern flair, and the inviting menu is fun to peruse (though pricey). Run by the same family since 1930, the restaurant has a trellised garden outside and intimate nooks inside. Aldo and sons will take care of you while Vincenzo—the Joe Cocker-esque resident mandolin player—entertains. Readers who show this book can choose a 10 percent discount on a fixed-price meal or a free *limoncello* if ordering à la carte. Reservations are smart (good vegetarian options, daily 12:00-23:30, closed Jan-Feb, air-con, Via Padre R. Giuliani 33, tel. 081-807-1082, www.lanticatrattoria.it).

## MIDPRICED RESTAURANTS

$$$ Inn Bufalito specializes in all things buffalo: *mozzarella di bufala* (and other buffalo-milk cheeses), steak, sausage, salami, carpaccio, and buffalo-meat pasta sauce on homemade pasta. The smartly designed space has a modern, borderline-trendy, casual atmosphere and a fun indoor-outdoor vibe (don't miss the seasonal specialties on the blackboard, Wed-Mon 12:00-23:00, closed Tue and Jan-March, Vico I Fuoro 21, tel. 081-365-6975).

$$ Ristorante Pizzeria da Gigino, lively and congested with a sprawling interior and tables spilling onto the street, makes huge, tasty Neapolitan-style pizzas in their wood-burning oven. Their *linguine gigino* and the seafood salad are favorites (daily 12:00-24:00, closed Jan-Feb, just off Piazza Sant'Antonino at Via degli Archi 15, tel. 081-878-1927, Antonino).

$$ La Cantinaccia del Popolo draws a spirited crowd anxious to taste Annalisa's cooking. Her husband Peppe seems well-fed, so you know the food is good. Peruse the counter of antipasti displayed under hanging prosciutto, but save room for delicious pasta that's stylishly served in large metal skillets (Tue-Sun 12:00-15:30 & 16:45-23:30, closed Mon, no reservations but Peppe pours free homemade wine while you wait, a couple of blocks past the train station at Vico Terzo Rota 3, mobile 349-955-6574).

With a Sea View: $$$ The Foreigners' Club restaurant (Terrazza delle Sirene) has some of the best sea views in town (with a sprawling terrace under breezy palms), live music nightly at 20:00 (May–mid-Oct), and affordable—if uninspired—meals. It's a good spot for dessert or an after-dinner *limoncello* ("snack" menu with light meals, daily, bar opens at 9:30, meals served 11:00–23:00, Via Luigi de Maio 35, tel. 081-877-3263). If you'd enjoy eating along the water (rather than just with a water view), see "Harborside in Marina Grande," later.

## CHEAP EATS

**Pizza:** There's nothing fancy about **$ Pizzeria da Franco,** Sorrento's favorite place for basic, casual pizza in a fun, untouristy atmosphere. Join the locals on benches eating hot sandwiches and great pizzas served on waxed paper in a square tin. It's packed to the rafters with a youthful crowd that doesn't mind the plastic cups. Consider their *saltimbocca,* a baked sandwich with top-quality prosciutto and mozzarella on pizza bread—splittable and perfect to go (daily 8:00–late, just across from Lemon Grove Garden on busy Corso Italia at #265, tel. 081-877-2066).

**Kebabs:** The little hole-in-the-wall **$ Kebab Ciampa** has a passionate following among eaters who appreciate Andrea's fresh bread, homemade sauces, and ethic of buying meat fresh each day (and closing when the supply is gone). This is your best cheap, non-Italian meal in town. Choose beef or chicken—locals don't go for pork—and garnish with fries and/or salad (Thu-Tue from 17:00, closed Wed, before the cathedral off Via Santa Maria della Pietà, at Vico il Traversa Pietà 23, tel. 081-807-4595).

**Picnics:** Get groceries at the large **Decò** supermarket (Mon-Sat 8:30–20:00, shorter hours Sun, Corso Italia 223) or at the **Carrefour** supermarket underneath Hotel Mignon (daily 8:00–22:00).

**Gelato:** Near the train station, **Gelateria David** has many repeat customers (so many flavors, so little time; they make 155 different flavors, but have about 30 at any one time). In 1957, Augusto Davide opened a *gelateria* in Sorrento, and his grandson Mario proudly carries on the tradition today, still making the gelato on-site. Before choosing a flavor, sample *Profumi di Sorrento* (an explosive sorbet of mixed fruits), "Sorrento moon" (white almond with lemon zest), or lemon crème (daily 9:00–24:00, shorter hours off-season, closed Dec-Feb, a block below the train station at Via Marziale 19, tel. 081-807-3649). Mario also offers gelato-making classes (€12/person, 5-person minimum, 1 hour, call or email ahead to reserve, www.gelateriadavidsorrento.it, info@gelateriadavidsorrento.it). Don't mistake this place for the similarly named Gelateria Davide, in the town center.

At **Gelateria Primavera,** Antonio and Alberta whip up 70 exotic flavors...and still have time to make pastries for the pope and other celebrities—check out the nostalgic photos in their inviting back room, proving this is a Sorrento institution (daily 9:00-24:00, just west of Piazza Tasso at Corso Italia 142, tel. 081-807-3252).

## HARBORSIDE IN MARINA GRANDE

For a decent lunch or dinner *con vista*, head down to either of these restaurants by Sorrento's small-boat harbor, Marina Grande. To get to Marina Grande, follow the directions from Villa Comunale on my self-guided Sorrento walk, earlier. It's about a 15-minute stroll from downtown. You can also take minibus #D from Piazza Tasso. Be prepared to walk back (last bus leaves at 20:00) or spring for a pricey taxi.

$$ **Trattoria da Emilia,** at the city-side end of the Marina Grande waterfront, is good for straightforward, typical Sorrentine home-cooking, including fresh fish, lots of fried seafood, and *gnocchi di mamma*—potato dumplings with meat sauce, basil, and mozzarella (daily 12:00-15:00 & 18:30-22:00, closed Nov-Feb, no reservations taken, indoor and outdoor seating, tel. 081-807-2720).

$$ **Porta Marina** serves fresh-as-can-be seafood in a modest location at the end of the port, with views every bit as good as more expensive places nearby. Servers will tell you the catch of the day—always the best option—but if grilled octopus is on the menu then think no more (daily, 12:00-21:30, Via Marina Grande 25, tel. 081-877-4781).

# Sorrento Connections

It's impressively fast to zip by boat from Sorrento to many coastal towns and islands during the summer—in fact, it's quicker and easier for residents to get around by fast boat than by car or train (see "By Boat," later, and the map on page 1043).

## BY TRAIN AND BUS

**From Sorrento to Naples, Pompeii, and Herculaneum by Train:** The run-down **Circumvesuviana commuter train** runs twice hourly between Naples and Sorrento with crowds, pickpockets, and no air-conditioning (Italian-only website at www.eavsrl.it). The schedule is available at the TI: Pompeii (30 minutes, €2.40); Herculaneum (50 minutes, €2.90); and Naples (70 minutes, €3.90). If there's a line at the train station, you can also buy tickets at the snack bar (across from the main ticket office) or downstairs at the newsstand. To confirm the latest departures, look for the electric schedule above the ticket window.

A more comfortable but less frequent alternative to the Circumvesuviana commuter train, the tourist-oriented **Campania Express train** runs from mid-March to October. It's less crowded, has air-conditioning, and provides some space for luggage (4/day,

€6 one-way to Pompeii, 25 minutes; €6 one-way to Herculaneum, 40 minutes; €8 one-way to Naples, 1 hour; online sales at http://ots.eavsrl.it or buy at the station). For more details, see "Getting Around the Region" on page 1014 of the Naples chapter.

**From Sorrento to Naples Airport:** Curreri buses run daily to the airport (€10, purchase online or pay driver, 8/day from 6:30-16:30, no service Dec 25 and Jan 1, a long 1.5 hours on winding roads, departs from in front of train station, tel. 081-801-5420, www.curreriviaggi.it). From Naples Airport to Sorrento, eight buses depart between 9:00 and 19:30.

**From Sorrento to the Amalfi Coast:** See page 1082.

**From Sorrento to Rome:** Most people ride the Circumvesuviana or Campania Express to Naples, then catch the Frecciarossa or Italo express train to Rome. Italo also offers a nifty but infrequent bus/train connection ("Italobus" from Sorrento to Naples, then train to Rome, 2/day, 3.5 hours, www.italotreno.it). Another option is the Sorrento-Rome bus: It's cheaper, although the departure times can be inconvenient (Mon-Sat at 6:00 and 17:00, Sun at 17:00; off-season Mon-Sat at 6:00, Fri-Sun at 17:00; 4 hours; departs Sorrento from Corso Italia 259B, by Bar Kontatto, a block from the train station, and runs to Tiburtina bus station in Rome; buy tickets at www.marozzivt.it—in Italian only, at some travel agencies, or on board for a surcharge; tel. 080-579-0111).

## BY BOAT

The number of boats that run per day varies: The frequency indicated here is for roughly mid-May through mid-October, with more boats per day in the peak of summer and fewer off-season. The specific companies operating each route also tend to change from season to season. Check all schedules locally with the TI, your hotel, or online (use the individual boat-company websites—see below—or visit www.capritourism.com, select English, and click "Shipping timetable"). Although some ferry-company websites sell tickets online, buying tickets at the port is easy (and keeps your departure options open, especially valuable if you're watching the weather); next-day tickets typically go on sale starting the evening before. All boats take several hundred people each and (except for the busiest days) rarely fill up.

**From Sorrento to Capri:** Boats run at least hourly. Your options are a fast **ferry** (*traghetto* or *nave veloce*, takes cars, 4/day, 30 minutes, Caremar, tel. 081-807-3077, www.caremar.it) or a slightly faster and pricier **hydrofoil** (*aliscafi*, over 20/day, 25 minutes, Gescab, tel. 081-807-1812, www.gescab.it). To visit Capri when it's least crowded, it's best to buy your ticket at 8:00 and take the 8:30 hydrofoil (try to depart by 9:45 at the very latest). If you make a reservation, it's not changeable. These early boats can be jammed, but it's worth it once you reach the island.

**From Sorrento to Other Points: Naples** (6/day, more in summer, departs roughly every 2 hours starting at 7:20, few or no boats on winter weekends, arrives at Molo Beverello, 35 minutes), **Positano** (mid-April-mid-Oct only, 4-6/day, 35 minutes), **Amalfi** (mid-April-mid-Oct only, 4-6/day, 1 hour).

**Getting to Sorrento's Port** (Marina Piccola): To walk, either hike steeply down directly from Piazza Tasso (find the stairs under the flags, 5-minute walk), or walk to the Villa Comunale public park (see my self-guided Sorrento Walk, earlier), where you can pay €1 to ride the elevator down (from the bottom, it's a 5-minute walk to the port). Otherwise, catch bus #B or #C from Piazza Sant'Antonino (specify that you're going to the *porto;* buses run 3/hour).

# Capri

Capri was made famous as the vacation hideaway of Roman emperors Augustus and Tiberius. In the 19th century, it was the haunt of Romantic Age aristocrats on their Grand Tour of Europe. Later it was briefly a refuge for Europe's artsy gay community: Oscar Wilde, D. H. Lawrence, and company hung out here back when being gay could land you in jail...or worse. And these days, the island is a world-

class tourist trap, packed with gawky, nametag-wearing visitors searching for the rich and famous—and finding only their prices.

About 12,000 people live on Capri (although many winter in Naples) and during any given day in high season, the island hosts another 20,000 tourists. The "Island of Dreams" is a zoo in July and August—overrun with tacky, low-grade group tourism at its worst. At other times of year, though still crowded, it can provide a relaxing and scenic break from the cultural gauntlet of Italy. Even with its crowds, commercialism, fame, and glitz, Capri is a flat-out gorgeous place: Chalky white limestone cliffs rocket boldly from the shimmering blue-and-green surf, and the Blue Grotto sea cave glows with reflected sunlight. Strategically positioned gardens, villas, and viewpoints provide stunning vistas of the Sorrento Peninsula, Amalfi Coast, Vesuvius, and Capri itself. And, if you study this chapter, you'll find that it's very well-organized for its many visitors.

## PLANNING YOUR TIME

This is the best see-everything-in-a-day plan from Naples or Sorrento:

- Take an early hydrofoil to Capri (from Sorrento, buy ticket at 8:00, boat leaves around 8:30 and arrives around 8:50—smart). You'll land at Marina Grande; yes, Capri's port has the same name as the small-boat harbor at Sorrento.
- At the port, select from three boating options: Enjoy the scenic circle-the-island tour with a visit to the Blue Grotto (1.5-2 hours); circle the island without Blue Grotto stop (1 hour); or just visit the Blue Grotto. (There are generally spaces available for departures every few minutes.)
- Arriving back at Marina Grande, catch a bus to Anacapri, which has two or three hours' worth of sightseeing.
- In Anacapri, see the town, ride the chairlift to Monte Solaro and back (or hike down), stroll out from the base of the chairlift to Villa San Michele for the view, and eat lunch.
- Afterward, catch a bus to Capri town, which is worth an hour of browsing.
- Finally, ride the funicular from Capri town down to the harbor and laze on the free beach or wander the yacht harbor while waiting for your boat back to Sorrento.

If you're heading to Capri specifically to see the Blue Grotto, be sure to check the weather and sea conditions. If the tide is too high or the water too rough, the grotto can be closed. Ask the TI or your hotelier. If the Blue Grotto is closed or you're not keen on seeing it, you can still enjoy a leisurely day on the island seeing the sights in Anacapri and Capri town. Or, for the same amount of time and less money, you can skip the Blue Grotto and enjoy circling the entire island by boat (an experience I find even more fun than the famed grotto).

Efficient travelers can see Capri on the way between destinations: Sail from Sorrento, check your bag at the harbor, see Capri, and take a boat directly from there to Naples or to the Amalfi Coast (or vice versa).

If you buy a one-way boat ticket to Capri (there's no round-trip discount), you'll have maximum schedule flexibility and can take any convenient hydrofoil or ferry back. (Check times for the last return crossing upon arrival with any TI on Capri, or at www.capritourism.com; the last return trips usually leave between 18:30 and 19:30.) During July and August, however, it's wise to get a round-trip ticket (ensuring you a spot). On busy days, be 20 minutes early for the boat, or you can be bumped.

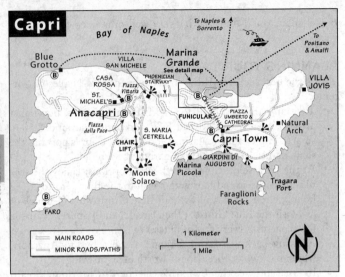

Starting your day as early as is reasonably possible is key to an enjoyable trip to Capri. Legions of day-trippers on big bus tours come from as far as Rome, combining with cruise-ship excursion groups to create a daily rush hour in each direction (arriving between 10:00-11:00, leaving around 17:00) and packing the island through the early afternoon. If you arrive before them, the entire trip to and into the Blue Grotto might take just a half-hour (10 minutes there, 10 minutes in the dinghy going inside, and 10 minutes back); arrive later and you might face a two-hour delay.

## GETTING TO CAPRI

For instructions on getting to Capri by **scheduled ferry,** see the "Connections" sections of the Sorrento and Naples chapters, and the "Getting Around the Amalfi Coast" section of the Amalfi Coast chapter.

Another option is to visit Capri by **tour boat.** Consider **Mondo Guide,** which offers my readers a no-stress, all-day itinerary for €90: You'll be picked up at your Sorrento hotel around 8:00 and driven to the port, where you'll board a small boat (maximum 12 people, shared with other Rick Steves readers) and be taken across to Capri to visit the Blue Grotto (optional entry fee to hop in one of the little rowboats to go inside). Then you'll continue to Marina Grande for about four hours of free time on the island—just enough to head to Anacapri for sightseeing and the Monte Solaro chairlift (island transportation and admissions on your own). Finally, you'll reboard the boat for a lightly narrated circle around the island and pass through the iconic Faraglioni Rocks (includes drinks, a snack, and—conditions permitting—a chance to swim from the boat). Considering the expense and hassle of doing all this on your own, the tour is a good value—you're basically paying about €20-30 extra for a less stressful, more personalized experience. The trip only goes if enough people sign up, and reservations are required—book online at MondoGuide.com. For details on Mondo and their tours, see page 970. **Tempio Travel**—based at the Sorrento train station—offers a similar trip at a similar price (tel. 081-878-2103, www.tempiotravel.com, or drop by their office).

## Orientation to Capri

First thing—pronounce it right: Italians say KAH-pree, not kah-PREE like the song (or the pants). The island is small—just four miles by two miles—and is separated from the Sorrentine Peninsula by a five-mile-wide strait. Capri has only two towns to speak of: Capri and Anacapri. The island also has some scant Roman ruins and a few interesting churches and villas. But its chief attraction is its famous Blue Grotto, and its best activity beyond the boat rides is the chairlift from Anacapri up the island's Monte Solaro ("the sunny mount").

### TOURIST INFORMATION

Capri's efficient English-speaking TI has branches in Marina Grande, Capri town, and Anacapri. Their well-organized website has schedules and practical information in English (www.capritourism.com). At any TI, pick up the free map or pay for a better one if you'll be venturing to the outskirts of Capri town or Anacapri.

The **Marina Grande TI** is by the Motoscafisti Capri tour-boat dock (Mon-Sat 8:30-18:15, Sun 9:30-17:15, shorter hours off-season, tel. 081-837-0634).

The **Capri town TI** fills a closet under the bell tower on Piazza Umberto I and is less crowded than its sister at the port (same hours as Marina Grande TI, WC and baggage storage downstairs behind TI, tel. 081-837-0686).

The tiny **Anacapri TI** is on the main pedestrian/shopping street, Via Orlandi, at #59 (Mon-Sat 8:30-16:15, closed Sun, shorter hours Nov-Easter, tel. 081-837-1524).

### ARRIVAL IN CAPRI

Get oriented on the boat before you dock, as you near the harbor with the island spread out before you. The port is a small community of its own, called **Marina Grande,** connected by a funicular and buses to the rest of the island. **Capri town** fills the ridge high above the harbor. The ruins of Emperor Tiberius' palace, **Villa Jovis,** cap

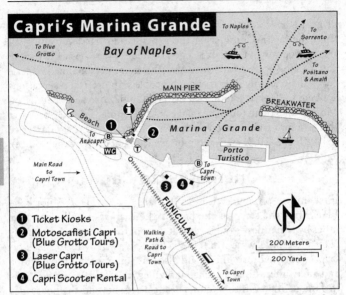

# Capri's Marina Grande

To Naples · To Sorrento

**Bay of Naples**

To Blue Grotto

MAIN PIER

To Positano & Amalfi

BREAKWATER

Beach

To Anacapri

**Marina Grande**

WC

Porto Turistico

Main Road to Capri Town

To Capri town

**FUNICULAR**

Walking Path & Road to Capri Town

To Capri Town

200 Meters
200 Yards

❶ Ticket Kiosks
❷ Motoscafisti Capri (Blue Grotto Tours)
❸ Laser Capri (Blue Grotto Tours)
❹ Capri Scooter Rental

---

the peak on the left. To the right, the dramatic *"Mamma mia!"* road arcs around the highest mountain on the island **(Monte Solaro),** leading up to **Anacapri** (the island's second town, just out of sight). Notice the old zigzag steps below that road. Until 1874, this was the only connection between Capri and Anacapri. (Though it's quite old, it's nowhere near as old as implied by its nickname, "The Phoenician Stairway.") The white house on the ridge above the zigzags is **Villa San Michele** (where you can go later for a grand view).

**Arrival at Marina Grande:** Remember that you're arriving with a boatload of other tourists with similar plans. You'll need some patience as you get your bearings. Find the base of the **funicular railway** (signed *funicolare*) that runs up to Capri town, and stand facing it, with your back to the water.

The fourth little clothing-and-souvenir shop to the right of the funicular provides **baggage storage** (€3/bag, look for the awning sign, daily 9:00-18:00, tel. 081-837-4575, shorter hours or closed in winter).

The ferry-terminal building in front of the Bar Grotta Azzura has ticket windows with counters for **funicular and bus tickets** (same price for both—don't line up without one) and for **boat tickets** to Naples and Sorrento. (Notice the grand electronic departure board on the terminal building listing all boats leaving in the next couple of hours.) Adjacent is the **stop for buses** to the rest of the island. Across the street is a pay **WC,** and a little farther on is Marina Grande's pebbly public beach.

Two companies offer **boat trips** around the island and to the

Blue Grotto: **Laser Capri** and **Motoscafisti Capri.** Motoscafisti Capri's ticket shed is along the pier; Laser Capri's office is halfway down the waterfront to the left at Via Cristoforo Colombo 69. Both offer similar services (see "Sights in Capri," later).

From the port, you can take a boat to the Blue Grotto or around the island, the funicular to Capri town, or a bus to various destinations on Capri. The steep paved footpath that connects the port area with Capri town starts a block inland from the ferry dock (follow the signs to *Capri centro;* I've heard it takes 30 minutes).

## HELPFUL HINTS

**Cheap Tricks:** A cheap day trip to Capri is tough, as you'll pay about €20 each way just to get there and about €30 to see the Blue Grotto. That's €70 already. But if you picnic and ride buses rather than enjoying restaurants and taxis, you'll find your time on the island itself to be relatively inexpensive. Many of Capri's greatest pleasures are free.

**Tread Lightly:** Be conscious of your personal impact on this island. More than 2.3 million annual visitors put a strain on local resources. Consider taking any trash out with you and carrying a metal water bottle.

**Best Real Hike:** Serious hikers love the peaceful and scenic three-hour Fortress Hike, which takes you entirely away from the tourists. You'll walk under ruined forts along the rugged coast, from the Blue Grotto to the *faro* (lighthouse). From there, you can take a bus back to Anacapri (3/hour). The TI has a fine map/brochure.

**Free Beach:** Marina Grande has a free pebbly beach (pay at the bar for a shower).

**Local Guides:** Capri resident **Anna Bilardi Leva** is licensed to guide both on the island and elsewhere around the region. She seems to know everybody and every trick on the island (groups of two to fifteen people: €150/half-day, €230/day, mobile 339-712-7416, www.capritourinformation.com, annaleva@ hotmail.it).

## GETTING AROUND CAPRI

**By Bus and Funicular:** Tickets for the island's buses and funicular cost €2 per ride. Think about how many tickets you'll need and save time by buying them all at once at the port kiosk. (Tickets are also available throughout the island at newsstands, tobacco shops, and official ticket offices.) The €10 all-day pass (available only at official ticket offices) isn't a good value for most visitors. Validate your ticket when you board.

Schedules are clearly posted at all bus stations. Public buses are orange, while gray and blue buses are for private tour groups.

Public buses from the port to Capri town, and from Capri town to Anacapri, are frequent (4/hour, 10 minutes). The direct bus between the port and Anacapri runs less often (2/hour, 25 minutes), but is worth the wait if you're following my suggested visit as outlined in "Planning Your Time" at the start of this section. From Anacapri, branch bus lines run to the parking lot above the Blue Grotto and to the lighthouse (3/hour). Buses are teeny (because of the island's narrow roads) and often packed, the aisles filled with people standing. At most stops, you'll see ranks for passengers to line up in (locals feel free to cut the line). If the driver changes the bus's display to read *completo* (full), you'll need to wait for the next one. But if you combine my recommended bus trips with the funicular at the end of your visit, wait times are significantly less.

**By Taxi:** Taxis have fixed rates, listed at www.capritourism. com (Marina Grande to Capri town—€17; Marina Grande to Anacapri—€28). You can hire a taxi for about €70 per hour—negotiate.

**By Scooter:** If you're an experienced scooter rider, this is the perfect way to have the run of the island. (For novice riders, Capri's steep and narrow roads aren't a good place to start.) **Capri Scooter** rents bright-yellow scooters with 50cc engines—strong enough to haul couples. Rentals come with a map and instructions with parking tips and other helpful information (€15/hour, €55/day, RS%—10 percent discount on rentals of 2 hours or more with this book; includes helmet, gas, and insurance; daily April-Oct 9:30-18:00, may open in good weather off-season, at Via Don Giobbe Ruocco 55, Marina Grande, mobile 338-360-6918, www. capriscooter.com).

## Sights in Capri

### ON THE WATER
You have three boat-tour options: circle the island with a stop at the Blue Grotto, circle only, or Blue Grotto only.

### ▲▲▲Capri Boat Circle (Giro dell' Isola)
For me, the best experience on Capri is to take the scenic boat trip around the island. It's cheap, comes with good narration and lots of curiosities, and there are plenty of departures from Marina Grande.

Both **Laser Capri** and **Motoscafisti Capri** run trips that circle the island and pass stunning cliffs, caves, and views that most miss when they go only to the Blue Grotto (€18, no one-way discount; Motoscafisti Capri—tel. 081-837-7714, www.motoscafisticapri. com; Laser Capri—tel. 081-837-5208, www.lasercapri.com). The circular tour comes with a live guide and takes about an hour (1.5-

2 hours with Blue Grotto stop). As you circle the dramatic lime-stone rock called Capri, you'll see quirky sights (a solar-powered lighthouse, tiny statues atop desolate rocks, holes in the cliffs with legends going back to Emperor Tiberius' times), pop into various caves and inlets, power through a tiny hole in the famed Faraglioni Rocks, hear stories of celebrity-owned villas, and marvel at a non-stop parade of staggering cliffs.

With both companies, you can combine the boat trip with a stop at the Blue Grotto at no extra charge (this adds about an hour; check schedules to find out which tours include the optional Blue Grotto stop). As the 10-minute ride just to the grotto costs €15 (no one-way discount), the island circle is well worth the extra three euros.

All boats leave daily from 9:00 until at least 13:00 (or later, depending on when the Blue Grotto rowboats stop running—likely 16:00 in summer).

### ▲▲Blue Grotto

Thousands of tourists a day visit Capri's Blue Grotto (Grotta Az-zurra). I did—early (when the light is best), without the frustration of crowds, and with choppy waves nearly making entrance impos-sible...and it was great.

The actual cave experience isn't much: a short dinghy ride through a three-foot-high entry hole to reach a 60-yard-long cave,

where the sun reflects brilliantly blue on its limestone bottom. But the experience—getting there, getting in, and getting back—is a scenic hoot. You get a fast ride and scant narration on a 30-foot boat partway around the gorgeous island; along the way, you see bird life and dra-matic limestone cliffs. You'll understand why Roman emper-ors appreciated the invulnerability of the island—it's surrounded by cliffs, with only one good access point, and therefore easy to defend.

Just outside the grotto, your boat idles as you pile into eight-foot dinghies that hold up to four passengers each. Next, you'll be taken to a floating ticket counter to pay the grotto entry fee. From there, your ruffian rower will elbow his way to the tiny hole, then pull fast and hard on the cable at the low point of the swells to squeeze you into the grotto (keep your head down and hands in the boat). Then your man rows you around, spouting off a few descriptive lines and singing "O Sole Mio." Depending upon the strength of the sunshine that day, the blue light inside can be brilliant.

The grotto was actually an ancient Roman *nymphaeum*—a retreat for romantic hanky-panky. Many believe that, in its day, a tunnel led here directly from the palace, and that the grotto experience was enlivened by statues of Poseidon and company, placed half-underwater as if emerging from the sea. It was ancient Romans who smoothed out the entry hole that's still used to this day.

When dropping you off, your boatman will fish for a tip—it's optional, and €1 is enough (you've already paid plenty). If you don't want to return by boat, ask to be let off at the little dock, where stairs lead up to a café and the Blue Grotto bus stop.

**Cost:** The €14 entry fee (separate from the €15 ride from Marina Grande and back) includes €10 for the rowboat service plus €4 for admission to the grotto itself. Though some people swim in for free from the little dock after the boats stop running (about 17:00), it's illegal and can be dangerous.

**Timing:** When waves or high tide make entering dangerous, the boats don't go in—the grotto can close without notice, sending tourists (flush with anticipation) home without a chance to squeeze through the little hole. (If this happens to you, consider the one-hour boat ride around the island instead.)

If you're coming from Capri's port (Marina Grande), allow 1-2 hours for the entire visit, depending on the chaos at the caves. Going with the first trip (around 9:00) will get you there at the same time as the boatmen in their dinghies—who hitch a ride behind your boat—resulting in less chaos and a shorter wait at the entry point.

If you arrive on the island later in the morning—when the Blue Grotto is already jammed—you could try waiting to visit until about 15:00, when most of the tour groups have vacated. But this may only work by bus (not boat). Confirm that day's closing time with a TI before making the trip.

**Getting There:** You can take the **boat** from Marina Grande (either as part of a longer circle-the-island tour-€18, or directly-€15, 10 minutes; see details on both options earlier), as most people do, or save money by taking the **bus** via Anacapri. You'll save almost €8, lose time, and see a beautiful, calmer side of the island (roughly 3/hour, 10 minutes; buses depart only from the Anacapri bus station at Piazza della Pace—not from the bus stop at Piazza Vittoria 200 yards away). If you're coming from Marina Grande or Capri town and want to transfer to the Blue Grotto buses, don't get off when the driver announces "Anacapri." Instead, ride one more stop to Piazza della Pace. At the Piazza della Pace bus station, notice the two lines: "Grotta Azzurra" for the Blue Grotto, and "Faro" for the lighthouse.

**Getting Back from the Blue Grotto:** You can take the boat back or ask your boatman to drop you off on the small dock next to the grotto entrance (for a small tip), from there you climb up the stairs to the stop for the bus to Anacapri (if you came by boat, you'll still have to pay the full round-trip boat fare).

## ANACAPRI TOWN AND NEARBY

More interesting than the island's namesake town, Anacapri has two or three hours' worth of sights. Though Anacapri sits higher up on the island ("ana" means "upper" in Greek) than Capri town, there are no sea views at street level in the town center.

When visiting Anacapri by bus, note that there are two stops: Piazza Vittoria, in the center of town at the base of the Monte Solaro chairlift; and 200 yards farther along at Piazza della Pace (pronounced "PAH-chay"), a larger bus station near the cemetery. Piazza Vittoria gets you closer to the main sights (chairlift and Villa San Michele), while Piazza della Pace is where you transfer to the Blue Grotto bus. When leaving Anacapri for Marina Grande, buses can be packed. Your best chance of getting on board is to catch the bus from Piazza della Pace (the first stop). Another option is to catch a bus to Capri town, visit sights there, then take the funicular down to Marina Grande. Bus tickets can be purchased at the "Moda Mare" souvenir store directly opposite the bus stop in Piazza Vittoria.

### Via Orlandi

Anacapri's pedestrianized main drag takes you through the charming center of town. It's just a block or so from either bus stop. (From Piazza Vittoria, the street is right there—just go down the lane to the right of the Anacapri statue. From Piazza della Pace, cross the street and go down the small pedestrian lane called Via Filietto.) Anacapri's **TI** is at Via Orlandi 59, near Piazza Vittoria.

To see the town, stroll along Via Orlandi for a few minutes. Signs propose a quick circuit that links the Casa Rossa, St. Michael's Church, and peaceful side streets. You'll also find shops and eateries, including good choices for quick, inexpensive pizza, *saltimbocca* (prosciutto and mozzarella on baked pizza bread—great for a filling picnic), *panini*, and other goodies. These two **$** options are both open daily in peak season: **Sciué Sciué** (same price for informal seating or takeaway, 50 yards below the TI at #73, tel. 081-837-2068) and **Pizza e Pasta** (takeaway only, lots of benches nearby, just before the church at #157, tel. 328-623-8460).

Of the sights below, the first two are in the heart of town (on or near Via Orlandi), while the next two are a short walk away.

## Casa Rossa (Red House)

This "Pompeiian-red," eccentric home, a hodgepodge of architectural styles, is the former residence of John Clay MacKowen, a Louisiana doctor and ex-Confederate officer who moved to Capri in the 1870s and married a local girl. (MacKowen and the Villa San Michele's Axel Munthe—see later—loathed each other, and even tried to challenge each other to a duel.) Its small collection of 19th-century paintings of scenes from around the island recalls a time before mass tourism. Don't miss the second floor, with more paintings and four ancient, sea-worn statues, which were recovered from the depths of the Blue Grotto in the 1960s and 1970s.

**Cost and Hours:** €3.50; discounted to €1 with ticket stub from Blue Grotto, Villa San Michele, or Monte Solaro chairlift; Tue-Sun 10:00-13:30 & 17:30-20:00; shorter hours April-May and Oct; closed Nov-March and Mon year-round, Via Orlandi 78, tel. 081-838-2193.

## ▲Church of San Michele

This Baroque church in the village center has a remarkable majolica floor showing paradise on earth in a classic 18th-century Neapolitan style. The entire floor is ornately tiled, featuring an angel (with flaming sword) driving Adam and Eve from paradise. The devil is wrapped around the trunk of a beautiful tree. The animals—happily ignoring this momentous event—all have human expressions. For the best view, climb the spiral stairs from the postcard desk. Services are held only during the first two  weeks of Advent, when the church is closed to visitors.

**Cost and Hours:** €2, daily 9:00-19:00, Nov and mid-Dec-March usually 10:00-14:00, closed late Nov-mid-Dec, in town center just off Via Orlandi—look for *San Michele* signs, tel. 081-837-2396, www.chiesa-san-michele.com.

## ▲Villa San Michele and Grand Capri View

This is the 19th-century mansion of Axel Munthe, Capri's grand personality, an idealistic Swedish doctor who lived here until 1946 and whose services to the Swedish royal family brought him into contact with high society. Munthe was gay at a time when that could land you in jail. He enjoyed the avant-garde and permissive scene at Capri, during an era when Europe's leading artists and creative figures could gather here and be honest about their sexual orientation.

At the very least, walk the path from Piazza Vittoria past the villa to a superb, free viewpoint over Capri town, Marina Grande, and—in the distance—Mount Vesuvius and Sorrento. Paying to enter the villa lets you see a few rooms with period furnishings (follow the one-way route, good English descriptions); an exhibit on Munthe; and one of this region's most delightful gardens, with a chapel, the Olivetum (a tiny museum of native birds and bugs), and a view that's slightly better than the free one outside. Throughout the gardens and the house, you'll see a smattering of original ancient objects unearthed here—and lots and lots of copies. A café (also with a view) serves affordable sandwiches.

**Cost and Hours:** €8, daily 9:00-18:00, closes earlier Oct-April, tel. 081-837-1401, www.villasanmichele.eu.

**Getting There:** From Piazza Vittoria, walk up the grand staircase and turn left onto Via Capodimonte. At the start of the shopping street, on your right, pass the deluxe Capri Palace Hotel—venture in if you can get past the treacherously eye-catching swimming pool windows (behind the pillars). After lots of overpriced shops, just before the villa, notice the Swedish consulate. In honor of Munthe, Swedes get into the villa for free.

### ▲▲Chairlift up to Monte Solaro

From Anacapri, you can ride the chairlift *(seggiovia)* to the 1,900-foot summit of Monte Solaro for a commanding view of the Bay of Naples. Work on your tan as you float over hazelnut, walnut, chestnut, apricot, peach, kiwi, and fig trees, past a montage of tourists (mostly from cruise ships; when the grotto is closed—as it often is—they bring passengers here instead). Prospective smoochers should know

that the lift seats are all single. As you ascend, consider how Capri's real estate has been priced out of the locals' reach. The ride takes 13 minutes each way, and you'll want at least 30 minutes on top, where there are picnic benches and a café with WCs.

**Cost and Hours:** €9 one-way, €12 round-trip, daily 9:30-17:00, last run down at 17:30; March-April until 16:00, Nov-Feb until 15:30, tel. 081-837-1438, www.capriseggiovia.it. Note that the lift gets more crowded with tour groups in the afternoon.

**Getting There:** From the Piazza Vittoria bus stop, just climb the steps and look right.

**At the Summit:** You'll enjoy the best panorama possible: lush cliffs busy with seagulls enjoying the ideal nesting spot. Even if skies aren't clear, the views are spectacular, with clouds surfing over the cliffs. Find the Faraglioni Rocks—with tour boats squeezing through every few minutes—which are an icon of the island. The pink building nearest the rocks was an American R&R base during World War II. Eisenhower and Churchill met here. On the peak closest to Cape Sorrento, you can see the distant ruins of Emperor Tiberius' palace, Villa Jovis. Pipes from the Sorrento Peninsula bring water to Capri (demand for fresh water here long ago exceeded the supply provided by the island's three natural springs). The Galli Islands mark the Amalfi Coast in the distance. Cross the bar terrace for views of Mount Vesuvius and Naples.

**Hiking Down:** A highlight for hardy walkers (provided you have strong knees and good shoes) is the 40-minute downhill hike from the top of Monte Solaro, through lush vegetation and ever-changing views, past the 14th-century Chapel of Santa Maria Cetrella (at the trail's only intersection, it's a 10-minute detour to the right), and back into Anacapri. The trail starts downstairs, past the WCs  (last chance). Down two more flights of stairs, look for the sign to *Anacapri e Cetrella*—you're on your way. While the trail is well-established, you'll encounter plenty of uneven steps, loose rocks, and few signs.

### Lighthouse near Anacapri

The lighthouse *(faro)*, at the rocky, arid, and desolate southwestern corner of the island, is a favorite place to enjoy the sunset. This area has a private beach, pool, small restaurants, and a few fishermen. Reach it by bus from Anacapri (3/hour, departs from Piazza della Pace stop).

## CAPRI TOWN AND NEARBY

This cute but extremely clogged and touristy shopping town is worth a brief visit, if only for window shopping.

### Piazza Umberto I

If you arrive by the funicular, it drops you just around the corner from Piazza Umberto I, the town's main square. With your back to the funicular, the bus stop is 50 yards straight ahead down Via Roma. The **TI** is under the bell tower on Piazza Umberto (see "Tourist Information," earlier). The footpath to the port starts just behind the TI (follow signs to *Il Porto*, 15-minute walk).

Capri town's main square is dedicated to the second king of Italy. Enjoy what's considered the "Living Room of Capri." Imagine the days when, rather than fancy cafés, the square was filled with a public market. Today, Capri town is traffic-free with only electric service minitrucks scooting here and there. While a coffee costs €1 at any bar, it's €5 at a table on the square.

To the left of City Hall (Municipio, lowest corner), a narrow, atmospheric lane leads into the medieval part of town, which has plenty of eateries and is the starting point for the 45-minute hike to Villa Jovis.

### Cathedral

Capri town's multidomed Baroque cathedral, which faces the square, is worth a quick look. Its multicolored marble floor at the altar dates from the first century AD—it was scavenged from Emperor Tiberius' villa and laid here in the 19th century.

### "Rodeo Drive"

The lane to the left of the cathedral (past Bar Tiberio, under the wide arch) is a fashionable shopping strip that's justifiably been dubbed "Rodeo Drive" by residents. Walk a few minutes down the street (past Gelateria Buonocore at #35, with its tempting fresh waffle cones—you'll smell them as you approach) to Quisisana Hotel, the island's top old-time hotel (formerly a 19th-century sanitorium). From there, head left for fancy shops and villas, and right for gardens and views. Between the lane and the sea

is a huge monastery (Certosa di San Giacomo, described later; access to the left).

### Giardini di Augusto

To the right and downhill, a five-minute walk leads to this lovely public garden (€1, daily 9:00-19:30, Nov-March until 17:30, free to enter off-season, no picnicking). While the garden itself is modest, it boasts great views over the famous Faraglioni Rocks—handy if you don't have the time, money, or interest to access the higher vantage points near Anacapri (Monte Solaro, Villa San Michele).

## Monastery of San Giacomo

One of the most historic buildings on the island is the Certosa di San Giacomo (€4, €3 combo-ticket with Giardini di Augusto at the garden entry, Tue-Sun 10:00-17:00, later in summer, closed Mon). The stark monastery has an empty church and sleepy cloister. But the finest piece of art on Capri is over the church's front entrance: an exquisite 14th-century fresco of Mary and the baby Jesus by the Florentine Niccolo di Tommaso. Today, the monastery hosts the **Museo Diefenbach,** a small collection of dark and moody paintings by eccentric German artist Karl Wilhelm Diefenbach, who walked around naked in Capri in the early 1900s, when this was a gay, political, and avant-garde place.

## Villa Jovis and the Emperor's Capri

Even before becoming emperor, Augustus loved Capri so much that he traded the family-owned Isle of Ischia to the (then-independent) Neapolitans in exchange for making Capri his personal property. Emperor Tiberius spent a decade here, AD 26-37. (Some figure he did so in order to escape being assassinated in Rome.)

Emperor Tiberius' ruined villa, Villa Jovis, is reachable only by a scenic 45-minute hike from Capri town. You won't find any statues or mosaics here—just an evocative, ruined complex of terraces clinging to a rocky perch over a sheer drop to the sea...and a lovely view. You can make out a large water reservoir for baths, the foundations of servants' quarters, and Tiberius' private apartments (fragments of marble flooring still survive). The ruined lighthouse dates from the Middle Ages.

**Cost and Hours:** €4, Wed-Mon 10:00-18:00, closed Tue, shorter hours and closed off-season—check at Capri TI.

# Capri Connections

**From Capri's Marina Grande by Boat to: Sorrento** (ferry: 4/day, 30 minutes, www.caremar.it; hydrofoil: up to 20/day, 20 minutes, www.gescab.it), **Naples** (roughly hourly, more in summer, hydrofoil: 50 minutes, arrives at Molo Beverello; ferries: 50-80 minutes, arrive at Calata Porta di Massa), **Positano** (mid-April-mid-Oct, 6/day, 30 minutes). Confirm the schedule carefully at TIs or www.capritourism.com (under "Shipping Timetable")—the last boats back to the mainland usually leave around 18:00-20:00. For a steep price, you can always hire a water taxi (weather permitting).

# AMALFI COAST & PAESTUM

*Amalfi Coast Tour • Positano • Ravello • Paestum*

With its stunning scenery, hill- and harbor-hugging towns, and historic ruins, Amalfi is Italy's coast with the most. The breathtaking trip from Sorrento to Salerno is one of the world's great bus or taxi rides. It will leave your mouth open and your camera's memory card full. You'll gain respect for the 19th-century Italian engineers who built the roads—and even more for the 21st-century drivers who squeeze past each other here daily. Cantilevered garages, hotels, and villas cling to the vertical terrain, and beautiful but out-of-reach coves tease from far below. As you hyperventilate, notice how the Mediterranean, a sheer 500-foot drop below, really twinkles. All this beautiful scenery apparently inspires local Romeos and Juliets, with the latex evidence of late-night romantic encounters littering the roadside turnouts. Over the centuries, the spectacular scenery and climate have been a siren call for the rich and famous, luring Roman Emperor Tiberius, Richard Wagner, Sophia Loren, Gore Vidal, and others to the Amalfi Coast's special brand of *la dolce vita*.

The two main Amalfi Coast towns (Positano and Amalfi) are pretty, but they're also touristy, congested, and overpriced. (Many visitors prefer side-tripping in from Sorrento.) Most beaches here are private, pebbly, and expensive. Check and understand your bills in this greedy region.

In Paestum, farther south, you can see one of the world's best collections of 2,500-year-old Greek temples, a worthwhile museum with artifacts from the site, and the remains of a Roman town.

# Amalfi Coast

The Amalfi Coast is one of those places with a "must see" reputation. Staggeringly picturesque and maddeningly touristy, it can be both rewarding and frustrating. As an antidote to intense Naples, its the perfect place for a romantic break—if done right and if you can afford it. These towns are the big three sights of the Amalfi Coast: Positano is like a living Gucci ad and has good overnight options; Amalfi evokes a day when small towns with big fleets were powerhouses on the Mediterranean; and Ravello is fun for that tramp-in-a-palace feeling.

## PLANNING YOUR TIME

On a quick visit, use Sorrento (see previous chapter) as your home base and do the Amalfi Coast as a day trip (skipping Paestum). But for a small-town vacation from your vacation, spend a few more days on the coast, sleeping in Positano.

Trying to decide between staying in Sorrento or Positano? Sorrento is larger, with useful services and the best transportation connections and accommodations. Tiny Positano is more touristy, but also more chic and picturesque, with a decent beach.

Naples or Paestum can also work as a base for an Amalfi Coast day trip, if you get an early start and the timetables align. From Naples, you have two options by public transport: train to Salerno, then bus (or boat) to Amalfi town; or, Circumvesuviana train to Sorrento, then bus to Positano and/or Amalfi. (You can go out one way and return the other.) From Paestum, you can take the train to Salerno, then the bus (or boat) to Amalfi or Positano.

## GETTING AROUND THE AMALFI COAST

The real thrill here is the scenic drive between Sorrento and Salerno. The stretch from Positano to Amalfi is the best. This is treacherous stuff—even if you have a car, you may want to take the bus or hire a driver. Brave souls enjoy seeing the coast by scooter or motorbike (rent in Sorrento).

Next, I've outlined your options by bus, boat, and taxi. Many travelers do the Amalfi Coast as a round-trip by bus, but a good strategy is to go one way by land and return by boat. For example, consider taking the bus along the coast to Positano and/or Amalfi, then catching the ferry back. Ferries run less often in

## Getting Around the Amalfi Coast

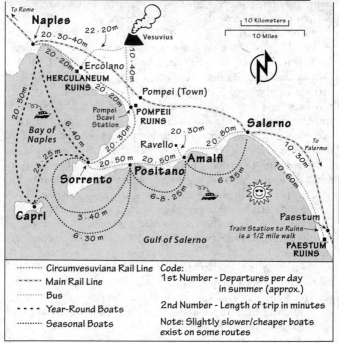

spring and fall, and some don't run at all off-season (mid-Oct-mid-April). Boats don't run in stormy weather at any time of year. If boats aren't running between Amalfi and Sorrento, you can change boats in Capri.

Looking for exercise? Consider an Amalfi Coast hike (see "Hikes" in the Amalfi Town section, later in this chapter). Numerous trails connect the main coastal towns with villages on the hills. Get a good map before you venture out.

### By Public Bus

SITA buses from Sorrento to Amalfi, via Positano, are the most common, inexpensive way to see the coast (for schedules, see www.sitabus.it or—easier to read—www.positano.com). In Sorrento, buses depart from in front of the train station beginning at 6:30; from 8:30 they run roughly every half hour until 17:00, then hourly until 22:00 in summer, until 20:00 in winter (50 minutes to Positano; another 50 minutes to Amalfi). To reach Ravello (the hill town beyond Amalfi) or Salerno (at the far end of the coast), transfer in Amalfi.

Individual tickets are inexpensive (€2-4). All rides are covered by the 24-hour Costiera SITA Sud pass (€10), which may not save you money but does save time buying tickets. Tickets are sold at tobacco shops and newsstands, not by drivers.

Line up under the *Bus Stop SITA* sign across from the train station (10 steps down, look for the sales desk under an umbrella). When checking the schedule, note that *Giornaliero (G)* means daily, *Scolastico (S)* means school bus, *Feriale (F)* denotes Monday-Saturday, and *Festivo (H)* is for Sundays and holidays.

Leaving Sorrento, grab a seat on the right for the best views. If you return by bus, it's fun to sit directly behind the driver for a box seat with a view over the twisting hairpin action. Sitting toward the front will also help minimize carsickness.

**Avoiding Crowded Buses:** Amalfi Coast public buses are routinely unable to handle demand during summer months and holidays (perhaps because the fares are so cheap). Generally, if you don't get on one bus, you're well-positioned to catch the next one. From Sorrento, aim to leave on the 8:30 bus at the latest—earlier if possible. Departures between 9:00 and 11:00 can be frustratingly crowded.

Note that an eight-seater minibus and driver costs about €300 for the day: If you can organize a small group, €40 per person is a very good deal. (For options, see "By Taxi," later.)

**When to Stop in Positano:** Summer congestion can be so bad—particularly in July and August—that some Amalfi-Sorrento buses don't even stop in Positano (because they fill up in Amalfi). Those trying to get back from Positano to Sorrento are stuck taking an extortionist taxi or hopping a boat...if one's running. When day-tripping from Sorrento to Amalfi, it's safest to make your Positano stop on the outbound leg, then come straight home from Amalfi, where the bus originates. Or, you can consider the hop-on, hop-off bus as an alternative.

## By Tour Bus

CitySightseeing's bright red hop-on, hop-off buses travel from Sorrento to Positano to Amalfi and back. While more expensive than public buses, they can be much less crowded and come with a recorded commentary. You'll pay €10 for your outgoing ride (buy tickets onboard), then €6 for the return trip (on the same day). Buses run hourly all day April-October, leaving the Sorrento train station at :45 past each hour starting at 8:45. Return trips from Amalfi leave at :15 past each hour (until 19:15—confirm locally). The trip takes about 1.5 hours, with a stop in Positano each way. Check out www.city-sightseeing.it (but don't be confused by their "two bays" tour of the Cape of Sorrento, which is not worth considering).

CitySightseeing also offers a second service on a smaller bus from Amalfi to Ravello. Tickets are €5 each way (buy onboard from driver). The trip takes 30 minutes, with departures at :15 and :45 past the hour beginning at 9:45. The last service of the day is between 16:00 and 17:00, so plan to leave Ravello by then. If you miss the last bus, a taxi back to Amalfi is about €50.

## By Boat

A few passenger boats per day link Positano and Amalfi with Sorrento, Capri, and Salerno (generally April-Oct only). The last daily departure can be as early as midafternoon and is never much later than 18:00. Check schedules carefully: Frequency varies from month to month, and boats may be cancelled in bad weather (especially at Positano, where there's no real pier). The companies operating each route change frequently, compete for passengers, and usually claim to know nothing about their rivals' services. The best sources for timetables are www.capritourism.com (under "Shipping Timetable") and www.positano.com (under "Ferry Schedules"). You can also check individual company websites (such as www.travelmar.it, www.alicost.it, and www.gescab.it). It's smartest to confirm locally: The region's TIs hand out flyers with current schedules. Buy tickets on the dock. For a summary of sample routes, frequencies, and travel times, see the "Getting Around the Amalfi Coast" map.

If you're going to Capri from Positano or Amalfi, save time and money by finding a boat that goes directly to the Blue Grotto (rather than dropping you in the port in Capri to catch another boat from there). Here's another useful trick: If no boats are going directly between Sorrento and Positano/Amalfi, you can usually still connect the two sides of the peninsula via Capri.

## By Taxi

Given the hairy driving, impossible parking, crowded public buses, and potential fun, you might consider splurging to hire your own car and driver for your Amalfi day.

The **Monetti family** car-and-driver service—Raffaele, daughter Carolina, cousin Tony, and Gianpaolo—have taken excellent care of my readers' transit needs for decades. Sample trips and rates: all-day Amalfi Coast (Positano, Amalfi, Ravello), 8 hours, €300; Amalfi Coast and Paestum, 10 hours, €450; transfer to

Naples airport or train station to Sorrento, €130. These prices are for up to three people; you'll pay more for a larger eight-seater van. Though based in Sorrento, they also do trips from Naples and longer excursions to Matera. Payment is cash only (as with most of the car services listed). Their reservation system is simple and reliable (Raffaele's mobile 335-602-9158 or 338-946-2860, "office" run by his English-speaking Finnish wife, Susanna, www.monettitaxi17.it, monettitaxi17@libero.it). Don't just hop into any taxi claiming to be a Monetti—call first. If you get into any kind of serious jam in the area, you can call Raffaele for help.

**Francesco del Pizzo** is another smooth and honest Sorrento-based driver. A classy man who speaks English well, Francesco enjoys explaining things as he drives (9 hours or so in a car with up to 4 passengers, €300; up to 8 passengers in a minibus, €340; mobile 333-238-4144, francescodelpizzo@yahoo.it).

**Anthony Buonocore,** an Amalfi native, specializes in cruise shore excursions, as well as transfers anywhere in the region in his eight-person Mercedes van (rates vary, special deals for early booking and in low season, tel. 349-441-0336, www.amalfitransfer.com, buonocoreanthony@yahoo.it).

*Rides Only:* If you're hiring a cabbie off the street for a ride and not a tour, here are sample fares from Sorrento to Positano: up to four people one-way for about €80 in a car, or up to six people for €90 in a minibus. Figure on paying 50 percent more to Amalfi. While taxis must use a meter within a city, a fixed rate is OK elsewhere. Negotiate—ask about a round-trip.

### By Shared Minibus

While hiring your own driver is convenient, it's also expensive. To bring the cost down, split the trip—and the bill—with other travelers using this book. Naples-based **Mondo Guide** offers a nine-hour minibus trip that departs from Sorrento and heads down the Amalfi Coast, with brief stops in Positano, Amalfi, and Ravello, before returning to Sorrento (€55/person). They also offer Rick Steves readers shared tours in Pompeii and Naples. For details, see page 970.

---

# Amalfi Coast Tour

The wildly scenic Amalfi Coast drive from Sorrento to Salerno, worth ▲▲▲, is one of the all-time great white-knuckle rides, whether you tackle it by bus, taxi, or shared minibus.

Gasp from the right side of the car or bus as you go out and from the left as you return to Sorrento. (Those on the wrong side really miss out.) Traffic is so heavy that private tour buses are only allowed to go in one direction (southbound from Sorrento). Summer traffic is infuriating. Fluorescent-vested police are posted at tough bends during peak hours to help fold in side-view mirrors and keep things moving. Here's a loose, self-guided tour of what you're seeing as you travel from west to east.

**AMALFI COAST**

**⊙ Self-Guided Tour:** Leaving **Sorrento,** the road winds up into the hills past lemon groves and hidden houses. The gray-green trees are olives. (Notice the green nets slung around the trunks; these are unfurled in October and November, when the ripe olives drop naturally, for an easy self-harvest.) Dark, green-leafed trees planted in dense groves are the source of the region's lemons (many destined to become *limoncello* liqueur) and big, fat citrons (*cedri,* mostly used for marmalade). The black nets over the orange and lemon groves create a greenhouse effect, trapping warmth and humidity for maximum tastiness, while offering protection from extreme weather (preserving the peels used for *limoncello*).

Atop the ridge outside Sorrento, look to your right: The two small islands are the **Li Galli Islands,** where some say the sirens in Homer's *Odyssey* lived. The largest of these islands was once owned by the famed ballet dancer Rudolf Nureyev; it's now a luxury residence, rented to wealthy visitors for upward of $100,000 per week (bring your own yacht or arrive by helicopter).

When Nureyev bought the island, the only building standing was the stony watchtower—the first of many you'll see all along the coast. These were strategically placed within sight of one another so that a relay of rooftop bonfires could quickly spread word of a pirate attack.

The limestone cliffs that plunge into the sea were traversed by a hand-carved trail that became a modern road in the mid-19th century. Fruit stands sell produce from farms and orchards just over the hill. Limestone absorbs the heat and rainwater, making this south-facing coastline a fertile suntrap, with temperatures as much as 10 degrees higher than in nearby Sorrento. The chalky, reflective limestone, which extends below the surface, accounts for the uniquely colorful blues and greens of the water. With the favorable climate, bougainvillea, geraniums, oleander, and wisteria grow like weeds here in the summer. Notice the nets pulled tight against the cliffs—they're designed to catch rocks that often tumble loose after heavy rains.

The dramatic, exotic-looking town of **Positano** is the main stop along the coast. The town is built on a series of man-made

## The Saracens

Throughout coastal Italy, you'll hear about the Saracens. But who were these people? To understand that, we have to go back in time and across the sea to 1492 Spain. That's when Ferdinand and Isabel—Spain's foremost Catholic monarchs—defeated the last Moorish stronghold of Granada. The conquered Muslims were allowed to settle in the mountains to the south. But over time, intolerance and tension between the two groups forced most Muslims across the Mediterranean to North Africa.

In the 16th century, modern-day Algeria, Tunisia, and coastal regions of Morocco and Libya formed a somewhat united coalition known as the Barbary States. This group of indigenous Berber tribes plus the displaced Moors chased from Spain were often referred to as Saracens, a term perhaps derived from Arabic, meaning "marauder." They raided Christian ships, capturing and reselling cargo and holding crews for ransom. Christian kingdoms paid bribes to keep shipping lanes open. The Barbary Coast Saracens were loosely aligned with the Ottoman Empire, but that wasn't much help when European powers (plus the United States in its first overseas show of strength) had enough of the raids and declared war. Saracen influence came to an end after their defeat in the Barbary War of 1815, but the Saracen legacy lives on along the Italian coast, with everything from watchtowers to restaurants named after them.

terraces, which were carefully carved out of the steep rock, then filled with fertile soil carried here from Sorrento on the backs of donkeys. You can read the history of the region in Positano's rooftops—a mix of Roman-style red terra-cotta tiles and white domes inspired by the Saracens (see sidebar).

If you're getting off here, stay on through the first stop by the round-domed yellow church (Chiesa Nova), which is a very long walk above town. Instead, get off at the second stop, Sponda, then head downhill toward the start of my self-guided Positano Walk (later in this chapter). Sponda is also the best place to catch the onward bus to Amalfi. If you're coming on a smaller minibus, you'll twist all the way down—seemingly going in circles—to the start of the walk.

Just south of Positano, **St. Peter's Hotel** (Il San Pietro di Positano, camouflaged below the tiny St. Peter's church) is just about the poshest stop on the coast. In the adjacent gorge, notice the hotel's terraced gardens (where produce is grown for their restaurant) above an elevator-accessible beach and dock.

Just around the bend, **Praiano** comes into view. Less ritzy or charming than Positano or Amalfi, it's notable for its huge Cathedral of San Gennaro, with a characteristic majolica-tiled roof and dome—a reminder of this region's respected ceramics industry. In spindly Praiano, most of the homes are accessible only by tiny footpaths and staircases. Near the end of town, just before the big tunnel, watch on the left for the big *presepe* (manger scene) embedded into the cliff face. This Praiano-in-miniature was carved by one local man over several decades. At Christmastime, each house is filled with little figures and twinkle lights.

Just past the tunnel, look below and on the right to see another Saracen watchtower. (Yet another caps the little point on the horizon.)

A bit farther along, look down to see the fishing hamlet of **Marina di Praia** tucked into the gorge *(furore)* between two tun-

nels. If you're driving—or being driven—consider a detour down here for a coffee break or meal. This serene, tidy nook has its own little pebbly beach with great views of the stout bluffs and watchtower that hem it in. A seafront walkway curls around the bluff all the way to the tower.

Just after going through the next tunnel, watch for a jagged rock formation on its own little pedestal. Locals see the face of the Virgin Mary in this natural feature and say that she's holding a flower (the tree growing out to the right). Also notice several caged, cantilevered parking pads sticking out from the road. This stretch of coastline is popular for long-term villa rentals—Italians who want to really settle in to Amalfi life.

Look down and left for the blink-or-you'll-miss-it fishing village that's aptly named **Fiordo** ("fjord"), filling yet another gorge. You'll see humble homes burrowed into the cliff face, tucked so far into the gorge that they're entirely in shadow for much of the year. Today these are rented out to vacationers; the postage-stamp beach is uncrowded and inviting.

After the next tunnel, in the following hamlet, keep an eye out for donkeys with big baskets on their backs—the only way to make heavy deliveries to homes high in the rocky hills.

Soon you'll pass the big-for-Amalfi parking lot of the **Grotta dello Smeraldo** ("Emerald Grotto"), a cheesy roadside attraction that wrings the most it can out of a pretty, seawater-filled cave. Passing tourists park here and pay €5 to take an elevator down to sea level, pile into big rowboats, and get paddled around a genuinely impressive cavern while the boatman imparts sparse factoids. Unless you've got time to kill, skip it.

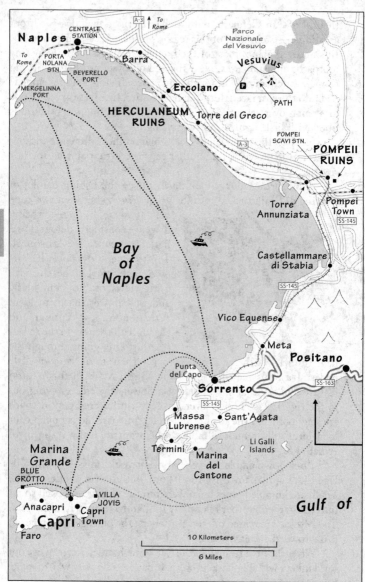

Now you're approaching what might be the most dramatic watchtower on the coast, perched atop a near-island. This tower guarded the harbor of the Amalfi navy until the fleet was destroyed in 1343 by a tsunami caused by an earthquake, which also led to Amalfi's decline (it was once one of Italy's leading powers).

Around the next bend you're treated to stunning views of the coastline's namesake town—**Amalfi**. The white villa sitting on the

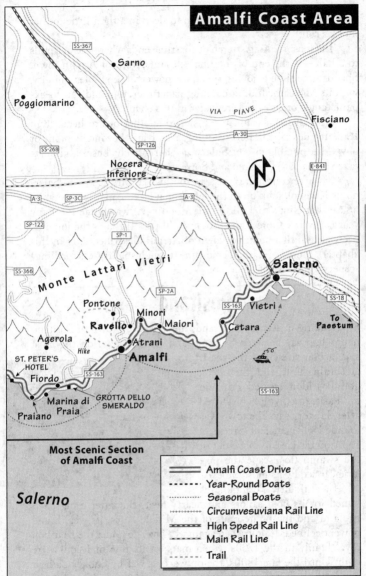

low point between here and there (with another watchtower at its tip) once belonged to Sophia Loren. Now look up to the very top of the steep, steep cliffs overhead. The hulking former Monastery of Santa Rosa occupies this prime territory. Locals proudly explain that the *sfogliatella* dessert so beloved throughout the Campania region was first created at this monastery. (Today it's a luxury resort, where you can pay a premium to sleep in a tight little former monk's cell.)

The most striking stretch of coastline ends where the bus pulls to a halt—at the end of the line, the waterfront of Amalfi town. Spend some time enjoying this once-powerful, now-pleasant city, with its fine cathedral, fascinating paper museum, and fun-to-explore tangle of lanes (covered later in this chapter).

From Amalfi, you can transfer to another bus to head up to **Ravello** (described later), capping a cliff just beyond Amalfi, or onward to the big city of **Salerno.** Alternatively, buses and boats take you back to Positano and Sorrento.

If you're continuing the trip southward (on the bus to Salerno or Ravello), look up to the left as you leave Amalfi—the white house that clings to a cliff (Villa Rondinaia) was home for many years to writer Gore Vidal. Soon you'll pass through the low-impact, pleasantly untouristy town of **Atrani** (described later in this chapter). From here, you'll enjoy fine (though slightly less thrilling) scenery all the way to Salerno.

# Positano

Specializing in scenery and sand, the easygoing town of Positano hangs halfway between Sorrento and Amalfi town on the most spectacular stretch of the coast.

According to legend, the Greek god Poseidon created Positano for Pasitea, a nymph he lusted after. History says the town was founded when ancient Greeks at Paestum decided to move out of the swamp (to escape the malaria carried by its mosquitoes).

In antiquity, Positano was famed for its bold sailors and hearty fleet. But after a big 1343 tsunami and the pirate raids of the Middle Ages, its wealth and power declined. It flourished again as a favorite under the Bourbon royal family in the 1700s, when many of its fine mansions were built. Until the late 1800s, the only access was by donkey path or by sea. In the 20th century, Positano became a haven for artists and writers escaping Communist Russia and Nazi Germany. In 1953, American writer John Steinbeck's essay on the town popularized Positano among tourists, and soon after it became a trendy Riviera stop. That was when the town gave the world "Moda Positano"—a leisurely *dolce vita* lifestyle of walking barefoot; wearing bright, happy, colorful clothes; and sporting skimpy bikinis.

Today, the village, a breathtaking ▲▲▲ sight from a distance, is a pleasant gathering of cafés and expensive stores draped over an almost comically steep hillside. Terraced gardens and historic houses cascade downhill to a stately cathedral and a broad, pebbly beach. Positano is famous for its fashions—and 90 percent of its shops are women's clothing boutiques (linen is a particularly popular item).

The "skyline" looks like it did a century ago. Notice the town's characteristic Saracen-inspired rooftop domes. Filled with sand, these provide low-tech insulation—to help buildings, in the days before central air, stay cool in summer and warm in winter. Traditionally, they were painted white in summer and black in winter.

For decades, it's been practically impossible to get a building permit in Positano. Landowners who want to renovate can't make external changes. Endless staircases are a way of life for the hardy locals. Only one street in Positano allows motorized traffic; the rest are narrow pedestrian lanes. While Positano has 4,000 residents, an average of 12,000 tourists visit daily from Easter through October. But because hotels don't take large groups (bus access is too difficult), this town—unlike Sorrento—has been spared the worst ravages of big-bus tourism. In winter, hotels shut down and the town once again belongs to the locals.

Consider seeing Positano as a day trip from Sorrento: Take the bus out and the afternoon ferry home, but be sure to check boat schedules when you arrive—the last ferry often leaves before 18:00 and doesn't always run in spring and fall. Or spend the night to enjoy the magic of Positano after dark. The town has a local flavor at night, when the grown-ups stroll and the kids play soccer on the church porch.

## Orientation to Positano

Squished into a ravine, with narrow alleys that cascade down to the harbor, Positano requires you to stroll, whether you're going up or heading down. The center of town has no main square (unless you count the beach). There's little to do here but eat, window shop, and enjoy the beach and views...hence the town's popularity.

**Tourist Information:** The TI is a block from the beach, in the red building a half-block beyond the bottom of the church steps (Mon-Sat 9:00-19:00, Sun until 14:00, shorter hours off-season, Via Regina Giovanna 13, tel. 089-875-067, www.aziendaturismopositano.it).

**Local Guide:** Positano native **Lucia Ferrara** (a.k.a. "Zia Lucy") brings substance to this glitzy town. During the day, she leads guided hiking tours, including the "Path of the Gods" above Amalfi town (up to 10 people, about 4 miles, 5 hours, €55/person, includes picnic). In the evening, if there's enough demand, she leads a Positano town

AMALFI COAST

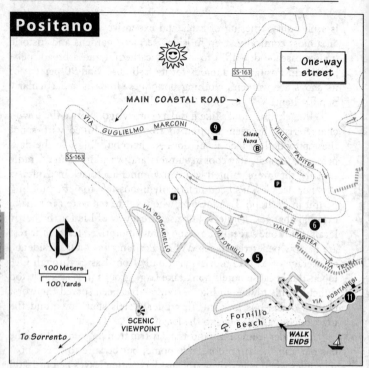

walking tour (3 hours, departs at 17:00, €30/person). She also offers food tours (mobile 339-272-0971, www.zialucy.com).

## ARRIVAL IN POSITANO

The main coastal highway winds above the town. Regional SITA buses stop at two scheduled bus stops located at either end of town: **Chiesa Nuova** (at Bar Internazionale, near the Sorrento end of town; use this one only if you're staying at Brikette Hostel) and **Sponda** (nearer Amalfi town). Although both stops are near roads leading downhill through the town to the beach, Sponda is closer and less steep; from this stop, it's a scenic 20-minute downhill stroll/shop/munch to the beach (and TI).

Neither bus stop has easy **baggage storage.** Positano does have porter services: A porter can meet you at the Sponda bus stop and watch your bags for €5 apiece—but you have to call them in advance (try Positano Porter, tel. 089-875-310). Another option is to get off at Chiesa Nuova and head for the Brikette Hostel, which offers day privileges for €10, including luggage storage, Wi-Fi, and showers. A last resort is to get off at the Sponda stop and roll your bags all the way down to Piazza dei Mulini, where the porters tend to hang out.

If you're catching the SITA bus from Positano, be aware that it

**AMALFI COAST**

may leave from the Sponda stop five minutes before the printed departure time. There's simply no room for the bus to wait, so in case the driver is early, you should be, too. Buy tickets at the tobacco shop in the town center (on Piazza dei Mulini).

If the walk up to the stop is too tough, take one of the dizzy little **shuttle buses** (marked *Interno Positano*), which constantly loop through Positano, connecting the lower town with the highway's two bus stops (2/hour, €1.30 at tobacco shop on Piazza dei Mulini, €1.80 on board, catch it at the convenient stop at the corner of Via Colombo and Via dei Mulini, heads up to Sponda). Collina Bakery, located off Piazza dei Mulini (as close as cars, taxis, and the shuttle bus can get to the beach), is just across from the shuttle bus stop, with a fine, breezy terrace to enjoy while you wait.

Coming from the **ferry,** you can give luggage to one of the porter services or lug everything uphill yourself. Follow crowds up wide stairs to the large church, then follow the trellis to Piazza dei Mulini. You'll be doing the reverse of my Positano Walk (described next).

**Drivers** must go with the one-way flow, entering the town only at the Chiesa Nuova bus stop (closest to Sorrento) and exiting at Sponda (a 20-minute one-way loop). Driving is a headache here. Parking is even worse.

**AMALFI COAST**

# Positano Walk

While there's no real sightseeing in Positano, this short, self-guided stroll downhill will help you get your bearings from top to bottom.
• *Start at...*

**Piazza dei Mulini:** This is the upper-town meeting point—as close to the beach as vehicles can get—and the lower stop for the little shuttle bus. **Collina Bakery** is a local hangout (in this small town, gossiping is a big pastime). Older people tend to gather inside, while the younger crowd congregates on the wisteria-draped terrace across the street.

Dip into the little yellow **Church of the Holy Rosary** (by the road), with a serene 12th-century interior. Up front, to the right of the main altar, find the delicately carved fragment of a Roman sarcophagus (first century BC). Positano sits upon the site of a sprawling Roman villa, and we'll see a few reminders of that age as we walk.

At the top of the town lane (across from the church) is a popular *granita* **stand,** where the family has been following the same secret lemon slush recipe for generations.

Now continue downhill into town, passing a variety of **shops**—many selling linen and ceramics. These industries boomed when tourists discovered Positano. The beach-inspired Moda Positano fashion label was born as a break from the rigid dress code of the 1950s. (For tips on shopping for linen, see "Shopping," under "Sights in Positano," later). Positano also considers itself an artists' colony, and you'll see many **galleries** featuring the work of area artists.

• *Wander downhill to the "fork" in the road (stairs to the left, road to the right). You've reached...*

**Midtown:** At **Enoteca Cuomo** (#3), butchers Pasquale and Rosario stock fine local red wines and are happy to explain their virtues. They also make homemade sausages, salami, and *panini*—good for a quick lunch. The smaller set of stairs leads to the recommended **Delicatessen grocery,** where Emilia can fix you a good picnic.

**La Zagara** (across the lane from the steps, at #10, with a leafy terrace) is a pricey pastry shop by day and a cocktail bar by night. Tempting pastries such as the rum-drenched *babà* (a southern Italian favorite) fill the window display. A bit farther downhill, **Brunella** (on the right, at #24) is respected for traditional quality, and Positano-made linens.

Across the street, the ritzy **Hotel Palazzo Murat** fills what was once a grand Benedictine monastery. Napoleon, fearing the power of the Church, had many such monasteries closed during his rule here. This one became a private palace, named for his brother-in-law, who was briefly the King of Naples. Step into the plush courtyard to enjoy the scene, with great views of the cathedral's majolica-slathered dome below. Continuing on, under a fragrant wisteria trellis, you'll pass "street merchants' gulch," where artisans display their goodies.

• *Continue straight down. You'll run into a fork at the big church. For now, turn right and go downstairs to Piazza Flavio Gioia, facing the big...*

**Church of Santa Maria Assunta:** This church, which sits upon Roman ruins, was once the abbey of Positano's 12th-century Benedictine monastery. Originally Romanesque, it was eventually abandoned (along with the entire lower town) out of fear of pirate attacks. When the coast was clear in the 18th century, the church was given an extreme Baroque makeover.

Step **inside** and find these items: In the first chapel on the left is a fine manger scene *(presepe)*. Its original 18th-century figurines give you an idea of the folk costumes of the age. Above the main altar is the Black Madonna, an icon-like Byzantine painting likely brought here from Constantinople by monks in the 12th century. But locals prefer a more romantic origin story for the gilded painting: Saracen pirates had it on their ship as plunder. A violent storm hit—sure to sink the evil ship. The painting of Mary spoke, saying, *"Posa, posa"* (lay me down), and the ship glided safely to this harbor. The pirates were so stricken they became Christians. Locals kept the painting, and the town became known as *Posa-tano* (recalling Mary's command).

To the right of the altar, a small freestanding display case holds a silver-and-copper bust of St. Vitus (along with his bones, now holy relics). He's the town patron, who brought Christianity here in about AD 300. In the adjacent niche (on the right) is a rare 1599 painting by Fabrizio Santafede of Baby Jesus being circumcised, considered the finest historic painting in town.

Back outside, you'll see the **bell tower,** dating from 1707. Above the door, it sports a Romanesque relief scavenged from the original church. The scene—a wolf mermaid with seven little fish—was a reminder to worshippers of how integral the sea was to their livelihood. Nicknamed "our pagan protector," it's a good example of how early Christians incorporated pagan elements into their worship. Notice the characteristic shallow, white "insulation domes" on rooftops in front of the church.

• *Backtrack up the steps, circling around the church. You'll likely see the entry to an underground Roman exhibit.*

The entire town center of today's Positano—from this cathedral all the way up to the Piazza dei Mulini, where we started this walk—sits upon the site of a huge **Roman villa complex,** buried when Mount Vesuvius erupted in AD 79. Positano excavated one small part of the villa, and a small museum provides views of a surviving fragment of a large Roman fresco.

Take the stairs down to two glass doors that offer a peek into the church's **crypt**—originally the early church's altar. According to local legend, the Benedictines sat their dead brothers on the stone choir chairs here to decompose and remind all of their mortality (pricey at €15, includes 30-minuted guided tour, open daily April-Oct 9:00-21:00, shorter hours off-season).

• *Continue descending the steps to the right (following beach/spiaggia signs). You'll eventually come to the little square with concrete benches facing the beach.*

**Piazzetta:** This is the town gathering point in the evening, as local boys hustle tourist girls into the nearby nightclub. Step down to beach level. Residents traded their historic baptistery font with Amalfi town for the two iron lions you see facing the beach. Around the staircase, you'll also see some original Roman columns, scavenged from the buried villa. Look up and admire the colorful majolica tiles so typical of church domes in this region.

Positano's **beach,** called Spiaggia Grande, is half public (straight ahead) and half private (to the left, behind the little fence). It's atmospherically littered with a commotion of fishing boats and recreational craft. The big kiosk on the beach sells excursions to Capri and elsewhere.

Looking out over the beach from this point, you can see three of the **watchtowers** built centuries ago to protect the Amalfi Coast from Saracen pirates: one on the far-left horizon, just below Praiano; a small one on the Li Galli Islands, ahead and right; and the rectangular one far to the right, marking the far end of Fornillo Beach. Defenders used these towers—strategically situated within sight of each other—to relay smoke signals. In more recent times, the tower on the right (near Fornillo Beach) was a hangout for artists, who holed up inside for inspiration. (The people of Positano pride themselves on being artists rather than snazzy jet-setters like those in Capri.)

As you face out to sea, on the far-left side of the beach (below Rada Restaurant) is **Music on the Rocks,** a chic club that's the only remaining piece of the 1970s scene, when Positano really rocked. While it's dead until very late, you're welcome to peek in at the cool troglo-disco interior, or go upstairs to the Fly Bar for the priciest cocktails in town.

• *Now turn right and wander across the beach. Behind the kiosks that sell boat tickets, find the steps to the path that climbs up and over, past a 13th-century lookout fort from Saracen pirate days, to the next beach. It's a worthwhile little five-minute walk through a shady ravine to...*

**Fornillo Beach:** This is where locals go for better swimming and to escape some of the tourist crowds. Via Positanesi d'America is the lane (lit at night) leading to the beach. It's named for the more than 50 percent of Positano's population that emigrated to America between the 1860s and the 1940s. (Some locals remember when priests used to say at Mass, "And now, let's pray for Positanesi Americani.")

• *Our walk is over. Time to relax. When you're ready to return, go back the way you came to the main beach. Although tempting, Via Fornillo continues straight up the cliffside with a whopping 200-plus stairs...not for the faint of heart.*

## Sights in Positano

### Beaches

Positano's pebbly and sandy primary beach, **Spiaggia Grande,** is colorful with umbrellas as it stretches wide around the cove. It's mostly private (pay about €12 to enter, includes lounge chair and umbrella), with a free section near the middle, close to where the boats take off. Look for the pay showers. The nearest WC is beneath the steps to the right (as you face the water).

**Fornillo Beach,** a less-crowded option just around the bend (to the west) of Spiaggia Grande, is favored by residents, with more affordable chair/umbrella rentals (€8). It has a mellow Robinson Crusoe vibe, with a sturdy Saracen tower keeping watch overhead. This beach has a few humble snack bars and lunch eateries. Note that its position, tucked back in the rocks, means it gets shade earlier in the day than the main beach.

### Boat Trips

Boats serving Positano pull up to the dock at the west end of Spiaggia Grande (to the right as you face the sea; booths sell tickets). Also consider renting a rowboat, or see whether they can talk you into taking a boat tour. Passenger boats run to Amalfi, Capri, Salerno, and Sorrento; see "Getting Around the Amalfi Coast" on page 1082.

### Shopping

**Linen:** Garments made of **linen** (especially women's dresses) are popular items in Positano. To find a good-quality piece that will last, look for "Made in Positano" (or at least "Made in Italy") on the label, and check the percentage of linen; 60 percent or more is good quality and 100 percent is best. Two companies with top reputations and multiple outlets are **Brunella** and **Pepito's** (each has shops on Via Colombo, near the top of town; along Viale Pasitea, a main drag; and along claustrophobic Saraceno Lane, near the bottom of town, parallel to the beach).

**Ceramics:** One of the oldest ceramics stores in Positano, **Ceramica Assunta** carries colorful Solimene dinnerware and more at two locations (Via Cristoforo Colombo 97 and 137).

**Custom Sandals:** Positano has a tradition of handmade sandals, crafted to your specifications while you wait (prices start at about €50). One good shop, La Botteguccia, faces the tranquil little square just up from the TI; around the corner, in front of the Capricci restaurant, you'll see Carmine Todisco, who loves to explain how his grandfather shod Jackie O.

### Nightlife

The big-time action in the old town center is the impressive club **Music on the Rocks**, literally carved into the rocks on the beach (opens at 23:00 mid-April-Oct, but the party starts even later; there's often a €15-30 cover charge on weekends and in summer, which includes a drink; closed off-season; Via Grotte Dell'Incanto 51, tel. 089-875-874, www.musicontherocks.it). For a more low-key atmosphere, café/pastry shop **La Zagara** morphs into a cocktail bar with music nightly in summer (Via dei Mulini 10, tel. 089-875-964, www.lazagara.com).

## Sleeping in Positano

Most of these hotels are all on or near Via Cristoforo Colombo, which leads from the Sponda bus stop down into the village (ideal for arrival by bus). Outside high season (May-Sept), prices go soft. Most places close in the winter (Dec-Feb or longer). Expect to pay more than €20 per day to park, except at Albergo California.

**$$$$ Hotel Marincanto** is a somewhat impersonal four-star hotel with 32 beautiful rooms and a bright breakfast terrace practically teetering on a cliff. Suites seem to be designed for a *luna di miele*—honeymoon (air-con, elevator, pool, stairs down to a private beach, pay parking, closed Nov-March, 50 yards below Sponda bus stop at Via Cristoforo Colombo 50, reception on bottom floor, tel. 089-875-130, www.marincanto.it, info@marincanto.it).

**$$$$ Villa Rosa** decorates its 12 spacious rooms plus one apartment with—you guessed it—roses. Most rooms have views plus a terrace, which is the perfect place to have your breakfast served (no elevator, Via Cristoforo Colombo 127, tel. 089-811-955, www.villarosapositano.it, info@villarosapositano.it).

**$$$$ Hotel Bougainville** rents 16 comfortable rooms, half with balconies. Everything's bright, modern, and tasteful (rooms without views are cheaper, air-con, small elevator, closed Nov-March, Via Cristoforo Colombo 25, tel. 089-875-047, www.bougainville.it, info@bougainville.it, friendly Marella).

**$$$$ Hotel Savoia,** run by the friendly D'Aiello family, has

39 sizeable, breezy, bright, simple, tiled rooms (RS%, most rooms with balcony or terrace, some cheaper nonview rooms, air-con, elevator, closed Nov-March, Via Cristoforo Colombo 73, tel. 089-875-003, www.savoiapositano.it, info@savoiapositano.it). Their breakfast room converts into a restaurant for lunch and dinner.

**$$$$ Hotel Vittoria** sits just west of the town center with 20 open, spacious rooms and arched ceilings that feel right out of Positano's 1950s boom era. Sprawling up a cliffside, they offer their own free porter service (tips appreciated). All rooms have balconies, most with views overlooking the town (buffet breakfast, uphill from Fornillo Beach on Via Fornillo 19, tel. 089-875-049, www.hotelvittoriapositano.it, info@hotelvittoriapostiano.it).

**$$$$ Hotel Il Gabbiano** lies west of the busy town center and has 19 simple but tasteful rooms plus one apartment. All have a view terrace. From here you can explore the many eateries downhill (past the curve) along Viale Pasitea without having to trek into the main part of town (elevator, Viale Pasitea 310, tel. 089-875-306, www.ilgabbianopositano.com, info@ilgabbianopositano.com).

**$$$ Albergo California** has 15 spacious rooms (all with lofty views), a grand terrace draped with vines, and full breakfasts. The Cinque family—including Maria, Bronx-born son John, and grandchildren Giuseppe and Maria—will welcome you (air-con, free parking, closed Nov-Easter, Via Cristoforo Colombo 141, tel. 089-875-382, www.hotelcaliforniapositano.it, info@hotelcaliforniapositano.it).

**$$ Residence la Tavolozza** is an attractive six-room hotel, warmly run by Celeste (cheh-LEHS-tay) and daughters Francesca (who speaks English) and Paola. Each cheerily tiled room comes with a view, a terrace, and silence (lavish à la carte breakfast extra, families can ask for sprawling "Royal Apartment," air-con, confirm by phone if arriving late, closed Dec-Feb, Via Cristoforo Colombo 10, tel. 089-875-040, www.latavolozzapositano.it, info@latavolozzapositano.it).

**$ Brikette Hostel** offers your best budget option in this otherwise ritzy town. Its 35 dorm beds are pricey by hostel standards, but you're in Positano. It has a great sun and breakfast terrace and a youthful ambience (private and family rooms available, breakfast extra, cheap dinners, air-con; day privileges for day-trippers, including luggage storage—€10; closed Nov-March but a few apartments without breakfast are available all year long; leave bus at Chiesa Nuova/Bar Internazionale stop and backtrack uphill 500 feet to Via G. Marconi 358, www.hostel-positano.com, hostelpositano@gmail.com, Cristiana). The hostel isn't reachable by phone; email instead.

# Eating in Positano

**On the Beach:** At the waterfront, several interchangeable restaurants with view terraces leave people fat and happy, albeit with skinnier wallets (figure €15-20 pastas and *secondi*, plus pricey drinks and sides, and a cover charge). Little distinguishes one place from the next; all are scenic, convenient, and overpriced. **$$$ Covo dei Saraceni** offers the best value on the beach, with good pizza and tables overlooking the action (daily, on the far

right as you face the sea, where Via Positanesi d'America starts).

**Near the Beach:** A local favorite for its great views, **$$$ Lo Guarracino** is on the path to Fornillo Beach, with good food at prices similar to the beachfront places (daily 12:00-15:30 & 18:00-22:30, closed Nov-March, follow path behind the boat-ticket kiosks 5 minutes to Via Positanesi d'America 12, tel. 089-875-794). **$$ Wine-Dark House,** tucked around the base of the stairs near the beach (and the TI), fills a cute little piazzetta at the start of Via del Saracino. They serve good pastas and *secondi*, have a respect for wine (several excellent local wines), and are popular with Positano's youngsters for their long list of sandwiches (Wed-Mon 10:00-15:30 & 18:30-22:30, closed Tue, Via del Saracino 6, tel. 089-811-925).

**Picnics:** If a picnic dinner on your balcony or the beach sounds good, sunny Emilia at the **Delicatessen** grocery store can supply the ingredients: *antipasto misto,* pastas, home-cooked dishes, and sandwiches made to order. She'll heat it up for you and throw in the picnic ware. Come early for the best selection (all sold by weight, daily 7:00-22:00, shorter hours off-season, just below car park at Via del Mulini 5, tel. 089-875-489). **Vini e Panini** (a.k.a. "The Wine Shop"), another small grocery, is a block from the beach a few steps above the TI. Daniela, the fifth-generation owner, speaks English and happily makes sandwiches to order. Choose between the "Caprese" (mozzarella and tomato) and the "Positano" (mozzarella, tomato, and prosciutto), or create your own. They also have a nice selection of well-priced regional wines (daily 8:00-20:00, until 22:00 in summer, closed mid-Nov-mid-March, just behind church steps, tel. 089-875-175).

**"Uptown":** The unassuming, family-run **$$$ Ristorante Bruno** is handy to my listed hotels on or near Via Cristoforo Colombo. While expensive, it has nice views and is worth considering if you want a meal without hiking down into the town center (daily 12:30-23:00, closed Nov-Easter, near the top of Via Cristoforo Colombo at #157, tel. 089-875-179).

# Amalfi Town

After Rome fell, the town of Amalfi was one of the first to trade goods—coffee, carpets, and paper—between Europe and points east. Its heyday was the 10th and 11th centuries, when it was a powerful maritime republic—a trading power with a fleet that controlled this region and rivaled Pisa, Genoa, and Venice. The Republic of Amalfi founded a hospital in Jerusalem and claims to have founded the Knights of Malta order—even giving them the Amalfi cross, which became the famous Maltese cross. Amalfi

minted its own coins and established "rules of the sea"—the basics of which survive today.

In 1343, this little powerhouse was suddenly destroyed by a tsunami caused by an undersea earthquake. That disaster, compounded by devastating plagues, left Amalfi a humble backwater. Much of the culture of this entire region was driven by this town—but because it fell from power, Amalfi doesn't always get the credit it deserves. Today its 5,000 residents live off tourism. The coast's namesake is not as picturesque as Positano or as well-connected as Sorrento, but it has a real-life feel and a vivacious bustle.

Though generally less touristy than Positano, Amalfi is still packed during the day with big-bus tours (whose drivers pay €80 an hour to park while their groups shop for *limoncello* and ceramics). Amalfi's charms reveal themselves early and late in the day, when the crowds dissipate.

## Orientation to Amalfi Town

Amalfi's waterfront is the coast's biggest transport hub. Right next to each other are the bus station, ferry docks, and a parking lot (€5/hour; if the lot is full, park in the huge Lunarossa garage, burrowed into the hillside just past town and just before the tunnel leading into Atrani). The waterfront hub is overlooked by a statue of local boy Flavio Gioia, the purported inventor of the magnetic compass.

Amalfi's **TI** is just up the main road, right before the post office and overlooking the beach (Mon-Sat 9:00-14:00 & 15:00-18:30, Nov-March Mon-Sat 9:00-14:00, closed Sun year-round, pay WC in same courtyard, Corso della Repubbliche Marinare

AMALFI COAST

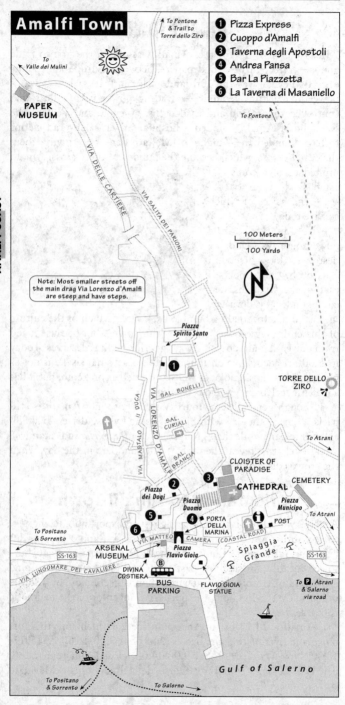

# Amalfi Town

1. Pizza Express
2. Cuoppo d'Amalfi
3. Taverna degli Apostoli
4. Andrea Pansa
5. Bar La Piazzetta
6. La Taverna di Masaniello

AMALFI COAST

To Pontone & Trail to Torre dello Ziro

To Valle dei Mulini

PAPER MUSEUM

To Pontone

VIA DELLE CARTIERE

VIA SALITA DEI PARIONI

100 Meters
100 Yards

Note: Most smaller streets off the main drag Via Lorenzo d'Amalfi are steep and have steps.

Piazza Spirito Santo

TORRE DELLO ZIRO

SAL. BONELLI

VIA LORENZO D'AMALFI

VIA MASTALO II DUCA

SAL. CURIALI

SAL. BRANCIA

To Atrani

CLOISTER OF PARADISE

CATHEDRAL

CEMETERY

Piazza dei Dogi

Piazza Duomo

Piazza Municipo

To Atrani

To Positano & Sorrento

PORTA DELLA MARINA

POST

(COASTAL ROAD)

VIA MATTEO CAMERA

ARSENAL MUSEUM

Piazza Flavio Gioia

SS-163

Spiaggia Grande

SS-163

DIVINA COSTIERA

BUS PARKING

FLAVIO GIOIA STATUE

To P, Atrani & Salerno via road

VIA LUNGOMARE DEI CAVALIERI

To Positano & Sorrento

To Salerno

Gulf of Salerno

27—about 100 yards from the bus station and ferry dock, next to the post office; facing the sea, it's to the left; tel. 089-871-107, www.amalfitouristoffice.it).

## HELPFUL HINTS

**Don't Get Stranded:** If you're day-tripping to Amalfi from elsewhere in the region, check locally to confirm when the last return bus or boat to Sorrento or Salerno leaves in the evening (in winter this can be as early as 19:00). Don't plan to leave on the last bus or boat of the day in peak season: If that bus or boat is full, your only way home might be a €100 taxi ride.

**Baggage Storage:** You can store your bag safely at the **Divina Costiera Travel Office** facing the waterfront square, across from the bus parking area (4 hours—€5, daily 8:00-20:00, closed Feb, tel. 089-871-181).

**Speedboat Charters:** To hire your own boat for a tour of the coastline from Amalfi (or to Capri), consider **Charter La Dolce Vita** (mobile 335-549-9365, www.amalficoastyacht.it).

# Sights in Amalfi Town

## AMALFI TOWN

Amalfi's one main street runs up from the waterfront through a deep valley, with stairways to courtyards and houses on either side. It's worth walking uphill to the workaday upper end of town. Super-atmospheric, narrow, stepped side lanes branch off, squeezing between hulking old buildings. If you hear water under a grate in the main street, it's the creek that runs through the ravine—a reminder that the town originally straddled the stream but later paved over it to create a main drag.

Before you enter the town, notice the colorful tile above the Porta della Marina gateway, showing off the trading domain of the maritime Republic of Amalfi. Just to the left, along the busy road, a series of arches marks the long, narrow, vaulted halls of Amalfi's arsenal—where ships were built in the 11th century. One of these is now the little Arsenal Museum.

Venture into town, and you'll quickly come to Piazza Duomo, the main square, with the cathedral—the town's most important sight—and a spring water-spewing statue of St. Andrew.

As you get farther away from the water, Amalfi becomes less glitzy and more traditional. The Paper Museum is a 10-minute walk up Via Lorenzo d'Amalfi, the main drag. On the way up to the museum, don't miss the huge, outdoor *presepi* (Nativity scenes) on your left. From the museum, the road narrows and you can turn off onto a path leading to the shaded Valle dei Mulini; it's full of paper-mill ruins that recall this once proud and prosperous industry. The ruined castle clinging to the rocky ridge above Amalfi is Torre dello Ziro, a good lookout point for intrepid hikers (see "Hikes," later).

As you return downhill, be sure to explore up the winding and narrow lanes and arcaded passages on either side of the main street.

### Arsenal Museum

This small, underground museum just across the road from the bus station tells a bit about Amalfi's maritime glory years. Stepping into the single long room under the dramatic vaulted stone ceiling, you can just tell that 1,000 years ago, they made ships here.

**Cost and Hours:** €4, daily 10:00-14:00 & 16:00-19:30, longer hours July-Aug, Piazza Flavio Gioia, mobile 334-917-7814.

**Performances:** Half of the arsenal space is a venue for performances of *Amalfi Musical*, a 1.5-hour musical bonanza loosely based on local history (English subtitles, Wed and Sat at 21:00, no performances Nov-April, www.amalfimusical.it).

### Cathedral

This church is "Amalfi Romanesque" (a mix of Moorish and Byzantine flavors, built c. 1000-1300), with a fanciful Neo-Byzantine facade from the 19th century. Climb the imposing stairway, which functions as a mini Spanish Steps-style hangout zone and a handy outdoor theater. The 1,000-year-old bronze door at the top was given to Amalfi by a wealthy local merchant who had it made in Constantinople. Visitors are directed on a one-way circuit through the cathedral complex with four stops: the cloister, original basilica, crypt, and cathedral.

**Cost and Hours:** €3, daily 10:00-17:00. The cathedral—but not the rest of the complex—can be entered free for prayer or discreet visits daily 7:30-10:00 & 17:00-19:30; it's closed 10:00-17:00 except as part of the paid visit; tel. 089-871-324, www. parrocchiaamalfi.com. There's a fine, free WC at the top of the steps (through unmarked green door, just a few steps before ticket booth, ask for key at desk).

**Visiting the Cathedral:** You'll follow a self-guided, one-way tour of the complex, beginning in a courtyard of 120 graceful columns—the **"Cloister of Paradise."** This was the cemetery for nobles in the 13th century (note their stone sarcophagi). Don't miss the fine view of the bell tower and its majolica tiles.

The original ninth-century church, known as the **Basilica of**

**the Crucifix,** boasts a fine 13th-century wooden crucifix. Today the basilica is a museum filled with the cathedral's art treasures. The Angevin Mitre (Mitra Angioina), with a "pavement of tiny pearls" setting off its gold and gems, has been worn by bishops since the 14th century. Also on display (waist-high, facing the altar) is a carved wooden decoration from a Saracen pirate ship that wrecked just outside of town in 1544 during a freak storm. The church is dedicated to St. Andrew, whom believers credit with causing the storm and saving the town from certain pillage and plunder.

Down the stairs to the right of the basilica's altar is the **Crypt of St. Andrew.** Just as Venice needed St. Mark to get on the pilgrimage map, Amalfi needed St. Andrew—one of the apostles who, along with his brother Peter, left their fishing nets to become the original "fishers of men." Under the huge bronze statue, you'll see a reliquary holding what are believed to be Andrew's remains (kneel at the back of the crypt for a better view). These were brought here from Constantinople in 1206 during the Crusades—an indication of the wealth and importance of Amalfi back then.

Climb the stairs up into the **cathedral** itself. Behind the main altar is a painting of St. Andrew martyred on an X-shaped cross flanked by two Egyptian granite columns supporting a triumphal arch. Before leaving, check out the delicate mother-of-pearl crucifix (right of door in back).

### ▲Paper Museum (Museo della Carta)

This excellent little museum—worth ▲▲▲ for paper enthusiasts—makes for a good excuse to break free from the crowds and walk up the main drag to a quieter, more local part of town. Paper has been an important industry here since Amalfi's glory days in the Middle Ages. Millworkers would pound rags into pulp in a big vat, pull it up using a screen, and air-dry each sheet (the same technique used to make artisan paper today—look for it at shops in town). At this cavernous, cool 13th-century paper mill-turned-museum, a multilingual guide collects groups at the entrance (no particular times) for a 25-minute tour. The guide recounts the history and process of papermaking and turns on the museum's vintage machinery. You'll see how the Amalfi River (which you can still hear rumbling underfoot) powered this important industry, and you'll learn the origins of the term "watermark." Kids can dip a screen into the rag pool and make a sheet of paper. It's amazing to think this factory produced paper through 1969 (when it was replaced by a modern facility up the valley).

**Cost and Hours:** €4.50; daily 10:00-18:30; Nov-Jan Tue-Sat until 15:30, closed Mon; a 10-minute walk up the main street from the cathedral—follow signs to *Museo della Carta* at Via delle Cartiere 23; tel. 089-830-4561, www.museodellacarta.it.

**AMALFI COAST**

## HIKES

Amalfi is the starting point for several fine hikes, two of which I've described here. The TI hands out photocopies of Giovanni Visetti's trail maps (or download them from his engaging website, www. giovis.com). The best book on local hikes is Julian Tippett's *Sorrento Amalfi Capri Car Tours and Walks* (2015), with useful color-coded maps and info on public transportation to the trailheads. Lucia Ferrara, a great guide based in Positano, leads hikes around Amalfi (see her listing on page 1093).

### Hike #1: Pontone

This loop trail leads up the valley past paper-mill ruins, ending in the tiny town of Pontone; you can get lunch there, and head back down to the town of Amalfi (allow 3 hours total). Bring a good map, since it's easy to veer off the main route. Start your hike by following the main road (Via Lorenzo d'Amalfi) away from the sea.

After the Paper Museum, jog right, then left to join the trail, which runs through the shaded woods along a babbling stream. Heed the signs that warn people to stay away from the ruins of paper mills (no matter how tempting they look), since many are ready to collapse on unwary hikers. Continue up to Pontone, where Trattoria l'Antico Borgo offers wonderful cuisine and a great view (Via Noce 4, tel. 089-871-469). After lunch, return to Amalfi via a steep stairway.

If you're feeling ambitious, before you head back to Amalfi, add a one-hour detour (30 minutes each way) to visit the ridge-hugging **Torre dello Ziro** (ask a local how to find the trail to this tower). You'll be rewarded with a spectacular view.

### Hike #2: Atrani

For an easier stroll, head to the nearby town of Atrani. This village, just a 15-minute stroll beyond Amalfi town, is a world apart; its 1,500 residents consider themselves definitely *not* from Amalfi. Leave Amalfi via the main road and stay on the water side until the promenade ends. Cross the street, continue a few more yards, then go up the whitewashed staircase just past the pizzeria. From here, twist up through old lanes to a paved route that takes you over the hill and drops you into Atrani in about 15 minutes.

With relatively few tourists, a delightful town square, and a free, sandy beach (if you drive here, pay for parking at harbor), Atrani has none of Amalfi's trendy resort feel. Piazza Umberto is the core of town, with cafés, restaurants, and little grocery stores that can make sandwiches. A whitewashed staircase leads up to the serene and beautiful town church (under the clock face).

To save time and sweat on the return walk, follow the promenade just above water level toward Amalfi. Then walk up through the restaurant terrace and find the big, long tunnel next to the parking garage—this will deposit you in the middle of Amalfi.

From Atrani, you could theoretically continue up to **Ravello** (described later in this chapter). But unless you're part mountain goat, you'll probably prefer catching the bus to Ravello from Amalfi town instead.

## Eating in Amalfi Town

**Quick Bites:** Walk five minutes up the main drag; on the right, past the first archway, is **$ Pizza Express,** with honest pies, calzones, and heated sandwiches to go (Mon-Sat 9:00-21:00, closed Sun, Via Capuano 46, mobile 339-581-2336). The **Cuoppo d'Amalfi** fried-fish stand at Piazza dei Dogi (described below) is another good option.

**On the Main Square, Piazza Duomo:** Several pricey places face the cathedral steps. The best of the bunch is tucked just around the left side of the grand staircase, up a smaller flight of stairs: **$$ Taverna degli Apostoli,** with colorful outdoor tables and cozy upstairs dining room in what was once an art gallery. The menu is brief but thoughtful, going beyond the old standbys, and everything is well-executed (daily 12:00-16:00 & 19:00-24:00, Supportico San Andrea 6, tel. 089-872-991). For dessert, the **Andrea Pansa** pastry shop and café, to the right as you face the cathedral steps, is the most venerable place in town—a good spot to try *sfogliatella* (the delicate pastry invented at a nearby monastery) and other desserts popular in southern Italy (daily 7:30-24:00).

**Near the Main Square, on Piazza dei Dogi:** If you walk straight ahead from the cathedral stairs, go up the little covered lane, and hook right at the fork, you'll pop out in atmospheric little Piazza dei Dogi. Slightly less trampled and more neighborhood-feeling than Piazza Duomo, this has several decent (if forgettable) restaurants aimed squarely at pleasing tourists. The **$ Cuoppo d'Amalfi** fried-fish shop, on the right as you enter the square, fills cardboard cones with all manner of deep-fried sea life. **$$ Bar La Piazzetta** has good prices at its tables right in the middle of the square. And tucked at the corner of the square leading to the port, **$$ La Taverna di Masaniello** is a bit pricier, with good food.

## Amalfi Town Connections

Amalfi is connected by bus and boat to all other nearby towns. If you're coming from Salerno, buy your boat ticket directly from the booth on the dock there. Boats also connect Amalfi to Positano, Capri, and Sorrento. SITA public buses originating in either Salerno or Sorrento stop in Amalfi (some terminate here; check with driver). CitySightseeing buses, whether coming from Sorrento or Ravello, terminate in Amalfi as well. For details see "Getting Around the Amalfi Coast" on page 1082.

# Ravello

The Amalfi Coast's version of a hill town, Ravello (a 30-minute bus ride from Amalfi town) sits atop a lofty perch 1,000 feet above the sea. It boasts an interesting church, two villas with stunning gardens, and breathtaking views that have attracted celebrities for generations. Gore Vidal, Richard Wagner, D. H. Lawrence, M. C. Escher, Henry Wadsworth Longfellow, Tennessee Williams, and Greta Garbo all succumbed to Ravello's charms and called it home.

The town is like a lush and peaceful garden floating in a world all its own. It seems to be made entirely of cafés, stonework, old villas-turned-luxury hotels, tourists, and grand views. Ravello feels like a place to convalesce.

## Sights in Ravello

To see the sights listed here, start at the bus stop and walk through the tunnel to the main square, where you'll find the Villa Rufolo on the left, the church on the right, and the **TI** down the street past the church (TI open daily 10:00-18:00, closes earlier Nov-April, 100 yards from the square—follow signs to Via Roma 18, tel. 089-857-096, www.ravellotime.com). Villa Cimbrone is a 10-minute walk from the square (follow the signs).

If you have time for only one villa, consider this: Villa Rufolo is easier to reach (facing the main square) and has a stunning terrace garden. Villa Cimbrone requires an up-and-down hike, but it's bigger and more rugged and offers even grander views in both directions along the coast.

### Piazza Duomo

The town's entry tunnel deposits you on the main square. Though Ravello is perfectly peaceful today, the weathered watchtower of Villa Rufolo—which once kept an eye out for fires and invasions—is a reminder that it wasn't always postcards and *limoncello*.

The fine umbrella pines on the square provide a shady meeting place for strollers ending up here on the piazza. Opposite the church is a fine view of the terraced hillside and the community of Scala (which means "steps"—historically a way of life there). The terraces—supporting grapevines and lemon trees—mostly date from the 16th century. Viale Wagner climbs to the top of town for sea views and ruined villas that are now luxury hotels. The town is essentially traffic-free.

## Duomo

Ravello's cathedral, overlooking the main square, feels stripped-down and Romanesque. The facade of the cathedral is plain because the earlier, fancy west portal was destroyed in a 1364 earthquake. The front door is locked; to enter, go through the museum on Viale Wagner, around the right side. Inside, you'll find tastefully restrained decoration and a floor that slopes upward. The key features of this church are its 12th-century bronze doors (from Constantinople), with 54 Biblical scenes; the carved marble pulpit supported by six lions; and the chance to get a close-up look at the relic of holy blood (in the chapel left of main altar). The geometric designs show Arabic influence. The humble cathedral museum, through which you'll enter, is two rooms of well-described carved marble that evoke the historical importance of the town.

**Cost and Hours:** €3 for the museum—which also gets you into the church, daily 9:00-19:00, Nov-April until 18:00.

## Villa Rufolo

The villa, built in the 13th-century ruins of a noble family's palace, presents wistful gardens among stony walls, with oh-my-God views. The Arabic/Norman gardens seem designed to frame commanding coastline vistas (you can enjoy some of the same view, without the entry fee, from the bus parking lot just below the villa). It's also one of the venues for Ravello's annual arts festival (July-Sept, www.ravellofestival.com) and music society performances (April-June and Sept-Oct, www.ravelloarts.org). Musicians perch on a bandstand on the edge of the cliff for a combination of wonderful music and dizzying views. Wagner visited here and was impressed enough to set the second act of his opera *Parsifal* in the villa's magical gardens. By all accounts, the concert on the cliff is a sublime experience.

**Cost and Hours:** €7, daily 9:00-20:00, Oct-April 9:00 until sunset, may close earlier for concerts, tel. 089-857-621, www.villarufolo.it.

**Visiting the Villa:** From Piazza Duomo, enter through the stout watchtower to buy your ticket and pick up the English booklet explaining the sight. Then, walk through part of the sprawling villa ruins. Check out the short video in the tiny theater at the base of the tower and the exhibit upstairs. The palace itself has little to

show, but the gardens and views are magnificent and invite exploration.

### ▲Villa Cimbrone

This villa offers another romantic garden, this one built upon the
ruins of an old convent. Located at the opposite end of Ravello, it
was created in the 20th century by Englishman William Beckett.
His mansion is now a five-star hotel. It's a longish walk to the end
of town, where you explore a bluff dreamily landscaped around the
villa. At the far end, above a sublime café on the lawn, "the Terrace
of Infinity" dangles high above the sea.

**Cost and Hours:** €7, daily 9:00-sunset, tel. 089-857-459,
www.hotelvillacimbrone.com.

**Getting There:** Facing the cathedral on Piazza Duomo, exit
the square to the right and follow signs. You'll climb up and down
(and up and down) some stair-step lanes, enjoying a quieter side of
Ravello, before reaching the villa at the point.

**Visiting the Villa:** Buy your ticket and pick up the free map/
guide of the gardens. Across from the ticket booth, duck into the
old monastery. Then pass the rose-garden terrace and head up the
"main boulevard," which leads straight to the stunning Terrace of
Infinity, with 360-degree views up and down the coast. If you have
the interest and energy, loop back along the more rugged downhill slope (facing the adjacent town of Scala). Tiny lizards scurry
underfoot, while mythological statues (Mercury's Seat, Temple of
Bacchus, Eve's Grotto) strike their poses before a stunning and serene backdrop.

### ▲Hike to Amalfi Town from Villa Cimbrone

To walk downhill from Ravello's Villa Cimbrone to the town of
Amalfi (a path for hardy hikers only—follow the TI's map), retrace
your steps back toward town. Take the first left, which turns into
a stepped path winding its way below the cliff. Pause here to look
back up at the rock with a big white mansion—Villa La Rondinaia,
where Gore Vidal lived for many years. Continue down the fairly
steep path about 40 minutes to the town of Atrani, where several
bars on the main square offer well-deserved refreshments. From
here, it's about a 15-minute walk back to Amalfi (see "Hike #2" on
page 1108).

# Eating in Ravello

Several no-brainer, interchangeable restaurants face Piazza Duomo
and line the surrounding streets. To enjoy this fine setting, just take
your pick. You can also grab a takeaway lunch at one of the little
groceries and sandwich shops that line Via Roma (between Piazza
Duomo and the TI). Enjoy your meal at the panoramic benches at

the far end of Piazza Duomo (facing the cathedral), or facing even better views just outside of town, near the bus stop and Ristorante Da Salvatore. (Picnicking isn't allowed inside the two villas.)

**$$$ Ristorante Da Salvatore,** near the Ravello bus stop (at the other end of the little tunnel from the Duomo), serves a serious sit-down lunch with great views. Pino, the English-speaking owner of this formal restaurant, serves nicely presented, traditional Amalfi cuisine from a fun, if pricey, menu. Their pasta with potatoes and calamari is a favorite. Be adventurous when ordering and share dishes. Pato, the parakeet, is learning English (Tue-Sun 12:30-15:00 & 19:30-22:00, closed Mon, Via della Repubblica 2, smart to call ahead for reservations—tel. 089-857-227).

## Ravello Connections

Ravello and the town of **Amalfi** are connected by bus along a very windy road. Coming from Amalfi town, buy your bus ticket at the Divina Costiera travel office facing the waterfront square, and ask where the stop for Ravello is (normally by the statue on the waterfront, just to the statue's left as you face the water). When returning from Ravello, line up early, since the buses are often crowded (at least every 40 minutes, 30-minute trip, €1.20, buy ticket in tobacco shop; catch bus 100 yards off main square, by the recommended Ristorante Da Salvatore). Another option to or from Ravello is a CitySightseeing shuttle bus (see "Getting Around the Amalfi Coast," on page 1082). Coming from Positano or Sorrento, you'll change buses in Amalfi. From Naples or Paestum, you have to change twice (in Salerno and Amalfi), making for a long day.

# Paestum

The archaeological park at Paestum (PASTE-oom) includes one of the best collections of Greek temples anywhere—and certainly the most accessible to Western Europe. Serenely situated, Paestum (worth ▲▲) is surrounded by fields and wildflowers. Not quite a village, it also has a bus stop, a church, a TI, a straggle of houses, and handful of eateries.

This town was founded as Poseidonia by Greeks in the sixth

AMALFI COAST

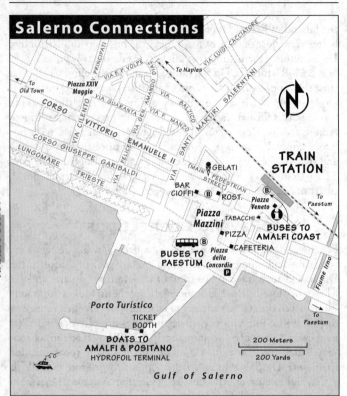

Salerno Connections

century BC and became a key stop on an important trade route. In the fifth century BC, the Lucanians, a barbarous inland tribe, conquered Poseidonia and tried to adopt the cultured ways of the Greeks. By the time of the Romans, who took over in the third century BC, the name Poseidonia had been simplified to Paestum. The final conquerors of Paestum, malaria-carrying mosquitoes, kept the site wonderfully deserted for nearly a thousand years. The temples were never buried—just ignored. Rediscovered in the 18th century, Paestum today offers the only well-preserved Greek ruins north of Sicily.

While most visitors do Paestum as a day trip (it's an hour from Naples by convenient direct train), it's not a bad place to overnight. Accommodations offer great value, and though it's a bit far, you could use Paestum as a base for day trips to Naples or the Amalfi Coast. There's a beach nearby, and hotels can help arrange visits to local buffalo-milk dairies.

**Tourist Information:** There's a small TI window at the train station (daily 8:30-18:30) and a bigger one next to the Paestum Archaeological Museum (daily 9:00-13:00 & 14:00-16:00, tel. 0828-811-016, www.infopaestum.it).

## GETTING THERE

Direct trains to Paestum run from Naples and Salerno; from elsewhere, you'll need to transfer at one of those two points. For those transferring in Salerno, see the map on the opposite page, which shows train, bus, and boat stops as well as a few handy eateries if you need to grab a bite. The helpful Salerno TI can answer any questions you might have (daily 9:00-19:30).

**From Naples:** Direct **trains** run from Naples' Centrale Station to Paestum for €7 (12/day, one hour, direction: Sapri or Reggio, only Intercity trains have a first-class section). Buy tickets online, or from the ticket windows or machines at the station. For a day trip from Naples, it's wise to get an early start—especially in warm weather. As of this printing, trains left Naples at 6:50, 7:35, 7:55, and 8:50, then not until 11:45 (confirm schedule on www.trenitalia.it). In the cooler shoulder season, consider arriving for lunch, visiting the museum, then seeing the temples bask in warm afternoon light.

**From Amalfi Town:** First take a bus (75 minutes) or boat (35 minutes) to Salerno, where you can catch the **train** on its way from Naples (30 minutes from Salerno to Paestum). You'll need to leave Amalfi early—8:00 at the latest—to make the last morning train. Buses from Amalfi terminate at the Salerno train station, but if you arrive in Salerno by boat, you'll walk from the boat dock a few short blocks up to the train station (about 10 minutes, mostly level; see map). Once in Salerno, buy your Paestum train ticket at ticket machines or the ticket office in the train station.

If you're in a pinch—for example, you've arrived in Salerno during the midday lull in the train schedule—you could take **local CSTP/BusItalia bus #34** from Salerno to Paestum (about hourly, fewer on Sun, one-hour trip). It seems convenient to the port (it departs from Piazza della Concordia—look for bus shelter between the big parking lot and the main road, no posted schedule), but you can't buy tickets nearby—the closest sales point is the tobacco shop a block in front of the train station. In Paestum, this bus drops you only slightly closer to the ruins than does the train.

**From Positano:** The extra 50 minutes by road to Amalfi, plus time spent changing buses there, makes a day trip from Positano to Paestum more difficult than from Amalfi town. It's possible, though (take a crack-of-dawn bus to Amalfi or the first ferry of the day to Salerno), especially in summer, when return buses from Amalfi run until late in the evening.

**From Sorrento:** The smart (if dull) approach is to go by Circumvesuviana train to Naples (70 minutes), catch the direct Naples-Paestum train, and return the same way. While it's technically possible to do one leg of the trip via an Amalfi Coast bus, this makes for a very long day marred by worry about making connections back. Other options are to rent a car or hire a taxi for the day. From Sorrento, Paestum is 60 miles and at least 3 hours (depending on traffic) via the Amalfi Coast road, but a smooth 2 hours by autostrada. To reach Paestum from Sorrento via the autostrada, drive toward Naples, catch the autostrada (direction: Salerno), skirt Salerno (direction: Reggio), exit at Battipaglia, and drive straight through the roundabout.

If you drive to Paestum, you'll see signs for *mozzarella di bufala*, cheese made from the milk of water buffalo. Try it here—it couldn't be any fresher.

*Arrival at Paestum:* If you arrive by **train,** cross under the tracks, exit the tiny station, and walk through the ancient city gate; the ruins are a half-mile walk straight ahead, up a dusty road. When you hit the street with hotels and shops, turn right to find the museum and site entrance. If you'd rather not walk, Patrizia Pecora runs a great team of local **taxi** drivers available for transport to hotels or to the ruins (€10 fixed rate, mobile 392-444-9020). **Buses** from Salerno stop near a corner of the ruins (at a little bar/café).

There's no official **baggage storage** at the train station or museum. If you're desperate, you can try nicely asking at one of the bars along the main road (they may want a small payment) or ask at a restaurant you've already patronized.

## ORIENTATION TO THE ARCHAEOLOGICAL PARK

**Cost:** €9, €10 with special exhibits, includes site and museum. The site alone is €7 on days when the museum is closed; the museum alone is €4 after dark on winter evenings, when the site is closed.

**Hours:** Museum open Tue-Sun 8:30-19:30 (last ticket sold at 18:50), closed Mon. Site open daily 8:30 to one hour before sunset (as late as 19:30 June-July, as early as 16:00 in late Nov-Dec, last site ticket sold 40 minutes before closing).

**Information:** Tel. 0828-811-023, www.museopaestum. beniculturali.it.

**Getting In:** The site and museum have separate entrances. The museum, just outside the ruins, is in a cluster with the TI and a small early-Christian basilica. Most visitors buy tickets at the museum and use the entrance across the street, but another ticket office and entrance are near the recommended Ristorante Nettuno (at the south end of the site). On days when the museum is closed, tickets are sold only at the site entrances.

**Local Guide:** For an insider's knowledge, **Silvia Braggio** specializes in Paestum and gives a fine two-hour walk of the site and museum (special rate for my readers—€100, arrange in advance, mobile 347-643-2307, www.silviaguide.it, silvia@silviaguide.it). She also offers walking tours of Pompeii and Herculaneum.

**Eating:** Several cafés and bars cluster around the museum (all open long hours daily in summer). **$ La Basilica Café,** facing a pretty little garden between the parking lot and TI, is the most straightforward and reasonable option, with good pizzas and other lunch fare (Via Magna Grecia 881, tel. 0828-811-301). **Ristorante Nettuno,** with standard tourist food and good temple views, is at the site's south entrance. They have a fine little glassed-in **$$ café** facing the ruins and a dressier, more expensive **$$$ restaurant** across the path (Via Nettuno 2, tel. 0828-811-028).

Another cluster of restaurants and bars sits north of the ruins, just outside the city wall along Via Tavernelle (a short walk from the museum). Away from the main entrance crowds, this strip of elegant eateries offers a good way to enjoy Paestum's peaceful atmosphere. **$$$ Bistrot 73,** run by hardworking chefs Roberto and Manuela, serves wonderful pasta dishes in a playful but sophisticated setting (at #48, mobile 342-526-1393). **$$ GinGin** serves regional wines and snazzy cocktails (at #38, open from 19:00, mobile 392-872-3016). **$$$ Antiche Mura** accompanies their fine grilled meats with an impressive wine list (at #20, tel. 0828-199-8535).

**Length of This Tour:** Allow two hours to see the ruins and the museum (about an hour for each). Which one you see first depends on your interest and the heat: You'll enjoy the coolest temperatures in the morning, but the best light and smallest crowds late in the day.

## BACKGROUND

While Paestum is famous for its marvelous Greek temples, most of the structures you see are Roman. Five elements of Greek Paestum survive: three misnamed temples, a memorial tomb, and a circular meeting place (the Ekklesiasterion). The rest, including the wall that defines the site, is Roman.

Paestum was once a seaport (the ocean is now about a mile away—the wall in the distance, which stretches about three miles, is about halfway to today's coastline). Only about a fifth of the site has been excavated. The Greek city, which archaeologists figure had a population of about 13,000, was first conquered by Lucanians (distant relatives of the Romans, who spoke a language related to Latin), and then by the Romans (who completely made it over and built the wall you see today).

AMALFI COAST

AMALFI COAST

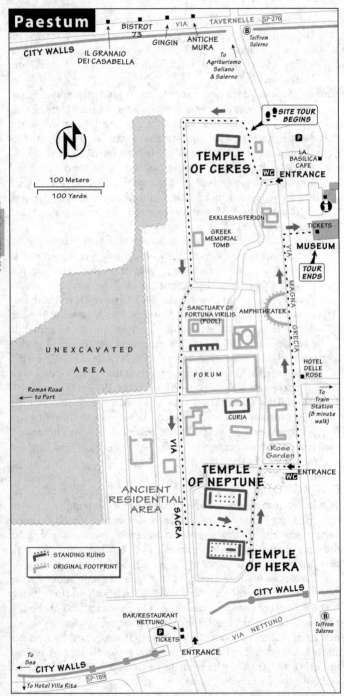

The remaining Greek structures survive because the Romans were superstitious—they respected sacred areas and didn't mess with temples and tombs. While most old Christian churches are built upon Roman temples (it tends to be what people do when they conquer another culture), no Roman temple is built upon a Greek temple. The three Greek temples that you'll see here today have stood for about 2,500 years.

## ❷ SELF-GUIDED TOURS

Although there are only scant descriptions at the site, the following self-guided tours provide all the information you need for both the site and the museum. Skip the museum bookshop's dull audioguide.

### Paestum Archaeological Site

This part of the tour starts at the entrance by the museum, visits the Temple of Ceres, goes through the center of the Roman town past the Greek Memorial Tomb, circles around the other two Greek temples, and then leaves the site to walk down the modern road to the Ekklesiasterion (which faces the museum).

• *Buy your ticket at the museum, then head to the right to find the site's north entrance. Once inside, stand in front of the...*

**Temple of Ceres:** All three Paestum temples have inaccurate names, coined by 19th-century archaeologists who based their "discoveries" on wishful thinking. (While the Romans

made things easy by leaving lots of inscriptions, the Greeks did not.) Those 1800s archaeologists wanted this temple to be devoted to Ceres, the goddess of agriculture. However, all the little votive statues found later, when modern archaeologists dug here, instead depicted a woman with a big helmet: Athena, goddess of wisdom and war. (The Greeks' female war goddess was also the goddess of wisdom—thinking...strategy...female. The Romans' masculine war god was Mars—just fighting.) Each temple is part of a sanctuary—an open, sacred space around the temple. Because regular people couldn't go into the temple, the altar logically stood outside.

The Temple of Ceres dates from 500 BC. It's made of locally quarried limestone blocks. Good roads and shipping didn't come along until the Romans, so the Greeks' buildings were limited to local materials. The wooden roof is long gone. Like the other two temples, this one was once painted white, black, and red, and has an east-west orientation—facing the rising sun. This temple's *cella* (interior room) is gone, cleared out when it was used as a Christian church in the sixth century. In medieval times, Normans scavenged stones from here; chunks of these temples can be found in Amalfi's cathedral.

Walk around to the back side of the Temple of Ceres. The capitals broke in a modern earthquake, so a steel bar provides necessary support. Each of the Paestum temples is Doric style—with three stairs, columns without a base, and shafts that narrow at the top to a simple capital of a round, then a square, block. While there were no carved reliefs, colorful frescoes once decorated the pediments.

As you walk away, look back at the temple. Traditionally, Greeks would build a sanctuary of Athena on a city's highest spot (like the Parthenon in Athens, on the Acropolis). Paestum had no hill, so the Greeks created a mound. The hill was more impressive in its time because the level of the Greek city was substantially lower than the Roman pavement stones you'll walk on today.

• *Follow the path down from behind the temple, and turn left to walk on the paving stones of Via Sacra toward the other Greek temples. After about 100 yards, to the left of the road, you'll see a little half-buried house with a tiled roof.*

**Greek Memorial Tomb** (Heroon): This tomb (from 500 BC) also survived because the Romans respected religious buildings. But the tomb was most inconveniently located, right in the middle of their growing city. So the practical Romans built a perimeter wall around it (visible today), added a fine tiled roof, and then buried the tomb.

There's a mystery here. Greeks generally buried their dead outside the city (as did Romans)—there are over a thousand ancient tombs outside Paestum's walls—yet this tomb was parked smack-dab in the center of town. When it was uncovered in 1952, no bodies were found inside. The tomb instead held nine perfectly preserved vases (now in the museum). Archaeologists aren't sure what the tomb's purpose was. Perhaps it was a memorial dedicated to some great hero (like a city founder). Or perhaps it was a memorial to those lost when a neighboring community had to evacuate and settle as refugees here.

• *Continue walking down Via Sacra, the main drag of...*

**Roman Paestum:** Roman towns were garrison towns: rectangular with a grid street plan and two main streets cutting north-south and east-west, dividing the town into four equal sections. They were built by military engineers with a no-nonsense standard design. New excavations (on the left) have uncovered Roman-era lead piping. City administration buildings were on the left, and residential buildings were on the right.

Shortly after the road turns into a dirt path, you'll come to a big **Roman pool** (on the left) that archaeologists believe was a sanctuary dedicated to Fortuna Virilis, goddess of luck and fertility. The strange stones likely supported a wooden platform for priests and statues of gods. Imagine young women walking down the ramp at the far end and through the pool, hoping to conceive a child.

The next big square on the left was the **Roman forum** and ancient Paestum's main intersection. The road on the right led directly (and very practically) to the port. It made sense to have a direct connection to move freight between the sea and the center of town.

Until 2007, the vast field of ruins on the right (between the forum and the next temple) was covered in vegetation. It's since been cleared and cleaned of harmful lichen, which produce acids that dissolve limestone. Study the rocks: Yellow lichen is alive, black is dead. Even the great temples of Paestum were covered in this destructive lichen until 2000, when a two-year-long project cleaned them for the first time.

• *Ahead on the left are the so-called...*

**Temple of Neptune and Hera:** The **Temple of Neptune** dates from 450 BC and employs the Greek architectural trick where the

base line is curved up just a tad to overcome the illusion of sagging caused by a straight base. The Athenians built their Parthenon (with a similar bowed-up base line) just 30 years after this. Many think this temple could have been their inspiration.

The adjacent **Temple of Hera,** dating from 550 BC, is the oldest of Paestum's three temples and one of the oldest Greek temples still standing anywhere. Notice the change 100 years makes in the architectural styles: Archaic Doric in 550 BC versus Classic Doric in 450 BC.

Archaeologists now believe the "Temple of Neptune" was actually devoted to a different god. Votive statues uncovered here

suggest that Hera was the focus (perhaps this was a new-and-improved version of the adjacent, simpler, and older Temple of Hera). Or perhaps it was a temple to Zeus, Hera's husband, to honor the couple together.

Together, the two temples

formed a single huge sanctuary with altars on the far (east) side. Walk between the temples, then hook right to get a good look at the front of the Temple of Hera. Notice how overbuilt this temple appears. Its columns and capitals are closer together than necessary, as if the builders lacked confidence in their ability to span the distance between supports. Square pillars mark the corners of the *cella* inside. Temples with an odd number of columns (here, nine) had a single colonnade crossing in the center inside to support the wooden roof. More modern temples (such as the Temple of Neptune) had six columns, with two colonnades passing through the *cella*. This left a line of vision open through the middle so that worshippers could see the big statue of the god.

By the way, in 1943, Allied paratroopers dropped in near here during the famous "Landing of Salerno," when the Allies (who had already taken Sicily) invaded mainland Italy. Paestum was part of their first beachhead. The Temple of Hera served as an Allied military tent hospital. From here, the Allies pushed back the Nazis, marching to Naples, Cassino, and finally to Rome.

• *Leave the site (using the exit straight ahead from the Temple of Neptune and a bit to the left) and turn left on the modern road...*

**Via Magna Grecia:** The king of Naples had this Naples-to-Paestum road built in 1829 to inspire his people with ancient temples. While he was modern in his appreciation of antiquity, his road project destroyed a swath of the ancient city, as you'll see as you pass by half of the small amphitheater.

• *Just past the amphitheater, you'll find the...*

**Ekklesiasterion:** Immediately across the street from the museum is what looks like a sunken circular theater. This rare bit of ancient Greek ruins was the Ekklesiasterion, a meeting place where the Greeks would get together to discuss things and vote. Archaeologists believe that the agora (market) would also have been located here.

• *Across the street is the...*

## Paestum Archaeological Museum

Paestum's museum offers the rare opportunity to see artifacts—dating from prehistoric to Greek to Roman times—at the site where they were discovered. These beautifully crafted works (with good English descriptions throughout) help bring Paestum to life. Not everything you see here is from Paestum, though, as the museum also collects artifacts from other nearby sites.

Before stepping into the museum, notice the proud fascist architecture meant to imitate the structure of the temples you've just seen. Though the building dates from 1954, it was designed in 1938. It seems to command that you *will* enjoy this history lesson. The exhibit is on several levels. You'll find mostly Greek pieces on the ground floor (artifacts from the Temple of Hera in front, frescoes from tombs in the back), Paleolithic to Iron Age artifacts on the mezzanine level, and Roman art on the top floor (statues, busts, and inscriptions dating from the time of the Roman occupation). While Roman art is not unique to Paestum, the Greek collection is—so that's what you should focus on.

• *Before exploring the collection, notice the display case (tucked into the far-right corner near the entrance) with the **huge book** turned to a page with a fine drawing by the Italian artist Giovanni Piranesi, showing his visit to Paestum in 1777. Then look for these museum highlights.*

**Temple Reliefs:** The museum's center room is designed like a Greek temple inner *cella* and used for temporary exhibitions. The large carvings overhead (known as metopes) that wrap around this inner sanctum once adorned a sanctuary of the goddess Hera five miles away. This sanctuary, called Heraion del Sele, was discovered and excavated in 1934. Some of the carvings show scenes from the life of Hercules. You'll get a chance to see the details later in this visit.

• *Along the back wall of this room, find the glass case holding nine perfectly preserved...*

**Vases:** One ceramic and eight bronze, with artistic handles, these vases were found in Paestum's Greek Memorial Tomb. Greek bronzes are rare because Romans often melted them down to make armor. These were discovered in 1952, filled with still-liquid honey and sealed with beeswax. The honey (as you can see in the display cases below) has since crystallized. Honey was a standard part of a funeral because, to ancient Greeks, honey symbolized immortality...it lasts forever.

• *Enter the room at the far end of the main hall, filled with ancient Greek...*

**Votive Offerings:** These were dug up at Heraion del Sele (not at Paestum) like the temple reliefs seen earlier. Such offerings are a huge help to modern archaeologists, since the figures that worshippers brought to a temple are clues as to which god the temple honored. These votives depict a woman with a crown on a throne—clearly Hera. The clay votives were simple, affordable, and accessible to regular people.

• *Now continue ahead into the large room (broken up by pillars and interior walls) that holds...*

**Relics from the Temples at Paestum:** This room displays smaller pieces. Displays tell in which temple each relic was found (videos unfortunately are only in Italian). The Temple of Ceres is often referred to as the Temple of Athena or as the northern *(settentrionale)* sanctuary. The Temples of Neptune and Hera are spoken of as the southern *(meridionale)* sanctuaries.

In a glass case nearby, find the seated statue of **Zeus.** This painted clay Zeus dates from 520 BC. The king of the gods was so lusty with his antics, he's still smirking.

Farther into the room, you can't miss the display case of a statue's **torso** emblazoned with swastikas—a reminder that this symbol (carrying completely different meanings) predated Hitler by millennia.

Across the room, look for the short fragment of a **frieze** with lion heads. Paestum's three temples were once adorned with decorations, such as these ornamental spouts that spurted rainwater out of lions' mouths. Notice the bits of the surviving black, red, and white paint. Reconstructions on the adjacent wall show archaeologists' best guesses as to how the original decorations might have looked.

• *Look out the museum's back window for a good, if distant...*

**View of Paestum's Walls:** The walls of ancient Paestum reach halfway to the mountain—a reminder that most of the site is still private property and yet to be excavated. The town up on the mountainside is Capaccio, established in the eighth century when inhabitants of the original city of Paestum were driven out by malaria and the city was abandoned.

• *Walk along the corridor at the back of the museum, which shows...*

**Objects from Tombs:** More than 1,000 tombs have been identified outside the ancient city's wall. About 100 were found decorated with frescoes or containing objects such as these.

• *At the far end of the corridor, turn left to see...*

**The Tomb of the Diver:** This is the museum's treasure and the most precious Paestum find. Dating from 480 BC, it's not only the sole ancient Greek tomb fresco in the museum—it's the only one ever found in southern Italy. Discovered in 1968, it has five frescoed slabs (four sides and a lid; the bottom wasn't decorated). The Greeks saw death as a passage: diving from mortality into immortality...into an un-  known world. Archaeologists believe that the pillars shown on the fresco represent the Pillars of Hercules at Gibraltar, which in ancient times defined the known world. The ocean beyond the Mediterranean was the great unknown...like the afterlife. The Greek banquet makes it clear that this was an aristocratic man.

• *After the Tomb of the Diver, the next room displays...*

**Lucanian Tomb Frescoes:** The many other painted slabs in the museum date from a later time, around 350 BC, when Paestum fell under Lucanian rule. These frescoes are cruder than their earlier Greek counterpart. The people who conquered the Greeks tried to appropriate their art and style, but they lacked the Greeks' distinctive light touch. Still, these offer fascinating glimpses into ancient life here at Paestum.

• *Beyond this room, you'll find yourself back at the entrance. Before you leave, go up the stairs by the bookshop for a glimpse at the mezzanine level, which focuses on prehistoric archaeology. Also see the temple friezes at eye level now, with explications of what's happening in almost every scene. Near the end of the left hall, check out the...*

**Film Footage from WWII:** A 10-minute continuous film loop, subtitled in English, tells the story of Allied soldiers' encounters with the ruins in 1943. You'll see footage of soldiers hanging up their laundry and shaving in the temples, which they actually safeguarded well. Part of the film focuses on excavations directed by a British archaeologist who was attached to the invading forces.

• *The back wall of the mezzanine displays* **bronze vases,** *mostly from Gaudo, a half-mile from Paestum.*

## SLEEPING IN PAESTUM

Paestum at night, with views of the floodlit ruins, is magic. Accommodations here offer great value. You can sleep in a mansion for the same price you'd pay for a closet in Positano. All listings have free parking.

**$$ Hotel Villa Rita** is a tidy, quiet country hotel set on two acres within walking distance of the beach and the temples. It has 22 rooms, a kid-friendly swimming pool, and attractive grounds with grassy lawns and a little soccer field (RS%, air-con, lunch or dinner available, closed Nov-mid-March, Via Nettuno 9, tel. 0828-811-081, www.hotelvillarita.it, info@hotelvillarita.it, Luigi). The hotel is a 10-minute walk west of the Hera entrance and public bus stop, and a 20-minute walk from the train station (they can usually pick you up if you're arriving with luggage).

**$ Il Granaio dei Casabella,** a converted old granary with 14 attractive, reasonably priced rooms, is a 10-minute walk from the ruins. It has a beautiful garden and pretty common areas, and four rooms have temple views (RS%, family rooms, air-con, closed Dec-Feb, just west of the bus stop closest to Salerno at Via Tavernelle 84, tel. 0828-721-014, www.ilgranaiodeicasabella.com, info@ilgranaiodeicasabella.com, hospitable Celardo family).

**$ Hotel delle Rose,** with 10 small, basic rooms with minuscule bathrooms, is near the Neptune entrance on the street bordering the ruins. It's an acceptable choice for those on a budget and is also the option closest to the ruins and the train station (RS%, family rooms, air-con, Via Magna Grecia 179, tel. 0828-189-0778, www.hotelristorantedellerose.com, info@hotelristorantedellerose.com, Luigi).

**Outside Town:** A great option for drivers, **$$ Agriturismo**

**Seliano** has plush public spaces, a pool, and 14 grand, spacious rooms on a peaceful, once-elegant farm estate that's been in the same family for 300 years (air-con, closed Nov-March; one mile north of ruins on main road—Via Magna Grecia—a small *Azienda Agrituristica Seliano* sign directs you down long dirt driveway; Via Seliano, tel. 0828-723-634, www.agriturismoseliano.it, seliano@ agriturismoseliano.it). They serve a fine lunch or dinner for guests and nonguests—made with produce fresh from the garden—and can also organize cooking classes. The place is run by Cecilia— an English-speaking baroness—and her family, including about a dozen nice and friendly dogs.

## PAESTUM CONNECTIONS

**By Train:** A dozen slow, milk-run trains per day head to Salerno (30 minutes) and Naples (one hour). In Salerno, you can change for the bus to Amalfi or walk down to the harbor to catch an Amalfi- or Positano-bound boat. You can buy train tickets at machines in the (unstaffed) Paestum station.

**By Bus to Salerno:** Buses depart from Paestum to Salerno roughly every hour (fewer on Sun; one-hour trip). Buy a ticket from one of the bars in Paestum, then go to either of the intersections that flank the ruins (see the "Paestum" map), flag down any north-bound bus, and ask, "Salerno?" From Salerno, you can continue on to Amalfi or Positano by boat or walk up to the train station to catch an Amalfi-bound SITA bus or a train.

# ITALIAN HISTORY

Italy has a lot of history, so let's get started.

### ORIGINS OF ROME (c. 753 BC–450 AD)

A she-wolf breastfed two human babies, Romulus and Remus, who grew to build the city of Rome in 753 BC—you buy that? Closer to fact, farmers and shepherds of the Latin tribe settled near the mouth of the Tiber River, a convenient trading location. The crude settlement was sandwiched between two sophisticated civilizations—Greek colonists to the south (Magna Graecia, or "Great Greece"), and to the north (Etruria—present-day Tuscany/Umbria) the Etruscans, whose origins and language have long puzzled historians (for more on the Etruscans, see page 654). Baby Rome was both dominated and nourished by these societies.

According to legend, when the son of an Etruscan king raped a Roman woman (509 BC), her defenders led a revolt, driving out the Etruscans and replacing them with elected Roman senators and (eventually) a code of law (Laws of the Twelve Tables, 450 BC). The Roman Republic was born.

### THE ROMAN REPUBLIC EXPANDS (c. 509 BC–AD 1)

Located at the midpoint of the peninsula, Rome was perfectly situated for trading salt and wine. Roman businessmen, backed by a disciplined army, expanded throughout the Italian peninsula, establishing a Roman infrastructure as they went. Rome soon swallowed up its northern Etruscan neighbors, conquering them by force and absorbing their culture.

Next came Magna Graecia, with Rome's legions defeating the Greek general Pyrrhus after several costly "Pyrrhic" victories (c. 275 BC). Rome now ruled a united federation stretching from Tuscany to the tip of the Italian peninsula, with a standard currency system of roads (including the Via Appia), and a standing army of a half-million soldiers ready for the next challenge: Carthage.

Carthage (modern-day Tunisia) and Rome fought the three bitter Punic Wars for control of the Mediterranean (264-201 BC and 146 BC). The balance of power hung precariously in the Second Punic War (218-201 BC), when Hannibal of Carthage crossed the sea to Spain with a huge army of men and elephants. He marched 1,200 miles overland, crossed the Alps, and forcefully penetrated Italy from the rear. Almost at the gates of the city of Rome, he was finally turned back. The Romans prevailed, and, in the mismatched Third Punic War, they burned the city of Carthage to the ground (146 BC).

The well-tuned Roman legions easily subdued sophisticated Greece in three Macedonian Wars (215-146 BC). Though Rome conquered Greece, Greek culture dominated the Romans. From hairstyles to statues to temples to the evening's entertainment, Rome was forever "Hellenized," becoming the curators of Greek culture, passing it down to future generations.

By the first century BC, Rome was master of the Mediterranean. Booty, cheap grain, and thousands of captured slaves poured in, transforming the economic model from small farmers to unemployed city dwellers living off tribute from conquered lands. The Republic had changed.

## CIVIL WARS AND THE TRANSITION TO EMPIRE (First Century BC)

With easy money streaming in and traditional roles obsolete, Romans bickered among themselves over their slice of the pie. Wealthy landowners (patricians, the ruling Senate) wrangled with the middle and working classes (plebeians) and with the growing population of slaves, who demanded greater say-so in government. In 73 BC, Spartacus—a Greek-born soldier-turned-Roman slave who'd been forced to fight as a gladiator—escaped to the slopes of Mount Vesuvius, where he amassed an army of 90,000 angry slaves. After two years of fierce fighting across Italy, the Roman legions crushed the revolt and crucified 6,000 rebels along the Via Appia as a warning.

Amid the chaos of class war and civil war, charismatic generals who could provide wealth and security became dictators—men such as Sulla, Crassus, Pompey...and Caesar. Julius Caesar (100-44 BC) was a cunning politician, riveting speaker, conqueror of Gaul, author of *The Gallic Wars*, and lover of Cleopatra, queen of Egypt. In his four-year reign, he reformed and centralized the government around himself. Disgruntled Republicans feared that he would ~~ke himself king. At his peak of power, they surrounded Caesar

# Italy Almanac

**Official Name:** Repubblica Italiana (Italian Republic)

**Locals Call It:** Italia

**Size:** 116,000 square miles, including the islands of Sicily, Sardinia, and others. Population is 62 million.

**Geography:** Italy is shaped like a boot, 850 miles long and 150 miles wide, jutting into the central Mediterranean. (By comparison, Florida is 500 miles long.) The terrain is generally mountainous or hilly, with the Alps in the north and a north-south "spine" of the Apennine Mountains. The highest point is Mont Blanc (15,771 feet), on the border with France. Outside the Alps, the highest point on the peninsula is Corno Grande (9,554 feet). Italy has 5,000 miles of coastline. Major rivers include the Po (the longest at 400 miles), Arno, Adige, and Tiber. Italy has three active volcanoes: Vesuvius, Etna, and Stromboli.

**Latitude and Longitude:** 43°N and 12°E (similar to Oregon and Maine).

**Regions:** Italy is divided into 20 regions (including Tuscany, Umbria, Veneto, and Lazio). Locally, there are some 8,200 "communes," each with a community council and mayor.

**Major Cities:** Rome (the capital, 2.8 million), Milan (1.3 million), and Naples (1 million).

**Economy:** The Gross Domestic Product is $2.3 trillion; the GDP per capita is $38,200. About 74 percent of the economy consists of service jobs (especially tourism), 24 percent is industry (textiles, chemicals), and 2 percent is agriculture (fruit, vegetables, olives, wine, plus fishing). There are 12,500 miles of train lines (mostly government-run) and 4,300 miles of expressway (autostrada).

**Government:** Italy is a republic, with three branches of government. The chief executive is Prime Minister Giuseppe Conte. The bicameral legislature is elected by (mostly) direct voting. Since World War II, the fragmented country has had 65 national governments.

**Flag:** Three vertical bands of green, white, and red.

**Italian Inventions:** Opera, cologne, thermometer, barometer, pizza, wireless telegraph, espresso machine, typewriter, batteries, nitroglycerin, yo-yos...and the ice-cream cone.

**Museums:** 3,800.

**The Average Gio:** The average Italian is 46 years old, has 1.4 kids, is nominally Roman Catholic, and will live to the ripe old age of 82 (1 in 5 Italians is older than 65). Every day, he or she consumes two servings of pasta, a half-pound of bread, and two glasses of wine. Despite Italian cuisine, Gio isn't fat—only 20 percent of Italians are considered obese.

The Roman Empire at its Peak: Pax Romana AD 120

Roman Empire

in the Senate on the Ides of March (March 15, 44 BC) and stabbed him to death.

Julius Caesar died, but the concept of one-man rule lived on in his adopted son. Named Octavian at birth, he defeated rival Mark Antony (another lover of Cleopatra, 31 BC) and was proclaimed Emperor Augustus (27 BC). Augustus outwardly followed the traditions of the Republic, while in practice he acted as a dictator with the backing of Rome's legions and the rubber-stamp approval of the Senate. He established his family to succeed him (making the family name "Caesar" a title) and set the pattern of rule by emperors for the next 500 years.

## THE ROMAN EMPIRE (c. AD 1-500)

In his 40-year reign, Augustus ended Rome's civil wars and ushered in the Pax Romana: 200 years of prosperity and relative peace. Rome ruled an empire of 54 million people, stretching from Scotland to northern Africa, from Spain to the Euphrates River. Conquered peoples were welcomed into the fold of prosperity, linked by roads, common laws, common gods, education, and the Latin language. The city of Rome, with more than a million inhabitants, was decorated with Greek-style statues and monumental structures faced with marble. It was the marvel of the known world.

The empire prospered on a (false) economy of booty, slaves, and cheap imports. On the Italian peninsula, traditional small farms were swallowed up by large farming and herding estates. In this "global economy," the Italian peninsula became just one province among many in a worldwide Latin-speaking empire, ruled by an emperor who was likely born elsewhere. The empire even survived the often turbulent and naughty behavior of emperors such as Caligula (r. 37-41) and Nero (r. 54-68).

## DECLINE AND FALL (AD 200-500)

Rome peaked in the second century AD under the capable emperors Trajan (r. 98-117), Hadrian (r. 117-138), and Marcus Aurelius (r. 161-180). For the next three centuries, the Roman Empire declined, shrinking in size and wealth, a victim of corruption, disease, an overextended army, a false economy, and the constant pressure of "barbarian" tribes pecking away at its borders. By the third century, the army had become the real power, handpicking figurehead emperors to do its bidding: In a 40-year span, 15 emperors were first saluted and then assassinated by fickle generals.

Trying to stall the disintegration, Emperor Diocletian (r. 284-305) split the empire into two administrative halves under two equal emperors. Constantine (r. 306-337) solidified the divide by moving the capital of the empire from decaying Rome to the new city of Constantinople (330, present-day Istanbul). Almost instantly, the once-great city of Rome became a minor player in imperial affairs. (The eastern "Byzantine" half of the empire would thrive and live on for another thousand years.) Constantine also legalized Christianity (313), and the once-persecuted cult soon became virtually the state religion, the backbone of Rome's fading hierarchy.

By 410, "Rome" had shrunk to just the city itself, surrounded by a protective wall. Barbarian tribes from the north and east poured in to loot and plunder. The city was sacked by Visigoths (410) and vandalized by Vandals (455), and the pope had to plead with Attila the Hun for mercy (451). The peninsula's population fell to six million, trade and agriculture were disrupted, schools closed, and the infrastructure collapsed. Peasants huddled near powerful lords for protection from bandits, planting the seeds of medieval feudalism.

In 476, the last emperor sold his title for a comfy pension, and Rome fell like a huge column, kicking up dust that would plunge Europe into a thousand years of darkness. For the next 13 centuries, there would be no "Italy," just a patchwork of rural dukedoms and towns, victimized by foreign powers. Italy lay in shambles, helpless.

## INVASIONS (AD 500-1000)

In 500 years, Italy suffered through a full paragraph of invasions: Lombards (568) and Byzantines (under Justinian, 536) occupied the north. In the south, Muslim Saracens (827) and Christian Normans (1061) established thriving kingdoms. Charlemagne, king of

HISTORY

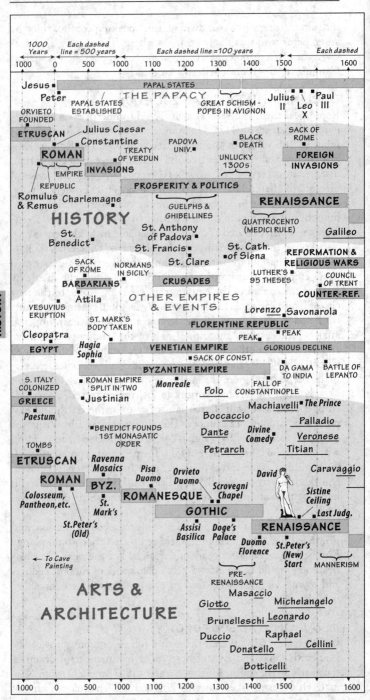

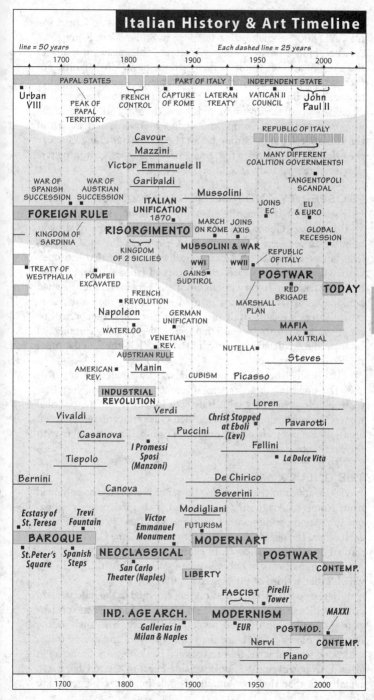

# Italian History & Art Timeline

line = 50 years          Each dashed line = 25 years

1700     1800     1900     1950     2000

PAPAL STATES          PART OF ITALY          INDEPENDENT STATE

Urban VIII
PEAK OF PAPAL TERRITORY
FRENCH CONTROL
CAPTURE OF ROME
LATERAN TREATY
VATICAN II COUNCIL
John Paul II

REPUBLIC OF ITALY

Cavour
Mazzini
Victor Emmanuele II
MANY DIFFERENT COALITION GOVERNMENTS!

WAR OF SPANISH SUCCESSION
WAR OF AUSTRIAN SUCCESSION
Garibaldi
TANGENTOPOLI SCANDAL

**FOREIGN RULE**
ITALIAN UNIFICATION 1870
Mussolini
JOINS EC
EU & EURO

KINGDOM OF SARDINIA
**RISORGIMENTO**
MARCH ON ROME
JOINS AXIS
GLOBAL RECESSION

TREATY OF WESTPHALIA
KINGDOM OF 2 SICILIES
**MUSSOLINI & WAR**
REPUBLIC OF ITALY

POMPEII EXCAVATED
WWI
WWII
**POSTWAR**
**TODAY**

GAINS SUDTIROL
RED BRIGADE

FRENCH REVOLUTION
MARSHALL PLAN

Napoleon
GERMAN UNIFICATION
**MAFIA**

WATERLOO
VENETIAN REV.
MAXI TRIAL

**AUSTRIAN RULE**
NUTELLA
Steves

AMERICAN REV.
Manin
CUBISM
Picasso

**INDUSTRIAL REVOLUTION**
Loren

Vivaldi
Verdi
*Christ Stopped at Eboli (Levi)*
Pavarotti

Casanova
Puccini

*I Promessi Sposi (Manzoni)*
Fellini

Tiepolo
*La Dolce Vita*

Bernini
De Chirico

Canova
Severini

*Ecstasy of St. Teresa*
*Trevi Fountain*
Modigliani

*Victor Emmanuel Monument*
FUTURISM

**BAROQUE**
**MODERN ART**

St. Peter's Square
Spanish Steps
**NEOCLASSICAL**
**POSTWAR**

*San Carlo Theater (Naples)*
LIBERTY
CONTEMP.

FASCIST
*Pirelli Tower*

**IND. AGE ARCH.**
**MODERNISM**
*MAXXI*

*Gallerias in Milan & Naples*
EUR
POSTMOD.
CONTEMP.

Nervi

Piano

1700     1800     1900     1950     2000

HISTORY

the Germanic Franks, defeated the Lombards, and on Christmas Day, AD 800, he knelt before the pope in St. Peter's in Rome to be crowned Holy Roman Emperor, an empty title meant to resurrect the glory of ancient Rome united with medieval Christianity. For the next thousand years, Italians would pledge nominal allegiance to weak, distant German kings as their Holy Roman Emperor.

Through all the invasions and chaos, the glory of ancient Rome was preserved in the pomp, knowledge, hierarchy, and wealth of the Christian Church. Strong popes (Leo I, 440-461, and Gregory the Great, 590-604) ruled like small-time emperors, governing territories in central Italy called the Papal States.

## PROSPERITY AND POLITICS (AD 1000-1300)

Italy survived Y1K, and the economy picked up. Sea-trading cities like Venice, Genoa, Pisa, Naples, and Amalfi grew wealthy as middlemen between Europe and the Orient. During the Crusades (e.g., First Crusade 1097-1130), Italian ships ferried Europe's Christian soldiers eastward, then returned laden with spices and highly marked-up luxury goods from the Orient. Trade spawned banking, and Italians became capitalists, loaning money at interest to Europe's royalty. Italy pioneered a new phenomenon in Europe—municipalities *(comuni)* that were self-governing commercial centers. The medieval prosperity of the cities laid the foundation of the Renaissance to come.

Politically, the Italian peninsula was dominated by two rulers—the pope in Rome and the German Holy Roman Emperor (with holdings in the north). Italy split into two warring political parties: supporters of the popes (called Guelphs, centered in urban areas) and supporters of the emperors (Ghibellines, popular with the rural nobility).

## THE UNLUCKY 1300s

In 1309, enticed by the fast-rising power of France, the pope moved from Rome to Avignon. At one point, two rival popes reigned, one in Avignon and the other in Rome, and they excommunicated each other. The papacy eventually returned to Rome (1377), but the schism created a breakdown in central authority that was exacerbated by an outbreak of bubonic plague (Black Death, 1347-1348), which killed a third of the Italian population.

In the power vacuum, new players emerged in the independent cities. Venice, Florence, Milan, and Naples were under the protection and leadership of local noble families *(signoria)* such as the Medici in Florence. Florence thrived in the wool and dyeing trade, which led to dominance in international banking, with branches in all of Europe's capitals. A positive side effect of the terrible Black Death was that the now-smaller population got a bigger share

# Church Architecture

History comes to life when you visit a centuries-old church. Even if you wouldn't know your apse from a hole in the ground, learning a few simple terms will enrich your experience. Note that not every church has every feature, and that a "cathedral" isn't a type of church architecture, but rather a designation for a church that's a governing center for a local bishop.

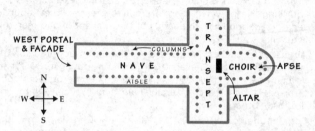

**Aisles:** The long, generally low-ceilinged arcades that flank the nave.

**Altar:** The raised area with a ceremonial table (often adorned with candles or a crucifix), where the priest prepares and serves the bread and wine for Communion.

**Apse:** The space beyond the altar, generally bordered with small chapels.

**Barrel Vault:** A continuous round-arched ceiling that resembles an extended upside-down U.

**Choir:** A cozy area, often screened off, located within the church nave and near the high altar, where services are sung in a more intimate setting.

**Cloister:** Covered hallways bordering a square or rectangular open-air courtyard, traditionally where monks and nuns got fresh air.

**Facade:** The exterior surface of the church's main (west) entrance, viewable from outside and generally highly decorated.

**Groin Vault:** An arched ceiling formed where two equal barrel vaults meet at right angles. Less common usage: term for a medieval jock strap.

**Narthex:** The area (portico or foyer) between the main entry and the nave.

**Nave:** The long, central section of the church (running west to east, from the entrance to the altar) where, in medieval times, the congregation sits or stands through the service.

**Transept:** In a traditional cross-shaped floor plan, the transept is one of the two parts forming the "arms" of the cross. The transept runs north-south, perpendicularly crossing the east-west nave.

**West Portal:** The main entry to the church (on the west end, opposite the main altar).

## Top 10 Italians

**Romulus:** Breastfed on wolf milk, this legendary orphan founded the city of Rome (traditionally in 753 BC). Over the next seven centuries, his descendants dominated the Italian peninsula, ruling from Rome as a Republic.

**Julius Caesar** (100-44 BC): After conquering Gaul (France), subduing Egypt, and winning Cleopatra's heart, Caesar ruled Rome with king-like powers. In an attempt to preserve the Republic, senators stabbed him to death, but the concept of one-man rule lived on.

**Augustus** (born Octavian, 63 BC-AD 14): Julius' adopted son became the first of the Caesars that ruled Rome during its 500 years as a Europe-wide power. He set the tone for emperors both good (Trajan, Hadrian, Marcus Aurelius) and bad (Caligula, Nero, and dozens of others).

**Constantine** (c. 280-337 AD): Raised in a Christian home, this emperor legalized Christianity, almost instantly turning a persecuted sect into a Europe-wide religion. With the Fall of Rome, the Church was directed by strong popes and so guided Italians through the next thousand years of invasions, plagues, political decentralization, and darkness.

**Lorenzo (the Magnificent) de' Medici** (1449-1492): Soldier, poet, lover, and ruler of Florence in the 1400s, this Renaissance Man embodied the "rebirth" of ancient enlightenment. Lorenzo's wealthy Medici family funded Florentine artists who pioneered a new realism in painting and sculpture.

**Michelangelo Buonarroti** (1475-1564): His statue of David—slayer of an ignorant brute—stands as a monumental symbol of Italian enlightenment. Along with fellow geniuses Leonardo da Vinci and

of the land, jobs, and infrastructure. By century's end, Italy was poised to enter its most glorious era since antiquity.

## THE RENAISSANCE (1400s-1600s)

The Renaissance (Rinascimento)—the "rebirth" of ancient Greek and Roman art styles, knowledge, and humanism—began in Italy (c. 1400) and spread through Europe over the next two centuries. Many of Europe's most famous painters, sculptors, and thinkers—Michelangelo, Leonardo, Raphael, etc.—were Italian.

It was a cultural boom that changed people's thinking about every aspect of life. In politics, it meant an eventual rebirth of Greek ideas of democracy. In religion, it meant a move away from Church dominance and toward the assertion of man (humanism) and a more personal faith. Science and secular learning were revived after centuries of superstition and ignorance. In architecture,

Raphael, Michelangelo mastered the visual arts of the Italian Renaissance: painting, sculpture, and architecture. Their innovations spread northward, influencing the rest of Europe.

**Giovanni Lorenzo Bernini** (1598-1680): The "Michelangelo of Baroque" kept Italy a major exporter of sophisticated trends. Bernini's ornate statues and architectural projects decorated palaces of the rising power brokers in France, even as Italy was reverting to an economically stagnant patchwork of foreign-ruled states.

**Victor Emmanuel II** (1820-1878): As the only Italian-born ruler on the peninsula, this king of Sardinia played a central role in Italian unification. Aided by the general Garibaldi, writer Mazzini, and politician Cavour (with a soundtrack by Verdi), he became the first ruler of a united, democratic Italy, in September 1870. (The preceding proper nouns have since come to adorn streets and piazzas throughout Italy.)

**Benito Mussolini** (1883-1945): An inspiration for Hitler, he derailed Italy's fledgling democracy, becoming dictator of a fascist state and leading the country to defeat in World War II. No public places honor Mussolini, but many streets and piazzas throughout Italy bear the name of Giacomo Matteotti (1885-1924), a politician whose outspoken opposition to Mussolini got him killed.

**Federico Fellini** (1920-1993): Fellini's films *(La Strada, La Dolce Vita, 8½)* chronicle Italy's postwar years in gritty black and white—the poverty, destruction, and disillusionment of the war followed by the optimism, decadence, and materialism of the economic boom. He captured the surreal chaos of Italy's abrupt social change from traditional Catholicism to a secular, urban world presided over by Mafia bosses and weak government.

it was a return to the balanced columns and domes of Greece and Rome. In painting, the Renaissance meant 3-D realism.

Italians dotted their cities with publicly financed art that celebrated Greek gods and emulated Roman-style domed buildings. They preached Greek-style democracy and explored the natural world. The cultural boom was financed by thriving trade and lucrative banking. During the Renaissance, the peninsula once again became the trendsetting cultural center of Europe.

## FOREIGN INVASIONS (1500s)

In May 1498, Vasco da Gama of Portugal landed in India, having found a sea route around Africa. Italy's monopoly on trade with the East was broken. Portugal, France, Spain, England, and Holland—nation-states under strong central rule—began to overtake decentralized Italy. Italy's once-great maritime cities now traded in an economic backwater, just as Italy's bankers (such as the Medici in Florence) were going bankrupt. While the Italian Renaissance was all the rage throughout Europe, it declined in its birthplace. Italy—culturally sophisticated but weak and decentralized—was ripe for the picking by Europe's rising powers.

Several kings of France invaded (1494, 1495, and 1515)—initially invited by Italian lords to attack their rivals—and began divvying up territory for their noble families. Italy also became a battleground in religious conflicts between Catholics and the new Protestant movement. In the chaos, the city of Rome was brutally sacked by foreign mercenaries (1527).

## FOREIGN RULE (1600-1800)

For the next two centuries, most of Italy's states were ruled by foreign nobles, who treated them as prizes in Europe's dynastic wars. Italy ceased to be a major player in Europe, politically or economically. Italian intellectual life was often cropped short by a conservative Catholic Church trying to fight Protestantism. Galileo, for example, was forced by the Inquisition to renounce his belief that the earth orbited the sun (1633). But Italy did export Baroque art (Bernini) and the budding new medium of opera.

The War of the Spanish Succession (1713)—in which Italy did not participate—gave much of northern Italy to Austria's ruling family, the Habsburgs (who now wore the crown of Holy Roman Emperor). In the south, Spain's Bourbon family ruled the Kingdom of Naples (known after 1816 as the Kingdom of the Two Sicilies), making it a culturally sophisticated but economically backward area, preserving a medieval, feudal caste system.

In 1720, a minor war (the War of Austrian Succession) created a new state at the foot of the Alps, called the Kingdom of Sardinia (a.k.a. the Kingdom of Piedmont, or Savoy). Ruled by the Savoy family, this was the only major state on the peninsula that was actually ruled by Italians. It proved to be a toehold to the future.

## ITALY UNITES—THE RISORGIMENTO (1800s)

In 1796, Napoleon Bonaparte swept through Italy and changed everything. He ousted Austrian and Spanish dukes, confiscated Church lands, united scattered states, and crowned himself "King of Italy" (1805). After his defeat (1815), Italy's old ruling order (namely, Austria and Spain) was restored. But Napoleon had planted a seed: What if Italians could unite and rule themselves like Europe's other modern nations?

For the next 50 years, a movement to unite Italy slowly grew. Called the Risorgimento—a word that means "rising again"—the movement promised a revival of Italy's glory. It started as a revolutionary, liberal movement—taking part in it was punishable by death. Members of a secret society called the Carbonari (led by

**Italian Unification**

NOTE: Dates indicate the year of annexation to the Kingdom of Sardinia. After 1861, this became the Kingdom of Italy.

SWITZERLAND

VENETIA (1866)

AUSTRIA

LOMBARDY (1859)

PIEDMONT

Venice

FRANCE

PARMA

MODENA

Florence

TUSCANY (1860)

STATES OF THE CHURCH (1870)

KINGDOM OF SARDINIA

Adriatic Sea

Rome

SARDINIA

Naples

KINGDOM OF THE TWO SICILIES (1860)

Palermo

SICILY

Mediterranean Sea

100 Kilometers
100 Miles

HISTORY

a professional revolutionary named Giuseppe Mazzini) exchanged secret handshakes, printed fliers, planted bombs, and assassinated conservative rulers. Their small revolutions (1820-1821, 1831, 1848) were easily and brutally slapped down, but the cause wouldn't die.

Gradually, Italians of all stripes warmed to the idea of unification. Whether a united dictatorship, a united papal state, a united kingdom, or a united democracy, most Italians could agree that it was time for Spain, Austria, and France to leave.

The movement coalesced around the Italian-ruled Kingdom of Sardinia and its king, Victor Emmanuel II. In 1859, Sardinia's prime minister, Camillo Cavour, cleverly persuaded France to drive Austria out of northern Italy, leaving the region in Italian hands. A vote was held, and several central Italian states (including some of the pope's) rejected their feudal lords and chose to join the growing Sardinian kingdom.

After victory in the north, Italy's most renowned Carbonari

general, Giuseppe Garibaldi (1807-1882), steamed south with a thousand of his best soldiers (I Mille) and marched on the Spanish-ruled city of Naples (1860). The old order simply collapsed. In two short months, Garibaldi had achieved a seemingly impossible victory against a far superior army. Garibaldi sent a one-word telegram to the king of Sardinia: *"Obbedisco"* (I obey). The following year, an assembly of deputies from throughout Italy met in Turin and crowned Victor Emmanuel II "King of Italy." Only the pope in Rome held out, protected by French troops. When the city finally fell—easily—to the unification forces on September 20, 1870, the Risorgimento was complete. Italy went ape.

The Risorgimento was largely the work of four men: Garibaldi (the sword), Mazzini (the spark), Cavour (the diplomat), and Victor Emmanuel II (the rallying point). Today, street signs throughout Italy honor them and the dates of their great victories.

## MUSSOLINI AND WAR (1900-1950)

Italy—now an actual nation-state, not just a linguistic region—entered the 20th century with a progressive government (a constitutional monarchy), a collection of colonies, and a flourishing northern half of the country. In the economically backward south (the Mezzogiorno), poverty and lack of opportunity led millions of poor peasants to emigrate to the Americas. World War I (1915-1918) left 650,000 Italians dead, but being on the winning Allied side, survivors were granted possession of the alpine regions. In the swirl of postwar cynicism and anarchy, many radical political parties—Communist, Socialist, Popular (Catholic), and Fascist—rose up.

Benito Mussolini (1883-1945), a popular writer for socialist and labor-union newspapers, led the fascists. ("Fascism" comes from Latin *fasci*, the bundles of rods that symbolized unity in ancient Rome.) Though only a minority (6 percent of the parliament in 1921), they intimidated the disorganized majority with organized violence by black-shirted fascist gangs. In 1922, Mussolini seized the government (see "The March on Rome" sidebar) and began his rule as dictator for the next two decades.

Mussolini solidified his reign among Catholics by striking an agreement with the pope (Lateran Treaty, 1929), giving Vatican City to the papacy, while Mussolini ruled Italy with the implied blessing of the Catholic Church. Italy responded to the great worldwide Depression (1930s) with big public works projects (including Rome's subway), government investment in industry, and an expanded army.

Mussolini allied his country with Hitler's Nazi regime, drawing an unprepared Italy into World War II (1940). Italy's lame army was never a factor in the war, and when Allied forces landed in

## The March on Rome

In October 1922, Benito Mussolini, head of the newly formed Fascist Party, boldly proposed a coup d'état, saying: "Either the government will be given to us, or we will take it by marching on Rome." Throughout Italy, black-shirted fascists occupied government buildings in their hometowns. Others grabbed guns, farming hoes, and kitchen knives and set off to converge on the outskirts of Rome. (Estimates of the size of the fascist band range from 300 to the 300,000 of fascist legend.) Mussolini sent the government an ultimatum to surrender. Though the fascists were easily outmanned and outgunned by government forces, the show of force intimidated the king, Victor Emmanuel III, into avoiding a nasty confrontation. He invited Mussolini to Rome. Mussolini arrived the next day (by first-class train), was made prime minister, then marched his black-shirted troops triumphantly through the streets of Rome.

Sicily (1943), Italians welcomed them as liberators. The Italians toppled Mussolini's government and surrendered to the Allies, but Nazi Germany sent troops to rescue Mussolini. The war raged on as Allied troops inched their way north against German resistance. Italians were reduced to dire poverty. In the last days of the war (April 1945), Mussolini was captured by the Italian resistance. They shot him and his girlfriend and hung their bodies upside down in a public square in Milan.

### POSTWAR ITALY

At war's end, Italy was physically ruined and extremely poor. The nation rebuilt in the 1950s and 1960s with Marshall Plan aid from the United States. Many Italian men moved to northern Europe to find work; many others left farms and flocked to the cities. Over time, Italy regained its standing among nations, joining the United Nations, NATO, and what would later become the European Union.

However, the government remained weak, changing on average once a year, shifting from right to left to centrist coalitions. Afraid of another Mussolini, the authors of the postwar constitution created a feeble executive branch; without majorities in both houses of parliament, nothing could get done. All Italians acknowledged that the real power lay in the hands of backroom politicians and organized crime—a phenomenon called *Tangentopoli*, or "Bribe City." The country remained strongly divided between the rich, industrial north and the poor, rural south.

Italian society changed greatly after the liberal reforms of the Catholic Church at the Vatican II conference (1962-1965). The once-conservative Catholic country legalized divorce and contraception, and the birth rate plummeted. In the 1970s, Italy suffered a wave of violence from left- and right-wing domestic terrorists and organized crime, punctuated by the assassination of former Prime Minister Aldo Moro (1978). In the early 1990s, the judiciary undertook a reasonably effective campaign to rid politics of corruption and Mafia ties. The Mafia still exists, but is much less powerful.

Italy entered the 21st century buoyed by a growing economy and living standards that were nearly on par with its European neighbors.

## ITALY TODAY

That turnaround made Italy a magnet for immigration, especially from Albania, North Africa, and Eastern Europe. The influx brought with it cheap labor but also pressures on social services and cultural norms. And then came the global recession. Like other European nations, Italy ran up big deficits, and by the end of 2011, its debt load was the second worst in the euro zone, behind only Greece. Bombastic media tycoon Silvio Berlusconi was forced to resign from his fourth stint as prime minister.

When Italians again went to the polls in 2018, they expressed their frustration with the severe austerity measures enacted to deal with the debt, throwing out the country's traditional centrist parties. The anti-establishment, anti-immigration 5-Star Movement got the largest vote, followed by the far-right, Euroskeptic League party. Political observers compared the election results to populist outcomes elsewhere, such as Brexit and the election of Donald Trump.

After months of haggling, the two parties agreed to a coalition government led by law professor Giuseppe Conte, but it's unclear how long this political marriage of convenience will last. Italy is used to political merry-go-rounds; it's had 65 governments since World War II. And while Italy remains the third-largest economy in the eurozone (and world's eighth-largest exporter), unemployment seems stuck at about 10 percent—with youth unemployment hovering around 30 percent.

As you travel through Italy today, you'll encounter a fascinating country with a rich history and a per-capita income that comes close to its neighbors to the north. Despite its ups and downs, Italy remains committed to Europe...yet it's as wonderfully Italian as ever.

To learn more about Italian history, consider *Europe 101: History and Art for the Traveler,* written by Rick Steves and Gene Openshaw (available at www.ricksteves.com).

# PRACTICALITIES

This chapter covers the practical skills of European travel: how to get tourist information, pay for things, sightsee efficiently, find good-value accommodations, eat affordably but well, use technology wisely, and get between destinations smoothly. For more information on these topics, see RickSteves.com/travel-tips.

## Tourist Information

Before your trip, scan the website of the Italian national tourist office (www.italia.it) for a wealth of travel information. If you have a specific question, try contacting one of their US offices (New York: Tel. 212/245-5618, newyork@enit.it; Chicago: Tel. 312/644-9335, chicago@enit.it; Los Angeles: Tel. 310/820-1898, losangeles@enit. it).

**In Italy,** a good first stop in every town is generally the tourist information office (abbreviated **TI** in this book). TIs are in business to help you enjoy spending money in their town, but even so, I still make a point to swing by to pick up a city map and get information on public transit, walking tours, special events, and nightlife. Anticipating a harried front-line staffer, prepare a list of questions and a proposed plan to double-check. While Italian TIs are about half as helpful as those in other countries, their information is twice as important.

Some TIs have information on the entire country or at least the region, so try to pick up maps and printed information for destinations you'll be visiting later in your trip.

Be wary of travel agencies or special information services that masquerade as TIs but serve fancy hotels and tour companies. They're selling things you don't need.

## Travel Tips

**Emergency and Medical Help:** For any emergency service—ambulance, police, or fire—call **112** from a mobile phone or landline. Operators, who generally speak English, will deal with your request or route you to the right emergency service. If you get sick, do as the locals do and go to a pharmacist for advice. Or ask at your hotel for help—they'll know the nearest medical and emergency services.

**ETIAS Registration:** Beginning in 2021, US and Canadian citizens may be required to register online with the European Travel Information and Authorization System (ETIAS) before entering certain European countries (quick and easy process, $8 fee, valid 3 years). A useful private website with more details is www. schengenvisainfo.com/etias.

**Theft or Loss:** To replace a passport, you'll need to go in person to an embassy (see below). If your credit and debit cards disappear, cancel and replace them (see "Damage Control for Lost Cards" on page 1050). File a police report, either on the spot or within a day or two; you'll need it to submit an insurance claim for lost or stolen rail passes or electronics, and it can help with replacing your passport or credit and debit cards. For more information, see www.ricksteves.com/help.

**US Embassies and Consulates:** Embassy in Rome—tel. 06-46741 for 24-hour emergency line, tel. 06-4674-2420 for non-emergencies, by appointment only (Via Vittorio Veneto 121). Consulates in Milan—tel. 02-290-351 (Via Principe Amedeo 2/10); Florence—tel. 055-266-951 (Lungarno Vespucci 38); and Naples—tel. 081-583-8111 (Piazza della Repubblica). For all, see http://it.usembassy.gov.

**Canadian Embassies:** Rome—tel. 06-854-441 (Via Zara 30); Milan—tel. 02-626-94238 (Piazza Cavour 3). For both, see www. italy.gc.ca.

**Avoiding Theft and Scams:** Although violent crime is rare in Italy, petty theft is common in large cities and heavily touristed sights. With sweet-talking con artists meeting you at the station and well-dressed pickpockets on buses, tourists face a gauntlet of rip-offs. Pickpockets don't want to hurt you—they usually just want your money and gadgets. Green or sloppy tourists are prone to scams.

Thieves strike when you're distracted. Don't trust overly kind strangers. Keep nothing important in your pockets, and be especially careful with expensive cell phones—maintain a firm grip when you're using one. Be on guard while boarding and leaving buses and subways. Thieves jam up the door, then stop and turn while others crowd and push from behind. You'll find less crowding and commotion—and less risk—on the end cars of a subway rather than the middle cars. Hold your bags in front with your arms over them. Sneaky thieves pretend to be teenagers on holiday, well-dressed businessmen, or tourists wearing fanny packs and toting cameras and even Rick Steves guidebooks. The best deterrent is to look confident and aware, not confused and afraid.

Watch out for fast-fingered moms with babies and groups of children picking the pockets and handbags of naive tourists. Be particularly aware of groups of young women who seem to have nothing to do. Pickpockets troll tourist crowds around major sights and at train stations. Watch them target tourists who are overloaded with bags or distracted with their phones.

Scams abound. When paying for something, be aware of how much cash you're handing over, demand clear and itemized bills, and count your change. Don't give your wallet to self-proclaimed "police" who stop you on the street, warn you about counterfeit (or drug) money, and ask to see your cash. If a bank machine eats your ATM card, check for a thin plastic insert with a tongue hanging out (thieves use these devices to extract cards).

If you feel you are being scammed or are in a situation that makes you feel threatened, use your camera to document the incident and call the police immediately. This alone may deter criminal behavior.

Don't be scared—just be aware and be smart, and you'll be fine.

**Time Zones:** Italy, like most of continental Europe, is generally six/nine hours ahead of the East/West Coasts of the US. The exceptions are the beginning and end of Daylight Saving Time: Europe "springs forward" the last Sunday in March (two weeks after most of North America), and "falls back" the last Sunday in October (one week before North America). For a handy time converter, use the world clock app on your phone or download one (see www.timeanddate.com).

**Business Hours:** Traditionally, Italy used the siesta plan, with people generally working from about 9:00 to 13:00 and from 15:30-

16:00 to 19:00-19:30, Monday through Saturday. Siesta hours are no longer required by law, so many shops stay open through lunch or later into the evening, especially larger stores in tourist areas. Shops in small towns and villages are more likely to close during lunch. Stores are usually closed on Sunday, and often on Monday. Many shops close for a couple of weeks around August 15.

**Watt's Up?** Europe's electrical system is 220 volts, instead of North America's 110 volts. Most electronics (laptops, smartphones, cameras) and new hair dryers convert automatically, so you won't need a converter, but you will need an adapter plug with two round prongs, sold inexpensively at travel stores in the US. Sockets in Italy and Switzerland only accept plugs with slimmer prongs: Don't buy an adapter with the thicker ("Schuko" style) prongs—it won't work. Avoid bringing older appliances that don't automatically convert voltage; instead, buy a cheap replacement in Europe.

**Discounts:** Discounts for sights are generally not listed in this book. However, seniors (age 65 and over), youths under 18, and students and teachers with proper identification cards (obtain from www.isic.org) can get discounts at many sights—always ask. Italy's national museums generally offer free admission to children under 18, but some discounts are available only for citizens of the European Union (EU).

**Tobacco Shops:** Known as *tabacchi* (often indicated with a big *T* sign), these Italian-style minimarts are ubiquitous across the country. They're handy places to pay for street parking and purchase such things as batteries, tickets for city buses and subways, and sometimes postage. If you aren't sure where to buy something, a *tabacchi* is a good place to start.

**Online Translation Tips:** Google's Chrome browser instantly translates websites; Translate.google.com is also handy. The Google Translate app converts spoken or typed English into most European languages (and vice versa) and can also translate text it "reads" with your smartphone's camera.

# Money

Here's my basic strategy for using money in Europe:
- Upon arrival, head for a cash machine (ATM) at the airport and withdraw some local currency, using a debit card with low international transaction fees.
- In general, pay for bigger expenses with a credit card and use cash for smaller purchases and tips. Use a debit card only for cash withdrawals.
- Keep your cards and cash safe in a money belt.

---

## Exchange Rate

**1 euro (€) = about $1.20**

To convert prices in euros to dollars, add about 20 percent: €20 = about $24, €50 = about $60. (Check www.oanda.com for the latest exchange rates.) Just like the dollar, one euro is broken down into 100 cents. Coins range from €0.01 to €2, and bills from €5 to €200 (bills over €50 are rarely used).

---

## PLASTIC VERSUS CASH

Although credit cards are widely accepted in Europe, cash is some-times the only way to pay for cheap food, bus fare, taxis, tips, and local guides. Some businesses (especially smaller ones, such as B&Bs and mom-and-pop cafés and shops) may charge you extra for using a credit card—or might not accept credit cards at all. Having cash on hand helps you out of a jam if your card randomly doesn't work.

I use my credit card to book and pay for hotel reservations, to buy advance tickets for events or sights, and to cover most other expenses. It can also be smart to use plastic near the end of your trip, to avoid another visit to the ATM.

## WHAT TO BRING

I pack the following and keep it all safe in my money belt.

**Debit Card:** Use this at ATMs to withdraw local cash.

**Credit Card:** Handy for bigger transactions (at hotels, shops, restaurants, travel agencies, car-rental agencies, and so on), pay-ment machines, and online purchases.

**Backup Card:** Some travelers carry a third card (debit or cred-it; ideally from a different bank), in case one gets lost, demagne-tized, eaten by a temperamental machine, or simply doesn't work.

**A Stash of Cash:** I carry $100-200 as a cash backup, which comes in handy in an emergency (such as when the banks go on strike or if your ATM card gets eaten by the machine).

**What NOT to Bring:** Resist the urge to buy euros before your trip or you'll pay the price in bad stateside exchange rates. Wait until you arrive to withdraw money. I've yet to see a European air-port that doesn't have plenty of ATMs.

## BEFORE YOU GO

Use this pre-trip checklist.

**Know your cards.** Debit cards from any major US bank will work in any standard European bank's ATM (ideally, use a debit card with a Visa or MasterCard logo). As for credit cards, Visa and

MasterCard are universal, American Express is less common, and Discover is unknown in Europe.

**Know your PIN.** Make sure you know the numeric, four-digit PIN for all of your cards, both debit and credit. Request it if you don't have one, as it may be required for some purchases in Europe (see "Using Credit Cards," later), and allow time to receive the information by mail.

**Report your travel dates.** Let your bank know that you'll be using your debit and credit cards in Europe, and when and where you're headed.

**Adjust your ATM withdrawal limit.** Find out how much you can take out daily and ask for a higher daily withdrawal limit if you want to get more cash at once. Note that European ATMs will withdraw funds only from checking accounts; you're unlikely to have access to your savings account.

**Ask about fees.** For any purchase or withdrawal made with a card, you may be charged a currency conversion fee (1-3 percent) and/or a Visa or MasterCard international transaction fee (less than 1 percent). If you're getting a bad deal, consider getting a new debit or credit card. Reputable no-fee cards include those from Capital One, as well as Charles Schwab debit cards. Most credit unions and some airline loyalty cards have low or no international transaction fees.

## IN EUROPE
### Using Cash Machines
European cash machines have English-language instructions and work just like they do at home—except they spit out local currency instead of dollars, calculated at the day's standard bank-to-bank rate.

In most places, ATMs are easy to locate—in Italy ask for a *bancomat*. When possible, withdraw cash from a bank-run ATM located just outside that bank. Ideally use the machine during the bank's opening hours so you can go inside for help if your card is munched.

If your debit card doesn't work, try a lower amount—your request may have exceeded your withdrawal limit or the ATM's limit. If you still have a problem, try a different ATM or come back later—your bank's network may be temporarily down.

Avoid "independent" ATMs, such as Travelex, Euronet, Moneybox, Your Cash, Cardpoint, and Cashzone. These have high fees, can be less secure than a bank ATM, and may try to trick users with "dynamic currency conversion" (see next page).

### Exchanging Cash
Avoid exchanging money in Europe; it's a big rip-off. In a pinch,

you can always find exchange desks at major train stations or airports—convenient but with crummy rates. Anything over 5 percent for a transaction is piracy. Banks generally do not exchange money unless you have an account with them.

## Using Credit Cards

Despite some differences between European and US cards, there's little to worry about: US credit cards generally work fine in Europe. I've been inconvenienced a few times by self-service payment machines that wouldn't accept my card, but it's never caused me serious trouble (I carry cash just in case).

European cards use chip-and-PIN technology; most chip cards issued in the US have a signature option instead. Some European card readers will accept your card as-is while others may generate a receipt for you to sign or prompt you to enter your PIN (so it's important to know the code for each of your cards). If a cashier is present, you should have no problems.

At self-service payment machines (transit-ticket kiosks, parking, etc.), results are mixed, as US cards may not work in some unattended transactions. If your card won't work, look for a cashier who can process your card manually—or pay in cash.

**Drivers Beware:** Be aware of potential problems using a US credit card to fill up at an unattended gas station, enter a parking garage, or exit a toll road. Always carry cash as a backup and be prepared to move on to the next gas station if necessary. When approaching a toll plaza, use the "cash" lane.

## Dynamic Currency Conversion

If merchants offer to convert your purchase price into dollars (called dynamic currency conversion, or DCC), refuse this "service." You'll pay extra for the expensive convenience of seeing your charge in dollars. If an ATM offers to "lock in" or "guarantee" your conversion rate, choose "proceed without conversion." Other prompts might state, "You can be charged in dollars: Press YES for dollars, NO for euros." Always choose the local currency.

## Security Tips

Pickpockets target tourists. Keep your cash, credit cards, and passport secure in your money belt, and carry only a day's spending money in your front pocket or wallet.

Before inserting your card into an ATM, inspect the front. If anything looks crooked, loose, or damaged, it could be a sign of a card-skimming device. When entering your PIN, carefully block other people's view of the keypad.

Don't use a debit card for purchases. Because a debit card pulls funds directly from your bank account, potential charges incurred by a thief will stay on your account while the fraudulent use is investigated by your bank.

To access your accounts online while traveling, be sure to use a secure connection (see the "Tips on Internet Security" sidebar, later).

## Damage Control for Lost Cards

If you lose your credit or debit card, report the loss immediately to the respective global customer-assistance centers. With a mobile phone, call these 24-hour US numbers: Visa (tel. +1 303/967-1096), MasterCard (tel. +1 636/722-7111), and American Express (tel. +1 336/393-1111). From a landline, you can call these US numbers collect by going through a local operator. European toll-free numbers can be found at the websites for Visa and MasterCard.

You'll need to provide the primary cardholder's identification-verification details (such as birth date, mother's maiden name, or Social Security number). You can generally receive a temporary card within two or three business days in Europe (see www.ricksteves.com/help for more).

If you report your loss within two days, you typically won't be responsible for unauthorized transactions on your account, although many banks charge a liability fee.

## TIPPING

Tipping in Italy isn't as automatic and generous as it is in the US. For special service, tips are appreciated, but not expected. As in the US, the proper amount depends on your resources, tipping philosophy, and the circumstances, but some general guidelines apply.

**Restaurants:** In Italy, a service charge *(servizio)* is usually built into your check (look at the bill carefully). If it is included, there's no need to leave an extra tip. If it's not included, it's common to leave about €1 per person (a bit more at finer restaurants) or to round up the bill. For more details on restaurant tipping, see page 1167.

**Taxis:** For a typical ride, round up your fare a bit (for instance, if the fare is €4.50, pay €5). If the cabbie hauls your bags and zips you to the airport to help you catch your flight, you might want to toss in a little more. But if you feel like you're being driven in circles or otherwise ripped off, skip the tip.

**Services:** In general, if someone in the tourism or service industry does a super job for you, a small tip of a euro or two is appropriate...but not required. If you're not sure whether (or how much) to tip, ask a local for advice.

## GETTING A VAT REFUND

Wrapped into the purchase price of your Italian souvenirs is a Value-Added Tax (VAT) of about 22 percent. You're entitled to get most of that tax back if you purchase more than €155 (about $170) worth of goods at a store that participates in the VAT-refund scheme. Typically, you must ring up the minimum at a single retailer—you can't add up your purchases from various shops to reach the required amount. (If the store ships the goods to your US home, VAT is not assessed on your purchase.)

Getting your refund is straightforward...and worthwhile if you spend a significant amount on souvenirs.

**Get the paperwork.** Have the merchant completely fill out the necessary refund document. You'll have to present your passport. Get the paperwork done before you leave the store to ensure you'll have everything you need (including your original sales receipt).

**Get your stamp at the border or airport.** Process your VAT document at your last stop in the European Union (such as at the airport) with the customs agent who deals with VAT refunds. Arrive an additional hour before you need to check in to allow time to find the customs office—and wait. Some customs desks are positioned before airport security; confirm the location before going through security.

It's best to keep your purchases in your carry-on. If your item isn't allowed as carry-on (such as a knife), pack it in your checked bag and alert the check-in agent. You'll be sent (with your tagged bag) to a customs desk outside security; someone will examine your bag, stamp your paperwork, and put your bag on the belt. You're not supposed to use your purchased goods before you leave. If you show up at customs wearing your new Italian leather shoes, officials might look the other way—or deny you a refund.

**Collect your refund.** You can claim your VAT refund from refund companies such as Global Blue or Planet with offices at major airports, ports, or border crossings (either before or after security, probably strategically located near a duty-free shop). These services (which extract a 4 percent fee) can refund your money in cash immediately or credit your card. Otherwise, mail the stamped refund documents to the address given by the shop where you made your purchase.

## CUSTOMS FOR AMERICAN SHOPPERS

You can take home $800 worth of items per person duty-free, once every 31 days. Many processed and packaged foods are allowed, including vacuum-packed cheeses, dried herbs, jams, baked goods, candy, chocolate, oil, vinegar, mustard, and honey. Fresh fruits and vegetables and most meats are not allowed, with exceptions for some canned items. As for alcohol, you can bring in one liter duty-

**PRACTICALITIES**

free (it can be packed securely in your checked luggage, along with any other liquid-containing items).

To bring alcohol (or liquid-packed foods) in your carry-on bag on your flight home, buy it at a duty-free shop at the airport. You'll increase your odds of getting it onto a connecting flight if it's packaged in a "STEB"—a secure, tamper-evident bag. But stay away from liquids in opaque, ceramic, or metallic containers, which usually cannot be successfully screened (STEB or no STEB).

For details on allowable goods, customs rules, and duty rates, visit http://help.cbp.gov.

# Sightseeing

Sightseeing can be hard work. Use these tips to make your visits to Italy's finest sights meaningful, fun, efficient, and painless.

## MAPS AND NAVIGATION TOOLS

A good map is essential for efficient navigation while sightseeing. The maps in this book are concise and simple, designed to help you locate recommended destinations, sights, and local TIs, where you can pick up more in-depth maps.

You can also use a mapping app on your mobile device. Be aware that pulling up maps or looking up turn-by-turn walking directions on the fly usually requires a data connection: To use this feature, it's smart to get an international data plan. With Google Maps or City Maps 2Go, it's possible to download a map while online, then go offline and navigate without incurring data-roaming charges, though you can't search for an address or get real-time walking directions. A handful of other apps—including Apple Maps and Navmii—also allow you to use maps offline.

## PLAN AHEAD

Set up an itinerary that allows you to fit in all your must-see sights. For a one-stop look at opening hours, see this book's "At a Glance" sidebars for each major city (Venice, Milan, Florence, Siena, and Rome). Most sights keep stable hours, but you can easily confirm the latest by checking with the TI or visiting museum websites. Or call sights in the morning and ask: "Are you open today?" (*"Aperto oggi?"*; ah-PER-toh OH-jee) and "What time do you close?" (*"A che ora chiude?"*; ah kay OH-rah kee-OO-day).

Don't put off visiting a must-see sight—you never know when a place will close unexpectedly for a holiday, strike, or restoration. Many museums are closed or have reduced hours at least a few days a year, especially on holidays such as Christmas, New Year's *(Capodanno)*, Italian Liberation Day (April 25), Labor Day (May 1), and Ferragosto (Feast of the Assumption, Aug 15). A list of holidays is in the appendix; check for possible closures during your trip. In summer, some sights may stay open late. In the off-season, hours may be shorter.

Going at the right time helps avoid crowds. This book offers tips on the best times to see specific sights. Try visiting popular sights very early or very late. Evening visits (when possible) are usually peaceful, with fewer crowds. Late morning is usually the worst time to visit a popular sight.

If you plan to hire a local guide, reserve ahead by email. Popular guides can get booked up.

Study up. To get the most out of the self-guided tours and sight descriptions in this book, read them before you visit.

## RESERVATIONS, ADVANCE TICKETS, AND PASSES

Given how precious your vacation time is, I recommend getting reservations for any must-see sight that offers them (see page 25).

To deal with lines, many popular sights sell advance tickets that guarantee admission at a certain time of day (for example, Florence's Uffizi Gallery or Rome's Vatican Museums), or that allow you to skip entry lines. Either way, it's worth giving up some spontaneity to book in advance. While hundreds of tourists sweat in long ticket-buying lines, those who've booked ahead are assured of getting in. In some cases, getting a ticket in advance simply means buying your ticket earlier on the same day. But for other sights, you may need to book weeks or even months in advance. As soon as you're ready to commit to a certain date, book it.

The advance-purchase price may be less expensive than what you would pay on-site. And many museums offer convenient mobile ticketing. Simply buy your ticket online and send it to your phone, eliminating the need for a paper ticket.

Some cities offer passes (e.g., Florence's Duomo sights comboticket or Siena's Acropoli pass) that save you time and money by covering admission to several sights. At some popular places (such as Venice's Doge's Palace), you can get in more quickly by buying your combo-ticket or pass at a less-crowded sight (the Correr Museum).

Booking a guided tour can help you avoid lines at many popular sights. So can knowing what days to avoid. State museums in Italy are free to enter (and more crowded) the first Sunday of the month from October through March and other days in peak season. Check museum websites for specifics and avoid free entry days when possible.

## AT SIGHTS

Here's what you can typically expect:

PRACTICALITIES

**Entering:** You may not be allowed to enter if you arrive too close to closing time. And guards start ushering people out well before the actual closing time, so don't save the best for last.

Many sights have a security check. Allow extra time for these lines. Some sights require you to check daypacks and coats. (If you'd rather not check your daypack, try carrying it tucked under your arm like a purse as you enter.)

**Photography:** If the museum's photo policy isn't clearly posted, ask a guard. Generally, taking photos without a flash or tripod is allowed. Some sights ban selfie sticks; others ban photos altogether.

**Audioguides and Apps:** Many sights rent audioguides with excellent recorded descriptions in English. If you bring your own earbuds, you can often enjoy better sound. If you don't mind being tethered to your travel partner, you'll save money by bringing a Y-jack and sharing one audioguide. Museums and sights often offer free apps that you can download to your mobile device (check their websites). And, I've produced free, downloadable audio tours for some of Italy's major sights, including those in Venice, Florence, Milan, Rome, Assisi, Naples, and Pompeii; look for the 🎧 in this book. For more on my audio tours, see page 26.

**Temporary Exhibits:** Museums may show special exhibits in addition to their permanent collection. Some exhibits are included in the entry price, while others come at an extra cost (which you may have to pay even if you don't want to see the exhibit).

**Expect Changes:** Artwork can be on tour, on loan, out sick, or shifted at the whim of the curator. Pick up a floor plan as you enter, and ask the museum staff if you can't find a particular item. Say the title or artist's name, or point to the photograph in this book and ask, *"Dov'è?"* (doh-VEH, meaning "Where is?").

**Dates for Artwork:** It helps to know the terms. Art historians and Italians refer to the great Florentine centuries by dropping a thousand years. The Trecento (300s), Quattrocento (400s), and Cinquecento (500s) were the 1300s, 1400s, and 1500s. The Novecento (900s) means modern art (the 1900s). In Italian museums, art is dated with *sec* for *secolo* (century, often indicated with Roman numerals), AC (*avanti Cristo*, or BC), and DC (*dopo Cristo*, or AD). OK?

**Services:** Important sights usually have a reasonably priced on-site café or cafeteria (handy places to rejuvenate during a long visit). The WCs at sights are free and generally clean.

**Before Leaving:** At the gift shop, scan the postcard rack or thumb through a guidebook to be sure that you haven't overlooked something that you'd like to see. Every sight or museum offers more than what is covered in this book. Use the information I provide as an introduction—not the final word.

## FIND RELIGION

Churches offer some amazing art (usually free), a cool respite from heat, and a welcome seat.

A modest dress code—no bare shoulders or shorts for anyone, even kids—is enforced at larger churches—such as the Duomos in Florence and Siena, Venice's St. Mark's Basilica, and the Vatican's St. Peter's—but is often overlooked elsewhere. If you're caught by surprise, you can sometimes improvise, using maps to cover your shoulders and a jacket for your knees. A few major churches let you borrow or buy disposable ponchos to cover up in a pinch. (I wear a super-lightweight pair of long pants rather than shorts for my hot and muggy Italian sightseeing.) If your heart's set on seeing a certain church, err on the side of caution and dress appropriately.

Some churches have coin-operated boxes that trigger lights to illuminate works of art. I pop in a coin whenever I can, to improve my experience (and photos), as a small contribution to that church, and as a courtesy to other visitors enjoying this great art. Whenever possible, let there be light.

# Sleeping

Extensive and opinionated listings of good-value rooms are a major feature of this book's Sleeping sections. Rather than list accommodations scattered throughout a town, I choose hotels in my favorite neighborhoods that are convenient to your sightseeing.

My recommendations run the gamut, from dorm beds to fancy rooms with all of the comforts. I like places that are clean, central, relatively quiet at night, reasonably priced, friendly, small enough to have a hands-on owner or manager, and run with a respect for Italian traditions. I'm more impressed by a handy location and a fun-loving philosophy than flat-screen TVs and a fancy gym. Most of my recommendations fall short of perfection. But if I can find a place with most of these features, it's a keeper.

Book your accommodations as soon as your itinerary is set, especially if you want to stay at one of my top listings or if you'll be traveling during busy times. See the appendix for a list of major holidays and festivals in Italy.

Some people make reservations as they travel, calling or emailing ahead a few days to a week before their arrival. If you're trying for a same-day reservation, it's best to call hotels at about 9:00 or 10:00, when the receptionist knows which rooms will be available. If you encounter a language barrier, ask the fluent receptionist at your current hotel to call for you. Some apps—such as HotelTonight—specialize in last-minute rooms, often at boutique or business-class hotels in big cities.

---

## Sleep Code

Hotels are classified based on the average price of a standard double room with breakfast in high season.

| | | |
|---|---|---|
| **$$$$** | **Splurge:** | Most rooms over €170 |
| **$$$** | **Pricier:** | €130-170 |
| **$$** | **Moderate:** | €90-130 |
| **$** | **Budget:** | €50-90 |
| **¢** | **Backpacker:** | Under €50 |
| **RS%** | **Rick Steves discount** | |

Unless otherwise noted, credit cards are accepted, hotel staff speak basic English, and free Wi-Fi is available. Comparison-shop by checking prices at several hotels (on each hotel's own website, on a booking site, or by email). For the best deal, *book directly with the hotel.* Ask for a discount if paying in cash; if the listing includes **RS%,** request a Rick Steves discount.

---

## RATES AND DEALS

I've categorized my recommended accommodations based on price, indicated with a dollar-sign rating (see sidebar). The price ranges suggest an estimated cost for a one-night stay in high season in a standard double room with a private toilet and shower, including breakfast, and assume you're booking directly with the hotel (not through a booking site, which extracts a commission). Room prices can fluctuate significantly with demand and amenities (size, views, room class, and so on), but relative price categories remain constant.

Taxes vary from place to place (figure €2-5 per person, per night). Some hoteliers will ask to collect the city tax in cash to make their bookkeeping and accounting simpler.

Room rates are especially volatile at hotels that use "dynamic pricing" to set rates. Prices can skyrocket during festivals and conventions, while business hotels can have deep discounts on weekends when demand plummets. Of the many hotels I recommend, it's difficult to say which will be the best value on a given day—until you do your homework.

**Booking Direct:** Once your dates are set, compare prices at several hotels. You can do this by checking Hotels.com, Booking.com, and hotel websites. After you've zeroed in on your choice, book directly with the hotel itself. Contact small family-run hotels directly by phone or email. When you go direct, the owner avoids the commission paid to booking sites, thereby leaving enough wiggle room to offer you a discount, a nicer room, or a free breakfast (if it's not already included). If you prefer to book online or are considering a hotel chain, it's to your advantage to use the hotel's website.

Booking directly also increases the chances that the hotelier will be able to accommodate any special needs or requests (such as shifting your reservation). Going through a middleman makes it more difficult for the hotel to adjust your booking.

**Getting a Discount:** Some hotels extend a discount to those who pay cash or stay longer than three nights. And some accommodations offer a special discount for Rick Steves readers, indicated in this guidebook by the abbreviation **"RS%."** Discounts vary: Ask for details when you reserve. Generally, to qualify for this discount, you must book direct (not through a booking site), mention this book when you reserve, show this book upon arrival, and sometimes pay cash or stay a certain number of nights. In some cases, you may need to enter a discount code (which I've provided in the listing) in the booking form on the hotel's website. Rick Steves discounts apply to readers with either print or digital books. Understandably, discounts do not apply to promotional rates.

## TYPES OF ACCOMMODATIONS
### Hotels

Double rooms listed in this book range from about €50 (very simple, toilet and shower down the hall) to €450 (maximum plumbing and more), with most clustered around €140 (with private bathrooms). Prices are higher in big or heavily touristed cities, and lower off the beaten path. Traveling alone can be expensive: A *camera singola* is often only 25 percent less than a *camera doppia*.

Some hotels can add an extra bed (for a small charge) to turn a double into a triple; some offer larger rooms for four or more people (I call these "family rooms" in the listings). If there's space for an extra cot, they'll cram it in for you. In general, a triple room is cheaper than the cost of a double and a single. Three or four people can economize by requesting one big room.

**Arrival and Check-In:** Hotels and B&Bs are sometimes located on the higher floors of a multipurpose building with a secured door. In that case, look for your hotel's name on the buttons by the main entrance. When you ring the bell, you'll be buzzed in.

Hotel elevators are common, though some older buildings still lack them. You may have to climb a flight of stairs to reach the elevator (if so, you can ask the front desk for help carrying your bags up). Elevators are typically very small—pack light, or you may need to send your bags up without you.

The EU requires that hotels collect your name, nationality, and ID number. When you check in, the receptionist will normally ask for your passport and may keep it for anywhere from a couple of minutes to a couple of hours. If you're not comfortable leaving your passport at the desk for a long time, ask when you can pick it up. Or, if you packed a color copy of your passport, you can generally leave that rather than the original.

# Using Online Services to Your Advantage

From booking services to user reviews, online businesses play a greater role in travelers' planning than ever before. Take advantage of their pluses—and be wise to their downsides.

## Booking Sites

Booking websites such as Booking.com and Hotels.com offer one-stop shopping for hotels. While convenient for travelers, they present a real problem for independent, family-run hotels. Without a presence on these sites, small hotels become almost invisible. But to be listed, a hotel must pay a sizeable commission... and promise that its own website won't undercut the price on the booking-service site.

Here's the work-around: Use the big sites to research what's out there, then book directly with the hotel by email or phone, in which case hotel owners are free to give you whatever price they like. Ask for a room without the commission markup (or ask for a free breakfast if not included, or a free upgrade). If you do book online, be sure to use the hotel's website. The price will likely be the same as via a booking site, but your money goes to the hotel, not agency commissions.

As a savvy consumer, remember: When you book with an online booking service, you're adding a middleman who takes roughly 20 percent. To support small, family-run hotels whose world is more difficult than ever, book direct.

## Short-Term Rental Sites

Rental juggernaut Airbnb (along with other short-term rental sites) allows travelers to rent rooms and apartments directly from locals, often providing more value than a cookie-cutter hotel. Airbnb fans appreciate feeling part of a real neighborhood and getting into a daily routine as "temporary Europeans." Depending on the host, Airbnb can provide an opportunity to get to know a

If you're arriving in the morning, your room probably won't be ready. Check your bag safely at the hotel and dive right into sightseeing.

**In Your Room:** Most hotel rooms have a TV, telephone, and free Wi-Fi (although in old buildings with thick walls, the Wi-Fi signal might be available only in the lobby). Simpler places rarely have a room phone. Pricier hotels usually come with a small fridge stocked with beverages, called a *frigo bar* (FREE-goh bar; pay for what you use).

More pillows and blankets are usually in the closet or available on request. Towels and linens aren't always replaced every day. Some hotels use lightweight "waffle," or very thin, tablecloth-type

local person, while keeping the money spent on your accommodations in the community.

Critics view Airbnb as a threat to "traditional Europe," saying it creates unfair, unqualified competition for established guesthouse owners. In some places, the lucrative Airbnb market has forced traditional guesthouses out of business and is driving property values out of range for locals. Some cities have cracked down, requiring owners to occupy rental properties part of the year (and staging disruptive "inspections" that inconvenience guests).

As a lover of Europe, I share the worry of those who see residents nudged aside by tourists. But as an advocate for travelers, I appreciate the value and cultural intimacy Airbnb provides.

## User Reviews

User-generated review sites and apps such as Yelp and TripAdvisor can give you a consensus of opinions about everything from hotels and restaurants to sights and nightlife. If you scan reviews of a restaurant or hotel and see several complaints about noise or a rotten location, you've gained insight that can help in your decision-making.

But as a guidebook writer, my sense is that there is a big difference between the uncurated information on a review site and the vetted listings in a guidebook. A user-generated review is based on the limited experience of one person, who stayed at just one hotel in a given city and ate at a few restaurants there. A guidebook is the work of a trained researcher who forms a well-developed basis for comparison by visiting many restaurants and hotels year after year.

Both types of information have their place, and in many ways, they're complementary. If something is well-reviewed in a guidebook and it also gets good online reviews, it's likely a winner.

PRACTICALITIES

towels; these take less water and electricity to launder and are preferred by many Italians.

Nearly all places offer private bathrooms, which have a tub or shower, a toilet, and a bidet (which Italians use for quick sponge baths). The cord over the tub or shower is not a clothesline. You pull it when you've fallen and can't get up.

Double beds are called *matrimoniale*, even though hotels aren't interested in your marital status. Twins are *due letti singoli*. Convents offer cheap accommodation but have more *letti singoli* than *matrimoniali*.

**Breakfast and Meals:** Italian hotels typically include breakfast in their room prices. If breakfast is optional, you may want to skip it. While convenient, it's usually pricey for what you get: a sim-

## Making Hotel Reservations

Reserve your rooms as soon as you've pinned down your travel dates. For busy national holidays, it's wise to reserve far in advance (see the appendix).

**Requesting a Reservation:** For family-run hotels, it's generally best to book your room directly via email or phone. For business-class and chain hotels, or if you'd rather book online, reserve directly through the hotel's official website (not a booking website). Almost all of my recommended hotels take reservations in English.

Here's what the hotelier wants to know:

- Type(s) of rooms you want and size of your party
- Number of nights you'll stay
- Your arrival and departure dates, written European-style as day/month/year (for example, 18/06/21 or 18 June 2021);
- Special requests (en suite bathroom, cheapest room, twin beds vs. double bed, quiet room)
- Applicable discounts (such as a Rick Steves reader discount, cash discount, or promotional rate)

**Confirming a Reservation:** Most places will request a credit-card number to hold your room. If you're using an online reservation form, make sure it's secure by looking for the *https* or a lock icon at the top of your browser. If the hotel's website doesn't have a secure form where you can enter the number directly, it's best to share that confidential info via a phone call.

**Canceling a Reservation:** If you must cancel, it's courteous—and smart—to do so with as much notice as possible, especially for

ple continental buffet with (at its most generous) bread, croissants, ham, cheese, yogurt, and unlimited *caffè latte*. A picnic in your room followed by a coffee at the corner café can be lots cheaper.

Hotels in resort areas may charge you for half-pension, called *mezza pensione*, during peak season. Half-pension means that you pay for one meal per day per person (lunch or dinner). If half-pension is required, you can't opt out and pay less. If it's an option, it can be worth considering, especially if they charge less per meal than you've been paying for an average restaurant meal (and provided the chef is good).

**Checking Out:** While it's customary to pay for your room upon departure, it can be a good idea to settle your bill the day before, when you're not in a hurry and while the manager's in.

**Hotelier Help:** Hoteliers can be a good source of advice. Most know their city well, and can assist you with everything from public transit and airport connections to finding a good restaurant, the nearest launderette, or a late-night pharmacy.

**Hotel Hassles:** Even at the best places, mechanical break-

From: rick@ricksteves.com
Sent: Today
To: info@hotelcentral.com
Subject: Reservation request for 19-22 July

Dear Hotel Central,

I would like to stay at your hotel. Please let me know if you have a room available and the price for:

• 2 people
• Double bed and en suite bathroom in a quiet room
• Arriving 19 July, departing 22 July (3 nights)

Thank you!
Rick Steves

smaller family-run places. Cancellation policies can be strict; read the fine print before you book. Many discount deals require pre-payment, with no cancellation refunds.

**Reconfirming a Reservation:** Always call or email to reconfirm your room reservation a few days in advance. For B&Bs or very small hotels, I call again on my day of arrival to tell my host what time to expect me (especially important if arriving late—after 17:00).

**Phoning:** For tips on calling hotels overseas, see page 1184.

downs occur: Sinks leak, hot water turns cold, toilets may gurgle or smell, the Wi-Fi goes out, or the air-conditioning dies when you need it most. Report your concerns clearly and calmly at the front desk.

If you find that night noise is a problem (if, for instance, your room is over a nightclub or facing a busy street), ask for a quieter room in the back or on an upper floor.

To guard against theft in your room, keep valuables out of sight. Some rooms come with a safe, and other hotels have safes at the front desk. I've never bothered using one and, in a lifetime of travel, I've never had anything stolen out of my room.

For more complicated problems, don't expect instant results. Above all, keep a positive attitude. Remember, you're on vacation. If your hotel is a disappointment, spend more time out enjoying the place you came to see.

## Bed-and-Breakfasts

B&Bs can offer good-value accommodations in excellent locations.

---

## Keep Cool

If you're visiting Italy in the summer, you'll want an air-conditioned room. Most hotel air-conditioners come with a control
stick that generally has similar symbols and features: fan icon
(click to toggle through wind power, from light to gale); temperature control (20 degrees Celsius is comfortable); louver
icon (choose steady airflow or waves); snowflake and sunshine
icons (cold air or heat); and clock ("O" setting: run X hours
before turning off; "I" setting: wait X hours to start). When you
leave your room for the day, turning off the air-conditioning is
good form.

---

Usually converted family homes or apartments, they can range
from humble rooms with communal kitchens to high-end boutique
accommodations with extra amenities. Boutique B&Bs can be an
especially good option, as they are typically less expensive than a
big hotel, but often newer and nicer, with more personal service.
Because the B&B scene is constantly changing, it's smart to supplement this book's recommendations with your own research.

Be aware that B&Bs can suffer from absentee management.
The proprietors often live off-site (or even in another town) and
may be around only when they are expecting guests. Clearly communicate your arrival time, and after checking in, be sure you have
your host's telephone number in case you need to reach them.

### Short-Term Rentals

A short-term rental—whether an apartment, house, or room in a
local's home—is an increasingly popular alternative, especially if
you plan to settle in one location for several nights. For stays longer
than a few days, you can usually find a rental that's comparable
to—and even cheaper than—a hotel room with similar amenities.
Plus, you'll get a behind-the-scenes peek into how locals live.

Many places require a minimum-night stay and have strict
cancellation policies. And you're generally on your own: There's no
hotel reception desk, breakfast, or daily cleaning service.

**Finding Accommodations:** Websites such as Airbnb, FlipKey,
Booking.com, and the HomeAway family of sites (HomeAway,
VRBO, and VacationRentals) let you browse a wide range of properties. Alternatively, rental agencies such as InterhomeUSA.com
or RentaVilla.com, which list more carefully selected accommodations that might cost more, can provide more personalized service.

Before you commit, be clear on the location. I like to virtually "explore" the neighborhood using the Street View feature on
Google Maps. Also consider the proximity to public transportation, and how well-connected the property is with the rest of the

city. Ask about amenities (elevator, air-conditioning, laundry, Wi-Fi, parking, etc.). Reviews from previous guests can help identify trouble spots.

Think about the kind of experience you want: Just a key and an affordable bed...or a chance to get to know a local? There are typically two kinds of hosts: those who want minimal interaction with their guests, and hosts who are friendly and may want to interact with you. Read the promotional text and online reviews to help shape your decision.

**Confirming and Paying:** Many places require you to pay the entire balance before your trip. It's easiest and safest to pay through the site where you found the listing. Be wary of owners who want to take your transaction offline; this gives you no recourse if things go awry. Never agree to wire money (a key indicator of a fraudulent transaction).

**Apartments or Houses:** If you're staying in one place for four or more nights, it's worth considering an apartment or rental house (shorter stays aren't worth the hassle of arranging key pickup, buying groceries, etc.). Apartment or house rentals can be especially cost-effective for groups and families. European apartments, like hotel rooms, tend to be small by US standards. But they often come with laundry machines and small, equipped kitchens *(cucinetta)*, making it easier and cheaper to dine in.

**Rooms in Private Homes:** In small towns, there may be few hotels or apartments, but an abundance of Airbnb rentals and some *affittacamere* (rental rooms). These can be anything from a set of keys and a basic bed to a cozy B&B with your own Tuscan grandmother. Renting a room in someone's home is a good option for those traveling alone, as you're more likely to find true single rooms—with just one single bed, and a price to match. Beds range from air-mattress-in-living-room basic to plush-B&B-suite posh. Some places allow you to book for a single night. While you can't expect your host to also be your tour guide—or even to provide you with much info—some may be interested in getting to know the travelers who come through their home.

**Other Options:** Swapping homes with a local works for people with an appealing place to offer (don't assume where you live is not interesting to Europeans). Good places to start are HomeExchange.com and LoveHomeSwap.com. To sleep for free, Couchsurfing.com is a vagabond's alternative to Airbnb. It lists millions of outgoing members who host fellow "surfers" in their homes.

## Agriturismi

*Agriturismi*—working farms that double as countryside B&Bs—began cropping up in the 1980s to allow small family farms to survive (as in the US, many have been squeezed out by giant agribusinesses). By renting rooms to travelers, farmers receive generous tax breaks that allow them to remain on their land and continue to grow food crops. These B&Bs make a peaceful home base for those exploring rural Italy, and are ideal for those traveling by car—especially families.

It's wise to book several months in advance for high season (late May-mid-Oct). July and August are jammed with Italians and other European vacationers; in spring and fall, it's mostly Americans. Weeklong stays (typically Saturday to Saturday) are preferred at busy times, but shorter stays are possible off-season. To sleep cheaper, try early spring and late fall. Most places are closed in winter (about Nov-Easter).

As the name implies, *agriturismi* are in the countryside, although some are located on the outskirts of a large town or city. Most are family-run. *Agriturismi* vary dramatically in quality—some properties are rustic, while others are downright luxurious, offering amenities such as swimming pools and riding stables. The rooms are usually clean and comfortable. Breakfast is often included, and *mezza pensione* (half-pension, which in this case means a home-cooked dinner) might be built into the price whether you want it or not. Most places serve tasty homegrown food; some are vegetarian or organic, others are gourmet. Kitchenettes are often available to cook up your own feast.

To qualify officially as an *agriturismo,* the farm must still generate more money from its farm activities, thereby ensuring that the land is worked and preserved. Some travelers who are enticed by romanticized dreams of rural Italy are turned off when they arrive to actual farm smells and sounds. These folks would be more comfortable with a countryside B&B or villa that offers a bit more upscale comfort (farmhouse B&Bs are still fine places to stay, even if they aren't working farms). In this book, I've listed both types of rural accommodations; if you want the real thing, make sure the owners call their place an *agriturismo.*

In addition to my listings, local TIs can give you a list of places in their area. For a sampling, visit AgriturismoItaly.it or search online for *agriturismo.* One booking agency among many is Farm Holidays in Tuscany (closed Sat-Sun, tel. 0564-417-418, www.byfarmholidays.com, info@byfarmholidays.com).

## Hostels

A hostel provides cheap beds in dorms where you sleep alongside strangers for about €25-30 per night. Travelers of any age are welcome if they don't mind dorm-style accommodations and meeting other travelers. Most hostels offer kitchen facilities, guest computers, Wi-Fi, and a self-service laundry. Hostels almost always provide bedding, but the towel's up to you (though you can usually rent one for a small fee). Family and private rooms are often available.

**Independent hostels** tend to be easygoing, colorful, and informal (no membership required; www.hostelworld.com). You may pay slightly less by booking directly with the hostel. **Official hostels** are part of Hostelling International (HI) and share a booking site (www.hihostels.com). HI hostels typically require that you be a member or else pay a bit more per night

# Eating

The Italians are masters of the art of fine living. That means eating long and well. Lengthy, multicourse meals and endless hours sitting in outdoor cafés are the norm. Americans eat on their way to an evening event and complain if the check is slow in coming. For Italians, the meal is an end in itself, and only rude servers rush you.

A highlight of your Italian adventure will be this country's cafés, cuisine, and wines. Trust me: This is sightseeing for your palate. Even if you liked dorm food and are sleeping in cheap hotels, your taste buds will relish an occasional first-class splurge. You can eat well without going broke. But be careful: You're just as likely to blow a small fortune on a disappointing meal as you are to dine wonderfully for €25. Rely on my recommendations in the various Eating sections throughout this book.

In general, Italians eat meals a bit later than we do. At 7:00 or 8:00, they have a light breakfast (coffee—usually cappuccino or espresso—and a pastry, often standing up at a café). Lunch (between 13:00 and 15:00) is traditionally the largest meal of the day. Then they eat a late, light dinner (around 20:00-21:30, or maybe earlier in winter). To bridge the gap, people drop into a bar in the late afternoon for a *spuntino* (snack) and aperitif.

## RESTAURANT PRICING

I've categorized my recommended eateries based on the average price of a typical main course, indicated with a dollar-sign rating (see sidebar). Obviously, expensive specialties, fine wine, appetizers, and dessert can significantly increase your final bill.

The categories also indicate the personality of a place: **Budget** eateries include street food, takeaway, order-at-the-counter shops, basic cafeterias, and bakeries selling sandwiches. **Moderate** eateries are nice (but not fancy) sit-down restaurants, ideal for a straightforward, fill-the-tank meal. Most of my listings fall in this category—great for a good taste of local cuisine at a reasonable price.

**Pricier** eateries are a notch up, with more attention paid to the setting, presentation, and (often inventive) cuisine. **Splurge** eater-

## Restaurant Code

Eateries in this book are categorized according to the average cost of a typical main course. Drinks, desserts, and splurge items can raise the price considerably.

**$$$$**  **Splurge:** Most main courses over €20
**$$$**  **Pricier:** €15-20
**$$**  **Moderate:** €10-15
**$**  **Budget:** Under €10

Pizza by the slice and other takeaway food is **$**; a basic trattoria or sit-down pizzeria is **$$**; a casual but more upscale restaurant is **$$$**; and a swanky splurge is **$$$$**.

ies are dress-up-for-a-special-occasion swanky—typically with an elegant setting, polished service, pricey and intricate cuisine, and an expansive (and expensive) wine list.

## BREAKFAST

Italian breakfasts, like Italian bath towels, can be small: The basic, traditional version is coffee and a roll with butter and marmalade. Many places have yogurt and juice (the delicious red orange juice—*spremuta d'arancia rossa*—is made from Sicilian blood oranges), and possibly also cereal, cold cuts and sliced cheese, and eggs (typically hard-boiled; scrambled or fried eggs are less common). Small budget hotels may leave a basic breakfast in your room (stale croissant, roll, jam, yogurt, coffee).

If you want to skip your hotel breakfast, consider browsing for a morning picnic at a local open-air market. Or do as the Italians do: Step into a bar or café to drink a cappuccino and munch a *cornetto* (croissant) while standing at the bar. While the *cornetto* is the most common pastry, you'll find a range of *pasticcini* (pastries, sometimes called *dolci*—sweets). Look for *otto* (an 8-shaped pastry, often filled with custard, jam, or chocolate), *sfoglia* (filo-dough crust that's fruit-filled, like a turnover), or *ciambella* (doughnut filled with custard or chocolate)—or ask about local specialties.

## ITALIAN RESTAURANTS

While *ristorante* is self-explanatory, you'll also see other types of Italian eateries. A trattoria and an osteria (which can be more casual) are both generally family-owned places serving home-cooked meals, often at moderate prices. A *locanda* is an inn, a *cantina* is a wine cellar, and a *birreria* is a brewpub. *Pizzerie, rosticcerie* (delis), *tavola calda* ("hot table") bars, *enoteche* (wine bars), and other alternatives are explained later.

I look for restaurants that are convenient to your hotel and

sightseeing. When res-
taurant-hunting, choose a
spot filled with locals, not
the place with the big neon
signs boasting, "We speak
English and accept credit
cards." Restaurants parked
on famous squares gener-
ally serve bad food at high
prices to tourists. Ventur-

ing even a block or two off the main drag leads to higher-quality food for less than half the price of the tourist-oriented places.
Locals eat better at lower-rent locales. Family-run places operate
without hired help and can offer cheaper meals.

Most restaurant kitchens close between their lunch and dinner service. Good restaurants don't reopen for dinner before 19:00.
If you arrive at opening time, most restaurants will be empty and
available—the main push of customers arrives later. Small restaurants with a full slate of reservations for 20:30 or 21:00 often will
accommodate walk-in diners willing to eat a quick, early meal, but
you aren't expected to linger.

When you want the bill, mime-scribble on your raised palm
or request it: *"Il conto, per favore."* You may have to ask more than
once. If you're in a hurry, request the check when you receive the
last item you order.

## Cover and Tipping

Avoid surprises when eating out by familiarizing yourself with two
common Italian restaurant charges: *coperto* and *servizio*. You won't
encounter them in all restaurants, but both charges, if assessed, by
law must be listed on the menu.

The *coperto* (cover), sometimes called *pane e coperto* (bread and
cover), is a minor fee (€1.50-3/person) covering the cost of the typical basket of bread, oil, salt, cutlery, and linens found on your table.
It's not negotiable, even if you don't eat the bread. And it's not a tip
(it goes to the owner)—think of it as entitling you to use the table
for as long as you like.

The *servizio* (a 10- to 15-percent service charge) is similar to
the mandatory gratuity that American restaurants often add for
groups of six or more. You can consider it a "tourist tax," as you're
most likely to encounter it in locations with lots of tourists. Because
the service charge is sometimes built into your bill, look carefully
at your check to see if you've already paid a tip—don't leave any tip
beyond this.

If there is no *servizio* on the bill, a common **tip** at a simple restaurant or pizzeria is €1 per person at the table (or simply round up

the bill). At a finer restaurant, leave a few euros per person. Don't leave the tip on the table; hand it directly to the server to make sure he or she receives it. Be prepared to tip with cash/coins, as credit/debit card receipts won't have a tip line as in the US.

## Italian Menu Courses

A full Italian meal consists of multiple courses (all described below). For most travelers, it's simply too much food—and the euros can add up in a hurry. To avoid overeating (and to stretch your budget), share dishes. A good rule of thumb is for each person to order any two courses. For example, a couple can order and share one *antipasto*, one *primo*, one *secondo*, and one dessert; or two *antipasti* and two *primi;* or whatever combination appeals.

Small groups can mix *antipasti* and *primi* family-style (skipping *secondi*). If you do this right, you can eat well in better places for less than the cost of a tourist *menù* in a cheap place.

Some touristy restaurants serve a *piatto unico,* with smaller portions of each course on one dish (for instance, a meat, starch, and vegetable).

**Antipasto:** An appetizer such as bruschetta, grilled veggies, deep-fried tasties, thin-sliced meat (prosciutto or carpaccio), or a plate of olives, cold cuts, and cheeses. To get a sampler plate of cold cuts and cheeses in a restaurant, ask for *affettato misto* (mixed cold cuts), *antipasto misto* (cold cuts, cheeses, and marinated vegetables), or *tagliere* (a sampler "board"). This could make a light meal in itself.

**Primo piatto:** A "first dish" generally consisting of pasta but also rice or soup. If you think of pasta when you think of Italian food, you can dine well here without ever going beyond the *primo.*

**Secondo piatto:** A "second dish," equivalent to our main course, of meat or fish/seafood. Italians freely admit the *secondo* is the least interesting part of their cuisine.

**Contorno:** A vegetable side dish may come with the *secondo* but more often must be ordered separately. Typical *contorni* are *insalata mista,* spinach, roasted potatoes, or grilled veggies. This can be an interesting, if overlooked, part of the menu. Vegetarians can skip the *secondo* and order several *contorni* to make a meal.

**Dolce:** No meal is complete without a sweet. On most menus you'll find typical Italian desserts such as tiramisu and *panna cotta* as well as local favorites.

## Ordering Tips

Seafood and steak may be sold by weight and priced by the *etto* (100 grams, 3.5 ounces) or the kilo (1,000 grams, 2.2 pounds). The abbreviation *s.q. (secondo quantità)* indicates an item is priced by weight (often used at antipasto buffets). Unless the menu indicates a fillet *(filetto)*, fish is usually served whole with the head and tail. However, you can always ask your server to select a small fish and fillet it for you. Sometimes, especially for steak, restaurants require a minimum order of four or five *etti* (which diners can share). Make sure you're clear on the price before ordering.

Some special dishes come in larger quantities meant to be shared by two people. The shorthand way of showing this on a menu is "X2" (for two), but the price listed could indicate the cost per person.

In a traditional restaurant, if you order a pasta dish and a side salad—but no main course—the server will bring the salad after the pasta (Italians prefer it this way, believing that it enhances digestion). If you want the salad with your pasta, specify *insieme* (een-see-EH-meh; together).

Because pasta and bread are both starches, Italians consider them redundant. If you order only a pasta dish, bread may not come with it; you can request it, but you may be charged extra. On the other hand, if you order a vegetable antipasto or a meat *secondo*, bread is often provided to balance the ingredients.

At places with counter service—such as at a bar or a freeway rest-stop diner—you'll order and pay at the *cassa* (cashier). Take your receipt to the counter to claim your food.

## Fixed-Price Meals and Ordering à la Carte

You can save by getting a fixed-priced meal. Avoid the cheapest ones (often called a *menù turistico*). Look instead for a genuine *menù del giorno* (menu of the day), which offers diners a choice of appetizer, main course, and dessert. It's worth paying a little more for an inventive fixed-price meal that shows off the chef's creativity. They're also frequently exempt from cover and service changes.

While fixed-price meals can be easy and convenient, galloping gourmets prefer to order à la carte with the help of a menu translator. When going to an especially good restaurant with an approachable staff, I like to find out what they're eager to serve. Sometimes I'll simply say, *"Mi faccia felice"* (Make me happy) and set a price limit.

| MENÙ PIZZA *(Pizza a scelta)* | MENÙ 1 |
|---|---|
| Pizza margherita + Drink | Spaghetti with tomato sauce *(Spaghetti al pomodoro)* Mixed salad *(Insalata mista)* Drink |
| € 8,00 | € 9,50 |
| **MENÙ 2** | **MENÙ 3** |
| Pasta with pesto sauce *(Pasta al ragù)* Chicken steak *(Costoletta di pollo)* Mixed Salad *(Insalata mista)* Drink | Tortellini ham cream *(Tortellini panna e prosciutto)* Sedanjine "piemese style" with spinach *(Sedanjine alla piemese con spinaci)* Drink |
| € 11,00 | € 12,50 |
| **MENÙ 4** | **MENÙ 5** |
| Tortellini bolognese style *(Tortellini alla bolognese)* Thinly cut grilled steak with rucola *(Tagliata con rucola)* Drink | Big salad *(Insalatona: tomo, mozzarella, lettuge e pomodori)* Drink |
| € 18,00 | € 6,50 |

## BUDGET EATING

Italy offers many budget options for hungry travelers.

Self-service cafeterias offer the basics without add-on charges. Travelers on a hard-core budget equip their room with a pantry stocked at the market (fruits and veggies are remarkably cheap), or pick up a sandwich or *döner kebab*, then dine in at picnic prices. Bars and cafés are also good places to grab a meal on the go.

## Pizzerias

Pizza is cheap and readily available. Stop by a pizza shop for stand-up or takeout (many pizza places sell whole pies meant for one person; *pizza al taglio* means "by

the slice"). Supermarkets usually have a pizza counter too.

Some shops feature *pizza rustica*—thick pizza baked in a large rectangular pan and sold by weight. If you simply ask for a piece, you may wind up with a gigantic slab and be charged top euro. Instead, clearly indicate how much you want: 100 grams, or *un etto*, is a hot and cheap snack; 200 grams, or *due etti*, makes a light meal. Or show the size with your hands—*tanto così* (TAHN-toh koh-ZEE; this much). They'll often helpfully cut it up into smaller pieces. If you want your pizza warm, say *"sì"* when they ask if you want it heated up (*riscaldare;* ree-skahl-DAH-ray). For a rundown of common types of pizza, see that section, later. Pizzerias also sell *cecina,* a savory crêpe-like garbanzo-bean flatbread—a cheap snack that pairs well with a glass of red wine.

## Bars/Cafés

Italian "bars" are not taverns, but inexpensive cafés. These neighborhood hangouts serve coffee, mini pizzas *(pizzette),* sandwiches, and drinks from the cooler. This budget choice is the Italian equivalent of English pub grub.

Many bars are small—if you can't find a table, you'll need to stand or find a ledge to sit on outside. Most charge extra for table service. To get food to go, say, *"da portar via"* (for the road). All bars have a WC *(toilette, bagno)* in the back, and customers—and the discreet public—can use it.

**Food:** For quick meals, bars usually have trays of cheap, premade sandwiches (*panini,* on a baguette; *piadini,* on flatbread; or *tramezzini,* on crustless white bread)—some are delightful grilled. (Others have too much mayo.) In bigger cities, they'll have a variety of salads ready to serve up from under the glass counter. To save time for sightseeing and room for dinner, stop by a bar for a light lunch, such as a ham-and-cheese sandwich (called *toast*); have it grilled twice if you want it really hot.

**Prices and Paying:** You'll notice a two- or three-tiered pricing system. Drinking a cup of coffee while standing at the bar is cheaper than drinking it at an indoor table (you'll pay still more at an outdoor table). Many places have a *lista dei prezzi* (price list) with two columns—*al bar* and *al tavolo* (table)—posted somewhere by the bar or cash register. If you're on a budget, don't sit down without first checking out the financial consequences. Ask, "Same price if I sit or stand?" by saying, *"Costa uguale al tavolo o al banco?"* (KOH-stah oo-GWAH-lay ahl TAH-voh-loh oh ahl BAHN-koh). Throughout Italy, you can get cheap coffee at the bar of any establishment, no matter how fancy, and pay the same low, government-regulated price (generally about a euro if you stand).

If the bar isn't busy, you can probably just order and pay when you leave. Otherwise: 1) Decide what you want; 2) find out the price by checking the price list on the wall, the prices posted near the food, or by asking the barista; 3) pay the cashier; and 4) give the receipt to the barista (whose clean fingers handle no dirty euros) and tell him or her what you want.

### *Tavola Calda* Bars and *Rosticcerie*

For a fast and cheap lunch, find an Italian variation on the corner deli: a *rosticceria* (specializing in roasted meats and accompanying *antipasti*) or a *tavola calda* bar (a "hot table" point-and-shoot cafeteria with a buffet spread of meat and vegetables; sometimes called *tavola fredda*, or "cold table," in the north of Italy). For a healthy light meal, ask for a mixed plate of vegetables with a hunk of mozzarella (*piatto misto di verdure con mozzarella*; pee-AH-toh MEE-stoh dee vehr-DOO-ray). Don't be limited by what's displayed. If you'd like a salad with a slice of cantaloupe and a hunk of cheese, they'll whip that up for you in a snap. Belly up to the bar; with a pointing finger, you can assemble a fine meal. If something's a mystery, ask for *un assaggio* (oon ah-SAH-joh) to get a little taste. To have your choices warmed up, ask for them to be heated (*riscaldare*; ree-skahl-DAH-ray).

### Wine Bars

Wine bars *(enoteche)* are a popular, fast, and inexpensive option for lunch. Surrounded by the office crowd, you can get a salad, a plate of meats (cold cuts) and cheeses, and a glass of good wine (see blackboards for the day's selection and price per glass). A good *enoteca* aims to impress visitors with its wine, and will generally feature excellent-quality ingredients for the simple dishes it offers with the wine (though the prices add up—be careful with your ordering to keep this a budget choice). For more on Italian cocktails and wines, see the "Beverages" section, later.

### *Aperitivo* Buffets

The Italian term *aperitivo* means a predinner drink, but it's also

PRACTICALITIES

used to describe their version of what we might call happy hour: a light buffet that many bars serve to customers during the predinner hours (typically around 18:00 or 19:00 until 21:00). The drink itself may not be cheap (typically around €8-12), but bars lay out an enticing array of meats, cheeses, grilled vegetables, and other *antipasti*-type dishes, and you're welcome to nibble to your heart's content while you nurse your drink. While it's intended as an appetizer course before heading out for a full dinner, light eaters could discreetly turn this into a small meal. Bars advertising *"apericena"* (*cena* means dinner) tend to have buffets hearty enough to pass as dinner. Drop by a few bars around this time to scope out their buffets before choosing.

## Markets, Groceries, and Delis: Assembling a Picnic

Picnicking saves lots of euros and is a great way to sample regional specialties. A picnic can even be an adventure in high cuisine. Be daring. Try the fresh ricotta, *presto* pesto, shriveled olives, and any regional specialties the locals are excited about.

**Markets:** For the most colorful experience, gather your ingredients in the morning at a produce market. Towns big and small have markets selling everything imaginable for a fantastic picnic, including cheese, meat, bread, sweets, and prepared foods. You'll often find street-food stalls tucked into the marketplace as well (note that many stalls close in the early afternoon).

**Groceries and Delis:** Another budget option is to visit a supermarket (look for the Conad, Carrefour, and Co-op chains), *alimentari* (neighborhood grocery), or *salumeria* (delicatessen) to pick up cold cuts, cheeses, and other picnic supplies. Some grocery stores, *salumerie,* and any *paninoteca* or *focacceria* (sandwich shop) can make a sandwich to order. Just point to what you want, and they'll stuff it into a *panino.* Almost every grocery store has a deli case with prepared items like stuffed peppers, lasagna, olives, or chicken, all usually sold by weight; if you want it reheated, remember the word *riscaldare* (ree-skahl-DAH-ray). And *rosticcerie* sell cheap food to go—you'll find options such as lasagna, rotisserie chicken, and sides including roasted potatoes and spinach. For more on *salumi* and cheeses, see those sections, later.

**Ordering:** A typical picnic for two might be fresh rolls, *un etto* (3.5 ounces) of cheese, and *un etto* of meat (sometimes ordered by the slice—*fetta*—or piece—*pezzo*). For two people, I might get *un etto* of prosciutto and *due pezzi* of bread. Add two tomatoes,

three carrots, two apples, yogurt, and a liter box of juice. Total: about €10.

If ordering *antipasti* (such as grilled or marinated veggies) at a deli counter, you can ask for *una porzione* in a takeaway container *(contenitore)*. Use gestures to show exactly how much you want. To set a price limit of 5 or 10 euros on what you order, say *"Da [cinque/dieci] euro, per favore."* The word *basta* (BAH-stah; enough) works as a question or as a statement.

Shopkeepers are happy to sell small quantities of produce, but it's customary to let the merchant choose for you. Say *"per oggi"* (pehr OH-jee; for today) and he or she will grab you something ready to eat. To avoid being overcharged, know the cost per kilo, study the weighing procedure, and do the arithmetic. Remember that a kilo is 2.2 pounds.

## ITALIAN CUISINE STAPLES

Much of your Italian eating experience will likely involve the big five: pizza, pasta, *salumi*, cheese, and gelato. Here's a rundown on what you might find on menus and in stores. I've included specifics on regional cuisine throughout this book. For more food help, try a menu translator, such as the *Rick Steves Italian Phrase Book & Dictionary,* which has a menu decoder and plenty of useful phrases for navigating the culinary scene.

### Pizza

Here are some of the pizzas you might see at restaurants or at a pizzeria. Note that if you ask for pepperoni on your pizza, you'll get *peperoni* (green or red peppers, not sausage); request *diavola*, *salsiccia piccante,* or *salame piccante* instead (the closest thing in Italy to American pepperoni).

**Bianca:** White pizza with no tomatoes

**Capricciosa:** Prosciutto, mushrooms, olives, and artichokes—literally the chef's "caprice"

**Funghi:** Mushrooms

**Margherita:** Tomato sauce, mozzarella, and basil—the red, white, and green of the Italian flag

**Marinara:** Tomato sauce, oregano, garlic, no cheese

**Napoletana:** Mozzarella, anchovies, and tomato sauce

**Ortolana** or **vegetariana:** "Greengrocer-style," with vegetables

**Quattro formaggi:** Four different cheeses

**Quattro stagioni:** Different toppings on each of the four quarters

**PRACTICALITIES**

## Eating with the Seasons Across Italy

Italian cooks love to serve fresh produce and seafood at its tastiest. Each region in Italy has its seasonal specialties, which you'll see displayed in open-air markets. To get a plate of the freshest veggies at a fine restaurant, request *"Un piatto di verdure della stagione, per favore."* ("A plate of seasonal vegetables, please.") Italians take fresh, seasonal ingredients so seriously that a restaurant cooking with frozen ingredients *(congelato)* must note it on the menu. Here are a few examples of what's fresh when:

**April-May:** Calamari (Venice), romanesco (similar to cauliflower), fava beans (Rome), green beans, artichokes

**April-May and Sept-Oct:** Black truffles

**April-June:** Asparagus, zucchini flowers, zucchini

**May-June:** Mussels, cantaloupe, loquats, strawberries

**May-Aug:** Eggplant, clams

**July-Sept:** Figs

**Oct-Nov:** Mushrooms, white truffles, persimmons, chestnuts

**Nov-Feb:** Radicchio (Venice), cardoon (wild artichoke), *puntarelle* (chicory shoots; Rome)

## Pasta

While we think of pasta as a main dish, in Italy it's considered a *primo piatto*—first course. There are more than 600 varieties of Italian pasta, and each is specifically used to highlight a certain sauce, meat, or regional ingredient. Most pastas in Italy are made fresh.

Italian pasta falls into two broad categories: *pasta lunga* (long pasta) and *pasta corta* (short pasta).

*Pasta lunga* can be round, such as *capellini* (thin "little hairs"), *vermicelli* ("little worms"), and *bucatini* (long and hollow), or it can be flat, such as *linguine* (narrow "little tongues"), *fettuccine* (wider "small ribbons"), *tagliatelle* (even wider), and *pappardelle* (very wide, best with meat sauces).

The most common *pasta corta* are tubes, such as *penne, rigatoni, ziti, manicotti,* and *cannelloni;* they come either *lisce* (smooth) or *rigate* (grooved—better to catch and cling to sauce). Many short pastas are named for their shapes, such as *conchiglie* (shells), *farfalle* (butterflies), or *cavatappi* (corkscrews).

Here's a list of common pasta toppings and sauces. On a menu, these terms are usually preceded by *alla* (in the style of) or *in* (in):

*Aglio e olio:* Garlic and olive oil

*Alfredo:* Butter, cream, and parmesan

*Amatriciana:* Pork cheek, *pecorino romano* cheese, and tomato

*Arrabbiata:* "Angry," spicy tomato sauce with chili peppers

*Bolognese:* Meat and tomato sauce

*Boscaiola:* Mushrooms and sausage

*Burro e salvia:* Butter and sage

*Cacio e pepe: Pecorino romano* cheese and ground pepper

*Carbonara:* Bacon, egg, cheese, and pepper

*Carrettiera:* Spicy and garlicky, with olive oil and little tomatoes

*Diavola:* "Devil-style," spicy hot

*Frutti di mare:* Seafood

*Genovese:* Basil ground with *parmigiano* cheese, garlic, pine nuts, and olive oil; a.k.a. pesto

*Gricia:* Cured pork cheek and *pecorino romano* cheese

*Marinara:* Usually tomato, often with garlic and onions, but can also be a seafood sauce ("sailor's style")

*Norma:* Tomato, eggplant, and ricotta cheese

*Pajata:* Calf intestines (also called *pagliata*)

*Pescatora:* Seafood ("fisherman style")

*Pomodoro:* Tomato only

*Puttanesca:* Tomato sauce with anchovies, olives, and capers

*Ragù:* Meaty tomato sauce

*Scoglio:* Mussels, clams, and tomatoes

*Sorrentina:* "Sorrento-style," with tomatoes, basil, and mozzarella (usually over gnocchi)

*Sugo di lepre:* Rich sauce made of wild hare

*Tartufi:* Truffles (also called *tartufate*)

*Umbria:* Sauce of anchovies, garlic, tomatoes, and truffles

*Vongole:* Clams and spices

## Salumi

*Salumi* (cured meats), also called *affettati* (sliced meats), are an Italian staple. While most American cold cuts are cooked, in Italy they're far more commonly cured by air-drying, salting, and smoking. (Don't worry; these so-called "raw" meats are safe to eat, and you can really taste the difference.)

The two most familiar types of *salumi* are *salame* and *prosciutto. Salame* is an air-dried, sometimes-spicy sausage that comes in many varieties. When Italians say *"prosciutto,"* they usually mean *prosciutto crudo*—the raw ham that air-cures on the hock and is then thinly sliced. Produced mainly in the north of Italy, *prosciutto* can be either *dolce* (sweet) or *salato* (salty). Purists say the best is *prosciutto di Parma.*

Other *salumi* may be less familiar. If you've got a weak stomach, avoid *testa in cassetta* (headcheese—organs in aspic) and *lampredotto* (cow stomach).

**Bresaola:** Air-cured beef
**Capocollo:** Peppery pork shoulder (also called *coppa*)
**Culatello:** High-quality, slow-cured prosciutto
**Finocchiona:** *Salame* with fennel seeds
**Guanciale:** Tender pork cheek
**Lonzino:** Cured pork loin
**Mortadella:** A finely ground pork loaf, similar to our bologna
**Pancetta:** Salt-cured, peppery pork-belly meat, similar to bacon
**Salame di Sant'Olcese:** What we'd call "Genoa salami"
**Salame piccante:** Spicy hot, similar to pepperoni
**Speck:** Smoked pork shoulder

## Cheese

When it comes to cheese *(formaggio)*, you're probably already familiar with most of these Italian favorites:

**Asiago:** Hard cow cheese that comes either *mezzano* (young, firm, and creamy) or *stravecchio* (aged, pungent, and granular)
**Burrata:** A creamy mozzarella
**Fontina:** Semihard, nutty, Gruyère-style mountain cheese
**Gorgonzola:** Pungent, blue-veined cheese, either *dolce* (creamy) or *stagionato* (aged and hard)
**Mascarpone:** Sweet, buttery, spreadable dessert cheese
**Mozzarella di bufala:** Made from the milk of water buffaloes
**Parmigiano-reggiano:** Hard, crumbly, sharp, aged cow cheese with more nuanced flavor than American parmesan; *grana padano* is a less expensive variation
**Pecorino:** Either *fresco* (fresh, soft, and mild) or *stagionato* (aged and sharp, sometimes called *pecorino romano*)
**Provolone:** Rich, firm, aged cow cheese
**Ricotta:** Soft, airy cheese made by "recooking" leftover whey
**Scamorza:** Similar to mozzarella, but often smoked

## Gelato

American ice cream and Italian gelato are similar but decidedly not the same. Gelato is denser and creamier (even though it has less butterfat than ice cream), and connoisseurs swear it's more flavorful.

A key to gelato appreciation is sampling liberally and choosing flavors that go well together. At a *gelateria*, ask, as Italians do, for a taste: *"Un assaggio, per favore?"* (oon ah-SAH-joh pehr fah-VOH-ray). You can also ask what flavors go well together: *"Quali gusti stanno bene insieme?"* (KWAH-lee GOO-stee STAH-noh BEH-nay een-see-EH-may).

Most *gelaterie* clearly display prices and sizes. But in the text-book *gelateria* scam, the tourist orders two or three flavors—and the clerk selects a fancy, expensive chocolate-coated waffle cone, piles it high with huge scoops, and cheerfully charges the tourist €10. To avoid rip-offs, point to the price or say what you want—for instance, a €3 cup: *"Una coppetta da tre euro"* (OO-nah koh-PEH-tah dah tray eh-OO-roh).

The best *gelaterie* display signs reading *artiginale, nostra produzione,* or *produzione propia,* indicating that the gelato is made on the premises. Seasonal flavors are also a good sign, as are mellow hues (avoid colors that don't appear in nature). Gelato stored in covered metal tins (rather than white plastic) is more likely to be homemade. Gourmet gelato shops are popping up all over Italy, selling exotic flavors. Unless it's a gelato emergency, avoid the chain called Grom—it's the Starbucks of gelato in Italy.

Gelato variations or alternatives include *sorbetto* (sorbet—made with fruit, but no milk or eggs); *granita* or *grattachecca* (a cup of slushy ice with flavored syrup); and *cremolata* (a gelato-*granita* float).

Classic gelato flavors include:

*After Eight:* Chocolate and mint
*Bacio:* Chocolate hazelnut, named for Italy's popular "kiss" candies
*Cassata:* With dried fruits
*Cioccolato:* Chocolate
*Crema:* Vanilla
*Croccantino:* "Crunchy," with toasted peanut bits
*Fior di latte:* Sweet milk
*Fragola:* Strawberry
*Macedonia:* Mixed fruits
*Malaga:* Similar to rum raisin
*Riso:* With actual bits of rice mixed in
*Stracciatella:* Vanilla with chocolate shreds
*Tartufo:* Super chocolate
*Zabaione:* Named for the egg yolk-and-Marsala wine dessert
*Zuppa inglese:* Sponge cake, custard, chocolate, and cream

## BEVERAGES

Italian bars serve great drinks—hot, cold, sweet, caffeinated, or alcoholic.

### Water, Juice, and Cold Drinks

Italians are notorious water snobs. At restaurants, your server just can't understand why you wouldn't want good water to go with your good food. It's customary and never expensive to order a *litro* or *mezzo litro* (half-liter) of bottled water. *Acqua leggermente effervescente* (lightly carbonated water) is a mealtime favorite. Or simply ask for *con gas* if you want fizzy water and *senza gas* if you prefer still water. You can ask for *acqua del rubinetto* (tap water) in restaurants, but your server may give you a funny look. Chilled bottled water—still *(naturale)* or carbonated *(frizzante)*—is sold cheap in stores. Half-liter bottles of mineral water are available everywhere for about €1. (I refill my water bottle with tap water.)

Juice is *succo*, and *spremuta* means freshly squeezed. Order *una spremuta* (don't confuse it with *spumante*, sparkling wine)—it's usually orange juice *(arancia)*, and from February through April it's almost always made from Sicilian blood oranges *(arance rosse)*.

In grocery stores, you can get a liter of O.J. for the price of a Coke or coffee. Look for *100% succo* or *senza zucchero* (without sugar) on the label—or be surprised by something diluted and sugary sweet. Hang on to your water bottles. Buy juice in cheap liter boxes, then drink some and store the extra in your water bottle.

*Tè freddo* (iced tea) is usually from a can—sweetened and flavored with lemon or peach. Lemonade is *limonata*.

## Coffee and Other Hot Drinks

The espresso-based style of coffee so popular in the US was born in Italy. If you ask for *"un caffè,"* you'll get a shot of espresso in a little cup—the closest thing to American-style drip coffee is a *caffè americano*. Most Italian coffee drinks begin with espresso, to which they add varying amounts of hot water and/or steamed or foamed milk. Milky drinks, like cappuccino or *caffè latte*, are served to locals before noon and to tourists any time of day (to an Italian, cappuccino is a morning drink; they believe having milk after a big meal or anything with tomato sauce impairs digestion). If they add any milk after lunch, it's just a splash, in a *caffè macchiato*. Italians like their coffee only warm—to get it very hot, request *"Molto caldo, per favore"* (MOHL-toh KAHL-doh pehr fah-VOH-ray). Any coffee drink is available decaffeinated—ask for it *decaffeinato* (deh-kah-feh-NAH-toh).

If you want a hot drink other than coffee, *cioccolato* is hot chocolate, and *tè* is hot tea.

**Cappuccino:** Espresso with foamed milk on top (*cappuccino freddo* is iced cappuccino)

**Caffè latte:** Espresso mixed with hot milk, no foam, in a tall glass (ordering just a "latte" gets you only milk)

**Caffè macchiato:** Espresso "marked" with a splash of milk, in a small cup

**Latte macchiato:** Layers of hot milk and foam, "marked" by an espresso shot, in a tall glass. Note that if you order simply a *"macchiato,"* you'll probably get a *caffè macchiato*.

## Ordering Wine

To order a glass of red or white wine, say, *"Un bicchiere di vino rosso/bianco."* House wine comes in a carafe; choose from a quarter-liter pitcher (8.5 oz, *un quarto*), half-liter pitcher (17 oz, *un mezzo*), or one-liter pitcher (34 oz, *un litro*). When ordering, have some fun, gesture like a local, and you'll have no problems speaking the language of the *enoteca. Salute!*

| English | Italian |
|---|---|
| wine | *vino* (VEE-noh) |
| house wine | *vino della casa* (VEE-noh DEH-lah KAH-zah) |
| glass | *bicchiere* (bee-kee-EH-ray) |
| bottle | *bottiglia* (boh-TEEL-yah) |
| carafe | *caraffa* (kah-RAH-fah) |
| red | *rosso* (ROH-soh) |
| white | *bianco* (bee-AHN-koh) |
| rosé | *rosato* (roh-ZAH-toh) |
| sparkling | *spumante/frizzante* (spoo-MAHN-tay/freed-ZAHN-tay) |
| dry | *secco* (SEH-koh) |
| fruity | *fruttato* (froo-TAH-toh) |
| full-bodied | *corposo/pieno* (kor-POH-zoh/pee-EH-noh) |
| sweet | *dolce* (DOHL-chay) |

***Caffè corto/lungo:*** Concentrated espresso diluted with a tiny bit of hot water, in a small cup

***Caffè americano:*** Espresso diluted with even more hot water, in a larger cup

***Caffè corretto:*** Espresso "corrected" with a shot of liqueur (normally grappa, *amaro*, or *sambuca*)

***Marocchino:*** "Moroccan" coffee with espresso, foamed milk, and cocoa powder; the similar *mocaccino* has chocolate instead of cocoa

***Caffè freddo:*** Sweet and iced espresso

***Caffè hag:*** Instant decaf

## Alcoholic Beverages

**Beer:** While Italy is traditionally considered wine country, in recent years there's been a huge and passionate growth in the production of craft beer *(birra artigianale)*. Even in small towns, you'll see microbreweries slinging their own brews. You'll also find local brews (Peroni and Moretti), as well as imports such as Heineken. Italians drink mainly lager beers. Beer on tap is *alla spina*. Get it *piccola* (33 cl, 11 oz), *media* (50 cl, about a pint), or *grande* (a liter).

# Regional Wines

In almost every part of Italy, you'll find wine varieties designed to go with the regional cuisine.

**Tuscany** (Florence, Siena, and Nearby): Many Tuscan wines are made with the native sangiovese grape, including the well-known Chiantis, which range from cheap basket-bottles of table wine (called *fiaschi*) to the hearty Chianti Classico. Vino Nobile di Montepulciano is a high-quality dry ruby red. One of Italy's top reds is the smooth Brunello di Montalcino; a cheaper, younger "baby Brunello" is Rosso di Montalcino. Pricey Super Tuscans blend traditional grapes with locally grown non-Italian grapes (such as cabernet or merlot). The best white choice is the crisp Vernaccia di San Gimignano; trebbiano and vermentino are other local white grapes. Sweet and syrupy, vin santo dessert wine is often served with a cookie for dipping.

**Veneto** (near Venice): Valpolicella grapes are used to make red table wines as well as rich red Amarone and sweet Recioto dessert wine (both made from dried—*passito*—grapes). Whites include Soave, Pinot Grigio, and Bianco di Custoza. If you like bubbles, try sweet, fizzy Fragolino or prosecco (connoisseurs say the best hails from Valdobbiadene).

**Umbria** (Assisi, Orvieto, and Nearby): Trebbiano is this region's main white grape; look for golden, dry Orvieto Classico. For reds, consider Sagrantino de Montefalco or Torgiano Rosso Riserva. Wines from the quality producer Lungarotti are worth trying.

**Liguria** (Italian Riviera, including Cinque Terre): This coastal region produces light, delicate whites from native bosco grapes. Sossese di Dolceacqua is a medium-bodied red. After dinner, try

A *lattina* (lah-TEE-nah) is a can and a *bottiglia* (boh-TEEL-yah) is a bottle.

**Cocktails and Spirits:** Italians appreciate both *aperitivi* (palate-stimulating cocktails) and *digestivi* (after-dinner drinks designed to aid digestion). Popular *aperitivo* options include Campari (carmine-red bitters with herbs and orange peel), Americano (vermouth with bitters, brandy, and lemon peel), Cynar (bitters flavored with artichoke), Aperol (bright orange bitters with herbal, citrusy undertones) and Punt e Mes (sweet red vermouth and red wine). Widely used vermouth brands include Cinzano and Martini.

*Digestivo* choices are usually either strong herbal bitters or something sweet. Many restaurants have their own secret recipe for a bittersweet herbal brew called *amaro;* popular commercial brands are Fernet Branca and Montenegro. If your tastes run sweeter, try any of these flavored liqueurs: *amaretto* (almond), Frangelico (hazelnut), *limoncello* (lemon), *nocino* (walnut), *sambuca* (anise), or a

the potent, amber-colored Sciacchetrà.

**Lazio** (Rome and Nearby): The majority of wines produced in this region are white, most often made with trebbiano or malvasia grapes; the most popular is Frascati. For a red, try the medium-bodied Torre Ercolana.

**Dolomites:** While beer is king here, look for reds like the robust Santa Magdalaner and fruity Lagrein Scuro, or whites like Pinot Grigio, Gewürztraminer, and Pinot Blanc. Nosiola is an aromatic local grape used for dessert and sparkling wine.

**Piedmont** (near Milan and the Lakes): This region specializes in bold, dry reds. Nebbiolo is the main red grape, used in big, tannic Barolo or its elegant "little brother," Barbaresco. For lighter, fruitier reds, try Barbera or Dolcetto. Whites include the dry Gavi and flowery Arneis. For bubbly wines, sample sweet Brachetto, semisweet Moscato d'Asti (slightly fizzy), or dry Asti Spumante.

**Campania** (Naples, Sorrento, and Nearby): Plentiful sun and volcanic soils provide great wine-growing conditions. Taurasi is an excellent ruby-colored, full-bodied red. Lacryma Christi ("tears of Christ") comes in both a medium-bodied red and a dry and fruity white. Campanian whites include the mineral Greco di Tufo and flavorful Fiano di Avellino.

**Sicily:** The main red is the full-bodied Nero d'Avola. Corvo, Regaleali, and Planeta are some established producers. White wines use indigenous grapes like grillo, inzolio, and catarrato. Try fruity Bianca d'Alcamo and dry Etna Bianco. Marsala is a (usually) sweet fortified dessert wine.

sweet Marsala wine. Grappa is a brandy distilled from grape skins and stems; *stravecchio* is an aged, mellower variation.

**Wine:** The ancient Greeks who colonized Italy more than 2,000 years ago called it Oenotria—land of the grape. Centuries later, Galileo wrote, "Wine is light held together by water." Wine *(vino)* is certainly a part of the Italian culinary trinity—grape, olive, and wheat. (I'd add gelato.) Ideal conditions for grapes (warm climate, well-draining soil, and an abundance of hillsides) make the Italian peninsula a paradise for grape growers, winemakers, and wine drinkers.

Even if you're clueless about wine, the information on an Italian wine label can help you choose something decent. Terms you may see on the bottle include *classico* (from a defined, select area), *annata* (year of harvest), *vendemmia* (harvest), and *imbottigliato dal produttore all'origine* (bottled by producers).

In general, Italy designates its wines by one of four official categories:

***Vino da Tavola*** (VDT) is table wine, the lowest grade, made from grapes grown anywhere in Italy. It's often inexpensive, but Italy's wines are so good that, for many people, a basic *vino da tavola* is just fine with a meal. Many restaurants, even modest ones, take pride in their house wine *(vino della casa)*, bottling their own or working with wineries.

***Denominazione di Origine Controllata*** (DOC) meets national standards for high-quality wine. Made from grapes grown in a defined area, it's usually quite affordable and good. Hundreds of wines have earned the DOC designation.

***Denominazione di Origine Controllata e Guarantita*** (DOCG), the highest grade, meets national standards for the highest-quality wine (made with grapes from a defined area whose quality is "guaranteed"). These wines can be identified by the pink or green label on the neck...and the scary price tag on the shelf. They're generally a good bet if you want a quality wine. (*Riserva* indicates a DOC or DOCG wine that's been aged for even longer than required.)

***Indicazione Geografica Tipica*** (IGT) is a broad group of wines that don't meet the standard for DOC or DOCG status, but have been designated as "typical" of a particular region.

# Staying Connected

One of the most common questions I hear from travelers is, "How can I stay connected in Europe?" The short answer is: more easily and cheaply than you might think.

The simplest solution is to bring your own device—mobile phone, tablet, or laptop—and use it just as you would at home (following the money-saving tips below, such as getting an international plan or connecting to free Wi-Fi whenever possible). Another option is to buy a European SIM card for your US mobile phone. Or you can use European landlines and computers to connect. Each of these options is described next, and more details are at RickSteves.com/phoning. For a very practical one-hour talk covering tech issues for travelers, see RickSteves.com/mobile-travel-skills.

## USING A MOBILE PHONE IN EUROPE

Here are some budget tips and options.

**Sign up for an international plan.** To stay connected at a lower cost, sign up for an international service plan through your

## Hurdling the Language Barrier

Many Italians—especially those in the tourist trade and in big cities—speak English. Still, you'll get better treatment if you learn and use Italian pleasantries. In smaller, nontouristy towns, Italian is the norm. Italians have an endearing habit of talking to you even if they know you don't speak their language—and yet, thanks to gestures and thoughtfully simplified words, it somehow works. Don't stop them to tell them you don't understand every word—just go along for the ride. For a list of survival phrases, see the appendix.

Note that Italian is pronounced much like English, with a few exceptions, such as: *c* followed by *e* or *i* is pronounced ch (to ask, *"Per centro?"* "To the center?" you say, pehr CHEHN-troh). In Italian, *ch* followed by *e* or *i* is pronounced like the hard c in Chianti (*chiesa*—church—is pronounced kee-AY-zah). Adding a vowel to the English word often gets you close to the Italian one. Give it your best shot. Italians appreciate your efforts.

For more tips on hurdling the language barrier, consider the *Rick Steves Italian Phrase Book & Dictionary* (available at www.ricksteves.com).

carrier. Most providers offer a simple bundle that includes calling, messaging, and data. Your normal plan may already include international coverage (T-Mobile's does).

Before your trip, call your provider or check online to confirm that your phone will work in Europe, and research your provider's international rates. Activate the plan a day or two before you leave, then remember to cancel it when your trip's over.

**Use free Wi-Fi whenever possible.** Unless you have an unlimited-data plan, you're best off saving most of your online tasks for Wi-Fi. You can access the internet, send texts, and even make voice calls over Wi-Fi.

Most accommodations in Europe offer free Wi-Fi, but some—especially expensive hotels—charge a fee. Many cafés have free hotspots for customers; look for signs offering it and ask for the Wi-Fi password when you buy something. You'll also often find Wi-Fi at TIs, city squares, major museums, public-transit hubs, airports, and aboard trains and buses.

**Minimize the use of your cellular network.** The best way to make sure you're not accidentally burning through data is to put your device in "airplane" mode (which also disables phone calls and texts), turn your Wi-Fi back on, and connect to networks as needed. When you need to get online but can't find Wi-Fi, simply turn on your cellular network (or turn off airplane mode) just long enough for the task at hand.

**PRACTICALITIES**

## How to Dial

### International Calls

Whether phoning from a US landline or mobile phone, or from a number in another European country, here's how to make an international call. I've used one of my recommended Florence hotels as an example (tel. 055-213-154).

**Initial Zero:** Drop the initial zero from international phone numbers—except when calling Italy.

**Mobile Tip:** If using a mobile phone, the "+" sign can replace the international access code (for a "+" sign, press and hold "0").

### US/Canada to Europe

Dial 011 (US/Canada international access code), country code (39 for Italy), and phone number.

▸ To call the Florence hotel from home, dial 011-39-055-213-154.

### Country to Country Within Europe

Dial 00 (Europe international access code), country code, and phone number.

▸ To call the Florence hotel from Germany, dial 00-39-055-213-154.

### Europe to the US/Canada

Dial 00, country code (1 for US/Canada), and phone number.

▸ To call from Europe to my office in Edmonds, Washington, dial 00-1-425-771-8303.

### Domestic Calls

To call within Italy (from one Italian landline or mobile phone to another), simply dial the phone number, including the initial 0 if there is one.

▸ To call the Florence hotel from Rome, dial 055-213-154.

Even with an international data plan, wait until you're on Wi-Fi to Skype, download apps, stream videos, or do other megabyte-greedy tasks. Using a navigation app such as Google Maps over a cellular network can take lots of data, so do this sparingly or offline.

Limit automatic updates. By default, your device constantly checks for a data connection and updates apps. It's smart to disable these features so your apps will only update when you're on Wi-Fi. Also change your device's email settings from "auto-retrieve" to "manual" (or from "push" to "fetch").

**Use Wi-Fi calling and messaging apps.** Skype, WhatsApp, FaceTime, and Google Hangouts are great for making free or low-cost calls or sending texts over Wi-Fi worldwide. Just log on to a Wi-Fi network, then connect with any of your friends or family members who use the same service. If you buy credit in advance,

## More Dialing Tips

**Italian Phone Numbers:** Italian phone numbers vary in length; a hotel can have, say, an eight-digit phone number. Italy's landlines start with 0; mobile lines start with 3.

**More Phoning Help:** See www.howtocallabroad.com.

| European Country Codes | | Ireland & N. Ireland | 353/44 |
|---|---|---|---|
| Austria | 43 | Italy | 39 |
| Belgium | 32 | Latvia | 371 |
| Bosnia-Herzegovina | 387 | Montenegro | 382 |
| Croatia | 385 | Morocco | 212 |
| Czech Republic | 420 | Netherlands | 31 |
| Denmark | 45 | Norway | 47 |
| Estonia | 372 | Poland | 48 |
| Finland | 358 | Portugal | 351 |
| France | 33 | Russia | 7 |
| Germany | 49 | Slovakia | 421 |
| Gibraltar | 350 | Slovenia | 386 |
| Great Britain | 44 | Spain | 34 |
| Greece | 30 | Sweden | 46 |
| Hungary | 36 | Switzerland | 41 |
| Iceland | 354 | Turkey | 90 |

PRACTICALITIES

with some of these services you can call or text anywhere for just pennies.

Some apps, such as Apple's iMessage, will use the cellular network for texts if Wi-Fi isn't available: To avoid this possibility, turn off the "Send as SMS" feature.

**Buy a European SIM Card.** If you anticipate making a lot of local calls or need a local phone number, or if your provider's international data rates are expensive, consider buying a SIM card in Europe to replace the one in your (unlocked) US phone or tablet.

In Italy, buy SIM cards at mobile-phone shops. You'll be required to register the SIM card with your passport as an antiterrorism measure (which may mean you can't use the phone for the first hour or two).

There are no roaming charges when using a European SIM card in other EU countries, though to be sure you get this "roam-

---

## Tips on Internet Security

Make sure that your device is running the latest versions of its operating system, security software, and apps. Next, ensure that your device and key programs (like email) are password-protected. On the road, use only secure, password-protected Wi-Fi hotspots. Ask the hotel or café staff for the specific name of their Wi-Fi network, and make sure you log on to that exact one.

If you must access your financial info online, use a banking app rather than accessing your account via a browser. A cellular connection is more secure than Wi-Fi. Avoid logging onto personal finance sites on a public computer.

Never share your credit-card number (or any other sensitive information) online unless you know that the site is secure. A secure site displays a little padlock icon, and the URL begins with *https* (instead of the usual *http*).

---

like-at-home" pricing, ask if this feature is included when you buy your SIM card.

### WITHOUT A MOBILE PHONE

It's less convenient but possible to travel in Europe without a mobile device. You can make calls from your hotel and check email or get online using public computers.

Most **hotels** charge a fee for placing calls—ask for rates before you dial. You can use a prepaid international phone card (*carta telefonica prepagata internazionale*—usually available at newsstands, tobacco shops, and train stations) to call out from your hotel. Dial the toll-free access number, enter the card's PIN code, then dial the number.   You'll only see **public pay phones** in a few post offices and train stations. Most don't take coins but instead require insertable phone cards, which you can buy at a newsstand, convenience store, or post office. Except for emergencies, they're not worth the hassle.

Some hotels have **public computers** in their lobbies for guests to use; otherwise you may find them at public libraries (ask your hotelier or the TI for the nearest location). On a European keyboard, use the "Alt Gr" key to the right of the space bar to insert the extra symbol that appears on some keys. If you can't locate a special character (such as @), simply copy and paste it from a web page.

### MAIL

You can mail one package per day to yourself worth up to $200 duty-free from Europe to the US (mark it "personal purchases"). If you're sending a gift to someone, mark it "unsolicited gift." For details, visit www.cbp.gov, select "Travel," and search for "Know Before You Visit." The Italian postal service works fine, but for quick transatlantic delivery (in either direction), consider services such as DHL (www.dhl.com).

# Transportation

Figuring out how to get around in Europe is one of your biggest trip decisions. **Cars** work well for two or more traveling together (especially families with small kids), those packing heavy, and those delving into the countryside. **Trains** and **buses** are best for solo travelers, blitz tourists, city-to-city travelers, and those who want to leave the driving to others. Smart travelers can use short-hop **flights** within Europe to creatively connect the dots on their itineraries. Just be aware of the potential downside of each option: A car is an expensive headache in any major city; with trains and buses you're at the mercy of a timetable; and flying entails a trek to and from a usually distant airport.

If your itinerary mixes cities and countryside, my advice is to connect cities by train or bus and to explore rural areas by rental car. Arrange to pick up your car in the last big city you'll visit, then use it to lace together small towns and explore the countryside. For more detailed information on transportation throughout Europe, see www.ricksteves.com/transportation.

## TRAINS

To travel by train affordably within Italy, you can simply buy tickets as you go. For travelers ready to lock in dates and times weeks or months in advance, buying nonrefundable tickets online can cut costs in half. Note that the Italy rail pass is generally not a good value, but if your travel extends beyond Italy, there are multi-country rail passes that might be worth checking into. For advice on figuring out the smartest train-ticket or rail-pass options for your trip, visit the Trains & Rail Passes section of my website at RickSteves.com/rail.

### Types of Trains

Most trains in Italy are operated by the state-run **Trenitalia** company (www.trenitalia.com, a.k.a. Ferrovie dello Stato Italiane, abbreviated FS). Ticket prices depend on the speed of the train, so it helps to know the differ-

PRACTICALITIES

# Italy's Public Transportation

To Innsbruck
San Candido
Brennero
SWITZERLAND
St. Moritz          Cast.
Locarno
Bolzano
Geneva      Lugano      Tirano      DOLO-
Men.                    MITES
Domo-        Varenna    Trento
dossola      Como       Riva
Chamonix    Stresa
Pré-Saint-              Bergamo    Vicenza
Didier      Gallarate
La Palud    Malpensa ✈  Milan      Desezano   Verona
Aosta                  Cremona
To Lyon &              Mantova
Paris
Modane      Torino                 Parma      Modena
Genoa       Santa                  Bologna
Margherita
To          FRANCE      Ligure
Paris       Finale      Vernazza   Florence
Marseille                          Lucca ✈
CINQUE      Pisa
TERRE
Ventimiglia             La Spezia  San
Livorno    Gim.
To          Nice       Ligurian             Volterra
Barcelona              Sea                   Poggi.
                                  Siena
Bastia
See Hill Towns         ELBA   Piombino
Public Transportation
detail map             Civitavecchia
C O R S I C A
(F R A N C E)
Mediterranean
Sea
Porto
Torres     Olbia
100 Kilometers
S A R D I N I A
100 Miles
Chilivani

To Cagliari    To Naples    To      To
Aeolian   Naples
To Tunis               Islands  & Rome
Milazzo    Messina
Palermo ✈              Villa San
Trapani     Cefalù             Giovanni
Marsala                        Reggio
SICILY     Calabria   To
Castelvetrano  Enna               Cagliari
Taormina
Agrigento              Catania ✈  Ionian
Sea        See
detail map
Mediterranean  Piazza             To
Sea        Armerina   Siracusa   Tunis
Same scale as main map  Ragusa

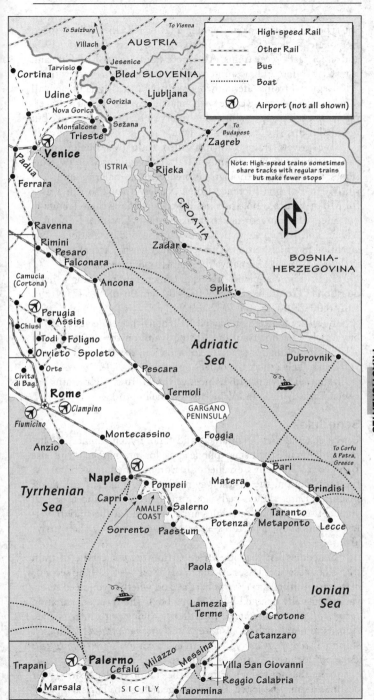

ent types of trains: pokey Regionale (R or REG); medium-speed Regionale Veloce (RV); fast InterCity (IC) and EuroCity (EC); and super-fast Frecce trains. All Frecce trains, many EuroCity and InterCity trains, and most international trains require reservations.

Regional trains offer only open seating (no assigned seats); all other classes of service come with an assigned seat. If you're traveling with a rail pass, you'll need to reserve a seat for any service but regional trains (see "Rail Passes," later).

The private train company called **Italo** (www.italotreno.it) runs fast trains on major routes in Italy. Italo is focused on two corridors: Venice-Padua-Bologna-Florence-Rome-Salerno and Turin-Milan-Bologna-Florence-Rome-Naples. They also run a useful Milan-Venice train. Italo has fewer departures than Trenitalia but offers discounts for tickets booked well in advance. In Naples, Milan, and Rome, some departures use secondary stations—pay attention to which station you need. Italo does not accept rail passes, but is a worthy alternative for point-to-point tickets.

Both train companies have call centers for answering general questions (**Trenitalia:** daily 7:00-24:00, tel. 06-6847-5475; **Italo:** daily 6:00-23:00, tel. 06-8937-1892).

Be aware that Trenitalia and Italo don't cooperate at all. If you buy a ticket for one train line, it's not valid on the other. Even if you're just looking for schedule information, the company you ask will most likely ignore the other's options.

Another private train company, **Thello,** runs night trains between Paris, Milan, and Venice (www.thello.com).

## Schedules

Check schedules at Trenitalia.it and ItaloTreno.it (domestic journeys only) or use their smartphone apps; for international trips, use Bahn.com (Germany's excellent all-Europe schedule website). At the train station, the easiest way to check schedules is at a ticket machine. Enter the desired date, time, and destination to see all your options. Printed schedules are also posted at the station (yellow posters show departures—*partenze;* white posters show arrivals).

Schedules list the time of departure *(ora),* the type of train *(treni),* and service classes offered *(classi servizi)*—first- and second-class cars, dining car, *cuccetta* berths, and whether you need reservations (usually denoted by an R in a box). The train's destination *(principali fermate destinazioni)* is shown, along with intermediate stops, and notes such as "also stops in..." *(ferma anche a...),* "doesn't stop in..." *(non ferma a...),* "stops in every station" *(ferma in tutte le stazioni),* "delayed..." *(ritardo...),* and so on.

Note that for today's trains on the station reader boards, your destination may be listed as an intermediate stop. For example, if you're going from Milan to Florence, scan the schedule and you'll notice that virtually all the trains that terminate in Naples or Salerno stop in Florence en route (but most terminating in Rome do not). The reader board also lists the track *(binario)* the train departs from. If you're not sure, confirm the *binario* with a ticket seller or railway official, or check monitors on the platform.

## Point-to-Point Tickets

Train tickets are a good value in Italy. Typical fares are shown on the map on page 1193, though ticket prices can vary for the same journey, mainly depending on the time of day, the speed of the train, and advance discounts.

**Classes of Service:** Frecce and Italo trains each offer several classes of service (e.g., Standard, Premium, Business, Executive) where all seats are reserved. Other trains offer standard first- and second-class seating (with first class costing up to 50 percent more than second). Buying up gives you a little more elbow room, a snack, or perhaps a better chance at seating a group together, if you're buying on short notice.

**Advance Discounts:** Ticket price levels are Base (full fare, easily changeable or partly refundable before scheduled departure), Economy (one schedule change allowed before departure, for a fee), and Super Economy or Low Cost (sells out quickly, no refunds or exchanges). For example, traveling Standard class from Rome to Florence on the fastest train costs €50 at Base fare, €36 at Economy fare, or €28 at Super Economy rate. Discounted fares typically sell out several weeks before departure. Fares labeled *servizi abbonati* are available only for locals with monthly passes—not tourists. Regional trains don't offer advance discounts or seat assignments, so there's little need to buy those tickets in advance.

**Speed vs. Savings:** For point-to-point tickets, you'll pay more the faster you go. Spending a modest amount of extra time in transit can save money. On longer, mainline routes, fast trains save more time and provide most of the service. For example, speedy Florence-Rome trains run about 3/hour, cost €50 in second class, and make the trip in 1.5 hours, while infrequent InterCity trains (only 1-2/day) cost €37 and take three hours.

**Age-Based Discounts:** Discounts for kids don't usually beat the Super Economy rate described above. If the cheapest tickets are no longer available, look for deals like "Bimbi Gratis" and "Offerta Famiglia." Other discounts for youths and seniors require purchase of a separate card (€40 Carta Verde for ages 12-26, €30 Carta Argento for ages 60 and over), but the ticket discount is so minor (10-15 percent respectively for domestic travel), it's not worth it for most.

## Buying Point-to-Point Tickets

You can buy tickets online, with a smartphone app, at train station ticket windows, from ticket machines, or at travel agencies. For long-haul runs or travel on a busy weekend or holiday, it can be cheaper to buy tickets in advance. But because most Italian trains run frequently and there's no deadline to buy tickets, for the most part I prefer to keep my travel plans flexible by purchasing tickets as I go. (You can buy tickets for several trips when you are ready to commit.)

It's easy to buy tickets **online** at Trenitalia.com or ItaloTreno.it. On either website, choose English and be sure to read the pricing info, as many of the cheaper tickets are not refundable or changeable. You can keep the ticket on your mobile device (either as a PDF or in a "ticketless" format with a booking code), or you can print it out.

Or download the Trenitalia or Italo app to your **smartphone**—both have English versions. If using the Trenitalia app to buy tickets, do so as a guest (a log-in isn't necessary—or possible—if you don't live in Italy).

If you instead go to the train station to buy tickets, you can avoid ticket-office lines by using the **ticket machines** in station halls. You'll be able to easily purchase tickets for travel within Italy, make seat reservations, and even book a *cuccetta* (koo-CHEH-tah; overnight berth). If you do use the **ticket windows** (e.g., to buy international tickets), be sure you're in the correct line. Key terms: *biglietti* (general tickets), *prenotazioni* (reservations), *nazionali* (domestic), and *internazionali*.

**Trenitalia**'s ticket machines are user-friendly and found in all but the tiniest stations in Italy. You can pay with cash (change given when indicated) or by debit or credit card (even for small amounts, but you may need to enter your PIN). Select English, then your destination. If you don't immediately see the city you're traveling to, keep keying in the spelling until it's listed. You can choose from first- and second-class seats, request tickets for more than one traveler, and pick seats, when applicable. Don't select a discount rate without being sure that you meet the criteria (for example, Americans are not eligible for certain EU or resident discounts).

To buy tickets at the station for **Italo** trains, look for a dedicated service counter (in most major stations) or a red ticket machine labeled *Italo*.

Some **international tickets** can't be bought online or from machines; for these tickets and anything else that requires a real person, you must go to a ticket window at the station. A good alternative, though, is to drop by a local travel agency. Agencies sell domestic and international tickets and make reservations. They

# Rail Pass or Point-to-Point Tickets?

Will you be better off buying a rail pass or point-to-point tickets? It pays to know your options and choose what's best for your itinerary.

### Rail Passes

A Eurail Italy Pass lets you travel by train in Italy for three to eight days (consecutively or not) within a one-month period. Italy is also covered (along with most of Europe) by the classic Eurail Global Pass.

Discounted rates are offered for seniors (age 60 and up) and youths (ages 12-27). Up to two kids (ages 4-11) can travel free with each adult-rate pass (but not with senior rates). All rail passes offer a choice of first or second class for all ages.

Rail passes are best purchased outside Europe (through travel agents or Rick Steves' Europe). For more on rail passes, including current prices, visit RickSteves.com/rail.

### Point-to-Point Tickets

Italian train tickets are relatively cheap, and most include seat reservations, making them the best deal for most travelers. Use this map to add up approximate pay-as-you-go fares for your itinerary, and compare that to the price of a rail pass plus reservations. Keep in mind that significant discounts on point-to-point tickets may be available with advance purchase.

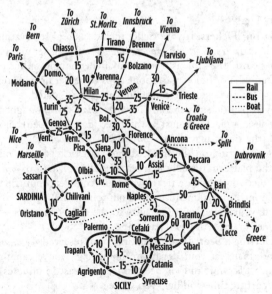

*Map shows approximate costs, in US dollars, for one-way, second-class tickets on faster trains.*

charge a small fee, but the language barrier (and the lines) can be smaller than at the station's ticket windows.

## Rail Passes

The single-country Eurail Italy Pass may save you money if you take several long train rides or prefer first-class travel, but for most people it's not a good value. Most train travelers in Italy take relatively short rides on the Milan-Venice-Florence-Rome circuit. For these trips, it can be cheaper to buy point-to-point tickets. Remember that rail passes are valid only on Trenitalia trains (not on Italo or Thello trains).

Furthermore, a rail pass doesn't offer much hop-on convenience in Italy, since even with a rail pass, seat reservations are required for InterCity, EuroCity, and Frecce trains (€5-10 each; make seat reservations at station ticket machines or windows). Most regional trains (such as Florence-Pisa-Cinque Terre service) don't require (or offer) reservations. Reservations for berths on overnight trains cost extra and aren't covered by rail passes.

If you're also traveling by train in other countries, consider a Eurail Global Pass. Although it covers most of Europe, prices can work for trips as short as three travel days or as long as three months. For more info, see the sidebar.

## Train Tips

**Validating Tickets:** If your ticket includes a seat reservation on a specific train *(biglietto con prenotazione),* you're all set and can just get on board. The same is true for any ticket bought online or with the Trenitalia or Italo smartphone apps (whether open or reserved seating); these tickets are considered already validated.

An open ticket (generally for a *regionale* train) bought from a ticket desk or machine must be validated (date-stamped) before you board (the ticket may say *da convalidare* or *convalida*). To validate it, before getting on the train, stamp your ticket in the machine near the platform (usually marked *convalida biglietti* or *vidimazione*). Once you validate a ticket, you must complete your trip within the stamped timeframe (usually about four hours). If you forget to validate your ticket, go right away to the train conductor—before he comes to you—or you'll pay a fine.

**Getting a Seat:** If you're taking an unreserved *regionale* train that originates at your departure point (e.g., you're catching the Florence-Pisa train in Florence), arriving at least 15 minutes before the departure time will help you snare a seat.

**Baggage Storage:** Many Italian stations have *deposito bagagli* where you can safely leave your bag for a standardized but steep price (€6/5 hours, €12/12 hours, €17/24 hours, payable when you pick up the bag, double-check closing hours; they may ask to pho-

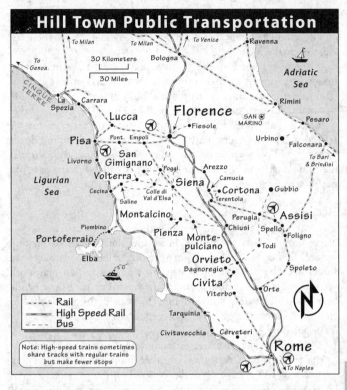

# Hill Town Public Transportation

tocopy your passport). Due to security concerns, no Italian stations have lockers.

**Theft:** In big cities, exercise caution and prudence at train stations to avoid thieves and con artists. If someone helps you to find your train or carry your bags, be aware that they are not an official porter; they are simply hoping for some cash. And if someone other than a uniformed railway employee tries to help you use the ticket machines, politely refuse.

Italian trains are famous for their thieves. Never leave a bag unattended. Police do ride the trains, cutting down on theft. Still, for an overnight trip, I'd feel safe only in a *cuccetta* (a bunk in a special sleeping car with an attendant who keeps track of who comes and goes while you sleep—approximately €40 or more).

**Strikes:** Strikes, which are common, generally last a day (often a Friday). Train employees will simply explain, *"Sciopero"* (SHOH-peh-roh, strike). But in actuality, a minimum amount of "essential" main-line service is maintained (by law) during strikes. When a strike is pending, travel agencies, savvy hoteliers, and remaining station personnel can check to see when the strike will go into effect and which trains will continue to run. Revised schedules may be posted online and in Italian at stations. See www.trenitalia.com, choose English, then "Information and Contacts," and then "In Case of Strike."

If your train is cancelled, your reserved-seat ticket will likely be accepted on any similar train running that day (either earlier or later than the original departure time) but you won't have a seat assignment. Tickets for cancelled trains should also be exchangeable without penalty ahead of the original departure time, or can be refunded (have an agent mark it "unused," and check refund deadlines). A rail pass works on any train still operating, but partially used rail passes can't be refunded—so make full use of any pass you have to continue your trip.

## BUSES

You can usually get anywhere you want in Italy by bus, as long as you're not in a hurry and plan ahead using bus schedules (pick up at local TIs or bus stations). For reaching small towns, buses are sometimes the only option if you don't have a car. In many hill towns, trains leave you at a station in the valley far below, while buses more likely drop you right into the thick of things. (If the bus stop or station is below town, sometimes an escalator or elevator helps get you up into town.)

Long-distance buses are catching on in Italy as an alternative to the train. Buses are usually cheaper, more modern, and often have free Wi-Fi. They're especially useful on routes poorly served by train. Some of the operators you'll see are Megabus (www.megabus.com), Flixbus (http://global.flixbus.com), and Marozzi (www.marozzivt.it). In general, orange buses are local city buses, and blue buses are for long distances.

Larger towns have a (usually chaotic) long-distance bus station *(stazione degli autobus)*, with ticket windows and several stalls (usually labeled *corsia, stallo,* or *binario*)—but to save time, buy your ticket at a travel agent or online, and print it out. Smaller towns— where buses are more useful—often have a central bus stop *(fermata)*, likely along the main road or on the main square, and maybe several more scattered around town. In small towns, buy bus tickets at newsstands or tobacco shops (with the big *T* signs). When buying your ticket, confirm the departure point *("Dov'è la fermata?")*.

Before boarding, confirm the destination with the driver. You are expected to stow big backpacks underneath the bus (open the luggage compartment yourself if it's closed). Upon arrival, double-check that the posted schedule lists your next destination and departure time.

Traveling by bus on Sundays and holidays can be problematic; even from large cities, schedules are sparse, departing buses are jam-packed, and ticket offices are often closed. Plan ahead and buy your ticket in advance. Most travel agencies book bus (and train) tickets for a small fee.

## TAXIS AND RIDE-BOOKING SERVICES

Most Italian taxis are reliable and cheap. In many cities, two people can travel short distances by cab for little more than the cost of bus or subway tickets. If you like ride-booking services such as Uber, their apps usually work in Europe just like they do in the US: Request a car on your mobile phone (connected to Wi-Fi or data), and the fare is automatically charged to your credit card. In Italy, however, Uber faces legal challenges, and may not be consistently available (for instance, Uber does not operate in Florence).

## RENTING A CAR

It's cheaper to arrange most car rentals from the US, so research and compare rates before you go. Most of the major US rental agencies (including Avis, Budget, Enterprise, Hertz, and Thrifty) have offices throughout Europe. Also consider the two major Europe-based agencies, Europcar and Sixt. Consolidators such as Auto Europe (www.autoeurope.com—or the sometimes cheaper www.autoeurope.eu) compare rates at several companies to get you the best deal.

Wherever you book, always read the fine print. Check for add-on charges—such as one-way drop-off fees, airport surcharges, or mandatory insurance policies—that aren't included in the "total price."

### Rental Costs and Considerations

Figure on paying roughly $250 for a one-week rental for a basic compact car. Allow extra for supplemental insurance, fuel, tolls, and parking. To save money on fuel, request a diesel car.

**Manual vs. Automatic:** Almost all rental cars in Europe are manual by default—and cars with a stick shift are generally cheaper. If you need an automatic, request one in advance. When selecting a car, don't be tempted by a larger model, as it won't be as maneuverable on narrow, winding roads or when squeezing into tight parking lots.

**Age Restrictions:** Some rental companies impose minimum and maximum age limits. Young drivers (25 and under) and seniors (69 and up) should check the rental policies and rules section of car-rental websites.

**Choosing Pick-Up/Drop-off Locations:** Always check the hours of the locations you choose: Many rental offices close from midday Saturday until Monday morning and, in smaller towns, at lunchtime. When selecting an office, plug the addresses into a mapping website to confirm the location. A downtown site is generally cheaper—and might seem more convenient than the airport. But pedestrianized and one-way streets can make navigation tricky when returning a car at a big-city office or urban train station. Wherever you select, get precise details on the location and allow ample time to find it. And be aware that most Italian cities have a "ZTL" (limited traffic zone) that's carefully monitored by cameras. If your drop-off point is near this zone, get clear directions on how to get there to avoid getting a big fine.

**Have the Right License:** If you're renting a car in Italy, bring your driver's license. You're also technically required to have an International Driving Permit—an official translation of your license (sold at AAA offices for about $20 plus the cost of two passport-type photos; see www.aaa.com). While that's the letter of the law, I generally rent cars without having this permit. How this is enforced varies from country to country: Get advice from your car-rental company.

**Picking Up Your Car:** Before driving off in your rental car, check it thoroughly and make sure any damage is noted on your rental agreement. Rental agencies in Europe tend to charge for even minor damage, so be sure to mark everything. Find out how your car's gearshift, lights, turn signals, wipers, radio, and fuel cap function, and know what kind of fuel the car takes (diesel vs. unleaded). When you return the car, make sure the agent verifies its condition with you. Some drivers take pictures of the returned vehicle as proof of its condition.

## Car Insurance Options

When you rent a car in Europe, the price typically includes liability insurance, which covers harm to other cars or motorists—but not the rental car itself. To limit your financial risk in case of damage to the rental, choose one of these options: Buy a Collision Damage Waiver (CDW) with a low or zero deductible from the car-rental company (roughly 30-40 percent extra), get coverage through your credit card (free, but more complicated), or get collision insurance as part of a larger travel-insurance policy.

Basic **CDW** costs $15–30 a day and typically comes with a $1,000-2,000 deductible, reducing but not eliminating your financial responsibility. When you reserve or pick up the car, you'll be offered the chance to "buy down" the deductible to zero (for an additional $10–30/day; this is sometimes called "super CDW" or "zero-deductible coverage").

In Italy, most car-rental companies' rates automatically include CDW coverage. Even if you try to decline CDW when you reserve your car, you may find when you show up at the counter that you must buy it after all (along with mandatory theft insurance, about $15–20 a day).

If you opt for **credit-card coverage,** you must decline all coverage offered by the car-rental company—which means they can place a hold on your card for up to the full value of the car. In case of damage, it can be time-consuming to resolve the charges. Before relying on this option, quiz your card company about how it works.

For more on car-rental insurance, see RickSteves.com/cdw.

## Navigation Options

If you'll be navigating using your phone or a GPS unit from home, remember to bring a car charger and device mount.

**Your Mobile Phone:** The mapping app on your mobile phone works fine for navigating Europe's roads, but for real-time turn-by-turn directions and traffic updates, you'll need mobile data access. And driving all day can burn through a lot of very expensive data. The economical work-around is to use map apps that work offline. By downloading in advance from Google Maps, City Maps 2Go, Apple Maps, Here WeGo, or Navmii, you can still have turn-by-turn voice directions and maps that recalibrate even though they're offline.

You must download your maps before you go offline—and it's smart to select large regions. Then turn off your data connection so you're not charged for roaming. Call up the map, enter your destination, and you're on your way. Even if you don't have to pay extra for data roaming, this option is great for navigating in areas with poor connectivity.

**GPS Devices:** If you want the convenience of a dedicated GPS unit, consider renting one with your car ($10-30/day). These units offer real-time turn-by-turn directions and traffic without the data requirements of an app. The unit may come loaded only with maps for its home country; if you need additional maps, ask. Also make sure your device's language is set to English before you drive off.

A less-expensive option is to bring a GPS device from home. Be sure to buy and install the maps you'll need before your trip.

**Paper Maps and Atlases:** Even when navigating primarily with a mobile app or GPS, I always make it a point to have a paper map, ideally a big, detailed regional road map. It's invaluable for getting the big picture, understanding alternate routes, and filling in if my phone runs out of juice. The free maps you get from your car-rental company usually don't have enough detail. It's smart to buy a better map before you go, or pick one up at a local gas station, bookshop, newsstand, or tourist shop.

## DRIVING

Driving in Italy can be scary—a video game for keeps, and you only get one quarter. Locals drive fast and tailgate as if it were required.

# Driving in Italy

m = miles   h = hours
Note: Your times may vary based on traffic, construction, and road conditions.

They pass where Americans are taught not to—on blind corners and just before tunnels. Roads have narrow shoulders or none at all. Driving in the countryside is less stressful than driving through urban areas or on busy highways, but stay alert. On one-lane roads, larger vehicles have the right-of-way.

**Road Rules:** Stay out of restricted traffic zones or you'll risk huge fines. Car traffic is restricted in many city centers. Don't drive or park in any area that has a sign reading *Zona Traffico Limitato* (ZTL, often shown above a red circle—see image). If you do, your license plate will likely be photographed and a hefty (€80-plus) ticket mailed to your home without your ever having met a cop. Bumbling in and out of these zones can net you multiple fines. If your hotel

zona
traffico limitato

🚶 7,30 - 19,30

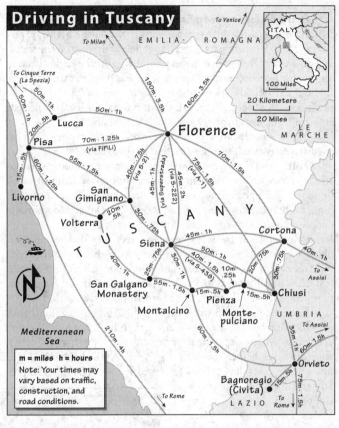

**Driving in Tuscany**

To Venice
To Milan
EMILIA - ROMAGNA
ITALY
100 Miles
20 Kilometers
20 Miles
LE MARCHE

To Cinque Terre (La Spezia)
50m · 1h
50m · 1h
Lucca
50m · 1h
Florence
160m · 3.5h
190m · 3.5h
20m · .5h
Pisa
70m · 1.25h (via FIPILI)
70m · 1.5h
15m · .5h
55m · 1.5h
60m · 1.25h
Livorno
San Gimignano
40m · .75h (via S-2)
45m · 1h (superstrada via S-222)
45m · 1h (via A-1)
7.5m · 1.5h
Volterra
20m · .5h
30m · .5h
T U S C A N Y
Cortona
Siena
45m · 1h
40m · 1h
25m · .75h
30m · .75h
30m · 1h (via S-438)
50m · 1.5h
20m · .75h
40m · 1h
San Galgano Monastery
55m · 1.5h
15m · .5h
10m · .25h
30m · .75h
40m · 1h
To Assisi
Montalcino
Pienza
15m · .5h
Monte-pulciano
75m · .5h
Chiusi
UMBRIA
To Assisi
Mediterranean Sea
210m · 4h
60m · 1.5h
35m · 1h
60m · 1.5h
Orvieto
m = miles  h = hours
Note: Your times may vary based on traffic, construction, and road conditions.
To Rome
Bagnoregio (Civita)
15m · .5h
75m · 1.5h
To Rome
LAZIO

PRACTICALITIES

is within a restricted area, ask your hotelier to direct you to parking outside the zone. (Although your hotelier can register your car as an authorized vehicle permitted to enter the zone, this usually isn't worth the hassle.) If you get a ticket, it could take months to show up (for more about traffic tickets in Italy, see www.bella-toscana.com/traffic_violations_italy.htm).

Be aware of typical European road rules; for example, many countries require headlights to be turned on at all times, and nearly all forbid handheld mobile-phone use. Seatbelts are mandatory, and children under age 12 must ride in child-safety or booster seats. In Europe, you're not allowed to turn right on a red light unless a sign or signal specifically authorizes it, and on expressways it's illegal to pass drivers on the right. Ask your car-rental company about these rules, or check the "International Travel" section of the US State Department website (www.travel.state.gov, search for your country in the "Learn about your destination" box, then click "Travel and Transportation").

**Drive Defensively:** Italians are aggressive drivers. Turn signals are optional. If a driver is tailgating you on the highway, pull to the side to let them pass, even if that means driving on the shoulder. If you're traveling in the right-hand lane on the highway, keep an eye out for slow-moving cars that appear out of nowhere. Also, if you brake quickly, it's customary to put on your hazard lights to warn the driver behind you. All this is normal for locals, who may colorfully gesture at you. Don't take it personally.

Motor scooters are very popular, and scooter drivers often see themselves as exempt from rules that apply to automobiles.

**Tolls:** You'll pay tolls for some stretches of freeway (autostrada; for costs, use the trip-planning tool at www.autostrade.it or search "European Tolls" on www.theaa.com). When approaching a tollbooth, skip lanes marked *Telepass;* for an attended booth, choose a lane with a sign that shows a hand or coins.

While I favor freeways because I feel they're safer and less nerve-racking than smaller roads, savvy local drivers know which toll-free *superstrade* are actually faster and more direct than the autostrada (e.g., Florence to Pisa). In some cases, if you have some time to spare, smaller roads can be worth the extra hassle.

**Fuel:** Fuel is expensive—often about $6.50 per gallon. Diesel cars are more common in Europe than back home, so be sure you know what type of fuel your car takes before you fill up. Diesel costs less, about $6 per gallon. Gas pumps are color-coded: green for unleaded *(senza piombo);* black for diesel *(gasolio).* You'll also see the term *benzina,* which is standard fuel. If you are unsure or need help, stop for full-service gas *(servito).* To fill up, say *"Pieno"* (pee-EH-noh). Autostrada rest stops can have full- or self-service stations (open daily without a siesta break). Many 24-hour stations are entirely automated. Small-town stations are usually cheaper and offer full service but shorter hours.

**Maps and Signage:** Learn the universal road signs (see illustration). Although roads are numbered

**STOP AND LEARN THESE ROAD SIGNS**

Speed Limit (km/hr)  •  Yield  •  No Passing  •  End of No Passing Zone

One Way  •  Intersection  •  Main Road  •  Expressway

Roundabout Ahead  •  Danger  •  No Entry  •  All Vehicles Prohibited

No Through Road  •  Restrictions No Longer Apply  •  Yield to Oncoming Traffic  •  No Stopping

Parking  •  No Parking  •  Customs or Toll Road  •  Peace

on maps, actual road signs give just a city name (for example, if you were heading west out of Venice, the map would be marked "route S-11"—but you'd follow signs to *Padua*, the next town along this road). Signs are inconsistent: They may direct you to the nearest big city or simply the next town along the route.

**Theft:** Cars are routinely vandalized and stolen. Thieves easily recognize rental cars and assume they are filled with a tourist's gear. Be sure all of your valuables are out of sight and locked in the trunk, or even better, with you or in your room.

**Parking:** White lines generally mean parking is free. Yellow lines mean that parking is reserved for residents only (who have permits). Blue lines mean you'll have to pay—usually around €1.50 per hour (use machine, leave time-stamped receipt on dashboard). Study the signs. Free zones often have a 30- or 60-minute time limit. Signs showing a street cleaner and a day of the week indicate which day the street is cleaned; there's a €100 tow-fee incentive to learn the days of the week in Italian.

*Zona disco* has nothing to do with dancing. Italian cars come equipped with a time disc (a cardboard clock), which you can use in a *zona disco*—set the clock to your arrival time and leave it on the dashboard. (If your rental car doesn't come with a *disco*, pick one up at a tobacco shop or just write your arrival time on a piece of paper and place it on the dashboard.) These are generally used in areas where parking is free but has a time limit.

Garages are safe, save time, and help you avoid the stress of parking tickets. Take the parking voucher with you to pay the cashier before you leave.

## FLIGHTS

To compare flight costs and times, begin with an online travel search engine: Kayak is the top site for flights to and within Europe, easy-to-use Google Flights has price alerts, and Skyscanner includes many inexpensive flights within Europe. To avoid unpleasant surprises, before you book be sure to read the small print about refunds, changes, and the costs for "extras" such as reserving a seat, checking a bag, or printing a boarding pass.

**Flights to Europe:** Start looking for international flights about four to six months before your trip, especially for peak-season travel. Depending on your itinerary, it can be efficient and no more expensive to fly into one city and out of another. If your flight requires a connection in Europe, see my hints on navigating Europe's top hub airports at RickSteves.com/hub-airports.

**Flights Within Europe:** Flying between European cities is surprisingly affordable. Before buying a long-distance train or bus ticket, check the cost of a flight on one of Europe's airlines, whether a major carrier or a no-frills outfit like Easyjet or Ryanair. Be aware that flying with a discount airline can have drawbacks, such as minimal customer service and time-consuming treks to secondary airports.

**Flying to the US and Canada:** Because security is extra tight for flights to the US, be sure to give yourself plenty of time at the airport. Charge your electronic devices before you board in case security checks require you to turn them on (see www.tsa.gov for the latest rules).

# Resources from Rick Steves

## Begin Your Trip at RickSteves.com

My mobile-friendly **website** is *the* place to explore Europe in preparation for your trip. You'll find thousands of fun articles, videos, and radio interviews; a wealth of money-saving tips for planning your dream trip; travel news dispatches; a video library of my travel talks; my travel blog; my latest guidebook updates (www.ricksteves.com/update); and my free Rick Steves Audio Europe app. You can also follow me on Facebook, Instagram, and Twitter.

Our **Travel Forum** is a well-groomed collection of message boards where our travel-savvy community answers questions and shares their personal travel experiences—and our well-traveled staff chimes in when they can be helpful (www.ricksteves.com/forums).

Our **online Travel Store** offers bags and accessories that I've designed to help you travel smarter and lighter. These include my popular carry-on bags (which I live out of four months a year), money belts, totes, toiletries kits, adapters, guidebooks, and planning maps (www.ricksteves.com/shop).

Our website can also help you find the perfect **rail pass** for your itinerary and your budget, with easy, one-stop shopping for rail passes, seat reservations, and point-to-point tickets (www.ricksteves.com/rail).

## Rick Steves' Tours, Guidebooks, TV Shows, and More

**Small Group Tours:** Want to travel with greater efficiency and less stress? We offer more than 40 itineraries reaching the best destinations in this book...and beyond. Each year about 30,000 travelers join us on about 1,000 Rick Steves bus tours. You'll enjoy great guides and a fun bunch of travel partners (with small groups of 24 to 28 travelers). You'll find European adventures to fit every vacation length. For all the details, and to get our tour catalog, visit www.ricksteves.com/tours or call us at 425/608-4217.

**Books:** *Rick Steves Italy* is just one of many books in my series on European travel, which includes country and city guidebooks, Snapshots (excerpted chapters from bigger guides), Pocket guides (full-color little books on big cities), "Best Of" guidebooks (condensed, full-color country guides), and my budget-travel skills handbook, *Rick Steves Europe Through the Back Door.* A complete list of my titles—including phrase books; cruising guides; travelogues on European art, history, and culture; and more—appears near the end of this book.

**TV Shows and Travel Talks:** My public television series, *Rick Steves' Europe,* covers Europe from top to bottom with over 100 half-hour episodes—and we're working on new shows every year (watch full episodes at my website for free). My free online video library, Rick Steves Classroom Europe, offers a searchable database of short video clips on European history, culture, and geography (http://classroom.ricksteves.com). And to raise your travel I.Q., check out the video versions of our popular classes (covering most European countries as well as travel skills, packing smart, cruising, tech for travelers, European art, and travel as a political act—www.ricksteves.com/travel-talks).

**Radio:** My weekly public radio show, *Travel with Rick Steves,* features interviews with travel experts from around the world. It airs on 400 public radio stations across the US, or you can hear it as a podcast. A complete archive of programs is available at www.ricksteves.com/radio.

**Audio Tours on My Free App:** I've produced dozens of free, self-guided audio tours of the top sights in Europe. For those tours and other audio content, get my free **Rick Steves Audio Europe app,** an extensive online library organized by destination. For more on my app, see page 26.

PRACTICALITIES

# APPENDIX

## Holidays and Festivals

In Italy, holidays seem to strike without warning, and every town has a festival honoring its patron saint. The following list includes selected 2020 festivals in major cities, plus national holidays observed throughout Italy. Many sights and banks close on national holidays—keep this in mind when planning your itinerary.

Before planning a trip around a festival, verify the dates with the festival website, the national tourist office (www.italia.it), or my "Upcoming Holidays and Festivals in Italy" web page (www. ricksteves.com/europe/italy/festivals).

In Italy, hotels get booked up on Easter weekend, Liberation Day, Labor Day, All Saints' Day, and on Fridays and Saturdays year-round. Some hotels require you to book the full three-day weekend around a holiday. During the Feast of the Assumption, a.k.a. Ferragosto (Aug 15), beach destinations are flooded with vacationing Italians. Cities empty out for much of August, and while tourist attractions remain open, shops and restaurants are often closed until September.

For festivals and events in the Cinque Terre, see page 341.

| | |
|---|---|
| **Jan 1** | New Year's Day |
| **Jan 6** | Epiphany |
| **Feb** | Carnevale, Venice (Mardi Gras, www. carnevale.venezia.it) |
| **Late Feb** | Carnevale Celebrations/Mardi Gras, Florence (costumed parades, jousting competitions) |
| **April 10-13** | Easter weekend; Scoppio del Carro fireworks in Florence on Easter Sunday |
| **April 19-22** | Vinitaly, Verona (wine festival, www. vinitaly.com) |
| **April 25** | Italian Liberation Day |
| **April 25** | Feast of St. Mark, Venice |
| **May 1** | Labor Day |
| **May 21** | Ascension Day |
| **Late May-early June** | Vogalonga Regatta, Venice |
| **June 2** | Anniversary of the Republic |
| **June 11** | Feast of Corpus Christi |
| **June 16-17** | St. Ranieri Day, Pisa |
| **June 24** | St. John the Baptist Day, Florence (parades, dances, boat races, and Calcio Storico, Renaissance ball game played on Piazza Santa Croce) |
| **June 29** | Sts. Peter and Paul Day, most fervently celebrated in Rome |
| **June-Aug** | Verona opera season |
| **Late June-early Sept** | Outdoor cinema season, Florence (contemporary films) |
| **July 2** | Palio horse race, Siena |
| **July (third weekend)** | Feast and Regatta of the Redeemer, Venice |
| **July-Aug** | Stresa Festival, Lake Maggiore (classical music) |
| **Aug 10** | St. Lawrence Day, Rome |
| **Aug 15** | Feast of the Assumption (Ferragosto) |
| **Aug 16** | Palio horse race, Siena |
| **Sept (first weekend)** | Historical Regatta, Venice |
| **Early Sept** | Festa della Rificolona, Florence (children's procession with lanterns, street performers, parade) |

| Sept 13 | Volto Santo, Lucca (luminaria procession and fair) |
|---|---|
| Sept 19 | St. Januarius Day, Naples |
| Sept-Oct | Chestnut festivals, most towns, mainly north of Rome (festivals, chestnut roasts) |
| Late Sept or early Oct | Musica dei Popoli Festival, Florence (ethnic and folk music and dances) |
| Mid-Oct | Castelrotto Music Festival (Kastelruther Spatzenfest), Dolomites |
| Nov 1 | All Saints' Day |
| Nov 21 | Feast of Our Lady of Good Health, Venice |
| Dec | Christmas market, Rome, Piazza Navona; crèches in churches throughout Italy |
| Dec 8 | Feast of the Immaculate Conception |
| Dec 25 | Christmas |
| Dec 26 | St. Stephen's Day |

# Books and Films

To learn more about Italy past and present, check out a few of these books and films.

## Nonfiction

*Absolute Monarchs* (John Julius Norwich, 2011). This warts-and-all illustrated guide to the most significant popes in history is a readable best seller.

*Ancient Rome: The Rise and Fall of an Empire* (Simon Baker, 2007). Baker chronicles the rise and demise of the great Roman Empire and its powerful leaders.

*The Architecture of the Italian Renaissance* (Peter Murray, 1969). Heavily illustrated, this classic presents the architectural life of Italy from the 13th through the 16th century.

*La Bella Figura: A Field Guide to the Italian Mind* (Beppe Severgnini, 2005). Severgnini strips down the idealized vision of Italy to reveal its more authentic self—at its best and its worst.

*Brunelleschi's Dome: How a Renaissance Genius Reinvented Architecture* (Ross King, 2000). The remarkable story of how the dome of Florence's cathedral was designed and built.

*Christ Stopped at Eboli: The Story of a Year* (Carlo Levi, 1945). Levi recounts the harsh yet beautiful existence he found in exile to a remote region of southern Italy during Mussolini's reign.

*City: A Story of Roman Planning and Construction* (David Macaulay, 1974). Macaulay's illustrated book about the Eternal City will please both kids and adults.

*A Concise History of Italy* (Christopher Duggan, 1994). Duggan's history starts with the fall of Rome but zooms in on the political difficulties of unified Italy over the last two centuries.

*Delizia!: The Epic History of the Italians and Their Food* (John Dickie, 2007). History buffs and foodies alike will enjoy this vibrant exploration of Italy's famed cuisine.

*Desiring Italy* (Susan Cahill, 1997). In this anthology, 28 women writers offer a mix of fiction, memoirs, and essays about the complexity and allure of Italy.

*Excellent Cadavers: The Mafia and the Death of the First Italian Republic* (Alexander Stille, 1995). This true account of Sicilian Mafia assassinations in the 1990s is as much thriller as it is history.

*A History of Venice* (John Julius Norwich, 1977). English Lord Norwich's engaging account spans more than a century, from Venice's fifth-century origins to the arrival of Napoleon.

*The House of Medici* (Christopher Hibbert, 1974). Florence's first family of the Renaissance included power-hungry bankers, merchants, popes, art patrons—and two queens of France.

*Italian Days* (Barbara Grizzuti Harrison, 1989). Harrison's appealing travel essays about Italy's varied regions cover everything from architecture to food to history.

*Italian Neighbors* (Tim Parks, 1992). Parks describes an Englishman's humorous and sometimes difficult attempt to live as a local in a small Italian town.

*Italian Renaissance Art* (Laurie Schneider Adams, 2013). In this well-written introduction to this pivotal period, Adams focuses on the most important and innovative artists and their best works.

*The Italians* (John Hooper, 2015). A veteran English correspondent in Italy probes the fascinating paradoxes of contemporary Italian life.

*Italy for the Gourmet Traveler* (Fred Plotkin, 1996). Plotkin, who's been described as an expert on everything Italian, shares his knowledge of Italy's culinary world in this food/travel guide.

*The Lives of the Artists* (Giorgio Vasari, 1550). The man who invented the term "Renaissance" offers anecdote-filled biographies of his era's greatest artists, some of whom he knew personally.

*Michelangelo and the Pope's Ceiling* (Ross King, 2003). The story behind the Sistine Chapel includes Michelangelo's technical difficulties, personality conflicts, and money troubles.

*Midnight in Sicily* (Peter Robb, 1996). Robb offers a good general

history of Sicily, covering its decadent pleasures and its literature, politics, art, and crimes.

*The Prince* (Niccolò Machiavelli, 1532). The original "how-to" for
gaining and maintaining political power, still chillingly relevant after 500 years.

*Saints & Sinners* (Eamon Duffy, 1997). Everything you always
wanted to know about the popes, but were afraid to ask.

*The Secrets of Rome: Love and Death in the Eternal City* (Corrado
Augias, 2005). Augias takes readers back through 27 centuries
of Roman history, secrets, and conspiracies.

*A Small Place in Italy* (Eric Newby, 1994). A young American couple tries to renovate a Tuscan farmhouse in the late 1960s.

*The Stones of Florence* (Mary McCarthy, 1956). McCarthy applies
wit and keen observation to produce a quirky, impressionistic
investigation of Florence and its history.

*Travelers' Tales Italy* (Anne Calcagno, 2001). Calcagno's guide is an
excellent compilation of travel writing.

*Under the Tuscan Sun* (Frances Mayes, 1996). Mayes' best seller describes living *la dolce vita* in the Tuscan countryside (and is
better than the movie of the same name).

*The Venetian Empire: A Sea Voyage* (Jan Morris, 1990). Morris brings
a maritime empire to life in this book that illustrates the city's
place on a larger historical canvas.

*Venice Observed* (Mary McCarthy, 1963). This snappy and engaging memoir details the Venetian ethos through the eyes of a
sharply critical writer.

## Fiction

*The Agony and the Ecstasy* (Irving Stone, 1958). Stone fictionalizes
Michelangelo's struggle to paint the Sistine Chapel (also a
1965 movie starring Charlton Heston).

*The Aspern Papers and Other Stories* (Henry James, 1894). An American editor travels to Venice in search of letters written to his
mistress. Other James works about Italy include *Italian Hours*
and *Daisy Miller.*

*Beautiful Ruins* (Jess Walter, 2012). This comedic romance, which
follows an Italian innkeeper's search for lost love over 50 years,
is the perfect beach read for the Cinque Terre.

*A Bell for Adano* (John Hersey, 1944). Hersey's novel about an
American major overseeing a town in WWII Sicily won him
the Pulitzer Prize in 1945.

*Birth of Venus* (Sarah Dunant, 2003). Dunant follows the life of a
Florentine girl who develops feelings for the boy hired to paint
the walls of the family's chapel.

*The Day of the Owl* (Leonardo Sciascia, 1961). This classic murder mystery set in a mid-20th-century Sicilian village is a fascinating window into the Mafia.

*Death at La Fenice* (Donna Leon, 1992). This chilling Venetian mystery and the others in Leon's Commissario Brunetti series reveal more about "real" Italy than many memoirs do.

*Death in the Mountains: The True Story of a Tuscan Murder* (Lisa Clifford, 2008). This fictionalized account of an unsolved murder reveals the hardship of early-20th-century Tuscan farming life.

*Death in Venice and Other Tales* (Thomas Mann, 1912). The centerpiece of this collection is an eloquent classic that explores obsession, beauty, and death in plague-ridden Venice (also a 1971 film).

*The Decameron* (Giovanni Boccaccio, 1348). Boccaccio's collection of 100 hilarious, often bawdy tales is a masterpiece of Italian literature and inspired Chaucer, Keats, and Shakespeare.

*Divine Comedy* (Dante Alighieri, 1321). Dante's epic poem—a journey through hell, purgatory, and paradise—is one of the world's greatest works of literature.

*The First Man in Rome* (Colleen McCullough, 1990). The author of *The Thorn Birds* describes the early days of the Roman Republic, in the first of a best-selling series of historical fiction.

*Galileo's Daughter* (Dava Sobel, 1999). Sobel's historical memoir centers on Galileo's correspondence with his oldest daughter and confidante.

*I, Claudius* (Robert Graves, 1934). This brilliant history of ancient Rome is told by Claudius, the family's laughingstock who becomes emperor himself. The sequel is *Claudius the God* (1935).

*I'm Not Scared* (Niccolò Ammaniti, 2001). A boy stumbles upon a terrible secret in an abandoned farmhouse in this thriller set in the 1970s Italian South.

*Invisible Cities* (Italo Calvino, 1972). Marco Polo tells of the fantastical cities he's seen...or is he just describing the many facets of his beloved Venice?

*Italian Journey* (Johann Wolfgang von Goethe, 1786). In his 18th-century collection of writings, Goethe describes his travels to Rome, Sicily, and Naples.

*The Leopard* (Giuseppe Tomasi di Lampedusa, 1957). Sicilian aristocrats see their world slipping away during the turmoil of the Risorgimento (also a 1963 movie starring Burt Lancaster).

*The Light in the Piazza* (Elizabeth Spencer, 1960). A mother and daughter are intoxicated by the beauty of 1950s Florence (also a 1962 movie and an award-winning Broadway musical).

*Lucrezia Borgia* (Maria Bellonci, 1939). In this historically based tale of court intrigue, a daughter of Pope Alexander VI navigates passions, plots, and controversy in Renaissance Rome.

*The Merchant of Venice* (William Shakespeare, 1598). In addition to *Merchant*, other Shakespearean plays set in Italy include *Romeo and Juliet* (Verona), *Much Ado About Nothing* (Sicily), *The Two Gentlemen of Verona*, and *The Taming of the Shrew* (Padua).

*The Neapolitan Novels* (Elena Ferrante, 2012-2015). This popular four-novel series traces two girls' coming of age in mid-20th-century Naples.

*The Passion of Artemisia* (Susan Vreeland, 2001). This novel is based on the life of Artemisia Gentileschi, one of the rare female post-Renaissance artists who gained fame in her own time.

*Pompeii* (Robert Harris, 2003). The engineer responsible for Pompeii's aqueducts has a bad feeling about Mount Vesuvius in this historical novel.

*A Room with a View* (E. M. Forster, 1908). A young Englishwoman visiting Florence finds a socially unsuitable replacement for her snobby fiancé (also a 1985 movie starring Helena Bonham Carter).

*The Sixteen Pleasures* (Robert Hellenga, 1994). Set during the 1966 floods in Florence, a young student discovers an erotic manuscript banned by the pope and lost for centuries.

*A Soldier of the Great War* (Mark Helprin, 1991). A young Roman lawyer falls in love with an art student, but World War I rips them apart.

*That Awful Mess on the Via Merulana* (Carlo Emilio Gadda, 1957). This detective story about a murder and a burglary in an apartment building in central Rome shines a harsh light on fascist Italy.

*A Thread of Grace* (Mary Doria Russell, 2004). This historical novel fictionalizes the story of how more than 43,000 Jews were saved by Italian citizens during World War II.

## Film and TV

*1900* (1976). Bernardo Bertolucci's epic tale of early-20th-century Italy follows the relationship between two young men—one rich (Robert De Niro), one poor (Gérard Depardieu).

*Ben-Hur* (1959). At the height of the Roman Empire, a Jewish prince is enslaved by a friend, and later seeks revenge in a stunning chariot race (the film won a record 11 Oscars).

*The Best of Youth* (2003). Beginning in the turbulent 1960s, this award-winning miniseries follows the dramatic ups and downs in the lives of two brothers over four decades.

*Bicycle Thieves* (1948). A poor man looks for his stolen bicycle in busy Rome in this inspirational classic of Italian Neorealism.

*Caterina in the Big City* (2003). A teenager whose family moves to Rome from a small town is the focus of this bitter comedy about the crisis of contemporary Italian society.

APPENDIX

*Cinema Paradiso* (1988). This Oscar-winning drama about a friendship between a film projectionist and a little boy is a compelling portrayal of post-WWII Sicily and a tribute to movies everywhere.

*La Dolce Vita* (1960). Director Federico Fellini tells a series of stories that capture the hedonistic days of early 1960s Rome.

*Enchanted April* (1991). Filmed in Portofino, this languid film follows an all-star British cast as they fall in love, discuss relationships, eat well, and take naps in the sun.

*The First Beautiful Thing* (2010). A man returns to his hometown in Tuscany to aid his dying mother, a woman determined to live life to the fullest while being a good parent to her children.

*Gladiator* (2000). An enslaved Roman general (Russell Crowe) fights his way back to freedom in Ridley Scott's Oscar winner.

*The Godfather* (1969). Francis Ford Coppola's famous film and its two sequels portray the multigenerational saga of a Sicilian family at the center of organized crime in New York.

*Golden Door* (2006). Poor Sicilian immigrants give up everything for a passage to America, but find a less-than-enthusiastic welcome at Ellis Island.

*Gomorrah* (2008). This mob drama, which reveals details about the Camorra (Neapolitan mafia), is not for the faint of heart.

*The Great Beauty* (2013). This thoughtful movie, named Best Foreign Film at the 2014 Academy Awards, showcases Rome in all of its decadence and splendor.

*The Italian Job* (1969). This classic English film features a crew of thieves attempting a high-stakes gold heist in Turin under the nose of the Mafia.

*Life Is Beautiful* (1997). In this tragicomic winner of three Oscars, a Jewish man from Tuscany finds imaginative ways to protect his son from the truth after they arrive at a Nazi concentration camp.

*Marriage Italian Style* (1964). A young Neapolitan prostitute (Sophia Loren) begins a lifelong on-again, off-again relationship with a cynical businessman in this Academy Award-nominated comedy.

*Mid-August Lunch* (2008). A broke Roman bachelor gets more than he bargained for when he agrees to take care of an elderly lady during a summer holiday to pay off a debt.

*Il Postino* (1994). Poet Pablo Neruda befriends his Italian postman, who uses a newfound love for Italian poetry to woo a local beauty.

*Quo Vadis* (1951). A Roman general falls in love with a Christian hostage in this epic that includes the burning of Rome, the crucifixion of St. Peter, and the madness of Nero.

*Roman Holiday* (1953). Audrey Hepburn plays a princess who es-capes her royal minders, falls for an American newspaperman (Gregory Peck), and discovers Rome on the back of his scooter.

*Rome* (2005-2007). This BBC/HBO miniseries focusing on Julius Caesar and Augustus intertwines the perspectives of aristocratic and ordinary Romans during the transition from republic to empire.

*Spartacus* (1960). In this epic directed by Stanley Kubrick, a gladiator (Kirk Douglas) leads a slave revolt in the last days of the Roman Republic.

*A Special Day* (1977). On the day of Hitler's visit to Rome, the wife of a militant fascist (Sophia Loren) has a fateful meeting with a persecuted journalist (Marcello Mastroianni).

*Tea with Mussolini* (1999). Franco Zeffirelli's look at pre-war Florence involves proper English ladies, a rich American Jew, and the son of a local businessman—all caught in the rise of fascism.

*The Wings of the Dove* (1997). Based on the Henry James novel, this romantic drama is a tale of desire that takes full advantage of its Venetian locale.

# Conversions and Climate

## NUMBERS AND STUMBLERS

- Europeans write a few of their numbers differently than we do. 1 = 1, 4 = 4, 7 = 7.
- In Europe, dates appear as day/month/year, so Christmas 2021 is 25/12/21.
- Commas are decimal points and decimals commas. A dollar and a half is $1,50, one thousand is 1.000, and there are 5.280 feet in a mile.
- When counting with fingers, start with your thumb. If you hold up your first finger to request one item, you'll probably get two.
- What Americans call the second floor of a building is the first floor in Europe.
- On escalators and moving sidewalks, Europeans keep the left "lane" open for passing. Keep to the right.

## METRIC CONVERSIONS

A **kilogram** equals 1,000 grams (about 2.2 pounds). One hundred **grams** (a common unit at markets) is about a quarter-pound. One **liter** is about a quart, or almost four to a gallon.

A **kilometer** is six-tenths of a mile. To convert kilometers to miles, cut the kilometers in half and add back 10 percent of the original (120 km: 60 + 12 = 72 miles). One **meter** is 39 inches—just over a yard.

| | |
|---|---|
| 1 foot = 0.3 meter | 1 square yard = 0.8 square meter |
| 1 yard = 0.9 meter | 1 square mile = 2.6 square kilometers |
| 1 mile = 1.6 kilometers | 1 ounce = 28 grams |
| 1 centimeter = 0.4 inch | 1 quart = 0.95 liter |
| 1 meter = 39.4 inches | 1 kilogram = 2.2 pounds |
| 1 kilometer = 0.62 mile | 32°F = 0°C |

## ROMAN NUMERALS

In the US, you'll see Roman numerals—which originated in ancient Rome—used for copyright dates, clocks, and the Super Bowl. In Italy, you're likely to observe these numbers chiseled on statues and buildings. If you want to do some numeric detective work, here's how: In Roman numerals, as in ours, the highest numbers (thousands, hundreds) come first, followed by smaller numbers. Many numbers are made by combining numerals into sets: V = 5, so VIII = 8 (5 plus 3). Roman numerals follow a subtraction principle for multiples of fours (4, 40, 400, etc.) and nines (9, 90, 900, etc.); the number four, for example, is written as IV (1 subtracted from 5), rather than IIII. The number nine is IX (1 subtracted from 10).

*Rick Steves Italy 2020*—written in Italian with Roman numerals—would translate as *Rick Steves Italia MMXX*. Big numbers such as dates can look daunting at first. The easiest way to handle them is to break them down into discrete chunks. For example, Michelangelo was born in MCDLXXV: M (1,000) + CD (100 subtracted from 500, or 400) + LXX (50 + 10 + 10, or 70) + V (5) = 1475. It was a very good year.

| | | | | | |
|---|---|---|---|---|---|
| M | = 1000 | XC = 90 | | IX = 9 |
| CM | = 900 | L | = 50 | V | = 5 |
| D | = 500 | XL = 40 | | IV | = 4 |
| CD | = 400 | X | = 10 | I | = duh |
| C | = 100 | | | | |

## CLOTHING SIZES

When shopping for clothing, use these US-to-European comparisons as general guidelines (but note that no conversion is perfect).

**Women:** For pants and dresses, add 36 in Italy (US 10 = Italian 46). For blouses and sweaters, add 8 for most of Europe (US 32 = European 40). For shoes, add 30-31 (US 7 = European 37/38).

**Men:** For shirts, multiply by 2 and add about 8 (US 15 = European 38). For jackets and suits, add 10. For shoes, add 32-34.

**Children:** Clothing is sized by height—in centimeters (2.5 cm = 1 inch), so a US size 8 roughly equates to 132-140. For shoes up to size 13, add 16-18, and for sizes 1 and up, add 30-32.

## ITALY'S CLIMATE

First line, average daily high; second line, average daily low; third line, average days without rain. For more detailed weather statistics for destinations in this book (as well as the rest of the world), check www.wunderground.com.

| J | F | M | A | M | J | J | A | S | O | N | D |
|---|---|---|---|---|---|---|---|---|---|---|---|

### Rome

| J | F | M | A | M | J | J | A | S | O | N | D |
|---|---|---|---|---|---|---|---|---|---|---|---|
| 55° | 57° | 63° | 68° | 75° | 84° | 90° | 86° | 81° | 73° | 64° | 59° |
| 37° | 37 | 43° | 46° | 55° | 63° | 66° | 64° | 61° | 54° | 46° | 39° |
| 24 | 22 | 24 | 21 | 24 | 26 | 28 | 31 | 24 | 23 | 22 | 22 |

### Florence

| J | F | M | A | M | J | J | A | S | O | N | D |
|---|---|---|---|---|---|---|---|---|---|---|---|
| 54° | 54° | 59° | 66° | 75° | 82° | 88° | 88° | 81° | 70° | 59° | 52° |
| 37° | 39° | 43° | 48° | 55° | 63° | 66° | 64° | 61° | 54° | 45° | 39° |
| 25 | 21 | 24 | 23 | 24 | 23 | 27 | 26 | 22 | 22 | 21 | 23 |

### Venice

| J | F | M | A | M | J | J | A | S | O | N | D |
|---|---|---|---|---|---|---|---|---|---|---|---|
| 42° | 46° | 53° | 62° | 70° | 76° | 81° | 80° | 75° | 65° | 53° | 46° |
| 33° | 35° | 41° | 49° | 56° | 63° | 66° | 65° | 61° | 53° | 44° | 37° |
| 25 | 21 | 24 | 21 | 23 | 22 | 24 | 24 | 25 | 24 | 21 | 23 |

### Naples

| J | F | M | A | M | J | J | A | S | O | N | D |
|---|---|---|---|---|---|---|---|---|---|---|---|
| 54° | 56° | 59° | 65° | 73° | 79° | 85° | 85° | 79° | 71° | 63° | 57° |
| 39° | 40° | 43° | 47° | 54° | 60° | 64° | 64° | 60° | 53° | 46° | 41° |
| 21 | 18 | 21 | 21 | 25 | 26 | 29 | 27 | 24 | 23 | 19 | 20 |

## Fahrenheit and Celsius Conversion

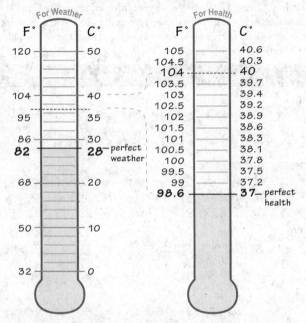

Europe takes its temperature using the Celsius scale, while we opt for Fahrenheit. For a rough conversion from Celsius to Fahrenheit, double the number and add 30. For weather, remember that 28°C is 82°F—perfect. For health, 37°C is just right. At a launderette, 30°C is cold, 40°C is warm (usually the default setting), 60°C is hot, and 95°C is boiling. Your air-conditioner should be set at about 20°C.

# Packing Checklist

Whether you're traveling for five days or five weeks, you won't need more than this. Pack light to enjoy the sweet freedom of true mobility.

## Clothing

- ❏ 5 shirts: long- & short-sleeve
- ❏ 2 pairs pants (or skirts/capris)
- ❏ 1 pair shorts
- ❏ 5 pairs underwear & socks
- ❏ 1 pair walking shoes
- ❏ Sweater or warm layer
- ❏ Rainproof jacket with hood
- ❏ Tie, scarf, belt, and/or hat
- ❏ Swimsuit
- ❏ Sleepwear/loungewear

## Money

- ❏ Debit card(s)
- ❏ Credit card(s)
- ❏ Hard cash (US $100-200)
- ❏ Money belt

## Documents

- ❏ Passport
- ❏ Tickets & confirmations: flights, hotels, trains, rail pass, car rental, sight entries
- ❏ Driver's license
- ❏ Student ID, hostel card, etc.
- ❏ Photocopies of important documents
- ❏ Insurance details
- ❏ Guidebooks & maps

## Toiletries Kit

- ❏ Basics: soap, shampoo, toothbrush, toothpaste, floss, deodorant, sunscreen, brush/comb, etc.
- ❏ Medicines & vitamins
- ❏ First-aid kit
- ❏ Glasses/contacts/sunglasses
- ❏ Sewing kit
- ❏ Packet of tissues (for WC)
- ❏ Earplugs

## Electronics

- ❏ Mobile phone
- ❏ Camera & related gear
- ❏ Tablet/ebook reader/laptop
- ❏ Headphones/earbuds
- ❏ Chargers & batteries
- ❏ Phone car charger & mount (or GPS device)
- ❏ Plug adapters

## Miscellaneous

- ❏ Daypack
- ❏ Sealable plastic baggies
- ❏ Laundry supplies: soap, laundry bag, clothesline, spot remover
- ❏ Small umbrella
- ❏ Travel alarm/watch
- ❏ Notepad & pen
- ❏ Journal

## Optional Extras

- ❏ Second pair of shoes (flip-flops, sandals, tennis shoes, boots)
- ❏ Travel hairdryer
- ❏ Picnic supplies
- ❏ Water bottle
- ❏ Fold-up tote bag
- ❏ Small flashlight
- ❏ Mini binoculars
- ❏ Small towel or washcloth
- ❏ Inflatable pillow/neck rest
- ❏ Tiny lock
- ❏ Address list (to mail postcards)
- ❏ Extra passport photos

## Italian Survival Phrases

| English | Italian | Pronunciation |
|---------|---------|---------------|
| Good day. | Buongiorno. | bwohn-**jor**-noh |
| Do you speak English? | Parla inglese? | **par**-lah een-**gleh**-zay |
| Yes. / No. | Sì. / No. | see / noh |
| I (don't) understand. | (Non) capisco. | (nohn) kah-**pees**-koh |
| Please. | Per favore. | pehr fah-**voh**-ray |
| Thank you. | Grazie. | **graht**-see-ay |
| You're welcome. | Prego. | **preh**-go |
| I'm sorry. | Mi dispiace. | mee dee-spee-**ah**-chay |
| Excuse me. | Mi scusi. | mee **skoo**-zee |
| (No) problem. | (Non) c'è problema. | (nohn) cheh proh-**bleh**-mah |
| Good. | Va bene. | vah **beh**-nay |
| Goodbye. | Arrivederci. | ah-ree-veh-**dehr**-chee |
| one / two | uno / due | **oo**-noh / **doo**-ay |
| three / four | tre / quattro | tray / **kwah**-troh |
| five / six | cinque / sei | **cheeng**-kway / **seh**-ee |
| seven / eight | sette / otto | **seh**-tay / **oh**-toh |
| nine / ten | nove / dieci | **noh**-vay / dee-**ay**-chee |
| How much is it? | Quanto costa? | **kwahn**-toh **koh**-stah |
| Write it? | Me lo scrive? | may loh **skree**-vay |
| Is it free? | È gratis? | eh **grah**-tees |
| Is it included? | È incluso? | eh een-**kloo**-zoh |
| Where can I buy / find...? | Dove posso comprare / trovare...? | **doh**-vay **poh**-soh kohm-**prah**-ray / troh-**vah**-ray |
| I'd like / We'd like... | Vorrei / Vorremmo... | voh-**reh**-ee / voh-**reh**-moh |
| ...a room. | ...una camera. | **oo**-nah **kah**-meh-rah |
| ...a ticket to ____. | ...un biglietto per ____. | oon beel-**yeh**-toh pehr ____ |
| Is it possible? | È possibile? | eh poh-**see**-bee-lay |
| Where is...? | Dov'è...? | doh-**veh** |
| ...the train station | ...la stazione | lah staht-see-**oh**-nay |
| ...the bus station | ...la stazione degli autobus | lah staht-see-**oh**-nay **dehl**-yee **ow**-toh-boos |
| ...tourist information | ...informazioni per turisti | een-for-maht-see-**oh**-nee pehr too-**ree**-stee |
| ...the toilet | ...la toilette | lah twah-**leh**-tay |
| men | uomini / signori | **woh**-mee-nee / seen-**yoh**-ree |
| women | donne / signore | **doh**-nay / seen-**yoh**-ray |
| left / right | sinistra / destra | see-**nee**-strah / **deh**-strah |
| straight | sempre dritto | **sehm**-pray **dree**-toh |
| What time does this open / close? | A che ora apre / chiude? | ah kay **oh**-rah **ah**-pray / kee-**oo**-day |
| At what time? | A che ora? | ah kay **oh**-rah |
| Just a moment. | Un momento. | oon moh-**mehn**-toh |
| now / soon / later | adesso / presto / tardi | ah-**deh**-soh / **preh**-stoh / **tar**-dee |
| today / tomorrow | oggi / domani | **oh**-jee / doh-**mah**-nee |

## In an Italian Restaurant

| English | Italian | Pronunciation |
|---|---|---|
| I'd like... | Vorrei... | voh-**reh**-ee |
| We'd like... | Vorremmo... | vor-**reh**-moh |
| ...to reserve... | ...prenotare... | preh-noh-**tah**-ray |
| ...a table for one / two. | ...un tavolo per uno / due. | oon **tah**-voh-loh pehr **oo**-noh / **doo**-ay |
| Is this seat free? | È libero questo posto? | eh **lee**-beh-roh **kweh**-stoh **poh**-stoh |
| The menu (in English), please. | Il menù (in inglese), per favore. | eel meh-**noo** (een een-**gleh**-zay) pehr fah-**voh**-ray |
| service (not) included | servizio (non) incluso | sehr-**veet**-see-oh (nohn) een-**kloo**-zoh |
| cover charge | pane e coperto | **pah**-nay ay koh-**pehr**-toh |
| to go | da portar via | dah **por**-tar **vee**-ah |
| with / without | con / senza | kohn / **sehnt**-sah |
| and / or | e / o | ay / oh |
| menu (of the day) | menù (del giorno) | meh-**noo** (dehl **jor**-noh) |
| specialty of the house | specialità della casa | speh-chah-lee-**tah deh**-lah **kah**-zah |
| first course (pasta, soup) | primo piatto | **pree**-moh pee-**ah**-toh |
| main course (meat, fish) | secondo piatto | seh-**kohn**-doh pee-**ah**-toh |
| side dishes | contorni | kohn-**tor**-nee |
| bread | pane | **pah**-nay |
| cheese | formaggio | for-**mah**-joh |
| sandwich | panino | pah-**nee**-noh |
| soup | zuppa | **tsoo**-pah |
| salad | insalata | een-sah-**lah**-tah |
| meat | carne | **kar**-nay |
| chicken | pollo | **poh**-loh |
| fish | pesce | **peh**-shay |
| seafood | frutti di mare | **froo**-tee dee **mah**-ray |
| fruit / vegetables | frutta / legumi | **froo**-tah / lay-**goo**-mee |
| dessert | dolce | **dohl**-chay |
| tap water | acqua del rubinetto | **ah**-kwah dehl roo-bee-**neh**-toh |
| mineral water | acqua minerale | **ah**-kwah mee-neh-**rah**-lay |
| milk | latte | **lah**-tay |
| (orange) juice | succo (d'arancia) | **soo**-koh (dah-**rahn**-chah) |
| coffee / tea | caffè / tè | kah-**feh** / teh |
| wine | vino | **vee**-noh |
| red / white | rosso / bianco | **roh**-soh / bee-**ahn**-koh |
| glass / bottle | bicchiere / bottiglia | bee-kee-**eh**-ray / boh-**teel**-yah |
| beer | birra | **bee**-rah |
| Cheers! | Cin cin! | cheen cheen |
| More. / Another. | Di più. / Un altro. | dee pew / oon **ahl**-troh |
| The same. | Lo stesso. | loh **steh**-soh |
| The bill, please. | Il conto, per favore. | eel **kohn**-toh pehr fah-**voh**-ray |
| Do you accept credit cards? | Accettate carte di credito? | ah-cheh-**tah**-tay **kar**-tay dee **kreh**-dee-toh |
| tip | mancia | **mahn**-chah |
| Delicious! | Delizioso! | day-leet-see-oh-**zoh** |

For more user-friendly Italian phrases, check out *Rick Steves Italian Phrase Book & Dictionary* or *Rick Steves French, Italian & German Phrase Book*.

# INDEX

INDEX

INDEX

# MAP INDEX

## Explore Europe

At ricksteves.com you can browse through thousands of articles, videos, photos and radio interviews, plus find a wealth of money-saving travel tips for planning your dream trip. And with our mobile-friendly website, you can easily access all this great travel information anywhere you go.

## TV Shows

Preview the places you'll visit by watching entire half-hour episodes of Rick Steves' Europe (choose from all 100 shows) on-demand, for free.

# ricksteves.com

## Radio Interviews

Enjoy ready access to Rick's vast library of radio interviews covering travel tips and cultural insights that relate specifically to your Europe travel plans.

## Travel Forums

Learn, ask, share! Our online community of savvy travelers is a great resource for first-time travelers to Europe, as well as seasoned pros.

## Travel News

Subscribe to our free Travel News e-newsletter, and get monthly updates from Rick on what's happening in Europe.

## Classroom Europe

Check out our free resource for educators with 300+ short video clips from the Rick Steves' Europe TV show.

# Audio Europe™

## Rick's Free Travel App

Get your FREE **Rick Steves Audio Europe**™ app to enjoy…

- Dozens of self-guided tours of Europe's top museums, sights and historic walks
- Hundreds of tracks filled with cultural insights and sightseeing tips from Rick's radio interviews
- All organized into handy geographic playlists
- For Apple and Android

With Rick whispering in your ear, Europe gets even better.

## Find out more at ricksteves.com

# Pack Light and Right

*Gear up for your next adventure at ricksteves.com*

## Light Luggage

Pack light and right with Rick Steves' affordable, custom-designed rolling carry-on bags, backpacks, day packs and shoulder bags.

## Accessories

From packing cubes to moneybelts and beyond, Rick has personally selected the travel goodies that will help your trip go smoother.

## Shop at ricksteves.com

## *Experience maximum Europe*

### Save time and energy

This guidebook is your independent-travel toolkit. But for all it delivers, it's still up to you to devote the time and energy it takes to manage the preparation and logistics that are essential for a happy trip. If that's a hassle, there's a solution.

### Rick Steves Tours

A Rick Steves tour takes you to Europe's most interesting places with great

# great tours, too!

## with minimum stress

guides and small groups of 28 or less. We follow Rick's favorite itineraries, ride in comfy buses, stay in family-run hotels, and bring

you intimately close to the Europe you've traveled so far to see. Most importantly, we take away the logistical headaches so you can focus on the fun.

### Join the fun

This year we'll take thousands of free-spirited travelers—nearly half of them repeat customers— along with us on four dozen different itineraries, from Ireland to Italy to Athens. Is a Rick Steves tour the right fit for your travel dreams? Find out at ricksteves.com, where you can also request Rick's latest tour catalog. Europe is best experienced with happy travel partners. We hope you can join us.

## See our itineraries at ricksteves.com

# A Guide for Every Trip

## BEST OF GUIDES

*Full-color guides in an easy-to-scan format. Focused on top sights and experiences in the most popular European destinations*

Best of England
Best of Europe
Best of France
Best of Germany
Best of Ireland
Best of Italy
Best of Scotland
Best of Spain

## COMPREHENSIVE GUIDES

*City, country, and regional guides printed on Bible-thin paper. Packed with detailed coverage for a multi-week trip exploring iconic sights and venturing off the beaten path*

Amsterdam & the Netherlands
Barcelona
Belgium: Bruges, Brussels,
   Antwerp & Ghent
Berlin
Budapest
Croatia & Slovenia
Eastern Europe
England
Florence & Tuscany
France
Germany
Great Britain
Greece: Athens & the Peloponnese
Iceland
Ireland
Istanbul
Italy
London
Paris
Portugal
Prague & the Czech Republic
Provence & the French Riviera
Rome
Scandinavia
Scotland
Sicily
Spain
Switzerland
Venice
Vienna, Salzburg & Tirol

HE BEST OF ROME

, Italy's capital, is studded with
n remnants and floodlit-fountain
s. From the Vatican to the Colos-
with crazy traffic in between, Rome
derful, huge, and exhausting. The
, the heat, and the weighty history

of the Eternal City where Caesars walked
can make tourists wilt. Recharge by taking siestas, gelato breaks, and after-dark
walks, strolling from one atmospheric
square to another in the refreshing evening air.

*Pantheon*—which
dome until the
2,000 years old
over 1,500).

Athens in the Vat-
s the humanistic

adiators fought
ther, entertaining

*ristorante*

## POCKET GUIDES

*Compact color guides for shorter trips*

Amsterdam
Athens
Barcelona
Florence
Italy's Cinque Terre
London
Munich & Salzburg

Paris
Prague
Rome
Venice
Vienna

## SNAPSHOT GUIDES

*Focused single-destination coverage*

Basque Country: Spain & France
Copenhagen & the Best of Denmark
Dublin
Dubrovnik
Edinburgh
Hill Towns of Central Italy
Krakow, Warsaw & Gdansk
Lisbon
Loire Valley
Madrid & Toledo
Milan & the Italian Lakes District
Naples & the Amalfi Coast
Nice & the French Riviera
Normandy
Northern Ireland
Norway
Reykjavík
Rothenburg & the Rhine
Sevilla, Granada & Southern Spain
St. Petersburg, Helsinki & Tallinn
Stockholm

## CRUISE PORTS GUIDES

*Reference for cruise ports of call*

Mediterranean Cruise Ports
Scandinavian & Northern European
 Cruise Ports

## Complete your library with...

## TRAVEL SKILLS & CULTURE

*Study up on travel skills and gain
insight on history and culture*

Europe 101
Europe Through the Back Door
Europe's Top 100 Masterpieces
European Christmas
European Easter
European Festivals
For the Love of Europe
Travel as a Political Act

## PHRASE BOOKS & DICTIONARIES

French
French, Italian & German
German
Italian
Portuguese
Spanish

## PLANNING MAPS

Britain, Ireland & London
Europe
France & Paris
Germany, Austria & Switzerland
Iceland
Ireland
Italy
Spain & Portugal

# Credits

## RESEARCHERS
For help with this edition, Rick relied on...

### Virginia Agostinelli

Virginia was born and raised in Abruzzo, in central Italy. After graduation she moved to Seattle, where she taught Italian studies at the University of Washington while finishing her doctorate. Besides travel and teaching, Virginia has a passion for Italian cinema and detective fiction. When not leading a Rick Steves' Europe tour, she spends her time in the Pacific Northwest swimming, reading, and sipping a cappuccino at the nearest coffeehouse.

### Trish Feaster

As a high-school Spanish teacher, Trish regularly led student trips in Europe, sharing her passions for language, history, culture, and cuisine. She now combines her love of teaching and travel as a Rick Steves' Europe tour guide, guidebook researcher, and language instructor. When not working in Europe, she binge-watches favorite shows, practices archery, and perfects her chocolate and caramel chip cookie recipe in her hometown of San Diego. You can follow Trish and her journeys at TheTravelphile.com.

### Cameron Hewitt

Born in Denver and raised in central Ohio, Cameron settled in Seattle in 2000. Ever since, he has spent three months each year in Europe, contributing to guidebooks, tours, radio and television shows, and other media for Rick Steves' Europe, where he serves as content manager. Cameron married his high school sweetheart (and favorite travel partner), Shawna, and enjoys taking pictures, trying new restaurants, and planning his next trip.

### Suzanne Kotz

Suzanne, an editor with Rick Steves' Europe, began her travel career riding in a station wagon with her six siblings from Michigan to Florida for spring break. Since then, she's broadened her destinations to include much of Europe and parts of Asia. A librarian by training and a longtime editor of art publications, she's happiest in her Seattle garden or when planning a meal for family and friends.

## Sarah Murdoch

Sarah, trained as an architect, abandoned her drafting board in 2000 to lead tours and research guidebooks for Rick Steves' Europe. Specializing in Italy, she occasionally speaks with her hands and drives like a Sicilian. She blogs about her life at adventureswithsarah.net and often writes about her passion for the perfectly packed bag. Sarah lives in Seattle but prefers to be out on adventures with her sons Lucca and Nicola.

## Robert Wright

Raised in Memphis, Robert funded his first dream trip to Europe in 1998 by selling his entire Star Wars collection—proof that where there's a will, there's a way. He fell in love with Spain and Portugal and returned many times, all while living in Argentina for 14 years. Robert recently married a *sevillano* and moved to Spain. He continues to enjoy Iberian architecture and loves uncovering forgotten connections between Spain and Portugal's intertwined history.

## CONTRIBUTOR
## Gene Openshaw

Gene has co-authored more than a dozen *Rick Steves* books, specializing in writing walks and tours of Europe's cities, museums, and cultural sights. He also contributes to Rick's public television series, produces audio tours on Europe, and is a regular guest on Rick's public radio show. Outside of the travel world, Gene has co-authored *The Seattle Joke Book.* As a composer, he has written a full-length opera called *Matter,* a violin sonata, and dozens of songs. He lives near Seattle with his daughter, enjoys giving presentations on art and history, and roots for the Mariners in good times and bad.

# Photo Credits

Avalon Travel
Hachette Book Group
1700 Fourth Street
Berkeley, CA 94710

Printed in Canada by Friesens
First printing December 2019

ISBN 978-1-64171-154-8

For the latest on Rick's talks, guidebooks, tours, public television series, and public radio show, contact Rick Steves' Europe, 130 Fourth Avenue North, Edmonds, WA 98020, tel. 425/771-8303, www.ricksteves.com, rick@ricksteves.com.

**Rick Steves' Europe**
**Managing Editor:** Jennifer Madison Davis
**Assistant Managing Editor:** Cathy Lu
**Special Publications Manager:** Risa Laib
**Editors:** Glenn Eriksen, Julie Fanselow, Tom Griffin, Suzanne Kotz, Rosie Leutzinger, Teresa Nemeth, Jessica Shaw, Carrie Shepherd
**Editorial & Production Assistant:** Megan Simms
**Editorial Interns:** Amelia Benich, Maxwell Eberle
**Researchers:** Virginia Agostinelli, Ben Cameron, Trish Feaster, Cameron Hewitt, Suzanne Kotz, Sarah Murdoch, Robert Wright
**Contributor:** Gene Openshaw
**Graphic Content Director:** Sandra Hundacker
**Maps & Graphics:** David C. Hoerlein, Lauren Mills, Mary Rostad
**Digital Asset Coordinator:** Orin Dubrow

**Avalon Travel**
**Senior Editor and Series Manager:** Madhu Prasher
**Editors:** Jamie Andrade, Sierra Machado
**Copy Editor:** Maggie Ryan
**Proofreaders:** Suzie Nasol, Denise Silva
**Indexer:** Stephen Callahan
**Production and Typesetting:** Lisi Baldwin, Rue Flaherty, Jane Musser
**Cover Design:** Kimberly Glyder Design
**Maps & Graphics:** Kat Bennett

# COLOR MAPS

*Italy • Venice • Florence • Tuscany & Umbria • Rome*

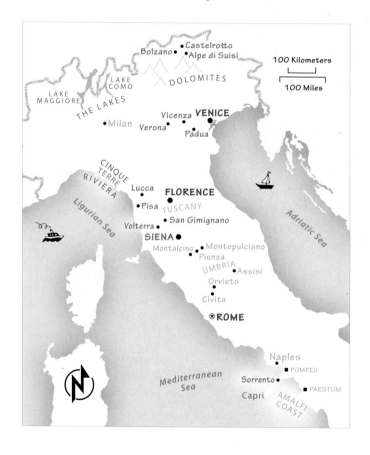

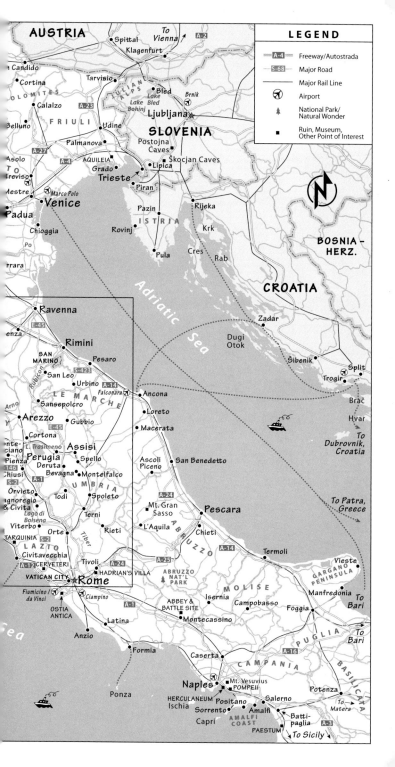

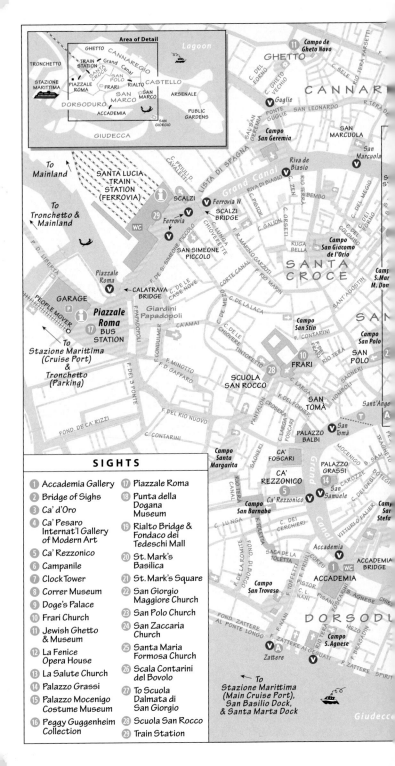

## SIGHTS

1. Accademia Gallery
2. Bridge of Sighs
3. Ca' d'Oro
4. Ca' Pesaro Internat'l Gallery of Modern Art
5. Ca' Rezzonico
6. Campanile
7. Clock Tower
8. Correr Museum
9. Doge's Palace
10. Frari Church
11. Jewish Ghetto & Museum
12. La Fenice Opera House
13. La Salute Church
14. Palazzo Grassi
15. Palazzo Mocenigo Costume Museum
16. Peggy Guggenheim Collection
17. Piazzale Roma
18. Punta della Dogana Museum
19. Rialto Bridge & Fondaco dei Tedeschi Mall
20. St. Mark's Basilica
21. St. Mark's Square
22. San Giorgio Maggiore Church
23. San Polo Church
24. San Zaccaria Church
25. Santa Maria Formosa Church
26. Scala Contarini del Bovolo
27. To Scuola Dalmata di San Giorgio
28. Scuola San Rocco
29. Train Station

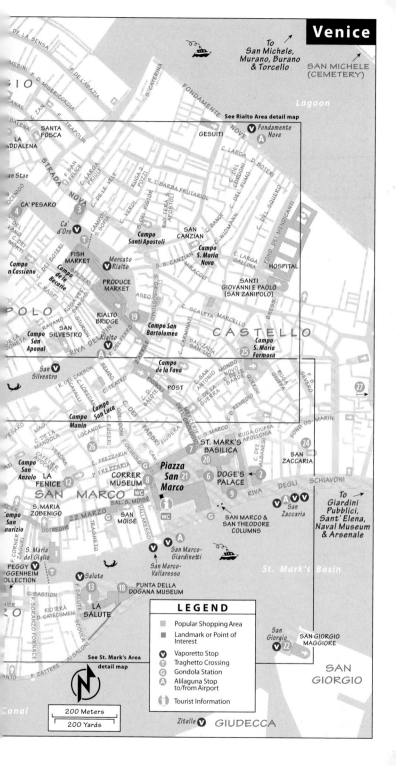

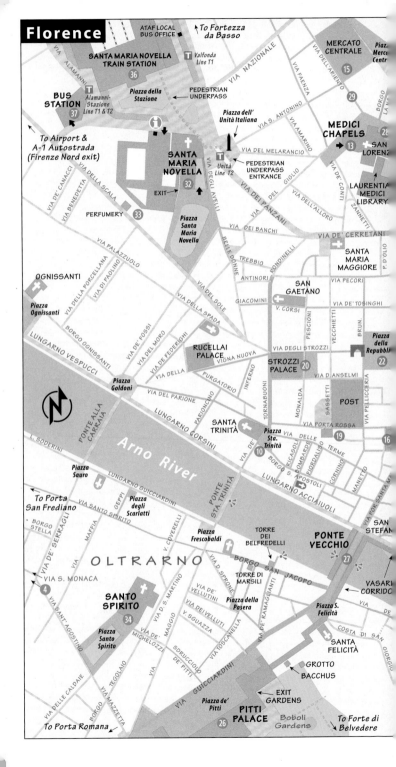

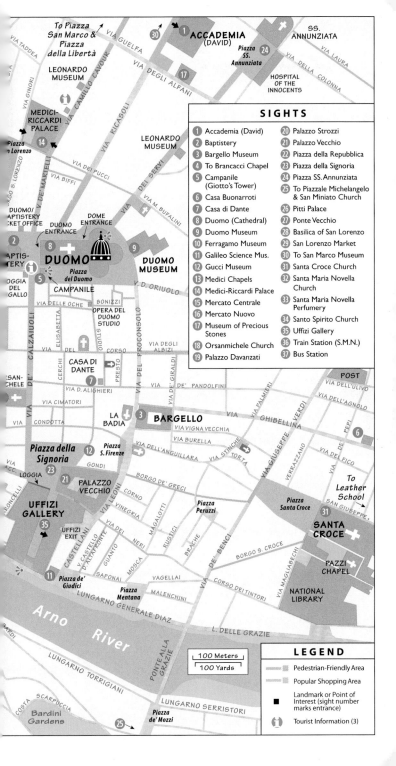

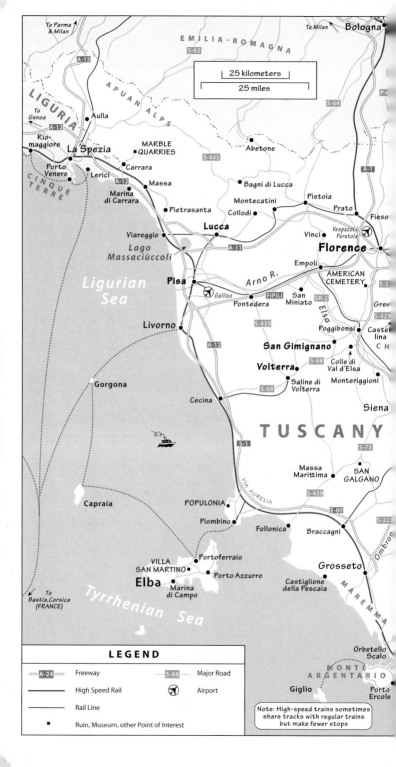

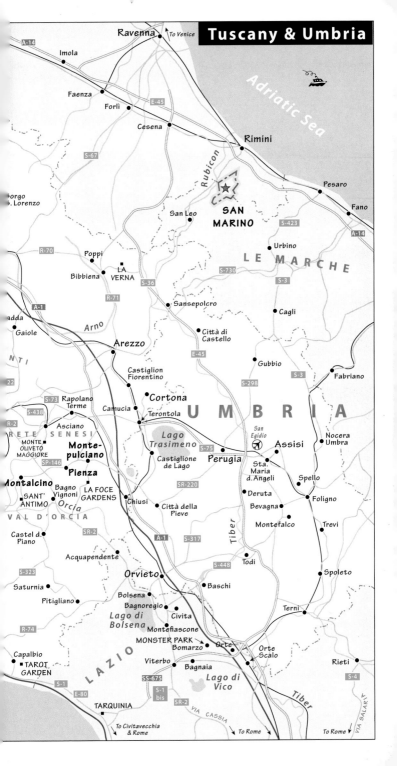

# Rome

To Olympic Stadium & Ring Freeway

**M** Lepanto

To Parco della Musica

Flaminio

VIA DI SAVO

Piazza del Pop

VIA ANDREA DORIA

VIA GIULIO CESARE

VIA LEONE IV

V. BARLETTA

VIA DEGLI SCIPIONI

GERMANICO

PONTE REG. MARGHERITA

L. IN AUGUSTA

VIA GANDIA

VIA COLA DI RIENZO

Ottaviano

VIA CICERONE

L. DEI MELLINI

PONTE CAVOUR

**M** Cipro

V. VENIERO

VATICANO

VIA BOEZIO

VIA VIRGILIO

Piazza Cavour

MAUSOLEI OF AUGUST

ARA PACIS

Piazza Risorgimento

VIA CRESCENZIO

VIA S. PORCARI

L. MARZIO

To Battistini

VATICAN MUSEUMS

ANCIENT CITY WALLS

CASTEL SANT'ANGELO

PALACE OF JUSTICE

L. PRATI

PONTE UMBERTO I

L. DI SCROFA

VATICAN CITY

SISTINE CHAPEL

VIA D. CONCILIAZIONE

L. CASTELLO

PONTE SANT'ANGELO

ST. PETER'S BASILICA

St. Peter's Square

BORGO S. SPIRITO

IN SASSIA S. VATICANO

PONTE VITT. EMANUELE II

LUNG. DI TOR DI NONA

VIA DEI CORONARI

SAN LUIGI

To Civita-vecchia

TUNNEL

V. PORTA CAVALLEGGERI

PONTE PR. AMEDEO

CORSO VITTORIO EMANUELE II

CHIESA NUOVA

Piazza Navona

PANTHEO

V. GREGORIO VII

V.D CROCIFISSO

V. INNOCENZO III

ANCIENT CITY WALLS

L. GIANICOLENSE

L. DEL SANGALLO

VIA DEL PELLEGRINO

VIA GIULIA

STA. ANDREA

To Via Aurelia & Ring Freeway

SAN PIETRO STATION

Campo de' Fiori

PONTE MAZZINI

LARGO ARGENTIN

VIA A. CERIANI

Parco Gianicolense

L. DEI TEBALDI

Palazzo Farnese

GH

VILLA FARNESINA

PONTE SISTO

L. DEI VALLATI

DEI CEN

BOTANICAL GARDEN

L. DELLA FARNESINA

L. RAFFAELLO SANZIO

PONTE GARIBALDI

Isola Tiberin

Piazzale Garibaldi

VIA DELLA SCALA

VIA AURELIA ANTICA

To Trastevere, Ostiense & Termini Stations

S. MARIA (TEMPIETTO)

STA. MARIA IN TRASTEVERE

VIA DELLA LUNGARETTA

TRASTEVERE

VIALE DI TRASTEVERE

PORTA PORTESE

ANCIENT CITY WALLS

PORTO RIPA GRAN

Tiber River

PONTE SUBLICIO

VIA PORTUENSE

L. TESTACCIO

TESTACCIO

VIA MARMORA

TESTACCIO MARKET

VIA NICOLA ZABAGLIA

VIA GALVANI

Monte Testaccio

## SIGHTS

1. To Ancient Appian Way
2. Ara Pacis
3. Arch of Constantine
4. Baths of Caracalla
5. Baths of Diocletian
6. Bocca della Verità
7. To Borghese Gallery
8. Campo de' Fiori
9. Capitoline Museums
10. Capuchin Crypt
11. Castel Sant'Angelo
12. Circus Maximus
13. Colosseum
14. National Museum of Rome
15. Palatine Hill
16. Pantheon
17. Piazza Navona
18. Porta Portese Flea Market
19. Roman Forum
20. St. Peter's Basilica
21. St. Peter-in-Chains
22. Santa Maria della Vittoria
23. Santa Maria in Trastevere
24. Santa Susanna
25. Sistine Chapel
26. Spanish Steps
27. Synagogue & Jewish Museum
28. Termini Train Station
29. Testaccio District
30. Trajan's Column, Market & Museum of the Imperial Forums
31. Trevi Fountain
32. Vatican Museums (Entrance)
33. Victor Emmanuel Monument
34. Villa Farnesina

1/2 Kilometer
1/2 Mile

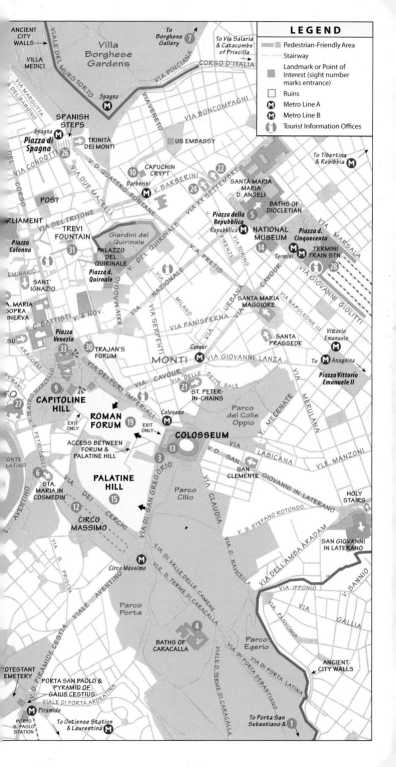

# More for your trip!
## Maximize the experience with Rick Steves as your guide

**Guidebooks**
Make side trips smooth and affordable with Rick's Venice, Florence, and Rome guides

**Phrase Books**
Rely on Rick's Italian Phrase Book & Dictionary

**Rick's TV Shows**
Preview your destinations with a wide variety of shows covering Italy

**Rick's Audio Europe™ App**
Get free self-guided audio tours for Italy's top sights

**Small Group Tours**
Take a lively, low-stress Rick Steves tour through Italy

# For all the details, visit ricksteves.com